THE DICTIONARY OF WELSH BIOGRAPHY
1941 – 1970

THE DICTIONARY OF WELSH BIOGRAPHY

1941-1970

TOGETHER WITH A
SUPPLEMENT TO
THE DICTIONARY OF WELSH BIOGRAPHY
DOWN TO 1940

PUBLISHED BY THE HONOURABLE SOCIETY
OF
CYMMRODORION

LONDON
2001

ISBN 0-9541626-0-9

Typeset and printed by
Cambrian Printers, Aberystwyth

CONTENTS

PREFACE

Four years ago it was my privilege to write a Preface to *Y Bywgraffiadur Cymreig, 1951-70.* Here is the English version. It could be said that the Cymmrodorion Society's greatest gift to Welsh scholarship has been the creation of a Welsh dictionary of biography on the pattern of the English monumental *Dictionary of National Biography*. After the memorable effort, largely under the inspiration of Sir John Cecil-Williams, of producing the first volume, down to 1941, and having seen its enthusiastic welcome, it was incumbent upon the Society to carry on with this great venture, first in Welsh and then in English. By now these volumes are an essential part of the very stuff of Welsh history, and the Cymmrodorion is firmly committed to their continuance.

Contributions, mainly a labour of love, have come from scores of scholars to whom we are deeply indebted, but we pay a special tribute for the skilled and dedicated work of the editors. Dr E.D.Jones of the National Library of Wales had completed most of the work on the Welsh version before he died in 1987, and he was ably assisted in this by Dr Auronwy James. The editorial work continued under the scholarly direction of the then National Librarian, Dr Brynley Roberts, and this volume is largely the fruits of his labours. The Society can only record its gratitude for his completing this arduous task, and for the fact that he is already engaged on the subsequent volume. Throughout this venture the National Library has given us an inestimable service.

We are also indebted to Mr Gwyn Davies for seeing the work through its printing and publishing, and to all those who assisted in translating and proof-reading. On behalf of the Society of Cymmrodorion I am proud to present another memorable chapter in the history of Wales.

EMRYS JONES
President

FOREWORD

Y Bywgraffiadur Cymreig hyd 1940, which appeared in 1953, was followed in 1959 by *The Dictionary of Welsh Biography down to 1940*, an English edition which also contained corrections, updates and additional entries. Though it did not prove possible to produce further volumes at ten-yearly intervals as had been originally intended, work on the project continued with the enthusiastic support and encouragement of the Council of the Honourable Society of Cymmrodorion after the publication of these two volumes. *Y Bywgraffiadur Cymreig, 1941–1950* was published in 1970 and *Y Bywgraffiadur Cymreig, 1951 – 1970* in 1997, both of which incorporated in appendices further updates, amendments and some new, additional articles.

The late Professor R. T. Jenkins, who had been involved in the Welsh National Biography project since 1937 and who had worked with Sir John Edward Lloyd, the first Editor, and with Sir William Llewelyn Davies, the Associate Editor, to produce the first Welsh and English versions, was responsible for much of *Y Bywgraffiadur Cymreig, 1941 – 1950*, especially the amendments. He retired from the editorship in 1965 but retained his active interest in the work up to his death in 1969. His colleague, and then his successor as Editor, was Dr E. D. Jones who completed the task of compiling and editing the entries and saw the book through the press. He immediately began work on the next proposed volume, gathering material and commissioning articles. He was the ideal choice as Editor – an experienced editor and leading archivist who was involved in many aspects of Welsh public and academic life – and he succeeded in bringing together the majority of the articles for *Y Bywgraffiadur Cymreig, 1951 – 1970* before his untimely death in March 1987, leaving, however, some articles yet to be written and a number to be edited. It was a matter of great regret that E. D. Jones did not live to see the fruits of his labours published. I was invited to become Editor some months after Dr Jones's death, and though I received unstinted support and co-operation both from Dr Jones's family and from Dr Auronwy James, his assistant, the publication of *Y Bywgraffiadur Cymreig, 1951 – 1970*, was inevitably delayed; and this, in turn, has led to a delay in the publication of the present volume.

The Dictionary of Welsh Biography, 1941 – 1970, is essentially an English version of the corresponding Welsh dictionaries. Most of the articles have been translated from the Welsh but others were written in English in the first instance. The amendments found in the appendices to *Y Bywgraffiadur Cymreig, 1941–1950* and *1951–1970* are included here, usually in the Supplement except where it has proved possible to incorporate them in the relevant article. The few articles in *Y Bywgraffiadur Cymreig hyd 1940* which were omitted from *The Dictionary of Welsh Biography down to 1940* are now included in the Supplement as are some further amendments and updates which were noted after the publication of the Welsh versions.

The Council of the Honourable Society of Cymmrodorion wishes to record its gratitude to His Royal Highness the Prince of Wales for his encouragement and practical support for this project, and wishes to acknowledge, once again, the generosity of the Pilgrim Trust and the valuable support of the Principality Building Society. I am grateful to all those who have assisted in the production of this work: to those who drew attention to omissions and suggested amend- ments, and to the volunteers who undertook the task of translating a number of the Welsh articles. Without their assistance this volume would have been delayed even longer. My two colleagues have shared fully in the preparation of this book and they have played an essential part in all aspects of its production. In particular, Mr Gwyn Davies has seen the work through the press, while Dr Auronwy James's experience as a researcher has been of great value. The responsibility for the errors which remain must, however, be laid at my door. I wish to thank Cambrian Printers (Aberystwyth) for their interest in the project and for their willing co-operation in this complex and protracted undertaking, but I owe the Council of the Honourable Society of Cymmrodorion a special debt of gratitude both for entrusting the editorship of *The Dictionary of Welsh Biography* to me and for their support and forbearance.

From time to time users of *The Dictionary of Welsh Biography* (and of *Y Bywgraffiadur Cymreig*) have expressed interest in having a list of contributors and their articles. I am very grateful to Dr Auronwy James for undertaking this task also and her valuable 'Contributors' Index' is included in this volume.

BRYNLEY F. ROBERTS

CONTRIBUTORS

A.ap G.	Arthur ap Gwynn (1902-87), Aberystwyth
A.D.F.J.	A.David Fraser Jenkins, London
A.E.	Aled Eames (1921-96), Bangor
A.H.D.	Arthur Herbert Dodd (1891-1975), Bangor
A.H.L.	Archibald Henry Lee, Cardiff
A.J.M.	Aubrey John Martin (1911-90), Llandysul
A.L.	Aneirin Lewis (1924-89), Cardiff
A.Ll.D.	Aled Lloyd Davies, Mold
A.Ll.H.	Arwyn Lloyd Hughes, Llandaff
A.Ll.-W.	Alun Llywelyn-Williams (1913-88), Bangor
Al.R.J.	Alwyn Rice Jones, St Asaph
B.A.M.W.	B.A.Mark Williams, Sidmouth
B.B.T.	Benjamin Bowen Thomas (1899-1977), Bangor
B.F.R.	Brynley Francis Roberts, Aberystwyth
B.G.C.	Bertie George Charles (1908-2000), Aberystwyth
B.G.J.	Benjamin George Jones (1914-89), London
B.G.O.	Benjamin George Owens, Aberystwyth
B.H.	Belinda Humfrey, Lampeter
B.L.J.	Bedwyr Lewis Jones (1933-1992), Bangor
B.Ri.	Brinley Richards (1904-81), Maesteg
C.A.G.	Colin Alistair Gresham (1913-89), Cricieth
C.B.	Clive Betts, Cardiff
C.D.	Christopher Dignam, Swansea
C.G.	Ceris Gruffudd, Aberystwyth
C.H.T.	Ceinwen Hannah Thomas, Cardiff
C.Ll.-M.	Ceridwen Lloyd-Morgan, Aberystwyth
C.P.	Cecil [John Layton] Price (1915-91), Swansea
D.A.B.	Douglas Anthony Bassett, Cardiff
D.A.E.D.	Dewi Aled Eirug Davies (1922-97), Cardiff
D.A.W.	David Alun Williams (1920-92), Cardiff
D.B.C.J.	David Brinley Clay Jones (1924-96), Chepstow
D.D.	Daniel Davies (1893-1961), Aberystwyth
D.E.J.D.	David Elwyn James Davies (1926-97), Swansea
D.E.P.W.	David Ewart Parry Williams (1900-96), Bangor
D.E.W.	Daniel Emrys Williams, Aberystwyth
D.G.R.	David Glanville Rosser, Caernarfon
D.I.	Dylan Iorwerth, Lampeter
D.J.	David Jenkins, Penrhyn-coch, Aberystwyth
D.J.D.	David Joseph Davies, Swansea
D.J.G.	David John Griffiths, Aberystwyth
D.J.M.	David James Morgan (1894-1978), Aberystwyth
D.J.Mu.	Daniel Joseph Mullins, Swansea
D.J.R.	David John Roberts (1910-96), Cardigan
D.J.Wr.	Dennis John Wright, Bangor
D.Je.	David Jenkins, Aberystwyth
D.Jo.; (De.J.)	Derwyn Jones, Colwyn Bay (Bangor)
D.L.D.	David Leslie Davies, Aberdare
D.M.J.	Derwyn Morris Jones, Swansea
D.M.Ll.	David Myrddin Lloyd (1909-81), Aberystwyth

D.O.E.	Dyfed Oswald Evans, Pwllheli
D.P.J.	David Peregrine Jones (1907-86), Tumble, Llanelli
D.R.ap T.	Dafydd Rhys ap Thomas, Bangor
D.R.Ho.	Deian R. Hopkin, London
D.T.	David Thomas (1880-1967), Bangor
D.T.D.	Daniel T.Davies, London
D.T.Ll.	David Tecwyn Lloyd (1914-92), Corwen
D.T.W.P.	David Trevor William Price, Lampeter
D.W.	David Williams (1900-78), Aberystwyth
D.W.H.	Donald Walter Hopkins, Swansea
D.W.P.	Dewi Watkin Powell, Cricieth
Da.Jo.	Dafydd Jones (1907-91), Ffair-rhos, Tregaron
De.J.; (D.Jo.)	Derwyn Jones, Colwyn Bay (Bangor)
Don. M.	Donald Moore, Aberystwyth
E.A.O.	Edwin Augustine Owen (1887-1973), Bangor
E.B.	Edouard Bachellery (1907-88), Versailles
E.D.J.	Evan David Jones (1903-87), Aberystwyth
E.E.L.J.	Elizabeth (Bethan) Eirliw Louis Jones, Wrexham
E.G.B.	Emrys George Bowen (1900-83), Aberystwyth
E.G.E.	Evan Gwyndaf Evans (1913-86), Llandudno
E.G.H.	Edward George Hartmann (1912-95), Wilkes-Barre, U.S.A.
E.G.J.	Emyr Gwynne Jones (1911-72), Bangor
E.G.Je.	Emlyn Glasnant Jenkins, Cardigan
E.L.E.	Evan Lewis Evans (1898-1978), Swansea
E.L.El.	Edward Lewis Ellis, Aberystwyth
E.O.R.	Emrys Owain Roberts (1910-90), London
E.O.W.	Euryn Ogwen Williams, Barry
E.P.E.	Emrys Peregryn Evans (1898-1981), London
E.P.R.	Enid Pierce Roberts, Bangor
E.R.M.	Edward Ronald Morris, Llanidloes (Llanfyllin)
E.W.J.	Emyr Wyn Jones (1907-99), Pwllheli (Liverpool)
E.W.R.	Eryl Wyn Rowlands, Llangefni
E.Wy.J.	E.Wyn James, Cardiff
El.G.J.	Elis Gwyn Jones (-1999), Cricieth
E.M.H.	Edward Morgan Humphreys (1882-1955), Caernarfon
Em.D.	Emlyn Davies, Cardiff
Em.W.J.	Emrys Wynn Jones, Aberystwyth
En.P.	Enid Parry (1912-98), Bangor
E.R.	Evan Roberts, Llandderfel
Er.E.	Eric Edwards, Wrexham
E.W.P.E.	Edward William Price Evans, Pontypool
F.J.N.	Frederick John North (1889-1968), Cardiff
F.P.J.	Frank Price Jones (1920-75), Bangor
F.M.G.	Francis Michael Gibbs, Swansea
F.W.J.	Francis Wynn Jones (1898-1970), Aberystwyth
G.A.E.	Gwilym Arthur Edwards (1881-1963), Oswestry
G.A.J.	Gwilym Arthur Jones (1925-98), Bangor
G.A.U.	Gwilym Arthur Usher (1915-78), Bangor
G.B.O.	Gwilym Beynon Owen, Bangor
G.C.B.	George Counsell Boon (1927-94), Penarth
G.E.	Gwilym Evans (1896-1983), Aberystwyth
G.E.J.	Geraint Elfyn Jones, Newtown
G.G.	Robert Geraint Gruffydd, Aberystwyth

G.H.	Graeme Holmes, Llandaff
G.H.J.	Geraint Huw Jenkins, Aberystwyth
G.H.W.	Gareth Haulfryn Williams, Caernarfon
G.I.L.	G.I.Lumley, Wrexham
G.J.	Gwyn Jones (1907-99), Aberystwyth (Cardiff)
G.Je.	Gwyn Jenkins, Aberystwyth
G.Jo.	Gerallt Jones (1907-84), Caerwedros, Newquay
G.L.R.	Graham Lloyd Rees, Aberystwyth
G.M.	Gwyneth Morgan (1916-98), Tonyrefail
G.M.G.	Griffith Milwyn Griffiths, Aberystwyth
G.M.R.	Gomer Morgan Roberts (1904-93), Llandybïe
G.P.J.	Gwilym Peredur Jones (1892-1975), Grange-over-Sands
G.R.	Glyn Roberts (1904-62), Bangor
G.R.H.	Glyn Rhys Hughes, Llanelli
G.R.T.	Gwilym Richard Tilsley (1911-97), Prestatyn
G.T.	Gildas Tibbott (1900-79), Aberystwyth
G.T.H.	Glyn Tegai Hughes, Newtown
G.T.R.	Griffith Thomas Roberts (1887-1977), Talsarnau
G.T.S.	G.T. Streather, Kettering
G.Tu.	Gwilym Tudur, Aberystwyth
G.V.-J.	Geraint Vaughan-Jones, Aberystwyth
G.W.	Glanmor Williams, Swansea
G.W.W.	Gareth W. Williams, Aberystwyth
Ga.R.	Garnet Rees (1912-90), Stamford
Ge.M.	Gerald Morgan, Aberystwyth
Gl.P.	Glyn Parry, Synod, Llandysul
Gw.D.	Gwilym Davies (1879-1955), Aberystwyth
Gw.E.	Gwynfor Evans, Pencarreg, Llanybydder
Gw.H.J.	Gwilym Henry Jones, Menai Bridge
H.ab E.	Hedd ab Emlyn, Wrexham
H.D.E.	Hywel David Emanuel (1921-70), Aberystwyth
H.D.J.	Hugh David Jones, Swansea
H.D.	Hywel David Lewis (1910-92), London
H.E.	Huw Ethall, Cardiff
H.E.H.	Hugh Emlyn Hooson, Llanidloes
H.G.W.	Herbert Gladstone Wright (1888-1962), Bangor
H.M.-J.	Huw Morris-Jones (1912-89), Bangor
H.M.S.	Harry Morrey Salmon (1891-1985), Cardiff
H.N.J.	Herbert Noel Jerman (1909-94), Newtown
H.O.	Huw Owen (1880-1953), Llanfair P.G.
H.P.M.	Hugh Pawley Mathew, Saffron Walden
H.T.Ed.	Hywel Teifi Edwards, Llangennech
H.W.	Huw Williams, Bangor
H.Wa.	Huw Walters, Aberystwyth
I.B.R.	Ioan Bowen Rees (1929-99), Bangor
I.C.P.	Iorwerth Cyfeiliog Peate (1901-82), Llandaff (St Fagans)
I.Ff.E.	Islwyn Ffowc Elis, Lampeter
I.G.R.	Ivor Gwynfil Rees (1909-89), Pennant, Ceredigion
I.Gl.R.	Ivor Glyn Rees, Hawarden
I.Je.	Islwyn Jenkins, Carmarthen
I.Ll.F.	Idris Llewelyn Foster (1911-84), Oxford
I.M.J.	Iwan Meical Jones, Aberystwyth
I.O.	Ifor Owen, Llanuwchllyn

I.S.J.	Ieuan Samuel Jones, Aberystwyth
Io. J.	Iorwerth Jones (1913-92), Gorseinon
J.A.D.	James Arthur Davies, Bangor
J.A.O.	John A.Oddy, King's Lynn
J.C.McL.	John Charles McLean (1875-1952), Cardiff
J.D.	John Davies, Cardiff
J.D.O.	John Dyfnallt Owen (1873-1956), Aberystwyth
J.D.V.L.	John Daniel Vernon Lewis (1879-1970), Machynlleth
J.E.	John Evans, (1877-1958), Felindre, Llandysul
J.E.C.W.	John Ellis Caerwyn Williams (1912-99), Aberystwyth
J.E.M.	John Ellis Meredith (1905-81), Aberystwyth
J.G.J.	John Graham Jones, Aberystwyth
J.G.W.	John Gwynn Williams, Bangor
J.H.	John Hughes (1896-1968), Dolgellau
J.H.H.	John Hrothgar Habakkuk, Oxford
J.J.E.	John James Evans (1894-1965), St. David's
J.K.E.	John Keith Evans, Caerwedros, Newquay
J.L.J.	John Lewis Jones, Mold
J.Ll.	John Lloyd (1885-1964), Llanbedr
J.Ll.T.	John Lloyd Thomas (1889-1974), Pontardawe
J.M.C.	John Martin Cleary, Cardiff
J.M.J.	John Morgan Jones (1903-89), Aberystwyth
J.O.S.	John Oliver Stephens (1880-1957), Carmarthen
J.R.R.	John Roderick Rees, Tregaron
J.R.W.	John Roberts Williams, Llan-rug
J.Ty.J.	John Tysul Jones (1902-86), Llandysul
J.W.Jo.	John William Jones (1884-1954), Blaenau Ffestiniog
Jo.G.J.	John Gwilym Jones, Wrexham
K.E.	Keri Edwards, Bargoed
K.E.J.	Kenneth Emlyn Jones (1911-83), Sketty, Swansea
K.R.	Kate Roberts (1891-1985), Denbigh
K.W.J.	Keith Williams Jones (1926-79), Bangor
L.D.	Lorraine Davies, Cardiff
L.N.H.	L.N.Hopper, Cardiff
Ll.G.C.	Llywelyn Gwyn Chambers, Bangor
Ll.P.	Llywelyn Phillips (1914-81), Aberystwyth
M.A.J.	Mary Auronwy James, Aberystwyth
M.B.D.	Margaret Beatrice Davies, Aberystwyth
M.E.	Megan Ellis (1906-2001), Aberystwyth
M.E.C.	Muriel E. Chamberlain, Swansea
M.E.	Margaret Ethelwynne Thomas (1906-89), Narberth
M.G.E.	Mary Gwendoline Ellis, Aberystwyth
M.H.D.	Margaret Helen Davies, Aberystwyth
M.H.J.	Marian Henry Jones, Aberystwyth
M.J.J.	Moses John Jones (1905-99), Mold
M.J.W.	Morgan John Williams (1910-95), Sketty, Swansea
M.M.W.	Margaret Mitford Williams, Llangefni
M.P.L.	Meilir Pennant Lewis, Bangor
M.R.	Maurice Richards (1921-89), Newtown
M.R.W.	Melfyn Richard Williams, Llanuwchllyn
Ma.B.D.	Mary Beynon Davies, Aberystwyth
Ma.E.C.	Mair Elizabeth Cole, London
Me.E.	Meredydd Evans, Cwmystwyth

N.H.W.	Nia Hall Williams, Llandaff
N.T.	Norman Percy Thomas (1915-89), Swansea
O.E.	Owen Edwards, Cardiff
O.E.R.	Owen Elias Roberts (1908-2000), Liverpool
O.P.D.	Owen Picton Davies (1882-1970), Bangor
O.W.J.	Owain William Jones (1922-95), Swansea
P.C.B.	Peter Clement Bartrum, Berkhamsted
P.J.	Paul Joyner, Aberystwyth
P.L.	Peter Lord, Aberystwyth
P.M.	Prys Morgan, Swansea
R.A.R.	Robert Alun Roberts (1894-1969), Bangor
R.B.W.	Richard Bryn Williams (1902-81), Aberystwyth
R.C.B.O.	Reginald Campell Burn Oliver (1908-93), Llandrindod
R.D.G.	Robert David Griffith (1877-1958), Old Colwyn
R.F.R.	Rhiannon Francis Roberts (1923-90), Aberystwyth
R.G.O.	Richard Griffith Owen (1890-1973), Bangor
R.H.M.	Richard Harding Morgan, Aberystwyth
R.I.A.	Richard Ithamar Aaron (1901-87), Aberystwyth
R.L.H.	Richard Leonard Hugh (1913-83), Gorseinon
R.L.J.	Richard Leslie Jones, Llandaff
R.M.	Roland G.Mathias, Brecon
R.M.J.	Robert (Bobi) Maynard Jones, Aberystwyth
R.O.	Robert (Bob) Owen (1885-1962), Croesor
R.O.G.W.	Robin O.G.Williams, Cricieth
R.P.P.	R. Palmer Parry, Llansannan
R.T.J.	Robert Thomas Jenkins (1881-1969), Bangor
R.Td.J.	Robert Tudur Jones (1921-98), Bangor
R.W.E.	Raymond Wallis Evans (1910-2001), Bangor
Rh.G.	Rhidian Griffiths, Aberystwyth
Ri.E.H.	Richard E.Huws, Aberystwyth
S.J.	Selwyn Jones (1906-81), Hirwaun
S.R.J.	Sally Roberts Jones, Port Talbot
S.R.W.	Siân Rhiannon Williams, Rhoose
T.A.L.	Thomas Arthur Levi (1874-1954), Aberystwyth
T.E.G.	Thomas Elwyn Griffiths, Caernarfon
T.E.J.	Tom Ellis Jones (1900-75), Bangor
T.G.D.	Thomas Gruffydd Davies, Seven Sisters, Neath
T.G.J.	Thomas Gwynn Jones (1904-90), Swansea
T.H.P.-W.	Thomas Herbert Parry-Williams (1887-1975), Aberystwyth
T.I.E.	Thomas Iorwerth Ellis (1899-1970), Aberystwyth
T.J.	Thomas Jones (1870-1955), Birchington
T.J.H.	Thomas James Hopkins (1919-87), Cardiff
T.J.M.	Thomas John Morgan (1907-86), Swansea
T.J.P.	Thomas Jones Pierce (1905-64), Aberystwyth
T.M.D.	Thomas Maelgwyn Davies (1904-66), Aberystwyth
T.M.R.	Thomas Mardy Rees (1871-1953), Neath
T.P.	Thomas Parry (1904-85), Bangor
T.R.	Thomas Richards (1878-1962), Bangor
T.R.O.	Thomas Richard Owen (1918-90), Swansea
T.Ro.	Thomas Roberts (1885-1960), Bangor
V.J.L.	Vyrnwy John Lewis, Farnham
W.A.W.	William Alister Williams, Wrexham
W.B.D.	William Beynon Davies (1908-87), Aberystwyth

W.C.R.	William Cyril Rogers (1911-95), Swansea
W.D.	Walford Davies, Aberystwyth
W.D.J.	William (Bill) David Jones, Cardiff
W.E.J.	William Emrys Jones (1894-1985), Bangor
W.G.	William Griffith (1816-1972), Rhyl
W.G.E.	William Gareth Evans (1942-2000), Aberystwyth
W.G.T.	William Gwyn Thomas (1928-94), Aberystwyth
W.J.S.	William James Smith, Reading
W.J.R.	William Joseph Rhys (1880-1967), Treherbert
W.L.	William Linnard, Llandaff
W.Ll. D.	William Llewelyn Davies (1887-1952), Aberystwyth
W.M.	William Morris (1889-1979), Caernarfon
W.M.R.	William Morgan Rogers (1934-99), Cardiff
W.O.W.	William Ogwen Williams (1924-69), Aberystwyth
W.P.W.	Wynn Powell Wheldon (1879-1961), Prestatyn
W.R.N.	William Rhys Nicholas (1914-96), Porthcawl
W.R.P.G.	William Richard Philip George, Cricieth
W.R.Wi.	W. R. Williams, Fairbourne
W.T.M.	Walter Thomas Morgan (1912-90), Aberystwyth
W.T.O.	William Thomas Owen (1914-2000), London
W.T.P.D.	William Thomas Pennar Davies (1911-96), Swansea
W.W.P.	Watkin William Price (1873-1967), Aberdare

ADDITIONAL ABBREVIATIONS

Alpine Jnl.	*Alpine Journal*
Ann. Roy. Coll. Surgeons	*Annals of the Royal College of Surgeons*
Baner	*Baner ac Amserau Cymru*
Bangor Dioc. Gaz.	*Bangor Diocesan Gazette*
Bapt. Rec.	*Baptist Record*
Biog. Memoirs Fellows R.S.	*Biographical Memoirs of Fellows of the Royal Society*
Blwyddiadur A	*Blwyddiadur yr Annibynwyr Cymraeg*
Blwyddiadur MC	*Blwyddiadur y Methodistiaid Calfinaidd*
Blwyddlyfr MC	*Blwyddlyfr y Methodistiaid Calfinaidd*
Braslun o Hanes Meth. Môn	Huw Llewelyn Williams (ed.), *Braslun o Hanes Methodistiaeth Galfinaidd Môn 1935-70* (1977)
Brec. & Radn. County Times	*Brecon & Radnor County Times*
Brit. Med. Jnl.	*British Medical Journal*
Bulawayo Chron.	*Bulawayo Chronicle*
C.C.C. Welsh Mus.	*Complete Catalogue of Contemporary Welsh Music*
Ca(e)rn. & Denb. Herald	*Ca(e)rnarvon and Denbigh Herald*
Camb. News	*Cambrian News*
Carms. Historian	*The Carmarthenshire Historian*
Cath. Dir. &c.	*(Complete) (Battersby's) Catholic Directory &c.*
Cylch. Cymd. Alawon Gwerin	*Cylchgrawn Cymdeithas Alawon Gwerin*
Cylch. Hanes Cymru	*Cylchgrawn Hanes Cymru (Welsh History Review)*
Dict. American Biog.	Allen Johnson, *Dictionary of American Biography* (1928-36, 1944, 1988)
Dict. Australian Biog.	Percival Serle, *Dictionary of Australian Biography* (1949)
Dict. Business Biog.	*Dictionary of Business Biography* (1986)
Dict. Lab. Biog.	Joyce M. Bellamy & J. Saville, *Dictionary of Labour Biography* (1972)
Dict. Scient. Biog.	*Dictionary of Scientific Biography* (1970)
DWB	*The Dictionary of Welsh Biography down to 1940* (1959)
Dyddiadur EF	*Dyddiadur yr Eglwys Fethodistaidd*
Dysg.	*Y Dysgedydd*
Ellis, *UCW*	E.L. Ellis, *The University College of Wales, Aberystwyth, 1872-1972* (1972)
Foley	H. Foley, *Records of the English Province of the Society of Jesus (1570-1800 circa)* (1877-79)
Geiriadur Bywgr.	Josiah Thomas Jones, *Geiriadur Bywgraffyddol o Enwogion Cymru* (1867-70)
Gen. Gymr.	*Y Genedl Gymreig*
Genh.	*Y Genhinen*
Glam. Hist.	*The Glamorgan Historian*
Gol.	*Y Goleuad*
Guy's Hosp. Gaz.	*Guy's Hospital Gazette*
Guy's Hosp. Reports	*Guy's Hospital Reports*
Hanes Meth. gorll. Meirionydd	R. Owen, *Hanes Methodistiaeth Gorllewin Meirionydd* (1891, 1899); H. Ellis (1928)
Herald Cymr.	*Yr Herald Cymraeg (a'r Genedl)*

Hist. Gwydir Family	Sir John Wynn, *The History of the Gwydir Family*, ed., John Ballinger (1927); ed. J. Gwynfor Jones (1990).
Jnl. Agric. Soc. UCW	*Journal of the Agricultural Society, University College of Wales, Aberystwyth*
Jnl. Brit. Grassld. Soc.	*Journal of the British Grassland Society*
Jnl. Royal Agri. Soc.	*Journal of the Royal Agricultural Society*
Jnl. Royal Inst. Chem.	*Journal of the Royal Institute of Chemistry*
Kelly's Handbook	*Kelly's Handbook to the titled, landed and official classes*
Le Neve, *Fasti*	John Le Neve, (rev. T. Duffus Hardy), *Fasti Ecclesiae Anglicanae* (1854)
Liv.D.P.	*The Liverpool Daily Post*
Lond. Welsh.	*The London Welshman*
Lives Fellows Roy. Coll. Surg.	*Lives of the Fellows of the Royal College of Surgeons, London, 1930-51, 1952-60*
Llyfr. Llen. Gymr.	Thomas Parry and Merfyn Morgan, *Llyfryddiaeth Llenyddiaeth Gymraeg* (1976)
Man. Guard., Manch. Guardian	*Manchester Guardian*
Mont. County Times	*Montgomeryshire County Times*
Munk's Roll	William Munk, *The Roll of the Royal College of Physicians of London, 1518-1700* (1878), *1701-1800* (1878), *1801-25* (1878); G.H. Brown, *Lives of the Fellows of the Royal College of Physicians of London 1826-1925* (1955); Richard R. Trail, *Munk's Roll, 5: Lives of the F.R.C. of Ph. of L. continued to 1965* (1968); Gordon Wolstenholme, *Munk's Roll, 6: Lives ... F.R.C. continued to 1975* (1982)
N. Wales Chronicle	*North Wales Chronicle*
N. Wales Obs.	*North Wales Observer*
N. Wales Times	*North Wales Times*
N. Wales Weekly News	*North Wales Weekly News*
Neath Guard.	*Neath Guardian*
Ormerod, *Cheshire*	George Ormerod, H*istory of the County Palatine City of Chester* (1882)
OPCS	Office of Population and Census Studies Indexes
Phil. Trans. Roy. Soc.	*Philosophical Transactions of the Royal Society*
Proc. Geologists Association	*Proceedings of the Geologists Association*
Proc. Phys. Soc.	*Proceedings of the Physical Society*
Proc. Roy. Soc.	*Proceedings of the Royal Society*
Radnor Expr.	*The Radnor Express*
Records Eng. Prov. S.J.	see Foley above
Rep. Brit. Assn. Adv. of Science	*Reports of the meetings of the British Association for the Advancement of Science*
S. Wales Argus	*South Wales Argus*
S. Wales Echo	*South Wales Echo*
S. Wales Evening Post	*South Wales Evening Post*
S. Wales Guardian	*South Wales Guardian*
S. Wales Voice	*South Wales Voice*
Swyn y Tannau	Meirionnydd Teachers' Services, no.4. Published by Meirionnydd Branch of the N.U.T., 1936.
Tr.,Traeth	*Y Traethodydd*

Traf. Cymd. Hanes Sir Ddinbych	*Trafodion Cymdeithas Hanes Sir Ddinbych*
Traf. Cymm.	see. *Trans. Cymm.*
Trans. Cymm.	*The Transactions of the Honourable Society of Cymmrodorion*
Trans. Liverpool Med. Inst.	*Transactions (Proceedings) of the Liverpool Medicine Institute*
Trans. R.S.A.	*Transactions of the Royal Society for the Encouragement of Arts, Manufacture and Commerce*
Trans. S. Wales Inst. Engineers	*Transactions of the South Wales Institute of Engineers*
Trys. Plant	*Trysorfa y Plant*
WHR	*Welsh History Review*
W. Wales Guard.	*West Wales Guardian*
West. Mail	*Western Mail*
West. Telegraph	*Western Telegraph*
Ww	*Who's who?*
Ww in America	*Who's who in America?*
WwFC	L.G. Pine, *Who's who in the Free Churches?* (1951)
WWP	*The Biographical Index of W.W. Price, Aberdare;* copies in NLW and Aberdare Public Library
Www	*Who was who?*
WwW (1921; 1933; 1937)	Arthur Mee (ed.), *Who's who in Wales* (1921; 1933; 1937)

THE DICTIONARY OF WELSH BIOGRAPHY

1941-1970

A

ALBAN, Sir FREDERICK JOHN (1882-1965), chartered accountant and administrator; b. 11 Jan. 1882, at ? Abergavenny, Mon., s. of David Alban and his wife Hannah. The mother d. at Abergavenny, 28 Sept. 1884. The father was a journeyman tailor and he d. at Hereford, 2 Jan. 1891. Consequently, the family was scattered. Two elder sons became shoemakers near Fleetwood. Frederick John was brought up by a Miss Williams at Lower Monk Street in Abergavenny until he was 16 years old. The children knew her as 'aunt', but it is not known whether she was a blood relation. Brought up under straitened circumstances, he attended the national school at Abergavenny until the age of 12, when he had to leave because the 'school pence' were raised to 6d. a week. He obtained a junior post at the office of Spicketts, solicitors, at Pontypridd where he gained proficiency in shorthand and typing. He strove to better himself by borrowing books and copying them in shorthand. He worked hard and allowed himself only four hours of sleep of a night. He was, however, a typically lively lad, and on different occasions he broke an arm and a leg which were not properly set, and damaged his eyes which affected his sight. He settled at Pontypridd and at the age of 17 was appointed clerical assistant to the Local Board of Guardians. Three years later he became accountant to the urban district council. In 1907 he obtained the first place in the final examination of the Institute of Municipal Treasurers and Accountants, achieving the same distinction in the finals of the Society of Incorporated Accountants and Auditors and of the Institute of Chartered Accountants. In 1909, he won the gold medal of the Society of Incorporated Accountants and Auditors. He was also a Fellow of the Institute of Chartered Accountants. For two years he was accountant to the United Water Board of Pontypridd and Rhondda, when he came to the notice of Thomas Jones (1870-1955, see below) who saw in him the making of a deputy accountant for the Welsh National Insurance Commission, a post which he held from 1912 to 1916, when he resigned to become secretary and controller of the Welsh National Memorial Association established by David Davies, aft. Lord Davies (1880-1944, see below) and his sisters, Gwendoline and Margaret (see below) to commemorate King Edward VII and to combat tuberculosis in Wales. He acted as accountant for the Ministry of Food in Wales, 1918-19. He resigned from his post with the Memorial Assoc. in 1922 but continued as its consultant on financial matters, and acted as financial consultant to local authorities. With Norman Ernest Lamb he established the firm of Alban & Lamb, chartered accountants, of Newport and Cardiff. He established the Accountancy and Secretarial Training Institute at Newport to provide a correspondence course and to publish concise handbooks to help students prepare for professional examinations, inspired by his own early experiences in his efforts to master the elements of his profession. He was consulting accountant to the Taff Fechan Water Board, and served on tri-bunals set up under the various Acts of Parliament concerning electricity, water and gas. He was chairman of the finance committee of the (then) Welsh National School of Medicine. He had retained an interest in medical administration from his period of service to the Memorial Association and had successfully persuaded Welsh local authorities to co-operate in the campaign against tuberculosis. The results of his wise and effective leadership were seen again in the fruitful relationship created between the Welsh Hospitals Board, the Medical School, and the Cardiff united hospitals during his chairmanship of the Board from 1947 to 1959.

He published a number of books on the administration of water undertakings, on matters relating to rating and local government finances, and income tax legislation. In 1954 he published *Socialisation in Great Britain and its effects on the accountancy profession.* He received many honours both within and outside his chosen profession. He was made president of the Society of Incorporated Accountants in 1947, and honorary life member of the Certified Public Accountants' Association of Ontario, and an honorary member of the Institute of Municipal Treasurers & Accountants, 1954. He was a J.P. for Glamorgan, was made a C.B.E. in 1932 and knighted in 1945. The University of Wales awarded him the honorary degree of LL.D. in 1956. He was a double silver medallist of the Royal Society of Arts. He was Grand Treasurer in the United Grand Lodge [of Freemasons] of England and Wales and Provincial Grand Master of the Mark Province of South Wales from 1950 until his resignation on account of ill health in 1963.

He m. 17 Aug. 1906, Alice Emily Watkins (b. at Ewyas Harold, 21 Oct. 1881), d. of James Watkins, wheelwright, and his wife Emily, late Woodhill, formerly Hughes. In 1906, she was a milliner at Crickhowell and after her marriage was of great assistance to her husband in secretarial work. They had six children, four sons and two daughters. Two of the sons and both daughters qualified in medicine, and the other sons in their father's profession. He d. 2 May 1965.

WwW (1937); *Www; West. Mail,* 3 May 1965; information from his eldest son, Vivian F. Alban.

E.D.J.

ALBAN DAVIES, DAVID (1873-1951), business man and philanthropist; b. 13 Apr. 1873 at Hafod Peris, Llanrhystud, Cards., youngest son of Jenkin Davies, master mariner, and Anne (née Alban) his wife. On leaving the local school at the age of 14 he worked on his uncle's farm at Hafod Peris, since the family had fallen on hard times. As his brothers had been sent to Llandovery College, he saved his earnings to enter Owen's School at Oswestry when he was 18 years old. On 28 Nov. 1899 he m. Rachel Williams of Brynglas, Moria, Penuwch, in Holy Trinity Church, Aberystwyth; they had 4 sons and a daughter. Davies and his wife went to London to work with Rachel's brother Evan who had a successful dairy business. David Alban Davies eventually bought Hitchman's Dairies, Ltd., which grew into a flourishing business under his direction. In 1933 he built Brynawelon, Llanrhystud and retired there, leaving the management of the business to two of his sons, Jenkin (see below) and David Harold. He d. 2 Dec. 1951 and was buried at Penuwch.

At the beginning of his career he vowed he would give the church 10% of his earnings. As a result, and in co-operation with other members, the Welsh Presbyterian Church, Moriah, Walthamstow, came into being and he helped provide it with a manse. He also built a school-room near his old home in Llanrhystud for the Presbyterian Church. He served the local community as a member of Walthamstow Borough Council for nine years. After returning to Wales he served as high sheriff of Cardiganshire in 1940 and became a member and alderman (1949) of Cardiganshire County Council, and served as chairman of its health and welfare committees. He was a founder-member and chairman of Aberystwyth and District Old People's Housing Society when it purchased Deva, a residence for old people which benefited greatly by his generosity. He was particularly interested in improvements in agriculture and donated £10,000 to the Department of Animal Health, U.C.W., Aberystwyth. He was president of the North Cardiganshire Farmers' Co-operative Society for a period. He also devoted his time to education, being the first chairman of the governors of Dinas Secondary Modern School, Aberystwyth, and a governor of U.C.W., Aberystwyth and of the University of Wales. At short notice he bought and pre-sented to U.C.W. 200 acres of land on Penglais estate to save it from building development. He was given an honorary degree of LL.D. in 1947. The following year his wife presented the first travelling library van to Cardiganshire County Council, to provide a service which was much appreciated by the public.

Llawlyfr Cymdeithas Ceredigion Llundain, 1952-3, 5-7; information from Mrs. Margaret Alban Davies, Aberaeron.

M.A.J.

ALBAN DAVIES, JENKIN (1901-68), business man and philanthropist; b. 24 June 1901, in Walthamstow, London, the eldest son of David Alban Davies (see above) and Rachel (née Williams) his wife, both of Cards. He was educated at Merchant Taylors' School, and gained a scholarship to St. John's College, Oxford, but could not afford to go there. He went to Cornell University, U.S.A., for two years to study agriculture and dairying and worked for a short while in American firms to study their business methods. He entered the family business in 1925 and in due course became chairman of Hitchman's Dairies, Ltd., which was selling 20,000 gallons of milk a day and employing over 500 men when it was sold to United Dairies, Ltd., in 1946. He was also a Lloyd's underwriter. On 6 Dec. 1939 he m. Margaret, daughter of John Davies, master mariner, Aberaeron and they had two sons. He d. 26 May 1968 at Brynawelon, Llanrhystud, Cards., his home since 1963.

He played an active part locally, becoming president of the Liberal Association and of the Rotary Club at Walthamstow and worked with the Association of Youth Clubs there, being himself a sportsman. When Moriah (Welsh Presb.) chapel, Walthamstow, became too small he insti-gated the building of a new chapel, Moriah, Leytonstone, which was a convenient meeting place for the many young Welshmen who flocked to London at that time. Several Welsh societies in London received generous donations from him. He did his utmost to further the Welsh language and was a founder-member of the London Welsh School which opened in Sept. 1961 in temporary premises in St. David's church hall. Later he provided a bus to take children to the Welsh class at Hungerford Road primary school in Islington before the class moved to Willesden Green. He had many years earlier, in 1948, founded a residential preparatory school for boys at Abermâd, Llanilar, Cards., where they were taught through the medium of Welsh up to the age of nine. The school remained open till about 1971. In 1965 he led a deputation to Patagonia. He served many institutions in Wales. As treasurer he gave valuable guidance to *Urdd Gobaith Cymru* (Welsh League of Youth) c. 1950, to U.C.W. (1954-68) and to Coleg Harlech (1957-68). He became chairman of the Council for the Protection of Rural Wales; was a member of the Councils of U.C.W. and N.M.W.; and Welsh rep-resentative of the Independent Television Authority for two terms, 1956-64. He made donations to *Urdd Gobaith Cymru*, contributed £10,000 to the building fund of U.C.W., Aberystwyth and provided a generous subven-tion towards the cost of producing *The Oxford book of Welsh verse*. His outstanding services to various aspects of Welsh life were recognised when he was appointed high sheriff of Cardiganshire in 1951 and was awarded an hon-orary LL.D. of the University of Wales in 1964.

West. Mail, 27 May 1968; information from his widow.

E.D.J., M.A.J.

ALYS MALLT – see WILLIAMS, ALICE MATIL-DA LANGLAND below.

AMANWY – see GRIFFITHS, DAVID REES below.

ANTHONY, DAVID BRYNMOR (1886-1966), school teacher and academic administrator; b. 28 Oct. 1886 at Kidwelly, Carms., the second s. of John Gwendraeth Anthony and Mary (née Harris), his wife. The father was a provision merchant, general draper and outfitter at Paris House, Kidwelly. David Brynmor attended the local Castle School before going to the county intermediate school at Llanelli. Entering U.C.W., Aberystwyth in Oct. 1905 he graduat-ed in 1908 with a class I in French and Romance philology, his studies including also history and Latin. From Oct. 1908 until Jan 1910 he taught at the *Collège de Garçons*, Cambrai, France, but with the help of a University of Wales post-graduate studentship he was able to leave his post and continue his studies at the Sorbonne and the *Bibliothèque Nationale*. In June 1910 he was awarded the degree of M.A. by the University of Wales for a dissertation on the poetry of the Parnassian group of French poets. In Jan. 1911 he was appointed to teach French at Holloway County High School, London.

He enlisted in the Royal Welch Fusiliers in Sept. 1914 and served overseas from Nov. 1915 to the end of Jan. 1919, at first in Belgium and France, and later in Italy. He rose to the rank of captain, and for his services was awarded the M.C., and bar, the Italian silver medal for valour, and the *Croce di Guerra*. At the end of the hostilities he was appointed to organise educational schemes for the troops in northern Italy, his continued stay in the country enabling him to learn Italian with great proficiency. He later (in 1920) qualified for a diploma in Italian awarded by the University of Florence.

He returned in 1919 to Holloway school and in Feb. 1921 was appointed registrar of the University of Wales. In addition to the usual duties of the registrarship he became in 1931 acting secretary of the Welsh National School of Medicine, pending the appointment of a full-time secretary. His duty as secretary of the art committee of the University gave him an opportunity to arouse and cultivate a greater awareness and appreciation of art in Wales. He became secretary and later chairman of the Contemporary Art Society for Wales and art remained a passion for him. He never lost his interest in France and in modern languages. He served as honorary treasurer of the Modern Language Association, as a member of its council, and as president of the South Wales branch. In 1936 he was nominated *Officier d'Académie* by the French government. During the years 1939-45 he was chairman of an organisation set up in Cardiff called Friends of Free France, and for services to the Free French Forces he was awarded, in 1947, the *Médaille de Vermeil de la Reconnaissance Française* by the French government. In 1964 he was promoted to the rank of *Officier de l'Ordre des Palmes Académiques* for services to France and French culture.

He resigned from the post of university registrar in 1945 and soon afterwards, in Feb. 1946, he was appointed chief inspector of the Central Welsh Board. The C.W.B. was merged into the new structure when the Welsh Joint Education Committee came into being: Brynmor Anthony transferred to the W.J.E.C. and continued with it up to his retirement.

His wife was Doris Musson, youngest dau. of George Tait Galloway Musson and his wife of Liverpool. They were m. on 24 Apr. 1918. There were two children, David Alan, and Lois Mary. He was made a freeman of the borough of Kidwelly in July 1924. He was an elder of Pembroke Terrace Presb. church, Cardiff, and was a member of the board of the Forward Movement of the Presbyterian Church of Wales. He believed firmly in the value of physical activity; he took his walks seriously and played golf regularly as a member of the Radyr Golf Club. During World War II he began to keep bees and came to have a large number of hives and to produce great quantities of honey. It is worth recording this personal detail for it symbolises his seriousness and industriousness – or better still, his 'busy-ness'. He died 24 Jan. 1966.

Personal details received from his daughter, Lois Mary Anthony.

T.J.M.

ANTHROPOS - see ROWLAND, ROBERT DAVID below.

ANWYL, JOHN BODVAN ('Bodfan'; 1875-1949), minister (Congl.), lexicographer, and author; b. 27 June 1875 in Chester, s. of John Anwyl, lay preacher, of the Anwyl family of Caerwys, Flints., and his wife Ellen (née Williams), whose family came from Llangwnnadl, Caerns. He entered the ministry and became minister of Elim (Congl.), Carmarthen in 1899. Owing to deafness he relinquished his church to take charge of the Deaf and Dumb Institute at Pontypridd, 1904-19. In 1914 he was responsible for the sixth edition of Spurrell's *Welsh-English Dictionary*; later, 1916, he edited the seventh edition of Spurrell's *English-Welsh Dictionary*. Both ran to several further editions. He was appointed (1921) secretary of the projected Welsh dictionary sponsored by the Board of Celtic Studies of the University of Wales. On retiring from the post, he settled in Llangwnnadl, Caerns., where he d., by drowning, 23 July 1949; he was buried in Penllech, Caerns., churchyard.

A younger brother of Sir Edward Anwyl (*DWB*, 12-13), he contributed extensively to the Welsh press. He edited reprints of *Drych y prif oesoedd* and *Gweledigaethau y Bardd Cwsc*, was author of *Y pulpud bach* (1924), *Yr arian mawr* (1934), *Fy hanes i fy hunan* (1933), and *Englynion* (1933), and prepared translations (into Welsh) of books published by the London Missionary Society.

Faner, 10 Aug. 1949; *West. Mail*, 27 July 1949; *Cymro*, 29 July 1949; *Llan*, 12 Aug. 1949; *Llusern*, 1949; *Www.*

T.H.P-W.

AP CEREDIGION – see LEWIS, DAVID below.

AP GWARNANT – see WILLIAMS, THOMAS OSWALD below.

AP HEFIN – see LLOYD, HENRY (1870-1946) below.

ARFRYN – see THOMAS, GEORGE ISAAC (1895-1941) below.

ARMSTRONG-JONES, Sir ROBERT (1857-1943), physician and alienist; b. 2 Dec. 1857 at Ynyscynhaearn, Caerns., s. of Thomas Jones, minister (Congl.), Eisteddfa, Cricieth, and Jane Elizabeth, dau. of Robert Jones, of the same place. Educated at Porthmadog grammar school, Grove Park school, Wrexham, U.C.N.W., Bangor, and St. Bartholomew's Hospital, he became M.D. (Lond.), 1885, F.R.C.S. (Eng.), 1886, and F.R.C.P. (Lond.), 1908. He specialised in mental diseases and was junior medical officer at the Royal Earlswood Institution, 1880-82, and Colney Hatch, 1882-88; resident physician and superintendent of Earlswood Asylum, 1888-93 and of the London County Council Asylum, Claybury, 1893-1916. He made a name for Claybury by developing modern methods of treating mental diseases. He was lecturer in mental diseases at St. Bartholomew's Hospital, consulting physician in mental diseases to the military forces, London and Aldershot commands, and Lord

Chancellor's Visitor in Lunacy. He served as temporary Lieut. Col. in the R.A.M.C. and was awarded the C.B.E. (Military division) in 1919. He was knighted in 1917. He assumed the additional surname of Armstrong in 1913. He was a J.P. and Dep. Lieut. of London and Caernarfonshire, and a member of the council and vice-president of the Hon. Soc. of Cymmrodorion. He m. in 1893, Margaret Elizabeth (d. May 1943), elder dau. of Sir Owen Roberts, London, and Plas Dinas, Caernarfon, and they had one s. (Ronald Owen Lloyd Armstrong-Jones whose son, Lord Snowdon, married Princess Margaret, sister of Queen Elizabeth II), and two dau. He d. 31 Jan. 1943.

Personal knowledge; *DNB*; *Www*.

E.M.H.

ASHBY, ARTHUR WILFRED (1886-1953), agricultural economist; b. 19 Aug. 1886, eldest son of Joseph and Hannah Ashby, Tysoe, Warwickshire. He was educated in the village school and after leaving at the age of twelve he helped his father (who appears to have been a very remarkable man and a local leader) until he was 23 years old, when he gained a scholarship at Ruskin College, Oxford, in 1909. He took a diploma (with distinction) in economics and political science. In 1912 following the award of a scholarship by the Board of Agriculture he went to the Institute for Research in Agricultural Economics at Oxford and then to the University of Wisconsin. There he studied the history of allotments and smallholdings and his book *Allotments and smallholdings in Oxfordshire* (1917) on this topic remains a standard work. He worked with the Board of Agriculture between 1917 and 1919, and during those years played a leading role in establishing the first Agricultural Wages Board. After a period on the staff of the Institute for Research in Agricultural Economics at Oxford, he went to Aberystwyth in 1924 as head of the new department of agricultural economics in the University College of Wales. He was made professor in 1929, the first chair in agricultural economics in Great Britain. He returned to Oxford as director of the Institute of Research in Agricultural Economics in 1946 and held the post until he retired in 1952.

Ashby was a prominent figure in a small group who pioneered agricultural economics as a separate area of study. During the years he spent at Aberystwyth he had an opportunity to reveal his talent in this field; he gave strong leadership both within the college and in agricultural circles outside. The education of young country people was important to him, and as a member of the committee which awarded scholarships to the sons and daughters of rural workers he had an opportunity to do his best for them over the years. With his practical experience of farm life and work he endeavoured as a member of the Agricultural Wages Board from 1924 onwards to maintain and deepen the good relationship between farmers and farm-workers. He also worked tirelessly to promote agricultural co-operation and supported the activities of the Welsh Agricultural Organisation Society. He played a great part behind the scenes in forming agricultural marketing schemes, including establishing the Milk Marketing Board, which more than any other initiative was responsible for bringing the agriculture of the lowlands of Wales (and the whole of the United Kingdom for that matter) out of poverty from 1933 onwards.

He contributed numerous articles on his subject to many journals, and his book (with Ifor L. Evans, 1897-1952; see below) in 1943, *The Agriculture of Wales and Monmouth*, is a mine of information on agricultural history for the period 1867 to 1939. He received an honorary degree of M.A. from the Univ. of Wales in 1923 and M.A. by decree in 1946 from the University of Oxford; he was elected a fellow of Lincoln College, Oxford in 1947. He was a justice of the peace, and was appointed a C.B.E. in 1946. In 1922 he m. Rhoda Dean Bland and they had one son. He d. 9 Sept. 1953, in Radcliffe Infirmary, Oxford.

DNB, 1951-60; Richard Phillips, *Pob un â'i gŵys* (1960); *Www, 1951-60*; personal knowledge.

Ll.P.

ATKIN, JAMES RICHARD, baron Atkin, life peer (1867-1944), judge; b. 28 Nov. 1867, in Brisbane, Australia, eldest s. of Robert Travers Atkin of Fernhill, co. Cork, a member of the Queensland senate. He was educated at Christ College, Brecon, and Magdalen College, Oxford, where he was made hon. Fellow in 1924. He was called to the Bar in Grays Inn, 1891, becoming a Bencher in 1906, and K.C. serving on the South Wales and Chester circuit, and building up a successful practice in common law and commercial actions; he was judge of the King's Bench division of the High Court with a knighthood in 1913, and a Lord Justice of Appeal in 1919. He served on many important bodies in connection with World War I (see *Who was Who*, 1941-50). He was chairman of the Irish Deportees Compensation Tribunal and of the Committee on Crime and Insanity, 1924; and president of the Medico-legal Society, 1923-27. He was a member of the councils of Christ College, Brecon and the University College of Wales, where he served as chairman of the Law department. He was also chairman of the Council of Legal Education.

Lawyers had a high opinion of his legal judgements, e.g. his judgement in the House of Lords in Liversidge *v.* Anderson defending subjects' rights in the face of official intervention, but his greatest service was his strong advocacy of making the teaching of law a part of the general scheme of education. To this end he delivered many lectures on law to schools. He favoured holding classes in universities to give education in law to lay students who did not intend to become lawyers, and with that in mind he wrote a Foreword to Edward Jenks, *Book of English Law* (1928), and was involved in its composition.

He was chairman of the group appointed by the Lord Chancellor to examine the position of legal education. He held that there was no reason why law should not have the same importance in general education as it had in the times of Fortescue, Locke and Blackstone. As a result of his efforts to extend legal education, the Legal Aid Act to give legal assistance to those who had not sufficient means was passed; it is to him that we owe the general sympathy which this movement received.

He was made a member of the Privy Council in 1919, and created baron in 1928; he was elected F.B.A. in 1938. He m. Lucy Elizabeth (died 1939), the eldest dau. of William Hemmant, Bulimba, Sevenoaks, formerly colonial treasurer, Queensland. Atkin lived for many years at Craig-y-don, Aberdyfi. He d. 25 June 1944.

Who's Who, 1943; personal knowledge.

T.A.L.

AWBERY, STANLEY STEPHEN (1888-1969), politician, local historian and author; b. 19 July 1888 at Swansea. He received most of his education at evening classes which he attended while he was employed at the port of Swansea. He spent 6 yrs. as secretary of the Swansea branch of the Dockers' Union before obtaining a full time post as trade union official in 1920 when he was appointed secretary of the Barry branch of the Transport and General Workers' Union. He became chairman of Swansea Labour Association in 1921 and chairman of Swansea General and Eye Hospital the following year. In 1928 he was elected president of the Welsh branch of the Independent Labour Party and served as president of Barry Trades Council.

He stood unsuccessfully as Labour candidate for the Clitheroe constituency in the general elections of 1931 and 1935. He was elected a member of Barry Borough Council in 1931, and became an alderman in 1939; he held his seat until he resigned in Nov. 1945, having served as mayor of Barry in 1941-42. He also served as Port Labour Inspector, South Wales Ports, during 1941-42. In March 1937 he was made a J.P. for Glamorganshire. He also became Deputy Sheriff for the county and in 1951 was elevated chairman of Glamorgan magistrates. In the 1945 general election he was elected M.P. (L.) for the Bristol Central constituency. He was re-elected with a large majority in 1950, 1951, 1955 and 1959, but decided to resign in 1964. He was a member of a parliamentary deputation to Malaya in 1948 and a member of the Select Committee on Estimates in 1950-51.

He was an enthusiastic prolific local historian and author of several important works including *Labour's early struggles in Swansea* (1949), *Let us talk of Barry* (1954), *Llancarfan: the village of a thousand saints* (1957), *The story of St. Athan and Aberthaw* (1959), *I searched for Llantwit Major* (1965), *St. Donat's Castle and the Stradlings* (1966), *The Baptists in Barry for 150 years* (1967), and *Fourteen talks about Barry* (1968). He also published many articles on aspects of local history.

He m. in 1911, and he and his wife Elizabeth Jane had two sons and three daughters. His wife d. in Apr. 1969 and he d. 7 May 1969.

Www; Dod's Parliamentary Companion; WWP; OPCS 1911.

J.G.J.

B

BANCROFT, WILLIAM JOHN (1871-1959), rugby player and cricketer; b. 2 Mar. 1871, son of William Bancroft, Carmarthen Arms, Waterloo Street, Swansea, the eldest of 11 children. He plied his craft as a shoemaker. He was born in Carmarthen but was brought up in the shadow of Saint Helen's sports ground, Swansea. He played for the local youth team, the Excelsiors, before playing his first game for Swansea on 5 Oct. 1889. After only 17 games, and without a trial, he was chosen to play for Wales against Scotland in Feb. 1890 after the first choice, Tom England of Newport, was injured. Bancroft proceeded to gain 33 caps in consecutive matches between 1890 and 1901, a record which was not broken until 1954, by Ken Jones (Newport). He was an incomparable back with the keen eyes and sure hands of a professional cricketer; he spent long hours perfecting his kick, and it was his penalty drop-kick which won the match against England in 1893, when Wales gained the triple crown for the first time ever. He led Wales to its second crown in 1900. He was one of the first to be employed as a professional player by Glamorgan Cricket Club (founded in 1888) in 1895 at £2 per week. He d. 3 Mar. 1959 at Swansea.

His brother, JACK BANCROFT (1879-1942), was a notable back for Swansea and Wales, winning 13 caps between 1908 and 1912.

J.B.G.Thomas, *Great rugger players* (1959); David Smith and Gareth Williams, *Fields of Praise* (1980); J.H. Morgan, *Glamorgan County Cricket* (1952); *S. Wales Evening Post* and *S. Wales Echo*, 4 Mar. 1959.

G.W.W.

BANKES, Sir JOHN ELDON (1854-1946), judge; b. at Northop, Fl., 17 Apr. 1854, s. of John Scott Bankes of Soughton Hall, a great-grandson of John Scott (Lord Chancellor Eldon); he was also a lineal descendant of John Wynne (*DWB*, 1106-7), bishop of St. Asaph, whose dau. Margaret m. Henry Bankes, and whose Soughton estate thus became the seat of the Bankes family. J.E. Bankes went to Eton and Christ Church (he rowed for Oxford), was called to the Bar in 1878, and took silk in 1901. In 1910 he became a judge of the High Court, and in 1915 a Lord Justice of Appeal and a Privy Councillor; he retired in 1927. Both before and after his retirement he devoted himself to public work; in Flintshire he was for 33 years chairman of the Quarter Sessions and an active member of the County Council, of which he was chairman in 1933; outside it, he was placed on numerous commissions or committees of inquiry – he was, for instance, chairman of the Departmental Committee on Education in Rural Wales, 1928. Politically, he was a Conservative, and had unsuccessfully contested Flint Boroughs in 1906. In religious matters, he was a prominent Anglican, interested especially in the problem of religious instruction in the schools. With Lord Sankey (see John Sankey, 1866-1948 below) he drafted the new constitution of the Church in Wales. He was honorary LL.D. (1921) of the University of Wales. He d. 31 Dec. 1946.

He had m. in 1882 Edith Ethelston (d. 1931), and they had two sons and two daughters.

Who's Who; and obituary notices in the press.

R.T.J.

BARSTOW, Sir GEORGE LEWIS, (1874-1966), civil servant, president of University College Swansea; b. 20 May 1874 in India, the son of Henry Clements Barstow, a civil servant, and Cecilia Clementina Baillie. The Barstows were long-established and prominent merchants in York. Following his marriage to the only daughter of Sir Alfred Tristram Lawrence, 1st Baron Trevethin, George Barstow established a home near Builth and a connection with Wales. Barstow graduated from Emmanuel College, Cambridge, in 1895-96 with first class in both parts of the classical tripos and then entered the civil service. In 1898, he joined the Treasury where he was involved, before World War I, in the conversion of the Navy from coal to oil fuel. During the war and up to 1927, Barstow was responsible within the Treasury for supply. In 1927, he was appointed the government director of the Anglo-Persian Oil Company. He was also a director of the Midland Bank and Chairman of the Prudential Assurance Company. In Wales, Barstow took a special interest in the Church in Wales and in higher education. He was principally responsible for reorganising the finances of the recently founded Church in Wales and for addressing its financial administration. He was a governor of Christ College Brecon and President of University College Swansea from 1929 to 1955. Appointed C.B. in 1913, Barstow was knighted in 1920. The University of Wales awarded him an honorary LL.D. in 1937.

In 1904, Barstow m. Enid Lilian Lawrence and they had two sons and a daughter. He d. at his home, Chapel House, Builth, on 29 Jan. 1966.

Www; WwW (1921) and (1937); *DNB*, 1961-70.

E.D.J.

BEBB, WILLIAM AMBROSE (1894-1955), historian, prose writer and politician; b. 4 July 1894 at Blaendyffryn, Goginan, Cards., s. of Edward and Ann Bebb. The family moved to Camer Fawr, near Tregaron, and Bebb attended Tregaron grammar school. He graduated in Welsh and History from U.C.W., Aberystwyth in 1918, and spent two years working for his M.A. In 1920 he went to Rennes University, but not finding there the facilities he had expected, he left after a few weeks for Paris, where he attended the lectures of Prof. Joseph Loth at the *Collège de France* and acted as Assistant in Welsh to Joseph Vendryes. He worked in Paris until 1925, when he was appointed tutor at the Normal College, Bangor, where he remained for the rest of his life, teaching Welsh, History and Scripture Knowledge at various times.

Ambrose Bebb published six books on the history of Wales from the earliest period till the sixteenth century. One of them, *Hil a hwyl y castell* (1946) was a course of lessons delivered on the radio in 1936. The other five form a sequence, though the dates of publication do not follow in chronological order. The first was *Ein hen hen hanes* (1932), the story of Wales from the earliest times till the fall of Llywelyn ap Gruffudd told in simple language for young children. The second was *Llywodraeth y cestyll* (1934), bringing the story down to the end of the fifteenth century. Then came *Machlud yr Oesoedd Canol* (1950), *Cyfnod y Tuduriaid* (1939) and *Machlud y mynachlogydd* (1937). These historical works are noteworthy for two reasons. First of all, the author made use of Welsh literary sources, as well as the more usual historical sources such as state papers, to understand and to elucidate the history of Wales, quoting extensively from published and unpublished collections of the works of the poets of the gentry. Secondly, these books are imbued with a patriotic fervour which ensures that a historical work by Bebb is not only a factual account of a period or of the men of note at the time, but also an attempt to arouse in the reader the enthusiasm felt by the author.

In three books which deal with the Welsh countryside when emigration to America was common the historian gave rein to his imagination. *Y Baradwys Bell* (1941) is an imaginary diary for the year 1841 kept by one of the author's ancestors, and *Gadael tir* (1948) is the story of the same man, again in diary form, until his departure for America in 1847. In both books use is made of letters sent from America and kept in the family; *Dial y tir* (1945) is a novel which tells how a number of men and women from Montgomeryshire, again including members of the author's family, emigrated to America at the end of the eighteenth and the beginning of the nineteenth centuries and how they fared there. In these three books there is a large element of historical fact.

Bebb had for many years kept a personal diary, and he was consequently well placed to comment on current events. Such comments are found in *1940, Lloffion o ddyddiadur* (1941) and *Dyddlyfr 1941* (1942). Similarly in *Calendr coch* (1946) he gives an account of his campaign as a *Plaid Cymru* candidate in the parliamentary election in 1945. These books are interesting because they present the author's immediate reaction to the events recorded without any of the distortions which lapse of time might cause.

Ever since his brief visit to Rennes in 1920 and his stay in Paris Bebb had been deeply interested in Brittany. He visited the country regularly and travelled extensively within it, so that he knew its topography thoroughly. He learnt the language, and he had some very good friends among the Bretons. He contributed extensively to *Breiz Atao*, the journal of the Breton nationalists. Through all this he not only gained a thorough knowledge of Brittany, its history, its customs and its religion, but also came to admire the Breton way of life and to sympathise with the aims of those who strove to preserve the country's culture. This led to the publication of three books: *Llydaw* (1929), *Pererindodau* (1941) and *Dydd-lyfr pythefnos, neu y ddawns angau* (1939), an account of his travels in Brittany during the last fortnight before the outbreak of World War II.

Though he thoroughly disapproved of the hostile attitude of France towards Brittany and its language, Bebb was a great admirer of France and its notable contribution to world culture. He had a wide knowledge of the country's history and its literature. This is evident in *Crwydro'r cyfandir* (1936), an account of a journey through France, Italy and Switzerland. During his stay in Paris he came to know Leon Daudet and Charles Maurras and other leaders of the reactionary and royalist movement known as *L'Action Française*, and they had a profound influence on his thinking. He read the movement's journal regularly on his visits to France.

One reason for Bebb's devotion to Brittany was that since his youth he had been an ardent nationalist. As a student at Aberystwyth he had edited *Y Wawr*, a student publication which had dared, during World War I, to champion the cause of conscientious objectors and to express approval of the 1916 Easter Week rising in Ireland, with the result that the College authorities had banned it. When he worked in Paris, Bebb used to send articles for publication in Welsh periodicals such as *Y Geninen*, *Y Llenor*, *Y Faner*, *Cymru* and *Y Tyst*. In these he discussed the future of the Welsh language, and as early as 1923 he argued the case for Welsh self-government. These articles played a significant part in creating an atmosphere conducive to the establishment of an independent Welsh political party. In Jan. 1924 he and G.J. Williams (1892-1963, see below) and Saunders Lewis met at Penarth, and decided to start a Welsh political movement. In Aug. 1925 a small group of ardent Welshmen met at Pwllheli, and established the Welsh Nationalist Party. The two movements were fused, and in June 1926 *Y Ddraig Goch* (the Party's monthly newspaper) was launched, the first page of the first number carrying an article by Bebb. He was the editor of the first few numbers, and remained a member of the editorial board till the outbreak of war.

During these fifteen years Bebb applied himself unsparingly to many kinds of activity on behalf of the Nationalist Party (as it was then called). He was president of the University College, Bangor, branch and of the Caernarfonshire Committee. As the party's candidate he won a seat on the Bangor Borough Council in 1939. He addressed innumerable meetings, and contributed to the press regularly on the principles of nationalism. He soon came to be regarded as one of the leaders of the movement.

But with the outbreak of war in 1939 he severed his connection with the other leaders. They maintained that Wales, lacking self-government, had had no opportunity to define its attitude to war, and that therefore a neutral position was indicated. It was Bebb's view, however, that the fate of France, which had so generously contributed to the culture of mankind and which he so dearly loved, was too important to be left to the mercy of German materialism and militarism. For some years he took no part in Welsh politics. In 1945, however, after considerable persuasion, he agreed to stand as the Nationalist Party's candidate in the general election held in July of that year.

Bebb had always been deeply religious. He thought very highly of the Welsh Sunday school, and published *Yr Ysgol Sul* in 1944. In his later years his concern for Wales had shifted from considerations of language and culture to anxiety about its spiritual condition. Hope lay for men and for nations not in political parties, but in the ideals advocated by the Christian Church. He expressed this standpoint in a series of articles in *Yr Herald Cymraeg* in 1953. (They were posthumously republished in book form, *Yr Argyfwng*, 1955). The same belief is forcibly expressed in the volume which he wrote to celebrate the centenary of his chapel in Bangor, *Canrif o hanes y Tŵr Gwyn* (1954). But this change of standpoint brought no change in the enthusiasm, conviction and sincerity which had always been a prominent feature of his character. As a prose writer Bebb had some marked characteristics. He liberally used words from his own dialect, and was fond of collocations and alliteration, thus creating an impression of energy and exuberance, all springing from the pleasure of writing or from a desire to convey a message, whether that be a description of a rural scene or the expression of some important principle which he wished to impress upon the reader's mind.

Bebb translated two works from French: *Geiriau credadun* (1923), Lamennais's *Paroles d'un croyant*, and *Mudandod y môr* (1944), *Le Silence de la mer*, by 'Vercors', a story of occupied France during World War II.

He m. Eluned Pierce Roberts of Llangadfan, Monts., in 1931, and they had seven children. He d. suddenly 27 Apr. 1955, and was buried in Glanadda cemetery, Bangor.

Leonard Clark, *Anglo-Welsh Review*, 17/40, 25; Saunders Lewis, *Gallica: essays presented to J. Heywood Thomas* (Cardiff, 1969); A.O.H. Jarman, *Genh.*, 6, 87; T.H. Lewis, *Genh.*, 21, 65-9; information given by his widow; [Gareth Miles in D. Llwyd Morgan, *Adnabod deg* (1977); Rhidian Griffiths, *Llyfryddiaeth Ambrose Bebb* (1982); Robin Chapman, *Ambrose Bebb* (1997)].

T.P.

BELL, ERNEST DAVID (1915-1959), artist and poet; b. 4 June 1915, s. of Sir (Harold) Idris Bell 1879-1967; see below) and Mabel Winifred (née Ayling). He received his education at a private school at Crouch End, London, and Merchant Taylors' School, where he was taught the classics and was given some instruction in art. He spent four years at the Royal College of Art, and gained the diploma. He joined the Egypt Exploration Society's expedition to the Sudan, and worked at Sesebi and Amarah in 1936-37 and 1937-38. After the outbreak of war in 1939 he spent some months at Llanfairfechan, Caerns., and then found employment with the cartographical section of the Admiralty, first at Bath and then at the National Library of Wales at Aberystwyth. He returned to London with the section, and remained there till the end of the war. In 1946 he was appointed Assistant Director (Art) under the Welsh Committee of the Arts Council, and in 1951 he became Curator of the Glynn Vivian Art Gallery, Swansea.

David Bell collaborated with his father on the translation of some of Dafydd ap Gwilym's poems which appeared in 1942 under the title *Dafydd ap Gwilym: fifty poems* as vol. 48 of *Y Cymmrodor*. He was the author of 24 translations. He provided the English words for *Wyth*

gân werin (Enid Parry) which appeared in 1947. In 1953 he published *The Language of Pictures*, a book (to quote the preface) 'not intended to increase anyone's knowledge of the world's masterpieces or of contemporary pictures ... but rather to enrich the experience of people, when confronted by a picture, with some understanding of what the painter is trying to say and how he says it.' He published *The Artist in Wales* (1957), an attempt to awaken a response to art in Wales. In 1959 his father published 17 original poems by David Bell written between 1938 and 1954, in a private edition of 65 copies, under the title *Nubian Madonna and other poems*.

He m. Megan Hinton Jones of Aberystwyth in 1944, and they had two sons. When he was 14 years of age David Bell contracted *encephalitis lethargica*, which left him slightly incapacitated throughout his life. He. d. 21 Apr. 1959.

There are some biographical details in the preface to *Nubian Madonna*; information supplied by his widow.
T.P.

BELL, Sir HAROLD IDRIS (1879-1967), scholar and translator; b. 2 Oct. 1879 at Epworth, Lincs., son of Charles Christopher Bell and Rachel (née Hughes). His maternal grandfather, John Hughes of Rhuddlan, was a Welsh speaker. Bell received his early education at Nottingham High School. In 1897 he won a scholarship to Oriel College, Oxford, and graduated in Classics. He spent a year at the Universities of Berlin and Halle studing Hellenistic history. In 1903 he was appointed an Assistant in the Department of Manuscripts at the British Museum. He was promoted Deputy Keeper in 1927, and Keeper in 1929, the post in which he remained until his retirement in 1944. In 1946 he went to live at Aberystwyth, naming his house Bro Gynin, a sign of his respect for the poet Dafydd ap Gwilym.

As a scholar Bell's special interest was in papyrology, the subject of two articles as early as 1907. At the same time he was also assisting in the preparation of catalogues of material in the British Museum; the fourth volume of the catalogue (1917) and the fifth (1924) were entirely his own responsibility. He thus acquired an extensive knowledge of the history of Egypt, and articles and bibliographies by him appeared regularly in learned journals, especially the *Journal of Egyptian Archaeology*. He also contributed to the *Cambridge Ancient History*. In 1935 he was appointed Honorary Reader in Document Papyrology in Oxford, a position he held till 1950. His standing as a scholar was now very high, and his knowledge of all kinds of documents – legal, social or literary – was unsurpassed. He was president of the International Association of Papyrologists from 1947 to 1955. He was elected corresponding member of several Continental and American learned societies, and was awarded honorary degrees by the Universities of Wales, Liverpool, Michigan and Brussels. In 1932 the British Academy elected him a Fellow, and he was President from 1946 to 1950. He was appointed O.B.E. in 1920 and C.B. in 1936, and knighted in 1946.

It was probably his awareness of his Welsh descent and his father's interest that prompted

Bell to take an interest in the Welsh language, which he began to learn when he was twenty-six years of age. The first result was a scholarly work, *Vita Sancti Tathei and Buched Seint y Katrin*, comprising a Latin text of the life of Tathan with an English translation, and a Welsh life of Katherine, with an introduction. The volume appeared in 1909 under the auspices of the Bangor Welsh Manuscripts Society. But it was not as a scholar that he chose to serve Wales. He always maintained that he was not a Welsh scholar, his aim being to provide the means for those who did not understand Welsh to be informed of the contents and quality of Welsh literature, especially Welsh poetry. His first effort in this direction was a volume of translations, *Poems from the Welsh* (1913), a joint production with his father, C.C. Bell. In 1925 father and son collaborated on another volume, *Welsh Poems of the Twentieth Century in English Verse*, with an introductory essay of 57 pages giving a summary of the history of Welsh poetry from the earliest times to the 1920s. Bell expanded this essay into a book of 192 pages and published it under the title *The Development of Welsh Poetry* in 1936.

Almost all the translations in these two volumes were from originals which were in the free metres, and the metrical pattern of the originals had been adhered to. In *The Development of Welsh Poetry* most of the examples cited had been rendered into English prose. The next step was to attempt to translate poems in the strict metres, and the result was *Dafydd ap Gwilym: fifty poems*, which appeared as volume 48 of *Y Cymmrodor* in 1942. Of these 26 are by Bell, and 24 by his son David (see above). The metre employed consists of lines of four stressed syllables rhyming in couplets, with variations in the number of unstressed syllables – a much more exacting pattern than that adopted by later translators. The style is 'poetic', often incorporating archaic expressions, which were justified by the occasional archaisms of the originals. The volume contains an introductory essay on the life and work of Dafydd ap Gwilym.

Bell's translation of *Hanes Llenyddiaeth Gymraeg hyd 1900* by Thomas Parry, was another aspect of his attempt to bring Welsh literature to the notice of people not conversant with the language. He added some explanatory notes and an appendix of 120 pages dealing with twentieth-century literature. It was published in 1955 under the title *A History of Welsh Literature*.

In 1926 Bell had visited Egypt to collect papyri for the British Museum. His account of the journey was translated into Welsh by D. Tecwyn Lloyd and published in two volumes entitled *Trwy Diroedd y Dwyrain* (1946). He also wrote two books for children – *Dewi a'r Blodyn Llo Mawr* (1928) and *Calon y Dywysoges* (1929), translated by Olwen Roberts, the wife of J. E. Jones (see below). In 1954 he published *The Crisis of our Time and other papers*, consisting of essays on the state of society, Welsh nationalism, the attitude of the Church in Wales towards Welsh culture, and his own religious experience as a convert from agnosticism to the Christian faith.

Bell was a man of great charm and courtesy, who retained his natural modesty in spite of his high status as a scholar and the honours bestowed upon him. His love of Wales was deep and sincere, and nothing gave him more pleasure than to have been awarded the medal of the Honourable Society of Cymmrodorion in 1946, and to have served as the Society's President, 1947-53. He d. 22 Jan. 1967.

He married Mabel Winifred Ayling in 1911. She d. a week before him. They had three sons.

Www; C.H. Roberts, *Proceedings of the British Academy*, 53 (1967). A list of Bell's works appeared in the *Journal of Egyptian Archaeology*, 1954, 1967.

T.P.

BELLEROCHE, ALBERT de (1864-1944), painter and lithographer; b. 1864 at Swansea and brought up by his stepfather, W.H.V. Millbank. Sir Frank Brangwyn (see below), his friend and staunch admirer of his work, bought for Brussels Museum the artist's 'The Fortune Teller'. Belleroche presented to the National Museum of Wales a collection of his works, including a full-length portrait of his mother. He devised a method of detecting forged watermarks in 1915. He d. 14 July 1944, at Rustington, Sussex. He and his wife Emilie Julie Visseaux had 2 sons and a daughter.

South Wales Echo and Express, 17 Aug. 1944; *Www*.

T.M.R.

BELLIS, MARY EDITH – see NEPEAN, MARY EDITH below.

BERRY (FAMILY), Lords Buckland, Camrose and Kemsley, industrialists and newspaper proprietors.

All three sons of JOHN MATHIAS BERRY (b. 2 May 1847 in Camrose, Pemb.; d. 9 Jan. 1917) and his wife Mary Ann (née Rowe, of Pembroke Dock), who moved to Merthyr Tydfil in 1874, were created peers. J.M. Berry worked on the railway and as an accountant before becoming an estate agent and auctioneer in 1894. He was the mayor when King George V visited the town in 1912. The foundation stone of a new Salvation Army Citadel in Merthyr was laid in memory of him in 1936 and he is also commemorated by the J.M. Berry Technical College which was built by his eldest son.

HENRY SEYMOUR BERRY, 1st Baron BUCKLAND (1877-1928) industrialist; their eldest son, b. 17 Sept. 1877 in Gwaelod-y-garth, Merthyr Tydfil. In 1892 he was a monitor at Abermorlais Boys' School and passed his examination to become a pupil teacher. Four years later he was a certificated assistant teacher there but left on 1 Sept. 1897 to work with his father. In 1915 he was asked to assist D.A.Thomas (Lord Rhondda; see *DWB*, 942-3) manage his estate, with the result that when the latter joined the cabinet in 1916 his numerous industrial companies were entrusted to the care of H.S. Berry. This proved to be a turning point in Berry's life. Within three years he became director of no fewer than 66 companies. These were mostly coalmines and shipping companies, including John Lysaght, Ltd. makers of galvanised sheets, with steelworks, rolling mills and colliery interests, which he had recently acquired in conjunction with his brother William Ewert Berry, D.R. Llewellyn (see Supplement below) and Viscountess Rhondda

(THOMAS, Margaret Haig, see below). This was the biggest industrial transaction in the history of Wales, involving five million pounds. He was chairman of the company until it became part of Guest, Keen and Nettlefold in 1920, of which he became chairman in 1927. He did much to reorganize GKN and introduced various management committees, but he was not a widely popular man, being resolutely opposed to trade unions, though he did not take part in the public statements of coalowners. His chief contact with the newspaper industry was as director of the *Western Mail* 1920-27. He m., 5 Sept. 1907, Gwladys Mary, eldest daughter of Simon Sandbrook of Merthyr Tydfil and they had five daughters. In 1922 he bought Buckland, Bwlch, Breck. and went there to live, subsequently becoming a J.P. for that county as well as for the borough of Merthyr Tydfil. He was a generous benefactor to his native town, to which he gave public swimming baths, a new wing to the hospital and many smaller gifts to assist underpaid pastors, ex-service men and other poor inhabitants of the borough. In 1926 he and his brothers granted Merthyr hospital £750 per annum for 7 years. He was also a benefactor of Brecon Memorial College, the university college at Cardiff, and the National Museum of Wales to which he was appointed a member of the Court of Governors shortly before his death. In 1923 he was granted the freedom of the borough of Merthyr Tydfil, and was created first Baron Buckland of Bwlch in 1926. He d. 23 May 1928 after a fall from a horse.

WILLIAM EWERT BERRY, 1st Viscount CAMROSE (1879-1954), newspaper proprietor and editor; the second son, b. 23 June 1879. When he was 14 years old he commenced five years' apprenticeship as a journalist on *The Merthyr Tydfil Times* and other south Wales newspapers before going to London to work as a reporter. He was unemployed for three months and never forgot this chastening experience when dealing with his staff in later years. In 1901, with a loan of £100 from his elder brother, he started an entirely new periodical, *Advertising World*. He then asked his younger brother, JAMES GOMER BERRY, to come to assist him with the second issue, thus starting a partnership which lasted over 35 years. Four years later the periodical was sold to enable them to set up a small publishing company, Ewart, Seymour and Co., Ltd.; they also acquired their first newspaper, *The Sunday Times*, which was losing money at the time. W.E.Berry was its editor-in-chief, 1915-36. In 1924, with Sir E.M. (later Lord) Iliffe they founded Allied Newspapers. The next big purchase was the Amalgamated Press in 1926, which included a large number of non-political periodicals, a book section, two printing works and the Imperial Paper Mills. The following year they bought Edward Lloyd, Ltd., one of the largest paper mills in the world, and also their first 'heavy' London daily newspaper, *Daily Telegraph*, with W.E. Berry becoming editor-in-chief. They now controlled 25 newspapers, and about 70 periodicals. Competition was fierce in the 1930s but instead of trying to attract readers with gifts, as other newspapers did, they decided to change the format of the *Daily Telegraph*, to maintain the quality of their news coverage, and to halve the price from 2d.

to a penny; the circulation doubled immediately to 200,000 and grew to well over a million copies by 1949. In 1937 the three partners decided to go their separate ways, the *Daily Telegraph, Financial Times* and the Amalgamated Press being taken by Lord Camrose. He was a distinguished-looking person, accessible, good-tempered and a gifted speaker. He maintained contact with his home town and in conjunction with his brothers rescued some local coal mines from closure, to their own loss. In 1936 he and his younger brother, then Lord KEMSLEY, presented a new clock tower to Merthyr parish church. He was director of several companies in south Wales and became a governor of Christ College, Brecon in 1929. He was the author of *London newspapers: their owners and controllers* (1939) and *British newspapers and their controllers* (1947). In 1905 he m. Mary Agnes, elder daughter of Thomas Corns, and they had four daughters, and four sons who also became directors of parts of the family business. In 1921 he was created baronet, first Baron Camrose of Long Cross, Virginia Water in 1929 and elevated first Viscount Camrose of Hackwood Park, Basingstoke in 1941. He d. 15 June 1954 in Southampton; a tablet has been placed in the crypt of St. Paul's Cathedral in memory of him.

JAMES GOMER BERRY, 1st Viscount KEMSLEY (1883-1968), newspaper proprietor; the youngest son, b. 7 May 1883. He was educated at Abermorlais school and was one of the first pupils to enter Merthyr Tydfil county intermediate grammar school. At his brother William's request he went to London when he was 18 years old to assist with *Advertising World* and his career for the next 36 years was closely connected with that of his brother, he too becoming director and chairman of many companies. When they divided the business, Lord Kemsley became chairman of Allied Newspapers, (renamed Kemsley Newspapers in 1943). The group owned 26 papers, the holding being maintained at much the same size over 22 years, making him the largest newspaper owner in the United Kingdom. From the start Lord Kemsley concentrated his energies on the *Sunday Times*, and once he was in sole command he became editor-in-chief and the circulation trebled. In 1947-49 he gave robust evidence before the royal commission on the press. He started the Kemsley editorial plan to train journalists and wrote the introduction to *The Kemsley manual of journalism* (1947). In 1959 he sold all his holdings in Kemsley Newspapers to Roy Thomson and went to live in Monte Carlo. As already mentioned, he too maintained connection with his native town. He succeeded his eldest brother as president of Merthyr General Hospital 1928-49, and received the freedom of Merthyr Tydfil in 1955; he was president of the Football Association of Wales 1946-60, and of the university college at Cardiff 1945-50. Among the many honours he received were hon. LL.D. degrees from the Universities of Wales and Manchester. He m. (1), 4 July 1907, Mary Lilian (d. 1 Feb 1928) daughter of Horace George Holmes, Brondesbury Park, London, by whom he had six sons and a daughter. He m. (2), 20 Apr. 1931, Edith, formerly wife of C.W. Dresselhuys. He was created Baronet in 1928, a week before his first wife died, first Baron Kemsley of Farnham

Royal in 1936, first Viscount Kemsley of Dropmore in 1945, and G.B.E. in 1959. He d. in Monte Carlo, 6 Feb. 1968.

Www, 1916-28; WwW (1921); West. Mail, 24 May 1928; David J. Jeremy, Dictionary of business biography (1984); DNB, 1951-60, 1961-70; Burke (105th ed.); WWP; Abermorlais Boys' School log book, 1886-1901, in Glam. Record Office, reference E/MT.

M.A.J.

BERRY, ROBERT GRIFFITH (1869-1945), minister (Congl.) and writer; b. 20 May 1869 in Llanrwst, Caern. s. of John and Margaret (née Williams) Berry, the father originally from Penmachno and the mother from Llannerch-y-medd. He received his education in the local British, national, and grammar schools. He was received into membership of Tabernacl (Congl.) church under the pastorate of Thomas Roberts (DWB, 881-2). He proceeded with a scholarship to Bangor university college, where he took the first part of the B.A. degree course of London University, and, in 1892, he entered Bala-Bangor Theological College. He contributed to the college magazine (of which he was the first editor) light and witty sketches of students and events. His only pastorate was at Bethlehem, Gwaelod-y-garth, Glam., to which he was invited 3 Aug. 1896. He m. 10 Aug. 1903, Hannah M. Watkins of Gwaelod-y-garth. They had one dau.

In 1911 R.G. Berry, as he came to be known, became prominent as one of the pioneers of the drama in Welsh. Amongst his plays are Asgre lân, Owen Gwynedd, Ar y groesffordd, and Y Ddraenen wen: shorter plays are Noson o farrug, Cadw noswyl, Dwywaith yn blentyn, and Yr Hen anian. He mastered the art of setting his plays, the techniques of live dialogue, and soon learnt what was required in the portrayal of characters. His plays which were based on the familiar everyday life of Wales, achieved great popularity and were acted in all parts of the country. He was particularly successful in writing in a style which became popular but in which genuine Welsh idiom was not travestied. He also wrote, from time to time, satirical essays and parodies which are marked by their lively criticism and astuteness. His collection of short stories, Llawr Dyrnu, contains memorable sketches of local characters. For his services to the literature of Wales he was awarded the degree of M.A. (honoris causa) by the University of Wales in 1925. He was chairman of the Glamorgan Congregational Union in 1943 and in 1944 he delivered at Newcastle Emlyn a memorable address – 'Arglwyddiaeth Crist' – from the chair of the Welsh Congregational Union. He d. 13 Jan. and was buried at Pen-tyrch cemetery, 16 Jan. 1945.

Tyst, 10 May 1944 and 25 Jan. 1945; Cymro, 19 Jan. 1945; Dysgedydd, Mawrth 1945; N.L.W. MS. 15508D.

J.D.O.

BEVAN, ANEURIN (1897-1960), politician and one of the founders of the Welfare State; b. 15 Nov. 1897 at 32 Charles Street, Tredegar, Mon., the sixth of the ten children of David Bevan and Phoebe, the dau. of John Prothero, a local blacksmith. David Bevan was a coal miner and a Baptist, he was fond of books and music and he exercised much influence on his son. Aneurin Bevan went to Sirhowy elementary school which he disliked intensely, and he left in 1910. Nevertheless, he borrowed books from the local Workmen's Library and read extensively on economics, philosophy and politics. He began to work underground in 1911, proved himself a skilled collier and developed an interest in the activities of the trades unions. An eye disease prevented him from enlisting for military service during World War I, and he achieved local renown as an opponent of the war. In 1916 he was elected chairman of the local lodge of the Miners' Union.

The award of a scholarship from the Miners' Union in 1919 enabled Bevan to spend the next two years at the Central Labour College in London where he broadened his horizons and became an effective debater. He returned to Tredegar in 1921 to face a period of unemployment. He was elected a member of the Tredegar Town Council in 1922, and secured a post as a checkweigher at a coal mine for several months before again re-joining the ranks of the unemployed. During the 1926 miners' strike Bevan was chosen as its agent by his trade union branch, and he proved himself a skilled organiser who spoke regularly at national conferences. He was elected a member of the Monmouthshire County Council in 1928, and in the following year he succeeded Evan Davies as the Labour M.P. for the Ebbw Vale division. He continued to represent this constituency in Parliament until his death.

Aneurin Bevan quickly proved himself an effective debater in the House of Commons, one who spoke regularly, especially on unemployment and matters relating to the coal industry. During the 1930s he launched particularly pungent assaults on Neville Chamberlain. Early in 1939 he was expelled from the Labour Party because of his support for Sir Stafford Cripps and the United Front movement, but was reinstated in December of the same year. He opposed the government throughout World War II, and was sharply critical of Sir Winston Churchill, the Prime Minister, and Ernest Bevin. In December 1944 he was elected for the first time to the Labour Party's National Executive Committee.

As Minister of Health in the 1945 Labour Government Bevan laid the foundations of the Welfare State. Every member of the National Insurance scheme was given free medical and dental care by the 1946 National Health Service Act. The hospitals were nationalised and regional boards set up to administer them. National taxation was to be used to finance the service. In his battle with the doctors which continued until 1948 Bevan proved himself especially patient and ready to compromise. The 1948 Local Government Act gave new responsibilities to the local authorities, notably to care for children and young people. The 1948 National Assistance Act swept away the old Poor Law and introduced comprehensive schemes for welfare services. In addition, Bevan, also serving as Minister of Housing, took steps to repair much of the damage caused to housing during the war, to provide prefabricated housing and to grant subsidies to local authorities to enable them to offer homes available for rent. He was critical of the government's expenditure on armaments and of its policies towards the U.S.A. and Russia.

Aneurin Bevan was appointed Minister of Labour in January 1951, but he resigned in April of the same year because of a disagreement with Hugh Giatskell over the intention to start levying charges in the health service. He assembled around him a number of M.P.'s who stood to the left in the political spectrum and who became known as 'Bevanites'. He remained popular amongst the electorate and the membership of the Constituency Labour Parties in the country, and he was still a member of the Shadow Cabinet. He was again ousted from the Labour Party for several months during 1955 following his challenge to Clement Attlee because of his attitude towards nuclear weapons. When Attlee resigned from the party leadership during the same year, Bevan stood for the vacant position, but was defeated by Hugh Gaitskell. He was elected party treasurer in October 1956, and he became Opposition Spokesman on colonial affairs and foreign policy. In 1959 he accompanied Gaitskell to Moscow, and in October of the same year he was elected deputy leader of the Labour Party as successor to James Griffiths. By this time his speeches in the Commons and his attitude in general were much less abrasive. Bevan published a large number of pamphlets and articles, especially in *Tribune*, and his book *In place of fear* which gave expression to his belief in Democratic Socialism appeared in 1952.

He m. in 1934 Jennie Lee who was Labour M.P. for North Lanark, 1929-32, and Cannock, 1945-70, and who stood firmly to the left within the Labour Party. There were no children. He d. 6 July 1960 at his home Asheridge Farm, Chesham, Buckinghamshire, and his remains were cremated at Croesyceiliog crematorium.

Www; DNB; Times, 7 July 1960; A. Bevan, *In place of fear* (1952); Vincent Brome, *Aneurin Bevan* (1953); John Campbell, *Nye Bevan and the mirage of British Socialism* (1987); Huw T. Edwards in *Aneurin*, I, no. I (1961); Michael Foot, *Aneurin Bevan*, 2 vols. (1962 and 1973); Mark M. Krug, *Aneurin Bevan: cautious rebel* (1961); Jennie Lee, *This great journey* (1963) and *My life with Nye* (1980); David Llewellyn, *Nye: the beloved patrician* (n.d.); Kenneth O. Morgan, *Labour people: leaders and lieutenants, Hardie to Kinnock* (1987); Patricia Hollis, *Jennie Lee: a life* (1998); [Dai Smith, *Aneurin Bevan and the world of south Wales* (1993)].

J.G.J.

BEYNON, ROBERT (1881-1953), minister (Presb.), poet and essayist; b. 8 Oct. 1881 in The Office, Pontyberem, Carms., son of Thomas and Anne Beynon. He began preaching in Soar chapel, and was educated for the ministry in Watcyn Wyn's school (Watkin Hezekiah Williams, *DWB*, 1076) in Ammanford; Pontypridd school; University College, Cardiff (where he graduated B.A.); and the Theological College, Aberystwyth. He was ord. in 1911, and was pastor of Carmel church, Aber-craf, in the upper reaches of the Swansea valley, all his life (1910-53). He m. Sarah Rebeca Thomas of Trehopcyn, near Pontypridd, and they had two daughters (one adopted).

As one of Watcyn Wyn's 'boys' he became interested in poetry writing, and one of his chaired poems 'Tyred, Canlyn Fi' was published in 1912. He won the crown at the national eisteddfod in Ammanford in 1922 for his *prydd-est*, 'Tannau Coll'. Some of his children's hymns were included in *Llyfr Emynau a Thonau'r Plant* (1947). His essays, which were published in 1931 under the title *Dydd Calan ac ysgrifau eraill* (2nd. ed. 1950), show considerable literary skill; and his genius as an essayist became evident again when he was editor of *Y Drysorfa* (1939-43). His selections from the Book of Psalms (1936) also revealed his artistry as a polished writer. He and Rhys Davies (one of the elders of the church) were co-authors of a history of Carmel (1921).

He was a very popular preacher throughout Wales, and the congregations doted upon the beauty of his turn of phrase and his terse, brilliant sayings. No doubt it was because of this that he was chosen to deliver the (unpublished) Davies Lecture on '*Y ffordd dra rhagorol*' in 1948. He was elected Moderator of the General Assembly (1952), but d. during his year of office. He d. 12 Feb. 1953, and was buried in Carmel graveyard, Aber-craf.

Blwyddiadur MC, 1954, 222; T. Beynon, *Allt Cunedda* (1955), 129; information from his relatives in Pontyberem; personal knowledge.

G.M.R.

BEYNON, TOM (1886-1961), minister (Presb.), historian and author; b. 3 June 1886 in Cenfu, Mynydd y Garreg, near Kidwelly, Carms., son of William and Elizabeth Beynon. At the end of his time in the local council school he went to work in Pontyberem in 1903, and was received as a member of Soar church where he began preaching at the height of the 1904-05 Revival. He was educated for the ministry in the Old College School, Carmarthen, in Newcastle Emlyn grammar school, and Bala Theological College. He was ord. in 1916 and was pastor of Tabernacl, Blaengwynfi, Glam. (1916-33), and Horeb and Gosen near Aberystwyth (1933-51). He m., 1922, Eleanor Annie Whittaker of Caerau, Maesteg.

He took an interest in the history of Wales, particularly the history of Calvinistic Methodism in Wales, and wrote regularly for *Y Goleuad*, *Y Drysorfa*, *Y Traethodydd*, and local papers such as *The Llanelly Mercury* and *The Welsh Gazette* (see his Bibliography in *Cylch. Cymd. Hanes M.C.*, 47). He was co-editor of *Y Pair*, the college magazine, when he was in Bala, and he edited the journal of the Calvinistic Methodist history society from 1933 to 1947, and contributed much to it. He was a member of the history committee of his Connexion from 1926 till his death, and was both secretary of the committee for a long period (1930-60), and keeper of the Calvinistic Methodist Archives in the N.L.W. He was also a member of the court of the National Library for many years.

He took a great interest in the Methodist 'fathers', particularly Howel Harris. He researched assiduously in Harris' diaries, publishing extensive excerpts from them in the journal mentioned above, and in his books. He wrote the history of Gyfylchi and Pontrhyd-y-fen chapels (1926), and of Morfa church, Kidwelly (1930); and many of his interesting essays were collected in five volumes: *Golud a mawl dyffryn Tywi* (1936); *Gwrid ar orwel ym Morgannwg* (1938); *Treftadaeth y Cenfu a Maes*

Gwenllian (1941); *Cwmsêl a Chefn Sidan* (1946); and *Allt Cunedda, Llechdwnni a Mwdlwscwm* (1955). The excerpts which he transcribed from the Trefeca diaries appeared in *Howell Harris, reformer and soldier* (1958); *Howell Harris's visits to London* (1960); and *Howell Harris's visits to Pembrokeshire* (which was published by his widow in 1966). These volumes are of particular value to those seeking information on the life and career of the reformer from Trefeca. He d. 10 Feb. 1961 at his home in Penparcau, Aberystwyth, and was buried in the cemetery at Mynydd y Garreg.

Trysorfa'r Plant, 1931, 57-8; *Treftadaeth y Cenfu*, 174 ff. and *Allt Cunedda*, 87, 92, 94, 100-5, 131; *Blwyddiadur y MC*, 1962, 256; *Cylch. Cymd. Hanes M.C.*, 45, 54-6; 47, 29-33; personal knowledge.

G.M.R.

BLIGH, STANLEY PRICE MORGAN (1870-1949), landowner and author; b. 15 Feb. 1870 in Brecon, only s. of Oliver Morgan Bligh and his wife Ellen (née Edwards of Clifton). The first Bligh to inherit the estate of the Price family of Cilmeri near Builth was Thomas Price Bligh: he was succeeded by his brother, Oliver Morgan Bligh, who kept a draper's shop in Brecon. They were a branch of the Blighs of Cornwall whose most distinguished member was William Bligh of the 'Bounty', vice-admiral of the Blue.

Stanley Bligh was educated at Eton and Trinity College, Oxford, became a member of the Inner Temple and was called to the Bar in 1895. Until he took over the management of the Cilmeri estate from his mother he practised on the S. Wales circuit. In 1895 he m. Matilda Agnes Wilson, dau. of Major John Wilson of the Royal Scots Greys, one of the survivors of the Charge of the Light Brigade. Bligh became interested in the theories of Sigmund Freud, and in order to attend the first conference of psychologists in Vienna in 1908 he acquired a knowledge of German. Under Freud's inspiration he wrote three books, *The direction of desire* (1910), *The desire for qualities* (1911), *The art of conversation* (1912), all published in Oxford. But for the outbreak of World War I, which called for all his energies in food production and land improvement, he would probably have published more. Following the setting up of the Welsh Plant Breeding Station in 1919, Cilmeri could be regarded as an extension of it, for the scientific workers there were willingly given facilities to hold numerous experiments into the improvement of poor grassland on the estate. R.G. Stapledon (1882-1960; see below) considered Bligh to be the most notable pioneer in the improvement of pasture in the country. The agricultural department of the University of Oxford kept a detailed account of all the costs of improvement of the Cilmeri land, and it is shown in the pamphlet *The improvement of upland grazings* by S.M. Bligh and F.J. Prewett in the series 'Progress in English farming systems' (1930), that the improvements were highly profitable.

Stapledon and Bligh became close friends and Stapledon regarded his meeting with him as one of the most important events of his life. He had a great influence on Stapledon's way of thinking. He taught him to see what lay behind facts. They had keen discussions on philosophy, psy-chology and agriculture, and would privately exchange poems with one another. For Bligh the pursuits of the country gentry were a waste of time; to them he was a crank or hermit, but for people like Charles Morgan (see below) and his wife, Hilda Vaughan, conversation with him was most inspiring. He had the rare gift of nurturing the minds of others. He was particularly interested in the philosophy of Plotinus. He had freed himself from a large number of social customs. For worship he had no use, but he found relief in composing metrical prayers, and there was a strong element of mysticism in his make-up.

Though a professed Liberal he took little part in politics, but he gave years of valuable service on the county council. When the fourth national conference, *circa* 1893, failed to reach agreement on the matter, Bligh erected his own memorial to Llywelyn ap Gruffudd on a site on his own land near the place where the prince is believed to have been killed in Dec. 1282.

He d. childless, 15 Jan. 1949, his estate was sold in 1950, and in accordance with his will the greater part of the proceeds went to endow scholarships worth £2,000 a year to boys and girls in Brecknocks. who wished to pursue courses of study or research in agriculture, co-operation or forestry.

S.M. Bligh, *Social therapeutics*, 1912; Charles Falkland, 'Portrait of a sage', *Listener*, 21 Sept. 1932; S.M. Bligh, 'The experience of a grassland apprentice', *Jnl. Agr. Soc., UCW*, 1933; R.G. Stapledon, *The land now and tomorrow*, 1935; *Brec. and Radn. Times*, Jan. 1949; R.G. Stapledon, *A survey of the agricultural and waste lands of Wales*, 1936; *Express and County Times*, Jan. 1949; Brecons. C. C., *Stanley Bligh memorial fund scheme*, 1957; Robert Waller, *Prophet of the new age*, 1962; personal knowledge.

G.E.

BOB TAI'R FELIN – see ROBERTS, ROBERT below.

BODFAN – see ANWYL, JOHN BODFAN above.

BOSTON, sixth BARON – see IRBY, GEORGE FLORANCE below.

BOWEN, DAVID ('Myfyr Hefin'; 1874-1955), minister (B) and editor; b. 20 July 1874, son of Thomas and Dinah Bowen of Treorchy, Glam., elder brother of Ben Bowen (*DWB*, 46) and Thomas (Orchwy) Bowen (father of the archdruid Geraint Bowen and the poet Euros Bowen), and of the mother of Sir Ben Bowen Thomas. Both parents had moved from Carmarthenshire to the coal industry in the Rhondda. The family's Welsh culture was safeguarded and fostered by the chapel life in Moriah (B), Pentre. David attended the Treorchy board school, and went to work in the Ty'n-y-bedw pit at the age of 12. His abilities were nurtured by the chapel, the small *eisteddfodau* and the remarkable success of his brother Ben. Compiling the latter's biography and collecting his poetry in 1903 helped his own gifts to mature. He began to preach during the 1904-05 Revival. He went to the preparatory school at Pontypridd and to the University College at Cardiff for the year 1908-09. He won the chair at the students' *eisteddfod* in Jan. 1909. He was called to the pastorate of Bethel, Lower Chapel, near Brecon and laboured there to restore Welsh as he had seen William Morris (*DWB*, 668) do at Noddfa, Treorchy. For this period of his life see his booklets *Oriau Hefin* (1902), *Emynau pen y mynydd* (1905), and *Cerddi Brycheiniog* (1912). In 1913 he moved to Horeb chapel, Five Roads, near Llanelli. He was Welsh editor of the *Llanelly Mercury* between 1915 and 1942, and of *Seren yr Ysgol Sul* from the same press, 1916-50. He established *Urdd y Seren Fore* in 1929, and the provision of reading material for children in Welsh was one of his chief aims. He was a member of the *Gorsedd* of Bards from 1897 until his death, and was president of the Llanelli Cymrodorion and the *Awen a Chân* literary circle. He was prominent in all Welsh cultural movements. He published five books on his brother, Ben, eight booklets of his own, and many contributions to the *Llanelly Mercury* and *Seren yr Ysgol Sul*.

He was twice married. (1) to Hannah Jones of Treorchy, in 1901. She d. young leaving one daughter, Myfanwy. In 1909 he m. (2) Elizabeth Bowen, Halfway, Llanelli, who d. in 1937 leaving two daughters, Rhiannon and Enid. He d. 22 Apr. 1955, and was buried in the new Horeb cemetery.

Information from his family and from his books.
G.R.H.

BOWYER, GWILYM (1906-65), minister (Congl.) and college principal; b. 7 Feb. 1906 at 74a Chapel St., Ponciau, Rhosllannerchrugog, Denb., s. of William Bowyer, miner, and his wife Sarah. He was the fifth of their six children. He received his primary education at the Council School, Ponciau, and then from 1920 to 1928 he worked in a grocer's shop, but received further education under the guidance of J. Powell Griffiths, minister of the English Baptist church, Grenville Williams, a teacher at the Council School, and especially R.J. Pritchard, his minister at Mynydd Seion, Congl. church, Ponciau, where he began to preach in 1923. Gwilym Bowyer entered Bala-Bangor College, where his elder brother Frederick was already a student, 27 Sept. 1928 and graduated B.A. with first-class hons. in philosophy in 1932 and B.D. in 1938. He was ord. in Soar, Cwmclydach, Rhondda, 12 Sept. 1935 and was subsequently minister at the Borough, London (1939-43) and Ebeneser, Bangor (1943-46). He began his work as principal of Bala-Bangor College in Oct. 1946 and remained in post until his death following a heart attack 5 Oct. 1965. He was buried 8 Oct. at New Cemetery, Bangor. He m. Prydwen Harrison of Penmaen-mawr 1 Oct. 1935 and they had three children.

Gwilym Bowyer's literary output was not extensive though he was a master of a lively Welsh style. He published *Yr eglwys wedi'r rhyfel* (Welsh Pacifist Pamphlets, 1944) and *Ym mha ystyr y mae'r Beibl yn wir?* (1954) and about 25 articles, sermons and reviews. His strength lay in the spoken word. He spoke quickly, forcefully and clearly and he was one of the most popular and influential preachers of his generation. He came to national prominence as an able broadcaster, gaining the ear of the public on radio with concise statements and keen

reasoning in series such as *Seiat Holi* (1946-49) and *Problemau bywyd* (1957-60), and he showed the same skills as one of the chairpersons of the series *Codi testun* produced by the television company T.W.W. between Sept. 1961 and March 1962. He contributed almost 100 broadcasts during his career, a severe strain on his physical resources.

He possessed a brilliant mind and a quick tongue. He was stronger in analysing and criticising than in constructing. As a theologian he tended towards rather conservative views and the thinkers who influenced him most were Augustine, Luther, Kierkegaard and his professor, J.E. Daniel (see below). Politically he was a radical, a convinced pacifist and a strong advocate for Welsh-medium education. He made a substantial contribution towards making it possible for theological students in the University of Wales to follow courses and take their examinations in Welsh.

W. Eifion Powell, *Bywyd a gwaith Gwilym Bowyer* (1968); *Portreadau'r Faner*, ii, 36-8; *Dysg.*, Nov./Dec. 1965; *Tyst*, 4 Nov. 1965.
R.Td.J.

BRACE, WILLIAM (1865-1947), miners' leader and M.P.; b. at Risca, Mon., 23 Sept. 1865, s. of Thomas and Ann Brace; ed. at Risca board school. When he was 12 years of age he began to earn his living as a collier at Risca colliery, and as he grew older he took a keen interest in labour problems. In 1890 he m. Nellie, dau. of William and Harriet Humphreys of Cwmcarn, Mon. In the same year he was appointed miners' agent for the local branch of the Miners' Federation of Great Britain. At that time one of the major controversies in the south Wales coalfield was the sliding scale arrangement for paying miners. At the head of those who favoured the sliding scale principle was William Abraham ('Mabon'; *DWB*, 1). Brace became the leader of the opposition movement, and the activities of the two men brought them into official and personal conflict. This antagonism led to successful legal proceedings for libel being taken by Abraham against Brace. At the conclusion of the miners' strike of 1898, however, the South Wales Miners' Federation was formed, with Abraham as president and Brace as vice-president of the executive council. In 1899 Brace, along with Abraham and John Williams, attended the annual conference of the Miners' Federation of Great Britain, to seek (successfully) the affiliation of the South Wales union to the national body. In 1901 he was asked to serve on a Royal Commission appointed to inquire into the coal reserves of the United Kingdom. Five years later he entered Parliament as Labour member for the South Glamorgan division, defeating Colonel Wyndham-Quin, later earl of Dunraven (W.H. Wyndham-Quin, see below). He continued to represent that constituency until 1918. During this period he maintained his connection with the South Wales Miners' Federation and in 1912 became its president. There was, however, by now, some opposition to his policies from amongst the miners on the grounds that he was not sufficiently radical. In 1915 he became under-secretary at the Home Office in the wartime coalition government, and the following year was appointed a member of the Privy Council. He remained a member of the government until the Labour Party withdrew from it in 1918. From 1918-20 he served as M.P. for the Abertillery division, and in the latter years he accepted the position of chief labour adviser to the Government Mines Department, a full-time post which necessitated his resignation as a M.P. In 1922 he was asked to serve as one of the four members of a Royal Commission set up by the government of South Africa to investigate economic conditions in that country after industrial unrest amongst the miners. He retired in 1927 and d. 12 Oct. 1947.

Ness Edwards, *History of the South Wales Miners' Federation*, 1938; L. Twiston Davies, *Men of Monmouthshire*, II, 1933; E.W. Evans, 'A history of industrial relations in the South Wales coalfield to 1912', University of Wales Ph.D. thesis, 1955; E.W. Evans, *Mabon; a study in trade union leadership*, 1959; Brinley Evans, 'A history of the Trade Disputes ... in the South Wales Coal Trade ...,' University of Wales M.A. thesis, 1944; *Www*, 1941-50; *West. Mail*, 14 Oct. 1947; *Times*, 14 Oct. 1947; *WwW* (1921).

G.M.G.

BRANGWYN, Sir FRANK FRANCOIS GUILLAUME (1867-1956), painter; b. in Bruges, Belgium, 13 May 1867, the third son of William Curtis Brangwyn (d. 1907 in Cardiff) and Eleanor (née Griffiths) his wife who hailed from Brecon. His father was a church architect and manufactured church furniture in Bruges but the family returned to London in 1875. Frank Brangwyn, who had very little formal education, learnt drawing in South Kensington Museum and entered the workshop of William Morris in Oxford Street in 1882. After two years there he earned his living as a travelling artist in England before going to the continent, the Middle East and South Africa. In 1896 he m. a nurse, Lucy Ray (d. 1924), and settled in Hammersmith, London, but they had no children. He d. in Ditchling, Sussex, 11 June 1956. He was regarded as the greatest decorator of his time, particularly of large buildings such as the Royal Exchange in London and the Missouri State Capitol, U.S.A. He specialised in painting large murals but also designed carpets and tapestries. In 1924 Lord Iveagh gave him a commission to paint murals for the House of Lords to commemorate the sons of peers who had lost their lives in World War I. After experimenting with scenes of war, which he found too morbid, he had the idea of depicting the wealth of the British Empire for which they had died, but when the work was barely half done the panels were rejected by the Lords and the large colourful pictures now adorn Swansea civic centre where the Brangwyn Hall was designed to accommodate them. A large collection of the drawings and cartoons which were made in the preparation of this work is in the Glynn Vivian Gallery, Swansea, but his pictures are to be found in many European cities, including Bruges where there is a gallery dedicated to his work, and in Australia. There is also a large collection of his work in the National Museum of Wales. He was the author of *Belgium* (1916) and *The way of the cross* (1935). He received many high honours both in the United Kingdom and on the continent; he was knighted in 1941.

DNB; T. Mardy Rees, *Welsh painters, engravers and sculptors, 1527-1911* (1912), 13; William de Belleroche, *Brangwyn talks* (1946) and *Brangwyn's pilgrimage* (1948); V. Galloway; *The oils and murals of Sir F. Brangwyn* (1962) and *Trivium*, 8, 1973, 121-6 for a reappraisal of the British empire panels.

E.D.J.

BRAZELL, DAVID (1875-1959), singer; b. Cesail Graig, Pwll, Llanelli, Carms., 23 Feb. 1875, son of John and Mary Brazell. He was reared in a musical family; his father (a collier) was fond of music, and two of his brothers, John and Thomas, were fairly well known musicians— John a tenor soloist, and Thomas a choir conductor and a precentor at the Independent chapel in Pwll. (David and John went on a tour in the United States for seven months with the Llanelli choir in 1909-10; John died on the ship *Mauretania* whilst returning to Britain from New York).

After leaving the elementary school at Pwll, he worked in the tinplate industry and studied music in Llanelli in his spare time, firstly with Maggie Aubrey and later with R.C. Jenkins, conductor of the Llanelli Choral Society who had been taught by Joseph Parry (*DWB*, 738). He served his apprenticeship as a singer in *eisteddfodau* and with the encouragement of R.C. Jenkins he went to the Royal Academy of Music in London in May 1901 where he studied for five years with Frederic King (singing), Frederic Corder (harmony and counterpoint), and Edgardo Levi (opera). He had a brilliant career as a student; he won six of the academy's medals, and he took a prominent part in performances of some of the principal operas there. When he finished his course in 1906 he was offered contracts with some of the main opera companies but although he joined the Carl Rosa Opera Company for a short period he chose to follow a career as a freelance professional singer.

He sang at concerts at most of the principal towns of Wales and England, as well as on the continent. He sang also in the national *eisteddfod* concerts and at the Harlech festival, and he became a favoured singer of some of the major composers of his time. At the request of Edward German he took the part of the Earl of Essex in his opera *Merrie England* in Bournemouth, and he was invited by Edward Elgar to sing at an early performance of his oratorio *The Dream of Gerontius*. Another composer who admired him was D. Vaughan Thomas (*DWB*, 943-4) who wrote and dedicated to him his well known song *Angladd y Marchog*, as well as his arrangement of *Y bwthyn bach to gwellt* ('Crych Elen', Thomas Lloyd, *DWB*, 589).

He had a delightful and rich baritone voice which was always well disciplined. As the style and quality of his voice were ideal for recording purposes, his name was one of the first to appear in the catalogues of gramophone companies. He started to record on wax rolls before the turn of the twentieth century and he continued to record on 78 disks for about half a dozen recording companies up to the 1930s. These disks included popular songs, selections from operas and oratorios and Welsh songs.

He was on friendly terms with many prominent and influential musicians. He inspired Katie Moss (in 1910) to write 'The Floral Dance' based on a Cornish air, a song that became a great favourite of the singer Peter Dawson. He m. in 1938 Catherine Hughes, headmistress of Coleshill school, Llanelli. He d. in Bryntirion Hospital, Llanelli, 28 Dec. 1959 and was cremated at Morriston.

Cerddor, May 1910, July 1910, and June 1911; *Welsh Music*, 3, Winter 1970, 8, 25; Peter Dawson, *Fifty years of song* (1951); the dates of his birth and death provided by his niece, Mrs. Morfudd Beynon, Pembre.

H.W.

BRITHDIR – see WILLIAMS, HUGH DOUGLAS, below.

BRUNT, Sir DAVID (1886-1965), meteorologist and vice-president of the Royal Society; b. 17 June 1886 at Staylittle, Mont., the youngest of the five sons and four daughters of John Brunt, a farm worker, and Mary (née Jones) his wife. Up to the age of ten David was a pupil at the village school, then in the charge of a single teacher who gave all his instruction in Welsh. In 1896 John Brunt moved his family to the south Wales coalfield where he subsequently worked as a coal miner. The family settled at Llanhilleth in Monmouthshire in surroundings very different from those to which they were accustomed on the open moorlands of mid-Wales. For the next three years David Brunt attended the local elementary school and quickly overcame the linguistic and other problems arising from larger classes and the absence of any special attention. In 1899 he was placed first on the list of those obtaining entrance scholarships to the Abertillery intermediate (later county) school and it was here that he first began to show exceptional brilliance in mathematics and chemistry. In 1904 he obtained a distinction in additional mathematics at Higher School Certificate level and as a result was awarded a county exhibition of £30 for three years. Later that year he obtained the top entrance scholarship of £40 for the same period at U.C.W., Aberystwyth. These scholarships allowed him to embark upon a university career. At Aberystwyth he studied mathematics, physics and chemistry. His teachers in mathematics included two distinguished professors then at Aberystwyth – R.W. Genese and G.A. Schott – both of whom became very proud of their pupil. In 1907 he left Aberystwyth with a first-class honours degree in mathematics and after a short break proceeded as a scholar in mathematics to Trinity College, Cambridge. Later he gained firsts in parts I and II of the Mathematical Tripos and in 1909 was elected to the Isaac Newton studentship at the National Solar Physics Observatory. After leaving Cambridge he spent a year as a lecturer in mathematics at the University of Birmingham and two years in a similar post at the Monmouthshire Training College, Caerleon. While he was at Caerleon, he married in 1915 Claudia Mary Elizabeth Roberts of Nant-y-glo, Mon., who had been a fellow student both at Abertillery and Aberystwyth. They had one son who died unmarried.

The real turning point in David Brunt's career came in 1916 when he enlisted in the Royal Engineers (meteorological section). In the war years he did important work related to atmospherical conditions at low levels in chemical warfare and at higher levels when he became meteorologist to the Air Force. He was often mentioned in despatches. He became an expert forecaster and after demobilisation he accepted an invitation to enter the Meteorological Office which in 1921 became the Air Ministry. He did not allow his official duties to interrupt his personal research, and he accepted Sir Napier Shaw's invitation to join him in his duties as part-time professor of meteorology at the Imperial College of Science and Technology, London. This led, after the retirement of Sir Napier Shaw, to Brunt becoming the first full-time professor of meteorology in Britain. He held the chair from 1934 to 1952 and two years later he was elected a Fellow of the college.

During his academic career he wrote 58 scientific papers and five important books – *Combination of observations* (1917), *Meteorology* (1928), *Physical and dynamical meteorology* (1934), *Weather science for everybody* (1936) and *Weather study* (1942). He was president of the Royal Meteorological Society, 1942-44, and received both their Buchan prize and Symons gold medal. He was president of the Physical Society, 1945-47. He had many interests closely related to meteorology in its wider application. He was chairman of the British Gliding Association, 1935-46, and chairman of the Electricity Supply Research Council, 1952-59. He was elected F.R.S. in 1939, and in 1944 was awarded its royal medal. He rendered great service to this famous scientific society as its very efficient secretary 1948-57, and as vice-president 1949-57. He received a knighthood in 1949 and K.B.E. in 1959.

Sir David Brunt was undoubtedly the most distinguished meteorologist in Britain in the first half of the twentieth century when the subject was changing from being almost a descriptive science to becoming a science increasingly based on mathematical concepts, and at the same time changing from a reliance on ground based observations to data from the upper atmosphere. He received the Sc.D. degree (Cambridge) in 1940, and later an honorary D.Sc. degree from the University of London in 1960, and a similar distinction from the University of Wales in 1951. He d. 5 Feb. 1965.

Portreadau'r Faner, i, 33-4; personal knowledge; [*Biog. Memoirs Fellows R.S.*, 11, 41-52; *Times*, 8, 23, 24 Feb. 1965].

E.G.B.

BRYANT, TOM (1882-1946), harpist; b. 22 July, 1882, at the Carpenter's Arms, Efailisaf, nr. Pontypridd, Glam. John Bryant (*DWB*, 56), his uncle, taught him to play the harp. He began to compete at *eisteddfodau* at a young age, winning many prizes. He took the first prize at the National *Eisteddfod* from 1891 to 1896. With Watkin Hezekiah Williams (*DWB*, 1076), and Robert Rees (*DWB*, 829), the former lecturing on folk-songs and the latter singing to Bryant's accompaniment on the harp, he travelled extensively in south Wales. He became an A.R.C.M. in 1906, and in the same year received King Edward VII's command to play the harp at the opening of a new dock in Cardiff. With the 'Golden Quartette' he held concerts at the principal towns of Britain. He wrote music for the harp, and composed variations on the tunes 'Merch y Felin' and 'Merch Megan'. He d. 13 Jan. 1946, and was buried in Tabernacl cemetery, Efailisaf.

West. Mail, 16 Jan. 1946; *Pontypridd Observer*, 19 Jan. 1946.

R.D.G.

BRYFDIR – see JONES, HUMPHREY below.

BRYTHONYDD – see WILLIAMS, DAVID PRYSE below.

BUSH, PERCY FRANK, (1879-1955), rugby player; b. 23 June 1879, in Cardiff. The family came originally from Penygraig. His father, James Bush, was an art teacher and one of the founders of the Cardiff rugby club in 1875. Percy Bush was educated at University College, Cardiff. He won 8 caps as an outside-half between 1905 and 1910. He was a remarkable character, full of humour and the unexpected on the rugby field. He was completely self-possessed and independent. He first played for Cardiff in Nov. 1899. He was a member of the British team in Australia and New Zealand in 1904, where he was considered to be one of the best outside-halves ever seen there. He scored 104 points on that tour, 17 of them in one match. He captained Cardiff in 1905-06, when they won every game except the one against the All Blacks, and Bush was held responsible for that failure. He played a key role in Wales' historic (3-0) victory over the All Blacks on Dec. 16th 1905. In 1907, he was the captain of Cardiff when they defeated South Africa 17-0. He won only 8 caps, because of the contrast between his style and that of Dickie Owen (Richard M. Owen, *DWB*, 720), the Welsh scrum-half. He was a schoolmaster until 1910, when he settled in Nantes, where he continued to play rugby. In 1918, he was appointed British Vice-Consul in that city. He returned to Wales in the mid-1930s, and was awarded the *Médaille d'Argent de le Reconnaissance Française* in recognition of his services to French relations with the Celtic nations. He d. in Cardiff on May 19, 1955. The pacifist, Ethel M. Bush, was his sister.

David Smith and Gareth Williams, *Fields of Praise* (1980); *West. Mail*, and *Times*, May 20 1955.

G.W.W.

C

CAMROSE, 1st VISCOUNT – see BERRY (FAMILY), WILLIAM EWERT BERRY above.

CARNEDDOG – see GRIFFITH, RICHARD below.

CARRINGTON, THOMAS (Tom), ('Pencerdd Gwynfryn'; 1881-1961), musician and printer; b. at Gwynfryn, Bwlch-gwyn, near Wrexham, Denb., 24 Nov. 1881, the son of John Carrington (a descendant of one of the families that migrated from Cornwall to work in the Denbighshire lead mines) and Winifred (née Roberts), a native of Bryneglwys. He spent his early years at Gwynfryn and was educated at Bwlch-gwyn school. After leaving school he was apprenticed as a printer at Hughes and Son, Wrexham. He m. Mildred Mary Jones, Minera, in 1905 and went to live in Coed-poeth where he followed his trade as a printer and as a music publisher. From his early childhood it was obvious that he had a special talent as a musician. At the age of nine he had been appointed organist at the Wesleyan Methodist church at Gwynfryn and he held that office for about fifteen years. He studied music in his spare time through the medium of tonic sol-fa and with Morton Bailey in Wrexham. Later he was organist for over fifty years at Rehoboth Wesleyan Methodist chapel at Coed-poeth and he became well known as an *eisteddfod* adjudicator, conductor and composer. He was music editor of *Y Winllan* and *Yr Eurgrawn* and he was secretary of the committee responsible for the music of *Llyfr Emynau a Thonau y Methodistiaid Calfinaidd a Wesleaidd* (1929). He was also a keen *eisteddfodwr* and he served as the general secretary of the 1933 National *Eisteddfod* at Wrexham. His most important musical compositions include *Concwest Calfari* (SATB anthem 1912), *Hen weddi deuluaidd fy nhad* (contralto/baritone solo 1910), and *Gwynfryn* and *Bryn-du* (hymn tunes). He was also the author of the handbook *Yr Ysgol Gân* (Gee, 1957) and *Doniau Da* (1955) that contains a number of his original tunes and songs, as well as arrangements of hymn tunes. He d. in his home at Coed-poeth, 6 May 1961. In 1963 a memorial plaque was unveiled in Rehoboth Chapel, Coed-poeth.

WwW (1937); *Cymro*, 29 Oct. 1959, 18 May 1961 and 31 Oct. 1963; *Eurgrawn*, Aug. 1961.

H.W.

CASSON, LEWIS (1875-1969), actor and theatrical producer; b. in Birkenhead, Cheshire, 26 Oct. 1875, son of Thomas Casson of Ffestiniog, Mer., and Laura Ann (née Holland-Thomas) his wife. After leaving Ruthin Grammar School he helped his father build organs, attending the Central Technical College, South Kensington, for a while, and subsequently entering S. Mark's College, Chelsea, to become a teacher. In 1903 he appeared as a professional actor at the Court Theatre, in *Man and Superman* and other plays. His career took a decisive turn when he joined Miss Horniman's repertory company at the Gaiety, Manchester, in 1907, for there he began

directing, and he also met Sibyl Thorndike, whom he m. 22 Dec. 1908 in Aylesford, Kent. They had four children.

During World War I he served as a sergeant in the Army Service Corps (1914-15) and major in the Royal Engineers (1916-19); he was wounded, and awarded the M.C. Having resumed his career in London, he directed jointly with the author, G.B. Shaw, the original production of *St. Joan* (1924), his wife playing the leading role. He and his wife toured South Africa in 1928, and the Middle East, Australia and New Zealand in 1932. In 1938 he produced *Henry V* at Drury Lane for Ivor Novello (see below), and also resumed his association with the Old Vic, directing Laurence Olivier in *Coriolanus*, and John Gielgud in *King Lear* (1940). That year he and his wife toured Wales in *Macbeth*, and subsequently by *King John*, *Candida*, *Medea* and *St. Joan*. They collaborated after the war, not only in London, where Lewis Casson came into his own as the leading man in J.B. Priestley's *The linden tree*, but also at festivals in Edinburgh and New York, and on four tours comprising dramatic recitals and contemporary plays in the Middle and Far East, India, Australasia and Africa. They celebrated the jubilee of their wedding by appearing in Clemence Dane's play, specially written for them, *Eighty in the shade* (1959). Lewis Casson had a rich, powerful bass voice, and was a versatile character actor as well as a celebrated producer. He played some hundreds of parts and continued to work until 1968.

As a dedicated member of his profession he was for many years one of its leaders, having built up the actors' trade union movement. He spoke fearlessly on the theatre and was elected president of the British Actors' Equity (1941-45), as well as drama director to the Council for the Encouragement of Music and the Arts (1942-44). In 1945 he was knighted, and he also received honorary degrees from the universities of Glasgow (1954), Wales (1959) and Oxford (1966). He lived at 98 Swan Court, London, but stayed occasionally at his inherited property, Bron-y-garth, Porthmadog, before it was sold in 1949. He d. 16 May 1969.

Www; John Casson, *Lewis and Sybil: a memoir* (1972); *Times*, 17 May 1969; *Genh.*, 27, 1977, 26-7.

M.A.J.

CECIL-WILLIAMS, Sir JOHN LIAS CECIL (1892-1964), solicitor, secretary Hon. Soc. Cymmrodorion and driving force behind the publishing of the *DWB*; b. 14 Oct. 1892 in Paddington, London, one of two children of John Cadwaladr Williams, a doctor, and Catherine (née Thomas) his wife. (The son adopted the hyphenated name of Cecil-Williams by deed-poll in 1935). The family came from Uwch Aled. He was educated first in London and, for a year or so, in the village school at Cerrigydrudion. Returning to London he attended the City of London School from where he went to Gonville and Caius College, Cambridge, where he read law and graduated

M.A. and LL.B. He registered in the Inns of Court OTC in 1914 and the following year joined the Royal Welch Fusiliers, serving in France and achieving the rank of captain. He was wounded three times. In 1920 he became a solicitor and practised in London, first alone and then in partnership. He retired in 1960.

He rapidly became known in London-Welsh circles as a man of great energy, for his enthusiasm for all things Welsh and as a first-class organiser. In 1934 he was elected honorary secretary of the Honourable Society of Cymmrodorion, following Sir E. Vincent Evans (*DWB*, 232). He held the post for nearly thirty years and made it his life work. Having a private income he was not wholly dependent on his practice as a solicitor, and consequently he was able to give much of his time to the Society and to other cultural and charitable activities. In all this he was eminently successful. He boosted the membership of the Society to nearly 2,000, many from overseas; and like his predecessor he attracted many of the most notable Welsh people of this period. In 1951, on its 250th anniversary, the Society was granted a Royal Charter. In the same year he was knighted and the University of Wales awarded him an honorary LL.D. Although he spent all his life in London, he retained the sweet accent of Uwch Aled and maintained a fluency in his mother tongue. He was acutely aware of the historical antecedents of the Cymmrodorion and of its status as a Society, and always strove to maintain the high ideal of its aims. In the words of Sir Thomas Parry-Williams, who was for a time President of the Society, Cecil-Williams maintained the office of secretary 'fiercely and untiringly to promote the welfare and protect the inheritance of Wales and the Welsh'.

Although Professor R.T. Jenkins (see below), together with Sir John Edward Lloyd (see below) and Sir William Llewelyn Davies (see below), deserve the praise for the form and content of the *DWB*, it is doubtful whether it would have been published without the efforts of Cecil-Williams. He never accepted that the project was too ambitious and too costly. With the help of his fellow officers he succeeded in raising the necessary money from county councils and organisations such as the Pilgrim Trust; and this guaranteed the publication in 1953 of the volume now acknowledged as one of the most important to appear in Wales in the twentieth century. He insisted on planning the first ten-year supplement in order to establish a precedent for publishing a continuing series.

He took a leading part in many cultural and charitable movements. He was a member of the Courts of the University of Wales, the National Library (and its Council) and the National Museum. He was a trustee of the Royal Welch Fusiliers Museum in Caernarfon castle, a member of the committee to celebrate the 350th anniversary of the founding of Virginia, and of the Goodwill Mission to the United States in 1957. He was president of the Southern Olympian Amateur Football League, 1951-59, and in 1959 was elected president of the Amateur Football Alliance. He was awarded the Hopkins Medal in New York in 1957, and in 1962 the Honourable Society awarded him its highest honour, the Cymmrodorion Medal. He was an honorary member of the *Gorsedd* of Bards under the name Seisyllt.

He married Olive Mary, only daughter of alderman Aneurin O. Evans of Denbigh, in 1935, and they had one son. Sir John died in London, 30 Nov. 1964 and the funeral service was in Golder's Green Crematorium, 5 Dec.

Trans. Cymm., 1964; *Times*, 1 Dec. 1964; *London Welshman*, Jan. 1965; personal knowledge.

B.G.J.

CELT – see HUMPHREYS, EDWARD MORGAN below.

CEMLYN-JONES, Sir ELIAS WYNNE (1888-1966), public figure; b. 16 May 1888 in Gwredog, Amlwch, Anglesey, son of John Cemlyn Jones, a solicitor from Caerphilly, and Gaynor Hannah, dau. of John Elias Jones, from Penmaen-mawr (and through his wife, of Gwredog, Amlwch), a prominent figure in the public life of Anglesey and an ardent Liberal. His father d. when he was a child and he was educated privately: at Mostyn School, Parkgate, Cheshire, at Shrewsbury School and in London. He became a barrister. In 1910-11 he and his aunt, his mother's sister, went on a journey round the world, the old 'grand tour', through the United States, Canada, Japan, Korea, China, etc. From 1912-14 he was private secretary to (Sir) Ellis Jones Ellis-Griffith (*DWB*, 215) in the Home Office, and between 1914-18 he served with the Royal Welch Fusiliers. He was an unsuccessful Liberal candidate for South Croydon in 1923 and for Brecon and Radnor in 1929. He served on numerous committees and public bodies, e.g. Anglesey county council from 1919 onwards (being chairman (1928-30) and alderman), the County Councils Association, the Milne Committee on water supplies, the Athlone Committee on the nursing services, the Rushcliffe Committee on nurses' pay, the Central Whitley Council for the health service, the court of the National Museum of Wales, and the council of the University College of North Wales, Bangor. During 1939-46 he was active in the work of the War Agricultural Executive Committee in Anglesey. He received a knighthood in 1941.

In 1931 he went on a 7000-mile journey through Russia with Frank Owen to capture the atmosphere of the country after the revolution for a novel on which they were collaborating; he described the journey in *Y Ford Gron*, Sept. 1931. The novel, *Red Rainbow*, was published in 1932. Under the pretence of writing a thriller, the authors sought to warn the British public of the threatening strength of Russia.

In 1914 he m. Muriel Gwendolin, daughter of Owen Owen, Machynlleth and Liverpool, the owner of large stores. They had two sons and a daughter. He d. 6 June 1966 and was buried in Amlwch.

Www; WwW (1937); the Gwredog papers in the library of the University College of North Wales, Bangor; information from Miss Gaynor Cemlyn-Jones, Menai Bridge, and Ellis Roberts.

B.L.J.

CERIDWEN PERIS – see JONES, ALICE GRAY below.

CHANCE, THOMAS WILLIAMS (1872-1954), minister (B) and principal of the Baptist College, Cardiff; b. 23 Aug. 1872, son of Thomas Chance (d. 5 Jan. 1873, 29 yrs. old) and Mary (b. Williams; d. 15 Aug. 1908, 79 yrs. old) of Erwood, Breck. He received his early education at Pen-rhiw school, but because of his father's early death he had to leave school when he was 11 years old to earn his living as a farm servant and maintain the family for the next 9 yrs., initially at Erwood and later in the neighbourhood of Cathedin. He was baptised 17 Apr. 1887 in Hephzibah church, Erwood, and at the urging of his pastor, John Morgan, he began to preach. He resumed his education, spending 2 yrs. at a grammar school held by Daniel Christmas Lloyd (Congl. minister), in his home, Hampton House, Glasbury, and then at the Baptist College and University College, Cardiff, where he graduated B.A. in 1898 with first-class honours in Hebrew, M.A. (1900) and B.D. (1916). In 1899 he was ord. minister of High Street (B) Church, Merthyr Tydfil. In Jan. 1904 he was appointed part-time lecturer in Church History at the Baptist College, Cardiff; and full-time professor and financial secretary in 1908. He became acting principal on the death of John Morlais Davies in Apr. 1928, but despite being recommended by the executive council to an enthusiastic meeting of nearly nine hundred church representatives in Cardiff on 20 Sept, he conceded the principalship to Thomas Phillips (1868-1936; *DWB*, 762-3) by only four votes, because, it was generally held, of his lack of knowledge of Welsh. After the death of Thomas Phillips, he was appointed to the post, July 1936, though not without much debate for some months in *Seren Cymru*. He remained head until he retired 30 June 1944 when he was made principal emeritus.

In addition to his academic abilities, he had business acumen and exceptional administrative gifts. One of his main achievements was to set the college's finances on a sound base, securing the freehold of the site as a gift, and ensuring that both the land and funds were available to build the residential hostel which he had long been advocating. He was dean of the Faculty of Theology of the University of Wales, 1928-32, and he was instrumental with others in helping to establish a Joint School of Theology at Cardiff in 1928, and in 1934 in designing a diploma course that met the requirements of non-graduate students preparing for the ministry.

He was a member of Albany Road Church, Cardiff, and enthusiastically supported the work of his denomination in the city, e.g. as chairman of the Cardiff Baptist Board for 21 yrs. He was also president of the East Glamorgan Baptist Association, 1934-35. He took a keen interest in the missionary work of the Christian Endeavour Movement, and was president of the Welsh National Christian Endeavour Union in 1906-07 and 1923-24, and president of the British C.E. Union in 1924-25. In June 1954, as a tribute to his long-standing service to the East Glamorgan Baptist Association, he received a gift of an oil portrait of himself, painted by Alfred Hall, Cardiff, which he later presented to the Baptist College. He edited and contributed three chapters to the biography of one of his predecessors, *The life of Principal William Edwards ...* (1934).

On 8 Aug. 1900 he m. Mary Maria, daughter of his first pastor, John Morgan (d. 8 Sept. 1922 aged 82) and Margaret his wife (d. 14 Apr. 1924, aged 74), and they had one son, Sidney Morgan Chance, South Park, Gerrards Cross, who was alive when his parents celebrated their golden wedding but d. before them. Thomas Williams Chance d. 22 Dec. 1954 after an operation in the County Hospital, Hereford, and was buried two days later in Hephzibah graveyard. His wife d. 22 July 1956, aged 81.

D. Mervyn Himbury, *The South Wales Baptist College (1807-1957)* (1957), 78, 89 ff.; annual reports of the Baptist College, Cardiff, particularly 1955, 7, 10-13; *Ser. Cymru*, 4 May, 28 Sept. 1928, 5 June 1936, 31 Dec. 1954 and 7 Jan. 1955; *West. Mail*, 23-24 Dec. 1954; *Baptist Times*, 6 Jan. 1955; *Dyddiadur B.*, 1956, 114-5; *Bapt. Hdbk.*, 1956, 322-3; *Www*; information from the Rev. W. George Evans, Whitchurch, Cardiff, Ivor Hayward, Cardiff, and E.C. Davies, Erwood.

B.G.O.

CHAPPELL, EDGAR LEYSHON (1879-1949), sociologist, a pioneer of town and village redevelopment, and writer; b. 8 April 1879 at Ystalyfera, Glam., son of Alfred Chappell and Ellen Watkins. Trained for the teaching profession at the University College of South Wales and Monmouthshire, Cardiff, he was for a time headmaster of Rhiw-fawr school, Pontardawe. In 1912 he joined Professor Herbert Stanley Jevons as a research assistant in economics, work which involved travelling and lecturing in south Wales as propagandist on behalf of the garden cities movement and town and country planning and writing articles and pamphlets on these and related subjects. In 1917 he became secretary of the Welsh section of the Industrial Unrest Commission set up by the War Cabinet, and, in 1918, special investigator for the Ministry of Agriculture into wages and conditions of employment of agricultural labourers in south Wales. From 1918 to 1921 he was an inspector under the housing department of the Ministry of Health, becoming, in 1921, Secretary of the South Wales Regional Survey Committee set up by the same Ministry.

Leaving the Ministry of Health he formed and managed building and land development companies in the Cardiff and London areas. He was one of the founders and for some years the secretary of the Welsh Housing and Development Association; he edited *The Welsh Housing Year Book* for 1916, 1917, and 1918. (For a list of companies with which he was connected see *Who's Who in Wales*, 1937). Later he devoted himself to local government affairs, serving on many councils (including the Glamorgan county council) and their various sub-committees; he was also a Privy Council representative on the Court of Governors of the National Library of Wales. In 1948, he was awarded the degree of M.A., *honoris causa*, by the University of Wales.

His main publications, apart from contributions to newspapers and journals (he was for a time editor of *The Welsh Outlook*) are: *Gwalia's Homes*, 1911; *Pithead and Factory Baths* (with J.A. Lovat-Fraser), 1920; *The Housing Problem in Wales* 1920; *History of the Port of Cardiff*, 1939; *Historic Melingriffith*, 1940; *The Government of Wales*, 1943; *Wake up, Wales, a*

Survey of Home Rule Activities, 1943; *Cardiff's Civic Centre, a Historical Guide*, 1946.

He m. Alice, dau. of Caleb Thomas, Ystalyfera, and they had one son. Chapell d. 26 Aug. 1949 at Cardiff.

WwW, 1937; *West. Mail*, 27 Aug. 1949.

W.Ll.D.

CHRISTY – see DAVIES, DAVID CHRISTO-PHER below.

CILCENNIN, VISCOUNT – see THOMAS, JAMES PURDON LEWES below.

CLEDLYN – see DAVIES, DAVID REES below.

CLWYD of ABERGELE, BARON – see ROBERTS, JOHN HERBERT below.

COOMBE TENNANT, WINIFRED MAR-GARET ('Mam o Nedd'; 1874-1956), delegate to the first assembly of the League of Nations, suf-fragette, Mistress of the Robes of the *Gorsedd* of the Bards, and a well-known medium; b. the only child of George Edward Pearce-Serocold and his second wife, Mary Richardson of Derwen Fawr, Swansea. In 1895 she married Charles Coombe Tennant, and they lived in Cadoxton Lodge, near Neath. She became, thereby, daughter-in-law to Gertrude Barbara Rich Collier and sister-in-law to Dorothy Coombe Tennant who married the famous explorer H.M. Stanley (*DWB*, 922-3; see Supplement. below).

During World War I she was deputy chair-man of the Womens' Agricultural Committee for Glamorgan, and she served as chairman of the War Pensions Commissions for Neath and district. She was appointed J.P. in 1920 and was the first woman to serve on the Glamorgan bench. From 1920-1931 she was an Official Visitor to Swansea Prison and was responsible for considerable improvements in the treatment of prisoners; for example, this remarkable woman fought for permission for prisoners in Swansea to use safety razors and not grow a beard. Consequently this policy was adopted throughout the United Kingdom.

In politics she was a fervent Liberal and greatly admired Lloyd George. In 1922 she was parliamentary candidate for the Forest of Dean, but failed to win the seat. Her connections with Lloyd George led to her appointment as one of the representatives in the League of Nations – the first woman in Britain to fulfil this role. But Winifred Coombe Tennant became a keen nationalist and prominent in *Gorsedd y Beirdd*. Under the bardic name 'Mam o Nedd' she became Mistress of the Robes, and in her will left the *Gorsedd* a sum of money, and to the National Library papers concerning the *Gorsedd*. She was chairman of the Arts and Crafts Section in the national *eisteddfod* of 1918 and in the same year she was appointed to a committee to explore the possibilities of a feder-al government for Wales. In addition to all this she was the mother of four children, Christopher, Daphne, Alexander and Henry. Daphne, however, lived for only eighteen months, and this shattering blow led her into spiritualism. This posed no problems as anoth-er sister-in-law, Eveleen, was married to F.W.H.

Myers who, with Henry Sidgwick, founded the Society for Psychic Research. Mrs. Coombe Tennant was welcomed as a very talented medi-um, but this was unknown outside a small circle of close friends until after her death. For years she acted as a medium to Sir Oliver Lodge and others such as Gerald Balfour, under the assumed name of 'Mrs. Willett'. There are many accounts of her work as a medium in the *Journal of the Society for Psychic Research*, and a collec-tion of post-mortem essays claimed to have been transmitted via another medium, Geraldine Cummings, in the book *Swan on a Black Sea* (ed. Signe Toksvig, 1970).

She was a colourful and warm personality who had sincere personal principles which she defended with vigour. She made a host of friends in her adopted country and had a great interest in Welsh culture, though she never completely mastered the Welsh language. She died 31 Aug. 1956 at her home in 18 Cottesmore Gardens, Kensington. She wished for neither flowers nor mourning at her funeral. On 17 Sept. a memorial service was held in All Saints by the Tower, where James Nicholas (see below) represented the Welsh Baptist Union and Sir John Cecil Cecil-Williams (see above) the Cymmrodorion.

Personal knowledge; *Times*, 1, 8 and 21 Sept. 1956; [Emyr Wyn Jones, *Trans. Cymm.*, 1996].

G.L.R.

COX, ARTHUR HUBERT (1884-1961), geolo-gist; b. 2 Dec. 1884 in Birmingham, s. of Arthur James Cox and his wife Mary. He was educated at Edward VI Grammar School, Birmingham, and then at Birmingham University where he graduated B.Sc. in 1904 and M.Sc. 1905, and subsequently gained the degrees of Ph.D. Strasburg and D.Sc. Birmingham. He was a F.G.S. and was awarded the Lyell Medal of the Geological Society in 1948. He began his career as a lecturer in geology at U.C.W., Aberystwyth in 1909 but went to King's College London the following year. He was a member of H.M. Geological Survey in 1917 but was appointed to the Chair of Geology at U.C.S.W., Cardiff in 1918 where he remained until his retirement in 1949. He worked on the geology of the Pembrokeshire coast and on Cader Idris, extending our knowledge of the volcanoes of the Ordovician Period, but he published most extensively on the geological structures of south Wales. He realised the potential economic importance of geological studies, e.g. research into the conditions of oil and mineral deposits, and his work on the incidence of silicosis was of particular significance. He played a leading role in the development of the National Museum of Wales.

He m. Florence Elizabeth Page in 1919. He d. at Cardiff, 14 Feb. 1961.

Www; Times, 20.2.61; *Nature*, 1961.

B.F.R.

CRAWSHAY, Sir GEOFFREY CARTLAND HUGH (1892-1954), soldier and social benefac-tor; b. 20 June 1892, s. of Codrington Fraser Crawshay, Llanfair Grange, Abergavenny, Mon., and great-great-grandson of the ironmas-ter William Crawshay I (*DWB*, 86-7). He was educated at Wellington College and spent a year at University College of South Wales, Cardiff. There followed a short apprenticeship at Cwmbran Ironworks and a period with a contracting firm. In 1914 he joined the 3rd Welch Regiment and was later commissioned to the new Welsh Guards, attaining the rank of captain. At the battle of Loos he was severely wounded and began a lifelong struggle against ill-health. Remaining with the Regiment until 1924, he founded both the Welsh Guards Choir and their rugby team which he captained. His enthusiasm for that game was evidenced by the sponsoring and promotion of Crawshay's XV which toured the west country every year and served as a nursery for young Welsh players and by his presidency of the London Welsh Rugby Club from 1924 onwards. His next interest was in politics: Liberal summer schools, the League of Nations, and several unsuccessful forays as a Liberal candidate for south Wales parliamentary constituencies. After 1930, however, he turned from active politics to social work.

Mounting unemployment in south Wales had led, through dispersed local initiatives, to a rapid growth of occupational centres and clubs for unemployed men. To provide a co-ordinated regional machinery for the guidance and encouragement of these scattered units, the South Wales and Monmouthshire Council of Social Service was set up in Feb. 1934. Its first Annual Report recorded 'The heavy task of establishing the machinery of the Council devolved upon Captain Crawshay, who gave practically full-time service as honorary secretary and chairman of the governing committee. These offices had to be given up in Dec. 1934, when he became district commissioner for the special areas in south Wales, representing in the coalfield areas the national commissioners charged by Parliament with the 'initiation, organisation, prosecution, and assistance of measures designed to facilitate the economic development and social improvement' of areas 'specially affected by industrial depression'. Most important of the economic measures was the provision of new factories for renting through the agency of Wales and Monmouthshire Industrial Estates, Ltd., of which Crawshay was director, 1936-45. As district commissioner, he continued a sympathetic interest in the Social Service Council, acting as a government representative thereon. Through his influence, generous grants were made from the Special Areas Fund to extend the Council's work into new fields, including a women's club movement, more district nursing, adult education, and library rehabilitation. A keen horticulturalist, he made available Government resources for two highly successful experiments in co-operative farming which enabled a number of ex-miners to return to the land. These were managed by the Welsh Land Settlement Society, Ltd., of which he was chairman. He also chaired the rural industries committee of the Monmouthshire Rural Community Council.

Special areas activities ceased with the outbreak of war in 1939, and 1940-45 Geoffrey Crawshay served as regional controller (Wales) of the Ministry of Aircraft Production, linking central government to firms in Wales making aircraft components and equipment. In 1945 he became chairman of the Welsh Board of Health, then embarking on vital post-war reconstruction tasks, including a new health service, a large housing programme, improved water supplies, extended social services, and local government supervision. He retired from this office on medical advice in Jan. 1952.

His educational interests, included membership of the Courts of the University College of South Wales, Cardiff, and of both the National Museum of Wales and the National Library of Wales. He gave enthusiastic attention to the National *Eisteddfod* and its reform, was a member of the *Gorsedd* under the bardic title 'Sieffre o Gyfarthfa' and until 1947 he was an impressive mounted herald bard. The University of Wales in 1953 conferred on him the honorary degree of LL.D. He was High Sheriff of Monmouthshire in 1939, a deputy Lieutenant and J.P. for the county, and a knight of the Order of St. John.

After his involuntary retirement he continued for another two years a losing battle with illness and d. suddenly at a Cardiff hotel on 8 Nov. 1954. The funeral was at Llanfair Kilgeddin church, Abergavenny. He was unmarried.

Geoffrey Crawshay touched Welsh life at many points, but to his contemporaries he was perhaps best known and most highly regarded for his generous support and encouragement of the youngster of promise in every field of interest.

Private research; *Ww*, 1947 and 1953; *West. Mail*, 9 Nov. 1954; Margaret S. Taylor, *The Crawshays of Cyfarthfa Castle* (1967).

L.N.H.

CRWYS – see WILLIAMS, WILLIAM (CRWYS) below.

CUDLIPP, PERCY (1905-62), journalist; b. 1905, son of William Cudlipp, a well known commercial traveller in south Wales, and Bessie his wife, of Lisvane Street, Cardiff. He was one of three eminent Welsh journalist brothers (Reginald became editor of *The News of the World*, 1953-59; and Hugh, editor of *The Sunday Pictorial*, 1937-40 and 1946-49, and chairman of Odhams Press, 1960). Percy was educated, as were the others, at Gladstone school and Howard Gardens High School, Cardiff. He entered journalism on *The South Wales Echo* at 14 as messenger and copy boy, and two years later became a reporter. Subsequently he worked on the *The Evening Chronicle*, Manchester, during which time he contributed articles and light verse to London newspapers which attracted much attention in Fleet Street. His career in journalism spanned 34 years, from junior reporter to editor and he created a particular niche in his first appointment as editor in his encouragement of specialist correspondents in an extended field of news and specialist coverage, a format which was adopted by most national and regional newspapers. He was drama critic and humorous columnist of *The Sunday News*, London, 1925-29, and special writer and film critic of *The Evening Standard*, London, 1929-31. In 1931 he was promoted assistant editor and became editor in 1933. His move to daily national newspapers came with his appointment as editorial manager of *The Daily Herald* in 1938, and then editor in 1940 (when he succeeded Francis Williams who became Prime Minister Attlee's press secretary at Downing Street in 1946) until 1953. His sojourn on *The Daily Herald* often subjected him to tense editorial restrictions which he resented and fought, but the paper, then the mouthpiece of the Socialist left, was obliged generally to support policies approved by the Trades Union Congress and the Labour Party. Under such strains he moved to the Liberal *News Chronicle* where he was a columnist, 1954-56. He again moved to be editor of *New Scientist* from its foundation in 1956. Fleet Street, the hub of British journalism, knew him as an accurate writer and a conversational wit whose instinctive mimicry of the famous was greatly appreciated.

He became a frequent broadcaster both on radio and television and his love of verse from his earliest days was reflected in his book, *Bouverie Ballads* (1955). He m., 1927, Gwendoline James and they had one son. He d. 5 Nov. 1962.

Www; *Times*, 6 Nov. 1962.

D.G.R.

CYBI – see EVANS, ROBERT below.

CYNAN – see JONES, Sir CYNAN ALBERT EVANS below.

D

DAGGAR, GEORGE (1879-1950), trade unionist and Member of Parliament; b. 6 Nov. 1879 in Cwmbran, Mon., s. of Jesse Daggar, mine worker, and his wife Elizabeth. The family moved to Abertillery and he was educ. at the British School there. He started work when he was 12 in the Arael Griffin pit, Six Bells, and threw himself into trade union work, being elected in his 20s vice-chairman of Number 5 Lodge, Arael Griffin. In 1911 he went to the Central Labour College, London as a student and in later years he was a popular lecturer on economic and industrial subjects in the Monmouthshire valleys. He attended the annual Labour Party conference in 1917, was elected a member of Abertillery urban district council in 1919 and miners' agent for the western valleys (Mon.) when he was also selected as a member of the executive council of the South Wales Miners' Federation. In 1921 he was elected Labour M.P. for Abertillery; he was re-elected unopposed in 1931 and 1935, and in the general elections of 1945 and 1950 he gained the highest percentage of votes of any candidate in Wales. He was a pleasant and compassionate person, exceptionally helpful in his dealings with his constituents, crowds of whom attended his surgeries when he returned to his constituency on Friday evenings. He was assiduous in his parliamentary responsibilities, and between 1929 and 1931 he was present in 525 out of 526 divisions. He belonged to the centre-left of the Labour Party and contributed regularly to parliamentary debates on matters such as safety in the mines, unemployment, the means test and pensions. He was a member of the Select Committee on Mining Subsidence, vice-chairman of the Parliamentary Labour Party and chairman of the Welsh Parliamentary Party. He m. Rachel Smith, seamstress, in 1915; they did not have children. He published *Increased production from the worker's point of view* (1921) and a pamphlet, *Has Labour redeemed its pledges?* (1950). He d. at his home in Six Bells 14 Oct. 1950.

Joyce M. Bellamy and John Saville (ed.), *Dict. Lab. Biog.*, 3 (1976), 54-55; *Times*, 16 Oct. 1950; *West. Mail*, 16 Oct. 1950.

J.D.

DAGGER – see REES, THOMAS WYNFORD below.

DALTON, EDWARD HUGH JOHN NEALE, BARON DALTON (known as Hugh Dalton; 1887-1962), economist and politician; b. at Neath, Glam., the son of Canon John Neale and Catherine Alicia Dalton, on 26 Aug. 1887. His father had been tutor to King George V when Prince of Wales and he was a Canon of St. George's Chapel, Windsor from 1885 until his death in 1931. His mother was the daughter of Charles Evans-Thomas of Gnoll House, Neath. Hugh Dalton was educated at Summer Fields, Oxford, and Eton before he entered King's College, Cambridge, where he was classed *junior optime* in the first part of the mathematics tripos in 1909. He went on to read economics under A.C. Pigou and J.M. Keynes, taking the second part of the economics tripos in 1910. One of his closest friends was Rupert Brooke. Under the influence of Keir Hardie, he joined the Fabian Society. He was called to the Bar in 1914. After World War I, during which he served in France and Italy, he became a research student at the London School of Economics.

Dalton published his *Principles of public finance* in 1923. By this time, he had entered the world of politics and he was elected M.P. for Peckham in 1924. He changed his constituency to Bishop Auckland which he won in 1929. He was Chairman of the Labour Party in 1936-37. During World War II he was appointed Minister of Economic Warfare and he was responsible for creating the Special Operations Executive, an organisation to strengthen internal resistance in the countries occupied by the Germans. Dalton was moved to the Board of Trade in 1942 and his efforts there led to the setting up of the Ministry of Fuel and Power and the National Coal Board. He prepared for peacetime by steering industry to depressed areas. After the Labour victory in 1945, Dalton became Chancellor of the Exchequer and he appointed J.M. Keynes as his personal adviser. Despite a number of achievements, his time as Chancellor was disappointing, on the whole, and it came to a sudden end when, at a weak moment, he revealed some of the contents of the 1947 Budget as he was on his way to the House to deliver his speech. By this time, Dalton was one of the leading figures in the Labour Party. He was appointed Chancellor of the Duchy of Lancaster in 1948. Dalton did not stand at the 1959 election and he was given a life peerage in 1960. He m. Ruth, daughter of Thomas Hamilton Fox, in 1914 and they had one daughter who died in early childhood. Dalton d. on 13 Feb. 1962.

His memoirs, *Call back yesterday* (1953), *The fateful years, 1931-45* (1957) and *High tide and after* (1962). *Times* 14, 17, 20 Feb. 1962; *DNB* 1961-70, 266-9. [Ben Pimlott, *Hugh Dalton* (1985)].

E.D.J.

DANIEL, JOHN EDWARD (1902-62), college lecturer and inspector of schools; b. 26 June, 1902, in Bangor, the elder of the two sons of Morgan Daniel (1864-1941), Independent minister, and Anna, his wife. J.E. Daniel was educated at Friars School, Bangor and nurtured in the classical tradition. In 1919 he won a scholarship to Jesus College, Oxford, and in 1922 he took a first class in Classical Moderations and the following year, a first class in *Literae Humaniores*, followed by a first class in divinity in 1925. In the same year, a 'fellowship' was created for him at Bala-Bangor College and on the death of Dr. Thomas Rees (*DWB*, 830-1), he was appointed a full professor on 28 July, 1926, to be responsible for the courses on Christian doctrine and the philosophy of religion. In 1931 he was freed from his work to study with Rudolph Bultmann in Marburg. He remained at Bala-

Bangor until Jan. 1946 when he was appointed a Ministry of Education inspector of schools with special responsibility for religious education and the classics. During this time, he lived first of all at Wick, Glamorgan and subsequently at Tŷ Gwyn, Botffari, Flint. He was killed in a road accident near Halkyn in Flintshire on 11 Feb. 1962 and his remains were interred in the New Cemetery at Bangor. He m. Catrin, daughter of Rowland Hughes (1870-1928), an Independent minister, and they had five children.

Possessing outstanding academic qualifications, Daniel was one of the most able theologians of his generation, combining wide knowledge, an unfailing memory and a superb analytical mind. He was strongly influenced by the teachings of Karl Barth and Rudolph Bultmann in the stirring days of their early efforts. He shared their challenging spirit and their keen criticism of current theological thinking, creating thereby fierce opposition. However, Daniel was the most able interpreter of the reaction against the liberal theology movement in Wales. Despite this, his literary contribution to this field was sparse. He published *Dysgeidiaeth yr Apostol Paul* (1933) and a handful of articles in various journals. He was not ordained but there was great demand for his services as a preacher because of the stirring power of his sermons which combined a broad culture with fiery conviction.

He was a staunch nationalist. He came to early prominence as one of the leaders of *Plaid Genedlaethol Cymru* which was established in 1925. He was a regular contributor to its newspaper, *Y Ddraig Goch*, and he stood as a candidate in four general elections. He was a vice-chairman of the party from 1931 to 1935 and he followed Saunders Lewis as its chairman in 1939 and held the office until Aug. 1943.

Daniel was notable for his broad culture, his exceptionally brilliant mind and the strength and richness of his grasp of the Welsh language, both orally and in writing, his zeal for everything that was good in Wales and for the Christian faith above all else.

Pennar Davies (edit.), *Athrawon ac Annibynwyr* (1971), 128-42; [D. Densil Morgan, *Torri'r seiliau sicr* (1993); *Tr.*, 1997].

R.Td.J.

DAVIES, Sir ALFRED THOMAS, C.B. (1861-1949), the first Permanent Secretary (1907-25) of the Welsh Department of the Board of Education; b. 11 March 1861 at Liverpool, son of William Davies, silk mercer; educated there and at the University College of Wales, Aberystwyth, he practised as a solicitor at Liverpool, 1883-1907, specialising in licensing law, and playing a prominent part in the temperance campaign in the city. He also served as secretary of various educational committees and trusts, and was from 1904 to 1907 a member of the Denbighshire County Council and its Education Committee. After his retirement from the Board, though he lived in England, he continued to interest himself in Welsh matters, founding the Ceiriog Memorial Institute at Glyn Ceiriog, and publishing (in addition to numerous pamphlets) two biographical volumes: *O.M.* (a memoir of Sir Owen M. Edwards; 1946) and *The Lloyd George I knew* (1948). He was knighted in 1918, and was Dep. Lieutenant for

Denbighshire and Buckinghamshire. Davies m. twice, and had three sons and a daughter. He d. 21 Apr. 1949 at Brighton.

Www, 1941-50; *Times*, 23 Apr. 1949.

R.T.J.

DAVIES, ANNIE (1910-70), better known as NAN, radio and television producer; b. 16 June 1910, in Llwyngwinau House, Tregaron, third of the six children of David and Elizabeth Davies. The family kept a butcher's shop in Tregaron at the time, but when she was about a year old they moved to farm Cefngwyddil in the parish of Llanbadarn Odwyn, and in 1919 to farm Pontargamddwr in the parish of Caron-is-clawdd. She was educated at Castell Fflemish elementary school from 1915 to 1923 when she went to Tregaron county school. In 1929 she went to U.C.W., Aberystwyth, and took her finals in history and Latin in June 1932, but graduated in 1933.

She was for a period on the staff of Cardiff city library before joining the B.B.C. in 1935 as secretary to Sam Jones. She assisted him in establishing the very fine tradition of Welsh radio broadcasting at Bangor. In 1946 she left the B.B.C. and returned to Cardiganshire as warden of the *aelwydydd* (youth clubs) of *Urdd Gobaith Cymru* in Tregaron and Pontrhydfendigaid. The following year she was appointed secretary of the *Urdd*'s monetary appeal, a year later head of the appeals department, and in 1949 head of the movement's programmes and planning department. A few months later she returned to Bangor as producer of radio talks, and in 1955 moved to the B.B.C. headquarters in Cardiff to the world of radio and later television.

In Cardiff she was responsible for editing the literary radio programme *Llafar*, and was the first producer (and later, editor) of the television magazine programme *Heddiw*, the first television programme to discuss national and international matters in Welsh. In 1965 this programme won the *Western Mail and Echo* prize for the best programme of the year in Welsh. She visited the Welsh colony in Patagonia and produced the first film of that country ever seen on television. She was responsible for a large number of programmes such as 'Nant dialedd', 'Shepherd's calendar', 'Bugail Cwm Prysor' and 'Prynhawn o Fai'. In 1969 she retired from the B.B.C., returned to Tregaron where she bought a house called 'Monarch'; she enjoyed only a few months' health there and d. aged 59 in Singleton hospital, Swansea, on 7 May 1970. She was buried in the graveyard of Bwlch-gwynt chapel, Tregaron, on May 11.

Personal knowledge, and details from her sister, Mrs. Jane Edwards, Ysbyty Ystwyth, and Oswyn Evans, Porthcawl.

O.E.

DAVIES, BEN (1878-1958), Independent minister; b. in Llanboidy, Carms., 12 April 1878, son of Thomas Davies, a worker on the Maes-gwyn estate, and his wife Sarah. After being apprenticed as a joiner, he went to Old College School, Carmarthen, in 1901 and he was admitted to the Presbyterian College there in 1902. He was ordained on 28 July 1904. He m. Sarah, the daughter of Benjamin and Mary Bowen of the parish of Eglwys Newydd, near Carmarthen who were in the lineage of Samuel Bowen, Macclesfield (1799-1877; *DWB*, 47). They had one daughter, Arianwen, and three sons, Elwyn, Alun and Hywel (see below).

He began his ministry in the churches of Siloh, Pontardulais, and Hen Gapel, Llanelli. In 1907 he went to Hermon, Plas-marl, Swansea and remained there until 1914. He served in Seion, Llandysul from 1914 to 1924. He moved to Capel Newydd, Llandeilo and remained there until his retirement in 1954 when he went to live in Sketty, Swansea. He d. 17 Sept. 1958 and was interred at Bwlchnewydd, Carmarthenshire.

He was chairman of the Union of Welsh Independents in 1947 and that year he went to America to attend the World Congregational Congress in Boston. He published three books: *Siôn Gymro* (1938), *Cofiant Tomos Llanboidy* (1953), and *Coleg Presbyteraidd Caerfyrddin a'r genhadaeth* (1957). He made regular contributions to the periodicals of his denomination: *Y Tyst*, *Y Dysgedydd*, *Cennad Hedd* and *Tywysydd y Plant* and also to *Y Genhinen*. Above all else his preaching was based on scripture, and his pleasant personality, his tall appearance and his melodious eloquence made him popular for many years in the churches of his denomination.

Tyst, 24 Sept., 2 and 9 Oct. 1958; personal acquaintance.

Io.J.

DAVIES, BENJAMIN ('BEN'; 1858-1943), singer; b. 6 Jan. 1858 at Pontardawe, Glamorgan – the family moved later to Cwmbwrla near Swansea – son of John and Hannah Davies. He won his first prize as a singer at the age of five. He sang alto in 'Côr Caradog' and won several prizes in *eisteddfodau*. In 1878 he won a scholarship which took him to the Royal Academy of Music where he gained several medals and became F.R.A.M. Appointed chief tenor to the Carl Rosa Company in 1885 he travelled with that company for three years; in 1885 also he m. Clara Perry, chief soprano of the company. In 1888 he returned to London and took part in nearly a thousand performances, e.g. *Dorothy*, a musical comedy; afterwards he was chosen by Sir Arthur Sullivan to sing in the opera *Ivanhoe*. He had become one of the most popular singers in Britain and was Queen Victoria's first choice as vocalist. He was invited to take part in all the musical festivals and in the chief concerts of London and the provinces. He went on tour to the United States twelve times, nine times to Germany, and once to Africa. On his eightieth birthday he was honoured by the Musicians' Club, London. His last public appearance was at Caernarfon in 1937 on the occasion of the royal visit to that town. He lived at Arkhill, near Bath, and d. in the Clifton Nursing Home, Bristol, 28 March 1943; he was cremated at Armo Vale cemetery, Bath.

Cerddor, March and Nov. 1898, Oct. 1899; *South Wales Post*, 1943.

R.D.G.

DAVIES, CLARA NOVELLO ('Pencerddes Morgannwg'; 1861-1943) musician; b. 7 Apr.

1861 in Canton, Cardiff, dau. of Jacob Davies and Margaret his wife, and named Clara Novello after Clara Anastasia (née Novello), whom Jacob Davies had heard singing. She received her musical education from her father, Dr. Frost, Frederick Atkins (Cardiff), and Charles Williams (organist of Llandaff Cathedral). She was appointed, when quite young, accompanist to the Cardiff United Choir and the Cardiff Blue Ribbon Choir, which took many prizes at the Crystal Palace, London, under her father's baton. In 1883, Clara Novello formed a ladies choir which held many successful concerts in Wales and England. In 1893 the choir won the prize in the World Fair, Chicago, the test pieces being 'The Lord is my Shepherd' (Schubert) and 'The Spanish Gypsy'. Afterwards they toured through part of the United States and gave several concerts in some of the chief towns of England and Wales on their return. In 1900 that choir was invited to sing in the Paris *Exposition*. Throughout the years some of Clara Novello's pupils succeeded in winning prizes in national *eisteddfodau*. In 1927 she began to experiment with her own particular method of voice-production and breathing, and in 1928 published an explanatory book entitled *You can sing*; this work was dedicated to her son, Ivor Novello (1893-1951; see below). She had a voice-training school in New York, and, in 1924, she formed the Novello Davies Artist Choir to take part in concerts. In 1928 the Welsh Ladies Choir was invited to sing at Windsor Castle; it also received a similar invitation on 26 Apr. to the Paris Exposition in 1937. The Choir rendered much service by raising funds for charitable purposes, especially during the two World Wars. An autobiographical work, entitled *The Life I have loved*, was published by Clara Novello in 1940. She d. 7 February 1943 and was cremated at Golder's Green, London.

F. Griffith, *Notable Welsh Musicians*; *Cerddor*, March 1896; *Www*, 1941-50.

R.D.G.

DAVIES, CLEMENT EDWARD (1884-1962), politician; b. 19 Feb. 1884 at Llanfyllin, Mont., the youngest of the seven children of Moses Davies, auctioneer, and his wife Elizabeth Margaret Jones. Educated at the local elementary school, he went to Llanfyllin County School when it opened in 1897. He went on to Trinity Hall, Cambridge, where he obtained first class in both parts of the law tripos (1906-07) and won a number of prizes. He took up a post as law lecturer in Aberystwyth in 1908-09 before he was called to the Bar at Lincoln's Inn. Davies joined the North Wales circuit in 1909 and transferred, within a year, to the Northern circuit. He was a successful lawyer and published, under the influence of his family background, books on agricultural law and on the law of auctions and auctioneers.

At the beginning of World War I Davies was appointed advisor on enemy activities in neutral countries and on the high seas. He moved to the Board of Trade where he dealt with trading with the enemy. He held the post of secretary to the president of the Probate, Divorce, and Admiralty division, 1918-19, and secretary to the Master of the Rolls, 1919-23. His experience in these posts together with his ready and favourable advice proved of great use to the Library authorities in obtaining the deposit of Welsh wills and the records of the Courts of Great Session at the National Library of Wales during the 1920s. From 1919 to 1925 he was a junior counsel to the Treasury and became a K.C. in 1926. He held the post of chairman of the Montgomeryshire Quarter Sessions from 1935 until his death. He was on the Board of Unilever 1930-41 and later acted as an adviser to the Board.

In 1929 Davies was elected Liberal M.P. for Montgomeryshire and he represented the county for the rest of his life. He joined the National Liberals in 1931 but rejoined the Liberal Party in 1941. During World War II he was a strong supporter of the coalition Government. He was leader of the Liberal Party from 1945 to 1956. He was zealous in his support for liberty and social justice. Davies was elected an honorary fellow of Trinity Hall in 1950 and a bencher of Lincoln's Inn in 1953. He was also made a freeman of Welshpool in 1955 and given an honorary LL.D. by the University of Wales in the same year. He d. on 23 March 1962 in London and he was buried in the graveyard at Meifod Church.

In 1913 he m. Jano Elizabeth (d. 27 Dec. 1969), the adopted daughter of Morgan Davies, a doctor with a popular practice among the London Welsh and who contributed frequently, under the pseudonym 'Teryll y Bannau', to Welsh newspapers. Clement and Jano Davies had three sons and a daughter; they lost three of the children, each at the age of twenty-four; a son and the daughter died in accidents; only one son survived. Jano Davies was a fine public speaker and she was of considerable assistance to her husband in his political career. She was the youngest head teacher of her time in London.

Times, 24 Mar. 1962; *DNB*, 1961-70, 278-9. [The papers of Clement Davies are held by NLW, see *N.L.W. Jnl.*, 23, 406-210; Lord Hooson, *Trans. Cymm.* 1997].

E.D.J.

DAVIES, DANIEL JOHN (1885-1970), Independent minister and poet; b. 2 Sept. 1885, at Waunfelen, a cottage in Pentregalar, Crymych, Pembs., a son of John Morris and Ann Davies. When his father was killed in a rail accident at Boncath station, his mother and her three sons moved to a house named Tŷ-canol, but the mother and the two brothers died soon after and the orphaned boy went to live with his mother's sister at Aberdyfnant, Llanfyrnach. There he was influenced by O.R. Owen, the minister of Glandŵr Independent chapel. He started to preach there at Whitsun, 1906. After a period at Old College School at Carmarthen he took an honours course in Hebrew at University College, Cardiff and graduated in 1913, followed by a theological course at the Memorial College, Brecon. The authorities at Brecon had prevented him from taking Welsh as his main subject at Cardiff. Despite this he won the chair twice at the college *eisteddfod*. He was ordained at Capel Als, Llanelli, in 1916 - a staunch pacifist in the middle of the Great War. He held strong radical views, politically and theologically, but he was no Boanerges. During his ministry six of the young men of Capel Als entered the ministry, one as a missionary who worked in Sudan.

He won the *cywydd* competition four times at the national *eisteddfod*. R. Williams Parry said of his poem *Ffynnon Fair* that he knew of no one who could write so easily and so effortlessly within the restrictions of *cynghanedd*. He was second to Gwenallt in the chair competition the year before winning in 1932 for his ode 'Mam' at the Aberavon National *Eisteddfod* in a competition of high quality. He adjudicated frequently at the national *eisteddfod* and he composed a number of acceptable hymns. He published a collection of his poetry, *Cywyddau a chaniadau eraill* in 1968. He held classes in *cynghanedd* in Llanelli.

Although he was shy by nature, he became one of the leaders of his denomination; he was shrewd and wise with an unforced sense of humour and a pleasing personality. He was elected to the chair of the Union of Welsh Independents and his address from the chair was published in the Union's annual report for 1957. He was one of the editors of the *Caniedydd Cynulleidfaol* which was published in 1960. He retired from his ministry at Capel Als in 1958. He d. 4 June 1970. His ashes were buried in Glandŵr cemetery. His likeable and talented wife, Enid, was the daughter of D. Stanley Jones (*DWB*, 1132), minister of the Independent chapel at Caernarfon.

Blwyddiadur A., 1971, 165; *Tyst*, June, 1970; personal knowledge; Maurice Loader, *Capel Als* (1980).

Io.J.

DAVIES, Sir DANIEL THOMAS (1899-1966), physician; b. in Nov. 1899 the son of D. Mardy Davies, minister (Presb.), Pontycymer, and Esther his wife. He was brought up in the Garw valley and was educated at Bridgend grammar school and the University College, Cardiff. Practical chemical pathology at Middlesex Hospital, London, owed a great deal to him after his appointment as pathologist there in 1927. He also made a great impression as medical registrar of the hospital before becoming a member of the staff of the Royal Free Hospital in 1930 where he did clinical work for 30 years and at St. John and St. Elizabeth hospital for 35 years (1930-65). He excelled as a teacher and was Bradshaw lecturer at the Royal College of Physicians. With Lionel Whitby, Graham Hodgson, Lord Dawson and others he did valuable research work on the use of Felton's serum in the treatment of pneumonia. His article on 'Gastric secretions of old age' which he published in conjunction with Lloyd James is considered a classic. He published several medical books, including a standard work on pneumonia and books on peptic ulcers and anaemia. He was a Fellow of the Royal Medical Society. In 1938 he became physician to the royal family. He was physician to King George VI and later to Queen Elizabeth and he continued to be physician to the Duke of Windsor, being one of his personal friends. He was also very friendly with well-known physicians such as Lord Dawson and Lord Horder. He was Lord Beaverbrook's personal physician and his medical adviser from the period when he was in the Ministry of Supply during World War II. In 1951 he received a knighthood. As a strict nonconformist he refused to join the national health service even though Aneurin Bevan (see above) was one of his closest friends. He read widely in English and Welsh literature and maintained close contact with Welsh life, being one of the original members of the Pantyfedwen Trust which was formed in 1957. He was an incomparable story-teller and conversationalist and spoke Welsh at every opportunity. He m. Vera, daughter of J. Percy Clarkson, and they had two daughters. He d. 18 May 1966 in his home in Wimpole Street, London.

Times, 19 May 1966; *Lancet*, 28 May 1966.

E.D.J.

DAVIES, DAVID of Llandinam (1880-1944), first BARON DAVIES (created 1932); b. 11 May 1880, only son of Edward Davies and Mary, dau. of Evan Jones, a Calvinistic Methodist minister who was closely related to John Jones of Talysarn (1796-1857; *DWB*, 478-9). He was the grandson of David Davies (1818-90; *DWB*, 116), the Welsh industrialist of the Victorian period, whose energy and enterprise he inherited. Educated at King's College, Cambridge, he entered the House of Commons at 26 years of age as Liberal member for Montgomeryshire, resigning his seat in 1929. In World War I, he raised and commanded the 14th Battalion, the Royal Welch Fusiliers, at home and in France until 1916, when he was appointed Parliamentary Secretary to David Lloyd George.

His name will be inseparably connected with his two main public interests – the Welsh campaign against tuberculosis and the international crusade for world peace. In 1911, together with his sisters, the Misses Gwendoline E. and Margaret S. Davies of Gregynog Hall, (see below) he founded the King Edward VII Welsh National Memorial Association which, under his direction, developed into a nation-wide scheme with many sanatoria and hospitals. The Llandinam family also endowed the University Chair of Tuberculosis at the Welsh National School of Medicine. From 1919 David Davies was equally tireless in the pursuit of international peace, carrying on the tradition of the Welsh pioneers Richard Price, Robert Owen, and Henry Richard. A founder of the League of Nations Union, he later gained prominence as the foremost advocate of strengthening the League of Nations by the creation of an International Police Force. In 1932 he established the New Commonwealth Society for 'the promotion of international law and order', writing several books on the right use of force, notably *The Problem of the Twentieth Century* (1930). In Nov. 1938, one of his ambitions was realised in the completion of the Temple of Peace and Health in Cathays Park, Cardiff.

For many years he was president of the University College at Aberystwyth and amongst his numerous benefactions was the endowment of the Wilson chair of International Politics, the first chair of its kind in Great Britain. He was also president and a generous patron of the National Library of Wales.

Though he had a wide range of industrial and commercial activities, essentially he was a countryman keenly interested in sport and at Llandinam he maintained foxhounds. He was an ardent supporter of the Royal Welsh Agricultural Society.

He was twice married. His first wife, who d. in 1918, was Amy, dau. of L.T. Penman of Broadwood Park, Lanchester; they had one son and one daughter. In 1922 he married Henrietta Margaret (Rita), dau. of James Grant Fergusson, of Baledmund, Scotland (d. 1948); they had two sons and two daughters.

Lord Davies d. 16 June 1944. In Sept. of the same year, his heir, Major DAVID DAVIES (1915-44) of the Royal Welch Fusiliers, second Baron Davies of Llandinam (b. 16 Jan. 1915), was killed on the Western Front. He m. Ruth Eldrydd, dau. of Major William Marshall Dugdale and his wife, of Llanfyllin, in 1939. They had 2 sons.

Personal information; *Www*, 1941-50.

Gw.D.

DAVIES, DAVID ALBAN – see ALBAN DAVIES, DAVID above.

DAVIES, DAVID CAXTON (1873-1955), printer and company director; b. at Lampeter, Cards., 8 Aug. 1873, s. of David and Margaret Davies (the oldest inhabitant of the town when she d. 28 Dec. 1937). Educated in his native town, he became manager of the Welsh Church Press at Lampeter, and (1909-19) of Grosvenor and Chater & Co., London; manager and director of William Lewis, Ltd., printers, Cardiff, and of Davies, Harvey and Murrell, Ltd., paper merchants, London. In 1935-36 he was president of the South Wales and Monmouthshire Master Printers Alliance. He was one of the founder members of Cardiff Rotary Club. In 1947 the University of Wales conferred on him an hon. M.A. degree for his services to the publication of books and periodicals about Wales, particularly those in the Welsh language. He d. 5 Nov. 1955, and a funeral service was held in St. David's Church, Cardiff, before cremation at Thornhill on 9 Nov.

WwW (1937); *West. Mail*, *Welsh Gaz.*, 6 Jan. 1938.

E.D.J.

DAVIES, DAVID CHRISTOPHER ('Christy'; 1878-1958); missionary and representative of the British Missionary Society (B.M.S.) in Wales; b. 16 July 1878 at Clydach, in the Swansea valley, Glam., second of the 10 children of John and Elizabeth Davies. He was brought up in a musical family; the father (who was employed in a local foundry) played the trombone with the Clydach brass band, and was deacon and treasurer of Calfaria (B) Church. The pastor of the church was T. Valentine Evans (father of Sir (David) Emrys Evans, see below) to whom Christopher felt greatly indebted. When he was 12 years old and had reached the top class at school he had to work for a year in the family grocer's shop before being apprenticed to a tailor at Ystalyfera, where he was baptised in Soar Church. At the end of his apprenticeship he worked in Swansea and Cardiff before entering the service of Colmers of Bath. There he became a member of Hay Hill Church, and in 1900 decided to enter the ministry. The week his father d. he had an interview for entry to Spurgeon's College. He commenced his course there in Jan. 1902. During the Christmas vacation of 1904 he came under the influence of Evan (John) Roberts' Revival (see below). While he was a student-pastor at Thorpe-le-Soken he felt a call to the missionary field, especially China, but the B.M.S. designated him for the Congo. After receiving medical instruction at the Livingstone Institution and spending some months at Brussels improving his French, he departed from London Aug. 1906 to go to his mission station in Yalemba in the Congo, near the mouth of the river Aruwimi. He soon mastered Heso, the language of the inhabitants. The natives called him Molembia, and revered him deeply. He also became proficient in Lingala, which was the common language of the inhabitants of the Upper Congo. He translated parts of the New Testament into both Heso and Lingala. He composed hymns in their languages and had them sung to Welsh tunes. In 1919 the Society transferred him to the rapidly growing city of Leopoldville. His task was to concentrate attention on the new arrivals of the Bangala tribe, who spoke Lingala. In 1933, because of his ill-health, he returned to Wales as a representative of the B.M.S. He arranged summer schools in various locations before being stationed for a period in the Theological College, Aberystwyth, and afterwards at Cilgwyn, Newcastle Emlyn. His good humour, his great sense of fun and enthusiasm greatly inspired those attending the summer schools. He retired in 1943 and spent the rest of his life at Mumbles, where he became a member of the Welsh (B) church, Capel Gomer, in Swansea.

In Nov. 1914 he m. Margaret Parker, a deaconess at Bloomsbury (B) Church. They had two daughters. He d. 4 May 1958, soon after being elected an hon. member of the B.M.S.

J. Williams Hughes, *D. Christy Davies* (1962).

E.D.J.

DAVIES, DAVID IVOR (1893-1951) – see NOVELLO, IVOR below.

DAVIES, DAVID JAMES (1893-1956), economist; b. 2 June 1893 at Cefnmwng, a small cottage near Carmel, Carms., the 3rd child of Thomas Davies, miner, and Ellen (née Williams). After attending local schools, he worked in several collieries and at Barry Dock (1907-12). In the meantime he continued his education in evening classes and through correspondence courses. In 1912 he emigrated to the U.S.A. and Canada where he worked in the mines and, with others, established the Northwestern Coal and Coke Co., Steamboat Springs, Colorado. He travelled widely in America and visited China and Japan; he also found time for boxing and studying law at the Universities of Seattle and Pueblo. In 1918 he joined the U.S. Navy and trained as an engineer but returned to Wales in 1919 (being discharged from the Navy in 1920). He worked for a short period as a collier in Llandybïe, until he was incapacitated by a serious accident in 1919. He utilised his enforced leisure reading and studying economics, politics and the history of the Working Class Movement. He was a founder member of the Labour Party in the Ammanford district. His attitude towards the relationship between socialism and nationalism changed completely in 1924 after he attended the International People's College, Elsinore, Denmark (where he met Noëlle Ffrench of Bushy Park, Co.

Roscommon, Ireland, whom he married, 2 June 1925) and the Folk High School, Vestbirk, Denmark. He came to believe that true internationalism was based on co-operation between free nations, while the advancement of the Welsh working class could only be secured in a free Wales. This point of view was expressed months before the Welsh Nationalist Party (now *Plaid Cymru*) was founded in 1925, while he was unaware of the existence of a nationalist movement in Wales. He returned from Denmark a convinced nationalist in favour of an economic policy of co-operation which placed ownership and control of the means of production in the hands of the workers themselves.

After an unsuccessful attempt at establishing a folk school in Ireland in 1924-25, he entered U.C.W., Aberystwyth, where he graduated (B.A.) in economics in 1928, M.A. (1930), Ph.D. (1931). He won several prizes at the national *eisteddfod* on political and economic subjects (1930, 1931, 1932 – an essay which was published as *The economic history of South Wales prior to 1800* (1933) – and 1933). He became a leading member of *Plaid Cymru* and rendered great service to the Party as a researcher and author of pamphlets and articles which he contributed regularly to all of the movement's publications, e.g. *The economics of Welsh self-government* (1931), *Towards an economic democracy* (1949), *Can Wales afford self-government?* (with Noëlle Davies, 1938, 1947), *Cymoedd tan gwmwl* (with Noëlle Davies, 1938), *Diwydiant a masnach* (1946). He was conscious of the necessity to reach out to the English-speaking population and took a prominent part in the decision to transfer the Party's head office from Caernarfon to Cardiff in 1944.

In 1932 he and his wife bought Pantybeilïau mansion at Gilwern, near Bryn-mawr, Mon., and attempted to establish a folk school there. Although they failed to realise their ambition, they were interested in the dispute concerning the legal status of Monmouthshire. They lost no opportunity in demonstrating that it had always been an integral part of Wales.

He d. 11 Oct. 1956 and was buried in Carmel (B) graveyard in the village where he was born.

Personal knowledge; D.J. Davies (with a memoir by C.H.T.), *Towards Welsh freedom* (1958).

C.H.T.

DAVIES, DAVID JOSHUA (1877-1945), dramatist; b. in Troedyrhiw, Llanwenog, Cards., 26 Dec. 1877, son of John Davies and Mary (née Evans) his wife. He was educated in Mydroilyn elementary school and the tutorial school in New Quay. He almost lost his sight there, but after recuperating he became an apprentice in an ironmonger's store in Swansea. He returned to manage the co-operative store at Llannarth. In 1910 he took a smallholding and later a shop and post office in Pontrhyd-y-groes, where he spent the rest of his life. He held important offices in his denomination (Meth.), and in the county council, where he became chairman of the education committee. He wrote a great deal to the local press on political topics, but his greatest distinction was to win the prize at the National *Eisteddfod* in Neath in 1918 for his very popular play *Maes y Meillion*. His play *Owen Glyndŵr* remains unpublished. He m.

Annie Davies, New Quay, 6 Apr. 1904, in St. Paul's Aberystwyth, and they had four children. He d. 8 Jan. 1945, and was buried in New Quay.

Information from his daughter, Mrs. J.T. Owen; personal knowledge.

G.R.T.

DAVIES, DAVID REES ('Cledlyn'; 1875-1964), schoolmaster, poet, writer, local historian; b. 6 Feb. 1875 in Glanrhyd, Cwrtnewydd, Cards. The house is now called 'Langro', and has a small plaque on it to mark his birthplace. He was one of the two sons of Evan Davies, blacksmith, and his wife Elizabeth (née James). He was educated in the village school and from the age of 14 until he went to U.C.W., Aberystwyth, in 1894, he was a pupil teacher there. At the end of his first term at college he gained one of the scholarships offered to the three best students in the education department, and at the end of two years he left with a first-class teacher's certificate. He first went to teach at Moelfre, Llansilin, near Oswestry and moved to Cofadail school, Cards., 9 May 1898. From 28 Feb. 1902 until he retired in 1935 he served as schoolmaster in his native village. A gifted schoolmaster, he was respected by his pupils and the local people. The recitation pieces which he composed for children were very popular and were published in *Tusw o flodau* (1925) for use in schools.

His major interests lay in writing poetry, and competing and adjudicating in *eisteddfodau*. He won many prizes at the National *Eisteddfod* including the chair at Corwen, 1919, and also at Mold, 1923. His entries showed a complete mastery of *cynghanedd* and of the Welsh language. He was president of the Unitarian Association in South Wales in 1920 and twelve of his hymns appeared in *Y Perlau Moliant*, though he rejected religion from the 1930s onwards. On behalf of the Cardiganshire Antiquarian Society he edited the words (collected mostly by J. Ffos Davies), and D.J. de Lloyd (see below) the music, of *Forty Welsh traditional tunes* (1929). He contributed regularly to *The Welsh Gazette* over a period of about 60 years, and also to *Yr Ymofynnydd, Y Genhinen* and *The Western Mail* (see Glyn Lewis Jones, *A bibliography of Cardiganshire, 1600-1964,* (1967) and the *Supplement, 1964-8* (1970) for a bibliography of much of his work). When he was 88 years old he published *Chwedlau ac Odlau* (1963), which portrays local characters and includes a selection of his own poems. But his main work, in collaboration with his second wife, was a local history, *Hanes plwyf Llanwenog* (1936; 2nd ed. 1939). They also wrote a history of the parish of Llanwnnen, parts of which were published in the *Welsh Gazette*.

He m. (1), summer 1895, Elizabeth Thomas, who d. 12 Feb. 1908 leaving three daughters and a son. He m. (2), 1914, Zabeth Susanah Owen, headmistress of Blaenau school, Gors-goch. He d. 29 Dec. 1964, five days after his wife.

Information from his grandson, Bifan Prys Morgan; *Ymofynnydd*, 65, 1965, 22-6; D.J. Goronwy Evans (ed.), *Deri o'n daear ni* (1984).

E.D.J.

DAVIES, DAVID TEGFAN (1883-1968), Congl.

minister; b. 27 Feb. 1883 in Capel Bach, a small-holding in Abergwili parish, Carms., where he was brought up by his grandparents, Dafydd and Hannah Dafis. It was to them, and the local inhabitants of the district of Peniel, that he was indebted for the vivid and vigorous language he spoke, full of words and expressions that are no longer in colloquial use. After leaving school he became a farm servant at Rhyd-y-rhaw, Peniel, and became a member of Peniel (Congl.) church, where he began to preach in Aug. 1903 under the ministry of H.T. Jacob (see below). He attended the Old College School at Carmarthen before going to Bala-Bangor College in 1905. On 13 Sept. 1908 he was ord. minister at Seion, Pontypridd, but moved to Addoldy, Glyn-neath, where he was inducted on 1 Jan. 1911. Finally he was inducted on 13 Sept. 1915 as minister of Gellimanwydd (Christian Temple), Ammanford, where he served for 50 years. He arrived at Ammanford during World War I and committed himself to his pastoral ministry in the district. He made friends with everyone; many went to him in tribulation and he visited everyone. He showed great concern about the unemployment and poverty of the 1930s and became chairman of the local Distress Committee. When Ammanford was adopted by the town of Wallasey, he was appointed a member of the consultative deputation that went there.

One of his many hobbies was astronomy. He knew the stars by name, and on many a clear night he observed them through his telescope outside his house; he became a Fellow of the Royal Astronomical Society. He also took an interest in gypsies, with whom he made friends. His published works – *O ganol shir Gâr, Cyn dringo'r Mynydd Du, Rhamantwr y De* and *Cyffro'r hen goffrau* – abound in old Carmarthenshire phrases, old beliefs and rural amusements, and reveal his vivid imagination and story-telling gifts. He was a well-received evangelical preacher but he gave most of his attention to pastoral duties. He travelled much on the continent of Europe, often travelling on cargo ships from Swansea. He also went on a preaching tour of the U.S.A. As president of the Union of Welsh Independents he delivered his address from the chair in Pwllheli in 1958 on 'The continuance of the Pentecost'. One of his many generous acts was his gift of £1000 to his denomination's Assistance Fund. He received an honorary D.D. (Oslo), and in 1965 he was awarded the O.B.E. in acknowledgement of his humanitarian acts and for his bravery on many occasions in rescuing persons in danger of drowning.

He m. (1), 10 Nov. 1908, Anna Twining, Richmond Tce., Carmarthen (d. 1933). He m. (2), 1934, Sarah Jane Davies, Wauncefen, Heol-ddu, Ammanford. He d. 10 Aug. 1968 and was buried in Gellimanwydd cemetery.

Tyst, 22, 29 Aug., 26 Sept., 2 Oct. 1968; *Blwyddiadur A*, 1969; Robert Ellis, *Lleisiau ddoe a heddiw* (1961); handbooks of the Union of Congregationalists at Ammanford, 1927 and 1959.

D.M.J.

DAVIES, DAVID THOMAS (1876-1962), dramatist; b. 24 Aug. 1876 at Nant-y-moel, Llandyfodwg, Glam., son of Thomas Davies and his wife Martha (née Thomas). He was educated at Gelli, Ystrad, Rhondda valley, and Thomas James's school, Llandysul, Cards. His father intended him for the ministry, but after graduating at the University College of Wales, Aberystwyth, in 1903, he became a teacher in the Central Foundation School, London. He served with the Royal Welsh Fusiliers in France during World War I, and in 1919 he was appointed an inspector of schools under the Ministry of Education and moved to live in Pontypridd. He retired in 1936 and moved to Porthcawl. He moved yet again to Swansea in 1954 where he d. 7 July 1962. He was buried in Glyntaf cemetery, Pontypridd. He m. Jane Davies at Trealaw, 29 July 1909 and they had one daughter.

D.T. Davies gained prominence as one of the Welsh social dramatists of the first half of the 20th c. He came into contact with John Oswald Francis (see below) while he was a student at Aberystwyth, and he had an opportunity to get to know contemporary English plays when he was a teacher in London. Ibsen's plays were popular in the London theatres and they provided a pattern for D.T. Davies and the new generation of Welsh dramatists like Robert Griffith Berry (see above), J.O. Francis and William John Gruffydd (see below). He wrote a number of full-length plays and many short plays: among his most important works are *Ble ma fa?* (1913), *Ephraim Harris* (1914), *Y Pwyllgor* (1920), *Castell Martin* (1920) and *Pelenni Pitar* (1925). He broke fresh ground with these plays by presenting a faithful portrayal and an honest evaluation of life. His works were very much in vogue during the 1920s when the Welsh drama movement was at its zenith in the valleys of south Wales and when drama companies and drama festivals were being established in the chapels and workers' institutes.

Menna Davies, 'Traddodiad llenyddol y Rhondda', University of Wales Ph.D. thesis (Aberystwyth, 1981), 259-82; R.M. Jones, *Llenyddiaeth Gymraeg 1902-1936* (1987), 529-32; information from his daughter, Sara Anne Davies; see also David Jenkins (ed.), *Erthyglau ac ysgrifau llenyddol Kate Roberts* (1978), 148-50; [Menna Davies in Hywel T. Edwards, ed., *Cwm Rhondda* (1995), 254-75].

H.Wa.

DAVIES, EDWARD TEGLA (1880-1967), minister (Meth.) and writer; b. 31 May 1880 at Hen Giât, Llandegla, Denb., fourth of the six children of William and Mary Ann Davies. His father was a quarryman, who was badly injured in Moel Faen quarry but continued to work there and subsequently in Mwynglawdd chalk quarry, to ward off destitution. In 1893 the family moved to Pentre'r Bais (Gwynfryn) and in 1896 to Bwlchgwyn. When he was 14 years old Edward became a pupil-teacher at Bwlch-gwyn school. Tom Arfor Davies, a young teacher at Bwlch-gwyn for a short period before his untimely death, awoke his interest in the history and literature of Wales. He experienced a religious conversion after attending a preaching festival at Coedpoeth, and decided to enter the ministry. In 1901 he became a probationer and after a year on the Ffynnongroyw circuit he entered Didsbury College, Manchester. He served his ministry at Abergele, Leeds, Menai Bridge, Port Dinorwic, Tregarth (thrice), Llanrhaeadr-ym-Mochnant, Denbigh, Manchester (twice), Liverpool, Bangor and Coedpoeth.

In 1908 he m. Jane Eleanor (Nel) Evans, Gwynlys Shop, Bwlchgwyn, and they had 3 children: Dyddgu, Arfor and Gwen. He retired in 1946 because of his wife's illness and moved to Bangor, where she d. in 1948. He d. 9 Oct. 1967, and was buried in Gelli cemetery, Tregarth.

Although he never had a Welsh lesson at school nor went to university, he became one of the most prolific writers in Welsh. He benefited from his friendship with Ifor Williams, T. Gwynn Jones, David Thomas (Bangor, 1880-1967; see all three below) and other writers. He was editor of *Y Winllan*, 1920-28; *Yr Efrydydd*, 1931-35; and the series, 'Cyfres Pobun', 1944-50. His boys' stories which appeared in *Y Winllan* were later published as books. The first, *Hunangofiant Tomi* (1912), became very popular. It was followed by *Nedw* (1922), *Rhys Llwyd y lleuad* (1925), and *Y Doctor Bach* (1930). He published many books for children on legendary and Biblical characters, and an adaptation of the Welsh translation of *Pilgrim's Progress* (1931). His imagination is given rein in *Hen Ffrindiau* (1927), and the fantasies, *Tir y Dyneddon* (1921) and *Stori Sam* (1938). Although criticised for moralising and allegorising in these, their inventiveness and narrative are still marvellous. His only long novel, *Gŵr Pen y Bryn* (1923), was initially serialised in *Yr Eurgrawn* and appeared in book form in 1923. Whatever its shortcomings, it is a milestone in the history of the Welsh novel because of its ordered plot and its penetrating study of a soul in anguish. It was translated into English by Nina Watkins as *The Master of Penybryn* (1975). He published only one other novel: the short satirical novel *Gyda'r Glannau* (1941). His short stories which appeared in magazines were collected together in *Y Llwybr Arian* (1934). Apart from a number of religious books for young people, his published works from 1943 onwards were mostly volumes of essays: selections, mainly, of his weekly articles in *Yr Herald Cymraeg* from 1946 to 1953 under the pseudonym 'Eisteddwr' and of his radio talks. *Rhyfedd o fyd* (1950) reveals his satire at its most scathing, while the powerful illustrations of a creative preacher are a prominent feature of *Y Foel Faen* (1951), and *Ar ddisberod* (1954). His autobiography, *Gyda'r Blynyddoedd*, was followed by a volume of further reminiscences, *Gyda'r hwyr*, and *Y Ffordd*, and *Y Dyhead* which contain some of his sermons. He published more than 40 books and booklets in all.

Tegla regarded himself as a rebel all his life. Although he was one of the most prominent preachers and one of the most influential men of his denomination, he did not refrain from criticising and satirising organizational systems, whether religious or secular. He was one of the early promoters of Biblical criticism in Wales and *Llestri'r Trysor* (1914), which was edited by his friend D. Tecwyn Evans (see below), and his preface to *Y Flodeugerdd Feiblaidd* (1940), caused quite a stir. But he was a Wesleyan through and through. He contributed articles on Wesleyan ministers to the *DWB* and an article on 'Welsh Wesleyan Methodism' in *The*

Methodist Church, A.W. Harrison (ed., 1932), as well as articles for *Y Geiriadur Beiblaidd*, and he was on the joint-committee of the Methodist hymn book, 1924-26. He was president of the Welsh Methodist Assembly in 1937. For many years he was a member of the council and executive committee of the National *Eisteddfod* and a frequent *eisteddfod* adjudicator. He received an honorary M.A. degree of the University of Wales in 1924 for his contribution to Welsh literature, and a D.Litt. in 1958.

E. Tegla Davies, *Gyda'r blynyddoedd* (1952); Islwyn Ffowc Elis (ed.), *Edward Tegla Davies, llenor a phroffwyd* (1956); Thomas Parry and Merfyn Morgan (ed.), *Llyfryddiaeth Llenyddiaeth Gymraeg* (1976), 245; personal knowledge from his daughter, Lady Dyddgu Elwyn Jones; [Huw Ethall, *Tegla* (1980); Pennar Davies, *E. Tegla Davies* (1983)].

I.Ff.E.

DAVIES, ELLIS (1872-1962), priest and antiquarian; b. 22 Sept. 1872, son of Ellis Davies, a gardener at Nannerch, Flints., but the family soon moved to Llaniestyn, Caerns. He was educated at Botwnnog grammar school, and in 1892 he gained an entrance exhibition to St. David's College, Lampeter, where he won prizes each year. After graduating in 1895 he was ord. and served as curate in Llansilin, and then in Old Colwyn and St. Giles, Oxford. Whilst at Oxford he graduated B.A. (1907) from Worcester College and took his M.A. in 1911. He also acted as chaplain to Jesus College and Radcliffe Infirmary. In 1909 he was appointed vicar of Llanddoged, Denbs., and rector of Whitford, Flints., in 1913, where he remained until his retirement in 1951. In recognition of his long and dedicated service to the Church he held a canonry at St. Asaph, 1937-46, and was chancellor of the diocese, 1944-47. Although he composed several hymn-tunes and chants he became more widely known in the field of archaeology. In 1913 he became a member of the Cambrian Archaeological Society and the same year he won a prize at the national *eisteddfod* at Abergavenny for a handbook on British and Roman remains in Denbighshire which was published in 1929 after further research. He also won a prize at the national *eisteddfod* at Corwen in 1919 for an essay on the place-names of Merionethshire. In 1956 the G.T. Clark Prize for research into Celtic history was awarded to him for his work on *The prehistoric and Roman remains of Flintshire* (1949). He was also author of *Llyfr y proffwyd Hosea* (1920), *Flintshire Place-names* (1959) and numerous articles in *Yr Haul*, *Y Llan*, *Dictionary of Welsh Biography down to 1940* and historical journals. He served as joint editor of *Archaeologia Cambrensis* for 15 years from 1925 and later as sole editor (1940-48). In 1929 he was elected F.S.A. and in 1959 the University of Wales conferred on him an honorary D.Litt.

He m. Mary Louisa (d. 27 May 1937), daughter of the Revd. David Davies, Llansilin. He d. 3 Apr. 1962 at Bryn Derwen, Caerwys, Flints., and was survived by 3 sons and 3 daughters.

Arch. Camb., 1962, 168-9; *Y Llan*, 13 Apr. 1962, 7; NLW Microfilm 302, St. David's College students.

M.A.J.

DAVIES, ERNEST SALTER – see SALTER DAVIES, ERNEST below.

DAVIES, EVAN THOMAS (1878-1969), musician; b. 10 Apr. 1878 at 41 Pontmorlais, Merthyr Tydfil, Glam., son of George (a barber whose shop was in South Street, Dowlais), and Gwenllian (née Samuel) his wife. He was brought up in Dowlais, but moved to Merthyr Tydfil in 1904. His parents were musical; his father was precentor in Hermon, Dowlais, for nearly a quarter of a century, and his mother was a good singer, a descendant of the same family as the song-writer, R.S. Hughes (*DWB*, 389). He was given private tuition and came heavily under the influence of Harry Evans (*DWB*, 235-6). He visited the U.S.A. with a party of singers from Wales in 1898, and after returning he came to be regarded as the leading musician in his native district, and as a worthy successor to Harry Evans, his tutor. He was organist at Pontmorlais chapel, Merthyr Tydfil, 1903-17, and a part-time singing teacher in Merthyr Tydfil secondary school, 1904-20, making his home in 'Cartrefle' near the school – the house where Harry Evans had lived.

After gaining his F.R.C.O. his services as a solo organist were in great demand, and he was said to have inaugurated about a hundred new organs in Wales and England. In 1920 he was appointed the first full-time director of music of the University College, Bangor, where he was responsible for numerous musical activities, and collaborated with (Henry) Walford Davies (see below), Aberystwyth, to enhance knowledge of music in a wide area under the auspices of the university's Council of Music. In 1943 he retired and moved to Aberdare, where he spent the rest of his life composing, adjudicating and broadcasting.

He first came into prominence as a composer after winning the first prize for 'Ynys y Plant' in the national *eisteddfod* held in London in 1909, and although he was not a very prolific composer, and tended to regard composing merely as a hobby, he had a beneficial influence upon Welsh music for more than half a century. Besides writing a few songs, he also composed part-songs, anthems and works for various musical instruments and instrumental groups, and about 40 of his tunes, chants and anthems are to be found in various collections of tunes. He recognised the excellent work on folk-songs that John Lloyd Williams (see below) had done before him at Bangor, and he was one of the first Welsh musicians to find sufficient merit in the folk-songs to arrange them for voice or instrument. His arrangements of over a hundred of these songs, (many of them produced when the composer was in old age) have great artistic merit. He also took an interest in Welsh national songs, and was co-editor with Sydney Northcote of *The National Songs of Wales* (1959). He m., 31 Aug. 1916, Mary Llewellyn, youngest daughter of D.W. Jones, Aberdare. He d. at home in Aberdare on Christmas Day 1969.

Cerddor, Nov. 1909; David Morgans, *Music and Musicians of Merthyr and District* (1922); *Cymro*, 7 Jan. 1970; *Welsh Music*, 3 (1970), No. 6, 2-10; Robert Smith (ed.), *A Catalogue of Contemporary Welsh Music*, No. 5 (1972).

H.W.

DAVIES, GEORGE MAITLAND LLOYD (1880-1949), Calvinistic Methodist minister and apostle of peace; b. 30 Apr. 1880, in Peel Rd., Sefton Park, Liverpool, son of John and Gwen Davies. He was christened G.M.Temple Davies; he himself was responsible for changing his name. One of his brothers was John Glyn Davies (see below). His father was a tea-merchant, whose roots were in Cardiganshire and Llŷn, his mother was a daughter of John Jones, Talysarn (*DWB*, 478-9). He was educated at Liverpool and entered the Bank of Liverpool at an early age. In 1908 he was appointed manager of the branch in Wrexham, where later he took a commission in the Royal Welch Fusiliers (territorials). He gave up his work in 1913 in order to become the secretary of the Welsh Town Planning and Housing Trust and about this time he resigned his commission; at the end of the year he took up full-time work, without pay, with the Fellowship of Reconciliation. On 5 Feb. 1916 at Finchley he married Leslie Eleanor Roy-de-Smith, sister of the novelist Naomi Royde-Smith; one child, Jane Hedd, was born to them. As a conscientious objector he was imprisoned more than once during the years 1917-19. In 1923 he was elected to Parliament, as a Christian Pacifist candidate, for the University of Wales; and as an unofficial envoy he carried out important work in the cause of peace – in arbitrating between David Lloyd George (see LLOYD GEORGE, David below) and Eamonn De Valera, for example. He was not returned in the following election and in 1926 he was ordained a minister in the Pres. Church of Wales. He was pastor of the churches at Tywyn and Maethlon from 1926 to 1930. He then responded to the appeal for help from the distressed areas of south Wales and spent the following years working among the unemployed in Monmouthshire and Glamorganshire, and in 1932 he moved to the Quaker Settlement at Maes-yr-Haf in the Rhondda. He retired to Dolwyddelan in 1946 and though his health was deteriorating he continued to preach and to address meetings. He died in tragic circumstances 16 Dec. 1949 and was buried at Dolwyddelan. He was a great and most unusual personality; a handsome man and an enchanting character. His circle of close friends included both the aristocracy and the poor of many nations. He consecrated his life to the ideals in which he believed so intensely – reconciliation between nation and nation and between person and person. He wrote a great deal to Welsh and English periodicals and newspapers. He published an account of his mission in *Pererindod Heddwch*, and of his family in *Atgofion Talysarn*. In 1950 a selection of his writings was published entitled *A Pilgrimage of Peace*.

Y Goleuad, 11 Jan. 1950; *Y Faner*, 21, 28 Dec. 1949; *Pilgrimage of Peace* (memoir by C.E. Raven); NLW J. Glyn Davies Papers; personal knowledge; [E.H. Griffiths, *Heddychwr Mawr Cymru*, 2 vols. (1967-8)].

J.E.M.

DAVIES, GLYNNE GERALLT (1916-68), minister (Congl.) and poet; b. in Liverpool 21 Feb. 1916, but brought up in Ro-wen, in the Conwy Valley, Caerns. He was educated at Ro-wen primary school and Llanrwst grammar school. He worked for a time in the office of Henry Jones, solicitor at Llanrwst. He began to preach in the Calvinistic Methodist connexion and followed further education at Clwyd College, the University College, Bangor, and the Theological College at Aberystwyth. He stood as a conscientious objector during World War II and worked on the land at home in Ro-wen. At the end of the war he became a Congregationalist, and, after a short period at Bala-Bangor College, was ord. He ministered to the churches of Peniel and Gerisim, Llanfairfechan, 1946-51; Ebeneser, Bangor, 1951-65; Salem, Colwyn Bay and Deganwy Avenue, Llandudno, 1965-68.

He served his apprenticeship as a poet in 'Pabell Awen', the bardic column of *Y Cymro* under the tutorship of Dewi Emrys (see David Emrys James, below) and came under the influence of R. Williams Parry (see below) at Bangor and Edward Prosser Rhys (see below) at Aberystwyth. He won many prizes at *eisteddfodau* including some at the National *Eisteddfod* In addition to his service as a caring and loved minister he became known to a wide circle in north Wales as an *eisteddfod* adjudicator, a weekly newspaper columnist, a broadcaster and a W.E.A. tutor. He published two volumes of poetry: *Yn Ieuenctid y Dydd* (1941) and *Y Dwyrain a Cherddi Eraill* (1945). A third volume, *Yr Ysgub Olaf* (1971), was published posthumously. He had been awarded the degree of M.A. of the University of Liverpool in 1958 for a thesis on the life and work of William John Roberts, Gwilym Cowlyd (*DWB*, 885), a work which was published by his widow under the title *Gwilym Cowlyd 1828-1904* (1976).

He m. Freda Vaughan Davies, Maesneuadd, Pontrobert and they had a son and a daughter. He d. at his home in Colwyn Bay, 13 June 1968, and was buried in Bron-y-nant cemetery, Colwyn Bay.

Personal knowledge; *Lleufer*, 24, no. 2 (1968), 7-12; preface to *Yr Ysgub Olaf*; *Blwyddiadur A*, 1969; *Baner*, 11 July 1968.

De.J.

DAVIES, GRIFFITH ('Gwyndaf'; 1868-1962), poet, tutor of poets and antiquary; b. 5 Feb. 1868 at Llwynpïod, a smallholding in Llanuwchllyn, Mer. His father Griffith Davies died before he was born, and his mother experienced great hardship in bringing up her two sons, Griffith and Thomas. After attending the local school, Griffith spent some time at the famous school of Owen Owen (1850-1920; *DWB*, 718) at Oswestry. He lived most of his long life farming Bryncaled, a farm near his birthplace. He m. (1) Elin Davies, Bryncaled, and (2) Kate Ann Jones, Bryn Coch, Llanuwchllyn, a descendant of John Jones ('Tudur Llwyd'), Weirglodd Gilfach, a local poet and antiquary. They had one daughter, Megan. Gwyndaf spent the last years of his life at Glan'rafon, a cottage at the foot of Carndochan. He was elected a deacon of Yr Hen Gapel (Congl.), Llanuwchllyn, and was a member and alderman of Merioneth county council for 40 years. He was a member of the Penllyn Historical Society and became vice-president of the Merioneth Historical Society. As a poet proficient in *cynghanedd* and in composing *englynion* he taught several generations of poets in the strict metres. He was an ardent supporter of *eisteddfodau*, became a member of the *Gorsedd* of Bards in 1911 and addressed his fellow poets from the *Gorsedd* Stone on several occasions. He wrote for the local press, and occasionally contributed articles to the *Tyst*, *Dysgedydd*, and *Geninen*. In 1910 he published a booklet containing his *awdl* to Michael D. Jones (*DWB*, 495). A posthumous volume of his works, *Awen Gwyndaf Llanuwchllyn* (1966) was edited by James Nicholas. He d. 4 Feb. 1962, the day before his 94th birthday, and was buried in the new cemetery at Llanuwchllyn.

Information from Megan Davies and Ifan Roberts; *Awen Gwyndaf*; personal knowledge.

I.O.

DAVIES, GWENDOLINE ELIZABETH (1882-1951), art collector and benefactress; b. Llandinam, Mont., 11 Feb. 1882; her father Edward (1852-98) was the only son of David Davies, 'Top Sawyer' (1818-90; *DWB*, 116). Her mother Mary, daughter of the Rev. Evan Jones, Trewythen, died in 1888 and three years later Edward married her sister Elizabeth (d. 1942).

Gwen Davies and her sister Margaret (see below) were educated at Highfield School, Hendon, and through foreign travel, particularly in France. They acquired Gregynog mansion near Newtown, just after World War I, intending it to become an arts and crafts centre for Wales. The one craft activity that came to fruition, largely through the energy of Dr. Thomas Jones (see below) was printing, and between 1923 and 1942 the Gregynog Press published forty-two titles in limited editions. Among the works, many of great beauty in typography and binding, eight were in Welsh and a good number of others had a Welsh connection. (The sisters themselves were not Welsh-speaking.) They began to buy paintings seriously in 1908 and, in the following fifteen years, built up notable collections, eventually given or bequeathed to the National Museum of Wales almost in their entirety. In their early purchases they were advised by Hugh Blaker (1873-1936), brother of their governess and sometime Curator of the Bath Museum, and among their more spectacular acquisitions were fine works by Corot, Millet, Cézanne, Monet and Renoir, and some Rodin sculptures. Gwen Davies was an amateur violinist of some accomplishment, and the musical side of life at Gregynog soon developed. A Music Room was built and an organ by Frederick Rothwell installed under the supervision of Sir (Henry) Walford Davies (see below), who was also chiefly responsible for the concerts, which culminated in the annual Festivals of Music and Poetry between 1933 and 1938. The sisters were members of the Gregynog Choir that sang on these occasions, and visitors included Elgar, Holst and Vaughan Williams. The National Council of Music for Wales had been to a considerable extent funded by the sisters, and their often very large charitable bequests also extended to many other musical, social, medical and educational institutions. At Gregynog, too, they welcomed many conferences on issues of the day, often in conjunction with their brother the 1st Lord Davies (David Davies, see above).

The life style of the sisters, rooted in a strong Calvinistic background, was in no way conventionally aristocratic. They were both reticent and modest and, for many years, strongly influenced by their formidable stepmother. Gwen was, however, the bolder and perhaps more imaginative personality, with some liking for luxuriance and variety, for instance in gardening. Though unassuming, they had ideals, together with the means and will to realise them.

Gwen Davies, who had been created a C.H. in 1937, d. in the Radcliffe Infirmary, Oxford, on 3 July 1951 and her ashes were interred at Llandinam.

I.Parrott, *The Spiritual Pilgrims* (1969); *Gregynog* (1977); J. Ingamells, *The Davies Collection of French Art* (1967); P. Cannon-Brookes, 'The Davies Sisters', *Apollo*, 109 (1979), 205, 221-6; T. Jones, *The Gregynog Press* (1954); M. Hutchins, *Printing at Gregynog* (1976); D. Harrop, *A History of the Gregynog Press* (1979); [Eirene White, *The Ladies of Gregynog* (1985); B. McIntyre, *Sisters select* (2001)].

G.T.H.

DAVIES, GWILYM (1879-1955), minister (B), promoter of international understanding, founder of the annual Goodwill Message from the Youth of Wales; b. 24 Mar. 1879 at Cwmfelin, Bedlinog, Glam. (where there is a memorial tablet to him), one of the sons of D.J. Davies, minister (B). He was a pupil teacher at Bedlinog when his father moved to the neighbourhood of Llangadog and he became a pupil at Llandeilo grammar school. He began preaching as early as 1895, and trained for the ministry at the Midland Baptist College, Nottingham, and at Rawdon College. There he won the Pegg Scholarship which enabled him to enter Jesus College, Oxford, where he graduated. Whilst at Oxford he edited *The Baptist Outlook*. In 1906 he was ord. minister at Broadhaven, Pembs., and the same year he m. (1) Annie Margaretta Davies but she d. 3 Dec. 1906 and their baby son d. four months later; they were buried in Cwmifor (B) cemetery, Maenordeilo, Carms. Subsequently he served as minister at Carmarthen, 1908-15; Abergavenny, 1915-19; and Llandrindod Wells, 1919-22. He was one of the founders in 1911 of the Welsh School of Social Services and showed initiative as secretary, chairman and president of the organisation. He had already gained prominence by his championship of the rights of boys from reformatory schools, who were not always justly treated by their employers.

In 1922 he retired from the ministry to devote himself to the cause of international peace. He joined with (Lord) David Davies (see above) in creating the Welsh council of the League of Nations Union with its headquarters at Aberystwyth; he was its director, 1922-45. Conferences were held annually (1922-39) at Gregynog on international education until the collapse of the League of Nations. During World War II the Welsh Education Committee under his direction was asked to draft a model constitution for an international education organisation. The draft submitted by Gwilym Davies greatly influenced the creation of UNESCO. He is probably remembered best for initiating in 1922 the peace message of the youth of Wales to the youth of the world which is now broadcast annually on 18 May. By chance he became the first person to broadcast in Welsh – on St. David's Day 1923. He made good use of radio, the cinema and the press. Many important articles by him appeared in *The Welsh Outlook*, *Yr Efrydydd*, and *Y Traethodydd*; some of the Welsh ones were collected in *Y Byd Ddoe a Heddiw* (1938). His article in *Y Traethodydd*, 1942, on the Welsh Nationalist Party aroused considerable controversy. Other publications include *International Education in the Schools of Wales and Monmouthshire* (1926), *The Ordeal of Geneva* (1933), *Intellectual co-operation between the Wars* (1943), and *The Gregynog Conferences on International Education 1922-37* (1952), as well as the annual reports of the Welsh national council of the League of Nations Union, 1923-39, and of the United Nations Association, 1943-46. He was appointed a C.B.E. in 1948, and the university of Wales conferred an honorary degree of LL.D. upon him in 1954.

He suffered from ill-health ever since his student days. He spent much of his life in Cardiff and Geneva, and his work took him to all parts of the world. On 24 Jan. 1942 he m. (2) Mary Elizabeth Ellis, Dolgellau (the second woman to be appointed an inspector of schools in Wales; she was granted permission to marry and to retain her post till 1943). They lived in 8 Marine Terrace, Aberystwyth. He d. 29 Jan. 1955 and his ashes were scattered at Lavernock Point, Penarth, where the first radio messages had been exchanged across water.

Ieuan Gwynedd Jones (ed.), *Gwilym Davies, 1879-1955* (1972); Gwilym Davies collection at N.L.W., 1955-72; information from D. Emrys Williams, Aberystwyth.

M.A.J.

DAVIES, HARRY PARR – see PARR-DAVIES, HARRY below.

DAVIES, HENRY JONES – see JONES-DAVIES, HENRY below.

DAVIES, Sir HENRY WALFORD (1869-1941), musician; b. Oswestry, Salop, 6 September, 1869, son of John Whitridge Davies and Susan (née Gregory) his wife. At the age of 12 he entered the choir of St. George's Chapel, Windsor, and became pupil-assistant to Sir Walter Parratt, 1885-90. In 1890 he won a composition scholarship at the Royal College of Music, and during these student days became organist of St. Anne's church, Soho, and later, Christ Church, Hampstead. In 1895 he was appointed Professor of Counterpoint at the Royal College but resigned in 1903. In 1898 he was appointed organist and director of the choir at the Temple Church, London, a post which he held with distinction for 20 years. Other important posts held by him were conductor of the Bach Choir; music director to the R.A.F.; organist of St. George's Chapel, Windsor, and Professor of Music at Gresham College, London. In 1919 he accepted the dual posts of Director of Music to the University of Wales, and Professor of Music at Aberystwyth university college, the latter post he relinquished in 1926. He was knighted in 1922, and on the death of Edward Elgar in 1934, King George V appointed him Master of the King's Musick. He was made a C.V.O. in 1932 and K.C.V.O. in 1937. His academic distinctions

were D.Mus. (Cantab.), D.Mus. (Oxford and Dublin) hon., LL.D. (Leeds) hon., F.R.A.M., F.R.C.O., F.R.C.M. He was a prolific composer and many of his longer works were performed at the Three Choirs Festivals. He was known all over the world by his broadcast talks and gramophone records. In 1924 he m. Constance Margaret, d. of William Evans, rector of Narberth and Canon of St. David's. He d. at Wrington, Bristol, 11 Mar. 1941.

Personal knowledge; *Times*, 12 Mar. 1941; H.C. Colles, *Walford Davies; Www*, 1941-50.

J.C.McL.

DAVIES, HUGH EMYR (1878-1950), minister (Presb.) and poet; b. 31 May 1878 at Brynllaeth, Aber-erch, Caerns., son of Tudwal and Annie Davies. He was educated at Pwllheli county school, Clynnog School, U.C.W., Aberystwyth and Bala College. He was ord. in 1909, and was a minister at Llanddona, Anglesey (1909-12), Lodge, Brymbo and Ffrith (1912-20), and Llanfechell, Anglesey (1920-29). He was an exceptional preacher, but it was as a poet that he gained prominence. He won a chair at Pwllheli when he was 16 yrs. old, and subsequently won 22 bardic chairs. He mastered the *cynganeddion*, but it was in the free metres that he excelled. His collected works were published in 1907 under the title *Llwyn Hudol*. His *pryddest* to 'Branwen ferch Llŷr' won the crown at the Caernarfon national *eisteddfod* (1906); and his poem, 'Owain Glyndŵr' won the crown at Llangollen (1908). He also won a chair at the American national *eisteddfod* in 1929. He adjudicated the competition for the crown many times at the national *eisteddfod*.

He m., 1910, Sydney Elizabeth Hughes of Bala, and they had a daughter. After retiring he lived at Holyhead and Menai Bridge. He d. 21 Nov. 1950 at Llandegfan.

WwW (1937); *Blwyddiadur MC*, 1951, 250-1; *Gol.*, 13 Dec. 1960.

G.M.R.

DAVIES, HUGH MORRISTON (1879-1965), probably the most outstanding pioneer of thoracic surgery in Britain; b. 10 Aug. 1879, the son of Swansea-born Dr. William Davies, a general practitioner at Huntingdon. Educated at Winchester and Trinity College, Cambridge, and University College Hospital, London, he obtained his initial qualifications in 1903, after being awarded some of the most prestigious prizes at the Medical School. He secured the degrees of M.Ch. and M.D. of Cambridge in 1907, the F.R.C.S. in 1908 and he was appointed assistant surgeon of the hospital the following year. After some fundamental research on nerve regeneration Davies turned his attention to radiological studies of diseases of the chest, and a visit to Berlin in 1910 awakened his interest in thoracic surgery. Two years later he was the first surgeon to diagnose a lung tumour by X-Rays, and he successfully removed it. There soon followed many new and progressive features of great therapeutic merit. The stage was set for a career of remarkable and even unique achievement. In Jan. 1916 when operating on a diseased chest he had the calamitous misfortune to infect his own right hand. The infection was particularly virulent and his life was in grave danger. Some of the most eminent medical men in London urged him to have the arm amputated. Davies refused. After extensive surgery his life was spared but the end-result was a clenched, distorted and useless hand, and fixation of the wrist and elbow. It was sadly evident that a meteoric career had been extinguished at the age of 37, and his retirement from the surgical staff of University College Hospital was inevitable.

The hospital offered him the post of radiologist, but in 1918 Davies, revealing enormous courage, decided to buy Llanbedr Hall Sanatorium, near Ruthin, where he could treat patients under his own direct supervision. The following year he published the first textbook in the English language on thoracic surgery. He discovered that many of his patients needed surgical treatment, and by a supreme effort of determination and perseverance he educated his left hand and the crippled right hand so that he could embark on major surgery of the chest once again. Within a few years Llanbedr Hall became a centre that was attracting world-wide attention. Davies was appointed thoracic surgeon to all the chest hospitals in Wales, and eventually his clinical responsibilities extended to Lancashire and Cheshire. His reputation was due to the fact that he uniquely embodied personally the wisdom and balance of a physician and the manual dexterity and innovative skill of a surgeon, combined with an unequalled experience in radiological interpretation. As a result of this impressive aggregation of talent his books and other publications were regarded as authoritative.

The outbreak of World War II added enormously to his responsibilities. He established the North West Thoracic Surgical Services at Broadgreen Hospital, Liverpool, and became its Director. Davies's clinical teaching and administrative guidance were of crucial significance, and of equal importance was his success in training a group of able young surgeons to follow him. His attachment to the Broadgreen Centre continued, in an advisory capacity, until he reached the age of eighty, and then he finally retired to his cottage at Llanarmon-yn-Iâl, where he continued to tend his garden in spite of increasing physical disability.

For over fifty years the value of his work was warmly recognised by his colleagues, and there was formal academic recognition as well. The University of Liverpool conferred upon him in 1943 the honorary Mastership in Surgery – Ch.M.; in 1954 he was awarded the Weber-Parkes Prize of the Royal College of Physicians; in 1961 he received a LL.D. from the University of Wales.

Davies was a man of small physique, with a bent frame and his head on one side. He looked almost frail and had a soft high-pitched voice, and yet he had tremendous energy and courage, and an inexhaustible capacity for hard work. He loved books, painting and music, and had an abiding affection for big, powerful and fast cars. He was a great and loveable man.

He m. Dorothy Lilian (d. 15 Oct. 1966 aged 88), daughter of Dr. W.L. Courtney, and they had two daughters. He d. at Llanarmon-yn-Iâl on 4 Feb. 1965.

Brit. Med. Jnl., 27 Feb. 1965; Lancet, 13 Feb. 1965;

Ann. Roy. Coll. Surgeons, 1965, 36, 246-9; Lives Fellows Roy. Coll. Surg., 1965-73, 99-100; Times, 5 Feb. 1965; Trans. Liverpool Med. Inst., 1965, 16-19; personal knowledge.

E.W.J.

DAVIES, HUGH THOMAS (1881-1969), musician, writer, and one of the pioneers of Cymdeithas Cerdd Dant Cymru; b. 5 Apr. 1881 at Y Felin Uchaf, Glanconwy, Denb., son of Richard Davies and his wife Eunice (née Williams). He m., 4 Sept. 1909, Margaret, daughter of Griffith R. Jones, minister (B) of Ffordd Las, Glanconwy, and they had five children, all of whom became interested in Welsh traditional cultural activities. As the surveyor for Conwy, H.T. Davies lived for some time in Liverpool and then at Glanconwy, but moved in 1919 to Tywyn, Mer., where he spent the rest of his life as an architect, surveyor and health officer. His chief interests were religion and music, and he made a significant contribution in his immediate circle and nationally in both fields. He was one of the founders of Cymdeithas Cerdd Dant Cymru on 10 Nov. 1934, and served as president of the Society and was its treasurer for 12 yrs. He was a national adjudicator, a prolific 'setter' of words and a composer of airs to which words could be set for penillion singing. He taught many parties, soloists and choirs in the art of singing to the harp (cerdd dant) who came to the fore at national eisteddfodau and cerdd dant festivals. His contribution in this field was appreciated by the members of the Society of which he was made an honorary life member. He d. 14 Mar. 1969.

Information from his daughter, Margaret Eunice Williams, Aberystwyth.

A.Ll.D.

DAVIES, HYWEL (1919-65), broadcaster; b. in Llandysul, Cards., 2 Feb. 1919, one of the four children of Ben Davies, Congl. minister (see above) and Sarah his wife. He was educated at Llandeilo grammar school and the University of Edinburgh, where he graduated M.A. with honours in English literature.

He first intended becoming a business man and was employed by the Lewis Co. of Manchester, but in 1942 he became an announcer and news reader for the B.B.C in London and subsequently editor of Welsh news. From 1946 onwards he was at Cardiff serving successively as organiser, deputy head and, from 1958 till his death, head of programmes. In 1961 a Ford Foundation scholarship enabled him to travel extensively in the U.S.A.

Hywel Davies was an excellent organiser and became well known throughout the U.K. as a radio broadcaster and later as an interviewer in television programmes. In 1959 he and the producer, David J. Thomas, won an award for their programme 'Out of this world' in an international competition in Monte Carlo. Again, in 1962, he was the interviewer in the programme 'It happened to me', which was successful in the same competition. He was praised for his television broadcasts from the International Eisteddfod at Llangollen and won the praise and admiration of viewers in every part of the U.K. for his work as interviewer in the series 'At home'. In Jan. 1965 the B.B.C. published the lecture which he delivered on 'The role of the regions in British broadcasting' in the series of lunch-time lectures in the B.B.C. headquarters in London. The same year he was honoured with an O.B.E. a few months before he d., 16 Oct. 1965. His widow, Lorraine, was organiser of 'Awr y plant' and chief producer on Radio B.B.C. Cymru.

Personal knowledge; *Portreadau'r Faner*, ii, 21-2.
O.E.

DAVIES, IDRIS (1905-1953), miner, schoolmaster and poet; b. 6 Jan. 1905 at 16 Field Street, Rhymney, Mon., the Welsh-speaking son of colliery winderman Evan Davies and his wife Elizabeth Ann.

After leaving the local school at the age of fourteen, for the next seven years he worked underground as a miner in the nearby Abertysswg and Rhymney Mardy Pits. After an accident in which he lost a finger at the coalface, and active participation in the General Strike of 1926, he became unemployed and spent the next four years following what he used to call 'the long and lonely self-tuition game'. He then entered Loughborough Training College and Nottingham University to qualify as a teacher, and eight years later gained the University of London diploma in history. Between 1932 and 1947 he taught in London County Council primary schools and in schools evacuated from wartime London to Pytchley (Northants.), Meesden (Herts.), Treherbert (Glam.) and Llandysul (Cards.). In 1947 he returned to his native Rhymney Valley to teach in a junior school at Cwmsyfiog, to read, broadcast, lecture and write until his death from cancer at 7 Victoria Road, Rhymney on Easter Monday, 6 Apr. 1953. He was buried in Rhymney Public Cemetery.

During his lifetime four volumes of his poetry were published: *Gwalia Deserta* (1938), written at Rhymney; *The Angry Summer: a poem of 1926* (1943), which he wrote in three months at Meesden; *Tonypandy and other poems* (1945), which he wrote during the short stay at Treherbert; and *Selected Poems* (1953), chosen by T.S. Eliot, who thought that the poems of Idris Davies had a claim to permanence as 'the best poetic document I know about a particular epoch in a particular place'. His work in both English and Welsh reflected the idealism and protest of a people during a time of great economic, social and religious change; in particular the inception, growth and decay of the old iron and coal town of Rhymney, Mon.

After his death over two hundred of his manuscript poems and a short verse-play, together with the typescripts of his comprehensive wartime diaries, were deposited at the National Library of Wales at Aberystwyth. Later, more of his unpublished poems and most of his prose – an unfinished novel, essays, lecture notes and some of his letters – were found. Some of this later material appeared posthumously in *The Collected Poems of Idris Davies* (1972); *Idris Davies* (1972), and Argo Record No. ZPL.1181: *Idris Davies* (1972).

His knowledge of poetry was immense, but he climbed on no bandwagon. He became the archetypal poet of the mining valleys of south Wales during the first half of the twentieth century.

Islwyn Jenkins, *Idris Davies* (1972); Islwyn Jenkins, *Idris Davies of Rhymney* (1986); personal acquaintance 1918-53; N.L.W. MSS.; private papers; [Dafydd Johnston, ed., *Complete Poems* (1994)].
I.Je.

DAVIES, IEUAN REES – see REES-DAVIES, IEUAN below.

DAVIES, JAMES KITCHENER (1902-52), poet, dramatist and nationalist; b. 16 June 1902, son of Thomas Davies of Pant-glas, Blaencaron, and Martha (née Davies) of Pantfallen, Tregaron, Cards. Their sons Thomas, John and James were born at Pantfallen; about a year later the family moved to Llain, Llwynpïod, a smallholding on the edge of Cors Caron, where their daughter Letitia was born. James attended the church school at Tregaron. When he was seven years old his mother d., and he was sent to Banbury for a period (having lost his Welsh on his return). The children were raised at Llain by an aunt, Mary Davies. In 1915 he went to Tregaron county school where everyone called him Kitchener because his father, with his moustache, resembled the British politician of that name. The father, of strong build, worked in Garw colliery and returned to farm the land each spring, summer and Christmas time. In 1919 the smallholding had to be sold when he re-m. and made his home in Blaengarw, and the aunt moved to Tonypandy. The experience of breaking up the home left a deep impression on the youth. For the final two years at school he lived in lodgings in Tregaron. This is when he received the help and lasting influence of the history master, S.M. Powell, who created in him, as in so many other well-known people of the area, a love for the history and culture of his neighbourhood and nation, and for drama and public speaking.

He left school in 1921 to become a pupil-teacher at Blaengwynfi and during 1922-25 he took a B.A. course in Welsh and education, with history, Latin and philosophy, at the University College, Aberystwyth. This was 'Aber' during the creative upsurge brought about by such students as Idwal Jones (*DWB*, 506-7). It was also the period of ex-servicemen and conscientious objectors (his friend Gwenallt (see David James Jones; 1899-1968 below) was there about the same time), and Kitchener's interest in the turmoil of politics and peace in Europe grew. He became secretary of the debating society and a member of the Students' Council, and led movements assisting continental students and the League of Nations which he represented at a month-long international school held in Geneva in 1925. After gaining his teacher's certificate in 1926, he spent the rest of his life teaching in several schools in the Rhondda valley. Soon after going there his aunt d., and in an essay he admits that this was as great a loss to him as losing his mother and leaving Llain had been.

If his childhood had a strong hold on him and his work, Rhondda was no less significant. He worked unsparingly for Welsh causes in the valley, a thankless task that nevertheless did not dis-hearten him. He led a strong campaign to establish the Welsh school there. He served in a host of national societies and organisations promoting culture, education and peace; he became particularly involved in organising adult education and lecturing. Poverty and economic conditions in the valley during the depression concerned him greatly, though there was no prominent position a nationalist could take in the workers' movements of his day; he helped with the social experiment in Maes-yr-haf during the war. He was a member of Bethania chapel, Tonypandy, and used to preach in the valleys, despite his dislike of the image and life of a preacher.

It was as one of the advocates of *Plaid Cymru* that he came into prominence. He was a masterly and influential speaker, with the gift to arouse people. He canvassed and held open-air meetings (often in the company of the inspired Morris Williams, and his wife Kate (Roberts), who lived for a while in the same street). He stood as a candidate for the county council, and also as a candidate for his party in east Rhondda in 1945, and west Rhondda in 1950 and 1951, shortly before he was taken ill. In 1940 he m. a Tonypandy grammar school teacher, Mair Rees of Ffos-y-ffin, Aberaeron, and they made their home in Aeron, Brithweunydd, Trealaw, where their three daughters Megan, Mari and Manon were born.

He enjoyed gardening, was good company, and read extensively. He steeped himself in the works of Williams, Pantycelyn (*DWB*, 1077-8), appreciated the works of Saunders Lewis and T.S. Eliot, and ensured that the poet was given a place in the theatre. He took an active interest in drama; he founded the Pandy Dramatic Soc., and produced and acted with the company during the 1930s; he became an adjudicator and lecturer, and broadcast many times. He contributed many articles to the Welsh and English press, usually on politics and drama. He was admitted as a member of the *Gorsedd* of Bards in 1945 for his contribution to Welsh drama. He regarded his own plays as literary experiments, being frequently the fruit of competition. His play *Cwm glo* (1935), about the shattered morals and relationships in a family during the depression, created a great stir. In the play the daughter departs to earn her living on the streets; denied the prize in Aberafan *eisteddfod* in 1932, people thronged to see it. His short play *Y tri dyn dierth* (1937) was an adaptation of one of Hardy's stories. *Susannah* (1938) was a one-act play based on the book in the Apocrypha, and *Hen wlad fy nhadau* (1939) a translation of a play by Jack Jones (see below). *Meini gwagedd* (1944; 2nd. ed. 1945) is a metrical tragedy about the hard life on Cors Caron; with its notable use of the rich language of the district, it is considered to be his best work prior to *Sŵn y gwynt sy'n chwythu*. He completed five other plays: *Dies irae*, a three-act play based on the story of Boudicca; *Gloria in excelsis*, a short radio play on the theme of Easter; *Miss Blodeuwedd*, a farce based on the folk-tale, written in conjunction with his wife; *Y fantell fraith*, in collaboration with his summerschool class in Harlech in 1942; and also *Ynys Afallon*, a partially-metrical play on the history of Wales, which he himself considered to be his most ambitious experiment.

He did not compose many poems. Nevertheless, it is as a poet that he is remembered because he left a message for his own age in his few poetical works, and in one poem in particular. *Meini Gwagedd* and the *pryddestau*

'Ing cenhedloedd' and 'Yr Arloeswr' present the theme which was definitively developed in 'Sŵn y gwynt sy'n chwythu'. This *pryddest* was commissioned, broadcast in 1952, and published posthumously in 1953. It was while he was in hospital, awaiting his second cancer operation, that he composed it, dictating its final form to his wife. It is a poem that shocks one, with the poet divesting himself of all his motives, as Pantycelyn had done, but here we have a new pitiless voice. It allows us to view a frightening pilgrimage into the presence of sanctity; and the author's plea to be spared his duty becomes the crisis of man in every age. It is regarded as one of the greatest Welsh poems of the 20th century, and Kitchener's name became synonymous with it, as with the Rhondda valley and *Plaid Cymru*.

He d. 25 Aug. 1952, and was buried in the cemetery of Llether Ddu, Trealaw. A plaque on the wall of Llwynpïod chapel in memory of him was unveiled on 3 Sept. 1977, and in 1980 an anthology of his chief works was published.

Documents and information mainly from his widow, and his sister; *Baner*, 23 Aug. 1944, 27 Aug. 1952; the introduction to *Sŵn y gwynt sy'n chwythu* (1953); *Lleufer*, winter 1953; *Barn*, Apr. and Aug. 1966; J.K. Davies, 'Adfyw', *Y Cardi*, 3 Aug. 1968, 14-18; Ioan Williams, *Kitchener Davies* (1985), complete bibliography; Mair Kitchener Davies, ed., *Gwaith J.K.D.* (1980).

G.Tu.

DAVIES, JENKIN ALBAN – see ALBAN DAVIES, JENKIN above.

DAVIES, JOHN DANIEL (1874-1948), editor and author; b. 12 Jan. 1874, at Gwynfryn, Aberderfyn, Ponciau, Denb., one of the seven children of Daniel Davies and his wife. Having completed his schooling he was apprenticed to David Jones, printer, at Rhosymedre, and afterwards to Richard Mills, printer of the *Rhos Herald*. He m. Mary Ellen, dau. of William Humphreys ('Elihu'), of Blaenau Ffestiniog, 25 Apr. 1900. He settled in Blaenau Ffestiniog and in 1906 became the editor and owner of *Y Rhedegydd*. He was a preacher with the Scottish or Sandemanian Baptists and had an unbounded admiration for J.R. Jones, Ramoth (*DWB*, 488; and see his article in *Y Geninen*, Apr. 1922). His poem on the temptation of Christ won a chair for him at the Penmachno *eisteddfod*. He did not compete for prizes after that, but devoted his energies to the composition of hymns, sermons, a catechism for children, and articles on a variety of subjects. His publications include *Emynwyr Gwynedd*, 1905, *Saith Canhwyllbren Aur* (sermons), and an account of the Scottish and Campbellite Baptists in Wales, which appeared in the transactions of *Cymdeithas Hanes Bedyddwyr Cymru*, 1940-1. He edited the Scottish Baptist periodical *Yr Ymwelydd* for many years. He d. 9 Apr. 1948 and was bur. in Bethesda cemetery, Blaenau Ffestiniog.

Y Rhedegydd, Apr. 1948.

J.W.Jo.

DAVIES, JOHN GLYN (1870-1953), scholar, songwriter and poet; b. 22 Oct. 1870 at 55 Peel St., Sefton Park, Liverpool, son of John and Gwen Davies. His father was a tea merchant, and his mother was a daughter of John Jones, Tal-y-sarn (*DWB*, 478-9); George Maitland Lloyd Davies (see above), Stanley Davies and Captain Frank Davies were his brothers. He was educated at the Liverpool Institute. He worked with the sailing boat companies Rathbone Brothers (1887-92) and The Cambrian (1892-95), with Henry Tate and Sons (1895-96) and then with the Mines Corporation of New Zealand (1896-98). After returning home (via the U.S.A.) he was persuaded by Thomas Edward Ellis (*DWB*, 214) and others to bring together a Welsh library at the University College of Wales, Aberystwyth, which could later form the nucleus of a National Library of Wales. He commenced the task at Aberystwyth in 1899, but after much labour he became dissatisfied with his terms of employment. In 1907 he was appointed to the staff of the library of the University of Liverpool and later as assistant to Professor Kuno Meyer in the Celtic department of the University. When Meyer retired in 1920, Glyn Davies was appointed head of the department and remained in that post until he retired in 1936; he lived at Mostyn and Denbigh. After retiring he lived at Cambridge, Llandegfan, Llannarth (Cards.), and at Llanfairfechan where he d. 11 Nov. 1953. He m., 18 July 1908, Hettie Williams, Newquay, Cards. and they had a son and three daughters.

Despite his undisputed abilities and his promising early work, his contribution to Welsh scholarship proved to be erratic and uneven. However, his songs for children in *Cerddi Huw Puw* (1923), *Cerddi Robin Goch* (1935) and *Cerddi Portinllaen* (1936), many of which are based on sailors' songs he had heard during his youth, bear the marks of a genius. His posthumous book of poems, *Cerddi Edern a cherddi ereill* (1955), contains many lyrics which will undoubtedly live. One could add that his reminiscences of the Welsh society he knew early in life, and his comments on it, are always interesting and very penetrating.

Hettie Glyn Davies, *Hanes bywyd John Glyn Davies* (1965); [his papers at N.L.W.].

G.G.

DAVIES, JOSEPH EDWARD (1876-1958), international lawyer; b. 29 Nov. 1876 in Watertown, Wisconsin, U.S.A., the son of Edward Davies, carpenter, and his wife, Rachel (*DWB*, 146), an evangelist and a poet known as 'Rahel o Fôn'. He spent part of his childhood in Anglesey and, as an university student, he spent each summer in Wales, part of the time with Evan Rowland Jones, the U.S. consul in Cardiff and a native of Tregaron, like Davies's grandfather. Later, he marked the connection with Tregaron by naming his home in Washington after the town; he hoped that the house would become a graduate school on international studies. He was called to the Wisconsin Bar in 1901 and he eventually became a noted international lawyer. He was a strong and close supporter of Woodrow Wilson and he stood unsuccessfully for Congress in 1918. He then retired from public life and devoted himself to his legal career. He was appointed ambassador to the Soviet Union in 1936, to Belgium in 1938, and again to the Soviet Union in 1943. He became ambassador in Britain in 1945 and attended the Potsdam

Conference. Davies was awarded nine hon. university degrees, including a LL.D. from the University of Wales, and he was a vice-president of Hon. Soc. of Cymmr. In 1946, he received the Medal of Merit, the highest civilian honour awarded by the U.S. government, and he received similar honours from the governments of ten other countries. He published articles in various journals between 1913 and 1947 as well as reports on industry, corporation tax and legal topics. His influential book, *Mission to Moscow* (1941), brought him wider fame.

He m. (1) Emlen Knight on 10 Sept. 1902 and they had three daughters: Eleanor, Rahel and Emlen. A wealthy man in his own right, he m. (2) Mrs. Marjorie Post who inherited 20 million dollars from her father. He d. 9 May 1958 and was buried in Washington Cathedral.

Www in America, 1951-60; *West. Mail*, 10 May 1958; [*American National Biography*, vol. 6, 156-158 (1999)].

E.D.J.

DAVIES, Sir LEONARD TWISTON (1894-1953), patron of the arts and of folk life studies; b. 16 May 1894, son of William L.T. and M.L. (née Brown) Davies of Chester. He was a great-grandson of Samuel Davies 'the first', a Methodist minister (*DWB*, 151) and his wife Mary (née Twiston). Out of respect for his great-grandfather, he wrote *The Rev. Samuel Davies (the first) and his times* (1932), which is an English version of the Welsh biography (1866). He was educated at Charterhouse and Liverpool University. He m. (1), in 1918, Mary Powell but the marriage was annulled; and (2), in 1924, Dorothy Savile Jackson of Brougton Park, Manchester; they had two sons and a daughter.

He spent two years with the Imperial Tobacco Co. and then three years in the army (1915-1918), when he was seriously wounded and discharged with the honorary title of captain. After farming in Herefordshire till 1924, he moved to Rockfield Park, Monmouth, where he lived for the rest of his life. He was high sheriff of Mon. in 1933; a member of Mon. county council for many years, president of Mon. Council for Rural Communities; justice of the peace; and active in many other spheres in the county. But he was more interested in the national institutions of Wales. He served as chairman of the Council for Social Services for Wales, as vice-commissioner of the St. John's Ambulance in Wales, and as a member of the court of the University of Wales. His service and generosity to both the National Library and National Museum of Wales were very remarkable. He was treasurer of the National Library of Wales and its vice-president when he died. He was president of the National Museum and the main instigator in establishing the department of Rural Life (1936) which led to the creation of the National Folk Museum (1947) (now Museum of Welsh Life) at St. Fagans. He made very many gifts to the Library and the Museum; he also worked hard and successfully to raise the levels of salaries in both establishments. In his last years he represented the Museum and the Library on the Standing Commission for British Museums and Art Galleries. In 1937 he was awarded an O.B.E. and knighted (K.B.E.) in 1939. He served as Deputy Lieutenant of

Monmouthshire, was a F.S.A. and received an honorary LL.D. of the University of Wales in 1947. Among his publications are *Men of Monmouthshire* (1933); (with Averil Edwards) *Women of Wales* (1935); *Welsh life in the eighteenth century* (1939); (with Herbert Lloyd-Johnes) *Welsh furniture: an introduction* (1950). He d. 8 Jan. 1953.

Personal knowledge. [Information from H. Lloyd-Johnes; L.T. Davies Deeds and MSS are at N.L.W.].

I.C.P.

DAVIES, LEWIS ('Lewis Glyn Cynon'; 1863-1951), novelist, local historian, schoolmaster; b. at The Tramway, Hirwaun, Aberdare, Glam., 18 May, 1863, the youngest son of Lewis and Amy Davies. His father was a refiner in the Crawshay Ironworks at Hirwaun. The son was educated at Penderyn elementary school, where he became a pupil teacher. He won a scholarship to Bangor Normal College, where he remained for 2 years (1881-82) and then returned to Hirwaun as headmaster of the local school from 1884 to 1886 when he became headmaster of Cymer School in the Afan valley. He retired in 1926. His public service included the chairmanship of the Glyncorrwg U.D.C. and of the Aberafan Juvenile Court. For several years he was the conductor of the Cymer-Afan 'drum and fife' band and of a similar band at Cwmparc (Rhondda Valley) and also of Blaenau Afan Male Voice Choir. He was an elder, precentor and organist at Hebron, Cymer. He was the composer of the well-known hymn-tune 'Cymer'. He adjudicated singing, reciting, essay and poetry competitions in hundreds of local *eisteddfodau* and also at the national *eisteddfod*. He lectured extensively on literary, historical and musical topics and for many years he taught the *cynganeddion* at the Welsh summer school at Llanwrtyd. He belonged to a noted generation of Welsh schoolmasters who were well versed in the arts. In all, he won about 30 prizes at the National *Eisteddfod* for short stories, novels for children, historical essays, novels, collections of folk-lore &c. His last prize was for an historical novel at the Dolgellau *eisteddfod*, 1949, when he was 86 years of age, frail and blind in one eye. He was second to D. Rhys Phillips at the Neath *eisteddfod*, 1918 for a comprehensive essay on the history of the Vale of Neath. For many years he was the columnist 'Eryr Craig y Llyn' in *Y Brython* and was a regular contributor to the newspapers of south Wales, both national and local. He won several chairs for poetry at local *eisteddfodau* and was an authority on the *tribannau* of Glamorgan. He shared the prize for a fine collection of these *tribannau* at the Bridgend *eisteddfod*, 1948, when he was 85 years of age. He was an authority on the history of the parish of Penderyn, and many articles were written by him on the history of the Afan Valley, Glyncorrwg, Margam, Blaengwrach, Neath Abbey, etc. Among his publications are *Radnorshire* (Cambridge University Press – 'County Series'), *Outlines of the history of the Afan districts, Ystorïau Siluria, Bargodion hanes* and four adventure novels, *Lewsyn yr heliwr, Daff Owen, Y geilwad bach* and *Wat Emwnt*. Many of his works remain unpublished.

He m. Celia Lewis of Pen-y-pownd, Cwmtaf, in 1886. He d. 18 May 1951 and was buried at the Cymer-Afan Cemetery. A memorial tablet was unveiled at Hebron Chapel alongside a similar tablet to his old friend, Sir William Jenkins.

Brinley Richards, *Hamddena* (1972); [T. Gwynn Jones in Hywel T. Edwards, ed., *Llynfi ac Afan, Garw ac Ogwr* (1998), 178-93].

B.Ri.

DAVIES, LOUIE MYFANWY – see THOMAS, LOUIE MYFANWY below.

DAVIES, MARGARET SIDNEY (1884-1963), art collector and benefactress, sister of Gwendoline Elizabeth Davies (see above); b. Llandinam, 14 Dec. 1884. Although many of her activities were joint ones with her sister, she was herself an amateur painter of ability. 'Miss Daisy', as she was generally called, was rather more conventional in her tastes than her sister, but after the latter's death she developed her collection of paintings to include Bonnard, Kokoschka, Sisley, Utrillo and others. She purchased work by contemporary British painters with the intention of laying the foundations of a travelling exhibition following their bequest to the National Museum.

She received an hon. LL.D. of the University of Wales in 1949, and in 1960 she made the major gift of her home Gregynog and its estate to the University for use as a residential conference and artistic centre. She herself remained in the hall as a tenant until her death in London on 13 Mar. 1963. Her ashes were buried at Llandinam.

For references see the article on her sister.

G.T.H.

DAVIES, MATTHEW WILLIAM (1882-1947), musician; b. at Neath, Glam., Aug. 1882 the son of Richard and Catherine Davies, Neath Abbey. As a child he learnt the Tonic Sol-fa, securing the A.C. certificate at the age of 12, and matriculating at 15. In 1890 he attended a course in London under Dr. David Evans (1874-1948; see below) and when the latter was appointed to the chair of music at the university college at Cardiff, his pupil aged 20 won a scholarship of £40 a year for three years at the college. He graduated Mus. Bac. in 1905 and B.A. in 1906. After a year of special training in London he settled as music teacher at Neath and was appointed organist and choirmaster of Bethlehem Green Calvinistic Methodist Church. He conducted the Neath Operatic Society for 36 years, and also the Neath Male Voice Choir. He was conductor of the choir when the national *eisteddfod* was held at Neath in 1934. He was in constant demand as an adjudicator and conductor at singing festivals. He composed a large number of part-songs, anthems, and hymn-tunes for children, and for congregational singing. He composed the hymn-tune 'Bethlehem Green' specifically for *Y Caniedydd Cynulleidfaol Newydd*, 1921. He d. 23 Nov. 1947, and was bur. in Lantwit juxta Neath cemetery.

Y Cerddor, Aug. 1907; [*Neath Guardian*, 28 Nov. 1947; H. Williams, *Tonau a'u Hawduron*, 1967].

R.D.G.

DAVIES, MORRIS ('Moi Plas'; 1891-1961), quarryman, local historian and researcher; b. 24 June 1891 in Plas Capten, Trawsfynydd, Mer., the son of William Davies, farmer, and his wife Ruth (née Humphreys). He was educated at the board school Trawsfynydd, but in common with many of his contemporaries his schooling was cut short and he left to work at home on the farm. He served with the Royal Welch Fusiliers in Palestine and France during World War I. Afterwards, and until his retirement in 1956, he worked at the Maenofferen, Oakeley and Llechwedd quarries, Blaenau Ffestiniog. His first act after retiring was to establish a local society to find work and improved living conditions for the injured.

It was the Rev. J. Dyfnallt Owen (see below) whilst a minister in Trawsfynydd between 1898-1901, who first encouraged him to take an interest in the history of his native district. He was to spend the remainder of his life conscientiously collecting material and researching into the subject. He wrote occasionally to Welsh newspapers like *Y Cymro*, *Y Dydd*, *Y Rhedegydd*, *Y Seren*, *Yr Herald Cymraeg a'r Genedl*, etc. He was regarded as the authority on the history of Trawsfynydd and vicinity. All his MSS., in accordance with his wishes, are lodged in the National Library of Wales – N.L.W. 17,843 – 932 (there is a selection of them on microfilm in the Merioneth Record Office). Morris Davies (or 'Moi Plas' as he was known locally), was a cultured, likeable and humorous person.

He was twice m.: (1) in 1919 to Kate Lewis, Cwm Cynfal, Ffestiniog (d. 1929), and four daughters were born to them; (2) in 1931 to Lizzie Jones, Tanygrisiau (d. 1968). He d. in Blaenau Ffestiniog, 16 Apr. 1961, and was buried in Salem cemetery, Trawsfynydd.

Information given by his eldest daughter, Naomi Roberts, Dolgellau; *Baner*, 6 Nov. 1958; *Camb. News*, 28 Apr. 1961; John Ellis Williams, *Moi Plas* (1969).

A.Ll.H.

DAVIES, NAN – see DAVIES, ANNIE above.

DAVIES, OWEN PICTON (1882-1970), journalist; b. 6 June 1882 at Waunffynhonnau, Trimsaran, Carms., son of Stephen and Anna Davies of Tre-lech. The family moved to Morlogws Uchaf, in the parish of Cilrhedyn in 1884. He was educated at Pen-y-waun school from 1886 to 1894 and spent the following two years at home on the farm, as he was too young to go to the Old College School in Carmarthen, which he entered in 1896. From there he went as an apprentice on the *Carmarthen Journal*, 1898, and in 1901 to the Rhondda Valley, as correspondent for the *Western Mail*. He moved to Cardiff in 1903 to become a sub-editor of that paper, and from there to Caernarfon in 1907 as editor of *Yr Herald Cymraeg* and the *Carnarvon and Denbigh Herald*, where he succeeded Daniel Rees (*DWB*, 823-4).

At the outbreak of war in 1914, he accepted the post of sub-editor on the *Western Mail*, and later, that of editor of the *Weekly Mail*. He remained in this post until 1949, with the exception of a few years as sub-editor of the *Western Mail* once more. He was appointed Director of Studies for the *Western Mail* in 1949, training young journalists until his retirement in 1952. He spent in all 54 years in journalism, and received the medal of the National Union of Journalists. In the early years of radio, he wrote many technical articles on the subject to the press. Later he wrote about 50 feature programmes in Welsh, on topics relating to Welsh history and literature, which were broadcast from Cardiff. In 1962 he published his reminiscences in *Atgofion Dyn Papur Newydd*.

In 1909 he m. Jane Jones, eldest daughter of Captain and Mrs. David Jones, Caernarfon, and they had one daughter. He d. on 10 Oct. 1970.

Personal knowledge.

En.P.

DAVIES, RHISIART MORGAN (1903-58), scientist and professor of physics; b. in Corris, Mer., 4 Feb. 1903, only son of the Rev. Rhys Davies (Congl.) who came from Gwynfe, and his wife. He was educated in Machynlleth and Dolgellau grammar schools, and won a scholarship to the university college at Aberystwyth in 1921. He graduated with first-class honours in physics in 1924, and was appointed a member of the research staff in H.M. Signals school at Portsmouth, but the following year he returned to Aberystwyth as an assistant lecturer in the physics department and was made a lecturer in 1928. In 1937 he obtained a D.Sc. (Wales) degree for important work on the measurement of dielectric and elastic constants under dynamic conditions. In 1938 he was awarded a Leverhulme research fellowship, which enabled him to work in Cambridge. During this period he developed an interest in stress waves, and became one of the leading specialists in this field. The results of his work were published in 1948 and this is now regarded as being basic to this branch of physics. He received a Ph.D. degree at Cambridge for his research work. He was released from his post during World War II to study under-water explosives for the Admiralty.

At the end of the war he returned to Aberystwyth college where he became professor of physics in 1946. Over the years he gathered a team of scientists to his department to study the innumerable problems relating to stress, and his department became world-famous. He served a successful term as vice-principal of the college from 1954 to 1956. He was visiting professor to the California Institute of Technology and the Reusselaer Polytechnic Institute, 1956-57. He contributed a large number of articles to various scientific journals, the most important being 'A critical study of the Hopkinson pressure bar' in *Trans. Roy. Soc.* in 1948. He was also co-editor and contributor to *Surveys in Mechanics* (1956), and was responsible for a series of radio lectures on modern science during the 1930s.

He had many recreations. He was organist and deacon for many years at Baker Street chapel, Aberystwyth. He kept a record of the hymns that were sung, so that the congregation seldom sang the same hymn more than twice a year. He was interested in the college sports and was treasurer of the town's football club. He m. in 1928 Elizabeth Florence, daughter of Thomas Davies, Aberystwyth, and they had one son who died young. He d. 18 Feb. 1958 aged 55.

Www; Courier, 4 Feb. 1956; *Dysg.*, June 1958; Ellis, *UCW*.

M.R.W.

DAVIES, RHYS JOHN (1877-1954), politician and trade union official; b. 16 Apr. 1877 at Llangennech, Carms., son of Rhys Davies, tin-plate worker, a native of Abergorlech, and Ann (née Griffiths), his wife, who came from Brechfa. In all she gave birth to 11 children, but died at the age of 34. Rhys John was educated at Church of England and British elementary schools at Llangennech. On leaving school he worked for three years as a farm labourer in the vicinity of his native village and then migrated to the Rhondda Valley, where he worked for 10 years in coalmines in Ferndale and Ton Pentre. In 1901 he was appointed cashier to the Ton Co-operative Society and during the four years he occupied this post he devoted himself to organising in south Wales the Amalgamated Union of Co-operative Employees. In 1906 he moved to Manchester to become a full-time official of that Union, which later became the Nat. Union of Allied and Distributive Workers. In 1910 he wrote jointly with a colleague, Joseph Hallsworth (who was later knighted and became a distinguished figure in the trade union world) a book entitled *The Working Life of Shop Assistants* dealing with the poor wages and bad working conditions of the workers in this industry. He was a recognised authority on social insurance and after the passing of the National Insurance Act of 1911 he concentrated on this aspect of his trade union activities, becoming secretary of the N.U.A.D.W. Approved Society. He was an early member of the I.L.P. and threw himself enthusiastically into trade union and labour activities in Manchester. In 1913 he began his ten-year stint on the Manchester City Council, serving on the Education Authority and on the City Insurance Committee. He became President of the Manchester and Salford Labour Party, of the Manchester and Salford Trades Council and of the Withington Divisional Labour Party. In 1918 he stood unsuccessfully as Labour candidate for West Salford, but was elected in a by-election for Westhoughton in 1921, a seat which he held till his retirement from parliament in 1951. In the 1924 Labour Government he was appointed Under-Secretary of State for Home Affairs. In this office he performed his duties efficiently and conscientiously, but he was not comfortable with ministerial office. He disliked the compromises with principles which the acceptance of office entailed. At the same time, his socialism was motivated more by his religious and humanitarian feelings than by theoretical or doctrinal considerations. He remained throughout his life an uncompromising pacifist. He was immensely popular in his constituency among people who admired his integrity and sincerity, even though they might not always agree with his views on temperance and pacifism. He was an able parliamentarian and a consummate master of the proceedings of the House. He was for many years joint-secretary of the British Group of the Parliamentary Union and was elected chairman of that body in 1945. In this and on other occasions he travelled widely throughout the world.

Though he had lived in Manchester for 45 years before returning to live in Porthcawl, he remained always in close touch with his native country. He was not only an eloquent speaker in Welsh, but was a frequent contributor to the Welsh language press, especially to *Y Cymro* and *Y Tyst*. He published a selection of those articles in two short books, *Seneddwr ar Dramp* (1934) in which he gives his impressions of foreign countries he had visited, and *Pobl a Phethau* (1943) which contains interesting biographical details and reminiscences. He also published in 1941 a pacifist pamphlet, *Y Cristion a Rhyfel* (Pamphledi Heddychwyr Cymru, III).

He was a keen musician and frequently acted as precentor at Bootle End, the Welsh Congregational chapel in Manchester, where he worshipped. He was also occasionally invited to conduct *cymanfaoedd canu* in different parts of the country. During the 1898 strike he organised a choir of 25 voices from the Rhondda to tour the country to raise money for the strikers' families.

In 1902 he m. Margaret Ann Griffiths, a domestic science teacher in Ton Pentre. They had three sons. A younger brother was the poet-preacher, Rev. T. Cennech Davies (1875-1944; see David J. Thomas, *Bywyd a gwaith Cennech Davies* (1949).

He died at Porthcawl, 31 Oct. 1954, his wife having predeceased him about a year before.

Www; WwW (1921, 1933, 1937); *Times*, 2 Nov. 1954; *West. Mail*, 1 Nov. 1954; Rhys J. Davies, *Pobl a Phethau* (1943); *WWP*.

W.T.M.

DAVIES, RICHARD ('Isgarn'; 1887-1947), farmer-shepherd and poet; b. at Y Trawscoed in the parish of Caron-is-clawdd, Cards., 29 Aug. 1887, and d. there 8 June 1947. He bequeathed the original manuscripts of his poetic compositions to the National Library of Wales; he left also to the Library a sum of money on condition that the Council should arrange for the publication of a selection from his manuscripts. This was done in 1949, the volume, *Caniadau Isgarn* having an introduction by T.H. Parry-Williams and an appreciation by S.M. Powell. He was deeply interested in local history and antiquities, and was buried, as he had wished, at Strata Florida.

Personal knowledge.

W.Ll.D.

DAVIES, RICHARD OWEN (1894-1962), scientist and professor of agricultural chemistry; b. in Ganllwyd, near Dolgellau, Mer., 25 May 1894, son of Owen Davies, Congl. minister, and his wife. He was educated at Dolgellau grammar school and the University College, Aberystwyth, where he obtained an M.Sc. degree in 1916. After five years as an industrial chemist with the Nobel Explosives Co., he was appointed assistant lecturer in agricultural chemistry at his old college, and lecturer in 1925. As a fellow of the Guild of Graduates of the University he studied nutritional problems in north America, and in 1939 he was appointed advisory chemist and head of the department of agricultural chemistry at University College, Aberystwyth. He had wide experience in teaching both college and extramural students, and could lecture with ease in both English and Welsh.

He was treasurer of the committee for coining words for the first Welsh agricultural magazine, *Gwyddor Gwlad*, which was published on behalf of the Welsh agricultural section of the Guild of Graduates of the University of Wales (1952-63). He was one of the first contributors to the journal, and often broadcast on 'Rural science' for schools and on 'The Farmers World' between 1935 and 1951. His researches dealt with problems relating to grassland and dairying, and he co-operated with the Welsh Plant Breeding Station. His articles appeared in a number of technical journals, and he wrote *Elfennau Cemeg* (1937), a chemistry textbook for schools. He was dean of the faculty of science (1950-51) and was appointed professor of agricultural chemistry in 1954, and retired with the rank of professor emeritus of the University of Wales in 1959. He served as external examiner in agricultural chemistry for the Institute of Chemistry from 1944 to 1954. He d. 25 Feb. 1962 and was buried in the public cemetery, Aberystwyth. He m. in June 1929 Dinah Myfanwy, daughter of James Evans, Mydroilyn, Llannarth. [She d. 15 Mar., within a few weeks of her 100th birthday on 10 Apr. 1987].

Jnl. Roy. Inst. Chem., July. 1962, 300; Ellis, *UCW*; information given by his widow [and her niece].

M.R.W.

DAVIES, ROBERT HUMPHREY ('Gomerian'; 1856-1947), correspondent of Welsh and English newspapers in U.S.A.; b. at Penygogwydd, near Dinorwig, Caerns., s. of Humphrey R. Davies and Janet (née Hughes). He was taken as a child by his parents to America, and lived for some years at Dam, near Slatington, Pa. When he was sixteen he was apprenticed as a compositor in the offices of *Y Wasg*, Pittsburgh, Pa., where, apart from fifteen months in New York and Utica, he spent the remainder of his long life. He m., 2 Feb. 1887, Annie Evans of Pittsburgh, Pa.

'Gomerian' was connected with many Welsh and English newspapers published in the U.S.A., and developed into a fluent writer in both languages. He wrote much to *Y Drych*; when *The Druid* began publication at Scranton, Pa., he soon became one of its chief correspondents. He was very active in Welsh circles in Pittsburgh; for fourteen years he was secretary of the St. David's Day Society and he was twice elected its president. He arranged several *eisteddfodau* and visited Wales to invite David Lloyd-George (see below) to attend the international *eisteddfod* to be held in the U.S.A. At the suggestion of Lloyd George he formed the American *Gorsedd* of Bards of which he became the recorder; he served, e.g. as recorder, of the *Gorsedd* held at San Francisco in 1915. He also was mainly responsible for the publication of the *Royal Blue Book* which contains an account of the proceedings of the international *eisteddfod* held at Pittsburgh in 1913. He d. at Pittsburgh in 1947.

The Cambrian (Utica), 1903, 430-2; *The Royal Blue Book of the Pittsburgh International Eisteddfod*, 1913, 73-5; *Y Drych*, 15 Nov. 1947; *WwW* (1921); personal knowledge.

R.O.

DAVIES, THOMAS ELLIS JONES – see JONES-DAVIES, THOMAS ELLIS below.

DAVIES, TOM EIRUG ('Eirug'; 1892-1951), Congl. minister, writer and poet; b. at Troed-y-rhiw, a farm in Gwernogle, Carms., 23 Feb. 1892, only son of John and Mary Davies. He worked on the farm until he was 18 years old, when he was encouraged to preach. He was educated at Gwernogle elementary school, Tremle preparatory school, Pencader, 1910-12, the University College and Bala-Bangor College (Congl.) in Bangor 1912-19. He graduated B.A. (honours philosophy) and B.D. The principal, Thomas Rees, referred to him as one of his brightest students. He gained an M.A. degree in 1931 for a thesis on the contribution of Gwilym Hiraethog (William Rees, 1802-83, *DWB*, 831-2) to the life and literature of his period.

He became minister of the churches in Cwmllynfell, 1919-26, and Soar, Lampeter with Bethel, Parc-y-rhos, 1926-51. He held classes under the auspices of the department of extramural studies of the University of Wales and many came to his home (particularly in Cwmllynfell) to prepare themselves for the ministry. He was a preacher and poet of very special talent – he won the crown twice – at the national *eisteddfod* in Aberafan, 1932, and Neath, 1934, and various other prizes (see the preface, 'Diolchiadau', to *Cerddi Eirug*). He adjudicated many times in the national *eisteddfod*, and was known as 'Eirug' in the *Gorsedd* of Bards.

He edited *Ffrwythau Dethol* (Ben Davies, Pant-teg) and *Cofiant Thomas Rees* (a biography of his old principal at Bala-Bangor). He also published a history of the church in New Testament times (1932), and a history of his two churches, Soar (1931) and Bethel (1940), and of Gwernogle (1949). He contributed articles to *Y Geiriadur Beiblaidd* (1926), and chapters on Philip Pugh and his predecessors in *Y Cofiadur*, 1937, and on the faith of the Congregationalists in *Ffyrdd a Ffydd* (1945). He edited *Y Dysgedydd* 1943-51, and his contributions showed him to be an astute thinker and writer on a range of topics. For a period his notes concerned 'Gwernogau' – his old area in Carms. These were collected under the title *Yr Hen Gwm* (1966), edited by one of his sons, Alun Eirug Davies. His poems were published posthumously in *Cerddi Eirug* (1966).

He m. in 1920 Jennie Thomas (a fellow-student at Bangor), the eldest daughter of R.H. Thomas, (Presb.) minister, Llansannan, and they had eight children. Both he and his wife had a long struggle with ill health in middle age. She d. in 1948, and he d. 27 Sept. 1951.

Personal knowledge and the sources cited.

G.Jo.

DAVIES, TREVOR OWEN (1895-1966), minister (Presb.) and principal of Trefeca College; b. 20 Nov. 1895 at Cae Adda, Llanwrin, Denbs., son of Owen Gruffydd Owen and Mary Winifred Davies of Cae Adda. His father was a brother of Richard Owen, Mynydd Ednyfed (father of Dame Margaret Lloyd George, see Lloyd George family below). He was educated at the village school, Machynlleth county school, University College, Aberystwyth (where he graduated in the classics), and Christ Church, Oxford (where he took an honours degree in theology). He was awarded a B.Litt. degree for his thesis on 'The Augustinian doctrine of grace and free will'. He began preaching in his home chapel before graduating, was ord. in 1925, and served the ministry in Bethel, Cilfynydd, Glam. (1925-26). He was appointed assistant lecturer in Trefeca College in 1926, and when the principal W.P. Jones d. he served as principal of the college till he retired in 1964. He m. in 1933 Olwen Jane, daughter of the Rev. Benjamin Phillips, Merthyr Cynog, and they had one son.

T.O. Davies was a prominent man in his denomination and in the public life of Brecknockshire. He was chairman of the United Colleges Board of his Connexion and was elected Moderator of the Association in the East in 1964. He was a member of the standing joint committee and of the education committee of Breck., and was appointed Justice of the Peace in 1950. For some years he gave extramural lectures under the auspices of the University Colleges of Cardiff and Aberystwyth, and the University of Birmingham. He d., 10 Apr. 1966, and was buried in Siloa cemetery, Merthyr Cynog.

Blwyddiadur MC, 1967, 259-60; information from his widow; personal knowledge.

G.M.R.

DAVIES, TUDOR (1892-1958), singer, b. 12 Nov. 1892 in Cymer, Porth, Rhondda, fifth son of David and Sarah Davies. Before taking up a musical career he worked in the mines and during World War I as an engineer in the navy. He was educated in the University College at Cardiff. He won a scholarship at the Royal College of Music in London, and sang in opera and held concerts in the U.S.A., Canada and Australia. In 1922 he joined the British National Opera Co. and remained with that company for the rest of his career. He portrayed Rudolfo in London in 1922, and in 1924 he sang the leading role in the first public performance of *Hugh the Drover* (Vaughan Williams) in His Majesty's Theatre. He was principal tenor in Sadler's Wells, 1931-41, and with the Carl Rosa Opera Company, 1941-46; and as a resident member of the company in Sadler's Wells he portrayed the leading role in the first English performance of *Don Carlos* (Verdi) in 1938. He was invited to sing in every one of the leading music festivals in Great Britain and America. He had a warm and virile voice, and always sang with dignity and sincerity. His voice was recorded between 1925 and 1930, and the part of *The Dream of Gerontius* (Elgar) which was recorded in Hereford cathedral in 1927 with the composer conducting is a notable example of his style. He m. the soprano Ruth Packer; and d. 2 Apr. 1958.

Www, 1951-60; *Welsh Music*, 3 (1970), 34-5; *Y Ford Gron*, Dec. 1934.

H.W.

DAVIES, WILFRED MITFORD (1895-1966), artist; b. Feb. 23, 1895 at Menai Bridge, Angl., the second son of Robert and Elizabeth Davies. The family soon moved to Star, between Llanfairpwll and Gaerwen, and he was brought up there. His early education was at Llanfairpwll elementary school, and the County

School, Llangefni. His plans to become an architect were scotched by World War I. After leaving the army, he spent four years at the Liverpool School of Art before starting work as a commercial artist in the city. He returned to live and work at Star on the death of his father. It was about this time – 1923-24 – that Ifan ab Owen Edwards (see below) asked him to provide illustrations for the monthly magazine *Cymru'r Plant*, and thus began more than forty years of work for *Urdd Gobaith Cymru*. His cartoon characters 'Toodles' and 'Twm y gath' became very popular; they appeared in Breton in 1936. He worked widely for Welsh publishers, illustrating volumes by Daniel Owen, E. Tegla Davies, Meuryn, John Ellis Williams and many others, and he was a cartoonist for Welsh newspapers and periodicals.

Apart from his commercial work, he was a noted artist in oils and watercolour, and his canvases, many of Anglesey and Snowdonia, are found in homes throughout Wales. He m. in 1925, Ellen Rowlands, daughter of Elias and Margaret Rowlands, Liverpool, and they had one daughter, Margaret.

He d. in Mar. 1966, and was buried at the town cemetery, Llangefni.

Personal knowledge; [W. *Mitford Davies*, Gwynedd Library Service exhibition brochure, 1980].

M.M.W.

DAVIES, WILLIAM (1874-1949), local historian; b. 6 Jun. 1874, at Plas Corniog, Llanegryn, Mer. Invalided early in life he was for ten years confined to bed from about the age of 13. When his health improved he was apprenticed as a tailor in Barmouth and Llanegryn. In 1907 he was appointed clerk to Llanegryn parish council and rate collector. In 1921 he kept a hotel in Oswestry, but returned to Llanegryn in 1928. He d. 19 Jun. 1949.

He contributed much to *Cymru, Yr Haul, Lleufer, Y Ford Gron, Heddiw, Y Dysgedydd,* and *Bathafarn*. He also helped J. Bodfan Anwyl (see above) in the preparation of the fifth edition of Spurrell's dictionary. His chief work was *Hanes plwyf Llanegryn*, published in 1948.

Personal knowledge.

W.Ll.D.

DAVIES, WILLIAM (1899-1968) botanist and grassland specialist; b. 20 Apr. 1899 in Norman Rd., London, eldest son of William and Margaret Davies, both of farming families from north Cards. He was educated in Sloane School, London, and after service in the army in 1917-18 he entered the University College of Wales, Aberystwyth, and graduated with first-class honours in botany in 1923. He was appointed to the staff of the Welsh Plant Breeding Station the same year, the beginning of the long and productive collaboration between him and R.G. Stapledon (see below). He was a plant geneticist at Palmerston North, New Zealand, 1929-31, and the choice of varieties to be developed for the grassland of that country was based on his work there. He visited Australia and had an opportunity to spend a year there in 1932-33. Between 1933 and 1940 he was head of the department of grassland agronomy at the Welsh Plant Breeding Station. He did not confine himself to experimental work, but made a survey of the grassland and waste lands of Wales which was published in *A survey of the agricultural and waste lands of Wales* in 1937, under the editorship of R.G. Stapledon and with the financial help of David Lloyd George (see below). Between Nov. 1936 and Mar. 1938 he made a detailed survey of the grassland of the Falkland Islands and his report, *The grasslands of the Falkland Islands*, was published in 1939. During 1938 and 1939 he and his assistants surveyed and carefully mapped the grassland of England. This survey was used as a guide in the campaign for ploughing grassland during World War II to grow more corn and other arable crops. This survey intensified his belief in a policy of ploughing up permanent grassland and reseeding it as leys which would be much more productive. This is when *Ley farming* (1941) was written in conjunction with R.G. Stapledon. Another consequence of the survey was the establishment of the Grassland Improvement Station in 1940 near Stratford-upon-Avon, with R.G. Stapledon as director and William Davies as assistant director. He was appointed director on the retirement of Stapledon in 1945, and he continued in that post after the work was moved in 1949 to a new centre near Hurley, in the Thames valley, namely the Grassland Research Institute. He remained there until he retired in 1964. He published very many articles in his own field, but his most important work is *The grass crop* (1952), in a volume which gathers his studies, thoughts and investigations regarding grassland in every part of the world during the preceding quarter of a century. He travelled widely to advise governments and international societies on research matters and developments in grassland, and he played a leading part in founding the British Grassland Society in 1945. He was its president on two occasions and an honorary fellow of the society for life. He was awarded the degrees of M.Sc. (1925) and D.Sc. (1945) of the University of Wales and was awarded an honorary D.Sc. degree by the University of New Zealand in 1956. He was honoured with the C.B.E. in 1964, and was an Honorary Fellow of the Royal Agricultural Society of England, and honorary life president of the European Grassland Federation.

He m. in 1928 Alice Muriel Lewis and they had one son. Davies d. 28 July, 1968, and was buried in the churchyard of Llanfihangel Genau'r Glyn, Cards.

Personal knowledge; *Www*; *Jnl. Br. Grassld. Soc.* 1968, 265-7.

LI.P.

DAVIES, WILLIAM ANTHONY (1886-1962), journalist; b. 1 March 1886 in Cwarter Coch, a thatched cottage in Cwmgrenig, Glanaman, Carms., third s. of the eight children of Daniel Davies and his wife. His father was a coalminer from Ysguborwen farm, Betws, and his mother was a native of Bryn, Llanelli. At 13 he joined his father and brothers in Gelliceidrim drift mine. He was a doorboy working with hauliers for some months but his father felt that this was too rough a life for the lad and he obtained work on the air pumps. In June 1900 he lost his left hand while cleaning powder from dynamite caps at home and he was blinded for several weeks. The accident changed his career from mining to journalism, and following the advice of his Sunday school teacher he mastered Pitman's short-hand. He joined the staff of the South Wales Press, Llanelli, and in 1903 he began to keep a diary in short-hand, a practice he retained throughout his life. He was 'Llyn y Fan' in the prose medal competition at the Llanelli national *eisteddfod* in 1962, when he was encouraged to publish the diary which he submitted. Selections, edited by J. Ellis Williams, appeared under the title *Berw Bywyd* in 1968. The original diaries were destroyed. In 1905 he moved to Cardiff to the *South Wales Daily News* becoming its political sub-editor and gossip writer. He joined the staff of the *Daily Sketch* in London in 1919 and then moved to the *Daily News* – the *News Chronicle* later, where he was sub-editor, night editor and assistant editor. His weekly column 'Llygad Llwchwr' became very popular and his love of Wales, its people and culture were apparent in it. He became one of Fleet Street's most brilliant executives but he retained his uncompromising radicalism and firm nonconformity throughout his life. His essays reveal his shrewd judgement of people and events. He had a sharp mind and was a staunch defender of the common man and of Welsh interests. One of his successes was to halt the spread of afforestation in the Teifi valley. He was a well-known *eisteddfod* supporter and was made an hon. white-robed member of the *Gorsedd* of Bards in Pwllheli in 1955. He followed the missionary campaigns of Stephen and George Jeffreys in Wales and London. He was bapt. in Llanelli and while he lived in London he worshipped at Spurgeon's Tabernacle, and did social work with the Salvation Army.

He m. (1) Margaret, dau. of William Trefor Davies, minister of Soar (Congl.), Llanelli in 1909; they had a s. and dau. His wife d. in 1953 a few weeks after his retirement to Cardiff where he became a member of Tabernacl church: and (2) Eirene Hughes, widow of T. Rowland Hughes (see below) and a fellow-member at Tabernacl, in 1958. After retiring he wrote regularly for a time for *Y Cymro* under the names 'Sguborwen' and 'Llygad Llwchwr'. He d. Sunday 4 Nov. 1962 in St. Winifred's Hospital, Cardiff and his ashes were buried in his first wife's grave at the Box cemetery, Llanelli.

Personal knowledge; *West. Mail*, 6 Nov. 1962; *Cymro*, 8 Nov. 1962.

D.T.D.

DAVIES, WILLIAM DAVID [P.] (1897-1969), minister (Presb.), college tutor and author; b. 18 Jan. 1897 in Glynceiriog, Denbs., only son of Isaac Davies, Presb. minister, and his wife. His father moved to Rhyd-ddu, then to Bryn-rhos, and finally to Bangor. The son was educated at Caernarfon county school and Friars School, Bangor. He gained a scholarship to Jesus College, Oxford, but his studies were interrupted by the war. Having registered as a conscientious objector, he served as an agricultural worker in Llŷn. Whilst there he began to preach at South Beach church, Pwllheli. After the war he returned to Oxford, where he gained a second class in classics, ancient history and philosophy, and a first class in theology. He gained a B.D. degree for research work, becoming the first Nonconformist to return to Wales with this Oxford degree. He was a scholar of his college and was offered a Fellowship and an appointment as tutor of theology at the University. But since he was intent on being a Presbyterian minister he could not accept their terms which required that he become a member of the Church of England.

In 1923 he was ord., and he served his ministry in the churches of Shirland Rd., London (1923-26), and Cathedral Rd., Cardiff (1926-28). In 1925 he m. Margaret Evelyn Palmer and they had a son. He was appointed professor of the history of religions and the philosophy of religion in 1928 at the Theological College, Aberystwyth, but resigned in 1933 following some unfortunate events. It became apparent that his mind was disturbed, and he displayed a split personality for the rest of his life. He moved from place to place and lived at Neath and Machynlleth, and he also lived in one or two other districts as a member of staff on the weekly newspaper, Y Cymro. He had charge of the churches in the pastorate of Llangadfan, Mont., but the few months he spent with them proved calamitous. Eventually he moved to Llandrindod Wells, where Ithon Road church gave him the opportunity to recover. He d. there 7 July. 1969. His friends and admirers raised a fund to place a monument on his grave.

W.D. Davies had a pleasant personality, he was a first-class scholar and a powerful preacher. He possessed particular qualifications required to meet the needs of the mid-twentieth century. He excelled also as an author who could readily draw upon all sources of learning and literature. He published some books on religious topics, namely Cristnogaeth a meddwl yr oes (1932), Datblygiad Duw (1934), and a penetrating and highly readable handbook on the Epistle to the Ephesians (1933). During his 'itinerant' period he took an interest in writing essays and poems – this is when he began to call himself W.D.P. Davies, though no-one knew what 'P' stood for. [He said 'P' was for 'Pechadur' (sinner), but it may have derived from his wife's maiden name.] He published Y diafol i dalu (1948), and Tannau telyn crwydrol (1953). Presbyterianism, and Wales in general, suffered a deep loss from the dualism which wrecked his personality.

Blwyddiadur MC, 1970, 277; personal acquaintance.

G.M.R.

DAVIES, WILLIAM HUBERT (1893-1965), musician; b. 24 May 1893 at Abersychan, Mon., and educated at West Monmouth Grammar School, Pontypool. At the age of fifteen he won a Sainton open scholarship to study the violin at the Royal Academy of Music; he was a pupil of Hans Wessely and later at Dresden of Leopold Auer. From 1919 to 1923 he was a member of the string trio which was formed by Henry Walford Davies (see above) at the University College of Wales, Aberystwyth, and in 1923 he was the leader of the Welsh Symphony Orchestra. Henry Wood heard him and persuaded him to join the Queen's Hall Orchestra in London. Between 1924 and 1934 he played there, at the Royal Opera House, Covent Garden, and with the London Symphony Orchestra. From 1927 he was also a violin and viola tutor, and a member of the string trio at the University College in Cardiff. He returned to the college at Aberystwyth in 1934 as tutor and leader of the college instrumental quartet. In 1950 he was appointed violin, composition and orchestral tutor at Cardiff College of Music and Drama. He composed many songs and choral and instrumental works, including work commissioned for the Düsseldorf Symphony Orchestra in 1945. He m. Hannah May Reynolds, and they had two sons. He d. at Cardiff 27 Oct. 1965.

West. Mail, 29 Oct. 1965; Robert Smith (compiler), *Seventh catalogue of contemporary Welsh music* (1981).

Rh.G.

DAVIES, WILLIAM LEWIS (1896-1941), specialist in analytical dairy chemistry; b. 23 Feb. 1896, the son of David (a farmer) and Jane Davies of Cwmlogin, Llansawel, Carms. He attended Llandeilo county school before joining the Royal Horse Artillery in 1914; he afterwards saw active service in France. He graduated B.Sc. (Wales) with first-class honours in chemistry from University College of Wales, Aberystwyth, then proceeding to Gonville and Caius College, Cambridge, where he graduated Ph.D. in 1924. In 1925 he was appointed advisory agricultural chemist at Reading University during which period he published papers on the nitrogenous compounds of fish meal and the proteins of green forage plants. Two years later he became biochemist at the National Institute for Research in Dairying, his field of research and investigation consequently becoming wider. He was joint author of a series of papers on the ripening of cheese, but the work which established him as a leading authority in his subject was *The Chemistry of Milk*, the first edition of which appeared in 1936. In recognition of his contribution to dairy chemistry University of Wales conferred on him in 1935 the degree of D.Sc. He was appointed in 1939 Director of Dairying Research to the Government in India and had the satisfaction of organising and seeing opened on St. David's Day, 1941, an active research centre, The Imperial Dairy Research Institute. He d. at New Delhi on 15 May 1941, and was buried at the Nicholson cemetery, New Delhi, a Celtic cross erected by the staff of the Institute marking his grave. His wife was formerly Miss Eleanor Unwin of Cambridge.

J.G.D., 'William Lewis Davies', *The Biochemical Journal*, 36 (1942), 543; information from his sister, Mrs. J. Thomas.

M.B.D.

DAVIES, Sir WILLIAM (LLEWELYN) (1887-1952), librarian; b. at Plas Gwyn Schoolhouse, near Pwllheli, Caerns., 11 Oct. 1887, the third child and younger son of William Davies and his wife Jane (Evans), both natives of Llanafan, Cards. His father, formerly the Earl of Lisburne's gamekeeper, was then similarly employed at Broom Hall, near Pwllheli. When he was five his father entered the service of Sir Osmond Williams, Castell Deudraeth, and the family moved to Minffordd,

Penrhyndeudraeth. He was educated at Porthmadog County School 1900-03 and at Penrhyndeudraeth pupil-teacher centre, where he was a pupil-teacher, 1903-06 before entering the University College of Wales, graduating B.A. (1909) with honours in Welsh and M.A. (1912) by virtue of a dissertation on 'Phylipiaid Ardudwy', a group of sixteenth and seventeenth century Ardudwy poets (*DWB*, 763-766). On leaving college he held various teaching appointments in elementary, secondary, and evening schools in north and south Wales and as a part-time lecturer at the University College, Cardiff. During World War I he served in the Royal Garrison Artillery and later as a commissioned officer in the Army Education Service.

In Sept. 1919 Davies entered upon his lifework when he was appointed first assistant librarian under (Sir) John Ballinger (*DWB*, 23-4) at the young National Library of Wales at Aberystwyth. When Ballinger retired in 1930 Davies succeeded him as chief librarian, a position which he held until his death. The task which faced him was a formidable one – to continue and develop the work, so successfully begun, of building up in Wales a national library which would rank among the great libraries of the world. His experience as Ballinger's deputy, his interest in Welsh history and literature, his bilingualism, his zeal and enthusiasm, together served him in good stead and his efforts were crowned with outstanding success.

Much of that success was achieved in connection with his collection and preservation of manuscripts and records. He was convinced from the outset that one of the National Library's most important functions was to collect and preserve the mass of manuscripts and documentary material relating to Wales which was scattered (often in a state of neglect) throughout the Principality and further afield – the raw material needed by present and future historians. He laboured indefatigably towards this end, his task being facilitated by the changing economic conditions which brought about the disintegration of large estates and the vacating of old country houses. The list of individual owners, institutions, and official bodies that responded to his diplomatic persuasion to transfer their records to the Library, either absolutely or on permanent loan, is a notable one. Of the approximately 3,500,000 documents housed in the Library when Davies died all but 200,000 or so were acquired during his period of administration. Extensive collecting and effective preservation, however, were not enough; adequate steps had to be taken to make the records available to researchers without undue delay. By substituting the production of handy, typewritten, brief-entry schedules and handlists for that of printed detailed calendars, and by subsequently introducing the compilation of subject-indexes to their contents, he greatly accelerated the rate at which individual collections were made available.

Since his concern for the preservation of records arose not from selfish motives but from a realisation of their historical value, he was always anxious to persuade other bodies to take steps to preserve records in their custody. He urged the various county councils of Wales to establish county records committees and gave to municipal, ecclesiastical, and other bodies and to individuals both valuable advice and practical assistance. He kept the Library in close touch with other bodies with similar aims through his membership of the Royal Commission on Historical Manuscripts, the Society of Antiquaries, the executive committee of the Council for the Preservation of Business Archives, and the British Records Association, of which he was a vice-president representing the interest of Wales.

The presentation of records was only one of several channels through which Davies rendered conspicuous service to Wales and its culture. As the National Library's principal administrative officer he was responsible for organising the lending of books to adult study classes throughout Wales, for operating in eleven Welsh counties the Regional Libraries Scheme for Wales and Monmouthshire, and for the selection, acquisition, and distribution of books for patients in the sanatoria of Wales. During World War II he established a national committee to provide Welsh books for men and women serving in the forces. He missed no opportunity, through lectures, broadcast talks, and publications, of bringing the Library into closer contact with the Welsh people. In 1937 he published *The National Library of Wales: A Survey of its History, its Contents, and its Activities*, whilst two years later he launched the publication of *The National Library of Wales Journal*, which he continued to edit for fourteen years. For varying periods he was honorary editor of the journals of the Welsh Bibliographical Society, the Cardiganshire Antiquarian Society, and the Merioneth Historical and Record Society; he was also associate-editor of *Y Bywgraffiadur Cymreig* and *DWB*. A member of numerous academic and cultural bodies, he was a leading spirit in every organisation promoting the intellectual life of the Principality. Endowed with exceptional organising ability, he was a hard and conscientious worker who was never satisfied with work of an inferior standard.

His manifold services were duly recognised by the conferment upon him of a knighthood in 1944 and of the degree of LL.D., *honoris causa*, by the University of Wales in 1951. In the year of his death he was High Sheriff of Merioneth.

Davies m. in 1914 Gwen, daughter of Dewi Llewelyn, grocer and baker, Pontypridd, and afterwards adopted the additional name of Llewelyn. There was one daughter of the marriage.

He d. at Sherborne House, Aberystwyth, 11 Nov. 1952, after and a long and painful illness. After cremation his ashes were scattered in the grounds of the great Library which he loved and served so well.

[*The Times*, 12 Nov. 1952; *Jnl. W.B.S.*, 7 (1953); *Trans. Cymm.* 1953; private information]; personal knowledge.

G.T.

DE LLOYD, DAVID JOHN (1883-1948), musician; b. 30 Apr. 1883, at Skewen, Glam., son of Morgan de Lloyd, an insurance agent. The family moved several times before eventually settling down at Penparcau, Aberystwyth. While they lived at Carmarthen David attended Pentrepoeth board school. From early childhood he showed remarkable musical ability. In

1894 J.S. Curwen attended the South Wales Tonic Sol-fa Conference held at Carmarthen and during the next two years took David with him on lecturing tours in England, Scotland and Ireland, to demonstrate the more advanced uses of the notation. From Aberystwyth county school (1896-99), he won the Ceredigion county exhibition to U.C.W., Aberystwyth, where he remained until 1905, graduating B.A. (hons. Hist.), 1903. In 1905 he became the first to gain the degree of B.Mus. in the University of Wales. It was felt he should be further encouraged, and a committee chaired by T.F. Roberts (*DWB*, 882) promoted a public testimonial amounting to £100 which enabled de Lloyd to spend the session 1906-07 at Leipzig.

He taught at schools in Woolwich, 1908-11, Llanelli, 1911-19, and took the degrees of B.Mus., 1913, and Mus. Doc., 1915, at the University of Dublin. He m. in 1911 Lilian Morgan of Aberystwyth. He often adjudicated at national *eisteddfodau*. In 1919 he returned to Aberystwyth as a lecturer in the music department when Sir H. Walford Davies (see above) came to occupy the vacant chair. The numerous extra-mural activities of the professor threw more work on to the shoulders of the lecturer and de Lloyd became responsible for the choral society, the college orchestra and the weekly concerts held by the department. He succeeded Sir Walford Davies in the chair in 1926. He d. 20 Aug. 1948, the day upon which his retirement from the college was to take effect.

He composed a large number of works and arranged other music. His principal works include *Gwenllian* (opera), 1924; *Tir na n'Og* a lyrical ode by T. Gwynn Jones (see below); *Gwlad fy Nhadau* (cantata); *Cân a Moliant* (Hymns and tunes – general editor H. Haydn Jones), *Saith o Ganeuon enwog Brahms* (with Welsh words by T.H. Parry-Williams); and *Forty Welsh traditional tunes*, issued by the Cards. Antiq. Soc.

Information supplied by Ifor L. Evans; personal knowledge.

S.J.

DEAKIN, ARTHUR (1890-1955), trade union leader; b. 11 Nov. 1890 at Sutton Coldfield, Warwickshire, the son of a shoemaker. His father d. when he was a child, his mother re-married and the family moved to live at Merthyr Tydfil. In 1904 he began work at the Guest, Keen and Nettlefolds steelworks at Dowlais. He was influenced by socialism, in particular by Keir Hardie, who used to address meetings at the factory gates. Although Deakin worked long hours, he read widely and attended evening classes. In 1919 he was appointed an official of the Dock, Wharf, Riverside and General Workers' Union which later became the Transport and General Workers' Union with its headquarters at Shotton in Flintshire. For fifteen years he served as a member of the Flintshire County Council, he became an alderman of the Council and served as its chairman. He also rendered service as a J.P. In 1932 Deakin was chosen as the general secretary of the General Workers' Group, and in 1935 he became personal assistant to Ernest Bevin, the general secretary to the T.G.W.U. When Bevin became a member of the Cabinet in 1940, Deakin to all intents and purposes took his place within the union. He was himself appointed general

secretary in 1945, an office which he held for ten years. He was influential, too, within the General Council of the Trades Union Congress, and he himself chaired the Congress in 1951-52. Deakin held a large number of posts on committees and public bodies, and he was one of the directors of the *Daily Herald*. He received the C.B.E. in 1943, became a C.H. in 1949 and he was chosen as a member of the Privy Council in 1954. He was a strong, forceful personality whose opinions carried great weight within Transport House. Yet he was also a moderate who fought courageously against the Communists and the extremists within the Labour Party. He d. 1 May 1955 at Leicester Royal Hospital six months before reaching retirement age.

Www; Times, 2 May 1955; *West. Mail*, 3 July. 1940, 24 Nov. 1945 and 2 May 1955; *WWP*.

J.G.J.

DEWI EMRYS - see JAMES, DAVID EMRYS below.

DEWI HIRADDUG – see EVANS, DAVID DELTA below.

DEWI MAI o FEIRION – see ROBERTS, DAVID JOHN below.

DIVERRES, POL (1880-1946), linguist, Celtic scholar, and sometime Keeper of manuscripts in the National Library of Wales; b. 12 Dec. 1880 at Lorient, Brittany, the son of Henri Diverres, lawyer and Breton folklorist, and Pauline Chauvlon. He was educated in the University of Rennes where he took his 'doctorat' in Celtic. He had almost completed his examination in medicine (a course which he had pursued at the specific request of his parents), when he decided to change to Celtic, which he studied at the *Collège de France* (under Jospeh Loth), the Sorbonne, and the *École des hautes études*, Paris. Coming to Wales in 1911 (as a member of the Breton *Gorsedd* of Bards) to attend the Carmarthen national *eisteddfod*, he shortly afterwards began his residence in this country which was to continue until his death. After taking his M.A. degree in the University of Liverpool in 1914 and after a short period as French master at Lewis' School, Pengam, Glamorgan, he was appointed Keeper of manuscripts and sub-librarian in the National Library of Wales (9 Sept. 1919); he relinquished this post in 1923 to join the French department in the newly-established University College of Swansea. He had a good Celtic library. His widow and son arranged for much of it, especially the Breton books and journals, to come to the National Library. His most important publications were *Le plus ançien texte de Meddygon Myddveu* ... (Paris, 1913) and *Le Siège de Lorient par les Anglais en 1746* ... (Rennes, 1931); articles in *Revue Celtique* and *Les Annales de Bretagne*.

Diverres m., in 1913, Elizabeth Jones ('Telynores Gwalia'), dau. of Hugh Jones ('Trisant'), Liverpool; they had one son. Diverres d. 25 Dec. 1946 at Swansea, and was buried in Sketty churchyard.

Personal knowledge.

W.Ll.D.

DIWYGIWR, Y – see ROBERTS, EVAN JOHN below.

DOFWY – see JONES, RICHARD below.

DUNRAVEN, 5th EARL – see WYNDHAM-QUIN, WINDHAM HENRY below.

DYFNALLT – see OWEN, JOHN DYFNALLT below.

DYNEVOR, seventh and eighth BARONS – see under RHYS, WALTER FITZURYAN below.

E

E.O.J. – see JONES, EDWARD OWEN below.

E.T. – see MORGAN, EDWARD below.

EAMES, WILLIAM (1874-1958), journalist; b. in Prestatyn, Flints., in 1874, the son of Griffith Eames and his wife Margaret Dowell from Prestatyn. His father was a carpenter who had been apprenticed in Liverpool after working, for a time, on the land in his native Anglesey. He settled in Barrow-in-Furness where he met his future wife as a fellow chorister in the choir conducted by Peter Edwards, 'Pedr Alaw' (*DWB*, 193). Margaret Eames insisted on returning to Prestatyn so that the child was born in Wales, although he was raised in Barrow for two years before the family moved to Maes-y-Groes, Prestatyn. William Eames was educated at the church school until he was 12 when he left to work with his father. However, at the age of 17 he became a pupil-teacher at the new British School in Prestatyn. In Oct. 1894, he was one of the first students at the education department of University College Bangor and he studied there for two years. When he had completed his course, he took a post as assistant teacher in the Wesleyan School at Dartford, Kent. He spent two years there and began to write for the press — *Illustrated Bits, Sketchy Bits* — and for John Hugh Edwards' (see below) *Young Wales*. He moved to a school in Surbiton and, after two years, accepted in 1900 a post at the Board School, Caernarfon, where he began to use the Welsh language in lessons, against accepted practice but with the support of Her Majesty's Inspectors of Schools. At Caernarfon, Eames established close relations with the leading figures of Welsh journalism, e.g., R. Gwyneddon Davies (*DWB*, 136, under John Davies, 'Gwyneddon'); Beriah Gwynfe Evans (*DWB*, 220-1); Daniel Rees (*DWB*, 823-4); T. Gwynn Jones (see below) and John R. Lloyd, the cartoonist and, later, his brother-in-law. Eames already had an interest in journalism and it is not surprising that the contacts he made at Caernarfon turned his mind towards journalism. When R. Gwyneddon Davies went to America for three months in 1902, he chose Eames to write, in his place, the leading article and a weekly column in the *North Wales Observer*. In Sept. 1902, Eames left teaching in order to succeed John Thomas, 'Eifionydd' (*DWB*, 954-5) as editor of *Y Genedl*, a post he held until 1907 when he was appointed one of the sub-editors on the *Manchester Guardian* which he joined in Jan. 1908. He kept his connection with the *Guardian* after he was appointed financial secretary to the Manchester Stock Exchange. He became the secretary of the Exchange in 1919. Together with the sons of C.P. Scott, he founded in 1920 the *Manchester Guardian Commercial Supplement*, a commercial weekly, which first appeared in June 1920 and became very popular, especially for its supplements, in the commercial world. This publication was issued up to 1939 and it gave publicity to Charles Tonge's suggestion that white lines should be painted on roads in order to control traffic. Eames settled in Prestatyn when he returned to Wales in 1931 and began to broadcast from the Bangor studios. Sir John Reith appointed him press secretary to the Ministry of Information in 1940; he moved to Cardiff where he became friendly with D.T. Davies (see above) and Caleb Rees (see below), school inspectors. He spoke frequently on the radio from Cardiff. In 1947, he was appointed M.B.E.

He m. on 25 July 1902 Jane Myfanwy Hughes, the sister of Howel Harris Hughes (see below) and the author of *Llyfr prydiau bwyd* (1932). As 'Megan Ellis', she was the editor of the women's pages in *Y Ford Gron* and she also broadcast from Bangor and Cardiff. Together, they wrote a novel, *Melin y ddôl* (1948). William Eames died at Colwyn Bay on 29 Sept. 1958; his wife had died at Cardiff on 23 June 1955.

W.W.P.; Genh., 10-15, 1959-65; *Prestatyn Weekly,* 4 Oct. 1958; OPCS deaths Oct.-Dec. 1958.

E.D.J.

EDWARDS, ARTHUR TUDOR (1890-1946), surgeon; b. Swansea, 7 Mar. 1890, elder son of William Edwards, J.P. Educated at Mill Hill School, St. John's College, Cambridge, and Middlesex Hospital, London, where he was awarded the Senior Broderip and the University scholarships. Qualifying as a doctor in 1913 he obtained the higher degrees of M.Ch. and F.R.C.S. 1915. He served in the R.A.M.C. during World War I and rose to the rank of major. He was appointed assistant surgeon to Westminster Hospital, surgeon to the Brompton Hospital for Diseases of the Chest, surgeon to Queen Mary's Hospital, Roehampton, and thoracic surgeon to the London County Council. His main interest in his first years lay in gastro-intestinal surgery, but he became a pioneer in thoracic surgery. Chest surgery was not truly established until he operated successfully on cases of bronchiectasis, bronchial carcinoma and pulmonary tuberculosis. He was the first surgeon in Britain to remove a lobe of the lung and to remove a lung, and one of the first to operate for carcinoma of the oesophagus. He resigned from Westminster Hospital in 1930 to organise a department of thoracic surgery at London Hospital. Edwards was regarded as a most skilful surgeon and fine teacher and he gained an international reputation. In World War II, he became civilian adviser in thoracic surgery to the War Office and R.A.F. He wrote numerous articles, and was a founder of the journal *Thorax*. He delivered the Harveian Oration (1939), on bronchiectasis. Edwards was the first president of the Association for the Study of Diseases of the Chest, president of the Thoracic Society, and Hon. Fellow of the American Society of Thoracic Surgeons. He was awarded hon. degrees by Grenoble and Oslo universities. He m. Evelyn Ime Ida Chichester, dau. of Dr Theo Hoskin, London. After a period of ill-health, he d. at St. Enodoc, Cornwall, 25 Aug. 1946.

Lancet (1946), 2, 365; *Brit. Med. Jnl. 2,* (1946), 2, 346, 444; *Brit. Jnl. of Surgery,* Oct. 1946; *Www.*

O.E.R.

EDWARDS, CHARLES ALFRED (1882-1960), metallurgist and principal of University College of Swansea; b. 23 March 1882, s. of Samuel and Elizabeth Edwards, Kitchener, Ontario, Canada. The family moved to Lancashire in 1884 and C.A. Edwards was apprenticed in 1898 in the Lancashire and Yorkshire railways foundry. Such was his interest in the properties of metals and alloys that he was appointed assistant to Dr. H.C.H.Carpenter at the National Physical Laboratory in 1905. In 1907 he was co-author with Carpenter of a report on the copper-aluminium alloys and was appointed a lecturer in Metallurgy at Manchester University. Between this date and 1910, when he returned to industry with Bolckow Vaughan and Dorman Long in Middlesborough, he published several papers on the heat treatment of steel and was awarded the degree of M.Sc. He was also far in advance of contemporary ideas in recommending the addition of oxygen to the air blown into iron blast furnaces, a practice which became common about fifty years later. Further research publications led to the award of a D.Sc. in 1913. In 1908 he married Florence Edith Roberts and their son was born in 1913. C.A. Edwards succeeded Carpenter as professor of Metallurgy in Manchester in 1914 and succeeded in combining government work on steel analysis and heat treatment with the development of an Honours School in Metallurgy.

In 1920 he became Head of the Department of Metallurgy and Vice-Principal at the newly established University College of Swansea. The first entrants were mainly young men who had seen military service and were rather older than the normal intake, but with the aid of three colleagues who were inspired to accompany him from Manchester these were persuaded to embark on serious study and some, later, on research. Edwards' earlier experience in industry and absorbing interest in the application of science ensured widespread and lively collaboration with local industry, especially steel and tinplate and led to the establishment of a research group supported by the South Wales Siemens Steel Association. There were numerous publications relating to the production of mild steel sheet and tinplate, including definitive work on the structure of steel ingots and the influence of heavy cold-rolling on the final sheet structure. He became Principal of the University College in 1926, but he retained the Chair of Metallurgy and found great pleasure in discussing teaching and research and giving lectures and publishing papers as a relaxation from his strenuous efforts in promoting the interests of the college. His election as a Fellow of the Royal Society in 1930 gave great pleasure to a wide circle of industrial and academic friends. His lectures on alloy structures in the early 1930s were again an example of his capacity to keep ahead of current ideas on an important topic. The outbreak of war in 1939 stopped work on the major scheme for the replacement of the temporary buildings erected in 1921 and for which Principal Edwards had been indefatigable in his efforts. His guidance during the difficult period which lasted virtually until his retirement in 1947 put the college into a favourable position to take advantage of subsequent opportunities for growth.

Even after retirement C.A. Edwards retained his interest in metallurgy and was for some years a consultant to a major south Wales steelworks. His somewhat retiring personality and diffidence in expressing opinions contrasted strongly with the evidence of his progression by personal effort and ability from an apprentice to a high academic level and the possession of the highest awards in his profession. A kindly and dignified person, he was capable of inspiring enthusiasm and lasting friendship and his loss was felt by many when he died on March 29, 1960.

Biog. Memoirs Fellows R.S.

D.W.H.

EDWARDS, DAVID MIALL (1873-1941), theologian and writer; b. 22 Jan. 1873 in Llanfyllin, Mont., son of William Edwards, grocer and gardener, and Jane Edwards. He began his education at the Board School, Llandderfel, and the grammar school, Bala, before proceeding with an Exhibition to the University College of North Wales, Bangor. As the University of Wales was not yet empowered to confer degrees, he sat for the Honours School of English in London University, and was awarded second-class Honours in 1896. He then proceeded to Mansfield College, Oxford, but being prevented by illness from sitting his examination on the completion of his three-year course, he accepted a call to Salem Congregational Church, Ffestiniog, and was ordained in 1900. This, however, did not prevent his returning to Oxford where he graduated in 1901 from Mansfield College with first-class honours in theology. Returning to Ffestiniog he remained there until 1904 when he became minister of Plough Chapel, Brecon. In 1909 he was appointed to the Chair of the Philosophy of Religion and Christian Doctrine in the Brecon Memorial College, where he remained until 1934 when, after a protracted and extremely courageous struggle, he was compelled to yield to ill-health and resigned from his Chair, continuing, however, active in many other directions until his death in 1941. His career as a teacher of theology, writer, and preacher was a notable one, and the influence of his work and personality was widely felt, especially in Wales where he carried his religious fervour into many social and cultural fields. His reputation as a theologian was established by his two books, *The Philosophy of Religion* (1929) and *Christianity and Philosophy* (1932), works for which he was awarded a doctorate by the University of London, and by his numerous contributions to learned journals. His first Welsh book, *Crefydd a Bywyd* (1915) was followed by numerous other books in which he discussed religious subjects with peculiar incisiveness and clarity, and thus prepared the way for his main literary work, *Bannau'r Ffydd* (1939) in which he strove, with much success, to provide a comprehensive interpretation of the main Christian doctrines in terms of modern life and culture. His contributions to Welsh journals were very extensive and he himself was editor of *Y Dysgedydd* (1915-18) and *Yr Efrydydd* (1920-28) and of the widely-read series of essays published by *Urdd y Deyrnas* under the title *Efengyl y Deyrnas*. In his philosophical and religious views Edwards owed much to personal idealism as represented in the work of James Ward, Pringle-Pattison, and W.R. Sorley, but he was subsequently much impressed also by Otto's *Idea of the Holy*. The most distinctive strain in his own thought is his insistence on the idea of the Holy as the basis of other values, but his work was notable, less for original developments of the positions he himself adopted, than for vigorous defence of them and criticisms of rival theories. His interest for posterity will owe much to his pioneer work in the art of writing a readable Welsh style on philosophical subjects. Welsh philosophy will always be greatly indebted to his work and example.

He m. 1914 Lilian Clutton Williams, of Manchester. He d. 29 Jan. 1941 and was b. at Brecon 1 Feb.

Dysgedydd, May, 1941; personal knowledge.

H.D.L.

EDWARDS, FANNY WINIFRED (1876-1959), schoolteacher, children's writer, and dramatist; b. 21 Feb. 1876 in Penrhyndeudraeth, Mer., a sister of the poet William Thomas Edwards ('Gwilym Deudraeth'; *DWB*, 201) and the youngest of the 12 children of William Edwards, master mariner, and his wife Jane (née Roberts). She was educated at Penrhyndeudraeth elementary school, becoming a pupil-teacher, afterwards a teacher until her retirement in Dec. 1944 thereby completing over fifty years' service. She did not marry, and d. in Ffestiniog, 16 Nov. 1959, and was buried in Nazareth cemetery, Penrhyndeudraeth.

She realised from her early days as a teacher that there was a dearth of suitable literature in Welsh for children and this prompted her to begin writing short stories which she could read to her pupils. (Sir) O.M. Edwards (*DWB*, 192-3) observed her at work whilst on a visit to the school and urged her to publish these stories. This was the beginning of her very successful career as a children's writer – a career which was to span nearly 60 years. She published more than 150 stories in *Cymru'r Plant* from 1902 onwards. (Her two short novels, *Cit* (1908) and *Dros y gamfa* (1926), appeared orginally in serial form in that monthly magazine.) She also contributed to *Cymru*, *Y Drysorfa*, *Y Winllan* and other denominational publications. Between 1925 and 1951 she published five collections of stories, sketches and pieces for recitation. She possessed the natural gift of the true story-teller and undoubtedly her host of publications filled a considerable gap in Welsh writing for children for many years. She also published 17 short, one-act plays, mostly for children, one of which was translated by Margaret Rosser under the title *Choosing a hat* (1951). She won twice in the national *eisteddfod* and was herself an adjudicator in the national *eisteddfod* at Dolgellau, 1949. T.H. Parry-Williams included one of her stories in his volume *Ystorïau heddiw* (1938). At the Llanrwst national *eisteddfod* in 1951 she was presented with the Sir. O.M. Edwards memorial prize in recognition of her outstanding and untiring service to *Urdd Gobaith Cymru* and to children's literature in Welsh. She gave faithful service to Nazareth (Presb.), Penrhyndeudraeth, and especially to the Sunday school there, through-

out her life. She took an active part in the North Wales Women's Temperance Union and she was a member of the council of the Merioneth Historical and Records Society until her death; she published work in the society's periodical (1951).

Information from her nephew, Trefor Edwards, London; *Trysorfa'r Plant*, 90 (1951), 52-4; *Baner*, 3 Dec. 1959, 26 March 1976; *Gol.*, 6 Jan. 1960; *Herald Cymraeg a'r Genedl*, 3, 10 Apr. 1961.

A.Ll.H.

EDWARDS, GWILYM ARTHUR (1881-1963), minister (Presb.), principal of the Theological College, Aberystwyth, and author; b. 31 May 1881 at Caernarfon, son of Owen Edwards, Presb. minister, a native of Llanuwchllyn (and cousin of Sir Owen M. Edwards, *DWB*, 192-3), and Mary (née Jones) his wife. The father emigrated to Australia to regain his health, but his wife d. before she could take her family to join him in Melbourne. The three sons were brought up by her parents in Dolgellau. He was educated in the county school, Dolgellau, and began preaching when fairly young. He was prepared for the ministry at the University College, Aberystwyth (where he graduated B.A. in 1903), and in Jesus College, Oxford (where he graduated in 1908). He was ord. in 1909, and served as minister of Zion, Carmarthen (1908-11), Oswald Rd., Oswestry (1911-17), City Rd., Chester (1917-23), and Tabernacl, Bangor (1923-28). In 1929 he was appointed professor at Bala College, and worked there with Principal David Phillips (see below) until 1939. From 1939 to 1949 he was principal of the Theological College at Aberystwyth. He was awarded an honorary D.D. degree by the University of Edinburgh. In 1917 he m. Mary Nesta, daughter of Richard Hughes, a veterinary surgeon in Oswestry; they had a son and two daughters. After retiring he returned to Oswestry, and d. there 5 Oct. 1963; he was buried in Llanycil graveyard.

He was a prominent member of his Connexion, being Moderator of the Association in the East in 1951, and of the General Assembly in 1957. He delivered the Davies Lecture in 1933 on 'The Kingdom of God in the light of the apocalyptic ideas of the Bible', [parts of which appeared in the *Monthly Treasury*], and a Welsh version was published in 1935. He wrote a great deal for *Cymru*, and the periodicals of his denomination. He published, among other works, two volumes of children's stories in Welsh (1921 and 1927); two volumes in Welsh on the Bible (1922; 1932), one on Christian doctrine (1953), a volume on the history of civilisation (1927), and *Athrofa'r Bala* (a history of Bala College, 1937). His work as a preacher, teacher, and author was charcterized by order and lucidity. He took an interest in education; he edited Sunday school textbooks for his denomination for years. He was also the literary editor of the Society for Religious Education in Wales and wrote a syllabus for religious instruction in the schools of Wales (1945-46). He took an interest in the School of Social Service for Wales, and wrote one of the booklets of that movement, *Hamdden yr adolesent yng Nghymru* (1929). The United Nations Organisation published another pamphlet of his, on Sunday school teachers and world peace (1934). He was a scholar with a clear, analytic mind, and paid great attention to detail.

WwW (1921), 107; *Blwyddiadur MC*, 1964, 276; William Morris (ed.), *Deg o enwogion* (1965), 77-84; personal knowledge.

G.M.R.

EDWARDS, HUW THOMAS (1892-1970), trade union leader and politician; b. 19 Nov. 1892 at Pen-y-Ffridd, Ro-wen in the Conwy valley, Caern., the youngest of the seven children of Huw Edwards, farmer and quarryman and his wife. He received very little formal education, but was brought up in a cultured and religious home environment. In 1907, at 14 years of age, he accompanied his father to work at the Penmaen-mawr slate quarry. He used to walk to work from the slopes of Tal-y-fan mountain to Penmaen-mawr. He displayed something of the adventurer's spirit when he ran away to south Wales to work in the coal mines of the Rhondda valley. He was at Tonypandy at the time of the 1911 strike. He used to box locally on Saturdays in order to supplement his meagre earnings. Edwards was severely wounded during World War I, but he returned to work in the coal mines and slate quarries of north Wales where he set up branches of the T.G.W.U. and the Labour Party. He was elected a member of Penmaen-mawr Rural District Council which he served as chairman. In the general election of 1929 he acted as agent to Thomas ap Rhys who opposed D. Lloyd George (see below) as Labour candidate for the Caernarfon Boroughs. While Edwards was unemployed in 1932 he was appointed a full-time trades union official when he succeeded Arthur Deakin (see above) as the Shotton area secretary of the Transport and General Workers' Union. From 1934 until 1953 he served as the T.G.W.U. area secretary for North Wales and Ellesmere Port. He was chosen J.P. for the county of Flint.

Huw T. Edwards became an important, influential figure in Welsh public life from the period of the Attlee government. As he was well known in both north and south Wales, and had extensive experience of the activities of Welsh local government, he was chosen as the first chairman of the Council of Wales and Monmouthshire in 1949. During the nine years which he spent in the post, he collaborated closely with Sir William Jones (see below) to produce important reports on devolution and on depopulation in the rural areas of Wales. He resigned from the Council in 1958 as a protest against the failure of the Macmillan government to implement the Council's recommendations in relation to the appointment of a Secretary of State for Wales and other administrative reforms. Edwards also chaired the Welsh Tourist Board for 15 years (and he headed a deputation to Russia), the Flintshire Education Committee and the Clwyd and Deeside Hospital Board. He served on the board of directors of Television Wales and the West and of the National Broadcasting Council of the B.B.C., and was a member of *Gorsedd y Beirdd* (his bardic name was 'Huw Pen Ffridd'), and of the Council of the National *Eisteddfod*, of the Wales Gas Board and of the National Assistance Board. He was one of the directors of Gwasg Gee, Denbigh, and a vice-president of the

Honourable Society of Cymmrodorion. He was described as 'the unofficial Prime Minister of Wales'. Edwards owned *Y Faner* for a few years after 1956 during a critical period in the history of the newspaper. He invested his own private money in it, and he fought for its existence in influential circles, ensuring its future until it was taken over by Gwasg y Sir, Bala.

Huw T. Edwards was a socialist through-and-through, and a member of the Labour Party throughout his life until Sept. 1959 when he joined *Plaid Cymru*, but he reverted to his former allegiance in 1965. He was the president of *Cymdeithas yr Iaith Gymraeg* (the Welsh Language Society). For many years he served as the chairman of the Flintshire Labour Party and the North Wales Labour Federation. Yet he won the respect and confidence of whose who leaned to the right in the political spectrum. On several occasions attempts were made to persuade him to stand as a parliamentary candidate on behalf of the Labour Party, but he refused each time.

Edwards took an interest in both poetry and prose writing. He published two volumes of autobiography in Welsh – *Dros y Tresi* (1956) and *Troi'r Drol* (1963). These were translated into English as *It was my privilege* (1962) and *Hewn from the rock* (1967). He also edited *Ar y cyd: cerddi gan Huw T. Edwards, Mathonwy Hughes, Gwilym R. Jones a Rhydwen Williams* (1962).

He was honoured by *Gorsedd y Beirdd* and the University of Wales (LL.D., *honoris causa*, 1957), but he refused to accept the M.B.E. and declined an invitation to be knighted at the Investiture of the Prince of Wales at Caernarfon castle in July 1969.

His wife Margaret d. in June 1966, and Edwards spent the last years of his life at the home of his daughter at Soughton. He d. 9 Nov. 1970 at Abergele hospital, and his remains were cremated at Pentrebychan, Wrexham crematorium. His papers were deposited at the National Library of Wales.

Alan Butt Philip, *The Welsh question: nationalism in Welsh politics, 1945-1970* (1975); H.T. Edwards, 'Why I resigned', *Wales*, Nov. 1958, and his volumes of autobiography; *Times*, 11 Nov. 1970; *West. Mail*, 11, 13 and 16 Nov. 1970; *Liv. D. P.*, 10 Nov. 1970; *Baner*, 12 Nov. 1970; D. Ben Rees (ed.), *Cymry adnabyddus, 1952-72* (1978); idem., (ed.), *Arolwg 1970* (1971); *Portreadau'r Faner*, i (1957), 19.

J.G.J.

EDWARDS, Sir IFAN ab OWEN (1895-1970) lecturer, founder of *Urdd Gobaith Cymru*; son of Sir O.M. Edwards (*DWB*, 192) and Ellen his wife and b. 25 July 1895 in Tremaran, Llanuwchllyn, Mer., though he was brought up in Oxford until the family returned to Llanuwchllyn in 1907. He went to Bala grammar school and U.C.W., Aberystwyth (1912-15). After serving as a soldier in France (1915-18) he entered Lincoln College, Oxford (1918-20) and graduated in history. In the meantime his parents died, and his father's last wish that Wales should be given better educational opportunities directed his steps thereafter. He returned to Wales as a teacher at Dolgellau grammar school 1920 and then as a part-time tutor in the Extra-mural Department, U.C.W., Aberystwyth in 1921, lecturer in the Education Department in 1933 and as director of extra-mural studies in 1946. He retired 2 yrs later so as to devote his whole attention to *Urdd Gobaith Cymru*.

After his father's death he felt compelled to continue his father's work. He edited *Cymru* (1920-27) and *Cymru'r Plant* (1920-50), with *Cronicl yr Urdd* as an appendix (1928-33), as well as inaugurating the magazine *Y Capten* (1931-32) for young people. It was his letter in the Jan. 1922 issue of *Cymru'r Plant* that led to the founding of *Urdd Gobaith Cymru*. He was a man of vision, but also a realist; he was a leader who had the gift of winning over all kinds of people to support and sponsor his progressive and ambitious plans, being always one step ahead of his age. He held the first *Urdd* recreational camp in Llanuwchllyn in 1928; later more permanent sites were obtained at Llangrannog (1932) and Glan-llyn (1950). He initiated the *Urdd* annual *eisteddfod* in 1929; athletic meetings in 1932; pleasure cruises in 1933; a camp for those learning the Welsh language and a football league to play for the *Urdd* cup in 1941; an international camp in 1948 and a Celtic camp in 1949. That year Pantyfedwen, Borth, Cards. was opened as a residential centre and thousands of young people and adults attended many kinds of interesting courses there. He accepted modern technology and used it as best he could for the benefit of Wales. He took photographs of *Urdd* activities and showed them on his 'magic lantern' in villages throughout Wales during the winter; in conjunction with J. Ellis Williams he made the first (partially successful) Welsh sound film, *The quarryman*, for a travelling cinema; and he became a director of Television Wales and the West, enabling him to persuade members of the board to become more favourably inclined towards the Welsh language. It was through his endeavours that the Welsh school was opened at Aberystwyth in 1939. Despite all criticism he considered this to be the most 'successful and valuable' project with which he had ever been associated. In addition to the magazines already named, he edited *A catalogue of Star Chamber proceedings relating to Wales* (1929), which gives some indication of the field – Welsh history – in which he would have desired to work had he not vowed to serve the *Urdd* to the best of his ability. He was co-author (with E. Tegla Davies, see above) of *Llyfr y bobl bach* (1924), a book for young children; author of *Yr Urdd 1922-43* (1943); a short autobiography *Clych atgof* (1961); a number of articles including 'The Welsh language, its modern history and its present-day problems' in *Hesperia*, 1951, 39-57. He gave notable service to numerous public institutions in Wales and London. He was a J.P. (1941-58); and he worked hard for the Parliament for Wales Campaign in the early 1950s. In 1947 he received a knighthood; *Urdd Gobaith Cymru* presented him with his portrait by Alfred Janes in 1956; he received the Cymmrodorion gold medal in 1956; and an honorary LL.D. degree of the University of Wales in 1959.

He m., 18 July 1923, Eirys Mary Lloyd Phillips, Liverpool, and resided at Neuadd Wen, Llanuwchllyn until 1930, and thereafter at Aberystwyth. They had two sons, Owen and Prys. He d. at his home, Bryneithin, 23 Jan. 1970, and was buried at Llanuwchllyn.

Norah Isaac, *Ifan ab Owen Edwards, 1895-1970* (1972); *Cofio Syr Ifan (1970)*; see Glyn Lewis Jones, *A Bibliography of Cardiganshire, 1600-1964* and *Supplement 1964-68* for his bibliography.

M.A.J.

EDWARDS, JOHN (1882-1960), politician and barrister; b. at Llanbadarn Fawr, Cards., on 28 Feb. 1882, the son of James Edwards, the minister at Soar Congregational Chapel, Llanbadarn, and his wife, Rachel Jones. The family had moved to Neath by 7 Jan. 1883 when his father became minister of Soar Chapel in that town. He was educated at the British School and the intermediate school at Neath. He won a scholarship to the University College of Wales, Aberystwyth, where he took a B.A. (London) degree. For some years, he was a schoolmaster in Aberdare. John Edwards served in France with the Royal Welch Fusiliers in World War I and was awarded the D.S.O.; promoted to lieutenant colonel; and twice mentioned in despatches. He played rugby for the London Welsh and Middlesex. He was elected the Liberal M.P. for Aberavon in Dec. 1918 but he lost the seat to Ramsay Macdonald in 1921. He stood as an independent candidate for the University of Wales seat in 1923 but George M.Ll. Davies (see above) was elected. He was called to the bar in Gray's Inn in 1921. He was the High Sheriff for Cardiganshire in 1942. Edwards had an interest in Welsh drama and published a play, *Galw'r môr* (1923), as well as a memoir of his father, *Edwards Castellnedd* (1935), and professional contributions to the *English and Empire Law Digest* and to legal journals.

He m. in London on 27 Oct. 1932, Gweno Elin, the eldest daughter of Joseph Davies Bryan and Jane Clayton, of Alexandria, Egypt; her father was a major benefactor of the University College of Wales, Aberystwyth (see under BRYAN, ROBERT, *DWB*, 56). They had two sons and a daughter. He lived at Llwyn, 11 West Road, Kingston Hill, Surrey and he d. at Surbiton Hospital on 23 May 1960. His ashes were buried at Aberystwyth.

Www; 'Will O' Whispers' column in *Camb. News*, 5 Sept. 1975; [information from his daughter, Rachel Davies, Llangynwyd].

E.D.J.

EDWARDS, JOHN HUGH (1869-1945), politician and writer; b. 9 Apr. 1869 at Aberystwyth, the eldest son of John Edwards, woollen merchant, and his wife. He was educated at the University College of Wales, Aberystwyth. A member of the Cardiganshire County Council for a period, he was elected (1910) as Liberal M.P. for Mid-Glamorgan, a seat which he held until 1922; from 1923 to 1929 he represented Accrington, Lancashire, again as a Liberal.

From 1911 to 1914 he edited *Wales: A national magazine*. He wrote much for the periodical press, particularly for the *British Weekly*. His published works are: *From Village Green to Downing Street, Life of D. Lloyd George* (London, 1908) – in collaboration with Spencer Leigh Hughes; *Life of David Lloyd George, with a short history of the Welsh People*, 4 vols. (London 1913-19); *David Lloyd George, the man and the statesman*, 2 vols. (New York, 1929), and another edition (London, 1930).

He m., 20 Apr. 1933, Doris, dau. of Sir Samuel Faire, Glenfield, Frith Park, Leicester. During the last years of his life he lived at Hindhead, Surrey; there he was actively connected with the Free Church Council and Ratepayers' Association affairs. He d. 14 June 1945 at Hindhead.

Who's Who, 1948; personal knowledge.

W.Ll.D.

EDWARDS, JOHN MENLOVE (1910-58), rock climber; b. 18 June 1910 at Crossens near Southport, Lancs., the youngest of the vicar's four children. He believed the Edwards family came from Wales though he did not know when: the grandfather was also a vicar and a pioneering socialist. Menlove was educated at Feetes College before entering Liverpool University where he graduated in medicine in 1933. There in 1930 he and his brother, Hewlett, founded the Rock Climbing Club. He soon became one of the leading figures during the second golden age of climbing in Snowdonia. He was the pioneer of the 'three crags' of Llanberis Pass and was the author of the Climbing Club handbooks on Cwm Idwal (1936); Tryfan (1937) and Lliwedd (1939) in collaboration with Wilfrid Noyce; and Clogwyn du'r Arddu (1942) with J.E.Q. Barford. Exceptionally strong, he also excelled as a venturous swimmer and rower. He enjoyed the challenge of 'poor conditions, poor rock and poor boots' on wet climbs such as those on Clogwyn y Geifr. The Alps did not interest him. His rare writings on the experience of climbing and the succint descriptions in his handbooks are highly regarded; his few poems are not as good. Most of his best work appeared in the books which are mentioned below.

Although he was a commendable psychiatrist in Liverpool, between summer 1941 and autumn 1942 he retired to Hafod Owen, above Nant Gwynant, to concentrate on the theoretical side of his work. He returned to posts in London but his ideas were not taken seriously. As a conscientious objector, an agnostic and a rejected homosexual, his loneliness led to paranoia and he retired to live near his sister near Canterbury in 1944. He was admitted to mental hospitals, including Denbigh (1949-50). On 2 Feb. 1958 he took his life by potassium cyanide. His ashes were scattered near Hafod Owen. He had been elected an hon. member of the Climbing Club and although one or two of his contemporaries were equally good (if not better) climbers, the atmosphere of the 1930s on the rock-face in Snowdonia is associated more with Menlove Edwards than anyone else.

Geoffrey Sutton and Wilfrid Noyce, *Samson, the life and writings of Menlove Edwards* (private ed., n.d.); Jim Perrin, *Menlove: the life of John Menlove Edwards* (1985); information from Dr. Emyr Wyn Jones.

I.B.R.

EDWARDS, NESS (1897-1968), trade unionist and Member of Parliament; b. 5 April 1897. He started to work in a coalmine when he was thirteen and when he was eighteen he was elected chairman of the Vivian Lodge. He joined the Independent Labour Party in 1915 and through his membership came into contact with the No

Conscription Fellowship; he refused to join the armed forces and consequently he was imprisoned in 1917. He attended the Central Labour College in London in 1919 where his fellow students included Aneurin Bevan (see above) and James Griffiths. In 1927 he became the full-time secretary of the Penallta Lodge and in 1932 miners' representative for east Glamorgan. In 1938 he became a member of the council of the British Miners' Federation, representing the South Wales Miners' Federation on that body. A year later, following the death of Morgan Jones, he was elected as the Labour Member of Parliament for Caerphilly, a seat he retained in subsequent general elections from 1945 to 1966, obtaining over 70% of the votes cast in all these elections. He was an ardent opponent of fascism and sharply criticised the Munich Agreement. He arranged for anti-Nazi colliers from the Sudetenland to escape from Germany in 1939; he visited the concentration camp at Buchenwald in 1945 and represented British colliers in the ceremony to unveil a memorial to the villagers of Lidice in Czechoslovakia. He was elected secretary of the parliamentary group representing coal mining areas in 1942 and chairman of the parliamentary group of Labour trade unionists in 1964.

Following the Labour Party victory of 1945 he became parliamentary secretary to the Minister of Labour. It was this administration that had the responsibility for demobilisation from the armed forces after the war; this was achieved more smoothly in 1945-46 than in 1918-19 and much of this is due to Ness Edwards. He was elevated to membership of the Privy Council in 1948. He was Postmaster General from 1950 to 1951 and was responsible for creating the greetings telegram. He opposed Gaitskell's appointment as leader of the Labour Party in 1955 and went to the backbenches for a period although he was, during the mid-1950s, prominent in opposing the plans of the Conservative government to set up commercial television.

Throughout the years he derided the idea of Welsh nationalism and he represented the tradition of international socialism nurtured by the Central Labour College. Despite this he had a lively interest in Welsh matters and he argued keenly in favour of reforming the way these were discussed in Parliament. He was proud of the industrial and socialist traditions of south Wales and for years his books (*The industrial revolution in south Wales* (1924), *The history of the south Wales miners* (1926) and *The history of the South Wales Miners' Federation* (vol. 1, 1938; the proofs of the second volume are in the library of Nuffield College, Oxford, but this has not been published) were the best available studies on these subjects. He d. 3 May 1968.

West. Mail, 4 May 1968; *Times*, 4 May 1968; H. Francis and D. Smith, *The Fed* (1980).

J.D.

EIRUG – see DAVIES, TOM EIRUG above.

ELFED – see LEWIS, HOWELL ELVET below.

ELLIS, MEGAN – see under EAMES, WILLIAM above.

ELLIS, ROBERT MORTON STANLEY (1898-1966), minister (Presb.), and author; b. 11 Apr. 1898 in a small cottage near the sea between Gronant and Prestatyn, Flints., son of John Edward and Emma Ellis. His parents moved to Birmingham, then to Mold, and Denbigh, finally settling in Glanaman, Carms. in 1905. He left Garnant school when he was 12 years old, and started working in a shop, and later in a coalmine and tin works. He was brought up as a Congregationalist, but he joined the Presbyterians in Bethania, Glanaman, and began preaching there. He was educated for the ministry in Newcastle Emlyn grammar school and in the Presbyterian colleges at Aberystwyth and Bala. In 1925 he was ord., and the same year he m. Martha Maud Davies of Brynmyrnach, Llanfyrnach, Pembs. He was minister of Abermeurig and Bwlchyllan churches, Cards. (1925-27), Saron, Llanbadarn Fawr in the same county (1927-30), and Caersalem, Tŷ-croes near Ammanford, Carms. (1930-66), together with Ebeneser church, Llanedi, for a period. During his period at Tŷ-croes he attended a course of study in the University College, Swansea, graduating B.A. He was elected moderator of the Association in the South in 1965.

He was well known throughout Wales as a preacher and especially as a lecturer. He lectured on such topics as 'Utgyrn Seion', 'Joseph Jenkins' and 'Philip Jones', and had a special talent of mimicking his heroes. His books, too, are about preachers: *Living Echoes* (1951), *Doniau a daniwyd* (1957), *Lleisiau doe a heddiw* (1961). In 1963 he published an entertaining biography, *Wrth gofio'r daith*. He d. 2 Nov. 1966, and was buried in Caersalem cemetery, Tŷ-croes.

Blwyddiadur MC, 1968, 279-80; R.M.S. Ellis, *Wrth gofio'r daith* passim; information from his widow; personal knowledge.

G.M.R.

ELLIS, THOMAS EVELYN SCOTT – see SCOTT-ELLIS, THOMAS EVELYN below.

ELLIS, THOMAS IORWERTH (1899-1970), educationalist and author; b. 19 Dec. 1899 in London, eight months after the death of his father, T.E. Ellis, M.P. (*DWB*, 214). His mother was Annie, daughter of R.J. Davies (see under DAVIES, ROBERT (1790-1841), *DWB*, 150), Cwrt-mawr, Llangeitho, Cards. He was educated at Aberystwyth grammar school, Orley Farm Preparatory School, Harrow, Westminster School (King's Scholar), U.C.W., Aberystwyth (open classical scholarship), Jesus College, Oxford (Welsh scholarship in classics). He graduated B.A. 1920, B.A. (Oxon.) 1924, M.A. (Oxon.) 1927, M. A. (Wales) 1930. He served in the Royal Artillery 1918. He was classics teacher at Cardiff High School, 1924-28; lecturer in classics University College, Swansea 1928-30; headmaster Rhyl County School 1930-40; lecturer in classics, St. David's College, Lampeter 1940-41, and at the University College, Aberystwyth 1941-46.

At the beginning of World War II he was appointed honorary secretary of the Committee to Safeguard Welsh Culture, the movement which was to become *Undeb Cymru Fydd* in 1941. He remained its secretary until 1967. He was High Sheriff of Cardiganshire 1944-45. He was a member of the University of Wales Court, the council of University College of Wales, Aberystwyth, the court and council of the National Library of Wales. He was Warden of the Guild of Graduates 1943-47, a member of the Governing Body of the Church in Wales and the Representative Body. He was treasurer of the Welsh Council of Churches 1961-66, and a member of the Honourable Society of Cymmrodorion. In 1967 he was awarded the honorary degree LL.D. by the University of Wales, and the following year was created O.B.E.

It was his indefatigable work as honorary secretary of *Undeb Cymru Fydd* which brought him into prominence in the life of Wales. He was the leader as well as the secretary. He visited the House of Commons frequently to lobby Welsh members of all parties on issues affecting Wales and its life. He travelled throughout Wales to address meetings on education in the Welsh language, broadcasting, television and the reorganisation of local government. He visited Welsh societies in England regularly and initiated the publication of *Yr Angor* as a liaison between them and Wales.

He edited three volumes of *The Letters of T.C. Edwards* (1952-53). He wrote a biography of his father, *Cofiant T.E. Ellis* (vol. i, 1944; ii, 1948), *Cofiant J.H. Davies* (1963), *Cofiant Ellis Jones Griffith* (1969); and *Ym môr fy esgyrn* (1955), a volume of essays on contemporary subjects. He was the author of *The Development of higher education in Wales* (1935) and a pamphlet *Blind guides?* (1942) under the pseudonym 'Timothy Stone', dealing with the future of the University of Wales. He was a member of the commission set up in 1960 to review the administration of the University of Wales. He was president of the Old Students' Association of U.C.W., Aberystwyth, in 1942.

At college in Aberystwyth he was greatly influenced by the Student Christian Movement and served on its central committee, and he was secretary of the Welsh Committee 1923-24. He was an active member of *Urdd y Deyrnas*, contributing articles to *Yr Efrydydd*. He was a member of the new council of The Institute of Christian Education and of the Welsh branch of the movement. In Aug. 1921 he attended the first Welsh Schoolboys Camp, which was organised on the lines of the S.C.M. camps. A natural leader, he was active in the movement for many years and kept in touch with it throughout his life. He organised boys' camps in Scotland and in Europe as well as in Wales. From his thorough knowledge of the Welsh countryside, gained by walking, cycling and travelling by car, he began writing travel essays, at first in *Y Ford Gron*, and then as books: *Crwydro Ceredigion* (1952), *Crwydro Meirionnydd* (1954), *Crwydro Maldwyn* (1957), *Crwydro Mynwy* (1958), *Crwydro sir y Fflint* (1959), *Crwydro Llundain* (1971), and *Dilyn Llwybrau* (1967).

He was a regular broadcaster in Welsh and English and was a member of the Welsh team of Round Britain Quiz (B.B.C.) for 20 yrs. He wrote scripts for radio and television and appeared on television. *Ateb parod* (1971), a book of questions and answers, is based on a television competition. The general knowledge questions and answers in the booklet *Canllawiau* (1942) first appeared in *Y Faner*. In the volume *Credaf* (ed. J.E. Meredith; 1943) he explains his conversion to Anglicanism from being a Calvinistic Methodist. He was confirmed at St. Asaph in Nov. 1936, and the following year he was licensed as a lay reader. He wrote regularly for *Y Llan*, and served as secretary to the Llan and Welsh Church Company for a short period. He contributed articles to *Yr Haul* (mainly as 'Timothy Stone'), *Y Llenor*, *Barn*, etc., and wrote many articles for *DWB*.

He m., 20 Apr. 1949, Mary Gwendoline Headley, and they had one son and one daughter. He d. at his home, 4 Laura Place, Aberystwyth, 20 Apr. 1970, and was buried at Llanfair, Harlech.

Www; [*Portreadau'r Faner*, i (1957), 9; *Baner*, 30 Apr. 1970; *Gol.*, 29 Apr. 1970; *Camb. News*, 29 Apr. 1970]; MSS in the author's possession; personal knowledge.

M.G.E.

EMANUEL, HYWEL DAVID (1921-1970), librarian and Medieval Latin scholar; b. 14 May 1921 in Burry Port, Carms., the son of William David Emanuel, schoolmaster, and his wife Margaret (née James). He was educated at Llanelli boys' grammar school and at the University College of Wales, Aberystwyth, where he graduated with honours in Latin in 1941. After five years' service overseas in the Royal Navy during World War II, he became, in 1947, an assistant keeper in the department of manuscripts in the National Library of Wales. From 1955 to 1968 he was a lecturer, and later a senior lecturer, in Medieval Latin and Palaeography in the U.C.W., Aberystwyth. In 1968 he was appointed librarian of the college, a post which he held when he died.

He was awarded the degree of M.A. of the University of Wales in 1950 for a thesis on 'The Latin life of St. Cadoc, a textual and lexicographical study', and in 1960 received a Ph.D. of the same university for his study of Latin texts of the Welsh laws. Further research in this field led to the publication in 1967 of his volume *The Latin texts of the Welsh laws*. His other publications include a chapter on these laws in *Celtic studies in Wales* (1963), and contributions to various works dealing with aspects of medieval studies. He also published articles on the Welsh laws and on other topics of medieval interest and made many contributions to the *Jnl. of the Nat. Lib. of Wales*. His appreciation of A.W. Wade-Evans (see below) was read to the Society of Cymmrodorion and published in *Trans. Cymm.*, 1965, 257-71.

He m. in 1947 Florence Mary Roberts of Burry Port, and they had a son and a daughter. He d. 20 Apr. 1970 in Aberystwyth.

Personal knowledge.

M.H.D.

ERFYL FYCHAN – see JONES, ROBERT WILLIAM below.

ERYR CRAIG Y LLYN – see DAVIES, LEWIS (1863-1951) above.

EVANS, ARTHUR WADE – see WADE-EVANS, ARTHUR WADE below.

EVANS, CARADOC (1878-1945), author; b. at Pant-y-croy, Llanfihangel-ar-Arth, Carms., 31 Dec. 1878, and christened David, son of William Evans, auctioneer, and Mary (née Powell). He spent most of his childhood at Lanlas, Rhydlewis, and attended the board school there before he was apprenticed to the drapery trade. He worked as a shop assistant for some twelve years – in Carmarthen, Cardiff and London. In London he attended classes at the Toynbee Hall and the Working Men's College in Crowndale Road and became an accomplished writer. He entered journalism as a free-lance journalist but held various editorial posts, most particularly with *Ideas* and *T.P's Weekly*. His first stories appeared in the *English Review*, 1914; his first volume was *My People*, 1915. This caused great offence to many of his countrymen, as did almost everything he wrote thereafter. His work includes five collections of short stories, *My People*, 1915, *Capel Sion*, 1916, *My Neighbours*, 1919, *Pilgrims in a Foreign Land*, 1942, *The Earth Gives All and Takes All*, 1946; five novels, of which the best is *Nothing to Pay*, 1930; a play, *Taffy*, 1923; and a posthumously published *Journal*. He also devilled for other writers. His best stories rank with the best of his time. In 1934-35 he returned to Wales and helped run a theatre at Aberystwyth. In 1939 he settled at Aberystwyth and then at New Cross. He was twice married, (1), to Rose Ware, 1907 (divorced 8 Mar. 1933), and (2), to Marguerite Helène ('Oliver Sandys'), dau. of Col. H.P. Jervis, in May 1933. He had no children. He d. 11 Jan. 1945 in Aberystwyth hospital.

West. Mail, 12 Jan. 1945; Oliver Sandys, *Caradoc Evans* (1946); G.H. Green, preface to *The Earth Gives All and Takes All*; N.L.W. Catalogue; [John Harris; ed. *My People* (1997); John Harris, ed., *Fury never leaves us* (1983); T. Ll. Williams, *Caradoc Evans* (1970)].

G.J.

EVANS, DAVID (1874-1948), musician; b. 6 Feb. 1874 in Resolven, Glam., s. of Morgan and Sarah Evans. He was educated at Arnold College, Swansea, and at University College, Cardiff, where he succeeded Dr. Joseph Parry, in 1903, as head of the department of Music, becoming professor in 1908. He gained early prominence in Wales as a composer, with the following works: *Llawenhewch yn yr Iôr*, a short oratorio, performed at the Caernarfon Festival, 1906; *The Coming of Arthur*, a dramatic cantata, performed at the Cardiff Triennial Festival, 1907, and the choral ballad 'Deffro! Mae'n Ddydd' and 'Carmen' (setting of a Latin ode), both of which were sung at the opening ceremony of the new University buildings, Cardiff, 1909. His unpublished incidental music to 'Alcestis' was written for a performance of the Greek play at Cardiff in 1928, and the short cantata 'Gloria' for the bicentenary celebration of Methodism in Wales. He made a deep, and lasting, impression on Welsh music. His outstanding success as a University teacher was matched by his loyalty to the traditional Welsh musical institutions, the *Cymanfa Ganu* and the *Eisteddfod*. He strove untiringly to raise musical standards throughout the country, and his *Moliant Cenedl*, a scholarly collection of the best hymn tunes, was a beneficial influence at the time. His editorship of *Y Cerddor* (1916-21) also revealed his thorough understanding of the musical scene in Wales. He actively encouraged orchestral music and he also proposed many reforms with regard to music at the *Eisteddfod*. His expertise in the field of religious music was widely recognised, and a number of his hymn tunes are to be found in the best English hymnals. He was chairman of the committee of experts responsible for the editorship of the *Revised Church Hymnary* and editor of *The Children's Hymnbook* (Blackie); and he was also largely responsible for the editing of the Welsh Methodist and Wesleyan *Llyfr Emynau a Thonau*. Some of his smaller compositions appeared under the pseudonym 'Edward Arthur'.

He m., 1899, Mary Thomas, Plas-y-coed, Morriston, and they had two sons. He d. 17 May, 1948.

Personal knowledge; *Www*, 1941-50.

D.E.P.W.

EVANS, DAVID (1886-1968), Professor of German and author; b. 18 Nov. 1886 in the Blaen-ffos area of Pembs., son of John Evans (d. 18 Jan. 1914, 81 yrs old) and Elizabeth his wife (d. 30 Jan. 1937, 86 yrs old) of Bwlchnewydd, parish of Castellan. He was educated at Cardigan intermediate school, where German had a prominent place in the curriculum, and after a fruitless period farming at home he entered the University College of Wales, Aberystwyth in 1907. He graduated with honours in German in 1910, and two years later gained his M.A. He then moved to Berlin as an English *lektor* and a student at the University where he became acquainted with the Celtic scholar Kuno Meyer. He was working there at the outbreak of World War I in 1914, and was interned for the next four years as one of about five thousand civilian prisoners in the comfortable surroundings of Ruhleben race-course. His major interest there was the Camp School, formed early in 1915, where he was head of Celtic studies and, to his great amusement later in life, president of the Irish Society. One of his students, initially, and then an assistant to him, was Ifor Leslie Evans (see below), later Principal of the University College, Aberystwyth.

After his release he was for some three months a teacher at Wrexham and then became a lecturer at the University of Birmingham until his appointment on 24 Sept. 1920 as an Independent Lecturer and Head of the Department of German at Aberystwyth. Despite the prevailing hatred towards Germany and its people, he succeeded in creating a particularly lively department and his name symbolised the new interest being awoken in the language. His success led the college in 1936 to establish a Chair of German and elevate him as Professor. He remained in the post until his retirement in 1952 when he was made Emeritus Professor.

In addition to translating *Detholiad o chwedlau Grimm* (1927) and *Detholiad o storïau Andersen* (1921, 1931) and also plays by Herman Heijermans (*Ahasfer*; *Y Gobaith da*) and Anatole France (*Y gŵr a briododd wraig fud*), he contributed numerous articles on German education, religion and contemporary problems and literature to Welsh periodicals. He published *A* *simplified German Grammar* (1948) and *Gofyniadau ac atebion i Lythyr Cyntaf Paul at y Corinthiaid* (1926), but his most important work which brought him into prominence generally was *Y wlad: ei bywyd, ei haddysg, a'i chrefydd* (1933), a searching survey of the fundamental values of rural life (for him, around Y Frenni Fawr) and a study for which there was a great demand for a second edition at the end of the year, partly because it was so enthusiastically recommended by David Lloyd George (see below) in a speech at Wrexham national *eisteddfod*.

David Evans was very active in the college at Aberystwyth. He was the prime mover in the introduction of a scheme of medical care for students, the first medical scheme to be instituted at any British university. He was president of the Old Students' Association in 1952, and the British Council representative at Aberystwyth for many years. He was an uncompromising Baptist, and a member, deacon and Sunday school teacher at Bethel, Aberystwyth.

He m., 30 Dec. 1920, Margaret James of Llandeilo; her father was an Inspector of Elementary Schools in Carmarthenshire and her mother had been a member of the 'Côr Mawr' conducted by Griffith Rhys Jones ('Caradog'; *DWB*, 465). His wife, too, was a graduate of Aberystwyth College in 1910, and by the time she met David Evans in Birmingham she had been appointed French teacher at Halesowen grammar school for girls. At Aberystwyth she actively supported several good causes, e.g. Friends of the Hospital and the R.S.P.C.A. Two sons and a daughter were born of the marriage. David Evans d. 26 Oct. 1968 in Bronglais Hospital, Aberystwyth and was buried in his mother-church at Blaen-ffos. His wife d. 29 Nov. 1973 aged 84 yrs. at her daughter's home in Camberley and was buried in Aldershot.

David Evans was of a companionable nature, kept rigidly to his principles, and made his views known, but occasionally he would not be bound by convention. As Principal Thomas Parry said at his funeral: 'in spite of the infinite variety of human nature, there will never be anybody exactly like David Evans'.

UCW Aberystwyth News Letter, 1969, 20-1 (Thomas Parry's tribute); *UCW Old Students' Association Annual*, 1969, 13-15; *Times*, 31 Oct. 1968; *Daily Telegraph*, 31 Oct. 1968; *Camb. News*, 1, 8 Nov. 1968, 7 Dec. 1973; *Ser. Cymru*, 10 Jan. 1969; *In Ruhleben camp* (later *Ruhleben camp magazine*) and copies of the prospectus of the Camp School, from David Evans' library, at N.L.W.; NLW MS 19979 (a letter from D. Lloyd George); D.Ll.G.'s personal copy of *Y Wlad* with notes, at N.L.W.; *Dragon* (U.C.W., Aberystwyth, magazine), 1929, 32-4, and 1931, 10; information from his son Roland D.W. Evans, Solihull, Birmingham, and the Rev. William Jones, Blaen-ffos; personal acquaintance.

B.G.O.

EVANS, DAVID CARADOG – see EVANS, CARADOC above.

EVANS, DAVID DELTA ('Dewi Hiraddug'; 1866-1948), journalist, author and Unitarian minister; b. in 1866 and brought up in Ochr-y-Marian, between Diserth and Cwm, Flints., one of seven children of Joseph Evans, miner, and his wife Ann. He was reared in poverty and began life as a farm servant at the age of ten. Later he worked on a newspaper, *The Rhyl Record*, and was also associated with *Y Faner* under Thomas Gee (*DWB*, 274). At 19 he went to London and took a leading part in establishing the first congregation of Welsh Unitarians in 1937, after which he maintained the connection until his death. Much of his later work was written in air-raid shelters after he had lost his home in war-time bombing. He spent the last years of his life in his sister's home in Diserth. He d. 22 May 1948 in Rhyl Memorial Hospital and was buried in Diserth churchyard.

In 1901 he was an assistant Unitarian missionary in Liverpool, and a year later became the editor of *Christian Life* (and *Unitarian Herald)* and made it a success until its merger with *The Inquirer* in 1929. The end of the *Christian Herald* was a great loss, as the appeal of *The Inquirer* was much narrower. Delta published a special issue in 1913 to celebrate the centenary of the Law of Trinity and 25,000 copies were sold within a week. He ministered in Southend-on-Sea, 1905-09, Portsmouth High Street, 1909-10, Woolwich, London 1913-17, Bermondsey, 1921-29 and Ilford, 1929-32. He visited the Unitarian Society's meetings in Cardiganshire and Glamorganshire.

Many of his articles appeared in *Y Gwyliedydd Newydd*, and issues of *Yr Ymofynydd* were sprinkled with his contributions, written under his name, Delta, DDE and Dewi Hiraddug. He also used the pseudonym Cadfan Rhys, Deiniol Ddu and An Old Sinner. Even Delta was an assumed name, his baptismal name being David. He wrote a weekly column for the *Kentish Independent* for years under the name, 'An Old Philosopher'. He wrote an article on *Phrenyddeg* (phrenology) in the second edition of *Y Gwyddoniadur Cymreig*, 1896.

He was a prolific writer. He wrote two novels, *Daniel Evelyn; Heretic*, 1913 and *The Rosicrucian*, 1918. Other works include *Pethau Newydd a Hen*, 1900; *The Ancient Bards of Britain*, 1906; *Hiwmor, Synnwyr a Halen*, 1937; *Rhedeg ar ôl y Cysgodion*, 1940; *Saviours of Men; An Argosy of Common Sense; At y Golygydd* (a collection of letters to the press 1937-42), *Days of Youth* – an autobiography in novel form; *Athrofa Mab y Saer; Jesus the Galilean; Ymdaith y Pererin*; and *Why do we Pray?* Many of his books are kept in Bangor University Library, and also a letter praising *Ymdaith y Pererin* together with a *cywydd* from T. Gwynn Jones (see below) (1942) and a letter praising *Rhedeg ar ôl y Cysgodion*. He was fluent in Esperanto and Hindustani. He was a fierce debater and a fiery character.

Ymofynydd, July 1948; recollections from Alwyn Thomas and Derwyn Jones.

A.J.M.

EVANS, Sir (DAVID) EMRYS (1891-1966), educationist and translator; b. 29 Mar., 1891, son of the Rev. T. Valentine Evans, Baptist minister, Clydach, Glam. He received his education at Ystalyfera county school and the University College of North Wales, Bangor, where he graduated with first-class honours in Latin in 1911 and in Greek in 1912. He took his Oxford

B.Litt. from Jesus College, and was elected a Fellow of the University of Wales. For a short period he was assistant master at Pentre secondary school and Classics master at Longton High School. In 1919 he was appointed Assistant Lecturer in Classics at University College, Bangor, and Professor of Classics at University College, Swansea, in 1921. He returned to Bangor as Principal in 1927, where he remained until his retirement in 1958. He served as Vice-Chancellor of the University of Wales for four terms – 1933-35, 1941-44, 1948-50, 1954-56. He was chairman of the Central Advisory Council for Education (Wales) 1944-46, and of the Schools Broadcasting Council (Wales); deputy-chairman of the Local Government Commission for Wales 1959-62; a member of the Welsh Advisory Committee of the National Trust and of the Welsh Committee of the Arts Council. He also sat on the Royal Commission on University Education in Dundee 1951-52. He was awarded the degree of LL.D. *honoris causa* by the University of Wales and the University of Liverpool. The city of Bangor made him an honorary freeman in 1958. He was knighted in 1952.

Sir Emrys published the following works: *Amserau'r Testament Newydd* (1926), *Crefydd a Chymdeithas* (1933), *Y Clasuron yng Nghymru* (the B.B.C.'s annual lecture in Welsh, 1952), and *The University of Wales, a historical sketch* (1953). His main contribution however was the series of translations into Welsh of Plato's works: *Amddiffyniad Socrates* (1936), *Phaedon* (1938), *Ewthaffron: Criton* (1943), *Gorgias* (1946) and *Y Wladwriaeth* (1956). Sir Emrys read widely and discriminately in Welsh and thus gained a mastery of the literary language, which he wrote with classical accuracy and an occasional touch of archaism, well suited to the translations from Greek, and, in accordance with the standards recognised at the time, to the translations of the books of the New Testament which were produced under the auspices of the University. Sir Emrys was a member of the panel responsible for translating Matthew, Luke and Acts. He also assisted with the translation of the New Testament into Welsh which appeared in 1975. As an administrator he was unobtrusive but firm.

He m. G. Nesta Jones of Pontypridd in 1927, and they had a son and a daughter. He d. 20 Feb. 1966.

Www; personal knowledge.

T.P.

EVANS, DAVID JOHN (1884-1965), minister (Presb.) and author; b. 1 July, 1884 at Bronfelen, Capel Seion, Cards., son of John and Ellen Evans. He was educated at Capel Seion elementary school, Pen-llwyn board school, Newcastle Emlyn grammar school, University College, Aberystwyth (where he graduated B.A.) and the Theological College, Aberystwyth (where he graduated B.D.). He was ord. in 1916, and served as minister of his mother-church at Capel Seion until his d. In 1943 he m. Mary Muriel Williams, Aberystwyth; he d. 1 May 1965. He came into prominence in 1926 when he published a handbook on the principal characters of the Old Testament – *Prif gymeriadau'r Hen Destament* – which had been rejected by his Association because of his liberal outlook. In 1935 he published *Hanes Capel Seion*, a very useful book of local history.

WwFC (1951), 340; *WwW* (1937), 57; *Hanes Capel Seion*; information from T.J. Davies, Cardiff.

G.M.R.

EVANS, Sir DAVID OWEN (1876-1945), barrister, industrialist and politician; b. 5 Feb. 1876 in Penbryn, Cards., son of William Evans, farmer, and his wife. He was educated at Llandovery College and the Imperial College of Science, London. In 1896 he entered the Civil Service and was attached to the Inland Revenue Department. He m. 1899, Kate Morgan. Whilst in the Civil Service he studied law and was called to the Bar at Gray's Inn in 1909. He practised as a barrister and published a book entitled *Law of Old Age Pensions: Finance Act 1909-10.* At the suggestion of Lord Melchett (then Sir Alfred Mond) he joined the Mond Nickel Company, Ltd. in 1916, later becoming Director of this company and a Vice-President of the International Nickel Co. of Canada, Ltd. In 1932, he was elected M.P. (Liberal) for Cardiganshire and he represented that constituency until 1945. He was greatly interested in Welsh institutions and was a member of the Council of the Honourable Society of Cymmrodorion, the National Library of Wales, and the National Museum of Wales. A keen musician and *eisteddfodwr*, he was president of the Council of the National Eisteddfod during the period when the new Constitution of the Council was adopted. To the University College of Wales, Aberystwyth, of which College he was Treasurer, he was a generous benefactor. He was knighted a week before his death on 11 June 1945.

Www; personal knowledge.

T.M.D.

EVANS, DAVID TECWYN (1876-1957), Meth. minister; b. 5 Dec. 1876 in Aberdeunant Uchaf, Llandecwyn, Mer., son of Evan and Catherine Evans. He was educated at Llandecwyn national school, Talsarnau board school (where he was also a pupil-teacher), the University College, Bangor, and the theological college at Didsbury, Manchester. He began preaching on Whitsunday 1894 when he was 17 years old, and quickly gained recognition. In 1902, at the beginning of his career, he went on a preaching tour of America, and again in 1913. He was minister at Aberdovey 1902, Llanddulas 1904, Portdinorwic 1907, Conwy 1910, Llanrwst 1911, Birkenhead 1914, Wrexham 1919, Rhyl 1922, Bangor 1925, Llandudno 1928, Tregarth 1931, Abergele 1936, Aberdovey 1939. In 1941 he became supernumerary and moved to Rhyl where he d. 27 Oct. 1957. He m. Nanna Stirrup of Llangefni, who d. 1925. He was awarded an M.A. degree of the University of Wales in 1927 for a thesis on the Welsh language, and an honorary D.D. (Wales) in 1951. He was Moderator of the Welsh Assembly in 1929-30 and chairman of the second North Wales district from 1936 to 1941.

He was one of the greatest 'princes' of the pulpit in his day, and his sermons were an unusual combination of scholarship, warmth

and eloquence. He was also a popular lecturer in Welsh on topics such as the Book of Job, the Book of Jonah, the Welsh Bible, Ann Griffiths (*DWB*, 303), and J. Puleston Jones (*DWB*, 487-8). Many of his lectures were published as booklets. He was a very faithful disciple of John Morris-Jones (*DWB*, 668-9) and did much to popularise the new Welsh orthography in lectures and journals and through his book *Yr iaith Gymraeg: ei horgraff a'i chystrawen* (1911) which was re-printed several times. He was editor of *Yr Eurgrawn* for twenty years (1931-51), which also gave him the opportunity to teach many to write correct Welsh.

He composed some hymns ('Duw a thad yr holl genhedloedd' being the best known), and translated hymns and poems, some of which appeared in *Bytheiad y nef a chaniadau eraill* (1927). He was co-editor (with E. Tegla Davies, see above) of *Llestri'r Trysor* (1914) and in 1920 published a translation of T.R. Glover's *Jesus of history*. He also published a commentary on I Corinthians (1926) for Sunday schools, a collection of prayers (1945), many sermons in magazines and books, and his memoirs, *Atgofion Cynnar*.

Atgofion Cynnar (1950); *Mins. of Methodist Conf.,* 1958; *Eurgrawn,* Winter 1976 (commemorative issue to D.T.E.).

G.R.T.

EVANS, EBENEZER GWYN (1898-1958), minister (Presb.); b. 31 May 1898 in Gellilenor Fawr, Llangynwyd, Glam., youngest son of Benjamin and Gwenllian Evans – the mother being of the stock of David Morris (1787-1858), Hendre (*DWB*, 658). He was educated in Maesteg elementary and county schools. He began working on his father's farm before becoming a schoolteacher for a period. He joined the army during World War I, and at the end of the war went to the University College, Aberystwyth (where he gained an honours degree in philosophy) and began preaching. He completed his education in the theological colleges at Aberystwyth and Bala. He was ord. in 1927, and served in the ministry in Rock Ferry (1927-30), Cathedral Rd., Cardiff (1931-36), Trinity, Swansea (1936-39), and Charing Cross Rd., London (1939-58). In 1927 he m. Enyd Jane Jones, daughter of Edward Jones ('Iorwerth Ddu'), minister, Maesteg, and they had two sons. He d. 23 July 1958.

He was a refined and powerful preacher in both English and Welsh, and consequently received many calls for his services throughout Wales. He was chairman of the Union of Free Churches of England and Wales (1957-58). He wrote in *Y Goleuad* and *Y Drysorfa*, and in 1951 published a history of the first hundred years of Charing Cross Rd. church.

J.M. Jones, *Hanes Eglwys Tabor, Maesteg* (1940), 29; *Gol.,* 6 Aug. 1959; *Blwyddiadur MC,* 1959, 263; *Drys.,* Jan. 1959; information from his son, Hywel I. Evans; personal knowledge.

G.M.R.

EVANS, ELLEN (1891-1953), principal of the Glamorgan Training College, Barry; b. 10 Mar. 1891 at 17 Dorothy St., Gelli, Rhondda, Glam., the daughter of John and Ellen Evans, both of whom came to the Rhondda from their native

Cardiganshire in 1871. Educated at Rhondda secondary school and at the Rhondda pupil-teachers centre, she entered the University College at Aberystwyth in 1911 and gained a degree in Welsh in 1914. Appointed a lecturer at the Glamorgan Training College in 1915, she was promoted to the post of Principal in 1923. Ellen Evans took a particular interest in the use of the Welsh language in schools and colleges; her books, *The Teaching of Welsh* (1924), based on her M.A. thesis; *Llawlyfr i athrawon* (1926); and *Cynllun Cymraeg* (1927) were of great assistance to teachers in the early days of the development of Welsh-medium education in schools. She published *Y Mabinogion i'r plant* in 4 vols. (1924); *Hwiangerddi Rhiannon* (1926); and *Y Wen Fro* (1931), a volume on historical places in Glamorganshire, to meet the need for Welsh-language texts for children.

Ellen Evans was a member of several public bodies. She was the only woman on the Departmental Committee on Education, 1925-27, and the first woman to be elected to the court of the Medical School (later, the University of Wales College of Medicine). She was a member of the executive committee of Coleg Harlech from its foundation in 1927 and later served as vice-president of the college; she was also a member of the courts of the university colleges at Aberystwyth and Cardiff and a vice-president of *Urdd Gobaith Cymru*. She was the first chairman of the Welsh branch of the Nursery School Association. A regular lecturer, *eisteddfod* adjudicator and broadcaster, Ellen Evans was an enthusiastic supporter of Welsh-medium schools and of Welsh culture in general. Ellen Evans, supported by other Welsh women strong in their support of Wales and the Welsh language, had an immense influence on thousands of students who came to the college at Barry. She was appointed C.B.E. in 1948. She d. 26 Sept. 1953 and was survived by three sisters.

Gymraes, 38, 41-4; *Www*; *West Mail*, 28 Sept. 1953.
E.D.J.

EVANS, ERNEST (1885-1965), county court judge, M.P.; b. at Aberystwyth, Cards., 17 May 1885, the son of Evan Evans, Clerk to the Cardiganshire County Council, and Annie Davies. Educated at Llandovery College; University College of Wales, Aberystwyth (*c.* 1902-05); and Trinity Hall, Cambridge (LL.B.), where he was President of the Union in 1909, Evans was called to the Bar in 1910 and he practised both in London and on the South Wales Circuit. He served with the R.A.S.C. in France during World War I and was promoted to the rank of Captain. From Nov. 1918 to Dec. 1920, he was a private secretary to David Lloyd George (see below). In 1921, M.L. Vaughan Davies, an out-and-out Tory who sat as the Liberal M.P. for Cardiganshire from 1895, was created a peer, with the title Lord Ystwyth of Tan-y-Bwlch. With Lloyd George's support, Evans fought the ensuing by-election against William Llewelyn Williams (*DWB*, 1085), the candidate chosen by the traditional liberals in Cardiganshire. He won the seat after a bitter battle which split the Cardiganshire Liberal Party for many years. At the 1922 general election, Evans' majority fell to 515 after a contest against Rhys Hopkin Morris (see below), who

stood for the Independent Liberals. At the 1923 general election, he lost the seat to Rhys Hopkin Morris in a three-cornered fight, with Lord Lisburne as the Conservative candidate. In 1924, he won the University of Wales seat in a contest against George M.Ll. Davies (see above), the Labour candidate, and he held this seat until 1942. Evans was made a K.C. in 1937 and from 1942 until his retirement in 1957 he held the post of a county court judge. He was a member of the council of N.L.W. and a vice-president of the Hon. Soc. of Cymmr. Evans specialised in agricultural law and he wrote, with Clement Edward Davies (see above), *An epitome of agricultural law* (1911) and, on his own, *Elements of the law relating to vendors and purchasers* (1915) and *Agricultural and Small Holdings Act*.

He m., in 1925, Constance Anne, daughter of Thomas Lloyd, draper, of Hadley Wood; at the time, her widowed mother was married to J.T. Lewis of London and Llanarth, Cards. Evans died on 18 Jan. 1965 at his home, Traethgwyn, Ffordd Tymawr, Deganwy, Caerns.

Www; *Camb. News*, 22 Jan. 1965; *Times*, 19 Jan. 1965.
E.D.J.

EVANS, EVAN (1882-1965), businessman; b. 8 Nov. 1882 in Glanyrafon, Betws Leucu, Cards., son of David Evans and Elizabeth (née Davies) his wife. He left Llangeitho school when he was only nine years old. At the age of 15 he went to work in his cousin's dairy in Marylebone with very little knowledge of English, but he attended night school in London to learn the language. By the age of twenty he owned his own dairy and later bought a farm, kept a hotel, had a car sales business and established Evan Evans Tours, Ltd., which had world-wide links. He took an active interest in the public life of the Borough of St. Pancras as a councillor 1922-59 and alderman 1935-45, mayor 1939-41, deputy mayor for five years, and J.P. He worked hard to provide a refuge for those who lost their homes during the air raids in 1940. He was a member of London County Council 1931-34 and was granted the freedom of the City of London in 1946. Elected an alderman in 1932, he served as secretary of Jewin (Presb.) Church from 1938 until his death, and was moderator of the Association in the South, 1961-62. He contributed towards the cost of publishing the book by Tom Beynon (see above) on Howel Harris in London. Under the bardic name 'Ifan Gwynfil' he became a member of the *Gorsedd* of Bards at Swansea national *eisteddfod*, 1964. On 19 Feb. 1936 he m. Nancy Meurig Davies in Jewin Chapel, and they had one son. He d. at his home in Guildford Street, 24 July. 1965, and was interred in the graveyard of Gwynfil Chapel, Llangeitho.

Information from his son, Dafydd Gwyn Evans; WWP. See also *Camden and St. Pancras Chronicle*, 30 July, 1965.
M.A.J.

EVANS, EVAN JENKIN (1882-1944), physicist and university professor; b. 20 May 1882 at Llanelli, son of David and Mary Evans. He received his early education at the county school, proceeding afterwards to the University College of Wales, Aberystwyth, where he graduated in 1902. He then went to the Royal College of Science, South Kensington, London where in 1906 he took the Associateship. He remained in South Kensington, becoming demonstrator first in astrophysics and later in physics, and at the same time conducting research in spectroscopy. He retained his interest in this branch of physics throughout his life. He moved to Victoria University, Manchester in 1908 and seven years later became senior lecturer in the physics department. His thesis for the degree of D.Sc. of the University of London in 1915 is an important contribution on the ionised helium series. In 1919 he became assistant director of the Manchester laboratories and was in charge of the department during Rutherford's absence on war work in 1917. He played for many years an important part in the training and building of Rutherford's school in Manchester. He m. Elmira, daughter of Captain Thomas and Mary Rees, New Quay, Cards., and they had 5 children.

In 1920 he was appointed to the Chair of Physics in the new University College of Swansea. Temporary accommodation was found for the department in the Technical College, while the new laboratories were being built. Evans gave much time to the design and equipping of the laboratories which were opened in 1922. Installed in the new laboratories he devoted his energies to building up a school of physics, laying great stress on training students in the methods of research, and particularly stressing the importance of accuracy of measurement. Many valuable contributions to scientific literature were made by students and members of staff under his stimulating leadership. He was a gifted and conscientious teacher. Towards the end of his life he became absorbed in the post-war problems of the universities. He d. 2 July 1944, at New Quay, Cardiganshire.

Personal knowledge; *Www.*

E.A.O.

EVANS, EVAN KERI (1860-1941), minister (Congl.); born at Pontceri near Newcastle Emlyn, Carms., 2 May 1860, s. of Evan Evans (1817-1902) and Mary, his wife, (1816-64). Apprenticed as a carpenter, he began writing poetry from an early age, winning a chair at an *eisteddfod* in Crymych when he was only 17 years old, and, it is said, was carried in it all the way home to Newcastle Emlyn. He began to preach at Tre-wen Independent church. After a term at the local grammar school he was in 1881 admitted to the Carmarthen Presbyterian College, where he showed remarkable ability as a student. In 1884, on securing the Dr. Williams Scholarship, he proceeded to the University of Glasgow, where he took his M.A. degree with honours in classics and a first class in philosophy. He was awarded the Ewing Scholarship in literature and the Ferguson Scholarship open to the four Scottish universities. He won the Clark Fellowship in 1890 and the Snell Exhibition tenable at Balliol College, Oxford, but as there was then no philosophy school at Oxford (except T.H. Green, see his life by Nettleship) he was granted a dispensation by the senate of

Glasgow University to hold it at Leipzig where Wilhelm Wundt was professor of philosophy. After spending a term there he was appointed assistant to Dr. Edward Caird at Glasgow. In 1891 he was appointed to the chair of philosophy at the university college in Bangor. He was appointed examiner for the degree of M.A. at Glasgow in 1894.

His health breaking down in 1896, he was in 1897 ordained minister to the Congregational churches of Hawen and Bryngwenith in Ceredigion. In 1890 he moved to the Priory Welsh Congregational church at Carmarthen, and the following year he was appointed professor of philosophy and Christian doctrine at his old college there.

He was deeply moved by the 1904-05 religious revival and he devoted himself to the work of the movement for deepening the spiritual life to such an extent that he neglected his lectures and had to resign his post at the college. Later on he was offered the principalship of the Memorial College at Brecon but he declined the offer. After the climax of the revival had passed, his brilliant literary talent reasserted itself and he published three biographies, that of his brother David Emlyn Evans (*DWB*, 226-7) in 1919, Joseph Parry (*DWB*, 738) in 1921, and David Adams (*DWB*, 3) in 1924. In 1938 his remarkable book *Fy mhererindod ysbrydol* appeared. An English translation, *My spiritual pilgrimage*, by T. Glyn Thomas, was published in 1961. He resigned from the ministry in 1938 and retired to Llanelli where he d. 7 June 1941. He was particularly gifted as a translator of hymns.

Oriel Coleg Caerfyrddin, 180; *Blwyddiadur yr Annibynwyr*, 1942; *Congregational Year Book*, 1942.

J.O.S., E.P.E

EVANS, GRIFFITH IFOR (1889-1966), surgeon and pioneer of the Christian Faith Healing Movement in Wales; b. 14 Feb. 1889, the son of G.T. Evans, a bank manager, Bryn Estyn, Rhyl, Fl., and his wife. He was educated at Ruthin School and Oxford, where he read history and economics at Lincoln College and then moved to Magdalen College to prepare for clinical medicine studies at St. George's Hospital, London. He had a very distinguished student career and was awarded a number of the chief prizes. He graduated in medicine in 1916. Following a period of three years war service with the R.A.M.C., he gained the M.A. and D.M. in 1919, and the F.R.C.S. in 1921. With such a remarkable academic record it is somewhat surprising that he did not seek a consultant post in one of the London hospitals. However he came to Caernarfon in 1926 to join Dr. Lloyd Roberts in general practice at 37 Castle Square. In 1931, as the result of publishing his book *Essays on familial syphilis*, he was awarded the gold medal of the Hunterian Society. He was appointed surgeon to the Caernarfon and Anglesey Infirmary at Bangor, but decided to retire from the post within a few years. His attempt to return to the staff as physician was not successful. During this period Evans was active in many spheres outside his practice. He had a good singing voice, he was an elder at Engedi chapel and a lay preacher. In 1942-43 he was president of the North

Wales Branch of the B.M.A., and in the same year he was High Sheriff of the County of Caernarfon.

He was a man of wide culture and was interested in philosophy and theology as well as the sciences. As the years went by Griffith Evans was increasingly attracted to the borderland between these disciplines and pure medicine. In time, and with the support of a number of friends, he established the Centre of Spiritual Healing at Caernarfon, and he was elected first chairman of the Healing Committee of his denomination. Thereafter his active interest extended to the London Healing Mission, and his support reached the stage that he decided to move to London, making his home at Melbury Road, Kensington, and becoming a member of Charing Cross Chapel in 1958.

By this time his close association with Spiritual Healing had apparently weakened his relationship with orthodox medicine. It was in the sphere of Christian healing that he maintained his interest, and in this area he centred his theoretical studies. He enriched his mind by wide reading, and he wrote quite extensively, mainly in English, in an attempt to distil the observations of contemporary experts. These issues have always presented serious medical and ethical problems but it was generally admitted that the vagueness and imprecision of his contributions were such that the articles were almost incomprehensible to doctors and laymen alike.

There is no doubt about the sincerity of his belief in the value of healing centres, nor in the thoroughness of his research, but it can scarcely be claimed that he succeeded in transmitting his enthusiasm to his professional colleagues, nor could their inherent conservatism be held entirely responsible for this lack of response. Without doubt the motivation for his work was the strength of his Christian belief, and the realisation of the effect of mind and emotion on the 'complete' health of the individual. Notwithstanding the distinction of the earlier years of his medical career, Evans could not avoid the influence of an obsessional element when analysing the results of his observations, and it is not improper to record that this tendency was recognised by his contemporaries long before he embarked on his work in the Healing Ministry.

He m. Dilys Eames of Bangor in 1916 and there were no children of the marriage. He d. 20 Sept. 1966 in London and was buried in Llanbeblig cemetery, Caernarfon.

Brit. Med. Jnl., 1966, 2, 1014; *Lives of the Fellows Roy. Coll. Surgeons*, 1965-1973; *Gol.*, 30 Nov. 1966; personal knowledge.

E.W.J.

EVANS, Sir GUILDHAUME MYRDDIN – see MYRDDIN-EVANS, Sir GUILDHAUME below.

EVANS, HORACE, 1st. BARON EVANS of MERTHYR TYDFIL (1903-63), physician; b. in Merthyr Tydfil, Glam., 1 Jan. 1903, the elder son of Harry Evans (*DWB*, 235-6) and his wife Edith Gwendolen (née Rees). Soon after his birth they moved to Dowlais, where his grandfather was a pharmacist, and later to Liverpool. He was educated at Liverpool College and after

his father's early death in 1914 he went to the Guildhall School of Music for four years and to the City of London School. Intent on reading medicine he entered the London Hospital Medical College in 1921 with a science scholarship. He qualified in 1925, graduated in medicine and surgery in 1928, and took his M.D. in 1930 when he became a member of the Royal College of Physicians and a fellow in 1938. This work merited his appointment as an assistant director of the medical unit in 1933, assistant physician to the London Hospital at Whitechapel in 1936 and physician in 1947. He worked under Arthur Ellis who instructed him in the traditional English clinical discipline and who brought him into prominence by selecting him as house physician to the medical unit. Subsequently he held appointments in surgery, obstetrics, pathology and anaesthetics, which gave him a broad basis for a career as a general physician. He specialised in the effects of high blood pressure and diseases of the kidneys, making a thorough study of Bright's disease, on which he published papers in medical and scientific journals. Years later he provided an authoritative revision of the section on diseases of the liver for Frederick William Price (ed.), *Textbook of the practice of medicine* (8th ed.; 1950). In addition he was consultant physician to five other hospitals and to the Royal Navy. It was through his influence that the Royal College of Physicians was moved from Trafalgar Square, having attracted the magnanimous financial support of the Wolfson Foundation towards the cost of erecting new buildings at Regent's Park.

He served the royal family as physician to Queen Mary in 1946, to King George VI in 1949 and to Queen Elizabeth in 1952, all of whom received him as a friend. He was knighted in 1949, and created a baron in 1957. In 1955 he delivered the Croonian lectures and was made hon. Fellow of the Royal College of Surgeons in 1961. The University of Wales conferred on him an hon. D.Sc. degree and he was made a freeman of his native town in Apr. 1962. He was not keen on open-air activities apart from horse-racing, on which he was an authority, and he often visited Monte Carlo.

He was regarded as the last of the great general physicians of his age, convinced of the need for personal physicians with a critical judgement based on broad general experience, and of the importance of treating patients as human beings. His presence in a patient's room or hospital ward left an immediate impression on every one who came into contact with him. His sympathy and understanding stemmed largely from his own family experiences.

He m. in 1929 Helen Aldwyth, daughter of T.J.D. Davies, Swansea and they had two daughters, the younger of whom they lost in tragic circumstances. He d. 26 Oct. 1963, and Lady Evans on 3 Dec. 1963 after a distressing illness.

Hubert John Evans (b. 1904), ambassador to Nicaragua 1952-54, was his brother.

WWP; *West. Mail*, 20 Sept. 1960, 28 Oct. 1963; *Brit. Med. Jnl.*, 2 (1963), 1133-5; *DNB*; see *Munk's Roll to 1965* for further references; *Statesman's yearbook for 1953, 1954* and *1955*.

E.D.J.

EVANS, HOWELL THOMAS (1877-1950), historian and schoolmaster; b. 6 Nov., 1877, at Cwmbwrla, near Swansea, the second s. of John Evans, steelworker, and Mary his wife. Educated at Swansea Grammar School, the University College of Wales, Aberystwyth, and St. John's College, Cambridge, he held the degrees of B.A. (Wales), B.A. (London), and M.A. (Cantab.) After teaching at Wellington College and Queen Elizabeth's Grammar School, Carmarthen, he was on the staff of the High School for Boys, Cardiff, from 1905 to 1917. In that year he was appointed Headmaster of the County School, Aberaeron, Cards., and held the post until his retirement in 1944. He wrote a number of history books, among them *History of England and Wales* (1909, 1910); *Making of Modern Wales* (1912); *Wales and the Wars of the Roses* (1915); *Once upon a time* (1929); *At Such and Such a time* (1931); *Long long ago* (1932); *The Age of Expansion* (1933). In 1940 he was President of the Welsh Secondary Schools Association, and for a period he was one of the representatives of the Headmasters of Secondary Schools upon the University of Wales Court.

Howell Evans was a man of wide interests, and refused to be confined within the limits of a teacher's professional life, considerable though his output of historical text-books was. In his presidential address to the Welsh Secondary Schools' Association (1940) he expounded his educational ideas, emphasising particularly the importance of individuality and the need to avoid the imposition of a colourless uniformity upon every pupil. He poured scorn on the prevailing tendency towards centralisation and rationalisation, and commended the public schools of England for maintaining the principle of independence in education; he gave it as his opinion that the powers of educational administrators were increasing, and should be curtailed. He was an enthusiastic gardener and an expert on chrysanthemums. He m. in 1904, Gwenllian Howells, of Briton Ferry, Glam., and they had four sons. He d. at Aberaeron, 30 Apr. 1950 and was buried in Cardiff.

Information from his family; *Welsh Secondary Schools Review*, 26, 1940; [Lyn Evans, *Portrait of a pioneer* (1982)].

T.I.E.

EVANS, IFOR (IVOR) LESLIE (1897-1952), principal of the University College of Wales, Aberystwyth; b. 17 Jan. 1897, son of William John Evans (see below) of Aberdare and Mary Elizabeth (née Milligan) his wife. He was educated at Wycliffe College, Stonehouse and studied in France and Germany where, in 1914, he was interned for the duration of the war at Ruhleben prison camp, where he learned Welsh and changed his given name Ivor to Ifor. He worked briefly in the coal trade in Swansea before going up to St. John's College, Cambridge, where he took first-class honours in economics and history. He was elected Whewell Scholar in International Law, and became university lecturer and Fellow of St. John's College (1923-34). A sometime member of staff of *The Economist*, he served on a League of Nations commission on economic conditions in Austria and travelled extensively in eastern

Europe and Africa. He published *The Agrarian Revolution in Rumania* (1924), *The British in Tropical Africa* (1929), and *Native Policy in Southern Africa* (1934).

In 1934 he became principal of U.C.W. Aberystwyth where he displayed outstanding gifts of creativity laced with prudence: he redeemed a substantial College debt, attracted valuable benefactions and made shrewd purchases of property. The long-range planning and initial development of new college buildings on Penglais hill was almost entirely his work. He spent little time in social contact with students but strongly supported schemes to promote their welfare and instituted an advanced system of joint consultation between the authorities and the student body. Deeply interested and involved in what he called 'the sacred cause of agricultural education', in which Aberystwyth specialised, he published, in collaboration with A.W. Ashby (see above), *The Agriculture of Wales and Monmouthshire* (1944).

He rendered outstanding service to the University of Wales as vice-chancellor (1937-39, 1946-48, 1950-52), chairman of the Press Board and, notably for years, as chairman of the Estates Committee when large sums derived from the disestablishment of the Welsh Church became available for investment. He played a leading part in establishing the Royal University of Malta (which honoured him with a D.Litt. degree) and the development of University College, Ibadan.

Masterful, courageous and occasionally ruthless, he had a wide experience of the ways of the world and a cultivated understanding of other people and languages, with which he combined a passionate interest in Welsh culture. He published several anthologies and translations into Welsh of literary works, among them *Emynau o'r Almaen, Y Cybydd* (Molière's *L'Avare*), *Blodau Hyfryd, Chwedlau La Fontaine, Ffordd y Deyrnas* and *Mawl yr Oesoedd* (an anthology of the hymns of Europe).

On 11 Nov. 1938 he m. Ruth Jolles of Hamburg, by whom he had a son and a daughter. He d. 31 May 1952.

A.D.R., 'Ifor Leslie Evans (1897-1952)', *Welsh Anvil*, 4, 9-12; *Www*; Ellis, *UCW*; *Camb. News*, 6 June 1952; [his papers, NLW ex 1837].

E.L.El.

EVANS, JAMES THOMAS (1878-1950), principal of the Baptist College, Bangor; b. 1 Mar. 1878 at Abercwmboi, Aberdare, Glam., son of William Evans and his wife Ann Williams. The family moved to Pont-y-gwaith, and it was there that the son began to preach. He spent some time at the Pontypridd Academy before his admission to the college and the university at Bangor in 1900, where he took an honours degree in Hebrew. He won the Dean Edwards prize and the George Osborne Morgan scholarship, and then proceeded to Leipzig to pursue a further course of study. He obtained the M.A. degree of the University of Wales in 1905 and the London degree of B.D. in 1910. In 1906 he was elected to succeed Dr. T. Witton Davies (*DWB*, 156-7) as professor of Hebrew at the Baptist College, and in 1923 followed Silas Morris (*DWB*, 666) as principal of the college. He published many articles, a commentary on the Book of Amos (1924), and was one of the assistant-editors of *Y Geiriadur Beiblaidd* (1926). He also published a useful handbook on Old Testament religion (*Llawlyfr ar grefydd yr Hen Destament*, 1928). He was president of the Arfon Baptist association, and he rendered valuable service to his denomination over many years in the churches of north Wales. He m. Annie Humphreys, 18 Sept. 1907. He d. 28 Feb. 1950 and was buried in Glanwydden cemetery.

Ser. Cymru, 24 and 31 March 1950; Edward Cefni Jones, *Hanes Coleg y Bedyddwyr*, 104-6; *Penodau yn Hanes Bed. Cym.*, 119; *Www*, 1941-50.

T.E.J.

EVANS, JANET (c. 1894-1970), journalist and civil servant; b. in London c. 1894, daughter of Thomas John Evans (*DWB*, 254) and Margaret (née Davies), 82 Addington Mansions, Highbury, both natives of Cards. She received private tuition before going to the Central Foundation Girls' School and subsequently attending courses held by London University. After obtaining comprehensive secretarial training she eventually became private secretary to the managing director of the exporting firm Amalgamated Anthracite Collieries, Ltd. in London. Despite being brought up in London, she took a deep interest in everything Welsh and was special correspondent on Welsh affairs to London newspapers. She travelled widely in Europe and twice went to America to visit relatives and give lectures to Welsh communities there. At the beginning of World War II she was for 2 years engaged in the intelligence section of the B.B.C. at Evesham, monitoring English broadcasts from foreign countries. During 1942-45 she travelled much in Wales as Woman Power Officer for Wales. She gave popular lectures, particularly on the London and American Welsh, and broadcast frequently in the series *Gwraig y tŷ*, Woman's Hour, and other programmes, c. 1947-54. She played a prominent part in Welsh social life in London, being the first woman chair of the London Welsh Association, and the first woman to be elected to the council of the Hon. Soc. of Cymmrodorion. She became president of the London Cardiganshire Society and served as sub-editor of the society's *Handbook*, 1936-39 and editor for five years when publication of the magazine was resumed in 1952. She did not marry. After retiring to Cardiganshire she d. 11 Dec. 1970 and her ashes were interred at Capel Erw, Cellan.

Trans. Cymm., 1970, part i, 138-40; *Camb. News*, 25 Dec. 1970; Janet Evans' papers at N.L.W.

M.A.J.

EVANS, JOHN (1858-1963); minister (Congl.) and professor at the Memorial College, Brecon; b. 12 May 1858 at Erwan Fach, Llangrannog, Cards., son of David and Eleanor Evans. He had very little formal education in childhood though he did for a while attend the school held by 'Cranogwen' (*DWB*, 829) at Pontgarreg. After the 1868 general election the family was ejected from their home because the father had voted for the Liberal candidate, and they moved to Pant-teg farm near New Quay. When he was 12 yrs. old he was apprenticed to a shopkeeper in

Llangrannog. Three years later he went to work in a grocer's and clothier's shop in Beaufort, Mon. About 1877 he decided to become a candidate for the ministry and delivered his first sermon in Maen-y-groes chapel, near New Quay. He went to the school kept by C.H. Hughes in the vestry of Tywyn (Congl.) chapel, New Quay, and in 1881 he became the first pupil of that school to be accepted by London University. He went to New College, London, where Samuel Newth was principal, to prepare himself for the ministry, graduating B.A. in 1884 and A.T.S. in 1886. He was an assistant teacher at the school of Watcyn Wyn (*DWB*, 1076) at Ammanford before being invited to minister at Painscastle and Rhos-goch churches, Rads., in 1887. In 1894 he moved to take charge of the English church in Glamorgan Street, Brecon. After the death of John Morris (*DWB*, 661), principal of the Memorial College in that town, in 1896, he was invited to lecture on Hebrew for a while there (while continuing as pastor of the church). When the faculty of theology was established in the University of Wales he was invited to lecture on church history for a year in 1901 and the invitation was renewed annually until he was appointed full time professor in 1905 and at the same time made financial secretary of the college (until 1942). He retained his chair until he retired in 1943 and received the title Professor Emeritus.

He accepted modern forms of scholarship in discussing the Bible and Christian history. His theological liberalism may be perceived in his commentary on Paul's First Letter to the Corinthians, *Epistol Cyntaf Paul at y Corinthiaid* (1926). He wrote an article on the Independents in the neighbourhood of Painscastle and Hay for *The history of Congregationalism in Breconshire and Radnorshire* (ed. Joseph Jones; 1912) and he was among the contributors to the Independents' *Llyfr Gwasanaeth* (1926). He also contributed to *Y Tyst* and *Y Dysgedydd*. He was chairman of the board of governors of Brecon grammar school, 1921-31. Through his quiet faith and gentle personality he came to be regarded as the college's unambitious and unjealous 'man of God'. Everyone knew of his love of Brecon and Brecknockshire and in 1957 he was honoured with the freedom of the borough. He preached for the last time in Tredomen chapel, near Brecon, 11 Nov. 1962. He was unmarried and d. 1 Jan. 1963 in his lodgings in Brecon, his home for many years. In a few months' time he would have reached the age of 105. He was buried in the town cemetery when snow lay heavy on the ground.

Congl. Year Book, 1963-64; *Blwyddiadur A*, 1964; reports of the Brecon Independent Memorial College, 1896-97, 1901-06, 1942-43; Pennar Davies (ed.), *Athrawon ac Annibynwyr* (1971), 20-30; information from D.W. Godfrey Evans, Llandysul, and Thomas Richards, Brecon; personal acquaintance.

W.T.P.D.

EVANS, JOHN DANIEL (1862-1943), a pioneer in Patagonia; b. in Mountain Ash, Glam., 1862. He accompanied his parents who went out to the Welsh colony with the first batch of emigrants in 1865 and became one of the finest horsemen in the country, a daring adventurer, and an able leader, so much so, that he was known as 'The Baceano'. He went out several times to explore the pampas, the most celebrated occasion being in 1883 when his party was attacked by Indians in the Kel-Kein valley and his three companions were killed before he himself miraculously escaped on his Malacara pony. He led a party to the Andes in 1885, when Cwm Hyfryd was discovered; he was one of the first settlers there in 1891. He spent the remainder of his life in Cwm Hyfryd and d. there 6 Mar. 1943 in his 81st year.

Eluned Morgan, *Dringo'r Andes*, 33-41; W. M. Hughes, *Ar Lannau'r Camwy*, 74-86; R. Bryn Williams, *Cymry Patagonia*, 98-105; *Straeon Patagonia*, 77-105; *Trans. of the Old Colwyn Nat. Eist.*, 1941, 87; A.F. Tschiffely, *This Way Southward* (1940), 73-6, 296-8.

R.B.W.

EVANS, JOHN JAMES (1894-1965), teacher and writer; b. 21 April 1894 in Tŷ Capel-y-Bryn (U), Cwrtnewydd, Cards., the son of Enoch Evans, Bwlchyfadfa, Talgarreg, and his wife, Mary Thomas, whose mother came from Llanwenog and who had moved to the chapel house when she lost her husband as a young man. John Evans, the minister at Capel-y-Bryn, had a great influence on J.J. Evans. He was educated at the village primary school to which David Rees Davies, 'Cledlyn' (see above), came as headmaster in 1902. Davies was of the same stock and he had a great influence on his pupil. The father was an engineer in a coal mine in the Aberdare area and he came home to see his family every month. Evans went in 1912 from Llandysul County School to the University College at Bangor where he obtained second-class honours in Welsh in 1915 and took his degree in the following year. In 1926, he was awarded an M.A. for a thesis on the influence of the French Revolution on Welsh literature which was published by Gwasg y Brython in 1928 (*Dylanwad y chwyldro Ffrengig ar lenyddiaeth Cymru*). He taught at schools in Hendreforgan and Llwynypïa before he served in World War I, first with the Royal Welch Fusiliers and then with the *Hood* Battalion, R.N.D. In 1920, he was appointed Welsh teacher at Fishguard County School where he remained until 1935 when he became the headmaster of St. David's County School. Evans was conscious, as a teacher, that the education of children should be founded on the national language, literature, history and traditions. The Unitarian traditions of the Cwrtnewydd district had left their mark and Evans had the gift of promoting reconciliation and of building bridges within society. He was a vice-president of the teachers' union, *Undeb Cenedlaethol Athrawon Cymru*, 1938-44. After his retirement in 1961, he was a member of Pembrokeshire County Council which gave him an opportunity to fight both for the place of the Welsh language in county schools and for a hospital at Haverfordwest.

Evans was especially devoted to the National *Eisteddfod* and he was secretary to the Literary Committee at the Fishguard *Eisteddfod* in 1936. He won his first *Eisteddfod* prize at Pontypool in 1924 for a Welsh reading-book on animals and birds, illustrated with quotations from Welsh poetry. At the Treorchy *Eisteddfod* of 1928, he won a prize for an essay on Morgan

Rhys (*DWB*, 846-7) and his times which was published by the University of Wales Press in 1935 (*Morgan John Rhys a'i amserau*). His handbooks on Welsh idioms and on *cynghanedd* were awarded prizes at the Cardiff *Eisteddfod* of 1938. *Llawlyfr y Cynganeddion* was published by the University of Wales Press in 1946 and reprinted in 1951. Evans also published *Cymry enwog y ddeunawfed ganrif* (1937), *Gramadeg Cymraeg* (1946 and 1960), *Dewi Sant a'i amserau* (1963), and *Diarhebion Cymraeg* (1965). He contributed several articles to the *Ymofynydd*.

Evans m., on 2 Jan. 1923, Eleanor, the daughter of T. Jones Davies, a Calvinistic Methodist minister at Taffs Wells, at Pembroke Terrace chapel, Cardiff. They had one son and a daughter. He d. at Haverfordwest Hospital on 30 Dec. 1965 and he was buried in the graveyard at St. David's.

WWP; information from his daughter.

E.D.J.

EVANS, JOHN JOHN (1862-1942), journalist; b. 9 Dec. 1862, at Llanberis, Caerns. He was educated at the local primary school but left to work in the quarry. He competed at literary meetings and took an interest in drama, being a member of the Llanberis company, the first Welsh drama company to be formed in Wales. During the Llanberis strike of 1886 he was told by Tecwyn Parry, minister of Gorffwysfa, who was responsible for the poetry column in *Y Faner*, that Thomas Gee (*DWB*, 274) required a young correspondent in his office. J.J. Evans secured the post and after settling in Denbigh he devoted his energies to his work and to master shorthand. He became a skilled journalist in both Welsh and English. He later became Thomas Gee's private secretary and during this period he contributed many articles to the Welsh encyclopaedia (*Y Gwyddoniadur Cymreig*). He afterwards became editor of *Y Faner* and later of the *North Wales Times*. He reported all the main meetings of the Vale of Clwyd for over half a century and represented *Y Faner* on his own at the national *eisteddfod* for many years. He attended the first meeting of the Denbighshire county council and was present at every meeting until his editorial duties tied him to his office. He acted for a long period as interpreter at the assizes and the quarter sessions. He was the Vale of Clwyd correspondent for the *Liverpool Daily Post*, *Liverpool Echo*, and the *Manchester Guardian*, for over fifty years. He m. Margaret Evans of Henllan in 1864, and they had seven children. He d. 22 April 1942 in Denbigh, as the result of an accident.

Personal knowledge.

K.R.

EVANS, JOHN RICHARDS (1882-1969), minister (Presb.) and author; b. 10 Jan 1882 in Manchester House, Pen-y-graig, Rhondda, Glam., son of William and Margaret Evans. He was educated in Cardiff High School, Porth secondary school, and, after beginning to preach, in the University College, Cardiff (where he graduated B.A.), and Trefeca and Aberystwyth theological colleges (where he graduated in theology). He was ord. in 1909, and served in the ministry in Bwlch, Brecks. (1906-10), and Bethlehem, Mountain Ash, Glam. (1914-39). He retired from pastoral care in 1939, and lived in Cardiff for the rest of his life. He m. in 1941 Anne May Thomas.

He was one of the leading Presbyterians of his day, being Moderator of the Association in the South (1952), and Moderator of the General Assembly (1955). He and Bishop W.T. Havard (see below) were the first presidents of the Council of Churches in Wales; he represented the churches in Wales in the first Congress of the World Churches Council. He also represented his Connexion in the Presbyterian Alliance. In 1938 he delivered the Davies Lecture *Cristnogaeth a'r Bywyd Da*, which was published in 1941. Prior to that he had published a useful textbook on the prophets, *Y Proffwydi a'u cenadwri* (1923). He wrote much for the *Goleuad*, *Y Drysorfa* and *Traethodydd*, being one of the editors of the latter from 1952 until his death. He d. 10 Feb. 1969, and was buried in the family grave, in Trealaw, Rhondda.

Traeth., 1969, 134-6; *Blwyddiadur MC*, 1970, 279-80; information from his widow (per M.R. Mainwaring, Cardiff); personal knowledge.

G.M.R.

EVANS, JOHN SILAS (1864-1953), priest and astronomer; b. 11 Mar. 1864, son of Evan Evans, Blaen-llan, Pencarreg, Carms. Educated locally he proceeded to the school kept by Alcwyn C. Evans (*DWB*, 219) at Carmarthen, and afterwards to the old grammar school, Lampeter. He gained the Phillips and Treharne scholarships to St. David's College, Lampeter, and graduated B.A., 1885 with honours in divinity, winning the Welsh and science prizes. He taught at a college in Coventry for a year, and was ordained deacon in St. Asaph in 1887 and priested in 1888. He was a curate of Diserth, 1887-90, and of Rhos-ddu, 1890-95; vicar of St. Asaph and vicar choral of the cathedral, 1895-1901; vicar of Gyffylliog, 1901-09; Llanrhaeadr-ym-Mochnant with Llanarmon Mynydd Mawr, 1909-38. He was proctor of the convocation of Canterbury, 1917-20, and was appointed canon of St. Asaph, 1928. He became a Fellow of the Royal Astronomical Society, 1923. He was a member of the British Astronomical Society and a member of the council of St. David's College, Lampeter, 1927-39.

He published *Seryddiaeth a seryddwyr*, 1923; *Marvels of the sky*, 1921; *Ad astra*, 1930; *Hanes Llanrhaeadr ym Mochnant*, 1940; and *Myfyrion min yr hwyr*, 1949.

He was in great demand as a special preacher and preached the sermon at Hereford Cathedral St. David's Day Festival, 1925, and St. Paul's London, 1939. He had an exceptional memory and he could conduct church services almost completely from memory. He was an authority on astronomy and lectured widely on the subject. He had the roof of the nave of Llanrhaeadr-ym-Mochnant church painted with stars and planets on a blue base. His other interests were folklore and local history. He never married. When he retired in 1938 he went to live in Aberystwyth so as to be within easy reach of the National Library of Wales. He called his home *Ad astra*. After he had returned to his old home in his native village he wrote the history of Pencarreg parish. He d. there, 19 April 1953, and was buried in the churchyard.

Official handbook of the Church in Wales, 1939, and the Church in Wales Office at Cardiff; *Y Llan*, 24 April 1953; *Welsh Gaz.*, 23 April 1953; *Hanes plwyf Llanrhaeadr-ym-Mochnant*.

M.G.E.

EVANS, JOHN VICTOR (1895-1957), barrister-at-law; b. 7 October 1895 at Cwmdare, Aberdare, Glam., son of Henry Howard Evans, general manager of the Cambrian Collieries in Mid-Rhondda, a prominent Baptist layman and Mary Ann Evans, his wife, who died shortly after her son was born. He was educated at the local elementary school in Cwmdare and at Christ College, Brecon. There followed war service in Egypt, France and Palestine, and after World War I he went to St. John's College, Oxford, where he read History and took a second-class honours degree in 1922. At Oxford he played a distinguished part in the Union Debating Society, being elected successively Secretary, Junior Librarian and in 1922 President of the Union; he was also President of the Dafydd ap Gwilym Society. After leaving Oxford he was called to the bar in 1924. He was an accomplished orator and in the general election of 1929 he contested Pontypridd as a Liberal, polling 37% of the vote and coming second to T.I. Mardy Jones in a three-cornered contest. He again entered the lists as the Liberal candidate in the Merthyr Tydfil by-election of 1934, coming second to S.O. Davies in a four-cornered contest, again polling a respectable vote of over 10,000. In 1930 he was appointed a lecturer in law at the University College of Wales, Aberystwyth, but resigned in 1935 to resume his bar practice. A man of deep religious convictions with a tender social conscience, he felt the urge to do something to alleviate the suffering of the unemployed in south Wales and accepted in 1936 the post of warden of the Aberdare Education Settlement, *Coleg Gwerin Cynon*, set up by the Council of Social Service. He had married in April 1927 Katherine Mary, daughter of the Rev. Henry Dawson of Streatham. Their only child, John, died suddenly in 1938. Evans had been very happy in his work at Aberdare but the loss of his son proved a shattering blow. In 1939 he resigned his post at the Settlement and returned to London. In the meantime World War II supervened and he took a post in the Ministry of Economic Warfare. In peace time he remained in the Civil Service and ended his career in the Ministry of Supply. He d. in his home in Dulwich Village 15 May 1957.

That he did not in many respects fulfil his early promise may be attributed in large measure to his greatly impaired health as a result of his sufferings in World War I. He overtaxed his strength by attempting to achieve at the bar and in politics more than his enfeebled constitution could stand.

B.B. Thomas, *Ddinas*, July 1957; *Aberdare Leader*, 8 Feb. 1936; WWP.

W.T.M.

EVANS, JOHN YOUNG (1865-1941), minister (Presb.), professor at Trefeca College and afterwards at the Theological College, Aberystwyth; b. 16 Nov. 1865, at Dowlais, Glam., the son of John Bennett Evans and Ellen his wife. He was educated at Merthyr Tydfil Grammar School and was a scholar of the University College of Wales, Aberystwyth, and Corpus Christi Oxford, graduating M.A. (London and Oxford) with first-class honours in classics and B.D. (London). He was appointed to a chair at Trefeca before completing his course at Oxford (1891), and he moved to Aberystwyth when the United Theological College was established there in 1906. He was responsible for the instruction of students in classics, English literature, the New Testament, and in later years church history. He was for many years examiner for Oxford Locals and the Central Welsh Board, and was dean of the University of Wales faculty of theology, 1922-26. He was the author of a Welsh commentary on St. Luke's Gospel, 1927, and wrote a great deal to newspapers and periodicals on classical, historical and religious subjects (see the list in *Who Was Who*, 1941-50). Following his ordination in 1897, he was Davies lecturer (*'Cymun Corff Crist'*), 1928, Moderator of the Association in the South, 1941-42; he d. before the end of his term, 26 Dec. 1941. He was a man of extraordinary knowledge in more than one field, but his ability to impart his learning was not commensurate with his knowledge, though no one was more ready to help students who sought his advice. He was an entertaining conversationalist, with a story and an apt saying constantly at his command and many of the characteristics of the old scholars were represented in him; he was fond of alliteration in articles, letters, and even in examination papers. He was one of a small group of Welshmen, including Sir Joseph Bradney (*DWB*, 48) who corresponded with one another in Latin. He had many of his poems in Welsh and in Latin printed for distribution among his friends. He m. Ellen, daughter of John Morgan, J.P., of Brecon, and they had a son and two daughters.

Cylch. Cymd. Hanes M.C., 27, 79-83; *Goleuad*, 1942; *Drys.*, 1942; *Www.*, 1941-50.

G.A.E.

EVANS, RICHARD THOMAS (1892-1962), Baptist minister and administrator; b. 8 Oct. 1892 at Penygraig, Rhondda Valley, Glam., son of David and Mary Evans (his father was killed in an accident in Abercynon colliery in 1924). His father was a prominent Baptist in the locality, especially so after moving to Abercynon, where he was a deacon at Calfaria chapel. In the second decade of the century he was a keen supporter of the campaign to establish a Support Fund for the denomination. R.T.E.'s mother was a member of the Wesleyan church, a sister of a minister in that denomination, John Edward Thomas (1875-1959). R.T.E. was baptised at a young age in Bethlehem, Trealaw, but it was in Calfaria, Abercynon that he was prepared for the ministry. He received his early education at Trealaw, and thereafter at secondary schools at Porth and Mountain Ash; he was a pupil-teacher and a teacher at Abercynon for a period before being accepted as a student in the University College and the Baptist College, Bangor. Because he never enjoyed the best of health throughout his life, it is unlikely that he would have been called up to undertake any type of military service during World War I. However, his pacifist stance was so strong that

he chose to leave Bangor, to be ordained on 23 May 1917 at Ainon and Tabernacl chapels, Bodedern. He returned to the college in the year 1919-20 to complete his B.A. degree and he was subsequently installed as minister at Porthmadog on 23 June 1920, at Newport, Pembs. on 14 June 1922 and at Ammanford on 26 May 1927. Within seven years he was chosen as the secretary of the Baptist Union of Wales and he was installed in that office during the annual conference held at Bethesda, Swansea, on 3 Sep. 1934. He retired on Easter Monday, 7 Apr. 1958 and in appreciation of his service he was elevated to be president of both the Welsh and English sections of the Baptist Union of Wales for the year 1958-59 (but without being required to deliver an address). He was given a generous testimonial in a public meeting in Swansea on 5 Dec. 1958. He continued to live in Swansea and it was at his home, 11 Gower Road, Sketty, that he d. on 13 Jun. 1962. In accordance with his own wishes, he was buried privately. In spite of perpetual bouts of ill health, he succeeded in leading safely the Baptists of Wales through a period of much change and re-organisation. It is considered that his prime achievement was to centralise all the activities of the denomination under one roof in the new office, Tŷ Ilston, that was opened in Swansea in 1940.

He m. 28 Mar. 1921 at Seion, Glanconwy, Maria Myfanwy (b. 27 Jun. 1893), the daughter of William Wallace Thomas (1832-1904), a native of Pentrefoelas and an Independent minister at Maes-glas, Holywell from 1873 until his retirement to Glanconwy in 1885. Her principal benefaction was to persuade the Baptist Women's Movement to establish the denomination's home for the elderly at Glyn Nest, Newcastle Emlyn. It was appropriate that she was invited to open it officially on 26 Sept. 1970 and that it was there that she spent the last eighteen months of her life, from Sept. 1978 until her death at Glangwili hospital on Monday 4 Feb. 1980. She was cremated at Parc Gwyn, Narberth, on 11 Feb. 1980. There was one son of the marriage, b. 16 May 1934.

Seren Cymru, 15 Jun. 1917, 30 Jul. 1920, 12 May, 28 Jul. 1922, 20 May, 10 Jun. 1927, 14 Nov. 1934, 20 Jun., 4 July, 5 Dec. 1958, 22, 29 Jun., 13 Jul. 1962, 9 Oct. 1970, 7 Mar. 1980; *Seren yr Ysgol Sul*, 1932, 2-6, 1934, 220; *Arweinydd Newydd*, 1935, 129-31; *Seren Gomer*, 1962, 94, 1966, 47-8; *Baptist Times*, 21 Jun. 1962; *Baptist Handbook*, 1963, 361; *Dyddiadur a Llawlyfr y Bedyddwyr*, 1963, 116-117; Gwilym Owen, *Da Was* (1966), 53-5; *Congl. Year Book*, 1905, 189; *WWP*; information from his widow and from Eilwen Jenkins, Capel Iwan.

B.G.O.

EVANS, ROBERT ('Cybi'; 1871-1956) poet, writer, and bookseller; b. 27 Nov. 1871 in Elusendy, Llangybi, Caern., one of the seven children of Thomas Evans, farmworker, and Mary (née Roberts). He was educated at the council school, Llangybi and after serving for a time on Eifionydd farms he was the local postman there for the greater part of his life. William Hugh Williams, 'Cae'r go', was his fellow postman. He also sold 'books of every sort, both scarce and valuable, old and new', and had a stall in the Market Hall at Pwllheli every

Wednesday. He wrote a very considerable amount of poetry, particularly *awdlau, marwnadau* and commemorative *englynion*. There is not a graveyard in Eifionydd that does not contain an example of his work. He published several books of his own poetry including *Odlau Eifion* (1908), *Awdl 'Bwlch Aberglaslyn'* (1910) and *Gwaith Barddonol Cybi* (1912). He was a regular competitor at local as well as provincial and national *eisteddfodau*, and he won many prizes including both chairs and crowns. His special interest lay in the poets of Eifionydd and he did useful service in publishing their works, particularly in *Lloffion yr ardd* (1911), the unpublished poetry of Robert ap Gwilym Ddu (Robert Williams, 1766-1850; *DWB*, 1067), and *Beirdd Gwerin Eifionydd* (1914), a selection of the poems of local poets from the end of the 17th century onwards. He was also a local historian, publishing *Ardal y cewri* (1907) dealing with the Llangybi district, and several other books on local characters. He lived at Bryn Eithin, Llangybi and d. 16 Oct. 1956. He was buried in the graveyard at Capel Helyg, Llangybi.

Information from Emrys Jones, Cricieth and personal knowledge.

C.A.G.

EVANS, THOMAS (1897-1963), alderman, education and hospital administrator; b. in Twyn Carno, Rhymney, Glam., 9 Sept. 1897, son of William Evans, miner, and Catherine, his wife; his father came originally from Hirwaun, Aberdare, though his roots were in Cardiganshire. Thomas was educated at elementary schools in Rhymney, but left at the age of 12 to work in a brickworks at Rhymney. He afterwards became a miner and worked for 14 years underground at the Rhymney, Oakdale and Pengam collieries till the 1926 coal strike, when he purchased a dairy and milk distributing business at Pengam. In 1927 he entered public life when he won a seat for the Labour party on the Gelligaer U.D.C., which he retained until he retired in 1950. He was for 15 years the leader of the Labour group on the council and was chairman on two occasions. In 1928 he won a seat on the Glamorgan county council, representing the Hengoed ward. His remarkable grasp of financial administration was soon recognised and in 1939 he was elected chairman of the county finance committee to which post he was re-elected 24 times in succession for the rest of his life so that he was popularly known as 'the chancellor of the exchequer' for Glamorgan. During the year 1952-53 he was chairman of the council, during which period the Welsh local authorities made him a public presentation in recognition of his long and distinguished services to local government in Wales.

But he did not confine himself to county administration. He was a member of the governing body and at one time chairman of Lewis' School, Pengam. For over 20 years he was chairman of the finance committee of the University of Wales Council and he was a member of the council of the Welsh National School of Medicine (as it was then known). His services to education were recognised by the University of Wales when he was awarded the honorary degree of LL.D. in 1958. His achievements in

hospital administration were also notable. In 1948 he was the first chairman of the Rhymney and Sirhowy hospitals management board. He was appointed chairman in 1955 of the board of governors of the United Cardiff hospitals, including the teaching hospital. At the time of his death he was vice-chairman of the Welsh Regional Hospitals Board and he had been chairman of its finance and establishment committee since 1952. In 1952 he was the last chairman of the now defunct Industrial Development Council for Wales and Monmouthshire; he was a part-time member of the South Wales Electricity Board and formerly represented the Gelligaer U.D.C. on the Rhymney Valley Drainage Board; he had been a Glamorgan county magistrate since 1936. In recognition of his outstanding services in public life, he was made a C.B.E. in 1956.

Despite the exacting demands of his public duties, alderman Evans was assiduous in his attendance at the services of his chapel, Nazareth Welsh Presbyterian Church, Glan-y-nant, Pengam, where he was an elder. He was a man of great dignity and integrity and a deeply committed Christian. It may truly be said that the chief motivation of his life of service to his fellowmen was rooted in his Christian faith.

In 1918 he m. Miriam Davies, schoolmistress, at New Tredegar, who predeceased him in 1953. There were three children of the marriage. One son, Rhys, a law student at Aberystwyth, a fighter pilot in the R.A.F. was killed on D-Day 1944. He d. 14 Jan. 1963.

West. Mail, 15 Jan. 1963; *S. Wales Argus*, 15 Jan. 1963; *Rhymney Valley Express*, 19 and 26 Jan. 1963; WWP; and information kindly supplied by his daughter Miss Nonn Evans.

W.T.M.

EVANS, THOMAS JOHN (1894-1965), local government officer and an administrator within the Baptist denomination; b. 30 Mar. 1894 in Carmarthen, one of twin sons of David Evans (d. 16 Aug. 1926 aged 55 yrs.), prison officer, and Mary Ann Evans (née Williams, d. 24 Dec. 1895 aged 25 yrs.). About three months after his birth the family moved to Shepton Mallet, where his father had taken employment, but following his mother's death the son returned to Carmarthen to be raised by his grandmother, Eliza Williams. His uncle David Evans Williams, M.A., (1876-1947), the Baptist minister of Salem, Blaenau, was a member of the same household. His uncle had a marked influence on his upbringing, and it was the nephew's privilege, in 1948, in association with E.T. Samuel, to produce a volume in his memory entitled, *Through suffering to triumph*, which commemorated his lifetime of affliction. He received his early education at Pentrepoeth Boys' Council School. On 17 Feb. 1908 he commenced his lifetime's work in the education finance section of the County Council offices at Carmarthen. His first post was as a junior clerk, culminating with his appointment, from 5 Nov. 1924 onwards, as Associate County Treasurer with sole responsibility for education. He retired a year early on 5 Apr. 1958 in order to facilitate the integration of the treasury functions within the County Council. He was married at Tabernacl, Carmarthen on 23 Nov. 1923 to Margaret Gwendoline Hodges (27 Jun. 1894 – 22 Mar. 1951), a childhood acquaintance in the church, who bore him one daughter. The small volume, *Gwen – A tribute of love and remembrance* (1951), that he published privately, was his personal tribute to his wife.

Throughout his life he gave remarkably active support to numerous good causes in the town of Carmarthen and in his church, where he was a deacon and church secretary (1921-64). His annual reports were punctual and detailed. One of his most important benefactions was to preserve the church records by placing them on deposit at the National Library of Wales (N.L.W. Dep. MSS. 746-71, 813-14, 817). His part in presenting to the National Library the diaries of two former ministers, Hugh William Jones, ('Yr Utgorn Arian', *DWB*, 468) and Evan Ungoed Thomas (NLW MSS. 1896-9, NLW Deposits 791-816, 827-66) was consistent with his efforts to preserve the sources of the history of Tabernacl church. He published the fruits of his own research many times in the literature of the denomination, e.g. in the programme of the annual conference of the Baptist Union of Wales held at Tabernacl in 1937, and in his volume *Fragrant memories: the story of two ministers, The Rev. John Thomas (1875-1891), The Rev. Evan Ungoed Thomas (1892-1930)* (1941). He was treasurer of the county association (1939-55), and thereafter the treasurer of the Union; the president of *Urdd y Seren Fore* 1936-37 and president of the Union of Young Baptists of Wales, 1952-58; president of the county association 1951-52 when he delivered an address from the chair on the subject 'In the midst of time'. In the November before his death he had been elevated to become the vice-president of the Welsh section of the union. The annual conference (the conference celebrating the centenary) had been invited back to its original home in Carmarthen. Throughout the years he was a fervent supporter of the Baptist Missionary Society. In 1959 it was he who was responsible for collection of the contributions from Wales towards the Thomas Lewis (1859-1929; *DWB*, 1140) memorial hospital in Angola and for organising a meeting to celebrate his centenary in his old home at Pontyfenni near Whitland. There is a clear indication of his radical nonconformist stance in his volume of tribute *Sir Rhys Hopkin Morris … The man and his character* (1958).

He spent the closing years of his life at the home of his daughter and son-in-law at Parson's Lodge, Clunderwen where he d. on 9 Mar. 1965. He was buried on 12 Mar. in Tabernacl graveyard. He had just completed his autobiography, *Golden strands: Some memories along life's pilgrimage* (1965). Tradition has it that the manuscript arrived at the printers on the morning of his death.

The sources noted above, *Seren yr Ysgol Sul*, 1936, 3-8, 1946, 2-5, 1948, 100-2, 1951, 151-2, 1952, 213-4; *Seren Fach*, 1962, 70-2; *Seren Cymru*, 27 Jun. 1958, 27 May 1960, 26 Apr. 1963, 17 Jan. 1964, 19, 26 Mar., 3 Sep. 1965; *Llythyr Cymanfa Caerfyrddin ac Aberteifi*, 1952, 4-18, 1965, 21-2; *Baptist Times*, 13 Jan. 1955, 18 Mar. 1965; *Carmarthen Journal*, 12, 19 Mar. 1965; *Welshman*, 12, 19 Mar. 1965; *Seren Gomer*, 1965, 36-8, 81; *Dyddiadur a Llawlyfr Undeb Bedyddwyr Cymru*, 1966, 120-1.

B.G.O.

EVANS, WILLIAM (1869-1948), minister (Congl.) and missionary in Madagascar; b. 31 Oct. 1869 in Y Meysydd, Landore, Swansea, s. of Thomas and Mary Evans. His father owned a small mine in the area. His mother was a member of the same Sunday school as Griffith John, China (*DWB*, 440-1) and he set his mind on serving in that country. His brother David was ord. minister in Rehoboth (Congl.), Brynmawr, in 1871. William was educ. at the private school run by his minister, W.S. Jenkins, and he afterwards attended St. Helen's Road Board School, Swansea. He worked for a while as weigher at his father's mine before being apprenticed as a chemist. He began preaching under the ministry of G. Pennar Griffiths (*DWB*, 304-5). He was a student in Watcyn Wyn's Gwynfryn School, Ammanford, and then went to Plymouth college (which later transferred to Bristol). He was accepted by the London Missionary Society to serve in Madagascar in 1898, and was ord. at Siloam, Pentre-estyll, Swansea, 18 and 19 June 1899. He m. Margaret, dau. of Revd. R.E. Williams, Ynyslwyd (Bapt.), Aberdare. On his arrival in Madagascar at the end of 1899 he was appointed minister of Ambatonakanga in the capital, a church established by David Jones of Neuaddlwyd (*DWB*, 453). Apart from some journeys to the north on behalf of the Society he spent his career serving churches – which numbered 57 at one time – in the capital, Antananarivo, and the surrounding districts. His early years on the island were dangerous and difficult because of the rebellion (1900-01) when many Christians and some missionaries were killed, but after this troubled time passed, Evans was particularly successful. He mastered the language to such an extent that he was invited to train preachers in oratory in the united college, this in addition to serving the London Missionary Society as director of the Imerina churches. He accomplished outstanding work bringing order to the life of churches young in the faith. His wife d. in June 1914 and he m. in Aug. 1918 a missionary with the Society of Friends, Phoebe Joyce Hall, a native of Penarth, a niece of Silvester Horne. He also carried out important work as secretary of the Intermissionary Congress of Protestant Missions from 1913 onwards. He published a new Malagasy translation of *Pilgrim's Progress* (the first translation was that by David Johns, 1796-1843; *DWB*, 442) and a revised edition of the Malagasy Bible to celebrate the centenary of the first translation in 1835. His masterpiece, however, was the Malagasy Biblical dictionary based on Hastings *Encyclopaedia*, a task which occupied Evans and his colleague, Revd. Henri Randzavola, for 21 years. One of the difficulties of this work was the need to create a theological vocabulary in a language lacking such a tradition. He edited Malagasy journals, e.g. *Teny Soa* ('Good words') and *Impanolo Tsaina* ('Counsellor'), all of which, together with other editorial work, reveal his mastery of the language.

He retired as a missionary at the end of 1936. He d. in Swansea 1 July 1948 and was buried in Bethel cemetery, Sketty.

D. Brinley Pugh, *Triawd yr ynys* (1954), 9-32; *Congl. Year Book*, 1949, 498; correspondence, etc., Mission Office, Tŷ John Penry, Swansea; *Tywysydd y Plant*, Sept. 1941.

I.S.J.

EVANS, WILLIAM ('Wil Ifan'; 1883-1968), minister (Congl.), poet and writer in Welsh and English; b. 22 Apr. 1883 in Vale View, Cwmbach, Llanwinio, Carms., son of Dan Evans, Congl. minister, later of Hawen and Bryngwenith and editor of the *Celt* for a period, and Mary (née Davies) of Cwmbach, Llanwinio. He graduated (B.A., 1905) in the University of Wales, and also went to Manchester College, Oxford. He was very able but did not seek a distinguished educational career; and although he was a cultured evangelical preacher, he had no desire to be a popular figure at preaching festivals. Indeed, he declined such engagements, but he was loved by the members of his pastorates. He ministered in Dolgellau, 1906-09, Bridgend, 1909-17, Richmond Rd., Cardiff, 1917-25, and Bridgend yet again, until 1949 when he was made Pastor Emeritus for the rest of his life. He m. Nesta Wyn, daughter of John and Catherine Edwards, Eirianfa, Dolgellau, 28 Dec. 1910, and they had four children: Elwyn, Mari, Nest, Brian. He d. 16 Jul. 1968.

He shone as one of the most versatile of the poets and writers of Wales. He was a playwright, newspaper columnist, broadcaster, lecturer, and a lyrical poet in both Welsh and English; he was also a musician and an excellent artist. He won some of the chief prizes at provincial *eisteddfodau* and the crown for a *pryddest* at the national *eisteddfod* three times: at Abergavenny in 1913 ('Ieuan Gwynedd'), Birkenhead in 1917 ('Pwyll pendefig Dyfed'), and at Pwllheli in 1925 for his best known poem to his childhood area ('Bro fy mebyd'). He adjudicated many times at the national *eisteddfod* and was Archdruid of Wales in the *Gorsedd* of Bards, 1947-50.

He was a prolific writer both in Welsh and English. Among his numerous published works are collections of poems: *Dros y nyth* (1913), *Plant y babell* (1922), *Haul a glaw* (1938), *O dydd i ddydd* (1927), *Y winllan las* (1936), *A quire of rhymes* (1943), *Unwaith eto* (1946), *Difyr a dwys* (1960); plays: *Dreams come true* (1916), *Etifedd Arberth* (1937); and prose: *Here and there* (1953), *Y filltir deg* (1954), *Colofnau Wil Ifan* (1962).

Personal knowledge; information from his son, Elwyn Evans; [*Barn*, Eist., 1983].

G.Jo.

EVANS, WILLIAM JOHN (1866-1947), musician; b. 29 Nov. 1866, at Aberdare, Glam. He was apprenticed to his father, Rhys Evans (*DWB*, 249) and worked with him in his tailoring business. He was given every encouragement at home to cultivate and develop his musical talent and he devoted himself wholeheartedly to the pursuit of music. After his appointment as organist of Siloa Chapel, Aberdare, he was called upon to give organ recitals in many parts of south Wales. He also became a regular adjudicator at *eisteddfodau* and soon acquired popularity as a conductor of singing festivals throughout Wales. He conducted hundreds of these festivals. At Aberdare he rendered valuable service to the musical life of the town by establishing an orchestra and holding concerts at which the choral works of the great masters were performed. His orchestra won the chief prize at the Pontypridd national *eisteddfod*. The Mountain Ash male voice choir was victorious

under his baton at the Albert Hall *eisteddfod* in London. He was co-editor of the Welsh congregational hymnal – *Y Caniedydd Cynulleidfaol Newydd*, 1921, and *Caniedydd Newydd yr Ysgol Sul*, 1930. Five of his own tunes were included in the former and his tune 'Rhys', composed in memory of his father for the Elvet Lewis hymn 'Rho im yr hedd', remains popular. Many musical compositions were performed by him and his father at Aberdare. He m. Mary Elizabeth Milligan sometime during Apr.-June 1895. After the death of his wife he retired from business and went to live with his son, Ifor L. Evans (see above), then principal of the University College of Wales, at Aberystwyth. He d. 12 Dec. 1947 at his son's home and was buried in Aberdare cemetery.

Y Cerddor, Aug. 1899, Aug. 1905, and Jan. 1917.

R.D.G.

EVANS-JONES, CYNAN ALBERT – see JONES, Sir CYNAN ALBERT EVANS below.

EVANS-WILLIAMS, LAURA (1883-1944), singer; eldest dau. of John and Ellen Evans, b. at Bryn Meirion, Henllan, Denb., 7 Sept., 1883. She was educated at Howell's School, Denbigh, and at the Royal Academy of Music, London. She began her career as a contralto, winning prizes at several *eisteddfodau*; at the Academy she studied under Edward Iles who developed her voice as a lyric soprano. She became widely known as a concert and oratorio singer; she was also a pleasing interpreter of operatic arias and particularly of Welsh songs, including folksongs. During World War I she toured extensively with Clara Butt. At the 1917 national *eisteddfod* at Birkenhead she had been invited to sing the Chairing Song, and when it was announced that the winner of the chair (Ellis H. Evans, 'Hedd Wyn', *DWB*, 229), had been killed in battle, she sang 'I Blas Gogerddan', which was particularly appropriate. Sixteen years later, at the Wrexham national *eisteddfod*, she sang the Chairing Song again, and received the unusual distinction of an encore. She was the first of all Welsh artists to broadcast from Savoy Hill. She visited the United States of America on a concert tour in 1926, and returned to Wales from London in 1940 to live at Colwyn Bay, where she taught singing till her death there on 5 October, 1944. She was buried at Henllan. She had married, in 1905, R.T. Williams, and she was survived by a daughter and a son.

Liverpool Post and Mercury, 14 Aug. 1933; *North Wales Weekly News*, 26 Oct. 1937; *Denbigh Free Press*, 14 Oct. 1944; information from her daughter, Mrs. Castle, Sutton Coldfield; personal knowledge.

T.I.E.

F

FAGAN, THOMAS WALLACE (1874-1951), agricultural chemist; b. 4 Feb. 1874 at Talysarn, Caerns., son of James Wallace and Katherine Fagan. He was educated in the local school, Denstone College, and Gonville and Caius College, Cambridge, and graduated in 1898. He was for a short period chemistry master in Abertillery secondary school (his successor in that post was Thomas Jacob Thomas, 'Sarnicol'; see below), and then went to study under the professors Dobbie and Winter at University College, Bangor. He was appointed lecturer in the Harper Adams Agricultural College, Salop, in 1904, and was afterwards lecturer in the department of agriculture of Edinburgh University. In 1919 he was appointed to the staff of the University College of Wales, Aberystwyth, as an adviser in agricultural chemistry under the Ministry of Agriculture for the counties served by the college. He became head of the department of agricultural chemistry of the college in 1924, as successor to J. Jones Griffith. He was promoted Professor in 1931 and retired in 1939.

In collaboration with the Welsh Plant Breeding Station between 1919 and 1939 Fagan became one of the leading British scientists studying the chemistry of grass and its conservation. He was a pioneer in this field and his articles, most of which were published in the *Welsh Jnl. of Agric.*, bear testimony to his ability, dedication and leadership as an agricultural scientist. His meticulous and accurate analyses were of inestimable value to plant breeders, and according to R.J. Stapledon (see below) Fagan laid sure foundations for understanding the innumerable factors affecting the nutritive value of grasses, clovers, and other grassland plants. He continued his researches to the end of his life, but did not receive the commendation which was due to him for his pioneering work, possibly because he was by nature unassuming, and reluctant to extol the value of his own researches.

He m. Helena Teresa Hughes, and they had one son. Fagan d. in Aberystwyth, 10 Feb. 1951, and was buried in the town cemetery.

Information given by J.H.W. Fagan; *Jnl. Agric. Soc. U.C.W. Aberyst.*, 1952, 33; Richard Phillips, *Pob un â'i gwys* (1970); personal knowledge.

LI.P.

FARR, HARRY (1874-1968), librarian; b. Cardiff, 11 June 1874, son of William Farr, a native of Salisbury, and Martha Rebecca (Harris), his wife. His mother died in Dec. 1875, after giving birth to twin sons who also died in the same month. It appears that William Farr enrolled after the death of his wife as a student in the Cardiff Science and Art School. The *Annual Report* for 1880-81 records that he was one of two senior students who had been appointed pupil teachers, and in the following session he was promoted to be art master. In the meantime his young son, Harry, was sent to Salisbury to be educated. He joined the staff of the Cardiff Free Library, as it was then called, in

1891, was appointed Assistant in charge of the Reference Department in 1896 and Deputy Librarian in 1901. In 1908 he succeeded as Chief Librarian John Ballinger (*DWB*, 23-4) who left to become the first Librarian of the National Library of Wales. During his 32 years' tenure of office Farr continued and extended the enlightened policies of his predecessor. Two new branch libraries were built at Gabalfa (1928) and Ely (1933), six older branches were extended and children's halls provided where such had not previously existed; public lending centres were provided in schools at Ely, Llanishen, Llandaff North and Rumney to serve areas which boundary changes had brought within the city's jurisdiction. In 1925 a bindery was established at the Central Library for the binding of periodicals and the repair and restoration of rare books and manuscripts. By 1940 the lending department of the Central Library had been rearranged and reorganised. When the collections of the Cardiff Museum, previously housed on the top floor of the Central Library were transferred to the National Museum of Wales, it was decided in 1923 to make use of the vacant space to establish a Research Room for the use of students and others wishing to consult the Library's manuscripts and rare books. The provision of these research facilities together with the construction of a fire-proof strongroom led the Master of the Rolls to recognise the Cardiff Central Library in 1931 as a repository for historical records. At the same time the policy of allocating part of the annual book fund for purchasing manuscripts, deeds, documents, prints and early printed books was vigorously pursued. N.R. Ker in his *Medieval MSS in British Libraries* (1992) lists 32 valuable MSS purchased by the Cardiff Library, 1920-36. In the acquisition of MSS and other expensive items Farr was greatly helped by benefactors who either donated or provided the funds to purchase valuable collections, for example, the famous Havod collection of MSS, the cost of the purchase of which was defrayed by Mr. Edgar Evans of Ely in 1918.

To Farr and his staff belongs the credit for organising the Welsh Book Festivals which were held each year from 1930 to 1939 in the City Hall Cardiff, usually in the weeks before and after St. David's Day. The productions of Welsh book publishers were put on display, books, prints and manuscripts from the Cardiff Library Welsh collections were exhibited, as well as valuable items lent by other libraries and private collectors. Each year a different aspect of Welsh life and letters was taken as a theme and catalogues were produced which served to bring to the attention of a wide public the richness of the Welsh cultural heritage.

A library service to hospitals in the city was commenced in 1931. In 1932 the Regional Library Scheme for Wales was inaugurated and thanks to Farr's efforts Cardiff was selected as the Regional Centre for Glamorganshire and Monmouthshire. Mention should also be made of the public lectures which he organised at the Cardiff Central Library and of the many book exhibitions he arranged, apart from the Welsh Book Festival already mentioned, in particular the Bible Exhibition in 1911, the Exhibition of Early Printed Books in 1913 and the Exhibition of Shakespeariana in 1923, all of which were accompanied by valuable catalogues.

Farr was a well-known figure in the Library world. He became an F.L.A. in 1910 and served on the Library Association Council. In the course of his career he wrote a number of articles and pamphlets on different aspects of librarianship including *Libraries in Rural Districts* (1909) and *Library Work with Children* (1910). He was recognised as a bibliographer of repute and an acknowledged authority on incunabula and early printed books, the editions of Shakespeare and the productions of private presses. He possessed a keen and lively mind and was not afraid to experiment. He even devised a decimal classification of his own, which was in use in the Library until the development of centralised cataloguing led to it being abandoned.

When Farr retired in 1940 the Cardiff City Library Service was recognised as one of the finest in the country and the Central Library as one of the great municipal libraries of Great Britain. But it was not only a municipal library. Its reference department, open till 9 o'clock in the evening, was used by readers beyond the confines of the city. Its Welsh collections served the needs of students throughout Wales.

Harry Farr m. in 1913 Elsie Olive Davies, a member of his staff, who predeceased him. They had five children, three sons and two daughters. He d. 19 Jan. 1968.

WwW (1921); *Jnl. W.B.S.*, 10, 2; *Brief Survey of the Library Movement in Cardiff*, 1932; typescript kindly lent by G.A.C. Dart, Farr's successor as chief librarian, of his 'The history of the Cardiff libraries, 1860-1974', staff records.

W.T.M.

FFRANCON-THOMAS, DAVID – see THOMAS, DAVID FFRANGCON below.

FFRANGCON-THOMAS, DAVID – see THOMAS, DAVID FFRANGCON below.

FINCH, Sir WILLIAM HENEAGE WYNNE – see WYNNE-FINCH, Sir WILLIAM HENEAGE below.

FISHER, FRANCIS GEORGE (1909-70), dramatist and producer; b. 26 Jan. 1909 in Bargoed, Glam. He was educated at Lewis' School, Pengam, and at University College, Cardiff, where he graduated in mathematics. For a short period he was a teacher in a missionary college in west Africa; then in 1932 a mathematics teacher (and later deputy headmaster) at Llangefni grammar school till his d. on 30 Jan. 1970.

He published a novel, *One has been honest* (1930), and poems and stories in *The Adelphi* and in *The Twentieth Century* in the 1930s; then he turned to drama and his play *The disinherited* was performed in Swansea Little Theatre in July 1939. He joined the navy during the war and while he was in Iceland he made efforts to learn Welsh from Caradar's booklet *Welsh made easy*. From then on he was intent on writing

plays in Welsh. He wrote at least five short plays between 1945 and 1952 and three long plays: *Catrin* (which won him a prize in the national *eisteddfod* at Dolgellau, 1949), *Y ferch a'r dewin* (1958) (which shared a prize in the national *eisteddfod* at Rhyl, 1953), and *Merch yw Medusa* (1951). He also translated Andre Obey's play, *Noa* (1951). However his most important contribution was to ensure that the drama society at Llangefni had a permanent home, with the creation of the Little Theatre which was opened in Pencraig, Llangefni in May 1953. He was made director of the theatre and realised his vision of an amateur theatre regularly presenting plays of truly professional standard in Welsh and English.

Taliesin, Aug. 1970, 123-5; Llywelyn Jones, *Francis George Fisher, bardd a dramodydd* (1983).

B.L.J.

FITT, MARY – see FREEMAN, KATHLEEN below.

FLEURE, HERBERT JOHN (1877-1969), geographer; b. in Guernsey, 6 June 1877, the son of John Fleure (1803-90) an accountant and Marie (née Le Rougetel) his wife. He was blind in one eye and his attendance at the States Intermediate School, Guernsey, 1885-91, was irregular because of poor health. Despite illness he continued his studies at home, learning from books and his natural environment; he passed the London matriculation examination in 1894 and London Intermediate B.Sc. in 1897. In Sept. 1897 he gained a scholarship to Aberystwyth, where he became a founder member of the Student Representative Council, published articles in the college magazine and obtained a first-class honours degree in zoology in 1901. The University of Wales awarded him a fellowship enabling him to go to Zürich, Switzerland, to study marine biology. Whilst there he mastered German (he was already fluent in French), and published the results of his research which gained him a D.Sc. degree (Wales). He returned to Aberystwyth in 1904 as a lecturer in zoology, geology and botany. He served as head of the zoology, geology and botany department 1908-10, head of the department of geology for a short period, and Professor of zoology from 1910 till 1917 when he was appointed the first (and only) Professor of anthropology and geography. He left Aberystwyth in 1930 to become the first Professor of geography of Victoria University, Manchester.

In 1905 he began an anthropological study of the Welsh people. He visited villages in all parts of Wales to make a survey and measurements, and give lectures. He reported on his progress to Section H (anthropology) of the British Association for the Advancement of Science in 1907 and (with T. Campbell James) published a report in the journal *Man*, the first of nearly 30 articles by him on anthropology. His epoch-making paper on the geographical distribution of anthropological types in Wales appeared in 1916. He published text books such as *Human geography in Western Europe* (1918), *The Peoples of Europe* (1922) and *Races of England and Wales* (1923), whilst his classic paper *Régions Humanies* which was published in Paris was widely translated. Between 1927 and 1956 he was joint author with H. J. E. Peake of the remarkable series of 10 vols. *The corridors of time* and in the meantime he published *French life and its problems* (1942) and *A natural history of Man in Britain* (1951 and 1959). He did much work for the teaching of geography in schools through his labours for the Geographical Association, of which he was secretary and also editor of its journal *Geography* for 30 years, 1917-47. He became president of many learned bodies, including the Cambrian Archaeological Association in 1924, while universities and scientific societies honoured him wherever he went; he was elected F.R.S. in 1936. But it was as a teacher that he was best remembered, his approach being thought-provoking rather than overlaid with facts.

In 1910 he m. Hilda Mary Bishop of Guernsey, formerly a student at Aberystwyth, and they had 3 children. On retirement in 1944 he moved to London and later to 66 West Drive, Cheam, Surrey, where he d. 1 July 1969.

Biog. Memoirs Fellows R.S., 16, 253-70 (see 271-8 for his bibliography); *Www*.

M.A.J.

FOSTER, IVOR LLEWELYN (1870-1959), singer; b. at Tramroad, Pontypridd, 1 March 1870, son of Ebenezer Foster and Sarah (née John) of Pen-y-graig, Rhondda, Glamorgan. He left school at the age of 12, and when he was 16 and working in a business with his uncle, William Richards, Dinas, Rhondda, he started to learn old notation in his spare time and competed in *eisteddfodau*. He won singing prizes at the Porth annual *eisteddfod* in 1892, 1893 and 1894, and twice on the baritone solo in the national *eisteddfod* (Caernarfon 1894 and Llanelli 1895). Following his success in Llanelli some of his friends in the Rhondda arranged concerts for him to help him to obtain tuition in music; he went to the Royal College of Music in London in May 1896 and he was there for four years studying voice with Henry Blower, harmony with James Higgs and opera with Villiers Stanford. He won a gold medal during his first year and before the end of the course Sir Hubert Parry said that he was one of the best baritones to have studied in the college. He portrayed the character Don Pedro in a performance of Standford's Opera *Much ado about nothing* at Covent Garden in 1901. Later he sang in the promenade concerts and in Boosey's ballad concerts in London and he appeared over 27 consecutive seasons in the Royal Albert Hall. He also sang in musical festivals, including the Cardiff festivals on three occasions and he recorded Welsh songs on the Winner label. After retiring from public performances he set up as a music teacher.

He m., 29 May 1897, Mary Ann Jones, Tonypandy (she d. 1971). He d. in his home at Porth-cawl 29 Mar. 1959 and was cremated at Llanishen, Cardiff. In 1962 his family gave £300 to set up memorial prizes in his name in the open baritone and the baritone under 25 competitions in the National *Eisteddfod*.

Www; Cerddor, May 1902; information from his son, Rupert Foster, Porth-cawl.

H.W.

FOULKES, ANNIE (1877-1962), editor of an anthology; b. 24 Mar. 1877 at Llanberis, Caerns. Her father, Edward Foulkes (1850-1917), was an official at Dinorwig slate quarry, a man of wide literary culture and author of a number of articles in Welsh periodicals on 19th-c. English writers: Robert Williams Parry (see below) wrote a sonnet in memory of him. She was educated at Dr. Williams' School, Dolgellau, and at *Collège de Jeunes Filles* in Saumur, France, 1896-97. She was a French teacher at Bray, Co. Wicklow, 1897, at Tregaron county school, 1898-1905, and Barry county school, 1905-18. In 1918 she was appointed Executive Secretary of the Appointments Board of the University of Wales, to succeed Robert Silyn Roberts (*DWB*, 878-9). At Barry she was a member of a literary circle which formed around Thomas Jones, C.H. (see below) and Silyn – the group behind the establishment of *The Welsh Outlook*. Thomas Jones believed there was a need for an anthology of modern Welsh poetry and suggested that Annie Foulkes should edit it. The anthology appeared in 1918 under the title *Telyn y dydd*, as one of the volumes of the series 'Cyfres yr Enfys'. It became very popular, particularly in schools – a fourth edition was published in 1929. Annie Foulkes d. unmarried at Caernarfon 12 Nov. 1862 aged 85 yrs.

The papers of Annie Foulkes and her father at Bangor College Library (Bangor MSS. 16040-16410, 16590-16668); *Caerns. & Denb. Herald*, 16 and 23 Nov. 1962 (under Caernarfon).

B.L.J.

FOX, Sir CYRIL FRED (1882-1967), Director of the National Museum of Wales, 1926-48; b. 1882 son of C. Fred Fox, F.S.A., Bursledon, Hampshire, and his wife. He was educated at Christ's Hospital, Horsham. After leaving school at 16 he was trained as a vegetable gardener, eventually moving to Worthing, Sussex, where he met Louis Cobett, a pathologist on the staff of the Royal Commission on Tuberculosis, who persuaded him to become a clerk on the staff of the Commission at Stanstead, Essex. When the commission finished its work, about 1912, some of its members set up a research station at Cambridge and Fox was appointed to take care of its administration until the Ministry of Agriculture took control of it. He was now without work and some of his friends at Cambridge arranged for him to register for a degree course at Magdalene College, Cambridge, but at the end of his first year, 'in a most unusual and skilful academic move' he did not complete his degree scheme but was transferred under the title 'pre-fellow' to carry out research work in the same college and to assist in the university museum of archaeology and anthropology. He gained his Ph.D. with work published as *The archaeology of the Cambridge region* (Cambridge, 1922).

In 1922 when R.E. Mortimer Wheeler, Keeper of the department of archaeology of the National Museum of Wales, Cardiff, was made Director of the museum, his former post became vacant. Although there was pressure to appoint an archaeologist with a Welsh background, Wheeler recommended Fox for the post and he was appointed. When Wheeler left in 1926 to take up a post in London, Fox was appointed in his place as Director of the National Museum of Wales.

During his time as Director, Fox continued to work in the field of archaeology and the Museum published several of his works, amongst them *The personality of Britain* (1932), *A find of the early Iron Age, Anglesey* (1946) and (with Lord Raglan) *Monmouthshire houses* (1951-54). He also surveyed Offa's Dyke, the results of which were published in issues of *Arch. Camb.* After his retirement the Museum published his *Pattern and purpose: a study of early Celtic art in Britain* (1958). He received many honours; amongst them, knighthood (1935), F.B.A. (1940), G.T. Clarke award (1946), president (1944-49) of the Society of Antiquarians of London and its gold medal (1952), honorary D.Litt. University of Wales (1947), president of the Museums Association (1933-34), president of the Cambrian Archaeological Society (1933), honorary fellow of Magdalene College, Cambridge (1953).

He married twice: (1) Olive Congreve-Pridgeon (d. 1932), they had two daughters; (2) Aileen Mary Scott-Henderson, they had three sons. After retiring, he lived in Exeter and died there 16 Jan. 1967.

Personal acquaintance; article by Sir Mortimer Wheeler, *Homage to Sir Cyril Fox*, 1-6 and a full bibliography, 502-12, in the *Festschrift, Culture and environment* (1963).

I.C.P.

FRANCIS, JOHN OSWALD (1882-1956), dramatist; b. 7 Sept. 1882, son of David Francis, Dowlais, Glam. and Dorothy (née Evans) his wife. He was one of the first pupils at Merthyr Tydfil Intermediate School and graduated at Aberystwyth and the Sorbonne, before becoming a school teacher at Ebbw Vale county school and later at Holborn Estate grammar school, London. After military service during World War I he entered the Civil Service and was an official of the National Savings Movement when he retired *c.* 1953, having received an M.B.E. for his work. But it is for his notable contribution to the revival of interest in drama in Wales that he is remembered. R.G. Berry (see above) and David Thomas Davies (see above) were contemporary playwrights. About 1910 he started writing plays for the Aberystwyth Old Students' Association. *The Poacher*, which was first staged in Aberystwyth in 1914, was a great achievement, showing his ability to create characters of the Welsh countryside. His comedy *Birds of a feather* had a remarkably successful run at the London Coliseum, 1914-18, and was performed in many parts of the world up to his death. *Howell of Gwent* (1934) was a massive historical piece which was performed in Wales and London by the Welsh National Theatre Company. One of his finest works was *The dark little people* (1922), though his best work was probably the full-length play *Change* (1913), a powerful drama of the industrial scene in Wales which won for him the Howard de Walden prize (see Scott-Ellis below). Many of his plays were translated into Welsh and he learnt to speak the language in middle-age. His essays were published in *The legend of Wales* (1924) and he wrote a short history of U.C.W., Aberystwyth. He was a distinguished dramatist

who could evoke laughter and tears in alternate moments but he was humble about his own gifts and was always surprised that his one-act plays should have won emphatic success on the British stage. The University of Wales conferred on him an honorary M.A. degree.

When he was over 70 years of age he took up the sport of gliding. He d. a bachelor on 1 Oct. 1956 at 13 Dingwall Gardens, Golders Green, London, where he lived with one of his sisters.

WwW (1921); *Ddinas*, Nov. 1954, Nov. 1956; *Times*, 2 Oct. 1956, 10; *Liv.D.P.*, 2 Oct. 1956.

M.A.J.

FREEMAN, KATHLEEN ('Mary Fitt'; 1897-1959), classical scholar and writer; b. at Cardiff 22 June 1897, only child of Charles Henry Freeman, Birkenhead, and his wife Catharine (née Mawdesley), Southport. She was educated at Canton High School for Girls and the University College of South Wales, Cardiff, where she graduated B.A. in classics in 1918, and was awarded her M.A. in 1922 and D.Litt. in 1940. She was appointed lecturer in Greek at the college in 1919, and first published her research in classical studies and then wrote a number of experimental novels. There was a clear interval in her published work between 1929 and 1936. When she resumed publication of serious works it was under the stress of war, her other energies having been directed at that time to the writing of detective fiction, which she published under the pseudonym of 'Mary Fitt'. During the war (1939-45) she lectured for the Ministry of Information and took part in the National Scheme of Education for H.M. Forces in south Wales. On 1 Oct. 1946, when a senior lecturer in her department, she resigned to devote her time to travel, research and writing. In 1951 she was elected Chairman of the Philosophical Society of Great Britain and in the same year was admitted to the Detection Club, a much-coveted honour amongst writers of detective fiction. She d. aged 61 on 21 Feb. 1959 at her home at Lark's Rise, St. Mellons.

As Kathleen Freeman she wrote: *The work and life of Solon* (1926), *The intruder and other stories* (1926), *Martin Hanner: A comedy* (1926), *Quarrelling with Lois* (1928), *This love* (1929), *It has all happened before, What the Greeks thought of their Nazis* (1941), *Voices of freedom* (1943), *What they said at the time: a survey of the causes of the second World War* (1945), *The murder of Herodes and other trials from the Athenian law courts* (1946), *Ancilla to the pre-Socratic philosophers, a complete translation of the fragments in Diel's Fragmente der Vorsokratiker* (1946), *The Greek way: an anthology* (1947), translations from verse and prose, *The Philoctetes of Sophocles: a modern version* (1948), *Greek city states* (1950), *God, man and the state: Greek concepts* (1952), *The paths of justice* (1954), *The Sophists* (1954) translated from the Italian of M. Untersteiner's *I sofisti*, *T'other Miss Austen* (1956) and *If any man build: The history of the Save the Children Fund* (1965) published posthumously.

Www; *West. Mail*, 23 Feb. 1959; *Times*, 24 Feb. 1959.

R.M.

FYNES-CLINTON, OSBERT HENRY (1869-1941), Professor of French and Romance Philology at the University College of North Wales, Bangor; b. 9 Nov. 1869, son of the Rev. Osbert Fynes-Clinton, rector of Barlow Moor, Didsbury. A graduate of St. John's College, Oxford, he was elected Taylorian Scholar of the University in Spanish in 1892. He was French master at King Edward's School, Aston, Birmingham from 1896 to 1904, when he was appointed Professor of French and Romance Philology at the University College of North Wales, a position which he held until 1937 when he retired and was appointed Professor Emeritus. A brilliant linguist, he devoted his leisure hours to a meticulous study of the Arfon dialect of Welsh, and in 1913 published *The Welsh Vocabulary of the Bangor District*, which secured for him a place of honour in the history of Welsh linguistics, being the only comprehensive phonetic study of the vocabulary of a Welsh dialect hitherto published. In recognition of his work the University of Wales in 1939 conferred on him the honorary degree of D.Litt. He d. 9 Aug. 1941.

Www, 1941-50; North Wales Chronicle, 15 and 22 Aug. 1941.

E.G.J.

G

GABE, RHYS THOMAS (REES THOMAS GAPE; 1880-1967), rugby player; b. 22 June 1880 in Llangennech, Carms. He played locally before representing Llanelli for the first time when he was 17 yrs. old. He won the first of his 24 caps (1901-08) on the wing against Ireland on 21 Mar. 1901. It was as a centre that he gained fame. He possessed all the skills; he was unyielding in defence, when attacking he ran straight and with determination. Deceptive, firm and boney, he was difficult to tackle. In 1901 he began a teachers' training course at Borough Road College, London, and played for a period with London Welsh. After travelling to Australia with the British team in 1904, he returned to be a teacher in Cardiff, and scored 51 tries in 115 games for the city's club before resigning in 1908. He made a key contribution to the historic Welsh win (3-0) against the All Blacks in 1905, and with Erith Gwyn Nicholls (*DWB*, 685), William ('Willie') Morris Llewellyn and Edward ('E.T.') Morgan (see below) he formed the most brilliant three-quarter line that ever played for Wales. He d. 15 Sept. 1967 at Cardiff.

W. Thomas, *A century of Welsh rugby players* (1980); David Smith and Gareth Williams, *Fields of praise* (1980); *West. Mail* and *Times*, 18 Sept. 1967.

G.W.W.

GAPE, REES THOMAS – see GABE, RHYS THOMAS above.

GARRO JONES, GEORGE MORGAN – see TREFGARNE, GEORGE MORGAN below.

GEORGE (FAMILY), Cricieth – see LLOYD GEORGE (FAMILY) below.

GEORGE, DAVID LLOYD – see LLOYD GEORGE, DAVID below.

GEORGE, WILLIAM (1865-1967), solicitor and public figure; b. at Highgate, Llanystumdwy, Caerns., 23 Feb. 1865, the youngest child of William George, schoolmaster (he d. 7 June 1864) and Elisabeth his wife (née Lloyd, 1828-1896), and a brother to David Lloyd George (see LLOYD GEORGE, David below), and Mary Elin. His father died before he was born and his uncle, Richard Lloyd, his mother's brother (1834-1917) had a profound influence on the formation of his character and on his attitude towards the world and its events. He was educated at the National School, Llanystumdwy, but his uncle and his mother refused to let him train as a pupil-teacher. The family moved to Cricieth in 1880. William George took articles in 1882 and succeeded in his final examination with honours and was fourth in the first class, a considerable achievement for one who had not received a college or high school education. He joined his brother in practice in the business that he established in Cricieth in 1885 and the partnership of Lloyd George & George became well known when they won the 'Llanfrothen Cemetery' case in the Appeal Court on 15 Dec. 1888. When David Lloyd George was elected to

Parliament in 1890 members were not paid a salary and William agreed that his brother should give most of his time to his political activities and he drew an income from the partnership for many years. It was William also who set up a home for his mother, Uncle Richard, his sister and himself, setting aside for the time any idea of marrying in order to fulfil these responsibilities. David's reliance on the partnership came to an end when he was appointed President of the Board of Trade in Dec. 1905 and William was then able to give more of his time to public affairs.

He was first elected to Caernarfon County Council in 1907 and he remained a member until 1967 and was chairman in 1911. He chaired the county education committee from 1916 to 1948 and as the chairman of the Central Welsh Board and a leader in educational circles in Wales he was able to implement some of the policies that he believed would protect the Welsh language and religion in Wales. He was ahead of his time in securing the status of Welsh in legislation and public administration; he translated the Insurance Act of 1911 into Welsh and published it as a booklet with a list of legal terms in Welsh as an appendix. He chaired the National Union of Welsh Societies that was set up in 1913 and during his period in office a national petition was arranged (1938) to try to obtain appropriate status for the Welsh language in the country, a campaign that led to the Welsh Courts Act 1942. He did much to encourage co-operation between county councils in Wales, particularly in education, and he was a firm believer in setting up a national educational council for Wales. He was a member of the deputation to the Minister of Education in 1920 to seek support for this policy. As Chairman of the Central Welsh Board, he made the suggestion that two pupils from secondary schools in every county should spend a week at the National *Eisteddfod* as guests of a fund that was set up with the proceeds from selling the offices of the Central Welsh Board in 1944.

He was the honorary solicitor of the court and council of the National *Eisteddfod* from 1937 to 1956 and he made every effort to unite the *Gorsedd* of Bards and the National *Eisteddfod* Society and he was elected a Fellow of the *Eisteddfod* in 1956. He also published material for children, *Llyfr y cyfarfod plant* (1908). He received an honorary LL.D. from the University of Wales in 1947 and the National *Eisteddfod* presented him with an address on vellum to mark his hundredth birthday. He was a member of Penymaes Chapel (Scottish Baptists, Disciples of Christ) and Berea (B) Cricieth and he received the Gee medal.

He was very able intellectually and he had the ability to express himself concisely and confidently. Without his self-sacrifice it is difficult to see how David Lloyd George could have developed into a professional politician so early in his career. The letters between them show that David placed great importance on William's judgement on current topics and that impression is reflected in his speeches. He published

My Brother and I (1958), *Atgoff a Myfyr* (1948) and *Richard Lloyd* (1934). He m. Anita Williams from Fishguard in 1910; she d. 1943. They had twin sons but one died in infancy. He d. at Cricieth 25 Jan. 1967 and he was buried at Cricieth public cemetery.

The sources named; W.R.P. George, *The Making of Lloyd George* (1976); William George papers in N.L.W.; personal information.

W.R.P.G.

GITTINS, CHARLES EDWARD (1908-70), educationalist; b. in Rhostyllen, near Wrexham, Denb., 24 Jan. 1908, son of Charles Thomas and Frances (née Rabbit) Gittins. He was educated at Bersham Boys' School, Wrexham, 1920-25, and at the University College of Wales, 1925-31. He entered energetically into student life at Aberystwyth, and became president of the Debates Union and of the Students' Representative Council. He graduated in 1928 with a well-merited first class in History, and then pursued the secondary school training course in the department of Education leading to the University of Wales Diploma in Education in 1929. From 1929 to 1931 he held the Eyton Williams postgraduate studentship which led to his Master's degree with a dissertation on 'Condorcet as an educationalist' in 1935. During this period he represented Wales three times at the Geneva Postgraduate School.

The years from 1932 to 1945 took him to the north-east of England, where he gained teaching and administrative experience as senior history master at King James' Grammar School at Bishop Auckland, 1932-38, being deputy headmaster from 1937, assistant officer for secondary and higher education for the county of Durham in 1938 and deputy director of education for the West Riding of Yorkshire in 1942. As tutor under the University of Durham he had experience of extra-mural and W.E.A. work.

In 1945 he became director of education for Monmouthshire and for the rest of his life he applied his rich academic training, his practical experience and his extraordinary energy unsparingly towards education and public service in Wales. From 1956 to 1970 he found a larger field for his leadership and influence as professor and dean of the faculty of Education at University College, Swansea. From 1966 to 1970 he was vice-principal of the college, and in order to devote his energies more fully to that office he gave up the headship of the department of Education over the last two years of his term. His tact and wisdom in the administration of college affairs won for him the admiration and the willing co-operation of students and staff. Under his guidance the department of Education grew in importance and widened its academic and training appeal. He became involved in national committees on youth activities and youth employment services. He was a member of the Welsh Joint Education Committee, the executive committee of the National Foundation for Educational Research, a governor of the National College for the Training of Youth Leaders, chairman of the Statutory Committee on Youth Employment, treasurer of the Standing Conference of Studies in Education, a member of the Local Government Boundary Commission for Wales

under the chairmanship of Sir Guildhaume Myrddin-Evans (see below), a member of the Swansea Art Galleries Committee, and a member of the Educational Advisory Council of the I.T.A., the Schools Broadcasting Council, the Welsh Committee of the Arts Council, etc. He acted as external examiner in education for several English universities. His inaugural lecture, *Educational Opportunity* (1957) was published and he edited *Pioneers of Welsh Education* (1954).

He was chairman of the Central Council on Education (Wales) which was commissioned by Sir Edward Boyle in 1963 to consider the whole subject of primary education in Wales. The report was published in 1967 in Welsh and English editions. It has become known as the 'Gittins Report' and is an important document in the history of Welsh education, which recommended the principle of a completely bilingual system of education in the schools of Wales in as much as the Welsh language is the medium for an important part of the historic tradition of Wales. Gittins always stressed the importance of the 'language of the hearth' and of the heart. Concurrently he was a member of the corresponding English Council under the chairmanship of Lord Plowden. Gittins firmly believed with Condorcet that 'education is the need of all' and that 'Society owes it equally to all its members'. He was made C.B.E. in 1968.

He m. on 28 Dec. 1934, Margaret Anne, dau. of John Lloyd Davies and Eliza Mary (née Wheale), in Llanfaredd church, Radnorshire, and they had a son and daughter. He d. as the result of an accident during a fishing trip at Oxwich Bay on 6 Aug. 1970, and was cremated following a funeral service at St. Teilo's church, Bishopston, Gower.

Information from his widow; *West. Mail*, 7 Aug. 1970; *Times*, 7 and 14 Aug. 1970.

E.D.J.

GLAN BARLWYD – see DAVID JONES under JONES, JOHN WILLIAM below.

GLAN RHYDDALLT – see LLOYD, ISAAC SAMUEL below.

GLANBERACH – see MORGAN, JOHN JENKYN (1875-1961) below.

GLASGOED – see HUGHES, OWEN (1879-1947) below.

GLENN, THOMAS ALLEN (1864-1948), soldier, historian, genealogist, and archaeologist; b. 8 Jan. 1864 in Pennsylvania, the son of Edward and Sarah Catherine Glenn, British subjects. Glenn had a distinguished military career both in America and in Britain. By 1903 he was a Lieutenant-Colonel in the American army, but he resigned from the U.S.A. services in 1905 and came to reside in Wales. He served as an officer in World War I and held a commission in the Home Guard in World War II. As an author he had an American period and a Welsh period, during both of which his genealogical works are noteworthy. After he came to live in Wales (at Newmarket, Meliden, Prestatyn, and, last of all, at Abergele) he shared his labours between archaeology (he was prominently connected with the Dyserth and District Field Club and the Cambrian Archaeological Association) and the history of some of the older Welsh families. In the latter work he was particularly skilled, for he was a tireless searcher into original records and a careful copyist. In addition, he possessed considerable ability as an amateur artist, as attested by his work in making armorial shields, etc.

Glenn m., 1904, Meenie Mary, dau. of Robert H. and Jessie Tothill; they had two daughters. He d. at Abergele, 30 Jan. 1948; his widow d. 4 Sept. 1949.

Besides articles in periodicals (*Archaeologia Cambrensis*, etc.) Glenn was the author of several books and monographs including *Merion in the Welsh Tract ... [Pennsylvania]* (Norristown, 1896); *Some colonial mansions and those who lived in them* (Philadelphia, 1st series, 1899, 2nd series, 1900); *Welsh Founders of Pennsylvania*, 2 vols., (Oxford, 1911); *Newmarket notes (Prestatyn Hundred, Flintshire)*, Parts 1 & 2 (Prestatyn 1911, 1912); *Northern Flintshire, historical, genealogical and archaeological*, Vol. I, Parts 1-3 (Horncastle, 1913); (with Lord Mostyn), *History of the Family of Mostyn of Mostyn* (1925); *The Family of Griffith of Garn and Plasnewydd in the County of Denbigh* (London, 1934).

Most of his genealogical and other manuscripts are in the National Library of Wales, N.L.W. MSS. 763-4, 1112-1114, 4417, 6341, 6737, 6990, 14015, etc.; personal knowledge.

W.Ll.D.

GLYNNE, WALTER – see WALTERS, THOMAS GLYN below.

GOMERIAN – see DAVIES, ROBERT HUMPHREY above.

GOODWIN, GERAINT (1903-41), author; the son of Richard and Mary Jane Goodwin, he was b. at Llanllwchaearn, Mont., 1 May 1903. He attended Towyn County School, and from 1922 to 1938 lived by journalism and authorship in London. In 1932 he m. Rhoda Margaret, dau. of Harold Storey. His first books were *Conversations with George Moore* (1929) and the semi-autobiographical *Call Back Yesterday* (1935). He then turned to fiction and Welsh subjects, with *The Heyday in the Blood* (1936), *The White Farm*, (short stories; 1937), *Watch for the Morning* (1938), and *Come Michaelmas* (1939). His stories of Wales and the Border are vivid and earthy. After his return to Wales he lived in Upper Corris and then in Montgomery, where he d. 10 Oct. 1941.

Personal knowledge; [Sam Adams, *Geraint Goodwin* (1975). Sam Adams and Roland Mathias, *Collected Stories* (1976)].

G.J.

GORE, WILLIAM GEORGE ARTHUR ORMS-BY – see ORMSBY-GORE, WILLIAM GEORGE ARTHUR below.

GREEN, CHARLES ALFRED HOWELL (1864-1944), second Archbishop of Wales, and eldest son of A.J.M. Green, clerk in Holy Orders, and Elizabeth his wife, was born at Llanelli, Carms., 19 Aug. 1864. On his mother's side he was a great-great-grandson of Peter Williams (1723-96; *DWB*, 1063). He was educated at Charterhouse and Keble College, Oxford, where he graduated B.A. in 1887 and M.A. in 1892. He was successively Librarian and President of the Oxford Union Society. He was ordained deacon in 1888 and priest in 1889, and served as curate and subsequently (1893) vicar of Aberdare until his appointment as canon of Llandaff Cathedral and Archdeacon of Monmouth in 1914. On the formation of the diocese of Monmouth in 1921 he became its first bishop, and was translated to Bangor in 1928. On the retirement of A.G. Edwards (*DWB*, 184) in 1934 he was elected Archbishop of Wales, which office he held till a month before his death on May 7, 1944. He was buried at Llandaff. He held the degrees of B.D. (1907), D.D. (1911), and D.C.L. (1938), of the University of Oxford and was an Honorary Fellow of Keble College. He was the author of *Notes on Churches in the Diocese of Llandaff* (1907) and *The Constitution of the Church in Wales* (1937). He m. in 1899 Katherine Mary, dau. of William Thomas Lewis, first Lord Merthyr (*DWB*, 564), who survived him.

Times, 8 May 1944; personal knowledge; [*Who Was Who*, 1941-50].

T.I.E.

GREEN, FRANCIS (1854-1942), antiquary; b. at Carmarthen, 15 Dec. 1854, the eldest s. of Francis Green, Oaklands, and his wife, Elizabeth (née Harries) of Tre-facwn near Tre-fin. He was educated at a Moravian school at Pendine, the chapter school at St. David's, and Shrewsbury School. After studying law in London, and working in his father's office, he emigrated to Canada in 1878 where he was engaged in farming until he returned to London to work in the office of *The Financial Times*. He returned to St. David's in 1907 and spent the remainder of his long life in antiquarian research in which he acquired a great reputation. He edited the *West Wales Historical Records*, and calendared *The Coleman Deeds* (1921), *The Crosswood Deeds* (1927) and *The Hawarden Deeds* (1931) in the National Library of Wales, but his calendar of the Peniarth Deeds remains unpublished. He contributed important papers on the history of Pembrokeshire in *Y Cymmrodor* and the *Trans. Cymmr*. Many of his manuscripts are preserved in the county library at Haverfordwest and there are copies in the National Library. He d. 6 Aug. 1942, at St. David's.

Information supplied by his niece, Miss Green of St. David's, and by the county librarian of Pembrokeshire; personal acquaintance.

J.J.E.

GREENLY, EDWARD (1861-1951), geologist; b. 3 Dec. 1861 in Bristol, the son of Charles H. Greenly and his wife Harriet. After attending Clifton College, Bristol, he spent some time as an articled clerk in the office of a London solicitor, but left so that he could study at University College London. He joined H.M. Geological Survey (Scotland) in 1889 but in 1895 he resigned and began his self-imposed and lifelong task, a new geological survey of Anglesey. He m. Annie Barnard in 1891 (she d. 1927) and they worked together on the task until its completion in 1910. *The geology of Anglesey*, two vols., was published in 1919 and the 1 inch map in 1920. The work was later extended to Arfon. He publ. (with Howel Williams) *Methods of geological surveying* (1930) and his autobiography, *A hand through time*, appeared in 1938. He was awarded the Lyell Medal of the Geological Soc. in 1920, the Medal of the Liverpool Geol. Soc. in 1933. He was made D.Sc. *hon. causa* Un. of Wales in 1920. He d. at Bangor 4 Mar. 1951.

Www; Nature, 167, 545-6.

B.F.R.

GRIFFITH, GRACE WYNNE (1888-1963), novelist; b. Feb. 1888 in Newborough, Anglesey, daughter of Captain W.G. Roberts. Elizabeth Ann Williams, author of *Hanes Môn yn y bedwaredd ganrif ar bymtheg* (1927) was her sister. She was educated in Caernarfon county school. In the early years of the 20th c. she was a nurse in Liverpool, and it was there that she met Griffith Wynne Griffith (see below); they were m. in 1914. She d. 1 May 1963. She came into prominence in 1934 when she shared a prize for a novel with Kate Roberts in the national *eisteddfod* at Neath, and it was published in 1935 under the title *Creigiau Milgwyn* – Kate Roberts' novel was *Traed mewn cyffion*. *Creigiau Milgwyn* was reviewed by T.J. Morgan who thoroughly criticised the novel and roundly condemned the adjudicator (Dr. Tom Richards, see below) for awarding her the prize.

Llenor, 1936, 48-55; Dafydd Jenkins, *Y Nofel* (1948), 23; information from her son, Huw Wynne Griffith.

G.M.R.

GRIFFITH, GRIFFITH WYNNE (1883-1967), minister (Presb.) and author; b. 4 Feb. 1883 in Brynteci, Llandyfrydog, Anglesey, son of John and Judith Griffith. He worked on his father's farm until he was 18 years old when he went to the school kept by Cynffig Davies (*DWB*, 124) in Menai Bridge, to prepare himself for the ministry. He was accepted as a candidate for the ministry by the Anglesey Presbytery in 1903. He was educated in the University College Bangor (where he graduated in philosophy), and in the Theological College at Bala (where he graduated in theology). He also went for a period (1909) to Jesus College, Oxford. He was ord. in 1911, and ministered in Bryn-du, Anglesey (1910-13), Douglas Rd., Liverpool (1913-23), Tabernacl, Porthmadog (1923-29), and Tabernacl, Bangor (1929-46). He m., 1914, Grace Roberts (see above), of Dwyran, Anglesey; they had two sons and a daughter. After retiring he lived in Llanfair Pwllgwyngyll. He d. 2 Feb. 1967 in his son's home, Huw Wynne Griffith, a minister (Presb.) in Aberystwyth, and was buried in Dwyran chapel graveyard, Anglesey.

He was an elegant and powerful preacher in his day, and became one of the leaders of his denomination. He was Moderator of the Association in the North (1952), and of the General Assembly (1959). He delivered the Davies Lecture in 1942, which was published in 1946 under the title *Datblygiad a Datguddiad*. He was chief editor of *Y Cyfarwyddwr* (1929-30), and an assistant editor of the same journal 1931-44. He was also editor of *Y Goleuad* (1949-57). He

was secretary of the committee which prepared the Welsh 'short confession of faith', and the book of services, *Llyfr gwasanaeth* (1958). He was a member of the committee for the new Welsh translation of the Bible, and of the Council and Court of governors of the University College, Bangor. He contributed articles to *Y Geiriadur Beiblaidd* (1926), and to *The Dictionary of Welsh Biography*. He published two novels, *Helynt Coed y Gell* (1928) and *Helynt Ynys Gain* (1939), and a number of other books: *Paul y cenhadwr* (1925), *Rhai o gymeriadau'r Hen Destament* (1927), *Y Groes* (1943), *The Wonderful Life* (1941), *Ffynnon Bethlehem* (1948), and a biography of Helen Rowlands (see below; 1961). During his last years he composed and translated many hymns, and published a collection of them, *Odlau'r Efengyl*, in 1959. Chapters of his autobiography appeared in *Y Goleuad*, and during the year of his death they were published under the title *Cofio'r blynyddoedd*. Despite all this activity his compositions as a preacher and author were always polished.

Cofio'r blynyddoedd (1967), passim; *Blwyddiadur MC*, 1968, 280-1; information from his son, the late Huw Wynne Griffith, Aberystwyth.

G.M.R.

GRIFFITH, RICHARD ('Carneddog'; 1861-1947), poet, writer, and journalist; b. 26 Oct. 1861, son of Morris and Mary Griffith in Carneddi, a small mountain farm in the parish of Nantmor, Caerns., and not far from Beddgelert. 'Carneddog' spent the whole of his life up to 1945 (when he and his wife went to live with their son in Hinckley, Leicestershire) in Carneddi, where his ancestors had lived for several generations. He was educated in local schools at Nantmor (under William Ellis) and Beddgelert (under George Thomas). He was a sheep farmer but he became better known as a poet, prose writer, and journalist. An *eisteddfod* competitor early in life, he also began to contribute to Welsh weekly newspapers, e.g. *Baner ac Amserau Cymru*, *Y Genedl Gymreig*, and *Yr Herald Cymraeg*, *c.* 1881; his weekly column ('Manion y Mynydd') in *Yr Herald Cymraeg* was very widely read over a number of years. He contributed articles and notes to *Cymru*, *Bye-Gones*, etc., wrote biographies of Richard Jones Owen ('Glaslyn'; *DWB*, 719), Richard Morris ('Yr Hên Lanc'), 'Tegfelyn', and John Jones ('Jac Glanygors'; *DWB*, 476); he prepared three selections for reciters (he often adjudicated in *eisteddfodau*) and also published *Blodau'r Gynghanedd, Cerddi Eryri*, and *Ceinion y Cwm*. He had an inexhaustible store of local lore, collected books and manuscripts (see NLW MSS. 7234-53 and 8404), and was always ready to give information to inquirers and to his numerous correspondents – he was, in short, an excellent example of the knowledgeable and cultured country-man writer. He m. 11 Jan. 1889 Catherine, dau. of Cadwaladr Owen, Nantmor and they had 2 sons. He d. 23 May 1947 at Hinckley and was buried at Beddgelert.

Personal knowledge; [*Brython*, 26 May 1921; E. Namora Williams, *Carneddog a'i deulu* (1985); photograph of Carneddog and his wife by Geoff Charles 23/25 May 1947, NLW Charles collection].

R.O.

GRIFFITH, ROBERT DAVID (1877-1958), musician and historian of Welsh congregational singing; b. 19 May 1877, in Cwm-y-glo, Caerns., son of Richard Griffith, a slate quarryman, and Jane (née Williams) his wife. His mother was a cousin of David Roberts ('Alawydd'; *DWB*, 861) and of John Williams ('Gorfyniawc o Arfon'; *DWB*, 1054). After moving to Mynydd Llandygái in 1885, the family returned to Bethesda in 1890, where he, too, obtained employment in Penrhyn quarry. Later he became an office clerk, and finally a commercial traveller until he retired. In 1928 he moved to Old Colwyn where he made his home for the rest of his life.

He received no higher education, but by cultivating himself he became an able musician and a diligent and successful researcher. In 1909 he formed a choir of 80 voices in Bethesda to perform with an orchestra some of the standard oratorios, and in 1921 Bethesda Choral Society was formed under his baton. He later conducted the Colwyn and District Choral Society (1929-36). He also took an interest in orchestral music; he was a zealous member of the Roland Rogers (*DWB*, 889-90) orchestra, and worked hard with the Gwynedd orchestra and Morfa Rhianedd youth orchestra.

Over a long period he was in demand as an adjudicator, a conductor at singing festivals, and a lecturer on musical topics. He also contributed regularly to *Y Traethodydd, Y Goleuad*, and *Y Drysorfa*, and wrote most of the articles about Welsh musicians in the *Dictionary of Welsh Biography down to 1940*. He was chosen to be musical editor of *Trysorfa'r Plant* when J.T. Rees (see below) d., and in 1951 was chairman of the Welsh Folk-song Society. He was mainly responsible for the annual selection of hymn-tunes for the Presbyterian singing festivals, and he served as secretary of the Presbyterian Church of Wales praise committee from its inception till 1958. He did not compose much, apart from a few religious pieces for children and the solo 'Y Sipsi'.

He began researching and writing about Welsh congregational singing about 1920, and contributed articles on the topic to *Y Cerddor*, commencing with the July issue, 1931. In response to an appeal by John Lloyd Williams (see below) he completed his researches to publish the results of his work as a book: *Hanes Canu Cynulleidfaol Cymru* (1948). In 1952 the University of Wales conferred upon him an honorary M.A. degree. He d. in his home in Old Colwyn, 21 Oct. 1958, and was buried in Bronynant graveyard, Colwyn Bay. Some of his manuscripts are preserved in the library of the U.C.N.W., Bangor.

Cerddor, Aug. 1920; *Trys. Plant*, Feb. 1942; J. Sutcliffe Smith, *Impressions of music in Wales* (1948); *Baner*, 6 Nov. 1958; [*Tr.* 2002].

H.W.

GRIFFITH-JONES, EBENEZER (1860-1942), Congregational minister and college principal; b. 5 Feb. 1860 at Merthyr Tydfil, son of the Rev. E. Aeron Jones and Mary Ann, dau. of David Griffiths (1792-1863; *DWB*, 303), missionary to Madagascar. Although he received the best education that was possible at the time he attributed his culture and scholarship mainly to the influence of his father. He went to Carmarthen Presbyterian College, 1875-78, and was an assistant teacher at Swansea, 1879-1880 before going to New College, London (1880-85), where he won many prizes and scholarships; he graduated B.A. (London) in 1882. He ministered in St. John's Wood, 1885-87, Park Chapel, Llanelli, 1887-90, Stroud Green, 1890-98, Balham, 1898-1907; he was principal of the Yorkshire United Independent College, Bradford, 1907-32. He was awarded the degree of D.D. (*honoris causa*) by the University of Edinburgh, was Chairman of the Congregational Union of England and Wales, and Chairman of the Council of Free Churches. He was the author of *The Ascent through Christ, Providence, The Master and his Method, The Economics of Jesus*, and of a large number of articles in theological and philosophical journals. He was a stout Nonconformist with definite opinions and a doughty debater on religious and public questions. He m. Carita (d. 1936) dau. of T. F. Stoner, Elstree, and his wife, and they had 2 children. He d. 22 March 1942.

H. Egl. Ann., v, 342; *Congl. Year Book*, 1942; N.L.W. MS 10328; *Oriel Caerfyrddin*; *Ww*, 1941; *Www.*

J.D.O.

GRIFFITH-JONES, WILLIAM (1895-1961), Independent minister and administrator; b. at Deiniolen, Caern., 2 Nov. 1895, the son of David and Mary Jones, members of Ebenezer Independent Chapel. The ministers at Ebenezer, J. Dyfnallt Owen (see below) and E. Wyn Jones, had a great influence on the young Griffith-Jones. When the family moved to Liverpool, he joined the English church in Great George St. During World War I, he served for two and a half years in Salonica, 1916-19. After his military service, he began to preach and also studied at Manchester University and Lancashire College, a theological college, between 1919 and 1924. Griffith-Jones was ordained in July 1924 at Freemantle Congregational Church, Southampton, where he served as minister until 1936. Besides his work in the church, he was active with the Free Churches and wrote for the press. From 1936 to 1951, he was the minister at the new Emmanuel Church in West Wickham. He became prominent in the Congregational Union of England and Wales and served on the board of the London Missionary Society. He was elected chairman of the London Congregational Union in 1949. He was the Moderator of the Welsh Congregational Churches from 1951 to 1961 and developed a close relationship with religious movements in Wales. At the same time, he was the chairman of the committee for maintaining the ministry with the Congregational Union of England. When he was elected chairman of the English Union in 1958, he became the third Welshman serving in Wales to be given that honour. As chairman, he delivered an address on 'The churches – their witness in the community'. He presided at the discussions which led to the union of Brecon Memorial College and the Congregational section of Carmarthen Presbyterian College; he was the first chairman of Swansea Memorial College.

Short in build, he had a lively mind and wide interests. He was also a powerful preacher, a careful administrator and an able chairman. He m. Annie Kathleen Speakman, 10 Sept. 1925, and they had a son and a daughter. He d. 10 July 1961, after a year-long illness.

Www; Blwyddiadur A., 1962.

E.D.J.

GRIFFITHS, DAVID REES ('Amanwy'; 1882-1953), poet and writer; b. 6 Nov. 1882 in Efail y Betws, near Ammanford, Carms., son of William and Margaret Griffiths (née Morris). One of his brothers was the Rt. Hon. James Griffiths, M.P. He was educated in Betws council school, and went to work in a coal mine when he was 12 years old. He was severely injured in an explosion in Pantyffynnon colliery, where one of his brothers was killed. After the explosion he began to take an interest in literature and competed in local *eisteddfodau*. His poems won him many chairs, and though he failed to win the prize, Cynan judged his poem to be the best in the competition for the crown at Aberafan national *eisteddfod* in 1932: it was published, with the second-best *awdl* by Thomas Parry, in *Cerddi'r Lleiafrif*. He won the prize for a sonnet in Neath national *eisteddfod* in 1934. His early poems were published in *Ambell gainc* (1919), and he edited *Ô lwch y lofa* (1924), a volume of poems by six Carms. colliers.

He left the mines in 1927 to become caretaker of Ammanford county school, where he influenced a number of the school's literary-minded pupils. He was responisble for the Welsh column in *The Amman Valley Chronicle* for many years, and contributed much to it on local matters. He also wrote the column 'O gwm i gwm' for *Y Cymro* for some years. He was elected a deacon of Gellimanwydd Congl. church, and published a tribute to his old minister (Rev. Isaac Cynwyd Evans) under the title *Gweinidog fy ieuenctid* (1945). He broadcast many times and took a leading role in the film *David*, a portrayal of his life. His poetical works – *pryddestau*, songs, sonnets and hymns – were published in *Caneuon Amanwy* in 1956, and were edited by the author of this note. Some of his hymns were published in *Y Caniedydd* (1960). He m. twice: (1) Margaret Morgan of Penygroes; and (2) Mary Davies of Crwys, near Swansea. The son of the first marriage was Gwilym, who had set his mind on taking holy orders in the Church in Wales but d. before realising his hopes. His father took him to South Africa in 1929 but he did not recover his health. Amanwy and his second wife had two daughters. He d. 17 Dec. 1953 in Middlesex Hospital, London, and was buried in Gellimanwydd cemetery, Ammanford. He was an excellent example of the culture of the folk of the anthracite district of Carms. in the first half of the 20th c.

'Camre'i yrfa' in *Caneuon Amanwy* (1956); *Genh.*, 1954, 88-93; personal acquaintance; [Huw Walters in Hywel T. Edwards, ed., *Cwm Aman* (1996), 131-72].

G.M.R.

GRIFFITHS, EVAN THOMAS (1886-1967), teacher, scholar and writer; b. 20 Feb. 1886, in Llanafan, Cards., the son of David and Anne Griffiths; he was baptised on 11 Mar. at Llanafan parish church. He received his early education at Llanafan primary school and the school's records note that he was a pupil-teacher, 1902-04, and a former pupil-teacher, 1905. In Sept. 1904, he was successful at the University of London's matriculation examination and entered the University College of Wales, Aberystwyth, in Sept. 1905. It is on record that, on his departure, the teachers and pupils at Llanafan school gave him a present of books. In 1909, he graduated with first-class honours in French and he was awarded, in 1914, an M.A. of the University of Wales for a textual study: 'The Map-cycle in Italy and especially of the Chantari di Lancilotto, with a short introduction on the history of the Arthurian tradition in Italy'. He also studied at a number of institutes on the continent. During his professional career, he was, in succession, a schoolteacher in London; a lecturer at the University of Manchester; a schoolteacher at Newport, Mon.; the headmaster of Llanfyllin County School; and the headmaster of Barry Grammar School. He retired in 1948 and spent some time, during his retirement, in Australia where he was awarded a D.Litt. degree by the University of Melbourne. He returned to Wales and settled first at Aberaeron and then at Llandre, near Aberystwyth. He d. at Bronglais Hospital, Aberystwyth, on 6 Nov. 1967.

Griffiths published two scholarly works which reflected his interest in French and Italian, i.e., *Oeuvres Poétiques de Jean de Lingendes* (Paris, 1916), and *Li Chantari di Lancilotto* (Oxford, 1924). He also published a number of books containing French exercises for students. In collaboration with William Ll. Davies (see above) he published *The Tutorial Welsh Course, Parts I and II* (in several impressions from 1914). However, he is remembered more for his adaptations and translations into Welsh from the Romance languages and which include the following: *Yr Hogyn Pren neu helyntion Pinocio* (from Italian, 1938); *Cerddi'r Trwbadŵr* (1954); *Calon* (from Italian, 1959); *Platero a minnau* (with T. Ifor Rees, from Spanish, 1961); *Atgofion dyddiau ysgol* (from Italian, 1965); *Cerddi estron* (from several languages, 1966); *Y Sgarff felen a storïau eraill* (from Italian, 1966), and *Y Diriogaeth goll* (from French, 1969). He also published a collection of short stories, *Storïau glannau Ystwyth* (1957). Typescripts and manuscripts of some of his writings are held by N.L.W.

Llanafan parish registers; Llanafan primary school registers; Register of deaths, North Cardiganshire Division; *University of Wales Calendar* (various years); catalogue of printed books, N.L.W.; Glyn Lewis Jones, *Llyfryddiaeth Ceredigion, 1600-1964* (1967); idem, *Llyfryddiaeth Ceredigion, 1964-68* (1970); *Camb. News*, 11 Nov. 1967; NLW Ms. 21689.

G.M.G.

GRIFFITHS, EZER (1888-1962), physicist; b. 28 Nov. 1888 at Aberdare, Glam., one of the nine children and the eldest of the six sons of Abraham Lincoln and Anne Griffiths. He was educated at Aberdare Intermediate School and the University College of South Wales, Cardiff, where he obtained first-class honours in physics, won a research scholarship and was awarded, later, a Fellowship of the University of Wales and a D.Sc. of that University. In 1915, Griffiths joined the National Physical

Laboratory at Teddington where, for the rest of his working life, he studied problems relating to heat. He became a leading authority on heat insulation, evaporation and related matters and his work was of great value to industry. He was a member of the team sent to Australia in 1923 to study the problems involved in transporting apples through the heat of the tropical zones to Britain. Seven years later he went to New Zealand to examine the problems involved in exporting lamb meat to Britain. He was also involved in studying problems linked to vapour trails made by aeroplanes, and he carried out research into the best method of adapting tanks for service in the heat of the Libyan desert during World War II. With R.W. Powell, he was awarded the Moulton Medal for their work on the evaporation of water from surfaces. He was elected F.R.S. in 1926 and appointed O.B.E. in 1950. He retired as the senior Chief Scientific Officer of the physics section of the National Physical Laboratory in 1953.

Griffiths never married and he d. at Teddington on 14 Feb. 1962. Among his publications are *Methods of measuring temperature* (1918; 2nd ed., 1925; 3rd ed., 1947); *Pyrometers* (1926); *Refrigeration principles and practice* (1951), and many scientific papers in his field.

His brothers included Edgar A. Griffiths, a physicist with the South African government, Jenkin Arthur Griffiths, the editor of the *Colliery Guardian*, and Roosevelt Griffiths, a lecturer in metallurgy at the University College, Swansea.

Biog. Memoirs Fellows R.S., 8; *WwW* (1937). [*DNB 1961-70,* 459-60].

E.D.J.

GRIFFITHS, IEUAN – see WILLIAMS, DAVID MATTHEW below.

GRIFFITHS, WILLIAM (1898-1962), bookseller; b. 6 June 1898 at Evanstown, Gilfach-goch, Glam., son of Joseph Griffiths and his wife Margaret Ann (née Williams). He received his early education at Abercerdin elementary school, Evanstown, 1903-11. He worked for some years as a collier and then went to live in London. He took an interest in music and became a student at the Guildhall School of Music, receiving tuition on the violin from teachers such as Jeffrey Pulver and Harold Fairhurst. He was a skilful violinist and played professionally until about 1931. He then joined Foyles, the booksellers in Charing Cross Road, where he was responsible for its Welsh department for about fourteen years. In 1946 he opened his own shop in Cecil Court (Leicester Square) where he established a Welsh bookshop with his three brothers. This was a successful business and he made the shop a popular meeting place for London-Welsh people and it was well known to Celtic scholars and other visitors from various parts of the world. He was prominent in London-Welsh life. He served as the chairman of the Council of the London-Welsh Society and as chairman of the Literary Circle of that society. He edited *Y Ddinas* from Nov. 1956 to Feb. 1959. He was a member of the Council of the Honourable Society of Cymmrodorion for many years and he was elected a member of the Bardic *Gorsedd* under the name of 'Gwilym Cerdin'. He m. Winifred

Irene, daughter of John Kent and his wife Sara (née Rogers) in the parish church of Mentmore, Bucks. 23 Sept. 1933 and they had one daughter. He died in a London hospital on 8 Oct. 1962.

Information from his brother Arthur; *Cymro,* 23 July 1948; *West. Mail,* 9 Oct. 1962, *London Welshman,* Nov. 1962; *Trans. Cymm.,* 1963, 146-7; *Ddinas, passim,* during his editorship; *WWP.*

G.M.G.

GRUFFYDD, WILLIAM JOHN (1881-1954), scholar, poet, critic and editor; b. at Gorffwysfa, Bethel, Caern., 14 Feb. 1881, son of John and Jane Elisabeth Griffith. He was educated at Bethel elementary school and Caernarfon County School, where he was one of the first entrants when the school was opened in 1894. He entered Jesus College, Oxford, in 1899, and read English Literature. In 1904 he was appointed Assistant Master at Beaumaris Grammar School, and in 1906 Lecturer in Celtic under Thomas Powel (*DWB,* 771) at University College, Cardiff. The years 1915-18 he spent as an officer in the navy, and on being demobilised he was appointed Professor to succeed Powel, who had retired in 1918. He remained in the chair until his retirement in 1946. In 1943 he successfully contested the University of Wales seat in Parliament as a Liberal, in spite of having been a prominent member of the Welsh Nationalist Party (as it was then called), defeating Saunders Lewis, the Nationalist Party candidate. He retained the seat until 1950, when university seats were abolished.

Gruffydd's main field of interest as a scholar was the Four Branches of the Mabinogi. As early as 1914 he published a substantial article in the *Transactions of the Cymmrodorion* under the title 'The Mabinogion'. His major contribution, *Math vab Mathonwy,* a discussion of the fourth branch, appeared in 1928, to be followed after a long interval by *Rhiannon* in 1953, in which the first and the third branches were investigated. The aim was to unravel the various strands that had formed the tales and discover how they were linked together.

Another aspect of Gruffydd's scholarship was his study of the history of Welsh literature. His first book was *Llenyddiaeth Cymru o 1450 hyd 1600* (1922), which, in spite of its title, dealt with the strict metre poetry only. Next came *Llenyddiaeth Cymru, Rhyddiaith o 1540 hyd 1660* (1926). Though 'a series of volumes on Welsh Literature' was promised, only these two appeared. They were very useful in schools and colleges. In 1929 Gruffydd edited a reprint of *Perl mewn Adfyd* by Huw Lewys (1595), and a bilingual booklet on Dafydd ap Gwilym appeared in 1935. He published four anthologies of poetry. The first was *Cywyddau Goronwy Owen* (1907). *Y Flodeugerdd Newydd* (1909) was a selection of *cywyddau* of the poets of the gentry, meant as a textbook for students rather than a meticulous work of scholarship. *Blodeuglwm o Englynion* (1920) included, in addition to the *englynion,* an introduction explaining a theory of John Rhŷs (*DWB,* 844) that the *englyn* was an adaptation in Welsh of the Latin elegiac couplet (a theory refuted by J. Morris-Jones (*DWB,* 668) in his *Cerdd Dafod*). In 1931 *Y Flodeugerdd Gymraeg* appeared, an anthology of poetry in the free metres of the period between the seventeenth and the twentieth centuries, with an introduction which is interesting for the light it throws on the principles of literary criticism adopted by the editor. Two lectures were published in pamphlet form – *Ceiriog* (1939) and *Islwyn* (1942).

Gruffydd was better known to his fellow-countrymen as a poet than as a scholar. He competed unsuccessfully for the crown at the national *eisteddfod* at Bangor in 1902 with a poem on the subject 'Trystan ac Esyllt', but was awarded the prize at the London *eisteddfod* of 1909 for his poem on 'Yr Arglwydd Rhys'. Love lyrics by him appeared in the periodical *Cymru* in 1900, and in the same year he and his friend R. Silyn Roberts (*DWB*, 878-9) published a collection of their poems under the title *Telynegion: Caneuon a Cherddi*, Gruffydd's own poems, followed in 1906. In 1923 *Ynys yr Hud a chaneuon eraill* appeared, containing poems written between 1900 and 1922. A selection of the poems which the author wished to preserve entitled *Caniadau* was published by the Gregynog Press in 1932. Gruffydd's poetry varies greatly in style and quality. The early works are often luscious, with echoes of Heine (and some translations) and of the English Romantic poets. There are also early examples, as in 'Cerdd yr Hen Chwarelwr', of his unaffected style. There are instances of steriotyped social comment, as in 'Y Pharisead' and 'Sionyn'. Later Gruffydd developed a more direct idiom and a more truly criticial attitude, as in 'Gwladys Rhys' and 'Thomas Morgan'. It is somewhat surprising that in his final selection for the Gregynog volume in 1932 he included examples both of cloying nostalgia and bitter onslaughts. His best poems are a valuable contribution to Welsh poetry, and the long poem 'Ynys yr Hud' is one of the outstanding products of the twentieth-century revival.

Gruffydd's prose is of a very high order. His style shows none of the striving after effect and the pedantic expressions found in the works of some writers of his period. His best work is *Hen Atgofion*, first published as articles in *Y Llenor* between 1930 and 1935, and in book form in 1936. Four additional chapters, but unfortunately no more, appeared in *Y Llenor* between 1936 and 1941. These reminiscences reflect the author's own personality, the men and women of his native parish and the Welsh people at a crucial time in their history, all conveyed with humour and keen discernment. In *Owen Morgan Edwards: Cofiant* (1937) Gruffydd found a subject and a time and place with which he was in full sympathy, and the work equals *Hen Atgofion* as an achievement.

Y Llenor was first published in 1922 as a quarterly with Gruffydd as editor, a role which he performed with distinction until 1945 when T.J. Morgan became co-editor until the periodical ceased publication in 1951. All the chief writers of Wales in a rich and productive period in the history of Welsh literature contributed. The editor himself was a frequent contributor of articles on literary criticism and of satirical commentaries on aspects of Welsh life. In 1926 he started his 'Editor's Notes', in which he expressed his views on all those topics which worried him and justified his description of himself as Wales's *enfant terrible*. Among the subjects discussed were the preservation of the Welsh language, religion, the Anglicisation of some class-

es in Welsh society, corruption in public life, political protest, broadcasting, education at all levels, and in particular the National *Eisteddfod*. He continually accused the local committees of the *Eisteddfod* of mismanagement, and criticised the prominence given to people who were out of sympathy with Welsh aspirations, and the growing use of English from the platform. When the reform of the *Eisteddfod* was taken in hand in 1935 and the Court and the Council established, Gruffydd played a prominent part in the discussions, and henceforth he was closely associated with the *Eisteddfod*, not only as adjudicator (of the crown poem usually) but also as a member of the Council and as President of the Court from 1945 until his death.

Gruffydd wrote three plays – *Beddau'r Proffwydi*, first performed by members of University College, Cardiff, in 1913, *Dyrchafiad arall i Gymro* (1914) and *Dros y Dŵr* (1928). His translation of Sophocles's *Antigone* was published in 1950. A full bibliography appears in the *Journal of the Welsh Bibliographical Society*, viii, 208-219, ix, 53-4.

He was awarded doctorates *honoris causa* by the University of Rennes (1946) and the University of Wales (1947), and the medal of the Honourable Society of Cymmrodorion (1946). His influence on several aspects of Welsh life was great, although his opinions were often the subject of controversy and disagreement, because they were sometimes forcibly expressed and were always the product of an independent mind, which was at times inconsistent. But he was remarkably consistent in his opposition to injustice and dishonesty, which accounts to some extent for the deep respect and affection in which he was held by his friends, and indeed by all who knew him.

He m. Gwenda, daughter of John Evans, minister, of Abercarn, in 1909. They had separated several years before his death. They had one son. Gruffydd d. 29 Sept. 1954.

Llenor, the Editor's memorial number, 1955; [T. Robin Chapman, *W.J.Gruffydd* (1992); Geraint Bowen, *W.J. Gruffydd* (cyfres Bro a Bywyd, 1994)].

T.P.

GWAENYSGOR, 1st BARON – see MACDONALD, GORDON below.

GWENALLT – see JONES, DAVID JAMES below.

GWILYM AMAN – see JONES, GWILYM RICHARD below.

GWILYM MYRDDIN – see JONES, WILLIAM below.

GWILYM RHONDDA – see THOMAS, WILLIAM PHILLIP below.

GWYNDAF – see DAVIES, GRIFFITH above.

GWYNFOR – see JONES, THOMAS OWEN below.

GWYNNE (FAMILY) of Kilvey, Swansea. RICHARD GWYNNE (1822-1907), schoolmaster; b. Swansea 18 Mar. 1822. He began his career as a compositor but in 1841 trained as a teacher at Gray's Inn Road Model School and

Norwood. The same year he began to teach at Kilvey (Infants) Copperwork School. He subsequently became the headmaster of the Kilvey Copperwork Schools and remained in that post until 1892. Under his headship the Junior School roll increased from under 40 to over 600 and the Kilvey Schools were consistently spoken of by the Inspectors as the best in the Swansea area. He was a keen student of geology and history and was for forty years vice-president of the Royal Institution of South Wales. In 1857 he m. Charlotte Lloyd (1825-1908), at one time the school-mistress of Kilvey. They had five sons and a daughter. When his friends applied for a pension for him in 1891 they pointed out that he had spent all his savings educating his sons. He d. at Langland, 28 November 1907, and was buried in Oystermouth cemetery.

Cambrian, 6 Dec. 1907, *Report on the State of Education in Wales*, 1847; L. Wynne Evans, 'Copper-Works Schools in South Wales during the Nineteenth Century', *National Library of Wales Journal*, XI (1959-60), 1-32; Grenfell Papers, Swansea University College Library.

Two sons achieved national fame:
Rt. Rev. LLEWELLYN HENRY GWYNNE (1863-1957), bishop, C.M.G. 1917; C.B.E. 1919; D.D. Glasgow 1919; LL.D. Cambridge, 1920; b. Kilvey, 11 June 1863. Educated at Swansea Grammar School and St. John's Hall, Highbury. Curate of St. Chad's, Derby, 1886-89, and St. Andrew's, Nottingham, 1889-92. While at Derby he played for Derby County Football Club, the only amateur in the team. Vicar of Emmanuel, Nottingham, 1892-99. In the latter year he went as a missionary to the Sudan, working for the C.M.S. In 1908 he became the first suffragan Bishop of Khartoum, then part of the diocese of Jerusalem. When World War I broke out he went to France as a volunteer chaplain and was appointed Deputy Chaplain General there in August 1915. He was frequently in the front line. One of his assistants, Dr. F.R. Barry, later Bishop of Southwell, describes him as a saint but adds, 'Yet in all my life I have never encountered anybody less like a saint in painted windows. A burly man, and a Welsh footballer, he was every inch masculine, a man's man.' After the war he could have had many preferments but he chose to return to the Sudan. When the diocese of Jerusalem was divided in 1920 he became the first Anglican Bishop of Egypt and the Sudan. He continued his work there until he was over eighty, finally retiring in 1946. He was responsible for the building of the Anglican cathedrals in Cairo and Khartoum and ministered to the 8th Army during World War II. He preached in Swansea in the 1950s. He d. 3 Dec. 1957.

Times, 4 Dec. 1957; *Www*, 1951-60; *Crockford*, 1957; F.R. Barry, *Period of my Life* (1970).

HOWELL ARTHUR GWYNNE (1865-1950), journalist, C.H. 1938; b. Kilvey, 3 Sept. 1865. Educated at Swansea Grammar School (Foundation Scholar) and in Switzerland. He was *The Times'* correspondent in the Balkans in the early 1890s. From 1893 to 1904 he was a special correspondent for Reuter's Agency. Whilst in their service he went to Ashanti in 1895,

accompanied Kitchener's expedition to Dongola in 1896, reported the Turko-Greek war of 1897 and Kitchener's expedition to Berber of the same year, and was in Peking at the beginning of the Boxer troubles from Jan. 1898 to May 1899. He was responsible for organising Reuter's services in South Africa during the Boer war. Immediately after the war he returned to South Africa with Joseph Chamberlain, who became a close friend. In 1904 he was briefly foreign director of Reuter's before becoming editor of the *Standard* from 1904 to 1911. He was then editor of the *Morning Post* until its merger with the *Daily Telegraph* in 1937. He was vehement in asserting the editorial independence of the *Morning Post* although he took a strong Tory line on foreign policy, the army and the empire. His personal friendships with Chamberlain, Kitchener, Sir Edward Carson, Haig, Kipling, Alfred Milner and others gave him a certain behind-the-scenes influence. *The Times* spoke of him as 'a talented Welshman' who was 'a little incongruous amid the sober compromises of the English political scene.' He published *The Army on Itself* (1904), and *The Will and the Bill* (1923), the latter a political satire. He m. Edith Douglas, daughter of Thomas Ash Lane, in 1907. There were no children. He d. 26 Jun. 1950.

Times, 27 Jun. 1950; *Www* 1941-50; *DNB Supplement, 1941-50*; W. Hindle, *The Morning Post 1772-1937* (1937); G. Storey, *Reuter's Century, 1851-1951* (1951) (includes photograph); Gwynne MSS, Bodleian Library, Oxford; Swansea Grammar School records, Swansea University College Library.

Two other sons also became clergymen:
RICHARD LLOYD GWYNNE (1859-1941); b. Kilvey, Feb. 1859; educated Swansea Grammar School and London College of Divinity; curate of Barrow, Cheshire, 1882-85, Winsley, Wilts., 1885-86 and St. John, Tunbridge Wells, 1891-1909, rector of Little Easton in the diocese of Chelmsford, 1915-37.

CHARLES BROOKE GWYNNE (1861-1944); b. Kilvey, July 1861; educated at Swansea Grammar School and Christ College, Cambridge, graduating B.A. 1884 and M.A. 1888. He was curate of Timperley, 1885-88 and Christ Church, Claughton, 1888-90; vicar of Holy Trinity with St. Matthews, Birkenhead, 1891-96, Bollington, 1896-1909, Neston, 1909-20, and rector of West Kirby, 1920-32. He was an honorary canon of Chester 1919-34 and canon emeritus thereafter. He was vicar of Wendover Ambo, near Saffron Walden, 1932-33. He was a proctor in Convocation and published *Criticisms on the Consecration Prayer in the New Prayer Book* (1931).

Crockford, 1941 and *Supplement* 1942-44.

M.E.C.

H

HALL, GEORGE HENRY (1881-1965), first Viscount Hall of Cynon Valley (created 1946), politician; b. 31 Dec. 1881 at Penrhiwceiber, Mountain Ash, Glam., son of George Hall (d. 1889), miner, a native of Marshfield, co. Gloucester, and Ann Guard, his wife (d. 1928) who came from Midsomer Norton, near Radstock, Somerset. He was educated at Penrhiwceiber elementary school, but on attaining his twelfth birthday, he was compelled to leave to take up work in the Penrhiwceiber Colliery, so that he could assist his widowed mother, who had been left with a large family to support. This was all the formal education he received. But a prolonged absence from work, following an accident in the colliery, gave him an opportunity for self-education and extensive reading. He worked at the coal face until 1911, when he was appointed colliery checkweighman and local agent of the S.W.M.F. In 1908 he won a seat on the Mountain Ash U.D.C., as the first Labour member for the Penrhiwceiber ward. He remained a member of this body for 18 years, during which he became chairman of both the U.D.C. and of the Education Committee. In the general election of 1922 he was returned as Labour member for the Aberdare division of the Merthyr Borough, defeating the sitting member C.B. Stanton (see below) and retained his seat with large majorities (twice unopposed) until he was elevated to the peerage in 1946. In the 1929 Labour Government he was given office as Civil Lord of the Admiralty. During the years 1931-35 he matured greatly as a parliamentarian. Hitherto he had concentrated mainly on the affairs of the coalmining industry of which he had an expert knowledge, but now, owing to the depleted ranks of his party, he was frequently called upon to speak from the front bench in debates on a variety of topics outside his previous range of interest. He was also a powerful propagandist for his party outside parliament; he waged a vigorous campaign in south Wales in the years 1934-35 against the Means Test regulations. In 1940 he was elected leader of the Welsh Parliamentary Party, but resigned when in May 1940 he took office in the wartime coalition as Parliamentary Under-Secretary of State in the Colonial Office. He was made a P.C. in 1942 and became successively Financial Secretary of the Admiralty, 1942-43 and Parliamentary Under-Secretary of State for Foreign Affairs under Anthony Eden, 1943-45. On the formation of the Labour Government in July 1945 he became Secretary of State for the Colonies and continued in this post until Oct. 1946, when he was made First Lord of the Admiralty. He had acquired a deep and abiding interest in the navy and was very happy in this office but owing to advancing years and indifferent health he decided to retire in May 1951. He was Deputy Leader of the House of Lords, 1947-51, and continued as Deputy Leader of the Labour peers till the end of 1953, when his active involvement in politics virtually ceased.

He was a first-class constituency M.P. Always courteous and approachable, he was ever ready to take up the grievances of his constituents. Aberdare owed a great deal to him for his efforts to attract new industries into the town during the dark days of the depression. In 1937 he was able to persuade a new company, Aberdare Cables, to establish their factory in Aberdare and he was eventually invited to join the board of directors. Thanks largely to his efforts Royal Ordnance Factories were established in Robertstown and Rhigos in 1940 and in 1945 the Hirwaun Trading Estate was founded. These developments helped to establish Aberdare as a centre of light industry, which was an inestimable boon for a town which had become too heavily dependent on coal.

He was awarded honorary LL.D. degrees by the University of Birmingham in 1945 (of which Anthony Eden was chancellor) and the University of Wales in 1946. Always a faithful member of the Church in Wales he was elected a member of its Representative Body.

Lord Hall was twice married: (1) to Margaret, d. of William Jones of Ynysybwl, 12 Oct. 1910. She d. 24 Jul. 1941. There were two sons of this marriage, one succeeded to the title and the other was killed on active service when serving as a First Lieutenant in the Royal Navy, 11 May 1942, and (2) Alice Martha Walker, dau. of Ben Walker of Brinklow, Rugby, in 1964. She was a member of the Leicestershire County Council.

He d. in Leicester Hospital, 8 Nov. 1965.

Aberdare Leader, 13 and 20 Nov. 1965; *Times*, 9 Nov. 1965; *Www*; Burke; *WWP*.

W.T.M.

HAMER, Sir GEORGE FREDERICK (1885-1965), industrialist and public figure; Kt., cr. 1955; C.B.E. 1948; Lord Lieutenant of Montgomeryshire and Custos Rotulorum 1950-60; b. 19 Mar. 1885, s. of Edward and Martha Hamer (née Matthews), Summerfield Park, Llanidloes, Mont.; m. Sybil Dorothy Vaughan Owen (High Sheriff of Montgomeryshire 1958), 3rd dau. of Dr. John Vaughan Owen and Emma Wigley Owen (née Davies), at St. Idloes parish church, Llanidloes on 1 July 1920; one dau. (Shirley, Lady Hooson). He was educ. at Llanidloes Grammar School and began his business career in 1902 when he joined the staff of his father's firm, Edward Hamer and Co., at Llanidloes. The firm farmed extensively and were pioneers in the Welsh mutton trade, being purveyors to three monarchs. In 1919 Sir George became sole proprietor of a firm of leather manufacturers bearing the name of his brother, T. Pryce Hamer, who was killed in action in France during World War I. Sir George became chairman of directors when the firm became a limited company in 1946, but relinquished the position in Jun. 1954 when there was an amalgamation with another firm, although he remained a director of the company. He was a member of Llanidloes Borough Council 1919-54, Mayor on eleven occasions; Alderman 1932; Hon. Freeman of the Borough 1948; Montgomery County Council 1929 (Chairman 1951-54 and 1956-58); Alderman

1949; Chairman Montgomeryshire Education Committee 1947-51; Member of Council for Wales and Monmouthshire 1949-54 and 1956-59; Chairman of Wales Gas Consultative Council and Member of Wales Gas Board 1949-58; Member of Central Advisory Council for Education (Wales) 1945-49; Member of B.B.C. Advisory Council for Wales 1946-49 and a member of the Welsh Joint Education Committee. J.P. Montgomeryshire 1932 and Chairman of Llanidloes Borough and Upper Petty Sessional Benches 1950-60; Chairman Montgomery County Magistrates' Committee. High Sheriff of Montgomeryshire 1949. County President Venerable Order of St. John for several years; President Montgomeryshire Boy Scouts' Association; President Montgomeryshire Playing Fields Association; Chairman Montgomeryshire Assessment Panel; Chairman of Governors Llanidoes Secondary School; Member of the Governing Body of each of the constituent Colleges of the University of Wales; Member of the University Court; Vice-Chairman Mid-Wales Police Authority; Member of the Court of Governors and Council of the National Museum of Wales; Member of the Court of Governors of the National Library of Wales; Member of the North Wales Development Council; Vice-President of the Industrial Association of Wales and Monmouthshire; Member of the General Committee of the Council for the Preservation of Rural Wales; Chairman of Llanidloes Boys' Club from its foundation in 1937. He became completely involved in the life of the community which he served in all its aspects but perhaps his most significant contribution was the firm and able leadership which he gave to the education service in the implementation of the 1944 Butler Education Act. His philosophy of education in the 20th century derived its inspiration from the two Liberal Members of Parliament for the county of Montgomery who played a significant part in the development of Intermediate and Higher Education in Wales in the 19th century – Lord Stuart Rendel (*DWB*, 834-5) and A. C. Humphreys Owen (*DWB*, 398). He d. on 3rd Feb. 1965 and was buried in Llanidloes.

Personal knowledge.

J.A.D.

HANSON, CARL AUGUST (1872-1961), first head of the bindery at the National Library of Wales; b. in 1872 in Oslo, Norway. About 1898 he came to London to seek work as a bookbinder and was employed by J. Zaehnsdorf in Shaftsbury Avenue. Three years later he joined the famous firm of Riviere and Sons, Regent Street, with whom he remained for ten years gaining considerable experience in repairing manuscripts and books. During this period he m. Edith Gwynne (1871-1950); they had four children. In 1911, the recently opened National Library of Wales urgently required an experienced craftsman to repair and rebind (where necessary) many of the rare manuscripts and books in the Peniarth and Llanstephan libraries which Sir John Williams (*DWB*, 1055-6) had donated as foundation collections. From three strongly recommended applicants Carl Hanson was unanimously appointed. The leaves of

many of the manuscripts written on paper were too fragile to be issued to readers, and consequently, in the case of hand-made paper, Hanson developed a process of splitting the damaged leaf and pasting the two halves to a new sheet of paper. He (and ultimately his staff) thus recovered many thousands of rare books and manuscripts, thereby enabling scholars to publish reliable and complete texts of a whole series of literary classics which proved indispensable for the development of modern Welsh scholarship. The University of Wales acknowledge his unique contribution in 1955 when he was awarded an honorary M.A. degree.

From his London days, Hanson was an ardent trade unionist, and within a year of his arrival at Aberystwyth he was elected vice-chairman of the North Cardiganshire Council of Trade Unions which he helped to establish. At the end of World War I he and a few friends formed a branch of the Labour Party and opened the first Co-operative Stores in the town. He took up his appointment at the National Library on 1 Jan. 1912 and did not retire until 30 Jun. 1959 when he celebrated his 87th birthday! He d. 26 Sept. 1961 and was buried in Llangorwen churchyard, Clarach.

Personal knowledge.

D.J.

HARKER, EDWARD ('Isnant'; 1866-1969), quarryman, poet and preacher (Congl.); b. 9 July 1866 at Nant-isaf (from which he took his bardic name), Bwlch-nant-yr-heyrn, Llanrwst, Denbs., the fifth of nine children (5 daughters and 4 sons) of John and Sarah Ann Harker. His great-grandfather, James Harker, had moved from Lancashire to work in the leadmine at Nant in the middle of the eighteenth century, but the family had come from Cornwall originally. He received only three weeks of formal schooling at the British School, Llanrwst, before going to work in the leadmines when he was nine. His father took an interest in writing poetry and he was a neighbour and friend of the poet-tailor Trebor Mai (Robert Williams, 1830-77; *DWB*, 1068) and it was said that he made Isnant's first suit. However he died when Isnant was 11 so it is unlikely that he had any great influence on the young boy. Gwilym Cowlyd (William John Roberts, *DWB*, 885) had only recently set up *Gorsedd Geirionydd* and a series of *eisteddfodau* on the banks of Llyn Geirionydd and it is against this background that the boy took seriously to learning the *cyng-aneddion*, mastering the handbook *Yr Ysgol Farddol* by Dafydd Morganwg (David Watkin Jones, *DWB*, 454-5), and to competing in *eisteddfodau*.

After giving up work at Nant, he worked for 15 years at Craig Ddu quarry at Blaenau Ffestiniog and for a further 15 years on the Gwydir estate. After this he worked at Cae Coch quarry, Trefriw. He retired in 1933. He composed many poems in the standard Welsh metres and won many prizes, 3 chairs, a crown and a gold medal, in *eisteddfodau*.

He contributed regularly to the poetry column of *Y Tyst* and to Welsh periodicals. A hymn by him is included in *Llawlyfr Moliant* (B). He was a deacon in Ebeneser, Congregational chapel, Llanrwst and, after that was closed, at Ebeneser, Trefriw. To celebrate his hundredth birthday in 1966, Ebeneser, Trefriw published a collection of his poetry entitled *Canmlwydd Isnant*. He was a recognised lay preacher in his denomination within North Arfon for many years, giving acceptable service to the churches of the Conwy valley.

He m. Jennie McGreggor in about 1910 and they lived at Tŷ Mawr between Trefriw and Llanrwst. She was the daughter of a forester on the Gwydir estate and she died in 1933. About 1950 Isnant went to live with his niece at Llanrwst. He became blind towards the end of his life but with his remarkable memory he was able to dictate his poems to his fellow-deacon, Gwilym Roberts, so that he could write them down. He recited his *cywydd* on the Conwy Valley to his niece Daisy Roberts and her husband, when he was 98. Two of his brothers had emigrated to search for gold in Denver, Colorado. He d. 15 March 1969 and was buried at the public cemetery, Trefriw.

Information from his niece, Daisy J. Roberts; *Tyst* 24 Apr. 1969, and *Genh*, 1969.

E.D.J.

HARLECH, 4th BARON – see ORMSBY-GORE, WILLIAM GEORGE ARTHUR below.

HARRIS, WILLIAM HENRY (1884-1956), priest, Professor of Welsh, St. David's College, Lampeter; b. 28 April 1884 at Pantysgallog, Dowlais, Glam., son of John and Anne Harris. He was educated at Merthyr Tydfil County School and St. David's College, Lampeter where he was Treharne and Senior Scholar, and English and Welsh (Creaton) Essay Prizeman. He graduated B.A. first-class honours in Welsh 1910, and proceeded to Jesus College Oxford as Meyrick Research Scholar in 1910. He gained a B.Litt. degree and the Powis Exhibition in 1913. In the same year he gained 2nd-class honours in Theology, B.A. 1914 and M.A. 1916. He was ordained deacon in 1913, became curate of Ystradgynlais and was ordained priest in 1914. He became assistant priest of Christ Church Swansea in 1917 and of All Saints, Oystermouth in 1918. He was appointed Lecturer in Theology in St. David's College, Lampeter, in 1919 and remained in that position until he was appointed Professor of Theology in 1940. He became Precentor in 1933 and was elected Canon of St. David's cathedral in 1937 and Treasurer in 1948. It was his appointment as Professor of Welsh in 1941 which gave him the most satisfaction. It is believed that he had been disappointed at not achieving this post earlier in his career.

He was one of the founder members of the St. David's Society which was formed to foster and establish the catholicity of the Church in Wales. He believed fervently in the Catholic faith and in the sanctity of the priesthood and no opposition could move him from his standpoint. The periodical, *St. David's Chronicle*, is better known by its later title, *The Faith in Wales*: *Y Ffydd yng Nghymru*. In 1931 he published penny pamphlets, *Yr Eglwys Gatholig* and *Gweinidogaeth yr Eglwys*. His commentaries on the Lesser Prophets were published by the SPCK on behalf of the Welsh Inter-Diocesan Sunday School Union between 1919-1924. He wrote on 'Gwyrthiau' in *Y Geiriadur Beiblaidd*, 1926.

He was knowledgeable in church music and was a member of the committee of *Emynau'r Eglwys* (The Welsh Church Hymnary) (1941, 1951) from its commencement in 1934 and was secretary from 1937. The book contains his translations of Latin and Greek hymns, as well as others from English. The book was the subject of some controversy because of its extreme Catholic standpoint. He was a member of the Liturgical Commission set up to revise the Book of Common Prayer, a director of the Llan and Welsh Church Press Company, and a member of the Provincial Press committee. He translated 'The Office of Compline' into Welsh *'Cwmplin, Gwasanaeth diwedydd'*, 1941.

His bardic name in the *Gorsedd* of Bards was 'Arthan'. He took a practical interest in Esperanto as a language for the League of Nations and held classes in it at the college in 1920. After his death in 1956 his revised edition of *Agoriad neu Allwedd i'r iaith gyd-Genedlaethol Esperanto* was published by G. Griffiths. The members of the St. David's College Welsh Society subscribed to its publication.

He was a popular preacher, drawing crowded congregations to St. Davids during his residence as Canon. He was twice Special Preacher at the Welsh Festival at St. Paul's Cathedral, London. As a man he appeared pale and unhealthy, with very poor eyesight, nevertheless he wrote prodigiously to periodicals and to the Welsh press. Apart from his tenaciously held religious beliefs, he was a kindly, courteous man with an unexpected sense of humour. He m. in 1924 Dorothy Clough (d. 22 Sept. 1980) and they had two daughters. He d. in hospital in London, 23 January 1956, aged 72 and was buried at Ruislip, Middlesex.

Y Llan, 2 Feb. 1956; *Church Times*, 27 Jan. 1956; *Welsh Church Yearbook* 1929; *WwW* (1933); *Emynau'r Eglwys*, 1951.

M.G.E.

HARRY, JOSEPH (1863-1950), schoolmaster and Independent minister; b. in Glandŵr near Swansea on 17 Aug. 1863. After studying at Arnold College, a preparatory school, he entered the Presbyterian College at Carmarthen. Although he had been raised a Calvinistic Methodist, his love of liberty brought him to the Congregational church at Priory Street and it was as a member there that he was received into the college in 1881. He left the college in 1884 and spent some time at the Lancashire College in Manchester. By 1887 he had returned to Carmarthen as a teacher under J.C. Thomas at Parcfelfed school. In 1888, he was ordained as the minister of the English congregational church, Mount Pleasant, Hirwaun. He resigned his ministry in 1892 when he won a science scholarship to the University College, Cardiff. He probably went with J.C. Thomas to Weston in 1894, but by 1895 he had returned again to Carmarthen where, with W. Roberts and T. Wedros Jones, he sought to keep the Old College School open. He was the headmaster of the school from 1885 to 1913 and he encouraged generations of young boys into the ministry and into the professions. He accepted the pastorate of Salem congregational church, Llandovery, in 1913 and he remained there until his retirement, on medical grounds, in 1922. Every spring, he lost his voice. After retiring, he lived with his daughter and her husband, Dan Davies, in Mansfield Road, Ilford. He was held in high esteem in Llandovery, as he had been in Carmarthen. On his departure from Llandovery, he was presented with a set of the *Encyclopaedia Britannica*. He took a leading part in the public life of the town of Carmarthen and he served as a member of the council and as a J.P. After he moved to London, he ministered at the congregational church in Thames Ditton from 1925 until his health forced him to give up this charge in 1930.

His chief interest, after he retired to England, was literary composition. He participated in *eisteddfod* competitions from early in the century and he took part in the debates held in the pages of *Y Tyst* on Welsh orthography. He won chairs and crowns at the Meirionydd, London, Powys and Birkenhead *eisteddfodau*. He was a frequent competitor for the crown and for the chair at the national *eisteddfod*. Some of his publications are the products of competition, e.g. *Orgraff y Gymraeg: llawlyfr i blant ysgol* (1925); *Anfarwoldeb* (1925), the poem which won the Crown at the Powys *eisteddfod* of 1925; *Priod-ddulliau'r Gymraeg* (1927), which won a prize at the Swansea *eisteddfod* of 1926; and, *Elfennau beirniadaeth lenorol* (second to the essay by D.J. Davies, Treorchy, at the Treorchy *eisteddfod* in 1928, but it was Harry's essay that Foyles chose to publish in 1929). He won a prize at the Pontypool *eisteddfod* for translating 3 lyrics from German into Welsh, and Cynan praised his lyrics at the Dolgellau *eisteddfod* of 1949. He was a thoughtful preacher but he shone as a teacher and guide of the young. He had an attractive personality which combined, in a natural manner, scholarship, patience and a sense of humour.

Between 1940 and 1949, Harry lived at Llandrindod but by 1950 he was back in London. He died on his holidays at Westcliffe-on-Sea, 23 June 1950, and he was buried in Surbiton.

Blwyddiadur A., 1951; *Congl. year book*, 1951; D. Edgar Jones, *Ysgrifau a cherddi* (typescript through the courtesy of the late Rev. Kenneth E. Jones; copy in NLW).

E.D.J.

HAVARD, WILLIAM THOMAS (1889-1956), bishop; b. 23 Oct. 1889 at Neuadd Defynnog, Breckn., 3rd son of William Havard, a deacon of Tabernacl (Congl.) chapel, Defynnog, and Gwen his wife. He was educated at Brecon county school; University College of Wales, Aberystwyth (graduated B.A. 3rd-class honours in history, 1912); St. Michael's College, Llandaff; Jesus College, Oxford (M.A., 1921). He was ord. deacon by John Owen (*DWB*, 714-5), Bishop of St. Davids in 1913, and a priest in 1914. He was curate of Llanelli, 1913-15. Between 1915 and 1919 he was chaplain to the armed forces. He was mentioned in despatches, 1916, and awarded the Military Cross, 1917. He was chaplain of Jesus College, Oxford, 1919-21, curate of Brecon, 1921-22, vicar of St. Paul-at-Hook, 1922-24, vicar of St. Luke, Battersea, 1924-28, vicar of St. Mary's, Swansea, 1928-34, canon in Brecon Cathedral, of East Gower, 1930-34. He was consecrated Bishop of St.

Asaph, Sept. 1934, on the resignation of A.G. Edwards (*DWB*, 184). After 16 yrs. he was translated to St. David's in 1950. He d. 17 Aug. 1956 and was buried at Brecon.

He was Select Preacher at St. Andrews University, 1943, Canterbury, 1946, and in 1951 he visited Yale University as special preacher and lecturer. He was chairman of the education council of the Church in Wales, visitor to St. David's College, Llandovery College, Trinity College, Carmarthen, and St. John's College, Ystrad Meurig. He was prominent in the religious education in schools movement. He encouraged greater co-operation between the Church in Wales and Nonconformist bodies. He had been brought up a Congregationalist and he was a member of Baker Street (Congl.) church, Aberystwyth, from 1908 to 1911, and after graduating in the University College he was confirmed in the Church in Wales. He was a powerful preacher in Welsh and English and was often invited to preach at the services broadcast on the Sundays previous to the national *eisteddfod*.

He gained fame as a rugby player at Aberystwyth, and won his cap for Wales against New Zealand in 1919, and he gained his rugby blue whilst at Oxford.

He m. in 1922 Florence Aimée Holmes, daughter of Joseph Holmes, Pen-y-fái, Llanelli, and they had 2 sons and 2 daughters.

Www; Haul, Oct. 1956; *Carm. Jnl.*, 24 Aug. 1956; information from the family.

M.G.E.

HAYCOCK, BLODWEN MYFANWY (1913-63), artist and author; b. at Glyndŵr, Mount Pleasant, Pontnewydd, Mon. on 23 Mar. 1913, the youngest of the three daughters of James David Haycock, miner (known locally as Jim Pearce) and Alice Maud, née Perry (both natives of Mon.) Educated at Cwm-ffrwd-oer primary school, Pontypool grammar school for girls and Cardiff Technical College (later Cardiff College of Art). Her skill as an illustrator in black and white, coupled with her early success with a lyric in English at the Port Talbot national *eisteddfod* of 1932, where W.H. Davies (*DWB*, 162) was the adjudicator, prompted her to reject a career as an art teacher and to take up one as a freelance journalist. From 1936 her poems and stories, illustrated with scraper-board drawings, appeared in *The Western Mail* and other newspapers and journals. On the outbreak of World War II she was in turn wages clerk in a munitions factory, assistant welfare officer in a factory in Cardiff's slumland, teacher, and information officer for the Institute of Agriculture at Usk. In 1943 she joined the B.B.C. in London: two of her radio plays were broadcast and her poems read over the air. Leaving the B.B.C. in 1945, she became a successful journalist in London, writing articles and poems, illustrating books, designing Christmas cards and becoming a member of the council of the Society of Women Journalists. In July 1947 she married Dr. Arthur Merion Williams of Borth (consultant anaesthetist at Redhill county hospital and the East Surrey group of hospitals) at the presbyterian church, Llanover, and lived after her marriage at Buckland, near Reigate, where she brought up their three children. Despite increasing ill-health, she continued to write and not infrequently read her poems on television. She d. on 9 Nov. 1963. The four volumes she published were *Fantasy and other poems* (1937), *Poems* (1944), *More poems* (1945) and (posthumously) *Mountain over Paddington* (1964). A fluent impressionistic poet, 'her imagery often touched with elfin whimsicality' (A.G. Prys-Jones), she used traditional forms with an effect which occasionally echoed W.H. Davies, leading 'Wil Ifan' (William Evans, see above) to call her 'Gwent's Second Voice'.

W.J. Townsend Collins, *Monmouthshire writers* (1945); *Some contemporary Anglo-Welsh writers* (1941); *West. Mail*, 14 Nov. 1963; information from Miss Gwladys Haycock.

R.M.

HELEN o FÔN – see ROWLANDS, JANE HELEN below.

HEMP, WILFRID JAMES (1882-1962), archaeologist; b. 27 Apr. 1882 in Richmond, Surrey, the only child of James Kynnerly Hemp and his wife, Alice Challoner (née Smith). Her sister had m. J. Lloyd-Jones, rector of Cricieth 1883-1922, and this gave Hemp a connection with north Wales, where he spent his summer holidays in Caernarfonshire. He was educated at Highgate School, London, and his first appointment was at the Principal Probate Registry, Somerset House. His main interest lay in history and heraldry; he was elected F.S.A. in 1913, and the same year he was appointed Inspector of Ancient Monuments for Wales in the Ministry of Public Works and Secretary to the Board of Ancient Monuments. After a short period of service in World War I, he was responsible for the important repair work on the castles of north Wales – Beaumaris, Caernarfon, Harlech, Denbigh and Ewloe, and he also excavated and restored the megalithic chamber tombs of Neolithic date – Capel Garmon in Denbighshire; Bryn Celli Ddu and Bryn yr Hen Bobl, on Anglesey. Meanwhile he was writing reports and guidebooks for these and on many other subjects. In 1928 he was appointed by Royal Warrant as Secretary to the Royal Commission on Ancient and Historical Monuments in Wales and Monmouthshire, and his Anglesey volume appeared in 1937. Work on the Caernarfonshire volume was halted by World War II, and Hemp retired in 1946. He joined the Cambrian Archaeological Association in 1911, and was its President 1955-56. He wrote many articles for *Archaeologia Cambrensis* (there is a list of over one hundred items under his name in the Index) and for other publications. He served on a number of committees in Wales. He was awarded an honorary M.A. degree by the University of Wales in 1932. He was an authority on Welsh heraldry and one of that small band of archaeologists who set the study of prehistory in Wales on a sound footing during the first half of the twentieth century. He m. Dulcia, daughter of Richard Assheton, in 1934, and in 1939 settled in Cricieth, where he d. 14 Apr. 1962.

Personal knowledge.

C.A.G.

HENEAGE, ALGERNON WALKER – see WALKER-HENEAGE-VIVIAN, ALGERNON below.

HEYCOCK, GEORGE REES – see REES, GEORGE below.

HOOSON, ISAAC DANIEL (1880-1948), solicitor and poet; b. 2 May 1880, at Rhosllannerchrugog, Denb., s. of Edward and Harriet Hooson. His father's family originally came from Cornwall. I.D. Hooson was educated at the Rhos board school and Ruabon grammar school. In 1897 he entered the service of Messrs Morris and Jones in Liverpool, where he stayed until 1904 when his father died. He was afterwards articled to a Wrexham solicitor and he remained there until the beginning of World War I. In the course of that war he served in the navy. On demobilisation in 1919 he settled as a partner in a firm of solicitors in Wrexham. From 1920 to 1943 he was Official Receiver in Bankruptcy in the Chester and North Wales area. He was a patron of *Urdd Gobaith Cymru*, and was a very useful member of the council of the National *Eisteddfod* and its committees. He wrote a good deal of poetry between 1900 and 1914 and his poems are found here and there in *Cymru*. Then he abandoned poetry for years and when he took it up again he was immediately recognised as one of Wales's premier poets. His favourite forms were lyrics and ballads and all his poetry is characterised by a sureness of touch and by charm of vision and expression.

He published *Y Fantell Fraith* (1934), an adaptation of the 'Pied Piper of Hamlin', *Cerddi a Baledi* (1936), *Y Gwin a Cherddi Eraill* (1948). He was awarded an hon. M.A. by the University of Wales in 1948. He d. 18 Oct. 1948.

W.R. Jones, *Bywyd a Gwaith I.D. Hooson* (1954); information from H. Ellis Hughes, Coedpoeth.

T.P.; A.Ll.H.

HOOSON, JOHN (1883-1969), teacher, scholar; b. in 1883 at Nant, a farmhouse in the Hiraethog area of Denbigh, son of Thomas Hooson and his wife Marged. The family moved to Maelor, Saron and then to Colomendy and Graig, near Denbigh. John Hooson was educated at Prion school and at the county school, Denbigh. He started to work on the farm but suffered from ill health. He returned to school and in 1903 won a scholarship to the University College of North Wales, Bangor where he graduated with honours in Latin (1906) and French (1907). Later he obtained the M.A. degree of the University of Wales. He continued his studies at the Sorbonne and the University of Berlin and travelled widely on the continent. He spent the whole of his professional life teaching French, German and Italian – at Taunton School, Somerset for eight years and then at the City of Westminster School for over thirty years. However his main interest was in the life and culture of Wales, particularly the social and economic life of Hiraethog and the Vale of Clwyd. He was an authority on the place-names of these areas and on their famous people – such as the Myddleton family, Galch Hill, Denbigh, the Salusbury family, Emrys ap Iwan, Thomas Jones, Thomas Gee of Denbigh and Owain

Myfyr as well as the connections of English writers, such as Dr. Johnson with the Clwyd valley. He lectured frequently in Welsh and in English at the London Welsh centre, London Welsh chapels and to societies in Hiraethog and the Clwyd valley. He contributed articles on his favourite subjects to publications such as *Y Ddinas, Y Drysorfa, Y Traethodydd, The London Welshman* and to local papers in Wales. He was prominent in London-Welsh religious life and he was an elder at Clapham Junction Welsh Presbyterian Church for many years. He m. Gwen Storey of Wynnstay, Denbigh and they had one daughter. He d. 19 July 1969 in London.

Personal knowledge.

H.E.H.

HOWARD, JAMES HENRY (1876-1947), preacher, author and socialist; born 3 Nov. 1876, in Swansea, son of Joshua George, and Catherine (née Bowen) Howard. His father claimed to be a direct descendant of John Howard, the prison reformer. He lost his parents when a child. For some time he was brought up in his mother's family and later he was put into the Cottage Homes at Cockett near Swansea. As an adolescent, he was taken in by a collier and his wife, Thomas and Mary Davies, Bonymaen, Llansamlet, and he was a collier himself for some time. He had received his early education in the school at Cockett, but when he decided to become a minister, he went for further education to Gwynfryn School, Ammanford, kept by 'Watcyn Wyn' (Watkin Hezekiah Williams, *DWB*, 1076) and then to the Academy at Newcastle Emlyn, kept by John Phillips, son of the famous Evan Phillips (*DWB*, 758). From there, he went to University College, Cardiff, and the college at Trefeca. He received a call to the Presbyterian Chapel (an English cause) in Terrace Road, Swansea, before he had finished his college course, and was ordained in the Association meeting in Porth in 1905. He was the minister of Terrace Road for only a short time before he moved to Tabernacl, Cwmavon, (1905-09), and then became the minister of Wilmer Road, Birkenhead (1909-15), the Presbyterian chapel (English) in Colwyn Bay (1915-27), Catherine Road, Liverpool (1921-41), and then received a second call to the English cause in Colwyn Bay in 1941. He remained there until 1947 when he resigned because of ill health. He m. Annie Matilda Davies, Ammanford, and they had a son and a daughter. During his ministry, especially in Liverpool, he did much social work and he was known as 'down and out Jim', because he was often seen joining the queue of the unemployed to have an opportunity of gaining knowledge of social problems. He was a fervent socialist, prominent in the Labour Party, and a personal friend of people like Philip Snowden, Ramsay MacDonald, Arthur Henderson and George Lansbury. He was a candidate for Labour in the parliamentary election of 1931. He was a convinced pacifist and gave a great deal of assistance to conscientious objectors in World War I, speaking in their defence and visiting them in military camps like the one at Kinmel Park. He was a popular preacher, especially with congregations in south Wales and though English was his first language, he

became a fluent speaker and writer in Welsh also. He emphasised the social aspects of the teachings of the Gospel and at one time was thought to be a fiery social reformer, but by the time he returned to Colwyn Bay in 1941 his opinions had cooled considerably.

He took great interest in the Poor Laws and was awarded an M.A. from the University of Liverpool in 1920-21, for a thesis on 'Phases of Poor Law policy and administration, 1760-1834, with special reference to Denbighshire and Caernarvonshire vestries'. In 1936, he was awarded a D.D. *honoris causa* by Princeton University, U.S.A. He wrote regularly for the press on religious and social topics, and published a number of books which were popular in their day, including an interesting autobiography, *Winding Lanes*. His most important publications are: *Y Bywyd llawn o'r Ysbryd (gan John Macneil), wedi'i gyfieithu gan y Parch J.H. Howard ... ynghyd â rhagymadrodd gan y Parch. J. Phillips ac A. Murray* (1906); *Cristionogaeth a chymdeithas, gyda rhagair gan y Gwir Anrhydeddus D. Lloyd George* (1914); *Life beyond the veil* (1918); *Which Jesus? Young Britain's choice* (1926); *Perarogl Crist: cofiant a phregethau y Parch. William Jones, Treforis* (1932); *Jesus the agitator: foreword by the Rt. Hon. George Lansbury* (1934); *Winding Lanes: a book of impressions and recollections* (1938).

He died in a private hospital in Colwyn Bay on July 7th, 1947, and was buried in Bron-y-nant cemetery, Colwyn Bay, on July 9th.

Winding lanes; Blwyddiadur MC, 1948; *Goleuad,* 10 Sept. 1944; information from his son, Ieuan Davies Howard; Brynsiencyn and personal knowledge.

De.J.

HOWARD DE WALDEN, 8th BARON – see SCOTT-ELLIS, THOMAS EVELYN below.

HOWELL, JOHN HENRY (1869-1944), pioneer of technical education in New Zealand; b. at Frampton Cotterell, near Bristol in 1869, third child of William Mends Howell (1838-1873), minister of the Congl. chapel there, a native of Narberth, Pembs., and his wife Harriet (née Brown); educated at Lewisham School (Caterham), his name appears twice on the school's roll of honour. At the end of his period at the school he won a scholarship to Cambridge, but it was insufficient to enable him to take advantage of it, and as his widowed mother could not augment it, he took teaching posts in private schools in Ilfracombe, London and Paignton. In Oct. 1889 he sat an examination for the Principal's Scholarship at Aberystwyth. He came second to T.K. Brighouse, but was offered a second scholarship of £30, £10 less than the Principal's, but he could not afford to stay in Aberystwyth. Principal Thomas Charles Edwards (*DWB*, 197-8) offered to lend him the deficiency. However, by taking private pupils and assisting at the Old Bank School in the town he did not have to borrow but he never forgot the principal's generous offer. By the end of the session he had completed the London B.A. course, and took a teaching post in a private school in London. Before the end of a year there he was recalled to Aberystwyth to assist Professor R.W. Genese and to start on a B.Sc. course. He then decided to earn enough to enable him to study physics in Germany, and to that end he went to teach in a private school at Clifton. In Oct. 1893 he entered the University of Strasburg and spent a winter there in great hardship. He accepted a post at a private school under the auspices of King's College in the Strand, attending afternoon classes at University College. He graduated B.Sc. with a first class in the final examination in 1897. In 1898 he arranged to settle in Cambridge to work under J.J. Thomson, but illness forced him to cancel the arrangements, and from Oct. 1898 to Apr. 1899 he was recuperating in St. Moritz and he spent the following summer in scientific research in Zurich. His medical advisers refused to allow him to return to Cambridge, and he again turned to Aberystwyth where he spent two years as science master in the county school, resuming also his earlier activities in the literary life of the town and his social work in Progress Hall.

He decided for reasons of health to emigrate to New Zealand and in the summer of 1901 he accepted a science post in Auckland grammar school. In 1905 he was appointed organiser of a scheme of night classes under the Christchurch Technical Association. He joined the Society of Friends in 1906. He took a special interest in the education of women and in 1911 he established a hostel to train girls in domestic science and child welfare. Sir Ernest Shackleton contributed half the proceeds of a public lecture to create the nucleus of a fund for this work. In 1913 the governors of the Christchurch Technical College (which had developed out of his work with night schools to be the first of the higher technical schools of New Zealand in 1907), decided to send him on a tour of western Europe and America to study higher education, but the outbreak of war in 1914 intervened and he was able only to visit Britain and America. As an uncompromising pacifist the war period was very difficult for him and attempts were made to dismiss him in spite of the outstanding success of the college under his supervision. He had started with 56 students but by 1919 he had charge of over 600 full-time and 1300 part-time students. When attacks on his pacifism in Christchurch were at their peak he was pressed to accept the post of principal of a new technical college in Wellington. He accepted the challenge and within five years the building was completed. By the time of his retirement in 1931 the number of students had reached 1033. He was the designer and builder of the technical colleges of Christchurch and Wellington, and the continuing growth of institutions of technical education in New Zealand was the work of his colleagues and students.

He m. in Sept. 1894 Nellie Wheeler, a prominent figure in socialist circles at Bristol, who shared fully his own ideals. They had no children, and when he d. on 20 Jun. 1944, he left a third of the residue of his estate to the U.C.W., Aberystwyth in memory of the principal who had befriended him in 1889.

He had two sisters, Esther Mary (Ettie) who was a deaconess in Dudley, 1897-1900, Manchester and Salford, 1900-02, and from 1902 to 1944 in the Whitefield Mission in Tottenham Court Road; and Mary Emma, who was at one time governess in the family of Sir Richard Martin in Llansamlet, a nurse in

Swansea hospital for a period from 1895, and in military hospitals in South Africa, India and Egypt; and matron of an infectious diseases hospital under the Egyptian government.

Information from Esther Mary Howell; *Dysg.*, Aug.-Sept. 1956.

E.D.J.

HOWELL, THOMAS FRANCIS (1864-1953), businessman and barrister; b. in London 22 Oct. 1864 son of James Howell and Fanny (née Davies Logan), later of Cardiff. He was educated at Cardiff, and at St. John's College, Cambridge (1883-87), where he obtained degrees in classics and law. Music, however, was one of his greatest interests at an early age, and he studied the piano, cello, singing and elocution at the Guildhall School of Music with the view of making this his career. The law triumphed, however, and he was called to the Bar at Inner Temple (1889) and practised for a time on the South Wales Circuit. On the death of his father in 1909, he took over management and control of the family business and Cardiff store founded by James Howell, and under his direction the store developed and became well known throughout south Wales, and beyond. He established himself as one of Wales' most prominent and successful businessmen in the first half of the twentieth century and retired in 1950. In 1913 he was admitted to the Livery of the Drapers' Company and became its Master in 1940. During World War I he was attached to the Contracts Department of the Admiralty and was its representative in Cardiff in 1918. A Justice of the Peace for Cardiff from 1935 he also undertook many other outside interests, including a governorship of Howell's School in Denbigh, and trusteeship of the Whitechapel Art Gallery. He continued to be active in musical circles, serving on many of the committees of the London national *eisteddfod* in 1940, and on various committees of the Cardiff Triennial Music Festival. He m., 1904, Edith Mary Millard and there were three children of the marriage. He d. in a Cardiff nursing home, 16 Nov. 1953.

WwW (1933); *West. Mail*, 17 Nov. 1953.

D.G.R.

HOWELLS, ELISEUS (1893-1969), minister (Presb.), and author; the only child of Eliseus and Jane Howells of Cefn Cribwr, Glam. His father was killed in an explosion in the Slip colliery, Parc Tir Gwnter, Cefn Cribwr, in Aug. 1892, and he was b. 8 Jan 1893 in Augusta St., Ton Pentre, Rhondda, the home of his uncle, William Howells and his wife, by whom he was brought up. He was educated in Ton Pentre elementary and secondary schools and then he went to Porth, Rhondda, to prepare himself to keep a business. He began preaching in Jerusalem chapel, Ton, in 1912, and went to Trefeca College in the same year. His course was interrupted by World War I, when he served with a Welsh company of the R.A.M.C. in France where his lungs were damaged by poison gas. He returned to Trefeca after the war, and completed his education in the Theological College at Aberystwyth. He was ord. in 1921, and ministered in Blaengarw, Glam. (1921-28), Hereford Welsh Church (1928-

31), and Lewisham, London (1931-46). After his home was destroyed and his library and papers were lost in an air raid he was called to Hermon, Bridgend, Glam., and was minister there from 1946 (and also of Soar, Ewenni from 1960) until his death. He m., 1922, Muriel, daughter of William Marwood, a minister in Hay, and they had two sons. He d. 16 Aug. 1969 and was buried in the public cemetery in Bridgend.

He was of unusual appearance, over six foot tall, with a rough, furrowed face, and he had an extraordinarily deep voice. He was an original and popular preacher; he spoke in the attractive dialect of Glam., and was in great demand for his service throughout the whole of Wales. 'Mr. Matthews of Ewenni' (*DWB*, 620) was a frequent reference in his sermons, and was the subject of lectures by him. He was Moderator of the Association in the South (1959), and of the General Assembly (1963). He delivered the Dr. John Williams, Brynsiencyn, Memorial Lecture and it was published by William Morris (ed.) as *Pregethu* in 1969. He wrote much to *Y Goleuad*, *Y Traethodydd*, to the journal of the Presb. history society and to *Y Drysorfa* – he was editor of the latter, 1959-63. He published *Hermon, Bridgend* (1949), a history of that church in English. For years he took an interest in the ancestors and descendants of Howel and Ann Harris (*DWB*, 339-40) of Trefeca, and the fruits of his work are to be found in NLW MS 20496 C.

Gol., 27 Aug. and 10 Sept. 1969; *Blwyddiadur MC*, 1970, 280-1; information from his widow (per Rev. J.W. Morris, Bridgend); personal knowledge and information.

G.M.R.

HOWELLS, GEORGE (1871-1955), principal of Serampore College, India; b. 11 May 1871 at Llandafal Farm, Cwm, Mon., the son of George William and Jane Howells. He received his early education at the Board School, Cwm, and later went to the Grammar School, Pengam. Having won the Ward Scholarship, he entered Regent's Park Baptist College, London. He graduated at the University of London, and then pursued his studies in Oxford at Mansfield and Jesus Colleges; Christ's College, Cambridge; and the University of Tübingen. He graduated at four universities, and received honorary degrees from the Universities of St. Andrews, Scotland; Serampore, India; and Wales.

Under the Baptist Missionary Society he went to India in 1895, and his chief responsibility was literary and educational work. In 1907 he was appointed Principal of Serampore College, and remained there for a quarter of a century. He re-established the college on the liberal foundations of William Carey, and preserved his highest ideals. From 1913 to 1929 he was a Fellow and examiner of the University of Calcutta, and in 1918 he was a member of the Bengal Legislative Council. He returned in 1932, and was lecturer in Hebrew at Rawdon Baptist College until his retirement in 1935. He d. 7 Nov. 1955 having made his home at Castleton, near Cardiff.

In 1913 he published *The Soul of India*, a series of lectures which he had delivered at the University of London in 1909. He wrote the major portion, and edited the whole, of *The*

Story of Serampore (1927) and contributed many articles to Indian periodicals, confining himself to education and theological problems.

Personal knowledge; *Www*.

Em.D.

HOWELLS, REES (1879-1950), missionary and founder of the Bible College, Swansea; b. 10 Oct. 1879 in Brynaman, Carms., 6th child of Thomas and Margaret Howells. He had few educational advantages and left Brynaman elementary school when he was 12 to begin work in a local tinplate mill. He emigrated to America in 1901 and worked in tinplate mills in Pittsburgh and Connellsville, Penn., where he was influenced by a Jewish evangelist, Maurice Reuben. He returned to Brynaman in 1904 and worked as a miner but attended evangelical conferences at Llandrindod and Keswick. Soon after marrying Elizabeth Hannah Jones of Brynaman, 21 Dec. 1910, he went to the Presbyterian College, Carmarthen, intending to enter the Congl. ministry but these plans were put aside when he received an invitation to become a missionary. He and his wife received training in colleges in Edinburgh and London and in 1915 they joined the South African General Mission with special responsibility for Rusitu mission station. After spending 5 years there they returned to Wales in 1920 and following a preaching tour in America in 1922 he decided to establish a Bible College in Wales, on the model of the Moody Bible Institute, Chicago, to train workers for the mission fields. Though he did not have the necessary capital – it is said that he possessed only 16 shillings at the time – he bought the Glynderwen estate in Swansea and the college was officially opened on Whit Monday 1924. He claimed to have paid for the venture by faith and prayers for financial contributions, and during the 1930s other Swansea estates were bought in Lower Sketty and Derwen-fawr, the buildings being adapted for use as a hospital and boarding school for the children of serving missionaries. The estate of John Dillwyn-Llewelyn (*DWB*, 171) in Penlle'rgaer was acquired at the end of the 1930s and he intended adapting the building as a school for Jewish refugees but the war thwarted this plan. Haile Selassie, emperor of Abyssinia (as it then was), spent a period in Penlle'rgaer on Howells' invitation in 1939 when he was exiled from his country by Benito Mussolini. In 1940 Howells published *God challenges the dictators*, a book which prophesied the end of the war and the fate of Adolf Hitler. His activities as Director of the Bible College expanded in the years after World War II and branches were established in Paris, Palestine and India. The story of his remarkable career, his consistent emphasis on the power of prayer and the manner in which he succeeded in putting the Bible College on firm foundations in spite of financial difficulties and lack of capital are testimony that he was an extraordinary character. He d. 13 Feb. 1950 and was succeeded by his son, Samuel Rees Howells, as Director of the college.

S. Wales Evening Post, 12 Feb. 1950; Norman P. Grubb, *Rees Howells, Intercessor* (1952); idem, *The intercession of Rees Howells* (1973).

H.Wa.

HUDSON-WILLIAMS, THOMAS (1873-1961), scholar and translator; b. 4 Feb. 1873, son of R. Williams, Caernarfon. He was educated at Friars School, Bangor, University College of North Wales, Bangor, and the University of Greifswald. In 1894 he took the degree of the University of London in Classics, French and Celtic, and the D. Lit. of the same university in 1911. He was appointed Assistant Lecturer in French and German at University College, Bangor, in 1896, and transferred to Classics in 1900. In 1904 he was promoted to the Chair of Greek, which he occupied until his retirement in 1940.

In Celtic studies he published 'Cairdius Aenias ocus Didaine (The love of Aeneas and Dido)', a Ballymote MS text which he edited with a translation and notes in Zeitschrift für celtische Philologie, 1898. His main contributions to Greek scholarship were The Elegies of Theognis (1910) and Early Greek Elegy (1926). In the Welsh language he published Groeg y Testament Newydd (1927) and Y Groegiaid Gynt (1932). He published two works of comparative linguistics, A Short Introduction to the study of Comparative Grammar (1935) and A Short Grammar of Old Persian (1936). Having learnt the Russian language in retirement, he translated some Russian classics into Welsh, Storiau o'r Rwseg (1942), Carcharor y Cawcasws, Tolstoy (1943), Cerddi o'r Rwseg (1945), Merch y Capten, Pushkin (1947). Two other translations were published posthumously: Pedair drama fer o'r Rwseg (1964) and Y Tadau a'r Plant, Turgeniev, (1964). He published an amazing number of translations and articles about foreign literatures in all the main Welsh journals and newspapers. There is a bibliography in the Journal of the Welsh Bibliographical Society, ix, 211-218. He published his reminiscences in Atgofion am Gaernarfon (1950).

He m. in 1905 Gwladys, daughter of W. Prichard Williams (DWB, 1086), and they had a daughter and two sons. He d. 12 Apr. 1961.

Www; personal knowledge.

T.P.

HUGHES, ARTHUR (1878-1965), writer; b. 2 Jan. 1878 at Bryn Melyn near Harlech, Mer., the son of John Hughes Jones, a physician, of Clwt-y-Bont, Caern. (who dropped the surname Jones) and his wife, Annie Harriet (née Jones; Gwyneth Vaughan, novelist; DWB, 371). He became a 'Welsh scholar' at St. David's College, Lampeter, where he graduated. He edited two anthologies of poetry which in their day were extremely useful to students, viz. Cywyddau Cymru, 1908 and Gemau'r Gogynfeirdd, 1910. His translation of one of Drummond's works, Y ddinas heb ynddi deml, appeared in 1904; the second volume of Drummond's works was edited by Gwyneth Vaughan.

His mother d. in 1910, and the following year he emigrated to the Welsh colony in Patagonia under the patronage of Eluned Morgan (DWB, 643), mainly because of a nervous complaint. He was given a home for a long period at the home of Barbara Llwyd (Mrs. J.O. Evans) and maintained his own 'batch', i.e. a bachelor's cottage, until his marriage, 10 Jan. 1918, to a widow, Mrs. H.M. Durrouzet, daughter of Erw Fair farm, and grand-daughter of W.E.

Williams, founder of the district of Treorci in Chubut. They had 3 daughters, two of them good poets, one of whom, Irma, became a chaired bard of the colony and editor of Y Drafod.

When he became deaf, he retired from public life and lived a hermit's life among his books. His influence on the Welsh mind and culture in the colony as a scholar, writer, poet and harpist was considerable, but his chief contribution was as a literary critic. He d. 25 Jun. 1965.

Personal knowledge; [Taliesin, 38, 6-23].

R.B.W.

HUGHES, DAVID ROWLAND ('Myfyr Eifion': 1874-1953), secretary of the National Eisteddfod; b. 9 Sept. 1874 at Maesglas, Holywell, Flints., son of the station-master William Hughes and Elizabeth his wife. He was educated at Porthmadog and Bangor elementary schools; Llandudno Collegiate School (1888-91); and the University of Wales colleges at Bangor (1891-92) and Aberystwyth, though he had to leave before completing his course to earn his living. He taught for a year at his old school in Llandudno before seeking employment in business. In 1894 he went to London, where he lived for 45 years before retiring from the staff of United Dairies, Ltd. and moving to Old Colwyn.

He was a leading figure in all aspects of life among the London Welsh, serving as joint secretary of the London national eisteddfod in 1909, and secretary of the Welsh Presbyterian Church in Falmouth Rd. He worked hard for Urdd Gobaith Cymru in the capital, and gave talks on the radio, as well as popular lectures. He was editor of Our Notebook, the staff magazine of United Dairies, Ltd. (1920-39); and, with John Williams (1872-1944; see below), he was joint editor (1926-38) of the London-Welsh periodical Y Ddolen, to which he contributed articles under the nom de plume 'Tafwys', 'A wayfarer', and 'Hafren'. After returning to Wales he was elected treasurer (1941) and president (1944-45) of Undeb Cymru Fydd. He was one of the pioneers and a founding member both of the Caernarfonshire and of the Denbighshire Historical Societies (1925-50). His main contribution was as secretary of the National Eisteddfod Association in 1935-36, and as joint secretary (1937-47) with Cynan (see Sir Cynan Albert Evans Jones below) after its amalgamation with the Gorsedd of Bards. It was his indomitable spirit that ensured the continuance of the Eisteddfod throughout difficult war years. It was he, too, who ensured – despite the shortage of paper – the publication of the monthly magazine Cofion Cymru (1941-46), as well as the six presentation books (1943-46) which were distributed free among Welsh men and women in the forces, and which were greatly appreciated by them (see D.R. Hughes MSS at N.L.W.). In 1943 he received an hon.M.A. degree of the University of Wales in recognition of his work.

He m., 4 Apr. 1903, Maggie Ellis of London, and they had three daughters. He d. 29 Aug. 1953, and was buried in Bronynant cemetery.

D.R. Hughes, Yma ac Acw (1944); E.H. Griffiths, Bywyd a gwaith D.R. Hughes (1965); WWP.

M.A.J.

HUGHES, EDWARD DAVID (1906-63), scientist and Professor of Chemistry in London University; b. in Ynysgain Bach, a farm near Llanystumdwy, Caerns., 18 Jun. 1906, youngest son of the nine children of Huw and Ann Hughes, who came from Llandecwyn, Mer. He was educated in Llanystumdwy primary school and Porthmadog grammar school. He was fortunate to have a notable science teacher in W.J. Hughes, and consequently secured a place for himself in the University College, Bangor, to read chemistry under Professor Kennedy Orton. In 1927 he gained a B.Sc. honours degree (1st class) in chemistry. During 1927-28, he was trained as a teacher, and the following year he returned to his old department as a research student. He took his Ph.D. degree in 1930 and was awarded the M.Sc. of London University in 1932 and D.Sc. (London) in 1936. That same year he was awarded the Meldola medal of the Roy. Inst. of Chemistry and also elected Ramsay Memorial Fellow. He was chosen to deliver the Tilden Lecture of the Chemical Society in 1945.

On the outbreak of World War II his department moved to the university colleges at Aberystwyth and Bangor, where it became mainly his responsibility. In 1943 he was appointed Professor of Chemistry at the University College, Bangor, and was dean of the faculty of science there 1946-48. In 1948 he returned to London as Professor of chemistry in University College, and in 1961 he was appointed head of the chemistry department which at the time had five professors. In 1949 he was elected F.R.S. He was the first to produce and use heavy hydrogen in the U.K., and he succeeded with the assistance of I. Dostrovsky and D.R. Llewellyn to build apparatus to separate oxygen isotopes on a large scale.

He held a number of posts during his period in London. He was honorary secretary of the Chemical Society, 1950-56, and vice-president, 1956-59; honorary secretary of the Chemical Council, 1953-55; Chairman of the Board of Studies in Chemistry and Chemical Industries, University of London, 1955-60; a member of the council of the Roy. Inst. of Chemistry, 1961 up to his death; governor of the Northern Polytechnic, 1950-60; honorary secretary of the Ramsay Memorial Fellowships Trust, 1949-61, and chairman of the Advisory Council from 1961. He was also dean of the faculty of science of University College, London, 1958-61. He wrote over 200 articles and scientific papers, most of which appeared in the *Jnl. Chem. Soc.*

In 1934 he m. Ray Fortune Christina, daughter of Llewellyn Davies, Brecon, and they had one daughter. He d. in University College Hospital, London, 30 Jun. 1963, after a short illness.

Www; Chemistry and industry, 18 Jan. 1964, 96-8; *Nature,* 200, 5 Oct. 1963, 19-20; *Eurgrawn,* 168 (1976), 16-19; *Biog. Memoirs Fellows R.S.,* 10, Nov. 1964, 147-82; *Gwyddonydd,* 1 (1963).

M.R.W.

HUGHES, EDWARD ERNEST (1877-1953), first Professor of history at the University College, Swansea, and a notable intermediary between the university and the public; b. 7 Feb. 1877 in Towyn, Mer., one of the 8 children of Owen, a policeman who ended his career as deputy chief constable of his county, and Catherine Hughes. He became blind in one eye and damaged the other in an accident as a child, a disability which he overcame to a large extent by developing his memory and hearing. He went to Bala grammar school, and lodged with the headmaster J.C. Evans, to whom he acknowledged his great indebtedness, as well as to the school. In 1895 he went to U.C.W., Aberystwyth, graduating with first-class honours in history in 1898. Then he went to Jesus College, Oxford, and graduated with second-class honours in modern history in 1902. He often talked of the kindness of Sir John Rhŷs (*DWB,* 844-5) to him and of his enjoyment of the meetings of the Dafydd ap Gwilym Society. His first appointment was as history master in Llanelli boys' secondary school; then in 1905 he moved to lecture in the history department of University College, Cardiff, where he acted as professor during the long illness of Professor Bruce. During these years, before the college had an extramural department, he began to lecture under the W.E.A. in Glam. and Mon. Welsh history was his favourite topic, and his aim was to give the cultured workers who had hardly ever heard any mention of it at school some notion of the past history of their country. Since his school days, according to R.T. Jenkins (see below), a school companion, he had been a gifted story-teller, and because the material for his lectures was of necessity in his memory rather than on paper, his style of lecturing was like that of a preacher so as to gain the attention of his audience. According to R.T. Jenkins (see below) he did more than anyone since O.M. Edwards (*DWB,* 192-3) to popularise the study of Welsh history.

In 1920, when the University College of Swansea was founded, he was persuaded by the new principal, Franklin Sibly (see below), to join him there as a Welshman who understood the needs of a college in a Welsh industrial district. For some years Ernest Hughes was the only lecturer in the arts faculty there, but his main task initially was to bring the new college to the notice of the public and obtain their support. He lectured on the history of Wales in the area which the college was to serve, and gave the proceeds of the lectures to the fund to establish the college library.

He continued to lecture in Welsh and English to external classes and cultural societies after a chair of history was established in 1926 – he had been an independent lecturer until then. During the whole of his period as history Professor in Swansea he insisted that every student in his department take a course in Welsh history. So great was his respect for the highest academic standards that he did not lecture on this topic himself in college but entrusted the work to Glyn Roberts (see below) who had the research qualifications that were impossible for him to attain with his poor and deteriorating eyesight. He restricted himself to his own special field, namely that of the constitutional history of England in the Middle Ages. He prepared those lectures with the help of his wife, who read for him. He lectured to the first-year students on Europe after the fall of Rome. Many of the colourful phrases, clearly enunciated in his melodious voice, remained in the memory of generations of his students.

He was chairman of Swansea Drama Co. for many years, as well as serving as actor and producer. He led the Union of Welsh Drama. He was chairman of the Swansea Orpheus Musical Soc. for years, and sang folk-songs well. He served on the councils of the National *Eisteddfod* and was drama adjudicator in the festival many times. He showed much zeal for the unity of the University of Wales and served regularly on its committees. He worked for *Undeb Cymru Fydd* during the difficult years of World War II and afterwards. He was a member of the court of governors of N.L.W. He presided over the Swansea and Llanelli branch of the Historical Association, fostering connections between the teaching of history in schools and in his college. Although he was not able to write much himself, he constantly urged others to do so. He collected material for the magazine *Y Beirniad* for Sir John Morris-Jones (*DWB*, 668-9) and supervised its finances.

When a studio was opened in Swansea by the B.B.C. he broadcast in English to the schools of Wales, and when the 'Welsh Interval' was provided he discussed the topics of the day in Wales for some years. He was a zealous Calvinistic Methodist and an excellent Sunday school teacher who attracted to his class in Trinity, Swansea, men of all ages and denominations. He continued to be active with cultural movements after he retired from his chair in 1944.

He d. 23 Dec. 1953 in Swansea and was buried in Llanycil churchyard. He m. twice: (1) in 1907, Sarah Agnes, daughter of William Thomas (coal merchant), Aberystwyth. She d. in 1918 leaving two daughters; (2) in 1920, Sarah (Sally), daughter of Thomas Evans, Abergavenny, who d. in 1967. They had two sons.

Sally Hughes, *Ernest Hughes* (private edition, 1967); R.T. Jenkins, 'Professor Ernest Hughes', *Jnl. W.B.S.*, Jul. 1954, 8, 4-8; R.T. Jenkins, *Edrych yn ôl* (1968); O. Llew Owain, *Hanes y ddrama yng Nghymru 1850-1943* (1948); information provided by his son, Owen Hughes, Aberystwyth; personal knowledge.

M.H.J.

HUGHES, EMRYS DANIEL (1894-1969), politician, journalist and author; b. 10 July 1894, the son of Rev. J.R. Hughes, 94 Henry Street, Tonypandy, Glam., minister (C.M.) and Annie (née Williams) his wife. He was educated at the council school at Abercynon, Glam., Mountain Ash secondary school and Leeds college of education. As a schoolmaster and journalist at Pontypridd and the Rhondda, he became an enthusiastic member of the Labour Party and came into close contact with Keir Hardie, M.P. In the general election of 1923 he stood unsuccessfully as the Labour candidate for the Bosworth division of Leicestershire. Between 1931 and 1946 he edited *Forward*, the newspaper of the Socialist movement in Scotland. Hughes gained a wide experience of the activities of local government, experience which proved of great benefit to him following his election as M.P. (Lab.) for south Ayrshire at a by-election in Feb. 1946. He continued to represent this division in Parliament until his death. He edited a Scottish edition of *Tribune* after World War II. Throughout the rest of his career

he stood on the left wing of the Labour Party, he remained on the back benches of the House of Commons, and he was considered a fiery rebel. He was deprived of the Labour Party whip from Nov. 1954 until Apr. 1955 after voting against the readiness of the Conservative government to accept German rearmament rather than abstaining in keeping with Labour Party instructions. He again lost the Labour whip between Mar 1961 and May 1963 after he had chosen to vote against the armed service estimates. He was an unwavering pacifist, and spent a year in Caernarfon gaol during World War I. Hughes was a regular visitor to Moscow, a close friend of the poet Samuel Marshak, and a constant opponent of the activities of N.A.T.O.

Emrys Hughes published a large number of biographies and other works, among them *Keir Hardie* (1950; new ed. 1957), a volume which gave him particular pleasure, *Winston Churchill in war and peace* (1950) and *Winston Churchill: the British bulldog* (1955), studies which revealed their author's loathing of their subject. He was also the author of *Pilgrim's progress in Russia* (1957), *Macmillan: portrait of a politician* (1962), *Sir Alec Douglas-Home* (1964), *Parliament and mumbo jumbo* (1966), *The prince, the crown and the cash* (1969), and *Sidney Silverman: rebel in Parliament* (1970), a volume which appeared posthumously. Hughes was always prepared to make use of his literary talents for the good of the Labour Party, and he published a number of Socialist and anti-war booklets.

He m. (1) in 1924 Nan, dau. of Keir Hardie. She shared his political philosophy and ideals, and her death in 1947 was a heavy blow to him from which he never fully recovered. He m. (2) in 1949 Martha, dau. of P.M. Cleland, a Glasgow schoolmaster. He made his home at Lochnorris, Cumnock in Ayrshire, and he d. 18 Oct. 1969 while still a member of the House of Commons. His remains were cremated at Masonhill crematorium. His papers were deposited at the National Library of Scotland.

Www; Dod's Parliamentary Companion; William Knox (ed.), *Scottish Labour leaders, 1918-39: a biographical dictionary* (1984); *Times, Guardian* and the *Glasgow Herald*, 20 Oct. 1969; WWP; OPCS 1911; information from Mrs. Beryl H. Griffiths.

J.G.J.

HUGHES, GARFIELD HOPKIN (1912-69), university lecturer and Welsh scholar; b. 13 Dec. 1912 at Hendy, Pontarddulais, Glam., son of John and Rachel Hughes. He was educated at Hendy council school, and Llanelli grammar school before going to U.C.W., Aberystwyth, in 1932, where he was awarded the Cynddelw Scholarship in 1934 and graduated with first-class honours in Welsh in 1935, and in English (class II, i) in 1936. Following a teacher training course, he was appointed student-assistant in the Welsh department at Aberystwyth in 1937; he was promoted assistant lecturer in 1940, lecturer in 1947, senior lecturer in 1960, and reader in 1968, serving as acting-head of the Welsh department, 1968-69. He gained his M.A. in 1939 for a thesis on the life and work of Iaco ap Dewi (James Davies, *DWB*, 129). He was a member of the language and literature committee of the Board of Celtic Studies of the

University of Wales, the committee of the Bibliographical Society of Wales, the Methodist Praise Committee, and of the Methodist History Society. In 1952 he m. Kathleen Jones, and they had one daughter. He d. in Brompton Hospital, London, 16 Sept. 1969, and was buried in Aberystwyth cemetery.

The field of study which first attracted him was the scholarship and culture of Carmarthenshire and Cardiganshire, as shown by his earlier publications, viz. *Iaco ap Dewi, 1648-1722* (1953); 'Ben Simon', *N.L.W. Jnl.*, 5; 'Halsingod Dyffryn Teifi', *Eurgrawn*, 1941. His wide reading and culture enabled him to place emphasis on the contemporary history and literature of the books and periods which he studied. He had recourse to his extensive knowledge of English literature when discussing the literature of Wales, as revealed particularly in his many reviews in *The Welsh Review, Traethodydd, Llenor* and *Llên Cymru*. But even though he took a great interest in the works of the early bards (*Gogynfeirdd*) and the Arthurian legend (topics on which he lectured), his main field of research became the history of Welsh prose from the Renaissance to the 18th c., with particular attention to the 17th c. He published *Rhagymadroddion 1547-1659* (1951); an edition of Theophilus Evans, *Drych y prif oesoedd*, *1716* (1961); *Theophilus Evans a Drych y prif oesoedd* (1963); *Gweithiau William Williams, Pantycelyn*, II, prose (1967); and numerous articles in Welsh journals, as well as a number of contributions to *The Dictionary of Welsh Biography*. His other main fields of research included the history of the Welsh Wesleyan Methodists and early Welsh hymnology. His wide reading was evident in all his work which was also characterised by discerning criticism and sound judgement.

Information from his widow; personal knowledge.

B.F.R.

HUGHES, GRIFFITH WILLIAM (1861-1941), accountant and musician; b. 22 Feb. 1861 at Cefn-mawr, Denbs., the son of Griffith and Ann Hughes. After attending the local elementary school and Ruabon grammar school he became a clerk in the office of the Wynnstay Colliery Company. In his youth he attended music classes conducted by J.O. Jones, Pen-y-cae, and Edward Hughes. In 1889 the Cefn-mawr choral society and a male-voice choir were formed and G.W. Hughes became conductor of both, conducting a variety of works; for a time he was also precentor at Capel Mawr (C.M.), Rhosllannerchrugog. He made a special study of the Tonic Sol-fa system, became a licentiate of the Tonic Sol-fa College, and in 1900, was elected to the Council of the College. In 1911 he was appointed stipendiary precentor at Princes Road Welsh C.M. chapel, Liverpool, where he laboured until his retirement in 1926 when he moved to Prestatyn. He composed several anthems and hymn-tunes, served as adjudicator, and conducted *Cymanfaoedd Canu*. He was one of the music editors of *Llyfr Emynau a Thonau y Methodistiaid Calfinaidd a Wesleaidd*, 1929. He d. 27 Sept. 1941 and was buried at Prestatyn public cemetery.

Cerddor, Nov. 1902.

R.D.G.

HUGHES, HOWEL HARRIS (1873-1956), minister (Presb.), principal of the Theological College, Aberystwyth; b. 7 Sept. 1873, in Brynteg, Llanfair Mathafarn Eithaf, Anglesey, son of J. Richard Hughes, a Presb. minister, and Jane his wife. He was educated at Beaumaris grammar school, the University College, Bangor (where he graduated B.A.), and the Theological College, Bala (where he graduated in theology – one of the first two to receive a B.D. degree of the University of Wales). He was ord. in 1901, and ministered in Penmachno (1901-03), Maenofferen, Blaenau Ffestinog (1903-07), Moriah, Caernarfon (1907-09), and Princes Rd., Liverpool (1909-27). In 1927 he was appointed principal of the Theological College, Aberystwyth, and remained there till 1939. After retiring he moved near Liverpool, taking charge of the Welsh church at Southport, 1939-50. In 1912 he m. Margaret Ellen, daughter of Griffith Roberts ('Gwrtheyrn', *DWB*, 864), Bala; they had three sons. He suffered from debility in his last years, and d. 23 Nov. 1956.

He was a powerful and influential preacher, who held many a memorable service during an Assembly or Association meeting. He became a person of influence in his denomination. He was Moderator of the Association in the North in 1943, and of the General Assembly during World War II, 1939-41. He was secretary of the committee on doctrine set up by the Presbyterian Church Commission for Re-construction after World War I, and he was one of the four who formulated the Shorter Declaration of Faith and Practice for the Presbyterian Church of Wales. His commentary on the Book of Amos (1924) was considered to be one of the best of the series published by his Connexion. He was gentle and gracious and was revered by his students and congregations as a saint and prophet.

WwW (1921), 195; *Blwyddiadur MC*, 1958, 247-8; William Morris (ed.), *Deg o Enwogion* (1965), 47-50; R.H. Evans, *Datganiad byr ar ffydd a buchedd* (1971), 40-3; personal knowledge.

G.M.R.

HUGHES, HYWEL STANFORD (1886-1970), cattle breeder, benefactor and Welsh nationalist; b. 24 Apr. 1886, at Mold, Flints., youngest child and only son of Owen Hughes, minister (Meth.), and his wife, Elizabeth. His sisters were leading members of the suffragette movement, particularly Vyrnwy, who achieved prominence as a journalist and *Daily Mail* columnist under the pseudonym Anne Temple. Both she and her sisters, Morfudd and Blodwen, became friends of Mrs. Pankhurst. One of their cousins was Sarah Pugh Jones, a well-known local historian and librarian at Llangollen. Hywel was educated at Grove Park grammar school, Wrexham, and Kinsgwood, Bath, a Methodist foundation. After leaving school he became a pupil with a veterinary surgeon at Llangollen, but in 1907 he sailed for Bogota, Colombia, to join two uncles, Ifor and R.J. Jones, both of whom were engaged in the import trade. Hywel Hughes soon displayed a high level business acumen and in time acquired 27,000 acres in the Honda region which he developed for cattle rearing. He expanded into coffee exporting and established offices in New York and elsewhere but as a result of the 1929-33 world economic recession his empire crashed. Lesser men would have abandoned any hope of recovery but he applied himself with singular determination, proven leadership and outstanding organising ability so that his interest had soon expanded into agricultural machinery, oil and cattle breeding. Although he had now turned from coffee exporting, many of his former employees held key positions in Colombia. He improved and developed cattle breeding and a second ranch, Poponte, was added to his expanding property.

In 1924 he m. Olwen Margaret Williams in Mile End chapel, London, with Thomas Charles Williams (*DWB*, 1074-5) officiating. B. in London, she was the daughter of Owen Williams, Gwalchmai, Anglesey, one-time High Sheriff of that county and a prosperous London draper. She was a niece of Sir Vincent Evans (*DWB*, 232-3). Their four children continued to farm in Colombia. Hywel Hughes never sought Colombian citizenship preferring always to emphasise his Welsh nationality. He was an enthusiastic member of *Plaid Cymru* and a generous benefactor. He actively supported *Urdd Gobaith Cymru* and allowed the movement to hold its first camp in 1929 at his home, Plas Tŷ'n dŵr, Llangollen. In 1931 he was elected a vice-president of the Company, *Cwmni Urdd Gobaith Cymru*. He was a member of the Hon. Soc. of Cymm., and at the Ebbw Vale national *eisteddfod* he was the leader of the Welsh from abroad, *Y Cymry ar Wasgar*. He was vice-president of the American *cymanfa ganu* at Cardiff in 1969. His benefactions and loyalty to Wales were recognised by the *Gorsedd* of Bards and he was admitted to the Druidic Order as 'Don Hywel'. His personality, facility in Spanish and undoubted reputation brought him into contact with many of the presidents and leading senators of Colombia. In 1955 he bought Drws-y-coed, Menai Bridge, and the mansion became a popular cultural and social centre for Welsh people from all parts of Wales and abroad. He greatly admired the life and work of Sir O.M. Edwards (*DWB*, 192-3). He retained his Christian faith and never abandoned his non-conformist principles. His aspirations may be summarised: to improve the standard of cattle breeding generally and to seek independence for Wales. He d. on 19 Mar. 1970 at Bogota and was buried there.

Information from Mrs. Olwen Hughes and Mr. Rolant Hywel Hughes; R.E. Griffith, *Urdd Gobaith Cymru*, 1 (1971).

G.A.J.

HUGHES, JANE MYFANWY – see under EAMES, WILLIAM above.

HUGHES, JOHN (1896-1968), musician; b. 16 Nov. 1896, in 6 Broad Street, Rhosllannerchrugog, Denbs., one of the 9 children of William Hughes and Catherine, his wife. He was educated in Grango School, Rhosllannerchrugog and then spent 8 years at Hafod colliery, near his home. He was deeply attached to music at an early age; he conducted local choirs, and studied harmony and counterpoint with Dr. J.C. Bridge, organist at Chester cathedral. In 1921 he went to the University College,

Aberystwyth, and after graduating in music in 1924 he stayed there an extra year to study Welsh literature under Thomas Gwynn Jones (see below). He was president of *Y Gymdeithas Geltaidd* (the Welsh society) at college. He became organist and choir-master at Noddfa Baptist church, Treorchy, 1925-42, before being appointed music organiser for Mer. – the first appointment of its kind in Wales – and made his home in Dolgellau.

By the time he retired in 1961 he had attained prominence as a conductor, adjudicator and lecturer. He succeeded in forming choirs in every part of Mer., and arranged a number of successful music festivals in the county. He conducted 50 performances of 20 different choral works between 1942 and 1961, and as a result of this activity the Dee and Clwyd Music Festival was established at Corwen in 1955 – a festival which he served as choirmaster for the first 8 years. He was also active with the *eisteddfod*; he was responsible for the musical aspects of the national *eisteddfod* at Dolgellau (1949), and prepared the choirs for the *eisteddfodau* in Colwyn Bay (1947), Llanrwst (1951), Dyffryn Maelor (1961) and Llandudno (1963). He served also as an adjudicator, and during the last years of his life he edited the Welsh translations in the music section of the National *Eisteddfod*.

He was a zealous Baptist, being elected president of the Welsh Baptist Union, 1963-64. He took a particular interest in hymnology, and was considered to be an authority on the history of church music. He edited *Llawlyfr Moliant Newydd* (1955) and *Mawl yr Ifanc* (1968), and was a member of the editorial board of *The Baptist Hymn Book* (1962). He also edited the music in *Llyfr gweddi a mawl i ysgolion* (1958) for the education committees of Caern., Mer. and Cards. Many of his original hymn-tunes, and his arrangements of hymn-tunes and carols, were included in his memorial programme, *Rhaglen goffa John Hughes, 1896-1968*, which gives a glimpse of the many aspects of his career as a musician, editor, researcher and scholar.

He was not a prolific composer, though he did write some hymn-tunes, such as 'Maelor' and 'Arwelfa', which became very popular. He revealed his real musical talent as a gifted choirmaster and conductor. He d. in a hospital in Cardiff, 14 Nov. 1968, and was buried in Rhosllannerchrugog cemetery.

H.J. Hughes (ed.), *Gŵr wrth gerdd: John Hughes, 1896-1968* (1973); *Welsh Music*, 3 (1969); *Cymro*, 1 Jun. 1961 and 21 Nov. 1968; information from his brother, Arwel Hughes, Cardiff.

H.W.

HUGHES, JOHN EDWARD (1879-1959), minister (Presb.) and author; b. 8 Jun. 1879 at Y Gronglwyd, Cerrigydrudion, Denbs., son of John and Jane Hughes. He was educated in the village school, Bala grammar school, University College of Wales, Aberystwyth (where he graduated B.A.), and Bala Theological College (where he graduated in theology). His co-digger at Aberystwyth was his second cousin, R.T. Jenkins (see below), later his brother-in-law. He began to preach in 1899, and was ord. in 1907. He was minister at Engedi, Ffestiniog (1906-12), and at Horeb, Brynsiencyn and Preswylfa, Llanddaniel, Anglesey (1913). He m. (1), 1907,

Ada Davies, Aberystwyth, who d. within a few yrs.; (2), 1920, Mary Jones of Porth Amlwch; there was one son of the first marriage, and three sons of the second marriage. He d. 10 Apr. 1959 at Anfield Hospital, Liverpool, and his remains were buried in Llanidan churchyard.

J.E. Hughes was a discerning theologian. His articles on the person of Christ in *Y Traethodydd* drew the attention of Dr. John Williams, Brynsiencyn (1854-1921; *DWB*, 1056), who persuaded Brynsiencyn church to extend a call to him. In addition to writing for the *Traethodydd*, *Y Drysorfa*, and *Goleuad*, he published a commentary on the Gospel according to St. Mathew in two volumes (1937-38). He also edited *Hanes dechreuad a chynnydd Methodistiaeth ym Mrynsiencyn* (1924). He was a powerful and substantial preacher. He strove to serve his denomination in many spheres, and was Moderator of the Association in the North in 1957.

H. Ellis, *Hanes Meth. Gorll. Meir.*, 3 (1928), 93 and 97; R.T. Jenkins, *Edrych yn ôl* (1968), 15; *Gol.*, 15, 22 and 29 Apr. 1959; *Blwyddiadur MC*, 1960, 267-8; H.Ll. Williams (ed.), *Braslun o hanes Meth. Môn* (1977), 224-6; information from his son, Medwyn Hughes, Llandegfan.

G.M.R.

HUGHES, JOHN GRUFFYDD MOELWYN (1866-1944), a Calvinistic Methodist minister; b. 30 May 1866; s. of Griffith and Elizabeth Hughes, at Tanygrisiau, Blaenau Ffestiniog, Mer. After leaving the board school he became a postman for a period, and then a clerk in a solicitor's office at Blaenau Ffestiniog. From there he went to Porthmadoc to the office of Messrs. William and David Lloyd George. He lived at the time at Pentrefelin and it was at Cedron chapel there that he began to preach. He was educated at Clynnog, Bangor, and Bala; and later, when minister at Cardigan, he went to Leipzig university where he graduated M.A., Ph.D. He was ordained in 1895. He m. Mya, dau. of Mr. & Mrs. Walter Lewis, Llangadog, and they had 6 children. He served ministries at Bethlehem Green, Neath (1894-96); Cardigan, (1896-1917); Parkfield, Birkenhead (1917-36). He delivered the Davies Lecture on 'Worship' in 1935 and was elected Moderator of the General Assembly for 1936. He was editor of *Y Drysorfa* from 1934 to 1938. He d. 25 Jun. 1944, a few months after his wife, and was buried at Llangadog.

He came to prominence initially as a poet, publishing four volumes of poems at an early age. In the second of these his well-known hymns 'Pwy a'm dwg i'r ddinas gadarn', and 'Fy Nhad o'r Nef, O! gwrando 'nghri', were first published. In addition to the poems he published *Yr Athro o Ddifrif*, 1903, *Cofiant a Phregethau'r Parch. Griffith Davies, Aberteifi* (jointly with Dr. J. Cynddylan Jones), *Llewyrch y Cwmwl, Anfarwoldeb yr Enaid, A New Method for the study of the German Language*, *Pedair Cymwynas Pantycelyn*, 1922; *Mr. Saunders Lewis a Williams Pantycelyn*, 1928, *Addoli*, 1935, *Pregethau Moelwyn*, 1925. He was very acceptable as a lecturer and preacher.

Drys., Sept. 1944; *WwW* (1937); [Brynley F. Roberts, ed., *Moelwyn: Bardd y Ddinas Gadarn* (1996)].

W.M.

HUGHES, (ROBERTS), MARGARET ('Leila Megáne'; 1891-1960), singer; b. in Bethesda, Caerns., 5 Apr. 1891, one of the ten children of Thomas Jones, a member of the Caernarfonshire police force, and Jane Phillip (née Owen) his wife. In 1894 the family moved to Pwllheli but her mother d. when she was 7 years old. Her father sacrificed much to give her a musical education. She had singing lessons for a period with John Williams, conductor of Caernarfon Choral Society, and in 1907 she made her first solo appearance singing 'Gwlad y delyn' (John Henry). Soon afterwards she received her first contract to sing in a concert, in Abersoch, for which she received an acknowledgement of 15 shillings. One of those who heard her sing in that concert was Harry Evans (*DWB*, 235), who prophesied that she would become a famous singer if she had a competent tutor.

In the Anglesey *eisteddfod* at Beaumaris in 1910 she entered a competition for the first time and won first prize for singing 'Gwraig y pysgotwr' (Eurgain), with Thomas Price (1857-1925; *DWB*, 793) and T. Osborne Roberts (see below) adjudicating. Also that year (against more than 50 competitors) she won the open contralto solo in the national *eisteddfod* at Colwyn Bay, and was highly praised by the adjudicator, David Evans (1874-1948; see above). Soon afterwards she was brought to the attention of George Power (a successful singing tutor in London) by Mrs. Ernest Taylor, who had heard her sing in Llanbedrog, and she later entered the Royal Academy of Music. In London (under the name Megan Jones) she came into prominence in ballad concerts, and was assisted by David Lloyd George (see below) and others to study for a further six years in Paris under the famous singer Jean de Reszke, who had been a student of Cotagni in Turin. After adopting the name Leila Megáne (on de Reszke's advice) she received her first professional contract, a two-year agreement to sing Massenet in the *Opera Comique*, Paris. The dress which she wore in the Paris opera is now in the Musuem of Welsh Life at St. Fagans. At the beginning of World War I she was in France and spent a period entertaining injured soldiers, which drew the attention of prominent politicians, among them Lord Balfour, Bonar Law and (Sir) Winston Churchill.

After singing in various opera houses in France and Monte Carlo she gained a five-year contract to sing in Covent Garden, where she made her début in *Therese* (Massenet) in May 1919, with Lloyd George and Melba, the famous singer, in the audience. In 1920 she sang for the first time in a concert in the Aeolian Hall, and for eight years she sang regularly in the Queen's Hall under the direction of Sir Henry Wood. After a successful tour of Europe, where she sang in La Scala (Milan) and Moscow, she was invited in 1923 to sing at the Metropolitan Opera House, New York. She m. (1) in New York, 21 Mar. 1924, T. Osborne Roberts who had accompanied her in concerts at home and abroad. They later made their home in Pentrefoelas. She popularised several songs composed by her husband, among them 'Y Nefoedd', 'Cymru annwyl' and 'Pistyll y llan'. She retired in 1939.

Leila Megáne had a rich, mature, contralto voice, and her performances were characterised by much warmth. Among the items which she recorded *circa* 1920-25 are selections from French opera (sung in French), works by Handel, Welsh songs, and Elgar's *Sea pictures*, with the composer himself conducting the performance.

She m. (2), 6 Oct. 1951, in Llanrwst, William John Hughes, Efailnewydd, one of her contemporaries who had performed in many concerts with her before she went to the Royal Academy of Music. In Pwllheli national *eisteddfod*, 1956, a scholarship bearing her name was established for young Welsh singers studying at the Royal Academy of Music. She d. suddenly in her home, Melin Rhydhir, Efailnewydd, near Pwllheli, 2 Jan. 1960, and was buried in Penrhos, Pwllheli.

'A Springtime of song' (her autobiography in typescript, dated 24 Jan. 1934, which was in the possession of Mrs. W.O. Jones, Holywell, in 1960); *Liv. D.P.*, 8 Oct. 1951 and 4 Jan. 1960; *Welsh Music*, 3, 8 (1970), 35; information from her daughter, Effie Isaura Osborne-Hughes, Pwllheli; Megan Lloyd Ellis, *Hyfrydlais Leila Megáne* (1979).

H.W.

HUGHES, MARY ANNE – see MARY ANNE LEWIS under LEWIS (FAMILY) below.

HUGHES, OWEN ('Glasgoed'; 1879-1947), railway official, businessman and poet; b. at Glasgoed, Cwm Prysor, Mer., one of the ten children of William and Mary Hughes. After a little education at Tŷ Nant and Upper Maentwrog school, he had to start working at the age of nine. In 1900, he moved to the Rhondda where he worked in the coalmines for 6 years. There, he came under the influence of the 1904-05 Revival as can be seen from his hymns. He returned to his birthplace in 1906 and won the chair at the Rhosesmor *eisteddfod* that year. He emigrated to Winnipeg where he lived for 20 years; he was a pillar of the Welsh church and of the St. David's Society. He worked as an official on the Canadian National Railroad before he established a successful business. He moved to California and, later, to Vancouver. He achieved some fame by winning cups and prizes in sport. He was able to speak and read eight languages. He took the bardic name of 'Glasgoed' from his home in Merionethshire. Between 1923 and 1940 he won more chairs and prizes for odes than any other person in America. He was a thoughtful poet and an outstanding master of *cynghanedd*. He m. Kate Elliss from Caernarfon and she died in 1941. Hughes d. on 29 Aug. 1947 and was buried in Vancouver. Manuscripts of his writings are held by N.L.W.

Genh., 4, 168-74.

E.D.J.

HUGHES, RICHARD SAMUEL (1888-1952), minister (Presb.), and college tutor; b. 18 Jun. 1888, in Tanycelyn, Rhostryfan, Caerns., son of Samuel and Mary Hughes. After the normal course in the village elementary school he worked for some years in a shop and then went to Clynnog School intent on the ministry. He won a scholarship to the University College, Aberystwyth (where he graduated B.A.), and graduated in theology in the Theological College, Aberystwyth. He was ord. in 1918, and

was minister of Calfaria, Porth, Glam. (1918-22), Fourcrosses, Llŷn, Caerns. (1922-24), and Garreg-ddu, Blaenau Ffestiniog (1924-30). In 1930 he was called to Clwyd College, Rhyl, and remained there till he d., serving initially as a tutor (under the Rev. R. Dewi Williams, see below), and thirteen years as principal. He left his influence on more than one generation of students in his care in Clwyd College. In 1919 he m. Jane Morris Jones, daughter of William Morris Jones (sometime chairman of Caernarfon county council); they had a son and daughter. He d. 16 Apr. 1952. He was considered to be a preacher of substance, of a prophetic nature. His particular interests lay in scriptural criticism and theological topics. His textbook on the Gospel according to St. Mathew was published in 1937.

Gol., 23 Apr. and 7 May 1952; *Blwyddiadur MC*, 1953, 228; information from his son, Professor Meredydd G. Hughes, Birmingham.

G.M.R.

HUGHES, ROBERT RICHARD (1871-1957), minister (Presb.), and author; b. 2 Jan. 1871, in Pont Myfyrian, a cottage near the railway, not far from Brynsiencyn and Gaerwen, Anglesey, son of Thomas and Margaret Hughes. He was educated in Llanidan British school; St. John's School, Menai Bridge; Oswestry High School; University College, Bangor (where he obtained a B.A. degree of the University of London); and Bala College. He was brought up in Brynsiencyn church under the ministry of John Williams (1854-1921; *DWB*, 1056), and when the latter was called to Liverpool he himself was called to succeed him for a short while (1896-97). He was ord. in 1898, and became minister of Ebeneser, Kingsland, Holyhead (1898-1913), Chatham St., Liverpool (1913-22), and Newborough (1922-47). In 1897 he m. Margaret Ann Lewis, Bootle; they had a son and daughter. He made his home in Holyhead after retiring, and d. there 23 Sept. 1957. He was buried in Maeshyfryd cemetery, Holyhead.

He was a man of influence in his denomination, becoming Moderator of the Association in the North (1940) and of the General Assembly (1946). He was a leading member of the Commission for Reconstruction of the Presbyterian Church of Wales, and was one of the four who formulated the Shorter Declaration of Faith and Practice in 1921. He was co-editor of *Y Llusern* for some years, and editor of *Y Goleuad* in 1931. He contributed articles to *Y Goleuad* and other periodicals of his denomination and published a standard biography of his old minister, John Williams, Brynsiencyn, in 1929. In 1931 he delivered the Davies Lecture, being an inquiry into man's belief in his own immortality, which was published in 1939 under the title *Dyn a'i dynged*.

Trys. Plant, 1931, 141-3; *WwW* (1921), 198; *Blwyddiadur MC*, 1958, 249; W. Morris (ed.), *Deg o enwogion* (1965), 41-6; R.H. Evans, *Datganiad byr ar ffydd a buchedd* (1971), *passim*.

G.M.R.

HUGHES, THOMAS HYWEL (1875-1945), Congregational minister, theologian, and philosopher; b. 10 July 1875, at Penclawdd,

Gower, son of Daniel and Ann Hughes. According to the Rev. W. Glasnant Jones, Swansea, Hughes worked for a brief period as a shoemaker in Gowerton before becoming a student at Gwynfryn Academy, Ammanford. Educated at New College and London University where he graduated B.A., (1st class hons. in Philosophy) and B.D. (1st class. hons. in Biblical Theology), he was ordained in Gunnersbury (1904) where he remained until 1911; he moved to Bishop's Stortford (1911-22), where he wrote his thesis on 'The Philosophy of Plotinus' for which he was awarded a D.Litt. degree by London University. In 1922, he was appointed Principal of the Scottish Congregational College, Edinburgh, where he served with great distinction until 1937. He gained his D.D. (Lond.) for a thesis on 'The Hebraic and Hellenic idea of God', and was awarded an honorary D.D. by Edinburgh University. Whilst he was Principal he also lectured on various subjects in theology, philosophy of religion, psychology and apologetics; he became lecturer in the Post-graduate School of Divinity, Edinburgh University, and examiner in the Divinity Faculty of London University.

Apart from his numerous articles in various English periodicals and journals, he published a number of works which are generally regarded as valuable contributions to theological studies, e.g. *The New Psychology and Religious Experience* (1933); *The Psychology of Preaching and Pastoral Work* (1939); *The Philosophic Basis of Mysticism* (1937); *Psychology and Religious Origins* (1936); *Psychology a Religious Truth* (1942); *The Atonement (modern theories of the Doctrine)*, the last being published posthumously.

He spent the evening of his life in retirement at Mount Grange, Penyrheol Drive, Sketty, Swansea, where he continued to preach until his death on 14 Aug. 1945. His wife Nina, dau. of Daniel Owen, pre-deceased him in 1940. There were no children.

Congl. Year Book, 1946; *Blwyddiadur yr Annibynwyr*, 1946; Scottish Congl. College Records, Edinburgh; *Www*.

J.D.V.L.

HUGHES, THOMAS ISFRYN (1865-1942), Wesleyan minister; b. 16 Oct. 1865 at Clocaenog, Denbs., s. of John Hughes, an enlightened layman and a strong theologian. He began preaching at the age of eighteen, was accepted for the ministry in 1887, and having studied for a term at the Handsworth theological college, he served the circuit of Abergele (1890), Llanfaircaereinion (1891), Rhyl (1893), Tywyn (1895), Coed-poeth (1896), Tre-garth (1899), Mynydd Seion, Liverpool (1902), Blaenau Ffestiniog (1905), Llanrhaeadr-ym-Mochnant (1908), Mynydd Seion, Liverpool (1911), Oakfield, Liverpool (1914), Porthmadog (1919), London (1922), Porthmadog (1925), and Beaumaris (1928). He retired in 1931 and d. at Trearddur Bay, Anglesey, 27 Dec. 1942. He m. 11 Sept. 1894, Catherine, dau. of Thomas and Margaret Jenkins of Aberdovey. He was Moderator of the Wesleyan Assembly in 1918. He contributed many articles (mainly on theological topics) to *Yr Eurgrawn Wesleaidd* ('Papurau Diwinyddol' 1911; 'Y Tu Hwnt i'r Llen', 1921-2; and other shorter series) under his own name and under the nom-de-plume 'Ifor Glyn', articles for *Y Geiriadur Beiblaidd*, a commentary on *Philippiaid a Philemon*, and a theological catechism, *Yr Arweinydd*.

Eurgr., 1904, 312-13, 1907, 74-5, 1943, 68, 101-07; *WwW* (1921).

G.T.R.

HUGHES, THOMAS ROWLAND (1903-49), poet and novelist; b. 17 Apr. 1903, at 20 Goodman Street, Llanberis, Caerns. s. of William Rowland Hughes and his wife May, dau. of Thomas Morydd Owen. He was educated at Dolbadarn primary school, Brynrefail county school, and the University College, Bangor, where he graduated in 1925 with first class honours in English and Welsh. In Sept. 1926 he became a teacher at the county school for boys in Aberdare, where he remained for two years. He took his M.A. and with a fellowship awarded by his old college he proceeded to Oxford where he obtained the degree of B.Litt. for research on English periodical literature in the 19th cent. He was lecturer in English and Welsh at Coleg Harlech, 1930-33. He m., 26 Aug. 1933, Eirene, dau. of Tom Williams, Ogmore Vale, and his wife. In the summer of 1934 he was appointed principal of the Mary Ward Settlement, London, and in 1935 organiser of feature programmes for the B.B.C. in Cardiff.

He won the chair at the Machynlleth national *eisteddfod* in 1937 for an ode 'Y Ffin' and that of the radio national *eisteddfod* (which was to have been held at Mountain Ash) in 1940, on an ode 'Pererinion'. About this time he composed his drama, *Y Ffordd*, on the Rebecca riots, which was translated into English: he was the first to write a radio play in Welsh. He also edited *Storïau'r Henllys Fawr*, a collection of short stories by W.J. Griffith (1938) (*DWB*, 302). He adapted R. Hughes Williams's *Yr Hogyn Drwg* as a radio play. About 1937 he contracted multiple sclerosis, but he continued to work for several years hoping for a recovery. During his illness he began to write novels. The first, *O Law i Law*, appeared in 1943 and it was clear that a novelist of extraordinary stature had made his appearance. This novel was followed by others, published every Christmastime – *William Jones* (1944), *Yr Ogof* (1945), *Chwalfa* (1946) and *Y Cychwyn* (1947). With the exception of *Yr Ogof* his novels are based on life in the slate quarries of north Wales, but *William Jones* also describes life in the Rhondda valleys during the Depression. At Christmas 1948, when he was very ill he published *Cân neu Ddwy*, a volume of poems. In 1949 the University of Wales awarded him the degree of D.Litt. *honoris causa*, and in the same year he was granted a civil list pension. He d. 24 Oct. 1949. The following summer an English translation of *O Law i Law* was published and it was very well received by some English critics. After Daniel Owen (*DWB*, 699) he was Wales's most productive novelist and a 'best-seller'. His work is characterised by gentleness, geniality, and kindness and by the courage of his chief characters.

Personal knowledge; date of birth from his sister; [see further Edward Rees, *Cofiant T. Rowland Hughes*, 1968].

K.R.

HUGHES, VYRNWY – see under HUGHES, HYWEL STANFORD above.

HUGHES, WILLIAM JOHN (1891-1945), school teacher and college lecturer; b. near Penfforddelen, Y Groeslon, Caerns., 10 Sept. 1891, s. of John Owen and Ann Jane Hughes, but his parents moved to Nantlle soon after his birth. The father was a quarryman and later a slate inspector. He was educated at the council school, Nantlle. At an early age he proved to be a gifted child, and he had a remarkably successful career at the county school at Pen-y-groes, 1904-08. He entered the University College at Bangor in 1909. He secured a high place in all his subjects throughout his course, and his name figured year after year in the list of students awarded scholarships for the excellence of their performance. He graduated B.A. in 1912 with second class honours in English, and gained a first-class Certificate of Education. In Sept. 1912 he proceeded to Nuremberg to pursue studies in French and German and methods of teaching these languages at *Le Cours de Langues Institute*. At the same time he taught English at German night schools. He spent a further six and a half years as a teacher in secondary schools – at Lisburn, Belfast, Jan. 1913 to 1915, Ilminster in Somerset to 1916, and Friars School, Bangor, to 1919. He was awarded the degree of M.A. in 1919 and his dissertation was published in 1924 under the title *Wales and the Welsh in English Literature from Shakespeare to Scott* (Wrexham). This was an attempt to trace and explain the attitude of English authors towards Wales and the Welsh. He researched his subject thoroughly and was able to present his conclusion clearly and interestingly. The chapters devoted to the tourers and antiquaries are of particular value, as are the two appendixes – the discussion on the relationships between the antiquaries of Wales and England in the 18th c. together with a comprehensive bibliography. In 1919 he was appointed lecturer in English language and literature at the Normal College, Bangor, a post which he held for the rest of his life. He was a man of wide culture and his students were deeply influenced by him.

In 1925 he m. Laura Binns, a tutor at the Normal College, and they had two daughters.

Between 1920 and 1930 he paid much attention to educational matters in Wales. He wrote articles on the topic for *Y Genedl*, *Yr Efrydydd*, and *Welsh Outlook*, and won a prize of £15 at the national *eisteddfod* at Holyhead, 1927, for an essay on the education system in Wales. He also tutored adult classes, and for many years served as assistant examiner in English for the Central Welsh Board. In the 1930s he began his involvement in the public life of Bangor. He served on the city council from 1932 to 1944, and was chairman of the general purposes committee from 1939 to 1944. He was of sound judgement, and had a clear mind, and his fellow members appreciated his guidance. He was not of a strong constitution. His health failed for a while in 1921, and deteriorated again towards the end of World War II. He d. 24 Apr. 1945, and was buried in Glanadda cemetery, Bangor.

Personal knowledge, and information from members of his family.

T.Ro.

HUGHES, WILLIAM ROGER (1898-1958), cleric and poet; b. 27 May 1898, son of John and Ann Hughes, Sain-y-gog, Llangristiolus, Anglesey. As a young man he worked for a few years in Liverpool. During World War I he served with the army in France and Egypt. He entered the University College of North Wales, Bangor, in 1922, and graduated in 1925. In the same year he was licensed as curate of Mold, moving to Holywell in 1929. In 1930 he was presented to the living of Llwydiarth, Mont., and to Bryneglwys-yn-Iâl in 1933, where he remained until his death. He was Rural Dean of Edeirnion and Canon of St. Asaph Cathedral. From 1930 till 1938 he edited *Yr Haul*. In addition to his duties as a parish priest he served the community as a Rural District councillor and as conductor of a well-known and successful choir. As a poet he won the chair of the Powys *eisteddfod* in 1930, and on more than one occasion came near to winning the national *eisteddfod* chair. In 1932 he published a small collection of his poems under the title *Cerddi Offeiriad*, containing two eisteddfodic poems and a number of lyrics which have the merit of being less subjective than many comparable poems of the period. He d. 5 Apr. 1958. He m. in 1929 Mabel Mansbridge of Gwernymynydd near Mold, and they had two sons and two daughters.

Yr Haul a'r Gangell, Winter 1958; personal knowledge.

T.P.

HUMPHREYS, EDWARD MORGAN (1882-1955), journalist, writer and broadcaster; b. 14 May 1882 in Dyffryn Ardudwy, Mer., eldest son of John and Elizabeth Humphreys. His brothers were Humphrey Llewelyn and John Gwilym. His mother was the niece of Edward Morgan (*DWB*, 642-3), Dyffryn, preacher and writer, and a cousin of R.H. Morgan (*DWB*, 650), Menai Bridge, pioneer of short-hand in Welsh. His great-grandfather was Richard Humphreys (*DWB*, 396-7), a preacher noted for his wit, a teetotaller and a pioneer in education. E.M.H. was educated at Barmouth and Porthmadog county schools. He began his career as a solicitor at Porthmadog but abandoned it because of his poor health and returned home to Maeldref, Dyffryn Ardudwy, where his father farmed. The family moved to Liverpool where he began to write and take an interest in journalism. He became a correspondent for the *Barmouth Advertiser* in 1904. After a short period on the staff of a Runcorn newspaper he had the experience of following the revival meetings of Evan Roberts (see below) as correspondent for the *Liverpool Courier*. His impressions also appeared in *Y Genedl Gymreig*. He became friendly with the evangelist but was not moved in the heat of the revival. He was also correspondent for the *North Wales Observer* under the editorship of William Eames (see above). When Eames joined the sub-editorial staff of the *Manchester Guardian* E.M.H. accepted an invitation to be editor of *Y Genedl Gymreig* and the English newspaper at the Caernarfon office, and in this period he became friendly with T. Gwynn Jones (see below) who worked at the time in the same office. He wrote English verse (including sonnets) and an occasional Welsh poem. In Jan. 1908 he was elected president of the Caernarfon Fabian Society. He was editor of *Cymru* for a short period and of *Y Goleuad* on two occasions. In 1918 he returned to *Y Genedl*, maintaining his connection with the paper until 1930 when he resigned to be a freelance writer. From 1919 he regularly contributed articles to the *Liverpool Daily Post* under the pen name 'Celt' and in 1927 he became special correspondent to the *Manchester Guardian*, contributing an uninterrupted series of reports from the national *eisteddfod* and other matters relating to Wales. He was a keen *eisteddfod* supporter and never missed the national event between 1919 and 1953. His eloquence and sonorous voice soon won him a place as a broadcaster. Despite his frail health he was a diligent and methodical worker and contributed a number of articles to the *DWB*. It was he who discovered the storytelling gift of W.J. Griffith, Henllys Fawr (*DWB*, 302). He served the Caernarfonshire Agricultural Committee as assistant executive officer, 1939-49, and continued to write and lecture in his spare time. He was a tutor with the Workers' Educational Association. He received an hon. M.A. (Wales) in 1927, and O.B.E. in 1953. He was a vice-president of the Hon. Soc. of Cymm., a member of the Welsh panel of the British Council and the Royal Cambrian Academy of Art. He was not prominent in the Presbyterian Church of Wales but he attached great importance to the dignity of the pulpit and he disliked untidiness. He was a member of Engedi church, Caernarfon, and was a well-known figure in the town because of his dignified appearance. He was diverting company and read widely. He m. Annie Evans, daughter of E.J. Evans, former minister of Walton Park Welsh Presbyterian church, Liverpool, but they had no children. He won the friendship of some of the leaders of the nation and D. Lloyd George (see below) thought highly of his opinion. R.T. Jenkins (see below) 'enjoyed a quarter century of pure friendship' with him.

He was one of the pioneers of the detective novel in Welsh and had the gift of composing acute biographical articles. He published *Dirgelwch yr anialwch* (1911); *Rhwng rhyfeloedd* (n.d.); *Yr etifedd coll* (n.d.); *Y llaw gudd* (1924); *Cymru a'r wasg* (1924); *Dirgelwch Gallt y Ffrwd* (1938); *Detholiad o lythyrau'r hen ffarmwr* (1939); *D. Lloyd George* (1943); *Ceulan y llyn du* (1944); *Y wasg yng Nghymru* (1945); *Gwŷr enwog gynt*, (1950), 2 (1953); *Profiadau golygydd* (1950); and *Gorse glen* (trans. of Hugh Evans' *Cwm Eithin*; 1948). He was an independent person and his life was a constant struggle against ill health. He wrote swiftly and concisely in Welsh and English. As John Eilian commented, 'having a sincere warm love towards the old country which his senses could comprehend – the excitement of Snowdonia, the peace of Merioneth and the sound of the western sea', that was patriotism to him. He d. 11 Jun. 1955 at Caernarfon. D. Tecwyn Evans (see above) another of his friends, officiated at his funeral. His remains were buried in the town cemetery.

Genedl, 23 May 1905, 21 Jan. 1908, 19 Jan. and 9 Feb. 1925; *Baner*, 15 Jun. 1955; *Cymro*, 16 Jun. 1955; *Herald Cymr.*, 13 Jun. 1955; *Traeth.*, Oct. 1955; *Genh.*, 1954-55, 1962-63; *Llenor*, 10, 1931; *Times, Man. G., Liv. D. P.*; E. Morgan Humphreys MSS. at the University College, Bangor, nos. 15747-65; information from R. Maldwyn Thomas.

G.A.J.

HUMPHREYS, EDWARD OWEN (1899-1959), educationalist; b. 2 Nov. 1899, in Hendre, Cefnddwysarn, Mer. He was educated in Sarnau school, Bala grammar school, and Bangor University College, where he graduated in chemistry and agricultural science in 1922. From 1923 to 1928, he taught in Banks Road elementary school, and Lister Drive Technical Institute in Liverpool. He was awarded an M.A. by Liverpool University in 1930 for a thesis on the influence of sociological conditions on schoolchildren. In 1928, he became a lecturer in the Normal College, Bangor, chiefly in Agricultural Science, and then, in 1935 he became Director of Education for Anglesey.

In Anglesey, he worked to realise his ideals. He believed passionately that as the result of the Welsh Intermediate and Technical Education Act of 1889 Wales lost a golden opportunity to establish a system of secondary schools which would fulfil the needs of every child and reflect the life of the whole community, being content instead to imitate English grammar schools and to provide for the needs of the few. Humphreys was determined to make a fresh start in Anglesey on the basis of the 1889 Act. In 1936, he obtained from the county education committee a declaration in favour of the principle of many-sided secondary schools to cater for every child. The next step was to persuade the authorities to put it into practice. When the Butler Education Act was passed in 1944 he saw his opportunity, and secondary education in Anglesey was reorganised to form four comprehensive schools – the first county to take this step. (See his article on 'Chwyldro Addysg Môn' in the periodical *Môn*, Aug. 1957). Because of his determination to see his vision come true, he is considered the 'creator of the comprehensive school'.

He was a co-editor of *Môn*, and a fervent supporter of Anglesey Rural Council, the Anglesey *Eisteddfod* Society, and the National *Eisteddfod*.

He d. on May 11th 1959, leaving a wife, two sons, and two daughters, and was buried in Llangristiolus.

Ben Bowen Thomas, 'The man who created comprehensives', *Education*, 13 June 1975, 658; Percy O. Jones, *Môn*, Oct. 1960.

B.L.J.

HUW MENAI – see WILLIAMS, HUW OWEN below.

I-J

IRBY, GEORGE FLORANCE, 6th Baron BOSTON (1860-1941), landowner and scientist; b. 6 Sept. 1860, eldest s. of Florance George Irby, 5th Baron Boston, and Augusta Caroline, dau. of the 3rd Baron de Saumarez. He was educated at Eton and Christ Church, Oxford, where he graduated with 2nd class honours in Modern History in 1882. From 1885 to 1886 he was lord-in-waiting to Queen Victoria. He had estates in Lincolnshire, Buckinghamshire and a seat at Lligwy, Anglesey. Throughout his life he devoted much of his leisure to branches of natural science, especially astronomy, botany and entomology, and was a Fellow both of the Society of Antiquaries and of the Geological Society of London. As president of the Anglesey Antiquarian Society and Field Club from its formation in 1912 to within a short time of his death, he took a keen interest in archaeological activities, and did much to facilitate the investigation of the Lligwy Romano-British village. He was also associated with the excavation at Segontium and Conovium (Caerhun). For his services to national culture the University of Wales in 1936 conferred on him the honorary degree of LL.D. He d. 16 September 1941.

Times, 17 Sept. 1941; *WwW* (1933); *Minutes of the Court of the Univ. of Wales*, 21 and 22 July 1936.

E.G.J.

ISFOEL - see JONES (FAMILY), Cilie, DAVID below.

ISGARN - see DAVIES, RICHARD above.

ISNANT - see HARKER, EDWARD above.

J.W. LLUNDAIN - see WILLIAMS, JOHN below.

JACOB, HENRY THOMAS (1864-1957), minister (Congl.), lecturer, writer and poet; b. in Treorchy, Rhondda, Glam., 14 Dec. 1864, second of the ten children of Thomas Jacob, blacksmith, and Ann (née Harries) his wife. He began preaching in Bethania church, and in 1885 went to Watcyn Wyn's school (W. Hezekiah Williams, *DWB*, 1076) in Ammanford before proceeding to Lancashire College, Manchester. He m., 20 Aug. 1890, Margaret Ellen Evans of Llandeilo, and they had two daughters and three sons. He was minister of Bethel, Trecynon, Aberdare, 1889-98, Peniel near Carmarthen, 1898-1912, and Tabernacl, Fishguard, 1912-34. He was a preacher of evangelical inclinations, with a graphic wit which secured attention and reinforced his message. He composed many poems during his early period, and occasionally thereafter. He was as famous as a lecturer as he was as a preacher; he was a master at portraying old characters; and he aroused interest and admiration throughout Wales. Among his lectures (in Welsh) were: 'My father's tale', 'The old collier', 'The old precentor', 'General Booth'. It was his interest in church missionary work, and his service to it, that prompted him to write *Dilyn y wawr*, and

a biography of Hopcyn Rees. He also published *Caneuon y bwthyn*, a history of Tabernacl church, Fishguard (1945), two booklets of catechisms for children in verse, and his reminiscences, *Atgofion H.T. Jacob* (published posthumously, 1960). He went on a journey to South Africa in 1922-23, and met Chief Khama, who heard him preach. He was elected vice-president of the Union of Welsh Independents in 1931 but had to assume the presidency in Jan. 1932 to complete Peter Price's (see Appendix below) term of office. His wife d. in 1950; he himself d. 18 May 1957 and was buried in Tabernacl cemetery, Fishguard.

Atgofion T.J. Jacob (1960).

G.Jo.

JAMES, DAVID EMRYS ('Dewi Emrys'; 1881-1952), minister (Congl.), writer and poet; b. 26 May 1881 at Majorca House, New Quay, Cards., son of Thomas Emrys James, a Congl. minister in Llandudno at the time, and Mary Ellen (née Jones), his wife, the daughter of a master mariner. The mother returned to New Quay to give birth to the child who was named David Edward, but the name Emrys was adopted later. When he was 7 years old his father received a call to be pastor of Rhosycaerau church, near Fishguard, and it was there that he spent his childhood. He received his early education in Henner school in the parish of Llanwnda, W.S. Jenkins' preparatory school, and Fishguard county school. He was apprenticed as a compositor and reporter in the office of *County Echo* in Fishguard. In 1896 the family moved to Carmarthen, and he had an opportunity to complete his apprenticeship on *The Carmarthen Journal*. The editor, Henry Tobit Evans (*DWB*, 236) gave him every encouragement to continue to write and to recite on stage as he had done since he was young. He was made sub-editor and editor of the Welsh column of the *Journal* before he was 20 years old, and was released to attend the Old College School as a part-time student under Joseph Harry (see above). During this period he began to preach. He went to the Presbyterian College in 1903. He served for a short while in the Welsh Free Church, Liverpool, founded by William Owen Jones (*DWB*, 529), before accepting a call to Bryn Seion, Dowlais, in 1907. In 1908 he went to the English church in Buckley, Flints. In July of that year he m. Cissie Jenkins in the English Congl. chapel in Carmarthen. He moved again in 1911 to Gelliwastad English church, Pontypridd. He was one of the most eloquent preachers of Wales before World War I; then in 1915 he became minister of Finsbury Park church in London, staying there till 1917. He joined the army, and by 1918 his name had disappeared from the *Congl. Yr. Bk.*

He began to loose interest in personal relationships and in his church, and spent years adrift, separated from his family — his wife and two sons. He settled down again in 1940-41 with his daughter, Dwynwen, in 'Y Bwthyn', Talgarreg, Cards., becoming a member of

Pisgah Congl. church and preaching occasionally in the neighbouring districts; he remained there for the rest of his life.

A charismatic person, around whom many stories gathered, he held Welsh literature and poetry classes here and there under the auspices of the W.E.A. movement for adult education, and 'Y Bwthyn' became the haunt of poets and writers. He was one of the masters of *cerdd dafod*, winning among many other prizes at the national *eisteddfod* the crown in Swansea, 1926 (for 'Rhigymau'r ffordd fawr'), and the chair four times - Liverpool, 1929 ('Dafydd ap Gwilym'); Llanelli, 1930 ('Y Galilead'); Bangor, 1943 ('Cymylau amser'); and Bridgend, 1948 ('Yr Alltud'). He was editor of the column 'Pabell awen' in *Y Cymro* from 1936 to 1952.

He d. at Aberystwyth hospital on 20 Sept. 1952, and was buried in Pisgah cemetery, Talgarreg. A memorial stone for him was also erected above the cliffs of Pwllderi, north Pembs.

Much of his work has been published: *Rhigymau'r ffordd fawr* (1926), *Rhymes of the road* (1928), *Y cwm unig a chaniadau eraill* (1930), *Ysgrifau* (1937), *Odl a chynghanedd* (a textbook on *cerdd dafod*; 1938), *Beirdd y babell* (ed.; 1939), *Cerddi'r bwthyn* (1948), and poetry pamphlets: *Y gwron di-enw* (poem at the *eisteddfod* in Anglesey; 1922), *Atgof* (second best poem at Pontypool; 1924), *Y gân ni chanwyd* (second best poem at Liverpool, 1929), *Daniel Owen* (*awdl* in the London *eisteddfod*; 1936).

Eluned Phillips, *Cofio Dewi Emrys* (1971); [T. Llew Jones, *Dewi Emrys* (1981)].

G. Jo.

JAMES, Sir DAVID JOHN (1887-1967), businessman and philanthropist; b. 13 May 1887 in London, one of the two sons of Cathryn (née Thomas) and John James. The family returned to the old home in Pantyfedwen, Pontrhydfendigaid, Cards. when the boys were young. In 1903 David John went to St. John's College, Ystrad Meurig, to prepare for the ministry but remained there for one term only. He returned to London to run the family dairy business and spent the rest of his life there and in Barcombe, Sussex. He m. Grace Lily Stevens on 24 Apr. 1924. Although he maintained a business interest in the dairy industry and in buying and selling wheat he is more particularly remembered as the owner of thirteen London cinemas. He built and opened the first London super-cinema in 1920, namely the Palladium, Palmer's Green. In the 1930s he sold them all apart from Studios 1 and 2, a rendezvous for the London Welsh for a period. He had been chairman of three companies before retiring in 1957.

During his life he donated substantial sums to the Nonconformist denominations and to the Church in Wales to improve the stipends and pensions of ministers, to St. David's College, Lampeter, to Pontrhydfendigaid village and to numerous other causes. In 1952 he founded the Pantyfedwen Trust which was administered from London. Its purpose was to promote religious, educational and charitable causes in Wales. This was abolished in 1957 when he founded the Cathryn and Lady Grace James Trust (named after his mother and his wife). In

1967 he founded a second Trust in the name of John (his father) and Rhys Thomas James (his brother who died young). Late in the 1950s Pantyfedwen *Eisteddfodau* were established in Pontrhydfendigaid (The James Family Eisteddfod), Cardigan (John James Memorial Eisteddfod) and Lampeter (Rhys Thomas James Eisteddfod). Sir D. J. James's main aim was to give individuals an opportunity to compete in *eisteddfodau* intermediate in standard between those of local *eisteddfodau* and the national *eisteddfod*. He participated in transferring the administration of the trusts to Aberystwyth but d. before the official opening of the Trusts' offices there in 1968.

He received an hon. LL.D. degree of the University of Wales in 1957, was knighted in 1959, became a member of the Order of the White Robe of the *Gorsedd* in 1965, and the following year he was granted the freedom of the borough of Aberystwyth.

His wife d. 20 Feb. 1963 and he d. 7 Mar. 1967 and they were buried in Strata Florida cemetery.

Sir D.J. James papers and reports of his life and work.

R.H.M.

JAMES, FRANK TREHARNE (1861-1942), solicitor, art connoisseur; b. at Merthyr Tydfil, Glam. He was admitted as solicitor in 1884, and was for forty years Clerk to the Merthyr Board of Guardians. Becoming a member of the Merthyr Town Council in 1904, he remained a member until his death; he was Mayor for the year 1907-08. Commissioned in the 3rd Volunteer Battalion of the Welch Regiment in 1890, he transferred to the Territorials in 1907 and retired with the rank of major in 1910. He was chairman of the Taf Fechan Water Board in 1925, 1926, 1941 and 1942. He took a very deep interest in the National Library of Wales (governor and a member of the Council) and in the National Museum of Wales where, besides being a governor and a member of the Council, he was also chairman of its Art and Archaeology Committee. He was also chairman of the Merthyr Museum Committee. He became a M.B.E. in 1919. He d. on 15 Feb 1942. A bronze bust of him, by Sir William Goscombe John (see below), is in the National Museum of Wales.

Personal knowledge.

A.H.L.
(revised by W.Ll.D.)

JAMES, JENKIN (1875-1949), first secretary of the University of Wales Council, and author; b. 28 Dec. 1875, in the parish of Llannarth, Cards. As a student of the University College of Wales, Aberystwyth, he obtained the B.A. degree of the University of London in 1895, and proceeded to the degree of M.A. of the same university in 1900. From 1897 to 1899 he taught at Beaumaris grammar school, and from 1900 to 1904 at Barry intermediate school. In 1904 he became clerk of the Cardiganshire education committee and director of education in 1908, a post which he held until 1920 when he was appointed director of education for the county borough of Barnsley. He was awarded the O.B.E. in 1920. In 1921 he became secretary of the University of Wales Council a post which he held until his retirement in 1945.

As secretary he was deeply involved in the establishment and the development of the University Press Board and the Board of Celtic Studies. The University of Wales conferred the degree of LL.D. *honoris causa*, upon him in 1946. He edited two small volumes of an anthology of the poems of Cardiganshire poets for the use of school children under the title of *Gemau Ceredigion*, 1914-15, and these were reissued as one volume in 1930. He was a devoted Sunday School teacher and compiled scriptural handbooks, such as *Gwerslyfr ar Hanes yr Iesu* (1918) and *Llawlyfr ar y rhan gyntaf o Actau'r Apostolion* (1920), and a number of articles and pamphlets. He was a member of the Cardiff panel which was responsible for the University of Wales translation of parts of the New Testament in the 1930s. He d. 31 Oct. 1949 at Heath Park Avenue, Cardiff and was buried in Aberystwyth.

WwW (1921); *Western Mail*, 2 Nov. 1949; *Y Goleuad*, 14 Dec. 1949; G.L.Jones, *Llyfryddiaeth Ceredigion 1600-1964*.

G.M.G.

JE AITSH - see JONES, JOHN HERBERT below.

JEFFREYS-JONES, THOMAS IEUAN (1909-67), scholar, lecturer, and warden of Coleg Harlech; b. 27 June 1909 in Rhymney, Mon., son of David Jones and Myfanwy his wife, daughter of Thomas Twynog Jeffreys (*DWB*, 430). He received his elementary education in Ystrad Mynach where his father was schoolmaster. Then he went to Lewis' School, Pengam, and in 1928 to the University College of South Wales and Monmouthshire in Cardiff. He graduated in 1931 with first-class honours in Economics and again in 1933 with honours (upper second class) in History. At college he won the Cobden and Gladstone prizes and was awarded a research scholarship to study the agriculture of Wales in the 16th and 17th centuries. In 1936 he obtained an M.A. degree for his thesis, 'The enclosure movement in South Wales during the Tudor and early Stuart periods', part of which was published in *Harlech Studies* (1938). In 1935 he was appointed tutor in Coleg Harlech to lecture on political history and economics. When the college closed in 1940 because of the War he became history master in Lewis' School, Pengam, for a year, before being appointed to the staff of the Extramural Department, Aberystwyth, to take particular responsibility for classes in Carms. In 1948 he was invited back as senior tutor to Coleg Harlech which had re-opened in 1946, and was elected warden of the college in 1960. He held a Leverhulme fellowship in 1958 and returned to his main topic of research, namely the history of agriculture in Wales. The fruits of his researches appeared in a number of articles in journals, but in the meantime he had been busy compiling two source-books for the historian, viz. *Exchequer Proceedings concerning Wales in Tempore James I* (1955) and *Acts of Parliament concerning Wales, 1714-1901* (1959). Adult education was very dear to him and he developed the educational facilities offered by Coleg Harlech by making it possible for resident students to sit

examinations for a diploma of the University of Wales in general studies, initiating a postal course for learners of Welsh, and designing a new block of buildings and securing the necessary finance for it. He was a Justice of the Peace and a member of several public bodies but the two great passions of his life were Welsh history and adult education. He d. 14 Jan. 1967. He m. Nancy Watkins in 1938 and had one son.

Information from his family.

J.E.C.W.

JEHU, THOMAS JOHN (1871-1943), geologist; b. in Brynafon, Llanfair-Caereinion, Mont., 19 Feb. 1871. He was educated at Oswestry High School and at Edinburgh University, where he graduated M.B., Ch.M., 1893, and B.Sc., 1894 at Cambridge he took a 1st class in both parts of Nat. Sc. Tripos in 1897-98 and 2nd class in Moral Sc. Tripos 1899; he graduated M.D. (Edinburgh) in 1902.

His first important research was a bathymetrical survey of the lakes of Snowdonia and eastern Caernarfonshire, published by the Royal Society of Edinburgh, 1902. He was appointed lecturer in Geology at St. Andrews University in 1903, and in 1914 Regius Professor of Geology and Mineralogy at Edinburgh, where he took a prominent part in the academic and scientific life of the city. His earlier work mainly related to the glacial deposits of Wales, and after settling in Edinburgh he made important contributions to Scottish geology, mainly in relation to the older rocks of the Highlands and the Hebrides. He was a member of the Royal Commission on Coast Erosion (1906), President of the Geological Society of Edinburgh (1917-18), and Fellow and Vice-President (1929-32) of the Royal Society of Edinburgh. He d. 18 July 1943 at Edinburgh.

Quart. Journ. Geol. Soc., 100, 1944, lxxi-lxxii; *Year Book of the Roy. Soc. Edinburgh*, 1942-43; *Www*; [information from C.P. Finlayson, Edinburgh].

F.J.N.

JENKIN, THOMAS JAMES (1885-1965), plant breeder and Professor of Agricultural Botany; b. 8 Jan. 1885 at Budloy, Maenclochog, Pembs., younger son of David and Sarah Alice Jenkin. After leaving the elementary school at Garn'rochor he worked on the farm with his parents and brother. He went to U.C.W., Aberystwyth, in Oct. 1907 to attend a short course in agriculture (one term), and returned for a follow-up course of two terms in 1908-09. He went to the Old College School, Carmarthen, in 1909 to attain university matriculation, and returned to the college at Aberystwyth in 1910, gaining a first-class honours B.Sc. degree in 1914 in botany. He was the agricultural organizer for Brecon and Radnor, 1914-15, and adviser in agricultural botany for the Board of Agriculture and Fisheries in the counties served by the University College of North Wales, Bangor, 1915-19, and in those served by Aberystwyth college in 1919-20. He joined the staff of the Welsh Plant Breeding Station in 1920, being senior research officer until he was elevated assistant director in 1940 and director and Professor of Agricultural Botany, 1942-50. He was acknowledged as the pioneer in the breeding of new and improved grass varieties and the techniques which he developed have been adopted world-wide. The first written mention of the need to establish an official plant breeding station is to be found in his honours thesis of 1914, and his paper, written jointly with R.G. Stapledon (see below) in *Jnl. Agric. Sci.*, 8 (1916), on indigenous grasses, was fundamental to much of the work which was done after establishing the Welsh Plant Breeding Station in 1919. In addition to his practical knowledge of agriculture as a farmer and agricultural adviser, he had an exceptionally keen eye to recognize the attributes of verdancy and of good cropping and the persistence of native grasses. His talent as a scientist and his dedication as a researcher enabled him to cross the various plants he had chosen, to select from among the offspring, and to develop better varieties in order to establish new productive and permanent pastures. An example of this is his perennial ryegrass S.23 which contributed immeasurably to the work of re-seeding productive pastures in the lowlands, sheepwalks and hill country from the 1930s onwards. In addition, his fundamental research work into the relationship within varieties and between varieties of grass, such as *Lolium*, *Festuca* and *Phallaris*, stand as an example of strict scientific dedication using a mere fraction of the apparatus and resources which became available to the plant breeder in the second half of the 20th c. After retiring in 1950 he published much of the fruit of his research into the genetics of grasses. He published several articles in this field in the *Jnl. of Genetics* and other scientific journals, as well as in the bulletins of the Plant Breeding Station. He contributed valuable articles in Welsh to *Gwyddor gwlad*, and to the journal of the agricultural society of the college at Aberystwyth. His short story '*Cawl*' in *Y Wawr*, 1917, the Welsh magazine of Aberystwyth college, is a treasure-house of Pembs. dialect. He was consultant director of the Commonwealth Agricultural Bureau for Pastures and Field Crops from 1942 to 1950, and he gave valuable service on the council and committees of the National Institute of Agricultural Botany in Cambridge. He was president of the Welsh Black Cattle Society, 1950-51, and he was the first recipient of the gold medal of the Royal Welsh Agricultural Society. He received the degrees of M.Sc. and D.Sc. of the University of Wales, was created a C.B.E. in 1950, and he was made honorary member of the Swedish Seed Association in 1961.

He m., 1919, Kate Laura Griffiths and they had two sons. He d. 7 Nov. 1965 in Aberystwyth and was buried in the public cemetery.

Personal knowledge; *Report of the Welsh Plant Breeding Station for 1965*; *Www*.

Ll.P.

JENKIN, ALBERT EDWARD (1895-1953), rugby player; b. 11 Mar. 1895 at Llanelli, Carms., he became the town's idol. His talent on the rugby field flowered when he played as full back for the 38th Division during World War I, but it was as a centre for Llanelli club that he came into prominence. Llanelli was the most successful club for a period during the 1920s, with men like Dai John, Ernie Finch and Ifor Jones in its ranks, but it was 'Albert' who inspired them. Although he was not tall (5 foot 8 inches) he weighed over

twelve and a half stone. He could sprint, had a powerful tackle, and a kick like a donkey from the hand and from the ground. He could time his pass to his wing perfectly. He was never selfish but he could change the course of the game on his own. Between 1920 and 1928 he won 14 caps for Wales, and could have won many more but for the foolishness of the selectors of that time. It was generally thought, both then and since, that he was one of the best centres Wales ever had. He captained Wales on his last international appearance, at the age of 33, against Ireland in 1928. He refused more than once an offer to play rugby league. He d. 7 Oct. 1953, and was honoured with a civic funeral by the borough of Llanelli.

J.B.G. Thomas, *Great rugger players* (1955); David Smith and Gareth Williams, *Fields of praise* (1980); *Llanelli Mercury*, 8 Oct. 1953.

G.W.W.

JENKINS, DANIEL (1856-1946), schoolmaster and devotee of Welsh literature and music; b. 7 Nov. 1856, s. of Griffith and Catherine Jenkins, Pentrefelin, Nancwnlle, Cards. He was educated at Bwlch-y-llan primary school, Holt Academy, and Bangor Normal College. He was appointed headmaster of Cilcennin school in 1877, and Llanfair Clydogau in 1878, both in Cards., and Llan-y-crwys school, Carms., in 1897 where he remained until his retirement in 1920. In 1898 he was elected to the Cardiganshire county council and became first secretary of the Vale of Aeron Bull Club in the same year. He was chairman of the Cardiganshire Beekeepers Association, and a member of the Welsh Cob Society from 1903, the Welsh Folk Song Society, the *Gorsedd* of Bards, etc He was a prominent figure on the national *eisteddfod* field and was universally known as the 'Archdruid of the field'.

He came from a noted family of local poets. With David Lewis he edited the works of one of them, *Cerddi Cerngoch*, 1904. He also published *Cerddi Ysgol Llanycrwys* in 1934. This consisted of a collection of poems made year by year by well-known poets for the celebration of St. David's Day at Llan-y-crwys from 1901 to 1920, with a short history of the parish. He m. in 1886, Elizabeth, dau. of William and Ann Williams of Llanfair Clydogau. He d. at Pentrefelin, the farmhouse where he was born, 18 Nov. 1946.

Information from his son, Mr. Ivor Jenkins.

I.G.R.

JENKINS, DAVID LLOYD (1896-1966), writer, poet and schoolmaster; b. at Foelallt, Llanddewibrefi, Cards., on 20 Nov. 1896, the son of William Jenkins, school attendance officer, and Betha Lloyd, his wife. He was educated at the village primary school before he entered Tregaron County school in Sept. 1909. He entered the University College, Aberystwyth in 1915 and obtained second-class honours in Welsh, with philosophy as an additional subject, in 1918. He was awarded a research scholarship which led to an M.A. degree for a thesis on the development of free-metre verse during the sixteenth and seventeenth centuries. In 1921, he obtained a Meyrick Scholarship at Jesus College, Oxford, but he did not take a degree at that university. He was a lecturer at the Barry summer school in 1922. He was a teacher at Lledrod primary school before he returned in 1924 to spend the rest of his working life at his old school at Tregaron, first as English master and, from 1945 to 1961, as headmaster. His cultural and gentle personality nurtured a love of both English and Welsh literature among his pupils.

He delighted, from early years, in Welsh poetry, both in the strict and in the free metres, and he was a master of *cynghanedd*. While a student, he contributed lyrics and essays to *Cymru* and to *The Dragon* as well as short stories and essays to *Welsh Outlook*, *Y Ford Gron* and *Cylchgrawn Cymdeithas Ceredigion Llundain*. He won prizes for essays at the National *Eisteddfod* in 1942 and 1943. He had been close to winning a chair until, finally, he won the chair at the Llandybïe *eisteddfod* in 1944 for an ode entitled 'Ofn'. He also translated some songs, e.g. *Prifwyl Pan*, 1925; 'Cwsg, cwsg, dlysaf un' (Blake), 1927; and 'Teg ei gwedd' from Handel's *Alcina*. In 1929, he wrote with S.M. Powell, the libretto for *Trwbadŵr*, with music by J.T. Rees (see below). He was an examiner for the *Gorsedd* of Bards and a member under the name of Moelallt.

The great interest in drama at Tregaron County School led him to publish *Y Trysor cudd: drama fer yn nhafodiaith canolbarth Ceredigion* (1921); *Ffortiynau*, a simple one-act comedy performed by the school's drama company in 1937; and *Gwanwyn, neu yr hen ŵr yn mynd i ffwrdd*, a translation of a one-act play by T.C. Murray. In 1948, he published a collection of his verses for children, *Awelon y bore* (Druid Press). His most important published work is *Cerddi Rhydd Cynnar (detholiad o farddoniaeth rydd Cymru'r XVIeg ganrif a dechrau'r XVIIeg)*, 1931, which is now a rare book. This work was based on his Master's thesis in the early 1920s and it is probable that the burdens of his teaching career hindered him from pursuing further scholarly research.

In politics he was a radical Liberal, serving for a time as president of the Cardiganshire Liberals and speaking on election platforms. He was an elder of Bwlch-gwynt Calvinistic Methodist Chapel where he served as the precentor and, on occasions, preached. Two of his hymns are included in the school's service book – the school hymn and the St. David's Day hymn.

He m. on 29 Dec. 1929, Arianwen Elizabeth Ann (Ane), the eldest daughter of Gruffydd Thomas Lewis, the school's headmaster, and they had a daughter. He d. 5 Aug. 1966.

Information from his daughter, Bethan Bennett; Glyn Lewis Jones, *Llyfryddiaeth Ceredigion*, II, 521-2; *Barn*, 55 (1967), 172-3.

E.D.J.

JENKINS, EVAN (1895-1959), poet; b. 2 May 1895, youngest of the 8 children of Thomas and Margaret Jenkins, Tynewydd, Ffair-rhos, Cards. His father was a miner who worked in the local lead mines, and farmed his smallholding in his spare time. Evan went to Pontrhydfendigaid elementary school in 1901, and to Tregaron county school in Oct. 1909, but when he left is not recorded. He failed to pass the medical examination for military service

during World War I but apparently worked in a munitions factory. In 1919 he went to the University College, Aberystwyth and graduated B.A. in 1921. It is said in *Cofiant Idwal Jones* (*DWB*, 506-7), by D. Gwenallt Jones (D. James Jones 'Gwenallt' see below), that he and Philip Beddoe Jones, composed *cywyddau* in a poetic contention when they were students of T. Gwynn Jones (see below). He taught for a period in Taliesin and Llanfihangel-y-Creuddyn schools. Being of poor health he left the teaching profession and in 1924 he became secretary to the Union of Cardiganshire Friendly Societies, a post which he held until 1948.

He was primarily responsible for encouraging the work of poets in the Ffair-rhos district and was a member of the Cardiganshire team in bardic contests. He won the South Wales bardic chair at Treorci on two occasions, the crown at the Anglesey *eisteddfod*, and prizes for lyrics, an *englyn*, a sonnet and a *cywydd* at national *eisteddfodau*. When the last of his sisters left the old home he moved to live with her and her husband at Ffynnon Fawr. About a year before his death he moved to live with his two sisters at Minawel, where he d. 2 Nov. 1959. He was buried in his brother John's grave in Strata Florida. His prize-winning collection of lyrics was included in the Cardiff national *eisteddfod*, volume of adjudications and winning poetry, 1938, 108-18. A selection of his poems was selected and edited by T. Llew Jones under the title *Cerddi Ffair Rhos* (1959).

Personal knowledge.

Da.Jo.

JENKINS, JOSEPH (1886-1962), minister (Meth.) and author; b. 4 Nov. 1886, in Tynewydd, Pontrhydygroes, Cards., his father being a cousin of Joseph Jenkins (1861-1929 (*recte* 1859-1929); *DWB*, 436) who was also a minister. He was educated in Ysbyty Ystwyth school and started work at the age of 13 in one of the local lead mines. He had a further period of education in Gwynfryn School, Ammanford, before going as a lay agent on the Llandeilo circuit. After being accepted as a candidate for the ministry, spending a year at Aberaeron, and going to Handsworth College, Birmingham, he served on the following circuits: Lampeter, Llandeilo, Machynlleth (twice), Tredegar, Aberystwyth, Beaumaris, Caernarfon, Pwllheli, Blaenau Ffestiniog. He became a supernumerary in 1959. Between 1926 and 1952 he published 14 story books for children, e.g. *Robin y pysgotwr*, *Straeon athro*, which were very popular, and also five plays, some of which were in great demand, such as *Dal y lleidr*. He published a textbook *Hanes yr Efengylau* in 1931 and edited *Y Winllan*, 1948-53. He was Moderator of the Welsh Assembly 1951 and an honorary member of the *Gorsedd* of Bards. He received the Sir O.M. Edwards Memorial Prize in 1947 for his contribution to literature; much of his work appeared in periodicals. He m. Mary Catherine Williams, Dafen, and they had a son and daughter. He d. 21 Apr. 1962.

Mins. of Methodist Conf., 1962, 213; [Mairwen and Gwynn Jones, *Dewiniaid Difyr* (1983)].

G.R.T.

JENKINS, ROBERT THOMAS (1881-1969), historian, man of letters, editor of *Y Bywgraffiadur Cymreig* and the *Dictionary of Welsh Biography*; b. 31 August 1881 in Liverpool, son of Robert Jenkins and Margaret (née Thomas). The family moved to Bangor when his father was appointed clerk to William Cadwaladr Davies, registrar of the new college (*DWB*, 161), but after the early death of his parents (his mother in 1887 and his father in 1888) he was raised by his mother's family at Bala; he always acknowledged a deep debt to his grandmother, Margaret, and to her husband, William Dafis, a coalmerchant. Profoundly influenced by the town of Bala, its craftsmen and his recollections of notable inhabitants, its sturdy Welsh culture, the old grammar school and the denominational colleges, it was thus natural for him often to rejoice that he had been baptized by Thomas Charles Edwards (*DWB*, 197-8). He was firmly grounded in Latin by John Cadwalader Evans, headmaster of the grammar school, and in 1898 he won a scholarship to Aberystwyth, where he specialized in English under Charles Harold Herford, who fired in him an abiding interest in the history of ideas and in the literature of the 18th cent. In 1901 he was placed in the first class. He tended to be critical of Aberystwyth for the remainder of his days and he left joyfully for Cambridge (where he was sizar at Trinity College). Owing to financial privation he was not very happy there either and it was Oxford which increasingly fascinated him during his maturer years. Although he had studied history and English at Cambridge, philology was his chief interest and after his examinations he was strongly urged to study the subject in Germany. Lack of funds obliged him to look for work. At first, because of a slight speech impediment, he hesitated before applying for a schoolmaster's post, but in the event he pursued this vocation with exceptional success from 1904 to 1930, at Llandysul (for some months), at Brecon from 1904 to 1917, and thereafter at the City of Cardiff High School for Boys. He lost none of his early love for the classics, English and French literature, but at Brecon he researched in earnest for some years into the origins of feudalism, equipping himself with a Cambridge LL.B. in order to understand Roman law. Although he discontinued his early research the knowledge he had acquired was of inestimable benefit to him and history henceforth became his main passion. In 1916 there appeared his first article in *Y Beirniad* on the Tudor period in Wales (the opening chapter in *Yr Apêl at hanes*), and from 1922 he contributed without intermission to *Y Llenor* until 1951. The Cardiff years were exceedingly fruitful. In 1928 there appeared a history of Wales in the 18th cent, *Hanes Cymru yn y Ddeunawfed Ganrif* (in the series entitled *Y Brifysgol a'r Werin*), which won him a secure place amongst Welsh historians, and in 1930 *Yr Apêl at hanes, Ffrainc a'i Phobl* and *Gruffydd Jones, Llanddowror*. In 1930 he was appointed independent lecturer in Welsh History at Bangor, though he did not become a professor until 1945, three years before his retirement. He accounted it a great privilege to be closely associated at Bangor with Sir John Edward Lloyd (see below) and here too he derived endless pleasure in the company of select, distinguished colleagues who met regularly to converse in lively, often mischievous fashion in the room of (Sir) Ifor Williams (see below).

In 1937 he became editor of the history and law section of the *Bulletin* of the Board of Celtic Studies, in 1938 assistant editor of *Y Bywgraffiadur Cymreig* and in 1947, after the death of Sir J.E. Lloyd, joint-editor with Sir William Llewelyn Davies (see above). The Welsh version appeared first in 1953 and when its English counterpart, *The Dictionary of Welsh Biography down to 1940*, was published in 1959, incorporating numerous corrections and additions, he was the sole editor. He had already given substantial service to the Hon. Soc. of Cymm. for, with Helen Ramage, he had prepared *A History of the Honourable Society of Cymmrodorion* to celebrate the bicentenary in 1951. He was Warden of the Guild of Graduates of the Univ. of Wales from 1940 to 1943 and a member of the Councils of the National Library and the National Museum of Wales. The degree of D.Litt. of the University of Wales was conferred upon him in 1939 and the LL.D., *honoris causa* (Wales), in 1956. In 1953 he was honoured with the Gold Medal of the Hon. Soc. of Cymm. In 1956 he was appointed C.B.E.

R.T. Jenkins was a many-sided man. His interests extended into various directions, including theology and architecture. France always remained close to his heart. As early as 1922, in an article in *Y Llenor*, he drew his countrymen's attention to the Catholic reaction in France. He had often travelled in France and he loved her fertile valleys and her tiny castellated towns, especially in those areas where the remains of Rome and of the middle ages were most marked. Yet his interest in Brittany was slight and Pan-Celtic ideas he considered bogus. His book on France and her people, *Ffrainc a'i phobl*, endures as an exceedingly readable introduction for the Welsh-speaking Welshman who wishes to understand the roots of French civilization. He had an unusually tenacious memory - rather like glue, he once said - but he was not overwhelmed by the detailed information always at his finger-tips. Indeed, he was never much enamoured of the formal apparatus of scholarship for his works aimed at a wider readership than a band of experts and he was loath to bewilder the ordinary, intelligent reader with the many footnotes which are handmaidens to other scholars. On the whole, *The Moravian brethren in north Wales* (1938) is rather an exception, though it is certainly very readable. His chief purpose was to discover the individual in his own habitat and to weigh the ideas and motives which impelled him to act as he did in fair weather and in foul. He compressed his astute remarks within the bounds of short paragraphs where others multiplied words over many pages. (Consider, for example, his treatment of conservatism in *Hanes Cymru yn y bedwaredd ganrif ar bymtheg* (1933), pp. 29-32, or of the differences between the old Dissenters and the Methodists in *Yng nghysgod Trefeca* (1968), pp. 22ff). Like Sir J.E. Lloyd, whom he so much admired, he had a thorough knowledge of the land and soil of Wales, and on foot, by bus or in a friend's car he measured by the pipeful the travels which were the firm foundation of his historical writing. Although it was for children that he wrote on the roads of Wales, *Y ffordd yng Nghymru* (1933), it would be difficult to find a better introduction to the history of Wales. He succeeded in conveying the magic and the flavour of the centuries, but his chief field was the 18th cent., especially Methodism. He was sufficiently close to that tempestuous movement to understand the fiery forces released by successive revivals and yet to remain sufficiently impartial and sound of judgement to reject the old denominational prejudices which had poisoned the history of religion in Wales until his own day. It is not surprising that it was this Methodist who was invited to write an account of a notable Congregational cause, the excellent *Hanes cynulleidfa hen gapel Llanuwchllyn* (1937). He has been compared to Macaulay, J.R. Green and Maitland, and although there is a grain of truth in each of these assertions, his own ideal was G.M. Trevelyan. Yet, at bottom he was unique and in Wales there has been no one like him. Nor should be lightly dismissed his work, together with William Rees (his former pupil at Brecon), in preparing *The Bibliography of the history of Wales* (1931), nor on any account his selfless commitment to *The Dictionary of Welsh Biography*. In addition to his editorial duties he wrote six hundred pieces, and both versions have guided our footsteps.

A number of essays appeared in *Casglu Ffyrdd* (1956), *Ymyl y ddalen* (1957), *Yng nghysgod Trefeca* (1968) and *Cyfoedion* (1974). It was the essay which appealed to him most, and doubtless his conversational style, his use of brackets and italics were more appropriate here than in other literary forms. During World War II he became convinced that it was his duty to prepare light literature for the public at large rather than scholarly studies. He cooperated happily with D.R. Hughes (see above) and others to prepare the monthly, *Cofion Cymru* distributed gratis to Welsh-speaking Welshmen who served in the armed forces throughout the world to keep them in touch with Wales and their heritage. He believed that he had contributed to every issue of *Cofion*, and his short stories appeared under the pseudonym Idris Thomas, which he also used to disguise his authorship of *Ffynhonnau Elim* (Llyfrau'r Dryw, 1945), where the conversation is in a south Wales dialect. His other novel was the splendid masterpiece *Orinda* (1943), which recreates the troubled atmosphere of the Commonwealth and Restoration and its effect upon a Fellow of Jesus College, Oxford. Shortly before his death there appeared a volume of his memoirs, *Edrych yn ôl* (1968), surely the most entertaining autobiography ever written in Welsh. As schoolmaster and lecturer he was peerless; learning and humour flowed from him and he won the affection of his pupils, 'my younger friends', as he called them. It was in Bangor that he spent the greater part of his life; there he reached his full maturity and there the recollection of him is at its sweetest and most fragrant. He d. 11 Nov. 1969, his remains being buried in Bangor cemetery. After a national appeal, the R.T. Jenkins memorial lecture was founded in the college in 1972.

He m. twice: (1) in 1907 to Mary Davies, Aberystwyth (who d. in 1946) and (2) in 1947 to Myfanwy Wyn Williams, Aberdare.

Alun Llywelyn-Williams, *R.T. Jenkins* (1977) and the sources listed there; G. Nuttall, *Trans. Cymm.*, 1977, 181-194; personal knowledge.

J.G.W.

JENKINS, THOMAS DAVID SLINGSBY - see SLINGSBY-JENKINS, THOMAS DAVID below

JENKINS, Sir WILLIAM ALBERT (1878-1968), shipbroker and politician; b. in Swansea 9 Sept. 1878, son of Daniel and Elizabeth Ann Jenkins. He m., 1906, Beatrice (d. 1967), daughter of Frederick and Elizabeth Tyler, Pirbright, Surrey. He was prominent in the Welsh coal industry as principal of William A. Jenkins and Company, Wholesale Coal and Coke Factors, and also as a shipbroker. He won recognition in many European countries for his commercial activities and his contributions to national and international charities and institutions. His political interests were not developed until after World War I when he was elected National Liberal Member of Parliament for Brecon and Radnor in 1922. He lost the seat in the 1924 General Election and afterwards concentrated his political attention on local government. In 1927 he was elected to the Swansea Borough Council on which he served until 1954, being mayor of Swansea 1947-49. He became president and custodian trustee of the South Wales Savings Bank and in 1949 was elected president of the Royal Welsh Agricultural Society. He was president of the Swansea and Central Wales Deaf and Dumb Mission, of the Deaf and Dumb Regional Association for Wales and of the Swansea Business Club. He was knighted in 1938 and his close association with the Order of St. John was recognised by his appointment to the presidency of the Swansea Order of St. John Council, F.I.C.S., and his appointment as Knight of St. John. He was made Knight Class 1 Order of Dannebrog (Denmark) in 1933; Gold Cross Royal Order George I (Greece) in 1938. France awarded him the Order of *Chevalier de la Légion d'Honneur* in 1949. He d. 23 Oct. 1968.

Www.

D.G.R.

JOHN, AUGUSTUS EDWIN (1878-1961), artist; b. 4 Jan. 1878, third child of Edwin William John and his wife Augusta (née Smith); younger brother of Gwendolen Mary John (see Appendix below). The family moved to Tenby from Haverfordwest, Pembs., after the d. of their mother in 1884. After being educated locally and at Clifton, Augustus John went to London in 1894, where he studied art at the Slade School for four years under Henry Tonks and Frederick Brown. He quickly began to make his name both as an artist and as a bohemian. Through his sister Gwen, who joined him at the Slade in 1895, he came to know a group of outstanding women students, including Ursula Tyrwhitt, with whom he fell briefly in love, and Ida Nettleship, whom he m. in 1901. Shortly afterwards he was appointed to teach art at the University of Liverpool; here their first child, David, was b. in 1902 and here too the artist met John Sampson, the University Librarian and expert on gypsies, who taught him Romany. Augustus John and his family subsequently spent periods travelling through Wales and England in gypsy caravans, and this inspired much of his work before World War I.

In the autumn of 1902 he met Dorothy McNeill, another friend of Gwen John; he gave her the gypsy name, Dorelia, and she became his most important model and lifelong inspiration. Dorelia returned from travelling in France with Gwen John to make a brief attempt at a *ménage-à-trois* in Essex, but Ida and Dorelia finally left to live in Paris, with their respective children, being joined there periodically by Augustus. After Ida's death in 1907, following the birth of her fifth child, Dorelia became the artist's *de facto* wife. From 1911 the family lived at Alderney Manor, Dorset, but in 1927 they settled permanently at Fryern Court, Hampshire, Augustus nonetheless spending much of his time at his studio in London. He d. at Fryern Court, 31 Oct. 1961.

The early period of his work is characterised by his exceptional drawings, notably of contemporaries, including his wives and sisters, as well as portraits in oils influenced by the Old Masters, and an experimental series of etchings. His visits to north Wales with another Welsh artist, James Dickson Innes (*DWB*, 1129), between 1910 and 1913, revealed a rich talent for landscape painting, and brought to the fore a more modern impressionistic idiom, also to be seen in his paintings of the south of France, where he spent long periods in the 1920s. After World War I, when he was briefly employed as a war artist in France by the Canadian government, Augustus John became increasingly successful as a portrait painter, so much so that his personal artistic interests could not develop fully. Hence many of his large figure compositions and imaginative pictures were left unfinished. He was made an R.A. in 1928, resigned in 1938, but was reinstated in 1940, and was awarded the O.M. in 1942 for services to art. Although he did not live permanently in Wales after 1894, he remained deeply attached to his native land, and supported the National *Eisteddfod* and Royal Cambrian Academy. A major collection of his pictures is held at the National Museum in Cardiff, and his personal papers at the National Library.

Michael Holroyd, *Augustus John: a biography* (1974); Malcolm Easton and Michael Holroyd, *The art of Augustus John* (1974); Augustus John, *Chiaroscuro* (1952); and *Finishing touches* (1964); Eric Rowan, *Some miraculous promised land*; *J.D. Innes, Augustus John and Derwent Lees in north Wales, 1910-13* (1982); [C. Lloyd-Morgan, *Augustus John Papers at NLW* (1996)].

C.Ll.-M.

JOHN, WALTER PHILLIPS (1910-67), minister (B); b. 31 January 1910 at Gilfach, Bargoed, Glam., the second of five children of the Rev. D.R. John and his wife, Susannah Mary (née Rees), both from Penygroes near Ammanford. The father was minister at Bargoed, Porth (Rhondda), Abercynon and the historic church at Rhydwilym. Walter P. John was educated at Mountain Ash Grammar School and the Baptist College and University College, Cardiff (1928-34), graduating in Arts and Divinity. Whilst in the grammar school he and R.E. Griffith established the first branch of *Urdd Gobaith Cymru* in south Wales at Abercynon.

He began his ministry at Tabernacl, Pontarddulais in September 1934 and in October 1938 he moved to London to take charge of the Welsh church at Castle Street, where he remained until his death on 15 March 1967. He m. Nansi, only child of Morgan A.

Jones, minister (B) at Whitland, Carms., and grand-dau. of Daniel Jones, his predecessor. Walter P. John achieved prominence early in his career as a cultured preacher, whose services were in great demand in his own and other denominations in England and Wales. He also mastered the art of broadcasting. Liberal in standpoint, he was zealous for mutual understanding and cooperation among the Christian bodies of Wales. A volume of his sermons *Rhwydwaith Duw* (1969) appeared posthumously and he was joint author with Gwilym T. Hughes of a history of Welsh Baptists in London, *Hanes Castle Street a'r Bedyddwyr Cymraeg yn Llundain* (1959).

Llawlyfr Bed., 1968; a tribute by Sir Ben Bowen Thomas in *Rhwydwaith Duw*; and personal knowledge.

M.J.W.

JOHN, Sir WILLIAM GOSCOMBE (1860-1952), sculptor and medallist; b. in Cardiff on 21 Feb. 1860, the son of Thomas John of Llantrithyd, Glam. and Elizabeth (née Smith) of Randwick, Glos. His father was a woodcarver to the third Marquis of Bute (*DWB*, 60) and William assisted him with carvings at Cardiff Castle from 1874. He attended Cardiff Art School 1871-1881 and was taught anatomy from 1876 by the local coach painter James Philpotts. John was influenced by the variety of excellent craftsmen working in Cardiff at this period and retained an interest in native Welsh artefacts. In 1913 he proposed that the National Museum of Wales collect 'peasant art and crafts'. He moved to London in 1881 working under Thomas Nicolls until 1886. John studied at Lambeth Art School and entered the Royal Academy school in 1884. In 1886 he began exhibiting at the Royal Academy annually until 1948. He won a gold medal in 1889 which provided funds for an extended tour to Europe and north Africa (c. 1890-91). He remained in Paris in 1891 where he studied in the studio of August Rodin. The Paris Salon honoured him with gold medals in 1892 and 1901. In 1899 he became A.R.A. and R.A. in 1909. He m. Martha Weiss in 1891 and they had one daughter. He d. 15 Dec. 1952.

After his return to London John was quickly established as an important figure in the New Sculpture Movement. He became a sculptor of national and international fame, executing numerous important commissions, receiving an honorary LL.D. from the University of Wales, the Cymmrodorion medal, H.A.R.I.B.A. and he was a member of various European academies. His important Welsh commissions included the altarpiece of St. John's, Cardiff, completed in Oct. 1891. In 1892 the third Marquis of Bute commissioned 'St. John the Baptist' for Regent's Park, which was completed in 1894. The Hirlas Horn was designed for the National *Eisteddfod* in 1898. Undoubtedly his two most important Welsh projects were the investitutre regalia and medals of 1911 and the seal, trowel, mallet and level for the foundation of the National Museum of Wales. He was knighted in 1911 and in 1913-16 was given the pre-eminent position of Welsh sculptors which was the commission to sculpt St. David for the City Hall, Cardiff. His fluent, brilliant style reflected his passion and vigour. He could execute designs for portraits, figures and emblematic subjects in Rodinesque Romanticism, Neo-Baroque and careful balanced classicism, Neo-Gothic and Celtic Revival styles. John was a truly national artist who seized the opportunity of a reawakening of Welsh identity to create a style and mood fit for the new capital, institutions and heroes of Wales. The National Museum of Wales and National Library of Wales have numerous pieces of his work and others are at the Royal Academy, Tate Gallery and the Imperial War Museum.

F. Pearson, *Goscombe John* (1979); *Teaching of art in Wales* (Cymmrodorion, 1925); *Welsh historical sculpture* (City of Cardiff, 1916); *Trans. Cymm.*, 1928-29, 202. See *DNB, 1951-60*; *Cymru*, 46, 1914, 100; NLW MSS 19979A, 20028B, 20471C (2975), 21482D; Cardiff Library MS 3.365.

P.J.

JONES (FAMILY), Cilie, Cards. A family of smiths, poets, musicians and preachers; they farmed Cilie, a farm of over 300 acres above the sea between Llangrannog and New Quay, Cards. Jeremiah Jones, the father (9 Apr. 1855 – 19 Feb. 1902) was a smith from a family of smiths in northern Pembrokeshire, a family which had, according to tradition, a close relationship to the poets of Cwmdu, near Newcastle Emlyn (see Siencyn Thomas, *DWB*, 965, and John Jenkin, *DWB*, 430-1). Jeremiah and his wife, Mary George (1853-1930) from the George family of Pembrokeshire, came to Blaencelyn in the parish of Llangrannog in 1876 to run the smithy. Their first eight children were born at the smithy; the family moved in 1889 to Cilie farm where the rest of the twelve children were born. Examples of Jeremiah Jones's poetry can be found in *Awen Ysgafn y Cilie* (1976). All his sons learned the blacksmith's craft, although the main occupation of the smithy at Cilie was dealing with horses and farm machinery. A number of the boys and girls, especially Tom, the third, and Ann, the sixth child, made an outstanding contribution to the singing in the area around Capel y Wig. Except for Tom, the other boys – Frederick; David ('Isfoel'); John ('Tydu'); Evan George ('Sioronwy'); and, Alun Jeremiah – were poets skilled in the strict and in the free metres and much of their work has survived (see below). Several anecdotes relating to the family can be found in *Ail gerddi Isfoel a hunangofiant byr* (1965), and in *Awen ysgafn y Cilie*.

FREDERICK CADWALADR (Fred; 1877-1948), Independent minister, writer and nationalist, was the eldest child; b. 3 May 1877 in the smithy house, Blaencelyn. After he left Pontgarreg school, he worked in the smithy and on the farm while he attended, intermittently, the tutorial school at New Quay between 1897 and 1899. That year, he went to Bala-Bangor College and to the University College, Bangor to prepare for the ministry. He obtained a B.A. degree in 1903 and a B.D. in 1910 after he had entered the ministry. He served as a minister in Moreia, Rhymney, 1906-17; Bethania, Treorchy, 1917-27; and, Bethel, Talybont, Cards., 1927-48. He was prominent in establishing Cymrodorion societies at Rhymney and at Treorchy; he was interested in social matters

and always placed an emphasis, from the platform or in the press, on the value of the Welsh language and the need to defend it. He was a county councillor in Cardiganshire from 1927 until his death in 1948.

He was a member of a group in south Wales which sought to establish a political party to work for self-government. Fred Jones was one of the six who gathered in Pwllheli in 1925 to found *Plaid Cymru*. For a long period, he was a popular lecturer on topics like 'Michael D. Jones', 'Homespun', 'Learn both', and 'Daniel Owen'. He was also an university external lecturer in the Rhondda and in Cardiganshire. He was noted at university as a writer of *englynion* and *cywyddau* as well as a lively and amusing companion; he was an original, powerful and bold preacher. He won the chair at the Gwent *eisteddfod* in 1913 for an ode on 'Llywelyn ein llyw olaf'; he served as an adjudicator at the national *eisteddfod*. He published a pamphlet on the Old Testament, *Llên a Dysgeidiaeth Cyfnod: I: Hanes Israel* (1929); he prepared entries for the *Geiriadur Beiblaidd* (1926); he left a manuscript which was published in 1977 under the title *Hunangofiant gwas fferm*; he published a short drama, 'Y ngŵr i' in *Y Llenor* (Oct. 1926); his *englynion* and light verse were published in *Awen ysgafn y Cilie*, 1976.

He m. (1) in 1906, Maud, the daughter of Rev. and Mrs. E.H. Davies, Llannon, Carms.; (2) Eunice, the daughter of Rev. and Mrs. D. Rhagfyr Jones, Treorchy, Glam. He d. 2 Dec. 1948.

DAVID ('Isfoel'; 1881-1968), the fourth child, was born in the smithy house on 16 June 1881. When his father died in 1902, most of the farm work fell on him and on his mother. He was a gifted smith and engineer. As a young man 'Dai Cilie' or 'Isfoel' became well known in his community as a poet, a composer of ballads, and a witty compère of *eisteddfodau*. He won prizes regularly at *eisteddfodau* for the *englyn*, *cywydd* and lyric. His *englynion* and verses written for special occasions became part of folk memory. Despite the frivolity and humour that characterised his verses, he wrote *cywyddau*, lyrics and, especially, memorial *englynion* with the hand of a master. He was made an honorary druid of *Gorsedd y Beirdd* and he named his retirement home, for himself and his wife Catrin (from Nanternis), 'Derwydd' [Druid]. They had one son and they both spent their lives in the Pontgarreg district, near Llangrannog. Isfoel was a frequent adjudicator at the national *eisteddfod* and, with his brother Alun, he directed the drama company, 'Cilie-Crannog'. In his later years, he published *Cerddi Isfoel*, 1958; *Ail gerddi Isfoel a hunangofiant byr*, 1965; and *Hen ŷd y wlad*, 1966. A selection of his work was published in *Awen ysgafn y Cilie*, 1976. He d. 1 Feb. 1968.

SIMON BARTHOLOMEUS (1894-1964), the youngest but one of the children, an Independent minister and a poet, was born at Cilie on 5 July 1894. He was a seaman in his youth but he returned to Cilie after falling into the hold of his ship in Buenos Aires harbour and breaking both legs, an accident which led to his spending 9 months in a local hospital. He entered the ministry after a course of study at the tutorial college in New Quay, University College, Bangor and Bala-Bangor College. He received a B.A. after interrupting his studies to serve with the Y.M.C.A. during World War I. He served as a minister at churches in Great Mersey St., Liverpool, 1922-27; Creigfryn, Carno, 1927-32 and Peniel near Carmarthen, 1932-62. He m., in 1923, Annie, the daughter of Mr. and Mrs. David Jones, the schoolmaster at Glynarthen. On his retirement, they went to live in Glynarthen, Cards., where he died on 27 July 1964. A popular preacher, he also conducted singing festivals when a young minister. At Peniel, he trained a dramatic company which achieved considerable success; he was an adjudicator of acting on several occasions.

From his college days until his death, he wrote poetry regularly. He won the crown at the Wrexham national *eisteddfod* in 1933 for a poem, 'Rownd yr Horn', and the chair at Fishguard national *eisteddfod* in 1936 for an ode 'Tyddewi', as well as lesser prizes at the National *eisteddfod*. He was an adjudicator at several national *eisteddfodau* and he was a chief bard in the *Gorsedd* of Bards under the name 'SB'. He published an outstanding, prize-winning ode, 'Yr unben', in 1935. After his death, his poetry and some of his prose writings were published in *Cerddi ac ysgrifau S.B. Jones* (1965).

Personal knowledge; [J.M. Jones, *Teulu'r Cilie*, 1999.]

G.Jo.

JONES, ALFRED ERNEST (1879-1958), psychoanalyst and Sigmund Freud's official biographer; b. 1st January, 1879, in Gowerton, near Swansea, Glam., the son of Thomas and Mary Ann Jones. He was removed from the local school to schools in Swansea, and from there he won a scholarship to Llandovery College. Subsequently, he became a student at University College, Cardiff, and University College, London, and while he was there, in 1900, he gained the diplomas of the Conjoint Board of the Royal Colleges (L.R.C.P., M.R.C.S.), and a year later, he obtained a London University degree in Medicine (M.B.) with honours and gold medals in Medicine and Obstetrics; and Sir John Williams (*DWB*, 1055-6) awarded him the University's Gold Medal in Obstetrics. Within five years, he obtained a series of postgraduate qualifications (M.D. with a gold medal, M.R.C.P., D.P.H.), but after several disagreements with the committees of the hospitals at which he worked, he had to resign. He spent some months visiting various clinics on the Continent before moving to Toronto as the head of a new psychiatric clinic. It was at his suggestion that the first international psychoanalytical congress was held in Salzburg in 1908, and there he read his famous paper on rationalization.

He was made an Associate Professor of the University of Toronto, and he did a great deal to accelerate the development of psychoanalysis in north America. In 1913, he returned to London without any hope of a university or hospital post, and it was there that he worked until he retired. In 1929, he offered evidence to the B.M.A. committee which led to their recommendation that Psychoanalysis should be recognised as an acceptable form of treatment. He formed the British Psychoanalytical Society, the Institute of Psychoanalysis and created the first psychoanalytical clinic in Britain. He was the President of the British Psychoanalytical Society (1919-1944), and the International Psychoanalytical Association (1920-24; 1930-49), the founder and editor of the International Psychoanalytical Library, and fifty volumes were published by the Library under his editorship. He founded the *International Psychoanalytical Journal*, and was its editor from 1920 to 1939. He was the international leader of the psychoanalytical movement for many years, and ensured that Freud was released from Nazi hands in 1938.

His interest in Welsh affairs was rekindled in the 1920s, and he became a keen member of the Welsh Nationalist Party soon after its formation, but to his great regret, he never learned to speak Welsh fluently. He is remembered as the person who did most to popularize Freud's work through the medium of the English language, and he published more than three hundred papers and a dozen books, but his pioneer work in psychoanalysis was not recognised outside his own field, and he had to wait almost until the time of his death before being elected a Fellow of his old college in London. Late in his life, he received many honours including the F.R.C.P. (1942), the D.Sc. (Wales) *honoris causa*, (1954), but long before that he had been elected an honorary member of several foreign psychoanalytical Societies.

In February 1917, he married (1) Morfydd Llwyn Owen (*DWB*, 716-7), and after her death in September 1918, he married (2) Katherine Jökl of Vienna in 1919.

He died on February 11th, 1958, and was cremated at Golders Green Crematorium, London. His ashes were buried in the grave of the oldest of his four children in the cemetery at Cheriton Church, Gower.

T.G. Davies, *Ernest Jones* (1979); Ernest Jones, *Sigmund Freud*, *I-III* (1953-57); Ernest Jones, *Free Associations* (1959); [Vincent Brome, *Ernest Jones* (1983)]; The Ernest Jones Papers (in the Inst. of Psychoanalysis, London).

T.G.D.

JONES, ALICE GRAY ('Ceridwen Peris'; 1852-1943), author; b. Dec. 1852 at Llanllyfni, Caerns. dau. of David and Ellen Jones. Her father was a brother of Rev. John Jones, Brynrodyn, and her mother a cousin of Rev. John John Roberts, 'Iolo Caernarfon' (*DWB*, 870). She was educated at Dolbadarn primary school and at the Swansea Training College, and was headmistress of her old school prior to her marriage in 1881 to Rev. William Jones, minister at Fourcrosses, Caerns. They had 4 children. She edited *Y Gymraes* from 1896 to 1919. She wrote a number of books for children, including *Caniadau Ceridwen Peris*. She played a prominent part in the establishment of the Treborth Home. She was one of the founders of the North Wales Women's Temperance Union, and was an active member of many committees. She moved to live at Cricieth in 1919. She d. at the home of her dau. at Bangor, 17 April 1943.

Y Goleuad, 28 Apr, 1943; *Y Gymraes*, Oct, 1919; *WwW* (1937).

M.B.D.

JONES, ARTHUR LLEWELLIN (1863-1947) - see MACHEN, ARTHUR below.

JONES, BENJAMIN (1865-1953), Chancellor of Bangor Cathedral; b. in Minffordd, Llangeinwen, Anglesey, May 17, 1865, son of Thomas Jones, a farm labourer and his wife Ann (née Williams). After a period of student-teaching in St. Paul's School Bangor he decided to enter the Church. He was educated 1889-90 in Bangor school of theology where reading, preaching and ministering (under the wing of the church hostel) were taught, and in 1890 became a member of Marcon's Hall, Oxford. He was ordained in Liverpool in 1894 by the Bishop of Sodor and Man and for two years was curate at Rushen, I. of M. In 1896 he returned to the see of Bangor as a curate in St. Ann's, Llandygái. In 1905 he was given the living of Penmachno by Lord Penrhyn and remained there until 1923 and his appointment as vicar of Llanfair-is-gaer (Port Dinorwic). He was promoted canon in 1930 and Chancellor of the Cathedral from 1937 from which he retired in 1940 having completed the period of appointment. He was Rural Dean of Arllechwedd, 1935-48. He restored the old and new church at Llanfair-is-gaer and built a new church hall in Port Dinorwic. He d. Dec. 16, 1953, and was buried in Llanfair-is-gaer. He left a widow; they had no children.

Throughout his career he was active with the Church's publications. He edited Yr Haul, 1913-20, and Y Llan, 1919-38, and was concerned with a project for a bilingual paper for the Church in Wales, Y Llan and Church News and the Church Family Newspaper. His service to the religious press during World War I and in the difficult times immediately after disestablishment was firm and wise. He was a member of the governing body of the Church in Wales from the beginning until 1951.

He was a talented musician and for many years was chairman of the music committee of the see. He established children and adult choirs and won many prizes. He was admitted to the Gorsedd of Bards under the name Heulog.

He was a tall, dignified figure, whose amiable personality demanded a hearing, and a born leader and counsellor. He was a natural debater, always ready to defend the right and not afraid of confrontation - even with archbishops. He assumed that the entire parish was in his care, was welcomed by all denominations and at home in every company. He was one of the founders of Clwb y Felin. 'Chancellor Ben' was a man of great stature in all ways.

Crockford; Llan, 25 Dec. 1953, Yr Haul a'r Gangell (Gaeaf 1954); North Wales Chronicle, 18 and 24 Dec. 1953; testimony of parishioners and personal knowledge.

E.P.R.

JONES, Sir CADWALADR BRYNER (1872-1954), a leading figure in Welsh agricultural education and eminent civil servant; b. 6 Apr. 1872, son of Enoch Jones, Cefnmaelan, Dolgellau, Mer., and Jane, the daughter of Lewis Jones, Maesbryner. He was educated at Dolgellau grammar school and Aspatria agricultural college; he received the degree of M.Sc. from Durham University and was a Fellow of the Highland and Agricultural Society of Scotland. He was appointed assistant lecturer at U.C.N.W., Bangor in 1893, responsible for extension classes in agriculture in north Wales. In 1899 he became lecturer at Armstrong (now King's) College, Newcastle-upon-Tyne. The University College of Wales, Aberystwyth set up its department of agriculture in 1890 – a year later than Bangor – and as in Bangor internal teaching was combined with extension work. The department fell into disarray on the departure of the first lecturer and in 1907 the college took the bold step of appointing Bryner Jones – well-qualified and experienced but still young – to a new chair of Agriculture. From then onward the department, together with the college farm (of which he was director) flourished and he became the undisputed leader of agricultural education in Wales. He also came to the forefront as an administrator. In 1912 the special needs of Wales began to be recognised. An arrangement was made whereby the development of two official schemes covering agricultural education and livestock improvement was entrusted to an Agricultural Commissioner, advised by an Agricultural Council for Wales. Bryner Jones was the obvious choice for appointment both as commissioner and chairman of the Council, the college wisely agreeing that he could carry out these duties while remaining Professor of Agriculture. The outbreak of War in 1914 dictated a change of emphasis, and Bryner Jones became increasingly involved in the work of the food production department of the headquarters. The widening experience and personal contacts he thus gained were later to be of great value to Wales.

In 1919 the Board of Agriculture was given a new title and wider duties; it became the Ministry of Agriculture and Fisheries. It set up a Welsh department at Aberystwyth, with Bryner Jones, who now resigned his professorship, as the first Welsh secretary. For the next twenty years he presided over a department which grew slowly but steadily as the ministry's work expanded. Nevertheless, it continued to regard agricultural education and advisory work at all levels together with livestock improvement as its main responsibility. One beneficial result of this policy and of the Secretary's leadership became evident during World War II. The all-important County War Agricultural Executive Committees in Wales were able to enlist an exceptional band of experienced and well-trained farmers and technical officers in the vital tastk of increasing food production.

A fine physique enabled Bryner Jones to remain fully active until his death. After the strenuous war years from 1939 to 1944, when he officially retired, he continued to act as the Minister's liaison officer and was chairman of Montgomeryshire committee from that time until 1947. But this was not the final chapter in his long career. From 1948 to 1953 he was deputy chairman of the newly formed Agricultural Land Commission for England and Wales and was chairman of the Welsh Agricultural Land Sub-commission. During this period the Sub-committee conducted a far-reaching survey of farming conditions in mid-Wales. The results were published in 1955 in The Mid-Wales Investigation Report. He also managed and began to rehabilitate the Glan-llyn section of the Wynnstay estate after its transfer in part settlement of death duties.

Ever since his arrival at Aberystwyth, Bryner Jones had taken a broad view of his responsibilities. Consequently, he was engaged in a range of activities which today are often assigned to full-time staffs. Thus he was president of the Welsh Mountain Sheep Flock Book Society from 1913 to 1919, while his keen interest in Welsh black cattle was recognised by his election to the Society's presidency in 1944-45. Another institution which owed a great debt to him was the National Show - now the Royal Welsh Agricultural Show. He acted as honorary director, 1908-10, was chairman of its council from 1944 to 1953, and became its president in 1954. His other life-long interests were Dr Williams' School, Dolgellau, to which he gave generous service for 25 years as chairman of the governors, and U.C.W., Aberystwyth. He was a member of the college council from 1920 till his death. He did much to ensure that the Welsh Plant Breeding Station, with George Stapledon (see below) as first director and Professor of Agricultural Botany, came to Aberystwyth. In recognition of his services to higher education the University of Wales awarded him the hon. degree of LL.D. in 1938. His official career was fittingly marked by the award of C.B.E. in 1920, C.B. in 1934, and a knighthood in 1947.

Sir Bryner was the author of the first Welsh book on the scientific principles of manuring, *Egwyddorion gwrteithio* (1907); he edited *Livestock of the farm* and numerous reports of agricultural experiments. He was a contributor to the *Welsh Jnl. of Agric.*, first published in 1925, on behalf of the Welsh Agricultural Education Conference of which he was chairman.

He was unmarried. He d. 10 Dec. 1954 and was buried at Brithdir, where his grandfather Cadwaladr Jones (1783-1867; *DWB*, 447) had been Congl. minister.

Ellis, *UCW*; U.C.W. archives; Ashby and Evans, *The Agriculture of Wales* (1943); Sir John Winnifrith, *The Ministry of Agriculture, Fisheries and Food* (1962); personal knowledge.

J.M.J.

JONES, Sir CYNAN (ALBERT) EVANS ('Cynan'; 1895-1970), poet, dramatist and *eisteddfodwr*; b. 14 Apr. 1895, the son of Richard Albert Jones and Hannah Jane (née Evans), Pwllheli, Caerns. He received his education at the elementary school and the County School at Pwllheli, and University College, Bangor (on a Baptist scholarship), where he graduated in 1916. In the same year he enlisted in the R.A.M.C., serving in Salonika and France as a member of the 86th Field Ambulance, and later as chaplain. After the war he entered Bala (CM) Theological College, and in 1920 he was ordained and inducted pastor of the Presbyterian church at Penmaen-mawr. In 1931 he relinquished his pastorate on appointment as Regional Tutor for Anglesey under the Extramural Department of University College, Bangor, and from 1936 until his retirement in 1960 he was Staff Tutor in the Department, specialising in Drama and Welsh Literature. He continued to accept preaching engagements regularly.

Cynan, as he was generally known, was a prominent figure in the life of Wales through his links with the National *Eisteddfod*. (He adopted the pseudonym Cynan on becoming a member of the *Gorsedd* of Bards, and retained it in his title on being knighted). He was appointed Recorder of the *Gorsedd* in 1935, and joint-secretary of the National Eisteddfod Council in 1937. From 1950 till 1954 and from 1963 till 1966 he held the post of Archdruid, the only instance of a person being elected to a second term in this office. Soon after his appointment as Recorder of the *Gorsedd* he initiated changes and reforms. Endowed with a keen sense of drama and pageant, he realised that the *Gorsedd* ceremonies were capable of being made attractive to the crowds. He brought order and dignity to the proceedings, and introduced new ceremonies, such as the flower dance. He renounced all the *Gorsedd's* former claims to antiquity and links with the Druids, and openly acknowledged that it was the invention of Iolo Morganwg (Edward Williams; *DWB*, 1033-4). He succeeded in gaining many new members, including some academics. In 1935 a start was made on the reorganisation of the *Eisteddfod* which resulted in the establishment of the Court and the Council, and in this Cynan played a prominent part. He was appointed President of the Court in 1967.

He was also prominent as a National *Eisteddfod* competitor. In 1921 he won the crown at Caernarfon with his poem 'Mab y Bwthyn', the story of a young Welshman's experiences in the 1914-18 war. So topical was the subject and so simple and straightforward the style and the versification that the poem attained immediate popularity. The subject of Cynan's second prize poem, 'Yr Ynys Unig' (Mold 1923), the story of Father Damien's mission to the lepers, made this an equally popular composition. His third crown poem, 'Y Dyrfa' (Bangor 1931), described a rugby match, the first time such a topic was attempted. The influence of contemporary English poets, especially John Masefield and J.C. Squire, is evident in these eisteddfodic poems, but it has been so thoroughly assimilated as to make the poems completely and distinctively Welsh. In the Pontypool *eisteddfod* in 1924 Cynan was awarded the chair for a poem 'I'r Duw nid adwaenir', which is a unique achievement in that the poem is in the metre known as 'tri thrawiad', which is not one of the recognised strict metres. He also adjudicated many times at the National *Eisteddfod*.

Cynan published the following volumes of poetry: *Telyn y Nos* (1921); *Y Tannau Coll*, the second best crown poem at the Ammanford national *eisteddfod* in 1922; *Caniadau Cynan* (1927); *Cerddi Cynan, y casgliad cyflawn* (1959), which included all the eisteddfodic poems, ballads, lyrics and translations of poems by English authors (not all of them acknowledged as such). The style is unaffected and the diction straightforward, in the manner of all the lyrical poets of the first quarter of the century. Many of the poems are based on the author's reaction to World War I and his own personal experience of it. On the other hand he was greatly inspired by the peace and tranquility of the Llŷn countryside. The narrative element, in the ballads and in the long poems, is more conspicuous in his work than in that of any other Welsh poet. In

1946 he published a short prose romance, *Ffarwel Weledig*, set in Macedonia.

Drama in Wales owes a great deal to Cynan. In 1931 he won the prize offered at the National *Eisteddfod* for a full-length play with his *Hywel Harris*. *Absalom fy mab* was the outcome of a commission which he accepted to write a play for the *eisteddfod* in 1957. He translated and adapted John Masefield's *Good Friday* and Norman Nicholson's *The Old Man of the Mountain*. But his most valuable contribution to the drama movement in Wales was through his lectures to extramural classes and drama festivals, his direction of performances, in which he himself sometimes took part as an actor, and his adjudications at the national *eisteddfod* in both the play-writing and play-performing competitions. He was for a period a tutor in a course arranged for young actors by Cwmni Theatr Cymru. He wrote and produced large-scale pageants, such as the historical pageant in Conwy castle in 1927, and the ones in Caernarfon castle in 1929 and 1930. In 1931 he was appointed reader of Welsh plays on behalf of the Lord Chamberlain, a post which he held till the abolition of censorship in 1968.

Cynan was awarded the degree of D.Litt. *honoris causa* by the University of Wales in 1961, and in 1963 was elected honorary freeman of his native town of Pwllheli. He was appointed C.B.E. in 1949, and knighted in 1969. He m. (1) Ellen J. Jones of Pwllheli in 1921, and there was a son and daughter of the marriage. His wife d. in 1962, and in 1963 he m. (2) Menna Meirion Jones of Valley, Anglesey. Cynan d. 26 January 1970.

Llwyfan, 5, Cynan memorial number (1970); personal knowledge and information supplied by Mr. Ernest Roberts; [Ifor Rees, *Cynan, Cyfres Bro a Bywyd* (1982); Bedwyr L. Jones, *Cynan, y llanc o dref Pwllheli* (1981); *Y Goleuad*, 24.4.1981; Dafydd Owen, *Cynan* (1979)].

T.P.

JONES, DAFYDD RHYS (1877-1946), schoolmaster and musician; b. 10 June 1877 in Maes Cornet, Drofa Dulog, Patagonia, one of the 10 children of Dafydd Jones and Rachel (née Williams) his wife. The father was among the first group to land on the beaches of Patagonia. He came from the Blaenporth area, Cards., of the same family as John Jones, Blaenannerch (1807-75; *DWB*, 480). His mother's family had emigrated from Bryn-mawr to the Welsh settlement in Rio Grande in Brazil and she was fluent in Portugese and Welsh. When that small settlement was dispersed they moved to Patagonia. The grandmother was a notable character in the religious history of the colony and was one of the founders of the Presb. church in Tre-lew. Her grandson inherited much of her adventurous spirit.

After attending the school of Richard Jones Berwyn (*DWB*, 33) the 15-year old youth was sent to Wales to be educated in Cardigan board school; Ardwyn school, Aberystwyth; and Newcastle Emlyn grammar school. Contemporaries at Newcastle Emlyn were William and David Davies of Pontrhydygroes with whom he spent part of his holidays, thus beginning his very long association with that area. He gained a teacher's certificate at Aberystwyth College,

and taught in Corris, Bryn-mawr, and Park Boys' School in Aberdare, before taking charge of Cwmystwyth school in Dec. 1902. At the end of March 1906 he returned to Patagonia to be first headmaster of the secondary school there. A few weeks earlier Eluned Morgan (*DWB*, 643) had visited Cwmystwyth school and addressed the pupils. Apparently there was a connection between this visit and his appointment as headmaster in Gaiman where he spent 8 influential and successful years. In 1914 he returned to Britain to teach in Hereford. G.J. Williams, the headmaster of Cwmystwyth school (and cousin of Professor Griffith John Williams, see below), was called for military service and replaced by temporary headteachers. In Jan. 1917 Dafydd Rhys Jones began his second term as headmaster of his old school, and remained there until the permanent headmaster returned at the end of Jan. 1920, and again for some weeks in April and May after G.J. Williams had taken a similar post in Pontrhydfendigaid. Dafydd Rhys Jones was then appointed headmaster of Ysbyty Ystwyth school and remained there until he reached retirement age in 1941.

He was an ardent supporter of *eisteddfodau*, and conductor of a well-known children's choir and a mixed choir from Pontrhydygroes and Ysbyty Ystwyth for over twenty years, winning many prizes. As a remarkable elocutionist he was in great demand at concerts, and he often served as music and literary adjudicator in *eisteddfodau*. He supported drama, being active on stage and as an adjudicator, and collaborated with his friend David Joshua Davies, the author of *Maesymeillion* (see above). He took a prominent part in the educational life of his county, becoming chairman of the Cardiganshire teachers' union. He was an approved lay preacher (Congl.), and a member of Baker Street (Seion) church, Aberystwyth. He had preached in Patagonia, and offered his services to all denominations. He was a firm nationalist, and worked for years on behalf of the New Wales Union as chairman of the Glennydd district. He did much to foster relationships between Wales and Patagonia. At his suggestion *Cymdeithas Cymry Ariannin* was formed during the national *eisteddfod* in Denbigh in 1939, and he was elected its president. After retiring he farmed Maesybeudy, Pontrhydygroes, and he took a particular interest in agriculture.

He m. twice: (1) in 1902, Jane daughter of John and Mary Morgan, Hafodnewydd, who d. in 1904; they had one daughter; (2) in 1927, Daisy, daughter of John and Jane Jones, London. He d. 9 Jan. 1946, and was buried in Ysbyty Ystwyth.

Baner, *Camb. News*, and *Welsh Gaz.*, Jan. 1946; Cwmystwyth school log books; information from Kathleen Hughes.

E.D.J.

JONES, DANIEL EVAN (1860-1941), author; b. 22 Sept. 1860, at Soar, Llangeler, Carms. s. of John Jones and his wife of Bargod Villa, Dre-fach. He was educated at local schools and by the Rev. W.E. Davies at the Pen-rhiw academy. In his youth he worked as a mason and bridge builder. Later he kept flannel and cloth factories in Dre-fach, Llandysul and Machen. He cultivated his literary interests from an early age. In

1899 he published *Hanes Plwyf Llangeler a Phenboyr*, a volume which shows minute and laborious research. The book was the subject of a Dyfed *eisteddfod* prize in August 1897. He also won the *Western Mail* prize for a translation of 'Ar lan Iorddonen ddofn' into English in competition with numerous entries. He d. 18 Aug 1941 at Llaintarad, Llangeler, aged 80, and was buried in the Pen-rhiw cemetery.

Personal knowledge; *Yr Ymofynydd*, Nov. 1898.

J.E.

JONES, DANIEL OWEN (1880-1951), minister (Congl.) and missionary in Madagascar; b. at Tŷ-gwyn, Rhiw-Siôn, Cwm-cou, Cards., near Newcastle Emlyn, 23 Feb. 1880, son of David and Rebecca Jones. He was educated at Tre-wen British School. At 16 years of age he began preaching in Tre-wen chapel under the ministry of David Evans (who later became his brother-in-law). He received further education at Newcastle Emlyn grammar school, the Old College School in Carmarthen and the Heath, Pontypridd. In 1897 he was accepted to the theological college in Brecon. He graduated with honours in Welsh at the University College, Cardiff, in 1902, returning afterwards to Brecon to study theology. In 1905 he was ordained to the Christian ministry at the English Congregational church at Stourbridge. After the death of his mother in 1909 he offered himself to the London Missionary Society, intending to go to China, but the Society felt that there was a need in Madagascar for a man of his qualifications. Perhaps they were also conscious of the long connection between Wales and the mission there. For a short period he went to France to learn French. His commissioning service was held in 1910 at Lyndhurst chapel, Hampstead, and he arrived at Madagascar at the end of Nov. that same year.

His first station was Ambohimanga, the old capital, where he ministered to eight churches and a school. On 1 May 1912, at Faravohitra Memorial Church, Antananarivo, he m. Hilda Victoria Smith, a member of the Anglican church at Watford, who had travelled out there in March to marry him. They had four daughters. He was moved to Ambopotsy in 1915 to superintend a wide circle of churches and to lecture on three mornings a week at the United Theological College. He returned to Wales for his first furlough at the end of ten years. On his return to the island he was moved to Antsihanaka to restart the missionary work which he had been obliged to stop when the French occupied the country, and to establish an academy for ministers at Imerimandroso to serve the north. A missionary hospital had been opened the previous year. He also superintended about 70 churches in the area around lake Alaotra. The women of the Welsh Congregational churches in the Swansea district bought a motor boat (named *Abertawe*) to make travelling easier, but the venture was unsuccessful owing to the luxuriant growth in the shallow water. In 1927 he was awarded the M.A. degree of the University of Wales for a dissertation on 'The Eschatology of the Celtic Church'. During his absence in 1926 the mission station at Imerimandroso was totally destroyed by a tornado. After it had been rebuilt, he established there a theological college to train ministers in place of the old academy. Three native teachers were appointed to help him, and three ladies to teach the women. Students came to the college from as far as Mandritsara, 200 miles away across the mountains. In 1930 he was made principal of the United Theological College in the capital, and he superintended a large circle of churches in three districts. After returning to Britain on furlough in 1939 he was prevented from returning until 1944, on account of the war. In 1947 he found himself in the middle of the bitter revolt against the French government. By then he had passed retirement age after 38 yrs. of diligent and dedicated service on the island. He d., three years after leaving the island, on 17 June 1951, and was buried in the churchyard of the Congregational church in Bushey. A memorial tablet to him was unveiled by his widow at Tre-wen chapel on 13 June 1956.

He was a kindly man with a good sense of humour, courteous in manner and totally dedicated to his work. He was a talented author and poet; he composed many hymns in Malagasi, and translated others from Welsh and English. He wrote a book on pastoral theology in Malagasi, which had a wide circulation, and also two commentaries on the Psalms. He made numerous contributions to ecclesiastical journals in Madagascar, and he was also the author of two books for children, *Ar lannau'r Llyn Mawr* (1929) and *Am dro i Fadagascar* (1950). In 1942 he contributed an article to the quarterly *Religion* on 'Primitive Cults and Beliefs in Madagascar'. He addressed the Union of Welsh Independents at Ammanford (1927) and Caernarfon (1949).

D. Brinley Pugh, *Triawd yr Ynys* (1954); *Tywysydd y Plant*, Feb., 1941; *Tyst*, 5 July 1951.

I.S.J.

JONES, DAVID GWYNFRYN (1867-1954), minister (Meth.); b. in Bryn-crug, Mer. 1 Nov. 1867. When he was seven, the family moved to Treorchy, but they returned to Bryn-crug two years later and he received a little education in the Board School there. At 12 he went to work in the colliery, but he sought more education in a private school in the Rhondda and later in a preparatory school in Cardiff. In 1890 he went to Dinas Mawddwy as a lay agent. After being received into the ministry in 1894 and appointed to Ashton-in-Makerfield, he served in the circuits at Ffynnongroyw (1897), Llangefni (1898), Bangor (1901), and Chester (1902). In 1904 his health broke down and he went to South Africa to seek a cure, becoming the minister of the non-denominational church in Cape Town. On his return he went to the circuits in Llandudno (1905), and Barmouth (1909), but became a supernumary for a year in 1911 because of ill-health, and in 1912 he moved to Flint Mountain where he lived for the rest of his life as a minister without charge. He was appointed editor of *Y Gwyliedydd Newydd* and remained in that post until 1940. He was the President of the Conference in 1924. From 1928 to 1934, he was the secretary of the first North Wales Province, and Moderator from 1934 to 1938. He was also secretary of the Bookroom for a while. He was in the first rank of the preachers of his time. In 1938 he became a supernumary and the Conference presented him with a testimonial. He held many other posts: editor of *Y Winllan*, secretary of the North Wales Free Church Council, a magistrate, a member of Flint county council, president of the North Wales Socialist Alliance, parliamentary candidate for Flintshire in 1922 and 1924. He was co-author of *Cofiant Glanystwyth*, and he edited *Odlau Moliant* for the Welsh church in Cape Town. He lectured widely and contributed regularly to Welsh periodicals. He m. Christiana Lloyd, and they had two sons. He d. on Dec. 18, 1954.

Minutes of Conference, 1955; personal knowledge.
G.R.T.

JONES, DAVID JAMES (1886-1947), Professor of Philosophy; b. 22 Dec. 1886 at Y Pandy, Pontardulais, Glam., son of William and Jane Jones. Educated at Gowerton, Cardiff University College, and Emmanuel College, Cambridge, he took firsts in Philosophy and Hebrew (Wales, M.A., 1912) and became a Fellow of the University of Wales. Ordained to the ministry of the Presbyterian Church of Wales in 1915, he was Chaplain to the Forces in France in World War I. He held pastorates in Brynmawr and Swansea. A breakdown in health in 1924 caused his retirement. In 1928 he was appointed tutor in Philosophy and Psychology at Coleg Harlech and, ten years later, Professor of Philosophy at Bangor University College. In 1916 he married Margaretta Roderick of Gwynfe, and they had two sons. He d. 23 July 1947, and was buried at Bangor.

To the passion which had characterized his preaching were later added, as the consequences of his prolonged fight against ill-health, a mature wisdom, contentment, dignity, and gentleness which made him a remarkable teacher. In his philosophy he sought to bring together the scientific standpoint with the Christian. In 1939 he published a penetrating study of Greek thought, *Hanes Athroniaeth: Y Cyfnod Groegaidd*; other publications include 'Nodiadau ar y Method Gwyddonol' in *Harlech Studies*, 1938, and articles in *Y Traethodydd* and *Efrydiau Athronyddol*.

Obituary notices in *Efrydiau Athronyddol*, 1947 and *Y Goleuad*, 13 Aug. 1947.
R.I.A.

JONES, DAVID JAMES ('Gwenallt'; 1899-1968), poet, critic and scholar; b. 18 May 1899 at Pontardawe, Glam., the eldest of three children of Thomas ('Ehedydd') Jones and his wife Mary. His parents were from Carmarthenshire and his consciousness of his roots was an important element in his personality, as is seen in his essay on Rhydycymerau in the D.J. Williams presentation *Festschrift* (ed. J. Gwyn Griffiths, 1965). The family moved to Allt-wen and Gwenallt was educated at local schools and Ystalyfera County School (where Kate Roberts was his teacher for a brief period). He was a pupil-teacher in 1916-17 dividing his time between Pontardawe elementary school and the 6th form in the county school. When he was conscripted to the army before taking his

Higher Certificate examinations, he stood as a conscientious objector on political grounds and he spent two years from June 1917 to May 1919, in Wormwood Scrubs and Dartmoor prisons. He went to the University College of Wales Aberystwyth in 1919, at a particularly brilliant time in the social life of that institution. He met there Idwal Jones (*DWB*, 506-7) whose biography he wrote in 1958. Following his degrees in Welsh and in English he was appointed Welsh master at Barry County School and then in 1927, lecturer in Welsh at Aberystwyth. He was promoted senior lecturer and subsequently reader (the first to be appointed to this new grade in Aberystwyth). He retired in 1966. He took his M.A. in 1929 and he was awarded a D.Litt. *honoris causa* by the University of Wales in 1967. He m. Nel Edwards in 1937 and they had one dau. He d. at Aberystwyth hospital 24 Dec. 1968. A memorial plaque was placed on his house Rhydymôr, Ffordd Rheidol, Penparcau, Aberystwyth, in 1997.

Gwenallt's first fields of research were the lives of the saints and rhetoric in bardic schools at the end of the middle ages (see *Yr Areithiau Pros*, 1934), and though he published studies such as *Y Ficer Prichard a 'Canwyll y Cymry'* (1946), *Blodeugerdd o'r Ddeunawfed Ganrif* (1936, 1947), he is best known as a literary historian of the 19th c. In addition to numerous articles on individual poets he published *Detholiad o ryddiaith Gymraeg R.J. Derfel* (1945), *Bywyd a Gwaith Islwyn* (1948), *Y Storm: dwy gerdd gan Islwyn* (1954). Nevertheless, his greatest contribution was as a poet and writer. He was among the first members of *Yr Academi Gymraeg* and the first ed. of its periodical *Taliesin* to 1964 (vol.9). His father had been his first teacher and he served his apprenticeship in local *eisteddfodau* and at college. His *awdl* 'Y Mynach' won the chair at the Swansea national *eisteddfod* (1926) but his awdl 'Y Sant', though adjudged the best at the Treorchy national *eisteddfod* (1928), was not awarded the chair. He won the chair with his *awdl* 'Breuddwyd y Bardd' at the Bangor national *eisteddfod* (1931). The poems, sonnets and longer narrative poems in his collections of verse, *Ysgubau'r Awen* (1939), *Cnoi Cil* (1942), *Eples* (1951), *Gwreiddiau* (1959), *Y Coed* (1969) are more personal and express the poet's deeply held convictions, his attitude to life and a complex personality. Running through his work are the threads of his attachment to Wales and her culture, and his meditation on the nature of evil which threatens the civilization of which the poet and his people are part. As his writing developed and his response to materialistic, industrial society and to the crisis in Wales grew more intense, his style became ever more uncompromising and rougher. His two novels, *Plasau'r Brenin* (1934) and *Ffwrneisiau* (1982), which draw on his experiences in prison and as a lad in the Swansea valley are not as successful as his poetry.

Gwenallt was committed and serious in everything which he undertook. He was one of the early members of *Plaid Cymru*, he was politically minded and keenly interested in current affairs (the result of sustained thinking about his personal experience in an industrial environment) and he experienced a difficult but triumphant spiritual pilgrimage as he revealed in his essay in *Credaf* (ed. J.E. Meredith, 1943).

Glyn Lewis Jones, *Llyfryddiaeth Ceredigion 1600-1964*, ii, 549, *(1964-68)*, 137, a list of his works; Lynn Owen-Rees, *Cofio Gwenallt* (1978); 'Rhai Atgofion', *Llais y lli*, 25 May 1966; *Traeth.*, Apr. 1969; *Baner*, Jan. 1969; *Eurgrawn*, summer 1969; Dyfnallt Morgan, *Gwenallt* (1972); J.E. Meredith, *Gwenallt, Bardd Crefyddol* (1974); Dafydd Rowlands, *Gwenallt* (cyfres Bro a Bywyd, 1982); R. Iestyn Hughes, *Llyfryddiaeth Gwenallt* (1983); Donald Allchin and D. Densil Morgan, *Sensuous Glory* (2000); Christine James, ed., *Cerddi Gwenallt, y casgliad cyflawn* (2001).

B.F.R.

JONES, DAVID JOHN TAWE (1885-1949), musician; b. in Rhyd-y-fro, Pontardawe, Glam. Educated at Swansea Grammar School and Cardiff University College, he was organist at Welsh Presbyterian churches in Llanrwst, Cardiff, Carmarthen and Holloway Road (London). He adjudicated and conducted extensively throughout Wales and in England and was Professor of Singing at the Guildhall School of Music during the latter part of his life. His compositions include many choral works and songs (for which he won many prizes at the national *eisteddfod*), together with some instrumental compositions. He held strong views concerning the lack of enterprize of Welsh choirs and the absence of any signs of progress in Welsh choral singing, and longed to hear a Welsh choir of the calibre of the Huddersfield Choir. The complete list of his compositions is too extensive to be included in this article.

He suffered a great deal from the effects of World War I when he was gassed and received a shrapnel wound in his head. Shortly before his death he completed a five-act opera, *The Enchantress*, based on the biblical theme of 'Jezebel' - the libretto by J. Dyfnallt Owen (see below) and an English translation by 'Wil Ifan' (William Evans, see above). The opera is scored for full orchestra. He d. at his home in Golders Green, London, 3 May 1949, aged 64, and was buried in Rhyd-y-fro. He was survived by his widow, Elizabeth.

Personal knowledge; [*Y Ddinas*, June 1949; *Y Darian*, 8 Sept. 1932; *Cymro*, 6 Aug. 1948].

J.H.

JONES, DAVID MORRIS (1887-1957), minister (Presb.) and professor; b. 14 March 1887 at Maes-y-groes, Maenan, Caerns., son of William Maurice and Elisabeth Jones. He was educated at the elementary and free schools in Llanrwst, the University College, Bangor (where he graduated with honours in Welsh and philosophy), Bala College, and Cambridge. He joined the armed forces in 1915, but was recalled from Salonica in 1916 to receive a commission as chaplain to the Welsh regiments in France; he was ord. the same year. He was awarded the M.C. for his bravery whilst administering to the wounded. He was minister of Gorffwysfa, Skewen (1920-24), Blaenau Ffestiniog (1924-29), and Trinity, Swansea (1929-34) before being appointed Professor of the philosophy of religion and history of religions at the Theological College, Aberystwyth, where he remained until he retired in 1953. In 1916 he m. Esther Ann Williams, Pwllheli, and they had two sons and two daughters. He d. 8 Oct. 1957, during his year of office as Moderator of the Association in the South.

Morris was a thorough scholar. He became president of the theology section of the Guild of Graduates of the University of Wales, and was the first editor of its periodical *Diwinyddiaeth*. The Davies Lecture (in Welsh) delivered by him in 1953 on 'God the Creator and God the Saviour' was not published. He published *Llên a dysgeidiaeth Israel hyd gwymp Samaria* (1929), *Efengyl Ioan a'i Hystyr* (1944), and a commentary on the first epistle to the Corinthians (1952).

Drys., Apr. 1957; *Gol.*, 16 Oct. 1957; *Blwyddiadur MC*, 1959, 266-7; information from his daughter, Buddug Morris Jones, London.

G.M.R.

JONES, Sir DAVID THOMAS ROCYN - see ROCYN-JONES, Sir DAVID THOMAS below.

JONES, EDGAR WILLIAM (1868-1953), educationalist and broadcaster; b. 13 Dec. 1868 at Llanrhaeadr-ym-Mochnant, Mont., the son of Richard Bellis Jones, schoolmaster, and Hannah (née Vaughan). He was educated at his father's school and later at the Northern Institute at Liverpool and at Oswestry High School under Owen Owen (*DWB*, 718). From 1885 to 1890, he was a student at U.C.W. Aberystwyth, returning after a period of teaching at Oswestry to read for the degree of M.A. (London) which he took in 1894. After a short period as Headmaster of Llandeilo county school (1894-99) he became headmaster of Barry county school where he remained until his retirement in 1933. He then became Adviser on Welsh matters to the B.B.C., where he organised school programmes and acted as secretary of the Religious Advisory Committee. He was at various times Clerk, Treasurer and Warden of the University of Wales Guild of Graduates, the only person to hold all three offices; a member of the Central Welsh Board, the only one to serve for its entire duration; and member of the Court and Council of the University of Wales, of Aberystwyth, of the University College of South Wales, and of the National Museum of Wales. In 1910 he was President of the Association of Welsh Secondary Schools. During World War I he became Officer commanding the Glamorgan Fortress Engineers with the rank of Major and was awarded the Military O.B.E. The University of Wales conferred on him the honorary degree of M.A. in 1922 and of LL.D. in 1951, and he received the Freedom of Barry in 1951.

He was a vigorous and imaginative headmaster and had an exceptional capacity to inspire loyalty and devotion among both pupils and staff. His personality enabled him to run a very flourishing and happy school with complete authority but without oppressive discipline. He had an extensive knowledge of archaeology and of the arts, particularly of painting, architecture and poetry; and there were hundreds of past pupils whose interest in culture was first awakened by him. He was also keenly interested in sport. At Aberystwyth he was the athletic champion and a member of the soccer team (which he captained) and of the first fifteen, and as headmaster there were few school games at which he was not present. On 22 Dec. 1894 he m. Ann Gwenllian, daughter of Thomas

Jones of Dowlais, and a fellow student at Aberystwyth. She was a lady of considerable ability who at the age of 20, went as a tutor to the grandchildren of John Hughes (1814-89; *DWB*, 382), the pioneer in the development of Russian metallurgy, at Yuzovka, in the Donets basin. They had three children, Gareth (*DWB*, 463) and two daughters. He d. 1 May 1953.

Information supplied by his daughter, Gwyneth; personal knowledge.

J.H.H.

JONES, **EDMUND DAVID** (1869-1941), schoolmaster and author; b. in Trawsfynydd, Mer., 9 Sept. 1869. His father died when the child was very young and he was brought up by a mother of great ability and his grandfather David Jones, a prominent figure with the Scottish Baptists. He acknowledged his debt to the headmaster of the village school and to his teachers at Blaenau Ffestiniog secondary school. In 1885 he went to Bala grammar school and in 1886 to the University College at Bangor where, in 1890, he graduated with honours in French in the University of London. In 1891 he obtained a teaching post in the Birkenhead Institute, but at the end of the year he returned to Bangor as a student-assistant in French. In order to prepare for the London M.A. degree he went to Oxford to attend lectures and to study in libraries without entering a college. Specializing in French and English he took the degree in 1894. Throughout his life he continued his studies, attending holiday classes of the *Alliance Française* in France. When the Barmouth intermediate school was established in 1894, he was appointed headmaster and held the post until his retirement in 1931. He started with only seven pupils in a dwelling house at Barmouth, but by 1900 he had succeeded, through a valiant local effort, to secure a new school near the sea and to make it a power in Arudwy. He was a pioneer schoolmaster; languages were his chief subjects and he placed great stress on phonetics, using the gramophone as an instrument to teach correct pronunciation. He was ahead of his time in the attention which he gave to Welsh and Welsh literature in his school, a standpoint he illustrated in the essay on 'The place of Welsh in the education of the future in Wales' which brought him the prize at the national *eisteddfod* held at Blaenau Ffestiniog in 1898. In the same vein he published in 1900 *Gemau Ceiriog i Blant*, a selection which remained very popular in Welsh schools for over a quarter of a century, reaching its 9th edition by 1927. Another subject very close to his heart was the role of fine art in education. He took care to secure reproductions of the work of the masters for the walls of his school. After retiring from teaching he undertook to compile what he called 'a survey of the development of art from the earliest times to the period of the Renaissance' which resulted in the publication of his illustrated volume, *Camre Celfyddyd*, in 1938. Other aspects of his interests are represented in the English volumes which he edited for grammar schools, e.g. a selection of poems by James Russell Lowell which he considered to be instrumental to lead children to appreciate beauty (*Select Poems ....* 1906); *Of King's Treasures*, 1907, from *Sesame and Lilies* by John

Ruskin, whose influence upon him as a Christian Socialist was marked; *Poems of Wales*, 1914, and two volumes in the 'World's Classics' - *English Critical Essays* (*nineteenth century*), 1916 and 1922, and *English Critical Essays* (*sixteenth, seventeenth, and eighteenth centuries*). He was a Sunday school teacher for many years in Barmouth, and, after his retirement, at Penuel chapel in Bangor, and he contributed a number of articles on difficult passages in the New Testament to *The Expositor*. He m. Claudia, youngest daughter of T.J. Morgan, Calvinistic Methodist minister at Pen-y-garn, near Aberystwyth. He d. following an accident, on 13 Feb. 1941, and was buried at the new cemetery on the Llandygái road.

Seren Gomer, 1942; *Liv.D.P.*, 20 Feb. 1941; *Y Cymro*, 22 Feb. 1941.

G.M.G.

JONES, **EDWARD ALFRED** (1871-1943), connoisseur of silverware; b. 1871, one of the four children of Thomas (d. 1877) and Mary Jones, Upper Cross Keys Inn, Llanfyllin, Mont. The mother moved to Porthmadog (c. 1895) and to Pwllheli (c. 1910). The son had private tuition before joining the Royal Welch Fusiliers but he did not pursue that path and resigned from the army. Having developed a deep interest in gold and silver antiques, he began to write to *Y Cymmrodor* and *Archaeologia Cambrensis* in 1904 and was a regular contributor for the rest of his life to journals such as the *Burlington Magazine* (e.g. 'Some old silver plate in the possession of Lord Mostyn', 1907), *The Connoisseur* (e.g. 'Welsh goldsmiths', 1941), *Apollo*, *The Athenaeum* and *Art in America*. *The church plate of the diocese of Bangor* (1906) was his first book, and it was soon followed by a number of books and catalogues dealing with gold treasures and silver plate of the churches of England and the Isle of Man, the colleges of Oxford and Cambridge, the royal collection in the Tower of London, and many private collections. After visiting museums and homes on the Continent, Russia and United States of America he published the fruits of his studies in *The old English plate of the Emperor of Russia* (1909), *The old silver of American churches* (1909), *Old silver of Europe and America, from early times to the nineteenth century* (1928) and other works. He was appointed Assistant Professor of Fine Art in Yale University, U.S.A., and received an hon. M.A. degree from four universities (Wales; 1918); he was elected a Fellow of a number of learned societies; received the freedom of the city of London; and became a member of the *Gorsedd* of Bards. He d. a bachelor in London 23 Aug. 1943.

Www; *Casglwr*, 32, Aug. 1987, 18-9; OPCS, July-Sept. 1871.

M.A.J.

JONES, **EDWARD OWEN** ('E.O.J.'; 1871-1953), journalist and writer of *englynion*; b. in May 1871 at Welford, Northants., where his father, 'Berwron', was a farm bailiff, but in 1875 the family moved to Llosg-yr-odyn, Y Gaerwen, Anglesey. He was apprenticed to the printer's trade at the Bangor office of the *North Wales Chronicle* in 1887; then in 1903 he succeeded Hugh Edwards as editor of *Y Clorianydd*, the

Anglesey weekly paper, at Llangefni, and held the post for 48 yrs. He was adept at writing *englynion* and competed at the national *eisteddfod* every year; he won the prize at Llandybïe national *eisteddfod* in 1944 for an *englyn* to the serpent: 'one of the poorest I ever made'. He d. 18 Sept. 1953.

Percy Hughes, *Ysgrifau a Cherddi* (1966), 27-30; *Gol.*, 14 Oct. 1953, 3.

B.L.J.

JONES, ELIAS HENRY (1883-1942), administrator and author; b. at Aberystwyth 21 Sept. 1883, eldest son of Sir Henry Jones (*DWB*, 466) and Annie (Walker). He was educated at Glasgow High School, Glasgow University, the University of Grenoble and Balliol College, Oxford, where he proceeded M.A. After being called to the Bar, he passed the Indian Civil Service administrative grade examinations, and in 1905 went to serve in Burma. He retired in 1922 as Financial Commissioner, settled in Bangor, north Wales, and for the next ten years was actively interested in the movement for international peace and in Welsh education. From 1927 to 1933 he was editor of *The Welsh Outlook*. In 1933 he was appointed registrar of the University College of North Wales, a post which he held until his death on 22 Dec. 1942.

E.H. Jones is best known as the author of *The Road to Endor*, the classic account of a cunning escape in World War I. Jones joined the Indian Army as a private soldier and was commissioned just before he was taken prisoner by the Turks after the fall of Kut-el-Amara. He then survived a march of 700 miles to Yozgad, during which one in every seven of the prisoners died, and he was in captivity for three years before he and a comrade, feigning madness, were repatriated only a fortnight before the Armistice. The book was reprinted seventeen times and then ran into three editions.

He m. in 1913 Mair Olwen, the youngest daughter of Dr Griffith Evans of Brynkynallt, Bangor (*DWB*, 235).

WwW (1937); information received from Mrs Jean Ware, daughter of E.H. Jones.

E.G.J.

JONES, Sir ELIAS WYNNE CEMLYN - see CEMLYN-JONES, Sir ELIAS WYNNE above.

JONES, ELIZABETH JANE LOUIS (b. ELIZABETH JANE LLOYD; 1889-1952), scholar; b. 28 Apr. 1889 at Llanilar, Cards., only child of John Lloyd, timber merchant, and his wife Elizabeth (née Edwards). She received her early education at the County School, Aberystwyth and proceeded to the University College, Aberystwyth where she graduated in 1911 with first class honours in Welsh. She was awarded a Fellowship by the University and continued to study for a further three yrs., mostly in London and Oxford libraries. During her time in London she and her close friend Morfydd Llwyn Owen (*DWB*, 716-7) were assisted by Sir John Herbert Lewis (*DWB*, 556) and his wife, Ruth (see below). In 1912 she won a prize and medal at Wrexham national *eisteddfod* for the principal essay on the history of the *Eisteddfod*. The following year she gained her M.A. degree

for a thesis on this topic. She was appointed a lecturer in Welsh and English in 1916 at Bangor Normal College. In 1917 she m. E. Louis Jones, a solicitor of Llanfyllin, son of Dr. Richard Jones, Harlech, and they had four children but two of them d. young. In 1928 she published with Professor Henry Lewis (see below), *Mynegai i farddoniaeth y llawysgrifau* (University of Wales Board of Celtic Studies, 1928). She d. 14 May 1952 at Wrexham, and was buried at Llanfyllin.

Personal acquaintance; *Welsh Music*, summer 1976, 5, no. 3, 99-100.

E.E.L.J.

JONES, ELIZABETH MARY ('Moelona'; 1877-1953), teacher and novelist; b. 21 June 1877, in Moylon, Rhydlewis, Cards., the youngest of the 13 children of John Owen (a carrier who took farm produce by horse and cart to the industrial centres of south Wales before taking the tenancy of the farm, Moylon) and Mary, daughter of Abraham Jones (who was also a carrier). One of the children d. young while the parents were in the cemetery at the burial of two others. Her eldest brother was Owen Rhys Owen (1854-1908), a Congl. minister whose name has become associated with Glandŵr. The family had to leave Moylon and take Llwyneos, a smaller, remote farm, and it was from there that she went to the elementary school in Rhydlewis. John Newton Crowther (*DWB*, 87) was the headmaster - an Englishman who learnt Welsh and became a Welsh poet; he also took a leading part in Hawen (Congl.) chapel where 'Moelona' became a member. At that time there was a flourishing literary and eisteddfodic tradition in the local churches and surrounding district, and her upbringing left a life-long impression on her. One of her contemporaries at school was D. Caradoc Evans (see Caradoc Evans above) and she was appointed pupil-teacher when they both applied for the post. As her mother d. in 1890, she had to care for her father along with her school duties, and so was unable to proceed to college as she had wished, but she secured her teacher's certificate at Rhydlewis. She was appointed teacher in Pontrhydyfen, Bridgend, and Acrefair before going to Cardiff in 1905.

She wrote her first novel, *Rhamant o Ben y Rhos* (1907), for Llwyn-yr-hwrdd *eisteddfod*; it was re-published as *Rhamant y Rhos* (1918). By that time she had profited from the cultural opportunities of the city of Cardiff, and attendance at meetings of the Anglo-French society where she became acquainted with the stories of Alphonse Daudet, describing life in his native locality. Eventually 'Moelona's' translations of Daudet's works were published in various magazines such as *Cymru* (1916) - Sir O.M. Edwards had encouraged her to write - *Y Wawr* (1917), and in a book, *Y wers olaf* (1921). Several essays and stories were published while she was in Cardiff, including *Teulu bach Nantoer* (1913) and *Bugail y Bryn* (1917).

In 1914 she began contributing a children's column to the weekly newspaper, *Y Darian*, under the editorship of J. Tywi Jones (see below), minister of Glais, whom she m. in 1917. She then took up lecturing for a while, but returned to writing essays, novels for children,

Welsh books for schools, girls' novels, such as *Breuddwydion Myfanwy* (1928) and *Beryl* (1931), as well as other books. These works are characterised by a love for her own language, and enthusiasm for the education and provision of opportunities for women. Some of her books, especially *Ffynnonloyw* (1939), reflect very effectively the social characteristics of the society in which she was brought up, though she merely intended relating a story rather than portray society.

In 1935 J. Tywi Jones retired and they moved to New Quay, Cards. He d. in 1948. 'Moelona' retained an interest in the chapel and *eisteddfod* until her death in New Quay on 5 June 1953. They had no children. She was buried in Hawen cemetery, Rhydlewis.

Bibliography in G. Lewis Jones, *Llyfryddiaeth Ceredigion 1600-1964*, 2 (1967); O.L. Roberts, *Cofiant y Parch. O.R. Owen* (1909); Alun R. Edwards, 'Gwasanaeth Moelona', *Welsh Gaz.*, 18 June 1953; [Mairwen and Gwynn Jones, *Dewiniaid Difyr* (1983); her papers in N.L.W.].

D.Je.

JONES, ELIZABETH WATKIN - see WATKIN-JONES, ELIZABETH below.

JONES, ENID WYN (1909-1967) a prominent worker in religious, social and medical fields in Wales and England; b. 17 January 1909 in Wrexham, Denb., daughter of Dr. David Llewelyn Williams (see below) and Margaret Williams. The family moved to Cardiff just before World War I, but she was brought up at Rhyl during the war. She was a pupil at the Welsh Girls' School, Ashford, from 1919 to 1926, and afterwards was trained as a nurse at Cardiff Royal Infirmary. On 9 September 1936 she married Emyr Wyn Jones of Waunfawr, Caernarfon, a physician and cardiologist at Liverpool Royal Infirmary; and there were two children of the marriage. Her home was at Llety'r Eos, Llansannan, and she spent a portion of her time in Liverpool. By virtue of her various offices she travelled widely throughout Wales and England.

Her work with the Y.W.C.A. involved Presidency of the Welsh Council, and Vice-Presidency of the British Council from 1959 to 1967, and she was also a member of the World Council and represented Wales at several conferences abroad. She was the President of the Women's Section of the National Free Church Council of England and Wales in 1958-59, and she was President of the Women's Branch of the New Wales Union in 1966-67. From 1955 to 1967 she was a Justice of the Peace for Denbighshire. She made a very substantial contribution in the field of medical and nursing administration as Vice-Chairman of the Nursing Advisory Council, Welsh Hospital Board; as a member of North Wales Mental Hospital and later Clwyd and Deeside Hospital Management Committees; and as a member of the Medical Executive Committee of Denbighshire and Flintshire, and of the Central Committee of the Royal Medical Benevolent Fund. She was County Vice-President and Commandant of the Denbighshire Branch of the British Red Cross Society.

She addressed many meetings throughout Britain on religious matters, social problems and pacifism. She was a member of the Society of Friends and the Presbyterian Church of Wales. She was an active member of the B.B.C. Religious Committee.

She d. 15 Sept. 1967 very suddenly during her flight home from Melbourne, where she had been representing Wales at the World Council of the Y.W.C.A. and she was buried at Llansannan.

E.W.J., *In Memoriam* (1968); E.W.J., 'Teyrnged Serch', *Traeth.*, Oct. 1969; E.W.J. (ed.), *Cyfaredd Cof* (1970); personal knowledge.

E.W.J.

JONES, Sir EVAN DAVIES (1859-1949), 1st baronet, of Pentower, Fishguard, civil engineer, Lord Lieutenant of Pembrokeshire; b. 18 April 1859, elder son of Thomas Jones, sea-captain, of Pentower, Fishguard, and Martha Philipps, his wife. He was educated at Fishguard national school, privately, and at University College, Bristol. Deciding to become a civil engineer he worked on the Severn Tunnel and the Manchester Ship Canal, eventually becoming a partner, and, later, managing director of Topham, Jones, & Railton, a firm which was responsible for work for government departments or public undertakings at Gibraltar, Fishguard Harbour, Singapore, the Aswan Dam (Egypt), and elsewhere. He was a member of the Institute of Civil Engineers and in the years 1935 and 1936 occupied the presidential chair of the Federation of Civil Engineering Contractors. During World War I he attained the rank of major (T.F.) in the Engineer and Railway Staff Corps of the Royal Engineers, was a member of the committee of three appointed to deal with the organisation of civilian labour for defence purposes in the London area, was Petrol Controller, 1917-18, Chairman of the Road Transport Board, 1918-19, and Commissioner for Dyes under the Board of Trade, 1917-19; he was also Controller of Coal Mines in 1919.

Sir Evan Jones (he was created a baronet in 1917) served his native county and Wales generally in a number of capacities. He served as High Sheriff of Pembrokeshire, 1911-12, became chairman of the Pembrokeshire County Council in 1926, was a Deputy Lieutenant and later (1932) became Lord Lieutenant of that county; he also represented the county in Parliament (as a Coalition Liberal) from December 1918 to October 1922. He gave excellent service to the Representative Body of the Church in Wales over many years (he served for some time as Chairman of its Finance Committee), to the University of Wales, and to the University College of Wales, Aberystwyth. His service to the National Library of Wales was notable both for its length and for its outstandingly devoted character. He was an original member (1907) of the Court of Governors and continued as member for over forty years, becoming in turn Chairman of the Building Committee (in the years when the building of the Library was proceeding stage by stage), Treasurer, and Vice-President. He qualified as a Life-Governor by virtue of his gifts to that institution, both selections from his own large private library of materials relating to Wales (for he was an assiduous collector of Pembrokeshire and non-Pembrokeshire material) and the purchase for the Library of the Compton House (Aberaeron) library and the Llywarch Reynolds (Merthyr Tydfil) collection and by his gift to the Library of his own very extensive collection of book plates of Welsh interest. A bust of him by Sir William Goscombe John (see above) (1924) and a portrait in oils (1939), are in the National Library. In 1927 the University of Wales conferred on him the degree of LL.D. (*honoris causa*); he was also an Officer of the Order of the Nile.

He married (1), 1884, Cecilia Ann Evans, dau. of Jacob Evans, St. Fagans, Glam., by whom he had three sons (two of whom lost their lives in World War I) and three daughters, and (2), Lily Ann Railton (d. 1945), dau. of James Railton, of Malpas, Mon. He d. 20 April 1949 and was buried at Fishguard.

Www; personal knowledge; *N.L.W.J.*, 6, 162-5.
W.Ll.D.

JONES, EVAN KENFFIG (1863-1950), minister (B), social and educational reformer; b. at Bryn Du, Kenfig Hill, Glam., 20 May 1863; student at the Pontypool Baptist College and University College Cardiff; he was ordained at Merthyr Vale in 1889, moved to Brymbo in 1891 and to Cefnmawr in 1913; retired in 1934. He was a zealous, uncompromising Baptist; he was secretary of the Denbigh, Flint, and Merioneth Association for years, and its president twice; president of the Baptist Union of Wales in 1928; president of the Baptist Missionary Society in 1934; he was the outstanding authority on the Circular Letters of the Welsh Associations (*Llythyrau Cymanfa*), as witnessed by his substantial contribution to *Traf. Cymd. Hanes Bed.* in 1922. In addition to all this he was one of the most active personalities in the public life of north Wales, alert, vigorous, full of enthusiasm. He was a member of the sometime Wrexham Board of Guardians, and a prominent member of the Denbighshire Education Committee; (in 1933 he published a valuable book on the history of the schools in the Cefnmawr district). He was an eager advocate of temperance, not only as a leader in the North Wales Temperance Union but as a persuasive pleader at Brewster Sessions ('Your Mr Jones is worth twenty of our men', said a prominent brewer to one of the temperance supporters). He was a sincere pacifist, and boldly carried his beliefs to the military tribunals and wrote numerous pamphlets in Welsh for *Cymdeithas Heddwch Cymru*. His chief literary works, apart from a number of articles in newspapers and periodicals, were *The Baptists of Wales and Ministerial Education* (1902), *Y Beibl a Dirwest* (1906), *A Short Sketch of the History of the Baptist Church of Llanidloes* (1908), *Hanes Cymdeithas Genhadol y Bedyddwyr* (1944); in 1941 he brought out *Hanes Eglwys Annibynnol Brymbo* (*Harwt a Bryn Seion*). In 1937 he received the degree of D.D. *honoris causa* from the University of Wales. He d. on 18 July, 1950.

Seren Cymru, 18 August 1950 (memorial issue); Oct 26, 1956.
T.R.

JONES, FRANCIS WYNN (1898-1970), statistician and writer; b. in Branas Lodge, Llandrillo, Mer., 15 Jan. 1898, second of 4 sons of Thomas Francis and Catherine (née Edwards) Jones. He received his early education at Bala grammar school but went to London, aged 16, to work as a Post Office clerk before joining the army in 1916. He was reported missing in March 1918 but was afterwards found to be a prisoner of war. He enrolled in the University College of Wales, Aberystwyth, in 1919 and graduated with first-class hons. in economics in 1923. He served the National Savings Movement in north Wales before being appointed statistician in the Ministry of Labour in London. He remained there until his retirement in 1959 and during that period he represented the Ministry in conferences and meetings worldwide. He was a leading figure in Welsh religious and cultural life in London, a member of Council and a vice-president of the Hon. Soc. of Cymmrodorion. He was made an O.B.E. in 1959. After retiring he was treasurer and vice-president of *Urdd Gobaith Cymru*, a member of the Court and Council of the Univ. Coll. of Wales and an elder in Seilo (CM) chapel, Aberystwyth.

Though he spent much of his life in London he lost none of his regard for Wales and her language. He remained faithful to Welsh culture and religion and never forgot his debt to his parents and his upbringing in Edeirnion. Small wonder that it was these interests that inspired his writing. In 1952, while living in Watford, he completed a narrative portrayal of his youth in his home area, published as *Godre'r Berwyn*. After retiring to Aberystwyth he accepted an invitation to write a history of his church and his *Canmlwydd Siloh Aberystwyth* (1962) is regarded as an exemplary church history. Towards the end of the 1960s he had the privilege and opportunity to contribute to the official commemoration of his hero and friend – and also his father-in-law – T. Gwynn Jones (see below), by researching and recording his vast published *oeuvre*. The intention was to publish a comprehensive bibliography but though he completed the task he died before its publication. *Llyfryddiaeth Thomas Gwynn Jones* was published by the University of Wales Press in 1989. In his preface the editor, D. Hywel E. Roberts, refers to the notable contribution made by F. Wynn Jones to whom the volume is dedicated. He published a host of articles in periodicals such as *Y Traethodydd*, *Y Ford Gron*, *Y Genhinen*, as well as official publications relating to his statistical work.

At a troubled time in the story of the Welsh language he fought quietly for its equal status and voluntarily translated a number of forms and documents before there was a general call for them.

He m. in 1926 Eluned, dau. of T. Gwynn Jones and his wife and they had a son and dau. He d. in Aberystwyth 21 Dec. 1970.

Personal knowledge.
N.H.W., Em.W.J.

JONES, GEORGE DANIEL (1877-1955), master printer; b. 1877 in Lampeter, Cards., the son of Daniel and Margaret (née Rees) Jones, Red Lion Fach, later of Harford Row, Lampeter, Cards. George was apprenticed to T.L. Davies, Caxton Press, Lampeter and thereafter joined the staff of a well-known firm of printers at Gloucester as an improver. Within a few years, on the advice of J. Gwenogvryn Evans (*DWB*, 245-6), he joined the Oxford University Press, and soon both worked a small hand press to print some of the first volumes of Early Welsh Texts which Gwenogvryn published privately. At the end of September 1909 George Jones moved to Aberystwyth to set up the new National Library's printing press and remained until September 1925 when he accepted the post of Works' Manager with the *Cambrian News*. Early in the 1930s he acquired The Montgomeryshire Printing and Stationery Co. in Newtown, and here he occasionally set some of the printing for the Gregynog Press. During this period he lost his only son and daughter - both teenagers. He retired to Aberystwyth towards the end of World War II and helped the *Cambrian News* during this critical period until shortly before his death 2 Sept. 1955. He was buried in Aberystwyth's Public Cemetery. His widow, Dorothy, survived him.

Personal research; *Cambrian News*, 9 Sept. 1955.

D.J.

JONES, GRIFFITH HARTWELL (1859-1944), cleric and historian; b. 16 April 1859, son of the Rev. Edward Jones (1826-92), vicar of Llanrhaeadr-ym-Mochnant. David Jones ('Dewi Fardd'), Trefriw (*DWB*, 450) was one of his ancestors and John Jones (1786-1865, see Supplement), printer of Gwyndod Wryf Press, Llanrwst, was his grandfather. He was educated at Shrewsbury School and Jesus College, Oxford. He was D.D. and D.Litt. of Oxford. From 1888 to 1893 he was Professor of Latin at the University College of S. Wales and Monmouthshire, and during that period he took Orders. In 1893 he was appointed to the Jesus College living of Nutfield, in Surrey, which he held until his retirement in 1940. He d. in London, 27 May 1944. He was unmarried. Hartwell Jones was the author of several historical works, including *The Dawn of European Civilization* (1903); *Celtic Britain and the Pilgrim Movement* (1912); and *Early Celtic Missionaries* (1928). Although he had lived most of his life in England he maintained a close relationship with Wales; for 20 years he was Chairman of the Council of the Honourable Society of Cymmrodorion - he was given the Society's medal in 1919 'in recognition of distinguished service to Wales'; he had been chairman of the National *Eisteddfod* Association, and a member of the Royal Commission on Ancient Monuments in Wales and Monmouthshire. He was disappointed not to have received preferment in the Church in Wales, where he thought he could have served Wales better; at one time it was thought he would have been appointed to a Welsh bishopric. His autobiography, *A Celt Looks at the World*, was posthumously published in 1946, and in that book he speaks frankly of his attitude towards personalities in the Welsh Church.

In his academic work the distinction he recalled with the greatest pride and pleasure' was his appointment as an examiner for the Chancellor's classical prizes and the Newdigate prize for English verse.

Trans. Cymm., 1919-20 and 1937; G. Hartwell Jones, *A Celt Looks at the World* (1946); [*WwW* (1937)].

E.M.H.

JONES, GWILYM CERI (1897-1963), minister (Presb.) and poet; b. 26 June 1897 at Newgate, in the parish of Llangunllo, Cards., s. of William and Ellen Jones. He was educated at Rhydlewis school, Llandysul grammar school, and the Theological College, Aberystwyth. He was ord. in 1922 and served his ministry at Cwm-parc (1922-28), Minffordd (1928-32), Llanwrtyd (1932-36), Port Talbot (1936-47), Clydach, Glam. (1947-58). He m., 1934, Mary Symmons, Swansea; they had a son. He d. 9 Jan. 1963 at Llansamlet.

He was in great demand as an original and astute preacher until a severe illness left him with impaired speech. He then turned his creative talents to writing poetry, specialising in the strict metres and having his work published in weekly newspapers and Welsh periodicals. He competed at the national *eisteddfod* and won prizes for *englynion* and a love-poem. At Pwllheli in 1955 he won the chair for his *awdl* to 'Gwrtheyrn'. The booklet, *Dwy Awdl*, contains an *awdl* by him on 'Bro'r Ogofeydd' and one by T.Ll. Jones; and a posthumous collection of his poems was published, entitled *Diliau'r Dolydd* (1964).

Blwyddiadur MC, 1964, 278-9; *Gol.*, 6 Feb. 1963; information from his sister; and personal acquaintance.

G.M.R.

JONES, GWILYM CLEATON (1875-1961), bank manager in Cape Town and Johannesburg; b. 25 March 1875 in Llanrug, Caerns., the second son of John Eiddon Jones (*DWB*, 485) and Sarah Jones. His father was a minister in the Presbyterian Church of Wales. He supported D. Lloyd George and in a letter of sympathy which the statesman sent to his widow from the National Liberal Club dated 16 Oct. 1903, he acknowledged that it was Eiddon Jones who had first asked him to stand in an election for the Caernarfon boroughs. Cleaton Jones was educated at Bala grammar school. He succeeded in the introductory examination of the Incorporated Law Society of England and Wales in 1889. By 1893 he had started working with Williams Company, Old Bank, Chester. He emigrated to South Africa (Cape Colony at the time) in Nov. 1902, soon after the death of his elder brother, Eiddon Rhys, of whom he thought highly. He joined the National Bank of South Africa, Ltd. He was promoted accountant and manager of the Cape Town office and later moved to a similar post in Johannesburg. When he retired on 25 Mar. 1936 he was the general assistant manager for South Africa in the Dominion, Colonial and Overseas Department of Barclays Bank. In July 1940 the Governor General appointed him honorary national treasurer of the National War Fund. He was also manager of the Heynes Mathew Co., Ltd. from 1937 until 1958. He acted as honorary treasurer of the Cape Western Regional Committee South African Institute of Race Relations. On the strength of his ability as an administrator as well as his legal knowledge, he was invited to serve on a sub-committee called to form a constitution for the Institute of Bankers of South Africa. He became a member of council of that body. He was a warm-hearted Welshman and a leading member of Johannesburg, Pretoria and Cape Town Welsh Societies. He was also prominent within the Methodist Church as a Sunday school superintendent, teacher, elder, secretary and president of the Welsh church in Cape Town. He displayed the same commitment in Johannesburg. He preached in Welsh and he supported the Cape Town *eisteddfod* from the outset. He was admitted to the *Gorsedd* of Bards under the name 'Ab Eiddon' in the national *esiteddfod* at Denbigh in 1939 and was one of the vice-presidents of the Hon. Soc. of Cymmrodorion. His youngest brother was John David Rheinallt Jones (see below), and he was an ardent admirer of his efforts as director of the South African Institute of Race Relations. He had four sisters. He m. (1) Esther Anne Davies, Llandeilo; one son and four daughters were born to them. Their son died in Alexandria, Egypt, in 1941 where he was serving as a captain in the Transvaal Scottish Regiment. After his wife's death in 1940 he m. (2) Mrs. Alice Lilian Williams, Johannesburg. Cleaton Jones died in Cape Town 30 Sept. 1961 and was cremated.

Information from his daughter, Mrs. Mair Lubynski, Camps Bay, Cape Town.

G.A.J.

JONES, GWILYM GWALCHMAI (1921-1970), musician; b. at Llanerfyl, Mont., 4 Jan. 1921, son of William Tomley Jones and his wife Miriam. He was educated at Llanerfyl primary school and at Llanfair Caereinion secondary school, and studied music privately with Maldwyn Price (*DWB*, 1146), Dr. Calvert (organ) and Powell Edwards (singing). He later followed a course in music at the Royal Manchester College of Music (1950-53) where he made a name for himself as a singer and won the college's Curtis gold badge, its highest honour for singing. He went on to study in the college's opera dept. (1953-54), and won the Imperial League of Opera prize (1954).

He taught (part-time) at Llanfair Caereinion secondary school (1954-57) before being appointed (1957) to the staff of the Royal Manchester College of Music. He was awarded an honorary fellowship by the college a few weeks before his sudden death (at Llanerfyl), 12 Jan. 1970. A memorial fund, bearing his name, was set up to enable promising Welsh singers to receive tuition at the college in Manchester.

He is remembered particularly as a successful teacher of singing, and as one who was enthusiastic for raising performing standards. After winning prizes himself at the national *eisteddfod* and the International *Eisteddfod*, Llangollen, he opened a studio for singing at Rhyl, Caernarfon and Wrexham (1954-57), and several of his pupils became well-known figures in *eisteddfod* and concert circles. Many of the students who were taught by him at the college in Manchester won international acclaim in the field of opera.

In the midst of his great activity as a college lecturer, he was much in demand throughout Wales as a conductor of singing festivals and as an *eisteddfod* adjudicator. He was also the founder (in 1959) of Cantorion Gwalia, which was regarded as an interesting experiment as every member of that party was an experienced soloist.

Personal research, together with additional information from Mrs. Glenys Jones, his widow, through Gwyn Erfyl, his brother.

H.W.

JONES, GWILYM RICHARD ('Gwilym Aman'; 1874-1953), musician, conductor of choirs and singing festivals, hymnist; b. in Siop y Bont, Brynaman, Carms., on 12 April 1874, the son of Richard Jones and his wife Elizabeth Mathew. The father, a successful baritone, came from Tŷcroes and settled, after his marriage, in Brynaman; his son grew up in the midst of the lively culture of that area during the heyday of Watcyn Wyn (Watkin Hezekiah Williams, *DWB*, 1076) and Gwydderig (Richard Williams, 1842-1917; *DWB*, 1066-7). Gwilym R. Jones was given music lessons by Joseph Parry (*DWB*, 738), then choirmaster at Ebenezer Independent chapel, Swansea. In Brynaman, there was a famous choir, conducted by John Jones (Pen-crug) and with David Vaughan Thomas (*DWB*, 943 and see Supplement below) as the accompanist; this rich musical tradition was an inspiration to a young musician like Gwilym R. Jones who was born to be a conductor of choirs. The first post he held was choirmaster at Weast Independent Church, Manchester, where he was conductor, for fifteen years, of a mixed Welsh choir and of a male voice choir in the city. In 1910, he was invited to become the organist and choir-master of the Christian Temple, Ammanford and he held this post, with outstanding success, for nearly 40 years. He was regarded as the ablest choral conductor who had been raised in the Amman valley. For 30 years, he was conductor of the Ammanford and District Choral Society which won the most important music prize at the Corwen national *eisteddfod* of 1919 and the Barry national *eisteddfod* of 1920. As a result of this success, the national *eisteddfod* came to Ammanford in 1922. At this *eisteddfod*, the choir achieved an outstanding success, under his baton and to the accompaniment of the London Symphony Orchestra, with a memorable performance, for the first time in Wales, of Bach's C Minor Mass. Another remarkable success occurred when the choir won the most important prize at three *eisteddfodau* on the same day in 1924 – Burry Port, Carmarthen and Clunderwen. Gwilym R. Jones was awarded a silver crown by the Clunderwen *eisteddfod* for his work as the conductor of the choir; this crown is now in the National Museum of Wales. The most successful piece performed by the choir was 'Ye nations offer to the Lord', from Mendelssohn's *Hymn of Praise*, which won them £1500 in prizes, at a time when prize money was small. Gwilym R. Jones was a born conductor of singing festivals and his musical accompaniment at the Christian Temple created a perfect atmosphere for worship and frequently encouraged the congregation to sing certain hymns to well-known tunes in an uplifting way. He trained very many soloists and musicians in the Ammanford area as well as acting as music teacher in the county school. A number of his pupils were prize-winners at the national *eisteddfod*. He trained Trevor Anthony, Tom Williams of Dafen and others. He was a gentleman through and through and his annual performances from the works of the great composers left a great influence in the Amman Valley. He was a member of *Gorsedd y Beirdd* and a skilled writer of *englynion*; some of his hymns are in modern hymnals. He m., on 16 April 1925, Blodwen, the daughter of Evan Jones and Jane (née Edwards) of Gellimanwydd, at the Christian Temple. He d. 3 Feb. 1953 and was buried in Gellimanwydd cemetery on the following Saturday.

Information from his widow; *Amman Valley Chronicle*, Feb. 1953.

E.D.J.

JONES, HARRI - see JONES, THOMAS HENRY below.

JONES, HERMAN (1915-64), minister (Congl.) and poet; b. 24 Jan. 1915 at 12 Caradog Place, Deiniolen, Caern., son of Hugh Edward Jones, undertaker and builder, and Elizabeth his wife. He was educated at the council school, Deiniolen, Brynrefail county school, the Normal College, Bangor, and he was accepted to Bala-Bangor College 29 Sept. 1938. He graduated with honours in Welsh in 1941 and M.A. in 1953. He did not complete his theological course as he accepted a call to Salem, Porthmadog, and was ordained there 21 July 1943. He moved to Jerusalem, Burry Port and was inducted there on 17 Nov. 1954. He remained there until his death in hospital at Bangor, 3 June 1964, as a result of a sudden heart attack. He was in great demand as a preacher, and in his preaching he belonged to the poetic and illustrative tradition.

He blossomed early as a poet, winning many prizes in local *eisteddfodau* before winning the crown at the national *eisteddfod* at Cardigan (1942) for a poem on 'Ebargofiant'. Simplicity, conciseness, skilfulness and lyricism characterized his poetry. He published *Hanes Eglwys Annibynnol Jerusalem, Burry Port, 1812-1962* (1962), and after his death the substance of his M.A. thesis, *Y Soned yn Gymraeg hyd 1900* was published (1967). On 14 Aug. 1946 he m. Ffion Mai, d. of David Thomas, Bangor (1880-1967; see below), and they had two sons.

Blwyddiadur A, 1965, 152-3; personal knowledge.

R.Td.J.

JONES, HUMPHREY ('Bryfdir'; 1867-1947), poet and 'compère' of *eisteddfodau*; b. 13 Dec. 1867, in Cwm Croesor, Mer., son of John Jones a smallholder and Mary (née Roberts) and grandson of Robert Roberts of Erw Fawr who founded the Sunday school at Llanfrothen. He lived practically the whole of his life in Blaenau Ffestiniog. After leaving school at the age of 12 he became a quarryman and eventually attained an official position. He learned the rudiments of poetry during his youth from Richard Jones Owen ('Glaslyn'; 1831-1909; *DWB*, 719) and before he was 20 yrs of age he had won several prizes. He was admitted to the *Gorsedd* of Bards in 1890. He won over 60 bardic chairs, and contributed regularly to *Y Geninen* and *Cymru*. He was a very successful *eisteddfod* 'compère' for many years, noted for his ready wit and control of large audiences. Two volumes of his poetry were published - *Telynau'r Wawr* and *Bro fy Mebyd a Chaniadau eraill*. He m. in 1893 Mary Eleanor Williams and they had 5 children. He d. 22 Jan. 1947.

Personal knowledge; [*WwW* (1937)].

W.E.J.

JONES, IDWAL (1899-1966), educationist and university professor; b. 31 December 1899 in Pen-clawdd, Glam., son of Llewelyn and Margaret (née Rees) Jones. After attending primary school at Pen-clawdd, and the County School, Gowerton, he went on to University College, Aberystwyth where he graduated B.A. with Honours in English in 1922. He gained his M.A. in 1924 with a dissertation on 'The Critical Ideas of Matthew Arnold, with special reference to French and German Criticism'. He took his Diploma in Education at King's College, London University.

He had teaching experience at Llanmorlais elementary school, Glam. from 1919; then at the Westminster City (secondary) school 1924-1925; and in 1924 he took evening classes at the Working Men's College, London. He was appointed as Assistant Lecturer in the Education Department of the University College, Swansea 1925 where he became Senior Lecturer 1930-1939, and for a period (1933-1934) was Acting Head of the department and College Correspondent to the Board of Education. From 1939-1960 he occupied the Chair of Education at the University College of Wales, Aberystwyth. He was the first Dean in the Faculty of Education at that college and established close academic links with Trinity College Carmarthen as well as with teachers and children within the wide Faculty hinterland. He was responsible for officially initiating the teaching of a subject (apart from Welsh) through the medium of Welsh in the University of Wales, and argued the case for this development with exceptional skill and perceptivity. He was an able committee-man: like all professors of Education he was weighed down with innumerable committees, but in such places he proved himself a generous and formidable advocate, completely unswerving in his stand for Welsh causes. Much of the success in establishing Welsh as a recognised medium of instruction at University level is due to him. Under his leadership the Department of Education at Aberystwyth developed as a significant international centre for bilingual studies. He himself lectured through the medium of Welsh on psychology in 1931, and was one of the pioneers writing on modern psychology in the Welsh language (e.g. 'Yr hunan o safbwynt seicoleg', 'Cyfraniad James Ward i seicoleg'; and 'Spearman' in *Efrydiau Athronyddol*. He did research into the history of Welsh education, and published work on Thomas Gee, 'The Voluntary System at Work' (in the *Trans. of the Cymm.*, 1933), the broadcast history lessons, 'Y plentyn a'r Eglwys', and 'Y Bardd a'r Athro'.

He possessed an inherent nobility of spirit, and even in his last days of illness he was a strikingly elegant and charming personality. On June 29, 1933 he married Kitty, daughter of Sir John Herbert Lewis (*DWB*, 556) of Plas Penucha, Caerwys; and this was no doubt what impelled him to compile the standard bibliography of Thomas Jones of Denbigh and to edit a new edition of that Methodist leader's autobiography in 1937. He was forced by ill-health to retire prematurely from his chair in 1960, due to an infirmity caused to a great extent by overwork during the war-years. He died January 3, 1966 at Caerwys and was buried in Colwyn Bay.

Official records at University College of Wales; information from Mrs Kitty Idwal Jones.

R.M.J.

JONES, JACK (1884-1970), author and playwright; b. 24 Nov. 1884, at Tai Harry Blawd, Merthyr Tydfil, Glam., the eldest of nine who survived of the fifteen children born to his mother, Sarah Ann, and his father, David, a miner. Educated at St. David's elementary school, Merthyr Tydfil, he left school at the age of twelve to work with his father at the coal-face. From 1902 to 1906, he was a regular soldier, serving in South Africa and India before resuming work as a miner at Merthyr Tydfil. In 1908, he married (1) Laura Grimes Evans of Builth Wells. By the outbreak of war in 1914 he was employed at a colliery near Pontypool because he found that his small wage as a bark-stripper at Builth was insufficient to keep himself, his wife, two sons and a daughter. As a member of the army reserve, he was called up immediately: he was mentioned in dispatches from France and later wounded. By 1921, the birth of two more sons had completed his family. In the same year his Miners' Federation lodge at Pontypool sent him as a delegate to the formation Conference of the British Communist Party held at Manchester: there he was chosen as temporary corresponding secretary for the South Wales coalfield. For months he sought to establish a branch of the Communist Party at Merthyr Tydfil, and in August 1921 he gave active support to the Communist parliamentary candidate for the Caerphilly constituency. When he was appointed full-time secretary-representative of the miners at Blaengarw in 1923 he joined the Labour Party, but criticism of his controversial first article for the press, 'The Need for a Lib-Lab Coalition', resulted, towards the end of 1927, in his resignation from the post at Blaengarw and he moved from Bridgend to Cardiff. After spending over a year as a member of Lloyd George's staff of speakers on the Liberal platform, in 1929 he was defeated in the election as Liberal candidate for Neath. Following a further few months as a speaker for the Liberals and a visit to Geneva as their observer at an International Labour Office conference, by 1930 he was unemployed. During the next five years he strove to earn his living in a number of ways — as a platform-speaker for Mosley's New Party, a salesman, a navvy, an assistant cinema-manager, an enumerator, and as a writer.

By 1939, he had become a naturalistic author of note among the Anglo-Welsh school of writers: his works had circulated widely — three novels (*Rhondda Roundabout*, 1934, *Black Parade*, 1935, *Bidden to the Feast*, 1938), a play (*Land of My Fathers*, 1937) and the first volume of his autobiography (*Unfinished Journey*, 1937). A short run of the stage-version of *Rhondda Roundabout* on Shaftesbury Avenue added to his fame. The film, *Proud Valley*, for which he wrote the dialogue and in which he took a small part, also appeared at this time. In Wales he was well-known to many audiences as a radio personality and as a speaker.

Most of his time during World War II was taken up with making speeches - sometimes with a brief introduction in Welsh - on behalf of the Ministry of Information and the National Savings Movement, and in preparing radio-scripts and articles.

He accepted a minor role in another film. Between August 1941 and the end of 1942, he undertook two exhausting lecture-tours in the United States and Canada, and later he visited troops on the European battlefronts, in Belgium and Holland in 1944, in Italy in 1945. He also produced *The Man David* (1944), 'an imaginary presentation, based on fact, of the life of David Lloyd George from 1880 to 1914'. In the general election of 1945 he supported the candidature of Conservative, Sir James Grigg. This was the fifth change in his political allegiance, but throughout his life his philosophy was based on left-wing ideas with a childlike religious faith.

From 1946 to 1951, he again applied himself to authorship with the publication of another two volumes of autobiography (*Me and Mine*, 1946 and *Give Me Back My Heart*, 1950), three new novels (*Off to Philadelphia in the Morning*, 1947, *Some Trust in Chariots*, 1948, and *River out of Eden*, 1951) and a play (*Transatlantic Episode*, 1947). His son, Lawrence, was killed in action in 1942; in 1946, his wife, Laura, died, and in 1948 his son, David. For his services to the community and his achievements in literature, in 1948 he was made a CBE. In the same year he became an adherent of the Moral Re-Armament Movement; he spoke in support of its ideals in Cardiff and at other centres in Wales; and in 1949 he spent three months in the United States promoting the cause.

Compared with much of his earlier work, his five novels of the 1950s *Lily of the Valley* and *Lucky Lear*, 1952, *Time and the Business*, 1953, *Choral Symphony*, 1955 and *Come Night: End Day*, 1956, reveal a sharp decline in literary standards. In 1954, he married (2) Gladys Morgan, a library-assistant in Rhiwbina. He was elected first president of the English section of *Yr Academi Gymreig*; and, in February 1970, he received an award from the Welsh Arts Council for his distinguished contribution to the literature of Wales. Still prolific in his writing, from 1956 to his death on 7 May, 1970, he continued to produce novels, plays, autobiography, biography; but none was published. The manuscripts are preserved in the National Library. Although his work varied widely in quality, *Black Parade* and *Off to Philadelphia in the Morning* have sufficient merit to make him an author of stature, while *Bidden to the Feast* and *Unfinished Journey* are two of the finest works in the whole of Anglo-Welsh literature.

Keri Edwards, *Jack Jones* (1974)

K.E.

JONES, JAMES IFANO (1865-1955); librarian and bibliographer; b. Oxford Str. Aberdare, Glam., 15 May 1865, according to *WWP*, but there is no record of his birth under this date in the Registry of Births and Deaths in Pontypridd; there is, however, a James Jones, son of Jane Jones of Harriet Street, b. 14 May, and a clerical error is possible. His father, Thomas Jones, was a miner and his mother came from Cwmtwrch. She was a sister of the Rev. J. Dyfnallt Owen's (see below) grandmother. He was educated at the Park Board School, Trecynon, popularly known as '*Ysgol y Comin*', which he left at the age of 11 to attend for one year a private school kept by Owen Rees in Seymour Street, Aberdare. He started work at the age of 12 as an apprentice in the printing works of the newspaper *Tarian y Gweithiwr*. In

1884 he joined as a compositor and proof reader the printing house of Jenkin Howell (*DWB*, 367-8). Meanwhile, he seized every opportunity for self-improvement. The great formative influence of his early years was the Sunday school at Gadlys Baptist chapel and the cultural activities associated with it. He became the secretary of the Aberdare and District Baptist Sunday School Union, he was keenly interested in music and acted as the chapel organist; he was an enthusiast for the drama and gained local fame as an actor and reciter. He was also politically active and became the secretary of the Aberdare Labour and Radical Association when it was formed in 1894. But it was his experience in the printing trade which gave him his detailed knowledge of the Welsh language which fitted him for the distinguished career on which he embarked when in November 1896 he went to work in the Cardiff Free Library, as it was then called, as a temporary assistant Welsh cataloguer. Over the following two years he cooperated with John Ballinger (*DWB*, 23-4), the Chief Librarian, in the production of a *Catalogue of Printed Literature in the Welsh Department* (1898) which has proved an indispensable tool for all who work in the field of Welsh studies and bibliography. His part in this work established his reputation as a bibliographer and he was appointed Assistant in Charge of the Reference Department in 1901. His knowledge of Wales and all things Welsh was remarkable and his helpfulness to scholars widely acknowledge. He took under his special care the Library's Welsh collections and became known officially as the 'Cardiff Welsh Librarian', though he was never officially accorded that title. Over the years his literary output was enormous. His bibliographical work included the bibliographical section of the *Bible in Wales*, which he published jointly with John Ballinger in 1906; *Bibliography of Wales*, a series of book lists which appeared periodically from 1899 to 1912; and his *A History of Printing and Printers in Wales and Monmouthshire to 1923*, published in 1925, for which the University of Wales awarded him an honorary M.A. degree. His historical works included his lengthy study of 'Dan Isaac Davies and the Bilingual Movement', which appeared in J. Vyrnwy Morgan, ed., *Welsh Political and Educational Leaders in the Victorian era*, 1908; *The Early History of Nonconformity in Cardiff*, 1912; and 'Sir Mathew Cradock and some of his contemporaries' in *Arch. Camb.*, 1919. He also wrote a biography *W.T. Samuel, ei fywyd a'i lafur*, in 1920. He entered the field of literary criticism when he wrote in the January and July 1902 numbers of *Y Geninen* an article entitled 'Llenyddiaeth hanner ola'r Ddeunawfed Ganrif'. From 1905 to 1929 he was the editor of the poetry and criticism column, 'Y Golofn Gymreig', in the *South Wales Weekly News*. But he was also a creative writer. In 1905 his prize play in the Bangor national *eisteddfod* of 1902 was published, entitled *Rhys ap Tewdwr Mawr* (a tragedy in three acts). He also published a number of poems, tunes, articles, reviews, and special bibliographies in Welsh and English periodicals. He was a keen *eisteddfodwr*, a member of the *Gorsedd of Bards* and an enthusiastic supporter of its supposed antiquity. From 1901 he frequently acted as an adjudicator in the

National *Eisteddfod*. He was himself a prizewinner for poetry and plays in 1902, 1904 and 1929. He was also in much demand as a popular lecturer to societies throughout Wales.

Ifano Jones retired from his post in the Cardiff Library at the end of 1925. It should be mentioned, however, that he had long laboured under a sense of grievance because he believed that his status in the Library had not been sufficiently recognised and that full credit had not been given for his achievements. According to his 'nephew', Dyfnallt, the biggest disappointment of his life was in not being invited to become the first Librarian of the National Library, when John Ballinger was appointed. The industry and versatility of this non-collegiate man, the outstanding Welsh bibliographer of his age, was truly remarkable. He was twice married: (1) to Nellie George, dau. of Thomas George, 'fineworker', 20 Jan. 1901 at Neath registry office. She died in 1911; (2) to Jessie Mary, second dau. of Thomas and Mary Charles, Havod House, Blaenavon, who d. 9 June 1953. He d. in his home in Penarth, 7 March 1955.

W.W. Price, 'James Ifano Jones, M.A.', *J.W.B.S.*, 8, 2; *WwW*, 1921 and 1937; *Www*, 1951-60; J. Dyfnallt Owen, 'F'Ewythr Ifano', *Tyst*, 17 March 1955; Cardiff Library Staff Records consulted by courtesy of the Librarian.

W.T.M.

JONES, JANE ANN - see THOMAS, LOUIE MYFANWY below.

JONES, JOHN CHARLES (1904-56) Bishop of Bangor; b. 3 May, 1904, the ninth child of Benjamin and Rachel Jones, Llan-saint, Carms. He was educated in Carmarthen Grammar School, and after graduating first class in Hebrew at University College Cardiff in 1926, he went on to Cambridge with a Hody Scholarship. He was at Wadham College, where he won the Junior LXX prize and the Pusey and and Ellerton scholarship in 1927. He graduated B.A. in 1928 with a first in theology, and M.A. in 1931. He was awarded a D.D. (Lambeth) in 1950. Chosen as Kennicot Scholar in 1928 he spent a year at Wycliffe Hall, Oxford. He was ordained deacon by the Bishop of St. David's in 1929 and priest in 1930. He was curate in Llanelli 1929-33 and in Aberystwyth 1933-34 with responsibility for students. In 1934 he entered the missionary field in the Bishop Tucker Memorial College, Mukono, Uganda, as tutor in theology. From 1939-45 he was warden and sole administrator at the college. With the assistance of his wife Mary, daughter of William Lewis of Carmarthen and a professional nurse, he established a section to educate the wives of native clergy. He returned to Wales in 1945 as vicar of Llanelli. He was enthroned as Bishop of Bangor, Epiphany 1949 – the first time this ceremony was performed in Welsh. He d. in Bangor on his way home from St. Winifred's School Llanfairfechan, Sat. 13 Oct. 1956, and was buried in Llandysilio cemetery 18 Oct. He left a widow and one daughter Ann, wife of Donald Lewis who became vicar of Swansea in 1977.

In the seven years he was Bishop he compressed a lifetime's work and influence. He brought new life to the diocese, and a unity and strength never seen before. He was known in the remotest parish, a bishop to all – 'belonging to us all' as one Methodist elder put it. In the summer of 1950 he led more than 4,000 people along the pilgrim route to Aberdaron. The exhibition of the treasures of the churches in the see, held in Bangor 3-5 March 1953, was an opportunity to bring everyone together as well as emphasising the traditions and the inheritance that extended over four centuries. The quarterly *Bangor Diocesan Gazette*, which he founded in July 1954, was another effort to unite the whole see.

He used to fly to the Middle East to visit the armed forces, and in 1954 he took part in a world-wide conference of Christian churches in Evanston, and in the conference of Anglican bishops in Minneapolis.

It is difficult for those who never saw his small, frail figure to appreciate his serene spirituality and the strength of his faith and vision.

Crockford; Llan, 19 and 26 Oct, 1956; *Haul a'r Gangell,* Winter 1956-57, 4-5; *North Wales Chronicle,* 19 Oct, 1956; *Bangor Diocesan Gazette,* Jan. 1957 (Memorial Issue); personal recollection.

E.P.R.

JONES, JOHN DANIEL (1865-1942), Congregational minister; b. at Ruthin 13 Apr. 1865, son of Joseph David Jones (*DWB*, 490-1), schoolmaster and musician; his mother was Catherine, dau. of Owen Daniel, Caethle, Tywyn, Mer., farmer. Owen D. Jones, head of an insurance firm, Sir Henry Haydn Jones, M.P. for Merioneth, and the Rev. D. Lincoln Jones were his brothers. Upon the father's death in 1870 the family went to live at Tywyn where he had at one time been a schoolmaster. The mother married, secondly, in 1877 the Rev. David Morgan Bynner, a Congregational minister at Chorley where they went to live. John Daniel was only 12 years of age when he left Wales and he spent his working life in England, returning to Merioneth when he retired in 1937. He had been reared with the Calvinistic Methodists by his grandparents and he bore characteristics of that persuasion throughout his life. He was educated at the Tywyn academy, Chorley grammar school, Owen's College, Manchester, where he took his M.A. (Vic.) degree, and at the Lancashire Independent College, where he was for a time assistant teacher, and was later, in 1912 and 1921, offered the principalship. He took the degree of B.D. at St. Andrews in 1889, and was ordained at Newland Church, Lincoln, in the same year. In 1898 he followed J. Ossian Davies (*DWB*, 141) as minister of Richmond Hill Church, Bournemouth, where he remained until his retirement to Bryn Banon, near Bala. He m., (1) Emily Cunliffe, of Chorley (d. 1917), and had a son, who d. in Africa, and a dau., Myfanwy, who d. soon after her father, and, (2) Edith Margery Thompson, of Bournemouth, in 1933.

He won for himself a remarkably honourable position in the religious life of England and his popularity endured till the end. He was made a Companion of Honour in 1927 and was awarded the degree of D.D., by the universities of St. Andrews, Manchester, and Wales. He was twice, 1909-10, 1925-26, chairman of the Congregational Union of England and Wales, Moderator of the Free Church Federal Council,

1921-23, and of the International Congregational Council, 1936-42. He was referred to as the Archbishop of Congregationalism.

He had his place among the chief celebrities of the pulpit in England in his day and possessed an enchanting gift which drew large crowds to listen to him. His church at Richmond Hill was considered to be one of the most renowned of nonconformist congregations in the whole country. It is probable it was as a leader and denominational statesman that he did his greatest work, and Congregationalism in England bore his image for a long time. He, more than any one else, did most for the maintenance of the ministry, though his schemes were considered by many to savour of Presbyterianism, if not of episcopalianism.

When he returned to spend the eventide of his life in his native land, it was difficult for him, who had so completely identified himself with the prosperous middle class in England, to come to terms with a new Wales, which had awakened to a consciousness of her nationhood.

He published some dozen books, mostly of sermons, and an autobiography.

He d. at Bala, 19 Apr. 1942, and was buried in Bournemouth.

J.D. Jones, *Three score years and ten;* D.F. Roberts, *Y Seren* (Bala) - an obituary note; *WwW,* 1941-50; *Congl. Year Book,* 1943, 417; Saunders Lewis, *Byd a Betws,* 13; *D.N.B.*

R.G.O.

JONES, JOHN DAVID RHEINALLT (1884-1953), philanthropist, founder and Director of the South African Institute of Race Relations; b. 5 July 1884 in Llanrug, Caerns., the youngest son of John Eiddon Jones (*DWB,* 485) and Sarah Jones. He was educated at Friars School, Bangor, but in 1897 became a boarder at David Hughes' grammar school, Beaumaris. It was there, in 1900, that he won a School Certificate in English, history, arithmetic, Latin, Welsh (with distinction). He emigrated to South Africa in Oct. 1905. According to G.J. Williams, Bangor (20 May 1905), he had a strong constitution and was an energetic person. He threw himself into philanthropic work becoming prominent in the effort to establish the South African Institute of Race Relations. He was its director from 1930 until 1947. That year he was appointed consultant on native matters to the Anglo-American Corporation. Prior to that he had been editor (1915) of *The South African Quarterly* and remained in post until 1926. In 1919 he was appointed secretary of the Witwatersrand Education Council – an unofficial body established by the *uitlanders* at the end of the preceeding century to promote education. He came into practical contact with the campaign to transform the South African School of Mines and Technology (1910) into a university college (1920). It was from this effort that the University of Witwatersrand was established (1922) [in Johannesburg]. Between 1928-30 Rheinallt Jones was assistant registrar of that university. In 1931 the university conferred an honorary M.A. degree upon him in recognition of his services to the university and of his work on behalf of racial problems. He is referred to in *African Studies* (5 Dec. 1953) as pioneering the idea of studying African life and institutions as an academic discipline. With the assistance of his wife and Professor Alfred Hoernlé, he emphasised the need to establish a department of Bantu studies within the university. That vision was realised. It was Rheinallt Jones who founded the journal *Bantu Studies* in Oct. 1921 and he became its editor. He lectured on native law in the department of Bantu studies from 1929 and was a guest lecturer on racial relations. In 1937 he was chosen as the first representative of the Africans of the Transvaal and the Orange Free State in the South African parliament. He also established the Inter-university Committee on African Studies to promote and co-ordinate research. He arranged a national conference of European and Bantu representatives in Cape Town in 1929 and that year, with the assistance of the Phelps-Stokes Institution and Carnegie Corporation (later), he established the South African Institute of Race Relations. This was an important event as henceforth it was possible to set up research and welfare plans on a firm foundation. He established the journal *Race Relations* and was its editor. In addition to this quarterly he was also involved with *Race Relations News* (monthly). He lost his parliamentary seat in 1942 to a candidate who had more radical views. In 1947 he accepted a post as counsellor on native affairs to the Anglo-American Corporation in South Africa without completely severing his work in connection with the Institute, though he had to resign as Director. In 1950 he was elevated president of the corporation and this gave him an opportunity to travel extensively throughout the continent of which he had become such an authority on its problems. He wrote many reports and detailed articles on every subject relating to racial and social problems. He had connections with the Jan H. Hofmeyr School of Social Work, the Y.M.C.A. and especially the Pathfinders (the South African scouts). He became the Chief-Pathfinder-Master in 1926 and in 1947 was honoured with the Silver Lion by the Chief Scout of South Africa. He was scout commissioner for Africa on behalf of the Chief Scout. In spite of the many calls on his time as a member of numerous committees he continued to maintain his connection with Wales and with his brother Gwilym Cleaton (see above) in particular. He visited Wales in 1936 and 1952. Rheinallt Jones' contribution towards improving relations between the coloured and white populations was truly remarkable. His wife, Edith Beatrice (née Barton) whom he m. in 1910, d. in 1944. He m. (2) Helen Clare Norfolk Francis (née Verley) in 1947. He d. 30 Jan. 1953 and his remains were buried in Braamfontein crematorium.

Www; Alan Paton, *Natal*; *African Studies*; Edgar H. Brookes, *R.J. – John David Rheinallt Jones* (1953); information from Mrs. Clare Rheinallt Jones, librarian of the South African Institute of Race Relations, and R. Musiker, librarian of the University of the Witwatersrand.

G.A.J.

JONES, JOHN EDWARD (1905-70), secretary and organiser of *Plaid Cymru*, 1930-62; b. 10 Dec. 1905 at Hafoty Fawr, Melin-y-Wîg, Mer., the third son of Rice Price Jones and Jane (née Williams). His father d. before J.E. was a year old, and his mother, assisted by his two eldest brothers, farmed the homestead afterwards. No doubt the splendid location of his home and the rich musical, literary and religious culture of the district bound him to Wales from a young age. One of his grandfathers was imprisoned during the tithe war.

He was educated in the primary school at Melin-y-Wîg – a name revived by him – 1910-18, and Bala grammar school, 1918-24, before entering the University College of Wales at Bangor in 1924. There he became secretary of the Students' Union and succeeded in making Welsh jointly official with English. He was a leading member of the society of the three G's – 'Y Tair G' – one of the three streams that united to found *Plaid Genedlaethol Cymru* – in Aug. 1925. He was appointed secretary of the college branch of the Party when it was formed in Nov. 1926, and topped the poll when he stood as a nationalist in a mock election. He graduated in 1927.

After he had taken a post as a teacher in London in 1928 a branch of the Party was founded there with J.E. again as secretary. As a result of his extraordinary organising talent the branch flourished and became the largest in the Party. He returned to Wales in 1930 as secretary and organiser of *Plaid Genedlaethol Cymru*. In Glan-rhyd (Presb.) chapel on 27 July 1940 he m. Olwen Roberts, the sister of John Iorwerth Roberts (see below), and they had a son and daughter.

He possessed a tough character, a strong mind and patience. The great strength of his personality was often camouflaged by his gentleness. In addition to his work as secretary of the executive committee of the Party, he organised the annual conference and summer school, and also rallies. He developed these into strong organisations but he also stimulated the formation of branches up and down the country. Apart from his responsibilities at local and parliamentary elections (he himself stood as a candidate in Caernarfon in 1950), he organised many special campaigns, such as those for radio and television, for a development corporation, against the extreme schemes of the Forestry Commission and against the appropriation of land in Wales by the War Office; the military camp at Trawsfynydd was twice surrounded by members of the Party. The campaign against the flooding of Cwm Tryweryn became very strong; but no doubt the campaign against the Bombing School in Llŷn in 1935 was the most notable, with the imprisonment of Saunders Lewis, Lewis Valentine and D.J. Williams. These numerous operations demanded great effort in gaining the country's support. He contributed more than anyone to the great feat of keeping *Plaid Cymru* together during World War II.

He took care of press releases and all publicity, and occasionally he had to shoulder most of the load in publishing the Party's papers, *Y Ddraig Goch* and *Welsh Nation*. More than a hundred books and pamphlets were published during his term as secretary. He also built up the St. David's Day Fund as the Party's main financial source.

He lectured and prepared television series on gardening, on which he was an expert. In addition to a valuable volume on the subject, he wrote a travel book about Switzerland. But his most valuable work is *Tros Gymru*, which is a mine of information on *Plaid Cymru* up to 1945. In addition to all this, he was the Sunday school teacher of a large class of young women in Heol y Crwys (Presb.) chapel, Cardiff.

In 1962 ill health compelled him to relinquish his post as secretary of *Plaid Cymru* and take a lighter position as its advisor. He was on his way home from the office, during the general election, when he d. suddenly, 30 May 1970. He was buried in Melin-y-Wîg cemetery. He is regarded as the chief architect of *Plaid Cymru*.

Personal knowledge; dates provided by his widow.
Gw.E.

JONES, JOHN HERBERT ('Je Aitsh'; 1860-1943), journalist and author; b. 29 May 1860, at Talsarnau, Mer., s. of Elizabeth and William Jones, a gardener at Cae'rffynnon mansion, and an elder at Bethel (Presb.) chapel, who had moved from Maesneuadd, near Llanaelhaearn. His only regular education was received at the village school. After service with a tailor at Porthmadog for a period, he went to Birkenhead to learn press compositing before going to Caernarfon in 1882 to take up a post at the office of *Yr Herald Cymraeg*. He returned to Merseyside in 1890 to work on the *Cymro*, owned by Isaac Foulkes (*DWB*, 267-8). That same year he m. Elizabeth Parry, from Caernarfon, and previously of Baladeulyn, Nantlle; they had three children. He was elected an elder at Parkfield Presbyterian chapel and did much to further the cause, and later became an elder at the churches at Woodchurch Road and Laird St., Birkenhead. He considered his labours as a contribution to his main task, namely to protect Welsh civilisation and culture in view of the dangers presented by the large cities. However, as he could not conscientiously support Isaac Foulkes on a contentious church matter affecting Liverpool and the surrounding areas at that time, he left *Y Cymro*. For a short period he became a compositor at Wrexham. Having already embarked on a literary career by writing at the end of his day's work weekly articles for *Y Genedl*, he came to an agreement with Hugh Evans (1854-1934; *DWB*, 238) in 1906 to take charge of a forthcoming weekly publication — *Y Brython* — which he edited until he retired in 1931. Afterwards he continued to deliver lectures frequently and visited the U.S.A. in 1932. In 1941 he went with his daughter and her husband to live at Pen-y-groes, Caerns., where he d. 23 Mar. 1943. He published a text (1915) of *Llyfr y Tri Aderyn* (Morgan Llwyd) and several books which included some of his own more important articles from *Y Brython*. His chief works are: *O'r Mwg i'r Mynydd* (1913), *Swp o Rug* (1920), and *Moelystota* (1932).

Personal knowledge.
G.P.J.

JONES, JOHN ISLAN (1874-1968), minister (U) and author; b. 17 Feb. 1874, son of Evan and Mary Jones, Tynewydd (later of Cornant and Melin Llys-faen), Cribyn, Cards. He went to schools in Cribyn and Llanwnnen (under David Thomas, 'Dewi Hefin', *DWB*, 942) until he was about ten years old. After being a farm servant and a stonemason with his father he attended the school of David Evans, minister (U) at Cribyn, (1896-98). He won a scholarship to Jesus College, Oxford, where he graduated in 1901 before proceeding to Manchester College, Oxford to prepare for the ministry. He won a Hibbert Scholarship which enabled him to go to the Universities of Marburg and Jena in Germany in 1904, but ill health caused him to return home before completing a Ph.D. degree course; he gained an M.A. degree in 1909. He spent the prime of his life as a minister (U) in England: Accrington (1906-09), Bolton (1909-17) and Hindley (1917-39), before retiring to his native district. He was at an advanced age when he was invited to be principal of Carmarthen Presbyterian College in 1945; he remained there for 3 yrs., ministering to Parcyfelfed (U) church at the same time. He was a man of strong convictions, proficient in the *cynganeddion* and a choirmaster. He published *A brief history of the Unitarian Church, Accrington* (1909), *Egwyddorion yr Undodiaid* (1948), and his reminiscences, *Yr hen amser gynt* (1958), which won him a prize offered by Ceredigion Education Committee. There are articles written by him in the *Ymofynydd* (1905-59), *Cymru*, and *Trans. Unitarian Historical Society* (see Glyn Lewis Jones, *A Bibliography of Cardiganshire, 1600-1964*). He d. a bachelor, 28 May 1968.

Ymofyn., 1901, 189; 1904, 192; 1906, 165; 1968, 81-7.
M.A.J.

JONES, JOHN JAMES (1892-1957), teacher, librarian, scholar and linguist; b. on 12 March 1892 in New Quay, Cards., the son of a saddler, Thomas Jones and Elizabeth, dau. of John Williams, Pendre, Llwyndafydd. He was educated at the Council School, New Quay and Aberaeron intermediate school (1906-10); he was a student teacher before entering the University College of Wales, Aberystwyth (1911-14). He graduated B.A. (Wales) with honours in Latin, and was awarded an M.A. degree for a thesis on *The native Italian element in early Roman religion*. He taught for nine years in English grammar schools - Stockton-on-Tees (1914-15); Whitchurch, Salop (1915-18); Ryleys School, Chester (1918-20); and Sir Thomas Rich's School, Gloucester (1920-23). Latin was removed from the curriculum at the school in Gloucester and he lost his post in consequence. Owing to a slight defect of his hearing, he left the teaching profession and returned to do further research in the Classics department at Aberystwyth. In 1926, he was appointed Assistant Keeper in the Department of Printed Books, National Library of Wales, promoted Deputy Keeper in 1928 and he was Head of the Department from 1950 until his death. He was recognized as a skilful bibliographer, a skill which he surely derived from his scholarship and discipline in the Classics. He married Elizabeth Mary, daughter of Isaac Davies, of New Quay, but there were no children.

He had a special aptitude for learning languages, and his thorough knowledge of Latin and Greek provided him with a firm foundation for learning other languages, such as French, Spanish and Italian. He had a good knowledge of German, Russian and Polish, and could read most of the other Slavic, Scandinavian, Hungarian, and, of course, Celtic languages. He was interested in the Eastern languages, such as Persian and Arabic, and he took up the study of Sanscrit and Pali to acquire first-hand knowledge of the religious literature of India. It was his mastery of Sanscrit that enabled him to translate the *Mahāvastu*, the scriptures of the oldest of the Buddhist sects, into English, and which was published in three volumes under the auspices of the Pali Text Society in 1949-56. According to Miss I.B. Horner, the Society's secretary, this first translation into any language is an outstanding contribution to Buddhist studies; he succeeded in overcoming and explaining the difficulties of the text, and translated it into a beautiful, flowing English style.

He contributed articles to Welsh periodicals on Celtic studies, religion and bibliography. He published Welsh translations of Breton and Russian short stories in *Yr Efrydydd*, 1935 and *Yr Haul* 1945, and Persian sayings in *Yr Efrydydd*, 1934. He published articles in *Yr Haul* (1942-4) on unascribed Latin hymns in the *Emyniadur* (the Welsh Anglican hymnal, 1897), contributed to the *Dictionary of Welsh Biography*, and wrote the introduction to the section on Welsh proverbs in *Racial proverbs ...* edited by S.G. Champion (Routledge, 1938).

His relaxations were chess and an occasional novel. He enjoyed watching football and cricket and was an enthusiastic bowls player. His hardness of hearing made conversation difficult for him and he developed interests such as these, which did not depend on conversational ability. He was a true gentleman, friendly, unassuming and respected by all who knew him. His wife died on 29 July, 1955, at the age of 64, and the third volume of the *Mahāvastu* is dedicated to her as a tribute to her patience and inspiration in the course of his work on the translation. He died suddenly on the 20th February, 1957, a few months before he was due to retire, and he was buried in the cemetery of Maenygroes Congregational chapel, near New Quay.

N.L.W. *Annual reports*; letters in the MSS. dept. of the NLW; *N.L.W. Jnl.* X, 1957, 119-20; *Times*, 26 Feb. 1957, personal knowledge and information from members of staff of N.L.W.

J.K.E.

JONES, JOHN LLOYD - see LLOYD-JONES, JOHN below.

JONES, JOHN MORGAN (1837-1946), minister (Congl.) and Principal of Bala-Bangor College, Bangor; b. 23 October 1873 at Albert Cottage, Cwmaman, Carms., the sixth child and second son of Joseph Jones, engineer, and Mary, his wife. After a course of education at the school in the Market Hall, he worked in the office of a local tinworks. He began preaching at New Bethel church, Garnant, under the ministry of the Revd. J. Towyn Jones in 1889 and subsequently became a student at the Gwynfryn Academy, Ammanford. In 1891 he was admitted to Brecon Memorial College and graduated with honours in English at Univ. College Cardiff in 1894. He began his theology course at Brecon in 1895 but moved to Mansfield College, Oxford, in 1896 and graduated B.A. in the theology schools in 1899. Then followed a year's

stay at the University of Berlin under the tuition of the church historian Adolf Harnack, the teacher who above all others made the most lasting impression upon him.

He was ordained minister of Tabernacle English Congregational church, Aberdare, in 1900 and played a prominent part in the public life of the town during his stay there. He was a Liberal member of the Town Council from April 1904 until April 1907 and formulated *A Scheme and Syllabus of Moral and Biblical Instruction* (Aberdare, 1905) for the day-schools of Aberdare. In 1902 he married Lucy Evans of Bridgnorth; two sons and one daughter were born of the marriage. In January 1914 he moved to Bangor to become Professor of Church History and English literature at Bala-Bangor Independent College. With the Principal, Dr Thomas Rees (*DWB*, 830-1), he took a leading role in publishing the pacifist newspaper *Y Deyrnas* from October 1916 to November 1919. When Thomas Rees died in 1926 he succeeded him as principal, a post which he held until his own death on 7 March 1946. His remains were buried in Glanadda Cemetery, Bangor.

Throughout his life he was deeply interested in education and was chairman of the north Wales branch of the Workers' Educational Association from 1926 to 1946. In the University of Wales he was Warden of the Guild of Graduates, 1930-33 and Vice-president of the University College of North Wales, 1944-46. In his denomination he was chairman of the North Wales Congregational Union 1933-34 and President of the Union of Welsh Independents, 1939-40.

He expressed his theological liberalism and his interest in public affairs in a host of articles and books. Important articles by him appeared in the *Celt*, *The Christian Commonwealth* and *Geiriadur Beiblaidd*. He contributed chapters to M.E. Sadler's *Moral Instruction and Training in Schools*, 1905; to *Welsh Political and Educational Leaders*, on David Rees, Llanelli; and on the Gospel according to St. Matthew to *The Story of the Bible*, 1938. He edited *Yr Efrydydd* from April 1928 until Sept. 1931 and the *Cofiadur* from 1923 to 1946. He also edited *Hanes ac Egwyddorion yr Annibynwyr*, 1939. His other publications were: *Y Tadau Pererin: eu Hanes a'u Neges*, Merthyr Tydfil, 1920; *Paul of Tarsus: the Apostle and his Message*, York, [1916]; *Dysgeidiaeth Iesu Grist* first published in 1921 by the Union of Welsh Independents and revised and reprinted at Cardiff, 1937; *The New Testament in Modern Education*, London, 1922; (with G.A. Edwards) *Diwinyddiaeth yng Nghymru* (Traethodau'r Deyrnas), 1924; *Traethodau'r Diwygiad* (Cyfres y Werin, Rhif 14) Wrecsam, 1926; *Y Bedwaredd Efengyl* (2 Vols.), Abertawe, 1930, 1931; *Y Testament Newydd: ei hanes a'i gynnwys*, Caerdydd, 1930; *Sgwrs: Cymdeithas Addysg y Gweithwyr*, Bangor, (1940).

D.J. Williams, *Hanes Coleg Bala-Bangor*, (unpublished); Sir J.E. Lloyd in *Congl. Year Bk.*, 1947, 464; *Dysg*, 1946, 107-111; *Drys.*, 1947, 59-63; *Tyst*, 1946, Mar. 12, 21, 28, Apr. 11; Minutes of Aberdare Town Council; information from Mr John Jenkyn Morgan, Glanaman; Mr C.E. Thomas, Bangor; Mrs E.W. Knight Jones and Revd. R.G. Owen, Bangor.

R.Td.J.

JONES, JOHN ROBERT (1911-70), philosopher and patriot; b. 4 Sept. 1911 in Pwllheli, Caerns., s. of William and Kate Jones. He was educ. at Troed-yr-allt school, Pwllheli county school, and then at Univ. Coll. of Wales, Aberystwyth where he graduated with 1st-class hons. in philosophy. He gained an M.A. with distinction and then went to Balliol College, Oxford, with a Univ. of Wales Fellowship, where he gained a D.Phil. He was appointed a lecturer in philosophy at his old college in Aberystwyth and remained there until his appointment as Professor of Philosophy at the University College of Swansea in 1952. He m. Catherine Julia Charles Roberts of Nefyn in 1943 and they had one daughter. He was visiting professor at Chapel Hill Univ., North Carolina, in 1961.

He began his career as a candidate for the ministry but turned to philosophy as his major academic interest after graduating, though he continued to preach throughout his life. He preached throughout Wales and gave addresses several times at meetings of the (CM) Association. His preaching was characterised by unusual passion which led many to refer to him as a prophet.

In his philosophical work he concentrated on three problems – the nature of the self, the nature of perception, the nature of universals. Of these the most important for him was the question of the nature of the self, and this was the subject of his first and of his last contributions to *Efrydiau Athronyddol*. Later in his career he was influenced by the ideas of Tillich, Wittgenstein and Simone Weil. During this period he delivered his television address *Yr Argyfwng Gwacter Ysbryd* ('the crisis of meaninglessness'), later published as a pamphlet which gave a new phrase to the Welsh language.

After moving to Swansea and seeing the decline of Welsh in the south Wales valleys his interest turned to the condition of Wales; and after his return from America where he had become aware of the lack of roots in the 1960s, he became increasingly concerned about the crisis of Wales and of Welsh. During his last years this was his main concern. He strongly opposed the 1969 Investiture and resigned as one of the editors of *Y Traethodydd* and as a member of the *Gorsedd* of Bards. He wrote *Prydeindod* ('Britishness') at this time and delivered several address to the Welsh Language Society. During the final months of his illness he prepared two books for the press, *Gwaedd yng Nghymru* and *Ac Onide*, both of which were published after his death. He d. 3 June 1970 at his home in Swansea and was buried in Pwllheli.

He published a number of books and pamphlets: *Yr Argyfwng Gwacter Ystyr* (1964); *Prydeindod* (1966); *Arwyddion yr Eiriolaeth* (from *Yr Ymofynnydd*); *Cristnogaeth a Chenedlaetholdeb*; 'Gweithredu Anghyfreithlon' in *Areithiau Eisteddfod Aberafan*; *Ni fyn y taeog mo'i ryddhau* (1968); *A rhaid i'r iaith ein gwahanu?* (1967); *Yr ewyllys i barhau* (1969); *Gwaedd yng Nghymru* (1970); *Ac Onide* (1970); Welsh articles on philosophy and religion in *Y Traethodydd*, 1933, 1943, 1949; *Credaf*, 1944; *Taliesin*, 1967; *Efrydiau Athronyddol*, 1938, 1939, 1947, 1950, 1951, 1957, 1961, 1969; *Diwinyddiaeth*, 1969; *Y Drysorfa* 1956; *Saith ysgrif ar grefydd* (ed. Dewi Z. Phillips), 1967; in English, *Religion as true myth* (inaugural lecture Univ. Coll. of Swansea, (1953); articles in *Mind*, 1948, 1950, 1954; *Philosophical Review*, 1949, 1951; *Philosophy*, 1950; *Philosophical Studies*, 1950; *Philosophical Quarterly*, 1951; *Aristotelian Society Symposium Suppl.*, 30 (1956), *Proc.*, 49 (1958-59); *Presidential Address*, 1967; *Analysis*, 1950; *Congregational Quarterly*, 1950; *Sophia*, 1970; and in *Religion and Understanding* (ed. Dewi Z. Phillips, 1967).

R.I. Aaron, 'John Robert Jones', *Efrydiau Athronyddol*, 1971; *Efrydiau Athronyddol*, 35, 1972; personal knowledge; [Dewi Z. Phillips, *J.R. Jones*, 1995].

Ma.B.D.

JONES, JOHN SHARE (1837-1950), veterinary surgeon; b. 25 Aug. 1873, son of Thomas Jones, Plas Kynaston, Cefn-mawr, Denbs. He was educated at the universities of Liverpool and London. He had a part in the foundation of the department or school of veterinary studies in the University of Liverpool. He was appointed Director of veterinary studies at that University in 1917, and Professor of Veterinary Anatomy in 1919. He was a Fellow of the Royal Veterinary College, and was President for one term. He was awarded the Steel memorial medal by that institution in 1928. He wrote a number of pamphlets and articles and acquired considerable fame in his field. He served on many committees, national and local, and was a member of the Wrexham Rural Council for many years. He was the Liberal candidate for the Oswestry constituency in the 1929 Parliamentary election. He d. 2 Dec., 1950.

The Times, 4 Dec. 1950; *Liv. D.P.*, 4 Dec. 1950; *Wrexham Leader*, 8 Dec. 1950; *WwW*, 1941-50; *WwW* 1921; information from H.H. Burchnall, Liverpool.

G.M.G.

JONES, JOHN THOMAS (1889-1952), missionary; b. at a farm called Ffos y Gaseg, in Llanegwad parish, near Carmarthen, 28 Feb. 1889, son of Thomas and Anna Jones. He was educated at Ysbyty national school. His father died when John was 15 yrs. old, and after leaving school he worked on the farm for several years. He began preaching in 1913, intending to offer himself for missionary work. To prepare himself he went to the Old College School, Carmarthen, and then to the Presbyterian College in the same town. He was imprisoned for two years as a conscientious objector and he suffered greatly. After the war he completed his college course, and after being accepted by the London Missionary Society as a missionary in Madagascar, he spent a further period of preparation at New College, London, and at Livingstone College to study the elements of medicine.

He was ordained to the ministry at Pant-teg, near Carmarthen (his mother church) on 4 and 5 July 1921. He m. Nurse Emily Bowen of Pembrey at King's Cross chapel, London, and they sailed for Madagascar on 9 May 1922, arriving at Tamatave on 11 June the same year. He worked in Mandritsara in the land of the Tsimihety in the north. As the first missionaries there were Christians from the Hova tribe (who had conquered the Tsimihety some time in the past), only a few had accepted the gospel. The country remained primitive and travelling was difficult. Jones was received warmly and his efforts were very successful. The secret of his success was his unstinting devotion and the gentleness of his personality. Training native leaders was of great importance to him, and he travelled long distances on foot from village to village. He and his wife had three children. After the birth of the last, Mrs. Jones fell ill and she d. in 1926 as she was being conveyed 200 m. over the mountains to Imerimandroso, where it had been arranged for a doctor from the capital to see her. (See *Tyst*, 17 June 1976, p.5). In Nov. the same year his youngest son died, and in less than six months his second son was killed when Imerimandroso was struck by a tornado.

He returned to Mandritsara, and on 7 Apr. 1927 he married Mlle. Madeleine Hipeau, a teacher and missionary under the auspices of the Paris Missionary Society, in the capital. After furlough in Wales he was appointed to work in another area because of his deteriorating health, but he continued to visit Mandritsara. By 1932 he was superintending 58 churches in Ambohimanga (near the capital, Antananarivo), 54 in Mandritsara and 25 in Anativolo. His health had deteriorated so much by 1943 that he was compelled to sever his connection with the north. After furlough in Wales and London he and his wife returned to Madagascar in Dec. 1946. But the revolt against France had made the Malagasy people suspicious of all Europeans. These were difficult and dangerous days, but for J.T. Jones they were an opportunity to serve as a   protector of those who were suffering and a peacemaker between warring tribes. He addressed the Union of Welsh Independents at Llanelli (1929), London (1937), Swansea (1945) and Bala (1951). He d. in Eltham, 4 Apr. 1952, having completed arrangements to return to Madagascar (against doctor's orders).

Brinley Pugh, *Triawd yr Ynys* (1954), 55-79; *Tyst*, 10 and 24 Apr. 1952; *Adroddiadau Cyfarfodydd blynyddol Undeb yr Annibynwyr Cymraeg* 1929, 1937, 1945 and 1951.

I.S.J.

JONES, JOHN TYWI (1870-1948), Baptist minister and journalist; b. 7 Jan. 1870 at Henllys Lodge near Llandovery, Carms., son of Thomas and Rachel Jones. He attended the British School at Llandovery and then went to work on local farms before moving to Glamorgan where he worked underground and on farms. He spent time in Aberdare, which was an important printing and publishing centre in that period and where there were 18 printing houses at the beginning of the 20th c., as well as periods in the Rhondda and Merthyr Tydfil. He began to preach at Calfaria Baptist chapel Aberdare where Rev. Thomas Price (*DWB*, 792), editor of the radical but short-lived newspaper *Y Gwron* was minister until his death in 1888. Through his own efforts Tywi Jones received further education at the Trecynon Seminary, Rees Jenkin Jones' (*DWB*, 503-4) school and proceeded to the Bangor Baptist college where Gwili (John Jenkins , *DWB*, 435-6) and E Cefni Jones were his contemporaries. He was ord. at Llanfair and Pentraeth, Angl., in 1897 and

remained there until 1906 when he received a call to Peniel, Glais, Swansea Valley. He ministered there energetically until the beginning of 1935.

From an early age he had contributed occasionally to *Tarian y Gweithiwr* published in Aberdare and in some sense a successor to *Y Gwron*; he later contributed regularly under the name 'Llewelyn'. Though a critic of political socialism, his Christian and liberal principles made him an unflinching advocate of workers' rights. He was a fervid supporter of the Welsh language and an ardent patriot. He became an early member of *Plaid Cymru*, a supporter of the *eisteddfod* and a member of the *Gorsedd* of Bards. Of the Welsh language he said: 'Nothing relating to the nation is more important than its language. The wealth of the life and ideals of a nation are enshrined in the language and literature. Poor indeed is the nation which does not possess a language worth preserving nor a literature worth nurturing'. And again, 'Our language is alive today ... It is sufficiently alive to live if Wales so wishes. If we neglect it, we will have broken our communion with the best of the nation's life in the post'. Increasing anglicization led *Tarian y Gweithiwr* to include some English reports. J. Tywi Jones formed the Tarian Publishing Co., Ltd. to safeguard the newspaper as a Welsh-language publication and he became the editor from 1914 until its demise in 1934. He was a convinced pacifist and a liberal in his theology.

He wrote a number of plays, some of which deal with the language and Welshness, e.g. *Dic Sion Dafydd* (1913), and stories for children and adults, together with some theological works, e.g. *Y Bedydd Ysgrythurol* (1900). He published numerous essays in *Seren Gomer* and hymns in *Llawlyfr Moliant*.

He m. twice: (1) Ellen, dau. of Herbert Davies, a tailor of Aberdare; she died in 1915; and (2) Elizabeth Mary Owen ('Moelona', see JONES, Elizabeth Mary below) in 1917. There were 2 dau. of the first marriage. He retired in 1935 and he and 'Moelona' moved to Newquay (Cards). He declared his support for *Plaid Cymru* in *Who's Who in Wales* (1937) and listed his leisure activities as gardening and climbing. He d. 18 July 1948 and was buried at Ainon cemetery, Birchgrove, Llansamlet.

Ser. Cymru, 30 July 1948; *Llawlyfr. Bed.*, 1949; [Noel Gibbard, 'Tywi yng Nghwm Tawe'. in Hywel Teifi Edwards, ed., *Cwm Tawe* (1993), 240-65; J. Tywi Jones papers at NLW, personal information from Noel Gibbard].

D.Je.

JONES, JOHN WILLIAM (1883-1954), author, collector of letters and papers, publisher, antiquary and folk poet; b. 5 Mar. 1883 at 4 Caerffridd, Tanygrisiau, Mer., son of David Jones, 'Glan Barlwyd', and his wife Ellen (née Roberts), Llwynogan, Llanedwen, Anglesey. He was educated at Glan-y-pwll school until he was twelve yrs. old, and then he spent a further two yrs. at the Higher Grade School in Blaenau Ffestiniog. In 1897 he went to work at the Oakley quarry where he laboured diligently for 53 yrs. until his retirement after injuring his hip. He married Maggie Jones, Minffordd, Oakley Square, Tanygrisiau, 11 June 1913, and they had one son. In 1936 J.W. Jones was elected an elder in Bethel chapel (CM), Tanygrisiau, and he was also a devoted and interesting Sunday school teacher for many years. He provided ready support for young boys and girls in his district who were fond of reading.

He was generally known as 'Joni Bardd' in his neighbourhood and he fulfilled the function of folk poet conscientiously. He had a burning interest in Welsh and English poetry, and particularly in collecting and publishing the work of some of the poets of his own and neighbouring areas. He edited some of the works of Ap Alun Mabon, *Gwrid y Machlud* (Blaenau Ffestiniog, 1941); Ioan Brothen, *Llinell neu Ddwy* (Blaenau Ffestiniog, 1942); Gwilym Deudraeth, *Yr Awen Barod* (Llandysul, 1943); Rolant Wyn, *Dŵr y Ffynnon* (Blaenau Ffestiniog, 1949) and R.R. Morris, *Caneuon R.R. Morris* (1951). One of his close friends was Ellis Humphrey Evans ('Hedd Wyn', *DWB*, 229) and he assisted J.R. Jones with the publication of *Cerddi'r Bugail*. He assisted with collecting the contents of *O Drum i Draeth* by Eliseus Williams ('Eifion Wyn', *DWB*, 1036) and with the preparation of biographies of Owen Griffith Owen ('Alafon,' *DWB*, 718) and John John Roberts ('Iolo Caernarfon', *DWB*, 870). He also assisted T. Gwynn Jones in collecting material for his book *Welsh Folklore and Folk-custom* (1930). He took particular delight in his friendship with T. Gwynn Jones (see below) and received several manuscripts from him, including the ode *Gwlad y Bryniau* after the bard himself had written it ('wedi i'r bardd ei hun ei hysgrifennu').

He lectured a great deal to literary societies on the poets of his locality and he collected many of the works of the poets and authors of Gwynedd, e.g. Alafon, Elfyn, Isallt, W. Pari Huws (*DWB*, 402), Gwilym Prysor, Carneddog (Richard Griffith, see above), Glaslyn (Richard Jones Owen, *DWB*, 719), Barlwydon, Gwilym Morgan, Awena Rhun, Glyn Myfyr, Llifon (William Griffith Owen, see under Owen Griffith Owen, *DWB*, 718), and others. He also ensured that the poets, authors and musicians of the locality were commemorated in a worthy manner. He arranged the erection of a gravestone for Robert Owen Hughes ('Elfyn', *DWB*, 390) and a memorial stone (a stone from Cwm Pennant) to 'Eifion Wyn.' With another friend and T. Gwynn Jones, he insisted on having a slate tombstone on the grave of Robert Roberts, '*Y Sgolor Mawr*', 1834-85 (*DWB*, 877) in Llangernyw churchyard. He was responsible for the memorial near the home of Thomas Lloyd (1841-1909; 'Crych Elen', *DWB*, 589) in Dolwyddelan – the money for this project came from a lady in America. He saw to it that a memorial stone was erected to Edward Stephen ('Tanymarian', *DWB*, 923) at Rhyd Sarn, Maentwrog, and he arranged a meeting to commemorate Morgan Llwyd (*DWB*, 594-5) and to unveil a memorial to him at Cynfal Fawr. He later collected and edited a substantial memorial volume, *Morgan Llwyd o Wynedd: Coffa Morgan Llwyd* (1952). He also collected money for the Sir O.M. Edwards (*DWB*, 192-3) memorial fund. He was a regular contributor to the newspapers and journals of his time: *Y Glorian*; *Y Rhedegydd* (a great deal, for many years); *Y Genedl* (he contributed a weekly column for some years – 'Nodion Meirion'); *Yr Herald Cymraeg* (many essays on poets and authors); *Y Brython*; *Y Faner*; *Y Dydd*; *Y Cymro* (in which the popular column 'Y Fainc Sglodion' appeared); *Cymru*; *Y Genhinen*; *Cymru'r Plant*; *Trysorfa'r Plant*; *Y Drysorfa Fawr*; *Yr Eurgrawn*; *Yr Haul*; *Y Goleuad*; *Seren Cymru*. Shortly before his death he saw the publication of *Y Fainc Sglodion: casgliad o rai o straeon y chwarel a'r capel* ...(1953). Over many years he sent various materials which were valuable (particularly to the social historian) to the National Library of Wales, including numerous scrap-books; hundreds of letters (some personal ones and some by notable Welsh people); manuscripts of the works of several poets and authors; various documents such as the accounts of local institutions, craftsmen and industries; minutes and reports of ecclesiastical and secular bodies; poems and election addresses – local and county; local folktales; programmes of *eisteddfodau*, concerts and literary societies; pictures of Ffestiniog people; memorial poems and cards. He sent similar materials to the library of the University College of North Wales in Bangor. He d. 6 Jan. 1954, at his home, and was buried with his wife (who had pre-deceased him twelve years previously) at Bethesda cemetery, Blaenau Ffestiniog. He was a notable example of a cultured common man, ready to help others, and motivated in all his activity by his concern for matters of culture.

Papers at N.L.W.; information from his son John Penri Jones and his daughter-in-law; *Trys. Plant*, 1941; personal acquaintance.

Me.E.

JONES, JOSEPH (1877-1950), principal of the Memorial College, Brecon; b. 7 August 1877 at Fronfelen, Rhydlewis, Cards., the son of Reuben and Jane Jones. The family moved in March 1882 to Cwmaman, Aberdare, and joined the Congregational church at Moriah Aman. His father lost his life in the colliery when he was 35 years old and, as a result, his mother ventured to manage a milk business and Joseph, the 12 year old son, was obliged, very reluctantly, to leave school for the coal mine. He began as a lamp-boy and subsequently worked as an engineer for a number of years. Soon it became evident that he had the makings of a scholar and preacher, and encouraged by the wholehearted support of the church at Moriah and its minister, the Rev. H. Aeron Davies, and the energetic, successful efforts of his mother in her milk business, Joseph Jones decided to leave the mine for the ministry. He began to preach and after a short period at the Higher Grade School, Aberdare and the Academy, under Dunmor Edwards, at Pontypridd, he entered the Memorial College, Brecon, in 1896.

Briefly, his college career was as follows: 1896-1901, University College, Cardiff; B.A., degree with Hons. in Greek; 1901-1904, Memorial College, Brecon; B.D., degree; the first Congregationalist to graduate B.D. (Wales); 1904-1907, Mansfield College, Oxford; an exhibition to Jesus College, First Class in the Hons. School of Theology and the Hall Houghton Junior Greek Prize open to all the colleges in the University. Before completing his course in Oxford, but already enjoying a reputation as a scholar, he was appointed in January 1907 to the New Testament Chair at the Memorial College, Brecon. He began duties in October 1907. At the close of his first year as professor, he was ordained to the ministry. In 1909, he married Miss Gwenllian de Lloyd, Aberystwyth. He was granted leave of absence by the college in 1911 to pursue special New Testament courses at Heidelberg. He spent his life in the service of the Memorial College; 1907-1943 as professor and, in 1943 on the retirement of Principal Thomas Lewis, he was appointed principal. He died suddenly at his home in Brecon on 28 April 1950 and was buried in the Brecon Public Cemetery.

Joseph Jones was endowed with exceptional gifts and came to prominence as a preacher, educationist, church statesman and social leader. It is hardly possible to record all the offices and positions to which he was called. He was very prominent in the life of Breconshire as a member of the County Council 1913-1948; chairman of the County Council 1940-1942; Alderman 1948-1950; chairman of the Education Committee 1919-1950. He was a Justice of the Peace of the Borough of Brecon. He became particularly prominent in the sphere of education. He served on various committees such as the Burnham, Hadow and Spens, and represented Wales on the Norwood Committee. He was a member of the County Councils Association and a vice-president of the Federation of Education Committees. He figured prominently on the councils of the University of Wales, a member of the Court, Council and of the governing bodies of several of the colleges. He was Dean of Divinity 1931-1934. A Liberal in politics. he contested the Welsh University Parliamentary seat in 1924, and was defeated by eight votes. In recognition of his great service to Welsh education, the University conferred on him the honorary degree of LL.D., in 1949. In that same year, he was appointed the first chairman of the Welsh Joint Education Committee.

He was very loyal to his denomination and to nonconformity. He had the gifts of the true church statesman. He was President of the Union of Welsh Independents in 1946 and served as the chairman of its Council for years. In 1950, he was elected Moderator of the Free Church Federal Council of England and Wales. He was a popular preacher and his services were in great demand. He had the gift of easy, fluent speech and a remarkable memory. His great interest was preaching, and the work dearest to his heart was that of interpreting the New Testament to generation after generation of young preachers.

He published *Esboniad ar Efengyl Mathew* (2 vols.) 1913-1914; *Cymrodoriaeth Gristnogol*, 1946; *Personal Christian Responsibility*, 1950. He edited for some time the Welsh monthly *Cennad Hedd;* was joint editor of *Brecon and Radnor Congregationalism*, 1912; contributed for many years the 'Letter from Wales' in the *Christian World*. He wrote articles for *Geiriadur Beiblaidd*, and to numerous periodicals.

Tywysydd y Plant, 1936; *Congl. Yr. Book*, 1951; Memorial College, *Reports*, 1896-1911; 1943; 1946; 1950; *Y Tyst*, May 1950; information from his widow and personal acquaintance.
                                                   D.J.D.

JONES, Sir LEWIS (1884-1968), industrialist and politician; b. 13 Feb. 1884, the eldest son of Evan and Margaret Jones, Tegfan, College Street, Ammanford, Carms. His father, who spent his whole life in the tinplate industry (he d. in 1934) was a devoted Congregationalist, and one of the first members of the Ammanford Urban District Council. Lewis Jones was educated at Ammanford secondary school and Reading University, where he spent five years. He earned his living as a schoolmaster at Reading until 1910 when he resigned his post in order to devote himself entirely to political work. From 1914 until 1917 he served in the Ministry of Armaments where he became secretary of the Priority Department. Jones was appointed secretary of the South Wales Siemens Steel Association in 1917, in which position he remained for 44 years until 1961.

In Oct. 1931 he was elected an M.P. (National Liberal, one of the supporters of Sir John Simon in the House of Commons) for the Swansea West constituency when he defeated H.W. Samuel (Lab.) (see below). He continued to represent this division until July 1945 when, against all expectations, he was ousted by Percy Morris (Lab.) (see below). He again stood in the same seat as a National Liberal and Conservative in the general election of Feb. 1950, but was unsuccessful. In 1933 he was chosen as a member of the National Health Insurance Joint Committee, and he became a J.P. for the borough of Swansea in 1934. He succeeded Clement Davies (see above) to serve as a Parliamentary Charity Commissioner between 1937 and 1945. Jones also served from 1952 as a member of the General Advisory Council of the B.B.C. He published a large number of articles and papers on economic and industrial matters. He acted as the Senior Vice-President of the Council and Court of Governors of University College, Swansea, and of the University of Wales, and he believed strongly in preserving the unified federal structure of the University. He was knighted in 1944 for his political and public work, and he was awarded the degree of LL.D. *honoris causa* by the University of Wales in 1954. Lewis Jones was a native Welsh-speaker, and was one of the first members of Gwynfryn Independent chapel, Ammanford, when it was founded in 1903. For many years he was a member of Swansea Cricket and Swansea Football Club.

He m. in 1911 Alice Maud, dau. of Frederick W. Willis of Bath. There were two sons. The younger was killed while on active service in India in 1947. Sir Lewis Jones lived at Highfield, Sketty, Swansea, and d. 10 Dec. 1968 aged 84.

Www; WwW (1937); *Dod's Parliamentary Companion, Times*, 12 Dec. 1968; *WWP*.
                                                   J.G.J.

JONES, LLEWELYN (1894-1960), minister (Presb.), editor and author; b. in 1894 at Llandegfan, Anglesey, s. of J.E. Jones, minister (Presb.) and his wife of that place. He was educated at Holyhead county school, the University College, Bangor (where he graduated B.A.), and Mansfield College, Oxford (B.Litt.). He gained an M.A. degree of the University of Wales in 1921 for his thesis on the hymnology of the Methodist Revival, with particular reference to the hymns of Williams, Pantycelyn. He was ord. in 1922, and served his ministry at Colwyn Bay (1922-24), Moriah, Utica, U.S.A. (1924-31), and Douglas Rd., Liverpool (1931-51). In 1951 he was appointed general secretary of the Presbyterian Missionary Society, and visited the mission fields in India, Pakistan and Brittany. In 1926 he m. Elizabeth Margaret Edwards, and they had two sons. He d. 24 Dec. 1960.

During the period he spent in Utica he published a history of Moriah. He gave great service to Welsh life on Merseyside, establishing centres for *Urdd Gobaith Cymru*, editing *Y Glannau* from 1944 onwards, and serving as a member of the editorial board of *Y Ffordd* (a journal for the youth of the Presb. church). He also published *Llawlyfr ar genhadaeth bersonol* (1939). His most important contribution, however, was *Aleluia gan y Parch, William Williams Pant y Celyn* (1926), a diplomatic edition of parts I-VI of *Aleluia*, 1744-47 by Williams, Pantycelyn (*DWB*, 1077-8), with a valuable introduction. Since copies of *Aleluia* are so very scarce, this volume is invaluable to students of William Williams' hymns.

WwFC, 346; *Gol.*, 8 Feb. 1961; *Blwyddiadur MC*, 1962, 259-60.

G.M.R.

JONES, MAI (1899-1960), pianist, composer and producer of light programmes on radio; b. 16 Feb. 1899 in Newport, Mon., the only child of Thomas John Jones, stationmaster of Newport and his wife Beatrice. When she was 8 yrs old D. Vaughan Thomas (*DWB*, 943-4) heard her playing the piano at an *eisteddfod* and he suggested to her mother that she had a brilliant future as a pianist provided she was sent to a competent teacher. At the age of 10 she was appointed organist of Mynydd Seion (Congl.) church, Hill Street, Newport, a post which she held for over 30 years.

She won the Caradoc Scholarship to study composition and piano playing at the University College, Cardiff, where her teacher David Evans (1874-1948; see above) described her as one of the best organists he had ever heard. She also showed an unusual skill as a pianist during this period, and this was recognised later when she was chosen to be one of the official accompanists for the national *eisteddfod* at Pontypool in 1924. After studying further at the Royal College of Music in London she pursued a professional career as a piano soloist in a concert party. She also came into prominence as a mimic as well as a singer and soloist on the accordion and she became a member of several notable groups in the entertainment world in London, including 'The five magnets', 'The Carroll sisters', and 'The three Janes'. She first broadcast from Savoy Hill with Jack Payne's band in 1928, and for the first time from Cardiff in 1932. She also broadcast from Belfast, Birmingham and Bristol in the 1920s. She joined the B.B.C. staff at Cardiff in 1941, and her name became known through her work as producer of many popular radio programmes, including 'Welsh Rarebit', 'Saturday Starlight', 'Merry-go-round' and 'Silver Chords'. Much of the music included in these series were her own compositions and these

broadcasts provided an opening for several artists who became prominent figures in English light entertainment. She wrote the music for the radio performance of *Twm Sion Cati*, the first Welsh pantomime ever broadcast on radio.

She was an inspired radio personality. She tried to base her work as producer on American patterns and standards, something new and unfamiliar in the early days of broadcasting. She had the advantage in her work of being able to compose quickly and sometimes impromptu. Her first song, 'Blackbirds', was published in 1925, and in 1927 her song 'Wondering if you remember' was included in the popular musical comedy *The gipsy princess*. She also wrote "Nos da/Good night" (1946), 'We'll keep a welcome' (1949), and 'Rhondda rhapsody' (the piano theme of the popular radio series 'Welsh Rarebit', 1951).

She m. at Newport in 1947, David (Davey) Davies of Garnant, a prominent singer and programme engineer for the B.B.C. in Wales (he d. in 1964). She retired from the B.B.C. in 1959, and d. at her home, 19 St. Mark's Crescent, Newport, 7 May 1960, and was buried in St. Gwynllyw churchyard.

Personal research; *Empire News*, 8 May 1960; *West. Mail*, 9 and 12 May 1960; additional information supplied by the B.B.C. and the Rev. Evan Davies, Crymych; [*Trans. Cymm*, 1991, 307-9; *West. Mail*, 10 Feb 1983, 5 Jan. 1988].

H.W.

JONES, MARGARET - see HUGHES, (ROBERTS), MARGARET above.

JONES, MAURICE (1863-1957), priest and college principal; b. 21 June 1863, at Trawsfynydd, Mer., 2nd s. of William Jones, shoemaker, and his wife Catherine. He was educated at the local school and with scholarships proceeded to Friars School, Bangor, Christ College, Brecon, where Dr. D. Lewis Lloyd (*DWB*, 576) was headmaster, and Jesus College, Oxford, where he graduated with 1st-class hons. in divinity, 1886. He gained the degrees of M.A. and B.D. in 1907, and D.D. in 1914. He was ordained deacon in 1886 and priested in 1887. He was curate of Caernarfon, 1886-88; assistant organising secretary of the Additional Curates Soc., 1888-89; curate of Welshpool, 1889-90. From 1890 to 1916 he served as chaplain to the Forces. During the South African war he served on the staff of Lord Roberts and Lord Kitchener. On leaving the army he accepted the benefice of Rotherfield Peppard, the gift of Jesus College, Oxford, and remained there till 1923, when he was appointed Principal of St. David's College, Lampeter. There were only 70 students there when he arrived and he worked steadfastly to increase their number. When he left in 1938 there were more than 200 students. They were mostly ordinands and the majority of them served the Church in Wales. He was made canon of St. David's in 1923, and was public examiner at Oxford 1921-22, and examiner for the B.D. degree of the University of Wales, 1922. As principal of St. David's College, Lampeter, he was a Fellow of Jesus College, Oxford. He was a member of the departmental committee which published the report *Welsh in education* *and life* in 1927. He was elected president of the Welsh National Council of the League of Nations Union, 1928.

He was a member of the *Gorsedd* of Bards with the bardic name of Meurig Prysor, and was treasurer of the *Gorsedd* from 1925 to 1938 when he was elected *Gorsedd* Bard. He was attendant druid from 1947 to 1957, and he narrowly missed election to the office of archdruid in 1955. In 1955 he was made a Fellow of the *Eisteddfod*. He was a member of the National Council of Music, and chairman of *Cymdeithas Caredigion Cerdd*. He was a vice-president of the Hon. Soc. of Cymmrodorion.

After he had completed his foreign service in 1908 he began to study the New Testament in depth and published his first volume, *St. Paul the orator*, in 1910. This was followed by *The New Testament in the Twentieth Century*, 1914; *The Epistle to the Philippians*, 1918; *The Four Gospels*, 1921; *The Epistle of St. Paul to the Colossians*, 1923. He contributed to many periodicals in Welsh and English. He was a renowned preacher. A short, slight man with red hair, he remained active and young in spirit to the end of his life. In 1940 and again in 1944 he was bombed out of his home in London. Failing to find a house, he accpted the living of Bradden, Northants, when he was 82 years of age.

He m. (1), in 1894, Emily, dau. of Col. C.M. Longmore, of Gosport; (2), in 1911, Jennie Bell, dau. of Sidney Smith, of Gosport. They had 3 sons and 2 dau. He d. 7 Dec. 1957 at his home, 27 Gravel Hill, Addington, Surrey, and was bur. in the churchyard there.

Www, 1951-60; *WwW*, 1933 and 1937; *Llan*, 21 Oct. 1955, 13 Dec. 1957; *Haul*, Oct. 1958.

M.G.E.

JONES, MEGAN - see HUGHES, (ROBERTS), MARGARET above.

JONES, MEIRION (1907-1970), educationist; b. at Llithfaen, Caerns., 30 July 1907, the son of Robert Owen Jones and Annie Jones. He attended Llithfaen primary school, Pwllheli grammar school, and Bangor Normal College, and served as a teacher at Corris primary school (1929-30), Blaenau Ffestiniog central school (1930-39), headmaster of Llandrillo primary school (1939-45), headmaster of Dyffryn Ardudwy primary school (1945-50), headmaster of Bala primary school (1950-70). In 1938 he married Jane, the daughter of Owen and Catherine Griffith, Derlwyn, Pwllheli. They had two daughters. In 1965 he received the M.B.E. for his services to education in Wales. He was one of the seven founder members of the Schools Council Welsh Committee. He was made a Druid at the Barry national *eisteddfod* 1968 for his service to Welsh culture. He was a member of the Council of *Urdd Gobaith Cymru*, and the Secretary of the *Urdd* National *Eisteddfod* at Blaenau Ffestiniog, 1936 and also at Bala 1954. He was Secretary of the *Urdd* Committee in Merioneth for many years. He was Honorary Secretary of the national *eisteddfod* of Wales at Bala, 1967 and Secretary of the committee responsible for the Welsh comic *Hwyl* for 20 years (1950-70). He was the author of two books, *Elizabeth Davies*, published by University of Wales Press (1960), and

a volume for children, *Am Hwyl* published by Gwasg Gee in 1967. As the Secretary of Penllyn Historical Society he was the instigator of memorials to Michael D. Jones (*DWB*, 495-6) and John Puleston Jones (*DWB*, 487-8). He was an elder of the Presbyterian Church of Wales for 27 years, and secretary of Capel Tegid, Bala. The imposing list of secretaryships indicates his outstanding skill as an able organizer. He died at his home, Llwynhudol, Bala, 11 March 1970.

Information by his widow, Jane Jones, and personal knowledge.

I.O.

JONES, OWEN THOMAS (1878-1967), Woodwardian Professor of Geology in the University of Cambridge; b. 16 April 1878, at Plasnewydd Farm, Beulah, Cards., near Newcastle Emlyn, the only son of David Jones and Margaret Thomas. He attended the British School in Tre-wen near Newcastle Emlyn and later entered Pencader grammar school. Up to this time O.T. Jones spoke Welsh only, and throughout his life continued to speak and write in Welsh with the greatest fluency. Already at his grammar school he was an outstanding pupil obtaining a first class in the College of Preceptors Certificate in 1894 and passing the Matriculation examination of the University of Wales with the same class in 1895. The following year he entered the University College of Wales, Aberystwyth with the Keeling Entrance Scholarship in Natural Science. His degree courses at Aberystwyth included mathematics, chemistry, botany and zoology and he obtained a first-class honours in Physics in 1900. He next entered Trinity College, Cambridge with an Open Exhibition and began taking a specialized interest in geology and mineralogy. He obtained a first class in the Natural Science Tripos Part I in 1902 and was awarded the Wiltshire prize in geology and mineralogy. The next year he gained a first class in Part II of the Tripos and became Harkness Prizeman in geology in 1904. Immediately after graduation, and realizing the importance of field work in geological studies, he worked with H.M. Geological Survey surveying the western extension of the south Wales coalfield in western Carmarthenshire and Pembrokeshire. In addition to his official duties he was engaged in considerable research studies on his own. These again were directed to Wales and in 1909 there appeared an important paper on the geological structure of the Plynlimon area in Mid-Wales. This work still remains the standard work on the Lower Palaeozoic rocks of Mid-Wales, and in many ways the standard work on the classification of these rocks the world-over. O.T. Jones was now a geologist of the first rank and was awarded the D.Sc. degree of the University of Wales in the same year. In 1909 also he was appointed to a lectureship in geology in his old college which he held for one session before becoming Professor of Geology there in 1910. In this year also he obtained the much coveted Sedgwick Essay Prize in Geology. He was a superb teacher and director of research and many generations of geologists are greatly indebted to him. The period following the cessation of hostilities in 1918 saw great changes in the British universities. Professional salaries remained at a low level and there were as yet no research grants so that men of O.T. Jones' standing had to find all the money necessary for their own private research from their own pockets. This was particularly serious in geology where extensive field work was involved. Dazzling offers of higher renumeration were made to him from universities near to Wales like Liverpool and Manchester, but his love for, and interest in the rural life of Wales was a deterrent. Finally he succumbed to the blandishments of the University of Manchester where he was appointed Professor of Geology in 1919 and remained until 1930 when he became Woodwardian Professor of Geology in the University of Cambridge.

During the fifty years between 1910 and 1960 O. T. Jones published numerous professional papers and books amounting often to more than one a year and covering virtually the whole range of geological studies from those relating to the geology of Wales to an examination of the great continental shelves of the British Isles and their geophysical problems. Studies of the geology of parts of North America were also involved while his work migrated from strict stratigraphy to include palaeontology and igneous intrusions. As always the geology of Wales and especially that of the Lower Palaeozoic rocks of Wales found its place in his later writings. It is interesting that while at Cambridge his interests had been shifting very much towards mineralogy and this facet of geology reached fruition in his work with the publication by H.M. Stationery Office in 1922 of the standard work on the lead and zinc mines in northern Cardiganshire and western Montgomeryshire. In this work, greatly used by modern researchers, every lode and every mine both large and small are studied in detail.

O.T. Jones was a Fellow and later President of both the Geological and Mineralogical Societies. In his capacity as foreign secretary of the Geological Society he was also in close contact with geological societies overseas, especially those of Belgium and the United States. He was now clearly the internationally known doyen of British geologists. He was elected a Fellow of the Royal Society and obtained its famous Royal Medal in 1956. In addition he had been awarded the Lyell Medal in 1926 and the Wollaston Medal of the Geological Society in 1945, while the University of Wales awarded him the honorary degree of LL.D. in 1958. In 1910 he m. Ethel May, dau. of William Henry Reynolds of Haverfordwest, and they had two sons and a dau. One son d. in an aircraft accident in 1945. O. T. Jones d. 5 May 1967.

Ellis, *UCW*; *Biog. Memoirs Fellows R.S.*, 13 (1967); his papers are in N.L.W.

E.G.B.

JONES, PERCY MANSELL (1889-1968), Professor of French; b. 11 April 1889 at Carmarthen, son of Arnaud Johnson Jones and his wife. Educated at Queen Elizabeth's Grammar School, Carmarthen, he went to U.C.W., Aberystwyth in 1908 gaining a first-class honours degree in French and later a master's degree. He then proceeded to Balliol College, Oxford, where he obtained his B.Litt.

A stimulating and influential teacher, he successively occupied posts as lecturer in French in Aberystwyth, University College of South Wales, Cardiff and Cambridge. He was appointed Professor of French in the University College of North Wales, Bangor in 1937 and in 1951 went to the University of Manchester as its first Professor of Modern French Literature. The University of Wales conferred on him an hon. D.Litt. degree in 1960, soon after his retirement. Mansell Jones was drawn to the study of modern French poetry; he was able, with his natural sensitivity and understanding, to illuminate his subjects in books like *Emile Verhaeren* (1926 and 1957) and *Baudelaire* (1952). His important new edition of *The Oxford Book of French Verse* (1957) displayed a sure taste in the choice of poems especially from Baudelaire onwards. Collections of essays on more general topics - *Tradition and Barbarism* (1930), *French Introspectives* (1937) and *The Background of Modern French Poetry* (1951) - reveal his interests in French thought and contemporary issues. In the 1950s he took a full part in the debates which were then raging on the role of the universities in the post-war world and especially the place of the humanities in a technological age. Mansell Jones, who suffered indifferent health throughout his life, was a bachelor with a host of friends. Known universally with affectionate admiration as 'P.M.' he was a welcome lecturer at universities where his humour, his humility, his affirmation of literary values and his pleasure in scholarship were fine examples to others. He d. on 24 Jan. 1968.

P. Mansell Jones, *How they educated Jones* (autobiography up to 1915; 1974) and 'Saunders Lewis: Sketches for a Portrait' in *Saunders Lewis: ei feddwl a'i waith*, ed. Pennar Davies (1950); L.J. Austin, Garnet Rees and Eugène Vivaver (ed.), *Studies in Modern French Literature presented to P. Mansell Jones by pupils, colleagues and friends* (1961).

Ga.R.

JONES, PHILIP (1855-1945), minister (CM); b. at 30, Cotton Row, Tai-bach, Glam., 19 Feb. 1855, son of Evan and Catherine Jones. He was brought up in Dyffryn Church, where he heard the old pulpit stalwarts of Glamorgan. He was educated at Trefeca, and was ordained at the Association in Aberystwyth in 1887. He held pastorates at Fishguard, Llandeilo Fawr (for two terms); Capel Newydd, Llanelli; and Penuel, Pontypridd. He spent his latter years at Porthcawl, where he d. 24 Sept. 1945. He was above all a preacher in the succession of the old Glamorgan preachers. He was most eloquent, with a dramatic style and an agile mind, and the old vocabulary of the Glamorgan dialect was alive on his lips. The ordinary people doted upon his eloquence. He preached regularly at the high festivals of his denomination for a long period, and was regarded as the last of the princes of the Methodist pulpit in south Wales. A small volume of his poems, with some hymns, was published in 1948.

Blwyddiadur MC, 1946, 173; W. Nantlais Williams (ed.), *Philip Jones: Pregethau ac Emynau*.

G.M.R.

JONES, RICHARD ('Dofwy'; 1863-1956), folk poet; b. at Fron-goch, Cemais, Mont., 3 May 1863. He received his only formal education at Dol-y-clwyd school, Cemais. He was apprenticed as a carpenter, but when he was twenty he and his brother went to farm Cwmeidrol, Cwmlline, where he remained for the rest of his life, with his wife and four children. Although a good musician and singer, he was primarily regarded locally as a poet. He mastered the rules of *cynghanedd* at an early age, and although no volume of his work was published, hundreds of his *englynion* and verses appeared in contemporary periodicals. He won his first prize for an *englyn* when he was twenty yrs. old, and the last when he was ninety. He was a 'character' in his own locality. He d. 18 Feb. 1956 and was buried in Cemais cemetery.

Personal knowledge.

G.R.T.

JONES, ROBERT (1891-1962), aerodynamicist; b. 7 Nov. 1891 at Tŷ Newydd, Cricieth, Caerns. the fourth child of John Jones and his wife Sarah Mary. He was educated at the local Board School and afterwards at Porthmadog County School. In October 1908 he entered the University College of North Wales with a small scholarship. His main course of study was in mathematics which he read under Professor G.H. Bryan, F.R.S., one of the founders of the science of aerodynamics. He also studied Welsh philology under Sir J. Morris-Jones (*DWB*, 668-9). An outstanding student, he won several prizes including the R.A. Jones prize in mathematics (1910). In 1911 he graduated with a 2nd-class honours degree in Pure Mathematics, following this with a 1st-class honours degree in Applied Mathematics in 1912. The award of a substantial scholarship (Isaac Roberts) enabled him to study for an M.A. which he gained in 1913, this being the first higher degree awarded by the University of Wales for a thesis in aerodynamics. The substance of his work was later published in the *Proc. Roy. Soc.* in a joint paper with Bryan (1915). From 1913 to 1916 he held an 1851 Exhibition Science Research Scholarship, studying firstly at the University of Göttingen (1913-14) and then at the National Physical Laboratory, Teddington. He subsequently joined the staff of the Aerodynamics Division of the N.P.L. remaining there until his retirement in 1953. On 17 Dec. 1918 he m. Madeline Broad; they had one daughter and lived at Ashford, Surrey. Throughout his life he was an active member of the Congregational Church, remaining close to Wales and her language. He d. 17 March 1962 at Stanwell.

Robert Jones' early work at the National Physical Laboratory was on the mathematical theory of aeroplane stability. Later he did much theoretical and wind tunnel work on airships and became one of the leading experts in the world on the stability of these craft. In 1923 he was awarded the R.38 Memorial Prize of the Royal Aeronautical Society for a classic paper on airship stability and in 1924 the University of Wales awarded him the degree of D.Sc., this being the first ever awarded for research in aerodynamics. Following the loss of the airship R. 101 Dr. Jones took a leading part in the wind tunnel work for the Commission of Enquiry

receiving personal thanks from the chairman, Sir John Simon, for his work. Allied to his work on airships he carried out investigations for the Admiralty on the stability of torpedoes. He also undertook some of the earliest research on the stability of parachutes. In 1931 the N.P.L. commissioned its Compressed Air Tunnel which enabled wind tunnel investigations to take place at high pressures (25 atmospheres). Dr. Jones took over supervision of the work of the tunnel and was associated with it until his retirement. Under his leadership work of fundamental importance was carried out, the special facilities of the tunnel enabling direct comparison to be made between results for small models and the full scale. In addition to papers in scientific journals, Dr. Jones was the author of some 60 substantial Reports and Memoranda issued by the Aeronautical Research Council.

Aeronautical Research Council R. and M., No. 2570; information from Miss Margaret G. Jones and Mr. Emrys Jones; University College of North Wales, Bangor, Manuscript Collection.

D.J.Wr.

JONES, ROBERT EVAN (1869-1956), collector of books and manuscripts; b. 22 May, 1869, one of seven children of John and Catherine Jones, High Street, Penrhyndeudraeth, Mer. His father was a grocer, and soon after Robert Evan's birth the family moved to Meirion House, Tanygrisiau, Blaenau Ffestiniog. He received his early education in the boys' school, Tanygrisiau and later spent five years there as a pupil-teacher before becoming an assistant teacher, and as assistant he moved to Glan-y-Pwll and Manod, both in the same district. In 1894 he won the Queen's Scholarship to the University College of Wales, Aberystwyth. He almost won the Cynddelw Scholarship and was given a special award for the high standard of his examinations in Welsh and History. At college he studied Welsh language and literature under Professor Edward Anwyl (*DWB*, 12-13), and was chairman of the Y *Gymdeithas Geltaidd* and one of the founders of the *eisteddfod*. In 1898, on completion of his course, he was appointed headmaster in Nantgwynant and later in Nantperis in Arfon. In 1910 he became headmaster of the council school in Tanygrisiau, his home, and he remained there until his retirement in 1932.

During his career as headmaster he was very active in establishing evening classes for adults, and his far-reaching influence in the society reflected his cultural interests and organisational talent. For a time he was active in the Liberal party in Meirionethshire, and the local M.P., Sir Henry Haydn Jones, was a close friend. Another friend, during a stint on the staff of *Yr Herald Cymraeg*, was T. Gwynn Jones (see below), and they corresponded regularly. In 1921 he was very active, with others, in establishing a memorial fund to O.M.Edwards (*DWB*, 192-3) of which he became secretary.

But he was best known as a collector of books and manuscripts. It is thought that he had more than ten thousand volumes in his personal library. More specifically he collected manuscripts and rare documents belonging to Charles Ashton (*DWB*, 15) and Thomas Edwards, 'Twm o'r Nant' (*DWB*, 196). He had an interesting collection of the letters of Peter Williams (1723-96; *DWB*, 1063) to his son Eliezer Williams (*DWB*, 1036) from 1798 onwards. His interest and knowledge of books and manuscripts was invaluable to students and researchers, particularly in Celtic studies. He also wrote copiously on Welsh bibliography and Welsh studies in periodicals and newspapers.

He married, 12 Aug. 1920, in Maentwrog Church, Sissie Hughes, dau. of Richard and Elizabeth Hughes, Llys Twrog, Maentwrog, and they had one daughter. He died 27 March 1956 and was buried at Maentwrog.

Information from his daughter.

Al.R.J.

JONES, ROBERT LLOYD (1878-1959), schoolmaster, children's writer and dramatist; b. 7 Dec. 1878 in Porthmadog, Caerns., the sixth of the ten children born to Robert Jones, master mariner, and his wife Elizabeth (née Williams). He was educated at the elementary schools in Porthmadog, Minffordd and Penrhyndeudraeth, the higher grade school, Blaenau Ffestiniog, the grammar school, Bala, and the Normal College, Bangor (1899-1901). He began his career as a teacher in his old school in Porthmadog and afterwards became headmaster of the elementary schools in Tremadog (1906-13), Trefor (1913-28) and Lloyd Street, Llandudno (1928-44). He took a keen interest in educational matters throughout his life and held a number of offices in the county branch of the National Union of Teachers. He was for a number of years a member of the governing body of John Bright School, Llandudno.

He began writing at a young age winning in many local *eisteddfodau* and as many as 13 prizes in the national *eisteddfod*. He is mainly remembered, however, as the author of the following adventure novels for children in Welsh: *Ynys y trysor* (1925); *Plant y Fron* (1926); *Atgofion hen forwr* (1926); *Capten* (1928); *Mêt y Môna* (1929); *Dirgelwch y Cwm* (1929); *Ogof yr ysbïwyr* (1933) and *Ym Môr y De* (1936). He learnt a great deal about life at sea from his father and spent much of his childhood on the busy Porthmadog quayside watching the ships and questioning the sailors. He read with zest the works of R.L. Stevenson, Ballantyne, Henty and others and all of this became raw material for his own novels later. He also contributed to *Cymru'r Plant* and to denominational publications such as *Y Drysorfa* and *Y Goleuad*. At the time his novels and stories filled a considerable gap in writing in Welsh for children. In addition he published 24 popular, short one-act plays in Welsh entitled: *Y pymtheg mil, Y walet, Y census, Nos Sadwrn, Y doctor, Yr etifedd, Y basgedi, Dau ben blwydd, Wyt ti'n cofio?, Arian modryb, Y troseddwr, Anghofio, Brawd a chwaer, Croeso, Y drws agored, Gweinidog Tabor, Y gwir a'r golau, Pan oeddym fechgyn, Rhiannon, Safle, Y scwlmis, Santa Clôs a'i fab, Y tair chwaer, Teulu'r Gelli*. It was he who was mainly responsible for forming the Drama Society of North Wales in Caernarfon in 1929, which was to function as a branch of the Welsh Drama Union. He served several times as an adjudicator in the *Urdd Gobaith Cymru* national *eisteddfod*.

He was twice m.: (1) in 1906 to Elin Alice Jones, Minffordd (d. 1942), and three sons were born to them; (2) in 1944 to Sarah Roberts, Bethesda (d. 1962). He d. at Tre-garth 3 Feb. 1959 and was buried at Coetmor cemetery, Bethesda.

Information given by his brothers, the late William and Goronwy Jones; *Lleufer*, 20 (1964), 27-30; [Mairwen and Gwynn Jones, *Dewiniaid Difyr* (1983)].

A.Ll.H.

JONES, ROBERT WILLIAM ('Erfyl Fychan'; 1899-1968) historian, litterateur and *eisteddfodwr*; b. New Year's Day, 1899, in Penygroes, Caerns., the younger son of Robert William Jones, Brynllwyni , quarryman and small-holder, and Jane his wife, the daughter of Robert Thomas, Drws-y-coed, Nantlle. Educated at Pen-y-groes county school, he entered the teachers' training dept at U.C.W. after World War I and taught for 2 yrs. in Birmingham. He was appointed head-teacher at Trisant, Cards., in 1922 and became headmaster of Llanerfyl endowed school in 1924. A Board of Education research scholarship (1928) enabled him to study Welsh social life in the 18c. under T.Gwynn Jones (see below) and the award of an Owen Templeman Scholarship allowed him to study under J. Glyn Davies (see above) at Liverpool University. He gained his M.A. in 1939 for a dissertation on 'The wayside entertainer in Wales in the nineteenth century' and he was appointed the same year headmaster of Berriew Road school, Welshpool. In 1944 he was elected a Fellow of the Royal Historical Society. He married in 1929 Gwendolen Jones of Aberystwyth and they had two sons. He served in the army in both world wars and was promoted to the rank of major.

He was deeply interested in the art of *penillion* singing and won the first prize at Swansea national *eisteddfod* for the *penillion* solo in 1926. He became a member of the *Gorsedd* the same year. In the field of Welsh culture he owed much to the influence of T. Gwynn Jones, the Francis brothers of Nantlle, and T.D. James ('Iago Erfyl'), the talented and scholarly rector of Llanerfyl in the 1920s. At Bala in 1934 he founded the *Cymdeithas Cerdd Dant* and he was the society's secretary until 1949 when he was chosen to be Recorder of the *Gorsedd*. He succeeded Geoffrey Crawshay ('Sieffre o Gyfarthfa', see above) as Herald Bard and was also Recorder and Chief Bard of the Powys *Gorsedd* for many years. Apart from his contribution to the *eisteddfod* and *Cymdeithas Cerdd Dant*, he held evening classes on Welsh history and literature for over thirty years and laboured untiringly to safeguard and advance the Welsh life of his adopted county.

He published *Bywyd Cymdeithasol Cymru yn y Ddeunawfed Ganrif* (1931) and a volume of poetry, *Rhigwm i'r Hogiau* (1949), as well as essays, articles and radio scripts etc. He died in Mynytho on 7 Jan. 1968, and was buried at Pen-y-groes.

Personal knowledge; family papers; *WwW* (1933, 1937); *WWP*; *Allwedd y Tannau*, 1968, 18-19; [correspondence in N.L.W.].

G.V.-J.

JONES, THOMAS (1870-1955), university professor, civil servant, administrator, author; b. 27

September 1870 in Rhymney, Mon., the eldest of the nine children of David Benjamin Jones, a shopkeeper, and his wife, Mary Ann Jones. He was educated in Rhymney Board School and Lewis' School, Pengam. At 14 he became a clerk at the Rhymney Iron and Steel Works. He was admitted to the University College of Wales, Aberystwyth in 1890 as a prospective candidate for the Calvinistic Methodist ministry. He migrated to Glasgow University in 1890 where he had a brilliant academic career. He was appointed to a lectureship there in 1901. From 1904 to 1905 he was lecturing in Ireland under the Barrington Trust and from 1906 to 1909 he was an assistant commissioner (research) to the Royal Commission on the Poor Law. For one academic session, 1909-1910, he was Professor of Economics in Queen's University, Belfast. He returned to Wales in 1910 as Secretary of the Welsh National Campaign against Tuberculosis. In 1912 he was appointed Secretary of the National Health Insurance Commission (Wales). He was transferred to London in 1916 as Assistant Secretary to the Cabinet, later becoming Deputy Secretary. He retired in 1930 to become the Secretary of the Pilgrim Trust. He became a Trustee in 1945 and Chairman from 1952 to 1954. From 1934 to 1940 he was a member of the Unemployment Assistance Board. He was appointed C.H. in 1929.

Jones was a man of exceptional drive and energy. Although he abandoned his intention of becoming a minister of the church, the social teaching of the Scriptures remained his chief inspiration. Thomas Charles Edwards (*DWB*, 197-8), Joseph Mazzini, Sir Henry Jones (*DWB*, 466) and Sidney Webb, successively influenced him greatly. Throughout his life, he sought to be a 'doer of the Word'.

He was one of the founders of *The Welsh Outlook* and its first editor (1914-1916), of the Gregynog Press in 1922 and the principal founder of Coleg Harlech in 1927. He, more than any other person, was responsible for the establishment of the Arts Council in 1939, or the Council for the Management of Music and the Arts as it was first known.

During his term of office in the Cabinet Secretariat he rendered great service during the Irish troubles in the negotiations that led to the 1921 settlement and likewise during the General Strike crisis in 1926. Three of the Prime Ministers whom he served, viz. Lloyd George (see below), Bonar Law and Stanley Baldwin placed great confidence on his judgement. His relations with Ramsay Macdonald were not so happy. He kept in close personal touch with Lloyd George and Stanley Baldwin throughout their lives. Both used him for confidential discussions, for example, during the attempts between 1935 and 1938 to improve Anglo-German relations. As the Chairman of the South Wales Coalfield Distress Committee and of the unemployment Committee of the National Council of Social Service his energy and insight gave effectiveness to efforts to mitigate the sufferings caused by industrial unemployment between 1929 and 1939. He was the Chairman of the York Trust (1934-40) and of the Elphin Lloyd-Jones Trust (1935-45). He served on many public bodies, for example the Councils of the University of Wales, the University College of Wales, Aberystwyth

(President, 1944-45), the National Library of Wales and the National Museum of Wales. He was Chairman of the Royal Commission on Ancient Monuments for Wales 1944 to 1948. He became a member of the Observer Trust when that was established in 1946.

He wrote and published many articles and pamphlets. His books include, the Everyman edition of *The Duties of Man*, Joseph Mazzini (1907), an edition of *Old Memories*, Sir Henry Jones (1938), *A Theme with variations* (1933), *Leeks and Daffodils* (1942), *Rhymney memories* (1938), *Cerrig Milltir* (1942), *The Native never Returns* (1946), *Lloyd George* (1951), *Welsh Broth* (1951), *A Diary with Letters* (1954), *The Gregynog Press* (1954), *Whitehall Diaries* Vol I and II (1969), edited by Keith Middlemas.

He received the honorary degree of LL.D. from Glasgow University (1922), the University of Wales (1928), St Andrews (1947) and Birmingham (1950). He was awarded the medal of the Honourable Society of Cymmrodorion in 1944.

He married Eirene Theodora Lloyd in 1902. There were three children of the marriage, Eirene Lloyd (Baroness White), 1909-99; Tristan Lloyd Jones, 1913-1990, Elphin Lloyd Jones, 1916-1928.

Thomas Jones suffered a serious fall indoors at his home in St. Nicholas-at-Wade, Kent, in June 1955 and died in a private nursing home in Golders Green 15 October 1955. He was cremated.

As a vigorous and resourceful administrator, he was regarded as one of the most unselfish and devoted benefactors of his time. He spoke and wrote Welsh but had grave reservations about Welsh political nationalism. His range of friends and acquaintances was exceptionally wide not only in Wales and the United Kingdom but throughout the Commonwealth and the United States of America. He was a tireless letter writer, most generous with advice and help to all and sundry, in every walk of society. No man had a higher sense of the value of time and he made excellent use of it.

The works noted above and personal knowledge; [E.L. Ellis, *T.J.: a life of Dr Thomas Jones* (1992); his papers in N.L.W.].

B.B.T.

JONES, Sir THOMAS ARTEMUS (1871-1943), journalist, judge and historian; b. 18 Feb. 1871 at 22, Lôn Abram, Denbigh, the sixth son of Thomas Jones, stonemason. At 11 years of age, he left the National School to work at the station bookstall, and while there, he taught himself shorthand. In 1886 he was appointed junior reporter on the *Denbighshire Free Press*, for which he reported the Tithe War. He left Denbigh in 1889 to work on newspapers in Herefordshire, East Anglia and Manchester. In 1896 he joined the Parliamentary staff of the *Daily Telegraph*, later transferring to the *Daily News*.

He studied Law in his spare time, and in 1898 became a student of the Middle Temple: he was called to the bar there in 1901, and the following year he joined the Welsh Circuit. He took part in the libel action Lord Penrhyn *v* W.J. Parry (1903) and the trial of Sir Roger Casement for treason in 1916. In 1909 he himself brought a libel action against Messers E. Hulton & Co. for using his name in a defamatory manner in the *Sunday Chronicle* (12 July 1908): the defendants carried the case to the House of Lords, but were unsuccessful, and the note normally inserted in novels to the effect that all characters in them are fictitious is the result of this action.

In 1919 he became a King's Counsellor and in 1928 he was appointed to represent Britain on the Claims Commission set up as a result of disturbances in Mexico. He was knighted for his service in 1931. In 1930 he was appointed Judge of County Courts in north Wales, an appointment he held until Oct. 1942. In 1938 he was elected chairman of the Caernarfonshire Quarter Sessions and in the same year he was awarded the degree of LL.D. *honoris causa* by the University of Wales. From 1939 until July 1941 he was Chairman of the North Wales Conscientious Objectors' Tribunal. He was a Parliamentary candidate (Liberal) in Macclesfield (1922), Swansea East (1923) and Keighley (1924).

In 1927 he married Mildred Mary, (eldest dau. of T.W. David, Ely Rise, Llandaff), who edited a volume of his articles published posthumously in 1944, under the title *Without my Wig*.

He contributed many articles to periodicals other than the newspapers by which he was employed, and they all reflect the experience of his humble beginnings and the deep impression which the radical-nationalist revival of the *Cymru Fydd* movement had upon him, as do also his pronouncements from the Bench. Some of these are listed below: in *Wales*, 1 (1894) he contributed two short stories which illustrate his childhood. In *Young Wales* (1902), 38, 210 and 265 he describes some of the Welsh M.P.s and the struggle against the Education Bill of 1902 in Wales: the principles which underlie those articles were seen again forty years later in his (English) Open Letter to Winston Churchill, published anonymously in *Y Cymro* 26 June 1943, calling for a Secretary of State for Wales. From the Bench, he announced that he would not imprison debtors who were unable to pay their debts, and he was a fierce opponent of the sharp, though legal, practices of some firms which operated hire-purchase agreements. But his chief work for Wales was his sustained effort to secure the right to use the Welsh language in the Courts. He heard cases in Welsh despite the prohibition against it in 27 Hen VIII 8 c. 26, and he did much in pronouncements from the Bench, and in articles and lectures, to support the Welsh Language Petition which secured the Welsh Courts Act of 1942.

He also argued in favour of restoring to Wales a National Judicature, and he discussed this matter in an article in *Welsh Outlook* Jan. and Feb. 1932. The same magazine, in April and Aug. 1932, contained articles by him under the *nom-de-plume* 'Demos' criticising the lay magistracy. Under the title 'Gwaliaphobia' and with the pen-name 'Rhydwen Aled', he counterattacked writers in the English press who decried Wales (*Welsh Outlook*, Oct. and Nov. 1932). The volume *Without My Wig* contains a number of his articles on legal matters and the fruits of his researches in Welsh history.

Among the posts which he held were the Readership of the Middle Temple and the Vice-Presidency of the University College of North Wales, Bangor. He d. 15 Oct. 1943 and was buried in Bangor Public Cemetery.

Information from Lady Artemus-Jones and personal knowledge.

                                                    F.P.J.

JONES, THOMAS GWYNN (1871-1949), poet, writer, translator and scholar; b. in Gwyndy Uchaf, Betws yn Rhos, Denbs., 10 Oct. 1871, eldest child of Isaac and Jane Jones. His father was a farmer and also a lay-preacher with the Calv. Methodists and a poet. The son began to add Gwynn (from Gwyndy) to his simple baptismal name Thomas about 1890 when, among other pen-names, he used Gwyn(n)vre ap Iwan (or ap Isaac). Apart from elementary education in Llanelian, Old Colwyn and Denbigh, and some instruction in Latin, Greek and mathematics from a neighbouring retired clergyman (to seek admittance to Oxford University, which did not prove possible because of ill-health), T. Gwynn Jones was self-taught. In 1891 he joined the staff of *Y Faner* under Thomas Gee (*DWB*, 274) and he remained in journalism until 1909. He left Denbigh in 1893 to join the staff of *Y Cymro* in Liverpool under Isaac Foulkes (*DWB*, 267-8) but returned to Denbigh in 1895 as sub-editor of *Y Faner* and to assist with Gee's recently established *North Wales Times*. He went to Caernarfon in 1898 to *Yr Herald Cymraeg*, *Papur Pawb* and the *Carnarvon & Denbigh Herald*. He fell ill in 1905 and spent some time in Egypt where he did some free-lance work in English. On his return in 1906 he lived in Denbigh, writing for newspapers, especially for *Papur Pawb*. In 1907 he went to Mold as editor of *Y Cymro*, then to Caernarfon in 1908 to the offices of *Yr Herald* and *Papur Pawb* before joining the staff of *Y Genedl Gymreig*.

In 1909 he was appointed a cataloguer at the National Library and spent the rest of his life in Aberystwyth and its neighbourhood. He was appointed a lecturer in Welsh at the University College of Wales, Aberystwyth, in 1913, and promoted to the Gregynog Chair in Welsh literature in 1919 – its only occupant ever – which he held until his retirement in 1937. He m. in June 1899 Margaret Jane Davies: they had a dau. and 2 sons. He d. at his home in Aberystwyth 7 Mar. 1949 aged 77 and was buried in Aberystwyth cemetery.

T. Gwynn Jones was influenced by Emrys ap Iwan (R. Ambrose Jones, *DWB*, 509-10) early in his career and inspired to look beyond the 19th c. for the foundations of Welsh literature. Ap Iwan strengthened his interest in languages and awoke in him the desire to look further than England for literature to read and study. Before the end of the 19th c. he was also influenced by Daniel Rees (1855-1931; *DWB*, 823-4). Jones's memorial essay in *Cymeriadau* (1933) reveals the close relationship and mutual influence of two remarkable men. Jones's interests in the Celtic languages was awoken in his early years, perhaps by his sympathy with the Irish struggle for Home Rule in the 1880s, and his interest in Ireland was deepened in 3 visits in 1892, 1908 and 1913, the last two affording him an opportunity to meet a number of scholars and writers who became close friends. These interests and contacts are reflected in *Iwerddon* (1919), *Peth nas lleddir* (1921), *Awen y Gwyddyl* (1922) and in many essays.

He obtained an M.A. (Wales) in 1914 for his dissertation 'Bardism and Romance'. His other main academic publications were: *Gwaith Tudur Aled* (1926), the fruits of many years' work; a detailed introduction to *Dwyfol Gân Dante*, Daniel Rees's translation of *Divina Commedia* (1903); *Cofiant Emrys ap Iwan* (1912); *Cofiant Thomas Gee* (1913); *Llenyddiaeth y Cymry* (1915) – vol. 1 only, to the Tudor period; *Traethodau* (1910); *Llenyddiaeth Gymraeg y Bedwaredd Ganrif ar Bymtheg* (1920); *Cultural Bases* (1921); *Welsh Folklore and Folk-custom* (1930, 2 ed. 1979).

He began writing poetry about the mid-1880s, mainly in the strict metres and many of his first efforts, including prize-winning local *eisteddfod* entries, were published in *Y Faner* and the *Abergele Visitor*, but his first separate publication was *Dyddiau'r Parch. Richard Owen* (1891), a booklet about half of which was the work of 'Gwynvre ap Iwan' and the rest by 'Gwilym Meredydd' (Revd. W.M. Jones). His satire 'Gwlad y Gân' appeared in *Cymru* (two cantos in 1896 and 1897) and in *Papur Pawb* (three cantos in 1898). This was his first substantial poem, and was later published in *Gwlad y Gân a Chaniadau Eraill* (1902). W.J. Gruffydd (see above) in 1949 referred to the poem as *juvenilia* but recalled its effect on him as a thunderbolt. In 1902 also his poem 'Ymadawiad Arthur' won the chair at the Bangor national *eisteddfod*, under the adjudication of John Morris-Jones (*DWB*, 668-9), a poem which secured for him a unique place in the emerging world of new Welsh poetry. He again won the chair at the national *eisteddfod* in 1909 for his poem 'Gwlad y Bryniau'. The 1902 poem was published in 1910, *Ymadawiad Arthur a Chaniadau Eraill*, but 'Gwlad y Bryniau' was not published again until the two *eisteddfod* poems and others appeared in the Gregynog Press selection *Detholiad o Ganiadau* (1926). This contained a number of Jones's well-known poems both old and new, e.g., 'Tir na n'Og' (1 ed. 1916); 'Madog' (1918, in *Y Beirniad*); Broseliàwnd' (1922); 'Anatiomaros' (1925); 'Gwlad Hud' (1919-25). His main works, prose and verse, were collected and published in 6 vols. by Hughes & Son, Wrexham, between 1932 and 1937. *Caniadau* (1934) contains more or less the same works as the Gregynog *Detholiad* but with the addition of 'Argoed' (1927), while *Manion* (1932) contains the poet's personal selection of the rest of his poetry. He continued to write, however, and under the name 'Rhufawn' he published in *Yr Efrydydd* in 1935-36 a number of poems, including 'Cynddilig', considered among the finest of his works. These poems were published in *Y Dwymyn* (1944).

His many translations combine his genius as a poet and his scholarly gifts. He translated works from many European languages, the best known being *Macbeth* (Shakespeare, *Papur Pawb*, 1902, separate publication 1942), *Dychweledigion* (*Die Gjengängere*, Ibsen, 1920), *Faust* (Goethe, 1922). His main translation from Welsh to English was *Visions of the sleeping bard* (*Gweledigaethau y Bardd Cwsc*, Ellis Wynne, Gregynog Press, 1940). In addition he published novels, plays, a travel book (*Y Môr Canoldir a'r Aifft*, 1913), reminiscences (*Brithgofion*, 1944), two books of children's verses (*Llyfr Gwion Bach*, 1924, *Llyfr Nia Fach*, 1932) and a variety of other works. Over a long period he wrote and translated words to be set to music. He was a regular adjudicator at the national *eisteddfod* from 1908 and was unfailing in his support as an adjudicator and lecturer at other *eisteddfodau* and societies. As a teacher he influenced generations of students. Upon his retirement in 1937 he was awarded *hon.* D. Litt. degrees by the two universities closest to his heart – Wales and Ireland – and made a C.B.E.

A special memorial number of *Y Llenor* (28, 2) was published in 1949. There is a good bibliography to 1937 in Owen Williams, *A bibliography of Thomas Gwynn Jones* (1938), with a supplement by David Thomas (1956). [Both are now superseded by D. Hywel E. Roberts, *Llyfryddiaeth Thomas Gwynn Jones* (1981)].

Personal knowledge and the sources noted; [see also David Jenkins, *Cofiant ... Thomas Gwynn Jones* (1973); W. Beynon Davies, *Thomas Gwynn Jones* (1970) and *Llyfryddiaeth* (1981), 219-78].

A. ap G., F.W.J.

JONES, THOMAS HENRY (HARRI; 1921-65), lecturer and poet; b. 21 Dec. 1921 at Cwm Crogau, Llanafan Fawr, Breck., eldest of the five children of Llywelyn Jones, a foreman roadman and Ruth (née Teideman) his wife. He attended Llanafan school five miles away, and Builth county school. In 1939 he went to U.C.W., Aberystwyth but joined the Royal Navy in 1941 and resumed his studies in 1946 to graduate with first-class honours in English in 1947 and gain his M.A. in 1949. He m. in 1946 Madeline Scott, a well-known potter, and they had three daughters.

He did not secure a post till 1951 when he began teaching at the Dockyard Technical School, Portsmouth, and lectured for the W.E.A. in the evenings. With no prospect of a suitable university post in Britain he emigrated to Australia in 1959 to become a lecturer at Newcastle College (University soon afterwards) where he gained a high reputation as a scholar and poet. Despite his successful academic career, he suffered from depression and drank heavily. Since his schooldays he wrote and read poetry aloud and had his work published in *Dock Leaves*, *Life and Letters*, *Dublin Magazine*, etc., and in *Quadrant*, *Meanjin*, etc. in Australia. He published three volumes of his poems, *The enemy in the heart* (1957), *Songs of a mad prince* (1960) and *The beast at the door* (1963); a critical study of *Dylan Thomas* (1963); and was editor of an Australian journal of studies in American literature. He demonstrated a mastery of language and developed his particular talent in poems which were appreciated in Australia and beyond. Both his war-time experience of losing friends at sea and the hard life of early childhood left an indelible mark upon him and he felt compelled to express his troubled feelings in verse. He regretted his ignorance of Welsh - his father's tongue, and yearned to return to his native land. Intense feelings of guilt and loneliness overcame him even in his most intimate relationship with his wife, and he was in a constant desperate search for his identity. He organized a week-long school in modern poetry and drama in Jan. 1965 but before the end of the course he was found drowned in a sea-side pool on 30 Jan. His ashes were brought to Wales and interred in Llanfihangel Brynpabuan churchyard. A collection of poems written in exile, *The colour of cockcrowing* (1966) and *The Collected Poems of T. Harri Jones* (1977) were published posthumously.

Julian Croft, *T.H. Jones* (1976); NLW MS. ex 499(i), 'Harri Jones'; *Planet* 49/50, 1980, 128-32; [P. B. Jones and Don Dale-Jones, *T. M. Jones* (2001)].

M.A.J.

JONES, THOMAS HUGHES (1895-1966), poet, writer and teacher; b. 23 Jan. 1895 in Tan-yr-allt, his mother's home in the Blaenafon area of Blaenpennal parish, Cards. He was one of the two children and the only son of Rhys Jones, farmer, and his wife, Ann Hughes. He was raised at Cefnhendre Farm, in the same parish, but, on the death of his mother when he was only six years old, his father moved to Blaenaeron Farm. Next to Blaenaeron was Dolebolion, farmed by John Rowlands, a cultured man – a local poet and a master of *cynghanedd*. Rowlands was the reputed father of Thomas Huws Davies (*DWB*, 156). The young Thomas Hughes Jones learned much in Rowlands's entertaining company. On Sundays, Jones went to his maternal grandparents and attended the services and Sunday school at Blaenafon Calvinistic Methodist chapel where he blossomed as a child with a ready answer during the public examination held at the close of the Sunday school and which required a sound knowledge of the Bible. He also excelled above his contemporaries at Tan-y-garreg elementary school, Blaenpennal, where his schoolteacher until 1903 was John Finnemore, followed by David Davies who persuaded Jones's father that the boy should go to Tregaron county school. He entered the county school in Sept. 1909, together with William Ambrose Bebb (see above), Evan Jenkins (see above), D. Lloyd Jenkins (see above) and Griffith John Williams (see below). All of these boys came under the influence of outstanding teachers, especially Samuel Morris Powell, to whom generations of pupils owed a great debt. At this time, Thomas Hughes Jones made a name for himself by winning chairs at local *eisteddfodau* for his poetry. He was given the nickname 'Tom (or, Twm), the poet' in Tregaron and the surrounding district. He did not neglect his school work; a wide reader and possessing of a remarkable memory, he obtained the Higher Certificate (Central Welsh Board) in English, Latin, Welsh and history. He entered the University College, Aberystwyth in 1913 and took a leading role in student activities. He was awarded the Cynddelw Scholarship in 1915 and graduated in 1916 with second-class honours in Welsh. He was an effective speaker in English and Welsh; he contributed verses to *Y Wawr*, the college's Welsh periodical which he edited in 1915-16. In the same year, he served as vice-president of the Celtic Society; at the time, a member of the university staff was always the president. The following year, he was elected president of the

Literary and Debating Society, but he was called up for military service in Nov. 1915. He served in France with the Welsh Guards. At the end of the war, he returned to Aberystwyth where he resumed his social activities and took up again the research work begun in 1916. He was the secretary of the Literary and Debating Society in 1919-20; president of the Students' Council, 1920-21; and editor of *The Dragon*, the college's periodical, 1921-22. This busy social life earned Jones considerable popularity among the students, but he did not neglect his studies and he was awarded an M.A. degree in 1922 for his thesis entitled 'Social life in Wales in the eighteenth century as illustrated in its popular literature of the period'.

He was appointed in 1922 to a post with the National Savings Movement in Cardiganshire – a rather prosaic occupation for one with such a lively personality. Within eighteen months, he left to become the secretary of the Liberal Party in Montgomeryshire where David Davies of Llandinam (see above) was the M.P. When Davies resigned in 1929, Thomas Hughes Jones became an administrator with the Council for the Protection of Rural Wales which was based at Aberystwyth. His duties involved travelling the length and breadth of Wales to promote, mainly through lectures, the preservation of the natural beauty of Wales. The new post gave him an opportunity to spend Sundays at home. When he worked in Montgomeryshire, he lectured to the small societies in the county and held a successful Sunday school class, as well as a reading class, at Bethel Calvinistic Methodist chapel in Newtown. He was made an elder there in 1936. He m. in 1934 Enid Bumford from Llanfair Caereinion, a college friend. He left his post with the Commission for the Protection of Rural Wales in 1932 for a part-time post, teaching Welsh, at Newtown grammar school. He also held external classes in Newtown. At the outbreak of World War II, a panel of teachers, with Jones as chairman and David Rowlands as Secretary, was established to consider improvements in the teaching of local history in schools. In 1941, the panel devised a syllabus for local history which was adopted by the Education Committee and distributed to every school in Montgomeryshire. The chairman's task was to arrange a programme to celebrate St. David's Day; this was held in every school and one of the county's worthies was the subject of each annual celebration. Jones was called upon to address meetings of teachers and the interest shown by school inspectors ensured that other counties became aware of the Montgomeryshire programme for local history. In 1946 an emergency training college for teachers was set up at Wrexham, which in time became known as the Cartrefle Education College; Jones was responsible for the course on Welsh-medium education. He was appointed deputy-principal of the College in 1956. Jones was in his element at Cartrefle College and the students later remembered him with great affection. He retired in 1962 and d. 11 May 1966.

He turned to prose writing during his military service and he is now known more for his short stories (especially the long short-story) than for poetry. For many years, he contributed stories and essays to Welsh periodicals, and in English to *Welsh Outlook*; he achieved a reputation in this field when he won the prose medal at the 1940 Mountain Ash national *eisteddfod* for his long short-story, 'Sgweier Hafila'. He was a frequent adjudicator for literature and drama at the national *eisteddfod;* together with B.T. Hopkins, another Blaenpennal man, he was on the panel of adjudicators for the crown at Cardiff in 1960. He reviewed books for *Y Faner, Lleufer,* and *Yr Athro.*

He published *Sgweier Hafila a storïau eraill* (1941); *Amser i ryfel* (1944); *Mewn diwrnod a storïau eraill* (1948); Gildas Tibbott edited *Atgofion a storïau eraill ynghyd â detholiad o ysgrifau, sgyrsiau a cherddi* (1971).

Information from his widow; *Atgofion a storïau eraill;* personal knowledge; [D. Ben Rees (ed.), *Cymry Adnabyddus*].

E.D.J.

JONES, THOMAS IEUAN JEFFREYS - see JEF-FREYS-JONES, THOMAS IEUAN above.

JONES, THOMAS ISAAC MARDY - see MARDY-JONES, THOMAS ISAAC below.

JONES, THOMAS IVOR (1896-1969), solicitor; b. July 13, 1896 at Caergai, Llanuwchllyn, Mer., the seventh child of John Morris and Jane Jones (the latter born at Cefngwyn, Llanuwchllyn). Educated at the village school, Llanuwchllyn, Bala County School and Towyn County School, which was then attracting pupils from a large area, he also owed much to the Rev. Owen Ellis, the Presbyterian minister at Llanuwchllyn, and Mrs Ellis. Articled to Thomas Davies Jones, his mother's brother, he was admitted solicitor in 1921, and joined his uncle's firm, T.D. Jones and Co. of Fleet Street, London, carrying on the practice after his uncle's death for the rest of his life. A faithful and hard-working member at Charing Cross Road Welsh Presbyterian church (in particular as a Sunday school teacher for many years), he was elected elder in 1930, he was soon Joint Secretary and for many years Treasurer. He was also Chairman, and for many years Treasurer, of the London Presbytery. Always interested in the welfare of young people coming to London, he was one of the founders of the Young Wales Association subsequently the London-Welsh Association, where he held many offices. He was Chairman of the Council in 1924 (the Association's fourth year), 1939 and 1946 and for many years one of the two Honorary Legal Advisers of the Association. He was one of the Trustees appointed by Sir Howell J. Williams in 1937, to hold the properties which Sir Howell had provided in Grays Inn Road for the purposes of a London-Welsh Centre, and retained that responsibility until his death. He was also active in many other London-Welsh interests, in particular *Undeb y Cymdeithasau* and the Welsh School, but above all perhaps in the Merionethshire Society. He assisted Sir Ifan ab Owen Edwards (see above) and Lady Edwards with legal work in the formation of *Urdd Gobaith Cymru,* and remained its legal adviser. He also assisted Sir David James (see above) with legal work and was a member of the Pantyfedwen Trust. He married Jane Gwyneth, the eldest daughter of Mr and Mrs Thomas Hughes, of Solway, Buarth, Aberystwyth. Never one to seek the limelight, he was a quiet man but with mischievous humour and a steadfast nature. He d. 29 March 1969, aged 72, and was buried at Llanuwchllyn.

Personal knowledge and information from his widow.

V.J.L.

JONES, THOMAS JESSE (1873-1950), a Welsh-American who took a special interest in the education of Afro-Americans and the peoples of Africa; b. 4 August 1873 in Llanfachreth, Anglesey, he emigrated at the age of 11 to the U.S.A. with his widowed mother, a brother, and two sisters, the family settling in Ohio with relatives. He went to the Universities of Washington and Lee (Virginia) and Columbia (New York), graduating M.A. and Ph.D.; he was also B.D. of the Union Theological Seminary. For seven years he was at the Hampton Institute, Virginia, one of the pioneer colleges for black students and it was there that he began to take the special interest in the education of Afro-Americans and Africans which characterised his life's work. After transferring to the United States Census Bureau he specialised in Negro statistics. In 1913 he began an investigation for the U.S. Bureau of Education and the Phelp-Stokes Fund; this resulted in two important volumes being published by the Bureau under the title *Negro Education in the United States.* One result of his experience with Y.M.C.A. work for black soldiers during World War I was the leading part he took in the formation of the Commission of Inter-Racial Cooperation after that war. He led two educational commissions to Africa which were undertaken by the Phelps-Stokes Fund at the request of British and American Missionary Societies and with the cooperation of the Colonial Office. The report on education in West, South and Equatorial Africa, published in 1922, led to the Colonial Office requesting him to make a similar study in East Africa; the report published in 1925 covered Kenya, Uganda, Tanganyika, the two Rhodesias, and Ethiopia (as they were then known). As a result of these reports the Colonial Education Department was set up. A dinner in honour of Jesse Jones was given by the British Government in 1925 at Lancaster House, London. Besides his work over 33 years for the Phelps-Stokes Fund, Jones undertook educational inquiries in Liberia (one result of this was the establishment of the Booker Washington Institute at Kakata); he also went to Greece and the Far East on behalf of the Near-East Foundation. In 1932 he was Carnegie Foundation lecturer in the universities of South Africa whilst in 1937 he headed a commission which studied the Navajo Indians in the United States. His educational theories are described by him in two books, *Four Essentials of Education,* 1926, and *Essentials of Civilization.* He d. early in 1950 at his home in New York.

Times, 17 Jan. 1950.

W.Ll.D.

JONES, THOMAS LLECHID (1867-1946), cleric, author and bibliographer; b. 4 Dec. 1867, at Tyddyn Uchaf, Llanllechid, Caerns., son of Hugh Jones and Catherine his wife. He was educated at the University College, Bangor and

St. David's College, Lampeter, where he took his B.A. degree in 1896. In the following year he was ordained deacon with licence to the curacy of St. David's, Blaenau Ffestiniog. He proceeded to priest's orders in 1899, and became curate of Llanllyfni in 1902. He became vicar of Ysbyty Ifan in 1906, vicar of Llysfaen in 1915, and rector of Llangynhafal (with Llangwyfan) in 1934. He m., 9 Jan. 1917, Elizabeth Dolben Jones. Upon his retirement in 1944 he went to live at Colwyn Bay where he d. 12 Aug. 1946.

He contributed much to the Church in Wales periodicals *Yr Haul, Y Llan*, etc. He was one of the most zealous members of the Welsh Bibliographical Society, becoming one of its vice-presidents. He contributed articles and notes on literary and bibliographical topics to the Society's Journal (see examples in vols iii-vi, and note particularly his series of five articles entitled 'Studies in Welsh Book Land'). He was a careful bibliographer and collected a good private library; some of his books and manuscripts went to the Library of the University College, Bangor, and others to the National Library of Wales. His most important work for the National *Eisteddfod* was his essay (1933) on the history of Catholicism in Wales in the seventeenth century.

Crockford, *Clerical Directory*, 1941; *North Wales Weekly News*, 15 Aug. 1946; *Jnl. W.B.S.*, VI, 215-16; *WwW* (1937).

W.Ll.D.

JONES, THOMAS MICHAEL - see MICHAELIONES, THOMAS below.

JONES, THOMAS OWEN ('Gwynfor', 1875-1941), librarian, dramatist, actor and producer; b. 19 Jan. 1875 in Pwllheli, Caerns., s. of William and Ellen Jones, New Street. He was educated at the town council school and then apprenticed in a local grocery shop. Between 1916 and 1917 he kept his own business at Caernarfon before being appointed county librarian on a salary of £130 per annum. This was the first county library established in Wales and was located in two rooms at Plas Llanwnda, Castle Street, Caernarfon. It appears that the appointment was a temporary one at first but Gwynfor visited the headquarters of the Carnegie Trust in Dunfermline for a while to equip himself for the new post, in a period when scant attention was paid to librarianship as a profession. Gwynfor excelled in the field of drama and he became famous throughout Wales as an actor and producer with his drama company, *Y Ddraig Goch*. He published a number of his own plays, *Y briodas ddirgel* (1915), *Trem yn ôl* (1920, 2 ed.), *Perthnasau* (1922), *Y llo aur a lloi eraill* (1925), *Eiddo pwy?* (1935), *Troi'r byrddau* (1935), *Tywydd mawr* (1939), and a book of short stories, *Straeon* (1931). He was good company with a stock of stories and traditions about *Y Maes* (Castle Square) in Caernarfon. He was a keen follower of *eisteddfodau* and he was a drama adjudicator at the national *eisteddfod* many times. His office at the library became a popular meeting place for leading literary figures in the area, like E. Morgan Humphreys (see above), Meuryn (R.J. Rowlands, see below) and Cynan (Sir Cynan (Albert) Evans-Jones, see above). He was one of the first to broadcast in Welsh from Manchester in the 1930s. He d. 22

Aug. 1941 and was buried in Llanbeblig cemetery, Caernarfon: his epitaph reads *'Actor da, Cymro da, Cristion da'* (A good actor, Welshman and Christian).

'Caernarfonshire and its libraries; development of the first County Library in Wales', *Trans. Caerns. Hist. Soc.*, 1972; O. Llew Owain, *Hanes y ddrama yng Nghymru 1850-93* (1948); local newspapers; [E. Wyn James in *Ysgrifau Beirniadol*, 23 (1997), 208-40].

T.E.G.

JONES, WATCYN SAMUEL (1877-1964), agricultural administrator and principal of a theological college; b. 16 Feb. 1877, son of Rees Cribin Jones (see Supplement below), Unitarian minister, and Mari Jones (the daughter of Watcyn and Mari Jones, Ty'n-lofft, Betws Bledrws), in a house in Bridge Street, Lampeter known as Glasfryn Stores. He was one of four children, but the other three died in infancy. His father, like many other Unitarian ministers of the time, ran a school, and perhaps the son received some of his early education at home in Ogmore House, a house that the family built in the same year as the son's birth. He was educated thereafter at Lampeter school (1890-92), Rev. David Evans's school at Cribyn (1892-94), and for a short time at Llanybydder grammar school, before he was accepted into the Presbyterian College, Carmarthen at the end of 1894. He displayed early scientific tendencies and it is said that he was the last student to sit examinations there in science, since the education syllabus of the old academy was confined to theology shortly after 1895. Before the end of that year, he decided to withdraw from the ministerial course (because he was not a fluent speaker, he said) to study for an arts degree at Aberystwyth (1895-1900). His course was interrupted because of his mother's illness; he moved to University College, Bangor in 1900 and gained a B.A. there in 1902, one of John Morris-Jones's (*DWB*, 668-9) first honours class. He gained a B.Sc. at the same college, pursuing additionally the new courses in agriculture and forestry and returned to Aberystwyth for another course in agriculture (N.D.D.). He was invited, with a scholarship, to be an assistant tutor at the School of Rural Economy at St. John's College, Oxford. He was recognised as an authority on the anatomy of trees, and he published a standard textbook, *Timbers, their structure and identification* (1924). He contributed on a similar subject to *Chambers' Encyclopaedia* 1927. He married Ada Sproxton in 1910.

In order to be close to his aged father, he returned to Wales in 1913, joining the civil service and becoming the chief inspector of the Welsh office of the Board of Agriculture with its head office at Aberystwyth. In this post he pioneered and developed agricultural education for a quarter of a century (1913-38) and under his supervision the four agricultural institutions in Wales were launched. In 1918 he received an M.A. degree from his college in Oxford and in the same year he was awarded an M.Sc. (Wales).

He retired from the Ministry of Agriculture in 1937, aged 60 years. In 1938 he accepted, with some hesitation, an invitation to succeed Rev. J. Park(e) Davies (*DWB*, 141) as the Principal of the Presbyterian College, Carmarthen. Although he had no theological qualification to teach there but having facility in Welsh and experience as a public speaker, he was, for a period of eight years, one of the most successful principals in the history of the college (1937-45). His students testified to his just discipline, his impartial thoroughness and gentlemanly and unassuming manner. He had great dreams for the future of the college at Carmarthen, but circumstances prevented him from realising them: he tried to combine the ample resources of the Unitarian colleges in England (Oxford and Manchester) with those at Carmarthen. He prepared plans and collected more than £3500 to extend the college, including a residential hall and a chapel. He hoped to see the development of the institution into a religious cultural centre for the ministers and laymen of Wales. He translated many of the Psalms, but they were not published. He was a Unitarian with 'a strong tendency towards humanism'; he was faithful at the Unitarian churches at Aberystwyth and Carmarthen.

As can be seen from his only Welsh book, *Helyntion hen bregethwr a'i gyfoedion* (1940), based on the story of his father, he was an able photographer and writer. He contributed regularly to Welsh periodicals, e.g. 'Rhyddid' namely his presidential address to the Unitarian Society, in *Yr Ymofynydd*, July 1924; 'Dosbarth Cymraeg (Syr) John Morris Jones', in *Y Geninen*, 1917; 'Pren, ei nodweddion, etc', in *Y Genhinen*, 1954. 'W.S.' and his wife retired to Landre, Aberystwyth. He died on 17 Oct. 1964 and his ashes were scattered on the family grave at Brondeifi graveyard, Lampeter. His wife died on 28 Jul. 1965.

Ymofynnydd, Nov. and Dec. 1964.

D.E.J.D.

JONES, WATKIN ('Watcyn o Feirion'; 1882-1967), postmaster, shopkeeper, folk poet, setter and tutor of *cerdd dant*; b. 12 June 1882 in Tŷ'r nant, Capel Celyn., Mer., son of Robert Jones and Elizabeth (b. Watkin). He kept a shop and Post Office in Capel Celyn and carried the post in the Capel Celyn and Arennig area for more than fifty yrs., walking about 15 miles every day. In his cultured home he brought up a family of singers. He had a rich voice, and much musical creativity, and, being well versed in harmony and counterpoint, he was an external examiner of the College of Tonic Sol-fa for many years. He was also proficient in *cynghanedd* and had the contents of *Cerdd Dafod* by Sir John Morris-Jones (*DWB*, 668-9) at the tips of his fingers. He won a number of bardic chairs at local *eisteddfodau*. He contributed significantly to making the art of singing to the accompaniment of the harp (*cerdd dant*) more widely known in the 1940s and 50s, travelling far and near to hold classes in setting words to folk tunes for *penillion* singing. During the same period he prepared settings for numerous less experienced *penillion* singers. For years he was the conductor of the Cwmtirmynach *cerdd dant* choir which won many prizes at *eisteddfodau*. He also composed many airs for *penillion* singing, such as 'Murmur Tryweryn' and 'Y ffrwd wen', which continue to be popular with present day verse-setters. He played a prominent part in founding *Cymdeithas Cerdd Dant Cymru*, being one of the three conveners of the

first public meeting at Bala on 10 Nov. 1934 which led to the founding of the society. He served as treasurer from the beginning until 1950. He m. Annie Thomas on 13 Apr. 1906 and they had seven children. He d. at Bod Athro, Dinas Mawddwy, 14 Feb. 1967.

Personal knowledge and research.

A.Ll.D.

JONES, WILLIAM ('Gwilym Myrddin'; 1863-1946), poet; b. Llwyndinawed farm, Cil-y-cwm, near Llandovery, Carms., 12 Apr. 1863, son of Evan Jones and his wife. His schooldays were restricted by the needs of the farm. In 1886 he m. Elizabeth Jones of Pumsaint and about the end of 1898 he left his native area and settled at Betws, Ammanford. For a time he was bailiff on a farm near Ammanford and later secured a post as lampman at the Pantyffynnon colliery. He resigned on health grounds in 1924. He was a keen *eisteddfod* competitor, and won the crown at the national *eisteddfod* held at Llanelli in 1930 for a poem on Ben Bowen (*DWB*, 46). In 1902 he published *Pryddest a Chân*, containing two poems entitled 'Porth y Nefoedd' and 'Angladd Crist', and two other pieces, and in 1938 'Y Ferch o'r Scer', and 'Peniel', containing two poems sent to the crown competition at the national *eisteddfod*, Cardiff, 1938. A number of his poems were collected and published under the title of *Cerddi Gwilym Myrddin* in 1948. He d. at Betws, Ammanford, 10 Jan. 1946.

West. Mail, 6 Aug. 1930; *WwW* (1937); *Y Faner*, 16 Jan. 1946; preface to *Cerddi Gwilym Myrddin*.

G.M.G.

JONES, Sir WILLIAM (1888-1961), administrator and politician; b. 27 June 1888, the son of Hugh and Mary Jones of Gellifor in the Clwyd valley, Denbs. He was educated in schools at Llanrwst and Denbigh, and began his career as a clerk in a solicitor's office. Jones became a solicitor himself in 1922, and was appointed to a post within the Denbighshire County Council. He served as Clerk of the Peace and as Clerk to the County Council from 1930 until 1949. He came to much prominence as Secretary to the Conference of Welsh Councils which discussed the Report of the Welsh Church Commissioners. In 1942 he became a member of the Advisory Council for Post-War Reconstruction in Wales and Monmouthshire, and from 1942 until 1945 he served as the Regional Controller for South Wales of the Ministry of Fuel and Power. He was also a part-time director of the Wales Gas Board, 1948-59, and a part-time director of the South Western Regional Coal Board from 1949. In the same year he served as a member of the Royal Commission on Capital Punishment. In 1952 Jones was appointed chairman of two influential sub-committees of the Council for Wales and Monmouthshire (committees responsible for government administration and for re-development in Wales), and he collaborated effectively with Huw T. Edwards (see above). He resigned from the Council in 1959 as a protest against the appointment of Henry Brooke, Minister for Welsh Affairs, as its chairman.

Jones was considered one of the most distinguished administrators in Welsh local government. He was a native Welsh speaker, a member of the Council of the Honourable Society of Cymmrodorion, and he served as a member of the Council and the Executive Committee of the National *Eisteddfod*. He received the C.B.E. in 1941, and was knighted in 1949.

He m. (1) in 1917 Charlotte Maud, dau. of Jos. Dykins. She d. in 1932. He m. (2) Ellen, dau. of Henry Bennett of Llanychan in 1942. He had two daughters. He d. 7 June 1961 at Hafod, Ruthin.

Www; WwW (1937); *Time*, 9 June 1961, 20b; *West. Mail*, 22 July 1942; *WWP*.

J.G.J.

JONES, WILLIAM (1896-1961), poet and minister; b. 24 Sept. 1896 at Trefriw, Caerns., son of Henry Jones, Congregationalist minister, and his wife Margaret (Madgie), dau. of William Jones, Presbyterian minister of Trawsfynydd. He was educated at Llanrwst county school (1908) and he entered Univ. Coll. of North Wales Bangor in 1914 and Bala-Bangor College 1914-16. He graduated in Welsh and Hebrew in 1917. He was ordained minister of Tabernacl church (Congl.), Betws-y-coed that year but returned to college to continue his studies during 1919-20 and 1923-24 but without taking a higher degree. He was minister of the English Congl. churches at Rednol and West Felton, Shrops. (1920) and Llanfair Caereinion. He resigned in 1937 and moved to his father's home in Tremadog where he had charge of Bethel (Presb.) church for a time though he was never formally its minister. He also assisted in the local branch of the County Library. He came to prominence as a poet during his college days. One of his best-known poems, the ballad 'Y llanc ifanc o Lŷn' appeared in *A Book of Bangor Verse* (1924). He was friendly with many well known literary figures such as R. Williams Parry (see below) and J.T. Jones, Porthmadog, and he won several prizes at national *eisteddfodau*. He published two collections of well produced lyric poems, *Adar Rhiannon* (1947) and *Sonedau a Thelynegion* (1950). He m. Jane (Jennie) Gertrude Williams of Coed-poeth in 1924. He d. at his home 14 Church St., Tremadog, 18 Jan. 1961 and he was buried in Bethel cemetery.

Blwyddlyfr MC, 1962, 260-1; *Gol.*, 8 Feb. 1961; *Cymro*, 20 Jan. 1961; *Barddoniaeth Bangor 1927-31*; his papers at University of Wales Bangor library, MSS. 16581-89; *Genh.*, 1961; Ifor Rees, *Ar glawr* (1983), 109-17; T. Arfon Williams in *Barddas*, 231/2 (1966), 24-34, 235 (1966), 8-17; Bedwyr L. Jones *Rhyddiaith R. Williams Parry* (1974), 123-6; *Taliesin*, 60 (1987), 49-54; information from Tomos Roberts and Derwyn Jones.

B.F.R.

JONES, WILLIAM ARTHUR (W. BRADWEN; 1892-1970), musician; b. at Caernarfon, 5 Apr. 1892, son of J.R. Gwyndaf Jones, proof-reader for *Y Genedl*, and Elizabeth Jones his wife. On his father's side he was related to Richard Jones, 'Gwyndaf Eryri' (*DWB*, 506), while his mother was the daughter of John Jones, 'Eos Bradwen' (*DWB*, 483). Because of his mother's family connections he was known as 'William Bradwen' when he was a child at school, and he chose to keep the name to the end of his life. He was brought up in a musical home; his mother gave

him piano lessons from an early age, and he later studied organ playing with John Williams, Caernarfon, and with Roland Rogers (*DWB*, 889-90), organist of Bangor cathedral. After short periods as organist and pianist to the Honourable F.G.Wynn at Glynllifon, Llandwrog, and from 1910 to 1915 as organist and choirmaster at Rug chapel, Corwen, he served with the Royal Welch Fusiliers in Palestine and Egypt, rising to the rank of lieutenant in 1918. In 1919 he was appointed (from among a hundred applicants) organist and choirmaster of St. Seiriol's church, Holyhead, a post which he held until Nov. 1951. From 1951 to the end of his life he was organist of Hyfrydle (Presb.) church, Holyhead. He won many diplomas in music, including A.R.C.M. (1920), L.T.C.L. (1921), L.R.A.M. (1922), A.R.C.O. (1925), F.R.C.O. (1927) and F.T.C.L. (1928), and as an accomplished pianist he became the official accompanist at the national *eisteddfod*. and in the county and provincial *eisteddfodau* for a very long time. But despite his undoubted skill as a pianist and organist, it was as a teacher and composer that he excelled and is remembered. For fifty years and more he gave private music lessons at Holyhead, and many of his pupils gained prominence as pianists and singers.

As a composer, he served his apprenticeship in the *eisteddfod* and he won about 25 of the chief prizes at the national *eisteddfod* for his compositions. His solo 'Paradwys y bardd' won a prize at the Liverpool national *eisteddfod* (1929), and his song 'Mab yr ystorm' at Aberavon (1932). At Wrexham national *eisteddfod* (1933) he accomplished the notable feat of winning seven of the main prizes in the music composition section. He played a prominent part in changing the nature of Welsh song in the second half of the 20th c., and through his experiments and those of a few of his contemporaries it was realised that the expressive rendering of the words could be enhanced by making the accompaniment an important and integral part of the song. Although he is chiefly remembered as a composer of songs, he also wrote part-songs, anthems, duets, works for the piano and string orchestra, several works for the piano, and pieces for the organ. (A complete list of his works appears in *Welsh Music*, vol. 5, no. 3, summer 1976). His MSS. were bought by the National Library of Wales in 1973.

He d. in hospital in Holyhead, 3 Dec. 1970, and was buried in St. Seiriol's churchyard, Holyhead.

Welsh Music, 5 (1976), no. 2, 34-40, no. 3, 43-9, and the sources noted there; G.I. Jones, *Meistr cerdd: bywyd a gwaith William Bradwen Jones* (1983); his baptismal name from the Rev. Dr. Llewelyn Jones, Holyhead.

H.W.

JONES, WILLIAM BRADWEN - see JONES, WILLIAM ARTHUR above.

JONES, (WILLIAM JOHN) PARRY (1891-1963), singer; b. 14 Feb. 1891 in Blaina, Mon., son of John Rees Jones, butcher, and Mary Jones (née Parry) his wife. At 11 yrs. of age he won a scholarship to Abertillery county school, but he left after 18 months owing to the family's financial circumstances, and went to work in the colliery.

After studying in evening classes and being appointed librarian at the Miners' Institute there, he joined the Blaina Choral Society and came to the notice of Norman McLeod, a teacher of voice production. He decided to follow a career as a professional tenor, and with the help of Lord Rhondda (David Alfred Thomas, *DWB*, 942-3) and others, he went to the Royal College of Music in London to study with Albert Visetti, Thomas Frederick Dunhill and Sir Charles Villiers Stanford. He later studied singing in Italy (with Colli), in Germany (with Charles Webber) and in England (with John Coates). He toured the U.S.A. and Canada, 1913-15, and was among those rescued when the liner *Lusitania* was sunk in May 1915. After the World War I, he became one of London's most versatile singers and his services were much in demand. He was appointed principal tenor with the D'Oyly Carte opera company (1915), with the Carl Rosa opera company (1920), and he sang many of the leading roles with the British National Opera Company (1922-28). He also appeared at the Old Vic and Sadler's Wells in the 1920s and 1930s, and by the time that he joined the management board at Covent Garden in 1955 he had had the honour of singing in the Royal Opera House during 19 international seasons there. He was also a leading member of Sir Thomas Beecham's opera company and he was invited to sing in the Henry Wood promenade concerts in 27 consecutive seasons. He also sang at the chief festivals in London and on the continent after 1919, including the festivals at Amsterdam, Copenhagen and Oslo (1945-54). He was honoured in being chosen to be the principal tenor at the Beethoven centenary festival, 1927, and the Schubert centenary festival, 1928. He was elected an honorary Fellow of the Royal College of Music, the Guildhall School of Music, and Trinity College of Music, and in 1962 he was awarded the O.B.E. for his notable services to music. For a time after retiring from singing he taught at the Guildhall School of Music and Trinity College of Music. He was endowed with an exceptionally good memory, and by the time of his death it is said that he had sung in performances of 70 operas and 80 oratorios. In 1917 he m. Hilda Dorothy Morris, Cirencester, and they had one son. He d. in London, 29 Dec. 1963.

Leslie Orrey (ed.), *The Encyclopaedia of Music* (1976); *Www*; *Welsh Music*, 1 (1960) and 2 (1964).

H.W.

JONES, WILLIAM PHILIP (1878-1955), minister (Presb.) and Principal of Trefeca College; b. 21 Nov. 1878 at Rock House, Tre-fin, Pembs., s. of Edward and Margaret Jones. His father d. when he was five yrs. old, and his mother returned to her native district of Nevern. He was educated at Nevern elementary school, and at Llandysul and Newcastle Emlyn grammar schools. He began preaching at the age of 15 at Gethsemane, Nevern, and entered the University College, Cardiff, to prepare himself for the ministry, graduating B.A. in classics. He proceeded to Trefeca College where he graduated in theology, and in 1902 he received the M.A. degree of the University of Wales for his thesis on 'The syntax of New Testament compared with Attic Greek'.

He was ord. in 1904, and the following year he m. Gwendolen Lewis, Fishguard; they had a son and two daughters. He served as minister of the church of Pen-towr, Fishguard (1903-06), Pen-ffordd and Gwastad (1906-10), Jerusalem, Pontrhyd-y-fen (1910-12), Bethlehem, Treorci (1912-15), returning to Pen-ffordd and Gwastad (1915-26). The first time he was at Pen-ffordd he established a church (Presb.) at Clunderwen. In 1926 he was appointed principal of Trefeca College, where he remained for the rest of his life. He was a good and successful tutor, and accomplished the great task of collecting thousands of pounds to establish a fund for the preservation of the old buildings at Trefeca. His handbook on the Gospel of S. Mark - in Welsh and English - was published in 1912, and a bilingual volume *Trevecca College 1842-1942* appeared in 1942. He contributed occasionally to *Y Goleuad*, *Y Lladmerydd* and *Cylchgrawn Cymdeithas Hanes y MC*. A prominent figure in his Association, he served as Moderator of the Association in the South in 1945. He d. Sunday, 3 July 1955, at the chapel house, Dyffryn, Taibach, where he was due to preach that day. His remains were buried at Fishguard.

Blwyddiadur MC, 1956, 257; W.M. Jones, *Pentour, Abergwaun* (1959), 43-4; *Gol.*, 27 July 1955; *Drys.*, 1945, 47-50; *WwW* (1921), 264; information from his daughter, Miss Gwyneth Jones, Fishguard; personal acquaintance.

G.M.R.

JONES, WILLIAM TUDOR (1865-1946), minister (U) and philosopher; b. 8 Sept. 1865 at Pontrhydfendigaid, Cards. Educated at the village school, he served there as teacher and at Goginan, Cardiganshire, for a few years. He decided to enter the Calvinistic Methodist ministry, and studied at Aberystwyth and Cardiff university colleges. Later he became minister of the Unitarian churches at Swansea (1899-1906), Wellington, N.Z. (1906-10), Islington (1910-15), and Bristol (1915-33). During his ministry at Swansea he studied for a period at Jena and came under the dominating influence of Rudolf Eucken. He afterwards became recognised as the foremost exponent and advocate of Eucken's philosophy of life, which seeks to disprove all materialistic interpretations of history, and stresses the reality of universal spiritual life as the only key to man's 'divine discontent' and ethical development. His own philosophy was an attempt at a further clarification and amplification of the idealistic trend of thought revealed in Eucken's *Activism*. He held the degrees of M.A. (Bristol) and Ph.D. (Jena). His publications include: translations of some of Eucken's main works and several expositions of Eucken's general philosophy; *Nature, Thought and Personal Experience* (1926); *The Reality of the Idea of God* (1929); *Contemporary Thought of Germany* (2 vols. 1930). He was also Editor of the Library of Philosophy and Religion and of the Library of Contemporary Thought.

His wife whom he had married in 1892, was Helen Clarke, of Northampton. He d. 12 June 1946 and was buried at Torquay, where he retired in 1933.

The Inquirer, July 1946; *Ww*, 1946; *N.L.W. Annual Report*, 1946-47.

D.D.

JONES-DAVIES, HENRY (1870-1955), farmer and pioneer of agricultural co-operation; b. 2 Jan. 1870, only son of Thomas and Elizabeth Davies, Bremenda, Llanarthne, Carms. He was educated at Queen Elizabeth Grammar School, Carmarthen, and in addition to farming he began at an early age to take a keen interest in public life. He was the first chairman of Llanarthne parish council, and at the age of 22 he was elected a member of Carmarthenshire County Council, becoming chairman of the council in 1902 and later chairman of the education committee. In 1908 he became County Land Agent for Carmarthenshire, and in the same year he became a Justice of the Peace for the county, and later chairman of Carmarthen County Petty Sessions.

But, without doubt, Jones-Davies's most significant contribution was as a pioneer of agricultural co-operation in Wales. In 1902, during his period as chairman of Carmarthenshire County Council, he acted as secretary of a deputation representing the three west Wales counties which went to Ireland to study agricultural co-operation organisations which had already been established there. Following that visit a Carmarthen Farmers' Co-operative Society was formed in 1903, of which he became the first secretary, and he soon became a prominent figure in the Agricultural Co-operative Society. He became a governor of that society in 1912, and continued to represent Wales at the society's headquarters until the Welsh Agricultural Organisation Society became an independent body in 1922. He was a life member of the W.A.O.S. and served as a Vice-president for a number of years and later as President from 1946-53. He was a member of the Development Commission for Wales from 1910-36, and it was largely for his services in that capacity that he was made a C.B.E. in 1936. He represented the Commission on the executive committee of the Irish A.O.S. from 1914-21.

In 1903 Jones-Davies married Winifred Anna, youngest daughter of Thomas and Elizabeth Ellis, Cynlas, Cefnddwysarn, Bala, and sister of Thomas Edward Ellis (*DWB*, 214), and they settled at Glyneiddan, Nantgaredig, Carms. There were two sons and one daughter of the marriage, the elder son being Dr. T.E. Jones-Davies (1906-60; see below). Henry Jones-Davies died 16 June 1955 and was buried at Nantgaredig.

Www, 1951-60; Elwyn R. Thomas, *Farmers Together* (1972), 46-8; personal knowledge.

M.E.

JONES-DAVIES, THOMAS ELLIS (1906-60), doctor and international rugby player; b. 4 March 1906, elder son of Henry and Winifred Anna Jones-Davies, Bremenda, Llanarthne, Carms. (see above). He was educated at Queen Elizabeth Grammar School, Carmarthen, St. George's School, Harpenden, Gonville and Caius College, Cambridge and St. George's Hospital, London. He was awarded the degrees of M.A. and M.D. (Cantab.), and F.R.C.P. and D.P.H. (London). After serving for some time as an assistant medical officer to London County Council he was appointed medical officer of health for Radnorshire in 1938. During World War II he served as an officer in the R.A.M.C., and later was appointed a consultant physician,

primarily as a heart specialist, at the West Wales Hospital, Carmarthen, a position he held for ten years until his death.

An all-round sportsman, he represented his hospital at rugby, tennis, cricket, and hockey, but it was as a centre three-quarter rugby player that he was best known. A Cambridge 'Blue', he played rugby for Llanelli, London Welsh, United Hospitals, Middlesex, and the Barbarians. He was selected to play for Wales on a number of occasions. He was also a member of the British touring team which toured New Zealand and Australia in 1930.

Like his father Dr. Jones-Davies played a prominent part in public life. He served as High Sheriff of Carmarthenshire in 1952-53, and was also a Deputy-Lieutenant and a Justice of the Peace for the county. For a number of years he was president of the Carmarthen Divisional Liberal Association and of the county branch of the British Legion.

In 1938 Dr Jones-Davies married Nesta, only daughter of Dr. and Mrs. Hector Jones, Maesteg, and there was one son of the marriage. T.E. Jones-Davies died 25 August 1960.

Carm. Jnl., 2 Sept. 1960; personal knowledge.

M.E.

JONES-PIERCE, THOMAS - see PIERCE, THOMAS JONES below.

JOYCE, GILBERT CUNNINGHAM (1866-1942), bishop; b. 7 April 1866, third son of Francis Hayward Joyce, vicar of Harrow-on-the-Hill. He was educated at Harrow School, and was a Scholar of Brasenose College, Oxford, obtaining a first class in Classical Moderations (1886) and in Lit.Hum. (1888). He took his B.A. in 1888, M.A. in 1892, B.D. in 1904, and D.D. in 1909. After studying in Germany he was ordained deacon in 1892 by Bishop Lewis of Llandaff, and was sub-warden of St. Michael's College, Aberdare, from 1892 to 1896, receiving priest's orders in 1893. From 1897 to 1916 he was Warden of St. Deiniol's Library, Hawarden, and from 1916 to 1922 Principal of St. David's College, Lampeter. He held a canonry in St. Asaph Cathedral from 1907 to 1914, and was chancellor from 1914 to 1927. After a year as archdeacon of St. David's, he was consecrated Bishop of Monmouth on 30 November 1928; he relinquished his see in 1940, and d. at Tenby 22 July 1942. He was buried at Tenby.

Joyce took a leading part in the life of the Church in Wales, and his counsel was also eagerly sought in educational movements. He was Pro-Chancellor of the University of Wales (which conferred on him the honorary degree of LL.D. in 1937) from 1934 to 1941, and President of the Welsh National School of Medicine from 1931 to 1937. He published *The Inspiration of Prophecy* (1910), and contributed to Hastings' *Encyclopaedia of Religion and Ethics*, etc.

The Times, 23 July 1942; Crockford's *Clerical Directory*; *Www*; personal knowledge.

T.I.E.

K-LL

KEMSLEY, 1st VISCOUNT - see BERRY (FAMILY), JAMES GOMER BERRY above.

LEACH, ARTHUR LEONARD (1869-1957), historian, geologist and archaeologist; b. at Tenby, 12 November 1869, elder son of John and Sarah Leach of Tenby. John Leach (1841-1916), having been a printer with the *Tenby Observer*, established his own printing and publishing business in the town and launched a successful rival local newspaper, to which his younger son Ernest H. Leach subsequently succeeded; both sons shared his antiquarian interests which may have been stimulated by his association with Edward Laws (*DWB*, 541-2). Arthur Leach's formal education was confined to the local National School and Trinity College, Carmarthen, where he qualified as a teacher in 1890, but in those academic subjects to which he contributed significantly he was of necessity largely self-taught. His teaching career (which he readily admitted he disliked) was entirely spent in south-east London, mainly at the Elementary School, Ancona Road, Plumstead. But school vacations often saw him back in Tenby, exploring and noting the antiquities of the area, and this pattern continued after his marriage on 23 December 1897 at St. Margaret's Church, Plumstead, to Sarah Currie (b. 1871) who had moved to Plumstead from the Liverpool area.

The first of his many publications appeared the following year, *Leach's Guide to Tenby*, published by his father to compete with the older *Mason's Guide* from the rival press; there were several later editions. From about this time also short articles by him on local history, antiquities and natural history began to appear in the *Tenby and County News*, his father's weekly newspaper, a practice which continued throughout his life, even after that paper had been absorbed by its rival; notes by him also appeared in the Woolwich local paper. His lifelong membership of the Cambrian Archaeological Association began in 1899, but influenced by Dr. Arthur Vaughan and E.E.L. Dixon his interest was directed rather more towards geology, and after attending lectures on this subject at the Woolwich Polytechnic (where he befriended another notable geologist, R.H. Chandler) he joined the Geologists' Association in 1905. The *Proceedings* of this Association for that year carried the first of many reports by him of its excursions to sites both in north-west Kent and in south Pembrokeshire (he was the organiser of its meetings in Tenby in 1909), and over the following thirty years or so more than forty papers and reports by him appeared in the *Proceedings* as well as others in which he was joint-author. He made an important contribution to the work of the Association, first as auditor and member of its Council, but most notably as General Secretary during the years 1913-18. His continued services were recognised by his presentation with the Foulerton Award in 1925 'for good amateur work', by his Vice-Presidency over many years, and ultimately by his election as President for 1932-34 (the topics of his two presidential addresses were the geology and scenery of his native area), and he was made an honorary member in 1943. He was elected Fellow of the more prestigious Geological Society of London in 1910 and received an award from the Society's Wollaston Donation Fund in 1926. His contribution to understanding the geology of south Pembrokeshire was acknowledged in Dixon's major study of that area, *Memoirs of the Geological Survey, Geology of the South Wales Coalfield*, Part XIII (1921).

Exploration of the Pembrokeshire cliffs as a geologist led to his archaeological discoveries (hearths, middens, etc. and flint implements) which were reported in a series of notes in *Archaeologia Cambrensis* and other journals such as *Nature* from 1909 to 1933. Of particular importance was his finding flint-working sites on submerged land and also his exploration of the habitation site at Nanna's Cave on Caldey Island which, though somewhat modified by more recent work, was meticulously recorded. In the early years of the 20th century he became involved in controversies that arose from evidence of early man in relation to recent (Pleistocene) geological features, his approach being characteristically factual rather than speculative. Holidays would often be spent visiting important archaeological sites in western and central France, on which he would subsequently give public lectures illustrated with his own lantern slides.

On retiring from teaching in 1929 he was able to undertake historical research on local history, using the resources of the British Museum and other repositories in London. The fruit of this was his most substantial work, *The History of the Civil War (1642-1649) in Pembrokeshire and on its Borders* (London, 1937), the publication of which, however, he had to subsidise himself. Though in large measure a documentary compilation, it showed a sure handling of the sources and has remained definitive (reviewed in *Arch. Camb.*, 93 (1938), 267-71 by Sir Frederick Rees). At the same time he was collecting material for a history of Tenby which unfortunately was never prepared for publication, although extracts often appeared as notes on various historical topics in the local newspapers.

In 1940 he settled in Tenby and was at once invited to become Honorary Curator of the museum there, an independent institution, subsequently acting also as its Secretary and Treasurer for fifteen years. To this work he devoted much of his time, while by lectures and regular press reports he kindled a greater public awareness and use of the museum. As early as 1918 he had produced a small publication *Some Prehistoric Remains in Tenby Museum* (second edn. 1931), and he now brought some expertise to the display of such material. As he was uniquely qualified to write an account of a neglected but significant Pembrokeshire antiquary, the Rev. Gilbert Smith (*Arch. Camb.*, 98 (1945), 249-54). The museum's collection of drawings prompted the publication of his *Charles Norris (1779-1858) of Tenby and*

Waterwynch, topographic artist (1949), incorporating a catalogue of Norris's works. The local museum's affiliation to the National Museum of Wales led to his membership of its Council, in which he also served on the Science Committee. In 1948 the University of Wales recognised his academic achievement by conferring on him the honorary degree of M.A.

His prolific writings, reflecting an inquiring and alert mind, were always precise and informative. Despite a rather severely academic and sceptical attitude, he could convey his enthusiasm for knowledge to others, especially to children although he had none of his own. He d. at Tenby on 7 October 1957, his wife having predeceased him in March of the previous year, and was buried in Tenby cemetery.

Tenby Observer, 11 Oct. 1957; *Proc. Geologists' Assoc.*, 69 (1958), 67-70; papers in Tenby Museum and personal knowledge.

W.G.T.

LEEKE, SAMUEL JAMES (1888-1966), Baptist minister; b. 28 Mar. 1888 at Tal-y-bont, Cards., son of Samuel Leeke (d. 14 Feb. 1943, aged 81) and Anne Leeke (née Williams, d. 31 Dec. 1937 aged 74). His parents married in Bristol on 20 Nov. 1884. His father was a carpenter by profession, a trade which he practised at sea, having sailed many times 'round the Horn'. The son's career started in the service of the Post Office, but as a consequence of the religious revival of 1904-05, he was persuaded in 1907 by his mother church, Tabernacl, Tal-y-bont, to begin preaching. After a preparatory course at the Old College School at Carmarthen, he was accepted in 1909 into the University College and Baptist College at Cardiff. In spite of his early disadvantages, he succeeded in obtaining the degrees of B.A. in 1912 and B.D. in 1915. He was ordained on 14 Feb. 1916 as the minister of Seion, Cwmaman, Aberdare, and he was subsequently installed as minister, on 16 Feb. 1925, at Siloam, Brynamman and on 5 Oct. 1931 at Bethesda, Swansea (on the occasion of the centenary of the re-location there of the church from Back Road). His preaching combined the passion of evangelism with breadth of learning. One of the notable features of his ministry was his unstinting care of his dispersed church during World War II, in spite of his own terrible suffering during the bombing raids on Swansea and the complete destruciton of his home at 12 Brooklands Terrace on Monday night, 17 Feb. 1941. He was married at Bethesda, Swansea, on 22 Sept. 1931 to Amy Gertrude Bryant, a member at Seion, Cwmaman, the daughter of William Bryant (who was killed in the colliery at Cwmaman in 1911) and Emily Bryant (who for half a century managed the Post Office at 3 Alexandra Terrace, Cwmaman). He died on 31 Dec. 1966 and was buried on 4 Jan. 1967 at Oystermouth public cemetery.

His name was legendary among his acquaintances as a collector of books of every kind, among them many first editions, and he will be remembered for his mastery of many languages, especially Hebrew. He contributed regularly to the denomination's literature, e.g. as early as 1917 to *Yr Hauwr* and especially in the 1930s to *Yr Arweinydd Newydd*, which dealt with the Sunday school syllabus. His most important work, *Llyfr y Proffwyd Eseia: detholion* has a similar context. This was published in 1929 by the Sunday School Union of the Baptist Union of Wales.

In 1929 he played a prominent part, with others, in the founding of *Urdd y Seren Fore* for the children of the denomination. He served that movement in more than one post including its presidency in the year 1939-40. He was also prominent as a member of the first committee and a lecturer at Ilston School, a preparatory school for theological students that was opened in Swansea on 8 Sep. 1934. He was the president of the Ystalyfera area District Meeting at the time of his move to Swansea. He was thereafter elevated to become president of the West Glamorgan County Association in 1949-50 (the subject of his presidential address was 'Looking back') and to the presidency of the Welsh section of the Baptist Union of Wales in 1961-62. (His address in Holyhead in 1961 was 'A call for new confidence and hope in the Gospel'.) He served for almost fifteen years as the Free Church chaplain at the general hospital in St Helen's Road, Swansea.

Seren Cymru, 24 Mar 1916; 6 Mar 1925; 16, 23 Oct 1931; 14, 21 Sep 1934; 28 Jul 1961; 13, 27 Jan, 3 Feb 1967; *Arweinydd Newydd*, 1932, 36 et passim; *Seren yr Ysgol Sul*, 1922, 310-316; 1934, 226-231; 1940, 2-7; *West Glamorgan Association Statement*, 1950, 7-16; *Seren Gomer*, Spring 1961, 7-11; *Llawlyfr y Bedyddwyr*, 1968, 116-117; *Baptist Handbook*, 1968, 366-7; *Seion Cwmaman: Canmlwyddiant yr Achos 1859-1959*, 13-15; Marian Henry Jones, *Hanes Siloam Brynaman* (1972), 61-5, 102 etc.; *Cambrian News*, 23 Nov 1934; 7 Jan 1938; 24 Feb 1943; WWP; personal information from his widow and her nephew, Peter Bryant, Walton-on-Thames.

B.G.O.

LEIGHTON, 1st BARON, of St. Mellons - see SEAGER, GEORGE LEIGHTON below.

LEILA MEGÁNE - see HUGHES, MARGARET above.

LEVI, THOMAS ARTHUR (1874-1954), professor of law; b. in Swansea, 18 Dec. 1874, s. of Thomas Levi (*DWB*, 543) and his second wife Margaret (née Jones). When he was two the family moved to Aberystwyth when his father became minister of Tabernacl (Presb.) chapel. Educated at Ardwyn grammar school he entered UCW Aberystwyth in 1891 graduating B.A. (Lond.). He entered Lincoln College Oxford in 1893 where he won the Carrington Prize for Law in 1897 and graduated with first-class Honours in Law. He took the B.C.L. postgraduate degree in 1900 and in the same year he was first in First Class in the Bar Final, with the Certificate of Honour. He was a member of the Inner Temple.

When the Law Faculty was opened at the University College of Wales, Aberystwyth, in 1901, he applied for the Chair of Law, despite the advice of the Vinerian Professor of English Law at Oxford, A.V. Dicey, that he should not throw away his brilliant gifts in such a remote and insignificant place (Levi had succeeded F.E. Smith (later Lord Birkenhead) as one of Dicey's star students). Nevertheless, Dicey supported him and he was appointed Professor of English

Law at Aberystwyth. W. Jethro Brown was appointed Professor of Constitutional and Comparative Law but left in 1906 for his native land, Australia, where he became a Chief Justice. Levi headed the Law Department thenceforward until his retirement in 1940.

Under his care the department became nationally known, both in universities and in legal circles. He set himself three objectives. First, to establish the small and financially fragile department in public acceptance in Wales and especially to win the goodwill of lawyers. He travelled widely in Wales, with joyous enthusiasm, lecturing to solicitors' articled clerks and winning financial and moral support from important societies. Secondly, he was eager to convince the University, its teachers and authorities of the value of law as a discipline which any self-respecting university must teach. He persuaded internationally known lawyers, academic and practising, to deliver public lectures at Aberystwyth, and attracted first-rate lecturers, many of whom headed Law Departments at larger universities later. Thirdly, in his own words, he was always concerned that university teaching of law was more than 'breeding pettifogging solicitors to work up vexatious litigation'. The Department had a 'duty to teach students the principles of public service, to train them to take part in communal life and inspire them with a high ideal of citizenship'. To some extent, he had to compromise. Roman Law was not part of the syllabus, despite its importance in the legal systems of many countries, nor was a great deal of the history of the Common Law taught, but Constitutional and International Law were taught, though perhaps too much time was spent in fields better taught in professional law schools, in order to make a good impression on practitioners.

Research and publications were not his world. He was rarely to be seen in the library (though he kept abreast of legal publications). He had in 1896 published an edition of Welsh poems (begun by his father), and various articles, one noteworthy one being on the Welsh Laws of Hywel Dda. But his college task, far above all else, was teaching. As a university teacher, he was unique and shining, in his delivery, voice and style. Law was never a dull topic in Levi's lecture room, students from other disciplines came to hear him and be entranced. The taking of notes was sternly discouraged, vivid examples cited to illuminate the most abstract legal doctrines and at the end he dictated a brief note of essential points - with never a note himself in any part of the lecture. He tended to deprecate the value of examinations but had a delightful talk on how to score marks in any legal paper. His power of holding an audience was also special. At Cambridge, Lord McNair, later President of the International Court of Justice, spoke of Levi's incredible talent to hold spellbound a most learned and sceptical audience of university teachers of law. A popular lecturer everywhere, a formidable debater in a debating society, his ability lay in his skill to produce almost uproarious laughter at the expense of his opponent's points and then drive home the deadly shaft. His deafness ruled out questions at lectures and debarred him from many wide contacts in the college life. He

arrived each morning with his driver, immaculate in his well-pressed navy blue suit, his hearing aid clipped to his head. He wore the barrister's gown, never academic robes. A bachelor, alleged to like and be liked by members of the other sex, there was, however, never a whiff of scandal.

A staunch Liberal all his life, modestly boasting that no General Election was fought adequately without his intensive participation - but in the lecture room, never a hint of party propaganda, though he was ready to parade his Liberalism in evening college talks where he was always a strong opponent of capital punishment and defects in the law. He was invited to stand as Liberal candidate for Cardiganshire and a number of constituencies in south Wales but he refused. He was an elder (from 1908) at Tabernacl Church.

His students knew him as 'Tommy' Levi but there was never a hint of disrespect in his presence, friendly though his demeanour always was. His great feat was to raise the University's Law Department to wide public esteem and broaden the outlook of the thousands of students who came to it from all parts of Wales and other countries, so that this Department stood as high in the regard of the academic world as any department in the University. He was not given any public honour to mark his contribution but his memory evokes a special kind of affectionate respect from his former students scattered throughout the world in many spheres of life.

He died at Aberystwyth on 24 Jan. 1954 and was buried in the public cemetery.

Among his publications are: *Casgliad o ganeuon Cymru* (1896); *The opportunity of a new Faculty of Law* (inaugural lecture) (1901); *Apêl at ddirwestwyr* (1916); *Legal education in Wales* (1916); 'The laws of Hywel Dda in the light of Roman and Early English law', *Aberystwyth Studies* (1928); 'The law department, University College of Wales', in Iwan Morgan, ed., *The College by the Sea* (1928); *The Story of Public Administration and Social Service. Suggestions for the formation of a school of public administration and social service, in connection with the University of Wales.*

Iwan Morgan (ed.), *The College by the Sea* (1928); Ellis, *UCW*; *Www* 1951-60; personal recollections.

E.O.R.

LEWES, EVELYN ANNA (*c*. 1873-1961), author; one of the three children of Major Price Lewes, adjutant of the Pembroke militia, and his wife Florence (née Kinnear, of Halifax, Nova Scotia); b. *c*. 1873 in Canada, but brought up at Poyston, Haverfordwest, Pemb., and educated privately. About 1902 the family moved to Tyglyn Aeron, Cards., one of the seats of the Lewes family who had taken a prominent part in Cardiganshire for the last four centuries as justices of the peace, high sheriffs and members of parliament. She moved to Eithinfa, Cliff Terrace, Aberystwyth *c*. 1928. She d. 4 March 1961 in hospital at Oswestry aged 87, and her ashes were buried in Trefilan, Cards.

She was a woman of great character and personality. She began writing poems, articles and stories for publication in 1896 when a poem appeared in *Wales*, and continued to do so until about 1940. Her work appeared in countless magazines including *The Gentleman's Magazine*, *c.* 1905, *The Field and the Queen, c.* 1905-14, *The Bookman, Fishing Gazette*, 1923-31, *T.P.'s and Cassell's Weekly*, 1927, *Every woman's world* (Toronto), *Western Home monthly* (Winnipeg), etc.; and in *The Western Mail, The Cambrian News* and other newspapers. Among her books are *Picturesque Aberayron* (1899), and *A guide to Aberaeron and Aeron valley* (1922). She taught herself Welsh and was a diligent reader (1924-33) of Lewis Glyn Cothi's works for a dictionary of the Welsh language, *Geiriadur Prifysgol Cymru*. Her translation of portions of the poems of Dafydd ap Gwilym appeared in *The life and poems of Dafydd ap Gwilym* (1915). Essays on 'Theatres of West Wales' and 'From Neuaddlwyd to Madagascar' (in Welsh) are among her MSS in the National Library of Wales. She became an authority on Welsh folklore. Her story 'Hywel of Claerwen' was published in the transactions of Bangor national *eisteddfod* 1902, and others appeared in *Dream folk and fancies* (1926). Her best known work, *Out with the Cambrians* (1934), is a record of outings with the Cambrian Antiquarian Society, of which she was a committee member for many years. She became a member of the *Gorsedd* in 1916 and was a member of the court of governors of U.C.W. and N.L.W. from 1940.

WWP; Evelyn Lewes MSS at N.L.W.; *Camb. News*, 24 March 1961; see Glyn Lewis Jones, *Bibliography of Cardiganshire 1600-1964* and *Supplement 1964-68* for a list of some of her articles.

M.A.J.

LEWIS, (FAMILY) of Llandysul, Cards., printers and publishers (Gwasg Gomer). (*DWB*, 1139-40, under LEWIS, John David).

DAVID LEWIS (1890-1943) was the eldest s. of John David Lewis and Hannah, his wife; b. 18 Apr. 1890, at Market Stores, Llandysul. He was educated at the local council and county schools, and was trained as a printer, at the Gomerian Press founded by his father, under the instruction of William John Jones, foreman printer at the press. After the death of his father in 1914, the heavy responsibilities of managing the press and the associated bookshop fell on his shoulders, as his brothers Edward and Rhys were serving in the armed forces. He was director of the Gomerian Press for the remainder of his life. He took an active part in the life of the community, following his father as treasurer of Pen-y-bont (B) church. He was also secretary of the Baptist singing festival in the Llandysul district, and was the first treasurer and president of the Llandysul Cymmrodorion Soc. He represented the southern part of the Llandysul parish on the Cards. county council. He was made Justice of the Peace, member of the Teifiside board of guardians, member of the governing bodies of the Llandysul county school, the National Library of Wales and the national council of *Undeb Cymru Fydd*. He was a member of the Welsh Baptist Historical Society, and like his father deeply interested in local history. He m. Mary Anne Hughes (see below) 9 Jan. 1939, and they lived at Dolanog, Llandysul. He d. 26 Aug. 1943.

EDWARD LEWIS (1891-1965), the second s. of

John David Lewis; b. 27 Aug. 1891 at Market Stores. Like his brother he was educated at the Llandysul council and county schools. Before World War I war he worked in his father's bookshop, and was later manager of the local labour exchange. Upon his brother's death he followed him as director of the Gomerian Press, county councillor, and treasurer of the Pen-y-bont Baptist church. He was treasurer of the Carmarthens. Baptist Association from 1955. He was made Justice of the Peace in 1946 and was made O.B.E. in 1956. In 1955 he was elected honorary member of the *Gorsedd* of Bards. He was president of the Llandysul Cymrodorion in 1938, when a tablet was unveiled at the Tregroes school in memory of Christmas Evans (*DWB*, 221-2). He was a member of the governing body of the Llandysul and Newcastle Emlyn secondary schools. He was a member of the WJEC and of the court of governors of the National Museum of Wales. He took a keen interest in local history and in local cultural and religious movements. He m. Lena Harries of New Quay, 27 Aug. 1927. He d. on Easter Sunday, 18 Apr. 1965.

The two brothers, through the Gomerian Press, made a great contribution to Welsh literature and their firm became a major Welsh publisher. They subsequently took over Gwasg Aberystwyth and the Caxton Press (Lampeter).

MARY ANNE LEWIS (formerly HUGHES; 1891-1960), wife of David Lewis. She was the only dau. of Timothy and Hannah Hughes of Plasnewydd, Llanllwni, Carms.; she had four brothers, John, William, David and Tim. (John became a lecturer in education at Aberystwyth and held chairs in the same subject at the universities of Witwatersrand and McGill, Montreal, where he d. in July 1977). Mary was b. 5 Feb. 1891 and was educated at the Llanllwni elementary and the Llandysul county schools. She proceeded to the U.C.W., Aberystwyth, and took a first-class honours degree in English in 1911. She was vice-president of the Students' Union. She held the posts of English mistress at Llandysul, 1912-18, and a lectureship in English at the Swansea training college, 1918-38. On 9 Jan. 1939, she married David Lewis (see above). At school and college she was an influential teacher. At Swansea she developed into a skilful producer of drama, and took a prominent part in Swansea's dramatic society. When she settled at Dolanog, Llandysul, she took great interest in the local dramatic society, and in the Cardigans. dramatic society. She adjudicated dramatic performances and compositions at national *eisteddfodau*. She translated *The Poacher* (J.O. Francis, see above) and *Jane Wogan* (Florence Howell) into Welsh. She d. 16 Mar. 1960 and was buried in Pen-y-bont Baptist church cemetery.

Personal knowledge; obituary notices in the local papers.

J.Ty.J.

LEWIS, ALUN (1915-44), poet; b. 1 July 1915 at Aberdare, Glam., s. of Thomas John Lewis, schoolmaster, and Gwladys Elizabeth (née Evans). He was educated at Glynhafod elementary school, 1920-26, Cowbridge Grammar School, 1926-32, University College of Wales,

Aberystwyth (B.A. with honours in History) 1932-35, Manchester University (M.A. with research in medieval history), 1935-37, and Aberystwyth again, 1937-38. He taught for a time at Lewis' School, Pengam, but without waiting to be called up joined the Army in May 1940. He had begun to contribute to literary journals in 1938, and in 1940-41 was a mover in the 'Caseg Broadsheets' venture. On 5 July 1941 he married Gweno Ellis of Aberystwyth. This same year appeared his first volume of poems, *Raiders' Dawn*, and in 1942 a volume of short stories, *The Last Inspection*. He was commissioned in October 1941, and a year later proceeded to India. On 5 March 1944, a lieutenant with the 6th Batt. South Wales Borderers, he died on active service on the Arakan front. A second volume of poems, *Ha, ha! Among the Trumpets*, was published posthumously in 1945; a selection of his letters to his parents and wife, *Letters from India* was published in 1946; and the uncollected short stories together with a reprint of the *Letters* in *In the Green Tree* in 1948. There was no issue of his marriage.

In the Green Tree (preface by A.L. Rowse, Postscript by Gwyn Jones); [Alun John, *Alun Lewis* (1970); John Pikoulis, *Alun Lewis, a life* (1983); Gwenno Lewis, ed. *Alun Lewis, letters to my wife* (1989); Ulrich Schäfer, *Alun Lewis, a bibliography* (1986); the *Collected Poems* appeared in 1994].

G.J.

LEWIS, BENJAMIN WALDO (1877-1953), Baptist minister; b. 7 Sept 1877 at Holyhead, Anglesey, the son of John (according to family tradition, but David according to the biographies) Lewis, (b. 29 Aug. 1829) from Bridell, and Anne Lewis (née Williams, in Feb. 1848 or 1849) from Fishguard. They married at Newport, Mon. on 31 Jan. 1871. His father was, according to tradition, of the lineage of a brother of Titus Lewis (*DWB*, 563) while his wife was the niece of Benjamin Davies (1826-1905; *DWB*, 111), his sister's daughter. His father was a stonemason who enjoyed a period of success in Cardiff *c*. 1850-75, but as the trade deteriorated he was forced to move to other places to seek work, at first at Holyhead and then, *c*. 1880 at the village of Broughton near Wrexham. In 1887 his father decided to visit the USA, where a son of his first marriage was living, in the hope of establishing a new life there, but he was taken ill on the voyage and he died shortly after arriving at Danville, Pa. on 27 May 1887.

Benjamin Waldo Lewis was baptised at Salem, Mass. within a week of his eleventh birthday, but less than three years later the family had moved back closer to the extended family in south Wales. They moved to Tylorstown and, in July 1891, enrolled as members at Hermon, Pontygwaith. There he was persuaded to begin preaching, at the same time as James Thomas Evans (see above), the principal of the Baptist College, Bangor. He began to earn his living in a colliery, at first underground and then in the smithy. After taking night-classes for some 7-8 years he was accepted for a period of about a year to 18 months at the Pontypridd Academy (again along with J.T. Evans and another of his friends, Ben Bowen, *DWB*, 46). From 1900-05 he went to the Baptist College and University College, Cardiff where he graduated

B.A. in 1905. From 1905-08 he attended the Presbyterian College, Carmarthen where he suffered a breakdown in his health in the middle of his B.D. course. He was ordained on 21 Jan. 1909 as the minister of Penuel, Carmarthen, where he had already enrolled in membership during his college days. This was his only pastorate until his retirement in 1946, when he was appointed honorary minister. During World War I, *c*. May 1915-Nov 1916, he was released by his church to work with the Y.M.C.A., first of all for some months at Dover and thereafter, for almost a year, in Malta. There he was promoted to become a 'Regional Leader', thereby being responsible for all the work of the Society on the island. He died at his home at Briarleigh, Longacre Road on 31 Dec. 1953, after a long illness which followed an accident at Borth the previous September. He was buried at Carmarthen public cemetery on 4 Jan. 1954.

He was married on 14 June 1922 at Zion English Presbyterian church, Carmarthen to Enid Mari Wheldon (b. 14 Mar. 1892), a native of Crickhowell, the daughter of Pierce Jones Wheldon and Louisa Arnaud Wheldon (née MacKenzie). Her father was the manager of the National Provincial bank and a brother of Thomas Jones Wheldon (1841-1916, *DWB*, 1015-6), who had settled in Carmarthen in 1900. She died 2 May 1963 at Glangwili Hospital, Carmarthen. There was one son of the marriage.

For very many years B.J. Lewis was an active supporter of a variety of movements and good causes in the town of Carmarthen and its environs, e.g. he was for 35 years a member and also the chairman of the governing body of Carmarthen hospital. When the National Health Service Act was enacted in 1947, he became a member of the Welsh Regional Hospital Board and chairman of the governing body of the West Wales hospital. He was a member of the governing body of Queen Elizabeth Grammar School from 1917 onward and its chairman in 1944. Until 1944 he was a member of the Carmarthen Borough education committee; a member of the County Library Committee; a member of the South West Wales branch of the Historical Society founded in 1931 and its chairman from the end of World War II until March 1950; chairman of the Community Council established in the town in 1932 to allay the distress of unemployment; the first chairman of the Carmarthen Christian Churches' Council; a member of the Carmarthen Arts Club; chairman of the committee of Baptist students of the Presbyterian College and a member of its board of Trustees. Throughout his life he was a student and collector of books; he conducted extra-mural courses under the auspices of the University College, Aberystwyth. He lectured at the Presbyterian College during the illness of J. Oliver Stephens (see below) in 1928-29. He contributed extensively to the literature of the Baptist denomination, e.g. a series of articles on the Baptists among the other denominations in *Seren Cymru* 1930, and between 1911 and 1937 intermittent lessons for the syllabus of the Sunday school for *Yr Hauwr* and *Yr Arweinydd Newydd*. He was elevated to become president of the Carmarthen and Cardigan Baptist Association in 1946-47 and the subject of his address was, 'Yr hyn a erys'. Politically, he was at first a Liberal, but at the general election of Dec. 1923, he turned publicly to the Labour Party, becoming a pioneer of the movement in the town and thereafter a close friend of Daniel Hopkin (1886-1951) who in May 1929 was elected as Member of Parliament for the county.

His wife was an able musician, and she, like her husband, was prominent in public circles, e.g. president and chairman of the Arts Club; a member of the Amateur Operatic Society in the town; a member of the South Wales Consultative Council of the National Assistance Board; a member of the management committee of the County Nursing Association; a member of the house committee of Kensington Hospital in Pembrokeshire and prominent in the work of the W.V.S.

NLW MS. 10328 (register of the Presbyterian College, Carmarthen); *Seren Cymru*, 5 Feb. 1909, 18, 25 July, 1, 8 Aug 1930, 17, 24 Mar 1939, 8 Jan. 1954; *Carmarthen Journal*, 29 Jan 1909, 8 Jan 1954, 10 May 1963; *Welshman*, 29 Jan 1909, 8 Jan. 1954, 10 May 1963; *Seren yr Ysgol Sul*, 1921, 310-314, 1937, 3-4; *Llythyr*, Carmarthen and Cardigan Association, 1927, 5-22, 1954, 19; *Llawlyfr y Bedyddwyr*, 1955, 115-116; *Baptist Handbook*, 1955, 330; Dewi Eirug Davies, *Hoff Ddysgedig Nyth* (1976), 205; WWP; personal information from his son.

B.G.O.

LEWIS, DAVID ('Ap Ceredigion'; 1870-1948), cleric, poet, and hymn-writer; b. at Llaethdy, Cilcennin, Cards., 24 Aug. 1870, s. of David Lewis, farmer, and Jane his wife. He was educated first at a private school at Llan-non, Cards., kept by J. Davies (afterwards vicar of Clynnog Fawr, Caerns.) and subsequently at St. David's College, Lampeter. There he won the Eldon Scholarship, for excellence in Welsh, and a Greek prize, and took the degree of B.A. in 1896. In Dec. of the same year he was made deacon by Bishop Richard Lewis of Llandaff, and licensed to the curacy of Ynys-hir, Rhondda. He received priest's orders in 1897, and in the same year went as curate to Cwm-parc and Treorchy. From there he went to Llanbryn-mair in 1900, and thence to Mallwyd in 1905. In 1906 he obtained a curacy at Llanllechid, and in 1915 he was appointed rector of Llansadwrn in Anglesey. He was appointed rural dean of Tindaethwy in 1937. He remained at Llansadwrn till his death on 19 Oct. 1948, and was buried there. There is a sanctuary lamp in the church there in memory of him.

Lewis was a frequent contributor to Welsh periodicals from the beginning of the century onwards, and for many years was the editor of the poetry column of *Y Llan*. His work also appeared in other Church publications, such as *Yr Haul*, *Y Cyfaill Eglwysig* and *Perl y plant*, and also in *Cymru* and *Y Geninen*. He was one of the literary editors of *Emynau'r Eglwys*, which appeared in 1942, and in that collection there are a number of his hymns, original and translated, and some carols. His work does not bear obvious marks of distinction, but it is fluent and pleasant, and characteristic of his period. His services were frequently in demand at local literary meetings; he was a pleasant and acceptable preacher, and a most likeable man. He m. Sarah Jane Ellis, of Llanllechid, Caerns., and they had a s. and a dau.

Hugh J. Williams, *Hanes eglwys Llanllechid*; *Llan*, 5 Nov. 1948; *Haul*, Jan. 1949; Llandaff diocesan papers in N.L.W.; information from his relatives, and from D.J. Mihangel Williams, rector of Llansadwrn.

T.I.E.

LEWIS, DAVID EMRYS (1887-1954), poet and journalist; b. in 1887 at Machynlleth, Mont., and educated at schools in the town. He began his journalistic work with the *Montgomeryshire County Times*. In 1916 he moved to Port Talbot as a representative of the *Cambrian Daily Leader*, and later joined the staff of the *Western Mail*. He was also a reporter for other papers in south Wales. He won the crown at Neath national *eisteddfod* in 1918 for his *pryddest* 'Mynachlog Nedd'. His wife, Margaret, was from Machynlleth and they had two sons. He suffered a grievous illness during his last years and d. at Gendros, Swansea, 12 Mar. 1954 aged 67.

West. Mail, and recollections of friends.

G.R.T.

LEWIS, DAVID JOHN ('Lewis Tymbl'; 1879-1947), Congl. minister, popular preacher and lecturer; b. at Mynydd-bach, a smallholding in the village of Hermon, in the parish of Llanfyrnach, Pemb., 28 Dec. 1879 the second son of the family of five children of Dan and Mari Lewis. His father worked at the Llanfyrnach lead mine until it closed and he had to go to Aberdare to find work, but following a serious injury he was unable to continue working. He d. aged 43 of lead poisoning. Despite this the children were given a good upbringing and the opportunity to make good; two of them achieved good posts in education and banking, but it was the preacher who was Mynydd-bach's most notable contribution to Welsh life.

David John received his early education in the elementary school at Hermon where Principal Thomas Rees (*DWB*, 830-1) had been a pupil ten years earlier. He entered the school on July 7, 1884; T.E. Nicholas was one of his contemporaries there. The headmaster at the time was John Davies from Felin-foel, a strict disciplinarian, who had succeeded Robert Bryan (*DWB*, 55-6) in 1883. [According to that article, Bryan had been headmaster at Whitland but that was merely the postal address of the school at Hermon]. The Sunday school at Brynmyrnach was more important to him in his development as a preacher than his day school. When he was 14 he was apprenticed as a tailor to Dafydd Jones, Brynawel, Hermon. He was one of nine apprentices noted for their talent. The discipline of this craft was to be reflected in the smart appearance of the preacher for the rest of his life. Religion and culture flourished in the area and under the firm influence of his mother, the inspiration of its literary figures, especially Brynach Davies and important ministers like John Stephens (Llwyn-yr-hwrdd), father of Professor J. Oliver Stephens (see below), O.R. Owen, Glandŵr and Ben Davies, Tre-lech (1840-1930; *DWB*, 110), he was fired with the desire to be a preacher.

After a period at Myrddin School (the Old College School), he entered the Memorial College, Brecon in 1901. After some difficulty with mathematics he was able to complete the entry criteria to the University of Wales and he started his degree course in the University College of Cardiff in 1903. He graduated with 2nd-class honours in Hebrew in 1905. For the next two years he followed the B.D. course at the Memorial College. He received full marks in the New Testament Greek paper in 1906 and special praise from the examiner on the philosophy of religion paper. He completed the second year of the B.D. in the summer of 1907 but by then the young enthusiastic church at Bethesda, Tumble, had, since February, called him to be their minister. He was ordained there July 3, 1907 and he remained there for the rest of his life, and became known as 'Lewis Tymbl'. He soon became a much loved figure in the Welsh pulpit, his magnetic personality almost greater in appeal than his sermons. These always covered a single topic and reached a climax to end with unexpected suddenness. He received many invitations to preach from all over Wales. His most famous and best known sermons were 'Do you wish to be made whole?' ('Roll up the mat'), 'Mary breaking the ointment box.' ('She broke the alabaster box'), 'Cast your bread on the surface of the water,' 'They departed into their country another way,' 'In the year that King Uzziah died I saw also the Lord.' His lectures were almost as popular as his sermons - 'The art of living,' 'David Livingstone' and 'Shon Gymro.' He preached from notes on postcards; he disliked writing anything in full and he did not like to be restricted to a script. This is why he refused to preach on the radio after one attempt.

He was President of the Union of Welsh Independents for 1945-46 and he delivered his address, 'Bwrw'r draul,' at Ebenezer, Swansea in June 1945. This was published in Ieuan Davies' biography of 'Lewis Tymble' and one of his sermons in *Llef y Gwyliedydd* (ed. E. Curig Davies, 1927). However, his lively personality could not be conveyed on paper.

He never married and he spent forty years in two lodgings in Tumble. He was taken ill in December 1946 and he underwent surgery in Cardiff. He was not allowed to preach subsequently and he d. 10 March 1947 in Morriston hospital. He was interred in Crymych cemetery on Sunday 16 March after the biggest snowstorm within living memory had prevented the funeral taking place the previous day. A memorial booklet was published.

Personal information; [Ieuan Davies, *Lewis Tymbl* (1989)].

D.P.J.

LEWIS, DAVID WATTS - see under LEWIS, GRUFFYDD THOMAS below.

LEWIS, DAVID WYRE (1872-1966), minister and administrator (B); b. 13 May 1872 at Felinganol, Llanrhystud Mefenydd, Cards., son of the poet and musician John Lewis ('Eos Glyn Wyre'; 1836-92; *DWB*, 556), Tŷ-mawr, and Jane (née Davies; 1844-1917), Felinganol, and nephew of the musician David Lewis (1828-1908; *DWB*, 550). He was educated in the church school in the village, and was apprenticed to a carpenter at Trawsgoed. Because of lack of work locally he moved to Maerdy, Glam., and then to Pen-y-graig, where he was baptised as a member of

Soar church, Ffrwdamws and began preaching. Following a short period at night school in Porth and 14 months at Severn Grove Academy, Llanidloes (1893-94), he was accepted by Bangor Baptist College, but he postponed commencing his course until Sept. 1895, spending the first year at the University College of Wales, Aberystwyth to matriculate, and the following four years at Bangor sharing the time between the University College and the Baptist College. On 3 July 1900 he was ord. minister of Nefyn and Morfa Nefyn churches, where he built a new chapel for the first and put the finances of the latter in order, and had 'totally inexplicable' experiences during the Revival of 1905. On 19 Apr. 1910 he was inducted minister of Calfaria church, Llanelli, where he came face to face with the disturbances of the railway strike in Aug. 1911. He moved 1 Sept. 1913 to Penuel church, Rhosllannerchrugog, where he carried out his most mature work and where he was required from the beginning, as in Llanelli, to assimilate his personal ministry with the social gospel which was gaining ground among the church members. He retired 7 Apr. 1946, but continued to live in the district.

He was an experienced conference man and a leading member of his denomination. He was secretary of Caernarfon Baptist Association, 1906-10, secretary of the Denbigh, Flint, and Merioneth Association, 1919-39, and took particular responsibility from 1934 onwards for the requirements of the Sustentation Fund. He was president of the Assembly (*Cymanfa*) twice (1930-31, 1954-55), and having previously addressed the Union (1910, 1920) he was elevated president 1938-39. He published his 1920 address, *Crist a'r werin* and the 1939 address, *Yr Eglwys a'i chyfle heddiw*. He was chairman of the Memorial Fund, the committee for the new hymnal, *Y Llawlyfr Moliant Newydd* (1955), and the Sustentation Fund committee (from mid-1950s until his d.), and organizer in Wales for the Re-organizing Fund (*Trysorfa Ad-drefniad*; 1944).

He was a prolific writer and published a short memoir in J. T. Rees (ed.), *Detholiad o donau, anthemau a rhanganau Dafydd Lewis, Llanrhystud* (1930), and *Yr eglwysi a'r Undeb. Y weinidogaeth a'i pherigl heddiw* (1939). He was at the forefront in the revival of *Seren Gomer* in 1909, was editor of the periodical, 1910-16, laying special emphasis on his 'notes on books', and his articles down to the 1930s include biographies of contemporary Baptists of Wales, reports of annual conferences and substantial essays on various topics. He contributed much to *Yr Hauwr* (later *Yr Heuwr*) and its successor *Yr Arweinydd Newydd*, from 1904 to the mid-1930s.

He was awake to the needs of the nation as well as his denomination. He was secretary of Llŷn and Eifionydd Temperance Association. Being a pacifist through and through, he was a member of the group which initiated *Y Deyrnas*, Oct. 1916, and secretary and recorder for the Peace Conference which was convened at Llandrindod 3-5 Sept. 1917. In 1940-41 he was chairman of the Committee for safeguarding Welsh Culture, and when it joined the National Union of Welsh Societies in 1941 to form the New Wales Union (*Undeb Cymru Fydd*) he was from the beginning a member of the Council and several committees of the new body and later chairman and president. The University of Wales conferred on him an hon. D.D. in 1961, and many considered him to be the most important Baptist of the 20 c. in Wales.

He m. (1), 13 Apr. 1904, Elizabeth Ellen Roberts (1896-1941), Holyhead; (2) 20 May 1946, Eleanor Thomas (b. Dodd), Pen-y-cae, Wrexham. Two sons were born of the first marriage. He d. 9 May 1966 at his home, Tŷ Cerrig, Pen-y-cae, and his ashes were interred in his first wife's grave in his mother-church, Salem, Llanrhystud.

N.L.W., MSS. from his library, particularly the main collection of 1969, which includes a holographic autobiography to 1914, see *Annual Report*, 1969, 28-9; for particulars of other collections, ibid. 1970, 32, and 1976, 45; NLW MSS. 8177-277, a collection of music, letters, etc., belonging to his father John Lewis and uncle David Lewis - see ibid., 1929, 23-4, and *Handlist of MSS*, iii, s.n.; NLW, a holographic family tree produced by E.T. Price, Llanrhystud; *Mynegiad* Caernarfon Association, 1905-06, 7-9; *Llythyr* Denbigh, Flint, and Merioneth Association, 1930-31, 3-13, 1938-39, 23 and 1954-55, 3-4; *Adroddiad* of annual Services of the Baptist Union of Wales, 1910, 56-63; *Adroddiad* of Baptist Union of Wales, 1938-39, 5-16, and 1965-66, 16; *Greal*, 1904, 305 and 1910, 136; *Ser. Cymru*, 27 July 1900, 8 Apr., 6 May 1910, 1 Aug., 12 Sept. 1913, 16 Mar. 1928, 1 Sept. 1939, 18 Apr., 16 May 1941, 3 May 1946, and 27 May, 3, 10 June 1966; *Ser. G.*, 1920, 259-69, 1939, 41-5, 1940, 41-7, 1961, 1-6, and 1966, 29-60 (memorial number); *Seren yr Ysgol Sul*, 1939, 198-203; *Genh.*, 1950-1, 205-8; *Deyrnas*, 1917, June 6-7, July 6, Aug. 6, Sept. 5-6, and Oct. 12; S. Rowley (ed. Lewis Valentine), *Hanes Eglwys Penuel Rhosllannerchrugog* (1959), 124-33, 159; *Undeb Cymru Fydd. Adroddiad blynyddol*, 1965-6, [4-5]; *Llawlyfr Bed.*, 1967, 115-6; *Bapt. Hdbk.*, 1967, 365; *Cefn Chronicle*, 6, 13 Sept. 1913; *Rhos Herald*, 20 Nov. 1943, 15 Apr. 1946, and 22 Apr. 1961; *Wrexham Leader*, 13, 20 May 1966; information from his daughter-in-law, Mrs. J.C. Lewis, Llanrhystud, and E.R. Morris, Llanidloes; personal acquaintance.

B.G.O.

LEWIS, EDWARD ARTHUR (1880-1942), historian, s. of Maurice and Elizabeth Lewis; b. at Nanty Mines, Llangurig, Mont., 6 Jan. 1880. Educated at Oswestry, Llanidloes, U.C.W., Aberystwyth, and the London School of Economics, he was appointed assistant-lecturer in Welsh history at U.C.W., Aberystwyth, 1910; professor of economics in 1912; first Sir John Williams professor of Welsh history in 1930. In 1925 he m. Elizabeth Thomas, vice-principal of Barry Training College, who d. in Dec. 1942. He d. suddenly 7 Jan. 1942.

A D.Litt. (Wales) and D.Sc. (London), he was responsible for several early pioneer works on Welsh agrarian and social history. *The Mediaeval boroughs of Snowdonia* (1912) established principles for later work on the growth of municipal institutions in Wales. Some years earlier there had appeared 'The decay of tribalism in North Wales' (*Trans. Cymm.*, 1902-3), an impressionistic study revealing considerable insight, together with some studies in Welsh commercial history (*Cymm.*, 14, *Trans. R.H.S.*, 17, 1903) which foreshadow the best known work of Lewis's later years - *Welsh port books* (Cymm. Rec. Ser., 12, 1927). Diverted from his main interest by teaching and academic preoc-

cupations Lewis never quite fulfilled his early promise, though he did much during his long tenure of the chair of economics to foster and encourage interest in Welsh history among successive generations of students. After returning to full-time research work in 1930, he concentrated on a variety of bibliographical projects, many of them still unfinished at the time of his death. Two calendars belonging to this phase of his career have been published - the second posthumously: *Early Chancery proceedings* (1937), and *Augmentation proceedings* (1950). Editions of valuable original material will also be found in various volumes of *B.B.C.S* and *W. Wales Historical Records*.

[*Welsh Gaz.*, 15 Jan. 1942.]

T.J.P.

LEWIS, EMLYN EVANS (1905-69), plastic surgeon; b. in Pennsylvania 10 Apr. 1905. While still young he was brought to Wales by his mother and he received his education at Monmouth School and then went to London to study medicine at St. Mary's Hospital. He was regarded there as the most brilliant student of his year and qualified M.R.C.S., L.R.C.P. in 1929 and F.R.C.S. in 1933. After acquiring extensive experience in general surgery he decided to specialise in plastic surgery. He gave exceptionally valuable service at the centre at Gloucester when treating airmen suffering from extensive burns received during World War I. The centre was transferred to St. Lawrence Hospital at Chepstow in 1948, and came under the administration of the Welsh Hospital Board. Lewis spent the remainder of his distinguished career in full charge of this Special Unit, and combined his responsibilities there with extra duties as consultant to various hospitals in Cardiff, including the Royal Infirmary. The excellent reputation of St. Lawrence Hospital extended throughout south and west Wales, and his skill and experience in the treatment of burns proved of inestimable value to miners and steel workers, who were particularly exposed to such hazards. He was an exceptionally talented pioneer and an untiring worker in his chosen field, and was greatly respected throughout the United Kingdom. Furthermore, he was a remarkably capable and determined administrator, and a persuasive lecturer.

Lewis was a man of short, stocky physique and an enthusiastic footballer - an activity that determined the shape of his nose. It was the recurrent damage to that organ that engendered his initial interest in plastic surgery. His kindness was legendary and his memory faultless. He was an avid collector of period clocks, and eventually became a very knowledgeable horologist. He was also a keen Freemason, being master of several lodges. He d. in Cardiff Royal Infirmary, 14 May 1969, and was survived by his wife (Mary Cooper, when he m. 28 Oct. 1939) and daughter.

Brit. Med. Journ., 1969, 2, 518, 829; *Lancet*, 1969, 1, 1107; *Lives of the Fellows R.C.S., England*, 1965-73; personal knowledge.

E.W.J.

LEWIS, GRUFFYDD THOMAS (1873-1964), schoolmaster and a leading layman in the Presbyterian Church of Wales; b. 3 Feb. 1873 at Pil-rhoth, Llan-gain, Carms., the only s. of David Watts Lewis, Presbyterian minister known generally as David Lewis, Llanstephan, and Elizabeth (née Harries) his wife. David Lewis was a native of Aberystwyth, son of Thomas Lewis who hailed from Llanrhystud. His mother's maiden surname was Watts, believed to be from the same stock as Isaac Watts (1674-1784), the English hymn-writer, but David Lewis did not use his second baptismal name. David Lewis began his career as a cabinet maker, but abandoned his craft to become a preacher. He was ordained at Llangeitho in 1875. He attained considerable popularity as a preacher, and James Morris (*DWB*, 660) devotes three chapters in his *Efengylwyr Seion* to his biography. His wife, Elizabeth, was the sister of T.J.Harries, founder of the drapery firm of Harries of Oxford Street, London. She managed the small farm of Pil-rhoth, thus allowing her husband to continue his itinerant preaching. He d. in 1896, aged 66, and she, who was of the same family as William Williams, M.P. (*DWB*, 1081-2), d. at an advanced age in 1933.

The son was named Gruffydd Thomas after an elder of that name, his father's bosom friend of Aberystwyth days. G. Tom., as he adopted for his usual signature, was educated at Llan-y-bri elementary school and at the Old College School at Carmarthen, from where he went with a scholarship to Llandovery College in 1889. He matriculated in the University of London in 1893, and won a scholarship to Sidney Sussex College, Cambridge, where he graduated *senior optime* in mathematics in 1896, taking his M.A. in 1900. He rowed in the first boat for his college. At the end of his course he was appointed second master at the Pembroke Dock secondary school, and was appointed headmaster of the Tregaron intermediate school which opened in the town hall in Sept. 1887. He was responsible for planning the permanent buildings which were modelled on those of Narberth School, and he placed the school on a sound footing and guided its development with great skill and enthusiasm until his retirement in 1937. He was a successful teacher and throughout his 'tenure of office' was responsible for the teaching of mathematics and scripture. Scripture was not given a prominent place in the curriculum but he made some use of it as a means of improving the English of some junior classes. He was a strong disciplinarian without being too severe. His puritanical attitudes were tempered by his sense of humour. Like the majority of teachers and parents in his time, material advancement was an aim to be encouraged in his pupils. He considered that the wholly Welsh catchment area of the school made it unnecessary to place much emphasis on Welsh education, and that the children needed a thorough instruction in English as that language was less familiar to them. He was a strong supporter of the annual Welsh *eisteddfod* at the school and he regarded the *eisteddfod* as a valuable element in the life and character of the school.

For the greater part of his period at the school most of the pupils from the neighbouring districts lodged in the town during the week, and at the week-night services at Bwlch-gwynt Presbyterian chapel where he was a thorough Welshman and an elder of the church since 1912 they saw a different side of their headmaster. He would impress upon the children who attended these meetings that they would be likely to do better in the school examinations, and he was proud of the number of ministers who entered the Christian ministry from the school.

He served on many key committees of the Calvinistic Methodist Connexion, and his services were acknowledged when he was elected to the chair of the South Wales Association in 1936-37, the centenary year of the death of Ebenezer Richard (1781-1837; *DWB*, 848) who made Tregaron a household name in Wales. He m. Annie, only child of John Thomas (1839-1921; *DWB*, 954) and his wife Ann (née Williams) of Llanwrtyd in the Water Street chapel at Carmarthen on 27 Dec. 1901. They had 5 daughters. She d. 10 June 1939, and he d. 20 July 1964. Both were buried in Bwlch-gwynt cemetery.

Information supplied by his grand-daughter, Bethan Bennett; *West Wales Guardian*, 27 Sept. and 4 Oct. 1935; *Treasury*, Feb. 1936; personal knowledge.

E.D.J.

LEWIS, HENRY (1889-1968), Welsh and Celtic scholar, university professor; b. 21 Aug. 1889, youngest son of William Lewis and his wife, in Ynystawe, Glam. He proceeded from Ystalyfera county school to university college Cardiff where he graduated in Welsh, and then to Jesus College, Oxford to study under Sir John Rhys (*DWB*, 844-5). He gained the degrees of M.A. and D.Litt. (Wales). He began his career as a teacher at his old school in Ystalyfera and then at Llanelli county school. During World War I he served as a sergeant in the Welsh Guards and 2nd Lieut. in the Royal Welch Fusiliers. From 1918 to 1921 he was an assistant lecturer in the Welsh dept., university college Cardiff, and he held the chair of Welsh at university college Swansea from 1921 until his retirement in 1954. In 1921, too, he m. Gwladys, youngest daughter of William Thomas and his wife of Treorchy. There were 2 daughters of the marriage.

It is difficult today to appreciate the difficulties facing the study of Welsh language and literature when Welsh degree courses were first established. Henry Lewis stands in the front rank of that handful of scholars who transformed the situation by editing essential texts, interpreting them and commentating on lexical, grammatical and syntactical features – work carried out in parallel with running a university dept. with the help of one or two lecturers. As early as 1921 he began to publish medieval Welsh translations of Latin texts: *Darnau o'r Efengylau* (*Cymmrodor*, 31), *Chwedlau seith doethion Rufein* (1925), *Delw y byd* (1928, with Pol Diverres) and especially *Brut Dingestow* (1942) with a valuable introduction for students of Welsh-Latin translations. He also edited and commentated upon the works of medieval Welsh poets, most importantly on Iolo Goch in *Cywyddau Iolo Goch ac Eraill* (1925, 1937) and *Hen gerddi crefyddol* (1931), a pioneering study of an important aspect of the poetry of the *Gogynfeirdd*. He edited some renaissance prose, e.g. *Hen gyflwyniadau* (1948) as well as some later texts, e.g. Glanffrwd, *Llanwynno* (1949), Hugh Jones, Maesglasau, *Cydymaith yr hwsmon* (1949), *Morgannwg Matthews Ewenni* (1953).

But to return to his main interests, he prepared, with Elizabeth J. Louis Jones (see above) an index to manuscript poetry (1928) and also edited (1927) the poetry in Peniarth MS. 53. The *Bulletin of the Board of Celtic Studies*, (the language and literature section of which he edited from 1950 to 1964), and to a lesser extent other scholarly journals contain, over a long period, numerous articles and notes by him. These are of fundamental importance and deal with Welsh from its earliest period in the work of the *cynfeirdd* and Old Welsh glosses and with the syntax and morphology of the language, topics he discussed in *Datblygiad yr iaith Gymaeg* (1931), *The Sentence in Welsh* (Sir John Rhys British Academy Lecture 1942) and *Yr elfen Ladin yn yr iaith Gymraeg* (1943). The comparative aspects of Welsh interested him as is seen in his grammars of Middle Cornish (1928, 1946) and Middle Breton (1922, 1935, and, in conjunction with J.R.F. Piette, 1966), and most particularly in his collaboration with Holger Pedersen in the translation and revision of the latter's masterpiece *Vergleichende Grammatik der Keltischen Sprachen* which appeared as *A concise comparative Celtic grammar* (1937, revised 1961).

Early in his career Henry Lewis was one of the editors of the *Cyfres y Werin a'r Brifysgol* series of translations and he had a hand in translating *Brenin yr ellyllon* (Gogol). He was a member of the editorial committee of the University of Wales Welsh Dictionary and he prepared the *Collins-Spurrell Welsh Dictionary* (1960). Other tasks which he undertook include membership of the editorial committee of *Y Caniedydd*, the hymnal of the Welsh Independents, orthographical revision of *Beibl y plant* (1929), *Y Testament Newydd* (1936), *Y Beibl* (1955), *Yr Apocrypha* (1959). He translated a number of government reports, thereby raising the standards of such translation. He was a member of several public bodies, committees and voluntary societies, e.g. Welsh Joint Education Committee, council (and Chairman) of Coleg Harlech, Clerk and Warden of the Guild of Graduates of the University of Wales, vice-president of the National Library of Wales, hon. Member of the Royal Irish Academy, a vice-president of the Hon. Soc. of Cymmrodorion. He was made C.B.E. in 1954 and awarded an hon. LL.D. by the University of Wales, and an hon. D.Litt.Celt. by the National Univ. of Ireland. He d. 14 Jan. 1968.

Www; E. Bachellery, *Études celtiques*, 12 (1968-69); Ben Bowen Thomas in *NLWJ*, 27 (1971), 121-35; bibliography by D. Ellis Evans, *Jnl. Welsh Bibl. Soc.*, 10, 144-52.

D.M.Ll.

LEWIS, HENRY GETHIN (1872-1945), merchant and financier; b. 5 Apr. 1872 at Pontlotyn, Glam., s. of James and Margaret Lewis. He went to Lewis School, Pengam, and later entered the office of an uncle who was at the head of the Bute Works Supply Co., Cardiff. He served here for 21 years, becoming a partner and, when the business was formed into a limited liability company, a director and its secretary. He compiled a series of tables which were published at Abergavenny in 1899 under the title of *Redemption hire, deferred purchase, and easy payment tables*; these were adopted as a standard by the Wagon Building and Financing Corporation. In 1911 he founded the firm of Henry G. Lewis and Co., Ltd., rolling-stock proprietors, and during World War I he supplied the Admiralty with wagons for coaling the Fleet. At the close of hostilities he was one of the largest wagon-hirers in Britain. His generosity kept pace with his success. In 1927 he bought the former residence of George Davidson, Wernfawr, Harlech, and presented it to the founders of Coleg Harlech. He also bought and gave to N.L.W. the E.C. Quiggin Celtic collection. He was High Sheriff of Glamorgan, 1920-21, a governor and treasurer of the University College, Cardiff, a governor and councillor of the N.L.W., and treasurer of the National *Eisteddfod* Association. In 1928 the University of Wales conferred on him the degree of LL.D. He m. in 1897, Ann, dau. of Jenkin Llewellyn of Penarth; they had eight children. Their home for many years was at Porthkerry, Barry, where Lewis d. on 9 Feb. 1945.

WwW; personal knowledge.

T.J.

LEWIS, HOWELL ELVET ('ELFED'; 1860-1953), Independent minister, hymn-writer, poet; b. 14 April, 1860, the oldest son of the twelve children of James and Anna Lewis, at Y Gangell, near Blaen-y-coed, Carms. Thomas Lewis (1868-1953; see below) was one of his brothers. His father's wage as a foreman farm-worker at Pencraig-fawr was small and was supplemented by keeping a shop in the home at Pant-y-Waun. Howell's opportunities for learning were restricted. He learnt the alphabet from the capital letters in his father's Bible and the home and the Sunday school nurtured him until he was eight when T.G. Miles opened a school in the chapel vestry. Howell soon showed his ability and he became a pupil teacher to his contemporaries. At no small sacrifice on his parents' part, he was sent to the grammar school at Newcastle Emlyn when he was fourteen. He started to preach and was known as the 'boy-preacher'. Whilst there he met E. Keri Evans (see above) who introduced him to the Welsh strict metres, *cynghanedd*, and E. Griffith Jones who introduced him to English literature. He took interest also in the local publication *Y Byd Cymreig* which was in the care of the Rev. John Williams. He started to compete under the pen-name of 'Coromandel'. Two years later he passed the entrance examination to Carmarthen Presbyterian College, the second out of fourteen applicants. He won every prize during his four years there and added German lessons to his other work at the College.

In 1880 he accepted an invitation to the pastorate of Buckley chapel, Flints., a church that was Welsh in spirit but English in language. After four years there he went to Hull that was English both in language and in spirit. It was during this period that he turned his mind and heart towards Wales and to delight in its prose and poetry. He composed poems and essays that won prizes in many *eisteddfodau*. The national *eisteddfod* in Wrexham in 1888 is testimony to his gifts. It was called 'Elfed's

Eisteddfod' as he won on the free-verse poem, 'Y Saboth yng Nghymru', the love poem, 'Llyn y Morwynion', and an essay on 'Athrylith John Ceiriog Hughes.' At that time he also wrote *The sweet singers of Wales* and *Emynwyr Cymru*. It was also the period when he composed a number of his popular hymns.

He returned to Wales in 1891 as minister of the English-language Park chapel, Llanelli. He devoted more of his efforts nationally. He won the national *eisteddfod* chair in 1894 on the subject 'Hunan aberth.' He was one of the editors of the Congregational hymnal, *Y Caniedydd Cynulleidfaol*, which was published in 1895, the same year that the National *Eisteddfod* was invited to Llanelli; *Caniadau Elfed* was also published and three years later *Plannu Coed*, a popular volume of sermons appeared. That year, 1898, he accepted a call to Harecourt, a well-known church in London with connections with Cromwell and David Livingstone. After several requests, he yielded to the insistence of Tabernacl chapel, King's Cross, in 1904 and he ministered there until his retirement in 1940 when he went to live at 'Erw'r Delyn', Penarth and became a member of Ebeneser chapel, Cardiff.

His ministry at Tabernacl covered three periods: (a) *The Revival* (1904-14) when Elfed devoted his talents to promoting and directing the religious enthusiasm of those years; (b) *The Deterioration* (1914-24). He drew up a 'covenant' with the members who had been dispersed because of the war so that their relationship with the church might be safeguarded; (c) *The Depression* (1924-40). Many Welsh people received help and work through Elfed during this difficult period and his message of hope was a great comfort to the many who had come to London to seek work.

His contribution to Welsh life and culture was acknowledged by the University, the *Eisteddfod*, the state and the church. He was the first person that the University of Wales honoured with three degrees, M.A. (1906), D.D. (1933) and LL.D. (1949). He received every honour that the *Eisteddfod* could bestow on him as a competitor, as adjudicator and Archdruid. The church also honoured him. The London Missionary Board called him to its chair on two occasions, 1910 and 1922, and he was also selected to be one of three representatives to visit Madagascar to celebrate the century of the arrival of the first missionaries. He was elected national president of the Free Churches in 1926 and chairman of the Congregational Union of England and Wales in 1933.

Elfed was also fortunate in his home life. He m. Mary Taylor of Buckley, in 1887. This was a happy marriage and they had seven children. However she died suddenly in 1918. He m. Elisabeth Lloyd five years later but she was in poor health and d. 1927. By 1930 Elfed assumed that his public life was coming to an end as his eyesight had failed completely and travelling became impossible for him. However, Mary Davies, one of the members of King's Cross, came into his life. They m. in 1930 and she gave him the opportunity to continue to minister in King's Cross and further afield. She enabled him to travel to preach and lecture until his death on 10 Jan. 1953. His ashes were interred in his home village of Blaen-y-coed.

Personal research; [Emlyn G. Jenkins, *Cofiant Elfed* (1957); Dafydd Owen, *Elfed a'i waith* (n.d.); bibliography in *Jnl. W.B.S.*, 8, 7-23].

E.G.Je.

LEWIS, IDRIS (1889-1952), musician; b. 21 Nov. 1889, at Birchgrove, Llansamlet, Glam., son of a coalminer. He took an interest in music at an early age, gaining a scholarship to study at the Royal College of Music in London when he was 16 years old, and he came into prominence as a pianist. After completing his musical education he toured India and the Far East, 1911-12, giving a series of piano recitals in some of the major cities there. Later he settled in London, where he became assistant musical director at Daly's Theatre, and musical director at the Lyric and Gaiety theatres (1915-27). He also served as organist at the Welsh chapel (Presb.) in Charing Cross (1923-26), and as conductor of the London-Welsh Choral Society. In 1927 he joined British International Pictures at Elstree, and as musical director for that company (1931-35) he was responsible for arranging music for a number of well-known films, 'Blossom Time' being among them, with Richard Tauber as soloist.

One of those impressed by that film was Sam Jones, who was at the time producer of Welsh programmes with the B.B.C., and after realising that Idris Lewis was a Welshman he succeeded in persuading him to join the B.B.C. in Cardiff, where he became musical director of the Welsh region (1936-52), the first to be appointed to that post. He d. at his home in Llandaff, 15 Apr. 1952, and his remains were cremated in Glyntaff.

He is an important figure in the history of Welsh music, chiefly because of his pioneering work in broadcasting orchestral concerts from Cardiff. He was also responsible for arranging several series of popular vocal programmes on sound radio, including 'Melys Lais' and 'Cenwch im yr hen ganiadau'. Although he was not a prolific composer, he arranged a number of works for male voice choirs, and some of the songs from his setting of 'Alun Mabon' (Ceiriog), which was first broadcast in 1935, remain popular on *eisteddfod* and concert platforms. He was the author of a useful volume *Cerddoriaeth yng Nghymru* (1945) which was translated into Welsh by Enid Parry.

His brother was D.H. Lewis, Llanelli, author of *Cofiant J.T. Rees*, and also of a number of articles on Welsh musicians which were published in *Y Genhinen* and other periodicals.

C.C.C. Welsh Music, 5, (1972); *Who's who in Music*; *West. Mail*, 16 Apr. 1952; information from Sam Jones in 1971.

H.W.

LEWIS, JOHN DANIEL VERNON (1879-1970), scholar, Independent minister, author, tutor and theological college principal; b. at Pentre Estyll, Swansea, 13 June, 1879, son of Thomas Jones Lewis and Ann Daniel his wife, originally of Glascoed Fach, Llanarthne. His parents emigrated to the U.S.A. when he was a young boy and his father soon afterwards undertook a course in Bangor theological college, Maine. He spent most of his subsequent life in the ministry in America, at Green's Landing, Mount Vernon and East Andover, except for a short period when he was the minister of the English Independent chapel at Porthcawl, Glam. Although his father tried to persuade his son to come to America more than once, he could not be induced to leave the home he had made with his grandmother and his aunt, Rachel Rees. The father died in Paxton, Connecticut in 1922.

The young man was interested in three things from his early days, the Sunday school, his school lessons and the *eisteddfod*. He was obviously talented and he won the recitation contest at the Llanelli national *eisteddfod* in 1895 with 78 competing. He did outstandingly well at school - the elementary school at Brynhyfryd and Swansea Grammar School. He won a scholarship to University College, Cardiff (1898-1901) and graduated B.A. with first-class honours in Semitic studies. He obtained the degree of B.D. Wales after studying at Brecon Memorial College (1901-04), only the second person to achieve this from one of the Welsh Congregational colleges. Whilst a student there he was awarded the essay prize at the 1903 National *Eisteddfod* on the subject, '*Perthynas daearyddiaeth Palesteina a hanes y wlad*' under the adjudication of Edward Anwyl (*DWB*, 12-13) and T. Witton Davies (*DWB*, 156-7).

Two important awards decided his future course of study; the Pusey and Ellerton Scholarship to Mansfield College, Oxford, followed by the Proctor Travelling Scholarship which gave him the opportunity of studying in Leipzig with Rudolf Kittel and other scholars. As well as completing the requirements of the Oxford M.A. he was nominated by Prof. D.S. Margoliouth, Prof. of Arabic, to be a member of the select group of the Royal Asiatic Society (M.R.A.S.). The University of Wales recognised his work and scholarship by awarding him an honorary D.D. in 1963.

He was called to Park Road Independent church, Liverpool in 1909. After ten years there he moved to the English church at Salisbury Park, Wrexham. In 1921 he was invited to Gibea chapel, Brynaman and he spent a fruitful period there (1921-35) until he returned to his old college at Brecon as a professor. He was an able and eloquent preacher, able to adjust easily to his congregation. He was offered the principalship of Camden College, Australia in 1932 but in that year he became a part-time lecturer in the Hebrew Department of University College, Swansea.

In 1934 he followed D. Miall Edwards (see above) in the Chair of Christian Doctrine and Ethics at Brecon. In 1943 he took responsibility for teaching Hebrew and Old Testament studies until his retirement in 1957. He was principal of the college from 1950-1952. He was the author of an authoritative book on the psalms which, although strongly recommended by the Clarendon Press, could not be published because of lack of funds.

He translated some of Karl Barth's sermons into Welsh and he was prominent in interpreting Barth's work as well as that of Brunner and Oscar Cullman in Wales. He lectured on their work to the students of Carmarthen Presbyterian College and to the Calvinistic Methodist churches in London. As well as being the dean of the Faculty of Theology in the University of Wales (1949-52), he was also an examiner for the B.D. degree (1932-36). He

wrote many monographs for *Y Geiriadur Beiblaidd* (1926) and articles for journals in Wales and England.

After retirement from the college in Brecon, he lived for a while in Aberllefenni before moving to Machynlleth. He died at his son's home at Machynlleth on 28 December 1970 and was buried in the cemetery at Machynlleth. After his death his papers were given to N.L.W. His main publications are: *Dysgeidiaeth y proffwydi* (1923); *The Word of God in theory and experience* (1943); *Crist a'r greadigaeth*, Chairman's address to the Welsh Union of Independents (1952); *Diwinyddiaeth heddiw a phregethu*, a radio lecture (1954); translation of *Lehrbuch der Neuhebräischen Sprache* (1956); editing *Requiem Mass in C Minor* Cherubini, with a translation from Latin into Welsh (1938); *Bydd melys fy myfyrdod: detholiad o lyfr y Salmau* (1949); *Llyfr y Salmau: cyfieithiad Cymraeg* (I-XLI), ... *gyda nodiadau ar y testun Hebraeg* (1967); *Mawl i'r Goruchaf, emynau a chyfieithiadau* (1962); editing *Grand Mass in C Minor* Mozart, with words in Latin and Welsh (1965); *Astudiaethau: y gelfyddyd o gyfieithu'r Ysgrythur*, Dyfnallt Memorial Lecture (1967); *Golud yr oesoedd*, sermons (1970).

Blwyddiadur A., 1972; Pennar Davies (ed.), *Athrawon ac Annibynwyr* (1971), 79-88; *Brecon and Radnor Express*, 23 August 1956.

E.L.E.

LEWIS, Lady RUTH (1871-1946), a pioneering collector of Welsh folk-songs, and advocate of educational, religious, temperance and philanthropic bodies; b. 29 Nov. 1871, at 16 Alexandra Drive, Liverpool, the third child of William Sproston Caine (*DNB*, 1901-50), and his wife Alice, the daughter of Hugh Stowell Brown, minister at the Myrtle Street Baptist church, Liverpool. When her father was elected M.P. for Scarborough, the family moved to London where she studied at Clapham Secondary School for Girls before entering Newnham College, Cambridge. She completed a degree course at Cambridge but, as the university did not award degrees to women, she received an M.A. from the University of Dublin. She worked for a few years, after she graduated, at the Caine Mission Hall in Vauxhall where she took an interest in temperance and in working with young women. She m. John Herbert Lewis (*DWB*, 556) in 1897 at Clapham; Thomas Gee (*DWB*, 274) officiated at the wedding. The married couple lived at Penucha Mansion, Caerwys, and at 23 Grosvenor Rd., London. A daughter, Kitty, was born in 1898 and a son, Mostyn, in 1901. She had attained a thorough knowledge of Welsh and the children were fluent in Welsh. The family were regular worshippers at Welsh chapels in Caerwys and in London. Ruth Lewis identified herself with Welsh life; she involved herself in public life and took a particular interest in her husband's work. She possessed a gift for public speaking which proved a great strength for a number of causes. She was frequently asked to address public meetings, especially at temperance meetings sponsored by *Undeb Dirwestol Merched Gogledd Cymru* (the North Wales Women's Temperance Union). She was generous both in her welcome and in her assistance, both at her home and at the Charing Cross Calvinistic Methodist chapel, to young

Welsh women who came to work in London.

During World War I, Ruth Lewis ran a canteen for soldiers in the borough of Westminster. This canteen was the first to stay open throughout the night in order to provide for soldiers arriving at Victoria Station. For this service, she was appointed O.B.E. She was appointed a J.P. in the borough and she became the first woman to sit on the Flintshire Commission of Peace; she appeared often on the Caerwys bench.

Because of her great interest in music, she was among the founding members of the Welsh Folk Song Society in 1906. At the beginning of the twentieth century, Ruth Lewis, Dr. Mary Davies (*DWB*, 143) and Mrs. R. Gwyneddon Davies, with the use of a phonograph, preserved many folk songs which were about to vanish from folk memory. She contributed on several occasions to the Society's journal. In 1927, she was responsible for revising the Society's constitution and she was elected president in 1930. At her own expense, she published a collection of Flintshire folk songs. She was elected a member of the *Gorsedd* of Bards. She was industrious in the Presbyterian Church of Wales, both in north Wales and in London. In recognition of their outstanding contributions to the life of the Church, an illuminated address was presented to Ruth Lewis and her husband in 1923. In the same year, they both spent nine months working as missionaries in Lushai where their daughter was a missionary.

After the death of her husband in 1933, Ruth Lewis was elected a member of Flintshire County Council for the Ysgeifiog and Caerwys districts. She was also a member of the courts of the university colleges in Bangor and Aberystwyth and of the courts and councils of the National Museum and the National Library. She took a great interest in Flintshire County Library and in the Women's Institute and she served as president of the Caerwys branch of the Institute and of the nursing society there. She d. 26 Aug. 1946 and was buried in the graveyard at Ddôl on 29 Aug.

Journal of Welsh Folk Song Society, passim; *Chester Chronicle*, 31 Aug. 1946; *Gymraes*, 1921; information from her daughter, Kitty Idwal Jones.

E.D.J.

LEWIS, THOMAS (1868-1953), Principal of Brecon Memorial College; b. 14 Dec. 1868 at Pant-y-waun, Blaen-y-coed, Carms., the fifth child of James and Anna Lewis, one of twelve children (although two died when young), including Howell ('Elfed', see above), the eldest. There were talented and gifted musicians on the mother's side of the family and this influenced Howell, the hymn-writer, and Thomas who had a good baritone voice and who, for a period, used to conduct singing festivals and *eisteddfodau* in the Brecon area. He inherited also physical strength and style which gave him the ability to excel in sport and football. The children were raised in a chapel culture and Thomas Lewis never lost his respect for Thomas Charles' *Geiriadur Ysgrythyrol* (*DWB*, 73-4). His childhood home was the small holding of Pen-lan in the parish of Cynwyl Elfed. His father used to conduct a weekly prayer meeting for young men in a cottage known as Cwmcafit.

He was educated at Cwmclynmaen board school until he was 14 when he went to live with his brother Howell at Buckley, Flintshire. After a period in the board school there he became a pupil at Alun School in Mold. He gained University of London matriculation in January, 1885 and that year he was admitted to University College, Bangor. In 1886 he enrolled at the Lancaster Congregational College, Manchester, and became a student at Owens College in Manchester. He graduated B.A. (London) in 1888 and M.A. (London) in 1890 with honours in classics. Between 1889 and 1894 he was a student at the Congregational College. He was successful in the scripture examinations of the University of London gaining the qualifications of A.T.S. and F.T.S. In 1893 he received the B.D. degree of the University of St. Andrews during the brief period when that University awarded the B.D. through examination only to students of some colleges. Also in 1893 he was able to study at the University of Marburg as part of his final year in the Congregational College. He won the Rees (1889) and Dr Williams (1892) scholarships and the Bles Prize in Hebrew from the University of Manchester (1893). At Marburg he had particular respect for Herrmann, an adherent of Ritschlian theology.

In 1894 he was appointed Professor of Hebrew in his college at Manchester where he remained until 1897 when he became Professor of Hebrew and Old Testament studies at Memorial College Brecon - the first of a new generation of teachers that moved Wales along the path of liberal modernism. He m. Flora (Augusta Flora Williams), daughter of Jacob Williams, Whalley Range, Manchester, in 1898 and they had three sons and three daughters. In 1907 he succeeded David Rowlands, 'Dewi Môn' (*DWB*, 895) as the principal of the Memorial College and governed there in a kindly fashion until his retirement in 1943.

He was the second to become dean of the Faculty of Theology of the University of Wales (1907-10) and in 1909 he went to Geneva to represent the faculty at the celebrations of the anniversary of the birth of Calvin. In 1920 he represented the Welsh Independents in the celebrations of the landing of the Pilgrim Fathers in Boston, U.S.A. He served on the education committee and on the county council of Brecknockshire, as a governor of secondary schools and in denominational and public circles. He was a county council alderman, 1930-48. He was Chairman of the Welsh Independents Union, 1936-37 and gave his address from the chair in 1937 in London on the relationship of the Old Testament to the New. He was chairman on two occasions of the South Wales Union of English Congregationalists.

He became pastor of the churches of Aber and Benaiah, Tal-y-bont on Usk in 1949. He d. in the manse of that pastorate on May 22, 1953, seven months before his brother 'Elfed'. He was buried in the town cemetery of Brecon in the presence of 'Elfed'. He had a deliberate, calm manner in the pulpit and in committee and he possessed wide and deep scholarship and his select library contained all the necessary source books. In his lectures he aided his students by purposeful repetition. He made a strong impression on all who attended his informal services in the college. Amongst all the teachers at Brecon College in his period he was the one who could best be described as a 'gentleman'.

He published *Llyfr y proffwyd Amos* (in the series *Llawlyfrau'r Ysgol Sul*, 1909), *Y Proffwydi a chrefydd yr Iddewon* (c. 1914 in the Old Testament series), *Llenyddiaeth a diwinyddiaeth y proffwydi* (1923) - according to Vernon Lewis, his best work, *Yr Hen Destament, ei gynnwys a'i genadwri* (1931), two translations of hymns and also articles in *The International Standard Bible Dictionary*, Hasting's *Dictionary of the Apostolic Church*, and *Geiriadur Beiblaidd*.

J. Vernon Lewis in *Athrawon ac Annibynwyr* (ed. Pennar Davies), 31-41; John Evans, *Dysg.*, 1937, 166-170; Arthur Jones, *Dysg.*, 1953, 188-190; *WwFC* (1951), 134-135; *Congl. year book*, 1954, 515; *Blwyddiadur A.*, 1954; *Coleg Coffa Reports* 1897-98, 1906-07, 1942-43, 1952-53; Information from R.N. Smart, Keeper of the Muniments, St. Andrews, W.E. Oxlade, Central Registry, University of London, S.H. Russell, Congregational College, Manchester; Emlyn G. Jenkins, *Cofiant Elfed* (1957); personal knowledge.

W.T.P.D.

LEWIS, Sir THOMAS (1881-1945), physician; b. 26 Dec. 1881, third of five children of Henry Lewis, mining engineer of Tŷ-nant, Taff's Well, near Cardiff, and his wife. He was educated privately at Clifton College; University College, Cardiff; University College Hospital, London, and became a student demonstrator in anatomy and physiology at Cardiff. He took an Hons. B.Sc. (Wales) in 1902, and qualified in medicine in 1904, gaining the University Medal and medals at the college and the D.Sc. (Wales) in 1905. He became assistant physician, and then consulting physician to University College Hospital, consultant in heart diseases to the War Office during World War I, and honorary physician to the Ministry of Pensions. He became F.R.C.P. in 1913, F.R.S. in 1918, giving the Croonian Lecture to the society in 1917, and was awarded its Royal Medal in 1927, the Copley Medal in 1941, the Conway Evans Prize in 1944, and was elected vice-president for 1943-45. He was appointed C.B.E. in 1920 and was knighted in 1921. He was offered (but declined) the chair of Regius Professor of Physic in Cambridge in 1932, and gave the Harveian Oration in 1933. He gained world-wide reputation as a physiologist and clinical scientist, and was awarded honorary degrees by the Universities of Wales, Liverpool, Sheffield, Birmingham and Michigan. He was a member or fellow of many foreign societies and universities. He became the first full-time clinical researcher for the Medical Research Committee (now Council) when the Department of Clinical Research was set up in 1916. A foremost research worker on the action of the human heart, he was one of the first to use the electrocardiograph. He was author of about 240 papers and 12 volumes on the heart, blood vessels and pain, books that saw many editions and were translated into a number of European languages. He edited *Heart* and founded and edited *Clinical Science*. He was a keen naturalist and bird photographer. He m. Lorna Treharne James of Merthyr Tydfil, 1916. They had three children, two girls and a boy. He d. at Rickmansworth, 17 March 1945 and was buried in the churchyard of Llangasty, Tal-y-llyn, Beckn.

Brit. Med. Jnl., 1945, 1, 461; full list of honours, books and papers in *Obit. Notices of F.R.S.*, 1945; [*Www*].

O.E.R.

LEWIS, THOMAS ARNOLD (1893-1952), insurance manager, treasurer of the Honourable Society of Cymmrodorion; b. 20 Apr. 1893, son of Captain Thomas Lewis and Elizabeth (née Jones) his wife, Manor Hall, Aberaeron, Cards. He was educated locally and at Ardwyn School, Aberystwyth, before joining an insurance firm, eventually becoming insurance manager of a branch of the Alliance Assurance Co. in the West End of London. He was a member of the Court of Assistants of the Worshipful Co. of Horners and received the freedom of the city of London. He served on the economic committee of the Road Research Fund and was an active member of the National Liberal Club, being the vice-president and a trustee at the time of his death. As a prominent figure in London-Welsh life he maintained an interest in Welsh matters, being elected vice-chairman of the Welsh Advisory Council of the National Trust, and High Sheriff of Cardiganshire in 1949. He assisted Sir John Cecil-Williams (see above) and Sir Wynn Wheldon (see below) with the financial aspect of the appeal launched in 1937 to publish the *Dictionary of Welsh Biography*, and he succeeded T.D. Slingsby-Jenkins (see below) as treasurer of the Honourable Society of Cymmrodorion in 1950.

On 8 Sept. 1924 he m. Eleanora Margaret Evans in Charing Cross Chapel, and they had two daughters. He d. at his home in Ealing on 24 Aug. 1952.

Personal knowledge.

Ma.E.C.

LEWIS, TIMOTHY (1877-1958), Welsh and Celtic scholar; b. 17 Feb. 1877, in a house called Noble Court near Nebo chapel in the village of Efail-wen, Cilymaenllwyd parish, on the border between Pembrokeshire and Carmarthenshire. He was the eldest son and third of seven children of Job and Mary Lewis. The father worked locally in Llwyn'rebol quarry but after the quarry owners failed to pay the workers for six weeks' work in 1880 he decided to go to the coalfield and he found work in a pit in Cwmaman, Aberdare. The family moved there a few years later and became members of Moriah Aman chapel (Congl.). The family was gifted: one son, Edward, became a school teacher in Cwmaman, an organist and conductor of the local 'Côr Mawr' [Cwmaman United Choir]; Daniel, another son, graduated at University College, Cardiff, and became minister of churches in the Clunderwen area, but d. aged 34; another son was Thomas John who graduated at University College, Bangor. He was a schoolteacher in Aberdare, and rose to be director of education for Aberdare. The poet, Alun Lewis (see above), was his son.

Most probably Timothy Lewis left school at the age of 13 and worked in the mines until he was 22. It is also likely that he had began preaching by then and set his mind on entering the ministry. In 1899 he was accepted as a probationary student at the Memorial College, Brecon, under whose sponsorship he had two years' preparatory education in an academy at Pontypridd until he entered University College, Cardiff, during autumn 1901. He graduated with honours in Welsh in 1904, and won the chief prize awarded to a student of Celtic during his second and third years. During the year 1904-05 he took a course for intending ministers at the Memorial College but he did not return to complete the course, presumably because neither the opportunity nor the encouragement was offered to him there to continue his study of Welsh.

In 1905 he won a scholarship worth £120 a year at Victoria University, Manchester, where he spent two years as a research student under Prof. John Strachan. He then obtained a scholarship to spend periods with Prof. Heinrich Zimmer at Berlin University and further periods in 1908-09 with Rudolf Thurneysen in Freiburg. Since Strachan had d. in Sept. 1907 Timothy Lewis was recalled from Berlin to prepare Strachan's book – *An introduction to early Welsh* – for publication by Manchester University Press. In the dispute and litigation between Strachan's trustees and J. Gwenogvryn Evans (*DWB*, 245-6) concerning the use, in the book, of Middle Welsh texts for which Gwenogvryn had the copyright, Timothy Lewis presented evidence on the facts of the case in favour of Gwenogvryn, and in consequence a warm and very close friendship developed between the young student and the latter. By Aug. 1908 the prospects for the future were dark, with his scholarship and savings depleted, but Evans and two 'anonymous' friends succeeded in raising sufficient funds to enable him to spend another semester with Thurneysen in Freiburg. No longer, he said, did he desire to return and prepare for the ministry, although he had been preaching in churches that had no minister during the intervals when he was not out of Wales, a practice he maintained till his last years. He was also a deacon of the Independent church in Baker Street, Aberystwyth, from 1914 till he retired in 1929.

Although he would have liked to have had a post in the newly established National Library at Aberystwyth, another opening came his way when he was appointed assistant lecturer in Welsh at the University College, Aberystwyth, under Sir Edward Anwyl (*DWB*, 12-13) in Jan. 1910. After Sir Edward d. in 1914, he collaborated with T. Gwynn Jones (see above) and T.H. Parry-Williams. He had obtained an M.A. degree of Victoria University, Manchester, in 1909 for his work on the Welsh of the laws of Hywel Dda; and in Sept. 1911 he m. Nellie Myfanwy (1885-1968), youngest daughter of Beriah Gwynfe Evans (*DWB*, 220-1) and they had two children, a son and a daughter.

At the end of 1915 he joined the army; he was called to the Royal Artillery in 1916, and fought near the Somme and Ypres in 1917 and 1918. He broke a bone in his arm on a raid and found himself by chance in the vicinity of the famous centre of learning in Peronne; he was discharged early in 1919. The following year was a difficult one for him. He had hoped to be appointed to the chair of Welsh at Aberystwyth, but during summer 1920 T.H. Parry-Williams was selected, which was a great disappointment to a man recently returned from the battlefield. However, he too was pro-

moted in his turn to a new post as reader in Celtic Palaeography, a position he held thereafter till he retired aged 65 in 1943. In 1924 he had hoped to be appointed to the Celtic Chair at Oxford but John Fraser (1882-1945) was chosen; after Fraser d. he desired to be appointed so as to secure a 'platform' for about five years from which to publish his theories since the University of Wales was not prepared to acknowledge them, but he was past the age of retirement by then. After retiring he continued to work on early Welsh literature – his favourite field – reading and collecting widely from out-of-the-way books and texts, especially from the works of scholars on the Continent. He planned a series '*Cyfres Hywel Dda*' in ten volumes but only two were published (by the author himself) namely *Beirdd a bardd-rin Cymru Fu* (1929) and *Mabinogi Cymru* (1931).

His early work on the vocabulary of the laws was highly commendable, but after gaining a foothold in the university he began to go his own way, particularly after the disappointment of not being appointed to the chair of Welsh. What made his perspective in much of his work unacceptable to scholars of Welsh of the University of Wales was that he was not satisfied with trying to explain the hypothetical philological derivation of words in the tradition of John Rhŷs (*DWB*, 844-5) and J. Morris-Jones (*DWB*, 668-9); but chose instead to search in the language itself, or in cognate or neighbouring languages for words which could have been borrowed into Welsh. Two of his central themes were that the characters of tales of the *Mabinogion* were not the old gods of the Celts but rather that the tales were stories about the plundering which had occurred along the coast of Wales in the ninth and tenth centuries by the Scandinavians; also that it was the stories of the Normans settling in Gwent and Glamorgan that constituted many of the tales of Arthur and the '*Coraniaid*'. In his volume *Beirdd a bardd-rin Cymru Fu* he tried to show that the analysis of J. Morris-Jones of the bardic system in his book *Cerdd dafod* was totally misleading since patterns for many of the Welsh metres and poetical terms are to be found in English and Medieval Latin. Some of his theses were mocked by some scholars and were totally ignored by others. However, many people wrote to him expressing their pleasure that he had defended 'Iolo Morganwg' (Edward Williams, 1747-1826; *DWB*, 1033-4) and the *Gorsedd* and that he was neither ashamed nor afraid of disagreeing with J. Morris-Jones and W.J. Gruffydd (see above). He corresponded regularly with many friends in the world of scholarship and particularly with Gwenogvryn Evans. The two families became close friends and in the 1920s Timothy Lewis took his family on many occasions to Gwenogvryn and his wife for a holiday.

He himself was an exceptionally charming man, as can be seen from the fact that he wrote to his father's aged sister at home in Cwmaman at least once a week for years. He could write interestingly on many topics and his mother-in-law wrote in a letter to him that he could have made an excellent newspaper correspondent. He d. 30 Dec. 1958 and was buried in Nebo graveyard in his home area of Efail-wen.

He published: *A glossary of mediaeval Welsh Law* (1913); *A Welsh leech book* (1914); *Beirdd a bardd-rin Cymru Fu* (1929); *Mabinogi Cymru* (1931), as well as a number of articles in *Aberystwyth Studies* and in periodicals such as *Wales*, *Y Wawr*, *Y Tyst*, *Y Ford Gron* and others. He also distributed studies under the title 'Aberystwyth Revisions' in duplicated typescripts.

Personal acquaintance; letters in the Timothy Lewis collection at N.L.W.; information from the family and from Principal Pennar Davies; [W. Beynon Davies in *N.L.W. Journal*, 21 (1979), 145-58].

W.B.D.

LEWIS, Sir WILFRID HUBERT POYER (1881-1950), judge; b. 9 Feb. 1881 in London, s. of Arthur Griffith Poyer Lewis, barrister-at-law, of Henllan, near Narberth, Pembs., and Annie Wilhelmine, his wife, and grandson of Richard Lewis, Bishop of Llandaff from 1883 to 1905. He was educated at Eton and University College, Oxford, where he graduated in history in 1903. He was called to the Bar by the Inner Temple in 1908 and served in the South Wales Circuit until 1914. Between 1914 and 1919 he served as an officer in the Army with the Glamorgan Yeomanry and was twice mentioned in despatches and awarded the O.B.E. After the war he settled in London, where he was eminently successful as a barrister. He specialised in ecclesiastical law and was chancellor of the dioceses of Llandaff, 1914-35, Monmouth, 1921-35, Manchester and Blackburn, 1929-35, and Worcester, 1930-35. In 1930, he became a junior counsel to the Treasury, and was in July 1935 appointed judge in the King's Bench division and knighted. On his first circuit in Wales he heard the case of the burning of the aerodrome in Llŷn at Caernarfon, when the jury failed to agree on a verdict. He served as J.P., chairman of Quarter Sessions, and Deputy Lieutenant of Pembrokeshire. He m. (1), in 1908, Margaret Annie (d. 1932), dau. of Sir John Eldon Bankes of Soughton Hall, Northop, Flints. (see above), and in 1934 (2), Elizabeth, dau. of Dr. David Barty King of London. He d. 15 Mar. 1950.

Times, 16 Mar. 1950; *Www*, 1941-50; *Concise D.N.B.*, 1941-50.

G.M.G.

LEWIS GLYN CYNON - see DAVIES, LEWIS above.

LEWIS TYMBL - see LEWIS, DAVID JOHN (1879-1947) above.

LLEWELYN, WILLIAM CRAVEN (1892-1966), colliery owner, companies director, agriculturalist and specialist in forestry; b. 4 June 1892 in Clydach, Swansea Valley, Glam., son of T. David Llewelyn. He m. Doris Mary Bell in 1932. There were no children of the marriage. He was educated at Arnold College, Swansea, and the Technical College, Swansea, and subsequently graduated at the University College of North Wales, Bangor. Initially he was particularly interested in a mining career and to this end studied mining privately under J. Henry Davies, but he then incorporated forestry and timber into his specialist studies and entered government service. In 1918-19 he was the Forest Statistical Officer in the Home-Grown Timber Department

of the Board of Trade. In this capacity he travelled extensively around the world, investigating timber regions in Central America, Central Europe and also Russia. In the immediate post-World War I period he reverted to his coal interests and engaged in colliery and timber undertakings. He widened his business activities to take in brick manufacturing, and also agricultural pursuits, and on the political side took a more active part in local Liberal Party affairs. He fought in two Parliamentary elections as Liberal candidate, in Chester in 1923 and Crewe in 1929. He was president of the Swansea Chamber of Commerce in 1944-45 and was appointed High Sheriff for Brecknockshire in the same year. Among his other public activities he was president of the Swansea Town Association Football Club and a member of the Farmers' Union of Wales. He compiled two important works in connection with forestry in Wales, *Afforestation of Wales* (1915) and *Forest soils of Wales* (1917). He d. 4 Jan. 1966.

Www.

D.G.R.

LLOYD, DAVID GEORGE (1912-69) , singer; b. at Trelogan, Fl., 6 Apr. 1912, son of Pryce (coalminer) and Elizabeth Lloyd. He left Trelogan school when he was 14 years old and was apprenticed to a carpenter at Diserth. He took an interest in singing when quite young, and he regularly competed at small *eisteddfodau* in Flintshire and the Vale of Clwyd. In an *eisteddfod* held at Licswm, 18 July 1931, when he won a competition for those who had never gained a first prize, John Williams, Bangor, the adjudicator, prophesied that he would have a brilliant future as a singer, and suggested that the people of Flintshire should help him obtain the musical education necessary to enable him to follow a career as a professional singer.

A number of local concerts were held to assist him, and he abandoned his trade in 1933 when he won a Sam Heilbut Scholarship to study at the Guildhall School of Music, London. There he studied under Walter Hyde and won some of the highest honours, including the Catherine Howard prize for tenors (1934), a gold medal of the school (1937), and a medal of the City of London Worshipful Company of Musicians (1938). During 1938-39 he came into considerable prominence when he sang Verdi and Mozart at Glyndebourne and when he was selected to sing some of the leading parts in music festivals in Sweden, Denmark and Belgium. In 1940 he sang Mozart at Sadlers Wells, and if the war had not upset his plans no doubt he would also have sung at La Scala Milan and in the Metropolitan Opera House in New York later that year.

During his period of military service (in the Welsh Guards, 1940-45), he was active broadcasting, recording and holding concerts throughout Britain, and because of his readiness at all times to sing Welsh items he won the ear and heart of his nation and was idolised in their homes. At the end of the war he sang in Verdi and Mozart festivals in the Netherlands (1946), and by 1954 he had had the honour of singing under the baton of some of the foremost conductors of his day. He also broadcast regularly for over a quarter of a century and some of the radio series in which he participated from Cardiff, such as 'Melys Lais', and 'Silver Chords', were extremely popular.

He had an accident in 1954 which seriously affected his distinguished career as a professional singer, and although he took to singing again in 1960 the quality of his voice had deteriorated after having spent long periods in hospital. In his prime he possessed a melodious voice, of a wonderful lyrical quality, and he paid particular attention to the words of the song he endeavoured to interpret. In England he won fame for his rendering of the works of Mozart, whereas in Wales he is remembered as a singer who immortalised popular Welsh songs and hymn-tunes.

A national testimonial of £1,800 was presented to him at a public meeting in Flintshire College of Technology, 25 Feb. 1961, and at Flint national *eisteddfod.*, 1969, a memorial fund was established bearing his name 'to offer practical assistance to some of our promising young people in the world of music'.

He d. unmarried in a hospital in Rhyl, 27 Mar. 1969, and was buried in Picton cemetery, near Gwesbyr.

Personal acquaintance; [see also Huw Williams, *David Lloyd (1912-1969): 'Llais a hudodd genedl'* (1985)].

H.W.

LLOYD, DAVID JOHN (1886-1951), headmaster; b. 6 Mar. 1886 son of Daniel and Jane Peregrine Lloyd, Swansea, Glam. He was educated at Swansea Grammar School, 1894-1904; University College, Cardiff, 1904-07, where he graduated in Classics; and Oriel College, Oxford, 1907-11, where he was an exhibitioner, gaining B.A. in 1911 and M.A. in 1914. From 1911-19 he was a teacher at Liverpool Collegiate School except for 1917-19 when he served with the R.N.A.S. and R.A.F. He was headmaster of the County School, Port Talbot, 1919-20, and Newport Secondary School, 1921-35. He moved to Wrexham in 1935 to be headmaster of Grove Park School, where he remained until his retirement in 1946 when he moved to Menai Bridge, Anglesey. He m. Olwen Beynon in 1914, and d. 2 Nov. 1951. They had 4 sons and a daughter.

During his headship at Grove Park School, where he succeeded J.R. Edwards, who was appointed headmaster at Liverpool Institute High School, he became very prominent in the field of education in Wales, and he was acknowledged to be an experienced and effective headmaster. He was a member of the Headmasters' Conference until the 1944 Education Act was passed, reducing the power of headmasters and school governing boards. He was also a member of the council of the Welsh Secondary Schools Association and the Headmasters' Association, which was of great benefit to the school. He was three times elected to represent the headmasters of secondary schools in Wales on the Burnham Committee. He was also associated with many good causes in the public life of the town of Wrexham.

Grove Park School was very successful during this period under the leadership of the learned and cultured headmaster who succeeded in winning the support of the governors and co-operation of his staff as well as the admira-

tion of his pupils. He sacrificed much to ensure that the school overcame the difficult problems which arose during World War II, particularly in the changes to school staff. There was a noticeable increase in the number of pupils in the Sixth Form, making Grove Park one of the schools with the largest Sixth Form in Wales. The headmaster took pride in the school's success both academically and on the playing field. Football was reintroduced into the curriculum in 1941 and the school cricket team won considerable fame in 1944 at the final match in the McAlpine cup competition. On the occasion of his retirement in 1946 the governors' tribute to him was entered in the school records.

Www; papers and records of Grove Park School at Wrexham Public Library and the Record Office, Ruthin; *The Wrexhamian*, 1935-46; *Wrexham Leader*, 1935-46; information from Mrs Anita M. Thomas, M.Ed., former teacher at Grove Park Grammar School for Girls, and E. Haddon Roberts, former headmaster of Grove Park Grammar School.

W.G.E.

LLOYD, ELIZABETH JANE - see JONES, ELIZABETH JANE LOUIS above.

LLOYD, HENRY ('Ap Hefin'; 1870-1946), poet and printer; b. 23 June 1870 in Tyddyn Ifan, Islaw'r Dref, Dolgellau, Mer., to David and Margaret Lloyd. He received some education in Arthog school, but more, he claimed, from the literary societies of the churches and the Good Templars. In 1878 he moved to Cwm Bwlchcoch, Dolgellau. After being an apprentice printer in the office of Y *Dydd*, he went to Aberdare in 1891 as a compositor in the office of Y *Darian*. In 1893, he moved to Merthyr, to the office of Y *Tyst*, and in 1902 returned to Aberdare, to the office of Y *Darian*, and the *Aberdare Leader*. Later, he established his own printing business where he remained until his retirement in 1940. He was editor of Y *Darian* for a while. He edited the poetry column of Y *Darian* for two years; he was a teacher of poets and an unfailing supporter of every Welsh and literary movement in his district, a local preacher (Wesleyan) for more than half a century, and a popular lecturer. He was an extremely able poet, and writer in the strict Welsh metres, and won the chair in many *eisteddfodau*, and hundreds of other prizes. He published 18 books – biographies, sermons, short stories, but chiefly of his own poetry. His *englyn*, 'Lliwiau'r Hydref', became famous, as did some of his hymns, such as 'Arhosaf yng nghysgod fy Nuw', and 'I bob un sy'n ffyddlon'. In 1896 he m. Sarah Ann Gravell, and they had 4 children. He d. on 14 Sept. 1946 in Aberdare.

Personal knowledge; [D. Jacob Davies, *Cyfoeth Cwm* (1965); *Cymro*, 23 April 1938; *Eurgrawn*, 1946, 36].

G.R.T.

LLOYD, ISAAC SAMUEL ('Glan Rhyddallt', 1875-1961); quarryman, poet and writer; b. 29 Jun. 1875 at Tŷ Newydd, Clegyr, Llanberis (the original name of the house was Penrallt), the son of William Lloyd and his wife Mary Hughes. He was educated at Llanberis elementary school, but he had little opportunity for further schooling because his mother died when he was only eight years old and he worked, from that time until he was sixty, in the slate quarries. He m. Margaret, daughter of John and Margaret Williams, in Llanrug Calvinistic Methodist chapel on 9 Nov. 1894 and they had two sons and two daughters. After his marriage, he endeavoured to improve his cultural background through wide reading and mastering *cynghanedd*. He wrote hundreds of *englynion* and verses. The rank of a bard was conferred on him at the Llanelli national *eisteddfod* of 1903 and he took the name of 'Glan Rhyddallt' in the *Gorsedd*. He was a weekly columnist with the *Herald Cymraeg* from 1931 until his death. Under the name of 'Mari Lewis', his daughter had begun her column a year before her father. He corresponded on a regular basis with Welsh Americans and he wrote an account of Goronwy Owen (*DWB*, 703), *Goronwy'r Alltud* (1947). He d. at Gallt y Sil Hospital, Caernarfon, on 7 July 1961 and he was buried in the graveyard at Llanrug Church on 11 July.

Information from his daughter, Mary Lloyd Williams.

E.D.J.

LLOYD, JOHN (1885-1964), schoolmaster, author and local historian; b. 11 July 1885 in Tŷ Gwyn y Gamlas, Ynys, Talsarnau, Mer., the seventh child of Evan Lloyd, farmer, and his wife Catrin (née Jones). He was educated at the board school Talsarnau; the intermediate school Barmouth; the grammar school Wigan (for a year only) and the University College of Wales, Aberystwyth (B.A., 1906 with second-class honours in Welsh; M.A., 1911). He was a teacher at his old school in Barmouth under Edmund D. Jones (see above) between 1907-19 and at the county school Tregaron, for the year 1919-20. In 1920 he was appointed a teacher at the grammar school Dolgellau, and headmaster in 1925, a post which he held until his retirement in Aug. 1946.

He is remembered as the co-translator with T.P. Ellis (*DWB*, 214-5) of *The Mabinogion* (1929) in two volumes. This was the second complete translation of the Mabinogion into English since Lady Charlotte Guest's (*DWB*, 322) version in 1838-49). Their translation was critically reviewed at the time by scholars such as W.J. Gruffydd (see above) and J. Lloyd-Jones (see below) but nevertheless it remained a useful work until the appearance in 1948 of a new translation by Gwyn Jones and Thomas Jones. He also published two school textbooks in Welsh entitled: *Detholiad o draethodau llenyddol Dr. Lewis Edwards* (1910) and *Llyfr Darllen ac ysgrifennu* (1913; a prize-winner at the national *eisteddfod* in Wrexham, 1912), as well as a textbook in Welsh for the use of Sunday schools, *Yr Eglwys Apostolaidd: Cenhadon cyntaf Crist* (1922). He supervized a number of editions of *The official guide to the Deudraeth rural district*. He took a special interest in local history and contributed between 1949-58 a number of articles on his beloved Ardudwy to the *Jnl. of the Mer. Hist. and Record Soc*. He also contributed to *Y Bywgraffiadur Cymreig 1941-50* (*DWB*). He lectured widely to local W.E.A. classes and occasinally, after his retirement, at Coleg Harlech. He was a dedicated headmaster and a painstaking researcher in all he undertook. He also served on many different committees and cultural bodies in Merioneth including the educa-

tion committee, the *Eisteddfod* Meirion committee and the county's *Urdd Gobaith Cymru* committee. He was amongst the founders of the county's Hist. and Record Soc. in 1939 and was made a vice-president. He was an elder in the Presb. Ch. of Wales consecutively at Talsarnau, Dolgellau and Llanbedr.

He m. 1925 Nancy Roden, Aberystwyth (d. 1980), and one dau. was born to them. He d. in Dolgellau 17 Jan. 1964 and was buried in St. Mihangel's churchyard, Llanfihangel-y-traethau.

Information given by his widow and members of his family; *Cymm.*, 40 (1929), 251-64; *West Mail*, 20, 24 June 1929; *Z/M/655/8-9* in Merioneth Record Office; *Liv. D.P.*, 20 Jan. 1964; *Camb. News*, 24 Jan. 1964; *Dydd*, 24 Jan. 1964; *Taliesin*, Dec. 1975, 75-85; *NLW Jn.*, 23, 434-8.

A.Ll.H.

LLOYD, Sir JOHN CONWAY (1878-1954), public figure; b. 18 Apr. 1878, in Dinas Mansion, Brecks., the only son of Thomas Conway Lloyd and his wife Katherine Eliza Campbell-Davys of Neuadd-Fawr, near Llandovery. His mother died when he was only four years old and he lost his father in 1893. He was educated at Broadstairs School, Eton, and Christ Church, Oxford. On a journey to the continent in 1899, he met Marion Clive Jenkins at Florence and m. her at Farnborough on 17 Feb. 1903. They had three sons and two daughters. In the autumn of 1903, they settled at his old home, Dinas, and he began to take part in the public life of Brecknockshire. He was a J.P. from 1900 and chairman of the Quarter Sessions in 1934; a member of Brecon Town Council from 1909; and a member of the County Council from 1913. He was made sheriff of Breconshire in 1906 and he was knighted in 1938. He began to take an interest in the militia during 1909. He was promoted to the rank of captain in the 3rd Regiment of the South Wales Borderers in April 1914 and he went, at the beginning of 1915, to France. He was wounded in May and was awarded the Military Cross. In 1919, he was appointed deputy provost marshal, with the rank of colonel, in the Army on the Rhine. Within a short time, he was able to resume life at Dinas, but he had to leave when the house was requisitioned by the Army in 1941 and he moved to Abercynrig.

He represented the County Council on several public bodies, e.g. the courts of the National Museum and the university colleges in Aberystwyth and Cardiff. He was a member of several committees and he was appointed chairman of the county Education Committee in 1950. He worked hard in 1936 to persuade the government to classify the A40 road as a trunk road. In 1946, he sought, without success, to maintain the separate identity of the Brecknock Constabulary; when it had been united with the Montgomeryshire and the Radnorshire constabularies, Lloyd became chairman of the new body until 1953. During World War II, he was a conscientious controller of the Air Raid Precautions (A.R.P.) in his county. Despite his English education, he developed a considerable interest in the history of his county and he tried to form an antiquarian society in 1924. At the time, he failed to obtain sufficient support and, in its place, a museum was established. When the funds proved insufficient to convert the English Congregational chapel in order to display the exhibits, he persuaded Lord Buckland (see above, under Berry Family) to donate £300 for the completion of the work as well as an annual donation for 7 years to help with the running costs. Lloyd was made secretary of the Museum and he obtained many items for the collection. He established the campaign to restore the historic buildings at Tretower. In 1952, he prevailed upon the County Council to raise a more worthy monument to Llywelyn ap Gruffudd (*DWB*, 597) at Cefn-y-bedd than the one raised fifty years previously by S.P.M. Bligh (see above), but he did not live to see the unveiling of the monument in 1956.

He d. 30 May 1954; his remains were cremated and the ashes were buried in the grave, at Mailleraye-sur-Seine, of his youngest son, John Richard, who lost his life when his aeroplane was shot down near Rouen on 22 June 1940. He lost his eldest son, Thomas Clive Conway, on board the *Thetis* on 2 June 1939, shortly before the outbreak of the war.

Brycheiniog, 1 (1955), 7-8; 4 (1958), 1-52.

E.D.J.

LLOYD, Sir JOHN EDWARD (1861-1947), historian, and first editor of *Y Bywgraffiadur Cymreig*; b. 5 May 1861 in Liverpool, s. of Edward Lloyd, J.P., and Mary Lloyd (née Jones). The family's ancestral home was Penygarnedd, near Pen-y-bont-fawr in Mont., and J.E. Lloyd never lost his feeling for this background nor his affection for the area. He was, at first, intended for the Congregationalist ministry, and for a considerable time he was a lay preacher in the denomination. It was natural that he should take a prominent part in the Historical Society of the Welsh Congregationalists when it was founded; and it was very natural too - and to him a subject of immense pride - that he should be elevated Chairman of the Union of Welsh Independents for 1934-35.

He went to college at Aberystwyth, and from there in 1881 to Lincoln College, Oxford. In 1883 he succeeded in obtaining a First in Honours Classical Moderations, and in 1885 he was placed in the First Class in the final examination in History. His career at Oxford was, thus, nearing its completion before the time of the famous group of Oxford Welshmen (like Owen M. Edwards (*DWB*, 192-3) who went up in Oct. 1884), and it was over before the Dafydd ap Gwilym Society was established in 1886; but of course, he very quickly associated himself with their aspirations. Indeed, in a sense he had anticipated them, for already in 1884, when he was only halfway through his degree course, had won the prize, at the Liverpool national *eisteddfod*, for a handbook on the history of Wales to 1282, an essay which was published in the *Transactions* of that *eisteddfod*.

He returned to Aberystwyth in 1885 as lecturer in Welsh and History. He remained there until 1892, and it was there, in 1889, that he prepared for the press *The Ancient Laws of Wales*, a volume written by Hubert Lewis (who had died in 1884; *DWB*, 554). But in 1892 Lloyd moved to Bangor as the registrar of the University College of North Wales and assistant to Principal Reichel in the department of History. Later on he used to describe humorously (but hardly strictly correctly) how he divided his workday at that time 'lecturer in the morning, registrar in the afternoon, and researcher in the evening'. He was an exact and organized registrar; he was remarkably prudent and patient, and as his experience grew he became an exceedingly useful committee member; there was none better at wording a resolution or an official document. He was thereafter a member of all kinds of committees in Wales (until the deafness of his later years affected his ability to respond in discussion). He was particularly useful when the University of Wales was reorganized in 1919; it was he, for instance, who drew up the constitution of its Board of Celtic Studies, and he served as its chairman until 1940. He was prominent in the activities of the Cambrian Archaeological Association and was twice its President. Reference has already been made to his prominence in the conferences of his denomination. And on no account should his service to the Society for the Utilization of the Welsh language be forgotten; he used to lecture in its summer schools for teachers and he wrote for it bilingual textbooks on Welsh history. He also played a part in the National *Eisteddfod* Association.

He continued as registrar of the college at Bangor until 1919, but he had already succeeded Reichel in the chair of History in 1899. This was the beginning of the most productive period of his career, the period that raised him to his true fame. He wrote regularly to the academic journals on topics in the history of Wales. In 1911 he produced his great standard work, *A History of Wales to the Edwardian Conquest*, which reached its third edition in 1939. It is no exaggeration to claim that this book was a turning-point in the study of Welsh history; it was the fruit of a thorough assessment of the sources, and a clear and readable exposition of the course of the history of the Age of the Princes. A few details were corrected by him (mainly in the *Bulletin* of the Board of Celtic Studies) and by other researchers, but the body of the work remains authoritative to this day. It brought him the degree of D. Litt., Oxford, 1918. In 1930 he was elected a Fellow of the British Academy (F.B.A.), and it was to that body that he delivered his Sir John Rhŷs Lecture on *The Welsh Chronicles*, which was published in 1930 - a notable example of the nature of its author's mind.

Almost to the end, Lloyd restricted himself, in his published work, to the period on which he had begun writing as far back as 1884. But he was persuaded to move to a later period when he was elected Oxford Ford Lecturer in 1931. He chose as his subject the history of Owain Glyn Dŵr (*DWB*, 691-2), and the work was published under the title *Owen Glendower* (the title was chosen by the press) in 1931. Once again the author's characteristics can be seen - the detailed scrutiny of sources and the clear narrative of the history of Owain's career. In 1930 he wrote a little book on the whole range of Welsh history in Benn's series, a Welsh version of which was published by Aberystwyth Press in 1943 under the title *Golwg ar hanes Cymru*. It would be a great mistake to assume that Lloyd was not truly well-versed in the history of his country after 1415. One need only glance at the collection of notes kept in the library of the University of Wales, Bangor, to see how extensive was his interest in the later periods, as was his knowledge of details (often very obscure). This information, the fruits of what he called 'pottering', was always available to inquirers both within the college and outside. Indeed, he had long grown to be the oracle, as it were, on the whole history of Wales; and to him everyone turned for advice and guidance in this field. He was, thus, the inevitable choice as editor of *The History of Carmarthenshire* in 1935. And when the Honourable Society of Cymmrodorion decided in 1937 to undertake the preparation and publication of *Y Bywgraffiadur Cymreig* he was invited to be editor and it was he who brought the project to the notice of the nation in a public meeting in Cardiff in 1938. It was rightly held that his name and reputation would guarantee the standard of the work.

He had extensive experience of this kind of work as he had contributed from 1893 to 1912 some 120 essays on famous Welshmen to the *Dictionary of National Biography*. He began his new task immediately: selecting names to be included and authors to write the essays, and he himself wrote over 60 essays under the first letters of the alphabet. But war broke out; the arrangements were postponed; and when it became safe to take up the task again in 1943, he felt that he could not now be involved with the correspondence and proof-reading and he chose to be called the Consultative Editor. But the consultation was by no means in name only, for he met weekly for some time after with his successor to review the progress of the work and to make valuable suggestions; and of course the work continued by his two successors, as far as possible, along the lines which he himself had drawn up.

But his health was now deteriorating, and he died on 20 June 1947. He was buried in the old cemetery at Llandysilio, on the island opposite Menai Bridge. He had been awarded many honours: knighted in 1934; honorary degree of D. Litt. of the Universities of Wales (1922) and of Manchester, and the freedom of the city of Bangor in 1941. He had a strong constitution and pleasant features: his stance was dignified when he addressed an audience, his voice clear and his language, whether in English or in Welsh, correct and formal, and he was always neatly dressed. He had been brought up in the heyday of the Victorian age and there is no doubt that the ideals of that age formed (or coloured) to a large extent his public conduct and his style of writing. He never sought to be 'popular', either on a platform or on paper. Consequently he was considered by some to be a 'distant' and formal person – and certainly he was not one with whom people dared to be overfamiliar. But in more intimate circles he was free, not infrequently humorous. Nevertheless, his dignity and refinement were always to the fore.

He married Clementina Miller of Aberdeen, a former pupil of his at Aberystwyth, in 1893; she died in 1951. They were survived by a daughter and a son.

J. Goronwy Edwards in *Proceedings of the British Academy*, 1955, and also *D.N.B. 1941-50*; Thomas

Richards, *Y Llenor*, October 1947; information from his daughter, Mrs Eluned Garmon Jones; personal knowledge. A long, but incomplete, list of Sir John's writings on very diverse subjects, not historical only, is in the *B.B.C.S.*, May 1948, 96-105.

R.T.J.

LLOYD, JOHN MORGAN (1880-1960), musician; b. 19 Aug. 1880, at Pentre, Rhondda, Glam., of a musical and religious family. His father, John Lloyd (an outfitter, who lived at Glan-y-don, Barry, and d. 1910) was of Montgomeryshire stock and was one of the chief founders of Penuel Welsh church (Presb.), Barry. His mother was a native of Treforest, grandchild of Benjamin Williams, minister of Saron, Pontypridd, and she was the first organist at Saron chapel, Treforest. Early in 1889 the family moved from Pentre to live in Barry and the musician spent the rest of his life there. He showed a leaning towards music very early in life and played the organ in Penuel, Barry, when he was 9 years old. He was educated at Lewis' School, Pengam, and received lessons in music from J.E.Rees, Barry. After leaving school he went to work for a short while in his father's shop but his heart was not in his work. Whilst still a school pupil he was chosen to be accompanist for Barry District Glee Society and in 1900 he was accompanist for the Royal Welsh Choir at the Paris Exhibition. He sat the first Oxford music examinations and having attracted the attention of David Evans (1874-1948; see above) he decided to study music with him at the University College in Cardiff, entering as a student in Jan. 1904.

After completing his course he became organist of Trinity church (English Presb.), Barry, for ten years, and from there he moved to Cathedral Road Church, Cardiff. In 1915 he joined the army, and was appointed a chaplain; he suffered bitter experiences at Vimy Ridge, Oppy Wood and Cambrai. In 1920 he was appointed lecturer at the University College, Cardiff, and later professor (as successor to David Evans (1874-1948; see above), a post he held till he retired in 1945. He had graduated in music at Trinity College, Dublin, in 1921, and gained his D.Mus. degree there in 1928. He d. at his home in Barry, 30 June 1960, and was buried in Merthyr Dyfan cemetery.

He did not write much music, but he composed a few short pieces such as the solos 'Dilys' and 'Alwen hoff', the madrigal 'Wele gawell baban glân', and part-song (SSA) 'Llyn y Fan', which are excellent examples of his style. His 'Arthur yn cyfodi' was performed during the Three Valleys Festival, 1936 and his 'Te Deum' for choir and orchestra was performed under his baton at Cardiff national *eisteddfod*, 1938.

He excelled as a teacher, and several leading composers, Grace Williams and Alun Hoddinott among them, were among his students.

Cerddor, Feb. 1919; *Trys. Plant*, Nov. 1939; *Who's who in Music*; *West. Mail*, 2 July 1960; *Y Drys.*, Sept. and Nov. 1960; information from the Registrar of University College, Cardiff.

H.W.

LLOYD, ROBERT ('Llwyd o'r Bryn'; 1888-1961), *eisteddfodwr*, entertainer and farmer; b. in

Penybryn, Bethel, Llandderfel, Mer., 29 Feb. 1888, the youngest son of John and Winifred Lloyd. He was baptized by Michael Daniel Jones (*DWB*, 495). He was educated at Sarnau school and after working for a period with his father on the farm, he m. in 1913 Annie Williams, Derwgoed, Llandderfel. Thereafter he farmed Derwgoed until he retired in 1944. In this connection, he was one of the first in Wales to stimulate interest in the experimental immunisation of cattle against tuberculosis (see Richard Phillips, *Pob un a'i gŵys* (1970), 86).

Throughout most of his life he acted as compère and adjudicator at countless *eisteddfodau* in north and mid-Wales; he was one of the promoters of the first national *eisteddfod* held by *Urdd Gobaith Cymru* at Corwen in 1929. Between 1938 and 1950 he was the witty compère of Parti Tai'rfelin (see Robert Roberts below), a group which held concerts in all parts of Wales and for Welsh societies in England. He also frequently took part in radio and television programmes.

He had the true story-teller's gift of narrating or writing a tale. This is evident in his autobiography *Y Pethe* (1955), the title of which later came to stand for the values and traditions that are associated with Welsh life at its best. In 1966 a volume of his letters was published, *Diddordebau*, which was edited by his nephew Trebor Lloyd Evans, and a collection of his articles for *Welsh Farm News* and other periodicals were published in *Adlodd Llwyd o'r Bryn* by his daughter, Dwysan Rowlands, in 1983. After retiring he visited many places to give lectures on country life and culture. There are descriptions of him by Robin Williams in *Y tri Bob* (1970) and in *Portreadau'r Faner* (n.d.). He d. 28 Dec. 1961 and was buried in Cefnddwysarn cemetery. In 1963 a 'Llwyd o'r Bryn prize' for recitation was established at the National *Eisteddfod* in memory of him.

Information from Dwysan Rowlands; personal knowledge.

D.T.Ll.

LLOYD, THOMAS ALWYN (1881-1960), architect and town planner; b. 11 Aug. 1881 in Liverpool, the son of Thomas and Elizabeth Jones Lloyd. The family came from a strong nonconformist tradition in Denbighshire, and Lloyd inherited a deep love for rural Wales and for Welsh culture. He was educated at Liverpool College and at the University of Liverpool where he studied architecture in the university's Architecture School. From 1907 to 1912, he was an assistant to Sir Raymond Unwin in the Hampstead Garden Suburb. He was appointed, in 1913, the consulting architect to the Welsh Town Planning and Housing Trust and he designed a number of new villages in England and Wales, e.g. in Fishguard, Llanidloes, Menai Bridge and Llangefni as well as St. Francis Church in Barry, St. Margaret, Wrexham, the Students' Union, Cardiff, and housing for the Forestry Commission and Coal Board. He was one of the founders of the Town Planning Institute in 1914. He entered into partnership with Alex J. Gordon in 1948. He became a member of the Cambrian Archaeological Association in 1919 and he was chairman of its general committee 1951-54 and President in 1958-59. With his wife, Ethel Roberts, M.A. (they m. in 1914),

he attended the Association's annual meetings, regularly. He was one of the founders of the Council for the Protection of Rural Wales in 1929 and served as chairman from 1947 to 1959. He was president of the South Wales Institute of Architects, 1929-31, and president of the National Housing and Town Planning Council, 1933-35. He served on the Minister of Health's Advisory Committee on Town and Country Planning, 1933-40; on Lord Reith's Consultative Panel on Reconstruction, 1941-42; on the Central Advisory Committee on Education (Wales), 1945-48; on the Royal Commission on Ancient Monuments (Wales), 1949-60; and, on the Postmaster General's Welsh Stamp Committee, 1957-58.

He published a number of books, *Planning in town and country* (1935); *Brighter Welsh villages and how we can achieve them* (1931); and, with Herbert Jackson, *South Wales outline plan* (1947), as well as a number of articles.

He was a J.P. and chairman of the Discharge of Prisoners Aid Society in Cardiff. He was awarded an hon. LL.D. by the University of Wales in 1950; elected F.S.A. in 1953; and appointed O.B.E. in 1958. His home was at Hafod Lwyd, Heol-wen, Rhiwbina, Glam., but he d. on his holidays at Torquay on 19 June 1960.

WwW (1937); *Www*; *Arch. Camb.*, 1960.

E.D.J.

LLOYD, WILLIAM (1901-67), tutor and setter of words to *cerdd dant* and composer of harp airs; b. 14 Feb. 1901 in Llansannan, Denbs., son of Richard Lloyd and Margaret his wife. The family moved to Glan Conwy when he was very young, and he was brought up there. He came to be known as William Lloyd, Cyffordd Llandudno, since he spent most of his life at Llandudno Junction working as a fireman on the railway and later as a train driver. His musical talent was fostered from an early age by Edwin Evans in Salem Chapel, Ffordd Las, and his interest was further developed under the influence of the Rev. D.H. Rees. In time, he gained the grade of A.T.S.C. He soon began to conduct choirs and local parties, and also the railway choir which competed many times in the national railway festivals in Birmingham. In the 1940s he and his colleague, Huw Hughes, began to take a serious interest in the old art of singing to the accompaniment of the harp and began setting verses to suitable airs for *penillion* singing. They both tutored and set verses for many singers. William Lloyd had duettists and parties in the districts of Eglwysbach and Llandudno Junction, and out of the *cerdd dant* party which he formed in 1962 Côr Meibion Maelgwn developed. In 1953 he won a competition in the national *eisteddfod* at Rhyl for composing a series of airs suitable for *penillion* singing. Realising the need for such airs, he proceeded to compose and publish a number of airs which became very popular, including 'Rhoshelyg' and 'Mwynen Eirian'. He adjudicated many times in the National *Eisteddfod*, and his artistic presentation of his musical compositions was a source of admiration for many. He m. Olive Lewis in Sept. 1929, and d. 20 Oct. 1967.

Personal knowledge and research.

A.Ll.D.

LLOYD GEORGE (FAMILY) The family was established by the marriage of David Lloyd George (see below) and Margaret Owen, 24 Jan. 1888. MARGARET OWEN was b. 4 Nov. 1864. She was made Dame Grand Cross of the British Empire in 1918. She d. 20 Jan. 1941. She came of a family rooted in the rural life and Methodist nonconformity of Eifionydd. Her father, Richard Owen, was a well-to-do farmer who acted from time to time as a valuer. He was also an elder of Capel Mawr (CM), Cricieth; a disagreement arose between the members which was settled when the minister, John Owen, and about half the membership, including Richard Owen, left Capel Mawr to establish Seion (CM) in Cricieth. Margaret was educated at Dr. Williams' School, Dolgellau; she was a faithful member of Seion chapel, Cricieth, throughout her life. She remained faithful also to those values which she was taught to respect in her nonconformist upbringing. Before their marriage D.Ll.G. and Margaret had a courtship which cut across denominational and social boundaries, and the story is now well known through books on the career of D.Ll.G. Bryn Awelon, Cricieth, was the family home between 1908, when it was built, and 1941 when Dame Margaret died. Because of D.Ll.G.'s political career the family also had before 1908 and thereafter until his death in 1945, several homes at different times in London and its environs. Dame Margaret's particular contribution was keeping the unity of the family under difficult circumstances and seeing that Welsh was the mother tongue of all five children.

1. RICHARD LLOYD GEORGE (1889-1968), 2nd Earl Lloyd-George of Dwyfor, the earldom created in 1945 a few weeks before the death of the 1st earl, David Lloyd George on 26 Mar. 1945. Richard was educated at Porthmadog secondary school and the University of Cambridge. He was an Associate Member of the Inst. of Civil Engineers; he was a major, Royal Engineers, in the two World Wars. He m. (1), 1917, Roberta Ida Freeman, dau. of Sir Robert McAlpine, 1st bart. They had one s. Owen, 3rd Earl Lloyd-George of Dwyfor (b. 1925) and one d. Valerie, Lady Goronwy Daniel. The marriage was annulled, 1933. He m. (2), 1935, Winifred Calve. He d. 1 May 1968, after a long illness.

He published, in 1947, *Dame Margaret - the life story of my mother*, a warm-hearted tribute to the memory of his mother, and in 1960, *Lloyd George*.

2. MAIR ELUNED LLOYD GEORGE (1890-1907). It is said that Mair Eluned was her father's most cherished child; he almost broke his heart when she died, 29 Nov. 1907, following an operation for appendicitis. She was a beautiful and talented girl, especially so in music; she used to entertain her parents by playing the piano and her father could not be reconciled to the fact that 'the white hand was under a crust of earth'. A beautiful marble statue of her by W. Goscombe John (see above) was placed over her grave in Cricieth cemetery.

3. OLWEN ELIZABETH (Lady Olwen Carey Evans; 1892-1990).

4. GWILYM LLOYD GEORGE (1894-1967), 1st Viscount Tenby, cr. 1957; privy councillor, 1941, J.P.; b. 4 Dec. 1894; educated at Eastbourne College and Jesus College, Cambridge (hon. Fellow, 1953); major Royal Artillery in 1914-18 war, M.P. (L) (1) 1922-24, (2) 1929-50, both terms for Pembs., (3) 1951-57 for Newcastle-upon-Tyne North (Nat. L. and Cons.). He held the following government posts: parliamentary sec. to the Board of Trade 1931 and 1939-41; Ministry of Food, 1941, Minister of Fuel and Power, 1942-45, Minister of Food, 1951-54 (Oct.), Sec. of State for Home Affairs and Minister for Welsh Affairs 1954 (Oct.) - 1957 (Jan.). He was cr. Viscount Tenby in the New Year's Hons. List, 1957. He was appointed chairman of the Council of Tribunals, 1961. He m., 1921, Edna Gwenfron, dau. of David Jones, Gwynfa, Denbigh; they had 2 s., and David, b. 4 Nov. 1922, became the 2nd Viscount Tenby.

During his term as Sec. of State for Home Affairs and Minister for Welsh Affairs he publicly announced on behalf of the Government that Cardiff was to be capital of Wales; he was made freeman of the city; the degree of LL.D. *honoris causa* of the University of Wales was conferred upon him. He was the first chairman of the Pantyfedwen Trust. He d. 14 Feb. 1967 and was buried in Cricieth public cemetery.

5. MEGAN ARFON LLOYD GEORGE (1902-66), youngest d. of D.Ll.G. and Margaret, his wife; b. 22 Apr. 1902. She was educated at Garrett's Hall, Banstead, and in Paris. She was elected M.P. for Anglesey (as a Liberal), 1929-31, and as Ind. Lib. 1931-45. At the General Election of 1951 she was defeated by Cledwyn Hughes (L). Between 1951 and 1957 she moved nearer the left in politics and joined the Labour Party. She was adopted as Lab. candidate for the Carmarthen constituency and was returned M.P. (Lab.) for that constituency in 1957. She held the seat until her death on 14 May 1966. She was buried in Cricieth cemetery in the family vault made when her sister Mair Eluned died. Her popularity and the respect for her was shown by the immense crowd which came to the cemetery on the day of her funeral, among them Gwynfor Evans who won the Carmarthen seat for *Plaid Cymru* at the by-election caused by her death.

On 1 July 1955 a conference of all parties and organisations was called under the auspices of the New Wales Union (*Undeb Cymru Fydd*) at Llandrindod to consider organizing a national petition for the campaign for a parliament for Wales; T.I. Ellis (see above), s. of T.E. Ellis (*DWB*, 214) and Ifan ab Owen Edwards (see above) were on the platform to support the campaign, and in proposing a resolution for the establishment of a committee to promote the petition and the campaign, M.Ll.G. referred to this and said that the three of them were three branches of 'old oaktrees which had their roots deep in the soil of Wales'. She was appointed to be president of the committee which was established to arrange the petition; she addressed many meetings throughout Wales. Her name and the fact that she had inherited much of her father's gift of oratory ensured large audiences for these meetings, and through her leadership she was responsible for removing much prejudice against the idea of a parliament for Wales. She was a member of the deputation which presented the petition with a quarter of a million signatures to the government in Apr. 1956. She was an active and conscientious M.P. on behalf of her constituents; but it is ironic that it was during the time that she was not an M.P. that she made her most substantial contribution to the politics of her time in Wales.

She was a member of Cricieth town council for many years, following her mother's example in this, and was chairman for a year; a J.P. like her mother before her, she also inherited much of her mother's love of the garden at Bryn Awelon, Cricieth, which she inherited after her mother's death. She was awarded the degree of LL.D. *honoris causa* by the University of Wales. She was unmarried but after her father received the earldom on 1 Jan. 1945, she became known as Lady Megan Lloyd-George; she was also made a C.H. shortly before her death. She was also a member of the *Gorsedd* of Bards; and for a time she was an active president of the Society for the Preservation of Rural Wales.

Www; the late Lady Olwen Carey Evans; and for information about the campaign for a 'Parliament for Wales', Elwyn Roberts, Bodorgan, Anglesey; personal knowledge; [Emyr Price, *Megan Lloyd George* (1983); Mervyn Jones, *A radical life: the biography of Megan Lloyd George* (1991)].

W.R.P.G.

LLOYD GEORGE, DAVID (1863-1945), the first Earl Lloyd-George of Dwyfor, statesman; b. 5, New York Place, Manchester, 17 Jan. 1863, s. of William George, Tre-coed, Pembs., and Elizabeth dau. of David Lloyd of Llanystumdwy, Caerns. On his father's death in Pembrokeshire in 1864 his mother moved with her chidlren to Llanystumdwy, to live with her brother, Richard Lloyd (1834-1917; *DWB*, 587). Lloyd George was educated at the Llanystumdwy National School and passed the Preliminary Law Examination in 1877, taking his final with honours in 1884. Beginning practice as a solicitor in Cricieth in 1885 he gained a reputation as a fearless advocate and eloquent speaker, and came into prominence in 1888 as solicitor for the defence in what became known as the Llanfrothen Burial Case, an action which he won on appeal. In Nov. 1888, he was adopted prospective Liberal candidate for the Caern. Boroughs; he was returned by a majority of 18, at the general election, 1890 (10 Apr.), taking his seat on 17 Apr. and making his maiden speech on 13 June. During his first period in Parliament his interests were mainly Welsh, especially disestablishment and land reform, and in 1894 he led a revolt of four Welsh members (himself, D.A. Thomas (*DWB*, 942), J. Herbert Lewis (*DWB*, 556) and Francis Edwards (*DWB*, 186)) against the Rosebery Government because of its attitude on Welsh disestablishment. In Wales during the same period he campaigned for the *Cymru Fydd* movement and for the amalgamation of the two Liberal Federations, north and south.

He opposed and criticised the conduct of the South African War (1899-1902) in Parliament and in the country; attempting to address a Liberal meeting in Birmingham in Dec. 1901, he was threatened by the mob and his life was in danger. He went through a period of great unpopularity, but was again returned in the 1900 election with an increased majority. Upon the introduction of Balfour's Education Bill in 1902 Lloyd George became the leader of the Radical and Nonconformist opposition to the measure, and in Wales he initiated the policy according to which the county councils refused

to administer the Act. When the Liberals came into power in 1905 he became President of the Board of Trade with a seat in the Cabinet, showing exceptional administrative ability with constructive talent and a gift for mediation in industrial disputes. In Oct. and Nov. 1907, he succeeded in averting a stoppage on the railways. Amongst the important measures for which he was responsible at the Board of Trade were the Merchant Shipping Act, 1906; the Patents and Designs (Amendment) Act, 1907; and the Port of London Act, 1908.

In Apr. 1908, when H.H. Asquith became Prime Minister, Lloyd George succeeded him as Chancellor of the Exchequer, and piloted through the House of Commons the Old Age Pensions Bill already introduced by Asquith. In 1909 he introduced his first Budget, designed to finance measures of social reform, and described as the most controversial budget of modern times. Its rejection by the Lords led to the passing of the Parliament Act in 1911. In Aug. 1910, Lloyd George made an unsuccessful attempt to form a coalition of Liberals and Conservatives. On 4 May 1911, he introduced a National Insurance Bill, which included both health and unemployment insurance and which received the Royal Assent in Dec. of the same year. In the 1911 Budget payment of members of Parliament was introduced. In a speech at the Mansion House on 21 July in that year Lloyd George warned Germany that Britain would not tolerate aggression in Morocco, a speech for which the Kaiser demanded his dismissal. On 29 June 1912, he launched his campaign for land reform, which included the setting up of a Land Enquiry Committee. In the same year a Select Committee of the House of Commons was set up to investigate allegations made respecting certain Ministers, including Lloyd George, in connection with share holdings in the American Marconi Co. All the persons involved were acquitted of acting otherwise than in good faith.

When war with Germany was declared in Aug. 1914, Lloyd George as Chancellor of the Exchequer had the task of stabilising the country's finances in difficult circumstances. In May 1915, on the formation of the first Coalition Government, he became Minister of Munitions. On the death of Lord Kitchener, Secretary for War, in May 1916, Lloyd George was appointed his successor. In Dec. 1916 Asquith resigned and Lloyd George became Prime Minister. One of the most important acts of his Premiership during the war years was the establishment of unity of command of the allied forces. In 1918, after the Armistice, he appealed to the country and was returned to power as head of the Coalition Govt. with a majority of 345 over all other parties. On 18 Jan. 1919, the Peace Conference opened, with Lloyd George as one of its three most prominent figures. In Dec. 1921 he succeeded in carrying the Irish Treaty through after prolonged negotiations. In Oct. 1922 the Conservative members of the Coalition Government resigned which made it impossible to carry on the Coalition, and Lloyd George resigned. Although he remained politically active for some years, he never again held office. In 1926 he set in train the Liberal Industrial Enquiry. In Jan. 1934, in a speech at Bangor, he outlined his programme for re-establishing national prosperity – the 'New Deal' policy – to be carried out by the Council of Action. From 1933 to 1936 he wrote his *War Memoirs*: his *The truth about the peace treaties* was published in 1938. In Aug. 1936, he visited Germany and met Hitler. When war came in 1939 he took no part in its direction but remained a member of the House of Commons till Jan. 1945, when he resigned his seat and was granted an earldom, taking as his titles Earl Lloyd-George of Dwyfor and Viscount Gwynedd. He was given the Order of Merit in 1919 and the *Légion d'honneur* in 1920. He was Constable of Caernarfon castle from 1908; hon. LL.D.(Wales) 1908, hon. Fellow of Jesus College, Oxford, 1910, hon. D.C.L., Oxford, and hon. LL.D. of Edinburgh, 1918, Sheffield, 1919, Birmingham, 1921. In 1944 he had come to his home, Tŷ Newydd, in Llanystumdwy, where he d. 26 March 1945. He was buried according to his own wishes in the wooded slope above the river Dwyfor near his home.

He m. (1), 24 Jan. 1888, Margaret (d. 20 Jan. 1941) dau. of Richard and Mary Owen of Mynydd Ednyfed, Cricieth. They had five children: Richard, (1889-1968), Mair Eluned (1890-1907), Olwen Elizabeth (1892-1990) (who m. Sir Thomas John Carey Evans), Gwilym (1894-1967), and Megan (1902-1966), (2) 23 Oct. 1943, Frances Louise, dau. of John Stevenson of Wallington, Surrey, his long-serving personal assistant and companion.

Malcolm Thomson and Frances Countess Lloyd-George, *David Lloyd George* (1948); David Lloyd George, *War Memoirs*, 6 vols (1933-6); [see other biographical studies by B. B. Gilbert (1987), Cyril Parry (1984), Emyr Price (1999) and John Grigg (1973, 1978, 1978, rev. eds. 1997, 1997, 1981); Stephen Constantine (1992); J. Graham Jones, *Lloyd George Papers at NLW and other repositories* (2001)].

E.M.H.

LLOYD-JONES, JOHN (1885-1956), scholar and poet; b. 14 Oct. 1885, s. of John and Dorothy Lloyd-Jones, Cartrefle, Dolwyddelan, Caerns. He was educated at Llanrwst grammar school and the University College of North Wales, Bangor. He graduated B.A. in 1906 and M.A. in 1909. He took the B.Litt. degree of Oxford University at Jesus College, and then studied under Rudolf Thurneysen at the University of Freiburg. He was appointed first head of the Welsh department at University College, Dublin, and held the post until his retirement in 1955. He acted as external examiner in Welsh to the University of Wales from 1916 till 1955.

As a scholar Lloyd-Jones first appeared as contributor of etymological and lexicographical notes in the *Bulletin* of the Board of Celtic Studies of the University of Wales and the *Zeitschrift für celtische Philologie*. In 1921 he won the prize at the national *eisteddfod* at Caernarfon for an essay on Caernarfonshire place-names, which he amplified and published in 1928 under the title *Enwau lleoedd sir Gaernarfon*. At the time this work was the only study of its kind in Wales done according to modern scholarly principles, and although there have been significant advances in place-names studies since then, the book is still useful. In 1924 Lloyd-Jones was asked by the Board of Celtic Studies to become responsible for the compilation of a glossary to the works of the

Poets of the Princes which the Board proposed to publish. The first fascicule appeared in 1931 in 96 large pages of closely packed print under the title *Geirfa barddoniaeth gynnar Gymraeg*. It was evident that the author had included many hundreds of words from the period before the Poets of the Princes, and also from the works of later poets and even from prose writers. With each fascicule the list of sources read increased. The seventh fascicule, the last to be seen through the press by the author, came out in 1952. The eighth and final part, which went as far as the word *heilic*, appeared in 1963. The glossary is a fine example of Welsh scholarship at its very best. In addition to the immense labour involved in collecting and arranging the material, it displays the author's extraordinary ability to deduce the meanings of words hitherto unknown. The detailed nature of the information given is remarkable; for example, twenty three men called Dafydd are recorded, and whenever possible each one is identified. The glossary is of inestimable value for the interpretation of the literature of the medieval period, and it is a great pity that the author's scheme of work did not allow him to complete the task. His Sir John Rhŷs Memorial Lecture delivered to the British Academy in 1948, 'The Court Poets of the Welsh Princes', was the result of the detailed knowledge of the poetry which he had gained by collecting material for the glossary.

Lloyd-Jones was highly regarded as a poet in the strict metres. He won the national *eisteddfod* chair at Ammanford in 1922 for his poem 'Y Gaeaf', a lyrical composition very skilfully constructed. Poems by him appeared in *Y Llenor* in 1930, 1942, 1949 and 1950, each one thoroughly traditional in spirit and in metre and of a high poetic standard. There is a collection of his poetry in his own hand in the library of the University College, Bangor. In 1925 the Gregynog Press published *Caneuon Ceiriog: detholiad*, edited by Lloyd-Jones with an introduction in the form of a critical essay on the poet's work. He was awarded the degree of D.Litt. *honoris causa*, by the University of Wales in 1948.

Lloyd-Jones was of a kind and gentle disposition. Although he had lived in Ireland for many years, he had lost none of those characteristics which his Welsh Nonconformist background had given him. He was one of the chief supporters of the Welsh Presbyterian chapel in Dublin till its closure.

He m. Freda Williams of Bangor in 1922. He d. 1 Feb. 1956 and he was buried in Bryn-y-bedd, Dolwyddelan.

Geirfa barddoniaeth gynnar Gymraeg, preface, pt. viii (1963); [*Baner*, 15 Feb. 1956; *Études celtiques*, 7 (1956), 482-3; *Tr.*, 111 (1956)].

T.P.

LLWYD o'r BRYN - see LLOYD, ROBERT above.

LOUGHER, Sir LEWIS (1871-1955), industrialist and politician; b. 1 Oct. 1871, second son of Thomas Lougher of Llandaff, Glam., and Charlotte, daughter of David Lewis, a farmer of Radyr Farm, Radyr, Cardiff. His family was deeply rooted in Glamorganshire; his father came from Wenvoe and his paternal grandfather from Garn-llwyd, Llancarfan. He was educated in Cardiff Secondary School and Cardiff Technical College, and was apprenticed to corn merchants. But Lewis soon entered the shipping business, and succeeded spectacularly as Cardiff developed into the world's chief port for exporting coal, until in 1910 he established the shipping company Lewis Lougher and Co., Ltd. having a fleet of ships in Bute docks, and he grew into a figure typifying Cardiff at the zenith of the city's mercantile power. He became chairman of a large number of shipping companies in Cardiff, Penarth and Barry, chairman of the federation of Bristol Channel shipowners in 1919, chairman of the Cardiff Chamber of Trade when the Chamber was particularly powerful, and an expert on the problems of exporting and handling coal as a member of the National Trimming Board.

He was a member of Glamorgan County Council from 1922 to 1949, a member and chairman of Cardiff Rural Council, and M.P. (C) for Cardiff East, 1922-23, and for Cardiff Central, 1924-29. His parliamentary career was notable in that he succeeded in getting an act of parliament on the statute book, namely the Road Transport Lighting Act, which he presented as a private member's bill in February 1927, and which to the present day requires that every vehicle shall have a white light at the front and red light at the rear.

He was J.P. for Glamorganshire, High Sheriff in 1931, and he received a knighthood in 1929. During the 1930s he was responsible for developing parts of Radyr through his land company and the building of Danybryn Estates. He was a leading member of the Freemasons, and contributed generously to all kinds of organisations and philanthropic causes in the Cardiff area.

He was a bachelor, and lived for a long time in a mansion called Dan-y-bryn, Radyr (now the Cheshire Homes), but about 1939 he and his unmarried sister Charlotte Lougher moved to live nearby in Northlands, Radyr, where he d. 28 Aug. 1955.

Who's who; *Www*; John Lougher, *The Loughers of Glamorgan* (1952, private circulation); personal acquaintance.

P.M.

LOVEGROVE, EDWIN WILLIAM (1868-1956), schoolmaster and an authority on Gothic architecture; b. in the first half of 1868, eldest son of Edwin Lovegrove, curate of Woodside, Horsforth near Leeds, and his wife. He was educated at Merchant Taylor's School, Crosby and was a scholar of New College, Oxford, where he graduated with first-class honours in Mathematics. He taught at Giggleswick, Yorks., Friars School, Bangor and Trent College before becoming headmaster of schools at Clee, Grimsby; Stamford; and Ruthin, 1913-30. He m. (1), 1899, Septima Jane Roberts (d. 30 Apr. 1928), sister of William Rhys Roberts (*DWB*, 885-6), and they had a son, Wynne, who fell at Dunkirk, and two daughters. He m. (2), Kathleen Agnes Sanders. After retiring he lived at St. Asaph, 1930-31; Chipping Campden, 1932-41; Abergavenny, 1942-45; and at Fownhope, Herefordshire until he d., 11 March 1956.

He was a valuable member of the Cambrian Archaeological Soc. (1913-56), and of other archaeological societies. He took a keen interest

in architecture and became an authority on the Gothic architecture of cathedrals and abbeys. He gave lectures on the topic and published his numerous detailed studies in journals such as *Arch. Camb.*, 1921-47; *Arch. Jnl.*; *Journal of the British Archaeological Association*; *Bristol and Gloucestershire Transactions*. Among the buildings he studied were the cathedrals of St. Asaph, St. David's and Llandaff; Valle Crucis abbey, Llanthony priory, and Rhuddlan friary.

WWP; Www.

M.A.J.

LYNE, HORACE SAMPSON (1860-1949), president of the Welsh Rugby Union, 1906-1947; b. at Newport, Mon., 31 Dec. 1860, son to Charles Lyne, mayor of the town in 1856 and 1884. He was educated in Plymouth and the Royal Naval College. By profession, he was a solicitor. At eighteen, he played as a back for Newport rugby club, but it was as a skilful forward that he found success, as the captain of the club in 1883-84, and being capped six times for Wales, 1883-85. In 1886-87, he was one of the founders of the International Rugby Board, as a representative of the game in Wales, and he served the Board without a break from 1887 to 1938. He served as the respected President of the Welsh Rugby Union longer than anyone else. He and Walter E. Rees (see below) between them steered the rugby affairs of Wales throughout the first half of the 20th century. He was prominent in the public affairs of Newport and was granted the Freedom of the town in 1934. In 1938, he was appointed Chancellor of the See of Monmouth, and he was a member of the Governing Body of the Church in Wales. He d. in May 1949 in Newport.

David Smith and Gareth Williams, *Fields of Praise* (1980); *West. Mail*, 2 May 1949; *South Wales Argus*, 7 May 1949.

G.W.W.

M

MACDONALD, GORDON, first Baron MAC-DONALD of GWAENYSGOR (1888-1966), politician; b. 27 May 1888 at Gwaenysgor, Prestatyn, Flints., son of Thomas Macdonald and Ellen (née Hughes), but the family soon moved to Ashton-in-Makerfield, Lancs., where he was brought up in a Welsh-speaking home. He left S. Luke's Elementary School, Stubshaw Cross, at the age of 13 and worked as a miner until the beginning of World War I, apart from a period as a student at Ruskin College, Oxford. In 1920 he was elected a member of the Wigan Board of Guardians of which he was chairman in 1929, and he became president of Bryn Gates Co-operative Society, 1922-24. In 1924 he was elected Miners' Agent for Lancashire and Cheshire in the Mineworkers Federation of Great Britain, a post which he held until he was elected M.P. (L) for Ince, Lancs., in 1929. He showed energy and balanced judgement during a difficult period for Labour members. Although he was a friend of Ramsay Macdonald, he did not support him in 1931. He became a whip of the Labour Party, and took a prominent part in debates on the coal industry and social matters. He was also Chairman of Committees in the House of Commons, 1934-41. In 1942 he resigned from Parliament on his appointment as manager for the Lancashire, Cheshire and North Wales region of the Ministry of Fuel and Power, and he was widely acclaimed for his work in this important post during World War II. In 1946 he received a knighthood and despite his inexperience he was nominated Governor of Newfoundland. The province was poor yet proud, and was in great financial difficulties, but Macdonald made a name for himself for his work among the fishermen, colliers and small farmers who called him 'the governor of the poor'. He steered the state to independence within the dominion of Canada and on the day of confederation in 1949 he returned to Britain and was elevated Baron of Gwaenysgor.

Though he held the post of Paymaster General during 1949-51, Commonwealth and international affairs interested him most. In 1950 he attended a meeting of the United Nations, and he was active in the preparations for an important conference in Australia on economic aid to countries of south-east Asia. From 1952-59 he was a member of the Colonial Development Corporation, a body which made an important contribution to the economic and social development of countries of the old empire when they were laying foundations for their independence.

After the fall of the Labour government in 1951 Lord Macdonald returned to Wales, where he became prominent in a number of societies and public bodies, and his dedication to the welfare of Wales became apparent. He took a great interest in religious and missionary societies, and he was elected president of the Band of Hope Union of Great Britain, 1951, and president of the National Society of the Blind. But it is as the first chairman of the National Broadcasting Council for Wales throughout the 1950s that he became best well known in Wales. He published speeches and radio addresses he had made in Newfoundland in *Newfoundland at the cross roads* (1949), and his parliamentary impressions, *Atgofion seneddol* (1953).

He m., 1913, Mary Lewis of Blaenau Ffestiniog and they had four children. He d. 20 Jan. 1966: his eldest son, Gordon Ramsay Macdonald (b. 1915), succeeded to the title.

Debrett; his memoirs; [*Prestatyn Weekly.*, 19 Jan. 1946, 3].

D.R.Ho.

McGRATH, MICHAEL JOSEPH (1882-1961), Archbishop of Cardiff; b. in Kilkenny in Ireland, 24 March 1882. He was educated at the local Christian Brothers' School and went from there to Rockwell College, Co. Tipperary. While there, his interest in the Irish language grew and he went on to gain a B.A. degree in the language in the National University of Ireland. Several years later, the same university awarded him the honorary degree of D.Litt. After graduation, Michael McGrath decided to become a priest. He entered St. John's College, Waterford, and on 12 July 1908, he was ordained a priest for the Catholic diocese of Clifton. He spent a number of years in that diocese, first as a curate at the cathedral in Clifton and then as parish priest at Fishponds, and at the Church of St. Nicholas in Bristol. His health at that period was uncertain and in 1918 it so deteriorated that he had to resign this parish and seek a period of leave of absence to try to regain full health. In 1921, his known interest in the Celtic languages led Bishop Francis Mostyn (*DWB*, 675) to invite him to work in Menevia diocese. This he accepted and went to serve at Flint and later at Bangor. In 1928, he was transferred to Aberystwyth, as parish priest and Rector of the small Catholic college in that town. During his stay in Aberystwyth, Michael McGrath followed courses in Welsh literature given by Thomas Gwynn Jones (see above) in the university college, and they became close lifelong friends. In 1935, on the death of Bishop Francis Vaughan, Michael McGrath was appointed Bishop of Menevia. He was consecrated on 24 Sept. of that year. On the death of Archbishop Mostyn, the man who had invited him to come to Wales, Bishop McGrath was translated to Cardiff. There he remained as archbishop until his death in St. Winifrede's Hospital on 28 Feb. 1961.

Among Archbishop McGrath's papers is a copy of a report he sent to Rome on 7 Mar. 1960. This report, prepared at the request of the Preparatory Commission of the Second Vatican Council, summarises the Archbishop's attitude to Wales and illustrates clearly his contribution to Welsh life. Writing of the Catholic community in Wales and answering the question, what is its future in Wales, he pointed out that the Catholic community was very largely of immigrant stock and with a large element whose forebears had come from Ireland. Though now settled in Wales for some generations, it had remained largely outside the cultural life of Wales. The most significant development in Wales since World War I, wrote the archbishop, was the decline of the Welsh language. Directly, this decline did not affect the life of the Catholic community to any great extent. Indirectly, however, it was a source of great danger for the future. He foresaw a continuing and accelerating decline of the language which would undermine the religious life of the nation and lead to widespread religious indifference. This indifference would undermine respect for family life and would lead to widespread divorce, to legalised abortion, to a lack of respect for life and property and to the abandoning of Christian standards in the relationships between the sexes. The significance of this analysis is not the accuracy of its vision of the future, striking as that is. Archbishop McGrath's special contribution to the life of the Catholic community in Wales and to the life of Wales was his clear insight into the importance of the Welsh language and its historic culture. He enabled many fellow Catholics to see that the two are inseparable and that their fortunes and continuance are essential to the religious health of the nation and even to the survival of the Christian religion in Wales.

Personal knowledge.

D.J.Mu.

MACHEN, ARTHUR (1863-1947), formerly JONES, ARTHUR LLEWELLIN, writer; b. 3 Mar. 1863. He spent his early years at Llanddewi Fach rectory, three miles north of Caerleon-on-Usk, Mon.; he attended Hereford Cathedral School until he was seventeen. After a period of near starvation in London, he enjoyed an independent income for a time and brought out some of his best early stories. He had already written a translation of Casanova and two imitative works, *The Anatomy of tobacco* and *The Chronicle of Clemendy*. In 1900 he acted with F.R. Benson's touring company. He entered journalism and two of his best-known works were originally published in the newspaper for which he worked. *The Bowman* (*Evening News*, 29 Sept. 1914) gave rise during World War I to the story of the Angel of Mons. The first of his autobiographical works, *Far off things* (1923), was printed under another title in the *Evening News* in 1915, and contains pleasing reminiscences written in a mellow spirit. Machen was celebrated for his stories of the other-world, fringing reality; terror is their keynote. *Hieroglyphics*, *The Hill of dreams*, and *The children of the pool* contain the best known of them. In his later years, Machen became a Roman Catholic. He m. twice, and had a son and daughter by his second wife. He retired to Amersham in 1929 and was noted as a conversationalist. He was awarded a Civil List pension in 1932. He d. 15 Dec. 1947.

The Times, 16 Dec. 1947; information from Leslie Millar; [D.P.M. Michael, *Arthur Machen* (1971) and see Meic Stephens, ed. *The New Companion to the Lit. of Wales* (1998)].

C.P.

MAM O NEDD - see COOMBE TENNANT, WINIFRED MARGARET above.

MARDY-JONES, THOMAS ISAAC (1879-1970), economist and politician; b. in 1879, the son of Thomas Isaac and Gwen Jones, Brynaman, Carms. His father and both his grandfathers were killed in coal-mining accidents. He received his early education at Ferndale board school, and began working in a local coal mine at 12 years of age. His wages had to support a family of six. He took advantage of the opportunity to study political and economic history at Ruskin College, Oxford for two years, and, after returning to south Wales, he acted as a 'missionary' for the College and succeeded in persuading the South Wales Miners' Federation to establish ten scholarships to enable working miners to follow college courses. Mardy-Jones also lectured on behalf of the Independent Labour Party in south Wales. He was promoted to the position of checkweighman in 1907. In the following year he suffered an eye accident, and in 1909 he was appointed a parliamentary agent to the South Wales Miners' Federation. He gave particular attention to the activities of local government and the rating system.

Mardy-Jones was elected an M.P. (L.) for the Pontypridd division in a by-election in July 1922 when he defeated the Liberal T.A. Lewis. He continued to represent this constituency until 1931, making his home at 16 Llantwit Road, Pontypridd. He visited India in 1927. He resigned from parliament in Feb. 1931 following accusations of allowing his wife the use of his M.P.'s railway travel voucher. He stood as an independent Labour candidate at Pontypridd in the general election of Oct. 1931, but received only 1110 votes.

Mardy-Jones attended a number of study courses in India, the Middle East and South Africa between 1928 and 1946. He served as the Staffing Officer of the Ministry of Supply, 1942-44, and as the Education and Welfare Officer with the British forces in the Middle East from 1945 to 1946. He became a popular public lecturer on foreign affairs and specialised on India and the Middle East. He was elected a F.R.Econ.S., and was appointed official lecturer to the National Coal Board on the economics of the coal industry. He published several volumes on the work of local government and ways of reforming the rating system including *Character, coal and corn - the roots of British power* (1949) and *India as a future world power* (1952).

He m. in 1911 Margaret, dau. of John Moredecai, St. Hillary, Cowbridge, Glamorgan. They had two daughters. He and his wife agreed to separate in Sept. 1933. He d. 26 Aug. 1970 at Harold Wood Hospital, Essex, at 90 years of age.

Www; Dod's Parliamentary Companion; Times, 27 Aug. 1970; *WWP*.

J.G.J.

MATHIAS, RONALD CAVILL (1912-68), trade union leader; b. 21 Sept. 1912 at Pontarddulais, Glam. He was educated at Gowerton Grammar School. From 1924 until 1945 he worked as a clerk for the Richard Thomas Co. (later Richard Thomas and Baldwins, Ltd.), iron and steel manufacturers in south Wales. In 1945 Mathias was appointed Merthyr and district organiser for the Transport and General Workers' Union. He became Cardiff district organiser, 1949-53, and South Wales Regional Secretary from 1953 until his retirement in 1967. In the same year he was appointed a full-time member of the National Board for Prices and Incomes. He held a number of public offices, among them Vice-Chairman of the Welsh Economic Council, secretary of the South Wales T.U.C. Advisory Committee, treasurer of the Welsh Council of Labour, and governor of the Welsh College for Advanced Technology, to name but a few. He became chairman of the Labour Party Wales in 1965. Mathias published a number of articles in journals, and he was a popular lecturer on economic and industrial matters. He received the M.B.E., in 1938 and the O.B.E. in 1967. He m. in 1938 Annie Ceridwen Hall; they had one daughter. He d. 15 Apr. 1968 at the beginning of a Mediterranean cruise and was buried at sea.

Www; Times, West. Mail and the *Liv. D.P.,* 18 Apr. 1968; *WWP.*

J.G.J.

MATTHEWS, NORMAN GREGORY (1904-64), chancellor; b. 12 Feb. 1904 at Swansea, only s. of William John and Agnes Amelia Matthews. He was educated at the Grammar School, Swansea, Jesus College Oxford where he held a Meyricke Exhibition, and gained B.A. (2nd-class hons. Theology, 1926, M.A. 1930), St. Stephen's House Theological College, Oxford, 1926. He was ord. deacon, 1927, served as curate of St. Dyfrig, Cardiff, 1927-35, and was ord. priest, 1928. In 1935 he was appointed the first Warden of St. Teilo's Hall of Residence, University College of South Wales, Cardiff. In 1940 he obtained the living of St. Saviour's, Roath, Cardiff. He was Llandaff Diocesan Missioner, 1936-40, and Examining Chaplain from 1938. He was Chaplain to H.M. Prison, Cardiff, 1940-45. In 1946, he was appointed canon of Llandaff cathedral and became Chancellor in 1952. He m. in 1953 Mary Laurella, eldest dau. of Walter Rees and Kathleen Olga Thomas, Whitchurch, Cardiff. They were fellow-students at Oxford. He obtained the living of St. Fagan in 1953, d. there 6 Aug. 1964 and was buried in Llandaff Cathedral graveyard.

He was a member of the Liturgical Commission of the Church in Wales from its inception, and a member of the Central Committee for the Training of Ordinands; he wrote a number of pamphlets on the call to the ministry. From 1942 he had been lecturing on English literature for the L.E.A. and the British Council. He was a frequent broadcaster and in 1957 he became a member of the Brains Trust on B.B.C. television. He wrote many articles in the press and in various journals on literary subjects and was a competent musician.

His influence was strong in the Church in Wales, where he was a talented preacher. A wit and a raconteur, he was considered one of the most brilliant clergymen in the Church in Wales of his day.

Www, 1961-70; *Handbk. of the Church in Wales,* 1959; *Llan,* 21 Aug. 1964; *Church Times,* 14 Aug. 1964; *West. Mail,* 7 Aug. 1964.

M.G.E.

MENANDER - see MORGAN, CHARLES LANGBRIDGE below.

MEREDITH, WILLIAM ('BILLY'; 1874-1958), footballer; b. 28 July 1874 in Chirk, Denbs., the son of James and Jane Meredith. He was one of ten children; his brother Samuel became a football player with Stoke City and Leyton and won eight international caps for Wales. But Billy was the most talented player of the family. He profited greatly from the early training he had received from his teacher at Chirk school, Thomas E. Thomas, the first executive president of the Welsh Football Association. His father worked as a machine operator at Parc Du Colliery, Chirk, and Billy himself worked there after leaving school. He joined the Northwich Victoria football club in 1893 and his skill as a nimble winger soon spread throughout the north. Manchester City persuaded him to join them and he played his first game for that team on 27 Oct. 1894. On the playing-field he could change a half chance into a goal: during the season 1898-99 he scored 36 goals in 33 games, and that record still stands for a winger to this day. In 1904 he scored the goal that won the F.A. Cup for Manchester City; he was the first Welshman to captain an F.A. cup-winning side. Because of financial problems, Meredith was transferred to Manchester United in 1907 for £50. He moved for more pay. Earlier, in 1901, he had m. a girl from Barnsley, Ellen Negus; they had two daughters. He was a constant inspiration to his new team: the First Division championship was won twice (in 1908 and 1911) and in 1909 Bristol City was beaten 1-0 in the final contest for the F.A. Cup at Crystal Palace. By the outbreak of World War I it seemed that his best days had come to an end. But he continued to play and in August 1921 he returned to Manchester City to reinspire the team for three years. On 29 April 1925 Billy Meredith, by then fifty years of age, left the game. Between 1894 and 1925 he had played 1,568 games and had scored 470 goals.

Meredith had had a brilliant international career. He had been first choice as right winger for Wales between 1895 and 1920. He had won 48 official caps – 20 against England, 16 against Ireland, and 12 against Scotland. He had scored a number of crucial goals for Wales, but he had to wait until his last game for Wales before experiencing the thrill of beating England (2-1 on 15 March 1920) on their home ground.

In many respects Billy Meredith was ahead of his time in both talent and intellect. He had a long and tough body; he was called 'Old Skin' by his friends. He looked very innocent, loitering along the flank wearing long loose trousers; one of his strangest whims was sucking a toothpick. But when the ball came his way, he glowed at once. He agonised backs mercilessly as they could not predict his next move. He had full awareness of the essentials of the game and experimented constantly while taking a penalty or corner kick. Though he was a shy man, he stood bravely for his rights on and off the field. He was not one to suffer personal injustice and laboured steadfastly in persuading authorities to acknowledge football as a profession and for players to be paid worthy salaries. In 1931 he returned to Manchester United to act as a trainer and after giving of his best in that capacity, he became a publican in the city. He d. at eighty-one years of age in Withington, Manchester, on 19 April 1958. Before World

War II there was no better Welsh footballer than Billy Meredith.

Information from Billy Meredith's daughter, Mrs. Lilian Pringle; E. Thornton, *Manchester City: Meredith to Mercer* (1969); P.M. Young, *Manchester United* (1960); P. Corrigan, *100 Years of Welsh Soccer* (1976); G.H. Jenkins, *Cewri'r Bêl-droed yng Nghymru* (1977); [J. Harding, *Football Wizard* (1985)].

G.H.J.

MERRETT, Sir HERBERT HENRY (1886-1959), industrialist; b. 18 Dec. 1886 in the parish of Canton, Cardiff, s. of Lewis and Elizabeth Merrett. He m., 1911, Marion Linda Higgins and they had two daughters and one s. He was educated at Cardiff; was Justice of the Peace for the county of Glamorgan and was High Sheriff of Glamorgan 1934-35. He was acknowledged a leading Welsh coal exporter of international repute whose career began in the Cardiff Docks with Cory Brothers; he became chairman of Powell Duffryn, Ltd. In 1935-36 he was president of Cardiff Incorporated Chamber of Commerce, and president of the British Coal Exporters' Federation 1946-49. His business and commercial associations within Europe were recognised by France with the award of *Chevalier de la Légion d'Honneur*, and he was knighted in 1950. *I fight with coal*, which he published in 1932, described his early skirmishes within the Welsh coal industry and his part in its troubled history. In his 'teens he won a reputation as a footballer and played for the Cardiff Corinthians, a prestigious amateur soccer team, and he subsequently qualified as a referee. He was appointed chairman of the Cardiff City Association Football Club in 1939 and with one short break, and despite his business involvement, he remained chairman until 1957. He was president of the Glamorgan County Cricket Club, chairman of the Post Office Advisory Committee for South Wales 1936, and a member of the Court of Governors of the University College of South Wales and Monmouthshire. He d. 3 Oct. 1959.

Www.

D.G.R.

MERTHYR TYDFIL, 1st BARON EVANS of - see EVANS, HORACE above.

MEURYN - see ROWLANDS, ROBERT JOHN below.

MICHAEL, JOHN HUGH (1878-1959), minister (Meth.), Professor in Methodist colleges in England and Canada, Biblical exegetist; b. 9 Aug. 1878 in Port Dinorwic, Caerns., son of Thomas and Kate Michael. He was educated at Friars School, Bangor, before entering the University College of Wales at Bangor, where he graduated B.A. in 1899. After being a lay preacher on the Caernarfon circuit, he was persuaded to offer himself as a candidate for the ministry with the Wesleyan Methodists. He was accepted and in 1900 he went to Didsbury College, Manchester, where he successfully completed a B.D. course. Then, in 1903, he was appointed an assistant professor at Headingley College, Leeds, where he remained for four yrs. As a minister he travelled in the circuits of

Wakefield (3 yrs.) and Eccles (3 yrs.) before going to Canada in 1913, having been appointed Professor of New Testament Studies at Emmanuel College of the University of Victoria in Toronto. During World War II he was joint-minister of Eaton Memorial church in Toronto, while continuing his studies with great success. In 1919 he received an hon. D.D. degree from Queen's University, Canada. Throughout his period in Victoria University he contributed regularly to theological periodicals, and of his published books perhaps the most important was his commentary to the epistle to the Philippians in the *Moffatt New Testament Commentary* series (1928). As a lecturer and preacher his delivery was eloquent and with conviction; he never lost his Welsh accent. The message could be severe but for his occasional flash of wit which made his lectures and sermons all the more effective. He shared the friendship of professors and famous men of his day, such as Reinhold Niebuhr, Albert Einstein, James Moffatt and Wilbert Howard, who was for a period one of his fellow-students at Didsbury. Another fellow-student at Didsbury was Edward Tegla Davies (see above) who described him as being well over six foot tall, broad, with a princely head, a firm yet gentle character and defender of the weak.

Having spent years in Toronto, he became a supernumerary there and continued to bring a blessing to many through his sermons and writings. He d. in Toronto, 6 Jan. 1959, having been a minister for 56 yrs.

Minutes of Methodist Conference, 1959, 191; *Who's who in Canada*, 1922.

Er.E.

MICHAELIONES, THOMAS (THOMAS MICHAEL JONES; 1880-1960), priest and owner of a gold mine; b. 1 May 1880 son of Thomas and Ellen Michael Jones, 24 Baptist St., Pen-y-groes, Caerns. He attended Pen-y-groes and Menai Bridge schools and was a lay student at Brecon Independent Theological College (1905-06). He took up journalism for a short period but in 1911 he was confirmed as a member of the Anglican Church in Wales at Llanllyfni and served as curate at Blaenau Ffestiniog (1917-20), Holyhead (1920-24) and Llanwnog (1924-29), before becoming rector of St. Beuno, Pistyll, Caerns., with Llithfaen and Carn-guwch churches (1929-60). In 1924 he published three booklets of English verse and the following year he composed verses to the 'Union Jack' for a competition. They were selected for publication by Empire Music Publishers, London and set to music by Arthur Selaw. Thomas Michaeliones was interested in archaeology and church history, publishing a number of pamphlets on the churches in Nefyn district in particular. He restored Pistyll church which had been closed for many years and made strenuous efforts to preserve the ancient church of Carn-guwch. He was an uncommon character, and one of his multifarious interests was prospecting for gold on the Craigwen smallholding which he bought in the Mawddach valley. He owned the Graigwen Gold Fields from *c.* 1938 until their closure in 1953. His offer to provide gold for Princess Elizabeth's wedding ring in 1947 was accepted.

He changed his name when he m. (1), in 1916, Janet Chadwick (d. 1940). They had three daughters and a son. He m. (2) Constance Mary Weighill in 1942 and they had a daughter. He d. 24 Apr. 1960 at his home, Gwerindy, Pistyll.

Taliesin, 1, 30-42; *Caern. and Denb. Herald*, 29 Apr. and 6 May 1960; *Herald Cymr.*, 2 May 1960; *Jnl. Merioneth Hist. Soc.*, 7 (1973-76), 170-1; Bangor diocese ordination papers B/0/1638 and 1678 at N.L.W.

M.A.J.

MILFORD, 1st BARON - see PHILIPPS, LAURENCE RICHARD below.

MOELONA - see JONES, ELIZABETH MARY above.

MOI PLAS - see DAVIES, MORRIS above.

MORGAN, ALFRED PHILLIPS (1857-1942), musician; b. 21 May 1857 at Rumney, Mon., s. of David Price and Levia Phillips Morgan. The family moved to Pwllgwilym near Cefn-bedd-Llywelyn, and later at Builth. He was educated at Builth Endowed School, and afterwards he went to Aberystwyth college for a music course under Dr. Joseph Parry (*DWB*, 738) and he received tuition at the Tonic Sol-fa College of Music. He won many prizes for composing tunes and singing (baritone) at *eisteddfodau*. He was appointed conductor of Builth Choral Society, and the choir won prizes at the national *eisteddfod* held at Liverpool, 1897, and at Blaenau Ffestiniog, 1898, and also at other important *eisteddfodau*. He composed music for the 'Te Deum', and 'The Lord's Prayer'. His tunes 'Treflys' and 'Dyfed' became popular, whilst his tune 'Cefn-bedd-Llewelyn' is still sung and is included in most hymnals. Anthems and a part-song by him were published in *Y Cerddor*. He became organist, choirmaster, and elder at Alpha Presbyterian church, Builth, duties which he carried out until his death. Under his baton the choir performed several works of the masters. He was a member of the joint committee for the *Church Hymnary*, and a member of Breconshire Education Committee. He d. 8 Feb. 1942, and was buried in Builth cemetery.

Cerddor, Nov. 1898; *Treasury*, June 1942.

R.D.G

MORGAN, CHARLES LANGBRIDGE ('Menander'; 1894-1958), drama critic, novelist, playwright; b. 22 Jan. 1894, youngest child of Sir Charles Langbridge Morgan, engineer, and Mary (née Watkins) his wife. His grandparents had emigrated from Pembrokeshire to Australia where his parents were married. He was trained in the Royal Navy from 1907 and became a naval officer, but he resigned in 1913 to lead a literary life, though he returned to serve in the navy during both World Wars. He entered Brasenose College, Oxford, 1919, and graduated, 1921. He then joined the staff of *The Times*, becoming well-known as its principal drama critic, 1926-39. He received many honorary degrees; was one of the select foreign members of *l'Institut de France*; was elected president of the English Association, 1953-54, and of the International Literary Congress for

Authors, 1954-56. With the exception of his first two novels, he produced a continuous sequence of literary masterpieces. His novels and plays were particularly artistic, of profound significance, and of great and varied narrative power. *Portrait in a Mirror* (1929) was awarded the *Femina-Vie Heureuse* prize; *The Fountain* (1932) the Hawthornden prize; and *The Voyage* (1940) the James Tait Black memorial book prize. A dramatised version of *The River Line* (1949) was produced at the Edinburgh Festival in 1952.

He lived most of his life in London. Possibly his closest connections with Wales came through his wife, Hilda Campbell Vaughan of Builth Wells, a novelist whom he m. 6 June 1923 and by whom he had a son and daughter (the Marchioness of Anglesey). His first play *The Flashing Stream* (1938) was written during a holiday spent at Llangorse Lake, Breck. Two long periods were spent in Pembrokeshire also, when *A breeze of morning* (1951) was written. He wrote a history of Macmillans (publishers) (1943); a collection of his lectures and essays was published posthumously in *The writer and his world* (1960). He d. 6 Feb. 1958.

WWP; Www; Eiluned Lewis, *Selected letters of Charles Morgan with a memoir* (1967); Henry Charles Duffin, *The novels and plays of Charles Morgan* (1959); D. Crystal, *The Cambridge Biographical Dictionary* (1994); see also *Times Literary Supplement Index*.

M.A.J.

MORGAN, DAVID JENKINS (1884-1949), teacher and agricultural officer; b. at Blaendewi, Llanddewibrefi, Cards., 23 Sept. 1884, the second child and eldest son of Rhys Morgan, minister of Bethesda church (CM) in the village, and Mary his wife (née Jenkins). On the last day of Aug. 1887 he entered the local board school, six days after his sister who was fourteen months his senior; he remained there until 14 May 1897. Tregaron county school was opened in the town hall three days later. His mother was one of the governors of the new school, and he started there on the first day. From Tregaron he went to college at Aberystwyth. He was appointed science master in his old school but returned to college to pursue a course in agriculture; he graduated B.Sc. in 1907. Afterwards he was appointed agricultural officer for Cardiganshire, a post which he occupied during the two World Wars. During his period as a teacher in Tregaron he co-operated with Samuel Morris Powell in writing, producing and acting in plays which depicted the history of the district; he usually played the part of the hero. After his appointment to the agricultural post, he settled in Lampeter and from there travelled to all parts of Cardiganshire, acquainting himself with its history and traditions. He gained the deep affection and trust of farmers. His vehicle, a Morgan three-wheeler, was a familiar sight along the highways and most remote by-ways of the county. His influence on the county's agriculture was enormous. His weekly essays in *The Welsh Gazette* under the title 'Pant a bryn' are a valuable source on the development of agriculture and social life in Cardiganshire during the first half of the twentieth century. They were written in a lively style. A selection of these essays was published in *Pant a bryn* (1953).

He m. 7 July 1915, Annie, daughter of John and Jane Jones, Tŷ-llwyd, Brynmawr (originally from Swyddffynnon). He d. suddenly on 18 May 1949 at Charing Cross Hospital, London. His body was cremated at Golders Green and his ashes were returned to Llanddewibrefi for burial.

Welsh Gaz., 26 May 1949; information from Mair Livingstone.

E.D.J.

MORGAN, EDWARD ('E.T.'; 1880-1949), rugby player; b. 22 May 1880 at Aber-nant, Cynon valley, Glam., and educated at Christ College Brecon and Guy's Hospital, London. Dr 'Teddy' (thus 'E.T.') Morgan scored the most historic try in the history of the game in Wales, if not the most remarkable one ever. It was his try which secured a 3-0 win for Wales over the All Blacks of New Zealand in Cardiff on 16 Dec. 1905. Not only was he exceptionally fast but he could deceive his opponents with a skilful dummy pass and sidestep. He could tackle and kick well. He came to the notice of the national selectors when he scored three tries for Newport against Blackheath in Oct. 1901. He is usually associated with the London Welsh and Guy's Hospital. He scored 14 tries in his 16 international matches between 1902 and 1908. 'E.T.' and William Morris Llewellyn (Pen-y-graig), a fellow-pupil at Christ College, formed the best partnership ever seen on the wings for Wales. In 1904 he scored in every international match and went on tour to Australia and New Zealand with the British team. He played against South Africa in 1906. He d. 1 Sept. 1949 in North Walsham, Norfolk.

His brother WILLIAM LLEWELLYN MORGAN (9 Mar. 1884 - 11 Apr. 1960) played rugby for Wales in 1910, as did his nephew William Guy Morgan, 1927-30.

David Smith and Gareth Williams, Fields of praise (1980); S. Wales Echo, 1 Sept. 1949; West. Mail and Times, 2 Sept. 1949.

G.W.W.

MORGAN, EVAN FREDERIC (1893-1949), 2nd VISCOUNT TREDEGAR, poet, artist, soldier, and statesman; b. 13 July 1893 at 33 Cadogan Terrace, London, only child of Courtenay Evan Morgan, 3rd Baron Tredegar and 1st Viscount of the 1926 creation (DWB, 637) and Lady Katherine A. Blanche Carnegie, daughter of the ninth Earl Southesk. The Honourable Evan Morgan, as he was known for the greater part of his life, was educated at Eton and Christ Church, Oxford. He was one of the founder vice-presidents of the Oxford Celtic Society. Following the tradition of his family he took a commission in the army, 27 June 1915, choosing, as might be expected, the Welsh Guards, but his health did not allow him to follow a military career. He was for a time private secretary to the Parliamentary Secretary at the Ministry of Labour, and to Sir George Riddell when he was representing the British Press at the Paris Peace Conference. After the war he acted as a liaison officer for Wales for the British Legion and was a patron of hospitals and philanthropic movements. He served as almoner for Wales of the Order of St. John. Soon after the War he was received into the Roman Catholic church and became a Knight of the Sovereign Order of Malta and of the Grand Cross of the Order of the Holy Sepulchre. He served Popes Benedict XV and Pius XI as Privy Chamberlain of Sword and Cape. For a time he was attached to the British embassy at Copenhagen. He was a Conservative and Unionist in politics, and he unsuccessfully contested the Limehouse constituency in Stepney in 1929. He was adopted Unionist candidate for the Cardiff Central constituency in 1931, but he withdrew in favour of the National Labour candidate. Though he was of a family that drew much of its wealth from the coal industry he was in favour of abolishing royalties on minerals.

He was an able and talented man. He painted much in his youth and exhibited his works at the Paris Salon. He was a knowledgeable collector of works of art, particularly of the period of the Renaissance in Italy. He published one novel, Trial by ordeal, 1921; and a number of volumes of poems, Fragments, 1916; At Dawn, poems profane and religious, 1924; The eel and other poems, 1926; The city of canals and other poems, 1929; Gold and ochre, 1917; Psyche: an unfinished fragment, 1920; and A sequence of Seven Sonnets, 1920. He was a Fellow of the Royal Society of Literature, where he read a paper on aspects of Christian mysticism in 1928. In 1935 he established the Tredegar Lecture for the Society in memory of his father, and he delivered the first lecture taking as his subject 'John Donne - lover and priest'. He was twice married: (1) in 1928 to the Honourable Lois Sturt (d. 1937), dau. of the 2nd Baron Allington, and (2) in 1939 the Princess Olga Dolgorouky, a marriage which was annulled in 1943. He d. at Honeywood, Horsham, 27 Apr. 1949 and the viscountcy lapsed with him. He was succeeded in the barony by his uncle, the Honourable Frederick George Morgan, 5th Baron Tredegar (1873-1954), and by family agreement the estate by his cousin, the Honourable (Frederick Charles) John Morgan, the 6th and last Baron Tredegar. The estate was dispersed but the last-named secured the preservation of the family archives by depositing them at the National Library of Wales on the understanding that they were to become the property of the Library should he, as he did, die without an heir.

Who's Who; Complete Peerage, xiii; N.L.W. and B.L. catalogues; personal knowledge.

E.D.J.

MORGAN, HERBERT (1875-1946), minister (B), university lecturer, and director of extra-mural studies; b. at Onllwyn in the Neath valley, 15 Sept. 1875, but at an early age moved with his parents to Porth in the Rhondda. He was educated at Porth, but owing to the family's straitened circumstances he was not able to continue his education. Instead he became a clerk with the Pontypridd Water Board, but his remarkable gifts could not be hidden, and, with the support of his neighbours and others, he was able to embark upon a successful academic career at the Pontypridd Academy, the Baptist College and the University College at Cardiff. He graduated with honours in philosophy and Greek, and in 1902 proceeded to Mansfield College, Oxford, where he took a degree in theology and won a scholarship which took him to the university of Marburg in Germany for further study. He accepted a call to the pastorate of the Welsh (B) church in Castle Street, London, in 1906, and in 1912 he left to undertake the pastorate of Tyndale church in Bristol. In the 1918 parliamentary election he contested the Neath constituency for Labour, but his pacifist views were unacceptable in the climate of that election, and Welsh Labour representation lost a figure of outstanding calibre. In 1920, however, he secured a post for which he was eminently fitted, that of Director of extra-mural studies newly established at Aberystwyth. He retired in 1940, having set the department on secure foundations.

He was in great demand as a preacher in Welsh and English, though not of the style regarded as 'popular', and as a lecturer. In 1945, the Welsh Baptist Union honoured him as their president. Though not himself a strict Baptist, during the year of his presidency he was loyal to the convictions of his denomination. He was keenly interested in the development of social services and his publications reveal this interest, e.g. *The Church and the social problem*, 1911, *Housing and public welfare*, 1912, *The Social task in Wales*, 1919, and *Christ and Caesar*, 1921, a joint study, with Nathaniel Micklem, of social responsibilities. His last work, *Reason and religion*, 1946, is a liberal theologian's reaction to the teaching of Karl Barth, which was gaining ground in some circles in Wales. He was a biblical scholar but this aspect of his learning is represented only by a Welsh commentary, with John Gwili Jenkins (*DWB*, 435-6) on portions of the Book of Isaiah, 1908, and articles in *Y Geiriadur Beiblaidd* (1926). He m. Mrs. James, a widow, who was a member of Tyndale church. He d. at Aberystwyth, 22 Sept. 1946, aged 72.

Efrydiau Athronyddol, x, 1947; *Seren Gomer*, xxxvii, no.1; W.P. John and G.T. Hughes, *Hanes Castle Street a'r Bedyddwyr Cymraeg yn Llundain*, 1959.

G.M.G.

MORGAN, IWAN JAMES (1904-66), extramural tutor and politician; b. 1904 at Tondu, Glam., the son of John James Morgan (1870-1954), the head teacher of Garw secondary school, 1909-35. He was educated at Bridgend County School and the University College of Wales, Aberystwyth, where he graduated with honours in economics in 1926. He was awarded the degree of M.A. in 1929 for a thesis on the 'Origins and Development of the University Movement in Wales in the Nineteenth Century'. Morgan lectured in night classes and extra-mural courses in several places in Wales, including Coleg Harlech, until his appointment in 1935 as tutor-in-charge of the Department of Extra-Mural Studies, University College, Cardiff. He remained in this position until his death. He became a popular lecturer and broadcaster on historical, international, economic and social subjects. He was a member of *Plaid Cymru* in the 1930s, but a disagreement with Saunders Lewis over his attitude towards Socialism led him to join the Labour Party. He was chosen as the Labour prospective parliamentary candidate for Cardiganshire in 1940, and stood against Roderick Bowen in 1945 and

1950. Morgan published in 1943 the pamphlets in *Attlee's Reply* following the response of the Deputy Prime Minister Clement Attlee to the demand for a Secretary of State for Wales. Throughout his life he was vehemently opposed to Communism. He edited the volume *The college by the sea* (1928), a collection of reminiscences of the University College of Wales, Aberystwyth. He also published a large number of articles in journals and newspapers on matters of national interest. In 1944 he was elected a member of the court of governors and council of the National Library of Wales.

He m. Esme Lewis, Caerau, Maesteg. He d. 1 Apr. 1966 at Cardiff Royal Infirmary.

WWP; *West. Mail*, 2 and 4 Apr. 1966, *University of Wales Calendars*.

J.G.J.

MORGAN, JOHN (1886-1957), Archbishop of Wales; b. 6 June 1886 at the rectory, Llandudno, Caern., youngest of the five children of John Morgan, Archdeacon of Bangor, 1902-24. Educated at St. George's National School, Llandudno, the Cathedral School, Llandaff, where he was soloist in the choir, Llandovery College and Hertford College, Oxford, (as an Exhibitioner), and Cuddesdon College. He graduated B.A., 1910, M.A., 1914, Honorary D.D. University of Wales 1934. He was ord. deacon in 1910 at St. Asaph, for the Bishop of Bangor, and was curate of Llanaber with Barmouth, 1910-12. He was ord. priest in 1911. From 1912-16 he was resident chaplain to the Bishop of Truro and honorary priest-vicar of Truro Cathedral. During 1916-19 he was temporary chaplain to the Forces, when he served in the Mediterranean, Kinmel and Shoreham. In 1917 he returned to Wales to be vicar-choral of St. Asaph Cathedral and vicar of St. Asaph. In 1919 he was appointed priest-in-charge of Llanbeblig and Caernarfon, and in 1920 on the implementation of the Welsh Church Act, he became vicar of the parish. Whilst he was there he served as chaplain to the prison and was rural dean of Arfon, 1928-31. In 1931 he was appointed canon of Bangor Cathedral and in 1933 he became rector of Llandudno. The following year he was elected Bishop of Swansea and Brecon, succeeding E.L. Bevan, and was consecrated in St. Asaph Cathedral on Whit Tuesday, by the Archbishop of Wales, Alfred George Edwards (*DWB*, 184), who had ordained him deacon. In 1939 he was translated to Llandaff in succession to Timothy Rees (*DWB*, 831) and in 1949 he was elected Archbishop of Wales to succeed David Prosser (see below). He d. at St. Thomas's Hospital, London, in June 1957 aged 71, and was buried at St. Asaph.

John Morgan was short in stature; a man, thorough in all his doings and meticulous regarding details, he demanded that all things should be seemly and in order, whether it was an ordinary service or a special occasion. He was an excellent administrator and abhorred disorder and slipshod ways in others. He could be a strict disciplinarian, like his father, but he could be gracious and merciful when the occasion arose. He regarded the office of bishop as a charge, and was unwilling to give way on matters of principle. In Brecon he fulfilled the office of dean as well as bishop and he laid sound foundations there for the cathedral ceremonies and music. At Llandaff, the administration of the diocese called for a strong arm and clear vision. War broke out soon after his appointment and the cathedral was ruined by enemy bombing. He was responsible for its re-building and subsequent re-consecration in the spring of 1957.

He was an accomplished musician and could play the organ since his boyhood days in Llandudno. He was chairman of the Bangor Diocesan Music Committee and in 1934 he was elected chairman of the committee which brought out the Welsh hymnbook *Emynau'r Eglwys*. From 1939 he was also chairman of the Music sub-committee. The words edition was published in 1941 and the music edition in 1951. During his term of office the Liturgical Commission was set up to revise the Book of Common Prayer.

His last public service was to consecrate G.O. Williams Bishop of Bangor at Llandaff on 1 May 1957. He returned to hospital that evening.

A shy man, only his close friends knew that he was a good raconteur, an excellent mimic, with the ability to use the Caernarfon town dialect.

Llan, 5 July 1957, 7 Apr. 1933, 13 Apr. 1934; *Haul*, Summer 1957; *Province*, Summer 1957; *Church Times*, 28 June 1957; *Www*, 1951-60; *Welsh Church Yearbk.*, 1936; *Emynau'r Eglwys* (1951); *Crynhoad*, May/June 1950; MS. T.I.E. in the author's possession.

M.G.E.

MORGAN, JOHN JAMES (1870-1954), minister (Presb.) and author; b. March 1870 at Glynberws, Ysbyty Ystwyth, Cards., son of David Morgan ('Y Diwygiwr'; 1814-83; *DWB*, 641) and Jane his wife. He was educated at Ysbyty Ystwyth board school, Ystradmeurig school, Thomas Owens's school, Aberystwyth and Trefeca College. He was ord. in 1894, and served his ministry at Cowbridge, Glam. (1893-95), and Mold, Flints. (1895-1946). In 1895 he m. Jeanetta Thomas, Llancatal, Vale of Glamorgan. After retiring he went to live with his daughter in Irby, Cheshire, where he d. 23 Jan. 1954.

All his life he enjoyed writing, and his work mostly historical, appeared in the periodicals of his denomination. He had a gift for recording the striking and pithy sayings and idiosyncracies of elders and preachers. He published several very useful biographies: *Hanes Dafydd Morgan a Diwygiad '59* (1906); *Cofiant Edward Matthews* (1922); *Cofiant Evan Phillips* (1930); and *Hanes Daniel Owen* (1936). At the end of his life he published his autobiography and reminiscences in three interesting volumes (1948, 1949 and 1953), under the title *A welais ac a glywais*.

Blwyddiadur MC, 1955, 247-8; *Gol.*, 10 March 1954; his biography of his father and his autobiography.

G.M.R.

MORGAN, JOHN JENKYN ('Glanberach'; 1875-1961); local historian and essayist; b. at Bodist Isaf, Glanaman, Carms., 10 Aug. 1875, s. of Jenkin and Angharad Morgan. He was educ. at Brynlloi British school, Glanaman, but began working in Mynydd pit, Cwmaman, when he was 12. He later worked in the Raven tinplate works Glanaman until his retirement in 1930. He m. Harriet, dau. of Thomas and Sarah Jones, Brynlloi shop, Glanaman, 5 Oct. 1901. She d. 25 Nov. 1956 at a service in Bryn Seion chapel, Glanaman: she was a sister of the ministers, W. Glasnant Jones, Dafydd G. Jones and E.Aman Jones. They had 4 children.

In an underprivileged age J.J. Morgan took advantage of every opportunity to develop his abilities. He was a cultured man and through his close friendship with Richard Williams ('Gwydderig', *DWB*, 1066-7) he became a keen follower of *eisteddfodau* and won many prizes, mainly for essays and handbooks of local history. He became a member of the *Gorsedd* of Bards at Llanelli in 1895 adopting the name Glanberach. He competed regularly at the national *eisteddfod* and was a sharp critic of adjudicators, especially if they were 'college people'. He gained prizes at the *eisteddfodau* in Ammanford (1922), Swansea (1926), Holyhead (1927), Denbigh (1939), Llanrwst (1951), Pwllheli (1955): some of these compositions are in the National Library. He was one of the Presidents of the Day at the Bridgend National *Eisteddfod* in 1948 and he was the oldest member of the *Gorsedd* following the death of Elfed (H. Elvet Lewis, see above) in 1953. He broadcast frequently and wrote articles on local history to Welsh periodicals. He collected a large library of material relating to the Amman valley and the surrounding area and he was active in every cultural movement in the district. He was secretary of the children's *eisteddfod* during the ministry of Rhys J. Huws (*DWB*, 401-2) in Bryn Seion chapel, Glanaman, a church in whose foundation he played a prominent part; he was librarian and secretary of the miners' reading-room in Glanaman. He published *Cofiant John Foulkes Williams* (1906), and *Hanner canrif o hanes Bryn Seion, Glanaman, 1907-1957* (1957). He d. at his home in Brynlloi, Glanaman, 18 May 1961 and was buried in Hen Fethel Cemetery, Cwmaman.

A.T. Davies, *Crwydro Sir Gâr* (1955), 285; *Tyst*, 8 June 1961; personal information.

H.Wa.

MORGAN, JOHN LLOYD (1861-1944), county court judge; b. 13 Feb. 1861 at Carmarthen, s. of William Morgan, minister (Congl.) and Professor at the Presbyterian College, Carmarthen, and his wife Margaret, dau. of Thomas Rees, Capel Tyddist, Llandeilo. He was educated at Tattenhall (Staffordshire) and Trinity College, Cambridge. He was a J.P. for Carmarthenshire, Pembrokeshire and Glamorgan, represented West Carmarthens. in Parliament (as a Liberal), 1889-1910, and was Recorder of Swansea, 1909-11. His biography of his father was published in London in 1886. He was generous to various religious causes, particularly to Union Street Chapel, Carmarthen, his father's church. He d. 17 May 1944 and was buried in the Union Street Chapel cemetery.

WwW (1933, 1937); *Report S. Wales Congl. Union*, 1944-45.

T.M.R.

MORGAN, MORGAN PARRY (1876-1964), minister of religion (CM) and powerful preacher; b.

8 July 1876, in Llanafan, Cards., the only son of David Morgan, Brynseir, Lledrod, Cards., and Catherine (née Parry) his wife, daughter of Morgan Parry, surveyor of the Trawscoed estate. When he was six years old the family moved to Pontycyme, Glam., where they became members at Bethel church (CM). He was educated at Pontycymer board school, but laid great stress on the influence of the Sunday school on his life. He attended Port Talbot academy around 1889-92, but like his father he had to return to the colliery. In 1894 he began preaching and went to the Rev. Dunmore Edwards' academy in Pontypridd. In 1896 he was accepted into Trefeca College. In 1900 he accepted a call to Blaenannerch, Cards. He was ordained in the Association held at Heol Dŵr church, Carmarthen, in Aug. 1901. The revival of 1904-05 had left a deep impression on Blaenannerch, the church and its young minister, and he in turn was a strong leader of his flock guiding them from the dangers of oversentimentality. He instructed them firmly in the scriptures by avoiding literal acceptance of the word and teaching them instead to become intelligent listeners. Though he spent the remainder of his life at Blaenannerch, he soon rose to become one of the foremost preachers of his day. He was in great demand at preaching festivals throughout Wales and 'M.P. Morgan, Blaenannerch', became a household name within the denomination. There were fiery elements in his sermons, but he took care to interpret his texts in detail and taught his flock in Biblical classes and in Cultural Society alike. Preaching, however, was his great passion in life. He delivered the Dr. John Williams Memorial Lecture in 1947; the subject of that lecture was 'Preaching'. He was moderator of the General Assembly in 1949.

He d. 27 Dec. 1964 and was buried in front of the chapel in Blaenannerch. He m., 17 Dec. 1901, Elizabeth Frances Jones, daughter of Samuel and Judith (née Hughes) Jones; they had one daughter.

D.J. Evans, *M.P. Morgan, Blaenannerch* (1976).
E.D.J.

MORGAN, TREFOR RICHARD (1914-70), company director; b. 28 Jan. 1914 at Tonyrefail, Glam. fifth child of Samuel and Edith (née Richards) Morgan. The father's family came from Peterston-super-Ely and the mother's from Llantwit Fardre. The father, a mason, died in the flu epidemic which swept the country in 1918. The mother struggled to raise the children in great poverty. Both sides of the family were committed Baptists, their forbears being among those who established the cause in Croes-y-Parc, Peterston-super-Ely, and a great-grandfather ministered in the Baptist chapel in Penuel, Pentyrch. His sole education was at the local school, and completely non-Welsh as was usual at that time. In later life he tried to correct his lack of education through evening classes in Welsh and Welsh history. He could not take advantage of the grammar school place he won at Cowbridge because the family was in such dire straits. He left school at 14 to work in the local mine in spite of precarious health, but because of the depression in coal-mining districts he had a variety of jobs in the following years.

He was always a fervent nationalist. His search for work led him to Pembrokeshire, where his nationalism was confirmed by his close friendship with D.J. Williams (1885-1970; see below) and his wife in Fishguard. In World War II he was a conscientious objector on nationalist grounds. In 1943 he married Gwyneth, daughter of Arthur and Mary (née Daniel) Evans of Aberdare, and they had four children.

He was a parliamentary candidate for *Plaid Cymru* in Ogmore in 1945 and in 1946, for Abertillery in 1955, and for Brecon and Radnor in 1966; and he stood as an independent nationalist in Merthyr Tydfil in 1950. According to an obituary in *Y Faner* he was one of the most effective speakers in *Plaid Cymru*; he dealt with critical issues with eloquence and conviction and could argue for nationalism with the best. But he was concerned that concentrating his efforts on elections, local or national, was not enough, and he sought to turn the principles he preached into practice. His basic tenet was the intrinsic value of the Welsh language and the need to create independent Welsh institutions. This is why he established an insurance and finance company with the aim of using any profit for two purposes; establishing small local industries and promoting the creation of Welsh schools throughout Wales. Cwmni Undeb began in Aberdare and succeeded in establishing a small trading estate in Hirwaun. In 1963 he founded *Cronfa Glyndwr yr Ysgolion Cymreig*, of which he was the first president. Its aim was to give financial help to parents and schools to enable children to attend Welsh schools set up by the parents themselves. The most important aspect of the trust was creating and maintaining nursery schools. Because of the reluctance of local authorities to offer secondary education in Welsh he founded a Welsh residential school in which every subject was taught through the medium of Welsh. Ysgol Glyndwr was opened in Bryntirion, Laleston near Bridgend, in Sept. 1968, but it came to an end soon after his death in Bridgend Hospital, 3 Jan. 1970. He was buried in Trane cemetery, Tonyrefail, 9 Jan.

Personal knowledge.
G.M.

MORGAN-OWEN, LLEWELLYN ISAAC GETHIN (1879-1960), army administrator in India; b. 31 Mar. 1879 son of Timothy Morgan-Owen, H.M.I., Llwynderw, Llandinam, Montg., and Emma (née Maddox). He was educated at Arnold House, Llandulas; Shrewsbury School; and Trinity College, Dublin. He joined the Carnarvon Militia in 1899 before entering the army in 1900 and serving with the 24th South Wales Borderers in the Orange River Colony and the Transvaal until the end of the South African war in 1902, being awarded two medals and five clasps. In 1904 he was employed with the West African Frontier Force and served with the mounted infantry in Northern Nigeria in 1908 before returning to his own regiment in 1910. During World War I he was sent to Gallipoli, was present at the Battle of Sari Bair, and eventually took part in the evacuation at Suvla and Helles Major. In 1916 he was appointed General Staff Officer of 13

Division and was posted to Mesopotamia, being mentioned five times in despatches during the second and third attempts to relieve Kut, and during the occupation of Baghdad in 1917. He went to India in 1920 on his appointment as assistant adjutant and Quartermaster General, first of the Waziristan Force, then at the headquarters of the Southern Command. From 1924 he was at the Army Headquarters and was appointed Deputy Director of Pay and Pensions in 1925, becoming Director of Organization in 1927. He left India in Apr. 1928. The following year he took command of 160 (S. Wales) Brigade, and of 9 Brigade at Portsmouth in 1931. During 1934-38 he was Major-General in Charge of Administration in the Eastern Command, and served the Royal Hospital, Chelsea, as lieut-governor and secretary, 1940-44. He was also colonel of the South Wales Borderers, 1931-44, and although he was away from his regiment for long periods he did much useful work as its colonel. As a former football player he was of particular service to the Army Football Association whose meetings he chaired during his time at the Horse Guards. He was awarded the D.S.O. in 1916, C.M.G. in 1918, C.B.E. for services during the Waziristan operations when he was again mentioned in despatches, and C.B. in 1934. In 1910 he m. Ethel Berry Walford (d. 1950) and they had one son. He himself d. 14 Nov. 1960.

WwW (1921); Www; Times, 16 Nov. 1960.

M.A.J.

MORRICE, JAMES CORNELIUS (1874-1953), priest and Welsh scholar; b. 10 Dec. 1874 at Porthmadog, Caern., s. of James Cornelius Morrice, engine driver, and his wife Margaret (née Thomas). He was educated at Porthmadog county school and University College Bangor (1897) where he graduated with first-class hon. in Welsh in 1900, the first to do so, it is claimed: he gained his M.A. with a dissertation on 'The poems of William Lleyn' in 1902. Ord. deacon in 1900 and priest in 1901 he served as curate in Mallwyd, Newport (Pemb.) and Amlwch (1902, 1903), chaplain in the training ship *Clio*, and a sub-canon of Bangor cathedral before being inducted rector of Ffestiniog and Maentwrog, 1910-12, and vicar of St. Mary's Bangor, 1913-20. He was vicar of St. Margaret's Oxford, 1920-26, and while he was there he gained his B.Litt. (1920) and D.Phil. (1923) from Corpus Christi. He was vicar of Holyhead, 1926-27, and served afterwards in various English parishes as listed in Crockford's.

He was a very productive scholar in the period after he left college. He edited the first vol. in the Bangor Manuscripts Soc., *Gwaith barddonol Howel Swrdwal a'i fab Ieuan* (1908) and in the same series *Detholiad o waith Gruffudd ab Ieuan ab Llewelyn Vychan* (1910), both editions based on British Museum (Library) MSS. His main work, *Barddoniaeth William Llŷn*, was published in 1908, followed by *A manual of Welsh literature* (1909) based on lectures he had given at University College Cardiff, 1902-03. Morrice was one of the first generation of editors of the work of the *cywydd* poets and though these editions have the shortcomings of their period he could have become an acknowledged editor and literary historian and he could

have followed a univesity career. He was nominated by the College Board for the chair of Welsh at St. David's College Lampeter in 1903 but the college Council did not accept the proposed arrangements. He was for a time lecturer in Welsh at University College Cardiff. *Wales in the seventeenth century* appeared in 1918 and his D.Phil. dissertation, *Social conditions in Wales under the Tudors and Stuarts*, in 1925.

He retired from the rectorship of Helmdon Brockley, Northants in Oct. 1951; he d. 22 Jan. 1953 in Bournemouth.

Crockford, 1951-52; *Www*; *WWP*; *Llan*, 31 Jan. 1941, 3; *Welsh Gossip*, 28 Nov. 1923; University of Wales Bangor records 16446; D.T.W. Price, *Hist. of St. David's University College* (1990).

B.F.R.

MORRIS, CAREY (1882-1968), artist; b. 17 May 1882 at Llandeilo, Carms., son of Benjamin and Elizabeth Boynes Morris. He attended Llandeilo county school, and soon rebelled against the Board of Education's mechanical method of teaching art. He went to the Slade in London, and excelled in the study of anatomy under the instruction of Henry Tonks. In 1911 he m. Jessie Phillips, and became a member of the numerous groups of artists who were working at Newlyn, Cornwall. With his wife, who was an author and editor, he moved to London, where he had a studio in Cheyne Walk, Chelsea. There he met prominent artists of the day, as well as writers and musicians. He himself played the cello at musical evenings. He frequently returned to Llandeilo and the Towy valley to paint, but enlisted in the army in 1914, and later obtained a commission in the South Wales Borderers. He suffered from the effects of gas in Flanders and his health was impaired for the rest of his life. He claimed descent from the Morrises of Anglesey (John, Lewis, Morris, Richard a William Morris, *DWB*, 661, 661-2, 663, 663-4, 666-7), and one of his interests after the war was the issue of art and craft at the National *Eisteddfod*. He saw the need for reforming the *Gorsedd* ceremonies, and wrote extensively on the topic. He published articles on art, such as 'Personality as a force in art' and 'Art and religion in Wales'.

He worked on landscapes and portraits throughout Wales, and his patrons include some aristocratic families. One of his close friends was Sir Joseph Bradney (*DWB*, 48), the historian of Monmouthshire. He illustrated books, particularly the children's books which his wife wrote, and he made the illustrations for *Taith y pererin*, an adaptation of *Pilgrim's Progress* by Edward Tegla Davies (see above). He d. 17 Nov. 1968 and was buried in Llandeilo churchyard.

Eirwen Jones, 'An artist in peace and war', *Carms. Historian*, 1978, 29-42.

El.G.J.

MORRIS, HAYDN (1891-1965), musician; b. 18 Feb. 1891, at Llanarthne, Carms., son of a coalminer, and the youngest of seven children, but he lost his parents (Richard and Rachel Morris) when he was young. He went to work in the New Cross Hands coalmine when he was 12 years old, and stayed there until he decided to devote himself entirely to music in 1916. He took an interest in music very early in life, and studied first under local teachers, and then under D. Vaughan Thomas (*DWB*, 943-4) at Swansea. After becoming A.R.C.M. in 1918 a concert was arranged to assist him to further his education. He went to the Royal Academy of Music in London later that year where he studied till 1922, gaining the Oliveria Prescott prize for composition and receiving the special commendation of Edward Elgar. He graduated Mus.Bac. in 1923, and received a D.Mus. degree of the University of New York in 1943.

He declined posts at the Royal Academy of Music and in Canada in 1923, and spent his career as organist and choirmaster in three churches in Wales, namely at the church in Union St., Carmarthen (until 1926), Soar, Merthyr Tydfil (1926-28), and Capel Als, Llanelli (1928-60). In Llanelli he was active as teacher, adjudicator, conductor and composer. He d. Dec. 1965 and was buried at Llanelli.

He was one of the three prominent composers of the period between the two World Wars who gained their apprenticeship through the National *Eisteddfod* (the other two were W. Bradwen Jones (see JONES, WILLIAM ARTHUR above) and W. Albert Williams (see below), and over a period of about 40 years he won more than 60 prizes in the composition section at the National *Eisteddfod*. He is regarded as one of the most versatile and prolific of Welsh composers of his day.

He published more than 450 diverse musical works, including operas, operettas, part-songs, cantatas, solos, and pieces for brass bands, piano, strings and orchestra. He was also author of several collections of melodies for the harp, ballads and songs, besides a useful handbook on *penillion* singing and a tutor on playing the piano (the only publication of its kind by a Welsh composer at the time) which he published at his own expense in 1924.

Personal research and information from his widow, Mrs. Eluned Morris, Llanelli.

H.W.

MORRIS, JOHN RICHARD (1879-1970), bookseller, writer; b. 13 Aug. 1879, son of Richard Morris, a quarryman who d. 6 March 1884 at Ebeneser, Llanddeiniolen, Caerns., and Jane his wife who remarried. He attended Penisa'r-waun and Llanrug schools, though the Sunday school and the Band of Hope also played an important part in his education. At eleven years of age he went to work on his uncle's smallholding for two years, and after seven years' employment in a slate quarry he ran away to become a collier in Ashton-in-Makerfield, Lancs., 1899-1910, when he was obliged to retire because of ill-health. Eventually he moved to Liverpool where he held various posts until he and Rolant Wyn opened a Welsh book-shop there. The business expanded to include typing, printing and publishing Welsh plays under the name 'Wyn Edwards and Morris'. They also translated the plays of Ibsen and others into Welsh, but the business failed during the depression. In 1933 J.R. Morris opened a very successful Welsh book-shop in Caernarfon which was sold when he retired aged 80. From 1939 onwards he lived at Hafod Lên, Bethel.

He was a member of a musical family and won prizes as a soloist, as well as a crown and many chairs for poetry. He was a prominent member of the Welsh community whilst living in England, as secretary of local *eisteddfodau*, a Sunday school teacher, conductor of a children's choir and a lay preacher. He became one of the founders of *Undeb y Ddraig Goch* in Liverpool in 1918, a movement supporting self-government for Wales. He held classes teaching *cynghanedd* and his papers at the National Library of Wales contain a large collection of *englynion*. His poems and articles appeared in many newspapers and periodicals. But he is best remembered as a bookseller; he attended countless auctions to buy books, many of which he sold to America. A notable aspect of his shop was its extensive stock of music - he published a catalogue of 800 Welsh solos - and he held in stock every Welsh play he could acquire. He was the author of a comedy, *Luned* (1928), and after retiring he wrote his autobiography, *Atgofion llyfrwerthwr* (1963) and a romantic novel, *Allwedd Serch*, which is among his papers at N.L.W.

He m. (spring 1905 ?) and he and his wife Elizabeth had two children who d. young. His wife d. 21 Sept. 1950; he d. 26 Apr. 1970 and was buried in Llanrug churchyard.

J.R. Morris MSS at N.L.W.; *WWP*; [Dafydd Islwyn, *Gen.*, 1973, 78-83].

M.A.J.

MORRIS, PERCY (1893-1967), politician and trade unionist; b. 6 Oct. 1893 at Swansea, the son of Thomas and Emma Morris. He was educated at Manselton elementary school and Dynevor secondary school, Swansea. He became involved in Labour politics in his youth, and was much sought after as an eloquent public speaker even during his schooldays. In 1908 he was appointed to an administrative post on the Great Western Railway and immediately became a vigorous trade unionist. Morris was elected a member of the Borough Council in 1927, became a council alderman, and in 1935 was elected chairman of its Parliamentary Committee. He served as deputy mayor in 1944-45 and mayor in 1955-56, and he was a member of a large number of its committees. In 1939 he was chosen J.P. for the town of Swansea. He served as treasurer of the Railways Clerks' Association, 1937-43, and as its president, 1943-53, and from 1941 until 1945 he was the Deputy Regional Commissioner for Civil Defence (Wales Region). During World War II he acted as president of the Swansea Labour Association.

Percy Morris stood unsuccessfully as the Labour candidate against Sir Lewis Jones (see above) in the Swansea West division in the 1935 general election. He was elected M.P. (Lab.) for the same constituency in 1945, and continued to represent Swansea West in parliament until 1959 when he lost his seat to the Conservative J.E.H. Rees by 403 votes. He was a member of the Parliamentary Delegation to the Far East in 1955. Morris was also a member of the National Assistance Board, 1961-66, served as its deputy chairman in 1965-66, and also as deputy chairman of the Supplementary Benefits Commission, 1966-67.

For many years he served as a member of the

Council of the University College of Swansea. He played an important part in the Labour politics of Swansea for more than 40 years. He was a committed Independent and a lay preacher, and between 1927 and 1945 he chaired the Carmarthen district of the South Wales Congregationalist Union. He became a freeman of the county borough of Swansea in 1958 and received the C.B.E. in 1963.

Morris m. (1) in 1920 Elizabeth, dau. of William Davies. She and Morris's sister and brother-in-law, were killed during the German bombing of Swansea in Jan. 1941. He m. (2) in 1956 Catherine Evans. His home was at 30 Lôn Cedwyn, Cwmgwyn, Swansea. He d. 7 March 1967.

Www; Dod's Parliamentary Companion; Times, 8 and 15 Mar. 1967; WWP.

J.G.J.

MORRIS, Sir RHYS HOPKIN (1888-1956), politician, stipendiary magistrate, first director of the Welsh Region B.B.C.; b. 5 Sept. 1888 at Blaencaerau farm, Caerau, Maesteg, Glam., son of John Morris (Congl. minister in Caerau) and Mary, dau. of Rhys Hopkin, Blaencaerau. He had one sister, Sarah, born in 1890. His parents died within three months of each other when he was 16 and he was then brought up by his uncle, another Rhys Hopkin. He was educated at home by his parents, the Cymmer Pupil Teacher Centre, and as a pupil teacher at Glyncorrwg school (under Lewis Davies, see above) in 1902. In 1910 he entered U.C.N.W., Bangor as a theological student, but read Philosophy instead, graduating in 1912 and serving as student President in 1911. He taught in Bargoed for a few months after leaving College but enlisted in the Royal Welch Fusiliers on the outbreak of war in 1914; he was commissioned and served throughout the war. He was twice mentioned in dispatches and awarded the M.B.E. (Military Division) for action in which he was severely wounded and carried shrapnel in his leg for the rest of his life.

On 11 Sept. 1918 he m. Gwladys Perrie Williams (b. 24 Nov. 1889) daughter of Elizabeth (author of *Brethyn Cartref* (1951), etc.) and W.H. Williams, Llanrwst, whom he met at Bangor. She completed her D.Lit. in the Sorbonne in 1917 and returned to spend the remainder of the war as south Wales organiser of the Women's Land Army. After demobilization Hopkin Morris read for the Bar at King's College, London, during which time he was supported by his wife who was head of the day continuation school at Debenham's. He was called to the Bar in the Middle Temple in 1920 and practised in the South Wales circuit. He assisted W. Llewelyn Williams (*DWB*, 1085-6) in his election campaign in Cardiganshire, upon whose death in 1922 he was invited to fight the seat for the Asquithian Liberals (the Wee Frees). He was not elected, but dented Ernest Evans' vote, was eventually returned for Cardiganshire in 1923 and remained as Member until 1932 when he applied for the Chiltern Hundreds on being appointed a Metropolitan stipendiary magistrate. In 1936, he became the first director of the B.B.C's new Welsh Region, where he showed his characteristic independence of mind during the difficult war years, and gave valuable encouragement to a number of young men and women who became prominent in Welsh radio and television broadcasting. He strove to maintain the right to broadcast Welsh programmes during the war. He remained at the B.B.C. until 1945 when Carmarthen West invited him to stand in the Liberal interest in the General Election. His was the only Liberal gain from Labour in that election and he kept the seat until his death, with increased majorities at every election. He took silk in 1946, was knighted in the New Year's honours list in 1954, received an honorary degree of Doctor of Laws of the University of Wales and was deputy chairman, Ways and Means, in the House. He was author of *Welsh politics* (1927) and *Dare or despair* (1950). He d. suddenly in his home at Sidcup on 22 Nov. 1956.

Lady Hopkin Morris published two books on education, *Welsh education in sunlight and shadow* (1918) and *The Northamptonshire composition scale* (1933), her thesis for a doctorate, *Li Biaus descouneüs de Renaud de Beaujeu* (1915) and *Le bel inconnu* (1929). She was chief external examiner for several county educational authorities. She d. 13 July 1958. They had one daughter, Perrie, b. 1923, who m. Alun Williams the B.B.C. commentator in 1944.

Personal knowledge; [see also Thomas John Evans, *Sir Rhys Hopkin Morris* (1958), John Emanuel and D. Ben Rees, *Syr Rhys Hopkin Morris* (1980); Sir Rhys Hopkin Morris papers at N.L.W.]

D.A.W., E.D.J.

MORRIS, ROBERT DAVID (1871-1948), itinerant bookseller and author; b. at Nant, Coedpoeth, Denbs., 18 Dec. 1871, the son of David and Hannah Morris. He left school early and went to work in a coalmine. After a few years as a collier, he opened a Welsh newspaper and book-shop in the High Street at Coed-poeth. In the 1920s he began to travel throughout north Wales, selling Welsh books which he collected from the Brython Press (Hugh Evans & Sons, Liverpool) and Hughes & Son, Wrexham. He and his little car became well known to hundreds of people in the rural areas, and he called regularly at out-of-the-way farms and cottages. He carried on until his death and was one of the last itinerant booksellers in Wales.

Though his formal education had been but slight, when he saw the need for popular literature in Welsh he resolved to meet the demand. In the preface to his second novel he drew attention to the reaction of young readers to the lack of Welsh novels which led them to prefer popular English novels. He saw the novel as the most effective means of winning them back to read Welsh. His first novel *Derwyn*, 1924, attracted many readers. It was followed by *Serch Gwalia*, 1925, *Merch y castell*, 1928, and *Llwybr y merthyr*, 1935. He published two comedies, *Ffordd Sera Parri* and *Gŵr Betsan Huws*, and a play, *Y Clwyf*, depicting the devastating effect of World War I upon a particular family. A large number of performances of his comedies were produced in all parts of Wales.

He had a passion for reform in Wales. He was one of the leaders of the I.L.P. in his district. He reacted against the system which made Welsh a language of religion and chapel and enthroned English as the language of education and trade. He insisted on speaking Welsh in the shops of

Wrexham which had adopted the new fashion. He dedicated his first novel to E.T. John, M.P. (*DWB.*, 440) in recognition of 'his zeal and efforts for Wales'.

For many years he was a Sunday school teacher of a class of young men at Salem, Coedpoeth. He taught those pupils to detest all wars, and inspired many of them with his vision of a more just world.

He m. (1) Elizabeth Roberts, of Nant, Coedpoeth, who d. in 1906; and (2) Elizabeth Hughes of Blaenau Ffestiniog. He d. 1 Aug. 1948, at the age of 77, and was buried in the Coed-poeth public cemetery.

Personal knowledge; *Porfeydd*, 1978.

D.M.J.

MYFYR EIFION - see HUGHES, DAVID ROWLAND above.

MYFYR HEFIN - see BOWEN, DAVID above.

MYRDDIN-EVANS, Sir GUILDHAUME (1894-1964), civil servant; b. 17 Dec. 1894, the second son of Rev. Thomas Towy Evans, minister (B.) at Blaenau Gwent, Abertillery, Mon., and Mary (née James) his wife. He was educated at Cwmtillery elementary school, Abertillery county school, Llandovery College and Christ Church, Oxford, where he graduated with first class honours in mathematics. He served as a lieutenant with the South Wales Borderers in France and Flanders during World War I and was seriously wounded. He was a member of Lloyd George's personal secretariat at 10 Downing Street in 1917, and assistant secretary to the War Cabinet in 1919. He held a number of key positions within the Treasury from 1920 until 1929 when he was appointed to the Ministry of Labour. Myrddin-Evans served as the Head of the Production Executive Secretariat at the War Cabinet Offices in 1941, and as adviser to the War Manpower Commission of the government of the U.S.A. in 1942. He also acted as adviser to the Canadian government. He returned to the Ministry of Labour and National Service as under-secretary in 1942 and deputy secretary in 1945. Between 1945 and 1959 he was the representative of the British government on the governing body of the International Labour Office which he chaired on three occasions. From 1955 until 1959 (when he retired) he was the Chief International Labour Adviser to H.M. Government. He was the chairman of the Local Government Commission for Wales in 1959 when he proved himself a popular and amiable but efficient colleague. The report of the Commission appeared in 1963. From 1943 Myrddin-Evans was a member of the Council of the Baptist Union of Great Britain and Ireland, and he served, too, as the secretary of the Bloomsbury Central Baptist Church in London. He was joint-author of the volume *The employment exchange of Great Britain* (1934). He received the C.B. in 1945 and the K.C.M.G. in 1947.

He m. in 1919 Elizabeth (who d. in 1981), the dau. of Owen Watkins of Sarn, Caerns. (Watkins, too, was a member of Lloyd George's personal secretariat during World War I). They had two sons. He d. 15 Feb. 1964 at his home 6 Chester Place, Regent's Park, London.

Www; DNB; Times, 17 and 24 Feb. 1964; *West. Mail*, 17 Feb. 1964; *WWP*.

J.G.J.

N

NANTLAIS - see WILLIAMS, WILLIAM NANTLAIS below.

NASH-WILLIAMS, VICTOR ERLE (1897-1955), archaeologist; b. 21 Aug. 1897 at Fleur-de-Lys, Mon., s. of Albert Henry and Maude Rosetta (née Nash) Williams. The father, a monumental mason, died when the children were quite young, and his widow took by deed-poll the surname Nash-Williams. Victor was educated at Lewis' School, Pengam, and University College, Cardiff, graduating B.A. with first-class hons. in Latin, 1922; M.A., 1923; awarded D.Litt., 1939; elected F.S.A. 1930; served on the council of the Society, 1953-54; and also on the Council of the Society for the Promotion of Roman Studies, 1932-35; president, Cambr. Arch. Assn., 1953-54, and editor of *Arch. Camb.* 1950-55. He was nominated a member of the Ancient Monuments Board for Wales in 1954, and a commissioner of the Royal Commission on Ancient and Historical Monuments (Wales) in 1955. He served in both World Wars (infantry, 1915-19; R.A.S.C. and latterly as Major in the Historical Section of the War Office, 1940-45); among other interests, he took particular pride in his membership of the Governing Body of the Church in Wales. In 1931 he m. Margaret Elizabeth, daughter of William Luck of Liverpool; they had two sons. He d. 15 Dec. 1955.

Nash-Williams spent his entire professional career in the service of the National Museum of Wales and of the University College, Cardiff. When Mortimer Wheeler whose early pupil he was, became director of the National Museum in 1924, Nash-Williams was offered the Assistant Keepership of the Department of Archaeology under Cyril Fox (see above); and when Fox in his turn became Director, Nash-Williams became Keeper of the department and also lecturer in archaeology at the College, a post conjoint with the keepership since Wheeler's arrival in 1920; Nash-Williams, however, was destined to be the last holder of both positions. His interests lay mainly in the Roman and Early Christian periods. He was an enthusiastic and indefatigable excavator, having imbibed Wheeler's early teaching, but developing no further: his best excavation-reports, thus, are his earliest – on Jenkins's Field and the Prysg Field, Caerleon, and on the baths, etc., and the defences of Caerwent. In connexion with Caerwent, he excavated at the Late Iron Age hillfort at Llanmelin and at Sudbrook promontory fort on the Severn coast; later, he re-excavated the Roman villa at Llantwit Major, and at the time of his death was engaged in an important series of 'digs' outside the legionary fortress of Caerleon. His earliest general publication in the Roman field was his *Catalogue of the Roman inscribed and sculptured stones found at Caerleon* (Nat. Mus. of Wales, 1935), in which his brother, Alva Harry, was co-author; his last such, *The Roman frontier in Wales* (Cardiff, 1954), 'severely factual' (H.J. Randall see below). In both these, he showed a decided ability to analyse, condense, and arrange diverse materials; and this character was exemplified to a greater and even more valuable extent in the one work of his which may justly be claimed to be a masterpiece, and into which the love and labour of many years, and the spiritual feeling of a devout Christian, also went: his *Early Christian monuments of Wales* (Cardiff, 1950). The memorial inscription on bronze at the Legionary Museum of Caerleon, now facing the great imperial inscription of AD 100 which he himself discovered, ends with these lines:

He was gracious in life, exact in scholarship, fearless in advocating what he believed to be the truth, unfailing in friendship, and selflessly helpful to his colleagues, his staff, and his students.

Obit. notice by H.J. Randall, *Arch. Camb.*, cv, 1956, 150-1; Nat. Mus. of Wales, *Forty-ninth Annual Report 1955-6*, 1956, 12-13; *Www.*

G.C.B.

NEPEAN (née BELLIS), MARY EDITH (1876-1960), novelist; b. at Llandudno, Caern. in 1876, daughter of John Bellis, a Caernarfonshire county councillor, and Mary, his wife. She was educated at home, studying art with Robert Fowler, and later showed her work at a number of exhibitions. She m. in 1899 Molyneux Edward Nepean, of a family of high-ranking civil servants, and resided in England, moving in literary circles in London. In 1932 she accused Caradoc Evans (see above) of libelling her in his novel *Wasps* (1933), and the book had to be altered before publication. She also took part in public life, being Commandant of a section of the Red Cross in Kent, and travelled in the Near East and the Balkans, taking a particular interest in the life of the gypsies of Transylvania.

Her first novel, *Gwyneth of the Welsh Hills* (1917), showed the influence of both Allen Raine (Anne Adalisa Puddicombe, *DWB*, 810) and Caradoc Evans. A further 34 light romantic novels followed, almost all with Welsh settings or characters, and she wrote one book based on her travels, *Romance and realism in the Near East* (1933), as well as much popular journalism. Her husband d. in 1948. She d. 23 March 1960 and was buried in the Great Orme cemetery, Llandudno.

Www; T.L. Williams, *Caradoc Evans* (1970), 93-4; *Llandudno and District Advertiser*, 26 March and 2 Apr. 1960.

S.R.J.

NICHOLAS, JAMES (1877-1963), Baptist minister; b. 12 Jan. 1877 at y Bryn, Cwmfelinmynach, Llanwinio, Carm., the son of Benjamin Nicholas (d. 10 Aug. 1931 aged 88) and Mary Nicholas (d. 23 Oct. 1900 aged 56). His father was a member of the Independent church at Llanboidy and his mother at the Baptist church at Ramoth, Cwmfelinmynach. It is recorded on the gravestone of his parents in Ramoth graveyard that they both came from Blaendyffryn. William Thomas, the Independent minister at

Llanboidy, influenced him greatly, but he became a member at Ramoth with his mother. He was baptized, aged 16, by the minister, D.S. Davies (Dafis Login) and he delivered his first sermon in April 1898. Following nine months at the Old College School at Carmarthen, he became a student at the Presbyterian College Carmarthen 1899-1901.

He was ordained as the minister of Moreia, Tonypandy on 14 Oct. 1901. He saw a recently founded church develop into a thriving cause, designing for itself a new place of worship in 1906. He also saw the Rhondda valley roused by the Revival of 1904-05 and the growth of the Labour Movement. Like William John, the secretary of Moreia, he was one of the few who tried to avoid the estrangement and separation that occurred between these two forces: for his own reaction to the situation see the articles *O fwg Morgannwg* by 'O.K.' that can be safely attributed to him in the period Oct 1907 - Mar. 1908 in *Y Piwritan Newydd* (the magazine of the Baptists of south-west Wales). He was temporarily released from his pastorate in 1915 to serve with the Y.M.C.A. in France but within a year he accepted an invitation to become the minister of Castle Street church, London. He was installed there on 26 Oct. 1916 with David Lloyd George (see above) presiding at the service. The next years were in many senses a memorable period in the history of the church, e.g. renovating the chapel building in 1924, sponsoring churches in distress in the Rhondda valley from 1928 onward, establishing churches in suburbs like Dagenham in 1928. A feature of his ministry lay in welcoming and succouring the host of young people who thronged to London in the years of the depression and, in his own words, 'being a friend to young Welsh people away from home', thereby swelling the ranks of the church, by 1931, to a membership of over 1000. He was also prominent in London-Welsh circles, e.g. he was the president of the Carmarthenshire Society 1954-56. He was elevated to become the president of the Welsh section of the Baptist Union of Wales in 1952-53 and the subject of his address in Llandudno was 'Yr Uchel Alwedigaeth'. Ill-health caused him to retire in 1934 and again in 1938 after having returned to the pastorate in 1937.

He died on 10 July 1963 at his home at 122 Rivermead Court, Hurlingham, and he was cremated on 13 July at Golders Green. Memorial services were held at Moreia, Tonypandy and at Castle Street on 18 July and at Ramoth, Cwmfelinmynach on 21 July 1963. He m. 18 Feb. 1936, Gertrude Thomas (née Crocker) of Epsom. She died on 9 Dec. 1942.

NLW. MS. 10329; *Seren Cymru*, 8 Nov. 1901, 24 Nov. 1916, 28 Aug. 1931, 15 Jan. 1943, 9 Nov. 1951, 12 Jan. 1962, 19, 26 July, 9, 16 Aug. 1963; *Greal*, 1906, 51-2, 1908, 163; *Seren Gomer*, 1953, 5-8; *Cymro*, 25 Jul. 1963; *Llawlyfr y Bedyddwyr*, 1964, 118-19; *Baptist Handbook*, 1964, 366; Walter P. John and Gwilym T. Hughes, *Hanes Castle Steet ... Llundain* (1959), 72-3, 81-2; *WWP*; information provided by Nansi Evans, Cwmfelinmynach.

B.G.O.

NICHOLSON, WILLIAM JOHN (1866-1943), minister (Congl.); b. 23 Dec. 1866, at 14 Vrondeg Street, Bangor, s. of William Nicholson

(*DWB*, 685). He was admitted to the Memorial College at Brecon in 1886 and he spent the first year at the University College, Cardiff. In May 1889 he was ord. minister of St. Paul's Church Swansea. In 1892 he became minister of Salem church, Porthmadog, and remained there until 1940, when ill health and defective eyesight forced him to retire. He was chairman of the Welsh Congl. Union, 1929-30.

Inheriting many of his father's gifts as a preacher, he reached the front rank at an early age and maintained his popularity to the end. He was a preacher by instinct and did not involve himself to a great extent with matters outside his pulpit; he was a cultured student, and did not allow his gifts to become his master; he possessed a sense of humour which made him an outstanding character among his fellow ministers. He d. 25 Nov. 1943 at the age of 77 and was buried at Porthmadog.

Tyst, 2, 9, 16 Dec. 1943.

R.G.O.

NORTH, FREDERICK JOHN (1889-1968), geologist, educator, historian of science and museum curator; b. in London in 1889 of a Welsh mother and an English father, he left school at 14 and learnt his geology in evening classes whilst working in a chemical factory and as a laboratory assistant (later a demonstrator) in King's College, University of London. He took an external degree, with 1st-class honours, at that University, before joining the staff of the National Museum of Wales where he served for 42 years, initially as assistant keeper of the Department of Geology and from 1919 to 1959 as Keeper; from 1959 to 1960 he was Honorary Keeper of the newly created Department of Industry.

His interest in geology and its allied sciences was catholic, as expressed in two hundred or so articles and twelve books. He excelled in compilative writing, as seen in books such as *The slates of Wales* (1925); *Coal, and the coalfields in Wales* (1926); *The evolution of the Bristol Channel with special reference to the coast of South Wales* (1929); *Limestones, their origins, distribution, and uses* (1930); *Studies in the origin of the scenery of Wales, 1 - The river scenery at the head of the Vale of Neath* (1930); and, with Bruce Campbell and Richenda Scott, *Snowdonia: The National Park of Wales* (1948). He paid particular attention to the study of maps: his published works include *Geological maps: their history and development, with special reference to Wales* (1928); *The map of Wales [before 1600 A.D.]* (1935); and *Humphrey Lhuyd's maps of England and Wales* (1937), which remains the definitive monograph.

He was one of the most active historians of geology of his time. Each of his compilative books contains a wealth of historical material and he also wrote monographs on a number of the nineteenth-century pioneers of geology - W.D. Conybeare (*DWB*, 81), Dean William Buckland, Charles Lyell and particularly H.T. de la Beche, founder of the Geological Survey of Great Britain, the Museum of Practical Geology and the Royal School of Mines. He contributed many items to *DWB*. He maintained an active interest in the history of industry in Wales, particularly the extractive industries, and in essence was the founder of the Department of Industry which was formed at the National Museum in 1958. He was always interested in the connection of geology with other subjects, as seen in *The stones of Llandaff Cathedral* (1958), *Sunken cities, some legends of the coast and lakes of Wales* (1957) and *Mining for metals in Wales* (1962).

He was a proficient curator who built up the Department of Geology at the National Museum and who wrote a great deal on the work of a museum curator, including a standard guide, *Geology in museums* (1939). He was a keen advocate of the museum profession - a long-serving Council member of the Museums Association, President in 1952-53, for many years Chairman of the Education Committee, architect of the Association's first Diploma, member of the Joint Committee with the Carnegie United Kingdom Trust; he was also a member of the National Co-operative Body for Museums for UNESCO. He was above all an ardent educator and proselytizer of his subject, an indefatigable lecturer, reviewer and annalist. He acted regularly as a consultant geologist for public bodies on water conservation projects and on quarrying ventures, and his contributions were recognised as President (and winner of the Gold Medal) of the South Wales Institute of Engineers, as an Honorary Fellow of the Institute of Quarrying and the Permanent Way Institute and as a member of a Committee on the slate industry appointed by the Ministry of Works.

He was awarded a D.Sc. by the University of London in 1920 for research work on fossil brachiopods, an O.B.E. in 1949 'for services to science in Wales', and an Honorary D.Sc. in the same year in the citation for which is stated: 'For him a museum is essentially an interpreter's house'.

He m. Ellen M. Pierce, Ticehurst, in May 1915. He d. 23 July 1968 at 19 Chargot Road, Cardiff.

Obit. Notice, Museums Association *Monthly Bulletin*, 1968; reference to his work on De la Beche in the foreword to *Henry de la Beche: observations on an observer* (Cardiff 1977); and a brief list of publications in *Amgueddfa, Bulletin of the Nat. Mus. of Wales* 15, Winter, 1973. Personal details from his dau., Laura North.

D.A.B.

NORTH, HERBERT LUCK (1871-1941), architect; b. at Leicester in 1871, s. of Thomas and Fanny North. He was educated at Uppingham school and Jesus College, Cambridge, where he took his B.A. In 1897 he m. Ida Maude Davies, and they had one dau. Settling at Llanfairfechan he became interested in the old buildings of Snowdonia. He published *The old churches of Arllechwedd*, Bangor, 1906, *The old cottages of Snowdonia* (1908, jointly with Henry Harold Hughes, *DWB*, 375) and *The Old Churches of Snowdonia* (1924, with H. H. Hughes). He d. 9 Feb. 1941.

Www, 1941-50.

G.M.G.

NOVELLO, IVOR (DAVID IVOR DAVIES till 1927; 1893-1951), composer, playwright, stage and film actor; b. at 95 Cowbridge Rd, Cardiff, 15 Jan. 1893, of a very musical family who soon

moved to Llwyn-yr-eos, 11 Cathedral Road, Cardiff, the only son of David Davies, rates collector, and Clara Novello Davies (see above). He attended Mrs. Soulez' school nearby and received musical tuition from his mother and (Sir) Herbert Brewer, Gloucester. His good soprano voice won him prizes at *eisteddfodau*, and a choral scholarship to Magdalen College School, Oxford, when he was 10 years old. He soon became a soloist with the college choir but never sang in public after his voice broke at the age of 16. He returned home as a piano teacher and accompanist at his mother's concerts but left for London a year later where he continued as her accompanist and composed ballads. In 1913 he moved to 11 Aldwych where he lived for the rest of his life, though he had a country home at Downley, Bucks., and later bought Redroofs, near Maidenhead. He d. suddenly 6 March 1951, a bachelor at the height of his fame.

Nearly the whole of his life was spent in a musical atmosphere. He was constantly busy, acting in films or plays - many of which were his own work - sometimes filming during the day, on stage in the evening, and every spare moment writing and composing new works, nearly every one more brilliant than the one before. He was only 15 years old when, as Ivor Novello, his first song, 'Spring of the year', was published. At the age of 21 he became famous for his war-time song 'Keep the home fires burning', the lyrics written by Lena Guilbert Ford. He wrote approximately 60 ballads and songs, including 'We'll gather lilacs'. In 1916 he joined the Royal Naval Air Force but failed as a pilot and was transferred to the Air Ministry. During this time he composed his first theatre score, for the show *Theodore & Co*. He was sent on a highly successful mission to Sweden in 1918 as an entertainer to nullify the effects of German propaganda in that country. After his release from the forces in 1919 he took the leading part in the London film *The Call of Blood*, and subsequently starred in about 16 other British and American films. His greatest desire to become a stage actor was realized in 1921 when he took a small part in *Deburaut. The Rat*, his first play (which was later filmed), proved a success for him as author and actor. He wrote and acted in numerous other plays before joining to musical plays, his most popular compositions of all, beginning with *Glamorous night* (1935), whilst his seventh and last, *King's Rhapsody* (1949), was his finest work in this field. There is no doubt that he drew the crowds when he was in the cast. See Sandy Wilson, *Ivor* (1975), for a remarkable list of his songs, plays, films and musical plays, his numerous performances on stage and in films, and his work as a producer and manager; also for references to earlier biographies. His bust was placed in the Theatre Royal, Drury Lane, and commemorative plaques mark both his birthplace and his London home, where he died.

Www; W. Macqueen-Pope, *Ivor: the story of an achievement* (1951); D.R. Davies collection, 52, at N.L.W.; NLW MSS 20972-3 for correspondence between Ivor Novello and Sir Edward Marsh; [James Harding, *Ivor Novello* (1996); and biographical studies by Paul Webb (1999), Graham Jones (1997)].

M.A.J.

O

O'NEILL, BRYAN HUGH ST. JOHN (1905-54), archaeologist; b. 7 Aug. 1905 in London, son of Charles Valentine O'Neill and Mabel Meliora (née Rowe). He was educated at Merchant Taylor's School and St. John's College, Oxford (M.A.); elected F.S.A. in 1935. He m. in 1939 Helen Evangeline Donovan of Bourton-on-the-water, Glos., who was also an archaeologist.

He was appointed to the Office of Works in 1930 as Assistant Inspector of Ancient Monuments and assigned to Wales in succession to C.A. Ralegh Radford, a post which he occupied until 1945, when he was made Chief Inspector of Ancient Monuments for England and Wales. He was responsible for advising on the conservation and presentation of ancient monuments in the guardianship of the State and of the scheduling of those worthy of preservation, by whomever owned. His office was in London, and in his fifteen years of Welsh duties he had no permanent residence in Wales. He joined the Cambrian Archaeological Association in 1931 and later served on its General Committee. Of his 200 listed publications, one third had to do with Welsh archaeology, and appeared mainly in *Archaeologia Cambrensis*, *The Montgomeryshire Collections* and publications of H.M.S.O. As inspector he had to write or commission authoritative guide books to ancient monuments of all periods. He specialised in mediaeval castles. He was an energetic excavator and is remembered in Wales for his work on the prehistoric hill-forts of Breiddin and Ffridd Faldwyn, Mont., and Titterstone Clee, Salop.

O'Neill had a life-long interest in coins and was a Fellow of the Royal Numismatic Society. He travelled widely and produced an officially-sponsored report on the coastal castles of the Gold Coast (now Ghana). He was secretary and editor of the Congress of Archaeological Societies. He was an industrious and conscientious worker, a zealous churchman and a keen follower of rugby. He d. 24 Oct. 1954 in Edinburgh.

E.M. Jope, 'Bryan H. St. John O'Neill: a memoir', 'The published works of B.H. St. J. O'Neill', and portrait in *Studies in building history*, ed. E.M. Jope (1961); *Antiquaries Jnl.*, 35 (1955), nos. 3,4, pp. 285-6; *Index to Arch. Camb. 1901-60*, 211; *Www*; personal knowledge.

Don.M.

ORMSBY-GORE, WILLIAM GEORGE ARTHUR (1885-1964), 4th BARON HARLECH; b. in London, 11 Apr. 1885, son of George Ralph Charles Ormsby-Gore (who became 3rd Baron Harlech in 1904) and Lady Margaret Ethel (née Gordon). The family home was Brogyntyn, near Oswestry, Salop. He was educated at Eton and Oxford and in 1913 he m. Lady Beatrice Cecil, a member of a prominent Conservative family.

In 1910 he was elected M.P. for the Borough of Denbigh by only eight votes but in 1918 he moved to a safer seat in Stafford and was a M.P. there until 1938 when he succeeded his father to the House of Lords. He became an expert on the Empire colonies and was Colonial Under-

Secretary from 1922 until 1929 apart from the short period when Labour was in power in 1924. In that year he headed the Commission that visited East and Central Africa. He was a member of the Cabinet, 1931-38, and in 1936 he was appointed Colonial Secretary, for which post his extensive experience in the field was invaluable. However, one of his chief political enemies, Neville Chamberlain, became Prime Minister in 1937 and the following year he resigned in bitter circumstances. He opposed the foreign policies of Chamberlain and he was a constant critic of the Nazis. In brief, he was a sincere and prominent politician although occasionally impulsive.

After retiring from political life he turned his attention to banking and to his interests in the arts. He had already published *Florentine sculptors of the fifteenth century* (1930), *A guide to the Mantegna cartoons at Hampton Court* (1935), and *Guides to the ancient monuments of England* (3 volumes). He and his father deposited a valuable collection of Brogyntyn manuscripts at the National Library of Wales and he was the President of the Library, 1950-58. He was also Pro-Chancellor of the University of Wales and Constable of Harlech and Caernarfon castles. He d. 14 Feb. 1964.

Obituaries from the Times, 1961-70, 350; *DNB*; John Harvey (ed.), *The diplomatic diaries of Oliver Harvey 1937-40* (1970).

G.Je.

OWAIN, OWAIN LLEWELYN (1877-1956), litterateur, musician and journalist; b. 3 July 1877 at Blaen-yr-yrfa, Tal-y-sarn, Nantlle Valley, Caerns., one of the eight children of Hugh Owen (*DWB*, 707) and his wife Mary. When Owain was young, the family moved to Bryn-y-coed in the same district. At twelve years of age the lad went to work to Gloddfa Glai quarry and to 'Cornwall' later. When he was aged fifteen he took to journalism and became a member of the editorial staff of *Y Genedl Gymreig* and *Yr Herald Cymraeg a'r Genedl* after they amalgamated. He retired in 1936 but continued to contribute to the Welsh and English press. He was an able journalist and a careful reporter. As he had literary and musical talent his articles on important national festivals were brilliant contributions in the journalistic press. He conducted singing festivals in Wales and England. He trained many musicians and adjudicated music in more than 550 *eisteddfodau*; he had copies of these programmes. He was a discerning book-collector and maintained that his library was even more extensive than that of Bob Owen (Robert Owen, see below). He had a small choir, 'Côr y Delyn Aur', which won many prizes in *eisteddfodau*. He was one of the founders of 'Clwb Awen a Chân' in Caernarfon and was its secretary. He took a keen interest in *Urdd Gobaith Cymru* in Caernarfon from the movement's early years, and it was he who took charge of its processions through the town on special occasions. He was an ardent supporter of the temperance cause as expounded by the

Rechabites and Good Templars. He published a number of biographies: *Fanny Jones* (1907), *Ieuan Twrog* (1909), *J.O. Jones (Ap Ffarmwr)* (1912), *T.E. Ellis* (1916), *Anthropos a Chlwb Awen a Chân* (1946), *Bywyd, gwaith ac arabedd Anthropos* (1953), articles in *Y Traethodydd* and *Y Drysorfa*, *Cerddoriaeth yng Nghymru* (1946), and the standard work *Hanes y Ddrama yng Nghymru 1850-1943* (1948) which is a shortened version of the essay that won him the prize in the national *eisteddfod* at Bangor in 1943. His first important prize in the national *eisteddfod* was for an essay entitled 'Gweithiau ac athrylith Llew Llwyfo' awarded at Colwyn Bay in 1910. R. Williams Parry (see below) won the chair for his ode 'Yr Haf' in the same *eisteddfod*. A procession was organised, lead by the Nantlle band, to welcome both home from that *eisteddfod*.

He m. (1) Claudia Roberts, 12 June 1916; one daughter was born to them. His wife d. 29 Nov. 1918. He m. (2) in 1921 Enid May Jones from Port Dinorwic. He d. at his home Bryn-y-coed, 10 Pretoria Avenue, Caernarfon, on 8 Jan. 1956 and left a widow and a son and daughter. He was cremated in Birkenhead.

Herald Cymr. a'r Genedl, 16 Jan. 1956; *Gol.*, 18 Jan. 1956.

E.D.J.

OWEN, Sir ARTHUR DAVID KEMP (1904-70), international administrator; b. 26 Nov. 1904, the eldest son of Edward Owen, minister of Crane Street church (B), Pontypool, Mon., who some months previously had moved from Bethel church (B), Tonypandy, and his wife Gertrude Louisa, daughter of Thomas Henry Kemp. (He had been a notable schoolmaster in Tal-y-bont, Cards., from 1865 to 1892 and a master in the Normal department of the University College of Wales from 1892 to 1894, after which he moved to become principal of the Merthyr Tydfil Teachers' Training Centre). The family moved from Wales in 1908 when the father was inducted as minister of Hope church, Hebden, near Leeds. David Kemp, as he was generally known, was educated at Leeds grammar school and the University. He graduated in economics and commercial studies, taking the M.Com. degree in 1929. He was assistant lecturer in economics at Huddersfield Technical College, 1926-29; director of Sheffield Social Survey Committee, 1929-33, secretary of the Civic Division, Political and Economic Planning (P.E.P.), 1933-36; co-director of the Pilgrim Trust Unemployment Enquiry, 1933-37; lecturer in citizenship, University of Glasgow, 1937-40; general secretary, P.E.P., 1940-41. In 1942 he became personal assistant to Sir Stafford Cripps in the office of the Lord Privy Seal and later in the Ministry of Aircraft Production. He was a member of the Cripps mission to India in 1942, and of the Reconstruction Department of the Foreign Office in charge of League of Nations affairs, 1944-45. He was a member of the U.K. Delegation at the International Labour Conferences held in Philadelphia in 1944 and in San Francisco in 1945. He became one of the leading administrators of the United Nations from 1946 until his retirement in 1969. He acted on the editorial board of the *Encyclopaedia Britannica* from 1959 to 1968. He was a steadfast believer in the principle of co-operation

between nations; his service to the United Nations at a time when that organisation was being set up was crucial. His efforts gained him general respect. His Welsh nonconformist ancestry doubtless influenced his ideals; there was a hint of a Welsh accent in his speech. Shortly before his death, he was made General Secretary of the International Planned Parenthood Federation.

He m. in 1933 Elizabeth Joyce, daughter of E.H. Morgan, Methodist minister. A son and a daughter were born to them. After their divorce in 1950 he m. Elizabeth Elsa Miller; they had two sons. He d. in St. Thomas' Hospital, London, on 29 June 1970, after being created K.C.M.G. that year. In addition to publishing his reports on the Sheffield survey in 1931-33, he published *British Social Services* in 1940 and a host of contributions to periodicals. He received honorary LL.D. degrees from the universities of Leeds in 1954, and Wales in 1969.

Www; DNB, 1964-70.

E.D.J.

OWEN, BOB, Croesor - see OWEN, ROBERT below.

OWEN, Sir DAVID JOHN (1874-1941), docks manager; b. in Liverpool 8 Mar. 1874 the son of R. Ceinwenydd Owen, minister (Presb.) and Elizabeth Jane (née Jones). He m. (1), in 1899, Mary Elizabeth (d. 1906) daughter of Captain William Owen, Caernarfon; and (2), in 1908, Marian Maud, widow of J.H. Thomas, Carmarthen, and daughter of Alderman William Williams of Haverfordwest; there were no children. He was educated at the Liverpool Institute and began his career in the service of the Mersey Docks and Harbour Board, Liverpool, and in 1904 became manager and secretary to Paul Brothers, Flour Millers, Liverpool and Birkenhead. In 1908 he was appointed assistant manager of Goole Docks and manager in 1915. Within the year he was made general manager and secretary to the Belfast Harbour Commissioners, a position he held until his appointment as general manager to the Port of London Authority in 1922, which post he held until 1938. During this period he served on many national organisations and became president of the National Confederation of Employers' Organisations. A member of the Royal Commission on Lotteries and Betting between 1932-33 and the Holidays with Pay Committee, 1937, he became chairman of the Merchant Shipping Reserve Advisory Committee of the Board of Trade in 1939. He was also chairman of the Anglesey and Caernarvonshire Agricultural Wages Committee and a member of the Central Advisory Water Committee. He was knighted in 1931. His long association with the major British ports enabled him to contribute to the understanding of their history by means of his publications: *A short history of the Port of Belfast* (1917), *History of Belfast* (1921), *The Port of London yesterday and today* (1927), and *The origin and development of the ports of the United Kingdom* (1939). He d. 17 May 1941.

Www.

D.G.R.

OWEN, DAVID SAMUEL (1887-1959), minister (Presb.); b. 12 Mar. 1887 at Ruthin, Denbs., son of Samuel and Harriet Owen. He was educated in the elementary schools at Ruthin and Abergele; Abergele county school; University College, Bangor (where he graduated B.A.); and Aberystwyth Theological College. He began to preach in 1905 in Bethlehem chapel, Colwyn Bay; he was ord. in 1913, and served as minister of Siloh, Llanelli (1913-15) before receiving a call to Jewin church, London, where he had a successful career and where he remained for the rest of his life. To his deep distress the beautiful chapel of Jewin was destroyed by bombs during World War II, and many of his church members returned to Wales; nevertheless, he continued to labour diligently among those who remained, though he did not live to see a new place of worship built on the site of the old. In 1913 he m. Gracy Jones, Glan Conwy and they had two sons and three daughters. He d. 26 Mar. 1959, and was buried in Bron-y-nant cemetery, Colwyn Bay.

A powerful and popular preacher, there was great demand for his services in Wales, where he served as Moderator of the North Wales Association (1954). From an early age he excelled as an elocutionist at *eisteddfodau*, and he adjudicated recitation competitions regularly for many years at the National *Eisteddfod*.

Www (1921), 347; *Gol.*, 1, 8 and 22 Apr. 1959; *Drys.*, Sept. 1959; *Blwyddiadur MC*, 1960, 270-1; G.M. Roberts, *Y ddinas gadarn* (1974), chapters 9-10; personal acquaintance.

G.M.R.

OWEN, EDWARD (1853-1943), journalist, barrister, and antiquary; b. at Menai Bridge, Anglesey, 9 Mar. 1853, only son of Edward and Sarah Owen, a former deputy chief constable of Anglesey, he was educated locally, and at a private seminary in Dublin. He was the first Welshman to enter the Civil Service by public examination and was appointed to the India Office *c.* 1873, where he remained until his retirement in 1913. During his stay of over sixty years in London, he spent almost all his leisure evenings working in the British Museum and the Public Records Office. He contributed regularly to the *Trans. Hon. Cymm. Soc.* and *Arch. Camb.*; the former society published his *Catalogue of the MSS. relating to Wales in the British Museum.*, Parts I-IV. In 1896, his work on changes in land tenure in mediaeval Wales appeared as an Appendix to the Royal Commission's *Report on Land in Wales*, followed by the publication (1910) of *Ancient tenures of land in North Wales and the Marches* jointly with A.N. Palmer (*DWB*, 727-8) of Wrexham. When the Royal Commission on the Ancient Monuments of Wales was established in 1908, he became its first secretary and editor of its volumes and inventories, and continued as such until about 1927. He was Reader in Welsh Mediaeval Antiquities at the University of Liverpool (1921-43), hon. M.A. 1921; and he received the Cymmr. Medal in 1923. He d. 8 Nov. 1943 aged 91 and was buried three days later in St. Seiriol's Churchyard, Holyhead, where his first wife and young daughter had been buried many years before.

Trans. Angl. Antiq. Soc., 1943, 19-20; *West. Mail*, 11 Nov. 1943; *WwW* (1921).

H.O.

OWEN, ELIZABETH MARY - see JONES, ELIZABETH MARY above.

OWEN, Sir GORONWY (1881-1963), politician; b. 22 June 1881 at Pen-llwyn, Aberystwyth. Cards., the youngest son of Abraham Owen and his wife Margaret (née Sylvanus Williams). He was educated at Ardwyn School, Aberystwyth, and the University College of Wales, Aberystwyth. He graduated M.A. He earned his living as a schoolmaster and lecturer primarily in London for several years before World War I. In 1914 he was one of the founder members of the London Welsh Battalion. Owen served in the army in France during the war, he was mentioned twice in despatches and was awarded the D.S.O. in 1916, attaining the rank of major and later brigade major. In 1919 he was called to the Bar at Gray's Inn, but it was apparent that his main interest lay in the world of finance, commerce and politics. He became a member of the London Stock Exchange, the director of several companies and a member of many commercial and trading organisations.

Goronwy Owen stood as the Liberal candidate for the South Derbyshire division in 1922, and was mentioned as a likely candidate for the University of Wales constituency. Elected for Caernarfonshire in 1923, he continued to represent the constituency in parliament until 1945. He became a member of David Lloyd George's (see above) family group of M.P.'s who opposed the formation of the national government in 1931. Between 1926 and 1931 he served as Liberal Party whip, and during Sept. and Oct. 1931 he held the position of Comptroller of the Household and acted as Liberal Party Chief Whip. He was defeated by Goronwy Roberts (Lab.) in the general election of 1945, and decided not to contest a parliamentary election thereafter.

Owen served as Deputy Lieutenant for Caernarfonshire in 1936, and was a member of the county countil for many years. He succeeded D. Lloyd George as an alderman of the council in May 1945. He was especially interested in the county's needs and problems, and was ever ready to devote his time to attempts to solve them. He chaired the Agricultural Wages Committee for Anglesey and Caernarfonshire and later for Montgomeryshire and Merionethshire. He was also chairman of the Territorial and Auxiliary Forces Association in Anglesey and Caernarfonshire. He acted, too, as his county's Army Welfare Officer. Owen was vice-chairman, 1954-55, and chairman, 1955-56, of the Gwynedd Police Authority, and the High Sheriff of Caernarfonshire in 1950-51. He was chosen J.P. for the county. He wrote a large number of articles in English and Welsh journals. He received the freedom of the Borough of Conway in 1943 and was knighted in 1944.

Owen m. in 1925 Margaret Gladwyn, the widow of Owen Jones, Glanbeuno, Caern. (it was he who erected the monument to Lloyd George in the Castle Square, Caernarfon) and the dau. of David Jones, coal merchant of Denbigh. She was a sister to Edna, the wife of Gwilym Lloyd-George (see above LLOYD GEORGE FAMILY). Goronwy Owen d. 26 Sept. 1963.

Www; *WwW* (1921) and (1937); *Times*, 27 Sept. 1963; *Dod's Parliamentary Companion*; *WWP*.

J.G.J.

OWEN, HUGH (1880-1953), historian; b. 8 May 1880 at Newborough, Angl., son of Hugh and Jane Owen. The family moved to Aigburth, Liverpool, in 1883. He was educated in St. Michael's Hamlet and Oulton schools, and the University of Liverpool. After gaining a teacher's certificate in 1901 he became a history teacher in London, Liverpool and Holywell schools before being appointed head of the history department at Llangefni school in 1918, a post which he held until he retired in 1944. A year after he returned to Anglesey he was elected editor of the transactions of the county's Antiquarian Society and Field Club and he was responsible for the periodical for the next twenty years. Between 1920 and 1949 he edited a number of Anglesey historical sources for inclusion in the periodical, such as the records of the Anglesey court of quarter sessions, 1768-88 (1924); Beaumaris bailiff's accounts, 1779-1805 (1929); a volume of Beaumaris borough records, 1694-1723 (1932) and the diary of Bulkeley Dronwy (1937). He also edited *Braslun o hanes Methodistiaid Calfinaidd Môn, 1880-1935* (1937); and, with Gwilym Peredur Jones, *Caernarvon court rolls, 1361-1402* (1951), and he published the following books: *The life and works of Lewis Morris (Llywelyn Ddu o Fôn) 1701-1765* (1951), *The history of Anglesey constabulary* (1952) and *Hanes plwyf Niwbwrch* (1952). The latter was a prize-winning essay in a competition at Dolgellau national *eisteddfod*, 1949, on the history of any Welsh parish. Not the least of his contributions, however, was his comprehensive index to J.H. Davies (ed.), *The Morris letters* (1907, 1909) which appeared in the periodical between 1942 and 1944, and his edition, *Additional letters of the Morrises of Anglesey* in two parts, *Y Cymmrodor*, 49 (1947, 1949).

The University of Liverpool awarded him a M.A. degree in 1914 for his thesis, 'Pre-Edwardian castles in north Wales'. In 1916 he was elected Fellow of the Royal Historical Society, and of the London Society of Antiquaries (F.S.A.) in 1924.

He m. in 1913 Marian Owen of Bethesda, Caerns., a teacher at Bangor county school. He d. 18 Mar. 1953 at Rhosyr, Llanfair Pwllgwyngyll.

Hugh Owen Papers at NLW; *Herald Môn*, 30 Mar. 1953; *Clorianydd*, 31 Mar. 1953; *Môn*, 1 (1954).

Gl.P.

OWEN, HUGH JOHN (1880-1961), solicitor, author and local historian; b. 5 Feb. 1880 in Pwllheli, Caern., the s. of John Owen, master mariner, and his wife Elizabeth (née Hughes). He was educated at Bala grammar school, Bala. After completing his articles with the firm of Robyns-Owen, Pwllheli, and on being admitted solicitor in 1903, he joined the legal department of London County Council. He served at home and in Greece with the R.A.O.C. during World War I and attained the rank of captain. He was appointed Clerk of the Peace and first full-time Clerk of Merioneth County Council in 1920, posts which he held with distinction until his retirement in March 1954. He was made Deputy Lieutenant of the county in 1949.

Without doubt one of his main interests was the study of local history and he always succeeded in transmitting his enthusiasm to others.

It was he who was mainly responsible for founding the Merioneth Historical and Record Society in 1939, of which he became a vice-president. He served as chairman of the Society's Council with devotion from its inception until his death. He was also prominent in establishing the Merioneth Record Office in 1952 and in the appointment of a county archivist. He represented Merioneth County Council on the Court of Governors of the National Library of Wales from 1934 until his death. He was a painstaking researcher and worked unceasingly on local records of all kinds, particularly on the records of the Merioneth quarter sessions court. He published five volumes: *The Merioneth Volunteers and local militia during the Napoleonic Wars* (1934); *Echoes of old Merioneth* (1944); *Sir Love's adventures in Spain* (1945); *The treasures of the Mawddach* (1950) and *From Merioneth to Botany Bay* (1952). He contributed between 1951-61 numerous articles in the *Jnl. of the Mer. Hist. and Rec. Soc.* His papers are kept in the Record Office in Dolgellau.

He was unmarried. He d. in Pwllheli 29 June 1961 and was buried in St. Hywyn's churchyard, Aberdaron.

Jnl. of the Mer. Hist. and Rec. Soc., iv, 1-2; Sir Edgar Stephens, *The Clerks of the Counties 1360-1960* (1961); *WwW* (1921); *The Times*, 1 July 1961; *Liv. D. P.*, 1 July 1961; *Camb. News*, 7 July 1961; *Y Dydd*, 7, 14 July 1961.

A.Ll.H.

OWEN, JOHN (1864-1953), minister (Presb. C.W.) and author; b. 17 Apr. 1864 at Pen-y-maes, Morfa Nefyn, Caerns., son of James and Margaret Owen. He worked in an office in Liverpool for six years, and began preaching in 1884. He was educated at Clynnog School, Bala College, and Oxford (where he graduated in 1892; M.A. in 1903). For a year he was a tutor at Bala College. He was ord. in 1892, and served as pastor of Gerlan, Bethesda (1892-1902), Bowydd and Blaenau Ffestiniog English church (1902-09), and Engedi, Caernarfon (1909-26). He m. Hannah Evans, Nantlle, but they had no children. He returned to Morfa Nefyn when he retired. He d. 1 Mar. 1953 at the Royal Infirmary, Liverpool, and was buried in Nefyn cemetery.

He was a prominent figure in the Presb. Church of Wales, being twice Moderator of the North Wales Association (1920 and 1949), and Moderator of the General Assembly (1926). He delivered the Davies Lecture in 1923, which was published under the title *Gwybodaeth y Sanctaidd* (1923). He contributed extensively to the periodicals of his denomination, and he was a columnist for *Y Goleuad* from 1930 onwards under the pseudonym 'Sylwedydd'; *Sylwadau Sylwedydd*, a selection of articles from this column was published in 1949. He also published *Cofiant a gweithiau David Roberts y Rhiw* (1908); *Rolant y teiliwr ac ysgrifau eraill* (1920); *Y Cyfundeb a'i neges: the Connexion and its message*, in English and Welsh (1935). He edited volumes of the sermons of John Williams, Brynsiencyn (*DWB*, 1056) (1922 and 1923), and Thomas Charles Williams (*DWB*, 1074-5) (1928 and 1929). He also published a textbook on the journeys of St. Paul (1902), and a commentary on the Gospel according to St. Luke (1927 and 1928). As general editor for the Presbyterian

Bookroom, Caernarfon, he guided for many years the passage of numerous works by other authors through the press. In 1950 he received an honorary D.D. degree of the University of Wales. A selection of his sermons (edited by William Morris) was published posthumously in 1957.

WwW (1921), 350; WwFC, 350; Drys., 1920, 121-3; 1926, 1-3; 1949, 59-63; Gol., 11 March 1953; Blwyddlyfr MC, 1954, 228-9.

G.M.R.

OWEN, JOHN, Y Fenni - see OWEN, OWEN JOHN below.

OWEN, JOHN DYFNALLT ('Dyfnallt'; 1873-1956), minister (Congl.), poet, writer, journalist and Archdruid of Wales; b. 7 Apr. 1873 at Coedffalde, Llan-giwg, Glam., at the foot of the Black Mountain, son of Daniel and Angharad Owen. His mother died when he was a year old and he was brought up by his paternal grandparents. He went to Cwmllynfell school and after a short period working in the mines he entered Parcyfelfed Academy (the Old College School), Carmarthen, and went to Bala-Bangor College in 1894. He was a close friend of Ben Bowen (DWB, 46) and other young poets. His interest in the eisteddfod persisted throughout his ministry in Trawsfynydd (1898-1902) where he was an influence on Ellis Humphrey Evans ('Hedd Wyn'; DWB, 229); and Deiniolen (1902-05) where he became acquainted with Thomas Gwynn Jones (see above) and William John Gruffydd (see above). He then moved to be minister of Sardis, Pontypridd (1905-10) and while he was there he won the crown at Swansea national eisteddfod in 1907 on 'Y Greal Sanctaidd', having been very close to winning at Rhyl in 1904. He m., 11 Aug. 1904, Annie Hopkin of Ystalyfera and they had two children. In 1908 Dyfnallt became a member of the Celtic Congress and maintained an interest in the Celtic countries thereafter. In 1910 he received a call to Lammas Street, Carmarthen where he remained until he retired from the ministry. In 1916 he went to Béthune in France as chaplain to the Y.M.C.A., and published Myfyrion a chaneuon maes y tân, an unique booklet of poems and meditations on his experiences on the battlefield. He wrote poetry only occasionally afterwards although he published a collection of poems, Y Greal a cherddi eraill (1946). He turned his attention to writing and to researching the history of Independent causes. Stephen Hughes (1912) (DWB, 390-1), 'Tomos Glyn Cothi' (Thomas Evans, 1764-1833; DWB, 252-3) (Y Dysgedydd, 1933) and 'Y Tri Brawd o Lanbrynmair' (Adroddiad Undeb yr Annibynwyr, 1928) were some of his heroes, and he wrote about them not so much to record events as to inspire a new generation. In 1927 he was appointed editor of Y Tyst, a position he enjoyed as a means of expressing his views on peace, anti-imperialism, nationalism and Christianity. In 1953, to celebrate his silver jubilee as editor, a collection of his essays was published in Ar y tŵr, a suggestive title conveying the editor as Isaiah's watchman guarding the city from the enemy, which is how he saw himself. He travelled widely in Poland, Italy, Switzerland, Bavaria and Brittany. He pub-

lished a book on his visit to Brittany, O ben tir Llydaw (1934) two collections of essays and articles, Min yr hwyr (1934) and Rhamant a rhyddid (1952), and also contributed numerous articles to the denominational press and The Dictionary of Welsh Biography. When World War II broke out he was in Danzig, and he published articles such as 'Wythnos yn Danzig', 'Arswyd y Gestapo' and 'Hitleriaeth gartref'. After the war he gave refuge in his home in Carmarthen to Ropaz Hemon the Breton writer who had escaped before his trial in Brittany. Dyfnallt was president of the Union of Welsh Independents in 1936 and received an hon. M.A. degree of the University of Wales in 1953. He was elected Archdruid of Wales at Rhyl in 1954. He was then eighty years old and had been enjoying his retirement in Aberystwyth since 1947. He d. 28 Dec. 1956, and his ashes were scattered on the Black Mountain. There was no flattery in the tribute given him in Y Cymro - 'one of the best loved of the Welsh'.

Geraint Elfyn Jones, Bywyd a gwaith John Dyfnallt Owen (1976). [See Emrys Jones in D. Llwyd Morgan, Adnabod deg (1977); Jnl. W.B.S., 11, 120-8, for his bibliography.]

G.E.J.

OWEN, JOHN JONES (1876-1947), musician; b. 2 May 1876 at Bryncoed, Tal-y-sarn, Caern., s. of Hugh Owen (DWB, 707) and Mary his wife, and a brother of Richard G. Owen ('Pencerdd Llyfnwy'; DWB, 719). He learnt to play the organ and the viola. He was conductor of the Nantlle Ladies Choir which took the prize at the Cardiff national eisteddfod of 1897. Appointed organist of Tal-y-sarn (CM) chapel, he succeeded his father as precentor there. Among his compositions which became popular were an anthem, 'Llusern yw Dy air i'm traed', a part-song 'Yr Afonig', and a children's song 'Lw-li-bei'. In 1921 he emigrated to the USA where he graduated Mus. Bac. and became organist and choirmaster of the Evangelical Church, Wilkesbarre; he also served as adjudicator, as conductor of cymanfaoedd canu, and as conductor of the Wilkesbarre Orpheus male voice choir. He d. 21 Apr. 1947 and was buried in Greenwood Mountain cemetery, Wilkesbarre.

Baner, Apr. 1947; Y Genedl a'r Herald, Apr. 1947.

R.D.G.

OWEN, LEONARD (1890-1965), administrator in India, treasurer of the Honourable Society of Cymmrodorion; b. at Bangor, Caerns., 1 Oct. 1890, son of David Owen, solicitor, and Mary (née Roberts) his wife. He was educated at Friars School and the University College of North Wales (1909-14), Bangor, where he played an active part in sport, was president of the literary and debating society and graduated B.A. with first-class honours in French in 1912 and M.A. 1914. He entered the Indian civil service in 1914 but World War I, in which he served in the Royal Field Artillery, delayed his taking up his appointment as assistant magistrate in Meerut until 1919, becoming district magistrate of Benares in 1924, settlement officer at Bara Banki in 1927, deputy commissioner for Kumaon division in 1934 and district magistrate at Cawnpore in 1936. He became chief government whip in the Indian Legislative Assembly (1935), and was made a C.I.E. in 1938 in recognition of his meritorious service to India. During World War II he worked in the Ministry of Home Security (1939-44), Ministry of Supply (1945), and Board of Trade (1946-52), subsequently devoting his time to humanitarian and cultural activities. He was chairman of the National Society for Epileptica, a member of the court of governors and the council of the National Library of Wales, and served the Honourable Society of Cymmrodorion as treasurer (1952-64). He had a great gift for translating Welsh poetry into English, some of which was published in *Trans. Cymm.* together with several valuable articles written by him on aspects of the history of north Wales. His transcripts of early north Wales taxation records are at the University College of Bangor and the National Library of Wales. He also translated very many articles from *Y Bywgraffiadur Cymreig hyd 1940* for inclusion in *The Dictionary of Welsh biography down to 1940*.

He m. in Bombay, India, in 1923, Dilys daughter of Joseph Davies Bryan (*DWB*, 56, under BRYAN, ROBERT) and they had one son and one daughter. He d. 4 Nov. 1965 at his home, 15 Ethorpe Close, Gerrards Cross, Bucks.

Www; D. Ben Rees, *Cymry adnabyddus, 1952-72* (1978); *Trans. Cymm.*, 1966, part 1, 238.

M.A.J.

OWEN, LLEWELLYN ISAAC GETHIN MORGAN - see MORGAN-OWEN, LLEWELLYN ISAAC GETHIN above.

OWEN, MARGARET - see MARGARET under LLOYD GEORGE (FAMILY) above.

OWEN, MORRIS BRYNLLWYN (1875-1949), minister (B), college professor, church historian; b. 15 Mar. 1875, at Crymllwyn Bach, Abererch, Caerns. After spending some time as a weaver in Wales and England, he went to the Holt Academy near Wrexham, and in 1897 was accepted as a student in the Baptist College at Bangor, taking courses also at the university college and graduating B.A. in 1903. In 1902 he was ord. as student-pastor at Llandegfan chapel. He followed his divinity studies at the Presb. College at Carmarthen, where he graduated B.D. in 1906. For part of the years 1906-07 he was minister at St. Mellons, near Cardiff; at the end of 1907 he was invited to become a professor at his old college in Carmarthen, responsible for classes up to 1912, in the Philosophy of Religion, and from that year until his death for Church History which gave him an opportunity to use his knowledge of the Greek and Latin Fathers: he was also the librarian of the college. In addition he was pastor (from 1925) of the Baptist churches at Felin-wen and Felin-gwm and editor of *Seren Cymru*, 1930-33. He was a quiet, shy, studious person but at the Baptist Union meetings at Caernarfon in 1937 he suddenly came to the fore with an address to the Hist. Soc. on the place of Christmas Evans in the history of his period, an address full of dry humour but revealing a deep knowledge of the social and economic background. This was printed in the *Trafodion* of the society for 1938

and was followed by an article in the *Trafodion* for 1945-47 on Baptists three centuries ago, a close study of the works of Thomas Edwards, author of *Gangræna*. In the early numbers of *Seren Gomer* for 1949 he had no less than eight contributions, the more substantial of them dealing with various aspects of the story of early Baptists both in England and Wales. But before the end of that same year five obituary articles to him had appeared in *Seren Gomer*, written by his fellow-professors, by old students, one by an old fellow-student of his, A.J. George. He d. 30 July 1949.

Seren Cymru, 12 Aug. 1949; *Seren Gomer*, 1949.

T.R.

OWEN, OWEN JOHN ('John Owen y Fenni'; 1867-1960), printer and publisher, choir conductor and *eisteddfod* compère; b. 1867 at Dolgellau, son of Dafydd Owain, compositor and reader in the office of *Y Dysgedydd* and *Y Dydd*, and Margaret (née Vaughan). He served his apprenticeship in the same office before moving to Abergavenny in 1887 to work as a Welsh compositor in Henry Sergeant's press. He took an interest in music, having learnt the rudiments of sol-fa in the Sunday school in Yr Hen Gapel, Dolgellau, where his father was the secretary. At Abergavenny he was a member of the Independent church, Castle St., where he became deacon and precentor. In 1897 he and his brother, Edwin Vaughan Owen (d. 22 Oct. 1950), bought the Minerva Press, and their office in Neville St. became a meeting place for members of the local Welsh-speaking community. Among the Welsh books published by the Owen Brothers is their father's biography (1907) and the works of Eluned Morgan (*DWB*, 643): *Dringo'r Andes* (1904), *Gwymon y môr* (1909), *Ar dir a môr* (1913).

On 9 Oct. 1909 John Owen m. Mabel Annie Dawson, and by that time he was well-known as a choir conductor, an elocutionist, witty public speaker and compère at *eisteddfodau*. He refused an offer to be a compère at the national *eisteddfod* in Abergavenny in 1913, but he regularly compered from the national *eisteddfod* platform afterwards (1920-37), and he was made a member of the *Gorsedd* of Bards. He was energetic, and his multifarious interests included astronomy, cycling, motoring, climbing mountains, painting, local history and playing the harp and he gave over fifty years' service as a lay preacher. He received the freedom of the town of Abergavenny in 1949, and O.B.E. a year later. When he d. 30 Dec. 1960 a tribute was paid to him as the 'Patron saint of Gwent'.

WwW (1937); personal research.

S.R.W.

OWEN, ROBERT (BOB OWEN, Croesor; 1885-1962), historian, bookworm and genealogist; b. at Pen-y-parc (Twllwenci, colloquially), Llanfrothen, Mer., 8 May 1885 [the son of Jane Owen, according to NLW MS 19295B] and brought up by his grandmother, Ann Owen, daughter of a weaver of Aberffraw, Anglesey. He left Llanfrothen elementary school at the age of 13 to work on the home-farm of Brondanw mansion. He worked for three years on farms in the district before being appointed a clerk in Park and Croesor quarry. He remained there for 30 yrs. until 30 Jan. 1931 when the quarry was closed because of the depression in the slate industry. After being unemployed for two and a half years he was appointed Workers Educational Association organiser for Caernarfonshire Rural District Council and later a W.E.A. lecturer.

Mixing with knowledgeable and cultured men in the quarry office proved the main educational influence on him and it was there that he developed an obsession with research. He collected an enormous library which spread to almost every corner of his home. He became well-known, particularly for his weekly column in *Y Genedl Gymreig*, 'Lloffion Bob Owen', 1929-37. He contributed to many newspapers and to about twenty different periodicals. His voluminous essays won prizes at the National *Eisteddfod* including one of about eight hundred foolscap pages in small handwriting or close type on emigration from Wales to the United States of America between 1760 and 1860, and one on the defunct industries of the Dwyryd and Glaslyn area, which was published in 1943.

Scholars considered him to be a serious researcher, an important genealogist and an authority on the history of the Welsh in America. He received an hon. M.A. degree of the University of Wales (the youngest ever at the age of 47) and later the O.B.E. for his contribution to the history and literature of Wales.

In June 1923 he m. Nell Jones from Caeathro, and they made their home in Ael-y-bryn, Croesor. They had two daughters and a son. He was a very popular lecturer with Welsh societies in all parts of Wales and in England. Because of his interest in people and their roots he tended to start hares and to follow their trail as he lectured. He was also accused of being an iconoclast because of his comments on well-known persons like Mary Jones of Bala and John Elias of Anglesey (*DWB*, 203-4). For his part, he contended that he created far more idols than he destroyed.

He was a colourful and marvellously fiery personality, a torrent of life, and as a consequence of his various eccentricities he became a legendary character in his own lifetime. He d. 30 Apr. 1962 and was buried in Llanfrothen New Cemetery.

Dyfed Evans, *Bywyd Bob Owen* (1977); Robin Williams, *Y tri Bob* (1970); NLW MS 19295B.

D.O.E.

OWEN, WILLIAM HUGH (1886-1957), civil servant; b. 16 Feb. 1886 at Holyhead, Angl., son of Thomas Owen. He entered the Marine Department of the London and North Western Railway in 1906, and later joined the personal staff of David Lloyd George (see above under LLOYD GEORGE, David), for whom he undertook several important missions. At the outbreak of World War I he joined the Royal Engineers and went to Canada in 1917 where he represented the War Office as director of inland waterways and docks. The work involved placing contracts for and the supervision of the building of auxiliary vessels for ocean, coastal and canal work, and also the purchase and charter of craft for similar work. He became lieut.-colonel in 1918 and was made a C.B.E. in 1919. Later he acted as special representative of the Comptroller of the Admiralty and subsequently represented the Ministry of Shipping. He played hockey for Wales against Ireland in 1910. He m. 8 Oct. 1919, Enid Strathearn, daughter of Sir John Hendrie, Lieutenant Governor of the Province of Ontario, and they had three daughters. He made his home at Montreal and d. 21 Feb. 1957.

Www; *Who's who in Canada*, 1922.

M.A.J.

P

PARCELL, GEORGE HENRY (1895-1967), musician; b. 18 Nov. 1895 in Carmarthen Road, Fforest-fach, near Swansea, son of Henry and Elisabeth Parcell. A miner like his father, he worked throughout his life in Garn-goch colliery, Gorseinon. From childhood he displayed a special talent for music and used his leisure time to develop his innate abilities. Despite the lack of any formal tuition or a tutor of any kind he was awarded two diplomas from the Curwen Memorial College, London: A.T.S.C (1950) and L.T.S.C. (1952). He was organist (1922-27) and precentor (1927-65) in Saron (Congl.), Gendros, near Swansea, and according to a report in the *Evening Post* his selection for the latter post, from nine applicants, was enthusiastically received. He was also appointed choirmaster of the Fforest-fach male voice choir. He composed over twenty hymn tunes, many of them such as 'David', 'Wig', 'Yr Allt' winning prizes in *eisteddfodau*, and one short anthem, 'Duw sy'n noddfa a nerth'; all were simple and well-crafted without being ambitious. They were fashioned for church congregations whose vocal resources were known to the composer. He named one of his best tunes 'Irene' after his wife and his hymn tune 'Marchog Iesu', on words by Williams Pantycelyn, 'Mae'r Iesu yn myned i ryfel', was highly esteemed in hymn-singing festivals both in Wales and the U.S.A.; it was recorded by Côr Godre'r Aran. A selection of his works was published as part of a special festival of praise held in Gendros 'as a mark of respect and indebtedness for his constant unpaid labour'. His home in 'Mile End' was a true academy of music with an ever-open door to welcome students free of charge. Under his influence Fforest-fach developed as a centre of musical culture of the first order. People flocked from far and wide to the annual concerts in Saron chapel to listen to the choir and to world-renowned artists performing the works of the masters. But above all, he taught generation after generation to master the tonic sol-fa thereby enabling them to sing hymns and anthems in four-part harmony. One cannot consider church music in Wales without being reminded of the contribution which he and others like him have made. In this context he represents a generation of benefactors whose importance cannot be exaggerated. He m. Irene Ackerman, 26 Dec. 1929; d. 8 March 1967 and was cremated in Morriston.

Predominantly based on the 'George Parcell File' held by the family; reports in the *Evening Post*; minutes book Saron Church, Gendros, and *Rhaglen Sul o Fawl*, 28 May 1950.

R.L.H.

PARR-DAVIES, HARRY (formerly DAVIES, HARRY PARR; 1914-55), pianist and composer; b. at Neath, Glam., 1914, son of D.J. and Rosina Davies (née Parr). He was educated at Dunraven school, Treherbert and Neath intermediate school. His musical talent became evident when he was a child, and he is said to have composed 30 songs and two operettas before he was 13 yrs. old. Seymour Perrott, the Neath

borough organist, provided his musical education, and Sir Henry Walford Davies (see above) urged him to make a career as a classical composer; but light music was more to his taste and he studied the works of Eric Coates and Edward German to perfect his technique. He introduced himself to the singer Gracie Fields and became her accompanist in Britain and on tour in Canada and South Africa. He composed the song 'Sing as we go' which Gracie Fields sang in the film *Shipyard Sally* (1939), and which gave the title to her autobiography; he also provided the music to Phil Park's words, 'Wish me luck as you wave me goodbye', which became popular at the beginning of World War II. For his song 'Smile when you say goodbye' he received an advance royalty of £1000, the highest sum paid at that time for a song. Among his stage shows were *Black velvet*, *The Lisbon story*, *Her Excellency*, and *Deaf Miss Phoebe*. He composed music for Gracie Fields' film, *This Week of Grace* (1933), and songs for other performers such as George Formby. He d. at home in Knightsbridge, London, 14 Oct. 1955, and was buried in Oystermouth cemetery near Swansea.

Times and *West Mail*, 15 Oct. 1955; *Neath Guard.*, 21 Oct. 1955.

Rh.G.

PARRY, HARRY - see PARRY, OWEN HENRY below.

PARRY, OWEN HENRY (HARRY PARRY; 1912-56), jazz musician; b. 22 Jan. 1912 at Caepella, Bangor, Caerns., the eldest son of Henry Parry, railway worker, and Emily Jane (née Rowlands). He was educated at Glanadda school and the Central School. He joined the department of physics, University College of North Wales, as an apprentice instrument maker. He showed an early interest in playing musical instruments and when twelve years old joined one of the district's brass bands. He was a member of St. Mary's Church choir, but was intent on playing instruments. He soon became adept at playing the tenor horn, *flügel* horn, cornet, violin as well as drums. He mastered the saxophone and was said to be Wales's champion player. He was an expert clarinettist – his favourite instrument – and was taught initially by Francis Jones (1904-86) of Port Dinorwic. He yearned to develop a more swinging musical style and experimented in that direction. His style was heard by some of the B.B.C.'s leading figures as he had by then joined some of England's main bands. Charles Chilton suggested that he should form his own instrumental group and that he should use the vibraphone instead of the trumpet. On 28 Sept. 1940 the sounds of the 'Radio Rhythm' Club sextet which he formed were heard for the first time. Miff Ferrie heard of him and it was from that association that the group 'Jackdauz' was formed. He held concerts in the Locarno, London, and shared platforms with musicians like Michael Flome, Louis Levy and Charles Shadwell. He joined the blind pianist, George Shearing, and the drummer, Ben Edwards, to form a trio which became very popular. It was his sextet which was the first to make a record in the 'Super Rhythm' series for the Parlophone company; his association with this company lasted for ten years. Many of his plans were shattered by World War II, but he resumed them later and formed a permanent orchestra in the Potomac, London. His compositions 'Parry Opus', 'Thrust and Parry', 'Potomac Jump', 'Blue for Eight', 'Says You' and the most popular, perhaps, 'Champagne' became household names amongst his followers. He appeared in five short films and was described by some critics as 'Britain's jazz king'. According to one of his contemporaries, he was the first from Wales and England to record a voice in instrumental style with the co-operation of his own band. The crowds flocked to listen to him in centres such as the Hippodrome, Birmingham; the Empire, Woolwich; and the Empire, Glasgow. His popularity waned during his tour of the Middle East and Egypt. After his return he presented the popular programme 'Housewives Choice'; he was also involved in the children's programme 'Crackerjack'. According to some columnists at the time, he died when he was on the brink of regaining his popularity, as he was the first to present 'swing' music to the layman. He was described by an *Evening Standard* columnist at the time as 'the third best clarinettist in the world'. His heroes were Benny Goodman, Artie Shaw, Benny Carter, Count Basie and Glenn Miller. Towards the end of his life he attempted to adopt a style similar to Miller. He counted Henry Hall, Roy Fox and Geraldo amongst his friends. His first wife was Gwen Davies. After a divorce he m. Jessie Bradbury, a professional singer, but that marriage failed. They were childless. He thought highly of his home town, but seldom had the opportunity to return there.

Harry Parry d. 11 Oct. 1956 in his room in Adam's Row, Mayfair, London. His ashes were buried in Golders Green crematorium, London.

Information gleaned from a family scrapbook in the possession of his sister, Eunice Taylor, Uxbridge, and her husband, Stan Taylor. This is now lodged at the Library of the University of Wales, Bangor. Some information also from his brother, Hugh P. Parry, Colwyn Bay.

G.A.J.

PARRY, ROBERT WILLIAMS (1884-1956), poet, univ. lecturer; b. 6 Mar. 1884 at Madog View, Tal-y-sarn, Caerns., son of Robert and Jane Parry (his father was a half-brother of Henry Parry-Williams, see Supplement below). He received his education at Tal-y-sarn elementary school, Caernarfon county school, 1896-98, and the new Pen-y-groes county school for one year. He spent three years, 1899-1902, as a pupil-teacher. He entered the University College of Wales, Aberystwyth, in 1902, but left in 1904 having taken part of the degreee course and trained as a teacher. He taught at various schools till 1907, when he became a student at the University College of North Wales, Bangor, and completed his degree. From 1908 till 1910 he was Welsh and English master at Llanberis (Bryn'refail) county school. He then returned to college at Bangor and spent some months in

Brittany working for an M.A. degree, which he gained in 1912 for a dissertation entitled 'Some points of contact between Welsh and Breton'. After a year, 1912-13, as schoolmaster at Cefn-ddwysarn, he left for Barry county school. In 1916 he was appointed English master at the Cardiff High School for Boys. He was in the army from Nov. 1916 till Dec. 1918. After demobilisation he returned to Cardiff, and in 1921 became headteacher of Oakley Park School, Mont. After a brief stay he left early in 1922 on being appointed lecturer at the university college, Bangor, to serve part-time in the Welsh Department and part-time in the Extra-Mural Department. He remained in this post till his retirement in 1944.

Williams Parry started his literary career as a strict-metre poet, having received instruction from two Tal-y-sarn poets, Owen Edwards ('Anant'), a quarry man, and H.E. Jones ('Hywel Cefni'), a shopkeeper, both of whom competed regularly at local *eisteddfodau* and published their successful *englynion* in periodicals, especially *Y Geninen*. As early as 1906 Williams Parry wrote an *awdl* on 'Dechrau Haf' for an *eisteddfod* at Ffestiniog. In 1907 he was a competitor for the chair at the national *eisteddfod* held at Swansea with an *awdl* on 'John Bunyan', but was unsuccessful. The following year he was awarded the chair at the Bangor students' *eisteddfod* for an *awdl* on 'Cantre'r Gwaelod', but was again unsuccessful at the London national *eisteddfod* on the subject 'Gwlad y Bryniau' in 1909. Success came however at Colwyn Bay in 1910 with the poem 'Yr Haf', the best known and admired of all the *eisteddfod awdlau* of the 20th c. Five long poems in so many years was a remarkable output, and the poet was never again to produce so much in the strict metres. In 1911 there were signs of a very different metrical development in the form of a sonnet in full *cynghanedd* to greet his friend G.W. Francis on his marriage. During World War I he wrote several sonnets - 'Pantycelyn', 'Mae hiraeth yn y môr', 'Cysur Henaint', 'Gadael Tir', and those which deal directly with the war, like 'Y Cantîn Gwlyb' and 'Y Ddrafft'. But he retained his love of *cynghanedd*, as can be seen in the memorial *englynion* to friends and acquaintances, and especially to those who fell in battle, like the famous sequence to Hedd Wyn (Ellis Humphrey Evans, *DWB*, 229).

The years between the wars were very productive. In the sonnet 'Adref', written in 1917, the poet vowed that he would renounce the allure of medievalism and reflect on matters of the present day. This he did, but to the exclusion of industrial conurbations, preferring the peace of the countryside and all that dwells in it, as in the poems 'Eifionydd', 'Tylluanod', 'Clychau'r Gog', 'Y Llwynog'. Another product of these years is the remarkable poem 'Drudwy Branwen', which embodies all the notable features of Williams Parry's work - a skilful versification, powerful imagination, and meaningful imagery. Towards the end of the period the poet's style underwent a change. He had long abandoned the verbal exuberance of 'Yr Haf', but carefully observed the refined language which he held was the hallmark of poetry. Now he modified his view and practice (largely under the influence of the poetry of his cousin T.H. Parry-Williams) and made use of the syntax and vocabulary of prose and of the spoken language. The sonnet 'Gwenci' is a good example. There was another change too, a change in the poet's reaction to human standards and behaviour. With satirical vehemence he condemned the materialism of the age. The initial impetus for this response was the anger which he felt at what happened following the fire at the bombing range in Llŷn in 1936, when Saunders Lewis was dismissed from his post. Much of this satirical writing was expressed in a new metrical form, sonnets whose rhythm depended on combining three-syllable feet with the traditional iambics.

Williams Parry was well versed in English poetry, and came under the influence of the Romantic poets, especially Keats. He had a great deal in common with the Georgian poets, whose imagery is sometimes reflected in his poems. But in spite of all influences, Williams Parry's acute observation, his independent outlook and his meticulous attention to the mode of expression created a body of poetry which has its own special features and is a unique contribution to Welsh literature. Two volumes of his poetry were published, *Yr Haf a cherddi Eraill* in 1924, and *Cerddi'r gaeaf* in 1952. Some poems not included in these volumes were published by T. Emrys Parry in *Barddoniaeth Robert Williams Parry*, (1973). The complete collection edited by Alan Llwyd appeared in 1998.

Williams Parry acted as adjudicator at many *eisteddfodau*, including the chief competitions of the National *Eisteddfod*. His adjudications were not a mere recital of errors and shortcomings, but a constructive attempt to improve the competitors' poetic sensibility and expression. He published articles in periodicals on various aspects of the poetic craft, commenting approvingly on all forms of lyrical poetry in particular, and the two masters of the formal lyric, Ceiriog (J. Ceiriog Hughes, *DWB*, 383-4) and Eifion Wyn (Eliseus Williams, *DWB*, 1036). His own prose shows a strength of conviction and also sharp wit. He was one of the best prose writers of his day. A selection of his prose appeared in *Rhyddiaith R. Williams Parry*, edited by Bedwyr Lewis Jones.

Williams Parry was of a retiring disposition, and never willingly joined a crowd, but he delighted in the company of a few real friends. He was a nationalist by conviction and was for a time chairman of the Caernarfonshire branch of *Plaid Cymru*, but his activities were limited, as he did not wish to be seen or heard in public. He m. in 1923 Myfanwy Davies of Rhosllannerchrugog. He d. 4 Jan 1956 and was buried at Coetmor cemetery, Bethesda. There were no children.

Meredydd Evans, 'Golwg ar waith Robert Williams Parry', *Taliesin*, 27 (1972), 76-96; 'Williams Parry: benthyciwr?' 39 (1979), 67-76; J. Gwilym Jones, *Crefft y llenor* (1977), 57-68; Alan Llwyd (ed.), *R. Williams Parry* (1979); [Bedwyr Lewis Jones, *R. Williams Parry* (1972); *R. Williams Parry* (1997)].

T.P.

PARRY, SARAH WINIFRED ('Winnie Parry'; 1870-1953), writer, and ed. of *Cymru'r Plant* from 1908 to 1912; b. 20 May 1870, dau. of Hugh Thomas (1841-?) and Margaret Parry (née Roberts). The family lived in Welshpool at the time of her birth, but left when she was but a few months old. At one time, her father was an inspector with an insurance company but he is said to have had literary interests also. Her mother published some poems in the strict metres under the pseudonym 'Gwenfron' (e.g. *Baner*, 19 Sept. 1860). At the time of the 1871 Census, Winnie, her mother and sister were staying with her grandfather, John Roberts, at Port Dinorwic, and it would appear that the family did not have their own home at this time. Margaret Parry d. aged 38 in 1876 in Croydon when Winnie was 6 years old, and she consequently went to live permanently with John Roberts and his wife, Ellen; she was, therefore, separated from her father, her brother and three sisters. Though there is evidence that English was her first language she was soon fluent in the colloquial speech of Port Dinorwic. No records of her attendance at the local primary schools have been found, but it is said that she was friendly with the daughter of the headmaster of the national school, so it is likely that she attended that school. She received no formal higher education, but it is said that John Roberts was a cultured man and that he had influenced his grand-daughter's inclinations. Her early years, it appears, were unhappy and lonely. Her father re-married in Swansea in 1877 a certain Martha Darroll, and by 1882 he and his entire family, apart from Winnie, had settled in South Africa, leaving her in Port Dinorwic. Shortly afterwards, her grandmother, Ellen Roberts, d. and Winnie, in a letter to John Glyn Davies (see above), states that she lived with her grandfather from the age of thirteen until her aunt came to live with them when she was nineteen.

In 1893, at the prompting of O.M. Edwards (*DWB*, 192-3) and Edward Ffoulkes she began to contribute occasionally to *Cymru*, *Cymru'r Plant*, *Y Cymro*, and even *The Cambrian* (Utica) and *Wales*. Her three books, *Sioned*, 1906, *Cerrig y rhyd*, 1907, and *Y ddau hogyn rheiny*, 1928, were mainly selections from her contributions to periodicals. She published one serial in *Y Cymro* in 1896, 'Catrin Prisiard', which did not appear later as a book. For a time in 1895-96 she corresponded with John Glyn Davies mainly on literary matters. He used to visit her on his trips from Liverpool to Llŷn; she borrowed books from him, and he helped her to learn French and German. When John Roberts d. in 1903, Winnie went for a short time to her uncle Owen Parry, CM minister at Cemaes, Anglesey. By the beginning of 1908 her father had returned for a time to Thornton Heath, Croydon, and it seems that Winnie went to live with him.

She edited *Cymru'r Plant* from Croydon between 1908 and the middle of 1912 when she gave up writing altogether (though *Cerrig y rhyd* was reprinted in 1915 and Foyle's published *Y ddau hogyn rheiny* in 1928). She never married, and in London she served as secretary first to a company of engineers and also for a time to Sir Robert J. Thomas (1873-1951; see below), M.P. for Anglesey, 1922-28. She adjudicated the short story at the 1932 national *eisteddfod*, but by then she had severed almost all connections with Wales. At the beginning of World War II E. Morgan Humphreys (see above) tried to persuade her to reprint *Sioned*, and the

B.B.C. tried to adapt some of her work for the Welsh Children's Hour. As late as 1949 she was still looking for a publisher for *Sioned*, but circumstances were difficult and by then she was old and infirm. She d. in an old people's home in Croydon on 12 Feb. 1953, and her friend, Hilda Álice Moore, arranged to have her buried in Croydon.

Sioned was undoubtedly her masterpiece and it won high praise from time to time (see E.M. Humphreys, *Yr Herald Cymraeg*, 9 Mar. 1953). It is said that R. Williams Parry (see above) thought highly of it and referred to it in his W.E.A. lectures (but see also Kate Roberts, *Baner*, 29 Apr. 1953).

Winnie Parry collection, N.L.W.; NLW 6647-59 (J. Glyn Davies); *Gen.*, 2 July 1895; E.M. Humphreys, *Her. Cymr.*, 9 Mar. 1953; Iorwen M. Jones, *Merched llên Cymru* (M.A. - Wales dissertation, 1935); Kate Roberts, 'Led-led Cymru', *Baner*, 29 Apr. 1953; Mair Ogwen, *Gymraes* 32, No. 8, Aug. 1928; Mairwen and Gwynn Jones, *Dewiniaid Difyr* (1983); E. Morgan Humphreys coll. at NLW; letters by Winnie Parry and her cousin F.E. Williams, Edinburgh; letters in the R. Gwylfa Roberts coll. UCNW; letters by Winnie Parry in the possession of Kate Roberts; 1871 Census, Frondeg, 18 Terfyn Terrace, Port Dinorwic; letters in the possession of the author from Alison Lane-Poole, Fovant, Wilts., step-niece to Winnie Parry, and Enfys Renshaw, Edinburgh, daughter of Winnie Parry's cousin; verbal information.

R.P.P.

PARRY, WINNIE - see PARRY, SARAH WINIFRED above.

PASCOE, Sir FREDERICK JOHN (1893-1963), industrialist; b. at Truro, Cornwall, 19 March 1893, son of Frederick Richard Pascoe. He m. in 1936 Margaret Esson, daughter of Col. F.J. Scott, and had one son and one daughter. He was educated at Exeter School and St. John's College, Cambridge (B.A. Mechanical Sciences). He entered industry as an apprentice at the Leeds Forge. During World War I he served as an officer with the Durham County Light Infantry in Europe and afterwards with the Indian Signal Service. He became one of Britain's leading industrialists between the two world wars, and afterwards. He first came into public notice as secretary of the Electric and Railway Finance Corporation, 1926-30, and shortly afterwards formed a connection with Wales and Welsh industry which was maintained until his death. He was affectionately described as the Cornish man with sufficient Celtic blood to give him an affinity with Wales and especially the south Wales valleys. In 1930 he became a director of British Timken, Ltd., and chairman and managing director from 1940 until 1959 when he became chairman of British Timken Division of the Timken, Roller Bearing Company, an organisation he had built up into a major industrial force of 7,000 workers from a few hundred employees. Among its subsidiaries was Aberdare Holdings (which also included Aberdare Cables, Ltd, Aberdare Engineering, Ltd., and South Wales Switchgear) which Sir John founded in 1955 and which brought up to 4,000 jobs to a depressed area of south Wales. A forthright Conservative he was chairman of the Kettering Conservative

and Unionist Association, 1948-53, and a Freeman of the City of London; he held membership of the National Council of Aims of Industry, and of the Regional Advisory Council for the Organisation of Further Education in the East Midlands, and was a Liveryman of the Worshipful Company of Tin Plate Workers alias Wire Workers, and the Fishmongers' Company. He was knighted in 1957 and d. 5 Feb. 1963.

Www; *West. Mail*, 7 June 1963.

D.G.R.

PASTOR DAN - see WILLIAMS, DANIEL POWELL below.

PEARCE, EVAN WILLIAM (1870-1957), minister (Presb.), and author; b. 2 Oct. 1870 at Llantwit Fardre, Glam., but the family moved to Pontycymer, where he began to preach in Bethel chapel in 1891. He went to Trefeca College on 14 Sept. 1892, remaining there for four years, and was ord. in 1897. He became minister in Broughton, Glam., but retired to look after a relative in Pontarddulais in 1902. Shortly afterwards he went to Bethel, Porthcawl, where he was minister for 25 yrs., retiring in 1927. He served as Moderator and secretary of East Glamorgan presbytery. On 31 March 1898 he m. Rachel James in Swansea and they had a daughter. He lived most of his life in Gorlan, Green Avenue, Porthcawl, and d. 30 Aug. 1957.

He took a great interest in local history and in the history of his own denomination, and was one of the first members of the Calvinistic Methodist Historical Soc. He wrote for the *Western Mail* and published *Beulah, Margam, 1838-1938, a historical sketch (1938)*, and a biography, *The Rt. Hon. George Swan Nottage, Lord Mayor of London, 1884-5 (1938)*.

Blwyddiadur MC, 1958; WWP.

M.A.J.

PENCERDD GWYNFRYN - see CARRINGTON, THOMAS above.

PENCERDDES MORGANNWG - see DAVIES, CLARA NOVELLO above.

PENCERDDES TAWE - see ANNE WATTS under PHILLIPS, DAVID RHYS below.

PHILIPPS, Sir GRISMOND PICTON (1898-1967), soldier and public figure; b. 20 May 1898, the only son of Major Grismond Philipps, Cwmgwili, Carms. He became a second lieutenant in the Grenadier Guards in 1917, was promoted captain in 1925, and retired in 1933. As lieutenant-colonel commanding the 4th Battalion of the Welch Regiment (Territorial Army) in 1939, he served throughout World War II, and was Honorary Colonel of the Welch Regiment (T.A.) from 1960-64. He was appointed Deputy Lieutenant of Carmarthenshire in 1935, a Justice of the Peace in 1938, and a county councillor in 1946. Having served as vice-lieutenant from 1936 to 1954, he became Lord Lieutenant of Carmarthenshire in 1954 and occupied that office until his death. He was a member of the Court of Governors and the

Council of the National Library of Wales and a member of the Council of the National Museum of Wales, 1945-52. He was chairman of the Historic Buildings Council for Wales from 1955 to 1967, and was also chairman of the Welsh committee of Television Wales and the West. Descendant of an ancient Carmarthenshire family (Philipps, *DWB*, 752), he was a man of tact and sympathy and was deeply interested in the history and antiquities, especially the county families and ancient buildings, of his own county in particular and of Wales in general. He was knighted in 1953.

He m. Lady Marjorie Joan Mary Wentworth-FitzWilliam, 2nd daughter of the 7th Earl FitzWilliam in 1925, from whom he was divorced in 1949. He d. 8 May 1967, leaving one son.

Who's who: Annual report of the Historic Buildings Council 1967; personal knowledge.

G.W.

PHILIPPS, LAURENCE RICHARD, 1st. BARON MILFORD and 1st baronet (1874-1962), philanthropist, industrialist, sportsman, and a member of one of the most prominent old gentry families of Pembrokeshire; b. 24 Jan. 1874, the 6th son of Canon Sir James Erasmus Philipps, 12th baronet of Picton, and the Honourable Mary Margaret Best, daughter of the Honourable the Rev. Samuel Best. Following his education at Felsted School and the Royal School of Mines he concentrated his career on the maritime trade and in time became the chairman of the Court Shipping Line which he himself established. He was a member of Lloyd's, director of several well-known companies such as Schweppes, Ltd. and Ilford, Ltd. and he was one-time chairman of Northern Securities Trust, Ltd.

He was created a baronet in 1919 and a baron in 1939, the third of the family to be raised to the peerage within one generation, being a brother to John Wynford Philipps (1860-1938), 1st Viscount St. Davids and of Owen Cosby Philipps (1863-1937), Baron Kylsant. He was a generous benefactor, particularly of the University College of Wales, Aberystwyth, to which he donated sufficient funds in 1919 to found the Welsh Plant Breeding Station which became world-famous in the fields of breeding plants and of grassland science and which was in addition of untold benefit to the country's agriculture. He donated £10,000 initially to establish the research station, with £1,000 annually for the next ten years towards its maintainance. Also, in 1944, he made provision for the payment of £800 annually for ten years to create The Milford Chair of Animal Health to conduct research which was closely allied to the work at the Plant Breeding Station. In recognition of his generosity the first laboratory to be built at the new centre at Gogerddan was named after him, The Lord Milford Plant Research Laboratory, when it was opened by Queen Elizabeth II in 1955. Another important example of his benevolence was his provision of a hospital at Rookwood, Llandaff, for former members of the Armed Forces suffering from paralysis.

He was elected J.P. for Hampshire in 1910, High Sheriff in 1915 and J.P. for Breconshire in 1918. He was a member of Aberystwyth College Council, 1922-57, and a life-governor, and in

1939 he recieved an hon. LL.D. degree of the University of Wales.

He took a keen interest in sport, especially in horse racing and in the work of organizing and managing races. He was elected a member of the influential Jockey Club, and he owned a number of horses which won him prizes. Later in life he transferred all these activities to the care of his third son, the Honourable John Perrot Philipps.

He m. in 1901 Ethel Georgina, J.P., the only daughter of Benjamin Speke, rector of Dowlish Wake, Somerset. They had four sons and a daughter. He d. 7 Dec. 1962, and was succeeded by his eldest son, the Honourable Wogan Philipps. His second son, the Honourable Richard Hanning Philipps, M.B.E., J.P., was Lord Lieutenant of Pembrokeshire 1958-74 and afterwards the first Lord Lieutenant of the new county of Dyfed.

Www; Burke, 1970 (105th ed.); Ellis, *UCW*; *Times*, 8 Dec. 1962.

D.J.G.

PHILLIPS, DAVID (1874-1951), minister (Presb.), philosopher and college principal; b. 1874 at Ffwrnes, Llanelli, Carms., son of Henry and Sarah Phillips. His father d. when he was young, and his mother moved with the family to Mountain Ash, Glam. He received his elementary education at Dyffryn boys' school, and went to work in a coal mine. In 1894 he won a miners' scholarship to study mining, but his tutors at the University College, Cardiff, persuaded him to take a degree course, and he graduated in 1898 with first-class hons. in philosophy. He won a scholarship to Trinity College, Cambridge, where he graduated first class in two branches of philosophy. He also spent a period at the University of Heidelberg. He began preaching before leaving Cardiff, but at the end of his university course he was appointed lecturer in moral philosophy at St. Andrews University, Scotland. On hearing of the religious revival in Wales, he returned home to see what was happening there. He was carried by the wave and was convinced that he should devote his life to the Christian ministry. He was ord. in 1905, and became pastor of the English church in Frederick St., Cardiff until 1908 when he was called by his denomination to the chair of Philosophy and History of Religions at Bala College (1908-27). From 1927 to 1947 he was principal of the college. He greatly influenced generation after generation of students at Bala, and after his retirement he was awarded honorary D.D. degrees by the Universities of Wales and St. Andrews. He m. Emily Treharne, and they had one son. He d. 6 Aug. 1951.

He was a very prominent figure in the life of his denomination. His Davies Lecture in 1919 on 'Intercourse with God' was not published. He served as Moderator of the North Wales Association (1938), and moderator of the General Assembly (1944). He was a member of the deputation which visited the missionary field of his denomination in Assam in 1935-36, and he provided his church with sound leadership in determining, at a critical time, their policy for future missionary work. He was gifted with exceptional intellectual faculties, and took an interest not only in philosophical matters, but also in defining and presenting the truths of the Gospel. He was one of the four who formulated the Shorter Declaration on Faith and Practice. He was somewhat reluctant to publish his work. When he was in Scotland he was sub-editor of the *International Jnl. of Ethics*, and during the same period he contributed an excellent article on the 'Ego' to the *Encyclopaedia of Religion and Ethics*. He published short monographs on the philosophy of Sir Henry Jones (1922), *Y Syniad o Dduw fel person* (1932) and *Christianity and the state* (1938). He was one of the editors of *Y Traethodydd* from 1932 until his d. The cream of his thoughts appeared in a collection of his writings in 1949 under the title *Ysgrifau athronyddol*.

Cambrian Daily Leader, 2 July 1925; WwFC, 351; *Gol.*, 29 Aug. 1951; *Blwyddlyfr MC*, 1952, 220-1; *Traeth*, Jan. and Apr. 1952; W. Morris (ed.), *Deg o Enwogion* (1959), 79-87; R.H. Evans, *Datganiad Byr ar ffydd a buchedd* (1971), ch. 2; information from his niece, Eluned Evans, Llandeilo; personal acquaintance.

G.M.R.

PHILLIPS, DAVID RHYS (1862-1952), librarian; b. 20 March 1862 at Beili Glas, Pontwalby, Glynneath, Glam., his grandfather's farm, the s. of David and Gwenllian (née Rees) Phillips, but he was brought up at Melincourt, Resolven, in the Neath valley. He was educated at the National School, Resolven and at private schools - Burrows School, Arnold College - in Swansea. After a period as a miner he became a compositor and proof-reader at Walter Whittingdon's printing office in Neath in 1893 and also acted as an auxiliary postman, but in 1900 he was appointed a reader at Oxford University Press. He was editor of the Welsh Bible in 1908 but more important, he followed courses in librarianship at Oxford Technical College. He returned to Swansea as Welsh Assistant in the Borough Library in 1905, having gained his Library Association diploma, and was responsible for cataloguing the Welsh section (including the collection of Robert Jones, Rotherhithe, *DWB*, 508-9). He was elected F.L.A. in 1913 and F.S.A. (Scotland) in 1920-21. He was promoted Borough Welsh and Celtic librarian and subsequently in 1923 joint-librarian with W.J. Salter until his retirement in 1939.

D. Rhys Phillips was nurtured in the literary and cultural societies of Resolven and Neath and he was inspired to research local history, to write entertaining articles to the Welsh press and to compete at *eisteddfodau*. He wrote a number of substantial essays on musical and biographical subjects at National *Eisteddfodau* in 1931, 1932, 1936, 1938, 1948, 1949 and he was active in many Welsh societies, including the Welsh Folksong Soc., National Eisteddfod Council, the *Gorsedd* Board; he was a keen Celtophile and was one of the supporters of the Celtic Congress in 1917, secretary until 1925 and a prime mover in establishing the Cornish *Gorsedd* in 1928. He published several articles on the development of the public library service but his main interest was in library and printing history. He was one of the founders of the Welsh Bibliographical Soc. in 1906, secretary from 1907 to 1951. There can be little doubt that his zeal and enthusiasm sustained the society and its journal. His own publications include: *Select bib-liography of Owain Glyndwr* (1915), *The romantic history of the monastic libraries of Wales* (1912), *Dr Griffith Roberts, Canon of Milan* (1917), *Lady Charlotte Guest and the Mabinogion* (1921), *The Celtic countries, their literary and library activities* (1915). It is very easy to draw attention to the faults in Rhys Phillips' work but he has an honourable place as one of the pioneers of modern Welsh bibliographical studies.

In 1918 he won a £100 prize at the Neath national *eisteddfod* for an essay on the history of the Neath valley. This was published in 1925 as *A history of the Vale of Neath*, the fruits of many years research and collecting documents and traditions of all kinds relating to the life of the community, a facsimile reprint appeared in 1994.

He m. twice, (1) Mary Hancock, who died April 1926, and (2) Anne Watts, 'Pencerddes Tawe', Dec. 1927. The son of the first marriage died in 1924, and there was a dau. of the second marriage. Rhys Phillips died at his home Beili Glas, 15 Chaddesley Terrace, Swansea, 22 March 1952.

D. Rhys Phillips papers at NLW and Swansea City Library; *Jnl. W.B.S.*, 7 (1952), 119-21, 122-24; *Jnl. W.B.S.*, 12 (1983-84), 43-50; WwW (1937); *Library Association Record*, 54 (1952), 189; Tom Davies, in Hywel Teifi Edwards, ed., *Nedd a Dulais* (1994), 218-38.

B.F.R.

PHILLIPS, EDGAR ('Trefîn'; 1889-1962), tailor, school-teacher, poet, and Archdruid of Wales, 1960-62; b. 8 Oct. 1889 in Rose Cottage. Tre-fin, Pembs., only child of William Bateman and Martha (née Davies) Phillips. His father was a sailor but after leaving the sea he was a baker in Porthcawl. Trefin's mother died in 1898 after she had been a patient for 5 yrs. in Saint David's Hospital in Carmarthen, and he was adopted by his father's sister, Mary, wife of John Martin, a sailmaker and formerly a sailor. English was the main language of the home and English was the language of the day-school, but thanks to the Sunday school he retained his Welsh. He tried to run away to sea when he realised that the family intended apprenticing him to a tailor. When his father re-married the family moved to Cardiff and the 11-yr. old boy entered Sloper Road school. The Welsh master, (Sir) John Rowland (see below), took an interest in him and arranged for him to borrow *Cymru* and other Welsh periodicals. His father and stepmother tried to wean him from his interest in the Welsh language, but his Welshness was reinforced when he had the company of Owen Morgan Edwards (*DWB*, 192-3) on a train journey to Pembrokeshire. When he was 14 yrs. old he returned to Tre-fin as an apprentice tailor to his uncle J.W. Evans, and as the workshop was a nursery for poets and a school in the *cyng-aneddion*, Trefin mastered *Yr Ysgol Farddol* (Dafydd Morganwg), the poets' primer. For a year after completing his apprenticeship he worked as a tailor in Letterston and Whitland. He returned to Cardiff to specialize in cutting and he became a tailor of ladies' wear. In 1912 he moved to London, working in several clothes shops before returning to Cardiff as master tailor in one of the largest shops in the city. In Aug. 1914 he opened a tailor's business in partnership with Trefor Roberts. He joined the Royal Garrison Artillery in 1915, becoming a bombardier. He was badly injured when one of the beams of a cellar fell on his head during an attack and he was moved from one hospital to another until his release from the army. He found temporary employment with Seccombes Company in Cardiff. With his health deteriorating he moved to the neighbourhood of Blackwood, Mon., and worked in a shop in Bargoed. In 1921 he went to Caerleon College and gained a teacher's certificate with distinction. He was Welsh teacher in Pengam primary school 1923-24 before being appointed Welsh master in Pontllanfraith secondary school where he taught until he retired in 1954. He was one of the pioneers of broadcasting in Welsh and his detective 'Bili bach' was a hero to children of that period. He was a regular competitor at *eisteddfodau*. Having already won 33 bardic chairs and a crown, he won the chair at the national *eisteddfod* in 1933 and he was Keeper of the sword of the *Gorsedd* of Bards from 1947 to 1960, when he was elected archdruid. He published *Trysor o gân*, poems for children in four volumes (1930-36), *Caniadau Trefîn* (1950) and *Edmund Jones, 'The Old Prophet'* (1959).

He m. three times: (1), Hannah Clement, a nurse of Tredegar, in 1915. She d. 24 Apr. 1943. They had one daughter. He m. (2), Violet Annie Burnell, schoolteacher, 13 Apr. 1946. The marriage was dissolved unopposed at Trefîn's petition Nov. 1950. He m. (3), Maxwell Fraser, 24 Oct. 1951. He d. 30 Aug. 1962.

Brinley Richards, *Cofiant Trefîn* (1963) [papers in N.L.W.].

E.D.J.

PHILLIPS, MORGAN HECTOR (1885-1953), headmaster; b. in the first half of 1885, youngest son of David Phillips, rector of Radyr, Glam. He was the brother of J. Leoline Phillips, Dean of Monmouth, and D. Rupert Phillips, chairman of Kibbwr magistrates. He had a brilliant career at Christ College, Brecon, where he won a scholarship in the classics to Jesus College, Oxford. He won fame for himself and his school on the rugby field. At Oxford he gained first class in Moderations and graduated in 1911. He was a schoolteacher at Fonhill (East Grinstead), Rossall University College School (London) and at Charterhouse. From 1915 until 1919 he was an officer in the Royal Fusiliers and R.A.S.C. In 1923 he was appointed Rector of the Royal College in Mauritius and Head of the island's Secondary Education Department. He worked there as a member of the Colonial Civil Service. In 1927 he represented the island at the Imperial Education Conference in London where he presented a paper on 'Teaching English in Schools'. He was also an examiner for the Civil Service and for the Schools Examinations Board of the University of Cambridge. In Mauritius he was also prominent on the playing field, showing particular interest in cricket, hockey and football.

He was appointed (from among 45 applicants) headmaster of Ruthin School in 1930. He took a great interest in rugby which had already been introduced into the school by his predecessor, Edwin William Lovegrove (see above), and he

managed to ensure that important rugby matches were played on the school field. Mystery remains concerning his resignation from the headship in 1935, which was attributed to ill-health. He moved to London where he held an educational appointment and later became director of a number of private companies.

He m. Jessie Whayman, daughter of A.E.P. Rae and they had a son. He made his home at Chorleywood, Hertfordshire, but d. at Holloway Sanatorium, Virginia Water, 3 Mar. 1953.

Clwyd Record Office, Ruthin; *The Ruthinian*, 1930-35; Old Ruthinian Association; *Denbighshire Free Press*, 14 Mar. 1953; information from Keith M. Thompson, the school historian.

W.G.E.

PHILLIPS, MORGAN WALTER (1902-63), general secretary of the Labour Party; b. in Aberdare, Glam., 18 June 1902, one of the six children of William Phillips, but he was brought up in Bargoed, Glam. He left school when he was 12 yrs. old to become a colliery surface worker. When he was 18 yrs. old he became a member of the Caerphilly divisional Labour Party, secretary of the party in Bargoed, 1923-25, and chairman of the Bargoed Steam Coal Lodge, 1924-26. After attending a two-year course in economic and social subjects at the Labour College, London, he became secretary of the Labour party in West Fulham, 1928-30. and later in Whitechapel, 1934-37. He also gained experience in local government as a member of the Fulham borough council, 1934-37. In 1937 he went to the party headquarters at Transport House as propaganda officer, being appointed secretary of the party's research department in 1941. As an able organizer, quick and unambiguous in his decisions, he soon rose to become secretary of the party, and general secretary in 1960. He was virtually the architect of the surge in the party's fortunes which resulted in six years of Labour government. Nevertheless, his organization tended to be blamed for the defeat in the 1955 general election. Despite the defeat of the Labour Party in 1959 his own reputation rose. His daily press conferences were one of the outstanding successes of the election. With an understanding of journalists, as of most classes of people with whom he came in contact, he answered questions with admirable conciseness. He kept the Labour Party from crumbling completely after the election by presenting a clear analysis of what had happened and constructive proposals for the future, many of which are included in his paper, *Labour in the Sixties* (1960). He also published *East meets West* (1954) and various political and economic pamphlets.

As one of the great international figures of the Labour movement he presided over a succession of conferences called by the International Socialist Committee from 1944 onwards and was chairman of the Socialist International from its formation in 1948 until he resigned in 1957. He was at the height of his career when he suffered a stroke in Aug. 1960, and had to retire a year later. He m. Norah Lusher in 1930 and they had a son and daughter. He d. 15 Jan. 1963 in London.

Www; *Times* and *West. Mail*, 16 Jan. 1963.

M.A.J.

PHILLIPS, PHILIP ESMONDE (1888-1960), Rear Admiral; b. 16 June 1888, younger son of P.S. Phillips, Crumlin Hall, Mon. He m. in 1933 Mrs Ellinor Curtis, daughter of Capt. Glen Kidston (the marriage was dissolved in 1950); there was one son. Phillips was educated at Britannia Royal Naval College, Dartmouth. He was awarded the D.S.O. and bar during World War I. In 1927 he became Chief Staff Officer to the Rear Admiral of Submarines. From 1935 to 1937 he was Second Naval Member of the Commonwealth Naval Board. From 1937 to 1938 he was Chief of Staff and Maintenance Captain, the Nore. He was placed on the Retired List as captain in 1938. The following year he was appointed A.D.C. to the King. With the outbreak of World War II in 1939 he was recalled to active service in the rank of Rear Admiral and served first as Flag Officer, Milford Haven and later as Senior British Naval Officer, Trinidad. He retired finally in 1945 and was appointed C.B. He was Deputy Lieutenant for Breconshire. He lived at Woodberry Cottage, Itchester, Sussex, and d. 27 Feb. 1960 at Chichester hospital.

Www; Navy list.

Don.M.

PHILLIPS, Sir THOMAS WILLIAMS (1883-1966), permanent secretary to the Ministry of Labour and National Service; b. 20 Apr. 1883, second son of Thomas Phillips, a schoolmaster at Cemaes, Mont., and Jane Ryder (née Whittington), his wife. In 1897 he entered Machynlleth county school where he gained numerous exhibitions and a B.A. degree of the University of London before leaving school in 1902 for Jesus College, Oxford, where he graduated with first-class hons. in classics (Lit. Hum.) and won the Gaisford Prize for Greek prose in 1905. He was called to the Bar at Gray's Inn in 1913. He joined the civil service in 1906 and went to the Board of Trade where he had a special responsibility for copyright matters. In 1919 he was transferred to the Ministry of Labour and soon rose to be deputy secretary of the department and permanent secretary in 1935. He was one of the chief architects of that large department, with responsibility for employment exchanges, unemployment insurance, and trade boards and industrial arbitration. The Ministry of Labour and National Service owed a great deal of its prestige to his work, and especially to his unobtrusive but extremely efficient leadership during World War II when it was brought closely into touch with all areas of employment in the country whilst mobilizing men and women for the forces and the production of munitions. In 1944 he was appointed permanent secretary of the new Ministry created to launch the new scheme of national insurance, and remained there for four years. He afterwards became chairman of many public bodies, including the Central Land Board and the War Damage Commission (1949-59). Seen as possessing shrewd judgement when dealing with complexities, he was a valued counsellor to a long line of ministers. Among his many honours was a knighthood (1936) and an honorary LL.D. of the University of Wales (1946). He was a prominent member of the Montgomeryshire Society in London.

In 1913 he m. Alice Hair Potter (d. 1965) and they had two sons and a daughter. He d. 21 Sept. 1966.

Burke; WwW (1921); Machynlleth County School: prospectus and list of successes (1905); Times, 24 Sept. 1966.

M.A.J.

PICTON-TURBERVILL, EDITH (1872-1960), worker for women's causes and author; b. in 1872 in the registration district of Hereford, a twin daughter and one of the large family of John Picton Warlow, later (1891) John Picton Turbervill of Ewenny Priory, Glam., and Eleanor (née Temple) his second wife. Soon after leaving the Royal School, Bath, she had her first experience of social service when she endeavoured to improve the conditions of the navvies working on the Vale of Glamorgan railway. She then made a study of the poor by living for a while as they did in Shoreditch, London. After six years' social work in India she returned home and became foreign secretary of the Y.W.C.A. Later, as vice-president of the movement for ten years, she travelled widely, and demonstrated her special capacity to organize and lead by raising a quarter of a million pounds for the wartime needs of the movement and arranging the opening of many of the Y.W.C.A. hostels. Soon after World War I she was invited to preach a sermon in a church in North Somercotes, Lincs., being the first woman to be allowed to do so in a regular service. She never ceased to advocate the entry of women into the full orders of the Church of England. She joined the Labour Party and was an unsuccessful candidate at the 1922 and 1924 general elections but was elected Member of Parliament for The Wrekin division, Salop, in 1929, and became the first woman to sit on the ecclesiastical committee of parliament. During her short stay of two years in parliament she introduced as a private member the Sentence of Death (Expectant Mothers) Bill which became law and enacted that no pregnant woman should be executed. She was one of a commission sent in 1936 to report on female child labour in Malaya and Hong Kong. Her minority report, advocating far more stringent ordinances than her colleagues proposed, was published in 1937 and the governments of Malaya and Hong Kong agreed to adopt her plans in principle.

Other published work includes: *The musings of a lay woman, Christ and woman's power, Christ and international life*, (with others) *Myself when young* (1938), *In the land of my fathers* (1946), and *Should women be priests and ministers?* (1953). She spoke and wrote with charm and force and made a wide circle of friends but she never married. In later years she lived near Cheltenham, having spent most of her life in Ewenny Priory and London. She d. 31 Aug. 1960 aged 88.

Edith Picton-Turbervill, Life is good: an autobiography (1939); Www; Times, 3 Sept. 1960; OPCS, b. July-Sept. 1872.

M.A.J.

PIERCE, JOHN (1889-1955), author, minister (Presb.) and schoolteacher; b. in Llandegfan,

Anglesey, 10 Aug. 1889. He was educated at Beaumaris grammar school; University College, Bangor, where he graduated B.A. in 1915; and Bala College. He was ord. in 1918 and called to the pastorate of Adwy'r Clawdd, but departed in 1921 when he was appointed Welsh master at Llangefni grammar school. He d. 19 Jan. 1955. He was author of several children's adventure books: *Tri mewn trybini* (1937), *Dan lenni'r nos* (1938), *Blacmel* (1946), 'Yr Ysbiwr' in *Storïau ias a chyffro* (1951).

Blwyddiadur MC, 1956; Mairwen and Gwynn Jones, *Dewiniaid Difyr* (1983); personal knowledge.

B.L.J.

PIERCE, THOMAS JONES (1905-64), historian; b. 18 Mar. 1905 at Liverpool to John and Winifred Pierce. He was educated at the Liverpool Collegiate School and Liverpool University where he graduated with first-class honours in the School of Medieval and Modern History in 1927. He was awarded the Chadwick Scholarship (1927), the Gladstone Memorial Prize (1928) and the degree of M.A. (1929). Following a brief period as a University Fellow he was appointed Assistant Lecturer in the department of History, University College of North Wales, Bangor, with additional duties in the dept. of extra-mural studies in 1930. In 1945 he was invited to take up the post of Special Lecturer in Medieval Welsh History at the University College of Wales, Aberystwyth, an appointment made jointly by the college and the National Library of Wales. He was promoted Research Professor in 1948 and elected F.S.A. in 1950. He was a researcher at the National Library (*Clenennau letters and papers* was published in 1947), a very effective lecturer at the college and in extra-mural classes and local societies, and he was active in other fields as editor of *Caernarvonshire Hist. Soc. Trans.* (1939-63), chairman of the society's Council (1962-64), secretary of the Cambrian Archaeological Association (1946-55), chairman of its general committee (1956-64), and its president (1964). He was High Sheriff of Cardiganshire 1960-61, and he was a keen Rotarian.

He m. Margaret (Megan) Williams in 1944 and they had one daughter and one son. They made their home at Brynhyfryd, Tal-y-bont, Cards. He d. in Aberystwyth 9 Oct. 1964 and was cremated at Anfield Crematorium, Liverpool.

T. Jones Pierce had been a pupil of William Garmon Jones at Liverpool but he was greatly influenced by John Edward Lloyd (see above) whose colleague he was at Bangor. In turn he himself inspired generations of young Welsh historians and was acknowledged to be one of the most creative Welsh historians of his day. He was a pioneer in the study of the problems associated with the decay of tribalism and the development of the landed estates. He published a number of studies of the social structure of Welsh rural communities in the middle ages and the changes in forms of land tenure. He was one of the first to analyse in detail the evidence of the Welsh Laws for the operation of *galanas* and *tir gwely*, and his demonstration of the dynamic, developmental elements in the medieval law-books and the exercise of the law in the courts shed much light on the complexities of medieval land tenure. His studies of 13th-century Gwynedd are essential for our understanding of the economic, political and constitutional development of that province. He did not succeed in completing a book on these themes but his major articles have been collected (together with a bibliography of his writings) by J. Beverley Smith, *Medieval Welsh society* (1974).

J.B. Smith, *op. cit.*; Glanville Jones, *Caerns. Hist. Soc. Trans.*, 26 (1965), 9-19; E.D. Jones, *Arch. Camb.*, 113 (1964); 170-2; J. Gwynn Williams, *Welsh Hist. Rev.*, 1965, 271-3.

B.F.R.

PODE, Sir EDWARD JULIAN (1902-68), accountant and industrialist; b. in Sheffield 26 June 1902, s. of Edward and Lilla (née Telfer) Pode, educated at Mount House, near Plymouth and in *H.M.S. Conway*, he served in the Royal Navy during World War I. In 1926 he entered on his life-work in Welsh industry when he joined Guest, Keen & Nettlefolds, Ltd. as district accountant at Dowlais. When the heavy steel interests of GKN and Baldwins, Ltd. were amalgamated he became secretary of the new company in 1930 and in 1938 took over the commercial managership as well. In 1943 he was promoted assistant managing director of Guest, Keen, Baldwins Iron and Steel Co., Ltd. Two years later he became managing director. Though personally opposed to the nationalisation of the steel industry, he was persuaded in 1947 to assume the directorship of the newly-formed Steel Company of Wales, being chairman from 1962 to 1967. Under his guidance it grew to be the biggest steel company in Europe, with the output of steel increasing from half a million to 3 m. tonnes per year. He was a member of the executive committee and later president (1962-64) of the British Iron and Steel Federation and became vice-president of the Iron and Steel Institute. He took a keen interest in saving fuel and wrote an article on 'Fuel efficiency in industry' in *Industrial Wales*, June 1952, becoming director and later chairman (1965) of the National Industrial Efficiency Service. He held numerous interests outside the steel industry, serving as chairman of the Development Corporation of Wales (1958) and of the Prince of Wales Dry Dock Co., Swansea, Ltd., and a director of Lloyd's Bank, Ltd. He held fellowships in his profession and an honorary diploma. His contributions to public life were acknowledged when he became High Sheriff of Glamorgan in 1948 and J.P. in 1951. In 1957 the borough of Port Talbot recognised his great contribution in raising the prosperity of the district by making him an honorary freeman. He was knighted in the New Year's List, 1959. His down-to-earth approach and his gift of getting directly to the heart of a problem, his readiness to take instant and firm decisions, and his ability to obtain the highest standards from those who worked under him, were qualities which contributed to his remarkable success in his profession. One of his hobbies was farming and he was as popular among the farmers in Bonvilston as among the town dwellers of Port Talbot. In 1930 he m. Jean Finlay, dau. of F. Finlayson of Gwynfa, Caswell, Swansea, and they had two children. He d. at his home, The Great House in Bonvilston, 11 June 1968, and he was buried in Bonvilston churchyard.

Www, 1961-70; *West. Mail*, 7 and 8 March 1957, 13 June 1968; *Times*, 13 and 18 June 1968; information from his son John Pode.

E.D.J.

POWYS, JOHN COWPER (1872-1963), novelist, poet, literary critic and popular philosopher, the only one of the eleven children of the Rev. Charles Francis Powys to lay special claim to his father's Welsh ancestry. As he narrates in *Autobiography* (1934), his father would announce his descent from 'Roderic Mawr, King of all Wales'. His father's ancestry can be traced back some six centuries to Powyses of Montgomery, and to, more recently, the first Sir Thomas Powys of Lilford (d. 1719). From his mother, Mary Cowper-Johnson, he derived the more literary blood of the poets John Donne and William Cowper. Born 8 Oct. 1872 in Shirley, Derbyshire, his father's first parish, but in 1879 the family moved to Dorchester, Dorset, then, in 1885, to Montacute vicarage, Somerset. He was educated at Sherborne School and Corpus Christi College, Cambridge, and in 1894 drifted into the post of lecturing at several girls' schools at Hove, Sussex. His first publication, 1896, was *Odes and Other Poems*. In the same year he m. Margaret Alice Lyon; they had one son; both wife and son predeceased him. In 1899, after a preliminary lecture on Sir John Rhys (*DWB*, 844-5) he was appointed peripatetic lecturer for Oxford University Extension and began his life of wandering, first in England and to pioneer courses at Dresden and Leipzig, then, from 1905, in America. He began his highly successful lecturing career in America with a winter tour under the auspices of the Philadelphia-based Society for the Extension of University Teaching; from 1909 to 1929 he lectured full-time in America (with summers in England), visiting all but two of the States. In 1914 his stage manager, Arnold Shaw, a Yorkshireman, turned publisher, and Powys's writing career began, with an essay on *The Menace of German Culture*. In two to three years he produced for Shaw his first two novels, *Wood and Stone* and *Rodmoor*, two volumes of literary criticism, *Visions and Revisions* and *Suspended Judgements*, and two volumes of poetry, *Wolf's Bane* and *Mandragora*, and his large part of *Confessions of Two Brothers* (with Llewelyn Powys) for another publisher. He went on writing, mainly philosophical works on 'the Art of Happiness', in trains and hotel rooms, until the publication of *Wolf Solent* (1929). Then in retirement in Upstate New York, he wrote *A Glastonbury Romance*, *Weymouth Sands* and *Autobiography*. In 1934 he returned to Dorset, and in 1935 he retired finally to north Wales, according to a wish cherished from youth, first to Corwen, then, in 1951, to Blaenau Ffestiniog, where he died, 17 June 1963 aged ninety-one. The Wessex novels carry Welsh characters and subjects, but in Wales he wrote the novels *Morwyn* (1937), *Owen Glendower* (1940) and his 'masterpiece' *Porius* (1951) set in a Wales of 499 A.D. His other notable works of this prolific period include books on his masters *Dostoievsky* (1947) and *Rabelais* (1948) and experimental fiction like *Up and Out* (1957), *Homer and the Aether* (1959) and *All or Nothing* (1960). He learned Welsh and corresponded with many distinguished Welshmen of letters; his non-fictional writings about Wales and the Welsh were collected in *Obstinate Cymric* (1947).

Personal research; see also Jeremy Hooker, *John Cowper Powys* (1973); and *Powys Review*; [some of his papers are in N.L.W.].

B.H.

PRICE, JOHN ARTHUR (1861-1942), barrister and journalist; b. 20 Nov. 1861, s. of John Price, Shrewsbury, lawyer, and his wife Amelia Ann. He was educated at Shrewsbury School and Balliol College, Oxford, graduating B.A. in 1881. He was called to the Bar at Lincoln's Inn in 1889, and specialised in ecclesiastical law. He practiced much as a journalist, writing to the *Saturday Review*, *Manchester Guardian* and other publications, and was for years on the staff of the *Church Times*. At Oxford he became acquainted with several other young Welshmen, including the historian John Edward Lloyd (see above) and became a convinced Welsh nationalist until the end of his life. A devout churchman, he pleaded for disestablishment because he believed that it would be better for the church itself. He gave an account of his conversion to Welsh nationalism and his connections with Welsh religious and political life in a series of reminiscences which he contributed to *Y Genedl Gymreig* in 1925. His articles on T.E. Ellis and Sir Ellis Griffith in *The Welsh Outlook* are amongst the best that were written about them. In 1941, he was appointed chancellor of the bishopric of Bangor. He m. 6 Sept. 1904, Emily Ann, dau. of Maurice Foster of Egryn Abbey in Ardudwy; she predeceased him. He d. 3 June 1942.

Personal knowledge; J. Arthur Price 'Atgofion', *Y Genedl Gymreig*.

E.M.H.

PRICE, WATKIN WILLIAM (1873-1967), schoolmaster, researcher; b. 4 Sept. 1873 at 261 Cardiff Road, Aberaman, Aberdare, Glam., son of Watkin and Sarah Price, a Welsh-speaking family from Breconshire. The father was a collier; apparently the family had moved to Aberdare by 1866. 'W.W.' was educated at Blaen-gwawr elementary school until 1886 when he went to work in the office of *Tarian y Gweithiwr* in Aberdare. Then he became a pupil-teacher in two local schools until 1895 when he entered Cardiff University College as a 'normal' student. In 1897 he was employed by Cardiff Schools Board. In 1900 he returned to the Cynon valley as a teacher in Dan Isaac Davies's (*DWB*, 112-3) old school, Ysgol-y-Comin (Park school), Trecynon, which was founded in 1848 in reaction to the vilification of the district in the Blue Books. Subsequently he was headmaster of Llwydcoed (1912), Cap Coch (1921) and Blaen-gwawr (1924) schools until he retired in 1933.

He spent almost all his life researching his local and county history and biography. He began in response to a competition set in the national *eisteddfod* in 1920 for an essay on the history and folklore of any Welsh parish. He never completed the work; but he collected and interpreted widely the history of one of the most important areas in Wales in the 19th c. His labours resulted in valuable essays, records and transcripts in fields varying from monastic to mining. One can but marvel at his feat in copying during 1941-43, in his old age, many hundreds of detailed pages from the complicated mining deeds of the district. He rescued an unique 1827-28 volume of drawings by the nieces of Anthony Bacon II (*DWB*, 19-20) which depicted the rural nature of east Glamorgan before it was despoiled by industry. His index of some 40,000 cards on persons, past and present, in Wales continues to be of use to researchers (copies are in the National Library of Wales and Cynon Valley Library). R.T. Jenkins invited him to contribute 30 articles to *The Dictionary of Welsh Biography*, several of them on some of the most important persons of old industrial Wales.

He was also a socialist pioneer; secretary of the Independent Labour Party at Aberdare 1900-08, and consequently one of the chief supporters of Keir Hardie when he was M.P. in 1906. There is a tradition that he was one of the most fervent members pressing for the nomination of Hardie in the meeting at Bethel, Abernant (Sept. 1900) to contest the general election in Oct. of that year. Eventually, however, he turned to *Plaid Cymru*, supporting Gwynfor Evans in the Aberdare by-election in 1954. Because of the luke-warm support of some of the chapels for Labour, 'W.W.' left Saron (Congl.) chapel, Aberaman, and joined the Welsh Unitarians meeting in Yr Hendy-cwrdd, Trecynon.

In 1901 he m. Margaret Williams, Henbant Hall, Llandysul, Cards. She d. in 1950. In 1952 the University of Wales conferred on him an hon. M.A. degree, and he was sometimes known as 'Bob Owen of the South' (see Owen, Robert above). He d. 31 Dec. 1967 leaving four sons and a daughter.

WwW (1937); *Old Aberdare*, 4 (1985) and the sources referred to there; *Casglwr*, Mar. 1983; *Aberdare parish magazine*, Mar. 1950; memoirs in *The Aberdare Leader* during Jan. 1968; biographical notes in Aberdare Central Library; his deposits there and at N.L.W. and Glamorgan Record Office.

D.L.D.

PROSSER, DAVID LEWIS (1868-1950), archbishop; b. 10 June 1868, s. of David Prosser of Tŷ Gwyn, Llangynnor, Carms. and Elizabeth, his wife. He was educated at Llandovery College and Keble College, Oxford, where he graduated with a third-class honours degree in history; he took his B.A. in 1891 and his M.A. in 1895. He was ord. deacon, 18 Dec. 1892, by Bishop Basil Jones of St. David's and licensed to the curacy of Holy Trinity church at Aberystwyth. He had his priest's orders from John Lloyd, suffragan Bishop of Swansea, 21 Dec. 1893. In 1896, he became curate of Christ Church, Swansea, where he remained until 1909, when he became vicar of Pembroke Dock. He was appointed Archdeacon of St. David's in 1920 and was consecrated Bishop of St. David's in succession to John Owen (*DWB*, 714-5) 2 Feb. 1927. In 1944, he was elected Archbishop of Wales to succeed C.A.H. Green (see above). He resigned the archbishopric in 1949. He d. 28 Feb. 1950, at Abergwili, where he was buried.

He wrote some devotional pamphlets, and

was awarded the degree of LL.D. *honoris causa* by the University of Wales in 1949.

Crockford's *Clerical Directory*, 1949-50; *Who's Who*; St. David's episcopal registers at N.L.W.; personal knowledge.

T.I.E.

PRYCE, FREDERICK NORMAN (1888-1953), museum curator; b. 19 Aug. 1888 in Welshpool, Mont., the s. of T.W. Pryce and his wife. Following his education at the local grammar school he entered the University College of Wales, Aberystwyth, where he graduated with a first class in Latin in 1908 and similarly in Greek in 1909. He was appointed to the staff of the British Museum in 1911, promoted Assistant Keeper in 1934 and Keeper of Greek and Roman Antiquities 1936-39. He served in the Middle East in World War I (and was mentioned in dispatches twice) and in intelligence in World War II. He was the editor of the *Journal of Hellenic Studies*, 1924-38, and the author of numerous papers on history and archaeology and of standard catalogues of classical antiquities.

He m. Ruby Sewell in 1925 and he d. at his home, 31 Erw Wen, Welshpool, 14 Oct. 1953.

Www.

B.F.R.

PRYSE (FAMILY), Gogerddan, Cards.
Sir Pryse Pryse, bart. (1838-1906) (*DWB*, 808) was succeeded by three of his sons: Edward (1862-1918); Lewes (1864-1946) who was primarily responsible for initiating the movement to found the Royal Welsh Agricultural Show; and George (1870-1948) who in turn was followed by his only son Pryse Loveden Pryse-Saunders (b. 12 Nov. 1896), the fifth and last baronet. Even before the end of World War I parts of the estate had been sold in order to meet increasing debts and family commitments. As he had no heir and very little prior association with north Cardiganshire, he found little difficulty in selling the mansion and the remaining estate of 3,839 acres to the Univ. Coll. Aberystwyth to accommodate its famous Welsh Plant Breeding Station. Sir Pryse thereafter resided at Glanrhydw, Carms., until his death in a London hospital 5 Jan. 1962.

Personal research; *Www*.

D.J.

PRYSE-SAUNDERS, PRYSE LOVEDEN - see PRYSE (FAMILY), Gogerddan above.

PRYSOR - see WILLIAMS, ROBERT JOHN below.

PUGH, EDWARD CYNOLWYN (1883-1962), minister (Presb.), author and musician; b. 21 June 1883 at Abergynolwyn, Mer., son of William and Mary Pugh. His parents moved to Trehafod, Rhondda Valley, Glam., in 1888. He was brought up there and became a coal miner after leaving school. Interested in music, he became a conductor of brass bands, and became an accomplished cornet player (in his day he was cornet player for the *Gorsedd* of Bards). During the 1904-05 religious revival he became a dedicated convert and began to preach in Siloam, Trehafod. He proceeded to further his education at Pontypridd Collegiate School, Trefeca College, and University College, Cardiff (where he graduated B.A.). He was ord. in 1917, and served his ministry with the Forward Movement at Pontypool and Tonyrefail, and in Wilmer Rd. English church, Birkenhead. In 1928 he emigrated to U.S.A. to take charge of the Welsh church in Chicago, and later the Welsh church in New York. He retired c. 1956 and returned to Wales. In 1917 he m. Jennet Jenkins of the Vale of Neath, and they had three daughters.

Cynolwyn Pugh was talented and contributed to periodicals in Wales and America. He won the prose medal at Ebbw Vale national eisteddfod (1958) for an autobiography which was published under the title *Ei ffanffer ei hun* (1959) (transl. by Nansi Pugh, *His own fanfare* (1999)). He d. in Cardiff, 22 Mar. 1962.

His autobiography; *Gol.*, 18 Apr. 1962; *Blwyddiadur MC*, 1963, 270; personal acquaintance.

G.M.R.

Q-R

QUIN, WINDHAM HENRY WYNDHAM - see WYNDHAM-QUIN, WINDHAM HENRY (1857-1952) below.

RADMILOVIC, PAUL (1886-1968), swimmer; b. 5 Mar. 1886 in Cardiff, of a Greek father and Irish mother, but he lived most of his life at Weston-super-Mare. He competed in five Olympic Games from 1908 to 1928 and won gold medals in three of them - for water-polo in 1908, 1912, 1920 and as a member of the British relay team in 1908. Had World War I not prevented the Games being held in 1916, Raddy - as he was called - must have won more gold medals and participated in more Olympics than any other swimmer. He won the Welsh 100 yds. championship 15 times between 1901 and 1922. In 1929, when he was 43 yrs. old, he won the Welsh 440 and 880 yds. championships. In 1967 he was honoured by the Hall of Fame at Fort Lauderdale, Florida, one of the few British competitors to receive one of the principal honours of the swimming world. He d. 29 Sept. 1968.

Pat Besford, *Encyclopaedia of Swimming* (1971).
B.L.J.

RAGLAN, 4th BARON - see SOMERSET, FITZROY RICHARD below.

RANDALL, HENRY JOHN (1877-1964), known generally by his many friends as Harry Randall, lawyer and historian; b. 13 Dec. 1877, at Bridgend, Glam., s. of William Richard Randall, a solicitor of that town, and his wife, Hannah (née Johnston). He was educated at Bradfield and was LL.B. (Lond.). He followed his father's profession and was admitted a solicitor in 1900, retiring from practice in 1962. He was secretary of the Bridgend District Law Society 1911-21; its president in 1928 and again in 1960.

He was notable not only in his profession but was a man of very wide interests, especially in the field of local history in the Vale of Glamorgan, where he lived all his life. He was a member of the Camb. Arch. Assocn., becoming its president in 1928 and was honorary treasurer 1936-51; a member of the Board of Celtic Studies for 22 years and of the Ancient Monuments Board for Wales until 1959; joint editor of the South Wales Record Society from 1929; F.S.A. and a member of its Council in 1949; and president of The Cardiff Naturalists' Society, 1946-47. He was a member of the Athenaeum Club. A further example of his sense of responsibility to the community was that he served as an officer in the Welch Regiment in the Volunteer and Territorial Forces from 1895 to 1918.

Noteworthy amongst his many legal papers was 'Law and geography' 1918, in the Evolution of Law series, vol. III, and 'Beginnings of English constitutional theory' 1919, in the Wigmore Celebration Legal Essays. His first published book, *History in the open air*, came in 1936, followed in 1944 by *The Creative centuries*.

In 1946 the Camb. Arch. Assocn. turned to him for an authoritative account of Roman Wales for its centenary volume of *Arch Camb*. and his able contribution 'The Roman period' filled that need very adequately. He continued to record his deep interest in his native county with, in 1955, his book *Bridgend: the story of a market town* and, in 1961, *The Vale of Glamorgan, studies in landscape and history*.

He was closely associated with the National Museum of Wales for nearly 40 years, having become a member of its Art and Archaeology Committee in 1925, then a member of the Court of Governors in 1937 and of the Council in 1938. He was treasurer of the Museum, 1952-62, and in that period made, perhaps, his greatest contribution in founding the 'Friends of the National Museum of Wales', of which he was chairman, 1954-64. His services to his native county and country were recognised by the conferment upon him, in 1963, of the degree of LL.D. by the University of Wales.

In 1916 he m. Olga Ruth Brewis; there were no children. He d. 4 Nov. 1964 at his home, 'Erw Graig', Merthyr Mawr, Bridgend, and a memorial service was held on 9 Nov. at St. Mary's Church, Nolton, Bridgend, followed by cremation.

Times, 9 Nov. 1964; *Arch. Camb.*, 113 (1964); *Ann. Report*, N.M. of Wales, 1964-65, p.11; Friends of the N.M. of W., 10th ann. Rep. 1-3; *Www* and personal knowledge.

H.M.S.

REES, CALEB (1883-1970), inspector of schools and author; b. in 1883 the son of Jacob and Mary Rees, Esgair-ordd, Whitchurch, Pembs. From the village school he went to Port Talbot Intermediate School where he gained a scholarship to Cardiff University College in 1899. There he won the Gladstone Memorial Prize, and graduated with first-class hons. in English in 1902. He continued his education at Manchester University where he won the Withers Prize before returning to Cardiff as a lecturer in the education department in 1908, gaining an M.A. degree the following year. In 1912 he was appointed inspector of schools for the counties of Brecon and Monmouth and the borough of Newport, later becoming deputy chief inspector for Wales. At the beginning of World War II he was seconded to the Ministry of information in Cardiff but his health failed and after recuperating he returned to his work as inspector of training colleges and university training departments. He m. in City Road chapel (Welsh Meth.), London, 28 Aug. 1922, Laura Gertrude Powell, medical officer of the Board of Health at Cardiff, and they made their home in 28 Clytha Park Road, Newport, Mon. Although he retired in 1943 to Island House, Laugharne, he was given the task three years later of interviewing young men, many ex-service men among them, for the teaching profession. He and his wife became members of his old church in Pen-y-groes, where he was elected a deacon. His wife d. 1 Jan. and he on 9 Jan. 1970.

He and his brother Stephen Morris Rees

were co-authors of a history of Pen-y-groes Congregational Church (1959). He also wrote a series of articles on education which appeared in the *Traethodydd* 1907-08; an article on teaching Welsh in schools in *Beirniad*, 1; the story of his great-uncle who emigrated to America in *Llenor*, 1933; as well as pamphlets on education.

WwW (1937); calendars of the University of Wales, 1900-13; *Cardigan and Tivy Side Advertiser*, 16 and 23 Jan. 1970; *WWP*; OPCS, b. registered July - Sept. 1883.
M.A.J.

REES, GEORGE (GEORGE REES HEYCOCK; 1873-1950), poet and hymnwriter; b. 20 Jan. 1873 at Dinas, Rhondda, (his parents hailed from Pontrhyd-y-fen and Pwll-y-glaw, Cwmafon, Glam.). Soon after his birth his parents moved to Pen-y-graig and it was there that he attended the elementary school before starting work in a coalmine. He undertook a course of instruction intending to qualify as a colliery official. He was admitted to church membership at Nazareth (CM), Williamstown, where his father was an elder. In 1900 he m. Kate Ann, dau. of Thomas Roberts, chief accountant at the Oakeley Slate Quarries, Blaenau Ffestiniog and for a time lived at Pont Rhondda, where he was elected an elder of his church. He moved to London to work in the milk trade. Here a milkman with the surname Maycock covered the same round and to avoid confusion George adopted his mother's surname Rees. Later on he moved to Abertillery in Gwent, where he was again chosen elder of a church. He returned to London to hold an important post with an insurance company. In 1941 he retired to Prestatyn. After the death of his wife in 1945 he went to live with his daughter and his son-in-law Prof. R.H. Evans, (Leeds University) at Headingley where he joined a Wesleyan church. He d. at Headingley 1 Sept. 1950 and was buried in Willesden Green cemetery, London, on 6 Sept. He won several prizes at national and other *eisteddfodau*: Pwllheli, 1925, Swansea, 1926, Treorchy, 1928, Liverpool, 1929, Port Talbot, 1930. He was best known for his *englynion* and his hymns. His hymn 'O Fab y Dyn, Eneiniog Duw' is regarded as one of the greatest Welsh hymns.

Trysorfa'r plant, Feb. 1938; *Eurgr.*, 1934; J. Thickens, *Emynau a'u hawduriaid*, 1961; *Gol.*, 6 Sept, 11, 25 Oct. 1950; *Ser. Cymru*, 21 Oct. 1973. The works of George Rees have been collected by Brynley F. Roberts, *O! Fab y Dyn* (1976).
R.D.G.

REES, Sir JAMES FREDERICK (1883-1967), Principal of the University College at Cardiff; b. 13 Dec. 1883 son of John Rees, Priory Hill and later of Hakin, Milford Haven, Pembs., a dock worker. He was educated in the local board school before gaining a scholarship to the local intermediate school on 24 Jan. 1898; he entered the University College at Cardiff in 1901, where he graduated with Class I in History in 1904. In 1908 he gained Class I in the school of Modern History at Lincoln College, Oxford. He became an assistant lecturer in History in the University College at Bangor, 1908-12, a lecturer for a short while in Queen's University, Belfast, and then a Reader in Economic History at Edinburgh University, 1913, until he became Professor of Commerce in Birmingham University in 1925. In 1929 he was appointed Principal of the University College at Cardiff, a post he held for 20 yrs. He was vice-chancellor of the University of Wales twice, 1935-37 and 1944-46, and Warden of the Guild of Graduates, 1950-53. After retiring in 1949 he went to Ceylon (Sri Lanka) University in 1953-55 as a visiting Professor in Economics, and served as head of the department of Economic History at Edinburgh University, 1956-58.

As a man of uncommon wisdom, insight and energy, he became a member of many industrial and constitutional committees. He was chairman of the Consultative Committee on the Welsh Problems of Reconstruction, 1942-46, and was a member of the commission on Reforming the Constitution of Sri Lanka, 1944-45 and of the Local Government Boundary Commission, 1946-49. He received honorary LL.D. degrees of the Universities of Wales, Birmingham and Edinburgh, and was knighted in 1945 when he was in Sri Lanka. In 1955 he served as High Sheriff for his native county, and was president of the Cambrian Archaeological Association, 1956-57.

He was the author of many books, including *A social and industrial history of England, 1815-1918* (1920), *A short fiscal and financial history of England, 1815-1918* (1921), *Studies in Welsh history* (1947); *The story of Milford* (1954), *The problem of Wales and other essays* (1960); and editor of *A survey of economic development with special reference to Great Britain* (1933), and *The Cardiff region: a survey* (1960). Many of his articles appear in history society journals, encyclopaedias, *Cambridge History of the British Empire* and *The Dictionary of Welsh Biography down to 1940*. Several of his public addresses have been published, among them *The dominion of Ceylon* (1949) and the B.B.C. Welsh regional annual lecture entitled *Of Welsh nationality and historians* (1951).

He m. in 1913 Dora Rose Lucile, dau. of Gethin Davies, Principal of the Baptist College, Cardiff and they had one son. He d. 7 Jan 1967 at his home, 11 Celyn Grove, Cyncoed, Cardiff.

Www; information supplied by the archivist at Haverfordwest.
E.D.J.

REES, Sir JOHN MILSOM (1866-1952), surgeon and laryngologist; s. of John Rees of Neath, Glam., b. 20 Apr. 1866. After studying at St. Bartholomew's Hospital, London, he qualified in 1889, and three years later took the F.R.C.S. (Edin.). Having taken up laryngology as his special subject he was appointed surgeon to the Ear, Nose and Throat Department of the Prince of Wales General Hospital, Tottenham, and he conducted his private consulting practice at Upper Wimpole Street. He became laryngologist to the Royal Opera House, Covent Garden, and to the Guildhall School of Music; in that capacity he was medical adviser to the most famous singers of the day - Madame Patti, Dame Nellie Melba, Kirsten Flagstad, Jan de Reszke and many others - and he was on terms of close friendship with them. Even more noteworthy was his long and distinguished service to the Royal Family; he was laryngologist to King

George V throughout the twenty-six years of his reign, and to Queen Mary, Queen Alexandra and Queen Maude of Norway. He was knighted in 1916, appointed K.C.V.O. in 1923, and promoted to G.C.V.O. in 1934. The University of Wales conferred upon him an honorary D.Sc. in 1931. Milsom Rees was officially associated with many of the leading London teaching hospitals as vice-president or governor, and he was also a member of the Court of the University of Wales. In addition he took an active part on the governing body of the British Postgraduate School, Epsom College, the Nuffield Provincial Hospital Trust and similar bodies. Apart from his remarkable success in professional spheres, he also achieved great distinction in many other fields. As a student he was an excellent cricketer, boxer and rugby player; later on he became a first-class golfer of international standing, and still later he took up big-game hunting with equal success. The account of his visits to Africa reveal in a striking manner his multifarious interests. His expert surgical craftmanship would be in demand for the local celebrities and native chieftains; his wise counsel would be sought on the question of providing new hospitals, and at times he gave generous financial assistance for their construction. Furthermore, he acquired extensive business interests there, in the form of coffee estates in Tanganyika and salt mines in Nyaza, and these proved very successful ventures.

Eventually he retired to Broadstairs where he maintained a practical and generous interest in education, and d. there 25 April 1952. He m. Eleanor, dau. of William P. Jones of Finchley, chairman of Jones Brothers, Holloway and of John Barnes, Ltd., in 1894, and they had a son and a daughter.

Br. Med. Jnl., 3 and 24 May 1952; *Lancet*, 3 and 10 May 1952; *Times*, 25 Apr. 1952.

E.W.J.

REES, JOHN SEYMOUR (1887-1963), minister (Congl.) and author; son of John Rees and Magdalen (née Evans) his wife, Glasgow House, Aberaeron, baptised on 22 July 1887. He was educated at Aberaeron; Pencader; The Old College School, Carmarthen (c. 1909-10); and Brecon Academy (1911-15), attending a degree course under its auspices in the colleges of the University of Wales at Aberystwyth (1911) and Cardiff (1912). He was minister at Ebeneser, Cefncoedycymer (1915-22), where he was ord.; Hermon, Treorci (1923-27) and Soar, Seven Sisters (1927-45), before being appointed secretary of the Cardiff Council of Christians and Jews (1945-63). He was a very popular preacher but declined an invitation to become pastor of a church in New York, U.S.A., *c.* 1922, and in Radnor Walk, London, in 1926. He gave his valedictory address to South Glamorgan Association in 1943 and gave many radio talks *c.* 1932 onwards.

He was known initially as a short-story writer. He won three crowns and 16 chairs in local and regional *eisteddfodau*, and first prize at the National *Eisteddfod* 28 times, mostly for essays and biographies, but the urge to include every detail stifled his literary skills, as in his essay on the history of the Welsh Language Society in 1952. He contributed to the periodical press for over 50 years; see Glyn L. Jones, *A bibliography of Cardiganshire 1600-1964* and the *Supplement* for a list of his articles in the *Dysgedydd, Cymru, Genhinen, Ymofynnydd*, etc. Other published work includes a one-act play, *Y Canfasiwr*, in *Y Ford Gron*, 5, no. 1, under the pseudonym J.C.M. Evans; and *The history of Ynysgau Church, Merthyr Tydfil* (c. 1958). He was a meticulous historian and about 50 volumes which were impeccably typed and neatly bound by him are preserved at the National Library of Wales (NLW MSS 18628-18865; 18866 correspondence). They contain collections of hymns, biographies of hymn-writers, poets, preachers (and Congregational ministers of South Glamorgan to 1939, in particular); and stories, history and notable figures of the Aeron valley, especially of Neuaddlwyd Academy. He also compiled indexes to *Y Beirniad* and the biographical dictionary of Josiah T. Jones (1867).

He m., Jan. 1924, Annie Owen, Dyffryn, Rhydlewis, Cards., who also gave valuable service to the church, and they had one son. He d. 17 June 1963.

Blwyddiadur, (Congl.) 1910-16, and 1964, 156; and the MSS mentioned above.

M.A.J.

REES, JOHN THOMAS (1857-1949), musician; b. 14 Nov. 1857 at Llwynbedw, near Cwmgïedd, Brecks.; s. of Thomas and Hannah (née Morgan) Rees. He had little schooling and began work as a pit-boy at the age of nine. Whilst working as a miner in Ystradgynlais, Rhondda Valley, and Aberdare, he acquired a sound musical discipline. He began to give music lessons when he was 17 (Daniel Protheroe, *DWB*, 801-2, was one of his pupils) and he mastered the sol-fa notation between 1876 and 1879 under the tuition of D. W. Lewis, Brynaman (*DWB*, 550-1). At twenty-one he gained some prominence as the composer of a cantata which he submitted for competition at a Treherbert *eisteddfod*. A modest fund raised by friends enabled him to study with Joseph Parry (*DWB*, 738) at Aberystwyth in 1879, but his financial resources were few and the outlook bleak until David Jenkins (*DWB*, 431) opened the way for him to teach sol-fa classes in Pen-y-garn. He went to Emporium, Kansas, in 1882 and gained his Mus. Bac. (Toronto) in 1889 (he later held a teaching appointment there, during a short visit to America). On his return to Wales in 1883 he settled at Pen-y-garn, near Aberystwyth, as tutor to an adult music class, conductor of rural choirs which performed oratorios and similar works, and subsequently as part-time lecturer at U.C.W. Aberystwyth and part-time music teacher at Tregaron county school. In 1895 he won the prize of £20 for the composition of a string quartet at the Aberdare national *eisteddfod*. He became known throughout the country as composer of a number of hymn-tunes and anthems, and as a conductor of *cymanfaoedd canu* and adjudicator at *eisteddfodau*. His predominant interest found expression in numerous compositions of a religious character which include: 'Duw sydd noddfa' (Aberdare national *eisteddfod* prize composition, 1890); 'Y Teulu Dedwydd' (cantata); 'Crist yr Andes' (children's cantata);

'Hosannah' and 'Christos' (settings of services for children). Other published compositions include his 'String Quartet' (1895); 'Y Trwbadŵr' (based on words from the poetry of Dafydd ap Gwilym) in association with S.M. Powell at Tregaron; and 'Hillsides of Wales' for violin and piano. He also edited a collection of hymn-tunes by David Lewis, Llanrhystud (*DWB*, 550), *Perorydd yr Ysgol Sul* (a collection of children's hymn-tunes and anthems), and was joint-editor of *Llyfr hymnau a thonau y Methodistiaid Calfinaidd* (1897) and *Emynau a thonau y Methodistiaid Calfinaidd a Wesleyaidd* (1927). He m. Elizabeth Davies of Pen-y-garn in 1881 (she d. in 1939); there were 8 children, 5 of whom were alive in 1955. He d. 14 Oct. 1949 and was b. at Y Garn cemetery.

Personal knowledge; D.H. Lewis, *John Thomas Rees* (1955).

D.E.P.W., E.D.J.

REES, RICHARD JENKIN (1868-1963), minister (Presb.); b. 10 Sept. 1868 at Riwel Isaf, Pen-y-garn, Cards., son of John and Catherine Rees, who moved to London when he was an infant. He was educated at the City of London School and Aberystwyth College (where he graduated B.A. of the University of London). He later proceeded to Mansfield College, Oxford, graduating with a first class in theology. Whilst at Aberystwyth he had intended becoming a solicitor, but under the influence of Dr Henry Drummond's mission at the college he decided to enter the Christian ministry and began to preach in Jewin chapel, London. He was ord. in 1893, and became pastor of Ala Rd. English church, Pwllheli (1892-94); Clifton St. church, Cardiff (1894-1903), and Tabernacl, Aberystwyth (1903-22). Having been invited to superintend the Forward Movement of the Presbyterian Church of Wales in Cardiff, he worked with diligence and success in that office until 1947. In 1894 he m. Apphia Mary James of Pen-y-garn; they had two sons and two daughters: Morgan Goronwy Rees, sometime Principal of Univ. Coll. Aberystwyth, was their second son. After retiring he lived with his children at Pwllheli, and near Oxford, and at Waltham Cross, London. He d. 30 Apr. 1963, and was buried in Cardiff.

He was one of the principal leaders of the Presbyterian Church of Wales in his time, being Moderator of the South Wales Association (1920 and 1954) and Moderator of the General Assembly (1927). He was an incomparable speaker, both in Welsh and English. He contributed occasionally to the press, but he was a gifted orator rather than a writer. He published a handbook (in English and Welsh) on 2 Samuel (1899), and a commentary on the letters of St. Paul to the Philippians and Colossians (1909).

WwW (1921), 397; *WwFC* (1951), 352; *Drys.*, 1927, 1-4; *Gol.*, 22 May 1963; W. Morris (ed.), *Deg o Enwogion* (1965), 35-40; *Blwyddiadur MC*, 1964, 397; personal acquaintance.

G.M.R.

REES, THOMAS (1862-1951), breeder of Welsh cobs; b. 31 Jan. 1862 one of the 10 children, 3 girls and 7 boys, of James Rees and Mary, his wife, who lived at Sarnicol, the cottage in Capel Cynon, Cards., in which Thomas Jacob Thomas (see below) was born in 1873. The Rees family moved to Dolau Llethi, Llannarth where Thomas at the age of 8 was a shepherd in summer, working for a time alongside Evan Pan Jones (*DWB*, 462-3), and attended school at Talgarreg in winter. In 1886 he m. Rachel, dau. of David and Catherine Davies of Vicarage, near Capel Ficer, Mydroilyn. They had five children but only three boys grew to manhood. Their married life began at Ffosiwan, Mydroilyn, and they started farming at Cefnfaes, Capel Betws, around 1894. Then they took over the larger farm of Cwmgwenyn, Llangeitho, where they remained from 1897 to 1914. They moved to Blaen-waun, a small farm in Penuwch, 1914-44, and to Bear's Hill, a smallholding nearby, in 1944. He d. there on 15 Jan. 1951 cared for by his grandson and grand-daughter, his wife having predeceased him in March 1936, shortly after celebrating their golden wedding. They are buried in the cemetery of Capel Gwynfil, Llangeitho.

At the age of 18, in 1880, he started keeping a stallion, called 'Bold Buck', s. of 'Cardigan Driver' owned by a Unitarian minister at Maesymeillion, Llanybydder. When he was a servant at Pantmoch, Pontsian, he bought a 6-year old cob 'Welsh Briton', from David Charles Jones, Abercefel, Llandysul which became one of the taproot sires of Welsh cobs. Those were the days of the trotting cobs. 'Welsh Briton's' time for the mile was 2 minutes 18 seconds. Three of his progeny were champion trotters at Alexandra Park, London, during three successive years, 1892-3-4, and this was considered a considerable achievement. 'Welsh Briton' was 21 when he died. He is one of four cob stallions buried in the land of Cwmgwenyn, Llangeitho. A further 6 stallions lie buried in Blaen-waun. Of these 10 stallions 7 were over 20 years of age.

Thomas Rees was keeping Welsh cobs long before the establishment of the Welsh Stud Book in 1902. He has 2 stallions and 2 mares registered in that first volume. He kept 3 sons of 'Welsh Briton' as stallions - 'King Briton', 'Briton Comet' and 'Britonian'. He kept Welsh cob stallions for 70 years. He led stallions himself and engaged others to do so. Even at 80 years temporarily re-entering the lists as he had given up 'travelling' years before, he took his black stallion 'Blaenwaun True Briton' round for one season, travelling three days a week.

His three sons followed in his footsteps. David Rees led his stallions round for 50 years and kept them for over 60 years, James Rees for a similar span and Harry Rees throughout his shorter life. Thomas Rees's stallions travelled as far as Glamorgan and Gwent, and on occasion into Gloucester, where Harry Hopton, the smith worked. They walked all the way. 'King Briton' was the first stallion which he travelled into England. The contribution of Thomas Rees and his sons to the Welsh cob is distinctive on three counts; (1) his stallions represented the oldest strain of Welsh cobs, (2) no one else gave such an aggregate of years to owning and leading cob stallions, (3) the family devoted itself exclusively to the Welsh cob even when a majority of breeders found it more profitable to keep other breeds. It has often been said that the Welsh cob would not have survived the lean years but for the contribution of Thomas Rees and his sons. He was made an honorary member of the Welsh Pony and Cob Society. John Roderick Rees, son of David Rees, inherited 'Rhosfarch Frenin' continuing the line of the family's cob stallions into its hundredth year.

He was a talented man despite his lack of early education, a keen reader, a genealogist and local historian and a fine story-teller. Though he spent the greater part of his life in the midst of Calvinistic Methodism as a member in Capel Gwynfil, he continued at heart to be an Independent, deriving great joy from Elfed's hymns. It was his Welsh cobs that kept his name alive, but he was also well-steeped in the culture of a vanishing world.

Family knowledge of his grandsons and grand-daughter, Tom Rees, Maggie Rees, John Roderick Rees.

J.R.R.

REES, THOMAS JAMES (1875-1957), director of education; b. 19 Mar. 1875, son of James and Mary Rees, Waun-wen, Swansea, Glam. He was a graduate (B.A.) of the University of London (1898) and, despite his lack of experience as a headmaster, was appointed from among 112 applicants director of education in Swansea in 1908, a post which he filled with distinction until he retired in 1943. In national education he became well known as a member of the advisory and consultative committees of the Board of Education. With his wide knowledge, he became a popular and eloquent speaker on educational problems, and was one of the best known figures in Welsh education as honorary secretary of the Federation of Education Committees in Wales and Monmouthshire. He was connected with numerous organisations, being a member of the Central Council for School Broadcasting, the council of the University of Wales, the Welsh National Council of Music, and the Welsh National School of Medicine. He was a J.P. and served as treasurer of the University College at Swansea. He was one of the founder members of Swansea Rotary Club, having been president of Rotary in Great Britain and Ireland, 1942-44. In 1943 he was appointed C.B.E. Among his published work is an address on *The appointment of head teachers* (1911) and reports on *The teaching of Welsh in elementary schools* (1914) and *The education problem in Swansea* (1918).

He m., 1902, Katie Davies, Gowerton, and they had two daughters. He d., 24 Dec. 1957, at his daughter's home, Brynfield, Reynoldston.

Wwo; Cambrian, 18 Sept. 1908; *Herald of Wales*, 9 Jan. 1943 and 4 Jan. 1958.

M.A.J.

REES, THOMAS MARDY (1871-1953), Independent minister, historian and author; b. Skiwen, Glam., in 1871, one of the six children of William Rees, collier, and his wife Mary. He attended the national school in the village and afterwards joined his father in the Fforest Fforchdwm colliery. Later, after moving to Resolven, they worked at Melin-cwrt Level. When the level closed they moved to Maerdy in the Rhondda Fach valley. The father and two of the boys, Thomas and John, were working in No. 2 pit on 23 Dec. 1885 when a tragic explo-

sion happened there, but the three were saved.

Thomas' public career as a reciter, orator, poet and narrator began early. He began preaching when he was eighteen years of age, at the request of Siloa, Maerdy. He attended Pentre secondary school, Rhondda, before moving on to Gwynfryn school, Ammanford. He won a scholarship for local boys from Maerdy tenable at the University College, Cardiff. He was accepted by examination into the Memorial College, Brecon. He was ordained in June 1896 at Bethel Newydd, Mynyddislwyn, Mon. It was there, tracing the church's history, that he took to historical research. This was to become one of his main interests in life. In 1899 he moved to Buckley, Flints., as pastor of the English church, and whilst there he took advantage of the resources of St. Deiniol's Library, Hawarden. He played an active role in local government as a member of the county council and as chairman of Flintshire education committee. He was a member of the deputation which went before the Commission on the Disestablishment and Disendowment of the Church. In 1906 he moved and took charge of Markham Square church, Chelsea. There he co-operated with Lord Monkswell in promoting children's welfare. In 1912 he returned to Wales to take charge of the English church at Gnoll Road, Neath, where he stayed until his retirement in 1946. On his retirement he was made honorary minister of the church.

He won many prizes in the national *eisteddfod*. He was secretary of the literary committee of the national *eisteddfod* at Neath, 1918. He was a member of the *Gorsedd* of Bards and lectured widely on historical subjects. On the strength of his research and publications he was elected F.R.Hist.S. in 1919. He published a number of books and booklets: *Y Lili fach wen a thelynegion eraill* (1903); *Breezes from the Welsh hills and other poems* (1906); *Notable Welshmen* (1908); *Ebenezer Jones, the neglected poet* ...(1909); *Ystoriau difyr* ...(1908 and 1909); *Mynachdai Cymru* ...(1910); *Welsh painters, engravers, sculptors (1527-1911)* (1912); *Difyrrwch gwŷr Morgannwg* ...(1916); *Hiwmor y Cymro* ... (1922); *A history of the Quakers in Wales and their emigration to North America* (1925); and *Seth Joshua and Frank Joshua* ... (1926). He was the editor of *The Official Guide to Neath* from 1922 to 1941. He also published pamphlets in Welsh and English on the results of the Act of Uniformity, 1662, and short histories of Maes-yr-haf church, Neath, and Bethel Newydd church, Mynyddislwyn.

He m. Margaret Williams who predeceased him by four years. They had four sons and one daughter. The eldest son, Alyn, d. before his father. He was the first secretary of the Consultative Council on Technical Education in south Wales. Kenneth was a bank manager in Croydon, Penry was headmaster of Basaleg grammar school, and Bryn was minister of the Congregational church in Muswell Hill, London.

He d. 2 May 1953 and was buried in the new cemetery, Llanilltud Fach, Glam.

Congl. year book, 1954; N.L.W. *Annual Report*, 1979, 5.

E.D.J.

REES, THOMAS WYNFORD ('Dagger'; 1898-1959), major-general; b. in 1898 at Holyhead, Angl., but spent his early years in Barry, Glam. where his father, T.M. Rees, was pastor of Bethel (Meth.). He m. 1926 Rosalie, eldest daughter of Sir Charles Innes and had one son (Peter Rees, M.P. (C), Dover), and one daughter. Acknowledged as one of Wales' finest soldiers during and between the two world wars, and a distinguished campaigner in Far East battles, he was acclaimed Captor of Mandalay in the Burma war. He was usually known as General 'Dagger' Rees and, to his troops, 'Pocket Napoleon' because of his diminutive height of 5 feet 5 inches, and 'Pete' because he was always with his men in the front line. He took his nickname, 'Dagger' from the symbol of his beloved Indian Division. He served in World War I (mentioned in despatches and awarded the M.C.) under General Allenby fighting the Turks, and as a young officer he won a reputation as a great fighting commander. Welsh-speaking he was also the master of many Indian dialects. Postwar he served in India 1920-37, and was made C.I.E. in 1931. In 1939 he was given command of the 3rd Battalion, 6th Rajputana Rifles and on the outbreak of World War II he was sent to Burma where, in 1940, he was twice wounded and awarded a bar to his D.S.O. and promoted colonel. He commanded the 10th Indian Division in Iraq and North Africa, 1942, and the 19th. Indian (Dagger) Division in Burma, 1944-45, being made C.B. in 1945 and promoted major-general in 1947. He was head of the Military Emergency Staff to the Emergency Committee of Cabinet, Delhi, Sept-Dec. 1947. Retiring in 1948 he became hon. col. of the 5th Battalion Welch Regiment (T.A.); honorary president of the Boys' Brigade (Wales); Deputy Lieutenant for Monmouthshire 1955; Civil Defence Controller, Cardiff sub-region of Wales; honorary LL.D. University of Wales; chief executive officer and general manager Cwmbrân New Town, Mon. He d. 15 Oct. 1959.

Www.
D.G.R.

REES, WALTER ENOCH (1863-1949), contractor and long-standing secretary of the Welsh Rugby Union; b. 13 Apr. 1863 at Neath, Glam., son of Joseph Cook Rees, builder and contractor. He was educated at Neath and Barnstaple. He began his very long career as a rugby administrator in 1888 when he became secretary of the Neath club. He was elected to the council of the Welsh Rugby Union in 1889, and in 1896 he succeeded William Henry Gwynn (Swansea) as secretary of the Union. No-one has served the W.R.U. longer than he. His influence and authority were proverbial, particularly in south Wales. He was elected a member of Neath town council in 1900, and mayor in 1905. In 1910 he was appointed joint-manager of the British rugby team to South Africa. The War Office granted him the title of 'Captain' in recognition of his work as a recruiting officer in west Glamorgan in 1916. Having served as secretary of the W.R.U. for more than half a century, he retired in 1948. He m., 8 Sept. 1898, Lizzie Leith Peters of Aberdeen, and they had at least one son and one daughter. He d. 6 June 1949 at Bridgend.

David Smith and Gareth Williams, *Fields of praise* (1980); *Playfair Welsh rugby annual 1949-50*; *Neath Guardian*, 10 June 1949.

G.W.W.

REES-DAVIES, IEUAN (1894-1967), musician and author; b. 15 July 1894 in Treorchy, Rhondda, Glam., and educated at Pentre school. He moved to London *c.* 1914 and attended Goldsmith College and the Royal Academy of Music. He became particularly interested in the status of music in schools, and gained a teacher's diploma, L.T.S.C. He also had certificates of L.R.A.M. and A.R.C.M. and was an honorary F.T.S.C. and F.T.C.L. He became a schoolteacher and headmaster in London, and organised classes for music teachers in the Literary Institutes. He was appointed a lecturer at the college which was established in Marylebone to instruct music teachers. He advised the educational authorities of London, Kent, Essex, and Surrey on music in schools. He became a teacher and examiner of the Trinity College of Music in London and a member of the council of the College of Tonic Sol-fa. He published many books and articles on musical education, specializing in aural tests and classroom singing. His works include *Transposition at the keyboard* (1933), *A sight-singing course for the non-specialist teacher* (1955), *Aural tests for schools* (1960), *Graded music reading* (1961) and *Music for C.S.E.* (1966). He composed tunes and part-songs; the best known of his works is his setting for male choir of a nursery song which is attributed to Charles I, 'Close thine eyes', and which was rendered into Welsh ('Cyn cau llygaid') by William Evans ('Wil Ifan', see above) and published by Curwen Press in 1938. He published also a bilingual anthology of poetry from his native district, *Caniadau Cwm Rhondda* (1928) which includes two of his own compositions, 'Y garreg fawr' and 'A nocturne on Tylacoch'. That same year, with the bardic name 'Ieuan', he became a member of the *Gorsedd* of bards during the national *eisteddfod* at Treorchy. He m. (1) Jean Macdonald Fitchet (d. 1938); (2) Barbara Lacey. Towards the end of his life he lived at Kingston-upon-Thames. He d. 28 Nov. 1967.

WwW (1937); *Who's who in music* (1935; 1962); *Cerddor*, Apr. 1934.

Rh.G.

RHONDDA, 2nd. VISCOUNTESS - see THOMAS, MARGARET HAIG below.

RHYS, CHARLES ARTHUR URYAN - see under RHYS, WALTER FITZURYAN below.

RHYS, EDWARD PROSSER (1901-45), journalist, poet and publisher; b. 4 March 1901 at Pentremynydd, Bethel (Trefenter), Mynydd Bach, Cards., s. of Elizabeth and David Rees, a blacksmith, from a family of smiths, the family moved later to Morfa Du. As a child he attended Cofadail primary school and proceeded to Ardwyn grammar school (Aberystwyth county school) in 1914. He was there only for some eighteen months as his health broke down and he was at home ill for about three years. Having recovered he went to work at the *Welsh Gazette* office at Aberystwyth and in 1919 he moved to

Caernarfon to the *Herald Cymraeg* office. He returned to Aberystwyth in 1921 and when *Y Faner* moved from Denbigh to Aberystwyth in 1923, he was appointed editor, a position which he held till his death on 6 Febr. 1945.

He began to dabble in poetry at an early age and he contributed verses to *Cymru'r Plant* when he was quite young. In 1924, at the national *eisteddfod* held at Pontypool, he won the crown for his poem 'Atgof', a poem which was unusual in its form and its content and which caused a stir at the time. He took the surname Rhys when he m. Mary Prudence Hughes, of Aberystwyth in 1928; they had one daughter. In 1928 he began to publish books and founded Gwasg Aberystwyth, a press which grew year by year and which was acquired after his death by J.D. Lewis & Sons, Llandysul. The Welsh Books Club which he also established flourished under his management.

In 1923 he published with J.T. Jones a joint volume of verse, *Gwaed Ifanc* (Hughes & Son). No further poems of his were published except in periodicals or on the radio until the appearance of *Cerddi Prosser Rhys* from Gwasg Gee in 1950. Though he was a good poet his name is more likely to live as editor and publisher. He was a member of *Plaid Cymru* from its inception and his nationalist spirit was soon manifested on the pages of *Y Faner*, though he was not given a free and unfettered run until *Y Faner* was moved back to its old home in Denbigh in Jan. 1939. Through his weekly column 'Led-led Cymru' in *Y Faner* he became friendly with many whom he would never have known in any other way. He was at heart a countryman, and was at his best writing about country characters and writers. As a publisher he attracted some of the leading Welsh writers to use his press for publishing their works. He also published school books.

Personal knowledge; [*Traeth.*, Oct. 1977, 181-5; Rhisiart Hinks, *Cofiant E. Prosser Rhys* (1980)].

K.R., E.D.J.

RHYS, ERNEST (PERCIVAL) (1859-1946), poet, author, and editor; b. 17 July 1859 in Islington, London, s. of John Rhys, a native of Carmarthen, who was a publisher's assistant in London, and Emma, dau. of Robert Percival, Hockerell, Herts. Soon after the birth of their son the parents went to live in Nott Square, Carmarthen, from where Ernest Rhys went to his first school; they afterwards proceeded to Newcastle-on-Tyne. It was from Newcastle-on-Tyne that Ernest Rhys was sent to the grammar school at Bishop's Stortford in his mother's native county, after which he attended a Newcastle-on-Tyne day school. Intended by his father for the university, Rhys chose instead to take up mining engineering as his profession. He spent some years at Langley, qualified, but then decided to go to London to pursue a career as an author. He left for London in Jan. 1886.

The name of Ernest Rhys will be inseparably connected with the editorship of J.M. Dent's 'Everyman's Library' in which by 1950, nearly a thousand works had been included; Rhys had previously begun (in 1886) to edit the 'Camelot Series' for the same publisher. Many of his original publications (and some of the works which he edited) deal with Welsh (or Celtic) poetry,

romance, and folklore; for lists see *Who's Who*, 1946; and the two autobiographical works named in the bibliography below. His wife Grace (d. 1929; dau. of Bennett Little, of Co. Roscommon, Ireland) was also an author, one of her works being *A Celtic Anthology*, 1927. Although he lived for the greater part of his life in London, Rhys and his wife spent much time in Wales. His (Saturday) 'Welsh Literary Notes' in the *Manch. Guard.* during the early years of the twentieth century were very widely read. Among Rhys's works of Welsh (or Celtic) interest were *The Fiddler of Carne*, 1896, *Welsh Ballads*, 1898, *The Whistling Maid*, 1900, *Lays of the Round Table*, 1908, and *The South Wales Coast*, 1911; he also wrote *Readings from Welsh History* which was at one time much used in Welsh schools. He d. 25 May 1946 in London.

Times, 27 May 1946; *Who's Who*, 1946; and two autobiographical works - *Everyman Remembers* (London, 1931), and *Wales and England Wed* (London, 1940).

W.Ll.D.

RHYS, WALTER FITZURYAN, 7th. Baron DYNEVOR (1873-1956); b. at Dursley, Gloucs., 17 Aug. 1873, son of Arthur de Cardonnel, 6th. Baron, and Selina Lascelles (of the Earls of Harewood). He was educated at Eton and Christ Church, Oxford. He returned to Dynevor Castle in 1898 on marrying Lady Margaret Child-Villiers, eldest daughter of the Earl of Jersey. Involvement in running the estate did not prevent his serving the Government as private secretary to the Secretary of State for India (1899-1903) and to the First Lord of the Admiralty (1903-05). He became Member of Parliament (C) for Brighton and Hove, 1910-11 (but resigned his seat on his elevation to the House of Lords). He assisted the Ministry of Munitions 1916-18, was a J.P., Carmarthenshire County Councillor 1919-35, chairman of the Land Union 1920-37 and Lord Lieutenant of Carmarthenshire 1938-48. The Depression hit the Dynevor and Neath Abbey estates hard, both being coal and steel-centred and the Dynevors are remembered for the charity, employment and other assistance offered to tenants and local people. Offering Dynevor Castle to the War Office in 1939 for use by the army prevented the seizure and destruction suffered by many other noble houses. Despite the army's quitting the estate after the war, failing health led to the stagnation and decline of Dynevor. Lord Dynevor was acutely aware of his Welsh heritage. He bore the ring at the investiture of Edward Prince of Wales in 1911, and in 1916 readopted the Welsh spelling of Rhys by Royal Licence. He wrote about his family and estate in *Trees at Dynevor* (1934) and *History of the two castles of Dynevor* (1935), he corresponded with Sir Cyril Fox (see above) regarding Newton House (Dynevor Castle) and he was concerned about preserving the park's ancient herd of wild white cattle. He d. 8 June 1956 and was buried at Llandyfeisant Church in Dynevor Park.

RHYS, CHARLES ARTHUR URYAN, the eldest son and 8th. Baron Dynevor (1899-1962), was b. 21 Sept. 1899, and was educated at Eton and the Royal Military College, Sandhurst. He was a captain in the Grenadier Guards Reserve of Officers, and served in the British

Expeditionary Force in Russia 1919. He was awarded the M.C. and the Order of S. Anne of Russia. He was Member of Parliament (C) for the Essex and Romford division, 1923-29. He became parliamentary private secretary to the Financial Secretary of the War Office (1924) and to the Under-Secretary of State for the Colonies (1926). In 1927 he was elevated to the position of parliamentary secretary to the Prime Minister, Stanley Baldwin, until he lost his seat. During the 1920s and 30s he became more involved in estate affairs, taking over the administration of the Neath Abbey Estate from his father. He was closely concerned with heavy industry as a director of Richard Thomas and Baldwin's tinplate works on the estate at Jersey Marine. 1931-35 he was Member of Parliament (C) for Guildford. During World War II he served in the Reserve of Guards and was the unsuccessful C. candidate for North Islington in the 1945 election. Farming in general and timber production in particular interested him (in 1954 he was a member of the Departmental Committee on Home Grown Timber). He began a programme of conifer planting and cropping on the Dynevor estate. After the war he persuaded his father to connect Dynevor to mains electricity and in the 1950s he began an extensive refurbishment of Dynevor Castle and the rationalisation of estate finances which involved the sale of estate properties. Reform was made more essential because of the death duties due following his father's death but Charles d. before the plan was realised. He had been a governor of the National Museum of Wales, president of the University College of South Wales and a member of the Welsh Advisory Committee on Civil Aviation. He m., 1934, Hope Mary Woodbine Soames and had one son. He d. 15 Dec. 1962.

Www, 1951-60, 1961-70; *Who's who*, 1956-62; *Debrett*, 1963; Walter Fitzuryan Rhys, *My reminiscences* (1934) and his works cited above; Dynevor estate papers at the County Records Office, Carmarthen; information from Richard Fitzuryan Rhys, 9th. Baron Dynevor.

C.D.

RHYS, WILLIAM JOSEPH (1880-1967), minister (B) and author; b. 12 Feb. 1880, son of Thomas and Esther Rees, Pen-y-bryn, Llangyfelach, Glam. He and his two brothers - M.T. Rees, Meinciau and D.H. Rees, Llandudno Junction - became ministers. His father was related to Morgan Rees who had been instrumental in establishing Salem Church, Llangyfelach in 1777, whilst his mother was of the lineage of Moses Williams, Llandyfân (*DWB*, 1060-1). On leaving school he worked in a grocer's shop in Abergwynfi, but after being urged to enter the ministry, he went to Gwynfryn School, Ammanford, in 1901 and Bangor Baptist College (1903-06), where he came under the powerful influence of the Revival. He became pastor of Horeb, Maenclochog, and Smyrna, Puncheston, Pembs. (1906-25), and Dinas Noddfa, Landore, Swansea (1925-47), finally retiring to Gelli, Rhondda.

He began taking an interest, it appears, in the history of his denomination when he was about fifty years old. For the 30 years following the publication in *Seren Gomer* (1934-35) of a histo-ry of the Baptists at Landore, he wrote articles regularly for *Seren Cymru*, *Trafodion Cymd. Hanes y Bedyddwyr*, and *Seren Gomer*, and supplied a chronicle of church events regularly to the latter periodical from 1954 until he had a stroke in 1966. He also contributed to *The Dictionary of Welsh Biography*. He won prizes both for his work on Baptist social leaders in Wales and for his voluminous essay on the life and work of James Spinther James (NLW MS 12603 D). He was commissioned to write a history of the Baptist College during its term at Llangollen and Bangor; and biographies of Welshmen who were trained at Bristol Baptist College. He published *A Brief History of the Baptists in Wales* (1956), and *Penodau yn hanes y Bedyddwyr Cymreig, 1649-1949* (1949), which is a valuable, reliable sourcebook on the history of his denomination. Histories of about 50 churches were written or edited by him, including a dozen or more standard works such as *Hanes Seion, Treforus, 1845-1945*, and the last one which he wrote, namely the history of Noddfa, Treorchy, where he was a member.

He m. (1), in 1910, Bessie Gwen Morris (d. 6 March 1960), Treorchy; and (2), 1961, Annie Lydia Williams, the widow of David Pryse Williams, minister (B), Treherbert (see below). He d. 22 Oct. 1967 at his home, Y Wenallt, 14 Bute St., Treherbert.

Llawlyfr Bed., 1969, 364, 377; *Ser. G.*, 59 (1967), 89-90; *Ser. Cymru*, 1 Dec. 1967, 5.

M.A.J.

RHYS-WILLIAMS, Sir RHYS (1865-1955), first Baronet created 1918, and a judge; b. 20 Oct. 1865 the eldest son of Judge Gwilym Williams (*DWB*, 1039-40) and his wife Emma (née Williams) of Miskin, Pont-y-clun, Glam. He went to Eton in 1880 and Oriel College, Oxford, and was called to the bar at the Inner Temple in 1890. He practiced for some years on the South Wales circuit, succeeding his father as chairman of the quarter sessions in Glamorganshire in 1906, an office they held for more than half a century. He became a judge in 1913. Early in World War I he obtained a commission in the Grenadier Guards but transferred to the Welsh Guards on its formation in 1915. He devised a means of preventing bombs from accidentally exploding and injuring the soldiers who carried them, but he himself was injured twice and mentioned twice in despatches, being awarded the D.S.O. in 1915 and a medal of the Order of St. Vladimir by Russia in 1916 for his gallantry. He spent the latter half of 1917 in the War Office, followed by a year in the Admiralty Office. He served as a Coalition Liberal M.P. for Banbury (1918-22), and during his brief period as parliamentary secretary to the Minister of Transport, Sir Eric Geddes, he drafted a bill unifying the railways into five main groups. In 1922 he became Recorder of Cardiff (till 1930). In conjunction with the chief constable, Lionel Lindsay, he had the responsibility of controlling the police through the difficult times during the long miners' strike and the general strike of 1926. As director of several companies he spent much time developing his business interests in the Rhondda valley, where he endeavoured to alleviate the effects of unemployment. He m. 24 Feb. 1921, and had two sons and two daughters but the eldest son was killed in action in World War II and he himself d. 29 Jan. 1955. He appended Rhys to his surname in 1938.

His wife was JULIET EVANGELINE, Lady RHYS-WILLIAMS (1898-1964), author; b. in Eastbourne 17 Dec. 1898, daughter of Clayton Glyn and his wife the novelist Elinor Glyn. Juliet left school in 1914 to join the Voluntary Aid Detachment, eventually becoming private secretary to Rhys Williams in 1919. In the 1930s she did valuable work for maternity services and child welfare in south Wales and served as chairman of Cwmbrân Development Corporation (1955-60). For her part in drafting and supporting the Midwives Act in 1936 she was created D.B.E. Although unsuccessful twice at elections, she served the Liberal Party as chairman of the Publications and Publicity Committee (1944-46). She supported European unity, being secretary and a leading member of the European League for Economic Co-operation. As chairman of the National Birthday Trust Fund she was active for many years in organising medical research, resulting in the production of the *Perinatal Mortality Survey Report* (1963). Among her best known publications are *Something to look forward to* (1943), delineating a scheme for social security, and *Taxation and incentive* (1952). She d. 18 Sept. 1964.

Www, 1951-60, 1961-70; *Times*, 25 Feb. 1921, 31 Jan., 1, 3, 4 Feb. 1955, 19 Sept. 1964; *West. Mail*, 31 Jan. 1955.
M.A.J.

RICHARDS, DAVID THOMAS GLYNDWR (1879-1956), Independent minister and principal of Coleg Myrddin, Carmarthen; b. 6 June 1879 at Nantyffyllon, Maesteg, Glam., s. of William and Martha Richards. He was educated at the Old College School, Carmarthen and the Carmarthen Presbyterian College (1902-1905, 1909-12), University College, Cardiff (1905-09). He won a Hibbert Scholarship to study in Cardiff, where he graduated with honours in Hebrew and gained a Berman Scholarship to complete his B.D. degree at Carmarthen. In 1912 he was ordained, without pastoral care of a church, in Saron, Nantyffyllon. In the same year he became a tutor at the Old College School, thereafter becoming principal in succession to Joseph Harry (see above). In June 1916 he went to France under the auspices of the Y.M.C.A. He returned to Carmarthen in Oct. 1917 to take up a teaching post at the grammar school. In 1919 the Old College School was re-opened (it had been closed for a period during World War I) under the name Coleg Myrddin and he was the principal until the closure of the college in 1946. In addition to his work at the college he was also the minister of Burry Port English Congregational church (1919-21), Nebo, Llanpumsaint (1921-1931), Elim, Ffynnonddrain, Carmarthen (1931-54).

He was an able teacher, learned in the classics, and 'Ysgol Glyndwr', as it was called, was instrumental in preparing some hundreds of young men from different denominations to gain entry to the theological colleges, apart from many others who were trained in commercial subjects which prepared them for secular employment. Coleg Myrddin can be regarded as the last of the small Independent academies. He took a firm stance in support of tem-

perance and the cause of peace in Carmarthen town. There was a fair amount of debate in the local and national press when he expressed opposition to boxing matches, which were staged in the town in the 1930s. He addressed the young people at the meetings of the Union of Welsh Independents at Llandeilo 1933 on 'Temperance in the light of the New Testament'. He contributed articles to the *Tyst* on his journey in South Africa (see the issues of 29 Oct., 5 and 12 Nov. 1936) and a sermon for the publication *Ffordd Tangnefedd* (pp. 93-101). He married in 1913, Elizabeth Parry of Carmarthen. He died on 17 July 1956.

Tyst, 26 July 1956.
D.A.E.D.

RICHARDS, ROBERT (1884-1954), historian and politician; b. at Tan-y-ffordd, Llangynog, Monts., 7 May 1884, the son of John Richards, slate quarryman, and his wife Ellen. He was educated at Llangynog elementary school, Llanfyllin county school and the University College of Wales, Aberystwyth. Between 1903 and 1906 he pursued degree courses in political science, Latin, French and philosophy obtaining a first-class honours in political science, but for some reason he did not take his degree. He spent the next two years at St. John's College, Cambridge, where he graduated with honours in economics. He was appointed lecturer in political economics in the University of Glasgow where he remained until, on the urging of Sir Henry Jones (*DWB*, 466), he moved to Wales as a first full-time lecturer in the department of extra-mural studies at the University College of North Wales, Bangor, in 1911. He held classes in economics, European history, and political science at Blaenau Ffestiniog, Llanberis, Bethesda, and Pen-y-groes. In 1916 he took a post in the War Office, and later under the Board of Agriculture, but returned to Bangor in 1919, holding classes in Cefn-mawr, Rhos, Llandrillo and Llanrhaeadr-ym-Mochnant. He was appointed head of the department of economics at U.C.N.W., Bangor, in 1921. In Oct. 1922 he was elected the first M.P. (L) for the Wrexham division. For a few months in 1924 he was Under-Secretary of State for India where he showed understanding and ability and won the sympathy of the Indians. He lost his seat in the general election of 1924, regaining it in 1929, losing it again in Nov. 1931 and winning it for the third time in June 1935, and holding it thereafter until the end of his life. Between 1931 and 1935 he was a lecturer in economics and political science at Coleg Harlech. During World War II he was head of the civil defence service for north Wales. In 1946 he led a parliamentary deputation to India where he won the respect and trust of Gandhi and Jinnah. He contributed a series of essays on India to *Yr Eurgrawn* in 1951. With Sir Ifor Williams (see below) he edited *Y Tyddynnwr*, 1922-23, writing much of the contents of the four parts of that short-lived journal himself. He was a historian by instinct and his main contribution in Welsh was *Cymru'r Oesau Canol* (1933). In the last years of his life he used to spend much of his time in the library of the House of Commons researching the history of monasteries in Wales. He did not succeed in having this work published, but a typescript remains in the N.L.W. He did, however, publish part of it, on the Cistercian abbeys, in *Trans. of the Denbighshire Historical Soc.*, vol. i (1952). [Another part dealing with the history of Cymer abbey was published posthumously in the *Jnl. of the Merioneth Historical and Record Soc.*, vol. iii, part iii (1959)]. With R.G. Lloyd he published booklets on the history of the churches of Llandanwg (1935) and Llanfair, near Harlech (1936).

He took an interest in antiquities [he was elected F.S.A. in 1940] and for ten years was chairman of the committee of the Cambrian Archaeological Association and its president in 1953. He was chairman of the Commission on Ancient Monuments, and was a member of Council of Hon. Soc. of Cymm. from 1936; he was made a vice-president in 1951. He was a zealous Methodist and was a Sunday school teacher in the chapel at Llangynog for years, never missing a Sunday at home if at all possible. He was a true Welshman, a man of the people and a modest gentleman. He declined the governorship of Malta, and the leaders of his party did not succeed in persuading him to be elevated to the House of Lords. It was characteristic of him that his maiden speech in parliament on 3 March 1923 dealt with the bill that sought to turn the Ceiriog Valley into a reservoir for Warrington. He was a hard worker; in spite of his political duties he continued as tutor in economics at Coleg Harlech. At the end of the war he was prevailed upon to accept the headship of the department of economics at Bangor. He was a staunch patriot, loyal to Wales, its history, literature and music; he was a fluent speaker, especially in Welsh.

He m. in 1918 Mary Myfanwy Owen (d. 1950) of Llangynog; they made their home in their native parish and stayed there all their lives. They had no children. He d. 22 Dec. 1954 and was buried in Peniel (CM) cemetery, Llangynog.

Www; Trans. Cymm., 1955, 73-8.

E.D.J.

RICHARDS, THOMAS (1878-1962), librarian and historian; b. 15 Mar. 1878 at Maes-glas, a smallholding near Tal-y-bont, Cards., son of Isaac Richards and Jane (née Mason). The family later moved to Ynystudur, near Tre'rddol. He received his early education at Tal-y-bont and Taliesin schools. He was a pupil-teacher for four years and, from 1897, was for two years a teacher at Alexandra School, Aberystwyth before entering the University College of North Wales, Bangor (1899-1903) where he graduated with honours in history under the well-known historian Sir John Edward Lloyd (see above). He was appointed a school-teacher at Towyn (1903-05), Bootle (1905-11), and Maesteg (1912-26). Thomas Shankland (*DWB*, 909) urged him to research the history of Puritanism in Wales in Lambeth Palace Library, the British Museum, the Public Record Office, and the Bodleian Library. The results of his study were published in a number of comprehensive volumes, *A History of the Puritan Movement in Wales, 1639-53* (1920), *Religious developments in Wales, 1654-62* (1923), *Wales under the Penal Code, 1662-87* (1925), and *Wales under the Indulgence,*

1672-75 (1928). As a result of this work he was recognised as the chief authority on the beginning of Nonconformity in Wales. He gained an M.A. degree of the University of Wales in 1914 and D.Litt. in 1924.

In 1926 he returned to Bangor as the librarian of his old college. He continued Shankland's work of collecting Welsh books and periodicals, and undertook the task of classifying and cataloguing them. He then opened up a new area by obtaining for the library records of north Wales estates and preparing comprehensive and highly readable catalogues of them. Through the enormous labour of Thomas Shankland and Thomas Richards the Bangor college library became a first-class research centre for students of the history of Wales.

Thomas Richards had the gift of noticing people's idiosyncrasies and seeing the amusing aspect of a situation. He was unrivalled as a raconteur and a popular lecturer and broadcaster. He published several books besides those already mentioned and contributed articles to various works (77 articles by him appeared in *DWB*). He wrote many articles for periodicals on the history of churches and personalities, sport and other topics. He was a deacon at Penuel (B), Bangor, and was honoured as president of the Baptist Union of Wales in 1957. He received the Medal of the Honourable Society of Cymmrodorion in 1958 and an hon. LL.D. degree of the University of Wales in 1959. In 1912 he m. Mary Roberts of Nantlle; they had two daughters. He d. 24 June 1962 and was buried in Bangor City Cemetery.

Thomas Richards, *Atgofion Cardi* (1960); *Rhagor o atgofion Cardi* (1963, including a bibliography by Derwyn Jones); Derwyn Jones and Gwilym B. Owen (ed.), *Rhwng y silffoedd* (1978); *Cymro*, 28 June 1962; *N. Wales Chron.*, 29 June 1962; *Barn*, Nov. 1962; *Ser. Cymru*, 6 July 1962; *Ser. G.*, summer 1978; *Traf. Cymd. Hanes Bed.*, 1979; *Genh.*, no. 29/2, 1979; [Geraint H. Jenkins, *Dr Tom* (1999)].

G.B.O.

ROBERTS, ARTHUR BRYN (1897-1964), trade unionist; b. 7 Apr. 1897, the son of William and Mary Roberts, Abertillery, Mon. He went to work as a collier at thirteen years of age. He won a scholarship to Ruskin College, Oxford, and in 1919 to the Central Labour College, London. He was appointed a checkweigher for Rhymney colliers in 1921 and five years later was appointed the representative of the colliers in the Rhymney Valley. He was general secretary of the National Union of Social Workers from 1934 to 1962 when he retired due to ill-health. The union grew considerably under his leadership. He was a representative at the American Labour Federation in 1942 and was one of the deputation of Labour unionists to China in 1954. For a period he was a member of a committee on social workers in the Mental Health Service and was prominent as a local government councillor in Wales. Although he was a very able man he did not rise to prominence amongst the Labour leaders as one might have expected. He published a number of pamphlets and books such as *At the TUC* (1947), *As I see it* (1957) and *The price of TUC leadership* (1961) in which he did not hesitate to criticise the organisation of the Labour movement.

He m. Violet Mary Sheenan in 1922, they had one son and two daughters. He d. 26 Aug. 1964 at his home in White Cottage, 11 Scotts Lane, Shortlands, Kent, after a long illness.

Www; Times, 27 Aug. 1964.

E.D.J.

ROBERTS, DAFYDD (1892-1965), chairman of Capel Celyn Defence Committee; b. 18 Aug. 1892 in Weirglodd-ddu, Capel Celyn, Mer., the youngest child of John and Margaret Roberts. He lived at Weirglodd-ddu for most of his life before moving lower down the valley to farm Cae Fadog. Besides farming he was one of the two postmen who carried the post in the area for more than 40 years. He was an elder in Capel Celyn (Presb.) for many years until the church was disestablished. When the threat came to drown the valley, he was elected chairman of the Capel Celyn Defence Committee and remained in that position until the final fateful hour arrived. He accompanied Gwynfor Evans and Dr. Tudur Jones to London and Liverpool to try to save the valley. He made every effort to prevent Liverpool Corporation destroying his heritage. He had been very active in the district all his life. When it was finally decided that the houses in the valley were to be demolished he moved to live in Bala. He d. 11 Oct. 1965 shortly before the official opening of the reservoir. He was buried in Llanycil church, near Bala, and was survived by Nell, his wife, and their son.

Personal knowledge; [Y Cyfnod, 15 Oct. 1965, 1].

J.L.J.

ROBERTS, DAVID ('Telynor Mawddwy'; 1875-1956), harpist, singer and author of handbooks on *penillion* singing; b. 1 Aug. 1875 at Llannerch, Llanymawddwy, Mer., the eldest of the seven children of Robert Roberts and Catrin (née Pughe). He was descended from highly cultured and musical families on both sides - his father descended from the versatile family of Bwlch Coediog, Mallwyd. When he was six years old he contracted measles, and became blind for the rest of his life.

His musical talent was nurtured at home and in the chapel, and his interest in poetry was roused at a very early age. He began to sing in public as a member of the Bwlch Coediog *plygain* party. It was from his two uncles, 'Eos Mawddwy' and 'Ioan Mawddwy', that he learnt how to set a stanza to an air, and he was steeped in the old oral settings which were sung in the homes of the Mawddwy district and which were part of the traditional *penillion* singing of the neighbourhood. He learnt the art of singing a round of *penillion*, and won prizes at the national *eisteddfod* at Blaenau Ffestiniog, 1898; Liverpool, 1900; and Llanelli, 1903. By that time he had learnt to play the harp as well as the fiddle, and he was invited to spend some time at Llanover under the tuition of 'Pencerddes y De' (Mrs. S. B. Griffith). He had a number of further successes at *eisteddfodau* as a harpist. After leaving Llanofer and marrying in 1909, he moved to Barmouth, and spent the rest of his life there entertaining visitors with his harp; and he served the district as a lay preacher. He tutored countless singers in

Merioneth. He published *Y Tant Aur* (1911), a booklet of 49 local oral pieces set to sol-fa. He realised that many of the settings were crude and lacking in imagination, and with the assistance of the Rev. P.H. Lewis, he revised them for the second edition (1915). These are far more accurate and musically imaginative. Again with P.H. Lewis, he published another important aid for harpists and singers, namely *Cainc y delyn* (1916), a handbook of airs presented in old notation for the harp, with words set to them. 'Telynor Mawddwy' was one of the key pioneers responsible for the revival of the old craft of singing to the harp in the early years of the 20 c., transforming the art from its old traditional oral form to the more consciously composed and written form of our time. Without *Y Tant Aur* perhaps the revival of the last fifty years would not have happened.

He and his wife Jennie had two sons and a daughter. He d. 21 Mar. 1956 at his home, Llys y Delyn, and he was buried in Llanaber church. A memorial bench was placed on the promenade in Barmouth by the *Cerdd Dant* Society to commemorate his unique contribution, and on it a couplet by W.D. Williams:

> Mainc adgof mwynhau cydgan
> Tonnau môr a'r tannau mân.

> ('A bench to recollect enjoying
> The song of the waves and the strings').

Personal knowledge and research.

A.Ll.D.

ROBERTS, DAVID FRANCIS (1882-1945), minister (CM) and author; b. 15 Nov. 1882, s. of Robert and Ellen Roberts, at 3 Libanus Terrace, Bontnewydd, Caerns. From the elementary school he went to Caernarfon county school, the University College, Bangor (1901-1904), Bala Theological College, and for a year to the universities of Berlin and Marburg. From 1908-1912 he was assistant lecturer in Hebrew at Glasgow University. Ord. in 1912 he was minister of Maenofferen, Blaenau Ffestiniog 1912-21, Fitzclarence St., Liverpool 1921-29, Capel Tegid and the English Church, Bala, and Llanfor 1929-45. On 18 Aug. 1921 he m. Sarah Ann Davies, eldest dau. of G.G. Davies, Glan-y-pwll Villa, Blaenau Ffestiniog. He contributed widely in Biblical studies, writing textbooks, *Hanes yr Hebreaid*, a commentary on *Haggai* and *Zechariah*, and numerous articles to denominational periodicals. He also contributed to the *International Bible Standard Encyclopaedia*. He was sub-editor of the *Geiriadur Beiblaidd*, and general editor of the *Geiriadur Diwinyddol* projected by the University of Wales whose publication was prevented by World War II. From 1929 to 1945 he was one of the editors of the *Traethodydd*, and served the theological section of the Guild of Graduates as secretary and president, making valuable contributions to the new translation of the Scriptures published by the University. He was secretary of the Sunday school committee of the General Assembly from 1932-37, secretary of the North Wales Association from 1936 to 1938 and again in 1940, Moderator of the North Wales Association in 1941. Later he was appointed secretary for north Wales of the Reconstruction Commission of his Church.

In all his varied work he was conscientious and thorough, combining great strength of conviction with sincerity and magnanimity of spirit. He d. at Bala 9 Sept. 1945 and was buried at Caeathro.

Drys., 1941, 99; Gol., 19 Sept. 1945; Seren, 22 Sept. 1945; Blwyddiadur, 1946, 176; notes provided by his daughter, [the late] Rhiannon Francis Roberts; personal acquaintance.

J.E.M.

ROBERTS, DAVID JOHN ('Dewi Mai o Feirion'; 1883-1956), journalist, folk poet, tutor and setter of cerdd dant; b. 14 May 1883 at Talweunydd, Blaenau Ffestiniog, Mer., son of David and Catherine Roberts. He began to take an interest in singing to the harp when he was very young, and as did a number of other youths from the neighbourhood of Blaenau, such as Ioan Dwyryd, Robert G. Humphreys, and W. Morris Williams, he used to frequent the cottage Llys y Delyn, Rhiwbryfdir, Blaenau Ffestiniog, where David Francis ('Telynor Dall o Feirion') lived in the early part of the 20th c. 'Dewi Mai', in company with his contemporaries, learnt from David Francis how to set a stanza to an air and how to handle cynghanedd. After living for a time in England, he returned to Merionethshire, for a while in the neighbourhood of Bala, before settling in the town of Dolgellau. There he earned his living as a journalist and undertook the task of teaching others to sing penillion. He prepared hundreds of settings of verses, and sent them by post to all parts of Wales, thereby arousing the interest of many who in their turn came to be prominent performers and setters of penillion. He published three volumes of settings, many of the poems they contain being written by him: Diliau'r plant (1913), Trysorau'r tannau (1935), Y Patrwm (1952). But despite his great contribution as a penillion setter and tutor, he made two other more important contributions which were essential cornerstones in the development of singing to harp accompaniment. Throughout 1933 and 1934 he wrote a weekly column in Y Cymro under the heading 'Cornel y delyn'. In it he dealt with every aspect of the ancient art, bringing it to the notice of the general public. He called for a national society to be formed to promote this ancient form of singing, and through his articles he prepared the way to secure the success of the society - Cymdeithas Cerdd Dant Cymru - when it was founded in Bala in Nov. 1934. After the society was founded, 'Dewi Mai o Feirion' formulated the first draft of the rules of Cerdd Dant which were adopted later by the society, and which remain to the present day as aids for penillion setters. His contribution to the development of the art of singing to the harp between 1920 and 1956 was crucial. He m. Kate Laura Ephraim and d. 27 Nov. 1956.

Allwedd y Tannau, 1956, 9-10; information from his son, D.G. Roberts, Rhyl.

A.Ll.D.

ROBERTS, DAVID OWEN (1888-1958), educationalist, b. 6 Oct. 1888 at 28 Church Row, Trecynon, Aberdare, son of Hannah (née Jones) and Gethin Roberts. He was educated at Llwydcoed Elementary School, Aberdare

County School and Bangor Normal College, 1907-09, where he gained his Teacher's Certificate. He became successively schoolmaster at Park School, Trecynon, Cwmdâr school and Abernant school, all in the vicinity of Aberdare. He taught Welsh, geography and music at Gadlys Central School, Aberdare, 1923-40, and was appointed headmaster of the school in 1940, a post which he retained until he retired in 1949.

In 1923-24 he established Undeb Athrawon Cymreig and was secretary of the Union until the end of World War II when Undeb Cenedlaethol Athrawon Cymru was set up. He was also a member of the editorial board of Yr Athro from its commencement in 1928 until his death. He published very useful textbooks facilitating the teaching of Welsh, namely Llwybr y Gymraeg 1, 2 and 3 and Priffordd y Gymraeg 1, 2 and 3 (both series pre-1930) and Cynllun Newydd yn y Gymraeg (1930), followed by Some Notes of Lessons for Teachers of 'Priffordd y Gymraeg' (1932). He contributed to Yr Athro a number of articles and notes on teaching Welsh and gave lectures in many localities on teaching children Welsh, particularly as a second language. He was the principal lecturer of the Union of Welsh Societies on bilingual teaching in schools, 1929-40. He received an hon. M.A. of the University of Wales in 1951 in recognition of his valuable contribution to education.

D.O. Roberts was very active in college and eisteddfod circles in Wales, in the National Book Festival, and in the musical life of the Cynon valley. He often gave radio talks drawing particular attention to the minority cultures and languages of Europe. His ideals were internationalist and pacifist and he strongly supported the cause of selfgovernment for Wales.

He m. Ann Edwards 23 Apr. 1917 and they had one son and one daughter. He d. 29 Aug. 1958.

Information from his son, Dafydd G.E. Roberts.

W.T.P.D.

ROBERTS, EMMANUEL BERWYN (1869-1951), minister (Meth.); b. 31 July 1869 in Y Nant, Rhewl, in the parish of Llantysilio, Llangollen, Denbs., one of the eleven children of Morris and Jemima Roberts. The family moved to Carrog, where Emmanuel was an apprentice shoemaker, but his mother died when he was 12 and the impoverished family left for Penygroes, where he and his father found work in Coedmadog, clearing rubble in a clay pit. There, he began to preach, and went to assist the Welsh Wesleyan minister in Hanley, Staffs., and worked in the steelworks and the coal mine there. In 1891 he went to the Corwen circuit as a lay-agent, living in Tŷ Nant, and then to a similar post in Dinas Mawddwy. In 1893, he went to Richmond College, and from there as a probationer-minister to Pen-y-cae, Ebbw Vale, in 1895, and to Treharris in 1896. In 1897, he was appointed assistant to the Revd. John Evans, Eglwys-Bach, Pontypridd, (DWB, 245) and it was he who insisted on giving him the middle name 'Berwyn', because he thought that no-one should be called 'Emmanuel'. From that time, he was always known by his new name. When John Evans died, he went to Pont-rhyd-y-groes, and in

1899, he was ordained in the first Conference of the Wesleyans in Machynlleth. He went to Corris in 1900, and there m. Annie Roberts, adopted daughter of David and Ellen Roberts, Waterloo House, Caernarfon. They had four children, 2 girls, who married Wesleyan ministers, and two sons, who became local preachers.

He served twelve circuits; he was secretary to the Second Province of North Wales from 1914 to 1933, Chairman of the Province from 1933 to 1936, and President of the Welsh *Cymanfa* in 1930. He came to early eminence as an expositor, and that was the chief characteristic of his preaching. His Commentary on Ephesians was published in 1902, that on the Epistles of Peter in 1904, and two volumes on the Gospel according to St. John in 1931. He d. in Colwyn Bay on 26 Jan. 1951.

Information supplied by his son, Selyf Roberts.

G.R.T.

ROBERTS, Sir ERNEST HANDFORTH GOODMAN (1890-1969), judge; b. in Pen-y-ffordd, Flints., 20 Apr. 1890, the only son of Hugh Goodman Roberts and his wife Elizabeth (née Lewis). He was educated at Malvern College and Trinity College, Oxford; he was president of the Oxford Union in 1914. During World War I he served with the Royal Welch Fusiliers and rose to the rank of captain. He served in Palestine. He was mentioned in despatches and was an officer in the military court. In the meantime he was called to the Bar (1916). He contested the Flintshire seat for the Conservatives in 1923 and won it in 1924, continuing as an M.P. until 1929. He was knighted in 1936 and was the Chief Justice of the High Court in Rangoon from that year until 1948. The following year he was made a King's Counsellor and was an Assize commissioner in a number of circuits eighteen times between 1949-55, and deputy chairman of Flintshire Quarter Sessions until 1961. He was a member of the Representative Body of the Church in Wales, 1916-36 and 1947-59, and chancellor of the dioceses of Bangor, 1947-59, and Chelmsford, 1950-69. He published *Principles of the law of contract* (1923). He was unmarried and d. 14 Feb. 1969 at his London home.

Www.

E.D.J.

ROBERTS, EVAN JOHN (1878-1951), 'Y *Diwygiwr*' (the Revivalist); b. 8 June 1878 at Island House, Bwlchmynydd, Loughor, Glam., s. of Henry and Hannah Roberts. He worked as a coalminer at Loughor and Mountain Ash when he was young, and became apprenticed to a blacksmith in 1902. He was an exceptionally gifted young man, attaining a high standard of culture through self-discipline. He had spiritual experiences at times, and he confessed to having prayed for thirteen years for a religious revival in Wales. At the close of 1903 he began to preach in Moriah, Loughor, and he was accepted as a candidate for the ministry by the Presbyterian Church of Wales. At the end of Sept. 1904 he entered the school kept by John Phillips, Newcastle Emlyn, to prepare himself for the ministry. Religious life was being awoken in south Cardiganshire at the time, following a series of conferences, similar to the Keswick conferences, which had been arranged by Joseph Jenkins (1861-1929; *DWB*, 436) and others to deepen the spiritual life of the churches. Evan Roberts had an experience that shook him to the core at one of these conferences (at Blaenannerch), and he was induced to return to Loughor to hold a mission before the end of Oct. Agitated meetings were held in the Loughor district, and in a short time - between Nov. 1904 and Jan. 1906 - a powerful religious awakening spread throughout Wales. He was the most prominent figure of the 1904-05 Revival (as it is called). Some leading personalities vigorously criticised him, and no doubt he did make some mistakes in the emotional heat of events and infectious enthusiasm of the meetings. He himself was absolutely sincere, and the stresses and strains of these months proved too much for him.

It is difficult to estimate the effect and influence of the Revival. Church membership increased enormously everywhere, and a new generation of leaders and ministers was raised in the churches. The awakening spread to other parts of Britain, and to the missionary fields as well. There were splits in some circles, one result being the formation of new religious bodies, such as the Apostolic Church, the 'four-square' Elim movement, and Pentecostal causes. The effects lasted a long time in some circles, although World War I counteracted them and extinguished them to some degree. Some of the effects can be traced down to the charismatic movements of more recent times. Some believe that the Revival also affected the growth of the young Labour movement between 1904 and 1914.

In 1906, fatigued and physically weak, Evan Roberts was cared for by Mrs Jessie Penn-Lewis, at her home in Leicester, and he also lived in London for a brief period. He retired from public view, though he took part occasionally at meetings in Wales during the period 1925-30. He received the succour of friends in Porthcawl, and in Rhiwbina, Cardiff, and he d. there 29 Jan. 1951. He was buried in the family grave in Moriah, Loughor. A monument to him in front of Moriah chapel was unveiled in 1953.

During his early period Evan Roberts composed many poems and hymns, a selection of which is to be found in his biography. A collection of his hymns was published in Aberdare in 1905, and when he lived in Leicester he published a booklet, *Gwasanaeth a milwriaeth ysbrydol* (1912).

T. Francis, in *Y Diwygiad a'r diwygwyr* (1906), 9-47; Vyrnwy Morgan, *The Welsh religious revival* (1909); D.M. Phillips, *Evan Roberts a'i waith* (1912, 10th ed. 1924); S. Evans and G.M. Roberts (eds.), *Cyfrol goffa Diwygiad 1904-1905* (1954), which includes a bibliography of the Revivalist and the Revival; Eifion Evans, *The Welsh revival of 1904* (1969); E.M. Humphreys, *Gwŷr enwog gynt* (1953), 100-9.

G.M.R.

ROBERTS, Sir GEORGE FOSSETT (1870-1954), soldier, politician and administrator; b. 1 Nov. 1870 at Aberystwyth, Cards., the third son of David and H. Maria Roberts. His father was a member of Aberystwyth Town Council for 44 yrs and served as mayor of the borough on three occasions. G.F. Roberts was educated at a private school at Cheltenham. He joined his father's company and was the managing director of the Trefechan brewery from 1890 until his retirement in 1935.

Roberts stood unsuccessfully as the parliamentary candidate (C) for Cardiganshire in 1910, and continued to support the Conservative Party throughout his life. During World War I he was the Staff Officer of the Embarkation Staff, and from 1921 until 1925 he led the 102nd Field Brigade of the Royal Artillery. In 1933 he was chosen as Honorary Colonel of the 146th Medium Regiment of the Royal Artillery.

He was elected a member of the Aberystwyth Town Council in 1902; he remained a member for 30 yrs. and served as mayor in 1912-13 and 1927-28. He chaired many council committees. He also served as a member of the Cardiganshire County Council for 20 yrs. Roberts also played an active part in the activities of the National Library of Wales; he was elected a member of the Court of Governors in 1914 and of the Council in 1919, and he served as treasurer from 1939 until 1944, when he was elected to succeed Lord Davies of Llandinam (see DAVIES, DAVID above) as N.L.W. President. He chose to retire from this position in 1950. He also served as vice-president of the University College of Wales, Aberystwyth. He was a prominent supporter, too, of the work of the Aberystwyth General Hospital, and he chaired the Mid-Wales Hospital Management Committee, 1948-51. Roberts was a member of a large number of local committees, was a prominent public figure in the Aberystwyth area and at Llanbadarn Fawr church. He won great respect because of his high principles, his kindness and generosity, and unfailing courtesy.

Fossett Roberts was awarded the O.B.E. in 1919, the T.D. in 1922, was knighted in 1935 and received the C.B. in 1942. He was awarded the degree of LL.D. *honoris causa* by the University of Wales in 1947. He was chosen a J.P. for Cardiganshire in 1906, served as High Sheriff in 1911-12, and as the county's Deputy Lieutenant from 1929.

He m., 29 Sept. 1896, Mary, the eldest dau. of John Parry, Glan-paith, Cards. She d. 26 May 1947. They had two daughters. They lived at Glan-paith, Rhydyfelin, Aberystwyth, and for a time at Laura Place in the town. He d. 8 April 1954 at Glan-paith, the funeral service was held at Llanbadarn church and his remains were buried at Aberystwyth cemetery. There is a bronze memorial plaque at the National Library of Wales.

Www; WwW (1933 and 1937); *Camb. News*, 16 Apr. 1954; *Times*, 10 and 14 Apr. 1954; *NLW Annual Report, 1953-54*; W.J. Lewis, *Born on a perilous rock* (1980); *WWP.*

J.G.J.

ROBERTS, GLYN (1904-62), historian and administrator; b. 31 Aug. 1904 at Bangor, Caerns., son of William and Ann Roberts, and educated at Friars School from 1915 to 1922 when he won a scholarship to the University College of North Wales, Bangor. He studied history under John Edward Lloyd (see above) and Arthur Herbert Dodd and graduated with first-class honours in 1925. He undertook research into the parliamentary history of the north Wales boroughs from 1535-1832 and in 1929 was awarded an M.A. as well as the Prince Llywelyn ap Gruffydd prize for his thesis which reveals the influence of Lewis Namier. In the same year he was appointed assistant lecturer at University College, Swansea where he remained until 1939 when he joined the Civil Service. By 1942 he was an assistant secretary in the Ministry of Supply and in 1944 was promoted deputy head of the mission to the U.S.A. to secure raw materials to meet the needs of Britain. A glittering career as a Government administrator lay ahead, but he decided to return to his old college in Bangor as Registrar. He played an indispensable part in the post-war reorganisation of the college and the number of students increased substantially. In 1949, on the retirement of Robert Thomas Jenkins (see above), the college in its wisdom invited him to fill the chair of Welsh History. However, he was in no way released from frequent administrative demands – he was dean of the faculty and vice-principal for two years on both occasions – and outside the college he was chairman of the University of Wales History and Law Committee of the Board of Celtic Studies and also of the Caernarvonshire Historical Society, a member of the council of the Historical Buildings of Wales and of the executive committee formed to advise the Master of the Rolls on the policy to be adopted when publishing public records. Despite such demands, he devoted himself more and more to his main subject and gradually his interests extended back from the eighteenth century to the Tudor period (at one time it was his intention to produce a volume on this period for *Cyfres y Brifysgol a'r Werin*), and eventually to the late Middle Ages. The difficult and troubled years post 1282 – with their compromise, submissiveness and co-operation on the one hand, rejection, challenge and rebellion on the other – held a special attraction for him. His publications on these complexities, ones which brilliantly illuminate the background of the Tudor dynasty, are his most mature contribution to this topic and provide a foretaste of the masterpiece which would have resulted had he lived. After his death a collection of his main articles was published under the title *Aspects of Welsh History* (1969).

Glyn Roberts possessed an incisive and analytical mind which led him patiently to unravel all complex problems before arriving at the heart of the matter and, in great measure, this accounted for his success as a teacher and administrator. He understood the motives of his fellow man better than most and detested over-respectability and affectation. Full of humour and a lover of amusing tales and ready witticisms he was fundamentally a likeable, gracious and kindly man.

M. twice (1): Mary Davida Alwynne Hughes on 6 Sept. 1933, and after her death (2): her sister, Caryl Eryl Hughes on 28 July 1954. He d. 13 Aug. 1962 in Menai Bridge and was buried in Llantysilio churchyard, Anglesey.

A.H. Dodd and J. Gwynn Williams (eds.), *Aspects of Welsh History* (1969) and the sources named there; *Trans. Caerns. Hist. Soc.*, 1963; personal knowledge.

J.G.W.

ROBERTS, GRIFFITH JOHN (1912-69), priest and poet; b. 2 March 1912, at Arwenfa, Afonwen, Caerns., s. of Edward and Catherine Roberts. He was educated at the elementary school, Chwilog, the grammar school, Pwllheli and University College of North Wales, Bangor, where he graduated B.A. (2nd-cl. hons.) in Hebrew 1934, M.A. 1936. In 1935-36 he was assistant lecturer in Semitic Studies, University College of N. Wales, Bangor. He began his studies as a ministerial candidate with the C.M. Church, but whilst at college he was confirmed into the Church in Wales. He was at Lichfield Theological College 1936-37 and was ord. deacon 1937 and served as curate of Rhyl, St. Asaph diocese. He was ord. priest in 1938. In 1941 he was appointed curate-in-charge of Llanefydd, and 1945-48 he was rector of Nantglyn. From 1948 to 1951 he was rector of Mellteyrn, Botwnnog and Bryncroes, diocese of Bangor, and became vicar of Blaenau Ffestiniog 1951-56. He obtained the living of Conwy with Gyffin in 1956.

According to one adjudicator, he was worthy of the crown at the national *eisteddfod*, Rhosllannerchrugog, 1945, for his *pryddest* 'Coed Celyddon'. He won the crown at the national *eisteddfod*, Colwyn Bay, 1947, for his *pryddest* 'Glyn y Groes' whilst his 'Awdl Goffa i R. Williams Parry' was highly commended in the *awdl* competition at the national *eisteddfod*, Llanelli, 1962. Later, he was the adjudicator in the *pryddest* competition on more than one occasion. He was a member of the *Gorsedd* of Bards. His anthology of poems 'Y Siaced Fraith' was staged at the national *eisteddfod* at Llangefni, 1957. In 1963 he was the chairman of the Literature Committee of the national *eisteddfod* at Llandudno, and he wrote a feature programme 'Y Llinyn Arian', portraying the Vale of Conwy, which was staged at that *eisteddfod*. He wrote a pageant, 'Deiniol Sant' 1959, which was performed at Bangor cathedral. His play, 'Goleuni y Byd' was staged at the parish church, Conwy, and was later performed at Bangor cathedral. In June 1967 he drew up a service to commemorate the 400th anniversary of the translation of the New Testament into Welsh, at Gyffin, the birthplace of Bishop Richard Davies (*DWB*, 147-8). When the Bishop of Bangor (John Charles Jones, see above) decided to lead a diocesan pilgrimage to Bardsey in 1952 he asked G.J. Roberts to arrange the route and to write the script giving the historical background. He was one of the small band who sailed over to the island a few days later. 'Enlli'r Pererinion' was the title of his radio *pryddest*. His voice was familiar throughout Wales when he began to broadcast regularly in the Sunday evening programme, *Wedi'r Oedfa*. He wrote a number of feature programmes for the B.B.C., e.g. Edmwnd Prys, Bishop William Morgan, Ieuan Glan Geirionydd, etc.

He was a lyric poet composing in the Christian tradition. His publications include: *Wrth y tân*, 1944; *Coed Celyddon*, 1945; *Gwasanaethau'r Plant* (trans.), 1953, *Hanes y Beibl*, 1954; *Cerddi* 1954; *Yr Esgob William Morgan*, 1955; *Llyfr y Siaced Fraith*, 1957; *Seintiau Cymru* (with E.P. Roberts), 1957; *Ymddiddanion Llafar*, 1961; *Sgyrsiau wedi'r Oedfa*, 1966; *Awdl Goffa i R. Williams-Parry*, 1967; *Ysgrifau*, 1968; *Cofnodion*, 1970.

He m. in 1942 Margaret Morris, dau. of Owen Morris and Elisabeth Williams, Morfa Nefyn, and they had two daus. He d. 13 Feb. 1969, and was buried at Abergwyngregin on the banks of the Menai Straits, as he had wished.

Bangor Dioc. Yr. Bk., 1968, *Llan*, 21, 28 Feb. 1959; *Baner*, 20 Feb. 1969; *Haul*, Spring 1969; *N. Wales Weekly News*, 20 Feb. 1969; information from his widow, personal acquaintance.

M.G.E.

ROBERTS, HUGH GORDON (1885-1961), surgeon and missionary; one of the sons of David Roberts of Dolenog, Llanidloes, Monts., and his wife Jane Sarah, daughter of Thomas Price Jones of Liverpool. He was born 16 July 1885 in Liverpool and was reared there. He was a great-grandson of David Roberts (1788-1869), a doctor in Bodedern, Anglesey (see *DWB*, 858), and Sir William Roberts, F.R.S. (1830-99), who was a prominent doctor in Manchester and London, was his father's uncle. Frederick Charles Roberts (1862-94), who died young of fever when he was a missionary doctor in Tientsin, was a cousin of his. It is not surprising, therefore, that he changed his mind in the middle of an accountancy course to become a missionary doctor. He graduated M.B., Ch.B., at the University of Liverpool in 1912 and M.D. in 1920. After his marriage to Katharine (d. 9 Jan. 1966), daughter of John Jones, Liverpool, in 1913 he went to work in the Khasia Hills, India. They had a son and daughter. He was a civilian surgeon in the capital, Shillong, during 1914-19, and was loaned to the Assam government by the Missionary Society (CM). This gave him an opportunity to quantify and understand the great needs of the province. Before his time the Mission had a travelling doctor, but after the war he returned to Wales to persuade the churches to build a hospital in Shillong. He himself donated £7,000 towards this and the hospital was opened in 1922. He was the superintendent and chief physician and surgeon there from the beginning until 1948 when he retired due to ill-health. More complicated operations were dealt with in the mission hospital than in all the state hospitals of Assam put together; his name became known throughout the province. With the assistance of Margaret Buckley and others he established a nursing school there. He was a member of Assam's Legislative Council, 1921-24, a prominent member of the Assam Medical Council, 1920-43, and president of the Assam Branch of the British Medical Association, 1932-33. He came to Britain in 1945 and was general secretary and editor of the Medical Missionary Association of London, 1946-48. He was strong enough to return to India in 1949 to supervise the building of a new hospital in Jowai, a gift from the Presbyterians of Wales to the Presbyterians of Assam. After the completion of the work in 1953 he returned to Britain, living in West Kirby and Eastbourne. He d. 20 Dec. 1961.

He was honoured with the C.I.E. in 1928, and was invested with the gold medal of Kaisar-i-Hind in 1925 and the King's Jubilee Medal in 1935. He was Moderator of the English Conference of the Presbyterian Church of Wales in 1937 and received an honorary LL.D. degree from the University of Wales in 1946.

P.A.C.F., 383; *Www; Blwyddiadur MC*, 1963, 270-1; John Hughes Morris, *The Story of our Foreign Mission* (1930), 54-5; see *Munk's Roll, iv*, 146-7 for a biography of Sir William Roberts; Mary I. Bryson, *Fred C. Roberts of Tientsin: or, for Christ and China* (1895); [Arthur Hughes in J. Meirion Lloyd (ed.), *Nine missionary pioneers* (1989)].

E.D.J.

ROBERTS, JOHN (1879-1959), minister (Presb.) and historian; b. 16 Oct. 1879 at Porthmadog, Caerns., son of John J. Roberts ('Iolo Caernarfon'; *DWB*, 870) and Ann, his wife. He was educated at Porthmadog board school, Bala grammar school and Jesus College, Oxford, where he graduated in classics, and subsequently in theology. (The University of Wales conferred on him an honorary D.D. degree towards the end of his life.) He was ord. in 1905, and served as minister at Aberdovey (1903-06), David St., Liverpool (1906-13), and Pembroke Tce., Cardiff (1913-38). He was called to serve as secretary of the Central Fund of the South Wales Association in 1938; ten years later the funds of North and South Wales were combined and he became the first secretary of the united Fund of the Presbyterian Church of Wales. In 1903 he m. Annie Jones Hughes, Porthmadog; they had four sons and two daughters. He d. 29 July 1959.

John Roberts was among the leading preachers of his time, even though his voice was not suitable for the pulpit (see R.T. Jenkins's opinion of him as a preacher in *Cyfoedion* (1976), 39-41). He was Moderator of the South Wales Association (1941) and Moderator of the General Assembly (1943). He delivered the Davies Lecture in 1930 on the philosophy of the history of the denomination, which was published in Welsh (1931), and in English under the title *The Calvinistic Methodism of Wales* (1934). (See again R.T. Jenkin's assessment of this work which placed him in the forefront of historians of the Presbyterian Church, *ibid.*, 41-2). He contributed numerous articles to *Y Goleuad*, and to the periodicals of his denomination. His most valuable contribution to his Connexion was to establish a new scheme for planning and sustaining the ministry. He developed into a first-rate organiser and administrator. He had a discerning and disciplined mind which made him master of everything he undertook. It is interesting to note that his hobbies were heraldry, reading *Who's who* and maps, and mastering railway timetables.

In addition to the references above, *WwW* (1921), 414; *WwFC*, 323; *Blwyddiadur MC*, 1960, 271-2; W. Morris (ed.), *Deg o Enwogion* (1965), 60-8; personal acquaintance.

G.M.R.

ROBERTS, JOHN HERBERT, BARON CLWYD of ABERGELE (1863-1955), politician; b. at 61 Hope Street, Liverpool, 8 Aug. 1863, the son of John Roberts, Liverpool and Bryngwenallt, Abergele (M.P. for the Flint Borough, 1878-92), and his wife Catherine Tudor, daughter of John Hughes (1796-1860, *DWB*, 382) minister (CM), Liverpool. He was educated at Trinity College, Cambridge, where he graduated B.A. in 1884 and M.A. in 1888. He published *A world tour* after spending a year (1884-85) travelling the

world, *Ymweliad â Bryniau Kasia* (second ed. 1888), and 'Tro yn yr Aifft' appeared in *Y Traethodydd*, 1896. He settled in Abergele and was an elder at Mynydd Seion chapel (CM) for sixty-eight years, but kept his connection with Liverpool for a while as a director of David Roberts, a company of builders and timber merchants which his grandfather had established.

As M.P.(Lib.) for Denbighshire West (1892-1918) he was one of a band of able young Welshmen like T.E. Ellis (*DWB*, 214) and David Lloyd George (see Lloyd George, David above). He took a particular interest in Indian affairs and the temperance movement. He was a member of the National Congress of India, and chairman of its British committee. He was president of the North Wales Temperance Association for many years, and a member of the Royal Commission on the Licensing Laws, 1896-99. It was his father who had presented the bill to close public houses in Wales on Sundays, and he attempted to add different legislation for Wales to strengthen the law. He supported measures for disestablishement and was a commissioner for the property of the Church in Wales from 1914. He was secretary of the Welsh Liberal Party and chairman, 1912-18. In 1922 he was a member of the Commission on voluntary hospitals in Wales. He was created a baronet in 1908 and elevated Baron Clwyd of Abergele in 1919. He journeyed regularly from Abergele to the House of Lords until he was over ninety years old. He did great service in public life of which the public was largely unaware.

He m. in Clapham chapel (Congl.), on 1 Aug. 1893, Hanna Rushton, daughter of William Sproston Caine, M.P. who had a great influence on him. They had three sons. He d. 19 Dec. 1955 at Tan-yr-allt, Abergele.

N. Wales Times, 31 Dec. 1955; G.E.C. (*Comp. Peerage*).

E.D.J.

ROBERTS, JOHN IORWERTH (1902-1970), schoolmaster and secretary of Llangollen International Eisteddfod, b. 8 Mar. 1902 in Warrington, son of William John Roberts, Presb. minister, and his wife Harriet, daughter of Edward Roberts, minister of Engedi (Presb.), Brymbo, onetime chairman of Denbighshire education committee. The family moved to Pontrhythallt, Llanrug, Caerns. in 1911 and he attended Penisa'r'waun school, and then Bryn-refail intermediate school (1914-19) and the Normal College, Bangor (1920-22). After teaching in several schools in Denbighshire, including Grango intermediate school, Rhos, and Penycae elementary school, he was appointed headmaster of Pentredwr school, near Llangollen, where he stayed till his retirement in 1964, having succeeded in converting his school into a model 'unofficial' Welsh school. He worked diligently as financial secretary of the New Wales Union and was an elder and secretary of Rehoboth chapel, Llangollen, for many years. As an ardent supporter of *eisteddfodau* he became associated with the Llangollen International Eisteddfod from its inception in 1947, and gave valuable service as secretary and chairman of the financial committee for a period. He was joint secretary of the Eisteddfod council when he died. Another of his interests was local history. He held classes on the topic for the Workers' Educational Association, and his lecture on the 1858 Llangollen *eisteddfod* to the Denbighshire History Society was published in the Society's journal in 1959.

He m. (1) Dilys Alwen Jones (d. 11 July 1965) in Rehoboth chapel, Llangollen, in Aug. 1934 and they had one daughter; and m. (2) Dilys Jones of Llangollen in King Street Presb. Chapel, Wrexham, in 1969. He lived at Isgaer, Birch Hill, Llangollen, when he d. suddenly on 17 March 1970 and was interred in Llantysilio cemetery.

Wrexham Leader, 20 and 27 March 1970; *Gol.*, 22 Apr. 1970; information from his sister Gwyneth Richards, Denbigh.

M.A.J.

ROBERTS, MARGARET - see HUGHES, (ROBERTS), MARGARET above.

ROBERTS, OWEN MADOC (1867-1948), minister (Meth.); b. in 1867, son of Captain O. and Elizabeth Roberts, Porthmadog, Caerns. He was brought up in Porthmadog and was educated there and at Menai Bridge Grammar School. He began to preach in his teens and after being accepted as an itinerant preacher he was accepted, in 1888, as a candidate for the ministry in the Wesleyan Methodist Church. At the end of his training at Didsbury College, Manchester, in 1891, he was appointed a minister on the Abergele circuit. He was ord. in 1904, on completion of his term of probation, and he subsequently served the Tre-garth, Caernarfon, Llanrhaeadr-ym-Mochnant, Llangollen, Conwy, Tywyn and Bangor circuits. In 1917 he was elected supervisor of the Book Agency in Bangor, where he remained for 21 yrs. He contributed articles regularly to the *Gwyliedydd Newydd*, *Y Winllan*, and *Yr Eurgrawn*, which he edited for a short period. He was the author of a number of books: *Llyfr y Proffwyd Amos* (1924), *Pobol Capel Nant y Gro* (1914), and *Bywyd Iesu Grist i'r ieuainc* (1937), and he was the biographer (1934) of Dr. Hugh Jones (1837-1919; *DWB*, 468). On behalf of the Wesleyans, he assisted in the publication of the joint hymnal of the two Methodist denominations in 1927, 1929. Besides supervising the bookshop, he also served in some Wesleyan district posts, and in 1920 he was president of the Wesleyan Methodist Assembly. In the same yr. he was elected a member of Bangor City Council, an Alderman for the last nine yrs. of his association with that Council. He was mayor of the city, 1935-37. As a supernumerary minister he continued to live in Bangor, where he was highly respected. He m. Margaret Jane Williams (d. 29 May 1939) of Caernarfon, and they had two daughters and a son. He d. 25 Oct. 1948, 81 yrs. old, and was buried in Llanbeblig churchyard, Caernarfon.

WwW (1937); *Minutes of Conference*, 1949; *Eurgrawn*, 141 (1948).

Er.E.

ROBERTS, RICHARD (1874-1945), preacher, theologian and author; b. 31 May 1874, s. of David and Margaret Roberts (née Jones). His father was minister of the CM church of Rhiw, Blaenau Ffestiniog, Mer. He was educated at the Liverpool Institute High School, U.C.W., Aberystwyth and Bala Theological college. He was a minister with the Forward Movement in the Cardiff area 1896-98. He became assistant and secretary to principal Thomas Charles Edwards, Bala, 1899-1900 (*DWB*, 197-8). He was minister of the Welsh church of Willesden Green, London, 1900-03. In 1902 he m. Anne Catherine Thomas and they had three dau. He was minister of St. Paul's Presbyterian Church, Bayswater, 1903-10 and Crouch Hill Presbyterian Church, 1910-15. In 1911 he was elected president of the Metropolitan Free Church Federation. One of the founders of the Fellowship of Reconciliation, he was its secretary, 1915-16. After migrating to America he held the pastorates of The Church of the Pilgrims, Brooklyn, New York, U.S.A., 1917-21; The American Presbyterian Church, Montreal, 1921-26; Sherbourne Church, Toronto, 1927-38. He was lecturer in theology at Emmanuel College, Toronto, 1929-32. He joined the United Church of Canada following the Union in 1925 and was Moderator of the United Church of Canada 1934-36. He and his wife moved to New York and it was there that he d. 10 Apr. 1945. He participated in the conferences of the Student Christian Movement, COPEC, and the Ecumenical Movement. In Autumn 1944 he delivered the Wood Lecture at the University of Mount Alison, Canada on 'Freedom and Society'.

He received the degree of D.D. from Victoria University, Toronto and the University of Vermont, U.S.A. In 1937 he received the same degree *honoris causa* from the University of Wales. He also received the degree of D. Litt. from the Univesity of Syracuse, U.S.A. As an author he contributed articles to *Cymru*, *The Hibbert Journal* and published many books among which are the following: *Robert Owen*, part I, 1907; part II, 1910 (part of a prize essay at the Liverpool national *eisteddfod*, 1900); *The Renaissance of faith*, 1912; *The Church in the Commonwealth*, 1916; *The Unfinished programme of democracy*, 1919; *The Jesus of poets and prophets*, 1919; *The Untried door*, 1920; *The New man and the divine society*, 1923; *The Gospel at Corinth*, 1924; *The Christian God*, 1928; *The preacher as man of letters*, 1930; *The Strange man on the Cross*, 1934; *The Contemporary Christ*, 1938.

WwW, 1941-50; *Gol.*, 18 Apr., 9 May, 18 July 1945; *Drych*, 15 May 1945.

D. Jo.

ROBERTS, RICHARD ARTHUR (1851-1943), archivist and editor; b. 13 May 1851 at Carmarthen, s. of J.N. Roberts and Margaret (née Jones) his wife. He was educated in private schools and in 1872 was appointed clerk at the Public Record Office. In 1879 he was called to the Bar by the Inner Temple. He was promoted assistant keeper at the P.R.O. in 1903, and from 1912 until his retirement in 1916 he was principal assistant keeper and secretary of the Office. From 1900 to 1919 he acted as Inspecting Officer (legal) under the provisions of the Public Record Office Act, 1887. He was secretary of the Historical MSS Commission from 1903 to 1912, and became a member of the Commission in 1912. He edited *The Court Rolls of the Lordship of Ruthin... of the Reign of King Edward the First* (London, 1893), *A Calendar of the Home Office Papers of the Reign of George III*, vol. III, 1770-72 (London, 1891), vol. IV, 1773-75 (London, 1899), and *A Calendar of the Inner Temple Records*, vol. IV (London 1933), vol. V (London, 1936). He took a prominent part in the editing of *A Calendar of the MSS of the Marquis of Salisbury*, vols. 4-12, published by the Hist. MSS. Comm. He was also the author of *The Episcopal Registers of the Diocese of St Davids 1397-1518*, vol. III, *A Study of the Published Registers* (London, 1920). He published two articles dealing with Welsh records, 'The Public Records relating to Wales' (*Cymm.*, 1889), and 'Welsh Records and a Record Office for Wales' (*Trans. Cymm.*, 1915-16). He m. Agnes, d. of Samuel Hallam in 1884, and they had a s. and three dau. He d. 2 Apr. 1943 at Orford, Woodbridge.

Times, 6 Apr. 1943; *Www*, 1941-50.

G.M.G.

ROBERTS, ROBERT ('Bob Tai'r Felin'; 1870-1951), folk singer; b. 1 Sept. 1870 at Tai'r Felin, Cwmtirmynach, Bala, Mer., s. of Cadwaladr and Betsi Roberts (née Rowlands, of Cae Gwernog, Capel Celyn). He followed his father as miller and farmer. He m. Elizabeth Jane Roberts of nearby Fron-goch farm. They had three children, Cadwaladr, Harriet and Morris. At Cwmtirmynach Presbyterian chapel he was precentor for nearly 50 years, Sunday school teacher, and was elected an elder in later years. He contributed to the rich culture of his neighbourhood by taking a prominent part at concerts, literary meetings and *eisteddfodau*; he often submitted entries for the *englyn* competition at the National *Eisteddfod*. Because of his notable voice and masterly style of presentation he was unique as a folk singer. In 1931 at Bangor national *eisteddfod* he was winner of the folk song competition. About this period 'Parti Tai'r Felin' was formed, its members being Robert Lloyd ('Llwyd o'r Bryn'; see above), John Thomas and his daughter, Lizzie Jane, Bob Roberts and his daughter, Harriet; this popular party entertained audiences throughout Wales, and also parts of England. From 1944 onward, he became the idol of the nation due to the impact he made when he sang on the B.B.C. radio series 'Noson Lawen' devised by Sam Jones. Decca and Teldisc companies made records of a number of his songs, and Sain company issued two long-playing records of his performances. In 1949 he took part in a film (made at Parc, Bala, and at London) the title of the Welsh version being *Noson Lawen*, and the English version *The Harvest*. The publicity given to the singing of the miller ensured the popularity and survival of songs such as *Mari Fach fy Nghariad*, *Moliannwn*, *Gwenno Penygelli*, etc. In 1959 Haydn Morris (see above) edited the book *Caneuon Bob Tai'r Felin*, which was published by Snell, Swansea. He d. 30 Nov. 1951 and was buried at Llanycil cemetery, near Bala. In 1961, Llwyd o'r Bryn's appeal for donations was instrumental in erecting a memorial to the singing miller on the roadside by the gate that leads to Tai'r Felin.

Personal knowledge; [Robin Williams, *Y Tri Bob* (1970)].

R.O.G.W.

ROBERTS, ROBERT ALUN (1894-1969), Professor of Agricultural Botany at University College, Bangor, and a naturalist; b. 10 Mar. 1894, at Glan Gors, Tan'rallt, Dyffryn Nantlle, Caerns., son of Robert Roberts (brother of Owen Roberts, father of Dr. Kate Roberts) and Jane Thomas. He received his primary education at Nebo school and won a scholarship to Pen-y-groes county school. For a period, he was a pupil teacher before securing a place in University College, Bangor in 1911. He was awarded a B.Sc. with honours in 1915 and completed his Ph.D. in 1927. His first appointment was as a science teacher at Botwnnog school (1915-17). He served with the Ministry of Agriculture from 1917 to 1919, and later as an agricultural botany consultant for the Ministry until 1921 when he was appointed to a lectureship in the Agricultural Botany department in the University College, Bangor. In 1926, he was promoted independent lecturer and head of the college's Agricultural Botany department. Between 1941 and 1944 he was seconded from his college post to become an administrative officer with the Ministry of Agriculture in Caernarfonshire. For a short period in 1944-45 he was one of His Majesty's Inspectors for rural schools, and this experience enabled him to contribute to the 1944 Education Act. In July 1945 he returned to University College of North Wales, Bangor and was appointed the first Professor of Agricultural Botany. He held this post until his retirement in 1960.

Alun Roberts worked diligently to establish a strong department in Bangor and developed his own incomparable style of imparting knowledge to his students. He contributed numerous articles and papers to scientific journals. For a decade he lectured on biological topics in tutorial courses and he and R.E.V. Roberts (see below) were the first members of the panel of naturalists on a well-known radio programme, *Byd Natur*. His wide knowledge of Wales led to many requests to serve on a host of national bodies and commissions such as the management committee of the Welsh National Folk Museum; the Agricultural Council for Wales; the council of the Wales Forestry Commission (1946-53); the Lord Carrington Council on Agricultural Education; he was first chairman of the Nature Conservancy (1953-56); the Welsh member of the Royal Commission on Common Land (1955-58); a member of the Nuffield Foundation team researching into Common Land in Wales and of the Water Resources Committee for Wales. From 1955-56 he was High Sheriff for the county of Caernarfon. In recognition of his contribution to agriculture he received a C.B.E. in 1962. He was to be awarded an honorary D.Litt. in July 1969 but died in the Caernarfon and Anglesey Hospital on 19 May 1969. His ashes were scattered on the slopes of the Cymffyrch, a stone's throw from his old home.

He was the author of numerous books, e.g. *Y tir a'i gynnyrch*; *Hafodydd brithion*; *Welsh Homespun*; *Y tyddynnwr-chwarelwr yn Nyffryn Nantlle* (Pen-y-groes Library Annual Lecture, 1968); *Yr elfen fugeiliol ym mywyd Cymru*

(Radio Lecture, 1968) and co-author of *Commons and Village Green* (1967).

He m. Jennie, daughter of Mr. and Mrs. John Morris Williams, Cae Mawr, Tan'rallt, in 1924, and they had one daughter.

Ww, 1969; *Y Gwyddonydd*, 2 (1964); Melfyn R. Williams, *Dr. Alun* (1977); personal information; his manuscripts in the Library, University of Wales, Bangor (MSS 20811 – 21046).

M.R.W.

ROBERTS, ROBERT ELLIS VAUGHAN (1888-1962), headmaster and naturalist; b. at Bryn Melyn, Rhyduchaf, near Bala, Mer., 24 Mar. 1888, son of William Roberts. Educated at Bala grammar school for boys and graduating in the sciences from University College, Bangor in 1909, he began his teaching career in Denbigh, Clocaenog, and Rhos-ddu, Wrexham, and in 1920 was appointed headmaster of Llanarmon-yn-Iâl primary school, one year after the retirement of the naturalist, Richard Morgan (1854-1939; *DWB*, 650). In 1942 he was appointed the first head of the elementary agricultural technical school at Llysfasi but in 1948 returned to the headship of Llanarmon-yn-Iâl school, a post which he held until his retirement in 1953.

Throughout his life he was a regular contributor to a number of Welsh and English journals incl. *Y Cymro*, *Yr Herald Cymraeg*, *Meirionnydd*, *Yr Athro*, *Llafar*, *Y Genhinen*, *Y Gymdogaeth*, *Countryside*, *Country Quest* and *Y Crynhoad*. He published '*Stalwm*, a play dealing with Welsh life past and present and also *Llyfr Blodau* (1952).

He became a member of the *Gorsedd* of Bards in 1923 where he was known as 'Vaughan Tegid'. He was also a member of the Welsh Folk Song Society and collected many songs, publishing some of them in *Chwe chân werin Gymreig* (1938). He was co-editor and contributor to the Chester and North Wales Natural Society from 1947-1954. He was awarded the Kinsey Memorial Medal in 1934 'for material contributions to several branches of natural science'.

He and Prof. R. Alun Roberts (see above) were the first experts on the Welsh radio naturalist programme *Byd Natur* which started in Jan. 1951. In the last decade of his life he was dealt a crushing blow when he lost his sight but despite this, he remained a panel member of *Byd Natur* until his death in Wrexham, 3 Mar. 1962. He was buried in Wrexham public cemetery. He m. Edith Mary Davies, Wrexham in 1921, and they had one son.

Melfyn R. Williams, *Gwyddonwyr Sir Ddinbych* (1973), 19-20; information from his son.

M.R.W.

ROBERTS, ROBERT MEIRION (1906-67), minister (Presb. C. of Wales and Presb. C. of Scotland), philosopher and poet; b. 28 Nov. 1906 at Station House, Llandrillo, Mer., son of Robert and Catherine Elizabeth Roberts. He was educated at elementary schools at Llandrillo and Pentre, near Chirk, Denbs.; Llangollen county school; University College, Bangor (where he graduated with first-class honours in philosophy), and at the theological colleges of his denomination at Aberystwyth and Bala. He began to preach in 1924 and was

ord. in 1933. He served as minister of Penuel, Ebbw Vale (1933-37) and St. David's, Belmont, Shrewsbury (1937-38). He was a tutor in philosophy and psychology at Coleg Harlech (1938-40) and a temporary lecturer at Bangor (1940). He served as an army chaplain (1940-46), minister of the Welsh church in Laird St., Birkenhead (1946-52), and army chaplain once again (1952-58). He joined the Presbyterian Church of Scotland in 1958, and was minister of Applegarth parish and Sibaldie, Dumfrieshire, until his d. In 1933 he m. Daisy Harper of Llanrwst and they had two sons and three daughters. He d. 11 Jan. 1967, and he was buried in Applegarth cemetery.

He took a life-long interest in philosophical studies, and whilst at Bala he found congenial company in the person of Principal David Phillips (see above) - he contributed a memoir of him to the volume *Deg o enwogion* (1959). He contributed articles fairly regularly on philosophical and theological topics to *Yr Efrydydd*, *Efrydiau Athronyddol*, *Y Traethodydd*, *Y Llenor* and *Y Drysorfa*. He was a member of the British Institute of Philosophy from 1929 onwards. He was also highly regarded as a poet, and much of his poetry is to be found in some of the above-named periodicals. He published two volumes of poetry, namely *Plant y llawr* (1946), and *Amryw ganu* (1965). One of his poems was selected for inclusion in *The Oxford Book of Welsh Verse* (1962).

WwFC (1951), 354; information from his wife and his sister Eurwen Jones, St. Dogmaels; personal acquaintance.

G.M.R.

ROBERTS, THOMAS (1884-1960), educationalist and scholar; b. 26 Dec. 1884 at Pandy, Llanuwchllyn, Mer., s. of John Roberts. He was educated at Llanuwchllyn school, Bala county school and the University College of North Wales, Bangor. He graduated with honours in Welsh in 1907, and took his M.A. degree in 1910. He was a school teacher at Abertyswg, Mon. 1907-08, and in a school in London 1908-10. He was then appointed Welsh tutor at the Normal College, Bangor, and was vice-principal from 1920 till his retirement in 1949.

As a scholar Thomas Roberts was interested in the works of the poets of the gentry throughout his life. The subject of his M.A. dissertation in 1910 was the poetry of Gruffudd ab Ieuan ap Llywelyn Fychan. In 1914 he published *Gwaith Dafydd ab Edmwnd* in the Bangor Welsh Manuscripts Society series. The work was based on many MS copies, but the editor did not attempt to produce a definitive text or to list variant readings. This was a busy time for Thomas Roberts, for there also appeared in 1914 *Cywyddau Dafydd ap Gwilym a'i Gyfoeswyr*, in which he collaborated with Ifor Williams (see below), being responsible for the introductions to the works of the contemporaries - Gruffudd ab Adda, Madog Benfras, Gruffudd Gryg and Llywelyn Goch - and for the texts of their poems. In the second edition, which appeared in 1935, Thomas Roberts added some poems and revised the introductions. In 1925 he took part in another joint effort, this time with Henry Lewis (see below) and Ifor Williams, to produce *Cywyddau Iolo Goch ac eraill*, in which Thomas Roberts dealt with Gruffudd Llwyd and Ieuan ap Rhydderch. The introductions were amplified and the text amended for the second edition in 1937.

There was a long interval till the appearance of *Gwaith Tudur Penllyn ac Ieuan ap Tudur Penllyn* in 1958. The pattern here is similar - a full introduction dealing with the life and background of the poets, a discussion of the authenticity of the poems, and one new feature, some comments on the poets' metrical usages. A standard text based on every available MS copy is provided, with detailed notes. This volume shows the editor at his best.

In addition to these works Thomas Roberts published several articles on his chosen field. In everything he did he was thorough and meticulous, and he always strove to maintain the highest standards of scholarship.

He m. Gwyneth Edwards of Llandudno in 1920, and they had one dau. He d. 25 Aug. 1960.

Information from the Normal College archives and from Mrs Llio Ellis-Williams; personal knowledge.

T.P.

ROBERTS, THOMAS OSBORNE (1879-1948), musician; b. 12 Feb. 1879 at Weston Rhyn, near Oswestry, Salop, s. of Evan Thomas Roberts and his wife Hephsibah Roberts; the family moved in 1890 to Ysbyty Ifan, Denb., to keep a shop. He was educated at the county school, Llanrwst, Salop School, Oswestry, the county school, Porthmadog, and the University College of North Wales, Bangor. He was articled to Major Barnes, agent of the Chirk Castle estate, and it was at Chirk that he began to study music and to learn to play the piano. He had begun to be in demand as an accompanist before he moved, in 1902, to Llandudno where he became organist of the English (B) chapel. He had by now decided to devote himself entirely to music. He wrote songs ('Y Mab Afradlon' and 'Good Shepherd') and a piece for male voice choirs ('Brwydr y Baltic') which was chosen as a test-piece at the Colwyn Bay national *eisteddfod* of 1910. Appointed organist of Castle Square English chapel, Caernarfon, he moved to that town; later he became organist and choirmaster at Moreia (CM) chapel in the same town. About this time he composed the songs 'Y Nefoedd', 'Pistyll y Llan', and 'Cymru Lân'. He wrote several hymn-tunes, among them 'Pennant'. His services were much in demand as accompanist and adjudicator. He d. at Wrexham Hospital, 21 June 1948, and was buried in Ysbyty Ifan churchyard four days later.

He had been married twice, his second wife being Leila Megáne (Margaret Hughes; see above).

Cerddor, Jan. 1911; *Baner*, June, 1948; [Huw Williams, *Thomas Osborne Roberts* (1980)].

R.D.G.

ROBERTSON, EDWARD (1880-1964), professor, linguist, and librarian; b. 1880, at Cameron, Fife, Scotland, son of John Robertson, the local schoolmaster. After atteding his father's school in Cameron and Madras College, St. Andrews, where he excelled in mathematics, he went to St. Andrew's University, graduated M.A. and

B.D., and proceeded to the universities of Leipzig, Berlin and Heidelburg; he also went to Syria for a year to learn Arabic. He returned to St. Andrew's for a year (1905-06) to assist the professor of Hebrew, and then became a Carnegie Research Scholar and Fellow before being a lecturer in Arabic at Edinburgh University (1913-21). He came to Wales as Professor of Hebrew and Semitic Languages at the University College, Bangor (1921-34), 'Jock', as he was called, was a popular teacher at Bangor, and he made a gallant attempt at mastering Welsh; he immortalized himself by making a tiny slip and calling Dr Thomas Richards (see above), the well-known College librarian, *llyfrgellydd*, a *llyfrgollydd* - 'book-loser'. He was vice-principal of the college (1926-28) and Dean of the Faculty of Theology (1922-34). He left Bangor for the Chair of Semitic Languages at Manchester University (1934-45), where he was also pro-vice-chancellor (1944); he was the Librarian of the John Rylands Library (1949-62). He gained a D.Litt. degree of St. Andrew's in 1913, and received a number of honours: he was Gunning lecturer at Edinburgh University (1929-32), had an hon. D.D. degree of the universities of Wales and St. Andrew, and LL.D. of the University of Manchester, and was made president of the Society for the Study of the Old Testament. His field was manuscripts in the Semitic languages, on which he published several studies; he also edited the *Bulletin of the John Rylands Library*. After retiring he emigrated to Canada to be with one of his two daughters, and he d. there 29 Apr. 1964.

Www; *Bull. of the John Rylands Library*, 45 (1963), 273-5; 47 (1964), 1-2.

Gw.H.J.

ROBINSON, GILBERT WOODING (1888-1950), professor of Agricultural Chemistry, world authority on soils; b. at Wolverhampton, 7 Nov. 1888, s. of John Fairs and Mary Emma Robinson. He was educated at Wolverhampton grammar school and Cambridge University where he was a scholar of Caius College (B.A. 1910). For two years he acted as demonstrator in the School of Agriculture at Cambridge and completed a survey of the soils and agriculture of Shropshire (1913). In 1912 he was appointed adviser in Agricultural Chemistry under the Board of Agriculture for the north Wales area at University College, Bangor, a post he held until the service was re-organised in 1946. In 1926 he was appointed Professor of Agricultural Chemistry at Bangor, and became a world authority on soils, his early research being on the palaeozoic soils of north Wales and on the mechanical analysis of soils. He built up a school of research in his dept. at Bangor, initiated a Soil Survey of Wales and trained many graduate surveyors for this work in Britain and overseas. He became the first director of the National Soil Survey of England and Wales from 1939 to 1946 when the service was transferred to Rothamsted. Robinson was a prominent figure in the International Society of Soil Science, he attended its first Congress in USA in 1925, and was president of its first Commission for several years. He travelled widely in Europe, West Indies, USA, and Africa, and in 1949 visited Australia and New Zealand as a delegate of the Royal Society to the Pacific Science Congress. He was devoted to Spain and its language, was hon. member of *Consejo Superior de Investigaciones Cientificas*, and held its medal of distinction. He was interested in the classics; he was President of the North Wales Branch of the Classical Association in 1928.

His book *Soils, their origin, constitution and classification* (1932) was the first English textbook on pedology. In 1937 he published *Mother earth* in the form of letters to R.G. Stapledon (see below) revealing his Virgilian outlook on the countryside, and wrote many technical articles to scientific journals. He received many honours - Cambridge Sc.D. in 1936, F.R.S. and C.B.E. in 1948. He was a J.P. for Caernarfonshire and served on the Departmental Committee on Rural Education in Wales (1928-30), the Central Advisory Council for Education in Wales, and as a devoted member of The Church in Wales he was Chairman of the Bangor Diocesan Religious Education Committee, and on the Governing Body of the Church in Wales from 1939. He was vice-principal of University College Bangor in 1947-48 and Dean of the Faculty of Science from 1948.

In 1913 he m. (1) Winifred Annie Rushworth of Louth, Lincolnshire, and they had one s. and three dau. In 1949 he m. (2) Mary Isabel, dau. of H.L. James, Dean of Bangor. He d. in Bangor on 6 May 1950.

Journal of Soil Science, 2, no.2, 1951; *Agricultural Progress*, 25, pt. I, 1951; *Obituary Notices of Fellows of the Royal Society*, vol.7, Nov. 1951; *Who's Who*.

R.A.R.

ROBINSON, THEODORE HENRY (1881-1964), professor, scholar and author; b. 9 Aug. 1881 at Edenbridge, Kent, son of W. Venis Robinson, minister (B), and his wife Emily Jane. He was educated at Mill Hill School; St. John's College, Cambridge; the Baptist College, Regent's Park, London; and Göttingen University. He was Litt.D. of Cambridge University and D.D. of London University. He was for a period Professor of Hebrew and Syriac at Serampore College, Bengal. He came to Wales in 1915, as a lecturer in Semitic languages at the University College, Cardiff, being promoted Professor at Cardiff in 1927, where he remained until his retirement in 1944. He was Dean of Theology of the University of Wales, 1937-40. A number of honours were bestowed upon him, including being Schweich lecturer (1926), having an hon. D.D. degree conferred on him by the universities of Aberdeen and Wales and D. Theol. of the University of Halle-Wittemberg, and receiving the British Academy's Burkitt medal for Biblical Studies. He made his name as the author of a number of standard books which were greatly needed in the field of Old Testament studies; among them were *Prophecy and the prophets in the Old Testament* (1923), *The decline and fall of the Hebrew kingdoms* (1926), *Hebrew religion* (1930) and *A history of Israel* (1932), the last two in collaboration with W.O.E. Oesterley. He published a number of books also on the Hebrew and Syriac languages. His other considerable contribution was his enormous labour for the Society for the Study of the Old Testament; he was its secretary for a very long

period (1917-46) and president twice (in 1928 and 1946). After retiring he went to live in Ealing, and d. 26 June 1964.

Www; H.H. Rowley (ed.), *Studies in Old Testament prophecy* (1950; a *Festschrift* on his 65th birthday), vii-ix, and his publications, 201-6.

Gw.H.J.

ROCH, WALTER FRANCIS (1880-1965), politician and landowner; b. 20 Jan. 1880, the second s. of William Francis Roch, J.P., Butter Hill, Pemb. (he d. 1889) and Emily Catherine (she d. 1938), the second dau. of Walter R.H. Powell, Maesgwynne, Llanboidy, Carm., M.P. (Lib.) for Carmarthenshire, 1880-85, and West Carmarthenshire, 1885-89. He was educated at Harrow. In 1908, at 28 yrs of age, he was elected M.P. (Lib.) for Pembrokeshire, and continued to represent the constituency in parliament until 1918. He had also become a barrister at the Middle Temple in 1913. Although he remained on the back benches, he was a prominent member of the Liberal governments, and in 1917 was chosen a member of the Royal Commission on the Dardanelles Campaign. He was mentioned as a possible future Prime Minister, but he chose to support Asquith rather than Lloyd George, a decision which put an end to his political career. Roch was the author of *Mr. Lloyd George and the War* (1920). In 1934 he was appointed J.P. for Monmouthshire.

He m. in 1911 the Hon. Fflorens Mary Ursula Herbert, the only dau. of Sir Ivor Herbert, M.P. for South Monmouthshire, 1906-17, and the first and last Baron Treowen. Roch and his wife spent the last 25 yrs of his life at Tŷ Nant, Llan-arth, Raglan, Mon., presiding over their estates at Llan-arth and Llanover. He d. 3 May 1965.

Www; *WwW* (1921) and (1933); *Times*, 5, 13 and 19 May 1965; *Dod's Parliamentary Companion*; W.R. Williams, *The parliamentary history of the Principality of Wales... 1541-1895* (1895); *WWP*.

J.G.J.

ROCYN-JONES, Sir DAVID THOMAS (1862-1953), medical officer of health and a public figure; b. in Rhymney, Mon., 16 Nov. 1862, the son of David Rocyn Jones, whose father, Thomas Rocyn Jones (*DWB*, 520-1) was a member of a famous family of bonesetters from Maenordeifi., Pembs. He was educated at Lewis School, Pengam, the University College of Cardiff and London, and graduated M.B. at the University of Edinburgh in 1897. He began his professional life in general practice at Abertillery. However, having obtained the D.P.H. at Oxford in 1904, he was appointed medical officer of health of Monmouthshire in 1907, and there he established an impressive service of preventive medicine, particularly in relation to tuberculosis. He was one of the five founders of the Welsh National Memorial Association that was formed to combat the then rampant disease.

He took an active part in the affairs of the University College of Cardiff, and served as its vice-president. He was much involved in the discussions that led to the establishment of the Welsh National School of Medicine (later University of Wales College of Medicine) as an independent institution. At first he was firmly opposed to the separation of the Medical School from the University College, but when this occurred he gave wholehearted support to the new venture. He served with distinction in various capacities on many public and professional bodies in Wales, such as the Welsh Regional Hospital Board, the British Medical Association and the St. John's Ambulance Brigade — he was a Knight of Grace of the Order. He was closely associated with the Welsh Rugby Union for forty-five years and was its president at the time of his death.

Rocyn-Jones, who was a county magistrate for many years, was appointed Deputy Lieutenant of Monmouthshire in 1947. He was knighted a year later, having been awarded the C.B.E. in 1920. He remained a staunch Congregationalist, and throughout his life was determined to strengthen the bonds between his native county and the other south Wales counties. He was always affectionately regarded as a 'character'.

In 1901 he m. Alla (d. 1950), daughter of Alderman S.N. Jones, of Abertillery. Two of their four sons became doctors; Gwyn succeeded his father as county medical officer of health, and Nathan, very appropriately in view of the family bonesetting background, became an orthopaedic surgeon in Cardiff. Another son was killed in Italy towards the end of the war. He d. 30 Apr. 1953.

Brit. Med. Jnl., 9 May 1953, 1054-5; *Lancet,* 8 May 1953, 954.

E.W.J.

ROGERS, RICHARD SAMUEL (1882-1950), minister (B), editor and writer; b. 12 Aug. 1882, at Pwll near Llanelli, Carms., s. of John and Elizabeth Rogers. He started preaching there at the age of 15 when he was a pupil at the county school. He won the Dan Isaac Davies prize and graduated with honours in Welsh at the University College, Cardiff. He won the college and other bardic chairs, but soon abandoned poetry for theology. He was ordained at Soar (B), Pontlotyn, in 1906, and served ministries at Rhos, Mountain Ash, 1908-1915, and at Gomer chapel, Swansea, 1915-48. He retired in 1948. His theological works include two volumes on eschatology - *Y Deyrnas a'r Ail Ddyfodiad*, 1914, and *Athrawiaeth y Diwedd*, 1934, the subject of his M.A. thesis. His commentary on the *Book of Revelations* appeared in 1944 and he published a volume of well-polished sermons entitled *A'r Drws yn Gaead* in 1948. He contributed much to periodicals and to *Y Geiriadur Beiblaidd*. His two useful works on the Welsh language, *Llyfr gloywi Cymraeg*, 1920, and *Camre'r Gymraeg*, 1926, became popular.

He was a member of the National *Eisteddfod* council, the *Gorsedd* of Bards, the B.B.C.'s religious advisory committee, and the Swansea public library committee. For a considerable period he was principal of the Ilston preparatory school, and was president of the Welsh Baptist Union for 1946-47. He edited the hymns for *Llawlyfr Moliant Newydd*, and was editor of *Seren Cymru* from 1936 until his death on 21 Feb. 1950.

Llawlyfr Undeb Bedyddwyr Cymru, 1951; *Seren Cymru,* March, 1950.

R.B.W.

ROWLAND, Sir JOHN (1877-1941), civil servant; b. 1 June 1877, at Penbont-fach, Tregaron, Cards., s. of John Rowland and Margaret, his wife. He was educated at the Technical College, Cardiff, and the University College of Wales, Aberystwyth. On leaving college in 1904 he taught at Cardiff, and identified himself with Welsh religious and cultural movements there. He attracted the notice of David Lloyd George (see above) and after serving as one of his private secretaries from 1905 to 1912 he was appointed a member of the Welsh Insurance Commission in 1911. He became Chairman of the Welsh Board of Health in 1930, retiring in 1940. He d. on 2 Jan. 1941, in Cardiff, and was buried there.

Rowland m., 1902, Mair, dau. of David Lewis of Llanafan, Cards.; they had three sons. He received the M.V.O. in 1911, C.B.E. in 1918, C.B. in 1922, and a knighthood in 1938.

Who's Who, 1941; *West. Mail,* 3.1.1941; *W. Gazette,* 9.1.1941; Percy E. Watkins, *A Welshman remembers* (1944).

T.I.E.

ROWLAND, ROBERT DAVID ('Anthropos'; ? 1853-1944), minister (CM), poet and writer; b. about 1853, the exact date and place not known. He was the adopted son of Robert and Beti Rowland, who lived in the village of Tyn-y-cefn, near Corwen. After some schooling he was for a time a stable-boy at Aber Artro, near Llanbedr, Mer., and afterwards apprenticed to a tailor. Not much is known about this period in his life; he seems to have worked at his trade in Shrewsbury and Rhosymedre, and probably in other places, but he went to Holt Academy when he was about twenty, and began to preach in 1873, entering Bala College the following year. During his time in Bala he was for a short period a teacher at the local school, and in 1877 he published his first book of verse, *Y Blodeuglwm.* He did not proceed to a pastoral charge at once, but entered journalism in Caernarfon, first on the staff of *Yr Herald Cymraeg,* and afterwards of *Y Genedl Gymreig,* being editor of the latter paper from 1881 and 1884. He also assisted Evan Jones, Caernarfon (*DWB,* 461-2), with the weekly *Amseroedd.* Ord. in 1887 he became the pastor of Beulah (CM) church, Caernarfon, in 1890, retiring in 1933. In 1912 he succeeded Rev. Thomas Levi (*DWB,* 543) as editor of *Trysorfa'r Plant,* resigning in 1932 when his services to Welsh literature were recognised by the grant of a civil list pension. He was a good preacher, but confined himself almost entirely to preaching in the smaller country churches. As a writer and poet he was known wherever the Welsh language was spoken; he had more than twenty books to his credit – collections of essays on books, people, and nature, some poetry and stories. His best works are *Y Pentref Gwyn,* early reminiscences, and *Y Ffenestri Aur,* a collection of essays. He was a regular contributor to many Welsh papers and magazines. From 1904 until 1914 he had written a weekly literary column for *Baner* and, despite his great age, was contributing a weekly article to the *Herald* up to the time of his death. As a prose writer he was descriptive, humorous and, when he chose to be so, incisive. As a poet he allowed sentiment to obscure a true lyrical gift. He was one of the wittiest men in Wales, and some of his sayings were long remembered. He d. at his home in Caernarfon, 21 Nov. 1944, and was buried in the town cemetery. He was twice married, but had no children.

Personal knowledge; *Liv.D.P.*, 22 Nov. 1944; *Blwyddiadur MC*, 1946.

E.M.H.

ROWLANDS, Sir ARCHIBALD (1892-1953), administrator; b. 26 Dec. 1892 at Twyn-yr-odyn, Lavernock, near Penarth, Glam., one of the three sons of David and Sarah (née Thomas) Rowlands, who kept a grocer's shop. He was educated at Penarth county school and from there proceeded in 1911 to the University College of Wales, Aberystwyth. At the end of his first year Professor Hermann Ethé foresaw a brilliant career for him in German, and he graduated with a first class in that subject in 1914; he took the same class in French in 1915. During his time in college he displayed the characteristics that led to his brilliant career. He was one of the most popular students of his time, a champion 100 yards runner, full back and captain of the rugby team (there is a sketch of him in the *Dragon*, XXVI, 221), an able oarsman and student President in 1914-15 (there is a photograph of him in his robes in the *Dragon*, XXVII, 18). Professor Ethé tried to persuade him to go on to Cambridge to study oriental languages but he chose to go to Jesus College, Oxford. He spent only a short time there as he joined the army and turned his back on academic life. He served in the Cyclists Corps and rose to the rank of captain and was mentioned in despatches. He was information officer in Baghdad and took part in planning the truce with the Turks in 1917. He won the M.B.E. (military).

In 1920 he joined the administrative department of the Civil Service and by 1937 was an assistant secretary. He was private secretary to three successive Secretaries of State in the War Office, Viscounts Hailsham and Halifax and Duff Cooper. He spent the year 1936 at the Imperial Defence College. In 1937 he went to India to take charge of defence expenditure there. He was called back to London in 1939 as Deputy Under-Secretary to the Air Ministry, and in 1940 was appointed first Permanent Secretary to the Ministry of Aircraft Production. Much of the praise for the success of that work during World War II is due largely to his inexhaustible energy and incisiveness. In Sept. 1941 he was on the Beaverbrook and Harriman mission to Moscow. In 1943 he was chosen to advise the Viceroy, Lord Wavell, on military arrangements in India faced with war against Japan. Following the famine in Bengal he was appointed chairman of the enquiry into the administration of the province. He won the admiration of the Indians. In 1945 he was appointed a financial member of the Governor's Working Party. He played a prominent part in the arrangement which led to the end of imperial government. In 1946 he was made Permanent Secretary to the Ministry of Supply, but for the last five months of 1947 he was on his third visit to India, this time as financial and economic adviser to Quaid-i-Azam Mahomed Ali Jinnah, the Governor-General of Pakistan.

This was another indication of the Indians' trust in his organising ability. The fruit of the advice he gave was seen in the centralisation of government in Karachi, though he foresaw that problems could arise in east Bengal. Until his retirement at sixty years of age in 1953 he was a member of the Economic Planning Board. He was regarded as the most brilliant and most constructive of his generation in Whitehall. When he retired from his posts he was invited by Beaverbrook to join the Board of the Express newspapers.

He had a strong and attractive personality. Though he was a hard worker himself who expected the same commitment from his assistants, he was loyal to them to the end. He was an easy person to warm to, without guile and a respecter of traditional ideals. He had no patience with impoliteness, ingratitude, niggardliness or taking unfair advantage; he was an interesting and humorous companion. His colleagues saw a poetic streak in him and an eloquence, they thought, that related to his Welsh background. He was made president of the Welsh Society in London. He was made K.C.B. in 1941 and G.C.B. in 1947.

He was m. in Swansea on 15 Sept. 1920 to Constance May Phillips, one of his college contemporaries and daughter of Phillip Walter Phillips, Controller of the port of Swansea. They were childless. He d. of a stroke at his home in Henley-on-Thames on 18 Aug. 1953, before realising his intention of retiring to the vicinity of Llangadog, his ancestral home. There he had hoped to tend his garden, to renew his relationships with his old friends in Welsh Wales, and find nourishment for his soul. Had his wish been realised he would, no doubt, have thrown himself into the national struggle alongside his old college friend, D.J. Williams (see below).

D.N.B.; *Www*; *Times*, 20, 24 Aug. 1953; D.J. Williams' tribute to him in *Baner*, 6 Apr. - 18 May 1955.

E.D.J.

ROWLANDS, EDWARD DAVID (1880-1969), schoolmaster and author; b. 25 Nov. 1880 at Ty'n-y-fron, Llanuwchllyn, Mer. s. of Ellis Rowlands and his wife Catrin (née Edwards). He was educated at the board school, Llanuwchllyn, the grammar school, Bala, and the Normal College, Bangor (1899-1901). He began his teaching career at Troed-yr-Allt school, Pwllheli (1901-08) and afterwards became headmaster of the elementary schools in Chwilog (1908-27) and Llandudno Junction (1927-45). As well as being a dedicated schoolmaster, he was also active in Welsh literary circles. He published the following works: *Prif-feirdd Eifionydd* (1914); *Dial y Lladron* (1934; 'a popular children's novel based on life in remote parts' — a prize-winner at the national *eisteddfod* in Port Talbot, 1932); *Bro'r Eisteddfod* (1947; publ. by the Committee of the National *Eisteddfod*, Colwyn Bay); *Dyffryn Conwy a'r Creuddyn* (1948) and *Atgofion am Lanuwchllyn* (1975; some inhabitants of his home area were responsible for publishing this volume). He also took an active part in the public life of the districts where he had lived and was Mayor of Conwy 1939-40. Some of his MSS. are in the library of Univ. of Wales, Bangor (20,663-8).

He m. in 1906 Jennie Ellen Jones, Caernarfon (d. 1950), and two children were born to them, a son and daughter. He d. in Llandudno 26 April 1969 and was buried in Conwy church-yard.

Information given by his nephew, T.E. Rowlands, Dolgellau; *Llên y Llannau* (1978), 55-6.

A.Ll.H.

ROWLANDS, JANE HELEN ('Helen o Fôn'; 1891-1955), linguist, teacher and missionary (with the CM); b. 3 April 1891 in Menai Bridge, Anglesey, the youngest child of Captain Jabez Rowlands, and his wife Martha. The father travelled the world on sailing ships. He was a man of wide interests and had an astute mind. The mother was a devotional and puritanical lady who ran a sewing business in the home, 1 Fair View Terrace. William, the eldest child, went into the ministry and became minister of some of the English churches of the Australian Presbyterian Church. He invented the Leeds Memory Method. The second child was Thomas John ('T.J.'), a scholar of Jesus College, Oxford, who graduated in classics. Though he was ordained in the Presbyterian Church of Wales, he turned to the episcopal church, becoming rector of Llandudno and canon of Bangor cathedral. The influence of her minister in Menai Bridge, Thomas Charles Williams (*DWB*, 1074-5), rested heavily upon Helen. She attended all the services and won prizes in the county scriptural examination. From Beaumaris grammar school she won a scholarship to the University College of North Wales and regis-tered there in Oct. 1908. Dr. Kate Roberts, her contemporary, refered to her 'unusual ability'. She won a second-class honours degree in French in 1911 and was awarded the George Osborne Morgan (*DWB*, 644) Scholarship which enabled her to proceed to Newnham College, Cambridge, but she stayed there for a term only. In a dilemma she returned home to dis-cuss matters with her minister. Between Sept. 1912 and June 1913 she taught French at her old school, spending the summer in France. In Sept. 1913 she was appointed a teacher at the girls' Central School in Newtown. This change was fateful as she threw herself into missionary activity, and gradually found herself becoming increasingly involved in church work.

In 1915 she decided to dedicate herself to the missionary field. She was accepted as a mis-sionary in the General Assembly in London in June 1915. She took a training course at St. Colm's College, Edinburgh, and on 23 Oct. 1916 sailed from Liverpool and arrived in Calcutta on 28 Nov. For ten years she served in the Sylhet district on the lowlands of Khasia and Jaintia, where the Hindu caste system was in force and respect towards women was low. By April 1918 she had been promoted headmistress of the Williams Memorial School for girls and had become fluent in Bengali. She showed unusual ability as a teacher and possessed organising skills. She decided to identify herself with the natives by adopting their dress, their customs and food. She frequented their Zenanas regu-larly. She preached in Bengali and taught the girls to knit and sew. The Sunday school flour-ished under her charge. In 1923 she went to Maulvi Bazaar and stayed there for two years.

She was invited to become headmistress of the language school in Darjeeling which was under the patronage of the Bengal and Assam Christian Council. Gandhi when he visited the school was amazed at her mastery of the lan-gauge. On the strength of her linguistic bril-liance she was seconded to study for the M.A. degree in Indian Vernaculars at the University of Calcutta. She was awarded the degree (first class) by examination in 1926 with a University prize (£200 worth of books) and a gold medal for her excellence in every subject. She was the most brilliant of the students. She stayed at the language school from 1925 to 1931.

She returned to Wales on furlough in 1930 and registered at the Sorbonne in Paris to study for a doctorate. (She had already spent 1928-29 at the University of Calcutta). By virtue of the excellence of her M.A. degree and on the spe-cial recommendation of Professor S.K. Chatterji, Calcutta, she was allowed to present her thesis within the year. He said of her, in a letter dated 15 April 1929, 'With her first-rate knowledge of Bengali and her intimate knowl-edge of the original texts, and her close associa-tion with Bengali life and culture, she is equipped for the work in a way which few for-eigners can expect to be ...'. She was awarded the degree of *Docteur de l'Université de Paris* for a thesis on the subject 'La femme bengalie dans la littérature du moyen âge'. There is a copy of this work in the library of the University of Wales, Bangor. She was offered chairs in Bengali by universities in Britain, America and India but declined them and returned to teach, direct and evangelise at Karimganj, Assam. She accepted an honorary professorship of English and Bengali at the Indian Government college in Karimganj. However, her name is mainly associated with Dipti Nibash (Home of Light), as it was there that she established a home for widows and orphans in need of care. There they made jam, cloth, handkerchiefs, stockings and grew rice as well as cultivating the land and producing silk. The women were trained to use the spinning-wheel and taught to be self-sufficient.

She was very supportive of the ecumenical movement which strove to establish a Presbyterian church for the whole of India. As a Swarajist she believed in church freedom and self-government, and succeeded in getting the women's work organised separately within the Assembly. She planned the Pracharikas (a women's evangelical order) and acted as the Assembly's clerk for twenty years. She was elected Moderator of the Assembly of the Lowlands. She was a regular contributor to the press especially *Y Cenhadwr*, *Y Goleuad*, *The Treasury*, not to mention her reports to the Foreign Mission. She published an English jour-nal jointly with the Rev. Lewis Mendus, *The Link*. She translated *Reality and religion, Search after reality* and *Sermons and sayings* by Sadhu Sunbar Singh into Bengali, and wrote a biogra-phy of the author. She composed two mission-ary plays, *Chumdra Hela* and *Dydd y pethau bychain*. She was friendly with Rabindranath Tagore and R. Kanta Sen and translated some of their poems into Welsh and English (see *Y Cenhadwr*, Feb. 1930). She d. suddenly in Karimganj on 12 Feb. 1955, and her grave is there in front of the chapel. The library of

Karimganj college is named 'Rowlands Hall' in her memory and there is a memorial to her in the chapel (CM) in Menai Bridge.

G. Wynne Griffith, *Cofiant cenhades* (1961); Evelyn Roberts, ed., *Pwy a'n gwahana? Llythyrau'r Dr. Helen Rowlands* (n.d.); *Cenhadwr*, Feb. 1930; *Gol.*, Feb. 1955; *Herald Cymr.*, Feb. 1955; *Blwyddiadur MC*, 1956; *Ddraig Goch*, Easter, 1964; *Baner*, Feb. 1955; *Vancouver Province*, March. 1955; *Cenhadwr*, memorial number, 1955; *Camb. News*, Feb. 1955; *St. Colm's college mag.; Glad Tidings*, March 1955; *Tyst*, Feb. 1962; *Juga Sakti*, Dec. 1958; information from Miss Evelyn Roberts, Morannedd, Porthmadog; [for her political involvement see Aled G. Jones, *Cymm. Trans*, 1997, 84-110].

G.A.J.

ROWLANDS, ROBERT JOHN ('Meuryn'; 1880-1967), journalist, writer, poet, lecturer, preacher; b. at Tŷ'n Derw, a smallholding at Aber near Bangor, Caerns., May 22, 1880, son of William and Mary Rowlands. When he was three years of age he met with an accident; he dislocated his thigh and as a consequence of unsatisfactory treatment he was lame for the rest of his life. His father died when he was six years old. He was educated at Aber National school at a time when the 'Welsh Not' was in force. Following a brief period as a shop assistant in Llanfairfechan he moved to Isaac Foulk's (*DWB*, 267) printing and publishing office in Liverpool; for a short time he also sold insurance policies in Porthmadog where he was a close friend of 'Eifion Wyn' (Eliseus Williams, *DWB*, 1036), Whilst in Liverpool he became a correspondent for *Y Darian* and *Yr Herald Cymraeg* and was subsequently responsible for the Liverpool edition of the latter. He played a prominent role in the Welsh life of Liverpool and was one of the founders of *Undeb y Ddraig Goch* and a promoter of its successful *eisteddfod*. In the 1921 national *eisteddfod* in Caernarfon he was awarded the chair for his ode 'Min y Môr', and in Nov. of that year he moved to Caernarfon as editor of *Yr Herald Cymraeg* and *Papur Pawb*. April 1937 saw the amalgamation of *Yr Herald* and *Y Genedl Gymreig* which were housed in adjacent premises. They became one paper in combination with *Papur Pawb, Y Werin a'r Eco* under the editorship of Meuryn until his retirement in March 1954. In 1923 he also followed 'Eifionydd' (John Thomas, *DWB*, 954) as editor of *Y Geninen*, continuing in that role until the periodical ceased publication in 1928. Following its revival in 1950 Meuryn became co-editor with S.B. Jones (1894-1964; see JONES (Family) above) until his death 2 Nov. 1967. At the time of his death he was a widower; he left 2 sons and 3 daughters. He was buried in Caernarfon cemetery.

He was a man of wide interests – a naturalist with a particular enthusiasm for medicinal herbs, a photographer, a chess player and in his youth, a billiards player. On Sundays he preached in Welsh Methodist churches and on week-nights he was a W.E.A. lecturer. He was the author of numerous books varying in content from adventure stories to poems and plays. (For a list of his works see David Jenkins, *Y Genhinen*, Winter 1967-68, the memorial issue to Meuryn.) Both as a journalist and an individual he was at all times a man of strong views and one who had a very great interest in writ-

ing correct and polished Welsh; he would drum the linguistic rules into his correspondents. For years he ran evening classes on Welsh prosody and when Dr. Sam Jones first presented *Ymryson y Beirdd* on the radio from Bangor Meuryn was one of the adjudicators and later the only adjudicator. His bardic name has been incorporated into Welsh as a new word, *meuryn* denoting the adjudicator in poetic contests. After retiring from the *Herald Office*, he assisted young poets through his poetry column, *Cerdd Dafod*, in *Y Cymro*.

Personal information; [Mairwen and Gwynn Jones, *Dewiniaid Difyr* (1983); *Herald Cym.*, 6 Nov., 20 Nov. 1967].

J.R.W.

ROWLEY, HAROLD HENRY (1890-1969), professor, scholar and author; b. 24 Mar. 1890 at Leicester, son of Richard and Emma Rowley. He went to Bristol Baptist College and Mansfield College, Oxford, graduating M.A. at Bristol, B.Litt. at Oxford and D.D. of London University. He won many prizes and scholarships, including the Houghton Syriac Prize. He was minister of the United Church (B and Congl.) at Wells, Somerset (1917-22) and a missionary in China (1922-30) where he was an Associate Professor at Shantung Christian University. He came to Wales in 1930 as a lecturer in Semitic languages at University College, Cardiff and afterwards was appointed Professor of Hebrew and Semitic Languages at the University College, Bangor (1935-45) and Dean of Bangor School of Theology (1936-45), and was respected as a hard worker and severe disciplinarian. He moved to the Chair of Semitic languages at Manchester University in 1945, where he was Dean of the Faculty of Theology of the University (1953-56), remaining there until his retirement in 1956. He was also president of the Baptist Union of Britain (1957-58). Among his numerous published works are: *Darius the Mede and the four world empires in the Book of Daniel* (1935), *The Relevance of the Bible* (1942), *The Relevance of Apocalyptic* (1944), *The Growth of the Old Testament* (1950), *The Biblical Doctrine of Election* (1950), *From Joseph to Joshua* (1950). He also published three collections of articles, *The Servant of the Lord* (1952), *Men of God* (1963) and *From Moses to Qumran* (1963), and he was editor of a number of books and of *The Jnl. of Semitic Studies* (1956-60). His work is characterised by extensive footnotes, which provide endless sources for researchers. In his day he was one of the most well-known Old Testament scholars throughout the world, as may be gathered from the honours bestowed upon him: honorary doctorates of the universities of Durham, Wales, Oxford, Manchester, Edinburgh, Uppsala, Zürich, Marburg, McMaster and Strasbourg; being made an honorary member of learned societies in several countries; a Fellow of the British Academy and awarded its Burkitt medal for Biblical studies. It was he, more than anyone, who succeeded in bringing Old Testament scholars into contact with each other after World War II; he was secretary of the Society for the Study of the Old Testament (1946-60), and its president (1950). In 1918 he m. Gladys B. Shaw and they had a son and three daughters.

He went to live in Stroud after retiring and d. there 4 Oct. 1969.

Www; Martin Noth and D. Winton Thomas (ed.), *Wisdom in Israel and in the Ancient New East (Supplements to Vetus Testamentum*, iii, 1955; a *Festschrift* on H.H. Rowley's 65th birthday), vii-x, and his publications, xi-xix.

Gw.H.J.

RUSSON, Sir WILLIAM CLAYTON (1895-1968), industrialist; b. 30 June 1895, s. of William and Gertrude Emma (née James) Russon, Selly Park, Warwickshire. His mother was Welsh but it is not known from what part of Wales she hailed. He was educated at the King Edward VI School, Birmingham and then he took an interest in radio and established a radio business of his own. He was an enthusiastic gardener and in 1932 he bought R. & G. Cuthbert of Waltham Cross, a company which specialised in growing and selling roses and other plants. By the start of World War II the company was also selling garden seeds and in 1940 moved to Dolgellau and then to Barmouth and finally, in 1942-43, to Llangollen. He had by this time become fully involved in the life of Wales and in 1944 became the first chairman of the North Wales Industrial Society and its president in 1947. He was High Sheriff of Merionethshire in 1947-48 and again in 1965-66. He took a prominent part in the establishment of the Llangollen International Eisteddfod and was its first president in 1947. He was chairman of the Committee for National Savings in Merionethshire from 1939-1947 and was honoured for this work by the award of an M.B.E. in 1946 and an O.B.E. in 1952. In 1958 he was president of *Gŵyl Gwerin Cymru* and a member of the Empire and Commonwealth Games Committee and was that year knighted for his contribution to the public life of Wales. He served on the Council for Wales from 1949 to 1963 and was chairman of its panel for the promotion of tourism. He was a member of the Wales Development Corporation from 1958 to 1963 and a chairman of several seed companies and of the Phostrogen company in Corwen. From 1960 onwards he served as an officer of the Order of St. John, becoming Commander in 1962 and Knight in 1968. He was also a Freeman of the City of London.

In 1931 he m. Gwladys Nellie, the daughter of Henry Markham of Dulwich and they made their home at Glanymawddach near Barmouth. He d. on 16 April 1968 and was buried at Caerdeon church cemetery.

Details supplied by his widow.

D.B.C.J.

S

SALMON, DAVID (1852-1944), training college principal; b. in the parish of Newport, Pemb., 30 Jan. 1852, s. of James and Martha Salmon. His forebears on both sides had for generations been farmers in the parish of Nevern. He was a pupil-teacher in Haverfordwest from 1865 to 1869, a student at the Borough Road (London) Training College in 1870-71, and a tutor at that college in the following session. From 1875 to 1891 he was headmaster of a board school in Belvedere Place, Borough Road, and was then appointed principal of Swansea Training College for women, where he remained until 1922. During a period of thirty years he greatly developed the scope and activities of that institution.

He produced over thirty publications, mostly school textbooks and editions of the English classics, some of which were widely used. He was greatly interested in aspects of Welsh history, on which he wrote numerous papers, notably 'A Welsh Education Commission (1846)', *Cymm.*, 1913; 'The Quakers in Pemrokeshire', *W. Wales Hist. Records*, 1923 and 1927; 'The Descent of the French on Pembrokeshire', *Ibid.*, 1929, (amplified and published separately in 1930); 'A Sequel to the French Invasion of Pembrokeshire', *Cymm.*, 1932. He wrote many notes on matters of local historical interest in the Pembrokeshire weekly newspapers. In 1919 the University of Wales conferred on him the honorary degree of M.A.

He m. in 1876 Mary Wiedhofft of London (d. 1925), and they had five children. He d. on 14 Dec. 1944 at Lampeter Velfrey in Pembrokeshire.

Private information.

D.W.

SALTER DAVIES, ERNEST (1872-1955), educationalist; b. 25 Oct. 1872, s. of Thomas Davies, minister (B) and president of the Baptist College, and his wife Emma Rebecca, Haverfordwest Pembs. He attended Haverfordwest Grammar School and U.C.W., Aberystwyth and entered Jesus College, Oxford, as a classical scholar. He was for a long period a leading figure in educational administration and thought in England. He began his career as a teacher, first at Glasgow Academy, 1895-96, then at Cheltenham Grammar School until he became an inspector for higher education in Kent in 1904 and rose to be director of education for that county in 1918, a post he held with distinction until he retired in 1938. In addition, he was educational adviser to the army in 1918 and to Maidstone prison from 1923 to 1938 and was elected president of several educational and library societies. His services were acknowledged when he was made a C.B.E. in 1932 and received an honorary M.A. degree of the University of Adelaide in 1937.

Even after his retirement he remained active and influential in the field of education. He served as a member of the committee on Higher Agricultural Education for the Ministry of Agriculture in 1940 and the Central Council for School Broadcasting until 1948, being chairman of the Rural Schools Committee. He also became chairman of many bodies including the Carnegie United Kingdom Trust (1946-51), of which he had been a life trustee since 1924.

Among his publications are *The Aim of Education* (National Adult School Union); *The Reorganisation of Education in England* (New Education Fellowship); *Education for Industry and for Life; Technical Education* (The Schools of England). He also edited *Kenilworth* and *The Fortunes of Nigel* by Scott for use in schools. As editor of *The Journal of Education*, the paper's respected reputation was upheld by him from 1939 to within a few months of his death at the age of 83.

He m., 1900, Evelyn May Lile (d. 1951) of Tenby and they had two sons. He d. 10 June 1955 at his home in 13 Chichester Road, East Croydon, Surrey.

Www; Times, 11 June 1955, 10f.

M.A.J.

SAMUEL, HOWEL WALTER (1881-1953), judge and politician; b. 1881 in Fforest-fach, Swansea, son of Thomas Samuel, a rollerman at Cwmbwrla Tinplate Works. He left Cockett elementary school at the age of 11 to work at Charles colliery, Fforest-fach. A colliery accident in 1906 left him lame and affected his health for the rest of his life. It was this accident that changed the course of his life, for he took to reading when he was bedridden. He recommenced work in Garn-goch pit 3, where David Rhys Grenfell (later a Member of Parliament for Gower) was one of his workmates. He took an interest in socialist activities and was one of the secretaries of Swansea Labour Society. In a Socialist holiday school in Caister-on-sea he met Harriott Sawyer Polkinghorne, a London schoolmistress. They were m. in 1911 and she strongly urged him to devote himself to his studies. Her efforts were rewarded when he was called to the Bar by the Middle Temple in 1915 and he was elevated a K.C. in 1931, recorder of Merthyr Tydfil (1930-33), and a judge on the Mid-Wales circuit in succession to Ivor Bowen (*DWB*, 46) in 1933. Following his appointment he and his wife moved to Llandrindod Wells. In the meantime he became the first Labour Member of Parliament for Swansea West, defeating Sir Alfred Mond by 115 votes in Dec. 1923, but losing the seat to Walter Runciman in Oct. 1924, regaining it in May 1929, and losing it once again by more than six thousand votes to Lewis Jones (see above) in Oct. 1931. He became one of the foremost barristers of his day in Wales. He gained prominence in workers' compensation cases and was chairman of the South Wales conscientious objectors' tribunal for some years. He was exceptionally competent and courageous, and had a great gift of friendship with people in all walks of life.

His wife d. in Swansea, 19 Aug. 1939, and he m. (2) in Llandrindod Wells, 24 Apr. 1941, Lady Annie Gwladys, widow of Sir Henry Gregg and daughter of David Morlais Samuel, Swansea. As 'Morlaisa' she was a member of the *Gorsedd*. He d. 5 Apr. 1953.

Www; Times, 7 Apr. 1953; *WWP*.

E.D.J., M.A.J.

SANDBROOK, JOHN ARTHUR (1876-1942), journalist; b. at Swansea, 3 May 1876, second son of Thomas Sandbrook and his wife Harriet Sarah (née Lotherington). He was educated at Swansea grammar school and became an outstanding personality in British journalism. He began his journalistic career at Swansea in 1892, becoming chief assistant editor of *The Western Mail* after serving in the Boer War (1899-1902) when he was awarded the Queen's Medal with five clasps. His series of dispatches to the *Western Mail* were among the most vivid reports which came out of South Africa at that time. In 1910 he was appointed editor of *The Englishman* in Calcutta. He collaborated in Reuter's description of the durbar in Delhi, Dec. 1911. In 1917 he was special correspondent in Mesopotamia; he was with the Indian press delegation on the Western Front in 1918; and he was at Waziristan and on the north-west frontier during the 1921 troubles. The following year he resigned his editorship and returned to Wales as chief associate editor of *The Western Mail*, succeeding Sir William Davies (*DWB*, 161) as editor in 1931.

A keen and sympathetic student of Welsh life he attended many national *eisteddfodau* and contributed reports daily of the proceedings. He took an active part in initiating public movements such as the erection of a national war memorial in Cathays Park, Cardiff. Until his death he concerned himself with making the 'Book of Rememberance' in the Temple of Peace a complete record of Welshmen who gave their lives in World War I. He lived at Beganston, Pencisely Rd, Llandaff before moving to Fairwater Rd, Cardiff. He was a cousin of Lady Buckland (see Berry family above) and d. a bachelor, 13 Feb. 1942.

WwW, 1933; *Western Mail*, 14 and 18 Feb. 1942.

M.A.J.

SANKEY, JOHN (1866-1948; BARON SANKEY, 1929; VISCOUNT SANKEY of Moreton, 1932), lawyer; b. at Moreton, Gloucester, 26 Oct. 1866, s. of Thomas and Catalina Sankey. Educated at Lancing and at Jesus College, Oxford, he was called to the bar in 1892, became a King's Counsel in 1909, was appointed a judge of the High Court in 1914, and a Lord of Appeal in 1928. In 1929 he became Lord Chancellor in the second Labour Government, and retained this office until 1935. He was chairman of the Coal Commission (1919) and a member of the Indian Round Table Conference, and his services were in great demand on many commissions and committees, legal, educational, and ecclesiastical (see the list in *Www*, 1941-50). He was a loyal and devoted churchman, and was largely responsible for the framing of the constitution of the (disestablished) Church in Wales. He was an honorary Fellow of Jesus College, Oxford, and in 1929 he received the honorary degree of LL.D. of the University of Wales. He was also an honorary graduate of the Universities of Oxford, Cambridge and Bristol. He died, unmarried, in London on 8 Feb. 1948, and was buried at Moreton.

His connexion with Wales began when he practised at Cardiff as a young barrister. There he became expert in cases under the Workmen's Compensation Act and gained a great reputation for brevity and conciseness in exposition. On the Bench his work was characterised by a deep humanity and a great concern for the dignity of the law, and on the Woolsack he made a notable contribution to political life by his dignity, his self-discipline, and his gifts of friendship. But above all else he will be remembered as a devoted Churchman and a sincere Christian.

Www, 1941-50; Hansard (Lords), 11 Feb. 1948; *Times*, 9 Feb. 1948.

T.I.E.

SARNICOL - see THOMAS, THOMAS JACOB below.

SAUNDERS, WILLIAM (1871-1950), minister (B) and educationalist; b. 24 May 1871 son of Thomas Saunders and Ann (née Thomas), 5 John St., Aberdare, but the family soon moved to Abercwmboi where his maternal grandfather was a leading member with the Baptists, and he was baptized there in 1883. The family moved yet again in 1887 to Ynysybŵl where William Saunders preached his first sermon in 1890. He was educated in Pontypridd Academy, and in 1892 he entered the Baptist college at Haverfordwest and Aberystwyth before becoming minister of Jerusalem, Rhymney (1895-99), Carmel (English Church), New Tredegar (1899-1901), and Noddfa, Pontycymer, where he remained for 44 years. He gained immediate popularity and soon demonstrated his ability to reconcile opposing factions. Not only was he an eloquent and powerful preacher, genial company and an unrivalled conference man, but he played an active role in many religious and secular movements. He was secretary of the Monmouthshire Union of Sunday Schools, the Welsh Baptist Young People's Union, and the Glamorgan Particular Baptists Association for over 15 yrs. He was a member of Glamorgan county council for over 40 years (1908-50), being chairman of the Council for two years and chairman of its elementary education committee. For his services to education the University of Wales conferred on him an hon. LL.D. degree in 1946. He and his wife Jane had a daughter, Eluned, who was a doctor in London. He d. 2 May 1950 and was buried in Pontycymer cemetery.

Llawlyfr Bed., 1951, 173; *Bapt. Hndbk.*, 1951, 361; *Ser. G.*, 1950, 117; *WWP*.

M.A.J.

SAYCE, GEORGE ETHELBERT (1875-1953), journalist and newspaper proprietor; b. in Llangua, Mon., Christmas Day 1875, s. of George Sayce and his wife Athel (née Miles). He was trained in journalism and pursued literary and commercial studies at King's College, London, gaining experience as a journalist between 1898 and 1914 chiefly in Yorkshire, where he became editor of *The York Observer*, *The Thirsk and District News*, and also *The*

Yorkshire Chronicle for a while. In 1914 he acquired the *Brecon and Radnor Express* and the *Radnor Express* and took over the *Brecon County Times* in 1933, incorporating it in the *Brecon and Radnor Express & County Times*. He was director of several commercial companies and was one of the founders of Builth Chamber of Trade. He took a prominent part in local government, being chairman of Builth urban district council and chairman of the Wye Valley Development Association. He did much to promote tourism and support games, especially golf. He also took an active interest in local hospitals and St. John's Ambulance as well as in elementary and higher education, being a member of the courts of the university colleges at Aberystwyth and Swansea. He was the first president of the North Breconshire Agricultural Society and became chairman of the Brecon and Radnor Liberal Association. He served twice as High Sheriff of Brecknockshire (in 1940-41 and 1947-48) and was Justice of the Peace (1932-50). To commemorate the end of World War II he donated a stained glass window to St. Mary's Church. He published his mother's poetry (*Poems by Athel Sayce*) in 1915; *Guide to Llandrindod Wells, Day with the blind*, and *Rambles in Yorkshire*.

In 1901 he m. (1) Eleanor Richards (d. 1910) and they had a son and three daughters. He m. (2), in 1914, May Walsh and they had a son and daughter. His last years were spent in Pontrilas where he d. 7 Oct. 1953 and was buried at Kenderchurch, Herefordshire.

Who's who, 1941; *Brecon and Radnor Express*, 15 Oct. 1953.

E.D.J.

SCOTT-ELLIS, THOMAS EVELYN (1880-1946), 8th BARON HOWARD DE WALDEN and 4th BARON SEAFORD, landowner and sportsman, writer, and patron of the arts; b. 9 May 1880, only son of Frederick George Ellis, 7th baron, and Blanche, eldest dau. and co-heir of William Holden, of Palace House, co. Lancaster. Educated at Eton and the Royal Military College, Sandhurst, he served in the Boer War, and afterwards in World War I. He succeeded, as 8th baron, in 1899. His descent from John Ellis, who was descended from a family of that name seated at Wrexham and who went to Jamaica in the reign of Charles II, is given in Debrett, Burke, and other works on the peerage; the additional name of Scott was adopted by the 8th baron in 1917. He m. 1912, Margherita Dorothy, dau. of Charles van Raalte, and they had 6 children. He lived for years at Chirk Castle, Denbighshire; in 1929 he bought the Old Hall at Croesnewydd, near Wrexham, which had been the home of his ancestors. He also spent some time at Llanina, Cards.

Besides being a patron of dramatists (in Wales and London) and musicians, e.g. his association with Josef Holbrooke in the production of *The Children of Don and Dylan*, he was himself a writer, the Arthurian cycle giving him the subject of his first play, and, later, the folklore of Wales providing him with material for operatic libretti. Among his works are: *Children of Don* (1912), *Pont Orewyn* (1914), *Lanval* (1915), *Dylan* (1919), *The Cauldron of Annwn* (1922), *The Cauldron of Annwn, including the*

story of Bronwen (1929), *Five Pantomimes* (1930), *Song of Gwyn ap Nudd* [1913]. He had previously published *Banners, standards, and badges: from a Tudor manuscript in the College of Arms*, and *Some feudal lords and their seals*, both in 1904. His last full-length play, which dealt with the emperor Heraclius and his relations with both Christianity and Islam, was produced in 1924. He was awarded the degree of LL.D. *honoris causa* by the University of Wales, was President of the Nat. Museum of Wales and a governor of the Nat. Library of Wales. In 1938 he became a trustee of the Tate Gallery. He d. 5 Nov. 1946 in London.

Burke, *Peerage* (1949); Debrett, *Peerage* (1938); *Times*, 6 Nov. 1949; NLW MSS 4970-6074; *Www*, 1941-50.

W.Ll.D.

SEAFORD, 4th BARON - see SCOTT-ELLIS, THOMAS EVELYN above.

SEAGER, GEORGE LEIGHTON (1896-1963; BARON LEIGHTON of St. Mellons, 1962); merchant and shipowner; b. 11 Jan. 1896 the youngest son of Sir William Henry Seager (founder of the shipping company W. H. Seager and Co.), and Margaret Annie (née Elliot), his wife, of Lynwood, Cardiff, brother of John Elliot Seager (see below). After leaving Queen's College, Taunton, at the age of 16 he travelled on the Continent and South America. At the beginning of World War I he was commissioned with the Artists' Rifles (London Regiment) and subsequently gave voluntary service with the secretariat of the Ministry of Food. He returned to Wales to join his father and eldest brother in the numerous family businesses. He paid particular attention to shipping and was soon looked on as an expert in this field. In 1929 he was economic adviser to the Government on a mission to Canada. He became director of numerous companies and was chairman of the Cardiff and Bristol Channel Shipowners' Association, the Chamber of Shipping of the United Kingdom, as well as of several committees concerned with the unemployed in Cardiff. He was also president of Cardiff Chamber of Trade. He gave valuable service and generous support to charitable societies particularly those associated with the education and well-being of seamen. He served as J.P. for Monmouthshire and was Deputy Lieutenant of the county from 1957 till his death. He received a knighthood in 1938, became a baronet in 1957 and a baron in 1962. In 1921 he m. Marjorie, daughter of William Henry Gimson, Breck., and they had two sons and two daughters. He lived at Marley Lodge, St. Mellons and d. 17 Oct. 1963.

Debrett, 1962, 775; *Www*; *WWP*; *Times*, 18 and 25 Oct. 1963.

M.A.J.

SEAGER, JOHN ELLIOT (1891-1955), shipowner; b. 30 July 1891, eldest son of Sir William Henry Seager and Margaret Annie (née Elliot), and brother of George Leighton Seager (see above). On 26 May 1922 he m. Dorothy Irene Jones of Pontypridd, and they had four children. Educated at Cardiff High School and Queen's College, Taunton, he joined his father's shipping companies where he gained experience of all levels of management and control of shipping and the equipping of merchant fleets. He soon became a director of a dozen or more shipping and industrial companies and chairman of several of them. For many years he was honorary adviser on ships' stores at the Ministry of Food. He became a J.P. and was High Sheriff of Glamorganshire, 1937-38. He took a keen and active interest in charitable work, especially on behalf of youth organisations and hospitals. He was thorough, meticulous and untiring in every task he undertook. During World War I he won the Military Cross while serving with the South Wales Borderers. He d. 8 Jan. 1955 at his home, Tŷ Gwyn Court, Cardiff.

Www; Times, 10 Jan. 1955.

M.A.J.

SEYLER, CLARENCE ARTHUR (1866-1959), chemist and public analyst; b. in Clapton, London, 5 Dec. 1866, eldest s. of Clarence Henry and Clara (née Thies) Seyler. He was educ. at Priory School, Clapton, University College London, and the City and Guilds technical college, Finsbury. He had brilliant teachers in Alexander W. Williamson, Sir William Ramsay, Sir Edwin Ray Lankester and Daniel Oliver. He was assistant to W.M. Tidy, water consultant to London Hospital and then to Sir William Crookes in Kensington. In 1892 he joined William Morgan, Ph.D., public analyst and metallurgical chemist at Swansea Laboratories which were specially equipped for the instruction of students in chemistry, metallurgy and mathematics. When Morgan died in 1895 he succeeded him as director of the Laboratories and for the next 47 years he was proprietor and director of the Orange Street and later of the Nelson Terrace Laboratories where he served as Public Analyst for Swansea County Borough and the counties of Glam., Carms., and Pembs. He was also retained as a private consultant to many industrial firms in south Wales and elsewhere. His inevitable involvement with the coal, gas, iron and steel, copper, zinc and other industries caused him to make the calorific value of coal a special study, and after reading his pioneer paper on the chemical classification of coal to the South Wales Institute of Engineers in 1900, he became in south Wales the recognised authority. After completing his World War I service with the R.A.S.C. he decided to pursue the analysis of coal by using the microscope. He had long decided that it was not a sufficient classification of coal 'species' to refer merely to their chemical components of carbon, hydrogen and oxygen, but that it was necessary to classify them petrologically and petrographically. He considered that the internationally accepted mineralogical classification used by Marie Stopes and other palaeobotanists did not go far enough because fundamentally it was lithological and if the remains of plant structures in each 'species' were to be properly assessed, the classification needed to be micro-petrological rather than just petrological. His idea of achieving this was to assess the homogeneity of the constituents which had definite optical properties and he succeeded in doing this by measuring the reflectance of polished samples of each 'species'

under a microscope which he fitted with Berek's photometer. 'Dry' examination of the crystallographic magnification he found to be unsatisfactory, and his remarkable final results were achieved by using Kuhlwein and Stach's microscopy in which the lenses were in contact with oils of known refractive values.

Prolonged painstaking observation enabled him to draw the internationally acclaimed Seyler Coal Chart from which information about volatile matter and calorific values could readily be extracted. For this highly specialised work the South Wales Institute of Engineers awarded him its Gold Medal in 1931 and in 1937 the Bar to it. In 1941 he was awarded the Melchett Gold Medal of the Institute of Fuel.

After much heart searching he left Swansea, the true town of his adoption over a period of 50 unbroken years, at the end of 1942, in order to become General Consultant to the British Coal Utilisation Research Association and head of its Coal Systematics and Petrology Dept. He served in both capacities until 1957 and his reputation internationally was evidenced by his election in 1955 as the first president of the International Committee for Coal Petrology. Retiring in 1957, he remained an Honorary Consultant to B.C.U.R.A. until his death.

His publications include: introduction to Greenwell and Elsden, *Analysis of British coal and coke* (1907); *Classification of Coal* (World Engineering Congress, Tokyo, 1929); *Petrography and the Classification of Coal*, I, II (1931, 1937); *Fuel technology* (1931); *Description of Seyler's Fuel Chart* (1933); *Selection of coals for steam raising* (1934); *Recent progress in petrology of coal* (Melchett Lecture, 1941); *Die Entwicklung der Kohlen-Petrographia* (1951); with W.H. Edwards, *The microscopical examination of coal* (1929); with Illingworth and Wheeler, *Report on explosions in anthracite stoves* (1924); and papers in the *Trans. of the South Wales Institute of Engineers*, and the Royal Society.

For his 'dilettante enjoyments', as he called them, after long weeks of laboratory work, he would apply his clear mind to difficult questions about the history of Swansea and Gower and offer lucid explanations of local placenames, in lectures to the Royal Institution of South Wales, Swansea, or in articles in *Arch. Camb.*, e.g. 'Early charters of Swansea and Gower' (1924, 1925); 'Stedworlango: the fee of Penmaen in Gower'; (1920); 'Seinhenyd, Ystumllwynarth and Ynysgynwraid: some place-names and folk-lore in Wales' (1950).

He was president of Swansea Rotary Club, 1929-30, of the South Wales Institute of Engineers, 1931-32, of the Royal Institution of South Wales, 1932-33, and a member of the Council of the National Museum, of the Cambrian Archaeological Association and of Surrey Archaeological Soc. He was B.Sc. (London) and was awarded an hon D.Sc. (Wales) in 1938. He was also F.R.I.C.

He m. Ellen Andrews in 1895 and they had 2 dau. Athène Seyler, C.B.E., the actress who died in 1990 aged 101, was his sister. C.A. Seyler died at his home, Gaywood, Chine Walk, Ferndown, Dorset, 24 July, 1959.

WwW (1937); *Www*; *Trans. S. Wales Inst. of Engineers*.

W.C.R.

SIBLY, Sir THOMAS FRANKLIN (1883-1948), geologist and university administrator; b. 25 Oct. 1883 in Bristol, s. of Thomas Dix Sibly and his wife Virginia (née Tonkin). He was educated at Wycliffe College, Stonehouse, and at St. Dunstan's, Burnham-on-sea, and gained a 1st-class hons. degree in experimental physics (Univ. of London) at the University College of Bristol in 1903. He turned to geology at Birmingham University and he was Exhibition Research Scholar at U.C. Bristol 1905-07; he graduated D.Sc. London in 1908. He was lecturer-in-charge of geology at King's College London 1908-13, Prof. of Geology, Univ. College Cardiff 1913-18, and Prof. of Geology at Armstrong College, Newcastle-upon-Tyne (University of Durham) 1918-20. He became the first principal of the University College of Swansea in 1920 and he played a crucial role in setting the new institution on a firm foundation. He was a firm and strong leader, a forceful advocate and a gifted administrator. It has been claimed that it was due to him that the new college was not allowed to harbour an inferiority complex in its relations with its older sister colleges in the University. In 1926 he was appointed Chief Officer of the University of London, a title changed at his appointment to Principal, and he became Vice-chancellor of the University of Reading 1929-46, where he did much to guide the development of the young university. His skills as a negotiator ensured that he was a leading figure in British university administration. He was chairman of the Committee of Vice-chancellors and Principals 1938-43, executive chairman of the Universities Bureau of the British Empire, and he served on the Advisory Council of the Dept. of Scientific and Industrial Research, and the Royal Commission in the University of Durham. Between 1905-1937 he published a series of articles on carboniferous limestones; he served on H.M. Geological Survey 1917-18 and he was chairman of the Geological Survey Board 1930-43. He was knighted in 1938 and he was awarded the degrees of D.Sc. Bristol, LL.D. *hon. causa* Wales, Liverpool and Bristol. He m. Maude Evelyn Barfoot in 1918 and they had 1 s. He d. in Reading 13 Apr. 1948.

Www; *DNB*; D. Emrys Evans, *The University of Wales* (1953); David Dykes, *The University College of Swansea* (1992).

B.F.R.

SIMON, JOHN ALLSEBROOK, 1st VISCOUNT SIMON of Stackpole Elidor (1873-1954), judge and politician; b. 28 Feb. 1873 at Manchester, son of Edwin Simon, Congl. minister from Stackpole, Pembs., and Fanny (née Allsebrook) his wife. He was educated at Fettes College, Edinburgh and Wadham College, Oxford. After graduating in the classics in 1896 he was elected Fellow of All Souls College, Oxford. In 1898 he won the Barstow Law Scholarship and was called to the Bar by the Inner Temple the following year. He was appointed a judge on the Western Circuit as early as 1908. His mind was ordered, his memory extraordinary and his power of presentation seldom surpassed, but his ambition was chiefly political. In 1906 he had been elected M.P. (Lib.) for Walthamstow, Essex, and he soon became a member of the

cabinet and was Secretary of State for Home Affairs (1915-16) when he resigned because he was opposed to the introduction of conscription. He returned as M.P. for Spen Valley, 1922-40. A speech he made in the House of Commons contributed markedly to the collapse of the miners' strike in 1926. In 1931 he entered the least satisfactory stage of his career when he became Secretary of State for Foreign Affairs, but was better placed as Secretary of State for Home Affairs, 1935-37, his second term in that office. This was followed by a period as Chancellor of the Exchequer, 1937-40. He served on several government commissions, and was chairman of the Indian Statutory Commission, 1927-30, which produced an historic report on the working of the 1919 act concerning the government of India. In 1940 he was elevated to the peerage and became Lord Chancellor, in which post he was pre-eminent. Many of his ensuing judgements are models of lucid and comprehensive expositions of the law. He m. (1), 1899, Ethel Mary Venables (d. 1902) and they had one son and two daughters; (2), 1917, Kathleen Manning (née Harvey); he d. 11 Jan. 1954. His publications include his memoirs, *Retrospect* (1952), and *Income Tax* (5 vols.; 1950).

Www; *Cymro*, 13 June 1952; *Times* and *West. Mail*, 12 Jan. 1954; *WWP*.

M.A.J.

SKAIFE, Sir ERIC OMMANNEY (1884-1956), brigadier and patron of Welsh culture; b. 18 Oct. 1884, son of Frederic and Josephine Skaife, Chichester, Sussex. He was educated at Winchester College, and Sandhurst. He joined the Royal Welch Fusiliers as a 2nd. lieutenant in 1903. During World War I he served in France, and while a prisoner in Germany he began to learn Welsh and improved his Russian. He became a major in 1918 and served in the War Office and in Waziristan before returning to the Welch Fusiliers as lieutenant colonel in 1929. From 1934 to 1937 he was military attaché in Moscow, and subsequently commander of the Welch Territorial Brigade, before joining the research department of the Foreign Office, 1941-44. He was author of *A Short history of the Royal Welch Fusiliers* (1924). He retired to Crogen mansion in Merionethshire, later residing at Dolserau, Dolgellau. He was an ardent *eisteddfodwr* and took a keen interest in Welsh culture. He was received as a member of the *Gorsedd* and was elected a vice-president of *Urdd Gobaith Cymru* in 1942. In 1946 he presented five harps, known as 'the Crogen harps' to the *Urdd* for young harpists to learn their craft. His Welsh speeches were unadulterated with English words, but he was not a fluent speaker and his Welsh had a strong English accent. As soon as Welsh books and periodicals came from the press he bought them and built up a large library. He was a member of the governing board of the Church in Wales and chairman of the Merioneth Conservative Society. He served as Deputy Lieutenant of the county, and was High Sheriff in 1956, the year he was knighted. He d., unmarried, 1 Oct. 1956, in Largos, while attending the Mod in Scotland as a delegate from the *Eisteddfod* and *Gorsedd*. On his gravestone in St. Mark's churchyard,

Brithdir, is a couplet in Welsh ('My heart was in Wales/ And in her soil are my remains').

Www; R.E. Griffith, *Urdd Gobaith Cymru*, I (1971), 262-4.

E.D.J.

SKEEL, CAROLINE ANNE JAMES (1872-1951), historian; b. 9 Feb. 1872 in Hampstead, where her family resided at 45 Downshire Hill, the sixth of the seven children of William James Skeel (1822-99) and Anne, his wife (1831-95). Her father, the son of Henry Skeel (d. 1847), a farmer, was born at Castle Hill in the parish of Haycastle, Pembs., and became a successful London merchant with offices in Finsbury Chambers in the city and a director of the South Australian Land Mortgage and Agency Co. Ltd. Her mother, a first cousin of her husband, was the dau. of Thomas and Martha James of Clarbeston, Pembs. Caroline was educated at a private school, then at the South Hampstead High School (*c*. 1884-87), the Notting Hill High School (1887-90), and Girton College, Cambridge (1891-95). She was a St. Dunstan's Exhibitioner and took a double first in classics (1894) and history (1895). She was awarded the Agnata Butler Prize in 1893 and 1894, and the Thérèsa Montefiore Memorial Prize in 1895. She was appointed to the staff of the history department of Westfield College, London, in 1895, was a lecturer there, 1895-1907, and after a period of absence because of ill-health became Head of Department 1911-19, Reader and Head of Department 1919-25 and University Professor of history 1925-29. She was a Fellow of the Royal Historical Society 1914-28, serving on the Council and the Publications Committee 1921-27, and a member of the Cymmrodorion Society, the Classical Association and the Historical Association. She was awarded the Henry Hutchinson Medal, 1914, and the degree of M.A. (Cantab.) 1926, and was Hon. Yerrow Research Fellow, Girton College, 1914-17.

Her first published work was *Travel in the first century A.D.* (Cambridge, 1901) originally written for the Gibson Prize in Girton College in 1898. She turned her attention to Welsh historical studies with the publication of her major work *The Council in the Marches of Wales: a study in local government in the sixteenth and seventeenth centuries* (London, 1904), her dissertation for the degree of D.Litt. in the University of London in 1903 where she was an internal student, 1901-03. This was supplemented by a number of articles and reviews in *Eng. Hist. Rev., Arch. Camb. Trans. Cymm., Trans. R. Hist. Soc., Shrops. Arch. and Nat. Hist. Soc., History, Camb. Hist. Jnl.*, most of which deal with the history of Wales and the Marches. Her second article on the Welsh woollen industry (*Arch. Camb.*, 1924) was both praised and criticised by A.H. Dodd which drew rejoiners from the author who was at the time hoping to produce a book on the Welsh woollen industry. She contributed a chap. on Wales under Henry VII to *Tudor Studies*, ed. R.W. Seton-Watson (1924), and to T. Auden, *Memorials of Old Shropshire* (1908). She gained the Gamble Prize in 1914 for an essay on the influence of the writings of Sir John Fortescue. She was also one of the editors of the S.P.C.K. texts for students and arranged the *Selections from Giraldus Cambrensis* and the *Selections from Matthew Paris*, Nos. 2-3 in that series (London 1918).

The importance of Caroline Skeel's contributions to Welsh historical studies is obvious from her publications and is still widely recognised, although some of the authority of her work has been eroded by later scholars. She broke much new ground in the fields of Welsh social and economic history at a time when these subjects were largely neglected. She was one of the first Welsh women to hold a university chair. Moreover, her services to her college and the University of London, both as a brilliant teacher whose lectures were famous for their humour and scholarship and as a member of university boards and committees, were readily acknowledged by her colleagues and students. After her retirement in 1929 she moved from Hampstead to 34 Heald Crescent, Hendon, where she lived modestly, almost frugally, dressed rather shabbily and quibbled with the tradesmen over pennies. Her neighbours looked upon her as a refined little lady who had known better times. She was in fact very wealthy. The only surviving member of her family (the others all died unmarried), she inherited the large fortunes left by her father and brother William Henry Skeel (d. 1925, leaving over £305,000). She d. on 25 Feb. 1951 and was cremated at Golders Green. Her estate was valued at £269,386 gross. In her will she bequeathed large sums to Church charities and the residue, amounting to over £50,000 net, to Westfield College, where the fine new library bears her name. After her death it was revealed that she had anonymously given away in her lifetime about £30,000 to poor families and charities.

Times, 23 March 1899, 13 Oct. 1925, 3 March 1951, 26 May 1951; *Daily Mirror*, 26 May 1951; *Girton College Register, 1869-1946* (1948); parish registers; private papers of Miss Dorothy Skeel Meyler and Major Francis Jones; archives of Westfield College per Dr. J. Sondheimer.

B.G.C.

SLINGSBY-JENKINS, THOMAS DAVID (1872-1955), secretary of a shipping company and philanthropist; b. 25 Dec. 1872, eldest son of Evan Jenkins, Bodhyfryd, Bridge Street, Aberystwyth, and Mary, his wife, but when he was two years old his father was lost at sea. He attended the local grammar school and worked in a solicitor's office in the town before joining the shipping company of Mathias and Son, Cardiff, where he became company secretary. He was a member of the board of the British Sailors' Society and made generous contributions to the society. His work often took him to Italy where he was awarded a medal by the king of that country in 1940 for fostering friendship between Italy and Britain. But he did not sever his connection with his native county. He became a J.P. and High Sheriff of Cardiganshire, and a member of the court of governors and council of U.C.W., Aberystwyth. He presented to the college a statue by Mario Rutelli of the Duke of Windsor as Prince of Wales (the only such large statue made) and an endowment to establish a scholarship for local pupils. He also served on the court and council of the National Library of Wales to which he was a generous benefactor. He donated the marble sculpture of

Sir John Williams (*DWB*, 1055-6) to the Library, and a bronze war memorial to Tabernacl (Presb.) church in the town (these also by Rutelli who was commissioned to erect the town War Memorial), desiring that the fund established by the members of the Church for the memorial be transferred to the local hospital to open a children's ward there. He served the Cymmrodorion Society as treasurer (1934-49) and vice-president, and contributed much towards publishing *Y Bywgraffiadur Cymreig hyd 1940*.

He changed his name to Slingsby-Jenkins on his m. (1), *c*. 1937, to Roma Beatrice Evlyn Marie Slingsby (d. 7 Feb. 1948), and they made their home in 9 Victoria Square, London and Devil's Bridge, Cards. He m. (2) in Italy Margherita Vita, grand-daughter of a friend, shortly before he d. at her home in Imperia, 5 Apr. 1955.

Trans. Cymm., 1955; *Adroddiad Tabernacl (MC), Aberystwyth*, 1921, 29; *Calendar of grants and probate*, 1948 and 1955; *Welsh Gaz.*, 7 Apr. 1955.

M.A.J.

SMITH, WILLIAM HENRY (BILL; 1894-1968) president of the Welsh National Opera Company; b. 9 Oct. 1894, the eldest of the three sons of William Henry and Eliza Smith, Cardiff. He attended Albany Road school before being apprenticed to the drapery trade. He began studying for a legal career by attending night classes at the technical college but following service as a gunner in World War I he joined a motor firm in London. Eventually, in 1932, he and David Bernard Morgan started a thriving business, Morsmith Motors Ltd., in Cardiff. He held important offices in the motor trade and gave valuable support to local sports, the Guild of Welsh Playwrights, Cardiff New Theatre Trust and the University College in Cardiff, but he is remembered particularly for his services to music. During the 1920s, after a visit to La Scala, Milan, when his interest in opera was roused, he became secretary of the Cardiff Grand Opera Society. It was not till 1946 that the Welsh National Opera Company held its first season in Cardiff, and when a board of management was formed two years later he was chosen as its chairman, an office he held for twenty years. The chorus at first rehearsed in a room over his showrooms. Having gained an early invitation for the company to perform at Sadler's Wells, he built up a large opera following in Wales, persuading the Arts Council to increase its grant tenfold and convincing businessmen and almost 60 local authorities to support the company. He was awarded the C.B.E. in 1953 for his services to music and an honorary LL.D. degree by the University of Wales in 1961. Shortly before he d. on 9 June 1968 he was appointed the first president of the opera company. He m. Elsie Allan in 1924.

Www; WWP; Welsh Music, 3, no.3 (1968), 3-4; *Times and West. Mail*, 10 June 1968.

M.A.J.

SNELL, DAVID JOHN (1880-1957), music publisher; b. 1 Aug. 1880 at 44 Dyvatty Terrace, Swansea, son of Henry and Eliza (née Lewis) Snell. In 1900 he established a business in Alexandra Arcade, Swansea, selling music,

musical instruments and records. Ten yrs. later, on the retirement of the publisher Benjamin Parry (1835-1910) who had worked in Swansea since 1878, Snell bought his stock and copyrights and thereby began his great lifework. In 1916 he paid £1150 to the widow of Joseph Parry (1841-1903, *DWB*, 738) for the stock and copyright of the works published by the composer, and about the same time he bought the business of David Jenkins (*DWB*, 431), Aberystwyth, who d. in 1915. During the 1920s he augmented his catalogue by buying the output of companies which had closed down and the works of composers who published their own compositions, republishing the whole under his own name. He purchased, among other items, the musical output of the publishers Isaac Jones (1835-99), Treherbert; Daniel Lewis Jones ('Cynlaw'; 1841-1916), Llansawel and Cardigan; John Richard Lewis (1857-1919), Carmarthen; the North Wales Music Co., Bangor; and the National Welsh Company, Caernarfon. By 1939 he had an extensive catalogue of fifteen hundred items, and he offered *eisteddfod* prizes to committees which chose his publications as test pieces. He republished popular works like 'Myfanwy' (Joseph Parry) and 'Yr hen gerddor' (David Pugh Evans, *DWB*, 227), but he also published new pieces of high standard, including 'Bugail Aberdyfi' (Idris Lewis, see above), 'Paradwys y bardd' (W. Bradwen Jones; see Jones, William Arthur above) and *Saith o ganeuon* and 'Berwyn' (D. Vaughan Thomas, *DWB*, 943-4). He also published books of *cerdd dant* settings by Haydn Morris (see above) and Llyfni and Mallt Huws. He lost a large proportion of his stock during the air raids over Swansea in 1941, but he continued to publish after the war. Unlike some of his predecessors in the field, Snell was a publisher only, and never printed any works. He was regarded as one of the keenest of businessmen, and was known as 'Mr. Music' in his native town. He m. in 1906 Elizabeth Evans (d. Apr. 1957) of Laugharne, and they had four sons. He d. 13 Jan. 1957.

MSS of Snell and Sons at N.L.W.; personal research.

Rh.G.

SOMERSET, FITZROY RICHARD (1885-1964) 4th BARON RAGLAN, soldier, anthropologist, author; b. 10 June 1885, eldest son of the 3rd Baron Raglan and Ethel Jemima Ponsonby, daughter of the 7th Earl of Bessborough. The 4th Lord Raglan succeeded to the title in 1921 as the great-grandson of the 1st baron who received the title in 1852 when Commander-in-Chief of the British Forces in the Crimea.

Lord Raglan was educated at Eton and the Royal Military College, Sandhurst and following the family tradition entered the Army. He joined the Grenadier Guards in 1905 and held the rank of Captain in 1914 and Major in 1919. His first post overseas was A.D.C. to the Governor of Hong Kong (1912-13). In the latter year he joined the Egyptian Army and remained in the Eastern Mediterranean Area until 1921, for the first six years with the Egyptian Forces and later from 1919 until he returned in 1922 he was a political officer in Palestine. In recognition of his services in Egypt he was made an Officer of the Order of the Nile.

The military phase may be considered as the first phase of Lord Raglan's life for it was followed in the 1930s by a second, though somewhat different, one. It is clear, however, that both phases are closely related. During his service with the Egyptian Forces he became deeply interested in the archaeology of ancient Egypt as well as the physical anthropology of the native troops, being, for example, particularly fascinated by the fine physique of the Nilotic negroes. These interests he developed on his return to Britain. In 1932 he took an active part, with his close friend C. Darryll Forde (then Professor of geography and anthropology at the U.C.W., Aberystwyth) in the excavations in that and later years conducted at the important Iron Age hill fort of Pen Dinas, outside Aberystwyth. By 1933 he was sufficiently advanced in anthropology to become president that year of Section H (Anthropology) of the British Association for the Advancement of Science, while during the two years (1945-47) his interests in social anthropology were recognized by his election to the presidency of the Folklore Society. Ten years later he was president of the Royal Anthropological Institute of Great Britain and had been elected a Fellow of the Society of Antiquaries of London. Meanwhile he turned his full attention to Wales and the archaeological field, occupying a succession of key positions at the National Museum of Wales, Cardiff. In 1947-51 he was chairman of the Museum Archaeology and Art Committee, in 1950-52, treasurer of the Museum, in 1952-57 vice-president and finally, in 1957-62, president.

Ever since his return to Britain he was not only an active member of many societies but interested in administrative duties in national institutions but also published a large number of important and interesting books and papers on archaeology and anthropology. In 1933 appeared *Jocasta's crime - an anthropological study*, and in the same year *The Science of peace* and followed in 1934 by *If I were dictator*. Two years later saw *The Hero - a study in tradition, myth and drama* followed three years later by *How came civilization?* After World War II there followed several studies in primitive religion; 1945 saw *Death and Re-birth*, 1949 *The Origins of Religion* and in 1964 *The Temple and the house*. While Lord Raglan became more and more closely associated with the National Museum he naturally became more closely associated with the director, Sir Cyril Fox (see above) and in the years 1951-54 a *Survey of Monmouthshire Houses*, I-III, prepared in collaboration with Sir Cyril Fox, appeared. This work was a survey of pioneer importance.

Lord Raglan's anthropological work has not been universally well received. This is largely due to the fact that the topics discussed are too contentious, complex and wide ranging to be dealt with within the confines of a single volume. The topics also present a temptation to provide simple solutions for highly complex situations, e.g. that men wear hats because they wish to be like kings who wear crowns. Many scholars too are of the opinion that Lord Raglan, an interesting and charming man, loved deliberately to provoke those who held strongly opposite views to his own and to watch with amusement their reactions, yet remaining on the most intimate personal terms with those who disagreed with him. His well-known views concerning the marked emergence of Welsh national feeling in post-World War II Wales is a case in point.

Behind his military, anthropological and archaeological interests and achievements there is yet another facet of Lord Raglan's life yet to be added, namely the long and devoted services which he rendered to the old county of Monmouth and to the whole of Gwent. He was a Justice of the Peace for the county as early as 1909 and served for twenty-one years (1928-49) as a member of the former Monmouthshire county council. He took a great interest in the Boy Scout movement and was county commissioner for Monmouthshire for twenty seven years (1927-54). He was deputy Lord Lieutenant for the county in 1930, becoming Lord Lieutenant in 1960. In 1923 he married the Hon. Julia Hamilton, daughter of the 11th Baron Belhaven. There were two sons and two daughters. The family home was at Cefntilla Court, Usk, Gwent. He d. 14 Sept. 1964.

Report of the British Association for the Advancement of Science, 1933; personal knowledge.

E.G.B.

SOULSBY, Sir LLEWELLYN THOMAS GORDON (1885-1966), naval architect; b. at Swansea, 24 Jan. 1885, son of James C. Soulsby, marine surveyor. He was educated at Jarrow-on-Tyne and apprenticed there to naval architecture at the works of Palmers' Shipbuilding Co. He worked for a while with John Thornycroft and Co., a firm specialising in naval destroyer construction at Chiswick, before returning to Jarrow for five years. He m., 1911, Margaret Dickinson; they had no children. His long and distinguished career in the ship-repairing industry began in 1912 when he went to Cardiff as assistant manager to Cardiff Channel Dry Docks and Pontoon Co. In 1919 he went to Newport as manager of C.H. Bailey Ltd., returning in 1928 to Cardiff as general manager of all the works of the Channel Co. operating in Cardiff, Newport, Barry and Avonmouth, until it was amalgamated with the Mountstuart Co. 3 years later. He then became general manager and eventually chairman (1947) of the combined enterprise, Mountstuart Dry Docks Ltd, retiring in 1961. He was also chairman of Stothert and Pitt Ltd., 1946-59, and of several societies associated with the docks. During World War II he was appointed by the Admiralty to the key post of regional director of merchant shipbuilding and repairs in the Bristol Channel and the north-west of England, 1941-47, and in recognition of his services he was knighted in 1944. He d. at his home, 77 Roath Court Road, Cardiff, 9 Jan. 1966.

Www; West. Mail, 10 Jan. 1966; *Times*, 11 Jan. 1966.

M.A.J.

SOUTHALL, REGINALD BRADBURY (1900-65), oil refinery director; b. at Bollington, Cheshire, 5 June 1900, son of the Rev. George Henry Southall, and Harriette his wife. He was educated at West Monmouth School. After spending a few years in the steel industry he joined the laboratory staff of the National Oil

Refineries, (subsequently the British Petroleum Refinery (Llandarcy), Ltd.), when the Llandarcy refinery came into operation in 1921 and he remained there except for short absences abroad. He saw the works grow to become the company's second largest refinery in the U.K., whilst he progressed from being works manager in 1942, to become a director in 1950. In 1960 he also became director of British Hydrocarbon Chemicals, Ltd., whose plant at Baglan Bay was fed by the Llandarcy refinery. He was a wise counsellor and was deeply involved with industrial organisations in Wales as a member of the Welsh Regional Board for Industry, director of the Development Corporation for Wales, 1958-64, chairman of the Welsh Advisory Water Committee, and member of the British Transport Docks Board, 1963-65. He was U.K. delegate to the International Labour Office of the Petroleum Industry Committee from its inception in 1947 to 1960.

He became a J.P. in 1954 and was president of the Swansea Chamber of Commerce, 1958-59. He showed a keen interest in scientific education and published various articles. He was vice-president of the University College of Swansea, 1956-64, and a governor of the Welsh College of Advanced Technology. He served on the Robbins committee on higher education, 1961-63, and became a member of the newly formed Central Training Council in 1964. In 1956 he was elected the first chairman of the Industrial Museum of South Wales. He received the C.B.E. in 1953 for his public services, and an hon. LL.D. of the University of Wales in 1962. In 1925 he m. Phyllis May Hemming. They had one daughter and lived at The Meadows, Bishopston, Swansea. He d. 1 Dec. 1965.

Www; Times, 2 Dec. 1965, 18f.

M.A.J.

STANTON, CHARLES BUTT (1873-1946), M.P. for the Merthyr and Aberdare constituency, 1915-1922; b. Aberaman, Aberdare, Glam., 7 Apr. 1873. On leaving school he was first employed as a pageboy with a family in Bridgend but later worked as a miner in his home town. He first came to public notice in the hauliers' strike of 1893, when, in one of the many skirmishes which occurred between the miners and the police, he was alleged to have fired a gun. He was charged and convicted of possessing a firearm without a licence and sentenced to six months imprisonment. He was prominent later in the coal strike of 1898 and in the London dock strike of the same year for he had sought work in the docks following the closure of the mines in Aberdare. He returned, however, and was one of the founder-members of the Independent Labour Party in the district in 1900, which invited Keir Hardie to be the successful candidate in the election of 1900. From 1903 to 1908 Stanton was a member of the Aberdare Urban District Council. On Hardie's death in 1915 Stanton was returned as member for the constituency in the by-election and stood as a supporter of the Government in its conduct of the war. He was opposed by James Winstone (*DWB*, 1088), then president of the South Wales Miners' Federation. He was re-elected in the general election of 1918, defeating T.E. Nicholas who stood as a pacifist candidate.

In 1919-20 Stanton was made High Constable of Miskin Higher and in 1920 he received the C.B.E. In 1929 he was defeated by G.H. Hall (see above), the official Labour candidate. He resided for the rest of his life at Hampstead.

He was a man of distinguished appearance and during the 1920s and 1930s he acted in a number of films, ironically enough taking the part of aristocrats or clergymen. He was married and had two s., one of whom was killed in 1917.

He d. in London, 6 Dec. 1946.

Private information; *Www*.

H.M.-J.

STAPLEDON, Sir REGINALD GEORGE (1882-1960), agricultural scientist; b. 22 May 1882 in Northam, Devon, youngest son of William and Mary Stapledon. He was educated at the United Services College, Westward Ho, and Emmanuel College, Cambridge, receiving his M.A. in botany in 1904. After working in the family's commercial office in Cairo for about two years he spent a year as a student on a large fruit farm in Kent. In 1908 he returned to Cambridge to follow a diploma course in agriculture, and this was the turning-point which led to his life's work into the study of grassland. From 1909-12 he was Prof. of Agricultural Botany in the Royal Agricultural College, Cirencester, and in this period his exceptional interest in grassland ecology became evident, particularly in relation to the impact of the dry summer of 1911 on the natural pastures of the Cotswolds. In 1912 he was appointed advisor in agricultural botany to the counties in the Aberystwyth college area (under the Agriculture and Fisheries Board), and this was the start of his long association with agriculture in Wales. One of his tasks during his first two years in that office was to undertake a review of the grassland of north Cardiganshire as a part of the comprehensive review of agriculture, geology and botany by C. Bryner Jones (see above), O.T. Jones (see above) and R.A. Yapp respectively. From 1916-18 he was director of the Official Seed Testing Station established during that period in London. Then, in 1919, he was appointed as the first director of the Welsh Plant Breeding Station and head of the Agricultural Botany department established in that period in University College of Wales, Aberystwyth. It was in the Plant Breeding Station between 1919 and 1942, in association with committed colleagues of his own choosing, that Stapledon accomplished his life's major work – work which enormously influenced the art, science and indeed the principles of grassland management throughout the world. The Agricultural Bureaux of the Empire (later the Commonwealth) were established in this period with Stapledon as director of the one for Grassland and Field Crops founded in Aberystwyth in 1927. In addition he was also the director of the Cahn Hill Improvement Scheme set up in 1933 to convert the results of minor experiments to improve the uplands of the hill-country of Cardiganshire into a large-scale practical project located on part of the Hafod Uchtryd estate in Cwm Ystwyth. In 1942 he left Aberystwyth to concentrate on his new post as director of the Grassland Improvement Station established in

Stratford-upon-Avon in 1940. On retirement from this office in 1945 he was consultant and one of the directors of Dunn's Farm Seeds at Salisbury until overtaken by frailty and profound deafness in his later years. Without doubt, in his time Stapledon was the most eminent agricultural scientist in the world as well as the foremost authority on grassland. Under his inspired leadership, the Welsh Plant Breeding Station at Aberystwyth became the most prestigious research establishment in Britain and abroad for grassland and plant breeding studies. He was honoured with a C.B.E. in 1932; in 1939 he was knighted and also became a Fellow of the Royal Society; he received an honorary D.Sc. from the Universities of Wales and Nottingham. He was awarded the gold medal of the Royal Agricultural Society for England, and was the president of the Fourth International Grassland Conference held in Aberystwyth in 1937. He published numerous scientific and agricultural articles and edited volumes on grassland and land improvement. His publications include: *Grassland, its improvement and management* (with J.A. Hanley, 1927); *A tour in Australia and New Zealand; Grassland and other studies* (1928); *The hill lands of Britain: development or decay?* (1937); *The plough-up: policy and ley farming* (1941); *Make fruitful the land: a policy for agriculture* (1941); *The way of the land* (1943); *Disraeli and the new age* (1943). But, without doubt, his masterpiece was his book *The land now and tomorrow* (1935).

He m. Doris Wood Bourne in 1913, but they had no children. He d. in Bath 16 Sept. 1960, and a memorial service was held in the Plant Breeding Station near Aberystwyth. The Stapledon Memorial Trust was established to enable young agricultural scientists from both England and Wales to undertake research in another Commonwealth country.

Personal knowledge; *Ww*; *Jnl. Brit. Grassland Soc.*, 15 April 1960; *Biog. Memoirs Fellows R.S.*, 7, 1961; Robert Waller, *Prophet of the New Age* (1962).

LI.P.

STEEGMAN, JOHN EDWARD HORATIO (1899-1966), author of books on art and architecture; b. 10 Dec. 1899 near Brentford, the elder son of E.J. Steegman, a naval doctor, and his wife Mabel (née Barnet). He was educated at Clifton College and King's College, Cambridge, where he graduated M.A. He was a cadet-officer in 1918 and a reporter for a short time before being appointed in 1925 as a lecturer and guide at the National Portrait Gallery in London; he was an assistant keeper there from 1929 to 1945. He was seconded to the British Council to work in Spain, Portugal, Iceland and Palestine during World War II. He settled in Cardiff after his appointment as Keeper of the department of art at the National Museum of Wales in 1945. He left in 1952 to become head of the Museum of Fine Arts in Montreal, Canada, where he remained until 1959. He was visiting professor at the University of Chicago in 1950. After his retirement he was in much demand as a lecturer in Europe, the Middle East, U.S.A., Canada, Australia and New Zealand.

During his period at the National Museum the department of art became an important centre for the study of the work of Richard Wilson

(*DWB*, 1087-8), and he gave encouragement to contemporary art in Wales. Before leaving the Museum he compiled a catalogue of the Gwendoline Davies (see above) bequest. He came to Wales as a specialist on British portraiture and his main contribution to the Museum was his survey of portraits in Welsh houses. His *Survey of portraits in North Wales houses* (1955) was published after he had left Wales; the survey of south Wales was completed by R.L. Charles and published in 1961. He published a number of articles and other books on art, including *Hours in the National Portrait Gallery* (1928) and *The artist and the country house* (1949). He himself was a watercolourist, and his only brother Philip was a portrait painter. He was unmarried and returned to live at 9 Sloane Gardens, London, but d. in Coffinswell, Devon, on 15 April 1966. He received the O.B.E. in 1952.

Www; information from A.D. Fraser Jenkins.

E.D.J.

STEPHEN, DOUGLAS CLARK (1894-1960), newspaper editor; b. at Leicester, 1894, s. of John T. Stephen; he began his career in journalism by helping his father report sport and general news for the Press Association. After training for five years on the *Leicester Mail* he joined the *Sporting Chronicle* at Manchester as a sub-editor, and worked on the *North Star* at Darlington for a short while before moving to work as a sub-editor on the *South Wales Echo* in 1916. He was appointed editor in 1922 at a time when intense rivalry between local newspapers resulted in the merging of *The South Wales News* with *The Western Mail*, and *The Evening Express* with *The South Wales Echo*. Under his direction *The Echo* grew in size, circulation and prestige. He demanded high professional standards and total integrity whilst giving encouragement, advice and support to successive generations of young journalists, many of whom later became well known Fleet Street personalities, Percy Cudlipp (see above) being one of them. In 1946 he was one of ten provincial editors who toured France at the invitation of the French Provincial Press. He was made a Fellow of the Institute of Journalists in 1951 and was president of the institute two years later. In 1955 he was elected to the board of directors of the Western Mail and Echo Ltd. He retired in 1957 but the following year, as assistant press officer to the Empire Games in Cardiff, he organised the press facilities which won world-wide journalistic tributes. He d. 4 June 1960 at his home, 7 Holmwood Terrace, Cyncoed, Cardiff, leaving a widow, Lucy Helena Stephen.

S. Wales Echo and *Times*, 6 June 1960; WWP.

M.A.J.

STEPHEN, ROBERT (1878-1966), schoolmaster, historian and poet; b. 30 Sept. 1878, in Penygroes, Caerns., son of Urias Stephen, railway signalman, and his wife, Anne. Robert received his early education in Penygroes, Clynnog, and the secondary school at Oswestry. He went to Bangor University College in Oct. 1896. He then taught in the elementary school, Cyffylliog, in 1899 and then returned to Bangor, where he graduated in

Welsh in 1903. He taught in London from 1903 to 1908. In 1907 he was awarded an M.A. of the University of Wales for a thesis entitled 'The Poetic Works of Bedo Aerddrem, Bedo Brwynllys, and Bedo Phylip Bach'. In 1908 he went as a teacher to a boarding school in Taunton, but left after a year because he was not offered a living-out post. In Jan. 1909, he was appointed a teacher in the grammar school at Pontypool (Jones' West Monmouthshire School), where he stayed until he retired in 1948. He was a very versatile man. He taught Welsh, history, geography, and mathematics. In Aug. 1913 he took a course in geography at the University College in Aberystwyth in order to be able to teach history and geography as a joint course. Professor H.J. Fleure (see above) said that he had a freshness of attitude only rarely found in teachers who had been out of University for more than ten years. When the chemistry and physics teachers went to the army in World War I he undertook the work of teaching these subjects through the school, taking a special interest in physics.

He was an enthusiastic *eisteddfod* competitor throughout his life. In the national *eisteddfod* in Llangollen in 1908, when the adjudicator was Sir Owen M. Edwards (*DWB*, 192-3), he won the first prize for a collection of the work of Guto'r Glyn. Sir Owen kept the work, intending to publish it, but it never appeared. In the national *eisteddfod* in Colwyn Bay, 1910, again under the adjudication of Sir Owen M. Edwards, Stephen shared the prize with the Revd. D.R. Jones, Cardiff, for the best collection of the unpublished work of any Welsh poet of Tudor times, with a short biography of the bard and critical notes of his work. It is not known what became of this work. In the national *eisteddfod* of Abergavenny, 1913, he shared the prize with Peter Williams (Pedr Hir, *DWB*, 1064) for a play in verse on the life and death of William Herbert of Raglan Castle, first Earl of Pembroke. He wrote poetry, in both the strict and free metres, and plays, throughout his life. He was also a skilled musician, and came from the same stock as Edward Jones Stephen ('Tanymarian', *DWB*, 923) and Robert Stephen ('Moelwyn fardd', 1828-79), who was a police officer in Conwy. He won the prize in the Ystradgynlais national *eisteddfod* in 1954, for a translation into Welsh of the libretto of *Princess Ju Ju*. His translation of the *Bohemian Girl* was performed in Penygroes, his native village, on 11 Dec. 1947. He published, at his own expense, about a dozen to twenty musical compositions. He was the General Secretary of the national *eisteddfod* of Pontypool in 1924, and General Secretary of the first musical festival held in Llandudno, in Oct. 1945, and many times afterwards. He was a member of the *Gorsedd*, under the bardic name, 'Robin Eryri'.

He was married twice: (1) to Alice Noel Jones, daughter of a sea captain from Borth-y-Gest. They had three children, (2) in Caxton Hall, London, on 8 Jan. 1942, to Mary Elizabeth Owen, widow of Captain Ralph D. Owen, army officer, and daughter of Edmund and Elizabeth Thomas, Gelli Haf, Maesycwmmer. The Gelli Haf family was very famous in Monmouthshire, and connected in some way with the family of William Thomas ('Islwyn', *DWB*, 972-3).

After his second marriage, he began to take interest in the lacquer industry of Pontypool. In 1947 he contributed an article on the industry in the periodical *Apollo*, and another in *Antiques* (New York, 1951). He contributed an article on the Allgood family to the *Dictionary of Welsh Biography*, 6. His manuscripts on the Allgood family, and the lacquer industry, are in the National Museum in Cardiff, and the remainder of his manuscripts are in the library of the University College, Bangor, excepting the manuscript of his collection of the work of the three Bedos, which is in the National Library.

He d. in his home in Colwyn Bay on Jan. 2nd. 1966.

Personal knowledge.

De.J.

STEPHENS, JOHN OLIVER (1880-1957), Independent minister and professor at the Presbyterian College, Carmarthen; b. at Llwyn-yr-hwrdd, Pembs., 12 May 1880, son of John Stephens, the Independent minister of Llwyn-yr-hwrdd and Bryn-myrnach, and Martha his wife. He was educated at Tegryn school, Cardigan county school and the Presbyterian College, Carmarthen (1900-02, 1906-09), University College Cardiff (1902-06), Cheshunt College, Cambridge (1909-12). He had a brilliant career, winning several scholarships and at the beginning of his preparatory course at the Presbyterian College, before he went on to University, one of the external examiners had referred to him as a young man of exceptional abilities. He graduated with a B.A. (with honours in philosophy), B.D. (Wales) and M.A. (Cantab.). At Cambridge he was a student of Sir James George Frazer. In 1912 he was ordained as a minister, without pastoral care of a church, at Llwyn-yr-hwrdd and in the same year he was appointed to the chair of Philosophy at the Presbyterian College. He was also responsible for teaching Christian doctrine, the history of religions and Christian ethics. He was instrumental in persuading the faculty of theology of the University of Wales to establish a course on Christian ethics independent of that on Christian doctrine. For a period of forty-five years as professor and teacher he introduced generations of students to a pattern of scholarship and culture that went far beyond the bounds of the subjects he taught.

He was learned in Welsh, English, German and French literature and as early as 1914 he pleaded for more attention to be given to the fine arts in Wales (see 'Y prydferth yng Nghymru', *Y Geninen*, Oct. 1914). In 1916 he received an invitation to become the minister of the church at Union Street, Carmarthen. He served that church for a period of forty-one years. He was the president of the Union of Welsh Independents, 1942-43 and the Dean of the faculty of theology of the University of Wales, 1955-57. He contributed widely to Welsh periodicals. In *Y Geninen*, apart from the reviews and the portraits of men such as George Essex Evans, Dewi Emrys, Dylan Thomas and Dyfnallt, there is a translation by him of a short story by Guy de Maupassant, 'Le Retour' (Jan. 1921); a warm appreciation of the contribution of Professor Edmund Crosby Quiggin, the Celtic scholar, and a study on the Celts and warfare (Summer 1956: a translation by D. Eirwyn Morgan of 'Keltic War Gods' that was published in *Religions*, July 1941). Through his regular contributions to *Y Tyst* he presented the thoughts and views of men like Henri Bergson, Nicolas Berdyaev, Karl Barth and Leonhard Ragaz. In the column 'Myfyrgell y Diwinydd' which he began in Feb. 1939, he discussed skilfully a host of subjects such as the early religion of Europe, the earliest European civilisation and the divine meaning of history. In *Y Dysgedydd* (Jan; Aug; Nov. 1955; July 1956) he dealt with the contribution of some of the foremost theological philosophers of Russia. One of his most notable contributions, 'The True Quality of Prayer', was published in the journal *Religions* (Oct. 1940). He delivered the Upton Lectures in 1940, choosing as his subject, 'The crisis in social psychology'. He also contributed articles dealing with sociology, the principles of Independence (Congregationalism) and with the Welsh of Australia.

In November 1927 he sailed to Australia to try to improve his health. He chronicled the story of his journey in 'A year in Australia' (*Y Dysgedydd*, Feb. 1931-Mar 1932) and in a travel book that is in the National Library of Wales (N.L.W. 20591) - two priceless sources for information about the Welsh connections of that continent. People sought to persuade him to make his home there, but he returned to Carmarthen and to Wales to enrich its life and culture as a professor, theologian and philosopher, and also to adorn it through the force of his enchanting personality. He died on 10 Mar. 1957.

D.L. Trefor Evans in *Athrawon ac Annibynwyr* (ed. Pennar Davies), (1971); Dewi Eirug Davies, *Hoff ddysgedig nyth* (1976), 211-5.

D.A.E.D.

STEPHENSON, THOMAS ALAN (1898-1961), zoologist; b. 19 Jan. 1898 at Burnham-on-Sea, Somerset, son of Thomas Stephenson, D.D., minister (Meth.) and his wife Margaret Ellen (née Fletcher). He was educated at Clapham; Wrexham; and Kingswood School, Bath, 1909-13. In 1915 he was admitted to the University College of Wales, Aberystwyth (where the family lived 1914-19) but was unable to take up his place because of ill-health. Professor Herbert John Fleure (see above) taught him privately, appointed him demonstrator, and obtained for him the sea anemones collected by the British Antarctic Expedition of 1910 which were the subject of his first paper, published in 1916. Though holding no initial degree he was allowed to submit published papers for the degrees of M.Sc. and D.Sc. He was elected a Fellow of the Royal Society in 1951. In 1922 he was appointed lecturer in zoology at University College, London, and he collaborated with his father during 1920-24 in the publication of articles on British orchids in *Journ. of Botany*. He was in charge of the reef section of the Great Barrier Reef Expedition of 1928-29 (*Reports*, vol. 3) and he made a major contribution to the understanding of the growth of reef-building corals. In 1930 he was appointed Professor of zoology at the University of Cape Town, South Africa, where he organised an extended survey of the distribution of marine plants and animals along the 1800-mile coast. In 1941 he became Professor of zoology at Aberystwyth and made pioneer studies of the

coast of north America in 1947, 1948 and 1952. He was a fine lecturer and his study of design and colour in nature together with his own artistic talent is evident in his illustrations to his two volumes, *The British sea anemones* (1928, 1935), and *Seashore life and pattern* (1944).

In 1922 he m. Anne Wood of Somerset and Barry who became a close collaborator in his research. He d. 3 Apr. 1961.

Www; *Biog. Memoirs Fellows R.S.*, 8, 1962, 137-46; see *ibid.*, 147-8 for a bibliography of his published papers.

M.A.J.

STONE, TIMOTHY - see ELLIS, THOMAS IORWERTH above.

STONELAKE, EDMUND WILLIAM (1873-1960), politician and a key figure in establishing the Labour Party in the Merthyr Boroughs constituency; b. 5 Apr. 1873 in Merchant St., Pontlotyn, Rhymney valley, Glam., last of the ten children of George and Hannah Stonelake. His mother (b. in Gloucester) had a strong influence on him. He was brought up in a non-Welsh and Anglican home: two attributes which set him outside the Nonconformist, Welsh-speaking, Liberal culture characteristic of the south Wales coalfield during the 19th c. He left school at the age of ten and began working underground at eleven after his mother, in their poverty, had altered his certificate of birth, but he had to leave the pit within a month when this was discovered, recommencing when he was 12. Towards the end of 1888 he and his widowed mother moved to live with an older brother at Aberdare because coalminers' wages were higher there, and he came into contact with the radical tradition of the valley. Stonelake said that the move had 'saved his soul'. About 1892 his public life began with a local friendly society and as a student in a class held by C.A.H. Green (see above), vicar of Aberdare. By 1895 Stonelake considered himself to be a Socialist, and he was elected to the committee of the Co-operative Movement, the Workers' Hall and his colliery lodge. Eventually he became chairman of the District Miners' Executive Council for Aberdare. He was one of the first students from Wales to attend Ruskin College in Aug. 1901. The experience made a lasting impression on him, but he returned in five months to the coalmine at Aberdare. He remained at the coalface until 1913 when he was elected by his fellow-workers in Bwllfa mine as safety inspector in the mine in compliance with the 1911 Mining Act. He was the first person in Britain to be elected thus, but his right was disputed by the company which was owned by the family of Sir D. R. Llewellyn (see Supplement below) until Keir Hardie secured his authority in the House of Commons. He was afterwards elected minimum wage representative for his fellow-workers, and he retained these posts until 1946. By 1897 he was a member of the Aberdare Socialist Society and was secretary of the local Trades Unions Council, 1902-29. At the suggestion of this Council in 1902 Labour candidates began to be nominated regularly for election to the local authority in Aberdare. In 1904 Stonelake was himself elected to the authority, and he was chairman of the local council, 1909-10. Stonelake and the Labour members pressed the authority to embark on a policy of public ventures. They initiated a public tram system and an electricity supply for house and street lighting; and as an education authority under the 1902 Act they opened a school for physically disabled children and those with learning difficulties (1913) and a baby clinic (1915). Stonelake himelf was most proud of the appointment of a health officer for the authority's schools in 1907, and later of a service to provide meals for pupils in need. He was also prominent in establishing Aberdare General Hospital (1915). Between 1904-14 he led a strong campaign against the poor condition of houses in the area. Consequently, the local council began to build houses shortly before the War and resumed the work in 1918. However a scandal concerning financial corruption among some of the council house officials between 1919-22 cost Stonelake dearly as chairman of the housing committee; although he had no part in the offence he lost his seat permanently on the authority in 1922. His innocence was confirmed by his appointment as J.P. in 1928 (an office he held until 1950). He was the co-ordinator in the effort to support about 10,000 miners and their families during their strike in 1926 which lasted six months after the General Strike ended. He was secretary of the Labour Party in the constituency (1929-45), and spent much of his time during the depression of the 1930s organizing the protests of the unemployed and preparing them for trials in the Court of Referees which constantly challenged their right to benefit payments.

He utterly despised C.B. Stanton (see above) for 'retreating from his party' and betraying Keir Hardie in the hour of need in 1914. Stonelake was the Representative for every candidate who stood in opposition to Stanton after Keir Hardie's death, and his comments on T.E. Nicholas and the 1918 election in particular are revealing. Stonelake was never a national figure, but he served leaders on the broader front. He worked hard to ensure that the Labour Party was deeply rooted in the south Wales coalfield. The span of his activity extended from the marginal days of the I.L.P. at the end of the 19th century up to the first time a Labour government obtained a secure majority under Attlee in 1945. His life is a classical example of the effort which gave the Labour Party supremacy in south Wales politics in the 20th c.

He m., in 1895, Rebecca Hobbs (d. 1950) and they had six sons and two daughters. He d. 5 Apr. 1960.

A. Mor-O'Brien (ed.), *The autobiography of E. Stonelake* (1981); *Aberdare Trades & Labour Council Jubilee Souvenir* (1950); *Morgannwg*, 26 (1982), 53-71; *Aberdare Almanack*, 1904-22; *WwW* (1921 & 1937); W.W. Price deposits at Aberdare Central Library; *Merthyr Express*, 8.8.1914; *Aberdare Leader*, 15.8.1914, 8.4.1922, 16.9.1922, 11.5.1929, 9.4.1960 and 7.5.1960; *Llafur*, 4, no. 3 (1986), 31-54; *Welsh History Review*, 14, no. 3 (1989), 399-416; information from his grandson.

D.L.D.

STRACHAN, GILBERT INNES (1888-1963), professor of medicine; b. in Bristol, Aug. 1883, the son of James Strachan and his wife Agnes (née Todd). He was educated at the high school and the University of Glasgow where he graduated

M.B., Ch.B., in 1910 and M.D. in 1913. He was at the London Hospital until World War I when he became a captain in the Medical Corps. He came to Cardiff in 1919 as an assistant pathologist to study abortions. He played a significant part in establishing a clinical school in Cardiff. He was appointed Professor of Obstetrics and Gynaecology at the Welsh National School of Medicine in 1932 and remained in post until his retirement in 1953. He was a fluent lecturer, though doctrinaire, he inspired his listeners and made a deep impression on generations of students. He worked indefatigably at the hospital and had a private practice. He pioneered the radium treatment of womb cancer and contributed extensively to the subject in medical literature. He wrote clearly and with ease on a number of subjects and published a standard textbook, *Textbook of obstetrics* (1947). He served the universities of Wales, Birmingham, Bristol and Oxford as an examiner in his subject. He went to Sydney and Melbourne in 1950 to lecture and to examine students on behalf of the Royal College of Obstetrics and Gynaecology of which he was a founder member; he became a vice-president in 1952-55. He took an enthusiastic interest in politics and the arts. He donated much of his fine collection of Spode porcelain and china to the National Museum of Wales. He received the C.B.E. in 1953.

He m. Olive, only daughter of F.E. Andrews, in 1920; they had one son. He made his home at 29 Cathedral Road, Cardiff, where he d. on 9 Dec. 1963.

Times, 14 Dec. 1963; [*Med. Directory*; *Www*].

E.D.J.

SYKES, MARY GLADYS - see under THODAY, DAVID below.

T

TANNER, PHILIP (1862-1950), folk singer; b. at Llangennith (Gower), 16 Feb. 1862. He was a weaver, born of a long line of weavers, and was the last to wear 'Gower tweed'. In his early days, he often acted as 'bidder' at weddings. He remembered a considerable number of old Gower folk-songs, and also the traditional 'reels' and 'hornpipies' of that countryside, and with his help these were recorded by the Gower Society. He d. 19 Feb. 1950, at Penmaen in Gower.

West. Mail, 20 Feb. 1950; *Baner*, 22 Feb. 1950.

R.T.J.

TEGLA - see DAVIES, EDWARD TEGLA above.

TELYNOR MAWDDWY - see ROBERTS, DAVID above.

TEMPLE, ANNE - see under HUGHES, HYWEL STANFORD above.

THICKENS, JOHN (1865-1952), minister (Presb.), historian and author; b. 9 Mar. 1865 at Abernantcwta, Cwmystwyth, Cards., son of David and Sarah Thickens. His father d. when he was young, and his mother moved with the family to Pentre, Rhondda Valley. There, in Nazareth chapel, he began to preach, and he trained for the ministry at Trefeca College. He was ord. in 1894, and that year he m. Cecilia Evans of Dowlais (sister of Sir David W. Evans); they had five daughters. He became minister of Libanus, Dowlais (1892-94), and Tabernacl, Aberaeron (1894-1907). Whilst there he spent much time with his uncle, his mother's brother, Joseph Jenkins (1861-1929; *DWB*, 436, and Supplement below) who was a minister at New Quay, Cards. The outcome of their collaboration was the series of conferences which were held in south Cardiganshire, precursors to the 1904-05 Religious Revival. He moved to London in 1907 as pastor of Willesden Green church, and remained there until he retired in 1945. He lived variously at Aberaeron, Neath and Llanwrtyd Wells, eventually settling in Leamington Spa, where he d. 29 Nov. 1952; his ashes were transferred from Cambridge Crematorium to Henfynyw churchyard, near Aberaeron.

He was a notable preacher at the height of his power, and at times had fiery meetings. He was a mystic by nature, and despite his great interest in theology, his favourite study was the history and hymnody of the mystics. He was prominent in the life of his denomination, serving as Moderator of the South Wales Association (1938) and Moderator of the General Assembly (1945). He published a commentary on the Acts of the Apostles in 1925 and delivered the Davies Lecture in 1934, which was published as a substantial volume in 1938 under the title *Howel Harris yn Llundain*. He steeped himself in the history and ethos of the Presbyterian Church of Wales; he was chairman of the History Committee (1939-52), and he contributed a great deal to its journal. His astute articles on the Methodist 'fathers' appeared in the beautifully produced booklet published by the London Presbytery in 1935 to celebrate the bicentenary of the Methodist Revival. He was editor of *Y Drysorfa* (1929-33), to which he contributed much, as well as to *Y Traethodydd* and *Y Goleuad*. He had the natural instinct and meticulousness of the true historian, always insisting on consulting original sources. He tended to be diverted by minutiae, and that possibly is the weakness of his Davies Lecture. His pedantic and over-grammatical style was also a stumbling block for many of his admirers. He was a member of the committee for the Welsh Methodist hymnal (1927). He researched much of the history of the hymnwriters and their works, and prepared a useful handbook to accompany the collection, *Emynau a'u Hawduriaid* (1947; 1961, 'new edition, revised, with additions', by Gomer M. Roberts). As much as he had written of his intended biography of his famous uncle, Joseph Jenkins, was published in *Y Drysorfa*, 1961-63.

Trys. Plant, 1938, 68-71; *Drys.*, 1938, 90-4 and Apr. 1953; *Gol.*, 31 Dec. 1952; *Blwyddiadur MC*, 1954, 232-3; S. Evans and G.M. Roberts (eds.), *Cyfrol goffa y Diwygiad 1904-1905* (1954), 22ff.; W. Morris (ed.), *Deg o Enwogion* (1965), 27-34; information from the Rev. D. Lewis Evans; personal acquaintance.

G.M.R.

THODAY, DAVID (1883-1964), botanist, university professor; b. 5 May 1883 at Honiton, Devon, the eldest of the six children of David Thoday, schoolmaster, and Susan Elizabeth (née Bingham) his wife. The family moved to London where he attended Tottenham grammar school, 1894-98, before entering Trinity College, Cambridge in 1902. He specialised in botany under the direction of H. Marshall Ward, A.C. Seward and F.F. Blackman, gaining first class in both parts of the Tripos in 1905 and 1906, and he won the Walsingham Medal in 1908. After serving as university demonstrator in botany at Cambridge for two years (1909-11) he was appointed a lecturer in Physiological Botany in Manchester University in 1911 and became Harry Bolas Professor of Botany in Cape Town University, South Africa in 1918. In 1923 he succeeded Reginald W. Phillips as Professor of Botany at the University College of North Wales, Bangor, where he remained until he reached the age of retirement in 1949. After retiring he became Professor of Plant Physiology at the University of Alexandria, Egypt, but returned to Bangor in 1955.

He obtained a Sc.D. degree at Cambridge, was elected F.R.S. in 1942 and received an hon. D.Sc. of the University of Wales in 1960. He published *Botany: a textbook for senior students* (1915: 5 editions) and many important articles in his field, including a series on succulent plants, *Kleinia articulata*, particularly on their acidic metabolism. His presidential lecture to the British Association, Section K, in 1939, on 'The interpretation of plant structures' was seminal.

He was assisted in much of his work by his

wife whom he m. 15 June 1910, and who, as Mary Gladys Sykes of Girton College and a research fellow of Newnham College, was author of a number of papers on botanical subjects. She was the daughter of John Thorley Sykes of Rossett, Denbs. They had four sons. His wife d. in 1943, and he d. at Llanfairfechan 30 Mar. 1964.

Biog. Memoirs Fellows R.S., xi (1965), 177-83; see ibid., 184-5 for a bibliography of his scientific papers, 1905-63; Times, 1 Apr. 1964.

E.D.J.

THOMAS, DAVID (1880-1967), educationalist, author and pioneer of the Labour Party in north Wales; b. 16 July 1880 son of David Thomas and his wife Elizabeth (née Jones), Quarry Cottage, Llanfechain, Mont. He was educated at Llanfechain and Llanfyllin schools with one term at Oswestry grammar school before going to work in a clothes shop in Llanfyllin. Soon afterwards he went to the British school there as a pupil-teacher (1895-99), later obtaining a post as uncertificated teacher at Pen-sarn, near Amlwch, at Bridgend, Glam., and then Walton-on-Thames. He took the opportunity to attend a class in London on Saturdays to prepare himself for an examination for a teacher's certificate. Afterwards he taught at Cradley; Rhostryfan (1905-09); Tal-y-sarn, Caerns. (1909-20); and Bangor Central School (1922-45). He worked on a farm near Wrexham during World War I as a conscientious objector and was for a short period (1920-22) secretary of the North Wales Labour Council, living in the neighbourhood of Newtown.

He worked energetically to form labour unions and branches of the Independent Labour Party in north Wales, assisting in founding the Caernarfonshire Labour Council in 1912 and the North Wales Labour Council in 1914. He took a leading part in the debate on Socialism in Yr Herald Cymraeg in 1908, followed by the publication of his first book, Y Werin a'i Theyrnas (1910), which left its influence on a number of unionists and Welsh Labour members. He took a keen interest in adult education. He was a tutor of classes held by the Workers' Educational Association in Caernarfonshire for a long period (1928-59), and he maintained an official connection with the society until his d. In 1944 he commenced the publication of Lleufer, the Workers' Educational Association periodical which he edited until 1965. He gained a M.A. degree for a dissertation on 'A study of a rural and maritime community in the nineteenth century, with special reference to the relation between agriculture and shipping' (Liverpool; 1928), and an hon. M.A. degree of the University of Wales in 1960.

He was a very effective speaker and radio broadcaster and he wrote many articles, pamphlets and books on a wide range of political, literary and historical topics, including: Y Blaid Lafur a Dinasyddiaeth y Gweithiwr (1912), Y Cynganeddion Cymreig (1923), Y Ddinasyddiaeth Fawr (1938), Hen longau a llongwyr Cymru (1949), Cau'r tiroedd comin (1952), Llafur a senedd i Gymru: ysgrifau, llythyrau a sgyrsiau (1954), a biography of Silyn (Robert Silyn Roberts) 1871-1930 (1956), and Ann Griffiths a'i

theulu (1963); also 'Glendid iaith', a weekly column on grammar in Y Faner (c. 1957-62). As a tribute to him he was presented with the volume, Ben Bowen Thomas (ed.), Lleufer y werin; cyfrol deyrnged i David Thomas, M.A. (1965), and his autobiography was published posthumously, Diolch am gael byw (1968). Some of his papers are kept at the National Library of Wales.

He m. 26 July 1919, Elizabeth Ann Williams, New Broughton (d. 1955 after a very long illness) and they had a son and a daughter. He d. at the home of his daughter, the widow of Herman Jones (see above), at 2 Pen-y-bryn, Burry Port, Carms. on 27 June 1967.

His autobiography; D. Ben Rees, Cymry adnabyddus 1952-72 (1978); WWP.

M.A.J.

THOMAS, DAVID EMLYN (1892-1954), politician and trade unionist; b. 16 Sept. 1892 at Maesteg, Glam., one of nine children. His father James Thomas was a native of Cilgerran, Pembs. and his mother hailed from Newcastle Emlyn, Carms. He spent short periods of his childhood at Cilgerran and Cardigan. He was educated at elementary schools at Maesteg, and attended evening classes in mining and mine surveying which enabled him to qualify as an engineer. In 1906, at 13 yrs. of age, he began working as clerk at the Oakwood and Garth collieries, he moved to a colliery at Llantrisant and then to the Caerau colliery, Maesteg. Thomas became a full-time official of the South Wales Miners' Federation in 1919 and served as secretary to Vernon Hartshorn (DWB, 344-45) and Ted Williams (see Williams, Sir Edward John below). In the same year he joined the Labour Party. He became the Aberdare area secretary of the S.W.M.F. in 1934, and he and his family moved to live in the area. In 1936 he was elected by an overwhelming majority as the miners' agent of the Merthyr and Aberdare valleys of the south Wales area of the N.U.M. as successor to Noah Ablett (DWB, 1113), and he became an advisory member of the south Wales area executive of the N.U.M. He became an authority on workmen's compensation.

On 5 Dec. 1946 at a by-election Thomas became M.P. (Lab.) for the Aberdare division in succession to George Hall (see above). He continued to represent this constituency in parliament until his death. He was re-elected with a majority of almost 28,000 votes in 1951. Emlyn Thomas was a quiet, modest individual - 'the gentle man in Welsh politics' - who always served his constituents conscientiously. He was elected chairman of the Welsh Parliamentary Labour group in the House of Commons in 1949-50. His political papers are in the custody of the National Library of Wales. He was a native Welsh-speaker, a deacon and a Sunday school teacher at Ebenezer Independent chapel, Trecynon, Aberdare. He was active in a number of cultural societies in the Cynon Valley, a member of Trecynon Choral Union and numerous eisteddfod committees. Gardening was one of his main interests.

He m. in 1923 Bessie Thomas (she d. 10 Sept. 1953), a schoolteacher at Maesteg. They had a son and two daughters. Following a heart attack he d. on 20 June 1954 at his home 65 Broniestyn Terrace, Trecynon, Aberdare.

Www; Dod's *Parliamentary Companion; West. Mail*, 31 Mar. 1936; *Merthyr Express*, 9 Aug. 1947; *Aberdare Leader*, 14 Dec. 1946, 19 Sept. 1953 and 26 June 1954; *Times*, 21 June 1954; *WWP*.

J.G.J.

THOMAS, DAVID FFRANGCON (1910-63), cellist; b. 19 Sept. 1910 at Plas-marl, Swansea, son of W. Roger Thomas and his wife. He was named Ffrangcon after the singer David Thomas Ffrangcon Davies (*DWB*, 119), one of his father's heroes. When he was eleven years old he began to learn to play the cello under Gwilym Thomas, Port Talbot, and within two years won a scholarship to the Cello School of Herbert Walenn in London. He won prizes at the national *eisteddfod* at Pontypool (1924) and Swansea (1926). After further study at the Royal Music Academy, where he won bronze and silver medals as well as the Ada Lewis Scholarship, he became a member of a number of orchestras, including the London Philharmonic Orchestra and the B.B.C. Symphony Orchestra. He also performed in the Wigmore Hall and in the Royal Opera House, Covent Garden. During World War II he served in the army and then he studied at Prague with Pravoslav Sadlo and Rafael Kubelik. He had an active career as a soloist in Britain and he travelled to Australia and the Far East. He formed a duet with the harpist Osian Ellis, broadcasting and recording for the Delysé company. He endeavoured to form a Welsh orchestra, and succeeded in holding concerts in 1954-55. He m. Dorothy C. Mallinson in 1941 and they had a daughter, Rosalind. He d. 10 Dec. 1963 in London and his ashes were interred in Nicholaston church in Gower.

WWP; *West. Mail*, 11 Dec. 1963; [*Y Ddinas* (London), 1, no. 5, Feb. 1947, 8].

Rh.G.

THOMAS, DYLAN MARLAIS (1914-1953), poet and prose writer; b. 27 Oct. 1914 in Swansea, s. of David John Thomas and his wife Florence Hannah (née Williams) who themselves came from rural, Welsh-speaking families in Cardiganshire, and Carmarthenshire. The father, a nephew of William Thomas 'Gwilym Marles' (*DWB*, 973), was from 1899 to 1936 English master at Swansea grammar school, which Dylan Thomas attended from 1925 to 1931. That was his only period of formal education and was followed by some fifteen months as junior reporter on the *South Wales Daily Post*. His early interest in English poetry had already borne fruit in the four notebooks in which he entered his first mature poems between 1930 and 1933. These notebooks were to be the major source of poems for his first three published volumes: *18 Poems* (London, 1934), *Twenty-five poems* (London, 1936), and *The map of love* (short stories and poems) (London, 1939). Publication of individual poems in London periodicals led to his first volume, and that in turn to his arrival in London in Nov. 1934. During the 1930s his work received increasing American as well as British attention and brought invitations to review books for leading London periodicals. Alternation between literary-social life in London and periods of greater actual creativity in Wales was to remain the pattern throughout

his career. A close friendship with the poet Vernon Watkins (see below) in Swansea started in 1935.

He met Caitlin Macnamara in 1936 and they were m. the following year. In May 1938 they moved for the first time to live in Laugharne, Carms., the village now most intimately associated with his name, and a deep influence on his later work in verse and prose. He had been awarded the American Blumenthal Poetry Prize, and was writing the autobiographical short stories that were to be published as *Portrait of the artist as a young dog* (London, 1940). The comic realism of these stories was in marked contrast to the macabre and surrealistic element in his earlier tales, which can be read in *A Prospect of the sea* (London, 1955). Continuation of autobiographical material in the form of a novel remained unfinished, but was published as *Adventures in the skin trade* (London, 1955). After the outbreak of World War II he started to write radio scripts for the B.B.C. and to take part in broadcast talks and readings. His popularity as a broadcaster remained to the end of his life, and the quality of his work for radio is reflected in the volume *Quite early one morning* (London, 1954). From 1942 to the end of the war he was employed as a script-writer for Strand Films in London. An example of his work in this medium is *The Doctor and the devils* (London, 1953).

The period of war had interrupted his writing of poetry, though towards the end of the war Wales became increasingly his major home. At Llangain and New Quay in 1944-45 a new period of poetic creativity started, the most productive since the early days in Swansea, leading to the publication of *Deaths and entrances* (London, 1946). At the end of the war, however, he also started to show interest in visiting America, and the need to earn a living (mainly through work for films and radio) meant having to be within reach of London. From 1946 to 1949 therefore the poet and his family lived in or near Oxford. He visited Prague in 1949 as guest of the Czechoslovakian government.

He moved to live in the 'Boat House' at Laugharne in May 1949, where his third child was born, and where Thomas hoped to establish a permanent home, helped possibly by visits to America where his reputation as a poet was now firm. The first of these visits was in Feb.-June 1950 and was followed by three more in 1952 and 1953. The individual work which occupied most of his time from 1950 onwards was the radio play *Under Milk Wood* (London, 1954), the main inspiration for which were the atmosphere and inhabitants of Laugharne itself. During the second American tour his last individual volume of poems was published, in America only, as *In country sleep* (New York, 1952). This completed the range of volumes that were to make up his *Collected poems 1934-1952* (London, 1952) and which won the award of the Foyle's Poetry Prize. The complications of heavy drinking and irresponsibility with money meant, however, that not even the profitable American visits were to remove the financial and personal insecurity which made the poet less and less productive of new work at home. He d. in New York on 9 Nov. 1953 and is buried at Laugharne.

Walford Davies, *Dylan Thomas* (1972); [J. Alexander Rolph, *Dylan Thomas: a bibliography* (1974); George M.A. Gaston, *Dylan Thomas: a reference guide* (1987); Ralph Maud, *Dylan Thomas in print* (1970); John Ackerman, *A Dylan Thomas Companion* (1994); and see many biographies, including Paul Ferris (1977), John Ackerman (1964, 1991), G.S. Fraser (1964), Constantine FitzGibbon (1965), Daniel Jones (1977); Walford Davies and Ralph Maud, *Collected Poems* (1994)].

W.D.

THOMAS, EVAN LORIMER (1872-1953), priest and scholar; b. 21 Feb. 1872, son of David Walter Thomas, vicar of St. Ann, Llandygái, Caerns., and his wife Anna ('Morfudd Eryri') (*DWB*, 944). He was educated at Westminster School and Jesus College, Oxford. Like his father, he was a scholar of his college. He was trained for holy orders in the Clerical School, Leeds. He served as curate of St. Mary's, Bangor, 1897-98, Wrexham, 1898-1900, Cuddesdon, Oxon., 1901-02, and Colwyn Bay, 1902-03. He m. Mary Rice-Williams, Holyhead in 1903 and they had a son. In 1903 he became Professor of Welsh at St. David's College, Lampeter. There he made every effort to ensure the position of the Welsh language in the curriculum and in the life of the college. He revived the honours course in Welsh, established a Welsh Library which included the Cenarth Collection which was bought by the college in 1904, and for the sake of the Welsh students he began *Cymdeithas y Brythoniaid*, a society which met every other Saturday evening in his house with not a word of English spoken. On Sunday afternoons he held a Welsh Bible class for the students. He moved in 1915 to be vicar of Holywell, and in 1922 to a similar post in the parish of Tywyn, Abergele. He published Welsh commentaries on St. Luke's Gospel in 1920 and 1922 and on 1 Corinthians in 1934. He became Archdeacon of Montgomery and vicar of Llansanffraid-ym-Mechain in 1938. He retired in 1944 and went to live in Llanfairfechan. He was a gentle and firm man who found pleasure in all kinds of sport, particularly through angling and in ornithology. He d. 9 Apr. 1953, and was buried in St. Seiriol's churchyard, Holyhead.

Www; St. David's University College archives.

D.T.W.P.

THOMAS, EVAN ROBERT (1891-1964), joiner and leader of the Welsh in Australia; b. 8 Jan. 1891 at Yspyty Ifan, Denbs., son of Robert E. Thomas and Jane his wife, but the family moved to Trefriw, Caerns., and he was educated in Llanrwst county school. He emigrated to Australia *c.* 1908. He was a joiner and a noted craftsman and many of his fine wooden panels are in the public buildings of Melbourne.

He knew the problems facing an immigrant and made a practice of meeting every ship arriving from Britain to ensure that any Welshman who landed had a place to go. He was an enthusiastic and indefatigable worker among the Welsh people. When he was secretary (1932-58) of the Cambrian Society which met once a month in St. David's Hall, Latrobe Street, Melbourne, the membership increased from about 30 to over 3000; he was president of the society 1958-59. He contributed a column to

the society's magazine, *The Cambrian*, while it existed (1939-46), and to *The Welsh Australian* before that (1938-39). He served as secretary of the Union of Welsh Societies from 1932 and, as secretary (1934-53) of St. David's Day Association, he organised the annual celebrations, being president in 1955. He kept in contact with Wales: he was elected vice-president of 'Welsh People in Exile' (Wales and the World) in 1960 and a vice-president of the Hon. Soc. of Cymm. in 1957. He m., 7 Aug. 1915, Gwladys B. Davies, Maryborough. They had five children and lived in Ael-y-bryn, 77 Murray Street, Caulfield, Victoria. He d. 6 Sept. 1964 and his funeral service was held in the Welsh chapel, Latrobe Street. He was buried in the new Cheltenham cemetery.

Who's who in Australia, 1962; Myfi Williams, *Cymry Awstralia* (1961), 160-3; *Traf. Cymm.*, 1964, part ii, 350; *Age* (Australian paper), 7 Sept 1964.

M.A.J.

THOMAS, GEORGE ISAAC ('Arfryn'; 1895-1941), musician and composer; b. at Spencer House, Llanboidy, Carms., 29 Nov. 1895, the son of Rhys Morgan and Margaret (née Jones) Thomas. He was educated at the University College, Cardiff (1920-22), and the Royal College of Music (1923-26). He became an A.R.C.M. as an accompanist in Sept. 1924, and A.R.C.O in July 1926. He passed the theory examination in 1927, but lost his health before completing the F.R.C.O course. He conducted the Ammanford and District orchestra from 1914 to 1922. He acted as the accompanist at the national *eisteddfod* at Ammanford in 1922, and as a harpist in Lady Brittain's ('Telynores y Golomen Wen') harp choir in the *eisteddfod* concert. During his stay in London he was organist of Charing Cross chapel (CM), and accompanied and conducted the London-Welsh Male Voice Choir. After returning to Wales he was organist of Bethany chapel, Ammanford. He conducted singing festivals, lectured and composed solos and hymn tunes. He d. 31 Dec. 1941 and was buried in the cemetery of the old chapel, Betws, on 3 Jan. 1942.

Information from this brother J. Emlyn Thomas.

E.D.J.

THOMAS, HENRY MORGAN STAFFORD (1896-1968), minister (Presb.) and poet; b. at Glenview, Melin Ifan Ddu, Glam., 13 July 1896, s. of Morgan and Margaret Thomas. His parents moved to Porthmadog and he commenced preaching at Tabernacl church. During World War I he was imprisoned as a conscientious objector. He was educated at Porth grammar school, University College, Cardiff (where he graduated), and Bala College. He was ord. in 1923 and served his ministry at Melingryddan, Neath (1923-26); Nazareth, Aberdare (1926-27); Holywell and Bagillt (1927-32); Maenan, Penmaen-mawr (1932-65, with Gatws, Bangor, 1956-65). In 1926 he m. Blodwen Griffith, Llanfair Talhaearn, and they had a daughter. He d. 6 Dec. 1968. He contributed much, in prose and in verse, to *Y Goleuad* and *Y Drysorfa*. He won prizes at the national *eisteddfod* for elegies to T. Gwynn Jones (1950) and Prosser Rhys (1952), and for a *cywydd*, 'Morgannwg', in 1956.

WwFC, 1951, 355; *Gol.*, 11 Dec. 1968 and 29 Jan. 1969; *Blwyddiadur MC*, 1970, 289-90; information from his daughter, Beryl S. Williams, Bangor.

G.M.R.

THOMAS, HUGH HAMSHAW (1885-1962), palaeobotanist; b. 29 May 1885, in Wrexham, Denbs., 2 s. and 3 child of William Hamshaw Thomas (men's outfitter) and his wife Elizabeth Lloyd. He was educated at Grove Park grammar school, Wrexham and went to Downing College, Cambridge, in 1904. Even at school he had acquired a serious interest in botany and fossil plants and he gained 1st class in pt. 1 of the Natural History tripos in 1906. He went on to take pt. 2 of the History tripos (2 cl.) in 1907 in preparation for the Civil Service. He took the Civil Service Entrance in 1908 but rejected the post offered him choosing to live as an independent scholar and researcher in Cambridge, supporting himself by teaching and coaching. He was appointed curator of the Botany School Museum 1909-23, and Sublector at Trinity College in 1912. He was elected a Fellow of Downing in 1914, and university lecturer in 1923. He served in the Royal Flying Corps in France and Egypt during World War I. He developed new techniques in aerial photography and also carried out research in the Aeronautical Dept. at Cambridge. He was twice mentioned in dispatches and was made an M.B.E. He also served in the R.A.F.V.R., engaged on aerial photographic interpretation, 1939-43.

He published his first papers on fossil plants in 1908 and continued his studies on the Jurassic flora of Yorkshire and plant morphology, much of it based on his own field collections rather than on museum collections. His most important and seminal paper, on the *Caytoniales*, appeared in 1925. This was a major contribution to one of the problems of fossil botany, the origin of flowering plants, though his ideas on morphology provoked a great deal of comment. His interests developed not only in the structure of fossil plants where his methodology of analysis was innovative, but also in the wider issues of evolutionary changes and the organization of the plant body so that his contribution to 'new' plant morphology is central. He became a historian of botanical ideas and played an important part in establishing the history of science option in the Natural History tripos. A modest, retiring and kindly man, he nevertheless achieved great distinction and in the Darwin-Wallace centenary (1958) he was judged to be among the 20 biologists of the world who had made the most outstanding contribution to knowledge of evolution and he was presented with a commemmorative medal. He was Pres. of the Linnean Society, of the botanical section of the British Association, of the British Soc. for the History of Science. He was awarded the Linnean Soc. gold medal in 1906, Sc.D. Cambridge 1926, and elected F.R.S. 1934.

He m. Edith Gertrude Torrance in 1923 and they had 1 s. and 1 dau. He d. in Cambridge 30 June 1962.

DNB; Biog. Memoirs Fellows R.S., 9 (1963); *Dict. Scient. Biog.*

B.F.R.

THOMAS, IDRIS - see JENKINS, ROBERT THOMAS (1881-1969) above.

THOMAS, IDRIS (1889-1962), minister (B); b. 1889, the eldest of the seven children of Jenkin and Ann Thomas, Cilfynydd, Glam. When he was six yrs. old the family moved to Moriah, near Aberystwyth, where his grandfather, Jenkin Thomas (*c*. 1824-65), had been a minister (B). He went to work in a shop in Aberystwyth when he was 13 yrs. old but 3 yrs. later he returned to the south, to Abercynon, where he was encouraged to begin preaching. He went to the Old College School, Carmarthen for 18 months, and to Bangor College (1911-14). In 1914 he was ord. minister of Seion, Nefyn and Caersalem, Morfa Nefyn, and soon became one of the most prominent preachers of his denomination. He moved to Dinas Noddfa, Landore, Swansea (1919-23); Rehoboth and Clawddcoch, Cilrhedyn, Carms. (1923-37)l and Tabernacl, Cefn-mawr, near Wrexham (1937-62). His sermons were well structured and had the power of conviction. He had a deep, pleasant voice and delivered his sermons in fluent, refined Welsh.

He m. in 1923 Nan Evans, Glanyrafon, Cenarth (who d. in a road accident, 28 Feb. 1936). His sister, Rachel Ann Thomas, who looked after him afterwards in Bro'r Awelon, Acrefair, was president of the Zenana in Wales. He d. 14 June 1962, soon after being elevated president of the Baptist assembly.

Llawlyfr Bed., 1963.

M.A.J.

THOMAS, IFOR OWEN (1892-1956), operatic tenor, photographer and artist; b. Bay View, Red Wharf Bay, Anglesey, April 10, 1892, third child and only son of Owen Thomas and Isabella (née Morris), a celebrated singer from Dyffryn Nantlle. The family moved to Pandy, Pentraeth, where he was educated in the village board school before being apprenticed to a carpenter. He began singing under the tuition of his mother and E.D. Lloyd of Bangor (1868-1922), winning a scholarship in 1914 to the Royal College of Music out of a field of 400. He left London in 1917 to study with Jean de Reszke in Paris and Benjamino Gigli in Milan.

The major concert halls of Britain had already welcomed the 'Welsh tenor' before he opened in La Scala Milan in 1925, moving to Monte Carlo and Nice before becoming chief tenor in the Paris Opera in 1927. In that year he was admitted as an honorary bard to the *Gorsedd* of Bards as 'Ifor o Fôn', before sailing to the United States.

Although he appeared with the Philadelphia Opera Company in 1928 he left the world of opera for the concert platform, broadcasting and recording for H.M.V. and Sanders. He became a great favourite with the American Welsh who dubbed him 'the second Evan Williams with a hint of Caruso'. He also sang with leading quartets before forming one himself - The Four Aces - with three other New York Welshmen. On the operatic stage he sang with Caruso (as his deputy), Chaliapin and McCormach in Milan and with Frances Alda and Kathryn Meisle.

His career as a solo artist was tragically

brought to an end in 1929 by asthma, an old complaint which had prevented his going to Llangefni Grammar School as a boy. Complete recovery proved elusive, in spite of spending 1931 in Italy, and although he sang occasionally in 1932 he eventually accepted a post as photographer for *Colliers Magazine* in 1933. Here he made a name for himself, especially for his portraits of F.D. Roosevelt and Winston Churchill, as well as a host of film stars. After retiring in 1948 he turned to painting in oils and watercolour, exhibiting in Britain and the United States.

He was a fervent Welshman - he Cymricised his middle name to Owain - and over the years he was host to scores of fellow Welshmen in his house in New York. He was considered one of the mainstays of Welsh culture in the city and in the Welsh Presbyterian Church, and conducted the Côr Merched Cymru in New York from 1944 onwards.

He died after a long illness, on his birthday, 1956, having returned from Wales the previous year. He was buried in Forest Lawn Cemetery, Delwanna, N.J. He married twice (1) Ceridwen Evans in 1920; a child from the marriage d. in 1922. The marriage was annulled and he married (2) Mildred Unfried, a professional pianist from New York, who survived him.

Drych, 1927-56; *Cloriannydd*, 1893-1956; *New York Times*, 11 Apr. 1956; Anglesey Archive Services, Llangefni; personal knowledge.

E.W.R.

THOMAS, IORWERTH RHYS (1895-1966), politician; b. 22 Jan. 1895, the son of David William Thomas, Cwm-parc, Glam. He was educated at a local elementary school, and in 1908, at 13 years of age, he began working at the Dare colliery, Cwmdare, Aberdare. He attended evening classes in economics and history in order to improve his education, and in 1918 he joined the Labour Party. In 1922 he was promoted to the position of checkweighman at Cwm-parc. He was a prominent figure within the South Wales Miners' Federation and the National Union of Mineworkers for more than 30 years, and held a number of offices in the Park and Dare Lodge, the largest in the south Wales coalfield. During the 1926 coalminers' strike Thomas was sentenced to three months imprisonment as the chairman of the Park and Dare Lodge as a result of his involvement in industrial disturbances. He was elected a member of the Rhondda Borough Council in 1928, chaired many of its committees and served as its chairman in 1938-39. He remained a member until 1951. He served, too, on a number of joint industrial councils for Wales and Monmouthshire, and was a member of the South Wales Electricity Board, 1947-49.

In 1950 he was elected M.P. (Lab.) for Rhondda West as a successor to Will John, and continued to represent the constituency until his death in 1966. He was much interested in economic and industrial matters. Thomas was a consistent opponent of Welsh nationalism, and fought tooth-and-nail against the Parliament for Wales agitation of the 1950s. He publicly attacked *Plaid Cymru* on several occasions, and in Oct. 1965 he was highly critical of the recommendations of the Hughes-Parry Report on the

Legal Status of the Welsh Language. In 1960 he supported the Conservative government's measure to open public houses on Sundays.

He m. in Oct. 1920 Annie Mary, dau. of D.J. Davies. She, too, was active in the Labour politics of the area. She died in July 1956. They had one son and one daughter. He d. 3 Dec. 1966 at his home 94 Park Road, Cwm-parc.

Www; Dod's *Parliamentary Companion*; *Times* and *West. Mail*, 5 Dec. 1966; *WWP*.

J.G.J.

THOMAS, JAMES HENRY (1874-1949), politician and Labour leader; b. 3 Oct. 1874 at Newport, Mon. Little is known of his early life except that he received his elementary education at Newport national schools and that he began his working life while very young as an errand boy in a chemist's shop and then as an engine cleaner in the Newport railway yard. Later he went to Swindon and worked as a fireman. He became interested in trade union activities and was elected to the Swindon town council where he gained valuable experience in public affairs. In 1904 he was elected president of the A.S.R.S.; he was re-elected in 1905. In the following years he was employed wholly as a trade union organiser in Manchester and then in south Wales.

In 1910 Richard Bell (*DWB*, 31-2) disagreed with the policy of the A.S.R.S. in affiliating to the Labour Party and resigned his office as secretary and his seat as Lib.-Lab member for Derby. J.H. Thomas was made assistant secretary of the union and was elected to succeed Bell in the Derby constituency, a seat which he held for 26 years. In 1911, while negotiating the settlement of a railway strike at Liverpool, he arranged for a number of smaller unions to combine with the A.S.R.S. to form the N.U.R., of which he became the general secretary in 1918.

During World War I war he gave much assistance in recruiting campaigns and visited the United States in 1917 as a member of the Balfour Mission. In the same year he was made a Privy Councillor. The post-war unrest led to many grave strikes on the railways, but Thomas was successful in arranging a settlement with the companies which doubled the rates of pay for his men together with an agreement to link such rates with the cost of living.

In 1920 and 1921 he was prominent in the Triple Alliance of railwaymen, miners, and transport workers to resist the use of armed force against the Soviet government. In 1924 he was made Colonial Secretary in the first Labour government. During this brief period of office he visited the West Indies, and developed a lifelong interest in colonial affairs.

He was a member of the executive committee of the Trades Union Congress which in May 1926 called a general strike of all its members. Thomas exerted a moderating influence which prevented a dangerous situation from getting out of hand and this resulted in the strike being ended with the promise that negotiation would be resumed, although the miners dissented strongly and were on strike for many months afterwards.

In 1929 Thomas was made Lord Privy Seal and Minister of Employment in the second Labour government. He was charged with the task of preparing measures to deal with the formidable rise in the numbers of unemployed men and women, a phenomenon which at the time was afflicting most industrial countries. In the hope of increasing Commonwealth trade Thomas visited Canada as a result of which an Imperial Economic Conference was organised which later led to the Ottawa agreements which established a preferential tariff area in the British Commonwealth. Despite his efforts, however, the number of unemployed increased and in 1930 he was appointed to the newly-formed Office of Dominion Affairs. In 1931 the Labour party was seriously divided on the measures required to meet the economic crisis and a section of the Government under the Prime Minister, Ramsay MacDonald, formed a National Government of all the main political parties. Thomas was a member and he retained his post as Minister for the Dominions. But his action caused great bitterness within the Union and he was dismissed from his post as secretary. However, he kept his seat at Derby in the elections of 1931 and 1935. During his later life he was more criticised by those whom he had once represented than by his political opponents. In 1936 a premature disclosure of certain financial changes in the Budget led to his resignation from Parliament and his retirement from public life.

He belonged to the right wing of the Labour movement and was much admired for his skill in conciliation and negotiation. He was President of the International Federation of Trade Unions, 1920-24. He received honorary degrees from Cambridge, LL.D. in 1920, and Oxford D.C.L. in 1926. He was a J.P. for the county of Kent and a governor of Dulwich College. He wrote *When Labour rules* in 1920 and *My story* in 1937. He m. Agnes Hill of Newport in 1898. They had two s. and two dau. He d. in London 21 Jan. 1949.

Times, 22 Jan. 1949; Philpott, *The Right Honourable J.H. Thomas*; J.H. Thomas, *My story*; Fuller, *The Rt. Hon. J.H. Thomas* (1936); *Who's who*, 1948.

H.M.-J.

THOMAS, JAMES PURDON LEWES (1903-60), VISCOUNT CILCENNIN, M.P.; b. 13 Oct. 1903, the son of J. Lewes Thomas, Cae-glas, Llandeilo, Carms., and his wife Anne Louisa (née Purdon). He was educated at Rugby School and Oriel College, Oxford. He was a candidate (C) for the Llanelli division in the general election 1929, but received little support; he was elected M.P. for the Hereford division in 1931 and kept his seat until 1955. He was parliamentary private secretary in a number of ministries, 1930-40, and was Lord Commissioner of the Treasury, 1940-43; Financial Secretary to the Admiralty 1943-45; and First Lord of the Admiralty, 1951-56. He was vice-chairman of the Conservative and Unionist Party, 1945-51, and chairman of the Governing Body of Rugby School, 1958. He was elevated Viscount Cilcennin in 1955 and knighted (K.St.J.) in 1958. His book *Admiralty House, Whitehall* was published three months after his death on 13 July 1960 when his title lapsed.

Www.

E.D.J.

THOMAS, JOHN (1857-1944), minister (B) and author; b. 25 June 1857 at Maesteg, Glam. A collier, he began to preach, in English, after he had been injured at work, and went to an academy at Aberafan and, in 1881, to the Baptist College, Pontypool. He won a scholarship (£30) to Bangor university college and at the end of the first session was awarded the Lord Penrhyn Scholarship (£50); he graduated B.A. and M.A., University of London. He ministered at Saledine Nook, Huddersfield (1887-93), Myrtle Street, Liverpool, 1893-1914 and Sutton 1915-20. He was lecturer in homiletics at Manchester College, and, after his retirement, he lectured at the Bible College, Swansea. He could preach in Welsh but in English he was one of the foremost preachers of his generation in England. He published volumes of sermons, books on the Old Testament and on philosophy, and volumes of poems, *The Iris and other poems*; *Psyche and other poems* and *Caniadau John Garth* (the only work in Welsh). He d. 20 Sept. 1944 and was buried at Gorseinon.

Ser. G., 1935, 47 and 1946, 1, [*Bapt. Hdbk.*, 1944-46, 330].

W.J.R.

THOMAS, JOHN EVAN (1884-1941), teacher and writer; b. at Penygroes, Caerns. July 1884. He was prize winner for six lyrics at the national *eisteddfod* of 1921. He edited *The Normalite*, 1909-10, was author of the Report of the teachers of Caernarfonshire to the Departmental Committee on Rural Education in Wales, 1928, of articles ('Y Gorffennol Di-farw') in *Y Winllan*, 1925, and articles and poems in *Cymru*, *Y Deyrnas*, *Y Dinesydd Cymreig*, etc. He was treasurer and one of the founders of the North Wales Labour Council, 1914-19. He was headmaster of Penmachno primary school, and tutor of extramural classes. He d. 1 Jan. 1941 at Penmachno.

Bangor MS. 8,703; *Cymru*, May 1915; *Dinesydd*, 2 May 1928; *Her. Cym.*, 21 Jan 1941.

D.T.

THOMAS, JOHN LUTHER (1881-1970), minister (Congl.); b. 23 Apr. 1881 in Bigyn Road, Llanelli, Carms., son of Thomas and Ann Thomas. The family moved to Pontarddulais where he attended the local school before beginning to work in the tin industry. In 1894 he was received as a member of Hope church, where he was encouraged to enter the ministry. He attended the school of Watcyn Wyn (Williams, Watkin Hezekiah, *DWB*, 1076) at Ammanford and Bala-Bangor College (1900-1903) before becoming minister of Seion, Conwy and Llandudno Junction (1903-21); Carmel, Tanygrisiau, Blaenau Ffestiniog (1921-30); Seion, Cwmafan (1930-45). He resigned because of his wife's illness and returned to Pontarddulais to his sisters at Gwynllys, Clayton Road, but he resumed his ministry, taking charge of the churches of Libanus, Cwmgwili and Llwyn-teg, Llan-non (1945-50) and Hendy, Capel Newydd, Pontarddulais (1950-58). Besides being noted for his clear preaching and his great pastoral labours, he worked diligently for the missionary society and edited the Welsh section of *The London*

Missionary Society Chronicle (1927-40), and was author of the pamphlet *Y bwlch lle bu'r Sul* (1942) for the Council of the Lord's Day Observance Society. He was also the author of a number of books, including: *Y byd a ddaw* (1918 and 1920); *Yr ynys aur; Hanes Iesu Grist* (1930); *Dyn rhyfedd y groes* (1947); and *Iesu penwyn* (1962). He wrote articles for *Y Geiriadur Beiblaidd, Y Dysgedydd, Y Tyst,* and other denominational periodicals. In 1921 he m. Anne Grace Williams, Conwy. Although his health was never robust, he had a long life. He d. 4 Feb. 1970 at his home, Lansdowne, Groves Ave., Langland, Swansea and his body was cremated at Morriston.

E. Lewis Evans, *Eglwys Hope, Pontarddulais* (1969), 69-70; *WWP.*

M.A.J.

THOMAS, JOHN ROWLAND (1881-1965), religious leader ad prominent merchant; b. 2 March 1881 at Penrhyndeudraeth, Caerns., son of Griffith and Ann Thomas. In 1883 Griffith Thomas and the family returned to Dwygyfylchi, Penmaenmawr – his old area. John Rowland attended Pencae school, Penmaenmawr, and won a scholarship to Friars School, Bangor, but after two years transferred to the new John Bright School at Llandudno. He went to work for a short period for the railway company at Llandudno Junction, and when he was 18, he became, for three years, an apprentice at the Cloth Hall shop in Bethesda. He then went to work in the silk dept. at the shop of Thomas Lloyd (of Llanybydder) in London. This was the start of the period that made him a world-famous specialist in silk. After Selfridges bought Lloyd's shop in 1914, he stayed with them for five years. From 1919-20 (18 months) he was assistant to the silk buyer at Harrods; from 1920-22 the silk buyer at Derry & Toms, Kensington; from 1922-30 silk buyer at Harrods; from 1930-35 chief silk buyer for the John Lewis Partnership, and from 1935-53 one of the company's Directors. As the silk dept. of John Lewis in London employed 130 men, and as the partnership had a number of shops across the country, 'J.R.', (as he was known by everyone), could be considered the leading silk buyer in Europe, possibly the world, and his work regularly took him to the continent.

He was equally energetic in London's religious and Welsh life. From 1902-1965 he was a member of Tabernacl, King's Cross Welsh Congregational Chapel, a deacon 1921-1965, and secretary 1940-53. He was also the editor of the Tabernacl periodical, *Y Lamp,* from its inception. During the depression of the 1930s, when people from Wales flocked to London, he was conscious of the need to have Welsh chapels in the suburbs for them. In June 1936, when he was the association's secretary he addressed the quarterly meeting on 'Extending the Boundaries', and a direct result was the establishment of a committee to undertake the work. Welsh Congregational chapels were established in Slough, Luton and Harrow. 'J.R.' was the person mainly responsible for establishing the cause at Harrow in 1937, and under his leadership the church quickly grew to 200 members. As he was elected its first deacon and then made a deacon for life, he was, for 28 yrs,

a deacon in two churches at the same time! He was also a leader in the Union of Welsh Independents. From 1941-52 he was its treasurer, from 1949-50 its President. His address from the chair, at Caernarfon, on the subject 'The Call to Move Ahead', displayed the same missionary zeal and religious restlessness which characterised him throughout his life. He was one of the energetic directors of the London Missionary Society. He promoted everything Welsh, and in 1925 was at the forefront establishing the London Caernarvonshire Society. Prominent (*c.* 1930) in establishing branches of *Urdd Gobaith Cymru* in several of London's Welsh chapels, he was one of the first Vice-Presidents of the *Urdd*. He was president of the Association of the Societies of London-Welsh Churches and a staunch life-long supporter.

In 1913 he m. Lily Anna Jones (d. 1964), a Welsh lady born in London. At their home, 'Y Nant', Dollis Hill, there was an open door for a host of Welsh people, especially ministers of the Gospel. They had 3 daughters; Morfudd, who married J. Idris Jenkins, the first minister of the Welsh Congregational church at Harrow; Gwyneth; and Eluned Marian, who emigrated to Toronto, Canada, and who was President of the North American Welsh National Gymanfa Ganu Association 1976-78. He d. 16 April 1965.

Dysg., Nov. 1932, July, August 1965; *Tywysydd,* Nov. 1935; *Y Ddinas,* July 1956; *London Welshman,* successor to *Y Ddinas,* June 1965; *Lamp y Tabernacl,* July 1965; *Gazette of John Lewis Partnership,* 24 April 1965; minutes *of Cyfundeb Eglwysi Annibynnol Llundain, 3.*

W.T.O.

THOMAS, JOSEPH MORGAN (LLOYD) (1868-1955), minister (U) and Free Catholic, councillor and public figure; b. 30 June 1868, one of the eight children of John and Elizabeth Thomas, Blaen-wern, Llannarth, Cards. (He took the name 'Lloyd', his mother's maiden name, when his brother of that name died.) He was educated at New Quay grammar school and Christ College, Brecon and completed his articles with Messrs. Walter H. Morgan and Rhys, solicitors, Pontypridd. He began to take an interest in religion and propagating Unitarian concepts, being one of the three who instituted the Unitarian cause at Pontypridd in 1892, where he served as its first secretary. He decided to enter the ministry and attended a course for that purpose at Manchester College (Unitarian), Oxford (1894-98); he received a call to Liscard Memorial Church (Free Christian), Chester, in 1898. He m. in 1899, Alice (headmistress of Pontypridd girls' school), daughter of David Evans, Bodringallt, Rhondda. They had a son and two daughters. He was minister of High Pavement Unitarian Church, Nottingham, 1900-12, and played a prominent part in establishing the Union of Social Service of the Unitarian movement, and was elected one of its first presidents. He spent the remainder of his years in the ministry in charge of the Old Meeting House, Birmingham, 1912-32. This was a successful yet turbulent period of his life when he was influenced both by the rationalism of L.P. Jacks, on the one hand, and the catholicism of W.S. Orchard on the other, two of his bosom friends. He continued to be a liberal Unitarian, but he had already published a pamphlet on *A*

Free Catholic Church (1907), containing ideas which were developed in a sermon which he delivered at Pontypridd the year he was inducted at Birmingham.

In 1916 he began publishing and editing the periodical, *The Free Catholic*, expounding and defending his catholic ideas. He was influenced by the 'new theology', and that same year he published his pamphlet, *Free Catholic? A comment on R.J. Campbell's 'Spiritual Pilgrimage'*. His church was also influenced by his theology, and in 1918 he published a pamphlet, *Tradition and outlook of the Old Meeting Church*, and another in 1921, *What the Old Meeting Church stands for*. No doubt it was his work on Richard Baxter's autobiography during these years that gave rise to his dream of establishing a catholic church to include 'every true Christian in the world'. He published an abridged version of *Reliquiae Baxterianae*, his major life's work, in 1925, with an introductory essay, notes and appendix; and in 1928, when the General Assembly of the Unitarian and Free Christian Churches was established, he and his church seized the opportunity to dissociate themselves from Unitarianism, which he considered to be too denominational, and establish a new denomination of an ecclesiastic and priestly spirit; he called himself a free Catholic priest, and adopted ecclesiastical usages, and compiled a comprehensive book of offices, *A Free Church Book of Common Prayer* (1929), with its contents ranging from the Nicene Creed to Martineau's prayers, as well as the Psalms and canticles (from the Authorised English Version) with complete notation, for the first time, for intoning them. For a short period Lloyd Thomas was not without his admirers and followers, including some ministers, and his high-church leanings became evident in some of the adornments of some Unitarian chapels (e.g. at Bromwich and Oldbury), but the new movement languished in its infancy, and in 1932 Lloyd Thomas retired from the ministry.

Although his dream of unifying the denominations did not materialise, he deserves to be called a pioneer in the field. He returned to his native heath and lived thereafter at 'Y Bwthyn', Llannarth, continuing to preach occasionally, lecture and expand his catholic ideas, as in his Dr. Williams Lecture at Carmarthen Presbyterian College (1941) on *Toleration and church-unity*. As a public figure, at this time, he served on Cardiganshire county council and as chairman of its highways committee; he promoted the success of the county's travelling library and was one of the chief founders of Ceredigion Library, and its first chairman. He served on the county's education committee, and as a member and chairman of the board of governors of Aberaeron county school. He supported Pauline Taylor, Blaen-wern, who had assisted him in editing the book of offices, to pioneer musical education in the county's schools, to establish pony-trekking activities, and ensure the continuation of Welsh breeds of stallions and cattle.

He was a perceptive prophet and visionary; conscientious and not afraid of espousing minority and unpopular movements. He supported the suffragette movement, publishing a pamphlet in its support and he chaired the fiery meetings of Chrystabel Pankhurst; he ventured to express some sympathy with the enemy during the Boer War; and during World War I he published a pamphlet, *The immortality of non-resistance and other sermons on the war*.

Although he was a modernist he warned against a narrow superficial modernism; his concept of education was to learn to think honestly, and he warned the authorities against glorifying scholarship at the expense of neglecting the crafts and manual work (cf. *What is education for?*, 1949). In his memorandum on religious education, which was written at the request of Cardiganshire education authority (1941), he recommended greater Christian influence, in an honest and tolerant spirit, predicting that a third World War (a war of ideas and ideals) could result in the decline of religion and the self-extermination of world civilisation. In his pamphlet, *The humanising of industry* (1919) he foresaw the problems of industry, and warned against mechanizing men, producing degrading matter, and excluding workers' representatives from boards of managers and directors; in a sermon which he published in 1944, *God and the land*, he foresaw social problems and warned against urbanising the country and destroying the roots of rural culture and Christianity.

He contributed regularly to periodicals, such as the *Hibbert Journal* and the *Free Catholic*, and to newspapers such as the *Welsh Gazette* and *Western Mail*. Towards the end of his life he became interested in the works of Kierkegaard. His published works include: *The autobiography of Richard Baxter*, abridged with notes, introductory essay and appendix (1925); *A Free Church Book of Common Prayer* (1929). His pamphlets include: *Dogma or doctrine?* (1906); *A Free Catholic Church* (1907); *The emancipation of womanhood* (1913); *Administration of the Lord's Supper or The Holy Communion* (1914); *The immortality of non-resistance and other sermons on the war* (1915); *Free Catholic? A comment of the Rev. R.J. Campbell's 'Spiritual Pilgrimage'* (1916); *Tradition and outlook of the (Birmingham) Old Meeting Church* (1918); *The crucifix - a sermon* (1918); *The humanising of industry* (1919); *A comprehensive Church. What the Old Meeting Church stands for* (1921); *Religious instruction in schools* (1941); *Toleration and church-unity* (Dr. Williams Lecture, 1941); *What is education for?* (1949); he edited *The Free Catholic* (1916-27).

He d. 2 July 1955 and his body was cremated at Glyn-taff on July 6. His wife d. in 1945. He was survived by his son and his two daughters. They presented calligraphic copies of his book of offices to the N.L.W.

Ymofyn., Aug. 1955.

D.E.J.D.

THOMAS, LAWRENCE (1889-1960), archdeacon; b. 19 Aug. 1889, s. of David and Elizabeth Thomas, Gelli-gaer, Glam. He was educated at Lewis' School, Pengam, St. David's College, Lampeter, where he gained B.A. (2nd-cl. hons.) Divinity 1911; St. Michael's College, Llandaff, and was ord. in 1912 and served as curate of St. John's, Canton. He was ord. priest in 1913. In 1914 he served as curate of Headington Quarry, near Oxford, and was also a student at St. John's College Oxford, where he gained B.A. (3rd-cl.

hons.) Divinity 1916, M.A. 1920. From 1916-24 he served as curate of St. John's, Cardiff. He obtained the living of Briton Ferry in 1924 where he remained until 1942, continuing his studies. He gained B.Litt. at Oxford in 1926; B.D. Trinity College Dublin in 1929 and D.D. 1930. In 1930 he published his standard work, *The Reformation in the old diocese of Llandaff*. In the same year he published *The life of Griffith Jones, Llanddowror*, a pamphlet prepared by the Llandaff Diocesan Sunday School Council to commemorate the bicentenary of the starting of the circulating schools in 1731.

He obtained the living of Bargoed in 1942 and was appointed canon of Llandaff cathedral in 1944. He moved to Aberavon in 1946 and when the archdeaconry of Margam was formed in 1948 he was selected to be the first archdeacon. An able administrator, he fulfilled his duties effectively. He resigned the vicarage in 1958. He m. in 1923, Beatrice Lilian Williams of Crickhowel and they had one dau. He d. 19 Oct. 1960 and was buried at Gelli-gaer.

He was an authority on the impact of the industrial revolution on the church in south-east Wales, but because of his onerous duties he was unable to find time to write a book on the subject. His main interests were in historical and antiquarian subjects. He contributed articles to the *DWB*. He was known for his forthright and unconventional induction charges to congregations. A distinguished character, he was well-loved by his people.

Www; *Hndbk. of the Church in Wales*, 1959; *Llan*, 11 Nov. 1960; *Church Times*, 28 Oct. 1960.

M.G.E.

THOMAS, LEWIS (1877-1955), pioneer of the art of *Cerdd Dant* (the art of singing to harp accompaniment) in south Wales in the first half of the 20th century; b. at Pontyberem, Gwendraeth Valley, Carms., 30 May 1877, the eldest of nine sons of William Thomas, a collier, and his wife, Jane. Lewis worked in the mines for a short period before being apprenticed and gaining his trade as a local shoemaker. In 1905 he m. Mary Emiah Jones, a teacher at Pontyberem, but originally from Llan-non, Llanelli. They had a son and two daughters. They built a house and an attached shop and for years he kept the shop and trained his apprentice shoemakers in a workshop at the rear. Later he was a rates collector for Llanelli Council. He and his wife were prominent in the cultural and social activities of the village. He was an *eisteddfod* enthusiast since his youth, competing at recitation, composing essays, hymn tunes, anthems for children, and choral works. Like some of his brothers he was interested in music and there was a small organ or harmonium at home. He won a certificate of the Tonic Sol-fa College in the examination which the movement held in the vestry of Caersalem Congregational chapel, where he was a member. About 1916-18, his musical interests turned to *Cerdd Dant*. A harp was bought and he had lessons from Telynores Elli, mastering the harp well enough to accompany his children where he had previously used the piano. Many professional musicans sought his help and found him very ready to share his knowledge. He began competing as a 'setter' of words to harp music

and his settings won at the national *eisteddfod* in Caerphilly (1950), Aberystwyth (1952), and Ystradgynlais (1954). The last, *Hwiangerddi gyda'r tannau*, was published by Snell & Co. in 1956. He contributed articles and settings to *Allwedd y tannau* and *Yr Athro*. For many years he regularly adjudicated *Cerdd Dant* at the national *eisteddfod*, the *Cerdd Dant* Festival and the *Urdd* National *Eisteddfod*. For his services he was made a member of the *Gorsedd* of Bards at the Llanelli national *eisteddfod* in 1930. He was a founder member of the *Cerdd Dant* Society and lectured at its first Summer School. He was its second President and was made an honorary member. He d. in Aberystwyth hospital 16 May 1955, and was buried in Llan-non church cemetery, Llanelli.

Information from his daughter, Lady Amy Parry-Williams; personal knowledge; *Allwedd y Tannau*; 15 (1956).

E.G.E.

THOMAS, LEWIS JOHN (1883-1970), missionary in India with the London Missionary Society; b. 2 Feb. 1883 at Llangefni, Angl., son of Cefni and Mary (née Williams) Thomas. The family moved to Rhiwbryfdir, Blaenau Ffestiniog, when he was five. After a period as a pupil-teacher and working on the railway, he moved to Corwen and then Birkenhead. There he came under the influence of the 1904-05 religious revival and began preaching; he had wished to become a missionary since he was a young man.

After attending Paton College, Nottingham, he was ordained at Jerusalem, Blaenau Ffestiniog, 12 Oct. 1911. He sailed for India 4 Nov. 1911 and worked hard as a superintendent of a large number of churches in the provinces where Telugu was spoken. He m. Hannah E. Mathews in Madras; they lived at Cuddapah, Kamalapuram, Goety and Jammalamadugu, and had a son and daughter. From 1927 to 1938 he was responsible for a seminary to instruct native evangelists, and from 1939 to 1949 he was secretary/treasurer of the Missionary Society. As an uncompromising Independent, he opposed the United Church, although he gave of his best in all co-operative activities.

He retired from missionary work in 1949, but accepted the care of St. Andrews Presbyterian Church, Bangalore, where their son Iorwerth was a missionary and head of a boys' grammar school. He lost his sight in 1954. His wife d. 13 May 1964 and he d. 17 April 1970 in Bangalore where they both were buried.

Personal research.

H.E.

THOMAS, LOUIE MYFANWY ('Jane Ann Jones'; 1908-68), novelist; b. 29 Feb. 1908 in Primrose Cottage, Holway, Holywell, Flints., only child of Walter Owen Davies, master saddler and his wife, Elizabeth Jane (née Jones). The mother d. 3 Feb. 1909 aged 26 and the grandmother helped to rear the child. The family moved to Yscawen, Rhuddlan, where the father obtained work as a grocer, and Louie Myfanwy was educated at the Church elementary school and Rhyl secondary school (1920-24) where she gained her Central Welsh Board

Senior School Certificate. She may have worked in Caernarfon, perhaps at a newspaper office, after having spent a period assisting her father in the shop (cf. the story 'Lol' in *Storïau hen ferch*). She was appointed a clerk in the education dept. of Denbigh County Council 17 Oct. 1927, later becoming secretary to J.C. Davies, Director of Education, and his successor Edward Rees. At this time she lived at Arwynfa, Borthyn, Ruthin, and by 1935 she is registered as living at Llwyni, Llanfair Road, Ruthin. The occupants are noted as Emily, Louise Myfanwy, Mary and William Henry Davies. W.H. Davies, a Meth. lay-preacher, was her father's brother, his wife was Mary and their dau. Emily. Myfanwy lived there for some years but was unhappy, being unable to share her uncle's narrow religion; he tended to be sanctimonious while she was more extravert. He used to asssert 'God will provide' while she claimed that it was her wages which provided. This is echoed in her story 'Helaeth fynediad' in *Storïau hen ferch*, 22.

Her relationship with her family in Llwyni is important, however, because of the frequent (but un-named) references to them in her work, especially *Y bryniau pell* and to a lesser extent, *Diwrnod yw ein bywyd*. Many of the situations and events in *Y bryniau pell* are autobiographical and she has many scathing references to preachers and ministers and to her own circumstances as an orphan and the subject of comment.

She m. Richard Thomas, Chief Clerk in the Education Dept. of Denbighshire County Council, at Bolton registry office 5 Apr. 1952 when she was 44. (Richard Thomas's sister and her husband lived in Bolton). The two lodged in Market Street, Ruthin, before moving to a flat in 6 Well Street. The marriage seems to have been a happy one: they did not have children but Richard Thomas had 2 daughters from his previous marriage. She suffered much ill-health. She had surgery in Cardiff but refused surgery for the cancer which she suffered. She was forced to resign because of her health in 1959. She and her husband moved to Carmel, Holywell in 1962 but she returned to Ruthin 2 years later, 2 months after her husband's death from lung cancer in Sept. 1964, to 115 Parcydre. In her obituary in *Y Faner*, 1 Feb. 1968, Kate Roberts says that Louie Myfanwy was unable to visit her husband in hospital and failed to be at his funeral because of the state of her health.

She had stayed for a time with Mrs. Bishop, Knapp House, Eardisland, nr. Ludlow, while she was recuperating after surgery. Mrs Bishop kept The White Swan and according to one account Louie Myfanwy found the spot by accident after asking a bus driver for a suitable place to stay. Whether the story be true or not, the location is significant in that it was here, apparently, that she began to write (but see the story 'Lol' in *Storïau hen ferch*). She had seen some pigs in a garden and began writing a children's story about them; this may have been the origin of stories, e.g. 'Siw a'r moch bach' in *Ann a Defi John*. See also the description of the cottage in *Diwrnod yw ein bywyd*.

Louie Myfanwy Thomas wrote under the name Jane Ann Jones, perhaps based on her mother's maiden name Elizabeth Jane Jones. However, she may never have known her mother's antecedents in any detail. She insisted on keeping her literary life a secret and an unremarkable and common name such as Jane Ann Jones would have prevented any suggestion of a connection. Kate Roberts in the obituary in *Y Faner* remarks: 'She kept the name Jane Ann Jones a secret between four of us for many years and no one knew who she was'. For a number of years none of her family, friends or office colleagues knew anything of her literary career. They knew she was an avid reader who often visited the local library to order new books reviewed in the *Liverpool Daily Post* but it was a surprise to many who knew her to learn that she was an author.

She won a £100 prize for a novel in a competition held by *Y Cymro* in 1953 (*Y Cymro*, 30 Oct. 1953): the adjudicators were Islwyn Ffowc Elis, J. Roberts Williams and T. Bassett. Her pen-name was 'Jini Jos' and it was announced that the winner was Jane Ann Jones: 'The secret is to be kept', said *Y Cymro*. She competed periodically at the national *eisteddfod* and submitted *Diwrnod yw ein bywyd* in the novel competition at the Dolgellau national *eisteddfod* in 1949 under the name Ffanni Llwyd (see D.J. Williams's adjudication in *Cyfansoddiadau a Beirniadaethau* (1949), 153). One of her short stories, 'Trwy ddrych mewn dameg', appeared in *Y Cymro*, 9 Apr. 1954, described as a skilful, concise, and intense story, and she wrote scripts and plays for the B.B.C. for some 10-15 years, giving up only when she was asked to change her style.

She published (under the name Jane Ann Jones) *Storïau hen ferch* (Gwasg Aberystwyth, 1937); *Y bryniau pell* (Gwasg Gee, 1949); *Diwrnod yw ein bywyd* (Hughes a'i Fab, 1954); *Plant y Foty* (George Ronald, Cardiff, 1955); *Ann a Defi John* (Gwasg y Brython, 1958). George Ronald, Cardiff, had intended publishing a children's series, 'Storïau Ann a Defi John' and it is interesting that a photograph of Jane Ann Jones appeared on the back cover of *Plant y Foty* with a list of her other titles. The secret was obviously out by 1955. She was remembered as a quiet, unassuming and able person, but others remarked that she believed that Kate Roberts had never taken favourably to anything she had written. Judging from her work, she was a woman with an independent mind and critical tendency. She d. in Ruthin hospital 25 Jan. 1968.

Personal research; *Baner*, 1 Feb. 1968.

H. ab E.

THOMAS, MARGARET HAIG, VISCOUNTESS RHONDDA (1883-1958), author, editor and chairperson of companies; b. 12 June 1883 in Bayswater, London, the only child of David Alfred Thomas (*DWB*, 942-3) and his wife Sybil Margaret, daughter of George Augustus Haig, Pen Ithon, Rads. She was taught initially by private governess at home. Then she was sent to Notting Hill secondary school, where she started a printed magazine, *The Shooting Star*, to which her relations contributed. From there she went to St. Leonard's School in St. Andrews, Scotland, where the Haig ancestors hailed from. She was at Somerville College, Oxford, for a short while, but was not happy there. She did not care either for the social life which London offered, preferring the solitude of

Radnorshire around Pen Ithon and the gentleness of Llan-wern, her home in Gwent. She did not learn any Welsh except for a short sentence which she used whilst canvassing in her father's elections in Merthyr Tydfil. She threw herself into her father's industrial interests, and acted as his secretary, which was useful in preparing her for the period when she had to take her father's place on industrial boards when government work weighed heavily on his shoulders, and after his death in 1918.

In 1908 she m. Humphrey Mackworth (baronet after his father's death in 1914) in Trinity Church near Caerleon, Mon. This was an ill-matched union. He was twelve years older than she was, with hardly any interests except in his hunting hounds – he was the master of the Llangybi pack; she was an avid reader, while he hardly ever opened a book; he was a Tory, she the daughter of a prominent Liberal, though out of a sense of duty she resigned from the council of the local Liberal Association on her marriage. They made their home in Llansoar, not too far from her parents' house. Within four months, in spite of her husband's dissatisfaction, she had thrown herself into the daring activities of Mrs. Pankhurst's followers by marching through Hyde Park with her cousin Florence Haig. She joined the Women's Social and Political Union and took part in the campaign for votes for women. She jumped onto the running-board of H.H. Asquith's car in St. Andrews. She learnt how to set pillar boxes on fire and was sentenced to a month's imprisonment in Usk for her acts in Gwent. Because of her refusal to eat, she was released after five days. She was the correspondent of the Newport branch of the movement.

She and her father were amongst those saved when the *Lusitania* was sunk by a German submarine in 1915. After returning home she was a commissioner for the national women's service in Wales and in 1918 was made chief recruiting officer of women in Britain. When her father d. she inherited the viscounty in accordance with the arrangement made by Lloyd George when her father was elevated to the title as there was no male heir. She herself presented a petition in 1920 to be summoned to the House of Lords, and though Lord Hewart and the Committee of Privileges were in favour, a large majority, under the leadership of Lord Birkenhead, voted against consenting to her request. To her the petition was an entirely natural development of her efforts on behalf of equality for women. Although she failed, she succeeded in the same year with a group of women of similar persuasion to form a company which published the influential weekly *Time and Tide* as a paper entirely independent of any sect or party which met the needs of a new post-war period. She edited it for the rest of her life; her stamp was upon it, though it was Helen Archdale who edited the first issues. It was through *Time and Tide* that she realised one of the dreams of her youth. She succeeded in drawing able and eminent contributors to the paper. In the midst of her busy life – she was a justice of the peace in Gwent and in 1926 was the president of the Institute of Directors, the demands of industrial management weighed heavily upon her and her health was fragile – she insisted on keeping a watchful eye on all the paper's contents for near-

ly thirty-eight years. Her great concern during the last months of her life was to secure a safe financial base for the paper, and she succeeded in her effort. She stood steadfastly for the freedom of the individual. To her every human being, man or woman, should be treated like an individual with an immortal soul. She published *D.A. Thomas, Viscount Rhondda* (1921), *Leisured Women* (1928), *This was my world* (1933) and *Notes on the way* (1937). She was president of the University College, Cardiff, from 1950 to 1958 and was awarded an honorary LL.D. degree by the University of Wales in 1955. She was divorced from her husband in 1923. They had no children and the title became extinct at her death at Westminster Hospital on 20 July 1958.

West. Mail, Times and *Time and Tide*, July 1958; *D.N.B.; G.E.C.*; see *WwW* (1921), 402 for a list of the companies of which she was chairman or president at the time.

                                                                E.D.J.

THOMAS, MORRIS (1874-1959), minister (Calvinistic Methodist), writer and historian, b. 8 July 1874, in Talysarn, Dyffryn Nantlle, Caerns., the son of Robert Thomas, quarryman, and his wife. The father d. when the Nantlle lake burst its banks, and 8 workmen were killed. Morris Thomas was only 12 years old, but at that age the boy had to go to work in the quarry. His minister, William Williams, saw that he was exceptionally able and gave him encouragement and instruction. He went to the college in Clynnog, and from there to the 'department' in the college in Bala. In Oct. 1901 he went to the University College of North Wales in Bangor and gained a 2nd-class degree in English, and a third class in Philosophy in 1905. He came under the influence of the 1904-05 Revival, and instead of completing the B.D. course, decided to become the minister of a congregation, though he was in Bala from 1905-07. He was ordained in 1908, and his first pastorate was at Aber and Y Gatws near Bangor. Later, he became a minister in Penmorfa, near Porthmadog, Trefeglwys and Llawr-y-glyn, Monts., and then Dolwyddelan.

He wrote extensively for the publications of his denomination. He won a prize in the national *eisteddfod* at Abergavenny in 1913, for a translation into Welsh of Robert Louis Stephenson's novel *Treasure Island*, and for a critical Essay on the 'Works and art of Islwyn'. In the national *eisteddfod* in Pwllheli, 1925, he shared a prize for his novel *Toriad y Wawr*, published in 1928 by Hugh Evans and Sons, Liverpool. The other winner was Lewis Davies, Cymer (see above), for his novel, *Wat Emwnt*, published by the same company in the same year. In the Bangor national *eisteddfod* of 1931, Morris Thomas won first prize with his novel *Pen yr Yrfa*, published in the office of the *Goleuad* in Caernarfon in 1932.

He was considered to be a good historian, and he was appointed to write the history of the Llŷn and Eifionydd Presbytery, left unfinished by Henry Hughes, Bryncir (*DWB*, 375). According to his own account, he tired of the work and the task of trying to make sense of Henry Hughes' notes, and he turned the work into a novel. *Toriad y Wawr* is a story of the early days of Methodism in the Llŷn peninsula in the days of 'Morgan y Gogrwr' (Morgan Gruffydd, see under Griffith Williams, 1769-1838; *DWB*, 1039). He wrote another novel, *Y Clogwyn Melyn*, which was never published. He used also to publish a short story in the Christmas number of the *Goleuad*.

His wife, L.M. Thomas, a native of Llanarmon Dyffryn Ceiriog, was a sister of Prof. Richard Morris of the College in Bala. She too wrote extensively for children, and contributed regularly to the periodicals *Trysorfa'r Plant* and *Y Gymraes*. Morris Thomas retired in 1945, and went to live in Tal-y-bont, in the Conwy Valley. He d. there in 1959.

Bangor MSS. 15135-15206, in the library of the University College, Bangor; *Goleuad*, 7 Oct. 1959; *M.C. Yearbook*, 1960; *Gymraes*, 37, 10, Oct. 1933; O.E. Williams, *Dringwn fel ein tadau: hanes eglwys Moreia, Dolwyddelan* (1980); personal knowledge.

De.J.

THOMAS, Sir PERCY EDWARD (1883-1969), architect and planning consultant; b. in South Shields, 13 Sept. 1883, the third son and fifth child of Christmas and Cecilia (née Thornton) Thomas. His father was a farmer's son from the Narberth district of Pembrokeshire who went to sea, and by the time Percy Edward was born he was captain of a sailing vessel. His mother came from Wedmore, Somerset. When the son was ten years old the family moved to Cardiff, attracted, like other similar families, by the flourishing coal trade. He was educated privately at Hasland House until his father died in 1897, when he was moved to Howard Gardens high school; but he had seen the world from a tender age with his father every summer and visited cities such as St. Petersburgh, Odessa, Istanbul, Genoa, Fiume and other ports. His early experiences must have coloured his later career. His father died at sea and was buried at Leghorn. His mother found the boy a place in a ship's office in Cardiff, but the work did not appeal to him. The vicar of Llandough took him to a phrenologist who concluded that he was suited to be an architect. He took articles in the office of E.H. Burton F.R.I.B.A. for five years, but by the fifth year he felt he should be paid, and accepted five shillings a week rather than be released from his articles. In a competition to design a school in Cardiff his entry was deemed better than that of his master, and he also won the architecture competition in the national *eisteddfod* at Llanelli in 1903. In Jan. 1904 he was given a post in Leigh, Lancashire, by J.C. Prestwich, but moved after a year to Bath as an assistant to R.A. Brinksworth. After two years he was searching for a more responsible post and answered an advertisement which had a box number only. To his surprise he found himself back with J.C. Prestwich, but as a chief assistant. He moved again in 1906 to Henthorne Stott in Manchester. He collaborated with Ivor Jones of Cardiff in open competitions, and in 1911 they won the prize for designing a technical college in Cardiff. This gave him the opportunity to return to Cardiff in 1913 in partnership with Ivor Jones. His career was interrupted by World War I, when he joined the Artists' Rifles at the end of 1915. He was commissioned in the 210 Field Co., R.E. and found himself at the

Somme, not in Egypt as he had hoped. He was promoted Staff Officer R.E. XIII Army Corps, was twice mentioned in despatches and won the military O.B.E.

Released from the army in Feb. 1919, he returned to his work in Cardiff. In the period between the wars he won many competitions for important commissions, e.g. police headquarters and fire station, Bristol, 1924, Newcastle, 1925 and Accrington, 1930; civic centres in Swansea, 1930, Tunbridge Wells and the town hall at Swinton and Pendlebury, 1934, the last two in collaboration with Ernest Prestwich of Leigh. In addition to these successes he had important commissions which included county offices for Glamorgan, the Temple of Peace – directly commissioned by Lord Davies (see David Davies above) – both in Cathays Park, Cardiff; county offices for Carmarthenshire and police headquarters and fire station for Worcester. He was now a recognised authority on planning and designing public buildings, and he was appointed planning consultant to Cardiff, Aberdeen, High Wycombe, Blackpool, and the Royal Borough of Kensington, as well as to the county councils of Flintshire and Shropshire. In 1935 he was invited to design the new campus of University College Aberystwyth and he was the architect of many of its buildings: the agricultural research laboratory, the swimming pool (where Forest of Dean stone was used against his advice) and the dairy science building. In 1935 the L.M.S. railway company asked him to redesign Euston station, but the outbreak of war put paid to these plans.

He was elected President of the Royal Institute of British Architects in 1935, and in 1939 was awarded their royal gold medal, one of the few architects to receive both honours. They awarded him the R.I.B.A. bronze medal in 1930, for James Howell's new shop in Cardiff, in 1935 for the Swansea Civic Centre, in 1938 for Swinton and Pendlebury Town Hall and in 1939 for the Temple of Peace. He was elected an honorary corresponding member of the American Architectural foundation in 1936, and was also President of the French and British Architectural Union. The partnership with Ivor Jones was dissolved in 1937 by mutual consent and he worked on his own until 1946 when he took his son Norman into partnership, and in 1952 enlisted William Marsden and Wallace Sweet.

World War II halted all public works and during this period Percy Thomas was immersed in government service in Wales, and continued to be so until the end of the 1950s. In 1940 the Lord Lieutenant of Glamorgan invited him to be regional officer in the Ministry of Supply, and when this ministry was taken over by Lord Beaverbrook he was made director. When the Ministry of Production was set up in 1942 he became regional director and chairman of the Welsh region, a post he held while the ministry existed. Sir Stafford Cripps invited him to continue as an independent chairman of the Welsh board and as a member of the National Productivity Advisory Council. He became one of the best-known figures on the Welsh industrial scene and was in great demand as chairman of meetings and committees on benefits and the problems of modern industry. Immediately after Anthony Eden's appeal for volunteers he joined the Local Defence Volunteers and was assistant to Col. Otto Jones in recruiting in Glamorgan. Later he was appointed a Lt. Colonel and Commander of the 22nd Battalion of the Glamorgan Home Guard. In 1943 he was elected president of the R.I.B.A. for the second time, the only precedent being Sir William Tite in 1867. He served the council for two years and was elected for a further year in 1945, thus holding the presidency for five years. He was mainly responsible for reconciling the interests of private practitioners and the official body of architects, who were by now in the majority, and in this way, incidentally, transformed the establishment from being London-based to being truly national.

He was responsible for much industrial design in post-war Wales, e.g. British Nylon Spinners great factory at Pontypool, new power stations at Aberthaw. As consultant architect to the Steel Company of Wales he was responsible, with W.A. Atkins, for the gigantic strip mills in Aberafan and Llanelli. He was consultant architect to the Ministry of Transport on numerous projects in Wales after the war, e.g. the Conwy by-pass bridge, the Severn bridge, and by-passes at Newport and Neath. He was also consultant architect to the Cardiff hospitals, the universities of Nottingham, Bristol and Wales, all British Electricity Authority's activities in Wales, and the Federation of British Industry's new headquarters in London.

He was an assessor on many major architectural competitions during this time, the most important being the T.U.C. headquarters in Great Russell Street and Coventry Cathedral. As consultant to the hospitals he was an assessor for the medical centre at the Heath in Cardiff. In 1952 he was appointed honorary colonel in the 109 Army Engineer Regiment (Glam.) R.E. (TA), a regiment in which his son was a senior officer.

He m. Margaret Ethel, daughter of Henry Turner of Penarth, in 1906, and they had one son and three daughters. She d. in 1953. In 1961 he was seriously ill, and after a brief period as consultant to the practice, he retired in 1963. His health was fragile for the rest of his life, and he d. Aug 19, 1969.

Besides his own specialised field, society benefited greatly from his brilliant services, and he received many honours, including a LL.D. from the University of Wales in 1937, and he was awarded a knighthood in 1946. He was a J.P. in Cardiff from 1946, Deputy Lieutenant for Glamorgan from 1945 and High Sheriff 1949-50. He edited a four volume work, *Modern Building Practice*, in 1936-7, and published an interesting autobiography, *Pupil to President*, privately in Leigh-on-Sea in 1963. It is said that his architectural style had three special qualities: symmetry, simplicity and sincerity.

Personal knowledge; *Pupil to President*.

N.T.

THOMAS, PERCY GORONWY (1875-1954), professor of English; b. 26 Nov. 1875 at Birkenhead, Cheshire, son of Josiah Thomas and Marianne (née Jones, of Llanfyllin), later of Liverpool, and grandson of John Thomas, minister (Congl.), Liverpool (1821-92; *DWB*, 953). He was educated at the University of Liverpool

and Caius College, Cambridge, and gained a Litt.D. of the University of Liverpool *c*. 1925. His first post was as assistant lecturer in English at the University College of North Wales, Bangor (1903-06) but he spent most of his life in the University of London as lecturer in English language and medieval literature at Bedford College (1923-42). He resumed contact with the University of Wales as external examiner during 1927-30 and he was external examiner to the University of London 1930-33. Despite his shyness, his students could not fail to realise the depth and breadth of his scholarship as he surveyed the linguistic changes from the fourth century onwards and presented them with glimpses into the realms of Germanic and Celtic lore. He was the editor of a number of medieval and sixteenth-century works and author of numerous volumes. His published works include: *A glossary of the Mercian hymns* (with H.C. Wyld, 1903); *Alfred and the prose of his reign* (1907); *Greene's Pandosto* (1907); *Introduction to the history of the English language* (1920); Middle English section in the *Year's Work in English studies* (1923 and 1924); *English literature before Chaucer* (1924); *Aspects of literary theory and practice, 1550-1870* (1931); and articles in *Modern Language Review*, and other learned periodicals.

He m., 22 Aug. 1918, Mary Pugh Jones, daughter of John Ivor Jones, Llangollen and Colombia, S. America, and they had two sons. They lived at Winfrith, 26 Forty Avenue, Wembley Park, Middlesex, where he d. 28 May 1954.

Www; WwW (1921); *Times*, 29 May and 9 June 1954.

M.A.J.

THOMAS, RICHARD (1871-1950), minister (CM) and writer; b. 8 Sept. 1871 at Llangefni, Angl. From Bala preparatory college he entered the University College, Bangor, where he graduated in 1901. After pursuing the theology course at Bala he was ordained in 1904, and was inducted minister of the Bontnewydd and Pen-y-graig churches in Arfon, where he remained for nearly 30 years. He was secretary of the board of governors of the Bontnewydd Home for orphans from 1904 to 1945 and was a governor until his death on 5 Apr. 1950.

His publications include *David Livingstone* (1912), *David Williams, y Piwritan* (1928), and *Cartre'r Plant* (1951). He won a National Eisteddfod prize for translations of legal terms into Welsh, and was for many years editor of the *Year-book* and *Diary* of his denomination.

Blwyddiadur, 1951; *Gol.*, 12 Apr. 1950; information supplied by his son.

R.B.W.

THOMAS, Sir ROBERT JOHN (1873-1951), politician and shipowner; b. 23 Apr. 1873, the son of William and Catherine Thomas, Bootle. He was educated at Bootle College, Liverpool Institute and Tettenhall College. He began working as a ship and insurance broker in the family business at Liverpool, and later became an underwriter at Lloyds. Thomas served as M.P. (Coalition Lib.) for the Wrexham division, 1918-22, stood unsuccessfully in Anglesey in 1922 before winning the seat at a by-election in Apr.

1923 held following the death of Sir Owen Thomas (*DWB*, 1150). He continued to represent Anglesey in Parliament until May 1929 when he resigned in order to be able to give more attention to his commercial interests. His successor in the constituency was Lady Megan Lloyd George (see LLOYD GEORGE FAMILY above). He was declared bankrupt in 1930 and was not discharged until 1935. Thomas was a member of the Anglesey County Council and served as High Sheriff for the county in 1912. He was the founder of the Welsh Heroes Memorial Fund to which he donated £20,000, and for many years he served as its honorary secretary. He also founded and equipped at Holyhead the Lady Thomas Convalescent Home for Discharged and Disabled Soldiers and Sailors. He was a native Welsh-speaker, a member of the Council of the University College of North Wales, Bangor, and for 15 yrs was the honorary treasurer of the Anglesey *Eisteddfod* Association. He was knighted in 1918.

Thomas m. in 1905 Marie Rose, dau. of Arthur Burrows. She d. in 1948. They had two sons and a daughter. His heir was Sir William Eustace Rhyddland Thomas (1909-57). He d. 27 Sept. 1951 at his home Garreg-lwyd, Holyhead, Anglesey.

Www; WwW (1921); *Times*, 28 Sept. 1951; *Dod's Parliamentary Companion*; *WWP*.

J.G.J.

THOMAS, Sir ROGER (1886-1960), pioneer of modern agriculture in India; b. 4 May 1886 at Pen-yr-ardd, Clunderwen, Pembs., the seventh of the eleven children of Lewis Thomas and Sophia (née James) his wife. He was educated at Narberth County School, and University College of Wales, Aberystwyth, where he gained 1st-class Honours in botany, with geology as a subsidiary subject. He was Victor Ludorum in sports, and ran for the college. Between leaving school at 16 and college, he taught as an uncertificated teacher at Pontyberem Primary and Narberth Board Schools, and at a private school in Taunton. After graduating in 1913, he was appointed a member of the Indian Agricultural Service and joined the Agricultural College of Coimbatore, South India, later becoming Deputy Director of Agriculture, Madras. In 1917 he went to Mesopotamia (now Iraq) as Deputy Director of Agricultural Research. He was a member of the Mesopotamia Expeditionary Force, with the rank of Captain, to enable him to carry out the work. He later rose to Colonel, and became Director General of Agriculture in 1920. In 1925 he resigned from government service, and spent some time travelling in the U.S.A., Egypt, Sudan, and Mexico, studying techniques of cotton growing. In 1927 he joined the British Cotton Growing Association at Khanewal, Punjab, India. In 1931 he bought land in Sind, and commenced farming in the area newly irrigated by the Sukkur Barrage, with the wider aims of improving farming generally, and cotton in particular. In Dec. 1944 he was appointed Minister for Agriculture, Sind Government. In 1945 due to pre-Independence political pressures he resigned, but remained as Advisor. In 1940 he was awarded the C.I.E., and in 1947 a knighthood. Both before and after World War II

he was a member of numerous committees in pre-partition India, and later Pakistan. His published works include: *Planning for agriculture in India* (1944); *Drainage and reclamation of irrigated lands in Pakistan, including a report on a visit to the U.S.A. and Egypt 1949* (1949); *Report on the draft of the Pakistan five-year plan* (1956).

In 1939 he m. Margaret Ethelwynne Roberts, of Ormskirk, Lancashire. They had one dau. He d. 19 Sept. 1960 and was buried at Blaenconin Baptist Chapel, Llandysilio, Clunderwen.

Personal knowledge.

M.E.T.

THOMAS, ROWLAND (*c.* 1887-1959), newspaper proprietor; b. *c.* 1887 at Oswestry, Salop, son of William Thomas and his wife. He was educated locally before entering the newspaper business, returning from World War I to succeed his father as director of the Caxton Press and chairman of Woodall, Minshall, Thomas and Co. Ltd., Oswestry, who originally produced only *The Border Counties Advertizer*. He founded the *Wrexham Leader* in 1920, later took over the *Montgomeryshire Express*, and in 1932 developed the Welsh language newspaper *Y Cymro* (formerly of Dolgellau) as a national weekly paper for Wales. In 1921 he acquired the Welsh book publishing company of Hughes and Son, and the Principality Press, Wrexham. Although he did not speak Welsh, he did all in his power to sustain the language. On the advice of a panel of leading Welsh scholars and authors he printed and published a constant supply of Welsh books, periodicals and newspapers, work which was recognized by his election as a member of the *Gorsedd* of Bards in 1947. He also developed the musical publishing activities of the press; both he and his wife, Elizabeth (née Parry), were organists of Oswald Road Chapel (Presb.), where he was an elder. He was a J.P. and became vice-chairman of the Oswestry bench. The publishing business had been transferred to his son Eric Lionel Thomas before he retired to live in Llandegfan, Anglesey. He d. suddenly, 17 May 1959, at Harrogate.

Thomas Bassett, *Braslun o hanes Hughes a'i Fab* (1946), 51-5; *Cymro*, 21 May 1959; *Times*, 19 May 1959.

M.A.J.

THOMAS, THOMAS JACOB ('Sarnicol'; 1873-1945), schoolmaster, writer and poet; b. 13 Apr. 1873 at 'Sarnicol', a cottage near Rhos-yr-hafod, Capel Cynon, Cards., the fourth of the five children of David Thomas, an agricultural labourer, and his wife Mary (née Jacob). He was registered as Tom, the name of the third child of his parents who had died in infancy. His first school was the board school at Capel Cynon which was locally known as Pantygiach and Clawddmelyn. He became a pupil-teacher there, but, following an altercation with his headmaster, he left to continue his education at Talgarreg school. Being a frail child his parents were advised to send him for a period to New Quay where there was a noted grammar school kept by C.J. Hughes. He stayed there for four years taking Department of Science and Art examinations. In 1891 he won a £20 scholarship at the University College of Wales, where he spent three sessions reading for the University of London B.Sc. degree. In 1894 he left for a teaching post in mathematics at the Hartley Institution in Southampton. In 1896 he obtained a post as science master at the Abergele intermediate school, where he found a more congenial atmosphere. During his stay at Abergele he took his final examination. In 1897 he migrated to the industrial valleys of south Wales, holding science posts at the following schools: Merthyr Tydfil, 1897-1901, Abertillery, 1901-13, Cyfarthfa Castle Boys', 1913-21. During his final year at Cyfarthfa he took the external B.A. degree of London University. In 1922 he was appointed first headmaster of the new Quakers Yard grammar school, Treharris, where he remained until his premature retirement owing to illhealth in Aug. 1931. The remainder of his life was spent in Llywel, Laura Place, Aberystwyth, where he found kindred spirits interested in literature and etymology with whom he could discuss the subjects which, despite his science training, were nearest to his heart. He d. 2 Dec. 1945, and was buried at Bwlch-y-groes (Congl.) chapel cemetery in his native neighbourhood. His wife survived him.

He won the chair at the Abergavenny national *eisteddfod* in 1913 with his ode 'Aelwyd y Cymro', and was in competition for the chair in London, 1909, Colwyn Bay, 1910, Wrexham, 1912, and Birkenhead, 1917. His *pryddest* at Bangor in 1931 was placed among the first three. He was one of the adjudicators of the *awdl* at Llanelli, 1930, and Bangor, 1943. He contributed much in prose and verse to the *Ymofynydd, Cymru, Y Geninen*, the *Western Mail*, the *London Kelt, Y Llenor, Y Ford Gron, Y Beirniad, Y Cymro*, and *The Merthyr Express*, for which he edited a Welsh column for many years. Many of his English poems appeared in the *Western Mail*, and he won several prizes for competitions in *John O'London* and *T.P's Weekly*. His chief publications were *Ar lan y môr a chaneuon eraill*, 1898, *Odlau Môr a Mynydd*, 1912, *Blodau drain duon*, 1935, *Storïau ar gân*, 1936, *Catiau cwta*, 1940, and *Chwedlau cefn gwlad*, 1944. He had a manuscript volume 'Odlau'r aelwyd', containing what he considered to be his best poems, ready for publication at the time of his death. The manuscript is at the National Library of Wales. He was notable for his skill as an epigrammatist and for his description of life and characters on his native heath around Banc Siôn Cwilt.

Ar Fanc Siôn Cwilt (ed. J. Tysul Jones), 1972; *Y Cardi*, 11 Oct. 1973.

E.D.J.

THOMAS, WILLIAM (1891-1958), under-secretary, Ministry of Housing and Local Government; b. 27 Nov. 1891, son of James and Catherine Thomas, Cymer, Rhondda, Glam. He was educated at Porth Secondary School and the University College at Cardiff where he graduated B.Sc. in 1911 and was demonstrator in physics there for a while. During World War I he served with the South Lancashire Regiment, and was on the General Staff (Intelligence) of the Egyptian Expeditionary Force. He was called to the bar at Inner Temple, 1928. He had joined the Civil Service in 1914, and eventually became a member of the Welsh

Board of Health, 1945-51, and under-secretary in charge of the Welsh Office of the Ministry of Housing and Local Government in Cardiff, 1951-54, when he retired. He contributed articles to *Y Fflam*, 1947, and the Welsh column of *The Western Mail* (e.g. 25 Nov. 1954) and was one of the editors of *Bro*, 1954. In 1925 he m. Mary Olwen Davies, Ynyshir, Rhondda and moved from Cymer in 1938 to 27 Maesycoed Road, The Heath, Cardiff. He d. 20 Apr. 1958.

Www; WWP.

M.A.J.

THOMAS, WILLIAM DAVIES (1889-1954), Professor of English; b. 5 Aug. 1889, son of William and Hannah Thomas, Abermule, Mont., where his father was a blacksmith and postmaster. He was educated at Newtown County School and at the University College of Wales, Aberystwyth, where he obtained a first-class honours degree in English in 1910. He was a valuable player in the college and town football teams. After a year as student assistant at Aberystwyth he proceeded to Jesus College, Oxford, gaining an M.A. in 1913. He was appointed lecturer at Trinity College, Toronto, Canada, becoming senior Professor of English at the University of Saskatchewan in 1919, after serving in France during World War I. In 1921 he returned to Wales as the first Professor of English language and literature at the newly founded University College at Swansea, a post he filled with distinction until his death. He helped nurture the college through its early life, being wise in committee, and serving as vice-principal of the college 1927-31. He was an excellent teacher, generous in encouraging his students, and a master at the art of examining, both at setting question papers and evaluating the scripts. He was sensitive to style and ideas, and wrote lively articles, full of grace and polish, but, being over-critical of his own work, very few of his writings were published. For many years he held highly successful extra-mural classes on English literature at Neath and elsewhere. He gave many radio talks on poetry and literature and various other topics. He m. Edith Mary, daughter of Richard Edwards, Maesycymer, and d. at home, 11 Clarendon Road, Sketty, Glam., 6 Mar. 1954.

WWP; West. Mail, 8 Mar. 1954; *Times*, 9 and 17 Mar. 1954.

M.A.J.

THOMAS, Sir WILLIAM JAMES (1867-1945), BARONET, coalowner, philanthropist; b. 10 Mar. 1867 at Caerphilly, Glam., s. of Thomas James and Jane Thomas. Orphaned at an early age he was cared for by his paternal grandmother during his schooldays at Mynyddislwyn and Pontypridd. He then entered the service of his grandfather, James Thomas (1817-1901), a pioneer of the coal industry in the Rhondda Fach valley, who at the age of 60 sank the Standard and Ynyshir pits. He left the greater part of his fortune to his grandson who displayed business acumen in the management of the mines and great consideration for the workers' welfare. Sir William, who was a director of the Great Western Railway, the Barry Dock and Railway and other companies, disposed of his mining interests in 1914 to the United National Collieries Ltd. Among his public gifts were £100,000 to the Welsh National School of Medicine, over £20,000 for the endowment of beds at the Cardiff Royal Infirmary, £5,000 to the Welsh National Memorial Anti-tuberculosis fund, £2,500 to the Welsh National Hospital for the treatment of wounded in World War I, and several thousand for other hospitals at Newport, Porth and Cardiff and for various religious causes. He was knighted in 1914 and created baronet five years later. He was a magistrate and Deputy Lieutenant for Glamorgan, High Sheriff in 1936 and member of the county council for many years. He became a Freeman of Cardiff in 1915, was awarded the honorary degree LL.D. by the University of Wales in 1931, and elected vice-president of the University College, Cardiff, in 1931.

He remained a member of Saron Welsh (Congl.) church, Ynyshir even after his removal to Cardiff. He m. in 1917 Maud Mary, eldest dau. of George Cooper, of Bexhill-on-Sea and deputy matron of Cardiff Royal Infirmary. Sir William d. 3 Jan. 1945 and was buried at the Cardiff Cemetery.

West. Mail, 4 Jan. 1945; Elizabeth Phillips, *A History of the pioneers of the Welsh coalfield* (1925); [*WwW* (1937)].

O.P.D.

THOMAS, WILLIAM JENKYN (1870-1959), schoolmaster and author; b. 5 July 1870, the son of John Thomas, Bryncocyn, Llangywer, Mer., and his wife Catherine who d. when William was a child, and the family moved to Plas Madog, Llanuwchllyn. He went to Friars School, Bangor, before matriculating as a sizar at Trinity College, Cambridge, in 1888; he had a scholarship in 1890 and graduated B.A. (class I part I in the classical tripos), and M.A. in 1896. After being a lecturer in classics at Bangor, 1891-96, he became headmaster of Aberdare county school. In 1905 he was appointed headmaster of the Grocers Company School at Hackney Downs, London, when it was taken over by London county council; he remained in post until his retirement in 1935. He took a prominent part in the Association of Headmasters. He was joint-secretary of the Incorporated Association of Headmasters, 1913-33; was made president in 1934 and re-elected for another year. He was a strong defender of his profession and did not hesitate to condemn any political interference in education, as when the governors of Pontypridd school refused to grant a holiday to the children on the occasion of a royal wedding in 1935, or when the Labour Party attempted to raise a committee in the same year to consider rewriting history books. He was harsh in his criticism of universities and the state for their reluctance in awarding worthy honours to teachers. David Lloyd George (see above) paid tribute to him in a preface to a souvenir booklet in celebration of his thirty years' headship at Hackney Downs. In 1893 he published a collection of *penillion* to be sung to harp accompaniment, and with E. Doughty *The new Latin Delectus* (1908-09). He edited an anthology of the poems of Sallust and Ovid in 1900, and two volumes for the 'Cameos of Literature': *The harp of youth, a book of poetry*

for school and home (1907) and *A book of English prose* (1909). With Charles W. Bailey he published *Letters to a young headmaster* (1927). Though he spent a lifetime in London he did not forget the needs of Wales. He edited *Cambrensia: a literary reading book for Welsh schools* (c. 1904), and published *The Welsh fairy book* (1907 and a number of reprints to 1995), *More Welsh fairy and folk tales* (1957), and a booklet *Heroes of Wales* (1912) based on sculptures in Cardiff City Hall. Some of his articles appeared in *Cymru* and *Wales* around 1894-95; and in *Wales*, 1911-15, there appeared a series of biographies by him entitled 'Forgotten Welshmen'. He addressed the Hon. Soc. of Cymmr. in 1941 on the same subject, urging the compiling and publishing of biographies of eminent Welsh persons [see *Trans. Cymm.*, 1941, 100-14]. For five years, if not more, he had appealed in lectures to the Guild of Graduates and on the radio for this project to be undertaken. [He contributed to *Bywg./DWB*]. He made his home at 38 Windsor Road, Finchley, and he and his wife had at least two sons. His wife, Marian Rose (née Dixon?), d. 22 Oct. 1936 and he d. 14 March 1959.

WWP; 1871, 1881 Census; [Juliette Wood, intro. to 1995 ed. of *The Welsh fairy book*].

E.D.J.

THOMAS, WILLIAM PHILLIP ('Gwilym Rhondda'; 1861-1954), colliery official; b. 27 Oct. 1861, son of Mary Thomas (née Phillips) and her husband of Treorchy, Glam. In 1874 he left the local school at the age of 12 to commence work as an office-boy with the Ocean Coal Co.; he rose to become general manager in 1926, retiring in 1933. He was director of the company 1927-37, and of many other coal companies besides. He was well known as an organiser of social and cultural activities. He was received into the *Gorsedd* of Bards under the pseudonym 'Gwilym Rhondda' at Cardiff national *eisteddfod* in 1883 for his literary and musical activities. He took an active part in religious affairs, being treasurer of the Welsh Baptist Association 1924-28, treasurer of the Union of Young Welsh Baptists, secretary of the Welsh Baptist Assembly of the Upper Rhondda District for more than 50 years and president of the Baptist Union in 1928-29. His great interest in the welfare of miners led him to organise very successful technical mining classes in the district. As secretary of Pentwyn hospital he organised the semi-national *eisteddfod* at Treorchy for 60 years, as well as drama festivals and other functions, in aid of the hospital. He served as J.P. and a member of Rhondda urban district council for over 25 years, being chairman 1913-14. He m., 1887, Elizabeth Devonald (d. 7 Aug. 1955). They had a son and two daughters and he retired to Hafod, Victoria Avenue, Porthcawl, Glam., where he d. 2 Aug. 1954 and was buried at Treorchy.

Llawlyfr Bed., 1955; *Adroddiad Noddfa (B), Treorci*, 1943 and 1955; *West. Mail*, 3 Aug. 1954; *WWP*; 1871 census, RG 10/5384.

M.A.J.

TILLEY, ALBERT (1896-1957), mace-bearer at Brecon cathedral and local historian; b. 8 Sept. 1896 at Norton Arms, Widnes, Lancs., one of the seven children of Edmund Valentine and Caroline (née Hawkins) Tilley. He was educated until he was aged fifteen at Simmer Cross school, Widnes. Then he moved to Liverpool and in 1914 joined the army. He was wounded on the Somme. He was sent to Brecon to recuperate where he met and subsequently married Constance Mary Watkins and settled there. They had one daughter. His wife d. in 1940. In Mar. 1923 he was appointed the first mace-bearer of the new cathedral in Brecon, an office which he held with dedication and remarkable dignity for thirty-three years until ill-health forced him to retire in Oct. 1956. He steeped himself in the history, traditions and architecture of the church. With strong encouragement from Gwenllian E.F. Morgan (*DWB*, 644-5) and Sir John Conway Lloyd (see above) he specialised in the history of the town and of his adopted county. He devoted himself to collecting material on local history, copying inscriptions in churches and cemeteries and other sources. He possessed an artistic talent and interested himself in the heraldry of the county and in the pedigrees of its families. Amongst his leisure interests was the collecting of majolica. He had special knowledge of the cathedral and its treasures, and his readiness to share his store of knowledge and his winning personality charmed thousands of visitors to the church during the period of his service. With great labour and skill he arranged a Christmas crib and Easter garden in the west corner of the church which was the object of general admiration for a quarter of a century.

He m. (2) 13 Sept. 1950, Doris Mary Davies. He d. 23 Sept. 1957, and was buried in Brecon cemetery following a funeral service at the cathedral on 25 Sept. His papers and MSS. were donated to the National Library by the Dean and Chapter of Brecon. It is a valuable collection of materials on the history, heraldry and geneology of Brecon and Brecknockshire.

Brecon and Radnor County Times, Sept., Oct. 1957; N.L.W. *Annual Reports*, 1964 and 1965; information from his widow.

E.D.J.

TOM NEFYN - see WILLIAMS, THOMAS below.

TOMLEY, JOHN EDWARD (1874-1951), solicitor; b. 3 Feb. 1874 son of Robert Tomley and Esther (née Weaver), Montgomery. He was educated at Montgomery and Shrewsbury; he was articled to Charles S. Pryce, former town clerk at Montgomery, obtaining honours in the solicitors' final examination in 1901, and became a member of the local firm of Pryce, Tomley and Pryce. He served as clerk to numerous public administrative bodies in Montgomeryshire and Shropshire. In 1950 he was president of the Association of Clerks to the Executive Councils of Wales. He was an active member of many bodies associated with public health and insurance, e.g., a member of the governors, council and various committees of the Welsh National Memorial Association which was concerned with the prevention,

treatment and abolition of tuberculosis. He took a prominent part in the inauguration of the Association of Welsh Insurance Committees, later becoming its president. He was also a member of the governing body of the Church in Wales. He was appointed a C.B.E. in 1920. His diverse interests are reflected in his published works: *Place names* (c. 1891), *Forms of religious worship*, *The old age pensions act*, *The Castle of Montgomery* (1923), *The de-rating act* (1928), and various statistical articles.

He m., 7 May 1902, Edith Florence Soley and had one son and two daughters. He lived at the Hollies, Montgomery, when he d. 14 June 1951.

WwW (1937); *Www*; *WWP*.

M.A.J.

TREE, RONALD JAMES (1914-70), priest and schoolmaster; b. 30 March 1914 at Garnant, Carms., s. of Frederick George and Susan Tree. He was educated at the church school Garnant, Dyffryn Aman county school and University College, Swansea, where he held a Powis Exhibition. He gained his B.A. 1st-class hons. in Philosophy 1937, M.A. 1939 and proceeded to New College, Oxford with an open scholarship and gained his B.A. with 1st-class hons. in Philosophy 1939: B.Litt. 1941. He was at St. Michael's College, Llandaff, 1939-40. Ord. deacon in 1940, he served as curate of Cwmaman, 1940-44 and was ord. priest, 1941. He was curate of St. Michael's, Aberystwyth, 1944-46 and acted as chaplain to the Anglican students in the University College. In 1946, he was appointed lecturer in Philosophy at St. David's College, Lampeter, and became professor in 1950. He was senior tutor and bursar in 1956. In 1957, he was appointed Warden and Headmaster of Llandovery College, succeeding G.O. Williams (later Archbishop of Wales). He was appointed canon of Mathry in St. David's Cathedral 1961. In 1966 he obtained the living of St. Mary's, Haverfordwest and was appointed director of religious education for the diocese of St. David's. He removed to St. David's when he was appointed Archdeacon of St. David's in 1968.

He published a number of articles on philosophical and historical subjects in *Efrydiau Athronyddol*, *Theology*, the *Jnl. Hist. Soc. of the Church in Wales*, *Province*, etc. He was a member of the editorial board of *Efrydiau Athronyddol* from 1949.

He played rugby football for his school and college and continued his enthusiasm for the game; his other hobby was carpentry. He was a genial character, at his best when tutoring students.

He m. in 1944 Ceridwen, dau. of G.E. Thomas, Gwauncaegurwen, and they had a dau. and a s. He d. 28 Nov. 1970 and was buried at St. David's.

Www; *St. David's Diocesan Year Book*, 1969; *Llan*, 11 Dec. 1970; *S. Wales Guardian*, 3 Dec. 1970; *West. Telegraph*, 3 Dec. 1970; personal acquaintance.

M.G.E.

TREFGARNE, GEORGE MORGAN, 1st BARON TREFGARNE of Cleddau (formerly GARRO-JONES, GEORGE MORGAN; 1894-1960), barrister-at-law and politician; b. 14 Sept.

1894 at Zion Hill House, Trefgarn, Pembs., son of David Garro-Jones, Congl. minister, and Sarah (née Griffiths). He was educated at Caterham School and served in the Denbighshire Yeomanry, 1913-14, and in France with the 10th South Wales Borderers and Royal Flying Corps., 1915-17, becoming an honorary captain in the Royal Air Force. In 1918 he went to America as advisory officer to the U.S. Air Service, returning as private secretary to Sir Hamar Greenwood (1919-21). A versatile and vigorous man, he was called to the bar at Gray's Inn in 1923 and was at the same time London editor of the *Daily Despatch*, resigning after two years when he became M.P. (L.) for South Hackney, 1924-29. In 1928 he went to Nigeria as a member of the Empire Parliamentary Delegation to inquire into trade conditions there. Late in 1929 he joined the Labour party (but rejoined the Liberals in 1958) and was the first Welshman to represent a Scottish constituency when he was elected M.P. (Lab.) for Aberdeen, 1935-45. Meanwhile he commenced practice on the South Wales Circuit in 1939. For three years he was parliamentary secretary to the Ministry of Production, 1942-45, and concurrently deputy chairman of the Radio Board, chairman of the Television Advisory Committee, 1946-49, and chairman of the Colonial Development Corporation from its inception in 1947, retiring in 1950 after the failure of the Gambia Egg Scheme. He was created a peer in 1947. He published *Jurisdiction of the railway rates tribunal* (1922), and his war experiences in *Ventures and visions* (1935). He m., 9 May 1940, Elizabeth Churchill, and had three sons and one daughter. He d. 27 Sept. 1960.

Www; Burke (1970); *WWP.*

M.A.J.

TREFÎN - see PHILLIPS, EDGAR above.

TREGONING, WILLIAM EDWARD CECIL (1871-1957), industrialist; b. 17 Feb. 1871, second son of John Simon Tregoning of Llanelli, Carms. and Sophia (née Morris, of Liverpool) his wife. He was educated at Harrow and Trinity College, Cambridge, before becoming a tinplate manufacturer and director of John S. Tregoning Co. Ltd (one of the first tinplate firms in Llanelli), St. David's Tinplate Co., Bynea Steel Works Ltd., and other companies. He was a founder member and trustee of the Welsh Plate and Sheet Manufacturing Association, a member of the International Tinplate Association and of the National Food Canning Council before World War II. He devoted much of his time, gifts and money to the Church in Wales, being a member of the governing body and treasurer and chairman of St. David's Diocesan Board of Finance from 1923. He retired in 1950 as J.P. for over 36 years, having been an outstanding chairman of the Llanelli magistrates court for many years.

In Oct. 1901 he m. Nancy, daughter of J. Beavan Phillips, and they had four sons and two daughters. He lived at Portiscliff, Ferryside, St. Ishmael, Carms., and d. 9 March 1957.

Iron and steel, 30, 1957, 158; *Llanelly Star*, 16 Mar. 1957; *WWP.*

M.A.J.

TREHARNE, BRYCESON (1879-1948), musician, b. in Merthyr Tydfil, Glam., in 1879. He studied at the Royal College of Music, London, and held teaching posts at Aberystwyth University College and in the University of Adelaide, Australia. He returned to Europe in 1911, spent some time in the Ruhleben prisoner of war camp, Germany, during World War I, and eventually (*c.* 1918) went to the U.S.A. From 1924 he taught music in McGill University, Montreal, Canada, but in 1928 he returned to the U.S.A., being for many years afterwards music editor to a Boston publishing company. Throughout the years he was an active composer and some of his solos, e.g. 'Môr o gân yw Cymru i gyd', became popular in Wales. A work by him, 'The Banshee', was performed in the 1938 national *eisteddfod*. He d. 4 Feb. 1948 in Long Island, New York.

Y Drych., 15 Feb. 1948; *Y Cerddor*, 1900, 62-4; *Gen.* Oct. 1951.

R.O.

TREHARNE, REGINALD FRANCIS (1901-67), Professor of history; b. 21 Nov. 1901 in Merthyr Tydfil, Glam., the son of Lewis Treharne and his wife Ethel Mary (née Hill) of Melksham, Wilts. He was educated at Ashton-in-Makerfield grammar school and the University of Manchester (B.A., 1922 and University postgraduate prize and studentship; M.A., 1923 and Langton Fellowship; Ph.D., 1925). He was appointed assistant lecturer at the University of Manchester in 1925, and was promoted lecturer in 1927. In 1930 he was appointed to the chair of history at the University College of Wales, Aberystwyth, where he spent the rest of his life and where he was much respected. He was elected F.R.Hist.S. in 1932. He was prominent in the Historical Association and was its president, 1958-61. He delivered the Raleigh Lecture to the British Academy in 1954. He held a Leverhulme Research Fellowship, 1946-47, and was visiting professor at the universities of Otago and Canterbury, New Zealand, in 1965. He was editor of *History* from 1947 to 1956. He published a number of standard books on history and numerous articles; amongst them *The Baronial plan of reform 1258 to 1263* (1932), *The Battle of Lewes in English history* (1964), *The Glastonbury legends* (1967), *Essays on thirteenth-century England* (1971), and editions of Muir's historical atlases. He was vice-principal of U.C.W. Aberystwyth, 1952-54, and again in 1957; he held the office with dignity. He was an excellent lecturer who did much to raise the standard of the college's department of history which had been quite low before his arrival there as a young man.

In 1928 he m. Ellen, daughter of Arthur Roberts, Tyldesley, Lancs. She was active in the life of the town and college and was generous in her hospitality to students. She was a Justice of the Peace for many years. They had one daughter. Professor Treharne d. 3 July 1967.

Www; personal knowledge; [for 'An Appreciation' of R.F. Treharne by Glanmor Williams, see pp. 1-8 of *Essays on thirteenth-century England* cited above].

E.D.J.

TREVOR, Sir CHARLES GERALD (1882-1959), inspector of forests; b. 28 Dec. 1882, son of Sir Francis Wollaston Trevor (of Trawscoed, Welshpool) and Mary Helen (née Mytton). He was educated at Wellington College and at the Royal Indian Engineering College, Coopers Hill. In 1903 he joined the Indian Forest Service as assistant conservator in Punjab. He was conservator of forests of the United Provinces in 1920 and became vice-president and Professor of Forestry at the Forest Research Institute, Dehra Dun., in 1926, later becoming chief conservator of forests in Punjab and North West Frontier Province, 1930-33. He was Inspector General of Forests to the Government of India, 1933-37, having represented India at the Imperial Forestry Conferences in Canada in 1923, Australia and New Zealand in 1928, and South Africa in 1935. He published a *Revised working plan for the Kulu forests* (1920); with E.A. Smythies, *Practical forest management* (1923); and with H. G. Champion, *A manual of Indian silviculture* (1938). In 1937 he received a knighthood and retired to Trawscoed Hall, Welshpool, Mont., where he took an active interest in his dairy and sheep farm, Fron y Fele, Guilsfield, and became the owner of a prize-winning flock of Kerry Hill sheep. He was prominent in the National Farmers' Union and all agricultural activities. For 17 years he served as a magistrate, and was High Sheriff of his county in 1941. In 1912 he m. Enid Carroll Beadon and had three daughters. He d. 20 May 1959.

Www; Montgomeryshire Express, 23 May 1959.

M.A.J.

TRUBSHAW, Dame GWENDOLINE JOYCE (1887-1954), public administrator and social worker; baptised 1 Apr. 1887, daughter of Ernest and Lucy Trubshaw, Ael-y-bryn, Felin-foel, Llanelli, Carms. During World War I she was responsible for the recruitment of women for war service and took a deep interest in their welfare, particularly those working in armament factories. She was chairman of South-West Wales War Pensions Committee and received a C.B.E. in 1920 for her services as honorary secretary to the Soldiers', Sailors' and Airmen's Families Association. She was elected a member of Carmarthen County Council in 1919 and later an alderman, and became its first woman chairman in 1937. She took great interest in local education, being governor of Llanelli County Schools and chairman of Llanelli School of Art. She was also very active in various health organisations, being a member of the Carmarthenshire Blind Society, and the West Wales Joint Board for Mental Defectives (of which she was chairman for four years), and when the Women's Voluntary Service was established she became the organiser for her county in 1939. In 1946 she was chairman of the Public Health Committee, having been a member for nearly 27 years, whilst in 1951 she became a member of the Central Health Services Council. She was created Dame of the British Empire in 1938. Her home was at Cae Delyn, Llanelli, but she d. in London 8 Nov. 1954.

WwW (1921); *Www; Carm. Jnl.*, 12 Nov. 1954; *WWP*.

M.A.J.

TRUEMAN, Sir ARTHUR ELIJAH (1894-1956), Professor of geology; b. 26 Apr. 1894 at Nottingham, son of Elijah Trueman and Thirza (née Cottee). He was educated at the High Pavement School, Nottingham (1906-11) and the University College of Nottingham. He graduated in 1914 with first-class honours in geology and was awarded the degrees of M.Sc. in 1916 and D.Sc. in 1918, for his resarch on Jurassic rocks and fossils. From 1917 to 1920 he was assistant lecturer in the University College, Cardiff, and then, 1920-30, head of the geology department in the new University College of Swansea; 1930-33 Professor of Geology and head of the department of geography at Swansea; 1933-37 Chaning Wills Professor of Geology at the University of Bristol; and 1937-46 Professor of geology at the University of Glasgow. 1946-49 he was deputy chairman and 1949-53 chairman of the University Grants Committee in the very important transition years of the universities from war to peacetime conditions with the resultant great expansion. He was chairman of the Geological Survey Board, 1943-54, again during the period of post-war expansion of the Survey, when work in the British coalfields was greatly intensified. In 1945-47 he was president of the Geological Society of London, and was awarded the Bigsby Medal of that Society in 1939, and their highest award, the Wollaston Medal, in 1955. Other distinctions which he gained were the Gold Medal of the South Wales Institute of Engineers in 1934, LL.D. *hon. causa* of the Universities of Rhodes, Glasgow, Leeds and Wales, Fellow of the Royal Society of Edinburgh in 1938 and F.R.S. in 1942. He was created K.B.E. in 1951.

His considerable research on Jurassic stratigraphy and palaeontology was internationally acclaimed, but he is best remembered for his work on the Coal Measures of Britain and especially on the use of the non-marine lamellibranchs. This work, *The Coalfields of Great Britain* (1954), made a considerable contribution to the development of both the exposed and concealed coalfields of Britain. He was interested in the popularization of science and wrote widely on the geology and scenery of England and Wales (1938, 1949).

He m. Florence Kate Offler in 1920 and they had one son, Dr. E.R. Trueman, a distinguished zoologist. He d. 5 Jan. 1956.

Proc. Geolog. Soc. London, no. 1541 (1956), 146-9; *Proc. Geologists Assoc.*, 68 (1957), 101-4; *Biog. Memoirs Fellows R.S.*, 4 (1958), 291-301 (see 302-5 for a bibliography of his books and published papers).

T.R.O.

TUDOR, STEPHEN OWEN (1893-1967), minister (Presb.) and author; b. 5 Oct. 1893 at Llwyn-y-gog, Staylittle, in the parish of Trefeglwys, Mont., son of Thomas and Hannah Tudor. He was educated at Newtown grammar school, and he served with the Welsh Guards in France during World War I. As a result of deep experiences he had during the war, he felt a call to enter the ministry. He went to University College, Aberystwyth (where he graduated with honours in philosophy), and to Lincoln College, Oxford (where he graduated with honours in theology). He won a David B. Mills

Scholarship which enabled him to continue his studies at the Union Theological Seminary, New York, U.S.A. He served for a period as student-pastor of Marsden church, Saskatchewan, Canada before returning to Wales. He was ord. in 1927 and became minister of Gaerwen and Pensarn Berw, Anglesey (1927-29), Tabernacl, Porthmadog (1929-35), and Moriah, Caernarfon (1935-62). During World War II he served as a chaplain in the army. After retiring, he moved to Colwyn Bay, supervising the churches at Llanddulas and Llysfaen. In 1927 he m. Ann Hughes Parry of Machynlleth; they had two sons and two daughters. He d. 30 June 1967 and his remains were buried at Llawr-y-glyn, Mont.

He was a prominent figure in the life of his denomination, being Moderator of the North Wales Association (1966). He delivered the Davies Lecture in 1959 on the Doctrine of the Incarnation, which was not published. He had an astute mind and developed deep convictions which he expressed with firmness from the pulpit and through the press. He contributed much to *Y Traethodydd*, *Y Drysorfa*, *Y Brython* and *Y Goleuad*, and was for years a regular columnist to the last two, writing a query and answer column, under the pseudonym 'Theophilus' in the latter. He published several books on religious matters: *Protestaniaeth* (1940), *Ein cymunwyr ieuainc* (1947), and *Beth yw Calfiniaeth?* (1957). He also wrote two detective stories: *Cyfrinach yr Afon* (1934) and *Tranc y Rheolwr* (1937), and before the end of his life he published a collection of essays, *Hen Raseli ac ysgrifau eraill* (1966).

Blwyddiadur MC, 1968, 289-90; *Gol.*, 26 July 1967; *Drys.*, 1966, 70; information from his widow.

G.M.R.

TURBERVILL, EDITH PICTON - see PICTON-TURBERVILL, EDITH above.

TWISTON-DAVIES, LEONARD - see DAVIES, Sir LEONARD TWISTON above.

V-W

VAUGHAN, HERBERT MILLINGCHAMP (1870-1948), historian and author; b. 27 July 1870 at Penmorfa, Llangoedmor, Cards., eldest son of John Vaughan and Julia Ann (Morris). He was educated at Clifton College and at Keble College, Oxford, where he graduated. Having private means he was able from his early youth to pursue his interests in the study of history and literature, and in authorship. He produced and published over a dozen books, besides articles, studies and reviews; three novels and other works remain in MS. His first book was *The Last of the Royal Stuarts* (1906), a life of Henry Benedict Stuart, Jacobite Duke of York and later Cardinal of York. From 1899 to 1910, when he was writing on Italian history and topography, he lived in Italy, mainly in Naples and Florence. A visit to Australia in 1912-13 led to the writing of *An Australasian Wander Year*. During World War I he lived at Plas Llangoedmor, engaged in various types of war service, mainly on committees in the county of Cardigan, and in writing works of fiction, particularly *Meleager: A Fantasy* (1916) and *The Dial of Áhaz* (1917). Two books by him were published privately, *Sonnets from Italy* (1919), and *Nepheloccygia: or Letters from Paradise* (1929).

In 1924, Vaughan went to live at Tenby where he wrote his best known work of Welsh interest, viz. *The South Wales Squires* (1926); he had previously written a national *eisteddfod* essay on 'The Welsh Jacobites' (published in *Cymm. Trans.*; 1920) and a study of Thomas Johnes of Hafod and his private press (*Cymm. Trans.*, two articles, 1911-12, 1919-20; *DWB*, 441-2); he was also a contributor to *West Wales Historical Records*, the *Journal of the Welsh Bibliographical Society*, *Western Mail*, *Welsh Outlook*, and some of the better known English Reviews.

Vaughan deserves to be commemorated also for his long years of devoted service (1916-48) to the National Library of Wales, both as member or chairman of some committees, and for his gifts to that institution. He gave to the Library the Oriental manuscripts collected in India by his great-grandfather, Benjamin Millingchamp (*DWB*, 633); on Millingchamp and the MSS. see his 'Life and Letters of the Venerable Benjamin Millingchamp' (now N.L.W. MSS. 13915-6) and H. Ethé, *N.L.W. Catalogue of Oriental Manuscripts* (1916). He was an authority on bookplates, helping to catalogue the Sir Evan Davies Jones collection and cataloguing for the National Library (1938) the Aneurin Williams collection. During his sojourn in Italy he had collected a large number of Italian books, some of them rare works; this Italian collection is now in the National Library. Just before he d. he wrote (not for publication) 'Memoirs of a Literary Bloke' (now N.L.W. MS. 14341) and 'Notes on the Life of Dorothy, Viscountess Lisburne' (N.L.W. MS. 14647), a member of a family with which he claimed kinship. He d. 31 July 1948 at Tenby.

N.L.W. Journal, 6, 166-9; *Who's Who*, 1948; personal knowledge.

W.Ll.D.

VAUGHAN, JOHN (1871-1956), general; b. 31 July 1871, the second son of John Vaughan, Nannau, Dolgellau, Mer. (he d. in 1900) and Elinor Anne, dau. of Edward Owen, Garthyngharad, Dolgellau. The family could trace its descent from the Welsh princes of the middle ages. Vaughan was educated at Eton and at the Royal Military College at Sandhurst. He joined the Seventh Hussars in 1891 and served in the Matabele relief expedition in 1896, in Mashonaland in 1897, and in the Sudan campaign in 1898. He was badly wounded during the South African War of 1899-1901, was mentioned three times in despatches, and was awarded an array of honours including the D.S.O. in 1902. He became a major in the 10th Hussars in 1904, and from 1911 until 1914 he served as commandant of the Cavalry School at Netheravon. During World War I he was given command of the Third Cavalry Brigade; he was mentioned in despatches, was awarded C.B. in 1915 and a bar to the D.S.O. in 1919. He also became a *Commander Légion d'honneur*. In 1919 he was chosen to command the First Cavalry Brigade, and retired from military life in the following year.

John Vaughan served as the Welsh President of the British Legion in 1932, was a zone commander of the Home Guard during World War II, and was Deputy Lieutenant of Merionethshire from 1943 until 1954. He also served as a J.P. for the county. He published a volume of reminiscences entitled *Cavalry and sporting memoirs* (1955), where he was harsh in his condemnation of David Lloyd George's (see above) leadership during World War I. He was much interested in fishing and hunting.

Vaughan m. on 22 Oct. 1913 Louisa Evelyn, eldest dau. of Captain J. Stewart, Alltyrodyn, Llandysul, Cards., and the widow of Harold P. Wardell, Brynwern, Newbridge-on-Wye. There were no children. They lived at Nannau. He d. 21 Jan. 1956 at his home after falling from his horse.

Www; *WwW* (1921, 1933 and 1937); *Times*, 23 and 26 Jan. 1956; Thomas Nicholas, *County families of Wales* (1875); *WWP*.

J.G.J.

VAUGHAN, WILLIAM HUBERT (1894-1959), railway guard and chairman of the Welsh Land Settlement Society; b. 21 Mar. 1894, son of Henry Charles and Catherine Vaughan, Rogerstone, Mon. He was educated at the Eastern School, Port Talbot, and, like his father and two brothers, was employed on the railway, where he served for 51 years, 34 of them as a guard. He became a well respected figure who undertook a remarkable variety of public voluntary work. He was a member of Port Talbot borough council, 1927-48, served as mayor of Port Talbot, 1941, became a J.P. in 1949 and was Deputy Lieutenant for Glamorganshire, 1957. He took an active interest in politics, serving as secretary to the Aberavon Constituency Labour Party from 1934 till his death. From 1939 he became a member of the Glamorgan Agricultural Executive, and was a member of the Welsh National Forestry Committee from 1945. In 1948 he was appointed a forestry commissioner, and as a member for Wales he did much towards the ambitious planting scheme in which he saw great hope for the country. As a member of the National Parks Commission from 1952 he became a prime mover in designating the Brecon Beacons an area of outstanding natural beauty. He was elected chairman of the Welsh Land Settlement Society Ltd. in 1953; he was appointed to the Welsh Advisory Council of the B.B.C. in 1957, and was a member of Milford Haven Conservancy Board, 1958, and of the Glamorgan River Board. He contributed many articles to national periodicals, and Trades Union and political journals. For service in both World Wars he was awarded several medals, and was appointed C.B.E. in 1958 for his public service. In 1921 he m. May Bishop, they had one daughter and resided in Wood Street, Taibach, and later at Groeswen Ganol, Port Talbot. He d. suddenly at Paddington Station, 17 Apr. 1959, on his way to attend a meeting of the Forestry Commission.

Www; Times, 20 and 22 Apr. 1959.

M.A.J.

VILE, THOMAS HENRY (1882-1958), rugby player; b. 6 Sept. 1882, in Newport, Mon. His rugby career was outstanding, as a player (8 caps for Wales, 1908-1921), referee (12 internationals, 1923-28), and administrator (president of the W.R.U., 1955-56). His playing career was extraordinarily long. He had his first chance with Newport in the third team in 1900. By 1902, he was a scrum-half in the first team. In 1904, he went with the British team to Australia and New Zealand. Because of the presence of Richard M. ('Dickie') Owen (*DWB*, 720) in the Welsh team, he had to wait until 1908 before gaining his first cap. He became captain of the Newport team in 1909, and the partnership between him and Walter Martin was one of the most brilliant ever known. He had an acute tactical mind. He steered Newport to their historic win (9 – 3) over South Africa in 1912. To his own, and everyone else's astonishment, he was recalled as captain of the Welsh team in 1921, when he was 37. He had a notable career as a soldier, businessman, and social administrator. He was High Sheriff for Monmouthshire in 1944. He d. in Newport on 30 Nov. 1958.

W.J.T. Collins, *Rugby Recollections* (1948); *S. Wales Argus*, and *West. Mail*, 1 Dec. 1958; *Times*, 2 Dec. 1958.

G.W.W.

VIVIAN, ALGERNON WALKER HENEAGE - see WALKER-HENEAGE-VIVIAN, ALGERNON below.

WADE, GEORGE WOOSUNG (1858-1941), cleric, professor, and author; b. 16 Aug. 1858 in China, son of Joseph Henry Wade of Shanghai, and educated at Monmouth School and Oriel College, Oxford (scholar). He took a first class in Classical Honours Moderations (1879) and a second class in Literae Humaniores (1882). He was made deacon in 1885 and ordained priest in 1886. After serving as curate of Basing, Hampshire,

from 1885 to 1888, he was appointed to the chair of Latin at St. David's College, Lampeter, and remained there for forty-four years, retiring from his chair and from the Senior Tutorship in 1932. He m. Rachel Elinor, dau. of the Rev. F.H. Joyce, and sister of Gilbert Cunningham Joyce, Bishop of Monmouth (see above). In 1934 he received the degree of D.D. (*honoris causa*) of the University of Wales, and he was also a canon of S. Asaph Cathedral. He d. at Monmouth on 15 October, 1941, and was buried there.

As a teacher at St. David's College for over forty years, Wade exercised a lasting influence on generations of alumni of the College and through them on the Church in Wales. In his teaching he laid great emphasis on thoroughness, and on the unity of all knowledge. In a farewell message to his students he expressed the hope that they would ever make progress in learning and true godliness.

His literary output was considerable. It included *Old Testament History* (first edition, 1901; twelfth edition, 1934); *New Testament History* (first edition, 1922; second edition, 1932): commentaries on Genesis, 2 Samuel, Isaiah, and most of the Minor Prophets: and *The Documents of the New Testament*, 1934. He was also much interested in topography and was wholly or partly responsible for the volumes in the Methuen *Little Guide* series in South Wales, Monmouthshire, Somerset, and Herefordshire.

Www; Foster, *Alumn. Oxon.*; *St. David's College, Magazine*, 1933: University of Wales, Court Minutes, July 1934.

T.I.E.

WADE-EVANS, ARTHUR WADE (ARTHUR WADE EVANS; 1875-1964); clergyman and historian; b. 31 Aug. 1875 at Hill House, Fishguard, Pemb., son of Titus Evans, master mariner, and Elizabeth (née Wade) his wife. He went to Haverfordwest grammar school and graduated at Jesus College, Oxford (1893-96) before entering the priesthood, being ord. deacon in St. Paul's Cathedral in 1898. By Deed Poll on 2 Sept. 1899 he assumed the surname Wade-Evans and soon afterwards m., 12 Oct. 1899, at St. George's, Hanover Sq., London, Florence May Dixon (d. 16 Jan. 1953). They had two daughters. After serving as curate in Ealing, Oakley Sq., Paddington Green, Cardiff, and English and Welsh Bicknor (1898-1909), he became vicar of France Lynch (1909-26). During this period he led a campaign for the disestablishment of the Church in Wales. He became vicar of Pottersbury with Furtho and Yardley Gobion (1926-32), and finally rector of Wrabness (1932-57) before retiring to Frinton-on-sea, Essex, where he d. 4 Jan. 1964.

He was a prolific writer, being author or editor of several books and numerous articles and letters in *Notes and Queries, Celtic Review, Beirniad, The Guardian, Western Mail, South Wales News* and many other journals and newspapers. He wrote on a wide range of topics such as the Welsh dialect of Fishguard, antiquarian problems and church plate (some papers were published as *Papers for thinking Welshmen* (1907)), but he made his most significant contribution as an historian of early Britain. He believed that the teaching of acknowledged historians of his age on the Saxon conquest and the flight of the Britons to the west - Wales and Cornwall - was erroneous and based on a misinterpretation of the nature of the text of *de excidio Britanniae* by Gildas (*DWB*, 277-9). In an effort to support his thesis he translated and made a thorough study of early historical documents and texts, publishing, most particularly, *Nennius's 'History of the Britons'* (1938), *Coll Prydain* (1950), and the fullest exposition of his views *The Emergence of England and Wales* (1956, 1959). He did much work on the history of the Celtic church, *Welsh Christian Origins* (1934), *Parochiale Wallicanum* (1911), a useful list of Welsh churches and chapelries, and on the lives of the saints in articles in *Y Cymmrodor* and *Archaeologia Cambrensis*. He provided a full analysis and translation of the Latin text in *Life of St. David* (1923) and published a number of Latin and Welsh texts with English translation in *Vitae sanctorum Britanniae et genealogiae* (1944). His *Welsh Mediaeval Law* (1909) remains a good text of '*Llyfr Cyfnerth*' (Cyfnerth's Book), and he contributed an article on Welsh law to *Encyclopaedia Britannica* (1929). Wade-Evans maintained his unorthodox theories and argued skilfully in their favour all his life. He was an acknowledged authority on Welsh and English hymnody, and his MS of a proposed hymnal, 'Proper hymns for the Christian year', is in the National Library of Wales with his other MSS and annotated volumes from his library.

An elder brother, JOHN THOMAS EVANS ('Tomos ap Titus', 1 Aug. 1869 - 10 May 1940), who was educated at Llandovery, London College of Divinity and St. John's College, Cambridge, was rector of Stow-on-the-Wold (1899-1939) and became well-known for his eight volumes on the church plate of England and Wales. Many of his MSS, too, are at N.L.W.

WWP; *Arch. Camb.*, 1964, 169-70; *Trans. Cymm.*, 1965, 257-271.

M.A.J., B.F.R.

WALKER-HENEAGE-VIVIAN, ALGERNON (1871-1952), admiral; b. 4 Feb. 1871, third son of Major Clement Walker Heneage, V.C., 8th Hussars, of Compton Bassett, Wilts., and Henrietta Letitia Victoria, daughter of John Henry Vivian of Singleton, Swansea. He m. (1) in 1912 Helen Mary, dau. of Capt. E. de V. du Boulay, late R.H.A. and they had three daughters (divorce, 1931); m. (2) in 1931 Beryl, dau. of T. Stanley, Cardiff. He assumed the name of Walker-Heneage-Vivian by Royal Licence in 1921. He was educated at Evelyn's and Stubbington, Hants. In 1886 he began a career in the Royal Navy, joining the battleship HMS *Triumph* as a midshipman under the command of Sir Algernon Heneage, a relative of his. He began to specialise in anti-submarine warfare when serving in HMS *Royal Arthur* in the Pacific. He gained speedy promotion, becoming commander in 1900. He served in various parts of the world, including north China. He was second-in-command of the naval contingent which was sent by HMS *Powerful* to defend Ladysmith in South Africa, and he was mentioned in despatches. The siege affected his health, and he was seriously ill afterwards. In 1907 he was promoted captain in command of the minelayer HMS *Hyacinth*, and in 1908 was given command of the First Squadron of Minelayers. At the beginning of World War I he took command of the battleship HMS *Albion* and soon sailed to the South Atlantic on a secret mission to transport gold bullion from South Africa to assist the war effort. This was followed by an assignment in the eastern Mediterranean to support the landings at Gallipoli (twice mentioned in despatches). During 1915-16 he was commodore commanding small vessels in the eastern Mediterranean, including 160 minesweepers. As commodore first class he was in charge of the allied barrage across the Strait of Otranto, 1916-17. Then he became Senior British Naval Officer in Italy and he was promoted rear-admiral in 1918. He was A.D.C. to the King, 1917-18. He retired from active service in 1920 after a long and distinguished career, in which his special contribution had been in anti-submarine warfare and defence against mines. He was promoted vice-admiral in 1923 and admiral in 1927.

On retirement he settled in Swansea, at first at Parc le Breos, Penmaen, an estate which he had been left by Graham Vivian. But, soon after, he inherited Clyne Castle on the death of Dulcie Vivian. Thereupon he added 'Vivian' to his surname. He played a full part in the commercial, social and cultural life of the area. He became director and chairman of his family business, Vivian & Sons Ltd. (involved in the production of non-ferrous metals), and chairman of the South-west Wales Savings Bank. He was a Justice of the Peace, Deputy Lieutenant of Glamorgan, and in 1926 High Sheriff of Glamorgan. He became Honorary Colonel of the 53rd (Welsh) division Training R.A.S.C. (T). He showed his interest in horticulture by the care which he lavished on his own gardens and by joining the Garden Society and the Rhododendron Society. He was a founder and first president of The Gower Society. He received many honours, including M.V.O. (1904), C.B. (1916), Officer of the *Légion d'Honneur*, Order of the Rising Sun (2nd class), and Grand Officer of the Crown of Italy. He was renowned for the warm welcome which he gave to the many important visitors who came to Clyne Castle. He d. 26 Feb. 1952. As a result of death duties it proved necessary to sell Clyne Castle (which was bought by the University College of Swansea) and many of its contents. His portrait was painted by Evan Walters (see below) in 1926, and by Margaret Lindsay Williams (see below) in 1931.

Www; Ralph A. Griffiths, *Clyne Castle, Swansea* (1977); *Navy list*; *Kelly's Handbook*, 1938.

Don.M.

WALTERS, DAVID (EUROF) (1874-1942), minister (Congl.) and writer; b. 27 May 1874 the eldest of the five children of John and Ann (née Dyer) Walters of Ty'n-y-coed, Betws, Ammanford, Carms. The father was a blacksmith and the family moved when David was five years old to Glais, near Clydach, Swansea Valley. He had his early education at the local board school where he became a pupil-teacher. The family were members at Seion, Glais, and his mother ensured that she took him to all the meetings held at that church. Another strong influence on him was his uncle Job Richards, 'Eilab', who had been a schoolmaster at the Llanelli copper works school and at Pontfathew (Bryn-crug today) near Tywyn, Mer., before embarking on a course at Bodiwan College, Bala, under the tuition of Michael Daniel Jones (*DWB*, 495-6) and John Peter (*ibid.*, 751), and becoming the first minister of Moriah (Congl.), Tŷ-croes.

Eurof Walters had for a time been a clerk with the Merthyr-Brecon Railway Company, before being apprenticed at Tracy's shop in Morriston as a jeweller and goldsmith (the explanation of his bardic name). He went to Gwynfryn School, Ammanford (see Watkin Hezekiah Williams, *DWB*, 1076), for half a year. He walked there from the home of his cousin John Dyer Richards, the eldest son of Job and Mary (née Dyer) Richards of Waun-lwyd, Saron, Llandybïe. The two cousins went to the Memorial College, Brecon, and Eurof pursued a degree course at the University College, Cardiff, where he obtained a first class in Hebrew and Greek. For three years successively he was awarded a scholarship. With the Dan Isaac Davies scholarship for three years he took an honours course in Welsh. He received a number of calls but decided to complete the B.D. course; he was amongst the first Welshmen to obtain that degree. He was ordained at Salem, Llandovery, where he stayed for five years, and was then minister of Market Square English church, Merthyr Tydfil, 1905-10. Afterwards he was a representative of the Bible Society, 1910-15, and travelled extensively in the Netherlands, Belgium and France. At the beginning of World War I he accepted a call to the church in Henrietta Street, Swansea, where he laboured for eleven years (1915-26) during which time the membership doubled there. His next pastorate was at Christ Church, Oswestry. In 1931 he moved to Tabernacl Welsh church, Belmont Road, Liverpool, where he threw himself into the Welsh religious and cultural life on Merseyside. He was awarded the M.A. degree of the University of Liverpool in 1933 for a thesis on Vavasor Powell (*DWB*, 777-8). He took an interest in bibliographical matters, was a member of the Welsh Bibliographical Society and a contributor to its journal. He was also a member of the *Gorsedd* of Bards. He was one of the founders of the Welsh Summer Schools under the Union of Welsh Societies, and was a tutor in Welsh literature for years. He won six *eisteddfod* chairs and many prizes in the national *eisteddfod*, e.g. an essay on Stephen Hughes (Birkenhead, 1917), an historical novel *Pwerau'r Deufyd* (Port Talbot, 1932). He wrote on the Sunday school syllabuses in *Y Tyst* and *Y Dysgedydd* and a number of Biblical commentaries. He was chairman of the Union of Welsh Independents in 1940-41.

He m. Catherine Eleanor (Kate), daughter of William Thomas, minister (Congl.) of Gwynfe, and Mary his wife; they had three children. In his latter years his health was impaired by the effects of the air-raids on Liverpool and also on Swansea where a great deal of the fruit of his scholarship and literary work was lost when Morgan and Higgs' bookshop was destroyed by enemy action. He d. at his home 12 Hampstead Road, Elm Park, Liverpool, on 24 Sept. 1942; his body was cremated at Liverpool crematorium.

WwW (1937); *Tyst*, 8 and 15 Oct. 1942.

E.D.J.

WALTERS, EVAN JOHN (1893-1951), artist; b. 6 Jan. 1893 in the Welcome Inn, Mynydd-bach, Llangyfelach, near Swansea, Glam., son of Welsh-speaking parents, Thomas Walters and his wife Elizabeth (née Thomas). After attending the village school at Llangyfelach, he became an apprentice painter-decorator at Morriston, Swansea. In 1910 he entered the Swansea School of Art, then under Grant Murray. He went on to Regent Street Polytechnic and the Royal Academy in London. Fearing that the World War would interrupt his work, he emigrated to America in 1916, but there he was called upon when America entered the war. Rejected for military service, he became a camouflage painter. After the war he returned to Swansea to resume his artistic career. He worked in oils, watercolour, pastel, crayon and pencil. At first his subjects were mainly portraits, but he also painted local landscapes and scenes, still-life and figures, and he designed schemes for interior decoration. In 1920 he held a one-man show in the Glynn Vivian Art Gallery, Swansea, where his work was noticed by a local philanthropist, Mrs Winifred Coombe Tennant, Neath (see under COOMBE TENANT above); this lady encouraged him with patronage and introductions. His work was in demand locally at a time when it was unusual to buy original art. At the Swansea national *eisteddfod* of 1926 he won a prize for a painting of Pennard castle, receiving high praise from his adjudicator, Augustus John (see above). His portraits often showed coal miners and local people, but he also had prominent figures sitting for him, such as David Lloyd George (see LLOYD GEORGE, DAVID above), Ramsay MacDonald, Lord Balfour, Rear Admiral Walker Heneage (later Walker-Heneage-Vivian; see above) and Archbishop David Lewis Prosser (see above). he also made numerous self-portraits. He had skill in capturing the likeness and personality of the sitter. His work was shown in Wales, London and Brighton. He could have continued as a successful portrait painter but for his restless desire to experiment. His picture of the Annunciation in modern dress displeased the critics. He then became obsessed with the theory of 'double vision': he claimed that an object appeared 'solid' to the viewer only when his eyes were focussed on it, and consequently other objects should be shown in double image. He followed the Impressionists in seeking to break down colours into their basic components. His 'blurred' pictures proved less popular, and his reputation waned. His last exhibition was held in the Alpine Club Gallery, London, in 1950. His last portrait was of Mrs Coombe Tennant, but she insisted that it should not be in 'double vision'. David Bell (see above) in his assessment of Walters declared that he had great talent, but never succeeded, in spite of conscious effort, in using his considerable powers to create an art acceptable to any large section of his contemporaries.

A shy country-boy at first, Evan Walters later affected a Bohemian image, with flowing hair and goatee beard. His marriage in 1935 to a student friend, Marjorie Davies, lasted but a few months. He was much attached to his parents and nursed them both in their last years. He d. in London on 14 March 1951 and was buried at

Llangyfelach. A number of his remaining works were left to the National Museum of Wales and to the Glynn Vivian Gallery. There are other examples in the National Library of Wales, Carmarthen Museum and Parc Howard, Llanelli.

David Bell, *Evan Walters memorial exhibition*, catalogue with biography (1952); Kirstine Brander Dunthorne, *Artists exhibited in Wales 1945-74* (1976); Michael Jacobs and Malcolm Warner, *Art in Wales* (1980); Erna Meinel, 'The visual wasteland', *The Studio*, Feb. 1955; Evan Walters, 'Binocular vision', *Artist*, xix, March-Aug. 1940, nos 1-6.

Don.M.

WALTERS, THOMAS GLYN (WALTER GLYNNE; 1890-1970), tenor; b. 4 Jan. 1890 son of David and Elizabeth (née Jones) Walters, Cefngorwydd, Gowerton, Glam., and was educated at Gowerton Grammar School. He was a bank clerk until he decided to take up a musical career, and won a scholarship to the Royal College of Music in London in 1910. He served in the Welsh Guards during World War I. In 1921, on the recommendation of Sir Landon Ronald, HMV's music advisor, he secured a recording contract with the company. He was one of the first singers in Britain to broadcast, and because his voice suited the microphone he had a successful career in that medium. He sang in the lyric concerts held by the companies of Boosey, Chappell and Cramer in London, and also with the Carl Rosa and D'Oyly Carte opera companies. He made very many recordings, excelling as a lyrical singer; he was known in particular for his rendering of ballads, but he was also a good tenor in oratorios, and in 1935 he recorded arias from Handel's *Messiah*. Among his Welsh records there are parts from *Blodwen* by Joseph Parry and ballads, some of which are to the vocal accompaniment of the Welsh Miners' Quartet from the Llanelli area. He took part in complete recordings of *The Yeomen of the Guard* by Gilbert and Sullivan and Coleridge-Taylor's *Hiawatha's Wedding Feast*. His disciplined singing, his pure tone, and his pleasant personality made him a very popular performer. In 1947 he retired and moved to Gower. He m. in 1921 Lena Evans, Pontarddulais, and they had children. He d. at home in Port Einon, Glam., 29 July 1970.

Welsh Music, winter 1970, spring 1971, autumn 1971, spring 1975; Landon Ronald (ed.), *Who's who in music* (1935).

Rh.G.

WARLOW, EDITH - see **PICTON-TURBERVILL, EDITH** above.

WATCYN o FEIRION - see **JONES, WATKIN** above.

WATERHOUSE, THOMAS (1878-1961), industrialist and public figure; b. 21 Mar. 1878 at Holywell, Flints., second son of Thomas Holmes Waterhouse, an industrialist of Bradford and Holywell. He was educated at Oswestry High School under Owen Owen (*DWB*, 718). At his father's death in 1902 the responsibility for the Holywell Textile Mills fell on his shoulders and between 1909 and 1957 he was successively manager, director and chairman of the company. In 1920 he was elected president of the Welsh Textile Manufacturing Association. From 1925 to 1935 he was a valued member of the Court of the University of Wales and especially of the University's committee to promote the interests of the ailing woollen industry. In 1943 he was elected chairman of the North Wales Industrial Development Council. He was very prominent in local government. In 1905 he was elected to Holywell urban district council and by 1919 he was on the county council, the main field of his public activity. He was created an alderman of the county council in 1931 and was a most effecive chairman, 1938-40. In 1920 he became J.P. and in 1945 vice-chairman of the court of Quarter Sessions. He was High Sheriff for Flintshire in 1942-43 and in 1945 he was appointed a C.B.E.

Always a staunch Liberal, he objected to those Liberals who joined the coalition under David Lloyd George (see above) in 1918 though by 1933 he won the warm commendation of Lloyd George for unequivocally affirming that it was the duty of a Liberal to leave the Coalition Government. During World War II he actively supported the campaign for a Secretary of State for Wales and his proposal to that effect was unanimously passed at a conference of local authorities at Shrewsbury in June 1943.

Thomas Waterhouse was a good example of a person of wholly English stock who became rooted in Wales, which he then served skilfully and tirelessly. Since there was no English Wesleyan cause at Holywell, the family joined the English Congregationalist Church to which they gave substantial support. Trim and dignified, Thomas Waterhouse had a clear mind; he was tough yet fair, and those who knew him well realised that he also had a warm heart and a lively sense of humour. A fearless, independent man, he upheld for over half a century the highest standards in the public life of his county and country. He m. Doris Helena Gough, Olton, Warwickshire, in 1915; they had four sons and one daughter. He d. 3 July 1961. There is a portrait of him in Clwyd county council office at Mold, and another at the home of his son, Sir Ronald Waterhouse, High Court Judge.

Www; David Lloyd George papers in the House of Lords (G/34/1/12); personal knowledge.

J.G.W.

WATKIN, MORGAN (1878-1970), scholar, university professor; b. 23 June 1878 at Pen-rhewllas farm, Mynydd Gelliwastad, Clydach, Glam., one of the 6 children of William and Barbara (née Rhys) Watkin. One of his brothers was William Rhys Watkin (see below). He attended Pen-clun elementary school, near Rhydypandy, and then began work, aged 11, as a door-boy in a colliery. In 1893 he was apprenticed for 3 years to a builder, John Griffiths, Pontardawe, where he made such an impression that he was paid at the 3rd-year rate at the end of the first year. He worked as a builder in Swansea and the Swansea valley, on the Elan and Clee reservoirs and in Birmingham. He learned French, German and Italian at evening classes. He spent a year in Crookley and used to walk the 4 miles to evening classes in Kidderminster. He gained the first prize in

French under F.E. Von Dembski and was placed first of 600 students in the Midland Counties Union of Educational Institutions. He mastered German and taught his teacher Welsh. He moved to Chatham where he was a stonemason in the naval dockyards and learned Latin in his leisure hours. In 1903 he became French teacher at the Birkenhead Institute and then moved to Lime School, Croydon. In 1905 he became French teacher at Howard Gardens School, Cardiff. He followed classes at the University College, Cardiff, and in 1910 graduated with hons. in French and Welsh. A university fellowship and the Gilchrist Scholarship enabled him to go to France as 'reader in English' in the Lycée Louis-Le-Grand and reader in English language and literature in the University of Paris. Joseph Vendryes, at the time professor of comparative philology at the university, employed him as a reader in Welsh. He studied Medieval Welsh with Joseph Loth, professor of Celtic at the Collège de France, and phonetics with Abbé Rousselot. He gained his M.A. (Wales) in 1913 for his dissertation on *Ystorya Bown o Hamtwn*, his *Licence ès Lettres* (Rennes) in 1914 and his Ph.D. *summa cum laude* (Zürich) in 1916. He was appointed to a lectureship in Welsh at Cardiff by Thomas Powel (*DWB*, 771-2) and (non-stipendary) special lecturer in French by Paul Barbier. From 1917 to 1920 he was professor of French and Italian at Johannesburg School of Mines and Technology, and was appointed in 1920 professor of French and Romance Philology at University College Cardiff. He held the chair of French at University College Swansea from 1948 to 1950. He was dean of the faculty of arts, Cardiff, 1923-25, vice-principal, 1931-33, and chief examiner in French and Italian for the Central Welsh Board for many years. He fought strenuously for the equality of Welsh and English in the University of Wales matriculation examinations and for bilingualism in the Welsh education system. He took particular interest in the Baptist College, Cardiff, and in Tabernacl Baptist church where he was elected an elder in 1926. He was an active member of the *Gorsedd of Bards* for over 70 years, serving as Administrative Druid from 1959 to 1964. Among the honours awarded him were *Officier de l'Instruction Publique*, Rennes, 1911; *Cavaliere della Corona d'Italia*, 1920; *Chevalier de la Légion d'Honneur*, 1932; *Commandeur des Palmes Académique*, 1965; *Docteur ès Lettres*, Rennes, 1962, D.Litt. (Wales) 1961.

He was a scholar of the foremost rank in two fields normally studied quite separately in his day, viz. Old French and Medieval Welsh literatures. He was one of the first to realise that the close relationship between the Norman lords and their French-language courts on the Marches and in south Wales and the Welsh lords and their courts had had important effects in both directions: not only did 'Celtic' tales (including Welsh Arthurian legends) have great influence on Old French Literature and consequently on all western European literatures, but French culture and language penetrated the Welsh aristocracy and literary circles. The majority of Old French words in Medieval Welsh were borrowed directly, rather than through the medium of English. This is particularly true in the case of Welsh texts (like *Ystorya*

Bown o Hamtwn) translated from Old French where the same French word appears in both versions. Morgan Watkin believed he could trace Old French idioms in the syntax of some Medieval Welsh texts. His mastery of palaeography also enabled him to see in the script of the main Welsh MSS., copied in Cistercian houses, the influence of the Old French script of the mother-abbeys. It must be acknowledged that Morgan Watkins's thorough knowledge of the Anglo-Norman background sometimes enticed him to go to extremes and to overstate the French influences on native Welsh texts such as *Culhwch ac Olwen*. The French origin of a Welsh word must also be rejected (however plausible the phonetics) if its Celtic cognates reveal its native origin. But, nevertheless, it is probably true that the great mass of French words borrowed into Welsh down to the mid-14th century came directly from French. Watkins's great achievement was to open wide a new window on an important aspect of Welsh literature which had long lain hidden. His successors can re-evaluate the evidence and assess his arguments, but they cannot be ignored.

His main publications are: 'The French linguistic influence in Mediaeval Wales', *Trans. Cymm.*, 1920; 'The French literary influence in Mediaeval Wales', ibid., 1921; with V.E. Nash-Williams (see above), 'A pre-reformation inscribed chalice and paten', *B.B.C.S.*, 3 (1925); 'Albert Stimmings Welsche Fassung in the Anglonormanische Boeve de Hamtone, an examination of a critique' in *Studies in French language and mediaeval literature presented to M.K. Pope*; 'Sangnarwy ac oed Kulhwch ac Olwen yn y Llyfr Gwyn', *B.B.C.S.* 13 (1949); 'Testun Kulhwch a'i gefndir Ffrengig eto', ibid 14 (1950); *Ystorya Bown de Hamtwn, cyfieithiad canol y 13 ganrif o La geste de Bown de Hamtone* (1958); 'The chronology of the Annales Cambriae and the Liber Landavensis on the basis of their Old French graphical phomena', *NLW Jnl.* (1960); *La civilisation française dan les Mabinogion* (1962); 'The chronology of the White Book of Rhydderch on the basis of its Old French graphical phenomena', *NLW Jnl.*, (1964); 'The Book of Aneirin, its Old French remanients, their chronology on the basis of the Old French language', *ibid.* (1965); 'The chronology of the Black Book of Carmarthen on the basis of its Old French phenomena', *ibid.* (1965); 'The Black Book of Chirk and the *orthographia gallica anglicana*, the chronology of the Black Book of Chirk on the basis of its Old French graphical phenomena', *ibid.* (1966).

He m. Lucy Jenkins, Hendy, Pontarddulais (a sister to John (Gwili) Jenkins (*DWB*, 435-6) at Tabernacl chapel, Cardiff in 1911. He d. 7 Sept. 1970.

Information from his son, Dr. Iestyn Watkin; personal knowledge.

E.B.

WATKIN, WILLIAM RHYS (1875-1947), Baptist minister; b. 10 Dec. 1875 in Ynys-Tawe, Glam., one of the six children of William and Barbara (née Rhys) Watkin: the father was one of the Grove family of Swansea, and the mother one of the Rhys's of Tŷ'n y Waun, and the Morgans of Cwmcilie. Professor Morgan Watkin (see above) was one of his brothers. He left the school at Pen-clun, Rhydypandy, at 12, and went to work in the local colliery and then in the tin works. After a short period in the Old College School, Carmarthen, he went to University College, Bangor, where he graduated in 1899 with honours in Welsh: and in 1909, he was awarded the degree of M.A. for his work on Bedo Brwynllys, the first Baptist minister to gain that degree in the University of Wales. He served as minister in Tabernacl chapel, Maesteg, from 1900 to 1910, and in Moreia, Llanelli from 1910 until his death.

He was the editor of *Seren Gomer* from 1921 to 1930, and from 1933 until 1947 (with John Gwili Jenkins, *DWB*, 435-6, for a year, and then with David Hopkins as co-editors). He was a notable administrator – he was President of his *cymanfa*, President of the Union of Welsh Baptists, 1939-40, and Chairman of the Baptist Missionary Society, 1944-45. He contributed many articles to *Y Genhinen*, *Seren Gomer* and to the transactions of the Historical Society of Welsh Baptists, as well as a volume on the history of the Baptists in Clydach, and one on the history of the parish of Llangyfelach.

His theology was that of the orthodox tradition of the old Nonconformity of the 18th century, but he became profoundly influenced by the *Cymru Fydd* movement, and believed firmly in the importance of the Welsh language – he held classes in Welsh in his church in Maesteg, a rarity at that time. He won the prose medal at the Llangollen *eisteddfod* in 1908, and, when the *eisteddfod* came to Llanelli in 1930 he was the secretary of the Literature Committee, and deputy secretary of the *eisteddfod*. He was a member of the *Gorsedd*, under the name of 'Glanlliw'. He was the chairman of the Poetry and Music Club of the town for many years, and during World War II he was Chairman of *Undeb Cymru Fydd* in the area. He owned a wide-ranging and valuable library, and was an authority on first editions.

On 12 Sept. 1905, in Tabernacl, Maesteg, he m. Jane, the daughter of David and Elizabeth (née Jenkins) Williams. She d. on 14 Dec. 1936 and he on 16 Dec. 1947, and they were both buried in the Box cemetery, Llanelli. They had one daughter.

Seren Gomer, March-April 1948; details from Enid Watkin Jones; and personal knowledge.

D.W.P.

WATKIN-JONES, ELIZABETH (1887-1966), author of children's books; born 13 July 1887 in Nefyn, Caerns., the only daughter of Henry and Jane Parry. Her father was a sea captain who was drowned in South America before his daughter saw him. She was educated in the school in Nefyn, Pwllheli county school, and in the Normal College, Bangor, and then became an infants teacher in Aberdare, Onllwyn, Porthmadog, Trefriw, and Nefyn. She m. John Watkin-Jones in Feb. 1916. After World War I, she lived for a short time in Merthyr before returning to Nefyn in 1920, when her husband was appointed headteacher there.

She started to write stories in English for children's publications, such as *Chicks' Own*, *Bubbles* and *Fairyland Tales*, before she turned to writing in Welsh. Between 1939 and 1949, she won many prizes in the National *Eisteddfod* for

novels and stories and short plays for children: she contributed often to *Tywysydd y Plant*, *Trysorfa'r Plant*, *Y Winllan*, *Cymru'r Plant*, *Yr Athro*, and especially to the comic *Hwyl*. She wrote many scripts for the B.B.C.'s programmes for children, and short plays for the children of Soar Independent chapel, Nefyn. In addition to *Pwt a Moi* (1953), *Onesimus* (1947), and three other books of short plays published in 1947, she published seven novels or historical stories for children – *Plant y Mynachdy* (1939) – (her own favourite), *Luned Bengoch* (1946), *Y Cwlwm Cêl* (1947), *Y Dryslwyn* (1947), *Esyllt* (1951), *Lois* (1955), and 'Lowri' in *Storïau Ias a Chyffro* (1951). Every one of these, with the exception of *Y Dryslwyn*, is set in Nefyn, and together they ensure for their author a place in the front rank of authors of books in Welsh for children.

She d. on 9 June 1966, and was cremated in the crematorium in Colwyn Bay, where her ashes lie.

Herald Cymr. 13 June 1966; Wenna Davies Hughes in *Athro Arfon*, No. 3, Dec. 1969, 30-2; information from H.J. Jones, Llangybi; [Mairwen and Gwynn Jones, *Dewiniaid Difyr*, 1983].

B.L.J.

WATKINS, Sir PERCY EMERSON (1871-1946); b. 3 December 1871 at Llanfyllin, Mont., son of Evan and Mary Watkins. One of ten children, he was educated at the local elementary school, and for five terms at the High School, Oswestry, under Owen Owen (*DWB*, 718). He then returned home to assist his father, but in 1896 was appointed first Clerk of the Central Welsh board. In 1904 he was appointed chief clerk to the Education Department of the West Riding of Yorkshire. In 1911 he returned to Wales to be Registrar at the University College, Cardiff, where he remained until 1913, when he became Assistant Secretary to the Welsh Insurance Commission at Cardiff. In 1925 he succeeded (Sir) Alfred T. Davies (see above) as Permanent Secretary of the Welsh Department of the Board of Education where he immediately established the good relationships which were very necessary if the Welsh Department at the Board, still immature, was to function effectively. Similarly in Wales he smoothed out the friction which had become acute between the Welsh Department in London and the Central Welsh Board in Wales. An important event during his tenure of office was the issue, in 1931, of a report on *Educational Problems of the Welsh Coalfield*; this led to great developments in adult education in south Wales. Watkins was ever a steadfast friend to all forms of adult education and was one of the moving influences in the establishment of Coleg Harlech in 1927. In 1927 a Departmental committee of the Board issued a report on *Welsh in Education and Life*. Watkins at once took measures to make the recommendations of this report well known and effective. He initiated surveys on the language situation in the schools, and encouraged the Board's inspectors to investigate the problem of Welsh and English teaching in the schools. As a result, two official memoranda were issued embodying suggestions to teachers on the teaching of Welsh and English in the elementary schools; these constituted the first firm attempt to provide teachers in Wales with principles which they might apply to the solution of this all-important matter. Watkins resigned his position at the Board in 1933 to direct, in south Wales, the work of the Council of Social Services. This involved great financial loss to him. With the same human sympathy, integrity and absence of self-seeking which always characterised him, he devoted the last ten years of his life to this work.

He married (1) (1898) Mary Jane Jones of Llanfyllin, and had one son. In 1930 he was knighted and received the honorary degree of LL.D. from the University of Wales. Lady Watkins died in 1939, and in 1941 he married (2) Lil Bush (née Lewis). He d. 5 May 1946. In addition to various articles and memoranda he published his autobiography in 1944 under the title *A Welshman Remembers*.

Percy E. Watkins, *A Welshman Remembers* (1944); personal knowledge.

W.P.W.

WATKINS, VERNON [PHILLIPS] (1906-67), poet; b. 27 June 1906, at Maesteg, Glam., only son and second child of William Watkins (a native of Taff's Well), manager of Lloyd's Bank, and Sarah Watkins (née Phillips) of Sarnau, Carms. Before Vernon was six the family had moved to Bridgend, to Llanelli and finally to Swansea. The boy entered Swansea Grammar School, but after one year was dispatched to prep. school at Tyttenhanger Lodge, Seaford, Sussex, and from there to Repton School, Derbyshire. Always, from a very early age, devoted to the English Romantic poets (for his Welsh-speaking parents had taught him no Welsh), he made of his last eighteen months at Repton a heroic golden age, and entry to Magdalene College, Cambridge, where he read French and German, proved a disappointing experience. Despite a successful examination, he went down after one year, irritated by the rigorously academic approach to literature, which he felt would be death to him as a poet, and proposed to his father, without prior notice, that he should travel in Italy for a year. William Watkins, whose resources had been strained by his son's residence at Cambridge, put him into Lloyd's Bank, Butetown, Cardiff, as a junior clerk. Two years later, in 1927, Vernon, overcome by 'grief' at the loss of the idyll of Repton and unable to adjust to the unliterary dullness of the adult world, had a nervous breakdown whose climax was a return visit to Repton. Six months in a nursing home at Derby were followed by transfer to the St. Helen's (Swansea) branch of Lloyd's Bank, so that he could live at home (which was then 'Redcliffe', Caswell Bay, and later 'Heatherslade' on Pennard Cliffs). The spiritual convalescence was to last a dozen years and the poetry which emerged (after visits to Germany in the early 1930s) was made from the 'grief'. It was devoted, dialectically, to 'the conquest of time', by which the poet meant, first, that nobody need be forgotten whom poetry could keep immortal, and, second (as a Neo-Platonic and a more fully Christian view developed, successively from his earlier Romantic pagansim), that all are immortal because all are 'justified' and that the present moment must be seen as the microcosm of all moments, past and future. Vernon

Watkins went on to become one of the very few metaphysical poets of the twentieth century and probably the most distinguished. Overshadowed in his lifetime by his meteoric friend Dylan Thomas (see above) whose letters he published in *Letters to Vernon Watkins* (1957), he was at one with him only in his belief in the primacy of poetry. But not even when Dylan failed to turn up as best man on the occasion of his wedding in London in 1944 (to Gwendoline Mary Davies, of Harborne, Birmingham, a colleague of his in the Intelligence Service) would Vernon break the friendship. He had developed an obstinacy of belief (in poets, for example, as 'good') that in personal relationships made of him a kind of unorthodox saint.

Vernon Watkins's volumes of poetry, exclusive of American editions and selections, were : *Ballad of the Mari Lwyd* (1941), *The Lamp and the Veil* (1945), *The Lady with the Unicorn* (1948), *The North Sea* (translations from Heine) (1951), *The Death Bell* (1954), *Cypress and Acacia* (1959), *Affinities* (1962) and *Fidelities* (published posthumously in 1968). *Uncollected Poems* (1969) and *The Breaking of the Wave* (1979) were put together from the vast mass of material the poet's demanding eye had left unpublished, and two new selections, *I That Was Born in Wales* (1976) and *Unity of the Stream* (1978), were made from the printed oeuvre.

Apart from war service (1941-46) in the R.A.F. Police and in Intelligence, Vernon Watkins lived all his adult life in Gower (after marriage at 'The Garth' on Pennard Cliffs), 'the oldest cashier', as he was fond of claiming, in the banking service. The recipient of many literary prizes, he was awarded a D.Litt. by the University of Wales in 1966 and became a Gulbenkian Scholar at University College, Swansea. He died 8 Oct. 1967 while playing tennis soon after his arrival in Seattle, U.S.A., for his second period (this time a year) as Visiting Professor of Poetry at the University of Washington. *The Times*, in reporting his death, revealed that his name was one of five or six under consideration for the Poet Laureateship.

Roland Mathias, *Vernon Watkins* (1974); Gwen Watkins, *Poet of the Elegiac Muse* (1973); Dora Park, *Vernon Watkins and the Spring of Vision* (1977).

R.M.

WEBBER, FRANK EDWARD (1893-1963) - see under WEBBER, Sir ROBERT JOHN below.

WEBBER, Sir ROBERT JOHN (1884-1962), managing director of Western Mail and Echo Limited; b. 14 Nov. 1884, the eldest son of Charles and Hannah Webber of Barry, Glam. He was educated at Barry County School and Cardiff Science and Art School. His first job was as a clerk in the general manager's office of the Barry Railway from where, in 1908 at the age of 24, he was one of 300 applicants for the post of private secretary in Fleet Street to George Riddell (later Baron Riddell), chairman of the *News of the World* and a major shareholder in the *Western Mail*. He won the post when, in answer to the question of what his recreations were, he replied, 'Work'. When the *Western Mail* needed an assistant manager for both the newspapers and the large printing business, Sir

George, then chairman of the company, suggested Robert Webber. In three years, aged 32, he was appointed general manager of the newspapers and of Tudor Printing Works and, within three months, to a seat on the board, and later a director for life and joint-managing director with Sir William Davies (editor 1901-31; *DWB*, 161) a position which he held for 32 years to 1955. In 1937, he was elected to the board of Allied (later Kemsley) Newspapers, owners of the *Western Mail*. Soon after his arrival in Cardiff, he had to cope with the strains of war on the company's two dailies, the *Western Mail* and the *Evening Express*. In 1928, he superintended the merger of Western Mail Ltd with David Duncan and Sons, publishers of Cardiff's rival newspapers, the *South Wales Daily News* and the *South Wales Echo*, with the intended closure of the loss-makers, the *Express* and the *News*; in the event, the combined company, whose merger was essentially impelled by Lord Rothermere's threat to open a third evening paper in the city, kept the *Express* in existence until 1930. He was closely involved with the decision to keep publishing the *Western Mail* during the general strike, using largely untrained staff. During his years with the *Western Mail*, he was described as a 'fair but hard taskmaster, although he wouldn't expect you to do anything he would not do himself'; he was praised for his encouragement of young journalists. He took a very prominent part in the commercial life of south Wales; he was a founder and president for 39 years, until his death, of Cardiff Business Club. A national figure in the newspaper industry (among other positions, president of the Newspaper Society 1926-27 and chairman of the Press Association in 1932-33), he was also much concerned with trying to breathe new life into south Wales during the Depression. In 1936, he was appointed one of eight directors of the new South Wales Trading Estate Co., Ltd. (which developed Treforest Trading Estate) and, in 1948, a director of Wales and Monmouthshire Estates Ltd. Among his schemes was one in 1937 for an arterial road from south to north Wales to employ workless miners, and stem emigration to England. He was a staunch supporter in the pre-war years of the then fledgling air and motor transport industries. (One of his later cars bore the number ANY 1). He was a Freemason; in 1947 he was elected president of Cardiff Central Conservative Association; and he was knighted in 1934. He m., 30 Dec. 1911, Jane Bennet Perkins, of Chepstow (d. 26 June 1963); they had one daughter (Joan Suzanne Prichard; d. in Toronto, 1983). He d. 18 Dec. 1962.

FRANK EDWARD WEBBER (1893-1963), general manager of Western Mail and Echo Ltd.; b. 8 Oct. 1893, the youngest of Charles and Hannah Webber's three sons. He was educated at Barry School and the University College, Cardiff. He enlisted in the army as a private in August 1914, commissioned in Aug. 1916 a lieutenant in the 2nd Batt. of the South Wales Borderers; he was twice wounded, leaving his left arm partly disabled. After demobilisation, he took his B.A. following study of classics, history and mathematics. In 1926, he became a fellow of the Chartered Institute of Secretaries, was appointed general manager of the Western

Mail and Echo in 1940, became a director in 1946, and vice-chairman in 1959. He retired in 1960. Keenly interested in education in Wales, he was a member of the Court of the University of Wales and the Council of University College, Cardiff. He was also very active in the business community and many good causes in south Wales. He was awarded an O.B.E. in 1946 for his work with the Cardiff Savings Committee. His wife Edith Clarissa (d. 1984) was a teacher and they had one son, David. He d. 21 Apr. 1963.

Www; *West. Mail* and *Times*, 19 Dec. 1962 and 23 Apr. 1963.

C.B.

WHEELER, Dame OLIVE ANNIE (1886-1963), Professor of Education; b. in 1886, daughter of Henry Burford Wheeler, Brecon. She was educated at Brecon County School for Girls and the University College of Wales, Aberystwyth, where she was president of the Students' Representative Council and graduated B.Sc. (1907); she received a M.Sc. degree (1911) and was elected a Fellow of the University of Wales. She went as a research student to Bedford College, London, and to the University of Paris, and obtained a D.Sc. degree in psychology (1916) at the University of London. Her appointment as lecturer in mental and moral science at Cheltenham Ladies College was followed by a lectureship in education at the University of Manchester, where she also served as dean of the Faculty of Education before moving to the University College at Cardiff. In 1925 she became Professor of Education there, and was for a period dean of the Faculty of Education at the college. She was particularly interested in the use of psychology in teaching methods. After working much with youth groups and student associations she became chairman of the Welsh Advisory Council on Youth Employment in 1947, and chairman of the South Wales District of the Workers' Education Association. She served on many educational committees and councils and was created D.B.E. in 1950 for services to education. Three years after her retirement in 1951 she went to Canada on a lecture tour. Her contribution to theories of education was known in many parts of the world through her numerous publications which include: *Anthropomorphism and Science* (1916), *Bergson and Education* (1922), *Youth* (1929), *Creative education and the future* (1936), 'The mind of the child' in *Nursery School Education* (G. Owen, editor, 1939), *The adventure of youth* (1945), part III of *Mental Health and Education* (1961); and papers in psychological and educational journals. She resided at Woodlands, Betws-y-coed Road, Cyncoed, Cardiff, and d. suddenly, 26 Sept. 1963.

Debrett; *Www*; *West. Mail*, 28 Sept. 1963.

M.A.J.

WHELDON, Sir WYNN POWELL (1879-1961), lawyer, soldier, administrator; b. 22 Dec. 1879, son of the Rev. Thomas Jones Wheldon (*DWB*, 1015-6) and Mary Elinor Powell, Bronygraig, Ffestiniog, Mer. He was educated at Friars School, Bangor, the High School, Oswestry, the University College of North Wales - he was the first secretary of the Students' Representative

Council, 1899 - B.A. 1900, and at St. John's College, Cambridge (B.A. and LL.B., 1903, M.A. in 1920). In 1906 he began his career as a lawyer in 63 Queen Victoria Street, London, EC. He joined a number of London's Welsh societies (among them the Hon. Soc. of Cymmrodorion) and soon became well acquainted with the city's influential Welshmen. He speedily and unhesitatingly enlisted in the army and served in the 14th Battalion of the Royal Welch Fusiliers in France from December 1914 until December 1918. As major and second in command, he was wounded, his bravery being mentioned in dispatches and recognised by the D.S.O. in 1917. He was Secretary and Registrar of Bangor College from 1919 until 1933 when he was appointed Permanent Secretary of the Welsh Department of the Board of Education. He retired in 1945 but there was no diminution of his public work, the following being but examples of his unremitting service: Chairman of the Welsh Committee, Festival of Britain, 1951; Chairman of the Council of School Broadcasting for Wales, member of the Court and Council of the University of Wales, Vice-President of the University Council of North Wales and President of the Cymmrodorion Society. In 1939 he was knighted, and appointed K.B.E. in 1952; the University of Wales conferred upon him the degree of *Doctor in legibus* (*honoris causa*) in 1947 and the Cymmrodorion Society its Medal in 1955. He died at Prestatyn on 10 Nov. 1961 and his will was proved on 18 Jan. 1962.

On account of his shrewdness and balanced judgement he was a splendid administrator and he was able to 'manage' affairs without fuss and bustle. He disliked pomp and vulgarity, and he never suffered fools gladly. Yet he was essentially a warm-hearted man and a true friend. He understood the feelings and aspirations of his countrymen, in committees and on the field of battle, in religion and in politics. He clung faithfully to the Calvinistic Methodist denomination; the chief beneficiary of his will (apart from the family) was Tabernacl, Bangor (his father's former church). [He was a leading layman in his denomination. His guidance and experience proved crucial in his chairmanship of the Commission on Education for the Ministry (1961), and also in the discussions which led to the setting up of the United Theological College, Aberystwyth].He was a handsome, dignified man, there is a pencil drawing of him by S. Morse Brown, a portrait by Kyffin Williams (1955), and a bust by Kustec Wojnarowski (1958) (in the Council Chamber of Bangor College, and another in the Clwyd Record Office, Hawarden).

He m. Megan Edwards, Canonbury, Prestatyn, daughter of Hugh Edwards, London, 31 July 1915. They had two sons, Huw Pyrs and Tomas Powell (who died a few months before his father) and two daughters, Mair and Nans.

Ww, 1961; *Www*, 1951-60; *Debrett*, 1961; *Times*, 13, 15 Nov. 1961; *Trans. Cymm.*, 1956, 11-17, 1962, 161-69. Personal knowledge. [His papers and diaries are in the Library of the University of Wales, Bangor; information from his daughter Mrs Mair Rees].

J.G.W.

WHITEHEAD, LEWIS STANLEY (1889-1956), secretary of the Representative Body of the Church in Wales; b. 12 Jan. 1889 in Stoke-on-Trent, son of George Whitehead. Four years later the family moved to Cardiff where he was educated at the High School. From 1910-16 he was manager of Rank Mills, Truro, and, indicative of his love of music, he became lay vicar choral of Truro and (later) Llandaff cathedrals. After serving with the Royal Flying Corps, 1916-19, he became assistant to Frank Morgan, Fellow of Keble College, Oxford, and secretary of the new Representative Body of the Church in Wales, whom he succeeded in 1935. Somewhat autocratic, like Frank Morgan, for his position gave him considerable power in administrative matters, he steered the Church in Wales through the difficult years of World War II and led a successful legal action against the Tithe Redemption Commission, 1943-44. He was recognized as the 'universal adviser' by the members of the 'Prayer Book and Nation Commission', 1946-49; he administered the Church in Wales appeal in 1952-53, and the purchase of Bush House, one of the more successful investments by the Church in Wales in the property market. The later years were clouded by the long illness of his wife, Ada Marie (née Thomas). He d. four months after her on 17 Dec. 1956. His articles in *Province* on 'Frank Morgan', 'Parsons' pay', and 'Bush House' are useful sources for the early history of the Representative Body.

West. Mail, 18, 20 Dec. 1956; *Province*, Easter 1950, Christmas 1950, Easter 1955; Denning, *Landmarks in the law* (1984).

O.W.J.

WIL IFAN - see EVANS, WILLIAM above.

WILDE, WILLIAM JAMES (JIMMY) (1892-1969), boxer, world flyweight champion (1916-23); b. 12 May 1892, at 8 Station Road, Pontygwaith, Tylorstown, Rhondda, Glam., the son of James and Margaret Wilde. When still young he showed considerable toughness in defending himself in street fights and when he began work at the local colliery, he worked with Dai Davies, an old mountain fighter, who taught him a great deal about boxing and invited him home to practice in the attic. When the family split, he lodged at Dai Davies's house and later married Lisbeth, his daughter. He was a frail, slight youngster, but nevertheless his ambition was to earn his living as a boxer. When he was 15 yrs. old, he had an accident at work and was unable to walk for more than a year, waiting for his leg to heal. He was given his first opportunity by Jack Scarrott, the owner of a boxing booth, although Jack, like others, expressed doubts about the future of someone only 5ft 2.5ins tall, who at that time weighed less than 6 stone. Throughout his unbelievable career of 864 contests (the figure most often quoted), his heaviest weight was 7st 10lb. In 1915, after persuading Ted Lewis to act as his manager, he left the pit to concentrate on a career in the professional ring. In Nov. 1914 he won the British flyweight championship by beating Joe Symmonds. In Jan. 1915 he lost his title to Tancy Lee in the 17th round. That was the first contest he lost, but within a year he had beaten Joe Symmonds to regain his title, and in Jan. 1916 got his revenge on Tancy Lee in the 11th round. The strength carried in his two fists by a person of such light weight amazed the specialists. Quality boxing, together with perfect timing and plenty of self-confidence, rather than any hidden strength, were Wilde's usual explanations. Late in 1916, by then an army physical training instructor, he beat Young Zulu Kid from the USA in the 11th round, to win the World Flyweight Championship. The 'Mighty Atom', the 'Tylorstown Terror', the 'Indian Famine' and the 'Ghost with a hammer' had reached the top. With the war over, three-round contests were arranged between the soldiers of Britain and America. The second night he was beaten by Pal Moore, and because of the arguments that followed, a second meeting was arranged, when he won over the 20 rounds. In Jan. 1920 he went on a boxing tour to the USA and easily beat all his opponents. In Jan. 1921 he was beaten in the 17th round by Pete Herman of the USA. The hope was that he would retire in good time, but for £15,000 he decided to visit New York to defend his title against Pancho Villa in June 1923. He had not been near the ring for a considerable time and was beaten by Villa in the 7th round. After retiring, he was connected with several unsuccessful ventures. In 1938 he wrote his autobiography *Boxing was my business*, and was for a time the *News of the World* boxing correspondent.

He was ill for the last four years of his life when he lost his wife and he died, 76 yrs of age, in Whitchurch Hospital, Cardiff, 11 March 1969.

Personal research.

W.M.R.

WILLANS, JOHN BANCROFT (1881-1957), country landowner, antiquarian and philanthropist; of Dolforgan, Kerry, Mont., J.P., F.S.A.; b. 27 May 1881 in Liverpool, only child of John William Willans (1843-1895), chief engineer of Liverpool Overhead Railway, and of Mary Louisa (1847-1911) née Nicholson, grandson of Benjamin Willans (1816-1895) of Blaina, Mon. He was educated partly by private tutors, including Sir Leonard Woolley, and partly at Haileybury. He lived in Kerry from 1894 onwards, after his father had bought the Dolforgan estate from the Waltons. He served in World War I on non-combatant duties mainly in Italy, and on his return he devoted himself to public service in Monts. He was High Sheriff of Montgomeryshire, 1917, J.P. from 1919, County alderman of Montgomeryshire, 1904-1907 and 1910-1919, member of Montgomery county council 1934 until his death, serving as chairman of the County Records Commiteee and County Library Committee. He represented Montg. C.C. on the Court of Governors of the University of Wales 1934-1957, of Univ. Coll. of Wales, Aberystwyth, 1907-1927, and of Univ. Coll. of North Wales, Bangor, 1936-1957, Life Governor of U.C.W., Aberystwyth, from 1919; member of Council 1914-1957: he represented U.C.W. on the Court of Governors of Nat. Mus. of Wales 1921-1957, and was a member of the Court of Governors National Library of Wales 1942-1957; member of Council 1945-1957.

His interests lay mainly in the antiquarian and genealogical fields, in the preservation of the national heritage and in his Unitarian faith. He was a Life Member of the Cambrian Archaeological Association from 1901 and of the Powysland Club from 1899, being its Chairman of Committee at the time of his death. He published a book *The Byways of Montgomeryshire* in 1905; this was kindly reviewed, albeit with helpful criticism, by Archdeacon D. R. Thomas (*DWB*, 943) in *Mont. Coll.* 1907. He contributed regular articles to *Mont. Coll* between 1910 and 1951, most of them recording his own researches into aspects of the history of the Kerry area. His constant, but always unobtrusive, philanthropy during his lifetime towards the causes which reflected his main interests - in his later years at some personal sacrifice - was considerable. It was not surprising, therefore, that his main residuary legatees should also reflect the same interests: the U.C.W. received £11,000, the N.L.W. £12,000, and the General Assembly of the Unitarian and Free Christian Churches a similar residual amount (this was in addition to some £3,500 in specific bequests to the Unitarian movement). An appreciation of his altruism would not be complete without a reference to his remarkable generosity to young students. Inspired by his close friend, Prof. H.J. Fleure (see above) he was never happier than when helping them financially with the background to their studies, by providing them with the means to undertake field work and often by taking them, entirely at his own expense, on cultural visits to places of interest in Europe. It is accordingly fitting that U.C.W. decided to perpetuate his memory by establishing the annual J.B. Willans Lecture at the College. He found his own recreation in walking, travelling, voracious reading and in his gardens and woods. Motivated as he was throughout his life by a deep social conscience, sense of public duty and religious faith, his contribution in his fields of interest to the cultural and educational life of Wales, and especially of Montgomeryshire, although always essentially reticent, was substantial. He was unmarried. He d. 12 Apr. 1957 at Salop Infirmary and was buried in Kerry churchyard.

Burke, *Landed Gentry*, 1937; *Mont. Coll.*, 54, 175-6; *Mont. County Times*, 20 April 1957; *South Wales Echo*, 5 Sept. 1957; personal knowledge, and the official records of the relevant authorities and institutions.

H.N.J.

WILLETT, Mrs - see COOMBE TENNANT, WINIFRED MARGARET above.

WILLIAMS, ALICE MATILDA LANGLAND (1867-1950), otherwise Alys Mallt, but more generally known as Y Fonesig Mallt Williams, author and celtophile; b. in Oystermouth, Gower (though some sources say in Aberclydach, Tal-y-bont on Usk, Brecks.), 4 Oct. 1867, fourth child of John James Williams, M.D. ('Brychan'), one of two sisters of William Retlaw Williams (see below). She came in her youth under the influence of Lady Llanover (*DWB*, 334, under Hall, Benjamin), and throughout her long life she retained her interest in Welsh and Celtic cultural and political movements. Her name with that of her sister GWENFRIDA ('Cate', 'Gwenffreda ferch Brychan'), is linked with that of Lady Llanover in a poem entitled 'An Diou Vag', which François Jaffrennou ('Taldir') composed after the national *eisteddfod* held at Cardiff in 1899, and published in *Gwerziou gant Abherve ha Taldir*, St. Brieuc, 1899. The two sisters were 'Y

Ddau Wynne', joint authors of the novels *One of the Royal Celts*, London 1889, and *A Maid of Cymru*, London 1901. Gwenfrida d. in 1914. As Maud Williams of Aberclydach (Llanfigan, Breckns.), Mallt was the second person to join *Urdd y Delyn* founded by Owen M. Edwards (*DWB*, 192) in 1896. For years this League offered prizes for *penillion* singing, harp-playing, reading Welsh books and speaking Welsh. Later she used to present prizes for the harp, under the name of *'Gwobrwyon Aberclydach'*, at national *eisteddfodau*. She was the founder and leader of *Ysbïwyr y Frenhines* in *Byddin Cymru* under the auspices of *Cymru'r Plant* from 1911 to 1916. The members took an oath to serve Wales with heart, mind, tongue and hand. By then she had moved to live at Plas Gwynnon Dôl in Llanarthne, Carms. In 1915 she moved again, this time to Plas Pantsaeson near St. Dogmaels, Pembs., where she spent the remainder of her life. She lived there with her younger brother, 'Jim', FREDERICK GEORGE ROBERTSON WILLIAMS, who had left Aberclydach when his elder brother inherited the estate. He first settled at Capel Isaf near Llandeilo, but in 1916 he purchased the Plas Pantsaeson estate and went to live there with his wife 'Daisy' or 'Modie', Hylda Marguerite, dau. of Major Penry Lloyd. Robertson Williams was interested in afforestation and as part of his endeavour to improve the estate he planted trees extensively. Like his sister Mallt he was conspicuous at Celtic gatherings on account of his dress modelled on the conjectured style of a Welsh lord of the thirteenth century. He d. at the age of 75 on 11 Jan. 1945 and his body was borne on a gambo to his resting place in Monnington churchyard. He is described in the inscription on his tombstone as *Hollgelt* ('a complete Celt'). His widow d. at the same house on 2 Feb. 1952. They had two sons and one daughter. The elder of the boys Ioan Penry Brychan, Robertson, co-operated with his aunt Mallt in the publication of a Welsh birthday book, *Llyfr Penblwydd*, in 1929. Mallt attended meetings of Welsh and Irish national movements zealously and stood firm for Welshness in speech and dress. In her annual address to *Ysbïwyr y Frenhines* she urged the members to imitate the zeal of the Irish, but after the Easter Rising of 1916 she was more subdued. Throughout the years she consistently supported the National *Eisteddfod*, *Urdd Gobaith Cymru* and *Plaid Cymru*. In her latter years her hundred pounds headed the list of subscriptions to the annual St. David's Day fund of the *Blaid*. She was a stalwart supporter of the campaign against the establishment of a training camp for the Royal Air Force at Porth Neigwl and Penyberth; and it was she who coined the name *Ysgol Fomio* ('bombing school'). She was a strict vegetarian and a disciple of Mary Baker Eddy. She d. 28 Oct., 1950 at Plas Pantsaeson and was cremated at Pontypridd; her ashes were scattered in the churchyard at Llansanffraid, Breckns. Her portrait can be seen on p.44 of *Cymru*, XXIX, 1905.

Cymru, Cymru'r Plant, passim; *Cardigan and Tivyside*, 26 Jan., 1945, 3 Nov., 1950; information from W.W. Price, Selwyn Jones, J.E. Jones, G.M. Roberts, and Maureen Patch; [Marion Löffler in *Planet*, no. 121 (1997)].

E.D.J.

WILLIAMS, ALUN OGWEN (1904-70), eisteddfod administrator and supporter; b. 2 Oct. 1904 in Well Street, Gerlan, Bethesda, Caerns., son of John Samuel Williams and Catherine (née Thomas) his wife. He was educated in Gerlan elementary school, Bethesda County School and Bangor Normal College (1922-24), from where he went to Llanfairfechan (1924-26) and Pwllheli (1926-36) as a teacher before being appointed headmaster of Pentre Uchaf (1936-42), Penmachno (1942-52) and Leeswood (1952-63) schools. Although he retired to Rhyl (Glan Ogwen, Grange Road) in 1963, he continued to teach Welsh in Offa's Dyke Comprehensive School, Prestatyn until 1965, He m. (1) Lil Evans (d. 2 Aug. 1968) in Llanbedr, Mer. in 1932 and they had one son, Euryn Ogwen Williams. He m. (2) Gwladys Spencer Jones in Colwyn Bay, June 1970 and moved to Noddfa, Erw-wen Rd., Colwyn Bay, but d. barely two months later on 4 Aug., in Ammanford where the national *eisteddfod* was held that year. He was cremated at Swansea 7 Aug. 1970.

He became well known as a young reciter and he was a reciter, actor and adjudicator of recitation all his life. He formed Parti Penmachno, a concert party which travelled through Wales and England during World War II and later. He was the party's compère and reciter. A member of the *Gorsedd* for 40 yrs., he served as chief marshal, its secretary for ten yrs. and as membership secretary of the *Eisteddfod* Court for a similar period.

Personal knowledge.

E.O.W.

WILLIAMS, ALYS MALLT - see WILLIAMS, ALICE MATILDA LANGLAND above.

WILLIAMS, BENJAMIN HAYDN (1902-65), education officer; son of Benjamin and Margaret Jane Williams; b. 9 Oct. 1902, at Rhosllannerchrugog, Denbs., Educated at Ruabon grammar school, he was a pupil-teacher, 1921-22, and then a student at Liverpool University. He gained a degree in science, with high honours in chemistry, and within two years graduated Ph.D. From 1927-31 he undertook research work with the Department of Scientific and Industrial Research in London. In 1931 he was appointed lecturer at Wrexham Technical College and was responsible for developing their chemistry department, specialising on the industrial side. In 1938 he came to the then Flintshire, as deputy Director of Education and became Director of Education in 1941. He was a member of the Court and Council of the University of Wales and a member of several sub-committees. He was Chairman of the Council of the National *Eisteddfod* of Wales 1960-64. He became well known as a pioneer of Welsh-medium schools, and with his characteristic energy established two Welsh secondary schools in Flintshire, the first two in Wales. He played a leading role in the campaign to promote Welsh television, and in 1961 became Chairman of the independent company *Teledu Cymru*, but the venture failed and came to an end in May 1963. In 1929 he m. Sarah Hughes of Rhosllannerchrugog and they had two children. He d. 29 May 1965.

Personal knowledge; *Liv. D.P.*, 31 May 1965; *West. Mail*, 31 May 1965.

M.J.J.

WILLIAMS, CHRISTMAS PRICE (1881-1965), politician and engineer; b. 25 Dec. 1881, the son of Peter Williams and Mary Price his wife, Brymbo Hall, Wrexham, Denbs. His father was the managing director of the Brymbo Steel Co. He was educated at Grove Park School, Wrexham, at Mold, and at Victoria University, Manchester, where he graduated B.Sc. (with honours) in science and M.Sc. He earned his living as an engineer at Sheffield, Warrington and South Africa, and held a number of important managerial positions. Williams undertook research work on the industrial potential of Canada. In 1924 he was elected M.P. (Lib.) for Wrexham following an electoral pact with local Conservatives, when he defeated the historian Robert Richards (see above). He was bitterly disappointed when Richards re-captured the seat in 1929, and his political career came to an abrupt end. He served as J.P. for Lincolnshire, was a Congregationalist and deeply interested in music.

He m. 23 June 1909, Marion, dau. of Thomas Davies, Brymbo. She was the author of a number of novels and plays. They lived at Sanddeth House, Gwersyllt, Wrexham, and briefly at 42B Courtfield Gardens, London. He d. 18 Aug. 1965.

Www; WwW (1937); Dod's *Parliamentary Companion; Liberal year book 1928; The Times Guide to the House of Commons 1929;* papers of Sir Henry Haydn Jones at N.L.W.

J.G.J.

WILLIAMS, DANIEL (1878-1968), minister (Meth.) and author; b. 17 June 1878, son of Richard Williams, a worker in the Penmaen Quarries, and his wife Anne, at Bodnant, Llanfairfechan, Caerns. He was educated at the village National School and spent two years at the Cynffig Davies School in Menai Bridge, before being accepted in 1901 as a ministerial candidate in the Methodist church. He served a pre-college year at Llanbedr, Mer., before starting his studies at Headingly, Leeds. After completing a successful period there, he was sent to Penisa'r-waun in the Caernarfon circuit, where he stayed for three years. Apart from two years, 1907-08, in the Manchester circuit, he spent all his time ministering to districts in north Wales, including Aberffraw, Corwen, Dolgellau, Llanfyllin, Llangollen, Penmachno, Rhydyfoel and Mold, where he stayed seven years. He retired from full-time work and became a supernumerary in 1943, making his home at Prestatyn, but returned to the regular ministry in 1948, and was superintendent of the Llangollen circuit for a year, retiring again and living there until he moved to Old Colwyn in 1952.

He was a gifted and popular preacher and in 1934 published *Gwerslyfr ar Efengyl Marc*. In addition to his considerable contribution to the religious life in Wales, Daniel Williams was well known as a writer and a historian of standing. He published five children's books, *Cario'r post a storïau eraill* (1932), *Dyrnaid o ŷd* (1924), *Llwyn y brain* (1930), *Pant y gloch* (1932), and *Plant y pentre* (1925); he regularly contributed to antiquarian journals. He was a keen *eisteddfod* supporter and in 1927 won a chair for a poem at the Whitsun *eisteddfod* in Penybont-fawr,

Monts. He also won the first prize on the principal essay, *'Teithi meddwl Ann Griffiths'* at the 1932 Powys Regional *Eisteddfod*. He had considerable literary success at the National *Eisteddfod* and between 1939-47 won seven prizes for essays or articles on a wide variety of subjects. In 1952 he was invited to deliver the annual lecture at the Methodist Assembly held in Llandeilo.

In 1909 he m. Annie Bartley Griffith, granddaughter of the Archdruid 'Clwydfardd' (David Griffith, 1800-94; *DWB*, 291), at Ebenezer chapel, Llandudno and they had three sons and a daughter. He d. 17 Mar. 1968 at his home, Bronygarth, Wynn Avenue, Old Colwyn, and following a private service at Bethesda Chapel, Old Colwyn, his remains were cremated at Colwyn Bay Crematorium.

Dyddiadur EF, 1969, 29-30; *Gwyliedydd Newydd*, 4 April 1968; *Liv. D.P.*, 19-20 March 1968; *The minutes of the annual conference Methodist Church* (1968), 194-5; J. Henry Martin and J. Bernard Sheldon, *Ministers and Probationers of the Methodist Church ... revised to 1 Sept. 1963* (1964), 331; Daniel Williams, 'Fy ngalwad i'r weinidogaeth', *Winllan*, 107 (1954) 201-5; [Mairwen and Gwynn Jones, *Dewiniaid difyr* (1983)]; information from Alun W. Francis, Caernarfon.

Ri.E.H.

WILLIAMS, DANIEL HOWELL (1894-1963), aerodynamicist; b. 27 June, 1894 at Ffestiniog, Mer., the son of Griffith J. Williams, schoolmaster (*DWB*, 1039), and his wife, Mary Helena. He was registered as Daniel John but later adopted his mother's maiden name, Howell. His father was later H.M. Inspector of Mines for north Wales. He was a nephew of Sir Richard J. Williams, Mayor of Bangor, 1913-20. He was educated at Friars School, Bangor and in October 1912 he entered the University College of North Wales with an Entrance Exhibition. His main course of study was in Mathematics which he read under Professor G.H. Bryan, F.R.S., one of the founders of the science of aerodynamics. An outstanding student he won several scholarships and prizes including the R.A. Jones Prize in mathematics (1914). Throughout his life he suffered from a weak heart and on this account was allowed to complete his studies despite the war. He graduated in 1917 with 1st-Class Honours in Pure Mathematics and 2nd-Class Honours in Applied Mathematics. For a short time he continued to work with Professor Bryan and Dr. Selig Brodetsky of Bristol on problems of aircraft stability. In October 1917 he joined the staff of the Aerodynamics Division of the National Physical Laboratory, Teddington, where he remained until his retirement. He was a prominent member of Kingston Congregational church being particularly active in Sunday school work. For many years he was treasurer of the London branch of Old Bangorians, returning frequently to Wales. He never married and d. 27 January 1963 at Teddington, where he lived with his sister Enid.

Dan Williams's early work at the National Physical Laboratory was concerned with theoretical and wind tunnel work on airships and in this he was associated with Dr. Robert Jones (see above). However, he soon moved away from this to the wind tunnel study of aircraft performance. At this time the general theories underlying the study of aircraft wings (aerofoils) were still the subject of controversy. In 1924 Dan Williams and L.W. Bryant carried out fundamental experiments which amongst other things provided verification of the law of Kutta and Joukowksy connecting the lift of an aerofoil and the circulation around it. This important work was later published in *Phil. Trans. Roy. Soc.* (1925). Following the loss of the airship R.101 in 1930 Dan Williams returned to work on airships. At the request of the Court of Inquiry he and A.R. Collar carried out a step by step calculation to determine the final flight path of the airship. This monumental labour occupied some 9 months using the relatively primitive methods of calculation then available and resulted in the award of the R.38 Memorial Prize of the Royal Aeronautical Society. Dan Williams also received the thanks of the Chairman of the Court of Inquiry, Sir John Simon, for his work. For much of his subsequent career he carried out experimental work using the Compressed Air Tunnel at the N.P.L. (see under Robert Jones above). In addition to papers in scientific journals he was author of 36 Reports and Memoranda issued by the Aeronautical Research Council substantially advancing the progress of aerodynamics.

Aeronautical Research Council R and M., No. 2570; *Old Bangorian* 1963; information from Miss Margaret G. Jones and Professor A.R. Collar; University College of North Wales, Bangor, manuscript collection.

D.J.Wr.

WILLIAMS, DANIEL JENKINS (1874-1952), minister (MC/Presb.) and official historian of the Welsh Calvinistic Methodist Church of America; b. Genesee Depot, Wis., USA, 22 Dec. 1874, the son of Robert H. Williams (b. near Gwalchmai, Anglesey, 1844), and Jane Mary (née Jenkins; b. Wisconsin, daughter of Welsh immigrants). Education: A.B. (U. Wis.), 1899; M.A. (U.Wis.), 1900; B.D. (Union Theol. Sem.), 1903; Ph.D. (Ohio State Univ.), 1914; D.D. (Carroll Col., Wis.), 1918; student of Celtic Literature, Oxford, 1904-05. Ordained by the Welsh Calvinistic Methodist Synod of Wisconsin, 1906. Pastor of churches: Arbor Vitae, Wis., 1905-07; Welsh CM, Columbus, O., 1907-11; 1st Presby., Oshkosh, Wis., 1911-15; 1st Presby., Wausau, Wis., 1915-20; 1st Presby., Cedar Rapids, Ia., 1920-23; Miami Ave. Welsh Presby., Columbus, O., 1923-33; retired to write official history of the Welsh Calvinistic Methodist Church of America, 1933-37; supply minister in Florida (winters) and in Wisconsin (summers), 1937 till death; moderator of the Presby. Synod of Wisconsin, 1915. Fluent in Welsh, he preached in Wales during recesses while attending Oxford, and preached in both English and Welsh throughout his career as a minister in the U.S. He was the author of: *The Welsh of Columbus, Ohio*; *A Study in Adjustment and Assimilation*, Oshkosh, Wis., 1913; *The Welsh Community of Waukesha County, Wisconsin*, Columbus, O., 1926; and *100 Years of Welsh Calvinistic Methodism in America*, Philadelphia, 1937. All three are valuable contributions to the history of the Welsh in the United States, and the latter is the official history of the Welsh Calvinistic Methodist Church of America

from its beginnings until its merger with the American Presbyterian Church in 1920. He died in Milwaukee, Wis., May 29, 1952.

Minutes of the Synod of Wisconsin, 1952; *Alumni Directory, Union Theological Seminary; Y Drych*, 15 Aug., 1952; letter from his son. Brig. General Robert Hugh Williams, 21 Jan. 1983; letter from his daughter-in-law, Alice Tuckerman Williams, Feb. 23, 1983.

E.G.H.

WILLIAMS, DANIEL POWELL ('Pastor Dan'; 1882-1947), founder and first president of the Apostolic Church, the only Welshman to establish a world-wide church; b. 5 May 1882 at Garn-foel, a smallholding near Pen-y-groes in the Amman valley, Carms., one of twelve children of William and Esther Williams. As the father lost his sight when Daniel was only ten years old, he had to leave school a few months later in order to increase the family's income in some way, but the lad's weekly wage as a door-man underground was small. When one considers the enormous work which he achieved in his life, his educational preparation was extremely limited, and as far as is known, his attendance at the village's elementary school was irregular. Of more importance than the school in his upbringing was the home and the church (Congl.) at Pen-y-groes under the able ministry of William Bowen who was inducted as pastor there, and at its sister-church at Milo, on 4 Feb. 1880. During the winter of 1904-05 the influence of 'Evan Roberts' Revival' spread vigorously from Loughor to the Amman valley, leaving more of its effect there than on any other district in Wales. The family of Garn-foel came heavily under the influence of the revival. Daniel and a deacon from the Baptist church began to hold revival meetings at Calfaria chapel, and on Christmas Day 1904 Daniel, his brother William and some friends went to Loughor, and it was there that Daniel experienced his conversion and blessing at the hands of the revivalist himself. The brothers and their friends, with William Bowen's ready support, held meetings in houses and in the halls erected in the surrounding districts following the revival. In 1906, Daniel, whilst at work underground, received a call to become a preacher, and in order to prove the genuiness of the call he set a fortnight to pass to await an invitation from his minister which came before the end of the period. He preached his first sermon on 1 Feb. and visited the churches of the district in turn; he was duly admitted as a regular preacher with the Independents.

Though two churches invited him to become their pastor, due to his lack of confidence at the time, he declined but continued to apply himself to the work. He did not experience strongly the passion of the second phase of the revival which broke out in the district in 1907-08, but in Aug. 1909, whilst on holiday in Aberaeron in the company of friends who had received the baptism of the Spirit, he too submitted on the hillside above the sea and he began to 'speak in tongues'. He hesitated for a while before leaving his denomination but resigned in 1910 when a rift developed in the church at Pen-y-groes between the more traditional members and the ones who had come under the influence of the revival. Those broke away with the minister to form the congregation for which Mynydd Seion chapel was erected in 1913, but Daniel did not cast his lot with them. Instead he joined a more extreme faction who had built 'the stone Hall' in Pen-y-groes in 1910 a non-denominational meeting place for the use of the revival's converts and where they could invite leaders of their own choice. These adherents attended pentecostal conferences, and it was in one of these at Belle Vue, Swansea, that Daniel began preaching in English, though his command of the language at the time was somewhat unsure. From these conferences came reports of the baptism of the Holy Spirit and of its signs, such as speaking in tongues and faith healing, and the idea of the imperfection of the church lacking an apostle or prophet in its ministry. In Feb. 1911 it was revealed to Daniel Powell through prophecy that a prophet would be called to co-operate with him, and the same night his brother, William Jones, was similarly convinced. It was he in due course who became the promised prophet. Contention arose amongst members of the hall, but for the sake of peace it was decided that those who cherished the vision of an 'apostolic church' should break away from the others. According to Rees Evans, *Precious Jewels*, the door of the hall was closed before them on the morning of 5 March, and after meeting in various buildings they erected for themselves a zinc building which they called *Pabell* or *Pabell y Cyfarfod* ('the tabernacle of the congregation'). The two brothers were the leaders. Contact was made with the Apostolic Faith Church in Winton, Bournemouth, where Daniel preached when he was on vacation there after a breakdown brought about through pressure of work. According to Rees Evans, William O. Hutchinson and three others from Bournemouth, including Mrs. Kenny, a lady who had the gift of interpreting prophecy, came to Pen-y-groes to lay their hands on the two brothers, one to be an Apostle and the other to be a prophet, though T.N. Turnbull says that it was at a conference in London in 1913 that Daniel Powell was called to the apostleship. Many calls were received by him from congregations in south Wales, and a small office had to be set up in Llwynhendy and afterwards in Pen-y-groes. They separated from the church in Bournemouth in 1915 because of a difference of opinion concerning ecclesiastical organisation. In 1916 the first part of the Apostolic Church's journal under Daniel Powell's editorship was published. The title of the first parts was *Cyfoeth y Gras: Riches of Grace*, but after two parts it was changed to *Cyfoeth Gras*. For years it was a bilingual journal, and the editor wrote much in prose and poetry in both languages for the journal, and also translated his brother's prophecies. The order of the languages in the title was changed in 1932 and soon the Welsh sub-title was dropped, but the articles in Welsh had become infrequent before then.

In 1916 the official legal constitution of the Apostolic Church was drawn up. Many of the Welsh pentecostal congregations were drawn in and the enormous work which this entailed fell on Daniel's shoulders. The two brothers visited Glasgow in 1918 and 1919, with the result that the Burning Bush Assembly there came into the Apostolic Church. The following year a congregation established in Hereford by Frank Hodges joined, and from there the movement spread to mid and south-west England. In 1922 The Apostolic Churches of God centred on Bradford joined; a missionary wing was established there, and through its activity the movement spread over the five continents.

In 1937 the various parts were united, the headquarters in Pen-y-groes, the missionary centre in Bradford, and the financial centre in Glasgow; Daniel Powell Williams was president of the church and chairman of the Council of Apostles and Prophets and the Executive Committee, with his home in Pen-y-groes. A constitution for the united church was agreed upon, and signed by the president before being presented to the High Court in London. From 1917 onwards an annual convention has been held in Pen-y-groes every Aug.; in 1933 the Apostolic Temple holding fifteen thousand was opened there. Daniel Powell Williams also played an important role in establishing the Biblical School of the Apostolic Church in Pen-y-groes in 1934. From 1922 to 1945 he travelled extensively a number of times to North America, Denmark, Norway, Estonia, France, Italy, Nigeria, Australia, New Zealand and India.

He m. (1) Elizabeth Harries of Llandeilo, and they had seven children; she d. 23 May 1918; (2) Mabel Thomas of Porthcawl. He d. on 13 Feb. 1947.

He published *The prophetical ministry* (1931); *The work of an evangelist*; and *The sanctuary of the Christian life*; and composed a number of hymns in Welsh and English.

Thomas Napier Turnbull, *Brothers in Arms* (1963) and *What God hath wrought: A short history of the Apostolic Church* (1959); Rees Evans, *Precious jewels from the 1904 revival in Wales*; Tom H. Williams, *Mining to ministering; Riches of Grace*.

E.D.J.

WILLIAMS, DAVID JAMES (1870-1951), schoolmaster; b. 18 Feb. 1870 in Caerphilly, Glam., one of the 13 children of Thomas Williams, collier, and his wife. Though he began work as a boy in the mines he showed early ability and in 1882 he won the Gelligaer Scholarship to Lewis' School, Pengam. The register of that school notes Bargoed Board School as his previous school and his father's address as Greenfield Terrace, Bargoed. He was placed in the middle school, and moved to the senior school in 1883-84 where he was second out of 24 in the summer examinations. He was at the top of the list of 27 in the 1885 summer examinations, having succeeded in the Cambridge Local Board the previous Christmas. He sat the same examination Christmas 1885 and in 1886 he won a scholarship to Llandovery College where his gifts as a mathematician flourished. He won a mathematics scholarship worth £80 a year for 4 years at Worcester College, Oxford, and gained prizes for his work in classics, divinity and mathematics. He took a first in mathematics in 1893.

Immediately after graduating he obtained a post at his old school in Pengam but soon moved to Tettenhall College, Wolverhampton. In 1895 he was appointed the first headmaster of the new county school in Bethesda, Caerns., a post which he held until his retirement in 1933. Religion was a major interest. He was a deacon at Bethesda chapel (Congl.) and then at Bethania, Bethesda. He contributed a great deal to the work of the Sunday school and he was one of the editors of the new, modern handbooks for children published by the Union of Welsh Independents. He was one of the secretaries of the Union from 1924 to 1927 and Chairman 1944-45. He was general secretary of Bala-Bangor College from 1932 to 1951 and over a period of some 20 years he compiled a biographical dictionary of all the professors and students of the college. There is a copy of the work at N.L.W.

He m. twice; (1) in 1897 Selina, dau. of John Evans, Minafon, Blackwood, Mon., and (2) in 1929 her sister Mary. He had a dau. and 3 sons. D.J. Williams was an unassuming man whose shyness concealed his great ability and his acquaintance with many prominent figures, but he left his mark heavily on the community in the Ogwen valley. He d. 1 Oct. 1951 and was buried in Coetmor cemetery, Bethesda.

D.J. Williams, *Hanes Coleg Bala-Bangor* (typescript); College *Report* for 1951-52; *Tyst*, 1 Nov. 1951, 6; information from the librarian, Lewis' School, Pengam.

R.Td.J.

WILLIAMS, DAVID JOHN (1885-1970), writer; b. at Pen-rhiw, a farmhouse in the parish of Llansawel, Carms., 26 June 1885, the elder child of John and Sarah (née Morgans) Williams. The family moved to Aber-nant in 1891 and he went to Rhydcymerau school, 1891-98. Between 1902 and 1906 he was a coalminer at Ferndale, Rhondda; Betws, Ammanford and Blaendulais. He resumed his education in 1906 at Stephens' School, Llanybydder. After being a pupil-teacher at Llandrillo school, Edeyrnion, Mer., 1908-10 he entered the Old College School, Carmarthen, 1910-11. In 1911 he went to the University College at Aberystwyth and after graduating and winning a Meyricke Scholarship in 1916 he proceeded to Jesus College, Oxford, where he graduated in 1918. After a term as temporary Welsh teacher at Lewis' Grammar School, Pengam, he became English and physical education teacher at Fishguard Grammar School, 1919-36, and then Welsh master there from 1937 until his retirement in 1945. In 1925 he m. Siân Evans, daughter of Dan Evans, minister of Hawen (Congl.) church, and Mary his wife, and sister of the poet William Evans, 'Wil Ifan' (see above). They made their home in the Bristol Trader, Fishguard, which became a meeting place for hosts of friends. D.J. Williams was elected an elder of Pentowr (Presb.) church in 1954. They had no children. His wife d. in 1965 and he d. with dramatic appropriateness on Sunday evening, 4 Jan. 1970, after delivering a patriotic address at a sacred concert held in Rhydcymerau chapel. He was buried with his wife in the graveyard of that chapel. A memorial tablet outside Aber-nant house was unveiled on 17 Sept. 1977.

Years before his death D.J. had become a legend among lovers of Welsh literature and among nationalists. He was one of the founders of *Plaid Cymru* in 1925, and with John Saunders Lewis and the Rev. Lewis Valentine he spent nine months in Wormwood Scrubs gaol during 1936-37 for setting fire to some of the huts of the Bombing School at Penyberth, near Pwllheli. That symbolic protest takes a central place in the mythos of the nationalist movement. He endeavoured all his life to campaign for a Free Christian Wales. He wrote hundreds of letters to the press and brought two of his heroes, the Irishman, 'A.E.' (George William Russell) and the Italian, Mazzini, to the notice of his fellow-Welshmen through his books: *A.E. a Chymru* (1929); *Y Bod Cenhedlig*, a translation with introduction of *The National Being* by A.E. (1963); and *Mazzini: cenedlaetholwr, gweledydd, gwleidydd* (1954). He also put on record some of the early history of *Plaid Cymru* in a pamphlet, *Codi'r Faner* (1968). Through all of these publications one feels the passionate single-mindedness that made him such a convincing advocate.

The same passion gives his creative literature its distinctiveness. With Kate Roberts he brought distinction to the Welsh short story and most of his published stories were collected together in *Detholiad o Storïau'r Tir* (1966). Some of his earliest stories, with a number of portraits and essays which are an index to his most important themes, are in *Y Gaseg Ddu* (1970). He sought to shame some of the most prominent writers of Wales who wanted no part in the battle to 'save the soul' of the nation, those who could 'stand aside limply without making any move to assist in the battle in any way - as though some moral paralysis has struck them'. How deficient they were, in contrast to the ancient prophets of Israel, unrepentant propagandists who gave being to a great literature. Wales needed 'writers under the passion of conscience' and it was as a propagandist and Christian nationalist that D.J. took to writing.

Basically he was a pastoral writer, the recorder of visual memories. He was in his middle age and early old-age when he produced the works which will be of lasting value. Like his hero, William Llewelyn Williams (*DWB*, 1085-6), he held a deep love for the rural life of Carmarthenshire, but he did not rest content with sentimentality. He saw the Wales that he found worth living and dying for mirrored in his native 'square mile'. Certainly he idealised it, but it is equally true that he showed the civilised, multi-talented, hardworking society which he had idealised in *Hen Wynebau* (1934) and *Storïau'r Tir Glas* (1936) gradually disintegrating in *Storïau'r Tir Coch* (1941) and *Storïau'r Tir Du* (1949) as 'the wretched new world' closed in on it. The same vision gave rise to his two autobiographical volumes, *Hen dŷ ffarm* (1953) and *Yn chwech ar hugain oed* (1959). *Hen dŷ ffarm* [transl. Waldo Williams, *The old farmhouse* (1961)] is his masterpiece, the story of cultivating the land of Pen-rhiw, creating a garden and orchard and then leaving because the hard work of winning the land brought ill-health and tensions within the family, preventing its continuation. Like every classical pastoral paradise, D.J.'s paradise, too, was destroyed, from within as well as from outside.

No man-made paradise can last, but man always needs a paradise to cherish. It is a fundamental need that is as old as existence, and his reaction to it makes D.J. Williams, at his best, one of the finest of Welsh storytellers. His achievement was acknowledged in 1957 when the University of Wales conferred on him an hon. D.Litt. degree. In 1963 he was elected President of the Welsh Academy.

John Gwyn Griffiths (ed.), *D.J. Williams, Abergwaun*, a tribute to him (1965); idem, *D.J. Williams, Abergwaun: Y Gaseg Ddu a gweithiau eraill* (1970); idem, *D.J. Williams 1885-1970: Bro a bywyd 5* (1983); Dafydd Jenkins, *D.J. Williams* (1973).

H.T.Ed.

WILLIAMS, DAVID JOHN (1886-1950), schoolmaster and author; b. at Corris 22 Aug. 1886, s. of H. Williams ('Ap Idris') and Sarah, his wife. Educated at Corris Board School, Towyn County School, Hull Municipal Training College (1913-15), 'D.J.' started teaching at Corris as monitor, afterwards pupil-teacher. He taught as Uncertificated Assistant at Newbridge (Mon.) 1905-08, Uncertificated Head at Cwm Abergeirw (1908-10), Bronaber (1910-13), as Qualified Assistant at Corwen (1919), as Qualified Head at Llawrybetws (1919-20), Llandderfel (1920-31), Llanbedr (1931-48). He retired 31 Aug. 1948. He m. Lena Williams of Llanuwchllyn in 1922. He d. suddenly at a meeting of Mer. Educ. Committee at Dolgellau 1 Feb. 1950 and was buried at Llanuwchllyn 4 Feb. 1950.

He published a large number of books for use in schools, such as *Cyfres Chwedl a Chân* (6 vols.); *Llyfrau Ysgrifennu Cymraeg* (6 vols.) He also made a comprehensive collection of books for children. He was co-editor of *Meirionnydd*, a magazine for the Merioneth branch of *Urdd Gobaith Cymru*; founder and editor of *Hwyl*, a Welsh comic for children. He won several prizes for literary work in the national *eisteddfod*, and he was a member of the *Eisteddfod* Council.

WwW (1937); personal knowledge.

J.Ll.

WILLIAMS, DAVID LLEWELYN (1870-1949), surgeon; b. 3 Feb. 1870 at Tal-y-bont, in the Vale of Conwy, where his father John Williams was Calvinistic Methodist minister. The family moved to Old Colwyn in 1882. Llewelyn Williams was educated at the Tal-y-bont primary school and at Old Colwyn (where he was a contemporary of Thomas Gwynn Jones; see above) and at a private residential school at Llandudno. In 1885 he was apprenticed in a chemist's shop in Rhyl, but at the age of 25 he entered Surgeons' Hall, Edinburgh where he had a brilliant career. He graduated in 1900 and after obtaining a fellowship of the Royal College of Surgeons, Edinburgh, by examination, he specialized in the field of public health. After holding posts in Edinburgh and Leith hospitals and as a ship's doctor with the P. and O. Line, he was appointed borough medical officer for Wrexham in 1905. He m. in 1906, Margaret Price of Rhyl, and they had two sons and a daughter. In 1907 he became county medical officer for Denbighshire, being the first holder of such a post in Wales. When the National Insurance Commission was set up in Wales in 1912 he was invited to serve as its deputy medical officer, and he moved to Cardiff. During World War I he joined the R.A.M.C., and served in France for a considerable period of time with a body of

men whom he himself recruited, *viz*. the 77th Medical Corps of the 38th (Welsh) Division. He won the M.C. for his gallantry in the battle of Mametz. After the war he returned to Cardiff, and was promoted to the office of chief medical officer of the Welsh Board of Health in 1920. He retired in 1935, and was honoured for his services with the award of the C.B.E. In 1939 he returned again to Old Colwyn. He d. in Liverpool, 12 May 1949 and was buried, with his wife who had predeceased him a year earlier, in the C.M. Chapel cemetery at Tal-y-bont.

Llewelyn Williams's chief contribution was in public health and in the organisation of medical education. He was a pioneer in his endeavour to convince local authorities and the Welsh people of the importance of preventive medicine. Much of the initial success of the health insurance scheme in Wales can be attributed to his labour and skill, despite great difficulties. He travelled widely in Wales to address meetings on health problems, temperance and morality, and wrote extensively in Welsh on these subjects. The results of his labours were not confined to Wales.

He worked hard in France during World War I in the interest of the medical welfare of people living on the edges of the battle-fronts, and his services were acknowledged with the awards of the *Médaille des Epidémies* and the *Médaille de la Reconnaissance Française*. He was equally enthusiastic in the cause of medical education. From the outset he was a zealous supporter of the movement to establish a school for the training of doctors in Wales, and when the Medical School was set up in 1930, he was made a member of its Council. Soon afterwards he was elected deputy chairman of the Council, an office which he held until his death. He was a member of the council of the Welsh National Memorial for the Prevention of Tuberculosis from its establishment in 1912. He was awarded the degree of LL.D. (*honoris causa*) by the University of Wales in 1947.

At one time Llewelyn Williams intended to become a missionary in India, and though this did not become possible, he retained throughout his life his interest in the Foreign Mission of the Presbyterian Church in Wales in Assam. He was one of the three commissioners sent to inspect the Mission Field in 1935, and he did much to bring the good work done in the field by the Mission's hospitals to the attention of his fellow-countrymen.

Personal knowledge; *Brit. Med. Jnl.*, 28 May 1949; *Who's Who*.

A.Ll.-W.

WILLIAMS, DAVID MATTHEW ('Ieuan Griffiths'; 1900-70), scientist, dramatist and inspector of schools; b. 3 May 1900 in Cellan, Cards., son of John Williams and Ann (née Griffiths), and younger brother of Griffith John Williams (see below). He left Cellan elementary school for Tregaron County School in 1911. In the Higher Certificate examination in 1918 he obtained the highest marks of all candidates in Wales in chemistry, for which his school was awarded special recognition. From Tregaron he proceeded to the University College of Wales and graduated B.Sc. with first-class honours in chemistry in 1921. After three years research work at Aberystwyth he became in 1924 the first student in the University of Wales to gain a Ph.D. degree. Previously only members of staff had attained that degree. He was chemistry master in Ebbw Vale Grammar School, 1924-26, before returning as a lecturer to the chemistry department in U.C.W., Aberystwyth. In 1932 he was appointed an inspector under the Ministry of Education and he served as inspector of schools in Gwent, Carmarthen and Swansea, later having responsibility over technical education and teacher training colleges throughout Wales. Mainly through his foresight and motivation the first Welsh school to be established by a local authority was opened in Llanelli in 1947. S.M. Powell, the English master at Tregaron, had fostered in him a love of literature and while at college encouraged by R. Idwal M. Jones (*DWB*, 506-7), he wrote two plays, *Lluest y Bwci* and *Ciwrat yn y pair*. Later he wrote *Dirgel ffyrdd*, *Awel dro* and others for the Swansea Drama Week Company, and at least eleven plays under the pen-name 'Ieuan Griffiths', including *Tarfu'r colomennod*, and *Dau dylwyth*. He also composed the music and words for an operetta which was performed in Newport in 1934. He m. Annie Rebecca Morris in Tre-wen chapel, Newcastle Emlyn, 6 Apr. 1939 and they had one daughter. He d. at home, 42 Palace Avenue, Llanelli, 29 Nov. 1970.

Llanelli Star, 5 Dec. 1970; *Gwrandawr*, Dec. 1970, p. vii; *WWP*.

E.D.J., M.A.J.

WILLIAMS, DAVID PRYSE ('Brythonydd'; 1878-1952), minister (B), writer, and historian; b. 1 Mar. 1878 and brought up in Y Wenallt, parish of Troed-yr-aur (Trefdreyr), Cards. His father Ivor Pryse Williams (1850-1920) was the son of the writer priest Benjamin Williams ('Gwynionydd'; 1821-91; *DWB*, 1026) and his mother Elizabeth the daughter of a Baptist family of Bethel church, Dre-fach Felindre, whose two brothers, David Phillip Jones (1850-84), Felin-gwm and Llanfynydd, and Samuel Jones (1875-1935), St. Mellons, were ministers. The son followed his mother to the Baptist fold, began to preach in 1903 and passed the denominational examinations with distinction the following year. In 1908 he entered the Dunoon Evangelical College (Baptist mainly) in Kirn, Argyllshire, and at the end of the two-year course he was ord., 21 May 1910, minister of Ffynnonhenri, and registered for two years as a part-time student at Carmarthen Presbyterian College under M.B. Owen (1875-1949; see above). He moved in 1913 to Philadelphia, Swansea (he was with the Y.M.C.A. in Kent for a short while during World War I), and thence to Libanus, Treherbert, in 1920 where he remained for the rest of his life, greatly influential and highly respected.

The first 30 years of his life were spent at home, writing and following *eisteddfodau* and researching the history of the country between Newcastle Emlyn and the sea in the parish of Penbryn, and despite frequent attacks of infirmity, undoubtedly the first ten years of the 20th c. were the most fruitful for his researches. He published a constant flow of poems, articles and notes in the Cardigan and Aberystwyth weekly papers and in periodicals such as *Seren*

Gomer, *Yr Athraw*, *Arch. Camb.*, *Byegones* and *Y Geninen*, but his essay on the History of Cenarth which won the prize under the adjudication of Sir John Rhys (*DWB*, 844-5) at Newcastle Emlyn *eisteddfod* in 1902 was not published. During this period he corresponded with a number of contemporary Welsh scholars. While at Treherbert he succeeded in safeguarding the official archives of the chapel and wrote *Canmlwyddiant Libanus ... braslun o'r hanes* (1950). From his early days he was active in rescuing the libraries of famous men and contemporaries, and at times using the material as a basis for biographies, e.g. his grandfather 'Gwynionydd'; David James, 'Defynnog'(1865-1928) (see Supplement below), Lewis Jones, the musician of Treherbert (d. 1882), William Evans Davies (1861-1945), Dre-fach, Rees Price (d. 1896), Cilfowyr, John Gomer Lewis (1844-1914) (*DWB*, 556), and David Price (1865-1931), both of Swansea, and Anthony Williams (1845-1913), Ystrad Rhondda; and also Rhys Jones Lloyd (1827-1904), the son of Bronwydd mansion, Llangynllo, the rector of Troed-yr-aur, and his troubled Independent neighbour Thomas Cynfelyn Benjamin (1850-1925), Pen-y-graig, upon whose grave in Llethr-ddu cemetery Trealaw D.P.W. played a part in arranging for a tomb-stone to be erected.

He m., 1 Oct. 1941, in Tabernacl, Cardiff, a member of his church, Annie Lydia, only daughter of David and Jane Morgan, Cedrwydd, Treherbert, deputy headmistress of Penyrenglyn Primary School and secretary of Treherbert Cymrodorion Society. He d. suddenly in Church Village Hospital, 27 Oct. 1952 and was buried in Glyn-taf Crematorium.

His manuscript collection, NLW MSS 15622-963 and 15985-16039, and photographs, 347-401, listed in a typescript catalogue; *Ceredigion*, 5 (1967), 347-401 (article on 'Gwynionydd' containing the family pedigree); Sidney Jenkins, *Hanes Eglwys y Bedyddwyr Ffynnonhenri* (1930), 60; NLW MS. 10330 (register of students at Carmarthen Presbyterian College), 261; *Ser. Cymru*, 21 Nov. 1952, 11 Feb. 1955, 20 Aug., 10 Sept, 1965; *Llawlyfr Bed.*, 1953, 180-1; *Bapt. Hdbk.*, 1954, 341; *Traf. Cymd. Hanes Bed.*, 1964, 40-1, 48-9, 1967, 38-48, 1976-7, 42, 1987, 45-56; *West. Mail*, 31 July 1965; *Rhondda Leader*, 1, 8 Nov. 1952, 6 Aug. 1965; information from his brother-in-law, Rev. T. Haydn Morgan, Ystradmynach.

B.G.O.

WILLIAMS, Sir EDWARD JOHN (TED; 1890-1963), politician; b. 1 July 1890 at Victoria, Ebbw Vale, Mon., the son of Emanuel Williams and Ada (née James) his wife. He was educated at Victoria voluntary school and Hopkinstown elementary school and in 1902, at 12 years of age, he began work at the Waunllwyd colliery, Ebbw Vale. He attended evening classes provided by Glamorganshire County Council in mining, political economy and book-keeping. He and his parents then moved to the Pontypridd area, and he served as secretary of his trades union lodge and as Minimum Wage Agent for the Great Western Collieries from 1909 until 1913. In the latter year Williams was awarded a scholarship to the Central Labour College in London where he spent two years. Thereafter, following his return to south Wales, he was a provincial lecturer for the college. In 1916-17 he faced a period of unemployment, returned to the coal mines in 1917, and was promoted checkweighman in the following year. In 1919 he was appointed miners' agent to the Garw district of the South Wales Miners' Federation in succession to Frank Hodges. From 1928 until 1931 he was a member of the Glamorganshire County Council, and in 1937 was appointed a J.P. for the county. He was unfailingly sympathetic towards those suffering poverty and hardship. Williams was elected M.P. (Lab.) for the Ogmore constituency in 1931 as successor to Vernon Hartshorn (*DWB*, 344-45). He was parliamentary private secretary to the under-secretary for the Colonies, 1940-41, to the financial secretary to the Admiralty, 1942-43, and to the parliamentary under-secretary of state for foreign affairs, 1943-45. He served as Minister of Information during 1945-46 (a post of Cabinet rank, although not within the Cabinet). He resigned from the House of Commons in 1946 following his appointment as High Commissioner of Australia, in which post he remained until 1952. He was granted an extension of a year in this position because of the respect which he had earned - an unprecedented step. Williams became especially interested in plans to encourage British people to emigrate to Australia. In 1950 he became a J.P. in New South Wales. In July 1952 he was appointed to a post in the Commonwealth Relations Office, and from 1953 until 1959 he served as a member of the National Industrial Disputes Tribunal. He published a number of articles in journals in south Wales and in miners' newspapers. He became a member of the Privy Council in 1945 and was created K.C.M.G. in 1952. He remained loyal to the Labour Party throughout his life.

He m. in 1916 Evelyn, dau. of David James, Pontypridd. They had two daughters. He d. 16 May 1963 at his home Canberra, 107 Grove Road, Bridgend, Glam., and his remains were cremated at Thornhill Crematorium.

Www; WwW (1937); *Dod's Parliamentary Companion; Times,* 18 May 1963; *West. Mail,* 17 May 1963.

J.G.J

WILLIAMS, ERNEST LLWYD (1906-60), minister (B), poet and writer; b. 12 Dec. 1906 at y Lan, near Efail-wen, Carms. He was educated at Brynconyn primary school, Llandysilio (where John Idwal Williams, father of his lifelong friend Waldo Williams, was headmaster) and at the county school in Narberth where he later began his career as an apprentice to a chemist. He was baptized in 1923 at Rhydwilym, and the traditions of that ancient church and the culture of the Prescelly district permanently influenced his literary work. After completing a course at Bangor Baptist College, 1928-31, he was ord. on 2 Sept. 1931 as minister of Tabernacl church, Maesteg. On 10 Sept. 1936 he was inducted minister of Ebeneser church, Ammanford, where he spent the rest of his life. He was highly esteemed as a minister and his services as a preacher were regularly sought at Baptist assemblies. He delivered an address (in Welsh) on 'This ministry' at the Assembly of the Baptist Union of Wales in 1943.

It was mainly his poetical works that brought

him into prominence - his winning poems at the national *eisteddfod,* particularly his *awdl* 'Y Ffordd' in 1953 and *pryddest* 'Y Bannau' in 1954. He published *Cerddi'r Plant* (1936), with Waldo Williams; and a selection of his poems in *Tir Hela* (1956); he composed poems for W. Rhys Nicholas (ed.), *Beirdd Penfro* (1961). One of his characteristics as a poet was his ability to experiment, without rejecting tradition. Two of his hymns appear in *Y Llawlyfr Moliant Newydd* (1955), and he was the author of the popular song, 'Pwy fydd yma 'mhen can mlynedd', in 1943. He was for a time editor of 'Colofn yr awen', a column for poets in *Seren Cymru,* and was a member of the Carmarthenshire team of poets for the contests of *Ymryson y Beirdd.*

He was also a prolific writer of prose, which may, possibly, prove to be more long-lasting. He published *Rhamant Rhydwilym* (1939), a useful sketch of the history of the cause (in conjunction with the secretary, John Absalom); *Hen ddwylo* (1941), containing portraits of,'characters' of his early days at the foot of the Prescelly hills; *Tua'r cyfnos* (1943), a prize-winning novel in a competition held by Llyfrau'r Dryw; a biography of *Thomas Phillips, 1868-1936* (1946), Principal of the Baptist College Cardiff (*DWB,* 762-3); *Dan y sêr,* a programme presented by *Urdd y Seren Fore* at the Assembly of the Baptist Union of Wales at Brynaman, 1948; and two travel books, *Crwydro Sir Benfro* (1958, 1960). He was also responsible for the weekly column, 'Yn y tŷ wrth y tân', in *The South Wales Guardian.*

On 11 Aug. 1936 he m. at Rhydwilym Eiluned James, Maenclochog, and they had a daughter. He d. suddenly on 17 Jan.1960, and was buried in Rhydwilym cemetery. A memorial service was held at Rhydwilym, 5 Feb. 1960, and a programme was performed at Maenclochog on 21 Mar. 1979 as a tribute to him.

Ser. Cymru, 23 Oct. 1931, 14 Aug., 25 Sept. 1936, 20 Apr., 13 Sept. 1943, 28 Mar. 1958, 22, 29 Jan. 1960, and 24 June 1966; *Ser. G.,* 1960, 17-22; *Cymro,* 28 Jan. 1960; *Baner,* 4 Feb 1960; *Llythyr* of the Carmarthenshire and Cardiganshire Association, 1960, 17-18; *Llawlyfr Bed.,* 1961, 118-9; *Bapt. Hdbk.,* 1961, 358; N.L.W., material from his library; Meic Stephens (ed.), *New Companion to Lit. of Wales* (1998), 790; information from his widow and his daughter; personal acquaintance.

B.G.O

WILLIAMS, Sir EVAN (1871-1959), BARONET and colliery owner; b. 2 July 1871, son of Thomas Williams, colliery owner, of Llwyn Gwern, Pontarddulais, Glam. Educated at Christ College, Brecon, and Clare College, Cambridge, he returned to Carmarthenshire in 1892 to assist in his father's colliery company. His election in 1913 as chairman of the Monmouthshire and South Wales Coalowners Association marked the beginning of a long period of prominence for him in the coal industry both in south Wales and in Britain in general. Serving on the 'Sankey' Coal Industry Commission in 1919, he was a key figure during the troubled years of 1919-21 and of 1925-26, principally because of his position as president of the Mining Association of Great Britain, a post to which he was elected in 1919 and which he was to hold for the record period of twenty-five years. He was a determined negotiator who was successful in securing district-based wages and hours of work instead of the national wage agreement canvassed by the Miners' Federation of Great Britain.

He remained in active control of his family business, Thomas Williams and Sons (Llangennech), Ltd., until the mid-1940s and became a director of some large industrial and commercial concerns such as Powell Duffryn, Rhymney Iron and Coal, Welsh Associated Collieries, Great Western Railway and Lloyd's Bank. He was also a vice-president of the Federation of British Industries and served on a number of official or technical organisations connected with the coal industry.

He m. in 1903 Charlotte Mary, daughter of David Lackie, J.P. of Montrose. There were no children. In 1922-23 he was High Sheriff of Carmarthenshire and subsequently he was Deputy Lieutenant and a J.P. for the county. He was created a baronet in 1935 and d. 3 Feb. 1959.

Dictionary of Business Biography, vol. 5; Mon. & S. Wales Coalowners' Assocn. Minute Books (at N.L.W.) MG12 *et seq.*; Julian Symons, *The General Strike*; *Colliery Guardian*, 197 (1959), 208.

G.H.

WILLIAMS, EVAN JAMES (1903-45), scientist; b. 8 June 1903 at Cwmsychpant, Cards., the s. of James Williams, mason and Elizabeth (née Lloyd), his wife. He proceeded from the primary school at Llanwenog to the county school at Llandysul, and from there to the University College of Swansea, where he took a first-class honours degree in physics in 1923. He pursued scientific researches at Swansea, Manchester and Cambridge, and had obtained the degrees of Ph.D. (Manc.), Ph.D. (Cantab.) and D.Sc. (Wales) by 1930. Between 1929 and 1938 he was lecturer successively at the Universities of Manchester and Liverpool, and he was for a session (1933-34) at the University of Copenhagen. In 1938 he was appointed to the chair of physics at Aberystwyth, but his career there was interrupted by the outbreak of war, and from 1939 to 1945 he was engaged in scientific research in connection with the armed forces. He was elected F.R.S. in 1939. He was a scientific officer at the Royal Air Force establishment at Farnborough, 1939-41, director of research for the R.A.F. Coastal Command, 1941-42, scientific adviser to the Navy on methods of combating submarines, 1943-44, and assistant director of research in the Navy, 1944-45. He d. 29 Sept. 1945. A list of his publications and an appreciation of his work as a scientist and of the significant part which he played in the battle against submarines are given by P.M.S. Blackett in *Obituary Notices of Fellows of the Royal Society*, vol 5, No. 15, 1947.

Www, 1941-50; *Times*, 2 Oct. 1945; *West. Mail*, 2 Oct. 1945 and 20 Sept. 1961; [J. Tysul Jones, ed., *E. J. Williams* (1970].

G.M.G.

WILLIAMS, GEORGE (1879-1951), company director and Lord Mayor of Cardiff; b. 2 Dec. 1879 at Haverfordwest, Pembs., the son of Frederick and Mary A. Williams, he was educated at Haverfordwest Grammar School. From 1920 to 1945 he was in business as a builder's

merchant and he was also a managing director of numerous companies, among them Williams and Borgars Ltd., Camrose Estates Ltd. and Whitehead's Electrical Inventions Ltd.

During the 1930s he was to the fore in the efforts to attract new industries into south Wales to alleviate the unemployment created by the decline of the staple heavy industries. He served as chairman of the National Industrial Development Council of Wales and Monmouthshire from its inception in 1931 and was the author of the scheme which led to the formation by the Government of the Special Areas Reconstruction Association and the building of advance factories. The Treforest Trading Estate was largely his idea and he also wrote numerous press articles on contemporary industrial and economic affairs.

The other major concern to which he devoted his public career was the city of Cardiff. First returned as a Liberal Councillor for the Penylan Ward in 1928, he became an Alderman in 1948 and served as Lord Mayor 1950-51. He chaired the Chamber of Trade, the estates committee and the airport committee, and he played an important part in the city's acquisition of Cardiff Castle and Pontcanna Fields. A leading champion of Cardiff's claim to be recognised as the capital of Wales, he purchased Parc Cefn Onn and later donated it to the city. He was made a C.B.E. in 1938.

In 1904 he m. Margaret Jones (d. 1942) and they had two sons and two daughters. He d. at Cardiff, 7 Oct. 1951.

Www; *S. Wales Echo*, 8 Oct. 1951; *West. Mail*, 9 Oct. 1951.

W.D.J.

WILLIAMS, Sir GEORGE CLARK (1878-1958), BARONET and county court judge; b. at Llanelli, Carms., 2 Nov. 1878, fourth child of Samuel and Martha Williams. His father was one of the owners of a company selling timber and of the largest tin works in the town at its industrial peak, namely the Old Lodge Works. An uncle and a cousin had been High Sheriffs of the county, and a relative, Samuel Williams, one of the doctors of the town, endowed postgraduate scholarships for students of the University of Wales. The family were zealous Independents and pillars of Park Church.

George Clark Williams received his early education at Llanelli and Bishop's Stortford public school. He went to Aberystwyth College and in 1898 gained a B.A. degree of London University. After serving his articles he qualified as a solicitor, and in 1902 joined the partnership of Roderick, Richards and Williams, Llanelli, where he remained for 6 yrs. until he decided to become a barrister. He was called to the bar in 1909 by the Inner Temple and he joined the South Wales and Chester Circuit, establishing himself in the busy chambers of Trevor Hunter of Swansea. After serving as an officer in the 4th battalion of the Welch Regiment throughout World War I, he resumed his work and built up a large practice specialising in matters relating to Workers' Compensation, gaining experience of great value to him on the bench in years to come. In 1934 he moved to London for a short period when he was made King's Counsel, but in 1935 he was appointed Judge of the County Court of mid-Glamorgan and he remained there for 13 yrs. until he took the post of deputy National Insurance Commissioner. He retired in 1950.

He was an unsuccessful parliamentary candidate (Lib.) for the Llanelli constituency in 1922 and he did not take further part in politics. He was Lord Lieutenant of Carmarthenshire, 1949-53. He was a member of the council of the University College, Swansea, from 1943 until his d. and vice-president of the college for the last two yrs. of his life. The University of Wales conferred on him an hon. LL.D. degree in 1956. The previous yr. he was created a baronet. He d. a bachelor on 15 Oct. 1958 and the title lapsed.

At one time, he had intended entering the ministry and although he turned to law, he maintained close links with the church throughout his life. His upbringing in a religious home influenced greatly his behaviour as a barrister and judge. His courtesy was proverbial and his patience in court or committee boundless. He was fond of children and was a generous benefactor. As a judge, he was magnanimous, a gift which was particularly apparent during World War II when he sat from time to time as chairman of some of the Tribunals for Conscientious Objectors in south Wales.

Www; Swansea College Council Report 1958-9; Principal Fulton's presentation at the Graduation Ceremony 1956; family particulars from his nephew, W.R. Rogers; reminiscences of Dr. Aled Rhys Wiliam and Dr. Urien Wiliam.

D.W.P.

WILLIAMS, GRIFFITH JOHN (1892-1963), University professor and Welsh scholar; b. at Cellan Court (the Post Office), Cellan, Cards. 19 July 1892, the eldest son of John and Anne (née Griffiths) Williams. His younger brother was Dr David Matthew Williams (see above). His father was a blacksmith by trade and since there were five acres of land attached to the house, he kept a couple of cows and a pig as well as being the local postman. He was precentor at Erw Independent chapel for over 50 years and also the church secretary. He died in 1931 at the age of 87. John Williams' father was a descendant of the Daviescs, a family of blacksmiths in the Aeron valley, G.J. Williams's mother also came from the Aeron valley, the daughter of Elizabeth Griffiths, who was said to have composed much poetry, though it appears that none of her work has been preserved.

He was educated at the council school, Cellan and on 20 Sept. 1905 he enrolled at Tregaron Intermediate School. He missed a year's schooling early in his career there, having to stay at home to allow his health to improve. That was when he began to help his father with postal deliveries and to take an interest in local history, reading all sorts of books concerning local and general history. There were in his home books such as *Y Gwyddoniadur, Hanes y Brytaniaid a'r Cymru; Cannwyll y Cymru, Difyr-Gampau Twm Shon Cati* and volumes that had been bound from issues of *Cennad Hedd* and *Diwygiwr*. His old teacher S.M. Powell maintained that the seed of the scholar that emerged later was planted during that year, when he was free of the burden of formal education. In 1911

he went to the University College of Wales, Aberystwyth as the holder of the Cynddelw Scholarship. He studied Mathematics, Latin and History, graduating with honours in Welsh in 1914. He spent the following two years as a teacher at Dolgellau County School (1914-15) and at Porth County School, in the Rhondda Valley (1915-16). Then he obtained a research scholarship and returned to Aberystwyth to study Middle Welsh texts, where he was awarded an M.A. degree for a dissertation on 'The verbal forms in the Mabinogion and Bruts'. In the meantime, with the encouragement of J.H. Davies (*DWB*, 140) and with the assistance of an additional scholarship he set about studying the Llanover manuscripts, which were donated to the National Library in 1917. That is how he began to take an interest in the life and work of Iolo Morganwg (Edward Williams, *DWB*, 1033-4), which became the main field of his research from then until the end of his life. At the national *eisteddfod* held at Neath in 1918, he won the main essay competition on the subject 'The Bards of Glamorgan to the end of the 18th century'. In 1919 he published articles about the work of Iolo in *Y Beirniad*. As a result he was awarded a fellowship of the University of Wales so that he could continue his studies in this field. He worked under the supervision of Sir John Morris-Jones (*DWB*, 668-9) at Bangor during the 1919-20 academic year and spent periods studying manuscripts at the British Museum in London, the Bodleian Library, Oxford and the Free Library, Cardiff, as well as parish records of the Vale of Glamorgan. During this period he also had to defend his scholarship in the public press in the face of fierce attacks by prominent people like W. Llewelyn Williams (*DWB*, 1085-6) who did not wish to hear the truth about the forgeries of Iolo Morganwg. The public bickering caused the organisers of the national *eisteddfod* at Caernarfon in 1921 to set one particular aspect of Iolo's Work, namely his connection with the sixteen *cywyddau* that were contained in the Appendix to *Barddoniaeth Dafydd ab Gwilym* (1789), as the main essay subject. These were the poems that Iolo sent to London to Owen Jones, 'Owain Myfyr' (*DWB*, 498-9) and William Owen [Pughe] (*DWB*, 815-6), the editors of the book, claiming that he had copied them from old manuscripts that had been kept safely in Glamorgan. The three adjudicators were John Morris Jones, T. Gwynn Jones (see above) and W. J. Gruffydd (see above). The only competitor was G.J. Williams who produced a lengthy and careful essay that proved conclusively that Iolo himself was the author of fourteen of the poems. He fully deserved the prize of £40.

The *Eisteddfod* successes of G. J. Williams demonstrated the important place of the National *Eisteddfod* in the life of Wales and its noteworthy contribution to the promotion of Welsh scholarship before the University became established. The *Eisteddfod* served as a catalyst for G. J. Williams, not only as a scholar but also as a poet. He spoke enthusiastically throughout his life about his first visit to the *Eisteddfod*, when his father took him to Carmarthen in 1911, immediately before going as a student to Aberystwyth. He enjoyed competing during the following ten years and he won in the Corwen *eisteddfod* of 1919 on the three lyric poems, the sonnet, the poetic composition for recitation and for the composition of verses for the harp. In Barry in 1920 he won for his lyric poem 'Gwladys Ddu' and his sonnet 'Llanilltud Fawr'. Indeed, during this period he was quickly becoming an important poet and among his papers there was a sizeable volume of poems in his wife's handwriting (see below). But he gave up writing poetry to concentrate on his research on Iolo and his work following his appointment in 1921 as a lecturer in the Department of Welsh at the University College, Cardiff. His later tendency was to look back on his poems as a boyhood amusement.

He threw himself into his work as a lecturer and in 1946 he succeeded W.J. Gruffydd in the Chair of Welsh, because by this time he had developed into one of the foremost Welsh scholars of his day. In order to separate the chaff from the wheat in the vast learning and abundant imagination of Iolo Morganwg, he set about mastering every aspect of knowledge about the Welsh language and its literary tradition. Consequently, he made a brilliant contribution in many fields. *Gramadegau'r Penceirddiaid* (1933) is a standard work on the grammar of poets in the middle ages with an authoritative preface on the manuscripts and the education of the bards. He undertook a thorough study of the work of the Welsh scholars of the Renaissance producing in 1930 editions of William Midleton's *Barddoniaeth neu Brydyddiaeth* (1593) and Henri Perri's *Egluryn Phraethineb* (1595). But his masterpiece in this field was his expert editing of Gruffydd Robert's Welsh grammar of 1567 (1939), a work that entailed research at the Biblioteca Ambrosiana in Milan and other libraries in Italy. He also made original contributions to the literature and learning of the 17th, 18th and 19th centuries. His publications include standard studies of the work of Stephen Hughes, Charles Edwards, Edward Lhuyd, William Owen [Pughe] and others. He drew attention to the important key role of London Welsh societies, especially the Cymmrodorion and the Gwyneddigion, in the development of the Welsh literature of the modern period. He showed how they were following the critical principles of Goronwy Owen and the classical movement of the 18th century and how they founded the modern *eisteddfod* as a means of producing literature and promoting scholarship.

He also maintained that *Gorsedd Beirdd Ynys Prydain* was Iolo's creation and that the antiquity that he claimed for it was fictional. Nevertheless, the *gorsedd* romanticised the *eisteddfod* and made it a popular movement among the common people in the second half of the 19th century, which had a profound influence on the growth of national consciousness and the development of literature and culture in Wales. Without doubt, G.J. Williams's work on the literary tradition of Glamorgan was his most substantial. In 1926 he published his winning essay of 1921 under the title *Iolo Morganwg a chywyddau'r Ychwanegiad. Traddodiad llenyddol Morgannwg* that appeared in 1948 was at first intended to be the preface to the biography of Iolo, but it grew into a volume in excess of three hundred pages. When he was on the point of making a serious attempt to construct a final

version of his revised biography, between 1953 and 1955, one of Iolo's descendants, Iolo Aneurin Williams (see below) donated to the National Library boxes of letters and pamphlets written by Iolo Morganwg. These had been in the possession of the family in Middlesborough and north-east England and in Kensington, but had been missing until a sister of Iolo Aneurin Williams inherited the house in which the family had lived before its sale to another family. She came across the manuscripts in a chest, which had been left in a shed in the garden before the sale of the property. After mastering this additional material, *Iolo Morganwg: y gyfrol gyntaf* appeared in 1956. Alas, this was the only volume of the planned biography that he wrote.

Although he retired from the Chair of Welsh at Cardiff in 1957, he did not wish to confine himself to concentrating on the completion of the biography of Iolo. He continued to edit *Llên Cymru*, the half-yearly journal that he was primarily responsible for founding in 1950 as a vehicle for publishing the product of research into the history of Welsh literature. In 1959 he delivered the O'Donnell lecture in the colleges of the University of Wales. His subject was 'Edward Lhuyd', a work that entailed much research at Oxford. He adjudicated at the national *eisteddfod* and lectured to local societies and in 1960 he was elected the first president of the Welsh Academy. He also gave much time to research into the history of individual works, by virtue of his membership of the editorial board of the Dictionary of the University of Wales. He took great pride in the fact that R.J. Thomas (1908-76), one of the most brilliant of his former students, had dedicated the whole of his career to serving the Dictionary as Editor and he was generous in giving him help and support. Also, between 1959 and 1961, he was chairman of the St Fagan's Folk Museum Committee taking great interest in the development of the Department of Oral Tradition and Dialects. However, during 1962 he had arranged all his transcripts, notes and indexes on Iolo and his works and was ready to commence work on the second volume. Iolo Morganwg was his chosen subject when he was invited to deliver the annual lecture of the B.B.C. Welsh Home Service before an audience in Cowbridge, Glamorgan, in the spring of 1963. Alas, he delivered it only to his wife in the quietness of his study, because as he was amending the wording of the final paragraph, he was taken ill at his desk and he died within a few days on 10 January 1963.

In 1922 G.J. Williams married Elizabeth Elen Roberts of Blaenau Ffestiniog, a fellow student in the college at Aberystwyth (1910-14) who taught Welsh at the girls' county school, Treforest, Pontypridd (1914-18) and at Ebbw Vale county school, Monmouthshire (1918-22). They had no children and she died in St. David's Hospital, Cardiff on 31 January 1979 after only a few days illness. She provided great support and practical help to her husband throughout his career, possessing a great concern for the Welsh language and the whole of the life of Wales. They both had a passionate desire to serve their country and their nation. They made their home from 1922 to 1933 at 9 Bedwas Place, Penarth, and it was there on 7 Jan. 1924, that Saunders Lewis and W. Ambrose

Bebb (see above) came together to found a 'new Welsh movement', to decide on fundamental principles and to choose W. Ambrose Bebb as President of the movement, Saunders Lewis as Secretary and G.J. Williams as Treasurer. This was the south Wales strand that joined with the strand from north Wales to establish the Welsh National Party (*Plaid Cymru*) at the national *eisteddfod* at Pwllheli in August 1925.

In 1933, they moved to Bryntaf, Gwaelod-y-garth, and in her will Mrs Williams left this house to *Plaid Cymru*. Additionally, in 1968 she presented a substantial sum of money to the National Union of Teachers of Wales in order to establish a trust to help disadvantaged children who were Welsh-speaking. The Charity Commission approved the objectives and over the years the 'Bryn Taf Trust' has assisted a number of children from different parts of Wales.

G.J. Williams was a lifelong avid collector of old Welsh books and he possessed a magnificent library that included treasures like his two copies of parts of William Salesbury's New Testament, *Y Drych Cristianogawl* (1585), Thomas Evans Hendre Forfudd's copy of the Grammar of Siôn Dafydd Rhys (1592) that had belonged to William Maurice of Llansilin, together with many other rare books from the 17th and 18th centuries. G.J. Williams's library and papers, together with his shelves, cupboards and desk are now in the National Library.

A list of his publications can be found in *Agweddau ar hanes dysg Gymraeg*, ed. Aneirin Lewis, Cardiff, 1969, 279-86.

Personal research; [Aneirin Lewis in *Dysg a dawn* (1992), ed. W. Alun Mathias and E. Wyn James, 30-37, 67-81; Ceri W. Lewis, *Griffith John Williams* (1994).]

A.L.

WILLIAMS, GWILYM IEUAN (1879-1968), minister (Presb.); b. 3 Oct. 1879 at Cardiff, son of John Williams and his wife, both of Merionethshire. After leaving school he worked in a shipping-office, but within a few years he began to preach at Heol y Crwys church. He was educated at the University College, Cardiff (where he gained an honours degree in English), and at the theological colleges of his denomination at Trefeca and Aberystwyth. He was ord. in 1909, and became minister of Tabernacl, New Quay, Cards (1908-20). During this period he was also a chaplain in the army, serving in Egypt and Palestine. In 1920 he received a call to Twr-gwyn church, Bangor, where he remained until 1966. In 1939 he m. Phyllis Roberts of Bangor. He d. 1 Feb. 1968. His ashes were transferred from Colwyn Bay Crematorium to the family grave in Cathays Cemetery, Cardiff.

He was a person of wide culture and interests, and he was prominent in the life of his denomination, being Moderator of the General Assembly (1948) and Moderator of the North Wales Association (1956). He was also chairman both of the Forward Movement and of the Praise Committee of his Connexion. He took a great interest in hymns and hymn tunes, and co-operated with E.T. Davies (see above) in translating and arranging several of the cantatas of J.S. Bach, such as *Aros di gyda ni* (1919),

Amser Duw, goreu yw (1922), *Iesu dyrchafedig* (1922), and *The Short Passion (St. Matthew's Gospel)* (1931, 1932 and 1933). Having learnt the rules of *cynghanedd* from Dyfed (Evan Rees, *DWB*, 825) who was one-time a lodger at his parents' home, he often composed *englynion*, &c. He contributed occasionally to *Y Drysorfa* and *Y Goleuad*. He was a prominent member of the society of Rotarians, being president of the Mersey and North Wales circle. He represented the society at conferences in America (1936) and Nice (1937).

Blwyddiadur MC, 1969, 309-10; *Drys.*, 1948, 143-5, 1956, 51-3; T. Bowen, *Dinas Caerdydd a'i Methodistiaeth* (1927), 60; information from Glenys Hughes Jones, Pen-y-groes, Arfon and Derwyn Jones, Bangor; personal acquaintance.

G.M.R.

WILLIAMS, GWLADYS PERRIE - see under MORRIS, Sir RHYS HOPKIN above.

WILLIAMS, HUGH (1862-1953), minister (Presb.), and Biblical commentator; b. in 1862 at Rhos-goch, Rhos-y-bol, Anglesey. He began to preach *c*. 1885-86 at Gorslwyd, and he superintended Rhos-goch church for many years. He was educated at Gwredog School, and as a protégé of the Gwredog family he entered Bala College. The principal Thomas Charles Edwards (*DWB*, 197-8) took an interest in him, and he became his private secretary for a period; he translated into Welsh the principal's Davies Lecture, *The God-man*. He visited Germany and learned German to a fair level. He returned to Anglesey and was ord. in 1897. Between 1901 and 1923 he published a series of eight or nine commentaries on New Testament books which proved to be very popular in Sunday schools. The Doctrine of Atonement was his field of study over many years and he delivered the Davies Lecture on that subject in 1945, publishing it in 1948 under the title *Grym y groes*. The University of Princetown, U.S.A., conferred on him a D.D. degree for his essays on the doctrine as discussed in that volume. He d. 25 Aug. 1953 at Amlwch, 91 years old.

H. Owen (ed.), *Braslun o hanes Meth. Calf. Môn (1880-1935)* (1937), 95, 341; *Blwyddiadur MC*, 1954, 233; H. Ll. Williams, *Braslun of hanes Meth. Galf. Môn* (1977), 103-4.

G.M.R.

WILLIAMS, HUGH DOUGLAS ('Brithdir'; 1917-69), teacher and artist; b. 7 June 1917 in 8 Albert Street, Upper Bangor, Caerns., son of David Thomas Williams and Mary Jane (née Williams) his wife, but was brought up in 4 Regent Street after the family moved there. He won a scholarship to Friars School when he was ten years old, and went from there to Manchester School of Art in 1936, where he gained a teaching diploma in art in 1941. He was president of the college Students Union, 1939-41. From college he went to Whitefield Grammar School as temporary teacher, and then to Birkenhead Secondary School in 1944 and King George V School, Southport, in 1945. He was appointed lecturer in art at Bangor Normal College in Apr. 1948, eventually becoming principal lecturer and head of the Art department. He m. Mair Eiluned Williams in Treharris 21 Aug. 1945, and they had two sons. He was a member of the *Gorsedd* of Bards and served for many years on the arts and crafts committee of the National *Eisteddfod* Council. Possibly his most important contribution to the *Eisteddfod* was to advocate to the local committee in Llanrwst in 1951 that they should prepare a separate pavilion for exhibiting the arts and crafts. With a few exceptions, that pavilion was used in every National *Eisteddfod* until 1975. He also designed some of the chief trophies of the *Eisteddfod* and suggested that lectures on art and craft be held in the Literary Pavilion. He illustrated a number of children's books (e.g. *Teulu'r cwpwrdd cornel* by Alwyn Thomas) and designed dust jackets for several other books. He d. 5 Nov. 1969.

Personal acquaintance; information from his widow. [A collection of his works is in N.L.W.]

El.G.J.

WILLIAMS, HUW OWEN ('Huw Menai'; 1886-1961), poet; b. 4 Rathborne Court, Caernarfon 13 July 1886, registered as the son of Elizabeth Williams and her husband William Williams, slate-quarryman, though it has been suggested that his natural father may have been one Hugh Owen. He left school at the age of twelve but continued to read widely and worked at various short-term jobs to help support himself and his mother. At the age of sixteen he went to work in the pits in Gilfach Goch, Glam., but did not move there permanently until he was 18, when he and his mother moved to Merthyr Vale to join his father. There he began to organise and address political meetings, and to write political articles for the *Social Democrat*, the *Social Review* and *Justice*. He soon lost his job because of his political activities but as he was now married with a young family, he accepted a job as a weigher (the employers' representative). This put an end to his political activities (though one of his sons, Alun Menai Williams, also became a political activist, fighting in the Spanish Civil War).

He began to write poetry during World War I; his work appeared in local papers such as the *Merthyr Express* and the *Western Mail*, and his first book, *Through the upcast shaft* was published in 1920; it was followed by *The passing of Guto* (1927), *Back in the return* (1933) and *The simple vision* (1945). Though he made many friends (including John Cowper Powys, see above) in London literary circles, he was often unemployed, and in 1949, when the Port Talbot Forum was active in helping him to obtain a civil list pension, he was living on £2.17s.0d. a week. In later years he lived in Penygraig in the Rhondda. His autobiography remains unpublished. He m. Ann in 1910 and d. 28 June 1961.

Glyn Jones, *The dragon has two tongues* (1968), 140-53; Gwyn Thomas, *A Welsh eye* (1964); R. Felstead, *No other way* (1989), 36-41; *Trans. Port Talbot Hist. Soc.*, II, i, 68; [research into family history by Huw Roberts].

S.R.J.

WILLIAMS, IESTYN RHYS (1892-1955), Director General Labour Relations Department, National Coal Board; b. 1892 at Cardiff, son of Augustus Frederick Williams, mining engineer,

he was educated at Roath Park Elementary School. In 1913 he joined the staff of the South Wales and Monmouthshire Coalowners' Association and was appointed as chief assistant to its Secretary, Finlay A. Gibson, in 1922, and as its Assistant Secretary two years later. In 1936 he became Joint Secretary, the first Welshman to occupy such an office with this organisation.

Widely regarded as being one of the most knowledgeable figures in the coal industry of his time, he earned his greatest reputation in the field of labour relations. He was an outstanding negotiator, much respected by coalowners and union officials alike, and served as joint secretary of the South Wales Conciliation Board. He was also either secretary or a member of numerous other mining organisations, notably the South Wales Committee of the Safety in Mines Research Board. His involvement in the industry in south Wales was matched by his championing of it during the inter-war depression. He wrote numerous promotional articles in the coal trade press and was joint honorary secretary of the south Wales 'Back to Coal' Movement.

Following the nationalisation of the coal industry in 1947 he was appointed chief executive officer of the Labour Relations Department of the National Coal Board. Later that year he became the department's Director-General, a position he held until his retirement in June 1954.

In 1917 he m. (1) Edith Ellen Diamond (d. 1934) and in 1935 he m. (2) Barbara Stamp. The father of three children, he d. suddenly while on holiday in Cornwall on 26 Aug. 1955.

Colliery Guardian, 1 Sept. 1955; *West. Mail*, 30 Aug. 1955; *WwW*. (1937).

W.D.J.

WILLIAMS, Sir IFOR (1881-1965), Welsh scholar; b. at Pendinas, Tre-garth, Caerns., 16 April 1881, the son of John Williams, slate-quarryman, and Jane, his wife. His maternal grandfather was Hugh Derfel Hughes (*DWB*, 378), and H. Brython Hughes (*DWB*, 377-8) was an uncle of his. After receiving his elementary education at Gelli and Llandygái schools, he entered Friars School, Bangor, in 1894, but stayed only for a year and a term owing to an accident which caused him severe back injuries and left him bedridden for some years. On regaining health he went in 1901 to the preparatory school maintained at Clynnog by the Calvinistic Methodist Connexion for candidates for the ministry, where J.H. Lloyd Williams was the master. From there in 1902 he gained a scholarship to the University College of North Wales, Bangor. He graduated with honours in Greek in 1905, and took honours in Welsh in 1906. Session 1906-07 he spent as Assistant to John Morris Jones (*DWB*, 668-9) in the Welsh Department and working for his M.A. degree. He was appointed Assistant Lecturer in 1907. In 1920 he was given a personal chair, with the title of Professor of Welsh Literature. On the death of John Morris-Jones in 1929 the personal chair was discontinued, and Ifor Williams became Professor of Welsh Language and Literature. He retired in 1947.

He became interested early in life in the study of spoken Welsh. He won the prize for an essay on the subject at the national *eisteddfod* held at Caernarfon in 1906, and lectured frequently on the topic to Welsh societies for many years. He was also interested in place names. In 1907 he contributed notes on local place names to *Y Gwyliwr*, which circulated in his native locality of Tre-garth and Bethesda. He collected material for a Welsh onomasticon, which however was never produced. But he kept up his interest for many years, and produced a very useful little book entitled *Enwau Lleoedd* in 1945. In 1949 at the request of I.A. Richards and O.G.S. Crawford he wrote on 118 of the names which occur in the 'Ravenna Cosmography' (*Archaeologia*, 1949).

Sir Ifor's aim in publishing his early books - *Breuddwyd Maxen* (1908) and *Cyfranc Lludd a Llevelys* (1909) - was a purely practical one, namely the provision of texts for the use of schools and colleges and similarly at a later date *Chwedlau Odo* (1926) and *Pedeir Keinc y Mabinogi* (1930). *Casgliad o waith Ieuan Deulwyn* (1909), which he edited for the Bangor Welsh MSS Society and which appeared in a limited edition of 200 copies, did not have the same aim. But he returned to his original purpose with *Cywyddau Dafydd ap Gwilym a'i Gyfoeswyr* (1914), produced in collaboration with Thomas Roberts (see above). He had long been interested in Dafydd ap Gwilym, having discussed his *floruit* in two articles in *Y Traethodydd* in 1909. This selection of Dafydd's poems was the first attempt to restore the text along scholarly lines. From this he proceeded, in a lengthy article in the *Transactions* of the Cymmrodorion 1913-14, to demonstrate how continental literature, through the *clerici vagantes*, had influenced Dafydd. Research into the activities of Dafydd's kinsman and friend, Sir Rhys ap Gruffudd, led to the poet who sang Sir Rhys's praise, Einion Offeiriad, author of the first treatise on grammar and prosody in the Welsh language (*Cymmrodor*, xxvi). Sir Ifor's studies in this field were new and original and made a valuable contribution to our knowledge of the background of Dafydd ap Gwilym's life and work.

It was the same desire to produce texts for the use of students that prompted the publication of *Cywyddau Iolo Goch ac Eraill* in 1925, jointly with Thomas Roberts and Henry Lewis (see above). Sir Ifor also edited the works of two poets which had been collected by two other scholars - Dafydd Nanmor (1923) by Thomas Roberts (of Borth-y-gest, not to be confused with the Thomas Roberts mentioned above), and Guto'r Glyn (1939) by J. Llywelyn Williams. He published many texts, both prose and verse, in the *Bulletin* of the Board of Celtic Studies. His linguistic pursuits led him to take a passing glimpse at sixteenth century scholars. William Salesbury's orthography and vocabulary were the subjects of two articles (*Y Traethodydd*, 1946, 1949). In another article he maintained that the date of publication of the first Welsh printed book was 1547, not 1546 as stated on the title page. (But in this he was mistaken, see *BBCS*, xxiii).

All these studies however were peripheral. The central topic of Ifor William's research was the *Hengerdd*, the poetry associated with the names of Aneirin, Taliesin and Llywarch Hen. It was this poetry, or subjects which shed some

light on it, that engaged his attention from the age of 25 until a few years before his death. After graduating in 1906 he took 'Y Gododdin', the poem attributed to Aneirin, the sixth century poet (*DWB*, 9) , as the subject of his M.A. dissertation, and published notes on the meanings of some obscure words as early as 1908 (*Y Geninen*, xxvi). There were also articles on the substance of the poem which contained a great deal of information that was new at the time (*Y Beirniad*, 1911, 1912).

But it was a dark and difficult field of study, and before it could be elucidated, the history of Wales and of northern Britain and the state of the Welsh language in the period between the sixth and the tenth centuries had to be examined in great detail. It was this that determined the pattern of Sir Ifor's scholarship throughout his life, a pattern that was both orderly and logical. As a result of a thorough study of Nennius's (*DWB*, 682-3, and see Supplement below) *Historia Brittonum*, in which is found the earliest reference to the 'Hengerdd' poets, he made certain important suggestions as to the interpretation of the work (*BBCS*, vi, vii, ix, xi). In a lecture to the Cymmrodorion (*Transactions*, 1946-47), he showed that some of Nennius's material is derived from folk tales.

It was of supreme importance to know the characteristics of the Welsh language in the early centuries, and this necessitated a very close study of all the contemporary linguistic evidence, such as the glosses found in some old Latin MSS. In following this trail Sir Ifor greatly extended our knowledge of Old Welsh. The best example of his highly perceptive approach to the language in its early period is his discussion of the 'Computus Fragment', a short treatise on the use of two astronomical tables (*B.B.C.S.*, iii). To interpret this piece of prose it was necessary to have not only wide linguistic knowledge but also astute understanding in order to grasp the significance of the background. The inscribed stones of the seventh and the eighth centuries also proved valuable evidence on the state of the language. As a result of these and other studies Sir Ifor gained an incomparable knowledge of the meaning of scores of Welsh words hitherto unexplained. Lexicographical notes by him appeared in various periodicals, especially in the *Bulletin* of the Board of Celtic Studies for thirty five years after the inception of that journal in 1921.

All this immense labour gave Ifor Williams the right to speak with authority on the 'Hengerdd'; he started with the easiest to interpret, namely the *englynion* once thought to be the work of Llywarch Hen. In 1933 he delivered the John Rhŷs Memorial Lecture to the British Academy, in which he set out his theory about the origin of the *englynion*. The theory was developed in 1935 in the volume *Canu Llywarch Hen*, which contained the text of the poetry with an introduction and copious notes. In view of Sir Ifor's interpretation of the poetry it was unfortunate that the book was called *Canu Llywarch Hen*, which implies that Llywarch was the author, whereas he was really one of the characters in the story. Furthermore, there is a large number of stanzas which have nothing to do with Llywarch, but rather with Cynddylan ap Cyndrwyn and his sister Heledd. Sir Ifor's theory is that the *englynion* are the remnants of sagas which were partly in verse and partly in prose, and preserved orally. They are nostalgic and elegiac, and tell the story of Llywarch, who is old and has lost all his sons, and of Heledd, who grieves over the devastated court of her brother Cynddylan. Both stories are dated around 850. (It should be said that some modern scholars do not accept this theory).

Ifor Williams's major achievement was the volume entitled *Canu Aneirin* (1938), in which he interprets the 'Gododdin' as a sequence of short elegies on the members of a small band of 300 men sent by Mynyddawg, lord of Edinburgh, to recapture Catraeth (Catterick today), which was in the hands of the men of Deira, but had formerly been an important civic and military centre. The expedition was a failure. The editor showed that the language of parts of the poem proved that it had been written down in the 9th or 10th century, and had been circulating orally long before that. He also showed that the facts which emerge in the poem are in accordance with what is known of northern England and southern Scotland in the 6th century. It is therefore fair to assume that the battle of Catraeth was fought about 600, and that the gist of the 'Gododdin' commemorates it.

As regards Taliesin (*DWB*, 930), Ifor Williams showed that a poet of that name sang the praises of the kings of Powys and of the North in the sixth century, and that about a dozen of his poems have survived. He also showed that a folk tale about Taliesin had developed early, and that it was current in Wales until the 16th century at least.

In addition to this valuable work on the early poetry, Sir Ifor interpreted some poems which fall in the 'gap' between the sixth century and the poets of the Princes, such as the elegy on Cynddylan, a poem in praise of Cadwallon, another in praise of the lord of Tenby, 'Armes Prydain', and the *englynion* in the Juvencus MS at Cambridge.

Radio gave Ifor Williams the opportunity to develop his special gift for writing short essays, presenting a scholarly topic in popular terms or philosophising in a light vein. Three collections were published – *Meddwn i* (1946), *I Ddifyrru'r Amser* (1959) and *Meddai Syr Ifor* (1968).

As a devoted scholar he very rarely undertook any public duties apart from serving on learned bodies - as Chairman of the Board of Celtic Studies, 1941-58, President of the Anglesey Historical Society, 1939-54 and of the Cambrian Archaeological Association, 1949. He received the medal of the Honourable Society of Cymmrodorion in 1938 and was elected a Fellow of the British Academy in the same year. He was knighted in 1947. In 1949 the University of Wales awarded him the degree of LL.D. *honoris causa*. He was a typical product of Welsh Nonconformity; he took preaching engagements on Sundays regularly for many years. He delivered lectures to Welsh societies in all parts of Wales, and as a lecturer, in public as well as in class, he was adept at keeping his audience interested. As a university teacher his great learning and his skill in presentation impressed and inspired his students.

He married Myfanwy Jones of Cae-glas, Pontllyfni, Arfon, in 1913, and there were two children, a daughter and a son. He d. 4 November 1965, and was buried at Brynaerau.

[Alun Eirug Davies, 'Bibliography'; *Studia Celtica*, 4 (1969); I. Ll. Foster, *Proc. Brit. Acad.* 53 (1969); Thomas Jones in A. T. Davies, ed., *Gwŷr Llên* (1948); *Tr.*, 136 (1981)]; personal knowledge.

T.P.

WILLIAMS, IOLO ANEURIN (1890-1962), journalist, author and art historian; b. 18 June 1890 in Middlesborough, Yorks., son of Aneurin Williams, M.P., ironmaster, and his wife Helen Elizabeth (née Pattinson). He m. in 1920 Francion Elinor Dixon of Colorado, U.S.A., and they had one son and two daughters. He was educated at Rugby School and King's College, Cambridge. From 1914 to 1920 he served with or in the army, chiefly in France, and retired as captain. He was a man of wide interests, covering literature, bibliography, art, folk songs and natural history. Like his father, he was a keen Liberal, and was twice unsuccessful Parliamentary candidate for the constituency of Chelsea. At first he worked as bibliographical correspondent for the *London Mercury* (1920-39), and then as art and museums correspondent for the *Times* (1936 onwards). He became an authority on the history of art in Britain and published a substantial and important book, *Early English watercolours* (1952). He discussed the Welsh aspects of this subject in an article 'Paul Sandby and his predecessors in Wales' in *Trans. Hon. Soc. Cymmrodorion* (1961, Part II (1962), 16-33). He was himself a discerning collector; he presented 24 of his pictures to the British Museum and bequeathed 65 more to the institution.

His literary work is to be seen in numerous publications: volumes of poems (1915 and 1919), a bibliography of John Masefield (1921), *Byways round Helicon* (1922), *Shorter poems of the eighteenth century* (1923), *Seven eighteenth-century bibliographies* (1924). He edited the plays of Sheridan (1926), and wrote an unusual handbook, *The elements of book collecting* (1927). Other works by him were *Poetry today* (1927), *Where the bee sucks* (1929) and *Points in eighteenth-century verse* (1934). He contributed to the *Dictionary of National Biography* and to the *Cambridge Bibliography of English literature*. He was vice-president of the Bibliographical Society in 1944, honorary secretary of the Folk Song Society - he wrote *English folk song and dance* (1935) - and vice-president of the Zoological Society of London. He wrote *Flowers of marsh and stream* (1946) and was an experienced field naturalist. He honoured the memory of his ancestor Iolo Morganwg (Edward WILLIAMS, *DWB*, 1033-4), a collection of whose papers he presented to the National Library of Wales, by taking a keen interest in Welsh matters, including the language, and he served on the Council of the National Museum of Wales and on the Welsh Committee of the Arts Council; he was made an honorary member of the *Gorsedd* of Bards (1960). He d. 18 Jan. 1962, and a tribute was paid to him by the *Times*, which referred to his tall, stooping, scholarly figure, indifferent to appearances. He was described as having Gladstonian rectitude, a stern radicalism and an almost fanatical support for temperance.

Www; *Times*, 19 Jan. 1962; personal research.

Don.M.

WILLIAMS, JOHN ('J.W. Llundain'; 1872-1944) slate merchant; b. in Tŷ Capel Rhostryfan, Llanwnda, Caerns., 22 Sept. 1872, the eldest of the seven children of John Williams, slate-quarryman, and Catherine his wife, daughter of Robert and Jane Jones, Llandwrog. One of his brothers was William Gilbert Williams (see below). John was educated in Rhostryfan Board School and began working in Braich quarry in July 1885 where he remained for about five years when water flooded the quarry. After a few months in Moeltryfan quarry he decided to try and improve his circumstances in Liverpool. He worked in a mill-stone factory, a ship repairer's foundry, a cotton storehouse, Morris Jones's warehouse, Laird shipyard, a smithy and a timberyard. In 1898 he was clerk to a builder in Neston but very unsure of his prospects there. He went to London and was employed as a foreman in a slate and roofing business in Jan. 1900. The business closed in 1904 but he secured a similar post with a company which was expanding. He m. Margaret Jane, second daughter of Edward Lloyd, Pen-y-fron, Derwen, Denbs., in Dec. 1900 and they had two daughters and two sons. In Sept. 1923, with his eldest son as clerk, he realised his ambition of setting up a business of his own as a slate merchant. He obtained a convenient yard for his roofing materials in three L.M.S. railway bridge arches near Queen's Park station. The venture proved successful with plenty of work between the two world wars when streets of new houses were being built.

During his early years in Liverpool he took an interest in the life associated with the chapels and the Welsh cultural societies, but temporarily lost touch. In London he became acquainted with several good Welsh writers and poets and his interest in the strict *cynghanedd* metres was kindled. He taught himself to play the piano and organ and took part in every aspect of the work in Willesden Green chapel, where he became a precentor and Sunday schoolteacher. He was firmly in favour of having Welsh spoken in Welsh society meetings in London. At his suggestion *Y Ddolen*, a newspaper for the London Welsh, was published in 1925, he himself being responsible for standards of language and grammar, with David Rowland Hughes (see above) as co-editor; its publication continued until Jan. 1941. John Williams gave lectures and held classes on *cynghanedd*; he wrote a weekly column 'Ymhlith Cymry Llundain' as well as articles on *cynghanedd* for *Y Brython*, 1934-38. His autobiography, *Hynt Gwerinwr*, includes some of his *englynion* and hymns.

He lived for a period in 4 Wrentham Ave., Willesden and Okehampton Road before returning to Wales *c*. 1940 and residing in Gwynfa, Llandwrog, Caerns., where he d. 30 May 1944.

John Williams, *Hynt Gwerinwr* (1943); WWP.

E.D.J.

WILLIAMS, JOHN HUW (1871-1944), newspaper editor; b. 28 Feb. 1871 at Caernarfon. Known by his bardic name of 'Leo', but in *Yr Herald Cymraeg* he wrote under the pen-name of 'Sgorfai'. He was one of the founders of *Y Dinesydd Cymreig* (1912), its editor until 1925,

and its manager until 1926. His articles, 'Senedd y Pentre', were very popular. He moved to Blaenau Ffestiniog (1926) as an official with the Independent Order of Rechabites, returning to Caernarfon (1942). He wrote a column 'Sibrydion yr Awel', in *Y Gwyliedydd Newydd*. He was an actor, author of the play, *Yr Hen Gojar* (1925), pacifist, temperance advocate, and local preacher. He d. 7 January 1944 at Caernarfon.

Eurgrawn, 1946; *Herald Cymraeg*, 17 Jan. 1944.

D.T.

WILLIAMS, JOHN JAMES (1869-1954), minister (Congl.) and poet; b. 8 Oct. 1869 at Taigwynion, near Tal-y-bont, Cards., the eldest of the twelve children of William and Elizabeth Williams. The father was a member at Bethel (Congl.) church, Tal-y-bont, and the mother at Pen-y-garn (CM) church. He attended Pwll-glas Sunday school and it was John Oliver, his teacher, who told him the time and place to hear 'the bells of Cantre'r Gwaelod'. He had his elementary education at Rhydypennau school. Due to the lack of work in the lead mines of the district his father had to turn to the coalfields, and was in Mountain Ash for some months during 1879-80. In 1882 the whole family settled in Penrhiwceibr and became members at Carmel chapel. They moved again to Ynysybŵl, and it was there at Tabernacl that the son began preaching. He worked in a coalmine before going to Pontypridd Academy under E. Dunmore Edwards. He was accepted in 1891 to the Memorial College, Brecon, spending the first year at the University College, Cardiff, where he was the best student of his class in Welsh literature and language. He was ordained at Bethania church, Abercynon, on 22 July 1895, and moved to Moriah church, Rhymney, in 1897. He accepted a call to Seilo church, Pentre, Rhondda, in 1903, succeeding Lewis Probert (*DWB*, 799-800). In 1915 he commenced his long ministry at Tabernacl, Morriston, where he stayed until his retirement in July 1944. He was one of the most popular preachers of his day and was elected chairman of the Union of Welsh Independents in 1935.

He began competing in the national *eisteddfod* early in the new century and won the chair twice, in 1906 at Caernarfon for an ode 'Y Lloer' (which immediately became popular because of its smooth, rhythmical lines) and in 1908 at Llangollen for an ode 'Ceiriog'. He adjudicated the chair competition for nearly a quarter of a century and was Archdruid for the period 1936-39. He wrote two scriptural plays in verse, *Ruth* (1909) and *Esther* (1911), set to music by James Davies. He wrote 'Cadair Tregaron' (1929), which appeared in *Straeon y Gilfach Ddu* (1931), in Glamorgan dialect portraying the colliers' life there. His last volume was *Y lloer a cherddi eraill* (1936). Some of his poems which were set to music became very well-known, such as 'Clychau Cantre'r Gwaelod' and 'Canu'r plant'.

He composed numerous hymns and was one of the editors of the hymns for the *Caniedydd Cynulleidfaol Newydd* (1921), and *Caniedydd newydd yr Ysgol Sul* (1930); he also assisted in preparing the *Caniedydd* (1960). It was he who edited the memorial volume to Hedd Wyn (Ellis

Humphrey Evans, *DWB*, 229), *Cerddi'r Bugail* (1918), and he was editor of 'Congl y Beirdd' in *Y Tyst*, 1924-37, and *Y Dysgedydd*, 1933-36. He received an honorary M.A. degree from the University of Wales in 1930.

He m. (1), 1899, Claudia Bevan of Mountain Ash. She died giving birth to a son who d. within a year and five months. He m. (2), 1903, Abigail Jenkins of Pontlotyn, sister to the mother of Sir Daniel Thomas Davies (see above). She d. 24 June 1936 when he was in Bangor passing the chairmanship of the Union to John Dyfnallt Owen (see above). He d. 6 May 1954.

Dysg., 1954, 157, 169-85; [Trebor Lloyd Evans, 'Y *cathedral anghydffurfiol Cymreig'* (1972), 95-122].

E.D.J.

WILLIAMS, JOHN JOHN (1884-1950), schoolteacher, education administrator, producer and drama adjudicator; b. 12 July 1884, in High Street, Caernarfon, the only child of John Williams and Anne (née Jones). The father was a quarryman. The mother ran a guesthouse for travellers; she d. when the child was only eight years of age. He received his early education at the town's Board School and afterwards at Llanrug British School. One of his contemporaries at Caernarfon central school (*c.* 1896-98) was Robert Williams Parry (see above) and they remained lifelong friends, J.J. being the poet's best man at his wedding. Other contemporaries were H.D. Hughes, minister (CM) and Dr. Arthur Owen. After a period as a pupil-teacher he entered the Normal College, Bangor, in 1905. He was awarded the teacher's certificate (first class) in 1907. The same year he went as an assistant teacher to Granby Street elementary school, Liverpool, and stayed there until his appointment as headmaster of Cefnfaes central school, Bethesda, in 1915 in succession to John Elias Jones. He spent fifteen fruitful years in that post and he threw himself into every aspect of the life of the district, encouraging generations of boys and girls to take an interest in literature, music and fine art. He established the flourishing *Clwb Awen a Chân* which was addressed by some of the nation's most prominent literati, musicians and historians. Sir Walford Davies (see above) took great interest in Cefnfaes school children's choir. Concerts of note and performances of operettas and plays were held there. But J.J. was also an excellent teacher, so much so that J. Glyn Davies (see above) went as far as comparing his method of inspiring children to Sanderson's at Oundle. In 1917 he began working on an M.A. thesis for the University of Liverpool under John Glyn Davies's supervision. His subject was 'Political elements in Welsh literature, 1788-1840'; he was awarded the degree in 1923. He had already turned his attention to the world of drama, immersing himself in the works of playwrights like Ibsen, Galsworthy, Strindberg and Shaw, besides the works of Welsh authors. He studied every aspect of theatre technique and associated himself with the drama company of the University College, Bangor, acting as producer for seven years. He inspired a generation of actors, playwrights and producers (Dr. John Gwilym Jones amongst them) who became in the course of time the leaders of Welsh drama. In the national *eisteddfod* at Holyhead in 1927

he was the liaison officer of the patron, Lord Howard de Walden (see Scott-Ellis, Thomas Evelyn above), when the translation by J. Glyn Davies and D.E. Jenkins (*DWB*, 431-2) of *Yr Ymhonwyr* (Ibsen) was performed with Theodore Komisarjevsky, a former administrative director and producer of the Opera Theatre and Moscow Ballet, producing. He adjudicated a number of times in the national *eisteddfod*, and wrote critical articles, mainly on educational subjects, to newspapers of the day. He discussed the works of Ibsen in the Welsh press and the novels of Daniel Owen in *Y Traethodydd*. His fervour for every aspect of culture was admired by persons like J.O. Williams, Ernest Roberts and Sir Idris Foster. He believed steadfastly in the ideals of Sir O.M. Edwards (*DWB*, 192-3), but Wales did not take advantage of the progressive ideas of this exceptional educationist and in 1930 he went as a schools' inspector to Birkenhead. In 1932 he was appointed the town's deputy Director of Education and remained in post until his retirement in 1949. He was responsible for arranging shelter in Merioneth and Montgomeryshire for hundreds of the town's schoolchildren during World War II. He acted on the Royal Commission appointed to review education in rural Wales, 1928-30. One of his closest friends since their student days at the Normal College was Fred Attenborough, Vice-chancellor of the University of Leicester, and father of the actor and film producer Lord Richard Attenborough who has acknowledged that he profited much from the advice given to him by J.J. at the start of his career in the theatre. He contributed articles to *Yr Athro*, *Y Brython*, *Y Genedl Gymreig*, *North Wales Observer* and the *Liverpool Daily Post*. His health was fragile but he had vivacity and humour. He possessed a charming personality, was an interesting conversationalist and an entertaining broadcaster. Amongst his other friends were William Garmon Jones (*DWB*, 528, the article by J.J.W.), E. Morgan Humphreys (see above) and Gwilym R. Jones. He possessed dignity and courtesy. He was described as a Welsh Christian Socialist. He enjoyed wandering in the rural parts of Wales and England. On the recommendation of Sir Wynn Wheldon (see above) he was interviewed for the post of first regional director for Wales of the B.B.C., but it was Sir Rhys Hopkin Morris (see above) who was appointed.

He m., 3 July 1937, Elsie May Evans of Llanystumdwy, an English teacher at St. Helens school at the time. There were no children. He d. 26 Dec. 1950 at 17 Ashburton Avenue, Claughton, Birkenhead, and was buried at Landican.

Information from his widow, and Ernest Roberts; letters from J. Glyn Davies, Fred Attenborough and Sir Idris Foster; *Gen. Gymr.*, 1920; *N. Wales Obs.*, 1920; *Y Brython*, 1925, 1938, 1939; *Traeth.*, 1936; *Athro*, 1951; *Liv. D.P.*, 29 Dec. 1950; *N. Wales Times*, 1951; *Baner*, 3 Jan. 1951; Theodore Komisarjevsky, *Myself and the Theatre* (1929).

G.A.J.

WILLIAMS, JOHN LLOYD (1854-1945), botanist and musician; b. 10 July, 1854 at Plas Isa, Llanrwst, one-time home of William Salesbury (*DWB*, 898), the eldest of seven children of Robert and Jane Williams. For five years, 1868-1872, he served as pupil teacher at the British School, Llanrwst, before going to the Normal College, Bangor, 1873-74; in 1875 he was appointed headmaster of the Board School, Garn Dolbenmaen, Caerns. In the mid-1890s he worked with Professor (Sir) John Bretland Farmer at the Royal College of Science, London, where he was Marshall Scholar, and from 1897 to 1912 he was assistant lecturer in Botany at Univ. College, Bangor. From 1912-15 he was Adviser in Agricultural Botany to the Board of Agriculture at Bangor when he was invited to the Chair of Botany at Aberystwyth, retiring in 1925. While in London he started his classic researches on the Brown Seaweeds – the life cycle of Fucus – the results of which were published in *The Annals of Botany* (1896) and *The Proceedings of the Royal Society* (1897). His best known work on Dictyota was completed in Bangor and published 1904-05, the double tides of the Menai Straits providing a factor of outstanding significance in his studies of rhythmic variations in the environment. It was not till 1921 that he published in the *Annals of Botany* his work on the fertilization process in marine algae, which he discovered simultaneously with Sauvageau though he had contributed papers on the topic to the British Association at Bradford in 1900 and Dundee in 1912.

He was President of Section K (Botany) of the British Assoc. for the Advancement of Science at Southampton in 1925. He was the leading expert on the arctic alpine flora of Snowdonia. From childhood his passion had been natural history and music. While at Garn Dolbenmaen he wrote operettas: his best known mature composition were *Aelwyd Angharad* and *Cadifor* with Llew Tegid (Lewis David Jones; *DWB*, 494) as librettist. He was eminent as a musical adjudicator, choir conductor and conductor of musical festivals throughout his life. He was prominent in establishing The Welsh Folk Song Society in 1906. He edited its journal and was an inspirational figure for many years. He also edited *Y Cerddor*. Jointly with Arthur Somerville he compiled the two volumes of *Welsh Melodies* (Boosey & Co.). He was awarded the D.Sc. degree of the University of Wales for his work on marine algae in 1908 and D.Mus. (*honoris causa*) in 1936. In his retirement he wrote his reminiscences *Adgofion Tri Chwarter Canrif* in four volumes, and *Y Tri Thelynor*. He also wrote *Byd y Blodau* published by Messrs. Morris and Jones, Liverpool. To the end he continued his researches into the origins and early development of Welsh Music.

He was married to Elizabeth Jones, daughter of Emanuel and Ann Jones of Tŷ Lawr, Cricieth, and they had two sons. He d. 15 Nov., 1945 at Peacedown St. John, Bath, Somerset and was buried at Cricieth.

Baner, 22 Nov, 1945; *Nature*, 157, 30 Mar. 1946; *Proceedings of the Linnean Soc. of London*, 158, pt. 1. Jan. 1947; *Liv. Daily Post*, 19 Nov. 1945; *Weekly Mail*, 24 Nov. 1945; [*Tr.* 155, 158-75; *Canu Gwerin*, 6, 40-6; 18, 3-26]..

R.A.R.

WILLIAMS, LUCY GWENDOLEN (1870-1955), sculptress; b. in 1870 at New Ferry, near Liverpool, daughter of Henry Lewis Williams, priest, and Caroline Sarah (née Lee), his wife.

Her father was the son of John Williams, Highfield Hall, Northop, Flints., but Gwendolen Williams can hardly be said to be Welsh from the point of view of her professional dedication. She studied art under Alfred Drury at Wimbledon Art College before proceeding to the schools of the Royal Academy where she worked under Lantèri. Her sculptures were first exhibited at the Royal Academy in 1893, and, until the middle of World War I, she worked successfully in Rome, where she built workshops for herself and for other artists. From childhood she suffered from backache which became arthritic, compelling her to abandon her work. After returning to England, she recovered her health in the mid-1920s, and in 1926 she completed her most important work from a Welsh standpoint, namely a bust of Robert Owen (1771-1858, *DWB*, 720-1) for Newtown Museum. She resumed her career and visited the U.S.A., but did not succeed in re-establishing herself among the most important sculptors of her time. She lived in London for the rest of her life. She specialised in light and romantic bronze statuettes, and was fond of portraying heads of children. She also executed a number of portrait commissions. The National Library of Wales has a good collection of her work, including a copy of one of her best items, 'Chasing the butterfly', and there are also examples in the National Museum of Wales. Her sculptures and watercolours have been exhibited at the Royal Academy, annual exhibition at Liverpool, in the Paris Salon, and in Rome. She d. 11 Feb. 1955.

N.M.W. archive; *Alumni Cantab. 1752-1900*, 491; see *Www* for a list of her exhibitons.

P.L.

WILLIAMS, LLYWELYN (1911-65), minister (Congl.) and politician; b. in Llanelli, 22 July 1911 one of the four children of William Williams and his wife Jessie (née Phillips). The father was a collier until he lost his health which caused him to spend the rest of his life as an insurance collector. The children were reared in a cultured home at 63 Marble Road. They were imbued with the principles of religion and education, a love of Wales and a commitment to social freedom. Olwen Williams, former headmistress of the Welsh school at Llanelli, was Llywelyn's sister. The children were heavily influenced by the society at Capel Als (Congl.) and undoubtedly the fine preaching of the minister, Daniel John Davies (see above), led two of them into the ministry. Llywelyn was educated at Stebonheath primary school and the boys' grammar school Llanelli. He went to the University College of Swansea with a scholarship and graduated in Welsh and philosophy in 1933. After a theological course at the Presbyterian College in Carmarthen, he was ordained minister in Bethesda, Caerns., in 1936. He left in 1943 for the Tabernacl, Abertillery, and within three years was called to succeed Howell Elvet Lewis (see above) at Tabernacl, King's Cross, London. In 1950 he was elected M.P. for Abertillery in a by-election following the death of George Daggar (see above). He won every election thereafter with a majority of over 20,000 votes. He had an opportunity in the House of Commons to channel his zeal for social justice and world peace in a wider context. His commitment to developing welfare in Wales continued as steadfastly as ever, and his brilliant speeches made a deep impression on his fellow-members. He represented Britain at the Council of Europe in Strasburg in 1954. He went on a lecture tour to America in 1955 and spoke on a variety of subjects including the campaign against famine, the Colombo Plan, the Welfare State in Britain, and the Council of Europe. In 1957 he argued for inviting Mao Tse Tung and Chou En-lai to Britain, and in 1958 he was one of the twelve M.P.s who toured the U.S.A. He was president of the Association of Old Age Pensioners in Wales in 1963, and was chairman of the Labour Group of Welsh M.P.s. Despite leading a busy life he contributed to the Welsh press – 'Y Wers Gydwladol' in *Y Cyfarwyddwr*, 1941-42, a tribute to Hugh Gaitskell in *Barn* in 1963, and 'Newyddion o'r Senedd' to *Y Cymro* in 1964-65. He was the author of *Hanes eglwys y Tabernacl, King's Cross, 1847-1947* (1947). He suffered a number of heart attacks from 1960 onwards.

He m. Elsie, daughter of Lord Macdonald of Gwaenysgor (see above) on 17 Aug. 1938 in Ashton-in-Makerfield; they had a son and daughter. He d. 4 Feb. 1965 after bequeathing his body to the Medical School, Cardiff for research; his remains were buried in the cemetery of Thornhill crematorium, Cardiff.

Blwyddiadur A, 1966, 153-4; *Www*; *Times*, 6 Feb. 1965; information from his sister, Olwen.

E.D.J.

WILLIAMS, MALLT - see WILLIAMS, ALICE MATILDA LANGLAND

WILLIAMS, MARGARET LINDSAY (1888-1960), artist; b. 18 June 1888, daughter of Samuel Arthur Williams, Barry Dock, Glam., who had a flourishing business as shipbroker in Cardiff, and Martha Margaret (née Lindsay) his wife. The daughter had private tuition before entering Cardiff Technical College where she won a gold medal for art. After a year working in Pelham school of art, London, she moved to the Royal Academy in 1906 where she was a brilliant student, winning 4 silver medals, a travelling scholarship, a landscape prize, and in 1911 a gold medal for her painting 'The city of refuge'. She received a number of important public commissions before she was thirty, including 'The Rt. Hon. Lloyd George, Prime Minister, unveiling the National Statuary at Cardiff', 1919, and 'The National Welsh War Service in Westminster Abbey', 1924. Among her early works are landscapes and titled paintings, some revealing an unusual and original imagination, such as 'The devil's daughter' and 'The triumph' which were exhibited in the Royal Academy in 1917. Nevertheless, she inclined more and more to portraiture after the war and among her sitters were clients as varied as Henry Ford, Field Marshall Slim and Ivor Novello (see above), as well as many members of the royal family.

Margaret Lindsay Williams worked for most of her life in London, but she was deeply committed to Wales and Welsh art. She was close to leaders of the national revival before World War I, when she portrayed Welsh topics as in her series of watercolours, 'Maidens of Llyn-y-fan'. She enthusiastically supported the National *Eisteddfod*, and W. Goscombe John (see above) was one of her friends. It is appropriate that Sir O. M. Edwards (*DWB*, 192-3) should be among the considerable number of Welshmen portrayed by her. It was she who created the image of him which remains in the minds of the public to the present day in the portait which she painted 26 yrs. after his death. Margaret Lindsay Williams was a member of the South Wales Art Society, the Honourable Society of Cymmrodorion and the *Gorsedd* of Bards. Examples of her work are at the National Museum of Wales and in private and public collections throughout south Wales. She d. 4 June 1960.

Www; N.M.W. archive; see her autobiography, 'Life was my canvas', *West. Mail*, 3-11 Oct. 1960, [Angela Gaffney, '*Wedded to her Art*' (1999)].

P.L.

WILLIAMS, OWEN HERBERT (1884-1962), surgeon and Professor of Surgery; b. 2 Jan. 1884 at Bodrwnsiwn, Llanfaelog, Anglesey, s. of Owen and Jane Williams, of a farming family. The father died before his son had reached his first birthday, and all his life he paid tribute to his mother's untiring efforts to secure an education for her son. After his primary education at Llanfaelog school he attended the grammar school at Beaumaris and then went to the University of Edinburgh to study medicine where he graduated M.B., Ch.B., 1906, and became an F.R.C.S. (Edinburgh) in 1909 and an F.R.C.S. (England) in 1923. His connections with the Royal Southern Infirmary, Liverpool started in 1908 and continued without break (apart for a period with the R.A.M.C. during World War I) until his retirement from his appointment as Senior Consultant Surgeon in 1945. During his early years at Liverpool University he was a lecturer in anatomy and later a lecturer and then Professor of Surgery from 1939 to 1945. He was a man of a kindly and gracious disposition and by virtue of his brilliant medical talents his name and that of the Infirmary became very well known throughout north Wales. He gave many years of service to the Wales Hospital Board and he took a prominent part in the affairs of the University College of North Wales, Bangor and was for a period a Vice-president. He also served on the Council of the Welsh School of Medicine. During his retirement he spent much of his time at Rhosneigr and he always regarded the Isle of Anglesey with much warmth and affection. In 1952 he was awarded an Hon. D.Sc., by the University of Wales.

In 1916 he m. Ethel Kenrick Thomas, dau. of William Thomas, a shipowner from Liverpool. She was able to give him the invaluable support needed because of the frailty of his health during the last thirty years of his life. They had a daughter and two sons. He d. on 6 March 1962 at his home in Liverpool and was buried in the cemetery at Bryndu, Llanfaelog on 10 March 1962.

Brit. Med. Jnl., 24 March 1962; *Lancet*, 24 March 1962; personal knowledge.

E.W.J.

WILLIAMS, PRYSOR - see WILLIAMS, ROBERT JOHN below.

WILLIAMS, ROBERT DEWI (1870-1955), minister (Presb.), headmaster of Clynnog School and writer; b. 29 Dec. 1870 at Llwyn-du Isaf, Pandytudur, Denbs., son of Isaac and Elizabeth Williams. He was a pupil at the local British School (Blaenau Llangernyw School, or Pandy School) and he had two months' education at the grammar school kept by his relative, Robert Roberts ('Y Sgolor Mawr', 1834-85, *DWB*, 877), at Llanfair Talhaearn; he subsequently attended a school at Llandudno and the preparatory school at Bala where he began to preach. After a period at the University College, Aberystwyth, he completed a four-year honours course at Jesus College, Oxford. He was ord. in 1900, and served as minister of Cesarea, Llandwrog, Caerns. (1898-1904) and Jerusalem, Penmaen-mawr (1904-17). In 1917 he was appointed headmaster of Clynnog School, and he retained the post when the school moved to Clwyd College, Rhyl, remaining there until he retired in 1939. He lived at Rhuddlan during the last years of his life. He was greatly respected by his students. It is clear that he was an excellent teacher with a deep knowledge of the classics and other subjects; he taught dozens of students - some of them rather unpromising - who had set their hearts on the ministry. He was a very acceptable preacher himself, and his vivid and pithy comparisons were long remembered. He was elected Moderator of the North Wales Association of the Pres. Church in 1950. He was also a fine writer, with a natural instinct for savouring words and sayings. His long short-story, 'Y Clawdd terfyn' was published in the first issue of *Y Beirniad*, and later published in *Clawdd terfyn, straeon a darluniadau* in 1912 (2nd. ed. 1948); he is considered to be the pioneer of this type of story in Welsh. He also wrote for periodicals, and some of his articles in *Y Drysorfa* were collected under the title *Dyddiau mawr mebyd* in 1973. In 1908 he m. Helena Jones Davies, and they had a son. He d. 25 Jan. 1955 at Rhuddlan.

Blwyddiadur MC, 1956, 265; *Gol.*, 9 and 16 Feb. 1955; *Drys.*, 1950, 59-62; W. Morris (ed.), *Ysgolion a Cholegau y MC* (1973), 61ff.; information from Alford Pritchard, Pandytudur; [W.J. Edwards, *Cerdded y clawdd terfyn* (1992)].

G.M.R.

WILLIAMS, ROBERT JOHN (PRYSOR; 1891-1967), collier and actor; b. 13 Apr. 1891 at Trawsfynydd, Mer. His father, Ellis, was a carpenter and d. young; his mother, Eliza, daughter of 'Eos Prysor', raised him and his sister with the scant assistance of the Board of Guardians. He was educated at Trawsfynydd British School but he left when he was ten yrs. old to earn his living as a farm-worker. When his mother re-m. the family moved to the coalmining valleys in the South, first to Abertridwr, where he began working underground in Senghennydd colliery, and subsequently in Abergorci pit, Treorchy. He was interested in music and drama and through his own exertions he became a precentor, an organist in the chapel (and local cinema, too, when he was short of money), and a prominent member of the opera company and drama company. At the Treorchy national *eisteddfod* in 1928 he met two people who were to influence his life greatly, namely Daniel Haydn Davies, who became a producer of school programmes for the B.B.C., and also one who became a lifelong friend, namely David Moses Jones, a collier and actor like himself. In 1936 Thomas Rowland Hughes (see above), the novelist and producer, invited both of them to take part in a radio play, and for the next 30 yrs. Prysor Williams's voice was among the most familiar on Welsh radio and television. He appeared also on stage, including performances in the Abbey in Dublin (*Birds of a feather* by J.O. Francis; see above) and in the Globe, London (*Rhondda roundabout* by Jack Jones; see above). He took part in five films; the best-known was *Blue scar* by Jill Craigie. He m. in 1917 Margaret Mary Walters and they had two daughters. He d. 13 Oct. 1967 at Treherbert and his remains were cremated at Glyn-taff.

Personal acquaintance and information from his daughter Betty Edwards, and Wyn Thomas, Cardiff.
L.D.

WILLIAMS, ROBERT ROLFE (1870-1948), a pioneer of Welsh-medium education; b. in 1870 in Llwyn-teg, Llan-non, Carms., son of Thomas Williams, minister (Congl.), and his wife Mary. He was educated at Bryndu Elementary School, and the Copper Works School, Llanelli. In 1880 his father accepted the pastorate of Soar Chapel, Clydach Vale, Rhondda, and Robert became a pupil-teacher with Thomas Williams ('Glynfab'), at the local school. He went to the University College, Cardiff (1892-94), before joining the staff of Ferndale Secondary School. He returned to Clydach Vale in 1896 as headmaster of his old school. He was widely acclaimed for his heroic leadership on 11 March 1910, when he was largely responsible for rescuing all but five of the pupils caught in the school yard when it was flooded by water from a disused coal-level at the head of the valley. He was awarded the Albert Medal for his bravery. Later that year he was appointed headmaster of Llwynypia School before being promoted Inspector of Schools. His flair for administration was greatly appreciated when he effectively re-organised the Authority's evening schools which catered for 20,000 students. In 1915 he became Assistant Director of Education for the Rhondda, and after World War I he increasingly concerned himself with the development of Welsh-medium education. In 1921, on his advice, five primary schools were designated bilingual schools. The Education Committee published his *Report ... on the teaching of Welsh in the bilingual schools of the Authority* (1925) and recommended that Welsh be the medium of instruction in these infant schools; that all the senior departments be conducted on the bilingual plan; that Welsh be included in the curriculum of the Secondary Schools as a subject of instruction, and as a medium of instruction in some other subjects. In 1926 a scheme was published to cover the needs both of pupils and of non-Welsh speaking staff. That the Education Committee was fully supportive of this revolutionary language policy was manifested in 1927 when it appointed its author to be Director of Education. Unfortunately his strength was heavily taxed; he suffered a severe breakdown in 1931 and had to retire before his plans were fulfilled. By the mid-1930s the Education Commiteee's enthusiasm for the Welsh language policy had waned and the scheme was dropped. The Council forfeited a unique opportunity to secure the rightful inheritance of the Welsh pupils attending the Valley's schools, and also of leading the country in the field of bilingual education. Consequently, there developed during the 1930s a clear break in the linguistic pattern of Welsh-speaking families with the younger generation increasingly losing the mother-tongue. Some of those children, fifty years on, became the most fervid supporters of the Welsh-medium Schools Movement.

R.R. Williams was a Fellow of the Geological Society, was made an O.B.E. (1932), and awarded an honorary M.A. degree by the University of Wales (1933). He was an active and valuable officer of many of the county's cultural societies. He m. (1) at Cardiff, 7 Dec. 1892, Esther John of Marian Street, Clydach, daughter of Benjamin John, collier; they had a son and two daughters. After their divorce he m. (2) Rachel Anne Jones, Tonpentre (d. 27 July 1970). He retired to Llwyn-teg, Llan-non. He d. 26 July 1948 and was buried in Llwyn-teg (Congl.) cemetery.

Private research with the assistance of Mrs Mary Price, Pontyberem.

D.J.

WILLIAMS, THOMAS ('Tom Nefyn'; 1895-1958), minister (Presb.) and evangelist; b. 23 Jan. 1895 at Bronolau, Boduan, Caerns., son of John Thomas, a well-known local poet in Llŷn, and his wife Ann Williams. The family moved to the vicinity of Nefyn, and established themselves later at Bodeilas near Pistyll where he was brought up. He left Nefyn Elementary School in 1909, and worked in the Eifl granite quarry. He joined the army in 1914, and saw action in the Dardanelles, France, Egypt and Palestine, suffering great hardship and being wounded. During his service in the Middle East he met David Williams (*DWB*, 1156), who was one of the army chaplains. He wrote poetry at that time and his friend, William Williams of Caernarfon, published a small collection of his poems under the title *Barddoniaeth o waith Twm Nefyn* (n.d.). He returned from the war an ardent pacifist. Some years later he published *Dagrau Cain - dagrau Crist* (1935), an essay against war, and the Fellowship of Reconciliation published a pamphlet of his, *At Suvla Bay; what a soldier learnt at Gallipoli* (n.d.). He began to hold evangelical meetings locally, and he was persuaded to become a candidate for the ministry. He went to Porth school in the Rhondda Valley to prepare himself for his vocation under the guidance of R.B. Jones before proceeding to the theological colleges of his denomination at Aberystwyth and Bala. He was ord. in 1925, and that same year he m. Ceridwen Roberts Jones of Coed-poeth, and they had children. He received a call to Ebenezer, Tumble, Carms., the anthracite coal district where there was much industrial and political unrest in the 1920s.

Tom Nefyn spent a stormy period at Tumble. His sermons on social matters - wages, the state of the coalminers' houses, &c. - drew much attention, and his ideas on the nature of the church and his doctrinal views were also rather new. Some of the leaders of South Carmarthenshire Presbytery doubted his ortho-

doxy and his case was brought before the South Wales Association. He insisted, from the floor of the meeting, that he be informed what were the doctrinal standards with which he was expected to conform. The case dragged on from one Association meeting to the next, and was given great publicity by the daily and weekly newspapers. Tom Nefyn himself published a lengthy manifesto (80 pp.) in 1928, under the title *Y Ffordd yr edrychaf ar bethau* and at the Treherbert Association (Apr. 1928) it was declared that his doctrinal views were at variance with not only the standards of the Connexion but also with the historical faith of the Christian church. He was asked to reconsider his position and conform with the standards of his Connexion or resign from the ministry. A number of prominent ministers and laymen of the Connexion appealed against the Association's decision, and a pamphlet of plea and protest was published under the names of five of the elders of Ebenezer. At the Nantgaredig Association (Aug. 1928) it was decided that he was to be barred from undertaking any ministerial duties, in the hope that he would be led to reconsider his position and have his place as a minister restored. His ministry at Ebenezer terminated at the beginning of September. Ebenezer church was disestablished and a church was re-established there for those who conformed with the terms of the Connexion. His supporters in Tumble came together and obtained the financial assistance of the Society of Friends to build a 'society house' in the village. Llain-y-Delyn was opened at the end of Nov. 1929, but his supporters were disappointed when Tom Nefyn decided, after a period of rest and contemplation at the Quakers' institution at Woodbrooke, Selly Oak, Birmingham, to be reinstated as a minister by his Connexion. He now felt ready to accept the 'Shorter Declaration on Faith and Practice' adopted by the Presbyterian Church of Wales and he was reinstated at the Porthcawl Association in Apr. 1931. (See *The Tom Nefyn Controversy*, a pamphlet published by the Welsh Review Co. Ltd., Tonmawr, Port Talbot (*c.* 1929); Tom Nefyn-Williams, *Yr Ymchwil* (1949); and E. P. Jones, *Llain-y-Delyn, Cymdeithas Gristnogol y Tymbl* (1970). In 1932 Tom Nefyn was called to be pastor of Bethel church, Rhosesmor, Fl., and he remained there until 1937. Subsequently he moved to Gerlan, Caerns. (1937-46); he had charge of the churches of Tarsis and South Beach, Pwllheli (1946-49) and of the churches of Edern and Greigwen, Llŷn (1949-58). All these years he evangelised in his own particulr style. No-one was more effective than he as a missioner, not only in chapels but in village halls, hospitals and public houses and in the open-air at fairs, on street corners and along the highways. He evangelised as he went along his way, singing, preaching and counselling. It was not easy for anyone to work with him, since he insisted on having his own way; it could be said that he was a lonely man although he loved his fellow-men passionately. He contributed much to *Y Goleuad*. Like his father before him, he enjoyed writing poetry, and his poems appear in *Yr Ymchwil* and in weekly papers. He d. suddenly on Sunday night, 23 Nov. 1958, after conducting a meeting in Rhydyclafdy chapel, and his remains were interred at Edern.

The sources referred to above, and also W. Morris (ed.), *Tom Nefyn* (1962); personal acquaintance; [Harri Parri, *Tom Nefyn: Portread* (2000)].

G.M.R.

WILLIAMS, THOMAS HUDSON - see HUD-SON-WILLIAMS, THOMAS above.

WILLIAMS, THOMAS OSWALD ('ap Gwarnant'; 1888-1965); Unitarian minister, author, poet and public figure; b. 10 May 1888, one of the four children of Rachel and Gwarnant Williams, farmer, poet and public figure of Gwarnant farm, in the parish of Llanwenog, Cards. He was educated at Cwrtnewydd school and Dafydd Evans's school Cribyn (1901-02); he was apprenticed as a pupil-teacher and, for a period of ten years he was a deputy-teacher at Blaenau school, Gorsgoch and Cwrtnewydd school. In 1911, 'without an hour of secondary education' he went to the University College, Aberystwyth, where he graduated B.A. in Welsh (with first-class honours) in 1915, a student, in his first years, of Professor Edward Anwyl (*DWB*, 12-13). He graduated with an M.A. in 1923 for a dissertation on 'The literary movement in west Wales in the early part of the eighteenth century, together with its religious connections.' He had charge of Capel y Cwm for a short time after leaving college and then, for three years, the churches at Brondeifi and Caeronnen, before receiving, in 1918, an invitation to become their official minister. He stayed there until his death in 1965.

During his college days he edited *Y Wawr*, the magazine of the Welsh students at Aberystwyth; he was the editor of *Yr Ymofynydd*, the Welsh-language magazine of the Unitarians in Wales, from January 1926 to December 1933 and in 1937, during the illness of his successor, Rev. T.L. Jones. He served on the consultative commiteee of *Yr Ymofynydd* until the end of his life. He contributed frequent articles under his own name as well as 'T.O.W.', 'O', 'Ap Gwarnant', 'E.W.O.', 'Na N.', 'Gwalch Ogwr' etc. He wrote a series about denominational giants, denominational homes and denominational chapels, publishing the latter part of this series as *Hanes cynulleidfaoedd Undodaidd sir Aberteifi* (1930). In the same magazine he published a series of critical articles on his contemporaries, 'Gwŷr blaenllaw yr enwad' under the pen-name 'Gwalch Ogwr'. He published *Hanes Caeronnen* in 1954 and the comprehensive volume *Undodiaeth a rhyddid meddwl* in 1963. He delivered many public lectures and at least one of his plays, *Gwyntoedd croes* was performed. He participated frequently in *eisteddfodau*; he twice won the chair at the inter-college *eisteddfod* and he came close to winning the chair and the crown at the National *Eisteddfod* on more than one occasion. He won many prizes for poetry at the National *Eisteddfod* and one for his essay on freedom of thought in Wales. He was acknowledged as a scholar and the beauty of his language and his ease of expression were proverbial. However, he did not escape criticism as one of the editors of the revised volume of the Unitarian hymnal *Perlau Moliant* which appeared in 1929 (see *Ymofynnydd* 1928, 195). Although he was not a musician, the 'music of heaven' was in his soul

and he composed many hymns. His style as a hymn writer was not dissimilar to that of Iolo Morganwg (Edward Williams, *DWB*, 1033-4), especially when his composition related to the world of nature or was for children, such as the hymns, 'Melys rhodio 'nglas y coedydd' and 'Anian wena 'nglas y dolydd'. He was the foremost historian of the Unitarians in Wales and no one succeeded in recording as much as he about the movement in order that 'the coming generation may know about our love for principle and truth'. As a good historian he was determined to get at the sources of information, but he kept an open mind when that knowledge was insufficient. He refused to believe that 'learned men had said everything' about Iolo Morganwg (*Ymofynnydd*, 1925, 139) and he looked forward to when he would have 'plenty of proof' to reveal another side of the expulsion from Llwynrhydowen church (*Ymofynnydd*, 1929, 111). He was a giant both physically and in terms of conviction. The same passion was displayed when he explained the logic of the arguments of his faith, as when he expressed his feelings about 'Jesus, the friend of a sinner'. He was never a student at a theological college, though there is reason to believe that he would have made a good teacher had he been given an opportunity, as he desired, at Carmarthen College. He was the president of the Unitarian Society of south Wales for two years (1923-25) and he was made an honorary member of the General Assembly of his denomination in 1963. He showed great ability during his public service in his town, his district and his county; he was a member of Lampeter Borough Council (1934-63) and mayor of the same local authority on four occasions (1940/41; 1941/42; 1950/51; 1959/60). He was granted the Freedom of the Borough in 1954. He represented the borough on the Court of Governors of the University of Wales and on Cardiganshire County Council in 1951, but he had previously been a co-opted member of the county education committee. He served as the chairman of many committees while a member of the county council including the benefits committee, the Cardiganshire planning committee, the planning committee of the Aberaeron and Lampeter district, the finance and general purposes committee, the elderly persons voluntary committee and the governors of Lampeter secondary school. He attempted to persuade 'the secondary schools of Cardiganshire to teach every subject through the medium of Welsh' and he succeeded in establishing 'Hafan Deg' home for the elderly to serve Lampeter and district.

His wife Daisy (née Thomas) died on 4 May 1965. They were the parents of two daughters. He died at Carmarthen hospital on 21 October 1965 aged 77 years and he was buried at Brondeifi graveyard, Lampeter.

Ymofynydd (memorial edition), Oct-Nov 1965; T.O. Williams, *Cae'ronnen* (1954), 47-8; *Yearbook of the Unitarian General Assembly* (1966), 105.

D.E.J.D.

WILLIAMS, THOMAS RHONDDA (1860-1945), Congregational minister; b. at Cowbridge, Glam., 19 June, 1860, one of three sons of Thomas Williams, a Calvinistic Methodist minister, who entered the ministry, two of them in the Congregational denomination and the other in his father's Connexion. He was admitted, as Thomas Rees Williams, to the Carmarthen Presbyterian College in 1877. He held pastorates at Bethania, Dowlais (1880), Gnoll Road, Neath (1884), Greenfield, Bradford (1888), and the Union Chapel, Brighton (1909). He resigned in 1931, spending the remainder of his life at Hove, where he d. 21 Nov. 1945. He published several books. He was considered to be a forward-looking preacher, and was an advocate of the 'New Theology' which was the subject of much discussion at the turn of the twentieth century. In 1930 he preached to the Assembly of the League of Nations in Geneva. The Chicago Theological Seminary conferred the degree of D.D. upon him, and he was chairman of the Congregational Union of England and Wales in 1929.

Oriel Coleg Caerfyrddin; WwW (1921); Congl. Yr. Bk., 1946.

R.T.J.

WILLIAMS, VICTOR ERLE NASH - see NASH-WILLIAMS, VICTOR ERLE above.

WILLIAMS, WILLIAM ('Crwys'; 1875-1968), poet, preacher, archdruid; b. 4 Jan. 1875 at 9 Fagwr Road, Craig-cefn-parc, Clydach, Glam., son of John and Margaret (née Davies) Williams. His father was a shoemaker and for some years the son learned the craft, but decided to change the course of his life and become a minister. He began preaching in Pant-y-crwys (Congl.) church, and after two yrs. in the school of Watcyn Wyn (Williams, Watkin Hezekiah, DWB, 1076), Ammanford, he entered Bala-Bangor College in 1894. Under the auspices of that college he was a student at the University College, Bangor for a year before embarking on his theological course. In 1898 he was ord. minister of Rehoboth (Congl.), Bryn-mawr, Brecon, which at that time was one of the Welsh churches of Monmouthshire Association. In the same year he m. Grace Harriet Jones (d. 22 Dec. 1937), a fellow-student at Bangor, and they had two sons and two daughters. In 1915 he accepted an invitation to succeed Dr. John Cynddylan Jones (DWB, 484-5) as the agent of the Bible Society in south Wales, and he retained the post until his retirement in 1940. Between 1946 and 1953 he was in charge of Rhyddings church (English Congl.), Swansea. He d. 13 Jan. 1968 and was buried in Pant-y-crwys cemetery.

He was prominent in the activities of the National Eisteddfod for many years. He won the crown in 1910 on the subject 'Ednyfed Fychan' and in 1919 on 'Morgan Llwyd o Wynedd'. But the pryddest 'Gwerin Cymru', which won him the crown in 1911, is his best-known work. He was elected archdruid in 1938 and held the office until 1947. The University of Wales conferred on him an hon. M.A. degree and he was honoured by Swansea Borough Council in 1968 when his bust was placed in the Town Library. He was one of the most prolific and popular poets of his time. He published four volumes of poetry: Cerddi Crwys (1920; 5 eds.), Cerddi Newydd Crwys (1924; 3 eds.), Trydydd Cerddi Crwys (1935), Cerddi Crwys, y pedwerydd llyfr (1944), and two selections of his poems (1953 and 1956). His recitation pieces for children and adults were very popular at eisteddfodau in the second quarter of the twentieth century, but he is chiefly remembered as the author of well-known lyric poems such as 'Dysgub y Dail', 'Melin Trefin', 'Siôn a Siân', 'Y Border Barch', and 'Y Sipsi'. He is one of the poets who succeeded in freeing himself from the fetters of the 'New Bard'. He also published A brief history of Rehoboth Congregational Church, Bryn-mawr, from 1643 to 1927 (1927), and two volumes of reminiscences, Mynd a dod (1941) and Pedair Pennod (1950). Among his surviving MSS. is the material for an English volume, 'Hither and thither', which corresponds, more or less, to Mynd a dod.

Blwyddiadur A, 1969; D. Ben Rees, Cymry adnabyddus 1952-72 (1978); Meic Stephens (ed.), New Companion to the Lit. of Wales (1998); personal acquaintance; [W.R. Nicholas, Crwys y Rhamantydd (1990)].

W.R.N.

WILLIAMS, WILLIAM ALBERT (1909-46), organist, music critic and composer; b. in Liverpool, 16 Jan. 1909, s. of Captain Richard Williams and Anne Williams, both from Marian-glas, Anglesey. His father drowned when Albert was 4 yrs. old and his mother d. when he was 15. His mother's sister, Mrs. Stanley Jones, Liverpool, then took care of him, his brother and sister. He began to have piano and organ lessons when he was very young, and he was appointed organist at Chatham St. Presbyterian chapel, Liverpool, when he was 16 yrs. old. Later he became organist at Douglas Road chapel and at the English Independent chapel in Great George St., Liverpool. On leaving school at the age of 16 he worked as a clerk to Liverpool city corporation. In 1940 he m. Glenys Jones from Church Village, Pontypridd. He continued as a music student under the instruction of W.H. Whitehall, Liverpool, and became A.R.C.O. and F.R.C.O. He prepared for the degree of Mus. Bac., but his plans were interrupted by World War II. At the end of the war he intended devoting himself entirely to the study of music and he was appointed music director for Cardiganshire, but the military authorities refused to release him. Shortly afterwards his health failed and he d. in Middlesex Hospital, 8 Jan. 1946. He possessed to a high degree a rare critical talent. He wrote critical articles on various aspects of music, particularly Welsh music, for Y Cerddor, Y Ford Gron, Y Brython, Y Faner, Y Cymro, Y Llenor, and the Western Mail. His writings show that he would have become an important music critic in Wales had he lived. His compositions demonstrate his very rich musical taste. He confined his compositions to vocal music - songs, part-songs for mixed voices, male voices and children, and a number of anthems.

Although he did not fully develop as a composer, he won many prizes at the national eisteddfod for composition. All his work demonstrates his perceptiveness, and a very clear promise of great things to come had he lived. Many of his works were published by the Gwynn Publishing Co., Llangollen, and the University of Wales Press; several of them were set as test pieces at the national *eisteddfod*. His early death was a great loss to music in Wales.

Personal knowledge.

J.H.

WILLIAMS, WILLIAM EMYR (1889-1958), solicitor and *eisteddfod* patron; b. 24 May 1889 at Llanffestiniog, Mer., the eldest of the 7 children of Rev. John Williams, minister of Engedi (Calv. Meth.) and Sarah Ann, dau. of Edward Hall, ship's captain and an elder at Tabernacl, Aberystwyth. The family moved to Dolgellau and then, when John Williams was appointed secretary to the Presbyterian Home Mission, to Wrexham. Emyr Williams was educ. at Grove Park grammar school, Wrexham, and University College of Wales, Aberystwyth, where he gained his LL.B. in 1911. He took an active part in several college societies, including the Liberal Society of which he was secretary.

On the outbreak of World War I he joined the Royal Welch Fusiliers and served as a lieutenant under Allenby in Palestine. His services were retained by the army for some months after the end of the war as judge of a military court dealing with unrest among the Egyptians who were seeking independence from British authority. On his return to Wrexham he became a partner with J.S. Lloyd in the firm of solicitors J.S. Lloyd and Emyr Williams. He m. Mary, dau. of J.E. Powell, Wrexham. Elected a member of the Wrexham borough council in 1923 he was mayor in 1933 and chairman of the executive committee of the national *eisteddfod* held in the town that year. He was deputy mayor on 7 occasions and elevated to the aldermanic bench in 1935. He was made an hon. Freeman of the borough in 1951 and served the council for 35 years. He was made C.B.E. in 1952 in recognition of his public services in several spheres, especially for his dedication to the success of the *eisteddfod*. At the time of his death he held offices on several national bodies. He served for some years on the Council of Wales, he was one of the prime founders of the Association of Welsh Local Authorities in 1927 and held the Presidency for a quarter of a century from 1933. He was a vice-president of the Hon. Soc. of Cymmrodorion. As a member of the Court he took considerable interest in the University of Wales, and the north-east Wales branch of the Guild of Graduates, of which he was president, received his enthusiastic support.

The progress of education in the Wrexham area was high on his list of priorities and he was elected chairman of the Education committee. His election as a governor of his old school, Grove Park, gave him particular pleasure and throughout his life he was a loyal member of Seion (Presb.) church, Wrexham, where he was senior elder and precentor. The Properties Board of the Presb. Church relied on his guidance as their hon. solicitor and secretary. The national *eisteddfod* also appreciated the guidance of Emyr Williams and he helped to resolve difficulties in more than one crisis. During the years prior to World War II the weakness arising from the dual control by the *Gorsedd* and *Eisteddfod* Association became more apparent.

Emyr Williams's 'vision and drive proved a great asset to the Joint Committee which strove for the fusion of the two societies into one governing body; his quiet firmness and legal acumen were invaluable in helping to frame a just, comprehensive and workable constitution for the Council in 1937'. Sir D. Owen Evans (see above) was elected chairman and Emyr Williams vice-chairman of the Council. During World War II he again came to the aid of the *eisteddfod* as chairman of the Emergency Committee responsible for organising the series of *eisteddfodau* for the period of the war. He became chairman of the Council on the death of Sir Owen Evans, an office which he held until his death. Followers of the *eisteddfod* mourned the loss of a great *eisteddfod* leader whose consistent firmness and dignified personality proved a tower of strength to the All-Welsh *eisteddfod*. 'He nothing common did nor mean'! In 1957 the Univ. of Wales conferred an hon. LL.D. on him.

The culture of the Llanbryn-mair area had considerable influence on his way of thinking and living, having spent many of his holidays since boyhood at Bontdolgadfan, the home of his grandfather, William Williams, 'Gwilym Cyfeiliog' (*DWB*, 1082-83). His choice of name, 'Emyr Cyfeiliog', on becoming a member of the *Gorsedd* of Bards was an indication of his attachment to that locality.

While following his profession as a solicitor, he dedicated his life to serve the community. He was an administrator by his very nature. A man of few words he would steer a discussion to the salient points of a problem with certainty and courtesy. He loved the arts. He delighted to place his administrative gifts at the disposal of the *eisteddfod* for he believed in it with all his heart as an instrument for fostering the arts in Wales and as an institution for promoting and safeguarding the use of the Welsh language.

He d., without issue, on 11 July 1958 and was b. at the public cemetery, Wrexham.

Personal knowledge.

G.E.

WILLIAMS, WILLIAM EWART (1894-1966), physicist and inventor; b. 3 Mar. 1894 at Bodgarad, Rhostryfan, Caerns., eldest on of Ellis William Williams (manager of Cilgwyn slate quarry) and his wife Jane, Llys Twrog, Y Fron. After attending local schools he entered Owens College, Manchester University, where he had Rutherford, Bohr and Darwin as tutors. He graduated with honours in physics in 1915 and gained his M.Sc. (Manchester) degree in 1926. After training with Barr Stroud Range Finder Makers, Glasgow (1917-20) he became responsible for developing polarimetric and spectroscopic instruments of high resolution for Adam Hilger Ltd., London. At the recommendation of Prof. O.W. Richardson (Nobel Prize winner) he was appointed lecturer at King's College, University of London (1920-39). Under the supervision of Appleton and Richardson he was awarded a D.Sc. (London) in 1934. For his contribution to the techniques of high resolution measurements in spectroscopy he was presented with the Duddell Medal by the Physical Society of London in 1935. He became a Leverhulme Fellow in 1936. In March 1938 he resigned and emigrated to South California and by 1946 he was an American citizen. His particular field was interferometry and he became a worldwide authority on the subject. His monograph, *Applications of interferometry* (1928, 1930, 1941, 1948, 1951) which was translated into several languages is considered a standard work. In 1949 he sold his personal laboratory at Pasadena to the U.S. Air Force. He was involved with the Northrop Company in the invention of a special type of window for the Mercury project. In 1952-53 he was the chief contractor for American Missile Control. In 1953, after a period of ill health and in collaboration with the physician, Dr Olive Hoffman, at Pasadena Institute of Research, he investigated the infra-red absorption spectra of steroids which led to the development of a new type of oximeter, but both of them d. before seeing the fruits of their labour. In 1958 he joined the Firestone Tyre Company (makers of the Corporal Missile). He contributed extensively to the *Transactions* of the Royal Society and the Physical Society of London; *Review of Modern Physics*, *Zeitschrift für Physik*, *Nature*. etc. Between 30 and 40 of his patents were accepted by various companies in the United Kingdom, Germany and other countries. He m. Sarah Ellen Bottomley, New Hey, Rochdale; they had no children. She was a linguist, and shared her husband's interest in music. He d. at Pasadena 29 Apr. 1966 and was buried in the family grave in Pisgah graveyard, Carmel, Caerns. He left a generous endowment to the University of South California to establish a scholarship to assist students of Welsh extraction to receive vocal and instrumental instruction there. His brother, Robert Arthur Williams, was Chief Conservation Inspector for Sydney Harbour, Australia. His youngest brother, Stanley Haydn Williams, Y Fron, spent more than fifty years as a minister of the Presbyterian Church in Wales.

Information from the Rev. Stanley H. Williams.
G.A.J.

WILLIAMS, WILLIAM GILBERT (1874-1966), schoolmaster and local historian; b. in Tŷ'r Capel, Rhostryfan, Llanwnda, Caerns., 20 Jan. 1874, son of John Williams, slate quarryman, and Catherine (née Jones) his wife. One of his brothers was 'J.W. of London' (see John Williams above). He left the local school when he was nine yrs. old to work in Cilgwyn quarry but returned as a pupil-teacher and won a scholarship to enter Bangor Normal College, 1892-94. He was appointed the first schoolmaster of Felinwnda school, Llanwnda, in 1895, and held a similar post at Rhostryfan from 1918 until he retired in 1934. He was a pioneering schoolmaster, using Welsh as a medium of education, and succeeding in arousing his pupils' interest in the history and culture of their neighbourhood. He described his method of teaching in *Y Cymro Bach* (1909). As a local and county councillor (1951-61) he held a prominent place in the public life of the county. He was elected an elder of Horeb (Presb.) in 1909, and Moderator of Arfon Presbytery, and he recieved a Gee medal *c*. 1962 for his work in the Sunday school over a very long period.

He was an historian of note who gave many lectures in the surrounding districts on local history, and he was one of the founders and president (1947-57) of Caernarfonshire Historical Society. He composed two historical plays in *cynghanedd*, countless *cywyddau* and *englynion*. Among his numerous booklets are *Cerddi gogan — beirdd newydd* (1904-06), *Hanes pentref Rhostryfan* (1926), *Breision hanes o 1688 hyd 1720* (1928), *Olion hynafol* (1944) and a volume of school songs. He printed and bound some of his booklets himself. Many articles written by him appeared in local periodicals and papers, particularly in *Y Geneдl*, where an occasional argument arose between him and his friend Bob Owen (see Owen, Robert, above), demonstrating the more disciplined and academic method of Gilbert Williams of studying history. He was also a contributor to *The Dictionary of Welsh Biography down to 1940*. A selection of his work was published (Gareth Haulfryn Williams, ed.) in *Moel Tryfan i'r Traeth* (1983). He received an hon. M.A. degree of the University of Wales in 1930 for his contribution to the history of the nation. Some of his MSS. are in the Caernarfon Record Office and the National Library of Wales. He d. a bachelor, 10 Oct. 1966, at his home, Tal-y-bont, Rhostryfan.

Herald Cymr., 17 Oct. 1966; *Gol.*, 7 Dec. 1966, 6; information from Mair Eluned Pritchard, Pontllyfni; see *Y Casglwr*, nos. 4, 5 and 12 for a bibliography of his pamphlets.
M.A.J., G.H.W.

WILLIAMS, WILLIAM JOHN (1878-1952), H.M. Inspector of Schools and Director of the Council of Social Service for Wales and Monmouthshire; b. 1878, the fourth son of Richard and Anne Williams, Hafod, Swansea. His brother Richard Trefor Williams, O.B.E., (who d. in 1932) was the Chief Inspector of the Ministry of Health at Cardiff. Educated at schools in Swansea and at the University College of Wales, Aberystwyth, where he graduated LL.B. and M.A., he was a schoolmaster at Gowerton County School, Bootle Intermediate School and Newport High School. He became a barrister at the Middle Temple in 1912, and an inspector of schools in the Welsh Department of the Board of Education in 1915. He played an important role in encouraging the use of the Welsh language in the elementary schools of Carmarthenshire. In 1933 he succeeded Dr. G. Prys Williams as Chief Inspector of Schools, and remained in the post until he reached retirement in Dec. 1944. He took particular interest in extra-mural studies, especially in the activities of the W.E.A. and the external department of Coleg Harlech. From 1945 until 1952 he served as the Director of the Council for Social Service for Wales and Monmouthshire which he had served as assessor since 1934.

Williams was a member of a large number of committees, among them the Welsh Committee of the Arts Council of Great Britain, the Welsh Committee of the British Council, the Welsh Committee of UNESCO and the B.B.C. Appeals Committee (Wales). He was also a director of the Welsh National Opera and a vice-president of Coleg Harlech, 1948-52. In 1943 he was awarded the degree of LL.D. *honoris causa* by the University of Wales.

He m. in 1906 Maud, dau. of David Owen, J.P., and Anne Owen of Morriston, Swansea.

They had one son. They lived at Llanelli and later at 4 North Road, Cardiff. He d. 23 Jan. 1952, and his remains were cremated at Glyntaff Crematorium.

Www; Cymro, 23 Nov. 1933; *Times,* 24 Jan. 1952; *Cardiff Times,* 25 Jan. 1952; *WWP.*

J.G.J.

WILLIAMS, WILLIAM JONES (1863-1949), civil servant, secretary of Kodak Limited, treasurer of Coleg Harlech and *Urdd Gobaith Cymru;* b. 21 May 1863 at Salford, Lancashire, the eldest of the 7 children of John Williams (1828-77), warehouseman, formerly of Tynygraig, Garthgarmon, near Llanrwst, and his first wife Ellen Williams (1838-74), formerly of Bethel, near Llandderfel, Mer. He was at Manchester Grammar School from January 1875 until December 1876 when he began to be employed on 21 December at 'Mr. Salmon's, Machinist, Manchester' at a wage of five shillings per week. He entered the Civil Service by examination, *c.* 1880, joining the Exchequer and Audit Department as a Second Division Clerk, and remaining in that service until 1900. In 1900, at the invitation of George Davison, late of Plas Wern Fawr, Harlech (now the home of Coleg Harlech), who had himself been in the Exchequer and Audit Department, Williams joined Kodak Limited as Secretary; he remained with that company until 1928. Before he had left the Civil Service he had taken by external examinations the degrees of B.A., and LL.B., London. He also qualified as a barrister as of the Middle Temple, but was never formally called to the Bar. While he was with Kodak Limited Williams travelled extensively in Europe (including Russia), South Africa, and Egypt, organising Kodak branches, etc., mainly in his capacity as an expert accountant. In his early years in London he was a member of Shirland Road CM Chapel; he was actively connected with the *Cymru Fydd* movement, and was a member of the Honourable Society of Cymmrodorion, and an early member of the Fabian Society. After his retirement from Kodak he became associated actively with several other societies, institutions, and bodies. Among these were Coleg Harlech (Treasurer, 1927-48, and subsequently Vice-President); *Urdd Gobaith Cymru* (Treasurer 1931-42), the Labour Party - he supported a Welsh Labour weekly *Y Dinesydd,* the Workers' Educational Association, the Caernarfonshire Historical Society, the Cambrian Archaeological Association. One major interest which he shared with his second wife, Mary Williams (1873-1942), of London and formerly Ruthin, whom he married in 1903, was mountaineering. He climbed in north Wales and the Alps with such pioneers as Owen Glynne Jones (see App.), Roderick Williams, J.M. Archer Thomson, and G.D. and A.P. Abraham; he had joined the Alpine Club in 1903 and was also a member of the Climbers' Club. He was a contributor to S.H. Hamer, *Dolomites* (1910, 2nd ed., 1926) and to Cassell's *Storehouse,* ed. by S.H. Hamer. He had a large private library and had throughout the years collected Welsh books and works on mountaineering. He d. 10 August 1949.

Alpine Journal, 57, Nov. 1950; information supplied by the late Dr. Thomas Jones, C.H.; *Aelwyd,* Oct. 1949.

M.B.D.

WILLIAMS, WILLIAM JONES (1891-1945), brother of Daniel Powell Williams (see above) and his companion as prophet on his travels; b. at Garn-foel, Pen-y-groes, Carms., 9 May 1891. He began attending revival meetings at the age of ten, and in a meeting held at Llanllian chapel (CM) Evan Roberts and Dr. D.M. Phillips laid their hands on him wishing him to be led into the ministry. He was called to serve the Apostolic Church as prophet, and travelled with his brother, and on his own, to many countries. He was a pastor to congregations in Pen-y-groes, Bradford, Llandybïe, Cardiff, and the Apostolic church in Edgware, London. He was for many years sub-editor of the *Apostolic Herald,* a missionary journal established in 1922 as the *Apostolic Church Missionary Herald;* the title was changed in 1931.

He m. (1) Mary Anne Evans of Llandeilo in 1912; they had three children. She d. 15 Nov. 1936, and in 1938 he m. (2) Elsie, daughter of John and Rachel Evans, Capel Isaac; they had one daughter. He d. 15 April 1945 in London and was buried in the cemetery of the Apostolic Temple in Pen-y-groes.

Thomas Napier Turnbull, *Brothers in Arms* (1963) and *What God hath wrought: A short history of the Apostolic Church* (1959); Rees Evans, *Precious jewels from the 1904 revival in Wales;* Tom H. Williams, *Mining to ministering; Riches of Grace.*

E.D.J.

WILLIAMS, WILLIAM MORRIS (1883-1954), quarryman, choir conductor, soloist and *cerdd dant* adjudicator; b. one of 7 children, 17 Jan. 1883 in Tan-y-fron, Tanygrisiau, Mer., s. of William Morris Williams, quarryman, and his wife Jane. His father was precentor in Bethel (CM) chapel, Tanygrisiau for 25 years and the son began to assist him when he was 17. He m. in 1905 Mair, dau. of Daniel and Mary Williams, Conglog, Tanygrisiau and they raised a musical family of 3 sons and 2 daughters. The family emigrated about 1909 to Granville, NY, and he formed a children's choir there but they returned to Tanygrisiau in 1911 because of his mother's ill health. He joined Moelwyn male voice choir, conducted by Cadwaladr Roberts, and he re-established the children's choir which he had set up in the village in 1905. A slack period in the quarries led to the family moving to Abertridwr in 1915, where he established a successful choir before returning to his native area in 1921. He obtained work in Maenofferen quarry where he remained until his retirement in 1941, during which time he established mixed choirs, children's and *cerdd dant* choirs. The mixed choir and amateur orchestra performed a number of oratorios, including *Messiah, Judas Maccabeus* and *Creation,* and he used the vocal resources of the church to present cantatas, the operetta *Esther* and the opera *Blodwen.* The augmented *Blodwen* company visited 14 areas in Gwynedd between 1945 and 1947. But the choir which made his name best known as a director and conductor was Tanygrisiau children's choir which won first prize in the chief children's choir competition at the national *eisteddfod* several times – Bangor 1931, Aberavon 1932, Neath 1934, Caernarfon 1935. At the first three the choir won, and held permanently the Iorwerth Glyndwr John Memorial Shield for their singing of arrangements of folksongs. The choir also won first prize at the *Urdd Gobaith Cymru* national *eisteddfod* at Colwyn Bay in 1934. The choir became well known throughout Wales in *eisteddfodau* and concerts, and was one of the first to broadcast a Welsh programme in 1936. W.M. Williams enjoyed *cerdd dant* and he was successful as a soloist at the national *eisteddfod* in Caernarfon 1921, Mold 1923, Pwllheli 1925. He gained first prizes with Barlwyd harp-accompaniment choir in the national *eisteddfod* in Ammanford 1922, Mold 1923, Pwllheli 1925, Treorchy 1928, as well as successes in *eisteddfodau* in north Wales 1922-25, and giving many concerts in Wales and England. He adjudicated *cerdd dant* in *eisteddfodau* in north Wales and the national in Ystradgynlais in 1954; he was one of the founders of the *Cerdd Dant* Society. He trained many individuals and groups in his locality, and served his church as precentor, secretary and Sunday school teacher for a long period. He d. 30 Dec. 1954 and was buried in Bethesda cemetery, Blaenau Ffestiniog.

Personal knowledge.

Me.E.

WILLIAMS, WILLIAM NANTLAIS (1874-1959), minister (Presb.), editor, poet and hymn writer; b. 30 Dec. 1874 at Llawr-cwrt, Gwyddgrug, near Pencader, Carms., the youngest of the ten children of Daniel and Mari Williams. He was educated at New Inn elementary school, and at the age of 12 he was apprenticed to his brothers as a weaver. He was brought up in New Inn church, where he began preaching in 1894. He was educated for the ministry at Newcastle Emlyn grammar school and Trefeca College. He took an interest in poetry at a young age and published a collection of his poems, *Murmuron y Nant* (1898), while he was a student. He won a bardic chair under the adjudication of Watcyn Wyn (Watkin Hezekiah Williams, *DWB*, 1076) at an *eisteddfod* in Ammanford in 1899, and he recieved a call soon afterwards to be pastor of the recently established church of Bethany in that town. He was ord. in 1901, and he laboured in Bethany from 1900 until his retirement in 1944 (having supervised also the small church of the Presbyterian Church of Wales in Llandybïe during the first years of the twentieth century). His ambition at that time was to preach at preaching festivals and succeed as a poet in *eisteddfod* competitions. He was joint-winner at Bangor national *eisteddfod* (1902) for composing six lyrics; he won the bardic chair at the Meirion *eisteddfod* in 1903, and the chair at the *eisteddfod* held in the Queen's Hall, London, in 1904. That year the religious Revival spread to Ammanford, and Nantlais was heavily affected by the stirring events. He determined to consecrate his life thenceforth to evangelising and fostering the spiritual life of the churches. He m. twice; (1) in 1902, Alice Maud Jones (granddaughter of the eccentric Thomas Job, Cynwyl), and they had three sons and two daughters; she d. in 1911; (2) in 1916, Annie Price (head-

mistress of Mountain Ash school and daughter of T. Price, minister of Brechfa). He d. 18 June 1959, and his remains were buried in front of the new chapel of Bethany.

After the Revival Nantlais became associated with the leading personalities who attended the annual evangelical conferences at Keswick and Llandrindod Wells, e.g. E. Keri Evans (above), R.B. Jones, W.W. Lewis, Seth Joshua (see Supplement below), W.S. Jones, W. Talbot Price, and in 1917 he established an annual conference of the same kind at Ammanford (see J.D. Williams, *Cynhadledd y Sulgwyn Rhydaman* (Ammanford, 1967). His labours at Bethany proved very successful; a schoolroom was built at Pantyffynnon in 1904, and another in Tir-y-dail in 1906 (a church was established there in 1911; see W.N. Williams, *Y Deugain Mlynedd Hyn* (Ammanford, 1921)). A beautiful new chapel was built at Bethany in 1930. Nantlais was elevated to the chair of the South Wales Association (1943), and he was Moderator of the General Assembly (1940). He corresponded for years with Eluned Morgan of Patagonia (*DWB*, 643), and at her earnest request Nantlais went on a preaching tour for three weeks in the Welsh colony in Patagonia in 1938 (see the correspondence between them in Dafydd Ifans (ed.), *Tyred drosodd* (1977)).

Although Nantlais refrained from competing at *eisteddfodau* after the Revival, he continued to write, consecrating his talents and his poetry thereafter to spreading the Gospel. He was one of the editors of *Y Lladmerydd* (1922-26), and editor of *Yr Efengylydd* (1916-33), and *Trysorfa'r Plant* (1934-47). He composed many hymns for children, indeed there was scarcely anyone more successful than he as a hymn writer for children. These hymns were published in three collections, *Moliant Plentyn*, part I (1920) and part II (1927), and *Clychau'r Gorlan* (1942). Many of his fine, inspired hymns are to be found in the present-day hymnals of all denominations. There is a collection of his best hymns in *Emynau'r daith* (1949), and in *Clychau Seion* (which he edited *c.* 1952). He also published (in collaboration with Daniel Protheroe (*DWB*, 801-2), David Evans (1874-98; see above) and J.T. Rees (see above) a number of children's songs, as well as other musical works. Even though he refrained from competing, he did not lose his gift as a lyrical poet, as was shown in his anthology of poems, *Murmuron Newydd* (1926), and his children's rhymes, *Darlun a chân* (1941). Before the end of his life, in recognition of his literary contribution, he was awarded an hon. M.A. degree by the University of Wales. There is an appreciation of him as a hymnist and poet, together with a list of all his publications in *Bwletin Cymdeithas Emynau Cymru*, I, no. 4 (1971), 77-99. He contributed extensively to the periodicals which he edited, and to *Y Goleuad*. There are chapters of reminiscences in the latter (1955), which were published in 1967 under the title *O Gopa Bryn Nebo*.

Add to the references noted above, *WwFC* (1951), 358; *Drys.*, 1944, 47-50; *Blwyddiadur MC*, 1960, 275-6; W. Morris (ed.), *Deg o Enwogion* (1965), 51-9; personal knowledge and acquaintance; [T. Gareth Jones in Hywel T. Edwards, ed., *Cwm Aman* (1996), 80-105].

G.M.R.

WILLIAMS, WILLIAM OGWEN (1924-69), archivist, university professor; b. in Llanfairfechan, Caerns., 12 Dec. 1924, the elder of the 2 sons of William Henry Williams and his wife Margaret (née Pritchard). He was educ. at Llanfairfechan national school, 1928-35, Friars School, Bangor, 1935-42, University College of North Wales, Bangor, 1942-47 (B.A., 1st.-class hons. History, 1945), Univ. of London, 1947-48 (diploma in archive elect studies, 1949); he was appointed archivist elect for Caernarfonshire 1 Aug. 1947 and county archivist in 1949, part-time lecturer in archive studies at Univ. College Bangor, 1954, lecturer in history (Welsh-medium) in Bangor, 1958-63, lecturer in Welsh history, Univ. College of Wales, Aberystwyth, 1963-65, senior lecturer, 1965-67, professor, 1967-69. He was assistant editor *Trans. Anglesey Antiquarian Soc.,* 1950-55, editor 1955-69. He possessed a sharp mind and was ready to accept responsibilities. He had the gift of gaining people's trust and was a person with natural courtesy who sought to avoid harm or hurt to any one. He enjoyed company and was gifted both as a lecturer and as a conversationalist.

As the first Caernarfonshire county archivist he succeeded in putting the fine archives of the county in order (as his *Guide to the Caernarvonshire Record Office,* 1952, shows) and also in popularising them. His article, 'County Records', which appeared as early as 1949 in *Trans. Caern. Hist. Soc.* is testimony to his mastery of the archives and his gift for presenting them in an intelligible and interesting way to lay people. This was by no means his most important contribution, for he published in 1956 his *Calendar of the Caernarvonshire Quarter Sessions Records, 1541-1558* with a masterly introduction describing the historical background of the documents. This is arguably the best analysis of the Tudor administrative and social order in Wales and gained for Ogwen Williams his M.A. (Wales) in 1956. Large portions of the introduction were re-issued as *Tudor Gwynedd* 2 years later. The *Calendar* reveals Ogwen Williams at his best as historian and archivist. He published several articles after the *Calendar,* among them 'The survival of the Welsh language, 1536-1614' (*Welsh Hist. Review,* 2, 1964) and 'The social order in Tudor Wales' (*Trans. Cymmrodorion,* 1967) but as his horizons broadened and he lost contact with original archives his grasp as a historian slackened. It is to be regretted that he did not seriously take up again the task of studying the Gwynedd gentry. He had a very important contribution to make in that field as his article, 'The Anglesey gentry as business men in Tudor and Stuart times' (*Trans. Anglesey Antiquarian Soc.,* 1948) suggests.

His family background, before his father became a shop-keeper in Llanfairfechan, lay in the quarry and quarrying areas but it was the world of the gentry which attracted Ogwen Williams's interest. His parents were staunch nonconformists but he turned to the Anglican church (under the influence of Archdeacon Henry Williams and others) for spiritual sustenance. His mother and father were strong Liberals but he tended towards a conservative frame of mind. He was strong enough to stand his ground on matters of vision and principle. He overcame physical disability (he was born

with defects in one eye and his hip, which kept him from military service though he volunteered in 1942) but he did not allow this to govern his mind, neither to detract one iota from his enjoyment of life nor to give the impression to others that it troubled him.

He d. in sad circumstances; he was found drowned on Ynys-las beach, near Aberystwyth, 3 May 1969. He was not married.

Archives of Gwynedd county council and University College, Bangor; obituary notices in *Trans. Caern. Hist. Soc.* (1969); *Welsh Hist. Rev.,* 4 (1969); *Trans. Anglesey Ant. Soc.* (1968-69); Dr. J. Aled Williams and personal knowledge.

                                                                                    K.W.J.

WILLIAMS, WILLIAM RETLAW JEFFERSON (c. 1863-1944), solicitor, genealogist, and historian. He was one of the remarkable children of Aberclydach, Llanfigan, Breckns. (see WILLIAMS, Alice Matilda, above). The father, John James Williams (d. 31 Mar. 1906), was a surgeon and a captain of the First Brecknockshire Rifle Volunteers, and a member of the *Gorsedd* of Bards as 'Brychan'. The mother's maiden name was Jane Robertson. The main feat of the eldest son, Howell Price, was to traverse the African continent from the Cape to Cairo in 1909-10. He d. in 1920. The second son, William Retlaw (which is Walter in reverse) became a solicitor in 1884, and had offices at Brecon and Tal-y-bont on Usk. There was a tradition of practising law in the family. The grandfather, Howell Williams, had m. a sister of Walter Powell, the senior partner in the firm of Powell, Jones and Powell. Though his name appears in the *Law List* under Brecon until 1929, and for another year under Tal-y-bont, it does not appear that William Retlaw practised much. Historical research was much more to his liking from an early age. At one time he ran a genealogical business and a trade in books on Wales at Tal-y-bont in close association with major booksellers such as Henry Blackwells of New York. He published privately a number of volumes on the history of the parliamentary representation of several counties and boroughs, beginning with *The Parliamentary History of the Principality of Wales, 1541-1895* (Brecon, 1895). A copy of this work with corrections and additions in his own hand intended for a second edition which was never published is preserved at the National Library of Wales (MS. 16363). This was followed by *The Parliamentary History of Hereford, 1213-1897* (Brecon, 1896); *The Parliamentary History of Worcester, 1213-1897* (Hereford, 1897); *The Parliamentary History of Gloucester, 1213-1898* (Hereford, 1898); and *The Parliamentary History of Oxford, 1213-1899* (Brecon, 1899). He left rough notes for a history of the parliamentary representation of Ireland. He published a history of the Courts of Great Sessions and their officers, *The History of the Great Sessions in Wales, 1542-1830,* together with the *Lives of the Welsh Judges* (Brecon, 1899), which is perhaps better known, from the lettering on its spine, as *The Welsh Judges.* He also published *Official Lists of the Duchy of Lancaster* (1901). These pioneer works are very useful, though not entirely reliable. It is possible that the author's untidy handwriting is partly responsible for some of the misprints in these books. N.L.W. MS 11029 contains a typewritten copy of lists which he compiled of officers of Welsh regiments, 1715-92. He edited and published a periodical entitled *Old Wales*, 1905-07, and contributed notes to *Old Welsh Chips*. He was married but had no children. He d. at his home, Brynoyre, Tal-y-bont, 20 March 1944, and was buried in Llansanffraid churchyard, Breckns.

Law Lists; Poole, Illustrated History and Biography of Brecknockshire, 113; Brecon and Radnor Times, 30 March 1944.

E.D.J.

WILLIAMS, Sir WILLIAM RICHARD (1879-1961), railway traffic inspector; b. 18 March 1879 son of Thomas Williams and Elizabeth Agnes his wife, Pontypridd, Glam. He m., 8 Apr. 1902, Mabel Escott Melluish but had no children. Known in railway circles as 'the man who achieved a schoolboy's ambition to run a railway', Sir William was educated in Cardiff and began his career with the Rhymney Railway Company in 1893 as a junior clerk. He was put in charge of the Traffic Department in 1905, and his great opportunity came when, on the grouping of the railways to form the major companies' network in 1922, he was appointed by the Great Western Railway as its Assistant Divisonal Superintendent at Cardiff. For his contribution to a lifetime of railway service in Wales and his civic service to Cardiff he received a knighthood in 1930. A year later he retired. He entered local politics in 1913 when he was elected to the Cardiff City Council, and was deputy Lord Mayor 1921-22. In 1928-29 he was Lord Mayor of the City of Cardiff and in 1954 was honoured with the Freedom of the City. He d. 28 June 1961.

Www.

D.G.R.

WILLIAMS, WILLIAM RICHARD (1896-1962), minister (Presb.) and Principal of the United Theological College, Aberystwyth; b. 4 Apr. 1896 at Pwllheli, Caerns., son of Richard and Catherine Williams, his mother of the lineage of Siarl Marc of Bryncroes (*DWB*, 614). He was educated at Penlleiniau church day-school and Pwllheli County School. He won a Mrs Clarke Scholarship, enabling him to enter University College, Aberystwyth, where he graduated with first-class honours in Greek and second class in philosophy. His father died in 1912, and he and his mother moved to Aberystwyth, becoming members of Tabernacl church where he began to preach. He served in the army for a period during World War I. He continued his education at Lincoln College, Oxford, where he graduated with a first class in theology. He ord. in 1921, and served as minister of Bethel, Gowerton, Glam. (1921-22) and Argyle English Church, Swansea (1922-25). He was appointed assistant lecturer at Aberystwyth Theological College (1925-27), and then became Professor of the Philosophy of Religion (1927-28), and of Greek and N.T. exegesis (1928-49). He was principal of the college from 1949 until he d. in 1962. In 1928 he m. Violet Irene Evans of Swansea, and they had a son. W.R. Williams d. 18 Dec. 1962.

He was a prominent figure in his denomination. He delivered the Davies Lecture in 1939 on 'The Missionary Spirit in the Early Church', which was not published. He served as Moderator of the General Assembly (1960), and Moderator of the South Wales Association (1962). He took an interest in the Sunday school and the Foreign and Home Missions, and was president of the Forward Movement for many years. He was one of the leading promoters of the ecumenical movement in Wales; he was the first secretary of the Council of Churches of Wales, and its president when he d. In 1961 he was elected chairman of the British committee of the Presbyterian Alliance. He was a member of the joint-committee which was appointed to prepare a new English translation of the Bible, and in 1961 he was appointed director of the committee which was established to prepare a new Welsh translation of the Bible. He contributed to the periodicals of his denomination and published three volumes of biblical commentary: *Arweiniad i Efengyl Ioan* (1930), *Yr Epistol at yr Hebreaid* (1932), and *Epistol cyntaf Ioan* (1943).

WwFC (1951), 358; *Blwyddiadur MC*, 1964, 284-5; *Drys.*, 1960, 114-7; 1962, 64-7; May 1963; information from his son, the Rev. Richard Williams; personal acquaintance.

G.M.R.

WILLIAMS-WYNN, Sir ROBERT WILLIAM HERBERT WATKIN (1862-1951) - see WYNN (FAMILY), Wynnstay below.

WILLIAMSON, EDWARD WILLIAM (1892-1953), Bishop of Swansea and Brecon; b. 22 April 1892, only son of Edward Williamson, a solicitor in Cardiff, and his wife Florence Frances Tipton. He received his education in the Cathedral School, Llandaff, Westminster School, where he was a King's Scholar, and Christchurch, Oxford where he gained B.A. (2nd-cl. Lit. Hum.) 1914, M.A. 1917. From Wells Theological College he was ordained deacon 1914 and served as curate of St. Martin, Potternewton, Yorkshire 1915-17. He was ordained priest 1916. He served as curate of Lambeth 1917-22 and was appointed Lecturer in St. Augustine's College Canterbury 1922-23. He was elected Fellow in 1923 and Honorary Fellow from 1936. He was appointed Warden of St. Michael's College, Llandaff 1926 and remained there until he was elected Bishop of Swansea and Brecon in November 1939. He was Hon. Chaplain to the Bishop of Llandaff 1929-31; Examining Chaplain 1931-39. He was canon of Caerau in Llandaff Cathedral 1930-37 and appointed Chancellor 1937-39. He was consecrated Bishop of Swansea and Brecon in Bangor cathedral 30th November by the Archbishop of Wales (Charles Green, see above).

Though he was not a Welshman, he loved Wales, its church and people. When he was invited early in 1953 to become one of the vice-presidents of the national *eisteddfod* at Ystradgynlais (1954) his letter of acceptance was written in Welsh. A few minutes before he died, during the meetings of the Governing Body of the Church in Wales at Llandrindod, he had made a powerful speech, deploring the exodus of young Welsh priests to England. He was at his best among the students at St. Michael's

College; his quiet charm and sound learning influenced generations of ordinands.

He was well versed in antiquarian subjects, and had begun to study ecclesiastical architecture when he was a boy. He travelled on the continent to pursue this interest and wrote about the subject with deep knowledge. He wrote a guide to Llandaff cathedral, *The Story of Llandaff Cathedral*, 1930, which went into five editions. He was a member of the Cambrian Archaeological Association and was elected President at Brecon in August 1957 for the session 1951-52. He delivered a lecture on this occasion, basing his remarks on the history of Welsh saints according to the BL Vespasian A XIV manuscript. He edited *The Letters of Osbert of Clare*, 1929. In 1946 he published *An Anatomy of Joy*, three sermons which he preached as the Select Preacher at Oxford in 1944-45. He was Select Preacher at Cambridge in 1951. In January 1953 he broadcast the Radio Lecture, *Henry Vaughan*, which was published by the B.B.C.

Although he was a shy, reserved bachelor, as a public speaker he could be both balanced and witty. Of attractive appearance, his saintliness was apparent to all who knew him. He died 23rd September 1953 and was buried at Brecon.

Crockford, 1948; *WwW*; *Province*, Autumn 1953; *Haul*, Autumn 1953; *Arch. Camb.*, 101 (1951); *Church Times*, 25 Sept., 2nd Oct. 1953; *West. Mail*, 3 Nov. 1939.

M.G.E.

WILLIS, ALBERT CHARLES (1876-1954), president of the Australian Labour Party; b. 24 May 1876 at Tonyrefail, Glam. He was educated at Bryn-mawr Board School, King's College, London and Ruskin College, Oxford. He was working as a coal miner in Glamorgan when he decided to emigrate to Australia in 1911. He secured employment as a coal miner, and developed a deep interest in the activities of the trade unions. In 1913 he was chosen president of the Illawarra Miners Association, New South Wales. From 1916 until 1925 he was the first general secretary of the Australian Coal and Shale Employees' Federation, and in 1923 he founded the Labour newspaper *Labor Daily* at Sydney, and acted as its managing director. Willis was also the president of the Australian Labor Party, New South Wales, 1923-25. He became a member of the Legislative Council of New South Wales in 1925 and served until 1933. In 1931 he was appointed Agent General for New South Wales, a position based in London, but he returned to Australia when his term of office came to an end the following year. In 1943 he secured a post in the Central Coal Authority, and from 1944 until 1947 he served as the Commonwealth Conciliation Officer and the Central Industrial Authority, a position established by the Coal Production (War Time) Act, 1944. He retired in 1947. He m. Alice Maud Parker. There were a son and two daughters of the marriage. They lived at Bryn Eirw, Gannon's Road, Burraneer Bay, New South Wales. He d. 22 April 1954 at a hospital at Cronulla near Sidney.

Www; *Times*, 24 Apr. 1954; *West. Mail*, 14 May 1931; *WWP*; [I. E. Young in *Journ. Rel. Hist.*, 2 (1962-63), 303-13].

J.G.J.

WOOD, MARY MYFANWY (1882-1967), missionary in China, 1908-51; b. 16 Sept. 1882 in London. Her father (Richard) was from Machynlleth and her mother (? Margaret) from Swansea; they had four children. Her parents became members at the Borough Welsh Congregational chapel in London and she was accepted into full membership there in 1896. She went to St. Mary's College, Cheltenham and whilst training to become a schoolteacher, the course of her life was determined after listening to W.B. Selbie at the Student Christian Movement's 1903 Summer School. During her period as a teacher in Herne Hill she followed courses at King's College and for a year devoted her free time to assist with the work at the Crossway Central Mission, London. In November 1903, she sailed for Siao Chang in north China and for seven years worked in the Girls' Residential School, also serving adjacent areas. Her 1915-16 year's leave was spent at a London college before returning to Peiping, where she was appointed headmistress of the Girls' Middle School. She made a significant contribution to the development in north China of the education of girls and she was co-opted to China's Consultative Council on the training of women. In 1921 the London Missionary Society released her for a short period to assist C.Y. Cheng and E.C. Lobenstine in organising China's National Christian Conference held in Shanghai in 1922. In 1926 she was appointed a lecturer in the women's religious education department at Peiping University and before returning there in 1923 as Head of Department, she visited New College, London, and United College and Columbia University, New York, to study methods of religious education and become familiar with developments in theology. She retired from the field in 1941.

Because of her knowledge of China and its language there were calls from several authorities for her services during World War II. In May 1945 she went to India with the Y.M.C.A., and before the end of the year reached the north of China by plane, arriving to see the plight of those suffering from the riots that had occurred there. She was expected to retire in 1943 but returned to her previous field at Peiping University. A year later the college was transferred and she followed the staff and students to Cheeloo University at Shantung. By 1951, despite her eagerness to stay in a country so dear to her, the safety of her friends was being endangered by her presence.

The policy of the new regime was to expel foreigners, but despite this, she welcomed the revolution, although she did not ignore its difficulties and dangers. Against her will, she left China in Aug. 1951.

For two years she undertook deputising work on behalf of the Missionary Society in the churches of England and Wales. In 1954, at 72 yrs. of age, she was ordained minister of the small church at Hambleden, near Henley. She worked diligently there for eight years and following retirement moved to Lomas House, Worthing, a Missionary Society home for missionaries after completion of their service. In July 1962, she was awarded an honorary M.A. by the University of Wales. She d. 22 Jan. 1967 in the Southern Hospital, Shoreham, and was cremated at Downs Crematorium, Brighton, 26

Jan. 1967. A memorial service was held at the Borough Chapel 2 Feb. 1967.

E. Lewis Evans, *Cymru a'r Gymdeithas Genhadol* (1945); *Tyst*, 26 Jan. 1967; N. Goodhall, *A history of the London Missionary Society, 1895-1945* (1954); *Congl. year book*, 1967-8; Minutes of the Board of the London Missionary Soc., 1967.

K.E.J.

WYNDHAM-QUIN, WINDHAM HENRY, 5th EARL DUNRAVEN and MOUNT-EARL (1857-1952), soldier and politician; b. 7 Feb. 1857 in London, the elder son of Captain the Hon. W.H. Wyndham-Quin (the second son of the Earl of Dunraven) and Caroline, dau. of Admiral Sir George Tyler, Cottrell, Glam. He was educated at Eton and the Royal Military College, Sandhurst. He joined the 16th Lancers in 1878 and, attached to the Inniskillin Dragoons, fought in the war against the Boers in 1881. In 1886 he attained the rank of captain, and served until 1889 as A.D.C. to the Hon. Robert Bourke, his wife's uncle, at Madras. From 1890 until 1894 he served as an adjutant with the Royal Gloucester Hussars, and was promoted major in the 16th Lancers in 1893. During the South African War in 1900, he was mentioned in despatches, and was awarded the Queen's Medal with three clasps and the D.S.O. He became a Companion of the Bath in 1903 and served as lieutenant colonel in the Glamorganshire Imperial Yeomanry.

Wyndham-Quin was elected M.P. (Con.) for South Glamorgan in 1895 when he defeated A.J. Williams, and he continued to represent this division in parliament until 1906 when he lost his seat to William Brace (see above). As a politician, he was extremely well-mannered and courteous. He served as High Sheriff for county Kilkenny in 1914 and commandant of the Lines of Communication in 1915. He was also one of the directors of the Great Western Railway Co. In June 1926 he succeeded his cousin Windham Thomas Wyndham-Quin (see Supplement below) as Earl of Dunraven. He also became a well-liked and popular character in south Wales. He was a member of the Court of Governors of the National Museum, and was president of the 1940 Bridgend national *eisteddfod*.

Wyndham-Quin published a number of works including *The Yeomanry Cavalry of Gloucester and Monmouth* (1898), *Sir Charles Tyler, G.C.B., Admiral of the White* (1912), *The Foxhound in county Limerick* (1919) and *A history of Dunraven Castle* (1926).

He m. 7 July 1885 Lady Eva Constance Aline Bourke, dau. of the 6th Earl of Mayo. She d. 19 Jan. 1940. They had two sons and a daughter. He spent his last years at his home Adare Manor, Limerick. He d. 23 Oct. 1952 at his home in Limerick aged 95. His heir was his elder son Richard Southwell Windham Robert, Viscount Adare (1887-1965).

Www; WwW (1921, 1933 and 1937); *Dod's Parliamentary Companion; The Complete Peerage; Burke's Peerage; Times*, 24 Oct. 1952; *West. Mail*, 14 Aug. 1895.

J.G.J.

WYNN (FAMILY), Wynnstay (*DWB*, 1100). The article in *DWB* takes the family history down to the 5th Baronet, Sir WATKIN WILLIAMS WYNN (1772-1840), and his two brothers, Charles and Henry, the trio nicknamed 'Pip, Squeak and Bubble'. Charles m. Mary, eldest dau. of Sir Foster Cunliffe and they made their home in Llangedwyn. Henry's wife was Hesther Smith, the dau. of Lord Carrington.

The title and estates were inherited by the eldest son of the 5th Baronet, Sir WATKIN WILLIAMS WYNN, the 6th Baronet (1820-85). He had been born in the family home in St. James's Square, London, 22 May 1820 and was educ. at Westminster School before going to Christ Church, Oxford, in 1837. When he entered into his inheritance in 1840 he was under-age to follow his father in the family seat for Denbighshire but he was elected M.P. in July 1841 and he retained the seat for the rest of his life. He did not make a name for himself in the House; it is said that he never made a speech there but voted consistently for his party. According to William Rees ('Gwilym Hiraethog', *DWB*, 831-32) he was not a fluent speaker and was halting in his speech. Nevertheless, he was well regarded as a landowner and benefactor in spite of the oppressive attitude of some of his agents and there is no doubt about his popularity among ordinary folk. As a mark of respect, for his memory, when he d., as one of the gentry, a countryman and patron of *eisteddfodau* the Denbighshire Liberals decided not to nominate a candidate for the vacant seat were the Tories to select his young successor to represent them. He was shown great respect throughout his life. There were great celebrations on the family estates when he was born. He was 12 years old when Princess Victoria and her mother stayed at Wynnstay and gave further distinction to the family. That was when the 'King's Head' hotel in Llangollen became the 'Royal Hotel'. There were even greater celebrations when he came of age in 1841. He m. his cousin Marie Emily, dau. of Sir Henry Williams Wynn, K.C.B., in St. James's church, London, 25 Apr. 1852. A tragedy, which brought a host of messages of sympathy from individuals and public bodies in Wales, occurred 5 March 1858 when a large part of Wynnstay mansion was burnt, destroying many treasures, including the valuable library of Welsh MSS. Among the messages received was an address from the Calvinistic Methodist Association in the North. The present house was rebuilt and Sir Watkin began to re-establish the library by purchasing the genealogical MSS. of Joseph Morris, Shrewsbury. He held his family's traditional offices in the administration of Denbighshire and Montgomeryshire, and with the 1st Denbighshire Volunteer Corps and the Montgomeryshire Yeoman Cavalry. He was the chief officer of the Free Masons in north Wales and he was responsible for establishing a number of lodges. There was a special room for them in Wynnstay. He had an interest in the National *Eisteddfod* and was called upon to preside as 'the Prince of Wales' on chairing day. He was accepted as a member of the *Gorsedd* of Bards under the name *'Eryr eryrod Eryri'*, the family motto which confirmed the eagles of Owain Gwynedd on his coat of arms. He was president of the Hon. Soc. of Cymmrodorion and such was his interest in the Welsh School at Ashford that a special memorial service was held for him in Ashford parish church. His health was frail in his last years. He regained a measure of health following a Mediterranean cruise on his yacht 'Hebe' in the winter and autumn of 1875-76. Sir William Jenner attended him in his last illness. He d. Saturday 9 May 1885 at Wynnstay and was b. in Llangedwyn the following Friday.

The younger of his two daughters d. when she was 14 but the elder, Louisa Alexandra (1864-1911) had m. her cousin HERBERT LLOYD WATKIN WILLIAMS-WYNN (1860-1944) on 26 Aug. the previous year. This nephew and son-in-law, therefore, succeeded to the title and estates as the 7th Baronet. He was b. 6 June 1860, second s. of Herbert Watkin Williams-Wynn, the younger brother of the 6th Baronet. He was educ. at Wellington School and Trinity College Cambridge where he took his B.A. He was M.P. for Denbighshire from May to Nov. 1885 but the constituencies were restructured before the general election in Dec. to create two constituencies in place of a single two-member seat. He stood as candidate in east Denbigh but was defeated by the Liberal candidate, George Osborne Morgan (*DWB*, 644) and though he stood again in 1886 and 1892 he was not successful and the Wynnstay family lost the representation which had been, in a sense, their heritage. He devoted himself, thereafter, to his local activities, serving his community faithfully for close on 60 years. He was elected to Denbigh county council as member for the Ruabon district in 1888 retaining the seat for the rest of his life. He was chairman of the quarter sessions, 1905, High Sheriff of Denbighshire, 1890 and Lord Lieutenant of Montgomeryshire. He served on the commission of peace in a number of counties; he was a member of the Territorial Army, raising a cavalry regiment during the South African War. He supported the ambulance service and was created a knight of St. John's. During World War I he established a munitions factory at Wynnstay and in 1939 he gave the stables and other buildings for government use. He had a deep interest in engineering and construction and he did much to improve his estates. Following his father and grandfathers he was Master of the famous Wynnstay hunt and a presentation was made to him in 1935 after 50 years in that office. For many years he held high office with the Freemasons and like his predecessors he set up many lodges. A keen churchman he was a member of the Governing Body of the Church in Wales and as a lay reader he took services in local churches as well as being a faithful member of the congregation at Ruabon parish church. He spent his life simply and unpretentiously amongst his people and like any other farmer he would work on the hay with his workers. He placed a large collection of estate papers in the National Library for safe keeping and invited the Library to collect and conserve other documents which were at risk when the army took over some of the buildings. At the same time he placed the Wynnstay MSS. in the National Library for safe keeping. He d. in Wynnstay, Sat. 24 May 1944 and was buried in Llangedwyn. He and his wife had divorced in 1898; she died in 1911. They had a son and 2 daughters.

His son, Sir WATKIN WILLIAMS-WYNN (1891-1949), the 8th Baronet, succeeded to the title. B. 26 Jan. 1891, he m., 14 Sept. 1920, Daisy, youngest dau. of John Johnson Houghton, Westwood, Neston. Inheritance tax severely affected the 100,000-acre estates and the 8th Baronet could afford to spend only brief periods at Wynnstay. He moved to Belan on the edge of the park and then to Llangedwyn. The Llwydiarth estate in Montgomeryshire was sold and Glan-llyn estate, Mer., was accepted by the Treasury in lieu of part of the inheritance tax and was transferred to the care of the Agricultural Land Commission to be administered by the Welsh Sub-commission. Plas Glan-llyn, Glan-llyn Isa house and some land were leased to *Urdd Gobaith Cymru* for use as a youth camp. Wynnstay was sold to Lindisfarne public school. The gentry period of the Wynns of Wynnstay thus came to an end. Though the 8th Baronet had had little connection with Wynnstay since his youth, he showed the same virtues as his father and grandfather when he came into his inheritance, and had the family circumstances been different, he would, without doubt, have faithfully continued the family tradition. He was educ. at Eton and Trinity College, Cambridge, where he graduated B.A. in 1913. He served with the Royal Dragoons in World War I and was wounded. He took up his father's social and religious activities in the community and local government. He was High Sheriff of Denbighshire and undertook the modernisation of the administration of what remained of the estate. He and his wife had a son and 3 dau. The death of his son in a fire in Barford camp, Barnard's Castle, 18 Jan. 1946, was a heavy blow. Sir Watkin died at Ruthin Castle, Monday 9 May 1949 and he was b. at Llangedwyn 12 May.

The baronetcy was inherited by his uncle, Sir ROBERT WILLIAM HERBERT WATKIN WILLIAMS-WYNN, Plas-yn-cefn (1862-1951), the 9th Baronet. The 5th Baronet had 2 sons, Sir Watkin Williams-Wynn (1820-85), the 6th Baronet, and Herbert Watkin Williams-Wynn, M.P. for Montgomeryshire 1850-62, who m. Anna, dau. and heiress of Edward Lloyd, Cefn Meriadog, Denbs. They had 3 sons, (1) Edward Watkin who was drowned near Windsor in 1888, (2) Sir Herbert Lloyd Watkin Williams-Wynn (1860-1944), the 7th Baronet, (3) Robert William Herbert Watkin Williams-Wynn who became the 9th Baronet. B. 3 June 1862 and educ. at Wellington School and Christ Church, Oxford, he joined the army, serving with the Imperial Yeomanry in the South African War 1900-01 and being mentioned in dispatches as well as winning the D.S.O. He was made hon. Capt. In 1900. He was a Lieut. Colonel and commander of the Montgomeryshire Yeomanry, 1906-1917, and went out with them to Egypt in 1916. He was commander of the South Egypt division from 1917 to 1919. He stood unsuccessfully as the Conservative candidate in Montgomeryshire in 1894, 1895 and 1900 against Arthur Charles Humphreys-Owen, Glansevern (*DWB*, 398). He was awarded a C.B. in 1923, K.C.B. 1938. He was Master of the Flint and Denbigh hunt from 1888 to 1946 and he also had an interest in the Wynnstay hunt. He m. in 1904 Elizabeth Ida, 2nd dau. of George W. Lawther, Swillington, Yorkshire, and they had

2 sons and 2 dau. He d. at his home, Plas-yn-cefn, 23 Nov. 1951.

He was succeeded by his son, Sir OWEN WATKIN WILLIAMS-WYNN, the 10th Baronet (1904-1988).

Www, 1941-50; 1951-60; *Burke; Wrexham Leader* on the relevant dates; *Baner*, 16 May 1885; *Wynnstay and the Wynns*, 1876.

E.D.J., B.F.R.

WYNNE-FINCH, Sir WILLIAM HENEAGE (1893-1961), soldier and landowner; b. 18 Jan. 1893, the second son of Lieut. Col. Charles Arthur Wynne-Finch of Foelas and Cefnamwlch, Caerns., and his wife Maud Emily (née Charteris). He was educated at Eton College and joined the Scots Guards (2nd Lieut., 1912; Captain, 1916; Major, 1923; Lieut. Col., 1931; Colonel, 1935). He served in World War I and was twice wounded and won the M.C. in 1916. He served in the Egyptian army 1919-25 and the Sudan Defence Force 1925-26 and was honoured with the Order of the Nile. He returned to act as commander of the second battalion of the Scots Guards, 1931-35. He served in World War II as a training officer attached to the Territorial Division in London, and as Lieut. Col. commanding the Scots Guards.

He took an intelligent interest in agriculture and in his estates; he was president of the Royal Welsh Agricultural Society. He was chairman of the Caerns. agricultural education committee and played an important role in establishing the College of Agriculture at Plas Glynllifon. In 1945 he was appointed Lord Lieut. of Caerns., and held office until 1960. As *Custos rotulorum* and Chief Magistrate he laid great stress on the preservation of the county's archives. He took a prominent part in establishing the county record office in 1947 and it was under his chairmanship of the County Records Committee that the *Calendar of the Caernarvonshire Quarter Sessions Records 1541-1558* was published in 1956. He was president of the Caerns. Historical Society from 1957 until his death. He fulfilled a number of other offices in the administrative and public life of the county. He was knighted in 1960 and d. on 16 Dec. 1961. He m. in 1929 Gladys, daughter of John J. Waterbury and his wife, of New Jersey, U.S.A. They had no children.

Www; Trans. Caerns. Hist. Soc., 23 (1962); *WWP*.

E.D.J.

Y

YORKE, SIMON (1903-66), the fifth descendant of that name from Simon Yorke (1606-82), wholesale grocer of Dover, grandfather of Earl Hardwicke; b. 24 June 1903, eldest son of Philip Yorke (1849-1922), Erddig, Denbs., and his second wife Louisa Matilda (née Scott). He was educated at Moorland House, Heswall; Cheltenham College; and Corpus Christi College, Cambridge. He graduated B.A. in forestry in 1927. In 1922 he inherited Erddig near Wrexham. He was High Sheriff for Denbighshire in 1937. Although he was a lieutenant in the Denbighshire Yeomanry, when World War II came he enlisted as a private soldier in the North Staffordshire Regiment. In accordance with his wishes he remained a sapper, without seeking or gaining promotion.

His relationship with his tenants was not a happy one. He refused them permission to have electricity nor a telephone on their farms. Although he was not a huntsman, he followed the hounds on his bicycle and he always knew where to find the fox. He was found d. of heart failure in Erddig Park, 7 May 1966, and was buried in Marchwiel churchyard. He was a bachelor and d. intestate. Erddig was inherited by his brother Philip Scott Yorke (1905-76).

Merlin Waterson, *The Servants' Hall* (1980); [Oliver Garnett, *Erddig* (1999)].

Jo.G.J.

YOUNG, JAMES JUBILEE (1887-1962), Baptist minister; b. 15 May 1887, the year of Queen Victoria's jubilee, s. of Thomas and Eunice Young (Revs. Jabes, Glasnant and Owen Young were his brothers). He was born in Maenclochog, Pembs., but he was brought up in Aberavon, Glam., and as a young man he moved to Tonypandy, Rhondda Valley, to work in a draper's shop. A member of Moreia Baptist church he began to preach there in 1906 and the following year enrolled at Old College School, Carmarthen. He was ord. minister of Capel Rhondda, Pontypridd in 1910 and he ministered later to churches in Felinganol (1914) and Seion, Llanelli (1931). He retired in 1957. His gifts as a powerful preacher were clear from the start and he became one of 'the princes' of the Welsh pulpit. He was regularly invited to preach at denominational meetings, and he preached at the St. David's Day service at City Temple, London in 1922, at Central Hall, Liverpool in 1923, and at the Welsh service at the Baptist Union of Gt. Britain in Cardiff in 1924. He was president of the Pembrokeshire meeting (*Cymanfa*) in 1929, and president of the Welsh Baptist Union in 1946. He d. 23 Jan. 1962 leaving a widow Mya (née Jones of Capel Rhondda) and one son.

Llawlyfr Bed., 1963; *Portreadau'r Faner*, 1, 7-9; record (Qualiton, DAF 212, 1969) preaching one of Christmas Evans's sermons.

B.F.R.

SUPPLEMENT AND AMENDMENTS TO DICTIONARY OF WELSH BIOGRAPHY DOWN TO 1940

ABEL, JOHN (1770-1819), Welsh Independent minister; b. in Llanybri, Carms, 1770, s. of William Abel, one of the founders of Capel Newydd in that village. It is said that he attended the Carmarthen Academy but this establishment was in Swansea at that time. In 1794 he succeeded David Davies (d. 1807, *D.W.B.*, 113) as minister of the small congregation at Capel Sul, Kidwelly and he also kept a school. John Abel was not orthodox, according to the Unitarian Wright, who visited Wales in 1816, and 'he was considered to be an Arian' who lent his chapel willingly to Wright. He d. on June 25th 1819.

H. Egl. Ann., iii, 336, 471; *Oriel Coleg Caerfyrddin*, 29, 246; *Monthly Repository, 1816; Trans. Cymm.*, 1928-29, 56.

R.T.J.

ADAMS, DAVID (*DWB*, 3). He d. 5 July 1922. See *Dysg.*, Sept. 1922.

AELHAEARN (*DWB*, 4). His father's name was Hygarfael.

ALLEN, EVAN OWEN (1805-52), writer; b. at Pant-y-llin, near Llanrwst, Caerns., the son of a farmer. He published in *Seren Gomer*. He also wrote poetry but none of this has been published. He d. Dec. 18th, 1852 in Ruthin.

Enw. F., 27.

R.T.J.

ANWYL (FAMILY; *DWB*, 12). Delete the reference to John, Benedictine martyr. See the article on John Roberts (1576-1610), *DWB*, 865.

BAKER, ELIZABETH (*DWB*, 23). Read *N.L.W. Jnl.*, iii (not ii), 80-101.

BALLINGER, Sir JOHN (*DWB*, 23-4), see now M.A. Bloomfield, *Sir John Ballinger: an annotated bibliography* (1998).

BARHAM, DIANA (*DWB*, 25). See also *Gower Memories* (1957), ed. Alicia Gower-Jones (autobiography of William Griffiths, 1788-1861, *DWB*, 309).

BAXTER, GEORGE ROBERT WYTHEN (*DWB*, 28). His father's dates are 1762-1841. He himself was b. at Monmouth and christened 14 June 1814. He entered an Oxford college but did not graduate there. He m. at Tenby, 5 June 1833, Martha Maria Caulfield (d. 1 Apr. 1875).

Mont. Colls., 59, 82-101.

BAYLY, LEWIS (*DWB*, 28-9). B. *c.* 1575, possibly the son of Thomas Bayly who was a curate at Carmarthen that year. He was at Abermarlais for a period and had the patronage of the family that lived there. He was parson of Llanedi, 1606-13. He gained a B.D. of Exeter College, Oxford, 1611, D.D., 1613.

Trans. Caerns. Hist. Soc., 28, 13-36.

BEBB, LLEWELLYN JOHN MONTFORD (1862-1915), cleric; the elder son of the Rev. William Bebb; b. in Cape Town, South Africa, 16 Feb.

1862. He was educated at Winchester and New College, Oxford; he graduated B.A. with first-class honours in classics and was appointed a fellow and tutor at Brasenose College. He was made vice-principal of that college in 1892. He was ordained deacon in 1886 and priest in 1887 and in 1898 he was appointed principal of St. David's College, Lampeter. He married Louisa Fraser of London in 1886 and they had four sons and three daughters. He was made an honorary canon of St. David's in 1910. He died 22 Nov. 1915 and was buried at Lampeter.

Foster, *Alumni Oxon; Cambrian News*, 26 Nov, 1915; *Welsh Gaz.*, 2 Dec. 1915.

T.I.E.

BEFIS, (Syr BEFIS LLÊN) (n.d.), poet; *Englynion* by him are found in NLW Bodewryd MS. 2 and NLW Sotheby MS. A1.

G.M.G.

BERGAM, Y (14 *c.*), poet, vaticinator. In the MSS he is known as '*Y Bergam o Faelor*' (Bergam from Maelor) and in an extent prepared for the Black Prince in 1352 reference is made, in connection with Pennant in Eifionydd, to *Gafael mab Bergam* (the holding of Bergam's son). His prophesies provided a source for the vaticinatory poems (*cywyddau brud*). See Enid Griffiths, *Early Vaticination in Welsh* (1937).

Personal research.

R.W.E.

BERRY, JOHN MATHIAS (1847-1917) – see BERRY (FAMILY) above.

BEVAN, SILVANUS (*DWB*, 35). It was in 1715 that he opened his shop at 2 Old Plough Court (Oxford Street). He m. (2), Martha Heathcote. He took a great interest in America; both he and his brother played a considerable part in establishing the first hospital at Philadelphia. His brother Timothy's dates are 1704-86.

BEYNON, THOMAS (1744?-1835; *DWB*, 37). B. at Greenmeadow, Llansadwrn, Carms., christened 26 Aug. 1745, son of Griffith Beynon and Rachel (Thomas) his wife. He was ord. priest at Hereford while he was curate at Cathedin. He was presented to the Bishop of Hereford by the Bishop of St. David's. There are strong reasons for believing that the Vaughan family of Golden Grove were his patrons. He d. 1 Oct. 1835 and was buried 8 Oct. at Llandeilo Fawr (Llandilo).

See the article by R.G. Thomas, *N.L.W. Jnl.*, ix, 354-64, for a list of books he read between 1763 and 1767.

BLAYNEY (FAMILY; *DWB*, 40). Read Morville for Morvil.

BLEDRI ap CYDIFOR (*DWB*, 41), fl. 1116-30.

BODVEL (FAMILY; *DWB*, 43a). Cwm, Llanrothal, had been established as headquarters of a new Jesuit province by Fr. John Salusbury in 1622, and was called the college of St. Xaverius. Fr. John Salusbury, d. in 1625 and Bodvel succeeded him as rector.

BODWRDA (FAMILY; *DWB*, 44a). Instead of

Naylor read Nayler. 'Crazy' is probably too strong a word.

BOLD, HUGH (*DWB*, 44). He became a lawyer's clerk at the Brecon office of John Philipps (of Tre-gaer near Llanfrynach – see Theophilus Jones, IV, 37). He m. twice. His first wife, Elizabeth, d. 31 Oct. 1781; and from this marriage the later Bolds of the shire are descended – see the history of the family by David Verey in *Brycheiniog*, 1960. He m., *c.* 1782, Dorothy, daughter of his old master John Philipps (many years after her father's d. in 1763); Dorothy d. in 1806 (Theophilus Jones, II, 95). In the original article his wife was erroneously called 'Johannah' – see the footnote on p. 76 of *Brycheiniog*, 1962, and also D. Verey's article in *Brycheiniog*, 1960; correspondence with D. Verey.

R.T.J.

BONAPARTE (*DWB*, 45). See B.F. Roberts, *Trans. Cymm.* (1996) and the references given there to Bonaparte bibliography.

BOWEN, D.E. (*fl.* 1840-80), editor, author and Baptist minister in U.S.A; b. in Glamorgan but moved to U.S.A. in his youth. He was a Welsh Baptist minister in Carbondale, Pennsylvania for a period. He came to prominence as the editor of *Y Gwyliedydd* (1843), the first periodical provided by the Welsh Baptists in the U.S.A., and its successor, *Y Seren Orllewinol* (1844). He may also have been responsible for editing *Y Beread* (1841), a fortnightly Baptist newspaper. He published *The Berean; or Miscellaneous Writings of the Reverend D. E. Bowen, Carbondale, Pa.* (Carbondale, n.d.); *a Lecture on the Life and Genius of the Reverend John Williams, Senior Pastor of the Oliver Street Baptist Church, New York* (New York, n.d.).

Y Seren Orllewinol, 1844, 10; Ashby MS in U.C.N.W., Bangor.

R.O.

BOWEN, DAVID (1774-1853), Felinfoel; b. at Bryn Bach, Felinfoel, Dec. 11th, 1774. He was baptised by Daniel Davies, Felinfoel, Carms. 14 May 1797 and he started to preach in 1798. He was ordained by Titus Lewis and Joshua Watkins, Carmarthen, on 25 Aug. 1806 to be joint-minister with Daniel Davies and he lived at Pantlludw. In 1831 Seion, Llanelli was formed as a church and Bowen was selected by the congregation to be its pastor. He spent the rest of his life in its service and he died on 18 Nov. 1853.

B. Humphreys, *Hanes Bedyddwyr Felinfoel* (1909).

M.B.O.

BOWND, WILLIAM (*DWB*, 47). John Moon not Moor – see the article on EVANS, HUGH (?-1656; *DWB*, 237). Instead of Bucknill read Bucknell.

BRADNEY, Sir JOSEPH ALFRED (*DWB*, 48). He also published *Noctes Flandricae* (London), a collection of poems and prose composed mainly in Flanders in 1917. Volume 5 of *History of Monmouthshire* (ed. Madeleine Gray) was published in 1993. See *NLWJ*, 14 (1965-66), 114.

BROWN, MIA ARNESBY (1867–1931), artist; b. in Cwmbran, Mon., daughter of Rev. Charles Smallwood Edwards and grand-daughter of Rev. Loderwick Edwards, vicar of Rhymney. She studied under Sir Hubert von Herkomer. She showed five pictures in the Royal Academy under her maiden name, Edwards. In 1913 in an exhibition of contemporary Welsh artists, two of her pictures drew attention – 'Mary reading' and 'The Garden Boy', the latter is now in the National Museum of Wales. She married, 1896, Sir John Arnesby Brown, R.A., artist. She died in 1931, aged 64.

Graves, *Royal Academy Exhibitors, 1769-1904.*

T.M.R.

BRUCE, CHARLES GRANVILLE (1866-1939), mountaineer and soldier; b. 7 Apr. 1866 in London, youngest s. of H.A. Bruce, 1st Lord Aberdare (*DWB*, 54) and his second wife, Norah. He went to Harrow and then Repton schools but unlike his brother W.N. Bruce (*DWB*, 54-5) he did not continue his education, obtaining his commission in the Oxfordshire and Buckinghamshire Light Infantry in 1887 through the militia rather than Sandhurst. After joining the 5th Gurkha Rifles in 1889 he mastered the skills of mountain warfare on the n.-west frontier of India. He was mentioned in dispatches three times and had been promoted major by 1913. In May 1914 he was appointed commander of the 6th Gurkhas and he was again mentioned three times in dispatches before being seriously wounded in Gallipoli. He was then sent back to India to lead an independent frontier brigade. Before being obliged to resign, as brigadier, in 1920 on health grounds, he had been twice mentioned in dispatches and had served in the Third Afghanistan War. He was appointed Hon. Col. of the 5th Gurkhas in 1931.

The basis of Bruce's success as a soldier was his remarkable mastery of the languages of the Gurkhas and their neighbours, his zest in their company and his proverbial strength. He is mainly remembered as one of the foremost pioneers in the Himalayas. He accompanied Conway on the first expedition to the Karakoram in 1892, and was with Younghusband in the Hindu Kush in 1893 and with Mummery on Nanga Parbat in 1895. In 1898 he explored the area around Nun Kun with his wife and 16 Gurkhas.

Bruce's true delight was in mountains under 20,000 feet, but having expressed a desire to see Everest since 1893, he arranged to make an attempt through Tibet with Longstaff and Mumm in 1907. The British Foreign Office blocked this and they went to Nanda Devi, succeeding in ascending Trisul (7,100 metres), the highest ascent until 1931. Bruce visited Nepal and Sikkim in 1908 and began to plan an ascent of Everest from the south. Permission again was refused but he planned and led the first two assaults (from the north) in 1922 when (General) John Geoffrey Bruce (b. 4 Dec. 1896, his cousin, son of Sir Gerald Trevor Knight-Bruce of St. Hilary, Glam.) broke the world record with an ascent of 8,300 metres, and in 1924 when Mallory and Irvine were lost on the final slopes. Bruce himself was unable to climb to great heights by now but according to

Longstaff he was an 'ideal leader'. In his time technical skill was not as important in the Himalayas as was the ability to be quite at home in the inaccessible highground and among the various groups of inhabitants. Bruce's greatest contribution, perhaps, was to discover the value of the native mountaineer, especially the Sherpa. From the beginning he insisted on training Gurkha soldiers to be mountain guides, and he brought some home to Cwmdare and to the Alps. He was elected president of the Alpine Club in 1923 and an hon. member of the Alpine Club of Switzerland (and of other clubs). He received the Gill memorial prize of the Royal Geographical Soc. in 1915 and the Founder's gold badge in 1925. He was awarded hon. doctorates by the universities of Wales (D.Sc.), Oxford (D.Sc.), Edinburgh (D.C.L.) and St. Andrews (LL.D.). He was appointed M.V.O. in 1903 and C.B. in 1918.

He published: *Twenty years in the Himalayas* (1910), *Kulu and Lahoul* (1914), *The assault on Mount Everest 1922* (1923), and *Himalayan wanderer* (1934). In this (p. 7) he says of his boyhood in Dyffryn, Cwmdare: 'I spent all my time running about the hills, and sucked in from my earliest time a love and understanding of mountain country without appreciating it at the time, my father being a most complete lover of his own valleys and hills.' Before joining the army he had walked with (Sir) Rhys Williams of Miskin 'from South to North Wales' and had become a 'worshipper of the wild Welsh mountain scenery' (p. 25). His teacher in rural matters was a farmer from the valley and according to Longstaff, Bruce used to sing Welsh airs with gusto.

He m. Finetta Madeline Julia, third dau. of Col. Sir Edward Fitzgerald Campbell in 1894. Their only child, a son, died young. Mrs. Bruce d. in 1932 and Charles Granville on 12 July 1939. A memorial to him was placed in Abbottabad (Pakistan) church in 1942 by the 5th and 6th Gurkhas.

Kenneth Mason, *Abode of snow: a history of Himalayan exploration and mountaineering* (1955); *DNB* 1931-40, 107; *Alpine Jnl.*, 52 (1940), 53 (1941-42); T.G. Longstaff, *This my voyage* (1950); Claire-Eliane Engel, *Les Batailles pour l'Himalaya, 1783-1936* (1936).

I.B.R.

BUCKLAND, 1st Baron (1877-1928) – see BERRY (FAMILY), HENRY SEYMOUR BERRY above.

CADWALADR, DAFYDD (*DWB*, 63). Instead of 'c. 1796' read *c.* 1795-6.

CADWALADR CESAIL (*DWB*, 63). In the bibliography instead of Hengwrt MS. 3 read Hafod MS. 3.

CAPELULO – see WILLIAMS, THOMAS (*c.* 1782-1855) below.

CECIL (FAMILY; *DWB*, 70). Read Northamptonshire for Lincolnshire.

CHERLETON (FAMILY; *DWB*, 74). The word 'possibly' in the last paragraph should be deleted.

CLIDRO, ROBIN (*DWB*, 886). See now Cennard Davies, 'Robin Clidro a'i ganlynwyr', M.A. diss., Un. of Wales Swansea, 1964.

COLLINS, WILLIAM LUCAS (*DWB*, 81). Add 'son of the Rev. John and Elizabeth Collins'. He was rector of Cheriton in Gower, 1840-67, not 1840-7.

CORBET, Sir RICHARD (1640-83), baronet and member of parliament; one of the CORBET family of Leighton, Montgomery, a son of EDWARD CORBET (who died before his father in 1653), and grandson of Sir EDWARD CORBET, the first baronet. He was educated at Christ Church, Oxford, 1658. He was Member of Parliament for Shrewsbury 1677-81 and chairman of the elections committee. He was a close friend of Lord William Russell whose execution in 1683 may have hastened Sir Richard's death. He was a Fellow of the Royal Society but this was in the period when the majority of Fellows were elected on social or political grounds. He married Victoria, daughter of Sir William Uvedale in 1663 and they had nine children. She died in 1679 and Sir Richard on 1 August 1683.

Foster, *Alumni Oxon; Mont. Coll.*, 1880, 345; 1892, 242.

R.J.T.

CORY, (B) (*DWB*, 83b, par. 2, 1. 6). Instead of (Richard), read (Herbert).

COX, JOHN ([1800]?-1870), printer, bookseller, and postmaster at Aberystwyth, Cards. G. Eyre Evans, *Aberystwyth and its Court Leet* (1902), provides a fairly complete list of the publications from the John Cox press. Among them were two newspapers - *The Demetian Mirror; or Aberystwyth Reporter and Visitants' Informant. . .*, which appeared once a week from 15 Aug. 1840 till 31 Oct. 1840, and *The Aberystwyth Chronicle and Illustrated Times*, a weekly paper published between 9 June 1855 and 22 Dec. 1855. The printing work from the Cox press was usually well produced.

W.Ll.D.

CRADOC, WALTER (*DWB*, 85, last line of the article). *The Saving Sight of God* was published in 1651 and not in 1655.

CYFEILIOG (*DWB*, 88). Read Brochwel instead of Brodrwch.

CYNWRIG ap RHYS (d. 1237), prince; son of (the Lord) Rhys ap Gruffydd (*DWB*, 838-9). Nothing is known of him other than the impression he made on Gerald the Welshman when he was travelling through Ceredigion with Archbishop Baldwin preaching the crusade. Gerald says that he was a tall, handsome young man with fair curly hair, dressed in the style of Welshmen of the period – a shirt and thin cloak and barefooted – but lithe and dignified in appearance. He survived to old age but left no mark on the history of the period.

Hist. W., 568, 577-8.

J.E.Ll.

DAFYDD ap HARRI WYN (*fl.* 1568), poet, a native of Edeirnion. It is said that he produced work of greater excellence than any poet who graduated at the Caerwys *eisteddfod* but he refused to graduate and destroyed all his work, describing it as vanity.

Enw. F.

E.D.J.

DAFYDD GAM (*DWB*, 101). In the bibliography read *Dwnn*, I (not ii).

DAVID (DEWI), St. (*DWB*, 107-8). Calixtus II granted the privilege of a blessing corresponding to one pilgrimage to Rome to 2 to St. David's. To the sources add *Wales*, 1944, 30-2.

DAVIES, BENJAMIN (1814-75; *DWB*, 111). See also Cooper, *From Stepney to St. Giles* (1960).

DAVIES, DAVID LLOYD ('Dewi Glan Peryddon', *DWB*, 118). For 'Ceinwen Morgan neu y Rian Ddiwylliedig' read ... 'neu y Rian Dwylledig'. Tecwyn Ellis, *Dewi Glan Peryddon a'i nofel fer* (2000).

DAVIES (or **CADWALADR**), ELIZABETH (*DWB*, 121). Instead of (*c.* 1795) read (*c.* 1795-6).

DAVIES, ELLIS WILLIAM (1871-1939), solicitor and politician; b. 12 Apr. 1871 at Gerlan, Bethesda, Caerns., s. of David Davies, a quarry official, and Catherine (Williams), Tyddyn Sabel, Bethesda. He was educated at Carneddi school, Bethesda, Liverpool College and a private school in Liverpool. After six years as a clerk in insurance offices at Wrexham and Sheffield he proceeded to qualify as a solicitor, gaining first-class honours in 1899 and a London Law Society prize. He established a solicitor's practice at Caernarfon, and lived there for rest of his life. In 1904 he was elected a member of Caernarfon County Council, later being made an alderman. He acted as solicitor for the North Wales Quarrymen's Union, and was director of several business companies.

In June 1906 he was elected M.P. (Lib.) for the Eifion division of Caernarfonshire, in succession to John Bryn Roberts (*DWB*, 1148), and retained his seat until 1918. During this period he was a member of the departmental committee on landed estates (1911), departmental committee on the jury system (1911), Lloyd George's land enquiry committee (1912), the Speaker's conference on reforming the electoral system (1916), the departmental committee concerned with the right of public authorities to make compulsory purchases of land (1917) and Lord Bryce's conference on reforming the House of Lords. At the general election held in Dec. 1918 he lost his seat, after a bitter campaign, to the official candidate of the Liberal and Tory coalition; the Labour candidate was also ahead of him. Then in Dec. 1923 he was elected M.P. (Lib.) for Denbigh division, and was subsequently appointed a member of the panel of chairmen of committees in the House of Commons in 1926. He resigned from Parliament in May 1929 because of ill health. During 1932 he became prominent and active in the discussions of the Presb. Church of Wales on formulating a parliamentary bill relating to the

Church. He joined the Labour Party in 1936 but resigned in Dec. 1938 because he disagreed with the party's foreign policy. He d. 29 Apr. 1939.

Ellis Davies worked hard and diligently in many spheres. His political activity was based on firm and single-minded radicalism. He had an alert and discerning mind, independent judgement and power of conviction. He read extensively and was endowed with a retentive memory. He contributed articles on politics, politicians and history to Welsh newspapers and periodicals; these testify to the breadth of his interests and the sureness of his thinking.

Www; newspaper articles; the diaries and personal papers of Ellis Davies.

I.Ll.F.

DAVIES, EVAN THOMAS (*DWB*, 124). To his works add *Pregethau, Erthyglau ac Areithiau* (1894). *Pregethau ac Anerchiadau* was published in 1899, not 1894.

DAVIES, GRIFFITH (1788-1855; *DWB*, 125-6). He developed a method of sharing earnings between partners in a bargain when some of them had been absent from work during the month. He was invited to become the first president of the Institute of Actuaries but declined. He was described as 'The father of the present race of actuaries'. One of the competitors for the post in the Guardian when Griffith Davies was appointed was Benjamin Gomperz who was already a Fellow of the Royal Society. It is said that there was objection to him because he was Jewish, and that Nathan Rothschild established the Alliance office for him! There is evidence to suggest that Telford had made errors whilst designing Britannia Bridge across the Menai Straits and that Griffith Davies had to re-do many of the calculations. He was active with the Calvinistic Methodists. He was a member of the Trefeca committee and it is said that he set the denomination's finances on a firm footing. He believed strongly in education. He was a member of the old London Mathematical Society until its demise, and a member of the committee of the Islington Literary and Scientific Society where he lived.

Ll.G. Chambers, 'Griffith Davies (1788-1855) F.R.S. Actuary', *Trans. Cymm.*, 1988.

Ll.G.C.

It should be added that he received the Royal Society of the Arts' large silver medal in 1820 for carving a sundial skilfully from a piece of slate. He was elected F.R.S. on 16 June 1831 (not 1832) A number of his papers are lodged at the Library of the Institute of Actuaries, amongst them *An investigation of the basis for calculating life contingencies &c*, i.e. twenty-four reports which he wrote in 1831, and *A paper on the construction of logarithms* (1849). Between 1829 and 1832 he was a member of the Cymreigyddion Soc. and in 1837 he was made an elder of Jewin church (CM), London. He was elected a Fellow of the Statistical Society of France in 1833. He was one of the interpreters of the Institute of Actuaries and was the first member to be elevated a Fellow of that institution. One of his accounting methods is still in use today. A hundred and five blocks of his key to *Bonnycastle's Trigonometry* are lodged at the N.L.W. as well as numerous letters from him. There are others also in the library of the University of Wales, Bangor.

Trans. R.S.A., 38 (1820); minutes of the Royal Soc. (1831); Library of the Inst. of Actuaries; papers in N.L.W., Univ. of Wales, Bangor, and the office of the Guardian Royal Exchange Assurance, London.

G.A.J.

DAVIES, JAMES (1767?-1860; *DWB*, 130). Instead of *Hist. Carms.*, ii, 243 read 253.

DAVIES, JOHN (1700?-92; *DWB*, 133). Read: He translated into English eight of Rowland's sermons, 1772, and, later, three others, 1774.

DAVIES, JOHN (1750-1821; *DWB*, 133). According to *Evang. Mag.*, 1826 (biography of Griffith Williams, pp. 457-61) he was curate at Cynwyl in 1774.

DAVIES, JOHN (Tahiti; 1772-1855; *DWB*, 134). His *History of the Tahitian Mission, 1799-1830*, ed. C.W. Newbury (Cambridge), was published in 1962.

DAVIES, JOHN ('Siôn Gymro'; 1804-84; *DWB*, 136). He began to preach on 1 July 1819 at Neuadd-lwyd school (Phillips, Thomas (1772-1842); *DWB*, 761-2).

DAVIES, JOHN ('John Davies, Taihirion'; 1825-1904), Welsh Independent minister; b. in Morriston, Glam. He was ordained in 1851 as the minister of churches at Taihirion and Efail Isaf, Glam. He instituted a new church at Bronllwyn in 1858. He gave up the pastorate of Taihirion in 1893 and that of Bronllwyn shortly after. He d. Sept. 16, 1904. He remained the minister of Efail Isaf until the end of his life and was buried in the cemetery of Tabernacl, Efail Isaf.

Although John Davies was a prominent member of his denomination and one of the directors of the London Missionary Society, his influence was felt principally in his own region and he was known as *Esgob y Fro* (the bishop of the community). He was active in promoting education and mainly due to his efforts, a British school was set up at Llantwit Fardre and he was for many years a member of the board of Pentyrch school. He published *Bras Llinelliad Hanesyddol o Gyfundeb Annibynol Dwyreiniol Morganwg* in 1879.

Tabernacl, Efail Isaf – Hanes yr Eglwys, 9-13, 22-5; *South Wales Daily News*, 19 Sept. 1904; *Y Tyst*, 28 Sept. and 5 Oct. 1904; *H. Egl. Ann.*, ii, 363-7.

T.H.L.

DAVIES, JOHN (1860-1939; *DWB*, 137-8). He was educated at Capel Dewi national school and at William Eilir Evans's school (*DWB*, 258), Llandysul.

DAVIES, JOHN (1882-1937), secretary of the South Wales District of the W.E.A., 1919-1937; b. 5 May 1882 at Bryn-bedd, Blaenpennal, Cards., s. of William and Jane Davies. The family moved in 1883 to the Rhondda valley where William Davies was killed in the Maerdy Pit explosion of 1885. John Davies was brought up by his widowed mother in the Cards. village of Llangeitho, one of the cradles of Welsh Calvinistic Methodism and the religious traditions of his boyhood home left a deep impression upon him. After attending the Llangeitho British school, he was apprenticed at the age of thirteen to a draper at Porth, Rhondda. Two years later his health broke down and for the rest of his life he was afflicted by a weakness of the chest which obliged him to spend lengthy periods of recuperation at Llangeitho, and he continued to visit the village whilst his mother was alive. He was often called upon to speak at the society at Capel Gwynfil, and his talks were always polished. He had returned to the Rhondda by 1898 and the six-month coal strike of that year awakened in him an interest in social and industrial questions. He became a voracious reader and was later to claim that he was the first to read the Porth public library's copy of *Das Kapital* from cover to cover. By 1903 he had left the Rhondda for Swansea where he was employed at Ben Evans's department store and was active in the Shop Assistants' Union. From 1904 to 1906 he worked in shops in London; there he developed a life-long interest in the problems of Welsh immigrants to English cities and, through his membership of Willesden Green CM chapel, he was strongly influenced by the Welsh religious revival of 1904-05. From 1906 to 1914 he lived in the Swansea valley where he was closely involved in the work of the Independent Labour Party. One of the founders of the Swansea Valley Socialist League, he was secretary of the Swansea Trades Council and, from 1909, a member of the staff of the socialist weekly, *Llais Llafur*. Rejected for military service, he worked from 1914 to 1917 with the Y.M.C.A. on Salisbury Plain. In 1917 he conducted research for Seebohm Rowntree on housing conditions in west Wales and in 1918 became the organiser of the Agricultural Labourers Union in Pembs. and Cards.

In Dec. 1919, out of 131 applicants, John Davies was appointed secretary of the South Wales District of the W.E.A., a post he held until his death in 1937. During the early years of his secretaryship, the Association was faced with severe financial problems and by 1922 he was owed six-months salary. He proved adept at soliciting funds from the wealthy while he was at the same time concerned that the Association should be seen, in the polarised atmosphere of the 1920s, to be aligning itself with working class causes – in 1926, for example, he was minutes secretary of the Cardiff Strike Committee and duplicated the local strike bulletin using the Association's equipment. Unorthodox in his administrative methods, he was rebuked by headquarters for not conforming to regulations over branch organisation. Nevertheless, under his guidance the work of the W.E.A. in Wales expanded rapidly, the number of students attending classes and courses rising from about 250 in 1919-20 to over 8,000 in 1937. In the struggle between the Association and the National Council for Labour Colleges for leadership of working class education in south Wales, the period of John Davies's secretaryship saw the W.E.A. drawing decisively ahead of the NCLC in its number of classes and members.

In addition to his work with the W.E.A., John Davies was joint secretary of the University of Wales Tutorial Classes Committee and was closely associated with Thomas Jones (1870-1955; see above) in the foundation of Coleg Harlech, serving on the council of the college from its inception. He was a member of the Committee on Rural Education in Wales established in 1927 by the President of the Board of Education. During the depression of the 1930s he was actively involved in efforts to relieve distress in the south Wales coalfield, serving as chairman of the executive committee of Community House, Senghennydd, and secretary of the South Wales Committee of the National Council for Social Service.

John Davies was one of the few socialists of the inter-war years to have an extensive personal knowledge of both industrial and rural Wales. His knowledge of Wales was considered to be encyclopaedic and in the later years of his life he put it to good use in the gossip column he contributed weekly, under the pseudonym 'The Watchman', to the Saturday issue of the Welsh edition of the *Daily Herald*. Although considered by some to be difficult and eccentric, John Davies possessed a genius for friendship, and enduring compassion for the deprived and an unquenchable faith in the possibilities of adult education.

In 1928 he m. Ruby Part of Somerset, national women's organiser of the Workers' Union. There were no children. He d. on 5 Dec. 1937 and was buried at Llangeitho. A memorial volume to him was privately printed by the Gregynog Press.

John Davies (Gregynog Press, n.d.); *South Wales Voice*, 11 and 18 Dec. 1937; *Y Llenor*, XVI, 4; Peter Stead, *Coleg Harlech, the first fifty years* (Cardiff, 1977); Richard Lewis, 'Leaders and Teachers, the origins and development of the workers' educational movement in Wales, 1906-1940' (Ph.D. dissertation, University of Wales, 1980).

J.D.

DAVIES, JOHN BREESE (1893-1940; *DWB*, 138-9), writer and a specialist in *cerdd dant*; b. 22 Feb. 1893 at Gwynfryn, Dinas Mawddwy, Mer., son of Thomas Tegwyn Davies, author of a history of *Dinas Mawddwy a'i hamgylchoedd* (1893). His mother, Elizabeth, was of the Breese family of Llanbryn-mair. He attended Dinas Mawddwy Elementary School and Dolgellau Grammar School until an illness kept him bedridden for five years and left him lame for the rest of his life. During his confinement he read extensively, thereby acquainting himself not only with the history and literature of Wales, but also with the languages and literature of other countries. During this period Sir Owen M. Edwards paid him a visit and urged him to write for his magazine, *Cymru*. He complied, and continued all his life to enrich Welsh literature, while at the same time he cultivated himself by attending summer schools in Wales and England and the extra-mural classes of Aberystwyth college in Dinas. He lived with his sister at Minllyn, Dinas Mawddwy (where they kept a shop), and both of them assiduously supported the culture of their district.

Many of his articles were published in *Cymru*, *Y Geninen*, *Yr Eurgrawn*, and *Y Cerddor*, and a selection of them were pub-lished in *Ysgrifau John Breese Davies* (1949). He wrote with a good style and economy of expression, showing artistic skill and many of the virtues of the true scholar. He was secretary of the literature committee for the national *eisteddfod* at Machynlleth in 1937, and his essay on the Dyfi district as an introduction to the list of competitions for that *eisteddfod* was a masterpiece of its kind. Even so, his greatest eisteddfodic achievement was to ensure that a competition for a Literature Medal be included from 1938 onwards. He worked equally energetically - as a tutor, adjudicator and conductor – to establish the highest standards possible for the traditional singing to harp accompaniment, and he and J.E. Jones were considered to be the chief benefactors of their day in this field. He was one of the founders of the *Cerdd Dant* Society and edited its magazine, *Allwedd y Tannau*, from its first issue till 1940. He was prominent in the life of his district, being a member of Mer. county council, chairman of the governors of Dolgellau Grammar School, president and secretary of the Council of Free Churches of Dyfi valley, and steward of Dinas Mawddwy Methodist circuit. He d. 4 Oct. 1940.

Personal knowledge; Robin Gwyndaf, 'Cyfraniad John Breese Davies i Gerdd Dant' in *Allwedd y Tannau*, 32 (1973), 10-24, a survey of a collection of his MSS. in the Museum of Welsh Life.

I.C.P.

DAVIES, JOHN DAVID (*DWB*, 139). Append to the bibliography – *Jnl. Gower Soc.*, VI.

DAVIES, JOHN LLEWELYN (1826-1916; *DWB*, 135 under John Davies, 1795-1861). He was one of the 31 founding members of the Alpine Club and one of the most successful of the early climbers of the Alps. With the guide Johann Zumtaugwald and other guides, he was the first to climb the Dom (14,942 ft.), the highest mountain entirely within Switzerland (on 11 Sept. 1858) and, in 1862, the Täsch-horn (14,700 ft.). He ascended the Finsteraarhorn as early as 29 Aug. 1857. He published only one article on mountaineering, 'An ascent of one of the Mischabel-Hörner, called the Dom' (*Peaks, Passes and Glaciers*, first series, 1859) but Leslie Stephen, one of his pupils and the best writer of his generation on mountains, thought highly of him.

DNB, 1912-21, 147; A.L. Mumm, *The Alpine Club register, 1857-1863* (1923), 85-7; *Alpine Jnl.*, XXX, 324-30.

I.B.R.

DAVIES, JOSEPH E. (1812-81). Welsh Calvinistic minister in America and author; b. at Cwm-Cati Fach, Llanarthne, Carms. He emigrated to America and landed in New York on 25 May, 1842. He entered the ministry in 1842 and was ordained at Danville, Pennsylvania. He was minister of the CM church at Hyde Park, Scranton, Penn. He published *Blwch Diwinyddol sef Corff o Dduwinyddiaeth ...* (Scranton and Utica; 1869-71) and *Crefydd y Byd Cristionogol*. He died at Hyde Park on 1 Jan. 1881.

Y Drych, 13 Jan. 1881.

R.O.

DAVIES, MOSES (*DWB*, 144). He was the father of William Davies, 'Mynorydd' (*DWB*, 160).

DAVIES, OWEN (1840-1929; *DWB*, 145-6). See *DWB*, 1054-5, which indicates that he would have been co-secretary of the Welsh Baptist Union, since John Rufus Williams also held the post from its foundation.

DAVIES, REES (*DWB*, 147). The 'Cromindee' ('Comb du') Congregation and the later (1744) 'Hanover' Congregation were one and the same (Isaac Thomas in *Y Cofiadur*, 1958, 12-13).

DAVIES, DAVIS, or **DAVYES,** THOMAS (*DWB*, 153b). For Katherine read Catherine.

DAVIES, WILLIAM (?-1593; *DWB*, 157-8). Read *Y Drych Cristianogawl* not *Cristionogawl*. Its authorship is uncertain. For a history of printing at Rhiwledyn see Geraint Gruffydd in *Jnl. W.B.S.*, VIII, 1-23, and *Argraffwyr cyntaf Cymru* (1972). Correct *fl.* John Griffith to 1548-87.

DAVIS, DAVID (1745-1827; *DWB*, 163-4). Instead of *God's Life in Man's Soul* read *The Life of God in the Soul of Man*. The memoir by 'Tau Gimel' (not Gimmel) was published in 1828, not 1824.

DAVIS, RICHARD (*DWB*, 164-5). On his gravestone at Rothwell parish church he is said to have died on 11 Sept., aged 56.

DEE, JOHN (*DWB*, 166). He was a grandson of Bedo Ddu of Nant-y-groes, Pilleth, Rads. and he retained his connection with the locality. He called Thomas Jones, 'Twm Shôn Catti' (*DWB*, 513, and see below) with whom he was acquainted, 'cousin'.

Joseph A. Bradney, *Radnorshire Soc. Trans.*, 3 (1933), 10. [On Dee see J. Roberts and Andrew G. Watson, *John Dee's Library Catalogue* (1990); P.J. French, *John Dee, the world of an Elizabethan magus* (1972); Gwyn A. Williams, *Welsh Wizard and British Empire: John Dee and Welsh identity* (1980).]

Ll.G.C.

DEFYNNOG – see JAMES, DAVID below.

DEWI ARFON – see JONES, DAVID HUGH below.

DEWI ELFED – see JONES, DAVID BEVAN below.

EAMES, ROLANT (1750-1825), musician; he lived in Penrhyndeudraeth, Mer. He made a major contribution as a teacher of singing and he visited the churches of Llanfrothen, Llanfair, Llanbedr, Llandanwg and Llanfihangel to teach the choirs; he was successful in celebrating and improving church music. People came to him from a wide area to receive music lessons. When the walls of Llanfrothen were being demolished prior to rebuilding, the old teacher's pitch pipe was found.

M.O. Jones, *Byw. Cerdd. Cymru.*

R.D.G.

EDWARDS (FAMILY), Cilhendre (*DWB*, 182). 'ancestor of the Heylins' should be deleted.

P.C.B.

EDWARDS, CHARLES (*DWB*, 184). *N.L.W. Jnl.*, 1961, 82 indicates that he was again at Llanrhaeadr in 1660.

EDWARDS, GEORGE ROWLAND (1810-94), soldier and enlightened landowner; b. in Ness Strange, Shropshire, the elder son of John Edwards (Justice of the Peace, Deputy Lieutenant, etc.) and Charlotte, grand-daughter of the 3rd Duke of Atholl. He was educated at Donnington School, Shropshire. When he was 16 he joined the East India Company. He returned before 1837 and became secretary to Lord Clive at the time of the Chartist riots in Montgomeryshire. He became known in Montgomeryshire as 'the man in the great coat with the heavy oak stick who would go at any fence.' He returned to India in 1839 and served in the 2nd Madras Cavalry. He retired from the army as a colonel in 1862 and returned to Shropshire. He married in 1847 Catherine Jane, the daughter of Major-General Armstrong, C.B., and in 1850 he inherited his father's estate – Ness Strange and Cefnymaes, near Oswestry. He was a good landlord who believed that all of his workers should have a portion of land to cultivate. He was a strong supporter of Jesse Collings' plan – 'three acres and a cow' – and he wrote extensively on this particular subject. He died on 3 March 1894 and was buried in the graveyard of Great Ness church.

Bye-Gones, 1894, 303.

R.O.

EDWARDS, JOHN ('Siôn Treredyn'; *DWB*, 187). It is not certain that Edward Fisher was the author of the *Marrow*.

EDWARDS, MIA - see BROWN, MIA ARNESBY 1867?-1931, above in the Supplement.

EDWARDS, PETER (PERCY); ('Pedr Alaw', 1854-1934; *DWB*, 193). His degree Mus.Bac. (Toronto) was received before 1906. After emigrating and taking holy orders he entered the ministry and served the churches of Westminster and Ideal, South Dakota, Monango and Lisbon, North Dakota, Malta and Roundup, Montana, and was assistant priest at the cathedral, Helena, Montana. He composed church music and conducted choral groups. Three of his sons were known in Wisconsin as 'the Welsh boy singers'. Among his friends were Daniel Protheroe (*DWB*, 801-2) and Bransby Williams. Some of his work is in the British Library and the National Library of Wales. His *Beatitudes* (1906), a sacred cantata, was dedicated to his friend, John Owen, Bishop of St. David's (*DWB*, 714-5). By this time he had adopted the name Percy Edwards.

Information from his son, Merlin D. Edwards, Minneapolis, and Huw Williams.

E.D.J.

EDWARDS, THOMAS DAVID (*DWB*, 198). B. 15 July 1874, according to *Gol.*, 24 Feb. 1989.

H.W.

EDWARDS, WILLIAM (*DWB*, 198-9). It is not absolutely certain that the church at Groes-wen ordained its ministers in 1745 – see *DWB*, 1022 under WILLIAM, THOMAS (1717-65), where it is said that William Edwards was given some kind of ordination about this time. His name appears as William Edward on the letter in support of the ordination of exhorters which was sent to the Caeo Association. This was dated 30 March 1745 at Eglwysilan.

H.E.A.C., II, 373-4.

EDWARDS, WILLIAM (1848-1929); *DWB*, 199). After *Cyfieithiad Newydd o'r Testament Newydd* read (four vols., 1894, 1898, 1913, 1915).

EDWIN (d. 1073; *DWB*, 201). For Gwerydd read Iwerydd.

EINION OFFEIRIAD (d. 1353; *DWB*, 203). There is now firmer information on Einion Offeiriad. One of this name was a priest in Llanrug. He d. in 1349. It is possible that his knowledge of this person led Thomas Wiliems to locate the author of the grammar in Gwynedd. But J. Beverley Smith, *Bull. Board of Celtic Studies*, 20, 339-47, argues strongly that the grammarian is to be identified with the Einion Offeiriad who was found guilty of being party to the murder of Iorwerth ab Iau by Gruffudd ap Morgan ab Einion in Mabwynion or Caerwedros in 1344. In the provost accounts of the commote of Mabwynion for 1352-53 an acre of land previously held by Einion Offeiriad is recorded in the escheat lands in the king's possession, and in the chamberlain's accounts for south Wales for 1354-55 a payment is recorded for sealing a deed dated the last day of January 1354 transferring land previously held by Einion Offeiriad in the commote of Gwidigada. It may be assumed that the same Einion had held lands in Mabwynion and Gwidigada. He probably died in 1353.

B.B.C.S., 20, 339-47; 10, 151; T. Parry, *The Welsh metrical treatise attributed to Einion Offeiriad*, Brit. Acad. Sir John Rhys Lecture (1961); [R. Bromwich, 'Gwaith Einion Offeiriad a barddoniaeth Dafydd ap Gwilym', *Ysgrifau Beirniadol*, 10 (1977), 157-80; Ceri W. Lewis in A. O. H. Jarman and G.R. Hughes, eds., *A Guide to Welsh Literature*, II (1979), 58-87, 88-111, and see R. Geraint Gruffydd, *Wales's second grammarian*, Sir John Rhŷs Memorial Lecture, British Academy (1995)].

E.D.J.

ELIS GOCH (n.d.), poet; nothing is known of his life. The only examples of his poetry found in the manuscripts are moral *englynion*.

Pen. MS 122 (62).

R.L.

ELISE JOHN Y GWEHYDD (The weaver) (n.d.), poet; nothing is known of his life. He was obviously a free-verse poet and there is one example of his work in Llan. MS. 42 (57), entitled 'Cyffes Elisse John y Gwehydd'.

R.L.

ELLIOT, Sir GEORGE (1815-93), BARONET, owner and developer of coalmines; b. at Penshaw, Gateshead, co. Durham, in March or June 1815, one of the six children of Ralph Elliot, under-manager of Whitefield colliery and his wife Elizabeth (née Braithwaite). At the age of 9 he began working 14 hours a day underground. When he was 19 yrs. old he went as a promising trainee to the office of Thomas Sopwith, underground inspector at Newcastle-upon-Tyne, returning to Whitefield within six months and becoming an overman. In 1837 he was made under-manager of the Monkswearmouth colliery, Sunderland – the deepest pit in England at the time – and manager in 1839.

In 1840 he bought, in partnership, Washington mine, and in 1843 he bought his first pit on his own at Usworth, and at Whitefield in 1864. He was appointed in 1851 chief consultant and engineer in the Marquis of Londonderry's mines in the Durham coal field. After resigning *c*. 1860 he bought Kuper & Co., Gateshead, makers of industrial wires which had almost become bankrupt in 1849. He went into partnership with Richard Glass, the inventor of submarine wire insulation, to recreate the company as Glass & Elliot, or from 1864 the Telegraph Construction & Maintenance Co., the company which made the first submarine wires between Europe and America (1866), and between India and Australia.

This is when he ventured into the coalfields of south Wales. He was responsible in 1864 for forming the partnership of Englishmen and Scotsmen who bought for £365,000 all the coal mines of the late Thomas Powell of 'Y Gaer', Newport, Mon. (*DWB*, 1146), from his sons, and established the Powell Duffryn Steam Coal Co. which grew to be the largest coal company in south Wales before it was nationalised in 1947. About 16 pits in Glamorganshire and Monmouthshire belonging to the Powell family came into the hands of the new company, and Elliot lost no opportunity in extending the business and buying coalmines near Aberdare. By buying the rich coalmine and ironworks of Crawshay Bailey (*DWB*, 20-1) in that neighbourhood, Powell Duffryn seized the nucleus of the old estate of the Mathews of Aberaman, a branch of the ancient family of Radyr and Llandaff (*DWB.*, 617-8), and gentry of the district before becoming extinct in 1788. There, in their mansion (which had been renovated extensively by a previous purchaser, Anthony Bacon, II, *DWB*, 19-20), Elliot lived at intervals; and there, after his day, Powell Duffryn made their headquarters.

Powell Duffryn proceeded under the leadership of Elliot and his successors to secure more coalmines in the Aberdare valley and other mines in the Rhymney valley. The company also developed railways in the Aberdare and Rhymney valleys to promote exports, and the coke, electricity and gas works. In 1920 P.D. gained ownership of the old Rhymney Iron Company and its extensive estate, and the company bought thousands of acres in the Llantrisant area. The company's foreign business was so vast by 1914 that a branch was established in Europe, *Compagnie Française des Mines Powell Duffryn*. This growth stemmed from Elliot's foresight and energy. He was acting manager of the company, 1864-77 and 1880-88; and chairman, 1886-89. Elliotstown, Rhymney valley, was named after him, and also streets in his and his wife's memory in Aberaman. In memory of his wife he paid for a new church there in 1882-83, and endowed a new church in Whitby, Durham, in 1886.

However, he was not free from opposition. The trustees of the Marquis of Bute were reluctant to grant him everything he sought, so he took an interest in the development of Newport docks to avoid Cardiff, over which they had a hold. He was the chief promoter of the Alexandra northern dock in Newport which was opened in 1875 and which gave a foundation for the subsequent growth of the town; he obtained parliamentary authority to lay the Pontypridd, Caerphilly & Newport Railway, 1878-83, to serve him in exporting coal. He was enthusiastic about the future of the coal industry to the last. Three months before his death he published a plan for a trust to hold all the resources of the industry in Britain, with the owners holding shares but sharing the profits with the workers and an insurance fund.

Elliot was also a prominent public figure. He was M.P. (C) for Durham North, 1868-80 and 1881-85; and for Monmouth, 1886-92. He was a Tory much to Disraeli's liking and was made a baronet in 1874 for services to his party and for his 'useful life'. Both of them shared an interest in Egypt. Elliot was there in 1874 and 1875-76 planning railways and as a financial advisor to the insecure government of the Khedive. In 1878 he went officially to inspect the island of Cyprus after Turkey had yielded it to Britain. He was Deputy Lieutenant for the counties of Durham and Monmouth and a J.P. for Durham, Monmouth and Glamorgan. In 1882 he received an hon. D.C.L. of the University of Durham, and he was president of the Association of Mining Engineers. He sponsored educational establishments and the Anglican church in the north of England and south Wales, and he was a prominent figure among the Freemasons. The Prince of Wales appointed him Provincial Grand Master of the Eastern Lodge of South Wales in Aberdare in 1877.

In 1836 he m. Margaret Green (d. 1880) of Rainton, Houghton-le-Spring, Durham. He d. 23 Dec. 1893, and was buried in Houghton churchyard. They had two sons and four daughters.

Sir George Elliot was succeeded to the baronetcy by his second son, Sir George William Elliot, in 1893 (his first son had d. in 1874) and he too was a M.P. (C), 1874-95, when he d. The title then passed to his son, Sir George Elliot, the third baronet, and in 1904 to the latter's brother, Sir Charles Elliot. The title became extinct at the d. of the fourth baronet in 1911.

Three particularly significant aspects may be perceived in Elliot's career. First, by rising from the lower ranks of society to its peak through his own endeavours he represents quite strikingly the energy and confidence of the Victorian Age in the industrial field. Second, he played an especially important role in the development of the south Wales coalfield, exemplifying the change which occurred as groups of English capitalists bought the companies and coalmines from several venturous native Welshmen who had preceded them. Third, his political career as a self-made man was an excellent example of the new Tory Party which Disraeli wanted to create. It was Elliot who was chiefly responsible for reducing the hours of work of an underground worker from 12 to 9 hours a day, and he was an important intermediary between the masters and workers during the great strike of 1871 in south Wales. In 1874 he maintained that he had devoted a great part of his life to the welfare of the working class; yet, he did not wish to be seen as a M.P. for that class – 'since there were other interests to be represented'.

Durham County Advertiser, 29.12.1893; *The Durham Directory*, 1882 and 1895; *Times*, 25.12.1893; William D. Lawson, *Tyneside Celebrities* (1873); Frank H. Rushford, *Houghton-le-Spring: a history* (n.d.); *History of the Powell Duffryn Steam Coal Co.* (1914); A. P. Barnett & David Willson-Lloyd, *The South Wales Coalfield* (1921); Charles Wilkins, *The South Wales Coal Trade* (1888); Elizabeth Phillips, *Pioneers of the Welsh Coalfield* (1925); W.W. Price in *Powell Duffryn Review* (1942-43) and *Old Aberdare*, 4 (1985); R. L. Galloway, *Annals of coal mining* (1904); A. Dalziel, *The Colliers' Strike in South Wales* (1872); Arthur C. Fox-Davies, *Armorial Families* (1895); M. Stenton, *Who's who of British members of parliament* (1976).

D.L.D.

ELLIS, JOHN (1760-1839; *DWB*, 209). The hymn-tune 'Eliot' appeared under the title 'Hill Street' in *Y Dysgedydd*, Jan. 1822.

H.W.

ELLIS, RICHARD (1865-1928), librarian and bibliophile (*DWB*, 210-1); see the article, *Trans. Cymm.*, 1977, on Ellis's career and his work on Edward Lhuyd (*DWB*, 565) which corrects and supplements the original entry. Ellis was born on 27 Dec. 1865. He was educated, probably, at a private grammar school in Aberystwyth run by David Samuel (*DWB*, 903) before he entered the University College at Aberystwyth in 1889. He was awarded a scholarship to Jesus College Oxford in 1893 but, for family reasons, he did not enter the college until 1898. He was again awarded a scholarship, on the recommendation of R.L. Poole, in 1899. He graduated B.A. in 1902 and M.A. in 1908. At Oxford, he began to work on the manuscripts and letters of Edward Lhuyd with the intention of publishing these papers. In 1908, he was appointed, in succession to J. Glyn Davies, the Welsh Librarian at the University College, Aberystwyth and he moved to the National Library when it opened in 1909. But he was not happy there and he returned to Oxford with a research scholarship in 1912. From 1916 to the end of World War I, he was the only assistant librarian at the Codrington Library in All Souls College. Early in the 1920s, Ellis returned to Aberystwyth. He spent a few weeks during 1927 in Dublin where he pursued his research on Lhuyd. For the same reason, he went to Oxford in July 1928 and there he died. In 1903, Ellis published his *Facsimiles of Letters of Oxford Welshmen* on Whatman paper. In addition to the facsimile 'broadside' published in 1904, he published another facsimile in 1907 – *Carol o gyngor yn galennig i'r Cymru 1658 Mathew Owen*. A selection of his English verse is published in the article cited above.

E.D.J.

ELLIS-GRIFFITH, Sir ELLIS JONES (*DWB*, 215). B. 23 May 1860. See his biography by T.I. Ellis, 1969.

EVANS (FAMILY of physicians). See under EVANS, WILLIAM (1735-1805), *DWB*, 256-7), and EVANS, WILLIAM (1734-1805) below.

EVANS, DAVID (*fl.* 1710?-45?), an early Independent minister in the Welsh Tract, etc. Pennsylvania, and author. Although it is not certain that he was born in Wales – some authorities say that he was a son of the Rev. William Evans, Pencader, Carms., who emigrated to America – he deserves notice as one of the earliest Welsh authors in America. At least three books by him were published, (a) *A Help for parents and Heads of families ... by David Evans, a Labourer in the Gospel at Tredyffren in Pennsylvania* (Philadelphia, B. Franklin, 1732); (b) *The Minister of Christ and his Flock* ...(Philadelphia, B. Franklin, 1732); and (c) *Law and Gospel, or Man wholly ruined by the Law and Recovered only by the Gospel. Being the Substance of some Sermons preached at Tredyffren in Pennsylvania ... 1734 and again at Piles-Grove in New Jersey in ... 1742* (Philadelphia, B. Franklin and D. Hall, 1748). He ministered to the church of Pencader, Pennsylvania, for seven years.

Y Cenhadwr Americanaidd, December 1878; *The Cambrian*, 1882, 118-9.

R.O.

EVANS, DAVID CLEDLYN (1858-1940), schoolmaster, geologist, antiquary; b. in Llanwenog, Cards. in 1858. At the age of 11 he was apprenticed to a stonemason but about five years later he prepared himself for the teaching profession. In 1876 he commenced teaching at Gwernogle, Carms., eventually becoming headmaster of St. Clears Council School (1889-1923) after short periods at Cwrtnewydd, Llwynrhydowen, Llandysul, Trefilan and Llanddowror. He taught both vocal and instrumental music, was a violinist, organist and choirmaster, adjudicated at *eisteddfodau* and was a gifted antiquarian and geologist. His notable paper on 'The Ordovician rocks of western Carmarthenshire' which he read before the Geological Society was published in *The Quarterly Jnl. of the Geological Soc.*, 1906. It included a coloured map of the area, several section-diagrams and a two-page list of fossils discovered in the Bala-limestone of Robeston Wathen and Sholeshook. He later examined the geology of the area from Brechfa to Glog and Llanybydder to Llangrannog, and discovered that the stones at Stonehenge were identical with those found on the Prescelly hills. On his map of the area he was able to delineate the boundary between Ordovician and Silurian rocks and although he did not complete his own account of this work, he allowed this important line of transition to be copied on to the geological survey map. He was elected Fellow of the Geographical Society and awarded an M.Sc. degree by the University of Wales in recognition of his work.

His wife d. *c.*1924; they had five children. He d. 11 June 1940 and was buried in Bethlehem cemetery, St. Clears.

Carms. Antiquary, 1941, 11-20; *Carm. Jnl.*, 21 June 1940, 8.

M.A.J.

EVANS, DAVID EMLYN (*DWB*, 226-7), son of Evan Evans (1817-1902) and his wife Mary (1816-84) both of whom were buried in the old cemetery at Tre-wen, Cwm-cou. Evan Evans's mother (née Peregryn) was of Huguenot stock and descended from the Francis family of Dinas Ceri and Cwmsylltyn and was a relative of Enoch Francis (1688/9-1740; *DWB*, 269-70); his father fought in the battle against the French at Fishguard in 1797, and the sword which he used was kept near the fireplace in the living-room at Brynderwen, Newcastle Emlyn, and subsequently used by Evan Evans when he took part in the Rebecca Riots. Evan Evans, a foreman in the Cyfarthfa steel works, used to frequent sales in old houses and farmhouses and built up a good library.

E.P.E.

EVANS, DAVID LEWIS MOSES – see MOSES-EVANS, DAVID LEWIS below.

EVANS, EDMUND (1791-1864), Wesleyan preacher; b. 9 July, 1791 at Aberdeunant, Llandecwyn, Mer. After lengthy consideration he became a member of the Wesleyan society in December 1815, was made an elder in April 1816 and started to preach in February 1818. He soon became a popular and influential preacher and was known as *Utgorn Meirion* (the clarion of Meirion). He refused an invitation to minister to the old cause of Cilgwyn (1837) choosing to remain a Wesleyan lay preacher. For some periods he was a stipended lay preacher on various circuits, collecting towards clearing the debt on chapels, and a peripatetic evangelist under the aegis of the North Wales regional meeting. He published articles in *Yr Eurgrawn Wesleyaidd* and edited a volume of sermons, *Dwfr y Bywyd* (*c.* 1855). He d. 9 October, 1864.

N.L.W. MS. 3505; *Yr Eurgrawn*, 1870, passim; 1871, passim; *Bathafarn*, i, 40-52; iii, 59.

G.T.Ro.

EVANS, EDWARD (b. 1582) theologian; a son of a cleric, born and educated at Llanrwst, Denbs., he entered Christ Church, Oxford, in 1598 at the age of sixteen. He graduated B.A., 16 February 1603-4 and M.A., 1606-7. Anthony Wood mistakes him for another cleric of the same name, also the son of a cleric but from Hampshire and a famous preacher in the University who published a book of sermons in 1615, *Verba Dierum or the Dayes report of God's glory ...*

DNB; Wood, *Athenae*, ii, 168; *Fasti*, i, 299, 307; Foster, *Alumni Oxon.*

W.T.M.

EVANS, EVAN (EVANDER) WILLIAM (1827?-74; *DWB*, 234). He is sometimes known as Evander William Evans. He was b. in Llangyfelach, s. of William and Catherine (née Howell) Evans. He studied theology in New Haven after graduating, and was principal of Delaware Institute, Franklin, New York, for a year. He left Marietta College in 1864 on account of his health and in order to improve his circumstances. He was very successful in the oil industry in West Virginia.

Bangor MSS 25616, 36485.

Ll.G.C.

EVANS, EVAN HERBER (*DWB*, 233). He was appointed principal of Bala-Bangor College in succession to Thomas Lewis (1837-92; *DWB*, 561-2) in 1892, not 1891. He had been reluctant to accept the principalship and after realising that he could not maintain both posts he relinquished his pastoral care of Salem, Caernarfon. He commenced his duties at Bangor in Jan. 1893, and delivered his valedictory sermon at Salem on 25 Feb. 1894.

EVANS, GRIFFITH (1835-1935; *DWB*, 235). His wife was the grand-daughter of Owen Jones of Gelli (1787-1828; *DWB*, 499).

EVANS, Sir GRIFFITH HUMPHREY PUGH (*DWB*, 235). He was a cousin of Griffith Evans above.

EVANS, JOHN (*c.*1680-1730; *DWB*, 240). His mother was the daughter of Colonel Gilbert Gerard (see *DWB*, 777, last two lines).

EVANS, JOHN, of Bala (1723-1817; *DWB*, 241). See a fuller discussion by G.T. in *Cylch. Cymd. Hanes M.C.*, 1961, 26-35, 53-60, and Goronwy Prys Owen, *Atgofion John Evans y Bala* (1997).

EVANS, JOHN (1768-*c.*1812; *DWB*, 242). Amend the volume number from xviii to xvii in the last line and in the bibliography.

EVANS, JOHN (1796-1861; *DWB*, 243-4). Among his pupils were Lewis Edwards (*DWB*, 191), Henry Richard (*DWB*, 849), David Charles Davies (*DWB*, 117) and Ieuan Gwyllt (John Roberts, *DWB*, 868-9). When Lewis Edwards kept a school in Aberystwyth he did not consider it to be in competition with but, rather, preparatory to Evans' school.

J.H. Davies, *Cymru*, 44 (1913), 45; D. Samuel, *Cymru*, 21 (1901), 191.

Ll.G.C.

EVANS, JOHN (1815-91; *DWB*, 244). His mother was a descendant of Edmwnd Prys, and his wife Mary, of Saethon, was a cousin of David Williams the M.P. (Letter from his grandson, the Rev. C. Beverly Davies, Hammersmith.)

EVANS, JOHN CASTELL (not 1845, 1844-1909; *DWB*, 1119), science teacher; b. 20 July 1844. He took a great interest in the traditions of his native area as indicated by three of his manuscript books which survive. He was a pupil and pupil-teacher at Bala British school, and he is said to have taught at Corwen school. From 1864 he was a schoolteacher at Devonport, where he m., in 1868, Jessie, daughter of William Henry Beal, and kept school on his own account. By 1871 he was at Harrogate. This narrow life thwarted his ambitions and he went to London and entered the Royal College of Chemistry. He studied the provision of technical education in Germany and he later took charge of chemical training in metalurgy [at the City and Guilds Technical College?]. He used ore which he himself had collected in Patagonia. Besides being an active officer among the Baptists, he also took up preaching. The title of one of his works should be corrected to *Physico-Chemical Tables* (1902).

N.L.W. MSS. 10567-8, [20,547C] and J. M. Rhys, 1 [MSS. 16653B ?]; *N.L.W. Journal*, xiv, i; [*Chronicl yr Ysgol Sabbothol*, 1881, 216; J. V. Eyre, *Henry Edward Armstrong*, 1958, 73-4, 286-7; information from Iolo Francis Roberts].

T.R., E.D.J.

EVANS, JOHN THOMAS ('Tomos ap Titus', 1869-1940) – see under WADE-EVANS, ARTHUR WADE (1875-1964) above.

EVANS, JOHN RHAIADORE (1790?-1850?); surgeon; b. in Glantanat Isaf, Llanrhaeadr-ym-Mochnant, and educated at Oswestry Grammar School. He was tutored by Hugh Roberts, a surgeon at Llanfyllin and then became Sir Benjamin Brodie's pupil. He became the chief medical officer of Bangor Hospital and subsequently a lecturer in surgery and one of the medical officers of the Middlesex Hospital and the Royal Metropolitan Infirmary. He was the author of a number of medical papers, e.g. *On the Remedial Evils attending the Life of the People; On Irritation of the Spinal Nerves; The remediable Influence of Oxygen on Vital Air.*

R. Williams, *Mont. Worthies.*

E.E.

EVANS, JONAH (1836-96), preparatory school tutor, and minister (Congl.); b. 7 Feb. 1836 in Llanfihangel, Carms. He enjoyed very few privileges early in life, and was a farm servant for years. He attended Carmarthen College, 1859-61, and opened a preparatory school at Llanybydder in 1861, before moving it to Llansawel under the name 'Sawel Academy'. He prepared students for the ministry and other callings. He was a prominent leader in establishing the Congregational church at Llansawel, and was ord. as minister there in 1870. He served the churches on Sundays, and lectured on 'Agriculture' throughout the country. He wrote *Cofiant Evan Jones, Crugybar, 1804-78* (Llandeilo, 1883), and *Y Berllan Ddiwinyddol*. He d. 31 March 1896.

Asaph; NLW MSS. 9257, 10326; *Not. W.*

J.D.O.

EVANS, LEWIS (*c.* 1700-56), cartographer; believed to have been b. in the parish of Llangwnnadl, Caerns. He became a land surveyor in Pennsylvania. In 1749 he published *A Map of Pensilvania, New Jersey, New York and the three Delaware counties*, including notes on thunder and lightning (revised ed. 1752). His most notable map is *A General Map of the Middle British Colonies in America* (1755); boundary disputes were decided on its authority and much use was made of it during the Seven Years War. In the *Analysis* which was published with the map the author expressed his opinion on the French claim to land which led to severe criticism in an anonymous article in *The New York Mercury*, 5 Jan. 1756, to which Evans responded within five days by publishing a second treatise. He had intended publishing maps of all the separate states, but he d. 12 June 1756 before completing the task; he was at the time in custody in New York on a charge of libel against the governor Robert Hunter Morris. His map was used unacknowledged many times between 1755 and 1814 by London map publishers. In 1776 it was published in America by Thomas Pownall with his *Topographical Description of North America* to aid Evans' family which was in straightened circumstances.

[He m. in 1743 Martha Hoskins (d. *c.* 1746) at Christ Church, Philadelphia and they had a daughter, Amelia (and possibly other children).]

Henry N. Stevens, *Lewis Evans his map of the Middle British Colonies in America* ... (2nd ed. 1920); *Dict. of American Biog.* (1931; amend his place of birth); C.A.W. Pownall, *Thomas Pownall* (1908); P.L. Phillips, *A list of Geographical Atlases in the Library of Congress* (1909-20); *Cat. of Printed Maps, Plans and Charts in the British Museum* (1885); [Lawrence Henry Gipson, *Lewis Evans* (1939); *Gwreiddiau Gwynedd*, Apr. 1987; *Casglwr*, 34, Mar. 1988].

M.G.L.

EVANS (née FRANCIS), MARY JANE ('Llaethferch'; 1888-1922), elocutionist; b. 3 Feb. 1888, in a house at Reed Row, Godre'r Graig, Swansea Valley, the daughter of Charles Francis, conductor of Ystalyfera Band, and his wife, Mary Ann Hutchings. Both Charles Francis and his father, George Francis, who came to Ystalyfera from the Caerleon district, Mon., were able musicians. The parents of Thomas Hutchings, Mary Ann's father and also a musician, came from Bristol to run a school in Swansea; after the father's death, the mother took charge of the 'College' School near Ystradgynlais. After travelling in many countries, Thomas Hutchings moved to Ystalyfera where he worked in the tinplate works. Through her mother, his wife was also from a musical family, the Anthonys of Cwmaman. Hutchings and his wife both worked, as children, in the tinplate works. When Mary Jane was five years old, her family moved to live with her mother's parents at Cwmtawe Villa where they kept a few cows and sold milk. The little girl carried two pitchers of milk to customers on her way to Panteg School because, at this time, her father worked at the Ynysmeudwy tinplate works. For this reason, she later took the name, 'Llaethferch' (Milkmaid). Despite a musical education given by local teachers, she showed little inclination for playing a musical instrument. William Asaph Williams gave her singing lessons but this again did not interest her because of her great love was reading and literature. She took part in recitation competitions and also participated in the quarterly meetings of the Sunday schools in the Panteg area. During the Revival of 1904-05, she was received as a member of Panteg Congregational church; she was among those members released in 1905 to establish a church in Godre'r Graig. On the initiative of her minister, Ben Davies (1864-1937; *DWB*, 110), she took lessons in recitation with David Thomas Jones. Mary Jane now began to recite at literary meetings and at *eisteddfodau*; she became famous as 'Llaethferch' and won many chairs and cups. In April 1909, she entered the Old College School, Carmarthen run by Joseph Harry (see above); in order to meet the fees, her family sold the cows. She was placed in a class of talented students and a special course on literature was arranged for her. Mary Jane preached for the first time at Godre'r Graig on

8 July 1909; she usually included a recitation with the sermon. In 1912, she took an examination in elocution and obtained the grade of A.E.V.C.M. at the Victoria College of Music. For a time, she taught at Tro'rglien School, Cwmtwrch, and attended the Royal Academy of Music in London for two terms in order to perfect her English, but lack of money cut this course short in Jan. 1916. She discovered an interest in drama and formed a drama company at Ynysmeudwy. She performed with Gunstone Jones and Gwernydd Morgan and also performed with her own company in *Gruffydd o'r Glyn* by Alarch Ogwy. Her delight in recitation competitions hindered her from rehearsing with the company. She turned to presenting dramatic recitations on her own or with a soloist so that she could obtain a respite and the audience given some variety. These recitations were very popular both in Wales and in parts of England between 1918 and 1922. The programmes contained rich and varied material both in English and Welsh. Her most popular piece in Welsh was 'Cadair Tregaron' by J.J. Williams (see above). In 1921, her writing paper described Mary Janes Evans as the winner of a crown, 11 cups, 68 chairs and 396 other prizes at *eisteddfodau*. She achieved little success as a reciter at the National *Eisteddfod*; she was given an award at Swansea in 1907 and acted as an adjudicator at Barry in 1920 and Corwen in 1921. She considered extending her tours to London, America and Japan but four years of performing throughout Wales proved too much for a constitution which was not strong. Mary Jane Evans d. on 25 Feb. 1922 at her home in School Street, Maerdy, Rhondda. Her body was carried to her parents' home at Wigfa near Ynysmeudwy on the following Thursday and she was buried in the graveyard at Godre'r Graig on Saturday, 4 Mar. For a period of less than four years, she appeared like a shooting star over the halls and chapels of Wales where she delighted many audiences and became, for that short period, the most famous woman in Wales.

Without telling her parents, she m. William David Evans on 5 Mar. 1919; he was a teacher in the Maerdy elementary school and had been discharged from the Army, suffering from the effects of poison gas at Ypres. A *penillion* singer to the accompaniment of the harp, he won prizes at the National *Eisteddfod*. He was the conductor of the Maerdy United Choir.

Ben Davies (ed.), *Llaethferch. Er Cof*, 1923.

E.D.J.

EVANS, THOMAS CHRISTOPHER ('Cadrawd'; *DWB*, 253-4). There are extensive collections of his MSS. dispersed between the N.L.W., the Cardiff Central Library and the Museum of Welsh Life, St. Fagans. See Brynley [F.] Roberts, *Cadrawd: Arloeswr Llên Gwerin*, being the Henry Lewis Memorial Lecture delivered at the University of Wales, Swansea, 1996.

A.Ll.H.

EVANS, WILLIAM (1734-1805; not 1735-1805; *DWB*, 256-7). He was baptised 31 Nov. 1734.

EVANS, WILLIAM DAVIES (1790-1872), inventor of a chess gambit; eldest son of John Evans, of the parish of St. Dogmaels and Mary Davis of the parish of Nevern, who, according to the parish records of Nevern, were married on 12 April 1787. They started life at the farm of Musland, St. Dogmael's. William Davies Evans was born on 27 January 1790.

It is almost certain that young Evans was educated at Haverfordwest Grammar School. Unfortunately the school records have been destroyed. In 1804 he went to sea and served in the navy until the Napoleonic wars ended in 1815. Transferred to the postal department, in 1819, he was the captain of a sailing packet, the *Auckland*, running between Milford Haven and Waterford. During this period he played a great deal of chess with a distinguished chess-player, Lieut. Harry Wilson, R.N. It was about 1824, in a steam postal packet, that he invented a game opening that is known the world over and in all the game's literature as 'The Evans Gambit'.

About 1826 Evans created a sensation in the chess world by introducing his opening in a famous game in London when he defeated Alexander McDonnell, the strongest player that Ireland ever produced.

In January 1840 Evans retired on a pension and spent his time at London chess clubs and travelling abroad. He died on 3 August 1872 at 29, Rue Christine, Ostend, Belgium, and is buried in the old cemetery in the town. The inscription on his gravestone reads: 'To the sacred memory of William Davies Evans, formerly Commander in the Post Office and Oriental Steam Services; Superintendent in the Royal Mail Steam Company, and inventor of the system of tri-coloured light for shipping. Also well known in the chess world as the author of the Evans' Gambit.'

Unfortunately, his age is wrongly given as 'eighty years and six months'.

Personal research and researches of W.R. Thomas, *British Chess Magazine*, 1928.

D.J.M.

EVANS, WILLIAM MEIRION (*DWB*, 259). He was buried in 'The Old Cemetery' in Ballarat.

C.G.

FOULKES, HENRY POWELL (1815-86), cleric and author; b. 2 January 1815 at Stanstead Bury, Herts., the second son of John Powell and Caroline Mary Foulkes. He was educated at King's School, Chester, Shrewsbury and Balliol College, Oxford, where he graduated B.A. 1837 and M.A. 1840. He was ordained deacon in June, 1839 with a title to the curacy of Halkin, Flintshire and in July of the same year he was ordained priest. He was given the living of Llandyssil, Mont. in 1857 and he was made Archdeacon of Montgomery in 1861, an office that carried with it a canonry in the cathedral. He was presented to the living of Whittington, Shropshire in 1879 and he stayed there until his death. He married Jane Margaret, the daughter of Edward Lloyd, Rhagad and they had one daughter who died when she was 14.

He was the author of several handbooks for use in Sunday schools. He read a paper on the history of the Church in Wales at the Church Conference in Leeds in 1872. He d. January 26, 1886 and was buried in St. Asaph cathedral.

Ceitho; Asaph; Enw. F; Thomas, *St. Asaph*; Foster, *Alumni Oxon; Bye-Gones*, 1886; S. Asaph diocesan records; N.L.W. MS. 9257.

G.M.G

FOULKES, HUMPHREY (*DWB*, 267). He d. 1737.

FOULKES, THOMAS (*DWB*, 268). His third wife Lydia was the daughter of Simon Lloyd; she was the sister of Simon Lloyd (1756-1836; *DWB*, 588).

FOXWIST, WILLIAM (*DWB*, 269). The will of William Foxwist, St. Albans, dated 1673, was proved that year. It is misleading to suggest that he d. soon after 1660.

G.H.W.

FRANCIS, MARY JANE – see EVANS, MARY JANE above in the Supplement.

GAMBOLD, (FAMILY; *DWB*, 273-4). Further information about this family has made necessary a revised entry. Changes are shown within square brackets.

[The name 'Gambold' (found in other parts of Britain) appears in the parish of St. Dogmaels, very early; it should be noted that part of the parish, which lies geographically in Pembs., belongs to the borough of Cardigan, across the river Teifi. A WILLIAM GAMBOLD was living in Cardigan in 1653 and was a member of the Court Leet. He appears to have had a son Hector, who in turn is believed (though the matter is not wholly clear) to have had two sons, TIMOTHY and WILLIAM (the grammarian below): Timothy had a son DAVID who died in 1761. David's descendants were his dau. ANNE who m. Benjamin Millingchamp, d. 1784, Comptroller of the Customs at Cardigan (see Benjamin Millingchamp, *DWB*, 633); and this branch of the Gambold family is henceforth associated with that post. WILLIAM, David's son, a freeholder in Cardigan (*West Wales Records*, III, 77, under 1760), was a naval purser. He lived in Beaumaris and this is why his name appears in the letters of the Morris brothers of Anglesey (Lewis, Richard, William, *DWB*, 661-62, 663-64, 666-67) and his exploits in skirmishes with smugglers in Anglesey and elsewhere are narrated. There can be little doubt that it was he who sheltered Lewis Morris in 1758 on his release from Cardigan jail. He was later captain of the customs-cutter *Pelham*. There are references in the *Morris Letters* – see the Index by Hugh Owen – and frequently in the Holyhead and London customs records to a GEORGE, himself a captain, perhaps an elder brother to William].

The eldest son of Hector Gambold above was WILLIAM GAMBOLD, the grammarian (1672-1728), a burgess of Cardigan in virtue of his ownership of the Nag's Head tavern. His son John states that he was born 10 Aug. 1672 'of reputable parents who gave him a good education to prepare him for orders in the Church' – but Foster, *Alumni Oxon.*, notes him as *pauper puer* and son of WILLIAM Gambold of Cardigan; [there is some confusion in the records of his first college, St. Mary Hall (now kept in Oriel College): there he is referred to as the son of 'William or Hector' and aged '18 or

20' when he matriculated there 26 May 1693.] He migrated to Exeter College (1694) but there is no record that he graduated. He was a friend of Edward Lhuyd (*DWB*, 565-67) who says that he provided him with additions for his notes to the Gibson ed. of Camden's *Brittania* (1695). He became rector of Puncheston with Llanychaer 1 Dec. 1709 (*West Wales Historical Records*, II, 226 and III, 250) but it would seem that he had been there previously, perhaps as curate, for in Nov. 1707 he was keeping school at Llanychaer. As early as 1707 Gambold was planning a Welsh dictionary, and this became his main occupation when an accident later disabled him from parochial work. It was finished in 1722 but Gambold failed to get money to publish it. In the *Morris Letters* (I, 114; II, 150, 233) there are references to Bishop Gambold trying to sell the MS. to the lexicographer Thomas Richards of Coychurch (1710-90; *DWB*, 854) – the Morrises characteristically tended to disparage the work. About 1770 the MS. came into the possession of another lexicographer, John Walters (1721-97; *DWB*, 1011-12) and it is now at the National Library. William Gambold published *A Grammar of the Welsh Language* in 1727, reprinted after his death in 1817 and several times afterwards. He d. 13 Sept. 1728.

[William Gambold's wife was Elizabeth; it is said that she was of the neighbouring parish of Letterston but her surname is not known.] The most celebrated of their 5 children was JOHN GAMBOLD (1711-71), Moravian bishop, b. 10 April 1711 in Puncheston. His career touches Wales only at intervals and it is reported fully by Alexander Gordon in *D.N.B.*; here the Welsh side of his life may be dealt with. He matriculated 10 Oct. 1726 from Christ Church where he came to know Charles Wesley and became one of the 'Oxford Methodists'. He graduated in 1730, was ordained in 1733 and appointed vicar of Stanton Harcourt, near Oxford; but in 1739 he met Zinzendorf and became increasingly drawn to Moravianism. He resigned his living in 1742, m. Elizabeth Walker in 1743 and returned to Pembrokeshire to keep school in Market Street, Haverfordwest (see *Cymm.*, 45, 28); but in 1744 he went to London and formally joined the Moravians – he became a bishop in 1753. Richard Morris had contacts with him in London (*Morris Letters*, II, 140-1, 221) and even his amused cynicism cannot help noting how the bishop 'despises riches, having thrown up a good living to take up his present way of life, where he has no income at all, and delights in appearing poor and slovenly' – his brother Lewis (ibid. II, 224) comments; 'such were the bishops of the primitive times'. In 1768 Gambold's health broke down, and he returned as pastor to the Moravian congregation at Haverfordwest where he d. 13 Sept. 1771 and was b. in the graveyard behind the chapel, [now closed].

Over and above his mission work Gambold was a considerable Greek and Patristic scholar. His theology was 'quietist' and mystical. He had not forgotten his native language. In 1760 he revised and saw through the press *Un Ymadrodd ar Bumtheg ynghylch Iesu Grist*, a translation of Zinzendorf's 'Berlin Discourses' by Evan Williams (1724-58; *DWB*, 1037); and in 1770 he published a Welsh Moravian hymn book, *Ychydig Hymnau allan o Lyfr Hymnau Cynulleidfaoedd y Brodyr* (*Cymm.*, 45, 112) –

three of the hymns were taken from Vicar Prichard (*DWB*, 795-6), the other 34 were Gambold's own versions of English Moravian hymns; it must be confessed that they are rather stiff.

[The order of the names of John Gambold's brothers in the original art. is faulty: see now *Journal of the Hist. Soc. Presb. Church of Wales*, Sept., 1961, for a more correct account based on their father's will. John was the eldest, b. 1711, followed by WILLIAM, see below, b. 1712 or 1713; HECTOR, b. in Puncheston, 1714, he emigrated to USA in 1742 and d. in Pennsylvania in 1788; GEORGE, see below; and a daughter MARTHA].

William never left the Methodist movement. He began to exhort in 1766; he travelled in north Wales (*Meth. Cymru*, II, 304) and he was a great friend of Howel Davies (*Journal of the Hist. Soc. of Presb. Church of Wales*, 4, 55; *DWB*, 127). Nevertheless, he was on the friendliest terms with the Moravians and interesting reminiscences of his about the religious history of Pembrokeshire have been preserved in a MS. formerly in the Moravian archives at Haverfordwest (see nos. 1 and 2, *Journal of the Hist. Soc. of the Presb. Church in Wales*, 4). He was farming near Llawhaden in 1770 and was alive in 1794. George d. in 1755. He too was, for a while, a Methodist. There is a letter from him to Howel Harris (*DWB*, 339-40) (T.L. 1256, Dec. 1744), and in 1748 he was an exhorter. He continued his brother's school at Haverfordwest and in turn he too became a Moravian, founding with John Sparks (*DWB*, 920) the society which was in 1763 to become the Moravian congregation at Haverfordwest.

References given in the text and the art. on John Gambold in *D.N.B.*; information from Mr. Jack Gambold, Indiana, one of the descendants of Hector, brother of the bishop; from the late Miss Lucy Williams, Holyhead; from Mrs. Dorothy Thompson (née Gambold), Leeds; from C.V. Appleton, Cardiff; and from Gen. R.S. Lewis, Rhaeadr.

R.T.J.

GLASCOED, see HUGHES, OWEN below.

GLYNNE, FAMILY of Hawarden (*DWB*, 281). John Glynne lived 1602-66.

GOUGE, THOMAS (*DWB*, 284-5). In the bibliograpy read A.G. Matthews not Mathews.

GOUGH (GOCH), MATHEW (MATHAU) (*c.* 1390-1450; *DWB*, 285). He was b. *c.* 1390. He was buried in the choir of S. Mary's of the Carmelite Friars in London. See further the article by Ynyr Probert in *Trans. Cymm.*, 1961, Pt. II, 34-44.

GRENFELL (FAMILY) Swansea industrialists, who originated from St. Just in Cornwall. They were related, through intermarriage with the St. Leger family, to Sir Richard Grenville of the *Revenge* and Richard de Granville, the founder of Neath Abbey. Sir Richard, a direct descendant of Richard de Granville (*Visitations of the County of Cornwall*, ed. J.L. Vivian), married Mary, daughter of Sir John St. Leger. PASCOE GRENFELL (1761-1838) married, as his 2nd wife, Georgina St. Leger, daughter of the 1st Viscount

Doneraile (of the 2nd creation), in 1798. Charles Kingsley, another relation by marriage, first traced the connection. The family were already prosperous merchants and bankers in the eighteenth century. In 1803 Pascoe Grenfell entered into a contract with Owen Williams to trade in copper and developed a business in London, Liverpool, Swansea and Flintshire. The firm of Pascoe Grenfell and Sons was founded in the 1820s. They owned the Middle and Upper Bank Copper Works in the Lower Swansea Valley and at their height employed 800 men. They ran a line of ships between Swansea and their Flintshire works on the River Dee. The Swansea works were sold to the neighbouring firm of Williams, Foster and Co. in 1892.

PASCOE ST. LEGER GRENFELL (1798-1879) Deputy Lieutenant, J.P., the eldest son of Pascoe and Georgina, came to live in Swansea in the 1840s and built Maesteg House at the foot of Kilvey Hill. He married, 1st in 1824, Catherine Ann Du Pre, the eldest daughter of James Du Pre of Wilton Park in Buckinghamshire and the grand-daughter of Josias Du Pre, Governor of Madras, and 2nd in 1847, Penelope Frances Madan, daughter of the Dean of Chichester. He was an active humanitarian who built model (by the standards of the times) houses for his workers, founded All Saints Church, Kilvey, and supervised the school taught by Richard Gwynne (see GWYNNE (family) above). He was chairman of the Harbour Trust and active in the development of Swansea docks. By his first wife he had four sons and five daughters: Madelina Georgina (1826-1903), Pascoe Du Pre (1828-1896), St. Leger Murray (1830-60), Arthur Riversdale (1831-1895), Gertrude Fanny (1834-1880), Elizabeth Mary (1836-94), Francis Wallace (1841-1925), Katherine Charlotte (1843-1906), Eleanor Catherine (1845-1928). MADELINA married Griffith Llewellyn (1802-88) at Baglan Hall in 1850. Llewellyn became rich from coal interests in the Rhondda and Madelina spent large sums on charity. She was responsible for the building of St. Catherine's Church, Baglan, and St. Peter's Church, Pentre, the restoration of St. Mary's Church, Aberafan, and the endowment of the Llewellyn Alms Houses at Neath and of Swansea Eye Hospital. (ELIZABETH) MARY was long remembered in Swansea for her public service. She trained as a nurse, intending to serve in the Franco-Prussian war, but returned to Swansea instead and devotedly nursed the poor. Contemporary newspapers said that 10,000 people spontaneously attended her funeral at Danygraig Cemetery in 1894. She was responsible for the foundation of St. Thomas Church in Swansea East, where a stained glass window is dedicated to her memory.

It was the 4th son, FRANCIS WALLACE, later Field Marshall Lord GRENFELL of Kilvey, who achieved national fame: P.C., K.C.B. 1886, G.C.M.G. 1892, G.C.B. 1898, LL.D. Edinburgh 1902, LL.D. Cambridge, 1903, and F.S.A. He was b. in London 29 April 1841 (the DNB is in error on this point) but spent his childhood at Maesteg House, educated at Milton Abbas School, Dorset, entered 60th Rifles (later the King's Royal Rifle Corps) in 1859 and served in Ireland during the Fenian troubles in the 1860s and subsequently in Malta, Canada and India. He went to South Africa in 1873 as A.D.C. to

General Sir Arthur Cunynghame. In 1875 he took part in the expedition which claimed Griqualand West (the site of the Kimberley diamond fields) for Britain and was one of the small party who recovered the body of the Prince Imperial, the only son of Napolean III, who was killed in a skirmish while serving with the British forces during the Zulu War of 1879. He took part in the British occupation of Egypt in 1882 and in April 1885 succeeded Sir Evelyn Wood as Sirdar (Commander-in-Chief) of the Egyptian army which had to be totally rebuilt after the events of 1882. He fought the Mahdi and his successor, the Khalifa, in several battles. The flag he captured in the battle of Toski in 1889 is in St. Peter's Church, Pentre. It was Grenfell's reconstituted Egyptian army which fought under Kitchener at the Battle of Omdurman in 1898. Grenfell, who had left Egypt for a War Office appointment in 1892, was back in Egypt in 1898 but was careful not to cramp the style of the famous Kitchener, whom he outranked. Grenfell was a keen amateur archaeologist and initiated important excavations at Aswan. Some of his finds are in Swansea Museum. From Egypt he went to Malta as Governor, 1899-1903, and to Ireland as Commander-in-Chief, 1904-08. There he had to deal with serious rioting in Belfast. He represented the British army at the coronation of the last Tsar, Nicholas II, in 1896 and wrote a book, *Three Weeks in Moscow*, about his experiences. He was raised to the peerage as Baron Grenfell of Kilvey in 1902 and made a Field Marshal in 1908. His later years were devoted to the Royal Horticultural Society, of which he was President, and the Church Lads Brigade. He continued to take an interest in Swansea and became a freeman of the town in 1889. He married 1st in 1887, Evelyn Wood, daughter of General Blucher Wood, who d. childless in 1899, and 2nd in 1903, Margaret Majendie, daughter of Lewis Ashunt Majendie, M.P. They had two sons and a daughter. His elder son, Pascoe (1905-1976), succeeded to the title on his father's death on 27 January 1925. He was buried at Beaconsfield, Buckinghamshire, after a large funeral at which the royal family was represented.

The last Grenfell to live at Maesteg House was KATHERINE (KATE), the daughter of St. Leger Murray Grenfell; she ran a school there. The house was demolished soon after World War I to make way for the Grenfell Park housing estate.

Two grandsons of Pascoe St. Leger, the youngest (twin) sons of his eldest son, Pascoe Du Pre, Francis (1880-1915), who won the V.C., and Riversdale (1880-1914) were killed in France and were the subject of a biography by John Buchan. The famous war-poet, Julian Grenfell (1888-1915), the son of Lord Desborough, the Olympic athlete, was a cousin. The twins and other members of the family are commemorated in All Saints Church, Kilvey.

Memoirs of Field-Marshall Lord Grenfell, 1925; Burke; *Cambrian*, 4 April 1879, 16, 23 March 1894, 15 June 1894; *Times*, 28 January, 2 February 1925; *DNB Supplement*, *1922-30*; Grenfell Papers, Swansea University College Library; Llewellyn Papers, Glamorgan Record Office, Cardiff; [Muriel E. Chamberlain, 'The Grenfells of Kilvey', *Glam. Hist.*, 9, 123-42].

M.E.C.

GREY, THOMAS (*DWB*, 287-8). He was granted a licence as a nonconformist preacher by the Cardiganshire court of quarter sessions on 30 July 1762. In the bibliography read Congregational Fund Board.

GRIFFITH, FAMILY of Carreg-lwyd (*DWB*, 288). William Griffith d. 1587 aged 71. Read *c*. 1516-87 as in the last paragraph in the article on Edmund Griffith (*DWB*, 291). John Griffith was alive on 10 June 1608. Delete 'christened'.

GRIFFITH, FAMILY of Cefn Amwlch (*DWB*, 288-9). John Griffith I was Sheriff of Caernarfon in 1604 and 1618, and M.P for the county from 1604 to (?) 1611; he d. before March 1628 – see M.F. Keeler, *The Long Parliament, 1640-1*, 197-8.
E.G.J.

GRIFFITH, ALEXANDER (*DWB*, 289-90). Read *Vavasoris Examen et Purgamen*. The last item in the bibliography should read: Salt MS. (Stafford) 2112 (393-6).

GRIFFITH, ELIZABETH (*DWB*, 292). See also J.M.S. Tomkins, *The Polite Marriage* (Camb. Univ. Press, 1938).

GRIFFITH, JOHN (fl. 1548-87; *DWB*, 293). Instead of Mary read Elizabeth as under William Aubrey (alias Awbrey; *c*. 1529-95; *DWB*, 17).

GRIFFITH, ROBERT (1847-1911; *DWB*, 298-9). He d. 8 Oct. 1909.

Moss Side church Report

GRIFFITHS, ANN (*DWB*, 303). Baptised 21 Apr. 1776; m. 10 Oct. 1804, Thomas Griffiths (1779-1808), and he d. 8 Apr. 1808. Her father d. *c*. Feb. 1804, and her mother in 1794; they had five children: (1) Jane, 1767, (2) John, 1770, (3) Elizabeth, 1772, (4) Ann, and (5) Edward, 1779. An extensive study of the children (and their descendants) has been made by David Thomas, *Ann Griffiths a'i theulu* (1963); Jane m. in 1794 Thomas Jones, Tŷ Cornel shop, Llanfyllin, and her grandson John Jones's daughter Margaret Jane Jones was the wife of the minister and writer Owen Jones (1833-99; *DWB*, 500-1); she d. in Jan. 1909. See further the biography, *Cofio Ann Griffiths* (Caernarfon, 1955), and John Ryan, *The hymns of Ann Griffiths* (1980), Siân Megan, *Gwaith Ann Griffiths* (1982), E. Wyn James, *Rhyfeddaf Fyth…* (1998).

GRIFFITHS, JOHN (1731-1811; *DWB*, 305). The parish of Llanglydwen and Castell Garw are in Carmarthenshire (Mr. Howell James, Norwich). Abergavenny Academy opened in 1757 and he went there that year.

GRIFFITHS, JOHN THOMAS (1824-95), mining engineer in U.S.A.; b. Christmas Day 1824 in the Brynengan area of the parish of Llanystumdwy, Caerns. He emigrated with his parents to New York in 1831 but because of cholera outbreaks the family moved within a year to Minersville, Pa. The son went to work in a colliery in Minersville and subsequently at Summit Hill, Carbon County. He helped to set up the Calvinistic Methodist church in Wilkesbarre. He composed some hymn tunes.

He d. 18 February, 1895.

Y Cyfaill (Utica), 1895, 232-5; *The Cambrian* (Utica), 1892, 157; *Y Drych*, March 1895.
R.O.

GRIFFITHS, RICHARD (*DWB*, 307). He seems to have leased rights to open levels rather than to have opened them himself; see E.D. Lewis *Hist. of the Rhondda Valleys*, p.39.

GRIFFITHS, VAVASOR (*DWB*, 308). He resigned from the Academy before 8 Dec. 1740. (Rev. Isaac Thomas, Bangor, in *Y Cofiadur*, 1958, 25).

GRIFFITHS, WILLIAM (1788-1861; *DWB*, 309). See also his autobiography *Gower Memories* (ed. Alicia Gower-Jones; 1957).

GROVE, Sir WILLIAM ROBERT (*DWB*, 310). See further Colin Matheson, *Glam. Hist.*, 9 (1973), 96-104.

GRUFFUDD ap NICOLAS (*DWB*, 313). See further the two detailed articles by Ralph A. Griffiths – 'Gruffydd ap Nicholas and the rise of the House of Dinefwr', *N.L.W. Jnl.*, xiii, 256-65, and 'Gruffydd ap Nicholas and the fall of the House of Lancaster', *Welsh Hist. Rev.*, ii, 213-31. The *fl.* can now be extended between *c*. 1415 and *c*. 1460. It is likely that he was b. before the end of the 14th c.

GRUFFUDD FYCHAN, Sir - see VAUGHAN, Sir GRUFFUDD (d. 1447), *DWB*, 1002.

GRUFFUDD NANNAU (*DWB*, 316). Amend the *floruit*; he was contemporary with Dafydd ap Maredudd ap Tudur, *fl.* 1460 (*DWB*, 98); they both wrote poetry to Dafydd ap Gruffudd Deuddwr (Pen. MS. 64, ff. 236 and 243), thus both were active in 1460. Note also that Ieuan Fychan of Pengwern (*DWB*, 412) d. *c*. 1458.

GRUFFYDD ap IEUAN ap LLYWELYN FYCHAN (*DWB*, 317). His will, dated 11 March 1553, was made at Henllan, Denbs., and was proved 3 May 1553.

GRUFFYDD, OWEN (*DWB*, 320). *Carolau a Dyriau Duwiol* was published in 1696. See the article on Jeremy Gruffydd (*DWB*, 319-20).

GWALLTER DYFI – see REES, EDWARD WALTER below.

GWERFULYN – see JONES, THOMAS ROBERT below.

GWILYM CARADOG - see William Caradawc Evans, 1848-78, under EVANS, DAVID, 1814-91, *DWB*, 226.

GWILYM GLAN LLWCHWR - see OWEN, WILLIAM below.

GWILYM GWYN (*DWB*, 327). Amend the *floruit* to 'end of 15 c.'

GWILYM MEUDWY - see OWEN, WILLIAM below.

GWYNFARDD BRYCHEINIOG (*DWB*, 330). Read *c*. 1090 not '1190'.

GWYNNE, RICHARD (1822-1907) – see GWYNNE (FAMILY) , Kilvey, Swansea, above.

HAMER, EDWARD (1840-1911; *DWB*, 335). B. 6 Feb. 1840 at Llanidloes, son of the shoemaker Meredith Hamer and his wife Ann. He d. at Bordesley, Birmingham, 24 Nov. 1911, aged 72.

E.R.M.

HANMER, FAMILY of Hanmer (*DWB*, 336-7). *Llwybr Hyffordd* was published in 1630.

HARRIS, GRIFFITH (*DWB*, 339). According to the family gravestone in Heol-y-dŵr (Water Street) chapel, Carmarthen, he was b. 15 July 1811, d. 1 Nov. 1892.

H.W.

HARRIS, HOWEL(L) (*DWB*, 339). Read Susanna not 'Susanah' as his mother's name.

HARRIS, JOSEPH (1704-64; *DWB*, 341-2). See 'Etifeddion Harrisiaid Trefeca' in R.T. Jenkins, *Yng Nghysgod Trefeca*, (1968). Eliza Anne was *one* of the daughters of Samuel Hughes, not the *only* daughter – her sister Amelia Sophia had d. in 1794. Her first husband (1804) was Roderick Gwynne, Buckland. He d. 20 Mar. 1808, and she m. William Alexander Madocks, 2 Apr. 1818

E.D.J.

Joseph Harris was author of several anonymous works on astronomy and mathematics and invented the 'New Azimuth Compass' and 'Forestaff'. Government ministers were often advised by him (unbeknown to many because of his shyness) and he received a pension of £300 per annum from the king from 1753. To a great extent he was responsible for standardising the U.K.'s weights and measures mid-18th c.

Cylch. Cymd. Hanes MC, 13 (1928), 85; J. Thickens, *Howell Harris yn Llundain* (1934), 9; Richard Bennett, *Blynyddoedd cyntaf Methodistiaeth* (1909), 37; *Report from the Committee appointed to enquire into the original Standards of Weights and Measures* (House of Commons 2 June 1758), 49 (12 Apr. 1759), 7.

Ll.G.C.

HARRIS, JOSEPH (Gomer; *DWB*, 342). Read *Bwyall* not '*Bwyell*'.

HARRIS, SOLOMON (*DWB*, 342). Read Timothy Davis (not 'Davies') twice. See Timothy Davis (1709-71; *DWB*, 164 and 165).

HARRIS, THOMAS (*DWB*, 342-3). It is not true to say that he was 'unmarried', though it is not known who his wife was, nor when she d. (see R.T. Jenkins, *Yng Nghysgod Trefeca*, p. 147).

HARRY, GEORGE OWEN (*DWB*, 343). The work of George Owen Harry's circle of friends is fully discussed by B.G. Charles, *George Owen of Henllys: a Welsh Elizabethan* (Aberystwyth, 1973), and the life and work of the antiquary is discussed in detail by E.D. Jones, 'George Owen Harry', *Pembrokeshire Historian*, 6 (1979), 58-75. On the basis of his evidence in a case in

1613-14 it can be assumed that he was born about 1553. He made his will (leaving a great deal of gear in the parish of Reynoldston, Gower) on 8 Feb. 1611-12 and he had probably died by summer 1614. E.D. Jones says that there is no evidence that Harry's work 'The Well-spring of True Nobilitie' was published as a book but that Thomas Salesbury published the portion which dealt with King James I's genealogy in London in 1604. However in 1956 Sir Michael Dillwyn-Venables-Llewelyn presented to the National Library a MS. of almost all of *The Well-spring*, a MS. (NLW 9853) which is a good copy made in the early 17th c. It is a reflection of George Owen Harry's antiquarian and historical interests.

George Owen Harry was one of the three children of Owen Harry who married three of the children of Thomas Lucas, The Hills, Reynoldston, Gower, which suggests a very strong association with that area. George Owen Harry says himself in the genealogy which he gave Lewys Dwnn in 1597 (Dwnn, *Heraldic Visitations*, i, 32-3) that his ancestors came, for the most part, from Llanelli, though his mother was the daughter of a man from Gower, married to a member of the Crump family whose home was in Sanctuary, Pen-rhys. In Gower it was believed that George Owen Harry was a native of the area, rather than of Carmarthenshire. In his description of Reynoldston for Edward Lhuyd in the 1690s (F.V. Emery, *Trans. Cymm.*, 1965, 103) Isaac Hamon says: 'In this parish Sr. Geo: Owen clerke, was born, called by some, George Owen Harry, he was the third son of Owen Harry Owen a freeholder of this parish'. In the genealogical MS. NLW Castell Gorfod 8, f. 141, *c*. 1700, containing notes gathered, perhaps, by Isaac Hamon, George Owen Harry is given as the 3rd son of Owen Harry of Reynoldston. It is likely that Isaac Hamon was well acquainted with George Owen Harry's grandson, John Owen, vicar of Pennard in Gower, who died in 1690. The genealogy in Castell Gorfod MS. 8 is probably based on William Bennett, Pen-rhys Castle's, book of genealogies which he compiled about 1630. The MS. is in the Royal Institution of South Wales (see the index to Bennett's book by G. Grant Francis, pp. 158, 188, 189). Here George Owen Harry is the fourth son of Owen Harry of Reynoldston and the two genealogies take the line back to Morris de Novo Castro or Morris Castell of Llanelli in the time of Edward II and naturally confirm that the three children of Owen Harry married the children of Thomas Lucas of Reynoldston.

These genealogies cannot be made consistent with that in Lewys Dwnn's book, but William Bennett's evidence cannot be totally disregarded since he lived in the same period as George Owen Harry, within a stone's throw of Reynoldston.

F.M.G., P.M.

HEILIN FARDD, poet - see HYWEL HEILIN (*fl.* 15th c.) below.

HEMANS (née BROWNE), FELICIA DOROTHEA (1793-1835), poet; b. in Liverpool 25 September 1793, a daughter of George Browne, merchant. When she was seven her familye moved to Gwrych, near Abergele, Denb. Her education was patchy but she read avidly and her progress and development were so exceptional that she was able to publish her *Juvenile Poems* in 1808 shortly after her fourteenth birthday. These poems were not well received but from then on she wrote and published almost continuously. She married Captain Alfred Hemans in 1812, and by 1818, the year they separated, she had borne him five sons. Other than for one short period, she lived in Bronwylfa, near Abergele, in her mother's house. A number of works belong to this period, *The Domestic Affections and Other Poems*, 1812; translations of the works of the Portuguese poet Camoens and others, 1818; *The Sceptic*, 1820; *The siege of Valencia*, 1823; *The Forest Sanctuary* and *Lays of Many Lands*, 1825. Her play, *The Vespers of Palermo*, was performed in Covent Garden, London, in December 1823 and with greater success in Edinburgh the following year. In 1825 she crossed the river Clwyd to Rhyllon and there she wrote *Dramatic Scene between Bronwylfa and Rhyllon*. After her mother's death two years later she went to live in Watertree near Liverpool. In 1831 she moved to Dublin; from then on she wrote mainly religious poetry. Her health had never been good and she died in Dublin 16 May, 1835. She was of a loving and gentle disposition and her poetry was tender and flowed gracefully and evenly, but it lacked strength and permanent value. Her collected works were edited by Mrs. Hughes in 1839 and by W.M. Rossetti in 1873.

H.F. Chorley, *Memorials of Mrs. Hemans* (two volumes), 1836; *Memoirs* by Hughes and Rossetti; *D.N.B.*; [Peter W. Trinder in Writers of Wales Series, 1984]

G.J.

HENRY VII (*DWB*, 346). There is a copy of Roland Velville's will, dated 6 June 1535, in N.L.W. MS. 1600, p. 94.

HERBERT (FAMILY) of Montgomery, etc. (*DWB*, 347-50). Sir Edward Herbert purchased the lordship of Powis in 1587 (see *DWB*, 778 under Powis).

HERBERT, WILLIAM REGINALD (WILLIAM REGINALD HERBERT HUDDLESTON from 1920; 1841-1929), sportsman, huntsman and rider of racehorses; b. 14 Feb. 1841, eldest son of William Herbert, D.L., Clytha, and Frances, daughter of Edward Huddleston, Sawston Hall, Cambs. He received private tuition in France before enlisting with the Royal Gloucestershire Hussars. He took the additional name of Huddleston when he inherited Sawston Hall estate, 1920-21. Having taken an early interest in racehorses he was highly regarded as one of the best riders of his day. From 1854 onwards he won several races held in the west of England, including the Cheltenham Grand Annual. In the history of sport he is famous as one of the first to introduce the game of polo into Britain. He was a founding member of the Hurlingham Club, and it was he, to a great degree, who was responsible for founding Ranelagh, an institution with which he maintained a connection for sixteen years. He was Master of the Monmouthshire Fox Hounds for 17 years; he was also a notable competitor at pigeon shoots, winning many prizes in both Britain and abroad. Among his other interests

were coach driving and sculling. In 1908 he published *When Diamonds were Trumps*, a book which relates much of the history of his life as a sportsman and which is ranked with the classic literature relating to his style of life. He served as Deputy Lieutenant of Monmouthshire, and d. 16 Oct. 1929.

Personal knowledge.

H.J.Ll.-J.

HEYLIN, ROWLAND (*DWB*, 356). Rowland Heylin was a member of the Heylin family of Pentreheilyn, Llanymynech, who claimed descent from Brochwel Ysgithrog. There was no relationship between this family and the Heylin family of Pentreheilyn, Ellesmere, who descended from Rhys Sais. See George Vernon, 'Life of Peter Heylin' in *The Historical and Miscellaneous Tracts of ... Peter Heylin* (1681). The reference to Rhys Sais (and *Powys Fadog* in the bibliography) should be deleted. Henry Heylin was, apparently, a cousin, not a nephew, of Rowland Heylin, and it is questionable whether Grono ab Heilyn was an ancestor of the family. See also the corrections to EDWARDS (Cilhendre), and HOLBACHE, DAVID.

P.C.B.

HIGGS, DANIEL (*DWB*, 356). Read Chadwick (not 'Chadwick').

HOLBACHE (HOLBECHE), DAVID (*DWB*, 359-60). Read 'of Pentre Heilyn, in Ellesmere' and delete the reference to HEYLIN, ROWLAND.

P.C.B.

HOPKINS, EVAN ([1801]?-1888), geologist; b. in Swansea. He spent his youth in the ironworks at Penydarren, Dowlais and Rhymney. In 1833 he went to South America to oversee gold and silver mines; he returned there later to research in the Andes and Panama; in 1852 he was in Australia as an advisor to a gold mining company. He was an expert on magnetic ores.

T. Iorwerth Jones in *Trans. Cymm.*, 1932-3 (which includes a list of his papers).

R.T.J.

HORSFALL TURNER, ERNEST RICHMOND (1870-1936), schoolmaster and local historian; b. 13 Jan. 1870 at Brighouse, Yorks., son of Joseph Horsfall Turner, who was also a schoolmaster and local historian. He was educated at his father's school and commenced his career as a teacher at that school. Later he graduated at London University. He taught at Blaenau Ffestiniog and Colwyn Bay before being appointed headmaster at Llanidloes County School in 1895. He learnt Welsh and then began to take an interest in local history and geography. Among other works he published *Wanderings in County Cardigan* (n.d.), and *The Municipal History of Llanidloes* (1908). These contain his own pen and ink drawings, since he was a skilful illustrator. Later in life, he became also an artist in watercolours. After retiring in 1932 he carried out much research into the history of the Chartist movement in Montgomeryshire and his manuscripts are now at the National Library of Wales. He was elected a member of Llanidloes town council in 1901, and was twice mayor of the town, 1908 and 1927-28. In 1897 he m. Annie, daughter of J.N. Crowther (*DWB*, 87), and they had a son who was town clerk at Aberystwyth. His wife d. in 1923. He d. at Llanidloes, 13 Mar. 1936, and was buried there.

Montgomeryshire County Times, 18 Mar. 1936; *Welsh Secretary Schools Review*, 1930; information from his son.

E.R.M.

HOWELL, DAVID (1797-1863), minister (Presb.); b. at Waunbrics, St. Clears, Carms., 31 March 1797, son of David Howell. Thomas Charles of Bala (*DWB*, 73-4) received him as a communicant of Bancyfelin society. He went to Swansea in 1814 as a tailor's apprentice. He became a member of Crug-glas church and began to preach there in 1817. In 1821 he was sent by his Connexion to Radnorshire as a missionary and he settled at Pen-y-bont. He was ord. at Llangeitho Association in 1824. He returned to Swansea in 1827 and m. Mary, daughter of his old master, John Cadwalader, a Calvinistic Methodist elder. He spent a short period at Carmarthen in 1840 and then moved to Llantwit Major in 1842 to take charge of churches in the Vale of Glamorgan. He returned again to Swansea in 1845 as pastor of Trinity church, where he exercised great influence till his d., 4 Aug. 1873; he was buried in Crug-glas graveyard. He was one of the chief Calvinistic Methodist leaders in Glamorgan throughout the 19th c. He was not a great preacher – he lacked fluency and his sermons were heavy – but he had a strong personality, and everyone considered him to be a devoted man of God. In addition to all this his energy and ceaseless industry made him a power and influence both within and outside the church.

Hugh Joshua Hughes, *David Howell: A Brief Memoir*, 1885; *Drys.*, 1919, 7-11; Samlet Williams, *Hanes Meth. Gorllewin Morgannwg*, 19; E. T. D., *Can-Mlwyddiant Capel y Trinity, Abertawe*, 12-6.

G.M.R.

HOWELLS, WILLIAM (1818-88; *DWB*, 370). Read John Harris (not 'Harries') Jones (see *DWB*, 486).

HUDDLESTON, WILLIAM REGINALD HERBERT - see HERBERT, WILLIAM REGINALD, 1841-1929, above.

HUGHES, DAVID (1800-49), Independent minister; b. in Amlwch, Angl., the son of a prosperous farmer. He received a good education locally and he also went to a school in Liverpool. He became a member of Tabernacl chapel, Liverpool under the ministry of John Breese and he started to preach there. He was a student at the Presbyterian College, Carmarthen, 1824-28 and he was ordained minister of Mill Street Chapel, Newport, 1 Jan. 1829. Ten years later he was inducted as minister at Trelech, Carm. on 11-13 June, 1839. He published a useful catechism for Sunday schools and he worked diligently for years on a general dictionary but this was not finished. He d. 20 Feb., 1849.

Oriel Coleg Caerfyrddin, 45; *H. Egl. Ann.*, iii, 397, 403-6; J.T.J., I, 544-7; N.L.W. MS. 10327.

J.D.O.

HUGHES, EDWARD ('Eos Maldwyn'; d. 1862), harpist; son of William Hughes, harpist, Llansantffraed, Mont. 'Eos Maldwyn' won a valuable harp at one of the *eisteddfodau* organised by Cymreigyddion y Fenni (Abergavenny). He d. of tuberculosis in Liverpool, 9 December, 1862.

Idris Fychan, 'Hanes canu gyda'r tannau', *Trans. Cymm.*, 1885; M.O. Jones, *Byw. Cerdd. Cymr.* (1890); R. Williams, *Mont. Worthies*; R. Griffith, *Llyfr Cerdd Dannau* (1913); Ceitho.

R.D.G.

HUGHES, HUGH ROBERT (*DWB*, 379). His wife was Florentia Emily Liddell, not 'Lidell'.

HUGHES, JANE (*DWB*, 380). According to the copy of John Hughes's register of baptisms of Capel Uchaf Pontrobert (in the D. Teifigar Davies collection of MSS in N.L.W.) it appears that she was the third child (and third daughter) of John and Ruth Hughes, and that she was b. 25 June and baptised 2 July 1811 by Evan Griffiths, Meifod, who had been recently ordained in June 1811 at Bala.

E.Wy.J.

HUGHES, JOHN (1791-?), musician. He was a servant at the Wynnstay Arms, Wrexham, in his early days. He learned to play several musical instruments and was appointed conductor of the band of the Denbs. militia. He won a prize at the Wrexham *eisteddfod* (1820) for the best arrangement of a Welsh air. He won the prize and medal at the Abergavenny *eisteddfod* of 1838 for the best Welsh madrigal and was the winner at the Liverpool *eisteddfod* (1840) for his variations on the tune 'Dynwared yr eos'. His 'Llanciau Eryri' was published in *Y Gyfres Gerddorol*.

M. O. Jones, *Byw. Cerdd. Cymr.*

R.D.G.

HUGHES, JOHN (1796-1860; *DWB*, 382). See not '(under Hughes, Charles)' but a separate article on Richard Hughes (1794-1871; *DWB*, 389).

HUGHES, JOHN (1873-1932; *DWB*, 1129). He was an official of the Great Western colliery at Pontypridd, not an official in the traffic department of the Great Western Railway. See Huw Williams in *Gol.*, 22 June 1990, 6.

HUGHES, ROBERT OWEN ('Elfyn'; *DWB*, 390). See O. Trevor Roberts, *Elfyn a'i waith* (1993).

HUGHES, STEPHEN (*DWB*, 390-1). His wife was Catherine, daughter of John Daniel, the second mayor of Swansea. See also *Y Cofiadur*, 31, pp. 35-9.

HUGHES, WILLIAM (1779-1836), engineer; b. at Penyclawdd, Mon. He was trained as an engineer, and gained considerable fame in his profession. Among the designs with which he was involved were the Ellesmere Canal, the Caledonian Canal, deepening the river Clyde, and dredging Lough Neagh. He d. in Northampton, 1836.

Asaph; NLW MS. 9260.

G.M.G.

HUGHES, WILLIAM ROBERT (1798?-1879), healer of cancer and cancerous warts; b. at Tanyrallt, in the parish of Abererch, Caerns., of a family reputed to have an exceptional ability to cure cancerous warts, etc. After marriage he moved to live at Mur Crysto, Llangybi, in 1821. He was a friend of David Owen ('Dewi Wyn o Eifion'; *DWB*, 700), Ebenezer Thomas ('Eben Fardd'; *DWB*, 944-5), and Robert Williams ('Robert ap Gwilym Ddu'; *DWB*, 1067). So great was his power that he became known as '*Dewin y Cennin*' (The leek magician). He emigrated to U.S.A. in 1845, settling in Columbus, Wisconsin. It was claimed that the first Welsh sermon in the state of Wisconsin was preached in his house. In America he continued to treat cancer and cancerous warts. He d. 15 Mar. 1879.

Y Brython (Tremadog), 1859, 221; 1860, 32; *Y Cenhadwr Americanaidd*, 1867, 374; 1879, 154; *Y Cyfaill* (Utica), 1879, 270-1.

R.O.

HUMPHREYS, DAVID (1813-66), minister (CM); b. 13 Oct. 1813, son of Edward and Elizabeth Humphreys, Glyndu, Llangynog, Monts. He began preaching with the Calvinistic Methodists in 1840, and was ord. 1848; he attended Bala College for a short while. He was a pleasant person and a commendable preacher. He m. a sister of Humphrey Evans, an elder at Llanrhaeadr-ym-Mochnant, where he spent the rest of his life. A skilful carpenter, he made a success of his business. The lands for building the British school and Bethesda chapel at Llanrhaeadr were donated by him. His family had poetic talent and his brother, 'Iorwerth Cynog', was an excellent poet. Although David Humphreys wrote much verse, only a temperance hymn, 'Babel gwympa', was published. He d. 25 Jul. 1866.

Ed.J.

HUW MENAI (*fl.* 16th c.), musician; at the *eisteddfod* held at Caerwys, 2 Jul. 1523, he graduated as a *disgybl disgyblaidd* - a pupil to pursue a course of instruction, having mastered the initial steps - but he rejected the grade.

M. O. Jones, *Byw. Cerdd. Cymr.*; R. Griffiths, *Cerdd Dannau*.

R.D.G.

HYWEL HEILIN or **HEILIN FARDD**; (*fl.* 15th c.), poet; nothing is known of his life. Some of his work is extant in manuscript, including two love poems and a *cywydd* in praise of Ieuan Llwyd of Glyn Aeron.

Jones and Lewis, *Mynegai*; *Blackwell*; *Em. W.*; W. Owen, *The Cambrian Biography*.

R.L.

HYWEL TUDUR – see ROBERTS, HOWELL below.

IAGO ERFYL – see JAMES, THOMAS DAVIES below.

IEUAN GYFANNEDD (*DWB*, 412). Amend the *floruit* to *c.* 1450-60. Phylip ap Rhys of Cenarth in the parish of St. Harmon, Rads., and his wife Gwenllian, daughter of Owain Glyn Dŵr, were the patrons.

IEUAN LLWYD SIEFFRAI (1575-1639 instead of *fl. c.* 1599-1619; *DWB*, 413). B. in 1575, s. and heir of Sieffrai ab Ieuan Llwyd, Dyffryn Ereithlyn, Eglwys-bach, Denbs., of the Lloyd family of Hafod Unnos (see John Lloyd (1749-1815; *DWB*, 583). On 12 July 1591, at Llandrillo church, Mer., when he was 16 years old and she only 11, he m. Margred, d. and sole heiress of Morus ap Siôn ab Elis of Palau. They had ten daughters and two sons, some born at Palau and others at Dyffryn. The eldest s., Sieffrai Llwyd (1607-26), was murdered at Dôl-y-cletwr, Rhiwedog, and the inheritance descended through the second son, Morus (b. 1619). Ieuan Llwyd Sieffrai, antiquary, genealogist and poet, was one of the literary gentry. He d. 8 July 1639, and was buried in Llandderfel cemetery.

Arch. Camb., 1885, 133-6; *Powys Fadog*, vi, 105-8.

E.D.J.

IFANS, ROBERT – see ROBERT ab IFAN, *DWB*, 1147.

ISAAC, EVAN (*DWB*, 418). He retired from Llandeilo Fawr, Carms.

JAMES, DAVID ('Defynnog'; 1865-1928) schoolmaster, educationist, organiser of summer schools, and author; b. 17 Aug. 1865 in Libanus in the parish of Defynnog, Brecs. He was the son of David James, Baptist minister and his wife Mary, sister of 'Myfyr Emlyn' (Benjamin Thomas, *DWB*, 938-9), the poet-preacher. They had four sons and four daughters. Defynnog was educated in Cynwyl Elfed, Carms., and Dinas, Pembs., where his father was minister. He was intent on becoming a teacher, and after a period as a pupil-teacher, was accepted as a certificated teacher. He was successful in the matriculation examination of the University of London (1889) and was awarded various certificates in a number of teaching subjects. He became a member of the University Correspondence College, Cambridge, and was successful in the Intermediate Arts examinations in Latin, Greek, French, mathematics and English. He won prizes, too, in the National *Eisteddfod*. In the *eisteddfod* at Merthyr Tydfil (1901) he won for his study of 'Kymric Literature' and in the *eisteddfod* at Bangor (1902) he was awarded first prize for his critical treatise on the novels of Daniel Owen. He was admitted to the *Gorsedd* of Bards; he also became a national adjudicator. He spent periods as a schoolteacher in Eglwyswrw, Cwmifor, Templeton, the Rhondda Pupil-teacher Centre, Dunraven and Treherbert (1908-26). Although he was a good mathematician, like his brother John, he turned his attention towards improving methods of teaching Welsh. When he was appointed secretary of the Welsh Language Society on 1 Oct. 1902, he took the opportunity to promote his mission throughout Wales. He applied himself to preparing reading books, teaching manuals, plans for language teaching and a children's dictionary. He contributed prolifically to *Cymru, Cymru'r Plant, Y Darian, Ysbryd yr Oes, Y Genhinen, Seren Gomer, The Welsh Outlook* and *The Welsh Leader*. More importantly it was he who started the Welsh Summer School in 1903. He was an excellent organiser and succeeded in inviting some of the nation's leading scholars to address members of the summer schools on methods of teaching Welsh and on literary history. He won the admiration and support of men like Sir Isambard Owen (*DWB*, 707-8), Sir O.M. Edwards (*DWB*, 192-3) and Sir J.E. Lloyd (see above). He was invited to join the Mosely commission on education in 1903 and visited the U.S.A. and Canada. He published a book based on his impressions entitled *American methods of organisation and instruction* (1908). He believed strongly in the direct method of language teaching and he (through the Society) recommended this to schools in Anglicised areas. His *Scheme of instruction in Welsh* which he produced jointly with H. Howells received the blessing of the Rhondda education committee. He could not tolerate lazy teachers who did not commit themselves fully to promote the language. The action of the departmental committee which looked into the place of Welsh in education and life (1925) in neglecting the mission and activities of the Welsh Language Society, saddened him, though consideration had been given to inviting Sir Isambard to serve on the committee. Defynnog was not content to be idle even after his retirement. He continued to write daily as editor of the Welsh column of the *South Wales News* until he was hindered by ill-health. He supported the establishment of a Secretaryship of State for Wales. He died on 1 Dec. 1928 in Swansea and was buried in Llethr Ddu cemetery, Porth, Rhondda. The newspapers were loud in praise of his kindness, generosity, dedication and zeal for the Welsh language. He m. Sarah Harries and they had one son. After her death he m. Sarah Williams on 7 Aug. 1920, a widow with three daughters. They had one son, David Geraint.

JAMES, JOHN. He was Defynnog's brother; director of education in Glam. 1903-1929. He had a brilliant academic career after having worked for a time in a grocer's shop in the Rhondda valley, Glam. At 16, as the holder of an open scholarship, he went to University College, Cardiff. Having taken a first-class degree (London Univ.) he went to Balliol College, Oxford, where he graduated with a first in mathematics. He gained a research B.Sc. degree and then proceeded to the Univ. of Erlangen, Germany, where he gained a Ph.D. in electronics. He did much to encourage the teaching of Welsh in the schools of Glam.

Gwilym Arthur Jones, 'David James (Defynnog) 1865-1928 in the context of Welsh education', *Trans. Cymm.*, 1978, 267-84 (with bibliography).

G.A.J.

JAMES, IVOR (1840-1909; *DWB*, 423), b. Ivor James, or IVOR BARNOLD ROBERT JAMES, as he called himself, 21 Sept. 1840, at Britannia, in the village of Rock, and the parish of Bedwellte, Mon., s. of Robert James and Mary (Arnold), his wife. Hence, on the distaff side, he had connections with the family of Llanthony and The Court, Llanfihangel Crucorney (see *DWB*, 13-14). The family moved to Llansamlet where the father was schoolmaster. Ivor James was a journalist in London for a while and he was also interested in reading documents at the British Museum before going to Cambridge. He m., c.

1870, Margaret Elborough Pruen, d. of Dr. Henry Pruen, rector of Ashchurch, Glos. Read E.R.G. Salisbury (not E.G.R.).

See also *South Wales Daily Post*, 14 Apr. 1909; W. Samlet Williams, *Hanes a Hynafiaethau Llansamlet* (Dolgellau, 1908).

P.M.

JAMES, JAMES ('Iago ap Iago'; 1818-43), poet; b. 14 Mar. 1818 at Defynnog, Breck., son of James James, merchant. He was educated at the village school and also privately. Despite having a weak constitution, he studied diligently and was considered to be a good linguist. He d. 30 July 1843 aged 25. His poetry was written in free metre, and some of his work, as well as articles, appeared in *Yr Eurgrawn* and other periodicals. His brother, Morgan James, wrote a short biography of him and collected his poetical works, in a volume edited by I. Jenkins, and published by Thomas Williams, Crickhowell, in 1844.

Daniel C. Lewis, *Hanes Plwyf Defynog*.

R.M.T.

JAMES, JOHN (d. 1705; *DWB*, 424). Instead of 'Happy Union' read 'Common Fund' or the Presbyterian Fund Board.

JAMES, JOHN (1815-51; *DWB*, 425). The Anglican newspaper *Y Cymro* was removed from Bangor to London in 1830 (not '1850').

JAMES, JOHN LLOYD (*DWB*, 425). His novel *Habakkuk Crabb* was published in Liverpool in 1901. It was later given a different cover and a new title – *Croesi'r Bont, sef anturiaethau H.C.*

JAMES, MARIA (1793-1868), poet; b. 11 Oct. 1793, possibly in north Wales. She emigrated with her parents to U.S.A. The family settled in Clinton, New York, and she spent most of her life, from the age of 10 onwards, as a maid servant. She exhibited considerable skill at composing poetry, and a collection of her works was edited by A. Potter and published in New York in 1839 under the title, *Wales and other Poems*. She d. 11 Sept. 1868 at Rhinebeck, New York.

NLW MS. 9261; *Asaph*; *Y Brython*, v, 158; *Enw. F.*; Cardiff Library catalogue.

G.M.G.

JAMES, ROBERT (*DWB*, 426). Read Dannville and Wilkes-barré.

JAMES, THOMAS DAVIES ('Iago Erfyl'; 1862-1927), clergyman, and popular preacher and lecturer; s. of Thomas James and his wife; b. at Manafon, Mont., 13 Aug. 1862. Soon afterwards the family moved to Wyddi-goed, Llanfechain, but his parents died when he was young and he was brought up by his grandparents at Garth Isaf, Rhosybrithdir, Llanrhaeadrym-Mochnant.

He began preaching with the Methodists at Rhosybrithdir, went to Didsbury College, Manchester, and after passing his examinations he was appointed an assistant on the Llanfyllin circuit, which at that time also included Llanfair

Caereinion. Shortly afterwards, perhaps under the influence of the family of his intended-wife (Emma Jones, Rhos-y-glasgoed, Meifod; m. Sept. 1890), he turned to the Church in Wales, and in 1888 entered St. David's College, Lampeter. He was ord. deacon at S. Asaph, 1891, and priest, 1892. He was curate of Llanfair Caereinion from Dec. 1891 to Oct. 1896; Northop, Flints., 1896-97; and chaplain of the Welsh church of St. Martin, Chester, from 1897 to 1901 when he was appointed by the Lord Chancellor to the living of Llanerfyl, Mont. (which was in the gift of the Crown), and he spent the rest of his life there. He succeeded 'Penfro' (William Morgan, see below) as Dean of Caereinion, 1918; he was elected member of Llanfyllin board of guardians, Llanfyllin district council, Montgomery county council and of the education committee.

The Methodists saw him as following in the footsteps of John Evans, Eglwys-bach (DWB, 245), and when he was curate of Llanfair Caereinion his sermons attracted large crowds to the church. His eloquence and his wit brought him fame as a preacher and lecturer in both Welsh and English, and he was in demand not only throughout Wales but also in Welsh centres in England. He preached in London during World War I, in Liverpool cathedral in 1927, and he had been invited to deliver a Welsh sermon in St. Paul's cathedral, London, in 1928. His most popular lectures were those on Robert Owen, Twm o'r Nant, Mynyddog, Ceiriog, Y Bardd Cwsg, Owain Glyndŵr and Ann Griffiths. He demonstrated his lectures (before the days of the lantern) with a series of his own pen and ink illustrations on large movable rolls. He was in great demand to compère eisteddfodau; he possessed a wealth of humorous stories, and was always ready with his repartee. He was a member of the Gorsedd of the Province of Powys, and at Carmarthen national eisteddfod, 1911, he became a member of the gorsedd under the name 'Iago Erfyl'. He contributed much to the local papers; for years he wrote the Welsh column, under the pseudonym Y Gigfran, in The Montgomery Express.

At one time he was a staunch Tory and vehemently opposed the disestablishment of the church, though when it came about he accepted it, recognising in it a greater freedom for the church and its officers. During World War I he changed his political views and became a socialist.

He was taken ill while preaching in Liverpool cathedral, and although he endeavoured to conduct services two Sundays after that, he had to yield. He d. at his daughter's home at Addiscombe, Surrey, 30 July 1927, and was buried in Llanerfyl churchyard, 3 Aug. He was as highly esteemed by the Nonconformists as by churchmen, and the following Sunday evening 7 Aug., when a memorial service was held in Llanerfyl church, every chapel and church in the vale of Banw was closed. In his funeral sermon the Reverend Canon J.R. Roberts, Llanfihangel (s. of Ellis Roberts, 'Elis Wyn o Wyrfai', DWB, 862-3) declared that he deserved to be reckoned among the chief stalwarts of the pulpit in Wales, together with the likes of John Elias (DWB, 203-4) and 'Williams o'r Wern' (William Williams, 1781-1840, DWB, 1081). He left a widow (d. Apr. 1939), a son and daughter.

Mont. County Times, 6 and 13 Aug. 1927; Montgomeryshire Express, 9 Aug. 1927; Brython, 11 Aug. 1927; Haul, 1927, 364, 387; Hist. Dioc. S. Asaph, I, 472; information from his son, Dr. Cernyw James, Llanfyllin; family acquaintance.

E.P.R.

JAMES, WILLIAM (1761-1845), minister (Congl.); b. on Palm Sunday [15 March] 1761 at Aberswn, Llanllwni, Carms. He became a member of Rhyd-y-bont church and began preaching when he was young. He kept school at Glyn Tawe, and then (1785-89) went to 'Carmarthen' academy, which was at the time located in Swansea. He was ord. minister of the churches of Watford and of Trinity, Cardiff, and lived at Ysguborwen farm. About 1826 he was persuaded to move to the town, relinquishing Watford and his farm. He d. 26 Feb. 1845, aged 84. His ministry showed little sign of success - the reason probably being that his sermons were exceptionally long, ranging from an hour and a half to two and a half hours.

J.T.J., i, 592; H. Egl. Ann., ii, 419-20; NLW MS. 10327.

R.T.J.

JEFFREYS, GEORGE (DWB, 429-30). On p. 430 delete '(q.v.)' after Ambrose Lewis.

JENKINS, JENKIN (DWB, 433-4). The Presbyterian Fund Board paid its last contribution to him as pastor at Llanfyllin on 2 June 1760 (Y Cofiadur, 1958, 19).

JENKINS, JOSEPH (1861-1929; DWB, 436). According to the christening register of Cwmystwyth chapel, he was b. 2 Nov. 1859 (not 27 Oct. 1861); registered at Lampeter, 3 Dec. 1859. His father was John Jenkins, lead miner, and his mother was Mary (née Howells); their home was Tan-y-chwarel (the Rev. Elwyn Pryse, Bow Street, who was brought up at Cwmystwyth, transcribed these records).

JENKINS, Sir LEOLINE (DWB, 436-7). In the bibliography read Codrington not 'Coddrington'.

JERMAN, HUGH (1836-95), artist and musician; b. Church Street, Llanidloes, Mont., 28 Sept. 1836, son of a carpenter, Richard Jerman and his wife Mary. He was educated in local schools and the National School before becoming a student at Battersea Training College, 1854-55, and then becoming a teacher. He taught in Lincolnshire, Connah's Quay, Kerry, Kirkby Fleetham and Wells in Yorkshire. In 1877 he returned to Llanidloes and established a private school, Severn Grove Academy, where he taught the sons of the richer town and country folk until 1890.

He was a talented musician who won many prizes at eisteddfodau. In the Conway national eisteddfod of 1861 he won first prize for an anthem, 'Deus Misereatur'. He conducted an accomplished choir in the town. He taught himself the violin and piano. But he became best known as an artist, skilled in oils and watercolours, and many of his pictures are in private collections. His best-known is 'The Glanyrafon Hunt', painted for Edward Bennett, brother of

Nicholas Bennett (*DWB*, 32) in 1885. There are three of his paintings in the National Library. He was also a very effective portrait painter.

In 1859 he married Elizabeth Salter of Kerry, and they had two sons and five daughters. One son, Richard Henry Jerman, 1866-1951, was also a gifted artist. His brother-in-law, Edward Salter, b. 1831, was a schoolmaster and artist and father of E.H. Langford Salter, 1870-1949, who established a music business in Neath and manufactured organs. He died May 8, 1895 and was buried in the parish cemetery at Llanidloes.

David Davies, *Musicians of Llanidloes*, 1931; personal knowledge.

E.R.M.

JOB, JOHN THOMAS (*DWB*, 439). See also *Traeth.*, cxxii, 95-103.

JOHN ap JOHN (*DWB*, 439-40). In the bibliography read Penney not 'Penny'.

JOHN, GWENDOLEN MARY (1876-1939), artist; b. in Haverfordwest, Pembs. 22 June 1876, the second child of Edwin William John and Augusta (née Smith) and the elder sister of Augustus John (see above). She was educated at Tenby, where the family moved after her mother d. in 1884. She continued to draw from childhood, and her first surviving oil paintings are a portrait of her younger sister Winifred (Tenby Museum) and a view of Tenby harbour. Following the example of Augustus she was sent to the Slade School of Art in London University (1895-98). This school was the most important source both of her friendships and her attitude to art, although this was learnt more from her fellow pupils than her teachers. She shared lodgings at first with Augustus, but was then on her own in the Fitzroy and Bayswater areas of London, and the apartments she later occupied in Paris and Meudon were of the same kind. Her appearance is recorded in self-portraits and in drawings by Augustus: medium height, slim and auburn-haired and dressed with an extreme neatness and a liking for jewellery and lace. Edna Waugh and Augustus recalled that she spoke with a soft, Pembrokeshire accent. The teaching at the Slade School was at odds with what in retrospect can be seen as her style as the Slade's method was based on a separation of drawing and painting with the emphasis on the former. Despite a few drawings in the style of Tonks, her tutor, the best of her early drawings are all portraits of her female contemporaries, particularly of Winifred John. In 1898 she stayed for six months in Paris to be taught at Whistler's school. Whistler's fastidious control of colour and his preferred subject of the single figure in an interior were both an example to Gwen John.

She returned to live in England, for the last time, until 1903. The New English Art Club exhibited her paintings, and although these seem to have been few she developed a skilful realist technique and a sense for the balance of tones similar to Whistler's. The occasion of her leaving Britain was a painting and walking expedition to France with Augustus's mistress Dorelia McNeill, unusual in that they travelled alone, and originally intended to get to Rome. In Feb. 1904 they arrived instead at Paris, where

they earned money as artists' models in Montparnasse. Gwen John's life in Paris from 1904 is recorded in letters to Britain, particularly a series to the painter Ursula Tyrwhitt (at the National Library of Wales) and by her copious letters to the sculptor Rodin, who became her lover from that year, after she had worked for him as a model. Her long affair with Rodin was not known to her contemporaries, and was only published in Michael Holroyd's biography of Augustus (1934), but is now known from the letters at the Musée Rodin published by Susan Chitty (1981). Until his death in 1924 she was supported by the New York collector John Quinn, who bought as much as the reluctant artist would part with, and who gave her an annual allowance. Subsequently some of her paintings were acquired by American museums.

Early in 1913 she was received into the Roman Catholic Church. She painted portraits of two nuns from a convent in Meudon, the town where Rodin lived, and where she had moved in 1911, and a series of copy portraits of the founder of their order. Her tiny gouaches of people in church and of children were painted in 'sets' of almost identical copies.

During 1918-24 she began to paint more frequently, exhibited at the salons, and made her outstanding and unique series of portraits painted with dry touches of thick colour in a harmony of close tones. Frequently her subject was a seated model, a young girl, in her apartment. Many of her notes (at National Library of Wales) are concerned with the perfection of her range of colours and their association with flowers.

Her reputation has risen steadily since her memorial exhibition at Matthiesen Ltd. in 1946. The Arts Council's retrospective exhibition of 1968 shown at London, Sheffield and Cardiff included in the catalogue the first detailed account of her work. At the same time as the feminist movement in criticism has revaluated women artists she has become recognised as one of the best twentieth-century British painters, and is also so regarded in America.

She d. 18 Sept. 1939 in Dieppe, where she had presumably gone with the intention of returning to Britain before the War. Her paintings were inherited by her nephew Edwin, who was also a water-colour painter. In 1976 the National Museum of Wales acquired from him the remainder of the collection, including more than one thousand of her drawings.

Susan Chitty, *Gwen John, 1876-1939* (1981); Cecily Langdale and David Fraser Jenkins, *Gwen John: an Interior Life* (1985); [see also: Mary Taubman, *Gwen John* (1985); Cecily Langdale, *Gwen John* (1987); Ceridwen Lloyd-Morgan, *Gwen John papers at the National Library of Wales* (1988)].

A.D.F.J.

JOHNES, ARTHUR JAMES (*DWB*, 441). Delete 'only' in the second line. The resistance to uniting the sees lasted from 1837 until 1846. See further the articles by Marian Henry Jones in *N.L.W. Jnl.*, X, 233-64, 329-64 ('The letters of A.J.J.') and XIV, 129-82 ('*Additional letters* of A.J.J. ...').

JOHNS, DAVID (*fl.* 1569-86, rather than 1573-87; *DWB*, 442). 'David ap John' was ord. deacon on 1 Nov. 1569, and priest ('David ap John, alias Johns') Christmas Day 1570. He was collated to Llanfair, 22 Sept. 1573 ('David John, clk.'). His successor, John Williams, was collated according to the Composition Book, 16 May, 1598, but on account of his plurality he was reappointed to Llanfair on 3 June 1603; he was S.T.P., i.e. D.D.

A.I. Pryce, *Dioc. of Bangor in the XVIc.*; additional information provided by E.D.J.

JONES, Sir ALFRED LEWIS (*DWB*, 445). See also P.N. Davies, *Sir Alfred Jones* (1978).

JONES, BASSETT (*DWB*, 446). Read Franeker (not 'Franecker').

JONES, BENJAMIN (1756-1823; *DWB*, 446). Read Griffiths (not 'Griffith'); see John Griffiths (1731-1811), *DWB*, 305.

JONES, CALVERT RICHARD (1802-77), pioneer photographer, artist and priest; b. 4 Dec. 1802 at Verandah, Swansea, Glam., son of Calvert Richard Jones. He was the third of his family to bear the name. His grandfather inherited part of the estate of 'the Herberts of Swansea' in the 18th c. He and his father (1766-1847) were prominent citizens of Swansea and benefactors of the town. He was educated at Eton, and Oriel College, Oxford, where he graduated first class in mathematics. After his ord. as a priest he held the livings of Loughor and Roath (Cardiff) for a period, but he spent much of his time travelling in Europe or pursuing his interests in art and music. At Oxford he was a fellow-student of Christopher Rice Mansel Talbot (*DWB*, 929), heir to the vast estates of Margam and Penrice, and they were close lifelong friends. Through the Talbot family of Penrice he came to know very early of the discoveries of their cousin William Henry Fox Talbot of Lacock Abbey, Wiltshire (*DWB*, 929), the inventor of the positive-negative method of making a photograph. Because of the practical problems associated with Talbot's process he first took to the daguerrotype process and completely mastered it by 1841. During the 1840s he collaborated with Talbot and with Frenchmen such as Hippolyte Bayard, and he was an important link between pioneers in France and England. By 1846 he had turned to Talbot's calotype process. His most well-known works are the calotype photographs he took at the end of the 1840s on the island of Malta, in Italy and around Britain, sending negatives to Talbot to have them printed and sold.

He inherited the Heathfield estate, Swansea, in 1847, and built streets which are now in the centre of the city, naming one Mansel Street in memory of his half-brother and another Portia Street in memory of his second wife. He left Swansea in 1853 to live for a time in Brussels before settling in Bath, where he d. 7 Nov. 1877. He was buried in the family chapel in St. Mary's Church, Swansea, but all was destroyed during World War II. He had one daughter of the first marriage and two of the second.

Before becoming a photographer Calvert Jones had shown that he was a skilful artist and his watercolours show a strong feeling for colour and form. He took a great interest in the sea and maritime objects, ships being his favourite subject for his paintings and photographs. He composed his pictures carefully but was venturesome and he considered his photographic work to be an artistic product. It was not until a century after his death that the clarity of his vision was recognised and he was acknowledged to be one of the most important pioneers of photography.

There are collections of his work in London at the National Science Museum, the Victoria and Albert Musuem and the National Maritime Museum, and in Wales at the National Library, Aberystwyth, and at the Glynn Vivian Gallery and in the collection of the Royal Institution, Swansea. His letters to Fox Talbot are in the Lacock Abbey collection.

Rollin Buckman, *The photographic work of Calvert Richard Jones* (1990); N.L.W. Department of Manuscripts; Cardiff MSS 2.839 (family pedigree); Lacock Abbey collection; Bath City Reference Library MSS 1010-1012 (his first wife's diary); [I.M. Jones, *Cymm. Trans.*, 1990, 117-72].

I.M.J.

JONES, DANIEL ANGELL (1861-1936), botanist and authority on ferns and mosses; b. 14 July 1861, in Liverpool. He was a schoolmaster at Machynlleth and Harlech. He acquired specialist knowledge of plants in Merionethshire and Caernarfonshire, and he was an acknowledged expert on British mosses. He won a prize at Blaenau Ffestiniog national *eisteddfod*, 1898, for an essay on the plants of Merionethshire. He rediscovered, on Cader Idris, in 1901, the plant known as hairy greenweed, which was presumed at the time to be extinct. He was one of the early members of the Moss Exchange Club, and when the British Bryological Society was formed he was appointed secretary of that society. Later he became president.

In 1918 he gained a M.Sc. degree of the University of Wales. Afer retiring in 1924 he lived in Cheltenham and Bristol. In 1925 he was elected a member of the Linnaean Society. He wrote 'The Flora of Dolgelley and the Neighbourhood' as an appendix to T.P. Ellis, *The Story of two Parishes, Dolgelley and Llanelltyd* (1928). He d. at Bristol, 6 Oct, 1936, and his collections of plants was distributed between the British Museum and the National Museum of Wales.

Liv. Daily Post, 10 June 1960; *The Merioneth Miscellany* (Merionethshire Historical and Record Society, 1955); *The North Western Naturalist*, xi, 374-5.
G.M.G.

JONES, DAVID (*DWB*, 450-1). Append to the bibliography *Cylch. Cymd. Hanes M.C.*, xlii, 12-21 ('Nodiadau ar David Jones, Llan-gan', G.M.R.).

JONES, DAVID ('Dewi Wyllt'; 1836-78?), musician; b. in 1836 at Mallwyd, Mer. His father was a weaver who gave him a good education. 'Dewi Wyllt' played the organ in Mallwyd church and at the age of 23 published a collection of 142 tunes under the title *Udgorn Seion*, which included works by Ambrose Lloyd, 'Owain Alaw' and 'Eos Llechid' (*DWB*, 584-5, 713-4, 146). The family moved from Mallwyd to

Caernarfon c. 1859. He was apprenticed as a medical practitioner to Dr. Jones, one of the doctors in the town, and he assisted a doctor at Ruthin before proceeding to Glasgow as a student. After passing his examination he established himself as a medical practitioner in Mold, where he lived until he d. c. 1878.

Y Cerddor, July and Aug. 1893.

R.D.G.

JONES, DAVID BEVAN ('Dewi Elfed', 1807-63), minister (B, and Church of Christ and Latter Day Saints – Mormons); b. 1807, son of John and Hannah Jones, Gellifaharen, Llandysul, Cards. and baptized 30 June 1807. He became a member of Pen-y-bont (B) church, in the parish of Llanfihangel-ar-arth, c. 1822, but was raised by Ebeneser church, Llandysul to preach. He ministered to Seion (B), Cwrtnewydd, Cards. (1841-46); Jerusalem, Rhymney, Mon. (1846-48); and Gwawr, Aberaman, Glam. from about the beginning of 1849. He completed the task of building Gwawr chapel for the church which had been incorporated in June 1848. Dewi altered the chapel lease, deleting the name of the Rev. Dr. Thomas Price (1820-88; DWB, 792) and a friend of his and adding his own name and that of a supporter. This was the beginning of the dispute between the two but underlying the disagreement was the accusation that Dewi used his standing as a Baptist minister to promote the tenets of the Saints; denigrating his fellow-ministers; denying the unity of the Trinity and the unique nature of the Bible on salvation; preaching the possibility of miracles directly from the hands of those who received the Spirit; teaching millenarianism and calling himself an apostle. It is not certain how or when Dewi came under the influence of Mormonism. But even before he left Rhymney it was rumoured that he fostered unorthodox ideas, leaning towards Unitarianism. An investigation was held by the Glamorgan Baptist Association at Aberdare, Nov. 1850, and he and the congregation of Gwawr were excommunicated from the Association. In 1851 Dewi went to William Phillips, president of the Saints in Wales, and received (with four others) Mormon baptism in the river Cynon, 27 Apr. 1851, in sight of a crowd of about 2,000, before returning to the chapel where he was inducted as a priest of the church of Latter Day Saints. This was a climax of the Mormon mission in Wales, leaving them with a chapel, a baptised minister and wide publicity. A legal controversy ensued between the Saints and the Baptists, and in the 1851 summer session of the Glamorgan assizes a verdict was reached in favour of the Baptists. In Nov. 1851 the Baptists organised a march of 2,000 supporters under the leadership of Price to repossess Gwawr chapel because Dewi Elfed had refused to surrender the building to them despite the court decision.

Dewi Elfed was sent by the Saints as an eloquent and well-known missionary through Glamorgan and Gwent to spread the faith. In Oct. 1852 he was appointed treasurer of the mission; and in Jan. 1853 he was appointed president of the Llanelli Assembly, with his son Aneurin as secretary. He moved to Swansea in Aug. 1854 on his appointment as president of the West Glamorgan Assembly. This coincided with the decision of Daniel Jones (1811-61, DWB, 449) to move the headquarters of the Welsh Saints from Merthyr to Swansea in Sept. 1854. Dewi Elfed's presidency came to an end in July 1855 when he was accused of financial fraud and was excommunicated. Although he was reconciled with this church and its leaders in Apr. 1856, he was never again given office in the administration of the Welsh Mission. Instead, advantage was taken of his indisputable gifts as a preacher and a keen debater and he was sent throughout south Wales to reinforce the faithful and seek new converts.

He was m. by 1833 and had five children. In May 1860 he emigrated with his wife and their two youngest children on board the William Tapscott from Liverpool to New York, where they stayed for two yrs. before travelling for four months across the prairie with other pioneer Mormons, arriving at Great Salt Lake Valley in Oct. 1862. He settled in Logan, about a hundred miles north of Salt Lake City, but d. of tuberculosis in May or June 1863.

He published Eos Dyssul (1838); Cân newydd yn dangos niweidiau meddwdod (n.d.); and Serch Gerdd (n.d.). His work appeared mainly in the Baptist and Mormon periodicals, (Seren Gomer and Udgorn Seion in particular); but the zenith of his literary career came undoubtedly with his later polemic prose, promoting the mission of the Saints and satirising Nonconformity in the fiery correspondence between him and Thomas Price in Yr Amserau and Udgorn Seion.

Dewi Elfed had his share of troubles and was one of the most colourful characters of the controversial Mormon mission in Wales in mid-19 c. Through his preaching, writing and debating and his hymns he contributed extensively to their missionary effort. But his chief contribution was his own conversion, since he was the only minister from among the main nonconformist denominations to become a member of the Saints. He was undisciplined, with the capacity to agitate both friend and foe. His life demonstrates the fierce enmity confronting the Saints in Wales at that time; but also the surprising dedication and discipline of the Welsh Mormon Mission in the middle of the 19 c.

D.L. Davies, 'From a Seion of Lands to the Land of Zion: the Life of David Bevan Jones' in Jensen and Thorp (ed.), Mormons in early Victorian Britain (1989), 118-141.

D.L.D

JONES, DAVID GEORGE (1780-1879), blacksmith, of Tir-Waun, Llanarthne, Carms. According to his epitaph, he was the author of the well-known verse 'Bydd myrdd o ryfeddodau'; see the discussion on p. 17 of Gomer M. Roberts's edn. (1961) of J. Thickens, Emynau a'u Hawduriaid.

R.T.J.

JONES, DAVID HUGH ('Dewi Arfon', 1833-1869), minister (CM), schoolmaster and poet; b. in Tŷ Du, Llanberis, Caern., 6th July 1833, to Hugh and Ellen Jones. He was the eldest of 4 children; one brother was Griffth Hugh Jones, ('Gutyn Arfon'; DWB, 465), composer of the hymn-tune 'Llef', written in memory of Dewi Arfon. When Dewi Arfon was about 5, he went to a school kept by Ellis Thomas, in Capel

Coch, Llanberis, and then to a school kept by John Evans, Ceunant Coch. He left school at 11, and went to work with his father in the quarry. He studied assiduously during his leisure hours and mastered the rules of poetry, music, arithmetic and English and Welsh grammar. In the spring of 1853, he caught a chill and was very ill in the early summer of that year. He returned to the British School, Dolbadarn, kept by David Evans (later the Revd. David Evans of Dolgellau), intending to become a schoolteacher. After consulting John Phillips, Bangor (1810-67; *DWB*, 759-60) he decided to go to Borough Road College, London, and to mark the occasion, a testimonial was presented to him in January 1856 by the Literary Society of Capel Coch, Llanberis. He went at his own expense to Borough Road, and after a year gained a teacher's certificate, second class. For four years after that, he was a teacher in the British School, Llanrwst. He became a close friend of Trebor Mai (Robert Williams, *DWB*, 1068) and other local poets. While in Llanrwst he became interested in poetry. He was the teacher when John Lloyd Williams, musician and botanist, was a pupil there.

Towards the end of this period, he began to preach. However, it was in Capel Coch, Llanberis, in 1861, that he was officially accepted by his denomination to be a minister, and in 1862, he went as a student to the school kept by Eben Fardd (Ebenezer Thomas, *DWB*, 944-5) in Clynnog. He was accepted as a minister to serve the whole circuit of the Arfon Presbytery in 1863. During Eben Fardd's illness he taught in the school, and he followed Eben Fardd in the post. He was ordained to the full work of the ministry in the Association held at Llangefni in June 1867. He was a better teacher than Eben Fardd, because of his lively manner while in school. A school building and a house were built for him, but he died before he could enter either.

His health was frail. He had to leave Clynnog, and return to Tŷ Du, Llanberis, where he died on Christmas morning, 1869. He was buried in the cemetery at Nant Peris, and money collected as a testimonial to him during his illness was used to erect a gravestone. A strange story is told about his death: between five and six in the morning, he called his sister and asked her to set the alarm clock to strike at 9, and, at exactly 9 o'clock, he died. He was considered to be a talented musician, though he was not a singer, and he was very popular as an adjudicator for music and poetry. He was considered to be a good poet, and, according to his obituary, his ode 'Tywylltiad yr Ysbryd Glân ar Ddydd y Pentecost' came high on the list in the competition in the Denbigh *eisteddfod* of 1860. but a quotation from the poem in the adjudication shows that he was 'Awenydd', the third of four competitors.

He excelled as a writer of *englynion*, especially epitaphs for gravestones, and his best-known *englyn* was his epitaph for John Jones (1796-1857), Talysarn (*DWB*, 478-9). This is not on John Jones's grave in the cemetery in Llanllyfni, but on the memorial column near Tanycastell, his old home in Dolwyddelan.

Gweithiau Dewi Arfon ... a chofiant ... gan y Parch. J. Owen, Penyberth, ed., Gutyn Arfon, 1878); Y

Gwyddoniadur Cymreig (2 ed.), 10, 538; *Asaph (Em. W.)*; Anthropos, *Camrau Llwyddiant: trem ar fywyd Dewi Arfon* (1901); William Hobley, *Hanes Methodistiaid Arfon* (1910); Carneddog, 'Tri Chyfaill', *Cymru*, 14 (1898), 176-178; *Y Drys*, March 1870, 114-115; G.H. Arfon (Gutyn Arfon), *Manion: penill, englyn ac adgof* (1919); Y Gwyneddigion, *Cyfansoddiadau Eisteddfod Dinbych 1860* (1862), 11; John Lloyd-Williams, *Atgofion tri chwarter canrif* (1941), 30.

De.J.

JONES, DAVID STANLEY (*DWB*, 1132), Pisgah, Talgarreg, not Brynrhiwgaled.

JONES, EDMUND (*DWB*, 455). In the second paragraph read Ty'n llwyn (not 'Ty-llwyn').

JONES, EDWARD (1761-1836; *DWB*, 457). See the full discussion, *Edward Jones, Maes-y-Plwm*, by J.E. Caerwyn Williams (Denbigh, 1962).

JONES, EDWARD (1790-1860), minister (Presb.); b. 11 Sept. 1790, son of Edward Jones, Rhiwlas, in the parish of Llanfihangel Genau'r-glyn, Cards., and Mary his wife. He was taught to be a saddler, and at the age of 20 he went to London, where he heard John Elias (*DWB*, 203-4) preach, and thence to Bristol. He returned to his native district and began to preach with the Calvinistic Methodists; he was ordained to the ministry in 1829. He excelled not so much as a preacher but as an educator and an expert on the property, constitution and discipline of his Connexion. He m. Mary, dau. of David Davies, Machynlleth, and sister of Robert Davies (1790-1841; *DWB*, 150). He d. 29 Aug. 1860, and was the first to be interred in Aberystwyth town cemetery.

John Evans, *Byr-gofiant am 49 o Weinidogion ymadawedig Sir Aberteifi*, 1894; *Drys.*, 1860, 360.

T.I.E.

JONES, EVAN ('Ieuan Gwynedd'; 1820-52; *DWB*, 460-1). He m. Catherine, third daughter of John Sankey, not at Tredegar, but at Marton on 11 Nov. 1845.

JONES, EVAN ('Gurnos'; 1840-1903; *DWB*, 462). The church at Treorchy was called Tabernacl. He had left the place before the erection of Bethania in 1876. His son (Giraldus) began to preach but did not continue. He was an accountant at a colliery (*Tywysydd y Plant*, 1940, 222).

JONES, EVAN ('Ieuan Buallt'; 1850-1928; *DWB*, 462). Extensive collections of his MSS are in the Museum of Welsh Life, St. Fagans – nos. 1793/1-654, 2038/1-137 and 2384/1-186.

A.Ll.H.

JONES, HENRY (d. 1592; *DWB*, 466). Read Benet's (not 'Bennett's').

JONES, HUGH ('Gwyndaf Ieuanc'; *fl.* 1812), poet, reputedly b. at Pen-y-groes, a smallholding in the parish of Llanwnda, Caerns. He was a carpenter by trade, and a Calvinistic Methodist. He took an interest in poetry and mastered the strict metres. Unfortunately only a few of his works are exant. His *awdl*, 'Arwyrain Amaethyddiaeth', in praise of agriculture which was composed for Tremadog *eisteddfod* in 1812, was published in *Cell Callestr*. Some of his compositions also appeared in the Welsh monthly periodicals. He is said to have moved towards the end of his life to live at Nantlle and d. there. It is not known whether he was buried there or at Llanwnda.

W. Edwards ('Wil Ysgeifiog')', *Cell Callestr*, 36; J. Jones ('Myrddin Fardd'), *Enwogion Sir Gaernarfon*.

R.L.

JONES, HUMPHREY OWEN (1878-1912; *DWB*, 468-9). Though he began climbing comparatively late in life he was in the front rank. According to Geoffrey Winthrop Young, the most famous climber of the day, he was an 'ideal comrade' whose 'climbing was a model of agile, accurate and elegant movement' (*On high hills*, (1947), 299). He appears to have visited Zermatt in 1906 and began rock-climbing seriously in Snowdonia the following year under the guidance of J.M. Archer Thomson, headmaster of John Bright School, Llandudno. Soon afterwards he was assisting that arch-climber to complete his pioneering of Lliwedd and his discovery of the climbing cliffs of Crib y Ddysgl, Llechog and Creigiau Gleision. Starting in 1907, Jones led a number of new climbs in Snowdonia which remain in vogue, including some 'very difficult' ones like Paradise on Lliwedd (1909) and some easy, popular ones like Criafolen on Tryfan (1910). In 1911 he created new climbs in the Cuillin with his sister Bronwen and Archer Thomson. (According to Young, Bronwen Ceridwen Jones – later Mrs. Mawson; 1890-1981 – was the first to show how a female climber could excel a male by means of measured steps rather than mere strength; she contributed the essay on climbing clothes for women in the first ed. of *Mountain Craft*).

Every summer from 1908 onwards Jones concentrated on the southern side of Mont Blanc, completing many first ascents, a number of them in the company of Young and the guide Joseph Knubel: among the most important were the Aiguille Blanche de Peuterey from the west (1909), the usual path up the Brouillard ridge (the pinacle of his pioneering work on Mont Blanc, according to Young), the western ridge of the Grandes Jorasses and the west face of the Grépon (1910) and L'Isolée (1912). His wife too was a skilful climber; she led the Pinacles' Ridge on Sgurr nan Gillean without male company. Jones was elected to the Alpine Club and the Mountaineers Club in 1910, serving on the committee of the latter. The little he contributed to the mountaineering journals was strictly factual be he read the works of Welsh authors like O.M. Edwards (*DWB*, 192-3). There is a memorial to him in Lewis' School, Pengam; La Pointe Jones is the name given to the north summit of Aiguille Blanche (4104 m.) in the Vallot *Guide* (1930 ed.).

N. Wales Chron., 16 and 23 Aug. 1912; G.W. Young, *On high hills* (1927); *Alpine Jnl.*, 27 (1913); W. Idris Jones, *Y Gwyddonydd*, 7, 4 (1969) – details of his work as one of the most important and fruitful chemical researchers of his day; Alan Hankinson, *The mountain men; an early history of rock-climbing in North Wales* (1977); John Shorter, 'Humphrey Owen Jones (1878-1912)', *Climber and Rambler*, 18, 2 (Feb. 1979); idem, 'Humphrey Owen Jones, F.R.S. (1878-1912), chemist and mountaineer', *Notes and records of the Roy. Soc. of London*, 33, 2 (March, 1979); information about his library from Dr. R. Elwyn Hughes, Cardiff.

I.B.R.

JONES, HUMPHREY ROWLAND (1832-95; *DWB*, 469). His father's name was Hugh Jones. His birthplace was not Gwarcwm Bach. His christening is recorded in the parish register on 10 Nov. as that of the son of Hugh and Elizabeth Jones of 'Trerddol alias Yniscapel'. He was born either in the home of his mother's parents, the Half-way Inn, Tre'rddôl, or in that of his father's parents, Ynyscapel. He was between 4 and 6 years of age when the family settled at Gwarcwm Bach sometime between 1836 and 1838.

Add *Papur Pawb*, No. 80, June 1982, 6; Eifion Evans, *Humphrey Jones a Diwygiad 1859* (1980), to the Bibliography.

E.D.J.

JONES, JOHN (Maes y garnedd; 1597?-1600; *DWB*, 472-5). On p. 474b read Ellis Wynne (not 'Wyn').

JONES, JOHN (1725?-96), musician; b. *c.* 1725. He was appointed organist at Middle Temple on 24 Nov. 1749, organist at Charterhouse (as successor to Dr. Pepusch) 2 July 1753, and organist at St. Paul's cathedral, Christmas 1755. He published some salm-tunes in 1785; one of these was sung when George III visited St. Paul's, 23 Apr. 1789, and also at the annual services for the children of the 'Welch Charity'. After hearing this salm-tune being sung, Haydn wrote in his diary: 'No music has for a long time affected me so much as this innocent and reverential strain.' He d. Feb. 1796 in London.

Grove, *Dictionary of Music*; M. O. Jones, *Byw. Cerdd. Cymr.*

R.D.G.

JONES, JOHN (1773-1853), cleric; b. 31 Mar. 1773, the eldest of the thirteen children of Thomas and Lowri Jones, Dolgellau, Mer. Thomas Jones was a businessman and financier, founder of the first bank in Dolgellau, and a relative of David Richards, 'Dafydd Ionawr' (*DWB*, 850-1). John Jones was educated in Dolgellau, Ruthin Grammar School and Jesus College, Oxford where he graduated B.A. in 1796 (M.A. in 1800). He was curate in Tremeirchion, 1797-99, and then in Llanyblodwel near Oswestry. While he was there he met Walter Davies, 'Gwallter Mechain' (*DWB*, 157), John Jenkins, 'Ifor Ceri' (*DWB*, 434) and others of the circle of 'literary parsons' and thereafter he became one of the circle. From Llanyblodwel he went to Wrexham as a curate but in 1811 he was ordained vicar of Llansilin parish. In 1819 he was appointed secretary of the Cambrian Society of the province of Powys but because of his move to the vicarage of Rhuddlan in 1820, he declined the post. But from then on he was prominent as a patron and adjudicator in the provincial *eisteddfodau*. In 1819 he m. Margaret Morris, heiress of Plas and Llanrhaeadr-yng-Nghinmeirch estate, Denbs. From Rhuddlan he moved to Llandderfel rectory in 1828 and remained there until 1840 when he moved once more to Llanaber parish, Mer. He retired in 1843 and went to live in Borthwnog near Pemaenpool where he spent the rest of his life. He d. 6 Apr. 1853 and was buried in Llanelltud churchyard.

He was a wealthy and generous person and was the Maecenas of the literary clergy. He also gave financial support and encouragement to Evan Evans, 'Ieuan Glan Geirionydd' (*DWB*, 231-2) and John Blackwell, 'Alun' (*DWB*, 39) at the commencement of their careers. He was a scholar and in 1834 he published the second edition of *British Antiquities Revived* by Robert Vaughan, Hengwrt (1662) (*DWB*, 1005-6). Occasional references in his letters reveal that he was also quite critical of the scholarship of John Williams, 'Ab Ithel' (*DWB*, 1052-3) affected by its Iolo mania and druidism. He paid for the monument to 'Dafydd Ionawr' in Dolgellau old churchyard and the 1851 edition of *Gwaith Dafydd Ionawr* was dedicated to him.

D. Tecwyn Lloyd, 'Dyddiaduron y Parch. John Jones, M.A.', *Jnl. Merioneth Hist. Soc.*, 1970, 148-72; D. Tecwyn Lloyd, 'Y Parch John Jones, M.A., Borthwnog', *Jnl. Merioneth Hist. Soc.*, 1971, 245-66.

D.T.Ll.

JONES, JOHN (1786-1865), printer and inventor; bapt. 7 May 1786, son of Ismael Davies (son of Dafydd Jones, Trefriw (1708?-85, *DWB*, 450)) and Jane, his wife. After Dafydd Jones d. in 1785, Ismael Davies continued working his father's printing press at Bryn Pyll, Trefriw. According to family tradition, John Jones was apprenticed to a blacksmith, but he also learnt the printer's craft, and from 1810 onwards there is a noticeable improvement in the output of Trefriw press which can be attributed to the work of John, although his name does not appear on the output (other than in *englynion* addressed to patrons and others) until 1817, when Ismael died. He m. Jane Evans in 1824; in 1825 he moved to 29, Station Road, Llanrwst, and again in 1836 to 30, Denbigh Road. He kept a paper and bookshop, and printed much miscellaneous work for the locality. Sometime (?before 1817) he constructed three presses to the Ruthven design, so called after its inventor, Alexander Ruthven, which he then used for all his printing work. He also learnt to cast his own type and used many of his own letters and characters for the rest of his life. Towards the end of his life he also invented a machine for cutting paper. This machine and examples of his type are at the Museum of Welsh Life, St. Fagan's, as well as many of the ballad illustrations; one of his presses is at South Kensington Science Museum. He was one of the most productive printers of ballads, and one of his itinerant booksellers was Thomas Williams, 'Capelulo' (see below). The Trefriw/Llanrwst press was responsible for printing the long series of almanacs bearing the title *Y Cyfaill* .... The imprint declares that they were printed in Dublin, but this was a ruse to avoid paying tax. When the tax was discontinued in 1834, the almanacs were openly printed at Llanrwst. John Jones printed the works of important contemporary authors such as William Williams 'Caledfryn', Robert Jones, Rhoslan, Ieuan Glan Geirionnydd, John Elias, Gwilym Hiraethog (*DWB*, 1083, 507-8, 231-2, 203-4, 831-2), as well as classical works such as *Drych y Prif Oesoedd*,

Egluryn Ffraethineb and a number of works by Twm o'r Nant (*DWB*, 196). He was also responsible for a number of periodicals and many odd, recreative or unusual booklets, such as a version of *Robinson Crusoe*, *Hanes Judas Iscariot*, *Hanes y Lleuad*, *Bywyd Turpin Leidr* and *Faunula Grustensis*, as well as *Gwaith Aristotle* (first printed by his brother Robert (1803-50) at Conwy in 1826; Robert also printed at Pwllheli and Bangor). John Jones produced the smallest books ever printed in Welsh; but his printing masterpieces were *Mawl yr Arglwydd* by John Ellis (1816) and *Gronoviana* (1860), the first edition of the complete works of Goronwy Owen (*DWB*, 703-4). These poems were collected by John Jones' son Edward (1826-81), father of Griffith Hartwell Jones, author of *Celtic Britain and the Pilgrim Movement* (1915) (see above). John Jones who was diverting company, was cultured and composed verse under the pseudonym 'Pyll'. After his d. 19 Mar. 1865, his son Owen Evans-Jones continued the business, without much enthusiasm, until his d. in 1887. His grandson J.J. Lloyd then owned it until 1935 when the shop was closed after the family had been in the printing trade over five generations from 1776 until 1935. Evan Jones (1830-1918), second son of John Jones, was a printer at Porthmadog.

Gerald Morgan, *Y Dyn a wnaeth argraff* (1982); personal research; NLW MSS. 12,004-12,021.

Ge.M.

JONES, JOHN (1807-75, printer; *DWB*, 480). Add to the bibliography *Trans. Denb. Hist. Soc.*, 17 Oct. 1969.

JONES, JOHN (1820-1907), minister (B) and historian; b. at Lower Trelowgoed Farm, Cefn-llys, Radnors., 10 May 1820, elder s. of the second marriage of James Jones, tenant farmer and pastor (1829-60) of Rock Chapel, Llanbadarn Fawr, in the same county. After scant formal local schooling he farmed with his father and after his confession of Christ in 1840 assisted him in his church work, including preaching. Four years later on the recommendation of William Jenkins, pastor of Dolau Baptist chapel, Nantmel, he was accepted as one of the 16 students preparing for the ministry under principal Thomas Thomas (1805-81; *DWB*, 966) at the Pontypool Baptist College. He was ord. in 1847 and was given the oversight of the churches at Gladestry and Evenjobb. A chapel had been built at the former through the efforts of his father in 1842, and one was built by John's efforts at Evenjobb in 1849. John also conducted a day school in Gladestry chapel, the salary derived from the Edward Gough charity. In 1849 he m. Anne Roberts (b. 1825 in Cheltenham but of a Methodist family) of Abbey Cwmhir. For a few years before her death she kept a girls' school in Kington. She and her husband had eight children, six of whom died young.

John Jones held pastorates at Usk (1850-53), Corsham, Wilts (1853-55), and Towcester, Northants. (1856-61). Late in 1861 he accepted the pastorate of Rock, vacant by his father's death in 1860, but he lived in Kington until, in 1867, a larger manse was built at Rock where until 1888 he lived with his second wife Anne (b. Rogers at Rotherhithe, Surrey, in 1825). He was instrumental in building chapels at Dolau, Llanfihangel Rhydithon, where he was pastor for 11 years, in 1870, and at Llandrindod Wells, where his second wife died in 1890 at the house into which they had moved from Rock two years earlier. In 1891 he gave up the Rock and devoted the rest of his pastoral life to his chapel in Llandrindod, until old age forced him to retire in 1897 to a less active life, though he conducted a service at the Friends' meeting house in Llandrindod within five weeks of his death on 1 March 1907. He left one daughter, Mrs. Annie E. Skewis (d. 1910) and a son.

He travelled widely in Wales and in England to collect funds to clear the debts of the chapels which he had helped to build. In Wales and the Border he was known as Jones the Rock, and was described as 'the nonconformist bishop of Radnorshire.' He published two slight volumes of sermons which are of no great merit. His only valuable written work was his *History of the Baptists in Radnorshire* on which he started before 1876, but was unable to finish, owing to the pressure of pastoral work until 1895. He relied on printed sources such as the works of Thomas Rees (*DWB*, 830) and Joshua Thomas (*DWB*, 956-7) for the early period, but for the period 1795 to 1895 he depended on his personal knowledge and on the reminiscences of his father and his own friends about the development of the Baptist cause in the county. Despite careless proof-reading and the lack of index the volume remains indispensable for students of the history of the Baptist cause in mid-Wales.

Jones, *History of the Baptists in Radnorshire*, (1895); *Bapt. Rec.*, 1906; Llandrindod Wells Baptist chapel archives from 1897; Population censuses, 1851 (Usk), 1861 (Towcester), 1871 (Llanbadarn Fawr, Radns.); *Hereford Times*, July 1876; *Radnor Express*, March 1907; correspondence with his descendants.

R.C.B.O.

JONES, JOHN (1837-1906), minister (Presb.) and writer; b. Dec. 1837, son of George Jones, Abercin (Abercain), Llanystumdwy, Caerns., see *Trans. Caerns. Hist. Soc.*, 1945, 46-8, 54, and the chart in J. E. Griffith, *Pedigrees*, 211 (although this particular branch of the pedigree is not included in it). He served in drapers' shops in Caernarfon and London, but he began to preach and went to Bala College in 1861. He was ord. in 1863, but apart from a short period (1872-78) when he was pastor of Capel y Graig near Bangor, he did not serve as a minister of a church. He m. a dau. of David Jones, Treborth (1805-68; *DWB*, 453). For some years after 1878 he was manager of a private (family) bank 'Pugh, Jones & Co.' in Bethesda, but returned to Pwllheli (where he had lived before going to Capel y Graig), and d. there 19 or 20 June 1906; he was buried at Glanadda, Bangor. He led a fairly prosperous life; he travelled much; he was interested in geology and geography, and wrote much on these subjects for the *Traethodydd*. He also published biographies of two eccentric ministers, Michael Roberts of Pwllheli (*DWB*, 873) and John Jones, Bryn'rodyn.

Myrddin Fardd, *Enw. Sir Gaernarfon*; *Gen.* (Gŵyl Dewi), 1907.

R.T.J.

JONES, JOHN (CYNDDYLAN; *DWB*, 484-5). B. 27 Feb. 1841. He was for some time a pupil at the school of John Evans (*DWB*, 243-4), Aberystwyth. He and John Rhys (*DWB*, 844-5) were both appointed pupil-teachers at Penllwyn because the schoolmaster could not choose between them. For a while he kept a school himself near the site of the town clock in Aberystwyth. His pupils were candidates for the ministry, young boys anxious to succeed in business and sailors. The revival of 1859 deeply affected him and soon afterwards he moved to London. There, under the stimulating influence of Owen Thomas (*DWB*, 960) and David Charles Davies (*DWB*, 117), he quite naturally became inclined towards the ministry. As the Calvinistic Methodists were reluctant to support his candidature, he entered Bala College in 1864 as a lay student. Nevertheless, he was not deterred from crossing swords with the Principal, Lewis Edwards (*DWB*, 191), on the topic of the Doctrine of Atonement. He went to Treveca College in 1865 and on completing a course in 1867 he accepted a call to serve as minister of the English Presb. church at Pontypool. He m. there but as his stipend was insufficient to maintain his family, even though he turned to journalism to supplement his income, he returned to London. In 1869 he took charge of the Congl. church in Offord Road, Pentonville, subsequently succeeding Thomas Jones (*DWB*, 518-9) as minister of Bedford Congl. church, Charrington Street, where Robert Browning and Alfred Tennyson occasionally heard him preach. According to the *Congl. Yr. Bk.* for 1875 he was 'late Bedford Chapel', having commenced his ministry at the English Presb. church in Frederick St., Cardiff on 15 Nov. 1874. His 'Non Con Quill' articles appeared during 1887-89. He was secretary of the Bible Society in south Wales from 1887 to 1909. In 1912 he went to America on a preaching tour. To his publications should be added his commentary, *Yr Epistol at y Colossiaid. Eternal Truth in the Eternal City* is an exposition of the Letter to the Romans. Studies of the first eight chapters of Genesis constitute *Primeval Religion. Luke* does not appear in the catalogues of the N.L.W. nor the B.L. as one of his series of *Studies*. He m. 3 times and left a son of the first marriage, E. Norman Jones, a Professor at Aberystwyth Theological College. To the bibliography add an article by his son on his centenary in *Y Drysorfa*, 1941, 171-6. [*West. Mail*, 20 Dec. 1913, marriage.]

E.D.J.

JONES, JOHN EIDDON (*DWB*, 485). Supporter of D. LLOYD GEORGE (see above). In a letter of condolence which he sent to his widow from the National Liberal Club 16 Oct. 1903 the statesman acknowledged that Eiddon Jones was the first to ask him to be an election candidate for Caernarfon boroughs.

G.A.J.

JONES, JOHN MATHER (1826-74), Utica, U.S.A., proprietor of *Y Drych*; b. 9 June 1826, at Bangor, Caerns. He emigrated to U.S.A. in 1849 and made his home in Utica, New York. He bought *Y Drych* in 1865 from John William Jones who thereafter became editor of the paper, being assisted by Thomas B. Morris

('Gwyneddfardd'). In 1866 John Mather Jones published a Welsh book on the history of the Civil War, which had been written by the two editors of *Y Drych* at his request. After the Civil War he founded a Welsh town, New Cambria, in Missouri, and in 1869, with James A. Whitaker, he bought an extensive tract of land in Osage, Kansas, where he founded another town, Arvonia. He was an enthusiastic opponent of slavery, and politically was a republican. He d. 21 Dec. 1874 in Utica.

NLW MS. 9262; *Not. W.; Y Drych*, 24 Dec. 1874.

N.C.J.

JONES, JOHN MORGAN (1838-1921; *DWB*, 486). *Pant*, i.e. at Cefncoedycymer.

JONES, JOSEPH (1799-1871), Catholic priest. The name of Joseph Jones is associated with Ysgeifiog, Fl. There, presumably, in 1799, he was b. and there also, or not far away, he spent part of his adult life. Like some others from the mining districts of Flintshire, he too in his youth moved to work in the lead mines at Minera where, at the time, there were better work opportunities for miners. At Minera he joined Pen-y-bryn church, one of the earliest of Welsh Wesleyan churches, where he became a leader. It could be that during his stay at Minera he began to preach for it is recorded that 'he began to preach when very young'. At the District Meeting held at Amlwch on 31 May 1824, he was received as an itinerant preacher in accordance with the custom and rules of the Wesleyan Church although he was not stationed that year. It was in the following year (1825) that he was sent to the Caernarfon circuit but before the end of the connexional year he had withdrawn from the itinerant ministry. He returned to Ysgeifiog, renewing his membership in the Holywell circuit. He kept school 'here and there', proof that he was a man of learning. As an accredited bard he took the bardic name of 'Caradog' and addressed an *eisteddfod* at Caernarfon with a sequence of *englynion*.

At a Quarterly Meeting in the Holywell circuit a complaint was brought against him for 'inclining towards Papacy' and although he firmly denied the accusation, the complaint was not without some credence for soon afterwards he joined first the Anglican Church before transferring his membership to the Catholic Church. Thereafter he was under the supervision of a Jesuit priest at Holywell, followed by a term at a college in France, before being appointed as missioner for his 'fellow countrymen in Wales', being the first Welsh missioner so to be appointed from among the Catholic priests. In 1847 he was at Abergele ministering to the Irish labourers constructing the railway from Chester to Bangor. There followed a term of ministry at Wrexham and Mold (living at Wrexham) and, in 1851, at Brecon where he was involved with the building of a new church. Later he ministered at Bangor, and was 'almost worshipped by the Irishmen' who were working on the railway extension to Holyhead. There followed a term at Dukinfield, Cheshire, (1860-1863), a year at Holyhead, then at Pant Asaph, and at Seacombe, before his last posting to Welshpool in 1870. He d. at Welshpool, 2

Dec. 1871 and was buried at Pant Asaph. An obituary was printed in *The Tablet*, 23 Dec. 1871. In his will (under the name of James Jones) there is reference to brothers William and Robert and sisters Mary and Sarah. He left money to the Catholic orphanage at Flint (?Holywell) and to the Catholic Clergy Fund, diocese of Shrewsbury.

Hugh Jones, *Hanes Wesl. Gymr.*, 1, 478, 2, 487, *Traeth.*, 1846, 361-3; Samuel Davies, *Cofiant y Parch. Thomas Aubrey* (1887), ccxxiii; *Cylchgrawn chwarterol cylchdaith Coed-poeth* 35 (2), 177; *Catholic Dir.*, 1846.

Er.E.

JONES, JOSEPH DAVID (*DWB*, 490-1). He m. Catherine Daniel in 1860. See *Three Score Years and Ten*, by his son.

JONES, LEIFCHILD STRATTEN LEIF (*DWB*, 519 under JONES, THOMAS, 1819-82). He went to Scotch College Melbourne before entering Oxford where he gained a M.A. degree in 1889. He became a member of the Privy Council in 1917; he was president of the United Kingdom Alliance (temperance movement) 1906-32, and president of the Liberal Council 1934-37. He changed his name to Leif-Jones 11 Jan. 1932.

L.G. Pine, *New extinct peerages 1884-1971*, 229; *Times*, 27 Sept. 1939; *Who's who British MP*.

Ll.G.C.

JONES, LEWIS (1808-54; *DWB*, 493). He was the son-in-law of the hymn-writer William Edwards, 1773-1853 (*DWB*, 199).

JONES, MARGARET ('Y Gymraes o Ganaan'; ?-1902); native of Rhosllannerchrugog, Denbs. She became well known for her travels in foreign lands. She spent a fairly long time in Palestine and in Morocco. A selection of her letters from Palestine to her family were published as *Llythyrau Cymraes o Wlad Canaan*, 1869, and a description of her experiences in Morocco appeared under the title, *Morocco a'r hyn a welais yno*, 1883. She settled in Australia, and m. a farmer from that country called Josey. She d. 18 Oct. 1902 in Red Bankes Plain, Queensland, Australia.

Asaph; NLW MS. 9263; *Y Tyst*, 10 Dec. 1902.

G.M.G.

JONES, MORDECAI (*DWB*, 496). He was the son of a nephew of Robert Jones, Rhos-lan (*DWB*, 507-8); see an article by J.E. Caerwyn Williams in *Trans. Caerns. Hist. Soc.* for 1964.

JONES, OWEN (1741-1814; *DWB*, 498-9). Read Upper Thames (not 'Thomas') Street.

JONES, OWEN (1833-99; *DWB*, 500-1). His wife was Margaret Jane Jones, Tŷ Cornel shop, Llanfyllin. She d. in Jan. 1909.

JONES, OWEN GLYNNE (1867-99), mountaineer and schoolteacher; b. 2 Nov. 1867 in 110, Clarendon St., Paddington, fourth of the six sons of David Jones, stonemason, and his wife Eliza (née Griffiths), both of Barmouth, Mer. His mother d. in 1882 (his father in 1890) and

Owen and his only sister Nellie (Margaret Ellen) made their home with a cousin and her husband, Alderman John Evans, 11 Brogyntyn, Barmouth, where Welsh was the language of the hearth. Owen probably went to school in Barmouth as well as London before winning scholarships to Finsbury Technical College and to the Imperial Institute (Imperial College) where he took his B.Sc. with first-class honours in 1890. After a period lecturing at the Institute, he was appointed science master of City of London School in 1892, the first to hold the post. He had applied for the chair of physics at U.C.W., Aberystwyth in 1891 and according to Sir Owen Saunders, F.R.S., his sister's son and professor of mechanical engineering at Imperial College of Science and Technology, London, 1946-67, Jones's research work was of great promise and significance.

In May 1888, knowing no more about organised climbing than he had absorbed from books on the Alps, Jones ascended the east ridge of the Cyfrwy on Cadair Idris alone. In Snowdonia, rock-climbing had hardly begun in earnest but in the English Lakes W.P. Haskett Smith and others had been climbing for about 3 years. Jones visited Wasdale in 1890 and came to the notice of some of the pioneers. As a result of his exceptional strength, his 'almost supernatural' climbing ability and his scientific outlook he soon excelled not only in leading new climbs but in developing the technique of rock-climbing. In 1894 he contributed a section on Cadair Idris and the Aran mountain to volume two of Haskett Smith's, *Climbing in the British Isles*; he then began to prepare his own more substantial and influential work, with its combination of instruction and adventure. In Apr. 1896, he called unannounced on the photographer brothers George and Ashley Abraham of Keswick, and persuaded them to come to the rocks to photograph his climbs. Jones's classic, *Rock-climbing in the English Lake District* (1897), was thus the fruit of a partnership with them, as was the Abrahams' book, *Rock-climbing in North Wales* (1906). The brothers had known that Jones was preparing another volume; some of his notes came into their possession after his death and they proceeded to 'put into effect our late friend's wish'. By this time George Abraham had married Jones's London-Welsh cousin, Winifred Davies, dau. of David Davies and a niece of 'Mynorydd' (William Davies, *DWB*, 160); as well as being a good climber trained by Jones, she had been to the universities of Wales (Bangor), London and Cambridge. It was she who ghosted George Abraham's numerous books on the basis of her husband's rough notes. But it was Jones's book that began the practice of grading climbs and popularising rock-climbing as such.

From 1891 onwards Jones visited the Alps annually. He made some important first winter ascents but never seems to have found a regular partner of the highest class, amateur or guide. He fell from the Ferpècle Ridge of the Dent Blanche on 28 Aug. 1899 when the leading guide collapsed upon him, and four of his party of five were killed. His grave is in Evolène and there are memorials in City of London School, in the English Church in Zermatt, and at the door of 11 Brogyntyn, Barmouth.

Jones served on the first committee of the Climbers' Club, founded in 1898, and was elected to the Alpine Club. He never seems to have been completely accepted by the select inner circle of English climbers, however, who considered him 'brusque and off-hand'. But Jones climbed often with his sister, his cousins, his fellow teachers, his fellow lodger in London, William Jones Williams (see above) and with the Abrahams (of Nonconformist background like himself) and their testimony is quite the contrary, while in Merioneth too he is remembered as a kind and cheerful man. As a teacher he was dedicated and inspiring. As a climber, he believed that all should climb and that all would be the better for it. By now a less patrician climbing world recognises him as the leading pioneer of the art of rock-climbing in the British Isles, from the point of view both of technique and attitude. He had intended climbing the highest mountains of the world; shortly before his death, he had invited G.W. Young to join him 'for Everest'. But his love of Cadair Idris was proverbial and he chided the English for mis-pronouncing Welsh names.

Kern Knotts Crack on Great Gable (1897) and Terrace Wall Variant on Tryfan (1899) are amongst his many notable first ascents; the most popular climb created by him is, however, the ordinary route on the Milestone Buttress of Tryfan, which reaches the A5 road near Llyn Ogwen.

Essays by Jones in *Alpine Jnl.*, 16, 18 and 19; W.M. Crook, memoir in *Rock-climbing in the English Lake District* (1900, 2nd ed.); reviews in *Alpine Jnl.*, 19, 385 and 20, 228; H.C. Bowen, *Alpine Jnl.*, 19, 583-5 and F.C. Hill, ibid., 590-3; the works of G.D. Abraham, especially *Mountain adventures at home and abroad* (1910); A.E. Douglas-Smith, *The City of London School* (1937), 294 and 313; Claire-Eliane Engel, *They came to the hills* (1952), a chapter on Jones; R.W. Clark and E.C. Pyatt, *Mountaineering in Britain: a history from the earliest times to the present day* (1957), a chapter; Ioan Bowen Rees, *Galwad y mynydd* (1961), a chapter; idem, *Mynyddoedd* (1975), 82-90; Alan Hankinson, *Camera on the crags* (1975), 1-21; idem. *The Mountain Men, an early history of rock-climbing in North Wales* (1977), 61-2, 70-80, 87-90, 157-9; BBC Wales television programme, 30 Oct. 1967; information from Nancy Harper (his sister's daughter), Megan Williams (daughter of his cousin, Mrs. John Evans) and Enid Wilson (daughter of George and Winifred Abraham).

I.B.R.

JONES, PRYCE – see PRYCE-JONES, Sir PRYCE below.

JONES, REES CRIBIN (1841-1927), Unitarian minister and teacher; b. at Talgarreg Mill, Cardiganshire, 9 Sept. 1841, one of four children. David Jones, his father, was from Rhandir, Talgarreg, and his mother was from Caer-foel, Ystrad. At one time a shepherd, he was educated at Dewi Hefin's school, Cribyn, John Davies's school at the Three Horse Shoes, Cribyn, Pont-siân school (1860-63), and the Presbyterian College, Carmarthen (1863-67). He conducted services occasionally at Cefncoedy-cymer Unitarian church and he was minister of the churches at Bridgend and Betws (1867-68), Cribyn (1869-76), Caeronnen (1871-1915), Ty'nrheol and Brondeifi (1874-1915) - the last three churches in the Lampeter district. During the period of his ministry (1867-1915) he was instrumental in founding the church at Ty'nrheol (1874) and building the chapel there and at Brondeifi (1876), together with a house and a schoolroom. He prepared eight young men for the ministry: J. Hathren Davies, D.J. Williams, T.J. Jenkins, E.O. Jenkins, D. Rhoslwyn Davies, J. Carrara Davies, J.E. Jones, D. Cellan Davies. Until 1879 he ran a school as well as ministering at Newton Nottage, at Cribyn and at Lampeter. He was a 'public figure' at Lampeter, serving as a member of the Local Board, School Board and the Board of Guardians. He was interested in spiritualism. Watcyn Samuel Jones (1877-1964, see above) was a child of his first marriage to Mari Jones (10 Jan. 1873). She died on 11 Mar. 1898. His second wife, Mary Ann, died on 8 Feb. 1945 and he himself died on 11 Aug 1927. His son dedicated his book, *Helyntion hen bregethwr a'i gyfoedion*, 1940, to his stepmother.

W.S. Jones, *Helyntion hen bregethwr a'i gyfoedion* (1940); *Ymofynydd*, memorial edition, Sept. 1927; Nov. and Dec. 1964.

D.E.J.D.

JONES, RICHARD ('Glan Alaw'; 1838-1925), minister (Presb.); b. 3 June 1838 in Llanfachraeth, Anglesey. Initially he was a shoemaker and poet. In 1875 he was called to serve the home mission at Millom, Cumberland, and stayed there for about 6 years. He moved from there to Holyhead where he continued to preach. In Jan. 1884 he was called to be pastor of Brynrefail church, Caerns. His culture was self-acquired for his path to the ministry led him neither to Clynnog school nor Bala College. Nevertheless, he was a refined thinker and understood several languages. He preached alongside the giants of his denomination, though it was as an expositor that he was most prominent. He m. twice, and raised a large family. He published two commentaries and a lecture, whilst a volume of his poetry and sermons was published posthumously by his children. He d. 4 Feb. 1925.

Canmlwyddiant Eglwys Brynrefail, 1848-1948; *Y Goleuad*, 11 Feb. 1925.

I.Ll.

JONES, RICHARD (1848-1915), itinerant bookseller; b. 24 August 1848 at Ty'n-y-fron, Clipiau, Aberangell, Mer., the son of Richard Jones, farmer, and his wife Lowri (née Hughes). His mother hailed from Cwmtirmynach, Bala. He originally intended to follow his elder brother, Robert, into the ministry, but because of his poor health and a lack of education he had to abandon this path. He was persuaded by friends to become an itinerant bookseller. He took to this suggestion and in due course became amongst the most well-known, and possibly the last, itinerant bookseller in north Wales. A bachelor, he travelled from his lodgings in Machynlleth, and later in Cemaes, to parts of Montgomeryshire and southern Merioneth. In the course of his career he walked hundreds of miles carrying his bag full of books on his back. He was always to be seen at his stall in Dinas Mawddwy fairs. He had business dealings with Thomas Gee and

Hughes and Son, Wrexham. Richard Jones always insisted on persons reading good literature, and he invariably read all the books himself first before recommending them to his customers. He distributed the popular Welsh periodicals of the day e.g. *Trysorfa'r Plant*, *Cymru*, *Cymru'r Plant*, biographies, theological books, etc. An appeal for a Subscription to acknowledge his service was launched in 1914. He was an exceptionally religious-minded person. He d. 18 November 1915 and was buried in Cemaes, Monts.

Information from his niece, the late Mrs. Annie Lloyd, Southerndown (formerly of Aberfan); Mus. of Welsh Life MSS 1755/36-37; *Cymru*, 50 (1916), 209-10, 62 (1922), 97-99; *Jnl. Merioneth Hist. and Record Soc.*, viii (1980), 447-49.

A.Ll.H.

JONES, ROBERT, Rhos-lan (1745-1829; *DWB*, 507-8). Mordecai Jones (see above and *DWB*, 496) was his nephew's son.

JONES, ROBERT ALBERT (1851-92), barrister and educationist; b. 16 Sept. 1851, s. of the Rev. John Jones, Pen-y-bryn, Wrexham, Denbs., and great-grandson of Robert Jones (*DWB*, 507-8), Rhoslan. He was a cousin of 'Ioan Maethlu' [John Maethlu Jones, 1839-66]. He was educated at Manchester Grammar School, and entered Corpus Christi, Oxford, in 1870, where he graduated B.A. with first class in Mathematics in 1874. He was called to the bar at Lincoln's Inn, 7 May 1879, and afterwards resided at Liverpool. He possessed independent means which enabled him to devote much of his time to public activities. With Robert Lewis, M.P., he was joint treasurer to the Executive Committee of the North Wales Liberal Federation, although he failed to agree with Gladstone on Ireland. He was deeply interested in land ownership, and published at his own expense *The Land question and a Land bill with special reference to Wales* (1887). A Welsh translation was published in 1888. He served on several committees, believing in, and arguing the case for free secular education. He was from the beginning a prominent member of the council of the Univ. College of North Wales, and travelled thousands of miles at his own expense on behalf of the college. He served the college without remuneration, and also contributed generously to its funds. He was offered the post of registrar, which he did not accept. With W.S. de Winton (Haverfordwest) he was joint secretary of the General Conference of Joint Education Committees for Wales and Monmouthshire. The concept of the University of Wales arose from this movement, and, to a large extent, R.A. Jones, who became secretary to the University Committee, was responsible for formulating the initial scheme for a Welsh university.

He was of a nervous and weak constitution, and performed most of his work in private; he disliked appearing in public. He d. 19 Oct. 1892 at his Liverpool residence and was buried at Toxteth cemetery, Liverpool. After his d. more than five hundred pounds were received towards a memorial fund, and the interest is still used for a higher mathematics prize at the University of Wales, Bangor.

He m., 26 Feb. 1890, Harriet Agnes Thompson, d. of Joseph Thompson, 'gentleman', of Willow Hall, Sowerby Bridge, Yorks. She d. 4 Nov. 1902, aged 47, and was buried at Toxteth cemetery.

Byegones, 1892, 239; *Not. W.* (T.M.R.); *Cymru*, v, 40; *Baner*, 26 Oct. 1892; *Gol.*, 27 Oct. 1892; personal knowledge.

Ll.G.C.

JONES, ROBERT AMBROSE ('Emrys ap Iwan'; *DWB*, 509-10). B. 24 Mar. 1848 (and his sister Priscilla 10 Dec. 1849) in one of the houses in Ffordd-las, Abergele. Emrys ap Iwan's mother was Maria Jones, daughter of Margaret Coates who was the daughter of George Coates, a miner in the copper works in Drws-y-coed (1769-72) before moving to Llanddulas to live. The French great-grandmother he was alleged to have is fictitious.

See W. Wynne-Woodhouse, *Hel Achau*, 1987.

JONES, SAMUEL (1681?-1719; *DWB*, 512). Read Roger Griffith (not 'Griffiths') twice. Malachi Jones was yet again in the vicinity of Hereford in 1704. The following additional details are: in William Davies, *The Tewkesbury Academy* (n.d. – c. 1905?): Jones moved to Tewkesbury during spring 1712. His house there was attacked in 1714 on the day George I was crowned. A satirical poem on Tewkesbury refers to him as 'Gamaliel sage, of Cambrian breed'. He was a Congregationalist and he did not have students supported by the Presbyterian Fund Board until 1714. He d. 11 Oct. 1719; according to his gravestone (outside the abbey chancel) he was 37 or 38.

Also, according to NLW MS. 10327 (Walter J. Evans), he had another nephew, Joshua (d. 1740), minister at Nailsworth and Manchester, and a niece who m. one Jackson and who had a son, Samuel – he was educated at Llwyn-llwyd, and, like his uncles, was minister at Nailsworth.

S.J. may have left Shrewsbury in 1704 and spent a year at Moorfields, under Chauncey, *before* going to Leiden (*Cofiadur*, 1958, 10, 20-1).

R.T.J.

JONES, SAMUEL (fl. 1715-67; *DWB*, 512). He d. 1767 (not 1764). The burial of the 'Rev. Samuel Jones' was recorded in the parish register of Llanedi on 10 August 1767.

JONES, THEOPHILUS (1759-1812; *DWB*, 513). His first wife, Mary was the dau. of Rhys Price of Porth-y-rhyd, Carms. She was buried in Myddfai churchyard.

G.M.R.

JONES, THOMAS ('Twm Shon Catti'; *DWB*, 513). According to the diary of John Dee (*DWB*, 166; above in the Supplement) he was b. 1 Aug. or 10 Aug. 1532 (J. Roberts and Andrew G. Watson, *John Dee's Library Catalogue* (1990, 45-46). Thomas Jones visited Dee in London in 1590 and Manchester in 1596, and they corresponded with each other in 1597: Dee called him 'my cousin'.

J.O. Halliwell, *The Private Diary of John Dee*, 1842; see also Dafydd H. Evans in D.P. Davies (ed.), *Coleg Dewi a'r Fro* (1984), 8-22; *Yr Aradr*, 7 (1996), 174-89.

JONES, THOMAS (*c.* 1622-82; *DWB*, 514). At the end of the article read Charlton (not 'Charleton').

JONES, THOMAS (1742-1803; *DWB*, 515-6). His 'Autobiographical Diary' was published by A.P. Oppé (ed.), 'Memoirs of Thomas Jones, Penkerrig, Radnorshire', *Walpole Soc.*, 32 (1951).

[See also R.C.B. Oliver, *The family history of Thomas Jones the artist of Pencerrig, Radnorshire* (1970).]

Ll.G.C.

JONES, THOMAS (1752-1845; *DWB*, 516). Read Loppington (not 'Lippington').

JONES, THOMAS (1756-1807; *DWB*, 516). There remains uncertainty as to his parents. According to the tradition recorded by Williams, *Mont. Worthies*, he was the illegitimate son of Owen Owen, Llifior, Berriew and there is an entry in Berriew register of baptisms 29 June 1756 'Thomas son of Catherine Evans of Llivior'. (Owen had married the heiress of Llifior.) In 1760 a case was brought against 'Catherine, wife of Mathew Jones of Trefeen, Kerry'; who had been in service in Tynycoed Llifior. However in Glansevern papers (NLW) 17840 there is a note concerning 'Jones of Trefeen illegitimate son of Davies of Ty'ncoed cousin to Miss Davies who married Owen "Welsh Uncle" to David Owen Senior Wrangler'.

Ll.G.C.

JONES, THOMAS (1777-1847), translator, schoolmaster and minister (CM); b. in Llanfwrog, Anglesey, in 1777. He was fortunate enough to receive some schooling with a cleric in his home area. He and two of his brothers, Rice Jones, Pen-clawdd, Glam., and Robert Jones, Congl. minister, Corwen, Mer., were preachers. In 1803 he and his wife, Margaret, moved to Ty'nyrefail, Llanynghenedl, Anglesey, where they had at least 8 children. He was elected an elder in Caergeiliog and began preaching with the Methodists in 1808. By 1816 he had moved to Penyrallt, Bodedern, and then to Llain-llwyd, Amlwch, where he died. He kept a school in Amlwch and published there a book on arithmetic, *Rhifiadur* (1827); he succeeded David Griffiths as master of the Nonconformists' school. During the last 20 years of his life he translated a number of English books, including some science volumes, for the monoglot Welsh reader. He published *Yr anianydd Cristionogol* (Thomas Dick, 1842), *Traethawd ar Ddaearyddiaeth* (1844) and theological works, e.g. *Scot ar y prophwydi*, and *Hanes gwaith y prynedigaeth* (1829). He d. 6 July 1847 aged 70, having been a preacher for 39 years. He was buried in his native parish of Llanfwrog.

Drys., 1848; *Enw. Ff.*; *Trans. Angl. Antiq. Soc.*, 1964, 39.

M.R.W.

JONES, THOMAS ('Gogrynwr'; 1822-54), doctor and musician; b. at Bronant, Dolgellau, Mer., 1822. His father was a druggist who gave him the best education and apprenticed him to a surgeon. After completing his educational course and performing his hospital work successfully, he spent some time in Liverpool, and subsequently at Wrexham and Corwen. When he was 32 years old he moved to Penstryt, Llandegla, and d. there in 1854. He left a manuscript volume of music containing tunes and the cantata *Gweddi Habacuc* which he had submitted to the Porthmadog *eisteddfod* in 1851. His letters which appeared in *Yr Amserau*, 1851, criticising the adjudication made by 'Tanymarian' (*DWB*, 923) at Bethesda *eisteddfod*, led to much agitation in musical circles.

M. O. Jones, *Byw. Cerdd. Cymr.*

R.D.G.

JONES, THOMAS LLOYD ('Gwenffrwd'; 1810-34; *DWB*, 520). 'Gwenffrwd' was, for a period, in the service of Thomas Jones (1802-51), a solicitor whose office was in Chapel Street, Holywell. It was not for a *pryddest* that he won a prize at Newmarket *eisteddfod* in 1829 but for a Welsh translation of 'Hymn of the Seasons' (Thompson). *Enw. Ff.* is correct, - it was from Denbigh that Gwenffrwd wrote a letter to R.L. Morris, Holywell, which was published in *Adgof uwch Angof*, and it was there that he wrote 'Llinellau' for *Y Gwyliedydd*, Aug. 1830. He was clerk to the solicitor William Jones ('Gwrgant'; 1803-86; *DWB*, 525) at St. Asaph before moving to Liverpool where he resided when he wrote the elegy to John Jenkins ('Ifor Ceri', 1770-1829; *DWB*, 434) which won at Beaumaris *eisteddfod*, 1832. It was from Philadelphia that he sent the poem 'Syniadau ar y Môr' which was published in *Seren Gomer*, Aug. 1833. He sent a poem in memory of his patron Archdeacon Beynon to the Gwent and Dyfed royal *eisteddfod* at Cardiff 1834. It did not win a prize, and the poet d. four days before the *eisteddfod* opened. (*Awenyddion Gwent a Dyfed*, London, 1834).

See Huw Williams, *Thomas Lloyd Jones* (1989).

JONES, THOMAS ROBERT ('Gwerfulyn', 1802-1856), founder of the charitable movement, the True Ivorites; b. in Maes Gwerful, Llannefydd, Denbigh, in 1802. He followed his trade as a shoe-maker in Ruabon, Cefn-mawr and Llansanffraid Glyndyfrdwy, where he m. Elizabeth, dau. of Evan Price, Baptist minister of Llanfyllin, in 1834. He established Welsh societies (*Cymreigyddion*) in all these areas and he was a regular contributor to the Welsh Baptist journals. He conceived the idea of setting up a society which would assist its members financially as well as safeguarding and nurturing the Welsh language. Robert Davies, 'Bardd Nantglyn' (*DWB*, 150) and William Owen Pughe (*DWB*, 815-6) expressed their willingness to be sponsors but both died before having an opportunity to help. Jones ventured and established a 'United and Gomerian Society under the sign of the Cross Guns' in Wrexham on 6 June 1836. There is little information about the society in its early period but by 1838 the membership of the first lodge was 252, 12 lodges had been opened in north Wales and the first lodge in south Wales (St. David's) was opened in Carmarthen on 24 Apr. that year. By June 1840 a misunderstanding had arisen between Jones and the movement and he left the Cross Guns lodge to set up a rival lodge. Consequently the St. David's lodge and the Union which had developed around it declared itself the chief lodge of the whole of Wales and a fierce contention arose between it and T.R. Jones and his followers. St. David's lodge won the day and in 1845 the movement's central office moved from Carmarthen to Swansea. 'Ivorism' (named after Ifor ap Llywelyn, or Ifor Hael, of Bassaleg, *DWB*, 414) was on the increase throughout Wales and the years between 1840 and 1850 were the golden period of the society. The Order had firm rules for its members regarding morals and behaviour, it nurtured the Welsh language and between 1850 and 1870 there was hardly a year without an Ivorite *eisteddfod*. This cultural activity puts the movement in a special category and assisting the poor and needy was not its only purpose. Though T.R. Jones established another lodge and claimed to have offices throughout Wales his influence waned after 1845. He spent the last two years of his life in Birkenhead where he died in May 1856 leaving a widow and 4 children.

Greal, July 1856, 165-67; *Ser. G.*, 1840, 303-5; *Ceredigion*, 1956-59, 25-26.

H.Wa.

JONES, THOMAS TUDNO (*DWB*, 521). Instead of Tŷ Cristin read Tŷ Cristion.

JONES, WALTER (?-1819), Cefn Rug, Corwen, Mer., commissioner under land enclosure acts. He was estate agent for Sir Robert Williames Vaughan (WYNN Family of Rug, *DWB*, 1099) which brought him into public notice in the county, e.g. as commissioner for the militia and trustee under the Barmouth Harbour Act (37 Geo, III. cap. 50). From 1806 onwards he served, almost continuously, as commissioner under the aegis of parliamentary acts dealing successively with land enclosure in the counties of Anglesey, Caernarfon, Merioneth and Denbigh; he was named in two other parliamentary acts but he declined to act. He d. 7 Apr. 1819.

Shrewsbury Chronicle, 23 Apr. 1819; *B.B.C.S.*, iii, 210-38.

A.H.D.

JONES, WILLIAM (1675?-1749; *DWB*, 522-3). In the bibliography read *History of the Island of Mona or Anglesey* (not 'Isle of Anglesey').

He was born in 1674 or 1675; the same year as the father of the Morris brothers of Anglesey (see Lewis Morris, *DWB*, 661, Richard Morris, *DWB*, 663-4, William Morris, *DWB*, 666-7). He d. 1 July, not 3 July, 1749, and was buried in St. Paul's church, Covent Garden on 7 July 1749. He was married twice: (1) to the widow of the merchant who employed him when he went to London. This might explain how he came by the money which he later lost; and (2) to Mary Nix on 17 Apr. 1731 when he was 56 and she was 25.

He left his mark on mathematics in several ways. The use of the symbol π to designate the ratio of the circumference of a circle to its diameter first appeared in his book *Synopsis Palmariorum Matheseos* (1706) and it was he, in his editions of Newton's works who used the dot as the differential sign in the calculus. In one of his papers in the *Trans. of the Royal Society* he created a rule for compound interest and many mathematicians of the period sought his opinion of their work.

In his will he left his library of some 15,000 works and over 50,000 pages of manuscripts, including hundreds of pages refering to those whom he knew and several of Newton's MSS. to the 3rd Earl Macclesfield, most of which remain in the earl's home, Shirburn Castle.

Hugh Owen (ed.), *Additional letters of the Morrises of Anglesey (1753-86)*, Cymmrodor, 49 (1947-49), 253; *General Advertiser*, 3 July 1749 (4585); Register of St. Paul's church, Covent Garden; Register of St. Lawrence Jewry and St. Mary Magdalen, Milk Street; D.T. Whiteside (ed.), *The Mathematical papers of Sir Isaac Newton* (1967), 400; S.J. Rigaud (ed.), *Correspondence of scientific men of the seventeenth century* (1841), 256; letters from D.T. Whiteside, Un. of Wales Bangor 2659A; Charles Hutton, *Mathematical Tables* (1785), 117.

Ll.G.C.

JOSEFF Y SEINAD – see JOSEPH JONES under JONES, THOMAS, 1811-66; *DWB*, 518.

JOSHUA, FRANK – see FRANCIS JAMES JOSHUA under JOSHUA, SETH below.

JOSHUA, SETH (1858-1925), minister (Presb.); b. 10 Apr. 1858 in Tŷ Capel, Trosnant Uchaf, Pontypool, Mon., son of George Joshua and Mary (née Walden) his wife. He m. Mary Rees, Llantrisant, in Neath, Glam., 23 Sept. 1883, and they had eight children (one son, Peter, was a minister and a popular evangelist in America; another son, Lyn, was responsible with Mai Jones (see above) for the radio programme 'We'll keep a welcome in the hillside'). Seth attended the local British School. He worked closely with his brother Frank (see below) founding the Mission Hall cause in Neath. He was a noted evangelist, travelling through Britain and visiting U.S.A. In 1893 he was ord. minister (Presb.) and worked with the Forward Movement, a branch of the Connexion's Home Mission, establishing evangelising centres in Glamorganshire and Monmouthshire. He d. 21 May 1925 and was buried in the Council cemetery, Llanilltud Fach, Neath.

A younger brother was FRANCIS JAMES JOSHUA (FRANK; 1861-1920), minister (Presb.); b. 15 Dec. 1861. He and Seth went to Neath in 1883 to hold an Evangelistic Campaign under the auspices of the Free Mission, Cinderford. In 1901 the Free Mission Church in Neath came under the auspices of the Calvinistic Methodists as a branch of the Forward Movement and he was ord. in the Cilfynydd Association (Presb.) in 1903. The whole of his ministry was spent in Neath where he raised a strong and flourishing church, and he became known in the town as 'St. Francis of Neath'. He d. 13 Sept. 1920 a bachelor and was buried in Llanilltud Fach churchyard, Neath.

T. Mardy Rees, *Seth Joshua and Frank Joshua, the renowned evangelists* (1926); see also centenary booklet of the Mission Hall, Neath; Howell Williams, *The Romance of the Forward Movement* (1949); John Morgan Jones, *Hanes Symudiad Ymosodol y Methodistiaid Calfinaidd* (1931); Annie Pugh Williams,

Atgofion am y Dr. John Pugh (c. 1944); Robert Ellis, *Living echoes of the Welsh revival 1904-5* (1951); reminiscences of Peter Rhys Joshua in *The Treasury*, 1978.

R.L.J.

KATHERYN of BERAIN (*DWB*, 531). Instead of 'N.L.W. MS. 5496' read 6495-6.

KENRY, 2nd BARON - see WYNDHAM-QUIN, WINDHAM THOMAS (1841-1926) below.

KYFFIN, EDWARD (*DWB*, 537-8). In the third par. read *Dafydh* (not '*Dafydd*') and Middelton (not 'Middleton').

LAUGHARNE, ROWLAND (*DWB*, 540-1). In the last par. his wife is said to be the daughter of Sir Thomas Button 'of Cottrell'. The first of the family to live at Cottrell was Sir Thomas's son through his marriage to the heiress of Rhys Meurug (Merrick) (*DWB*, 628-9) of Cottrell.

LEIF-JONES, LEIFCHILD STRATTEN – see LEIFCHILD STRATTEN (LEIF-) JONES (*DWB*, 519) under JONES, THOMAS (1819-82); and JONES, LEIFCHILD STRATTEN LEIF above.

LEWES, ERASMUS (1663?-1745), cleric; the sixth and youngest son of Captain John Lewes (below), Gernos, in the parish of Llangunllo ('Llanvayer' according to Foster, *Alumni Oxon.*), Cards. He entered Jesus College, Oxford, 22 Feb. 1683/4, aged 20, graduating in 1688. He became vicar of Roch, Pembs., 16 June 1692, and vicar of Brawdy, Pembs., 5 Mar. 1694. In 1695 he became rector of Betws Bledrws and vicar of Lampeter, Cards. S. R. Meyrick (*Hist. of the County of Cardigan*) quotes the inscription on his memorial tablet in Lampeter church; he is said to have d. 19 Feb. 1744/5 aged 82. English sermons in his handwriting are in NLW MS. 510, some of them written in 1693; NLW MS. 744 contains general notes written by him in English and in Latin.

His father, JOHN LEWES, deserves to be remembered because it was 'at the request of the Reverend Captain Lewes of Gernos' that Moses Williams (*DWB*, 1060) undertook the task of translating Vickers's *Companion to the Altar* into Welsh. It was published in London in 1715 under the title *Cydymmaith i'r Allor, Yn dangos, Anian ac Angenrheidrwydd Ymbaratoad Sacrafennaidd, Modd y derbynniom y Cymmun Bendigedig yn Deilwng.*

See also NLW MS. 1626; *W. Wales Hist. Records*, iii, 265-6; Foster, *Index Ecclasiasticus*; J. Ifano Jones, *Hist. of Printing and Printers in Wales*, 36.

W.Ll.D.

LEWIS of CAERLEON (*DWB*, 545). He was a physician to Elizabeth, widow of Edward IV, Margaret Countess Richmond and Henry Tudor. He did much to promote the marriage of Henry to Elizabeth daughter of Queen Elizabeth. The final reference to him is in the Treasury rolls 1493-94. He compiled mathematical and astronomical tables relating to eclipses of the sun and the moon.

D.N.B., P. Kibre, *Isis*, 43 (1952), 100.

Ll.G.C.

LEWIS, HUGH DAVIES (1866-1937) - see under LEWIS, Sir ALFRED EDWARD, *DWB*, 548.

LEWIS, JOHN (?-1616; *DWB*, 554-5). In the light of the detailed article by Ffransis G. Payne in *Radnorshire Soc. Trans.*, xxx (1960) the entry in *DWB* needs to be revised. It is unlikely that he is the John Lewis who entered Lincoln's Inn. It is more probable that he is the person who entered the Inner Temple, 20 Aug. 1568. There is no certainty when he was called to the Bar. Like other members of his family, he was a Catholic recusant, and he was excommunicated by the Bishop of St. David's (*Exch. Proc.*, 151/34/8, Jas. 1).

LEWIS, LEWIS WILLIAM ('Llew Llwyfo'; *DWB*, 557-8). He was the second of six children. At the age of eight he worked in the Parys copper mines. The draper to whom he was apprenticed in 'Siop Goch', Dean-street, Bangor (1845) was Edward Evans, father of Llewellyn Ioan Evans (1833-92; *DWB*, 247); when Evans emigrated to America (April 1850), Llew went to work with John Lewis, clothier at Holyhead, and he married there. Later, he opened a shop at Pen-y-sarn (not Tal-y-sarn), and was there when he published *Awên Ieuanc* (1851). He kept a school at Llanallgo for a short while, but in 1852 he went to live in Llaneilian, as a weigher in a storehouse at Porth Amlwch – before the end of 1852 he went to Holywell, to the office of *Y Cymro*; afterwards he went to Wrexham as some kind of 'visitor' for the parish priest; then he went to a clothiers shop in Liverpool. When John Lloyd (see under Lloyd, Evan and John, *DWB*, 1141) began publishing *Y Cronicl Wythnosol* (not *Yr Amserau*) in 1855 Llew was appointed editor. This *Cronicl* ceased in 1857, and Llew returned to the *Cymro* at Holywell; but was soon on the staff of *Y Gwron* at Aberdare, under Josiah T. Jones (1799-1873; *DWB*, 491-2). He quarrelled with his employer before the end of the year, but continued with the *Gwladgarwr* to the end of 1858. Then he was employed by Thomas Gee (1815-98; *DWB*, 274); and was at Denbigh in 1862. During 1863-65 he lived at Rhyl, but was back again at Denbigh by May 1866. He moved to Newport, Mon., in 1867 as editor of *Y Glorian*, in succession to Glasynys (Owen Wynne Jones, 1828-70; *DWB*, 501). In September 1868 he sailed to America, on a singing tour; he was also for a short period editor of *Y Wasg* (Pittsburg). He returned in 1874, and by 1875 he worked in the *Herald* office at Caernarfon. His whereabouts thereafter are obscure; it is not certain whether he went to America a second time; he worked some time or other on *Gwalia* at Caernarfon, but by July 1885 that ceased and he is found writing to several persons (such as W.J. Parry, 1842-1927; *DWB*, 742) seeking employment or financial support. His health deteriorated. He was maintained at Llan-rug for some years by friends. On his return from Liverpool *eisteddfod* (1900), he stayed with his son at Rhyl, and d. there 23 Mar. 1901; he was buried at Llanbeblig. Append to the sources for his history: *Adgofion Llew Llwyfo o'i Ymdaith yn America, ganddo ef ei hun* (Hugh Humphreys, Penny books, second series, no. 63), and letters at N.L.W. and the library of the University College of North Wales; [Hywel Teifi Edwards, *Llew Llwyfo: arwr gwlad a'i arwrgerdd* (1999); E. W. Rowlands, *Y Llew oedd ar y llwyfan* (2001)].

B.L.J.

LEWIS, WILLIAM HOWELL (1793?-1868), minister (Congl.); b. at Carmarthen, 1793?, a relative of Sarah Lewis, the first wife of David Peter (*DWB*, 750-1). He began to preach in Lammas St. chapel, Carmarthen; he entered Carmarthen College in 1814, aged 21, and remained there until 1818. He became a minister at Narberth, Pembs., 1818-21, being concurrently assistant tutor at the college school 'about two years or more'; at Glastonbury, Som., 1821-47; and Usk, Mon., 1847-50. After retiring, he went to live in Bristol; he was there from 1858 to 1865. In 1863 he presented several of the MSS. of Philip Henry (*DWB*, 346-7) to the Presbyterian College, Carmarthen, as well as a rare edition of Stephanus's Greek Testament. He wrote *Memoirs of the Life and Labours of the Reverend David Peter*; and d. in 1868.

Memoirs of ... David Peter; Hanes Eglwys Heol Awst; records of the Presbyterian Board.

J.D.O.

LEWIS, WILLIAM JAMES (*DWB*, 564). He was a tutor in Cheltenham College 1870-71 and for a period from 1862 he was one of the editors of *Messenger of Mathematics*.

Proc. Roy. Soc. A, 111 (1926), xliv; *Nature*, 117 (1926), 628.

Ll.G.C.

LEWIS, WILLIAM MORRIS (1839-1917), minister (Presb.); b. 9 May 1839 at Fishguard, Pembs., son of the Rev. Enoch Lewis and his wife. He was educated at the seminary of Dr. George Rees; Bala College; Normal College, Swansea and Trefeca College. He began to preach in 1856, and was ord. in 1863. In 1859 he m. Lettice Maria Lloyd, and they settled in Tŷ Llwyd, near Treffynnon, in the parish of Llandeloy, Pembs. They built Treffynnon chapel near their home, and were very supportive of the cause. He was Moderator of the South Wales Association in 1893-94. In his day he was considered to be a theologian and Biblical scholar of some standing. He corresponded with scholars like Adolf Harnack and H.M. Gwatkin; he was friendly also with Thomas Charles Edwards (*DWB*, 197-8). He contributed extensively to *Y Traethodydd*, *Y Drysorfa* and to English periodicals. He published his Davies Lecture on repentance – *Edifeirwch* – which was delivered at the General Assembly, 1900. His Welsh commentary on the Epistle to the Hebrews was translated into German, and W.M. Ramsay acknowledged that he had presented a strong case for Paul being its author. He d. 26 May 1917, and his remains were buried in Treffynnon cemetery.

Monthly Treasury, Nov. 1901; *Blwyddiadur MC*, 1918; G.M. Roberts, *Capel Treffynnon* (1967).

G.M.R.

LEWIS, Sir WILLIAM THOMAS (*DWB*, 564). Robert Thomas took a lease on Waun Wyllt in 1824. He d. 19 Feb. 1833. He had already (1830) formed business connections with London – so it is not literally true to say that his widow was the 'mother of the Welsh coal trade'.

LEWIS LLOYD, EMMELINE (1827-1913), one of the first women to climb in the Alps; b. 18 Nov.

1827, second daughter of Thomas Lewis Lloyd of Nantgwyllt (the manor house in Elan valley where Shelley stayed in 1812 but which is now under the waters of the Caban Coch reservoir) and his wife Anna Eliza Davies, the daughter of Treforgan near Cardigan. After leaving home, Emmeline farmed and bred mountain ponies at Llandyfaelog Fach near Brecon. With her enthusiasm for fishing, otter hunting and roaming the hills, she was regarded as something of a character, and she was a noted raconteur as she talked about her travels and exploits. Her main claim to fame is that she regularly climbed in the Alps during the sixties and seventies of the nineteenth century. There were only some half-dozen women climbers in Europe during this period and, apart from Lucy Walker of Liverpool (1835-1916), it is doubtful whether any of them went in for climbing before her. Lucy Walker always climbed with her father and her brother but Emmeline's usual companion was another woman, Isabella Straton. She also climbed with her younger sister, Bessie, who m. William Williams, the vicar of Llandyfaelog. Her usual guide, Jean Charlet of Argentière, spent a year as a groom at Nantgwyllt; years later he m. Isabella Straton. Few details are available about Emmeline's ascents but she was the eighth woman to climb Mont Blanc and on 22 Sept. 1871, (at the age of 44) she made the first ascent of the Aiguille du Moine (3412 m. or 11,194 ft.) near Chamonix with Isabella and the guide Joseph Simond. The two ladies also climbed Monte Viso with Jean Charlet that year. The two had made an unsuccessful attempt on the Matterhorn as early as 1869, 4 yrs. after the tragic first ascent. She d. 22 Sept. 1913, at Hampstead Hill Gardens, London, and is buried at Llansanffraid Cwmteuddwr, where there is a memorial to her in the church.

Radnor Expr., 2 Oct. 1913; Herbert M. Vaughan, *The South Wales Squires, a Welsh picture of social life* (1926), chapter XIV; Ronald Clark, *The Victorian Mountaineers* (1953), 178-81; *Guide Vallot: La Chaine du Mont Blanc*, 3 (1965); Nea Morin, *A Woman's Reach* (1968), Appendix 2: A survey of some notable feminine ascents; information from Major General Robert S. Lewis, Rhayader (great-nephew).

I.B.R.

LEWIS, WYNDHAM (1780-1838), M.P.; b. 7 Oct 1780, son of the Rev. Wyndham Lewis, Greenmeadow, Tongwynlais, Glam. He was M.P. for Cardiff, 1820-26; Aldeburgh (Suffolk), 1827-30; and Maidstone from 1835 until his d. 14 Mar. 1838. His widow, in 1839, became the wife of Benjamin Disraeli.

W. R. Williams, *Parl. Hist of Wales.*

R.T.J.

LLAETHFERCH – see EVANS, MARY JANE above.

LLEWELLYN, Sir DAVID RICHARD (1879-1940), BARONET, coalowner; b. 9 Mar. 1879 at Aberdare, Glam., the eldest s. of Rees and Elizabeth (née Llewellyn) Llewellyn, Bwllfa House: his father was general manager of the Bwllfa & Merthyr Dare Collieries, a post afterwards held by his son, William Morgan Llewellyn. D.R. Llewellyn was educated at Aberdare and Llandovery College before following a course in mining engineering at University College, Cardiff (1901-03). He went to USA for 2 years to gain more experience and on his return he began to acquire local pits and then more widely in south Wales, pioneering the use of new coal-cutting machines which he had seen in America. In 1916, as chairman of the Gwauncaegurwen Coalmining Company, he became associated with Henry Seymour Berry, Lord Buckland (see above under BERRY, FAMILY) and the Cambrian Combine, and consequently he had a part in the development of the anthracite coalfield. He became a director of many enterprises in the coal trade, especially the Vale of Neath, Amalgamated Anthracite Collieries, Guest, Keen & Nettlefold, and chairman of the Welsh Associated Collieries and later vice-chairman of the United Powell Duffryn Associated Collieries (under the chairmanship of Edmund Hann). By about 1920 it could be claimed that he owned or managed about 1/7 of the south Wales coalfield. He played an important part in the development of management methods in the coal industry and the growth of amalgamated companies. He was an influential figure in the regional Coalowners Association (especially about 1925-30) and he was acknowledged as a leader with moderate views. Both he and his brother W.M. Llewellyn mixed with their workers and they retained their personal and local links.

While his home was in Aberdare (Goytre, Llewellyn St., then Fairfield House) he was an active member of the Town Council (chairman 1920), High Constable of Miskin and a prominent Liberal and Unitarian (at Hendy-cwrdd, Aberdare). He was treasurer of University College, Cardiff 1922, and president 1924. The baronetcy was created in 1922 and he was awarded an hon. LL.D. by the University of Wales in 1929. He moved to The Court, St. Fagans. His chief hobbies were hunting (both he and his brother were masters of the Bwllfa hunt) and horses. He m. Magdalene (dau. of Henry Harries, 'Afonwy', Baptist minister of Treherbert) in 1905 and they had 4 sons and 4 daughters. (Following the death of their eldest son Rhys the baronetcy was inherited by the second s. Henry (Harry) Morton who became a leading equestrian figure). He d. at his brother's house, Tynewydd, Hirwaun, Glam., 15 Dec. 1940.

Dict. of Business Biography; WwW (1921), where his companies are listed; *Times*, 16 Dec. 1940; *Aberdare Leader*, 21 Dec. 1940, 1, 6.

B.F.R.

LLINOS MORGANNWG – see SUSANNAH WESLEY REES (née DAVIES) under REES, BOWEN below.

LLOYD (FAMILY) of Dolobran (*DWB*, 570-2). On l. 20 from the bottom of p. 571a read 1685 (not '1665'), and on l. 17 Bull Street (not 'Lane'). See a MS. Memoir of her father, Charles II, by Elizabeth Pemberton at Friends' House, London.

LLOYD (FAMILY), Maesyfelin (*DWB*, 572-3). FRANCIS LLOYD m. once only (d. 1669). He was survived by his wife, Mary (née Vaughan). She d. at St. Martin-in-the-Fields; her will was proved in London 31 Dec. 1677. Bridget Leigh was the mother of the three children of Francis Lloyd (the two sons, and his daughter, Frances). Bridget m. after Francis d. (and not later than 1676) one John Farrington.

Peterwell documents at N.L.W.

M.A.J.

LLOYD (FAMILY), Hafodunos, Denbs., and Wigfair, Fl. - see LLOYD, JOHN (1749-1815), *DWB*, 583.

LLOYD, DAVID (1805-63; *DWB*, 578). According to *Oriel Coleg Presbyteraidd Caerfyrddin* he was appointed tutor in classics in 1833 and principal in 1835.

LLOYD, EMMELINE LEWIS – see LEWIS LLOYD, EMMELINE above.

LLOYD, GEORGE – see under LLOYD, Sir WILLIAM below.

LLOYD, Sir RICHARD (1606-76; *DWB*, 587). Another member of the family (not to mention, for the time being, David Owen, 'Dafydd y Garreg Wen', *DWB*, 699) deserves some attention. A comparison of the charts in J. E. Griffith (*Pedigrees*, 330, 353, 269) shows that Sir Richard Lloyd had a sister Margaret who m. Richard Anwyl of Parc. Their daughter was Barbara, who was alive in 1707 and who m. twice, the second time to one surnamed Parry, sometimes identified with Jeffrey Parry of Rhydolion, forefather of the Parrys of Madryn, which cannot be correct since the latter died while she was still married to her first husband. Her first husband, as demonstrated by Nannau MS. 3452 in the library of University of Wales, Bangor, was Hugh Lloyd (not 'Richard' as given by Griffith) of Deneio and Nefyn. Their third son (fifth son according to some) was RODERICK LLOYD (d. 1730) of Hafodwryd, Penmachno, Caerns., who entered Lincoln's Inn in 1684 (and who spent most of his life there), and became (as had his uncle Richard Anwyl) Clerk of the Outlawries in the Court of Common Pleas. It is often said that he was protonotary to his famous neighbour, Sir Robert Price (*DWB*, 790) of Giler, but his name does not appear in the lists of W. R. Williams (*The Welsh Judges*). Nevertheless, it is obvious that there was a close relationship, throughout his career, between the two. He is commemorated in Penmachno by the school, almshouses, and the charitable gifts (including Welsh books for the poor) which he donated to his parish; see his will (Nannau MS. 3448, at Bangor), and also Lowe, *The Heart of Northern Wales*, ii, 437-40, and *Gweithiau Gethin*, 250, 253-4. He m. in 1703, Anne, widow of Robert Pugh of Pennar or Pennard, Penmachno (a lawyer of Middle Temple), and left a daughter, another Anne, who m. in 1730 Edward Williams of Meillionydd. Their daughter, yet another Anne, by her marriage to Robert Howell Vaughan (Griffith, *op. cit.*, 201), brought Roderick Lloyd's property to the Hengwrt-Nannau family, which is why his papers are among the Nannau papers in the library at Bangor, papers (particularly Nannau MSS. 3444-

60) which complement and rectify, to some extent, the charts of J. E. Griffith. Roderick Lloyd d. May 1730, and was buried 30 May in Lincoln's Inn chapel. A daughter of his wife's first marriage to Robert Pugh was Anne Pugh, who m. John Wynne (*DWB*, 1106-7), Bishop of St. Asaph; the bishop's name is seen with Sir Robert Price and others among the executors of the will of Roderick Lloyd.

P. H. Lawson in *The Cheshire Sheaf*, Jan. and Feb. 1937; and the other references given above.

R.T.J.

LLOYD, SIMON (*DWB*, 588). Lydia, who m. Thomas Foulkes, was the dau. of Simon Lloyd (1730-64) and thus the sister of Simon Lloyd (1756-1836).

LLOYD, Sir WILLIAM (1782-1857), soldier and one of the first Europeans to reach the peak of any Himalayan snow-capped mountain; b. 29 Dec. 1782, eldest son of Richard Lloyd, a banker of Wrexham, Denbs., and his wife Mary, and great-grandson of Thomas Lloyd the lexicologist (*DWB*, 1141). He was educated in Ruthin School and then, between 1798 and 1825, he served in the army of the East India Company, attaining the rank of major in the Bengal Infantry. He was captain of the Residency Guard at Nagpur between 1806 and 1820. He gained eminence not only in battle (in 1817 he was wounded four times in the Mahratta War) but also as a cartographer. In 1822 he went on a long journey through the foothills of the Himalayas as far as Boorendo Pass (or Buan Ghati) on the western boundary of Tibet, partly in the company of the most famous pioneer in this area, Alexander Gerard (1792-1839) of Aberdeen and his brothers Patrick and James. After camping in the snow at the foot of the pass and spending an uncomfortable night on the pass itself, Lloyd was the only one to proceed to the western peak of Boorendo (16,880 ft.) on 13 June, and see 'an assemblage ... of all the mountains in the world'. It is doubtful whether any others but the Gerard brothers had been on a mountain as high as this before. More importantly, this was the first time for almost anyone to climb a snow peak in the Himalayas merely for the sake of doing so rather than as part of the task of surveying. Even more importantly, Lloyd forestalled the Alpine climbers of the middle of the century by leaving a live, romantic record of his experiences. 'I had longed ardently to see them, to be upon them, to know them', he said of the Himalayas, 'The very impulse brought back to me my schooldays among the purple hills of the Vale of Clwyd.' In 1840, he published two volumes in London edited by his son George which include 'The narrative of a journey from Cawnpoor to the Boorendo Pass', based on his journal, as well as shorter items by Alexander and James Gerard. A one-volume second ed. was published in 1846. After retiring, Lloyd returned to Wrexham to live on Bryn Estyn estate, to captain the Denbighshire Hussars Yeomanry and play a prominent part on behalf of the Whigs in the political and social life of the district. He received a knighthood in 1838 and was appointed hon. Lieutenant Colonel in 1854. He d. 16 May 1857 and was buried in the old

Llandudno churchyard – he had a residence in the town.

It is believed that GEORGE LLOYD (1815-43), b. 17 Oct. 1815, was his illegitimate son of an Indian mother. George, at the age of seven, was with his father during the first weeks of the 1822 campaign but was left behind in Kotgarh. He also roamed in the Alps with his father. In addition to editing his father's work, he edited *An account of Koonawur in the Himalaya* (1841), relating all of Alexander Gerard's travels. He is said to have published a book of poems. He d. 10 Oct. 1843, near Thebes in Egypt, after an 'accident with a gun'.

R.H. Phillimore, *Historical records of the survey of India*, 2, 1800-15 (1950), 417, and 3, 1815-30 (1954), 42 and 451-2; Ioan Bowen Rees, *Mynyddoedd* (1975), 90-3; D. Leslie Davies, 'Sir William Lloyd of Bryn Estyn', *Trans. Denbighshire Hist. Soc.*, 25 (1976) and 26 (1977).
I.B.R.

LLWYD, ANGHARAD (*DWB*, 593). Beaumaris *eisteddfod* was held in 1832 (not '1833'). Add to bibl. articles by Mary Ellis, *Flints Hist. Soc. Publ.*, 26 and 27.

LLWYD, ROBERT (*DWB*, 595). Read *The Plaine Mans Path-way* (not '*Plain Pathway*').

LLYWELYN ap CYNFRIG DDU o FÔN, or **LLYWELYN DDU O FÔN** (*fl. c.* 1460-1500?), poet. About three examples of his work have been identified.

Jones and Lewis, *Mynegai*; NLW MS. 11087 (49); *Blackwell*; *Em. W.*; W. Owen, *The Cambrian Biography*.
R.L.

LLYWELYN ap GRUFFYDD or LLYWELYN BREN (*DWB*, 598-9). See also the article by Ralph Griffiths, 'The Revolt of Llywelyn Bren, 1316' in *Glamorgan Historian*, II, 186-96.

LLYWELYN ap IORWERTH (*DWB*, 600). John, husband of Llywelyn's daughter Helen, was not son of Ranulf, Earl of Chester, who had no sons, but his nephew. He was John le Scot, s. of David, Earl of Huntingdon, and his mother was Maud, sister of Ranulf.

LOYD, LEWIS (*DWB*, 604). Read Lob (not 'Dobb') Lane.

MADOCKS, WILLIAM ALEXANDER (*DWB*, 607). He went to Oxford in 1790 (not '1700'). He d. 29 Sept. 1828 and was buried in Paris. Add to the bibliography: Elizabeth Beazley, *Madocks and the Wonder of Wales*, and the chapter entitled 'Etifeddion Harrisiaid Trefeca' in *Yng Nghysgod Trefeca* by R.T. Jenkins. See under HARRIS, JOSEPH, above in the Supplement.

MADOG ap GRUFFYDD (*DWB*, 607). Delete (q.v.) after Gruffydd Maelor II.

MADOG ap MAREDUDD (*DWB*, 608). His wife was the daughter of Gruffydd ap Cynan (not 'Owain Gwynedd').

MANSEL (FAMILY; *DWB*, 611-2). See further the article by Glanmor Williams on Richard Mansell (1487-1559) in *Glam. Hist.*, VI, 33-51.

MARC, SIARL (*DWB*, 614). See also *Trans. Caerns. Hist. Soc.*, xxvi, 65-7.

MATHEW (FAMILY; *DWB*, 618). Recent research into the history of the family descended from Sir David Mathew of Llandaff and his grandson Sir William Mathew of Radyr reveals that since the Irish Mathew line became extinct with the death of Francis James Mathew, 2nd Earl of Llandaff in 1833 (his sister Lady Elizabeth died in 1842), the Welsh branch alone survives.

The descent is through William Mathew of Whitchurch, son of Edmund Mathew of Radyr, High Sheriff of Glamorgan in 1592 and younger brother of the George who founded the Irish family. William is stated to have been Mayor of Cardiff in 1644 and succeeded Sir Anthony Mansell as Governor of the garrison in Cardiff Castle for King Charles I. His son Capt. Thomas Mathew served with their kinsman Sir Edward Stradling under Prince Rupert and in 1648 was taken prisoner after the Battle of St. Fagans. He was one of the eleven officers sent on board the *Admiral Crowther* to await execution. Three of the officers were shot out of hand but Mathew escaped with others and rode to Pembroke Castle which was still held by the Royalists.

In 1818 when the family estates were disentailed and sold by Francis James Mathew, 2nd Earl of Llandaff, a small portion of Llandaff Manor was purchased by Captain Thomas's great-grandson, Anthony Mathew of Tŷ Mawr, Whitchurch.

The ancient arms of the family, recorded at the 1530 Heraldic Visitation of Wales for Sir William Mathew of Radyr, are now borne by Hugh Pawley Mathew of Thunderley Hall, Saffron Walden, Essex, twelfth in descent from Sir William. [See M. P. Siddons, *The development of Welsh heraldry*, II (1993), 371].
H.P.M.

MATHEW ap LLYWELYN GOCH (*DWB*, 618). Correct the *fl.* to the middle of the 16th. c. Olfyr ap Tomas was from Neuadd-wen, Llanerfyl. His wife was from Llangedwyn.
E.P.R.

MATTHEWS, ABRAHAM (1832-99), (MATHEWS, *DWB*, 618), minister (Congl.) and one of the pioneers of the Welsh settlement in Patagonia; b. at Llanidloes, Mont., Nov. 1832, son of John Matthews, weaver, and Ann Jones, but brought up by Edward and Ann Lewis, farmers living nearby who moved to Blaencwmlline, in the parish of Cemaes. At 12 yrs. of age he was apprenticed to a factory in Cwmlline for three yrs., becoming a craftsman working around Montgomeryshire and south Merionethshire. When 22 yrs. old he decided to maintain himself as a student of the master of Cemaes British School because he had had no formal education as a child. He left Llanwnnog (Congl.) church, where he had been a member since his conversion at the age of 17, and joined Samah (Congl.) church. He began to preach there before entering Bala College (1856-59) where he came under the influence of Michael D. Jones (*DWB*, 495-6). He was ord. minister of Horeb, Llwydcoed (1859-65) and Elim, Cwmdâr (Cynon valley, 1859-60), and was minister of Adulam, Merthyr Tydfil (1861-65). In May 1863, at Ynys-gau chapel, Merthyr, he m. Gwenllian Thomas, sister of one of the chief figures in the Welsh settlement in Patagonia, John Murray Thomas.

His public life did not diminish the ardour for establishing a Welsh settlement which had gripped him ever since he had been at the feet of M.D. Jones. In May 1865 he resigned from his pastorates to join the first party which sailed from Liverpool that month in the *Mimosa* to found a Welsh settlement in Patagonia. He arrived at New Bay on 28 July 1865 and landed at Porth Madryn. All the settlers were in very straightened circumstances, and Matthews became seriously ill after crossing the prairie between Porth Madryn and the Camwy valley. Life was so hard by the end of 1866 that Matthews and seven others went to Buenos Aires to seek government assistance to move the Welsh settlers to the province of Santa Fe. The minister for Home Affairs, Dr. Rawson, pressed them to spend another year on the banks of the Camwy, and in Apr. 1867 three of the eight returned to seek the views of their fel-low-Welshmen. Edwyn Roberts and R.J. Berwyn wanted to stay; but Matthews thought it wise to move. Most of the settlers agreed with him, and the three were sent back to the capital to procure a ship to carry them all from there. In the hamlet of Patagones they happened to meet Lewis Jones (1836-1904; *DWB*, 493), who per-suaded Matthews to change his mind and return to the Camwy valley. He persuaded the majority to stay there for another year and at that critical hour saved the great venture from disintegrating. By that time he was the chief (if not the only) public figure there. He farmed the land to support his family; but he strove volun-tarily for years to minister the churches in the Camwy valley, particularly those at Trerawson, Glyn Du, Moriah and Tair Helygen. It is said that the only stipend he received for his min-istry to the first emigrants was their assistance in enclosing the land near the river bend where he established himself. He called his home *Parc yr Esgob* (the bishop's field), and he was known as *esgob y Wladfa* (the Bishop of the settlement).

He saw the need for new blood and new spir-it if the settlement in Patagonia was to survive. He went to Wales in Jan. 1873, to U.S.A. in Aug., and to Wales a second time in Nov. until Apr. 1874 to give lectures and renew enthusi-asm for the venture. As a result two groups were raised in 1874, one being carried by the *Electric Spark* of New York (33 persons) and the other by *Hipparchus* of Liverpool (49 persons); and also parties from Wales in 1875 which brought 500 emigrants to reinforce the original settlers and treble the population. He visited Wales twice again, in 1889-90 and 1891-94 when he took charge of Severn Rd. Chapel, Cardiff (1893) and wrote *Hanes y wladfa yn Patagonia* (1894). This is the most comprehensive and objective history written at that time on the sub-ject.

He was a member of the first elected Council in the Welsh settlement and one of the key speakers in discussions with Buenos Aires, and he was on the committee of Oneto (representing the government of Argentine) to control assis-tance to the Welsh settlement in 1875-76. He con-stantly promoted opening new Welsh elemen-tary schools in the Camwy valley and was J.P.

three times. He was also a member of the com-mittee that steered the Welsh opposition to the central government order that every native over 18 yrs. old should be drilled on Sundays; and he was arrested along with all the other committee members by local officers in Feb 1899 as a result. He was editor of *Y Dravod*, 1896-99. He d. 1 Apr. 1899 and was buried in Moriah cemetery where he had been a minister for twenty years. He left a widow, two sons and two daughters.

One of his grandchildren is the historian Matthew Henry Jones, Trelew, author of two books on the history of that town: *Trelew: un desafio Patagonico* (1981; 1989).

Bangor, MS 8060; *Y Gwladgarwr*, 1865-74; *Y Dravod*, Apr. 1899; *Tyst*, May 1899; *Tarian y gweithiwr*, Aug. 1899; A. Matthews, *Hanes y wladfa yn Patagonia* (1894); Lewis Jones, *Y wladva Gymreig yn Ne America* (1898); R. Bryn Williams, *Y Wladfa* (1962 and 1969); personal research.

D.L.D.

MAURICE and **OWEN** (*DWB*, 621-2). On p. 622 delete Sir before William Owen. He was buried at Selattyn, 11 Oct. 1670.

MAURICE, HENRY (1634-82; *DWB*, 622-3). The second part of *Cannwyll y Cymru* was published at the end of 1659 or the beginning of 1660. See under Rhys Prichard (*DWB*, 795-6).

MAURICE, MATHIAS (*DWB*, 624). He d. 1 Sept. 1738; his widow Elizabeth d. 8 Oct. 1771, 73 years old. (Minutes of the congregation in Rothwell; see N. Glass, *The Early History of the Independent Church at Rothwell* (Northampton, 1871). N.L.W. and Bala-Bangor College library.

He published a number of English books, including *Monuments of Mercy* (1729), *A modern question affirmed and approved* (1739).

G.T.S.

MAURICE, Sir WILLIAM (*DWB*, 624-5). On p. 625 correct 1606 to 1600.

MEREDUDD ap RHYS (*DWB*, 627-8). In l. 3 read 'the books of pedigrees'.

MERRICK, RICE or **RHYS MEURUG** (*DWB*, 628-9). He d. 1 March 1586/7. See also T.J. Hopkin's article on him in *Morgannwg*, VIII, 5-13.

MEYRICK or **MERRICK** (FAMILY), of Hascard (*DWB*, 630-1). Sir Roger Williams d. in 1595 (*DWB*, 1069).

MEYLER, JAMES (1761-1825), minister (Congl.); b. in 1761 at Penysgwarn, Llanwnda, Pembs. He was well educated in his youth, and served as a solicitor's secretary for a while. He became a member of Rhos-y-caerau church, where he began to preach. He went to Wrexham academy under Jenkin Lewis (*DWB*, 554), and after com-pleting his course he received a call from his mother-church of Rhos-y-caerau and was ord. there on 20 Oct. 1795. He took a leading part, with others, in establishing English causes in the English parts of Pembrokeshire. On account of his knowledge of the law, and his particular abil-ity to plead the cause of the suffering, he was considered to be a wise leader both within and outside the church. He was a person of cultured mind, of mature and sound judgement, and a preacher who was greatly admired. He d. in 1825 aged 64.

H. Egl. Ann., iii, 35; J.T.J., ii, 263-4.

J.D.O.

MILLER, WILLIAM HALLOWES (*DWB*, 633). He had to take an M.D. degree in 1841 to satisfy the college statutes which required tutors to be medically qualified or clerics. He was elected F.R.S. in 1838 and secretary of the Royal Society in 1856. He was active on the commission to review the standard weights and measures of the United Kingdom in 1843 and he was a member of the *Commission internationale du Mètre* in 1870.

Proc. Roy. Soc., 31 (1881), ii; S. Markelyne, *Nature*, 22 (1880), 247.

Ll.G.C.

MILLINGCHAMP, BENJAMIN (1756-1829; *DWB*, 633). He was the son of Benjamin Millingchamp and grandson of Joseph Millingchamp.

MILLS, ROBERT SCOURFIELD - see VAUGH-AN, ARTHUR OWEN (Owen Rhoscomyl; 1863-1919), *DWB*, 1001 and below.

MINIMUS - see ROBERTS, JOHN (1808-80), *DWB*, 1148.

MORGAN (FAMILY), of Llantarnam (*DWB*, 635). William, Earl of Pembroke, d. 1570 (not '1601').

MORGAN, DAVID (1779-1858; *DWB*, 641). His wife was Mary Hughes (1782-1826). Their daughter, Ann, m. Thomas Bynner, Llanfyllin, draper, and they had a son who m. Catherine, daughter of Owen Daniel, Caethle, Tywyn. Her second husband was Joseph David Jones (*DWB*, 490-1).

MORGAN, EDWARD (1783-1869; *DWB*, 642). A fuller discussion and bibliography by G.M.R. in *Cylch. Cymd. Hanes M.C.*, 1962, 13-22.

MORGAN alias **YONG,** JOHN (d. 1504; *DWB*, 646-7). His pedigree is in Pen. MS. 131, p. 255; the pedigree on p. 251 is that of a different person. The bishop's mother descended from the Dwnns.

P.C.B.

MORGAN, JOHN (1743-1801; *DWB*, 648). A list of priests in the Bangor diocese (1778) notes Morgan, curate of Llanberis, as being aged 38. He may, therefore, have been born in 1740. NLW Cwrtmawr MS. 56B has the name 'John Morgan, Gorsvawr, Lledrod', perhaps indicating his birthplace. (Info. from G. T. Roberts).

R.T.J.

MORGAN, MAURICE (*DWB*, 649). Correct the number of the Bronwydd MS. to 7170.

MORGAN, RICHARD HUMPHREYS (*DWB*, 650). The first edition of *Phonographia* was published in 1876. The second edition was published in 1878.

MORGAN, Sir THOMAS (*c.* 1542-95; *DWB*, 652). It is not correct that he did not return to England between 1574 and 1593; official records at the P.R.O. indicate that he and Sir Roger Williams were recalled when the Armada threatened.

MORGAN, WILLIAM (*c.* 1545-1604; *DWB*, 656). It is unlikely that Morgan was a pupil of Tremellius, who was a tutor at Cambridge from 1550 to 1553 only, though he did visit London for a period in 1565. However, Morgan could have used Tremellius's Latin translation of the Old Testament, which was published in Frankfurt in 1575 and reprinted in London in 1579-80.

G.W.

For Morgan's use of Tremellius's Old Testament and his methods as a translator see Isaac Thomas, *Yr Hen Destament Cymraeg, 1551-1620* (1988) and *Y Testament Newydd Cymraeg, 1551-1620* (1976). For Morgan's status as a scholar see also R. Geraint Gruffydd, 'The Translating of the Bible into the Welsh Tongue,' 1988.

MORGAN, WILLIAM (1750-1833; *DWB*, 657). B. 26 May 1750. He was apprenticed to two apothecaries in London and was a student at St. Thomas' Hospital. He returned to Bridgend in 1772 to take up his father's practice after his death. He went to London in 1773 where he may have kept a school for a while. He was appointed to the Equitable 17 Apr. 1774.

He valued the Equitable in 1775, the first office to be valued, and the Equitable in 1800 was the first office ever to add a bonus on payment made on a policy. In addition to his work with the Equitable he advised the Scottish Widows office when it was set up. It is likely that he was the first to produce X-rays when he passed electricity through an almost airless tube.

His son Arthur was an actuary at the Equitable from 1830 to 1870 and was an F.R.S. Another son, William, who d. young was an assistant actuary briefly and a grandson, William, was an assistant actuary from 1870 to 1892.

Peter H. Thomas in *Glamorgan Historian* (1963), 89; Maurice Edward Ogborn, *Equitable Assurances* (1962); Sir Herbert Maxwell, *Annals of the Scottish Widows Fund Life Assurance Society during one hundred years, 1815-1914* (1914), 34; William Morgan, *Philosophical Trans. of the Royal Soc.* (abridged), 15 (1781-1785), 699; J.G. Anderson, *The birth-place and genesis of Life Assurance* (1940), 43; and see also Walford's *Insurance Cyclopaedia* (1973), ii, 630.

Ll.G.C.

MORGAN ELFAEL (ELFEL) (*DWB*, 639). He was buried at Presteigne, 25 Aug. 1563. See F.G. Payne, *Crwydro Sir Faesyfed*, II, 17.

MORGAN MWYNFAWR (*DWB*, 639). Read Onbraus (not 'Onbrans').

MORRIS, JOHN (1813-96; *DWB*, 661). 'its present buildings' i.e. at Brecon, as of 1953.

MORRIS, RICHARD (*DWB*, 663-4). According to the papers of the late Iolo A. Williams, Richard went to London on 1 Aug. 1722 and Lewis on 7 May 1723.

MORRIS, WILLIAM (1783-1861; *DWB*, 667). He is described as William Morris, 'Minister of the Gospel', Clydau, in his bond dated 22 Aug. 1822 to marry Lettice Morris, Llansteffan.

MORRIS, WILLIAM (1812-86; *DWB*, 667-8). According to the 1851 Census he lived at 47 High Street, Holywell, and he describes himself as a bookseller aged 35 employing six workers. [O.P.C.S. index to deaths reported Oct.-Dec. 1886 lists William Morris aged 74 of the Superintendent Registrar's District of St. Asaph.]

MOSES, DANIEL LEWIS (1822-93; *DWB*, 672). For Daniel read David and see MOSES-EVANS, DAVID LEWIS below.

MORRIS ap ROBERT - see ROBERTS, MORRIS, d. *c.* 1723, *DWB*, 873.

MOSES, EVAN (*DWB*, 672-3). See also *Cylch. Cymd. Hanes M.C.*, 1962, 5-13.

MOSES(-EVANS), DAVID LEWIS (1822-93; *DWB*, 672). He was known colloquially as Dafydd Moses but about 1860 he added the surname Evans after researching his family history, and this was the surname used by the 5 or 6 youngest of his 9 children, 4 sons and 5 daughters. His dau. Mary was the step-mother of J. Lloyd Thomas, headmaster of Llanfyllin grammar school, and the mother of Dafydd Arafnah Thomas, a minister. See T.J. Morgan's article on the *eisteddfod* poets of Cwmaman and the Swansea valley in *J.W.B.S.*, 9, 162-85, for his role as a teacher of poets in the area and the comments of Watcyn Wyn (Watkin Hezekiah Williams, *DWB*, 1076) and Gwydderig. [See also Huw Walters, *Canu'r pwll a'r pulpud*, 94-103]. Gwydderig (Richard Williams, 1842-1917, *DWB*, 1066-7) bequeathed his manuscripts to T. Moy Evans, one of D.L. Moses-Evans's sons, headmaster of St. David's College school Lampeter before becoming a solicitor in Ammanford: he edited a volume of stories, *Hirnos Gaeaf*. Another s., John M(oy) Evans, was a prominent solicitor in Swansea, a town council member and chairman of the library committee and of the Royal Institution. He was president of the South Wales Unitarian assembly and edited series of articles in the *Cambrian Daily Leader*. Other sons were D.L. Moses-Evans, a solicitor in Ystalyfera, and E. Tudor Moses-Evans, vicar of Monkton, Pembs. and canon of St. David's.

J.Ll.T.

MOSTYN (FAMILY), Mostyn Hall (*DWB*, 675). The second baronet, Sir Edward Pryce Lloyd, m. Elizabeth, third daughter of Sir Roger Mostyn. The Mostyn estates came into the possession of Elizabeth's husband, not into the possession of Elizabeth's son.

MUNGO – see KENTIGERN (*DWB*, 1139).

MYDDELTON (FAMILY; *DWB*, 675-8). Sir Thomas was constable of Denbigh castle in 1597 (*Hist. MSS. Comm.*, Cecil, vii, 185); 676, Hugh was apprenticed, 2 Apr. 1576, to the goldsmith Thomas Hartob (Goldsmith's Co. Register); 677b, par. 2, l. 18, 24 July (not '28').

NASH, JOHN (*DWB*, 681-2). According to Sir John Summerson, keeper of Soane Museum, and author of *John Nash, Architect to King George IV* (1935), he was b. in London, his father being a millwright at Lambeth. He claimed to be of Welsh blood, but was related to the Nash family of Worcestershire. Add to bibl. *John Nash; a complete catalogue* (1991); R. Suggett, *John Nash, architect in Wales* (1995).

NENNIUS (*DWB*, 682-3). An English translation was published by A.W. Wade-Evans (1938); also text and translation by John Morris, *Historia Brittonum and the Welsh Annals* (1980). Important discussions by David N. Dumville are found in his *Histories and Pseudo-Histories of the Insular Middle Ages* (1990) and contrast P. J. C. Field in *Studia Celtica*, 30 (1996), 159-65.

NICHOLAS, THOMAS; (*DWB*, 684). Read Hereford (not 'Herefords.') in l.8.

NORRIS, CHARLES (*DWB*, 686). He was the son of John Norris, Hughenden, Buckinghamshire, by his mistress, Deborah Busby. The second husband of Catherine Lynch was Sir John Norris, not John Norris, Hughenden.

OSBWRN WYDDEL (*DWB*, 689). Delete 'either Einion ab Osbwrn or'.

OUDOCEUS (EUDDOGWY) (*DWB*, 689). Instead of Burig read Buddig. The second 'u' in Anauued represents 'v'.

OWAIN ap GRUFFYDD (fl. 1260; *DWB*, 690). Read Senena (not 'Senana').

OWEN (FAMILY), Glansevern (*DWB*, 695). DAVID OWEN (1(b)) was bapt. 16 Sept. 1754 and WILLIAM OWEN (1(c)) 22 Aug. 1758 in Berriew church. The father was described as a 'gent. of Keel' and the family owned much property in the area. Before David went to Cambridge he attended his uncle's school at Warrington. In Cambridge he won the principal Smith Prize in 1777 and gained his M.A. degree in 1780. He d. 10 Dec. 1829. William went to Jesus College, Oxford, for a short period between attending Warrington school and Trinity College. He d. 10 Nov. 1837.

Alumni Cantab. (1951), 611, 614; Berriew parish registers at N.L.W.

Ll.G.C.

OWEN (FAMILY), Plas Du (*DWB*, 697-8). Delete 'educated at Lincoln's Inn (21 April 1556),' top of p. 697b. It is incorrect to say that Robert Owen was canon of Mantes (*sic*). According to Chambois (*Repertoire Historique ... du Diocese du Mans*, vol. II, p. 68), he was elected canon of Le Mans on 23 April 1588. He d. there on 9 Nov. 1629, 'very old'.

A.H.D.

OWEN, HENRY (1716-95; *DWB*, 704-5). He was b. in Dyffrydan, about 3 miles from Dolgellau. His mother's name was Jonet(te).

Dolgellau parish registers in N.L.W.

Ll.G.C.

OWEN, HUGH (1639-1700; *DWB*, 706). In the bibliography read *Nonconformist's Memorial*, as in the body of the article.

OWEN, JOHN ('Owain Alaw'; 1821-83; *DWB*, 713-4). His son, W[illiam] H[enry] Owen, [studied at the Royal Academy, London, and] was the organist of St. Bartholomew's church, Dublin. He lost his life in a railway accident near Abergele, 20 Aug. 1868, when he was only 23 years old. [WWP; *Llan*, 14 Apr. 1939, 3.]

OWEN, MARY (*DWB*, 716). B. at Ynys-y-maerdy, daughter of David and Mary Rees.

OWEN, MORFYDD LLWYN (*DWB*, 716-7). B. 1 Oct. 1891. Her mother's name was Sarah Jane Owen. She m. in Feb. 1917 the psychiatrist Alfred Ernest Jones (see above). Add to the bibliography *Gol.*, 10 Aug. 1960, and Rhian Davies, *Eneth ddisglair annwyl: Never so pure a sight* (1994).

OWEN, WILLIAM (1750-1830; *DWB*, 723). Read Milborne (not 'Milbourne') Port each time.

OWEN, WILLIAM ('Gwilym Alaw'; *DWB*, 723). His dates are 1762-1853. See Huw Williams, *Tr.*, 1982.

OWEN, WILLIAM ('Gwilym Meudwy', or 'Gwilym Glan Llwchwr'; 1841-1902), rhymester and tramp; b. in Aber Cenfi, Llandybïe, Carms. 23 July 1841, s. of William and Sarah Owen. The family hailed from Montgomeryshire and the father was a weaver in Cil-y-cwm, Llanwrda and Llandovery before moving to a woollen factory in Cwmllwchwr in 1836. According to Watcyn Wyn (*Y Diwygiwr*, 1902, 262) William Owen was the great-grandson of John Owen (1757-1829), Machynlleth (*DWB*, 712), author of the long poem *Troedigaeth Atheos*. Gwilym Meudwy was apprenticed to a carpenter in Trap, near Llandeilo, in 1856 but he returned to his father and the woollen mill after 3 years. His father d. in 1865 and his mother in 1877, and Gwilym Meudwy was a tramp for the rest of his life. He spent his summers at the spas in Llanwrtyd and Llandrindod, returning to Brynaman, Llanelli and Swansea over the winter. He used to sell the products of his muse on these annual pilgrimages and he kept the printers of Aberdare, Llandeilo, Ystalyfera, Llanelli and Ammanford busy for a period of 30 years. Between 1879 and 1902 he published about 18 pamphlets containing a variety of material such as temperance debates, conversations, ballads and tracts, but he made his name primarily as an elegist. He composed scores of memorial verses for leading Nonconformists and politicians as well as ballads in memory of those killed in colliery accidents. The quality of these verses is, to say the least, mediocre, but Gwilym Meudwy deserves recognition as one of the last of his kind to make a living by selling his poems and ballads. He d. in Ammanford 21 June 1902 and was buried in the family grave in the cemetery of the parish church, Llandybïe. One of his brothers was Joseph Pugh Owen, schoolmaster of Torrington Square, London; another was John Owen who m. a sister of D. Avan Griffiths, minister of Troedrhiwdalar (Congl.). William Pugh Owen, a priest in Melbourne, Australia, and Dr. John Griffith Owen, a doctor in Kingston-upon-Thames, were the children of that marriage. Edmund Owen Rees of San Francisco, British Consul in Nicaragua, was the rhymester's nephew, his sister's son.

Casglwr, 8 Aug. 1979 (with a list of his works); G.M. Roberts, *Hanes Plwyf Llandybïe*, 235; *S. Wales Guardian*, 21 Aug. – 11 Sept. 1975.

H.Wa.

OWEN, WILLIAM HENRY (1845?-68) – see under OWEN, JOHN (1821-83) above.

PAMPLIN, WILLIAM (1806-99), botanist; b. in Chelsea, 5 Aug. 1806. In 1827 he published a list of the rare plants of Battersea and Chelsea. He wrote a great deal for the *Magazine of Natural History* and became editor of *The Phytologist* in 1855; he married Caroline Hunneman, the dau. of the owner of the journal. Frequent visits to north Wales deepened his affection for the area and after retiring in 1864 from his business as a publisher and bookseller he settled in Llandderfel, Mer., where he built a house (Pen-y-llan) and lived for the rest of his life studying the botany and birds of the countryside. His wife d. in 1876, and he m. Margaret Parry of Blaen-y-cwm, Bethel, Llandderfel, in 1878. He d. 9 Sept. 1899 and was b. in Llandderfel.

Yr Haul, Nov. and Dec. 1939; *Jnl. of Botany*, Dec. 1899 (where it is incorrectly stated that he was b. in Wandsworth); *Jnl. Merioneth Hist. and Record Soc.*, 1 (1949) and 2 (1950). Some of his MSS. are in N.L.W. and others in the Univ. of Wales, Bangor.

E.R.

PARRY, JOHN (1776-1851; *DWB*, 736). It was not he, but his son John Orlando Parry, who composed 'Flow gently, Deva'.

PARRY, JOSHUA (*DWB*, 738). Add that his son Caleb was a distinguished physician on account of his work on angina, and on exophthalmic goitre (of which he provided the first description). He was a great friend of Edward Jenner.

E.W.J.

PARRY-WILLIAMS, HENRY (1858-1925), schoolmaster and poet; b. 11 June 1858, the son of Thomas and Mary Parry, Gwyndy, Carmel, Caerns. He was a half-brother of Robert Parry, father of the poet R. Williams Parry (see above) and of Richard Parry, father of Thomas Parry (1904-85). As a young man he adopted the surname of his paternal grandfather, Henry Williams, in addition to his own. He received his elementary education at Bron-y-foel school, and stayed on for five years as a pupil-teacher. He then attended Holt Academy under James Oliver Jones. He spent the last four months of 1876 as a temporary teacher at Loveston school, near Narberth, Pembs. In 1877 he entered Bangor Normal College, and on completing the course in 1879 he was appointed schoolmaster at Rhyd-ddu, where he remained until his retirement in 1923.

Parry-Williams's poetry, of which he wrote a good deal, was in accordance with the standards of his age. Three long poems in the free metres won prizes at local *eisteddfodau* (see *Y Geninen Eisteddfodol*, 1892, 1893, 1897). He was successful at the national *eisteddfod* held at Colwyn Bay in 1910 with nine lyrics on the subject 'Y bywyd pentrefol'. His main productions were poems to celebrate various happenings in his own locality, and a few lyrics (see *Cerddi Eryri*, ed. Carneddog). As schoolmaster he made the study of Welsh literature an integral part of the syllabus, a very unusual initiative in those days, especially in an elementary school. The pupils were taught something about the various schools of Welsh poetry throughout the centuries, and about the chief prose writers up to the eighteenth century. This Parry-Williams regarded as being educationally sound and the means of ensuring that his pupils took pride in their nation's achievements. Another unusual practice of his was to receive in his home during the summer months Continental scholars who wished to learn Welsh. This began in 1899 with Professor Heinrich Zimmer of Greifswald University, and there followed some of the best-known Continental Celticists, such as Herman Osthoff of Heidelberg, Rudolf Thurneysen of Freiburg, and A.G. van Hamel of Utrecht.

Parry-Williams m. Ann Morris, Glangwyrfai, Rhyd-ddu, in 1885, and they had two daughters and four sons (one of whom was T.H. Parry-Williams, 1887-1975). He d. on Christmas Day 1925 and was buried at Beddgelert.

Personal knowledge; *Y Genhinen*, xxviii, 66-70; *Cymru*, xx, 112-4; *The place of Welsh in the curriculum of Elementary schools: An address delivered by Mr. Parry-Williams, Rhyd-ddu, to the Carnarvonshire Teachers' Association on Saturday, April 8, 1911* (This pamphlet was printed at the *Herald* Office, Caernarfon, but without a publisher's name).

T.P.

PECOCK, REGINALD (*DWB*, 743-4). In the bibliography read V.H.H. (not 'N') Green.

PENRY, DAVID (1660?-1722; *DWB*, 746). He was the son of William Penry, Cwrt y Ceidrym, and Margaret, his wife (Alcwyn Evans). The conventicle was held in Gwernchwith farmhouse. Since his will was proved on 26 April 1722 it is highly likely that he died earlier that year, so change the year of death from ?1721.

PENSON, RICHARD KYRKE (*DWB*, 747). He was b. 19 June 1815, in Overton, Flints. not Oswestry. His mother was Frances (née Kirk) and his wife was called Clara Maria. He lived at Cilyrychen, Llandybïe, Carms., in 1871.

PERRI, HENRY (*DWB*, 747). Read 'pronuntiatio' (not 'pronuntiato').

PERROT (FAMILY; *DWB*, 747-9). Top of p. 748a, correct 'Edward VI valued ... Bath' to 'by 1547 he had been knighted'. Bottom of 748b, replace 'In spite of his attainder' by 'In spite of the Act of Attainder under which Perrot was punished,'.

A.H.D.

PERROT(T), THOMAS (*DWB*, 749-50). Amend Roger Griffiths to Roger Griffith as in the article upon him (*DWB*, 299).

PHILIPPS, Sir JOHN (*DWB*, 755). Catherine, the second wife of Sir Erasmus Philipps and the mother of Sir John, was the daughter of Edward Darcy by his wife Elizabeth, daughter of Philip

(Stanhope), first Earl of Chesterfield. She d. 15 Nov. 1713.

PHILLIMORE, EGERTON GRENVILLE BAGOT (*DWB*, 755-6). On 'Welsh Aedoeology' see *Studia Celtica*, 6 (1971), 99-102.

PHILLIPS, DANIEL (1826-1905), minister (Congl.) and lecturer; b. in 1826 at Swansea, Glam. He lost his parents when he was young. He went to work in Ebbw Vale, and in 1848, with about 50 other Welsh people, emigrated on the *Georgia* to U.S.A., arriving in New York in May and Pittsburg in June. He worked in Pittsburg for some time, preaching and preparing himself to enter college. In 1856 he graduated at Amherst College. He preached regularly among the Congregationalists from 1859 to 1894, serving his last ministry at Huntington, Mass. He was a powerful preacher and a very popular lecturer on themes relating to Wales, its history, customs, and, particularly, on the role of the Welsh in the development of U.S.A. Some of his lectures were published from time to time in *The Cambrian*. He spent his last years revising his lectures, and writing for Welsh and Welsh-American periodicals. He d. in 1905.

Asaph; The Cambrian, 1905, 358.

D.J.

PHILLIPS, DAVID (1812-1904; *DWB*, 757-8). B. 14 Dec. 1812.

PHILLIPS, REGINALD WILLIAM (1854-1926), botanist; b. at Talgarth, Brecks., 15 Oct. 1854, son of Thomas Phillips, registrar. He was educated at the Normal College, Bangor (he was later tutor there) and at St. John's College, Cambridge, where he graduated in 1884 with first class in science; he subsequently gained a D.Sc. degree of London University for research work on seaweed. He returned to Bangor in 1884 as a lecturer in biology at the University College; in 1888 he was promoted professor in that subject, but in 1894 he was appointed to the chair of botany, which he retained until retirement in 1923. He was an able administrator and took a prominent part in educational movements in the University College of North Wales. He d. 2 Dec. 1926.

Www; calendar of the University College of North Wales, Bangor.

R.T.J.

PIERCE, WILLIAM (*DWB*, 767). Read Congregational Library rather than 'Memorial Hall library'.

POWEL, DAVID (*DWB*, 770-1). See *N.L.W. Jnl.*, XIII, 398, where Prof. Melville Richards, on the basis of a deed of transfer of land dated 26 Oct. 1558 at N.L.W., concludes that the year of birth of Dr. Powel should be at least as early as 1540.

POWEL, JOHN (*DWB*, 771). According to Owen Williams, *Awduron Sir Ddinbych*, he was b. in 1731.

PREECE, Sir WILLIAM HENRY (*DWB*, 781). His *grandfather* was headmaster of Cowbridge school. William Preece's *father* went to

Caernarfon (1815), as a schoolmaster; he then went to work with Lloyd's Bank, and subsequently on the Stock Exchange. W.P. was b. at Bryn Helen, Caernarfon.

PRICE (FAMILY), Rhiwlas; (*DWB*,781-2). Cadwaladr ap Robert (alias Cadwaladr Price) d. in 1554: a metrical version of the year appears in a memorial *cywydd* in NLW MS. 436, p.39.

PRICE, EDWARD (*DWB*, 785). Hengaer-uchaf, where he d., is not in the parish of Llangwm, but at Llawr-y-betws in the old parish of Llanfor.

PRICE, JOHN (1734-1813) (*DWB*, 787). His father Robert Price was vicar of Llandegla from 1731 to 1737, and then of Llangollen until his death in 1771. He was buried 9 Sept.

PRICE, PETER (1864-1940), Independent minister; b. 11 July 1864 at Dewisbren-isaf, a smallholding about 3 miles from Dolgellau, Mer., the eldest of ten children of Thomas and Jane Price. Thomas Price was the eldest son of Peter and Catherine Price, Fronolau, a prominent farmhouse on the steep road from Dolgellau to Gwanas crossroads. This is the neighbourhood of the indentured land, famous in the history of the Quakers in Merionethshire in the 17th and 18th centuries. When the Quakers departed from Tyddyn-y-Garreg and the chapel that they had erected nearby, it was Peter Price, Fronolau, who was a deacon at the Independent church at Dolgellau, under the ministry of Cadwaladr Jones (1783-1867; *DWB*, 447), who was mainly instrumental in securing that chapel for the Independent denomination. It was rented in 1847, and bought in 1854, and named Tabor. The whole family was associated with Tabor and they claimed that they were from the same lineage as Edmwnd Prys (*DWB*, 804-5). Peter Price, Dewisbren-isaf was heavily influenced by the Quakers.

His parents moved to Plas-y-Brithdir when Thomas Price opened a business selling flour in Dolgellau. For a short time before leaving to help his father, Peter Price was educated at Dolgellau Grammar School, the headmaster of which at the time was S.S.O. Morris, a Cambridge scholar. He began to preach at Tabor in 1881. He became a student at University College, Aberystwyth and studied philosophy under Thomas Charles Edwards (*DWB*, 197-8). He left in 1885, but in the autumn of the same year, he was at Bangor, at the University College, where he gained his matriculation certificate and a scholarship of £10. He left the college in 1887, in the middle of his degree course, to become the minister at Ebeneser, Trefriw and he was ordained there on 14 and 15 Dec 1887. In 1896 he was installed as the minister at the recently founded church at Great Mersey Street, Liverpool. He was accepted at Cambridge University (without affiliation to any college) in October 1897 and within a year he had enrolled at King's College Cambridge, where he graduated with honours in philosophy in 1901. He received the degree of M.A. in 1939. He took up his ministry again in 1901. He married Letitia Williams, Tŷ Gwyn, Llanrwst in January 1902.

He moved to Bethania, Dowlais in the sum-mer of 1904, a church with over 600 members, where the musician Harry Evans (*DWB*, 235-6) was the organist. The Revival of 1904 was exciting the country by this time. The revivalist Evan Roberts (see above) visited Bethania. Peter Price was disturbed and, in a somewhat long and pretentious letter in the *Western Mail* on 31 Jan. 1905, he ventured to criticise the Revival and especially Evan Roberts's methods. Thereafter, in the religious history of Wales, Peter Price's name was associated with this protest and the agitation which followed it. In October 1910 he was installed as minister at Bethlehem, Rhosllannerchrugog. He spent 10 industrious years there organising various educational courses and addressing political meetings. One of his most zealous supporters was Dr Caradog Roberts (*DWB*, 860). He went to the USA in 1913 and shortly afterwards received the honorary D.D. from the University of Washington. He moved to minister at Baker Street, Aberystwyth, in November 1920 and generations of students of the University College there were unceasing in their praise of the extent and beneficial effect of his influence on their lives. He retired in 1928, owing to the ill health of both his wife and himself. They set up home in Swansea, Llanfairfechan and Prestatyn where he died on 1 July 1940; he was buried in Prestatyn cemetery.

Peter Price was a strong man with powerful opinions and passionate feelings, who was revered by his admirers but who also made enemies easily; a powerful preacher and an influential minister; a pacifist and an original character. He published two pamphlets, *Tarian yr ynfyd (Defence and delusion)*, 1936, *Y Fuddugoliaeth ddiarf* (from *Y Dysgedydd*), 1937.

West. Mail, 31 Jan. 1905; R.H. Davies, *Y Gloch Goll* (1947); Penry Jones, *Peter Price* (1949); D.J. Roberts, *Cofiant Peter Price* (1970); *Alumni Cantab.*, 1752-1900, V.ii, 194.

D.J.R.

PRICE, RICHARD (*DWB*, 789-90). He gave a great deal of help to John Howard in the preparation of his book *The State of Prisons*. After the death of Thomas Bayes in 1761, he edited his papers on the principles of probability. This apparently led to Price's interest in the principles of insurance and premiums. He was a consultant to 'A society of equitable assurances on Lives and Survivorships', (subsequently The Equitable Life Assurance Society). He was responsible for ensuring that the Equitable was the first ever office to ensure that premiums depended on the age of the assured and that they were sufficient to meet future commitments. He was supportive of the idea of pensions for the elderly and sickness benefits; in 1789 a House of Commons committee invited him to prepare tables for these purposes.

For a period he was a tutor at the Nonconformist Academy that was established in Hackney in 1768, and he discussed matters like premiums and Newton's *Principia* with some of the students there.

Carl B. Core, *Torchbearer of Freedom; The influence of Richard Price on eighteenth-century thought* (1952); Maurice Edward Ogborn, *Equitable Assurances* (1962); Caroline E. Williams, *A Welsh family from the begin-*

ning of the 18th century, (1893), 63; [There is a bibliography of Price's works by D.O. Thomas, J. Stephens, P.A.L. Jones (*Bibliography ... 1993*); B. Peach and D.O. Thomas have commenced the work of editing and publishing his correspondence, 1983-1994].

Ll.G.C.

PRICE, THOMAS (TOM; 1852-1909), Prime Minister of South Australia; b. at Maelor View, Brymbo, near Wrexham, Denbs., 19 Jan. 1852, s. of John and Jane Price. A year later they moved to the Everton district of Liverpool. The parents became members of the Welsh Wesleyan church at Burrough's Gardens before moving to a new chapel in Boundary Street. There the child Tom received his religious instruction and throughout his lifetime he acknowledged his indebtedness to that church and especially to the Sunday school where he became teacher and superintendent. After school-days he became, like his father, a stonemason and when he had completed his apprenticeship, undertook a share in his father's business. He m., 14 Apr. 1881, Anne Elizabeth, dau. of Edward Lloyd and a cousin of Sir Alfred T. Davies (see above). Struck by ill-health, Tom Price and his wife, decided to emigrate to Australia with their child and landed at Adelaide in May 1883.

In Australia, Tom Price was first employed dressing stones for the Parliament Buildings where he himself, ten years after landing in the country, became a Member of Parliament under the banner of the Labour Party. He became secretary of the Masons and Bricklayers Society and was, in time, chosen as the leader of the Parliamentary Labour Party. In 1905 he was elected Prime Minister, the first Labour Premier in South Australia and he maintained his position until his death. He became a fluent platform speaker and in this respect, as well as in appearance, he was often likened to Lloyd George (see above). He was an ardent Welshman and never despised his nationality. A man of his time, he was a total abstainer. Even when he was Prime Minister he did not conceal the fact that he had, throughout his lifetime, been a member of a temperance society. He will not be counted among the greatest of statesmen but in his day he fulfilled many worthy projects for the good of his community. He maintained contact with the Wesleyan church as a local preacher and he brought up his seven children in the same religious traditions. He d. 31 May 1909 and was buried in a cemetery at Adelaide.

The Centenary History of South Australia; Percival Serle, *Dict. of Austral. Biog.*; *Australian Christian Commonwealth*, 4 June 1909, 8-9; T.H. Smeaton, *From Stone Cutter to Premier* (n.d.); *Eurgrawn* 169 (1977), 154-9.

Er.E.

PRICE, THOMAS SEBASTIAN (*DWB*, 793). It appears that his father was John Price, Llanfyllin, who is described as a papist and father of papists and papist priests in the papers for Compounding in 1652.

PRICE, THOMAS WALTER (alias THOMAS GWALLTER; 'Cuhelyn'; *DWB*, 793-4). Price was

in California by 1858 and moved to Victoria, Vancouver Island, beginning of 1859 leaving his wife to sell the business. After another period in California in 1860 he and his wife arrived in Cariboo, about 300 miles north of Vancouver, in 1862 (he taught 'Tal o Eifion' the rudiments of poetry there in 1863) and returned to the east in 1865. He d. 13 May 1870 (*Y Drych*, 26 May 1870, 11 Aug. 1870). See Alan Conway, 'Welsh miners in British Columbia', *British Columbia Historical Quarterly*, 1957-58, 51-74.

G.I.L.

PRICE, WILLIAM (1800-93; *DWB*, 794). William Price was apprenticed to Evan Edwards and became a student at Bart's and at London Hospital, qualifying as a L.S.A. (Sept. 1821) and M.R.C.S. (Oct. 1821). He did not participate in the Chartist march on Newport. There is no evidence that he met Heine. He visited Boulogne in 1861. It was before Justice Stephen that the trial was held at Glamorgan assizes, on the double charge: (i) of attempting to cremate the body instead of burying it, (ii) of attempting to cremate the body so as to prevent an inquest being held. Gwenllian Llewelyn was the mother of three of his children. His body was cremated but not exactly in accordance with the instructions given in his will.

See further John Cule, 'The eccentric Dr. W. Price of Llantrisant', *Morgannwg*, VII, 98-119; Bryan Davies in David Smith, ed., *A people and a proletariat* (1980), 72-93.

PRICHARD, JAMES COWLES (1786-1848) – see under PRICHARD, THOMAS below.

PRICHARD, RHYS (*DWB*, 795-6). Witham is the present form of 'Wytham'. Rhys Prichard had a son, Samuel, whose daughter, Elizabeth, m. Thomas, son of Roger Mainwaring, Bishop of St. David's. Rhys Prichard's work was first printed during or before 1658. The 1659 edition indicates that this was the second time that this part was printed. See the article by Eiluned Rees in J.W.B.S., X, 36-41; [also Nesta Lloyd, *Cerddi'r Ficer* (1994)].

PRICHARD, ROWLAND HUW (*DWB*, 799 under PRITCHARD). There is greater warrant for the version without 't'. He went to Holywell in 1880, and was buried there in St. Peter's church.

PRICHARD, THOMAS (1764-1843; *DWB*, 796). He had a son, JAMES COWLES PRICHARD (1786-1848), physician, philologist and anthropologist; see D. Lleufer Thomas in *D.N.B.*, and G. Penrhyn Jones in *Y Genhinen*, summer 1963.

PRICHARD, THOMAS JEFFERY LLEWELYN (d. 1862, not 1875; *DWB*, 796-7). Initially Jeffery Llewelyn was a pseudonym (see some of his translations of Welsh poems in *Cambro-Briton* (1819-20), 393-4) which he combined with his baptismal name in *Welsh Minstrelsy*. He was, apparently, b. at Builth in 1789 or 1790, son of Thomas Prichard, 'lawyer', and Anne, his wife. He moved around a great deal – to London where he came into contact with some prominent Welshmen *c.* 1819, Aberystwyth, Abergavenny, Builth (where he m. Naomi Jones in 1826 and stayed until *c.* 1839). He catalogued

Llanover library 1841-54 but d. in great poverty at Swansea in Jan. 1862, aged 72. See articles by Sam Adams in *Anglo-Welsh Rev.*, 23 (1974), 21-60, *Brycheiniog*, 21 (1984-85), 52-63, and his monograph in the Writers of Wales series (Univ. of Wales Press), 2000.

PRITCHARD, EVAN (*DWB*, 798). Delete 'his cousin', and see *Trans. Caerns. Hist. Soc.*, XXVI, 52-71, for a full account by Thomas Parry.

PRITCHARD, ROWLAND HUW – see under PRICHARD above.

PRYCE (FAMILY), Newtown Hall (*DWB*, 802). In the bibliography read G.E.C., *the Complete Baronetage*, 1902; Burke, *Extinct...Baronetage*, 1838.

PRYCE-JONES, Sir PRYCE (PRYCE JONES until 1887; 1834-1920), pioneer of mail order business; b. Pryce Jones, Newtown, Monts., 16 Oct. 1834, second son of William Jones, solicitor, and Mary Ann Goodwin, whose father was a cousin of Robert Owen, the social reformer (*DWB*, 720-1). After being apprenticed at the age of 12 to a Newtown draper, he established his own business in 1859, in which year he m. Eleanor Rowley Morris. He began his mail order business by sending patterns to the local gentry, then lists and ultimately catalogues to all classes of people all over the world, inviting orders by post. From the early 1860s he displayed Newtown's famous Welsh flannel at Welsh National *Eisteddfodau*, and at great exhibitions in the world's greatest cities – Paris, Brussels, Berlin, Vienna, Melbourne, and Philadelphia among them – gaining many awards and attracting a large volume of orders, ultimately claiming over 300,000 customers worldwide, Florence Nightingale, Queen Victoria, and practically every royal household in Europe among them. He made extensive use of the railways to distribute his goods, developing his own parcel post system and advising the government when it introduced the Post Office Parcels Act 1882. In 1879 he opened a magnificent new Royal Welsh Warehouse near the railway station at Newtown.

He was knighted in Queen Victoria's Jubilee Honours 1887, and changed his name to Pryce Pryce-Jones. He represented the Montgomery Boroughs as Conservative M.P. 1885-86 and 1892-95. He was High Sheriff of the county in 1891. He d. at Newtown 11 Jan. 1920, and was buried in Llanllwchaearn churchyard.

The Biograph (1880), 206-8; various issues of the *Montgomeryshire Express*.

M.R.

PRYS, ELIS (*DWB*, 805-6). He d. 8 Oct. 1594. See Plas Nantglyn MS. 1 at N.L.W., and *Arch. Camb.*, 1915, 120.

PRYS, SIÔN (*DWB*, 807). The genealogy of the family of Llwyn Ynn is to be found in Lloyd, *History ... Powys Fadog*. See also NLW add MS. 9B, 413.

PUGHE, JOHN (*DWB*, 814), b. 8 Sept. 1814. See J.H. Cule in *Annals of the Royal Coll. of Surgeons of England*, 37 (Oct., 1965), 245-57.

PUW (FAMILY; *DWB*, 818-9). Robert Puw (d. *c.* 1629) was the second son of Huw son of Reginald son of Ieuan of Penrhyn Creuddyn, Caerns. He was a student at Middle Temple, 30 Nov. 1567 (*Register of Admissions to the Middle Temple*, I, 32). It should be noted that it was not he (ll. 7-10), but his uncle, his mother's brother, Robert ap Hugh ap Robert of Cefnygarlleg (of the lineage of Bryn Euryn), who was M.P. for Denbighshire in 1559, High Sheriff for the same county in 1562 and before that, in 1560 for Caernarfonshire.

Trans. Caerns. Hist. Soc., 1957.

PYLL, see JONES, JOHN (1786-1865) above.

QUIN, WINDHAM THOMAS WYNDHAM – see WYNDHAM-QUIN, WINDHAM THOMAS (1841-1926) below.

RAINE, ALLEN – see PUDDICOMBE, ANNE ADALISA (1836-1908), *DWB*, 810-1.

REES, ABRAHAM (*DWB*, 823). He was for a period before 1753 in Pencerrig, Llanelwedd, with John Evans, private tutor of Thomas Jones, the artist (1742 1803; *DWB*, 515-6; above). According to Thomas Jones when he was a fellow-pupil of his in Llanfyllin in 1758 he was 'deeply engaged in Hebrew, Algebra, Logarithms and Fluxions' – at the age of 15! He is said to have been the last nonconformist minister in London to wear a wig during services. He maintained his connection with Wales by attending Congregationalist festivals and preaching in Welsh.

A.P. Oppé (ed.), 'Memoirs of Thomas Jones, Penkerrig, Radnorshire', *Walpole Soc.*, 32 (1951), 4; S. Rees in *Cymru*, 25 (1903), 217; *DNB*.

Ll.G.C.

It would be more accurate to describe Abraham Rees as one of the trustees of Dr. Williams's Fund rather than a director of the fund.

REES, BOWEN (1857-1929), missionary; b. 16 Mar. 1857, at Ivy Bush Inn, Llandybïe, Carms., youngest of the six children of Jacob Rees, stone mason, and his wife Margaret, daughter of the publican Richard Bowen. The family moved to Ystalyfera, Glam., and he began working in a smithy when he was nine yrs. old. He set his heart on being a missionary after hearing an address by Thomas Morgan Thomas, 'Thomas of Africa' (*DWB*, 967), in 1879. After attending Bala College (1880-84), he was ord. at Pant-teg (Congl.) chapel, Ystalyfera, 22 May 1884 and was sent by the London Missionary Society to Lake Tanganyika. After a short intensive course at the medical school of the University of Edinburgh, he was transferred to Ndebele-land, and settled at Inyathi during March 1888. Between 1892 and 1918 he and his wife, Susanna Wesley (née Davies, the soprano 'Llinos Morgannwg', b. Merthyr Tydfil 5 July 1863, daughter of an iron worker; d. Swansea 9 Apr. 1933) were the only missionaries there – she too was of Ystalyfera and had been a preacher on a Methodist circuit since she was 22 yrs. old. They m. in Cape Town, 9 Mar. 1890: they had seven children but three d. young at Inyathi. Since King Lobengula (and his successors) protected their lives when Britain attacked their country in 1893, and spared them from the massacre at the beginning of the 1896 Rebellion, and continued to support them afterwards, their mission flourished over a district the size of Dyfed. Bowen Rees tried to protect the Ndebele from the rapacity of the British South Africa Co.: he provided information for the Quaker John Ellis, M.P., a member of the Committee for Investigation into the Jameson Raid, and gave evidence to the Aborigine Protection Society in a legal case which decided, in 1918, that the company had no right to the land of the Ndebele. He was very broad-minded, allowing the Ndebele to believe in the Gospel and its new teaching without abandoning altogether their old tradition: the fact that the Congregationalists are still in force in their midst is attributed to his and Susanna's attitude, besides their very long service. Bowen Rees was appointed a tutor at the preachers' training college at Tiger Kloof near Vryburg, South Africa, in 1918, but retired to Swansea in 1922, and d. there 7 Mar. 1929 and was buried at Oystermouth, Glam.

D.G. Williams, *Y Parch. Bowen Rees, Pant-teg ac Affrica* (c. 1939); *Tyst*, 14 Mar. 1929; *Cymro*, 10 Apr. 1929; *Gwyliedydd Newydd*, 27 Apr. 1918; N. Bhebe, *Christianity and Traditional Religion in Western Zimbabwe* (London, 1979); Marieke Clarke, 'Land, Missionaries and the Road to the North; aspects of the origins of Nkayi District, 1893-1918'; Terence Ranger, 'Violence and Memory: Zimbabwe, 1896 to 1996', *BZS Zimbabwe Review*, 96 (1995), 5-7; Ioan Bowen Rees, 'Surviving the Matabele Rebellion', *Planet*, 120 (1996-97), 82-91; 'Cenhadon olaf Lobengula', *Tyst*, 1, 8 Awst 1996; L.M.S. correspondence at SOAS library, London; personal knowledge and family MSS., some at Gwynedd Record Office, Caernarfon.

I.B.R.

REES, EBENEZER (1848-1908), printer and publisher; b. 1848 in Sirhowy, Mon. He was orphaned and brought up by relatives of his mother – David Clee and his wife in Cwmtwrch. He received little education and commenced work in one of the local collieries when he was seven years old. He left Cwmtwrch aged 18 years and worked in coalmines in Aberdare and Mountain Ash, returning to the Ystalyfera district in 1868 when he married Jane, the daughter of Dafydd and Rachel James (she died on 18 Sept. 1916). Labour trade unionism was growing in the valleys of Glamorgan at this time and Ebenezer Rees was prominent in this movement in the upper Swansea valley. He was dismissed and persecuted because of his convictions and he fled to Carbondale, Pennsylvania in 1869. He returned to Wales in 1872 and kept a bookshop for a time until in 1877 he opened a printing works in Ystalyfera. He established a new weekly newspaper, *Y Gwladwr Cymreig* in 1885. The first edition appeared on 22 January but it terminated on 24 September of the same year. D. Onllwyn Brace, Ystalyfera (*DWB* 47), J. Dyfrig Owen, Glantwrch and J.T. Morgan (Thalamus) were each, in turn, his editors. Ebenezer Rees had a great interest in social issues and he was prominent in the labour movement in the Swansea valley at the turn of the century. He was also friendly with the

socialist leaders of the time such as Keir Hardie, R.J. Derfel (*DWB*, 168) and John Hodge. In his office was printed and published *Cwrs y Byd* 'to investigate society in its various aspects' from January 1891 to 1895. Among other periodicals published by him were *Yr Oes Newydd* (1886) and the *Cenhadwr* (1894-97), two of the publications of the Swedenborgians in Wales. He also printed the *Celt* for a period.

Probably his most important contribution was to establish on 22 January 1898, *Llais Llafur* (later the *South Wales Voice*) as a weekly newspaper to serve the industrial areas of West Glamorgan and the east of the former Carmarthenshire. This publication was a vehicle for promoting the Labour movement in these districts. The last issue appeared on 2 December 1971. Ebenezer Rees published scores of ballads and pamphlets, the majority of which contained the works of minor poets and authors from the Swansea and Aman valleys. He died at his home in Ystalyfera on 30 September 1908 and he was buried in the graveyard of Beulah, Cwmtwrch.

Llais Llafur, 10 Oct. 1908; *Llenyddiaeth fy Ngwlad*, 41, 175; *S. Wales Voice*, 12 Aug. 1965.

H.Wa.

REES, EDWARD WALTER ('Gwallter Dyfi'; 1881-1940); bank manager and bearer of the *Gorsedd* sword; b. 8 Oct. 1881 son of Richard Rees ('Maldwyn', d. 1927) and Jane (née Jones) his wife, of Medical Hall, Machynlleth, Mont. He was educated at Machynlleth county school before becoming a bank clerk, and eventually manager of Barclay's Bank in Cardigan and later in Carmarthen (1926-40). On 8 Dec. 1914 he m. Frances Anne Rees, Goleufryn, Whitchurch, Glam., and d. 24 Apr. 1940, leaving two sons and a daughter. He was secretary of the Cardigan Cymrodorion Society which he founded and was a member of several other cultural societies. He was also secretary of Carmarthen national *eisteddfod*, 1911, and bearer of the sword of the *Gorsedd* of Bards from 1913 until 1940. He edited the Cardiganshire and Pembrokeshire column in the *Cardigan and Tivyside Advertiser* for a period. In 1938 he was elected treasurer of the Welsh Bibliographical Society; he himself owned a good collection of old Welsh books and manuscripts.

WWP; *Cardigan and Tivyside Advertiser*, 28 May 1926.

M.A.J.

REES, HENRY (1837-1908) - see under REES, WILLIAM (1802-83) below.

REES, JOHN (1770-1833; *DWB*, 826). Read William Huntington (not 'Huntingdon').

REES, THOMAS (1825-1908), minister (CM); b. 2 Aug. 1825 in the schoolhouse at Defynnog, Breck., son of Morgan Rees, schoolmaster of the free school, and Margaret, daughter of David Jones, shoemaker. As a boy he attended Brychgoed (Congl.) chapel with his mother and was educated at his father's school and Ffrwd Fâl Academy under the tuition of William Davies (1805-59; *DWB*, 159) who became the greatest influence on his life. He returned home when he was 16 and immediately started preaching by holding meetings at neighbouring farms. He lived at Tredegar for a time and became a member of Salem (CM), Sirhowi. Following the death of his sister in 1843 and his father in 1844 he returned to Defynnog and was chosen to be one of the early pupils at the Calvinistic Methodist College at Trefeca when he studied under David Charles (1812-78; *DWB*, 72). He was ord. at the Association in the South in Llanelli 4 Aug. 1852 and began his ministry in Hay. He returned to Defynnog in Aug. 1853 and became minister at Crickhowell from Dec. until 1868, living at 4 Tower St. In the following period he did much of his early writing whilst awaiting another ministry. In Nov. 1872 he became minister of Pontmorlais Church, Merthyr Tydfil, having by this time become a highly regarded member of the Calvinistic Methodist Church.

In 1873 he delivered the address on 'The nature of the Church', in 1883 he delivered the charge to the ordinands, 1886 he was Moderator of the Association in the South and in 1893 Moderator of the General Assembly. He retired in 1888 to devote his time to the Church and to writing. He was author of two biographies: *Cofiant y diweddar Barch. Ebenezer Williams, Aberhonddu* (1882) and (with D.M. Phillips) *Cofiant a phregethu y diweddar David James, Llaneurwg* (1895). Several volumes of his sermons were published and he was a contributor to *Y Traethodydd*, *Y Drysorfa*, *Y Cylchgrawn*, *The Treasury* and *The British Quarterly Review*. Dr. R. Tudur Jones said of him that 'he was a man of considerable learning and a distinguished figure amongst Calvinists'. He received the degree of D.D., New York, in 1894. He was described by a contemporary as a powerful preacher, a strict teetotaller, 'a bit of a wag' and a kindly man.

He m., 4 Nov. 1852, Sarah Williams, Glanyrafon, Llangors, and they had six children. He d. 8 June 1908 at his home, Ty'n-y-garn, Cefncoedycymer and was buried at Cefn Coed cemetery. His library was valued at £1,000.

Blwyddiadur MC, 1909, 253-4; *Drys.*, 1895, 145-8, 1908, 433-6.

I.Gl.R.

REES, WILLIAM ('Gwilym Hiraethog'; 1802-83; *DWB*, 831-2). HENRY REES (1837-1908) was his son; he began preaching in 1856. He attended Brecon College (1859-62), and became a minister at Chester (1862-85), and Bryngwran, Anglesey, from 1885 until his retirement in 1897. He d. 24 Feb. 1908. His biography and some of his sermons were published by R. P. Williams in 1909.

R. Hughes, *Enwogion Môn*; *Y Dysgedydd*, 1908, 185 and 1909, 315; see also E. T. Jones in *Ser. G.*, 1936, 151.

R.T.J.

RICHARDS and **HUMPHREYS** (FAMILIES; *DWB*, 850). 30 Sept. 1785 was the date of the marriage which brought them together. Also, 1689 (not 1698) was the date of the marriage of Grace Vaughan and John Humphreys.

RICHARDS, HENRY BRINLEY (*DWB*, 852). He was b. in Lower Market Street, Carmarthen. His mother was the daughter of John Brinley, Swansea (see F. Jones, *God Bless the Prince of Wales*, Carmarthen, 1969).

RICHARDS, THOMAS (1859-1931), Member of Parliament and secretary of the South Wales Miners Federation; b. 8 June 1859 at Beaufort, Ebbw Vale, Mon., s. of Thomas and Mary Richards. He was educated at Beaufort British School, and began work at a colliery when he was twelve years old. He played a prominent part in the work of the miners' unions in the Ebbw Vale area, and was a member of the Sliding Scale Association. In 1891 he was elected a member of Monmouth county council, and was made an alderman in 1904 and chairman of the council in 1924. When the South Wales Miners Federation was formed in 1898 he was appointed secretary, a post he held until he d. In 1904 he was elected Labour Member of Parliament for West Monmouthshire and he represented that constituency until 1918, and the constituency of Ebbw Vale from 1918 until he retired in 1920. He became a member of the Privy Council in 1918. For about two years, 1929-31, he was president of the Miners Federation of Great Britain. In 1880 he m. Elizabeth Eleanor Thomas. He d. 7 Nov. 1931 and was buried in Cardiff cemetery.

Www; *West. Mail* and *Times*, 9 Nov. 1931; L. Twiston Davies, *Men of Monmouthshire* (1933); Ness Edwards, *History of the South Wales Miners Federation* (1938).

G.M.G.

RICHARDS, WILLIAM (*DWB*, 855-6). He entered Bristol Baptist Academy in 1775 and was there for one year only.

J.A.O.

ROBERTS, ABSALOM (*DWB*, 859). Read St. Grwst (not 'Crwst').

ROBERTS, CARADOG (*DWB*, 860). Read Herr Johannes Weingartner (not 'Weingarter').

ROBERTS, EDWARD STANTON 1878-1938), schoolteacher and scholar; b. 11 March. 1878, in 'Edeyrnion', Cynwyd, near Corwen, Mer., s. of Robert and Martha Roberts. His father, a shoemaker, ensured the recording of local events and traditions, according to Hugh Evans (1854-1934; *DWB*, 238) in *Cwm Eithin*, who called him *cofiadur pennaf yr ardaloedd* (chief recorder of the areas).

Stanton Roberts was educated at Cynwyd Board School where he became a pupil-teacher from 1892 to 1896. He was awarded a Queen's Scholarship to the Normal College, Bangor, where he studied from 1896 to 1898, gaining a first-class certificate. For two months of 1898 he taught at the Victoria senior school in Harrington, Cumberland, before moving to Ponciau school, Rhosllannerchrugog, where he stayed from 1898 to 1905. He taught at Longmoor Lane Council School Liverpool, in 1905-06 and then became assistant headmaster at Glanadda school, Bangor, in 1907. In Oct. of the same year he enrolled as a student to U.C.W., Aberystwyth, where he won a number of prizes and was awarded an honours degree in Welsh in 1911. As a student he lodged in the same house as T.H. Parry-Williams. In 1917 he gained an M.A. degree for his work on William Salesbury's 'Herbal' (*DWB*, 898). From 1912 to 1915 he worked as a transcriber of manuscripts and editor for the Guild of Graduates at the National Library of Wales, Aberystwyth, before World War I interrupted his work there. He returned to teaching and became headmaster of schools at Pentrellyncymer 1916-1920, Cyffylliog 1920-31 and Gellifor from 1931 to his death in a bicycle accident on 26 Aug. 1938, on a road near Birmingham. He was buried at Cynwyd Cemetery. In 1919 he m. Annie, d. of Robert and Alice Roberts, Cefn Post, Llanfihangel Glyn Myfyr. They had three children.

Stanton Roberts was a good scholar and, according to some, one of the best palaeographers in Wales at the time. He was also a poet and writer of *englynion* (strict-metre quatrains). A very close friend of his, from Aberystwyth days, was poet Thomas Gwynn Jones (see above) who bore witness to Stanton Roberts' mildness and bravery as well as to his wide culture. During World War I, Stanton Roberts had to face several military tribunals as a conscientious objector which later had a detrimental effect on his career. After being an elder (CM) for several years, he joined the Quakers in 1930 mainly because of his disappointment at the major denominations' attitude towards war. Nevertheless, he carried on as a Sunday school teacher in Gellifor (CM) chapel. He greatly influenced the children who came under his care and worked extensively with *Urdd Gobaith Cymru*.

He published an essay on T.H. Parry-Williams in *Yr Ymwelydd Misol*, Nov. 1912, and the preface to the Corwen National *Eisteddfod List of subjects*. In 1916 his M.A. dissertation *Y Llysieulyfr meddyginiaethol a briodolir i William Salesbury* was published. He copied and edited editions of Llanst. MS 6 (1916), Pen. MSS 67 (1918), 57 (1921). Pen. MSS 53 and 76, which he copied, were published in 1927.

Denb. Hist. Soc. Trans., 20, 1971; personal letters and papers and information from the family; [*Brython*, 1 and 8 Sept. 1938].

D.I.

ROBERTS, FOULK ('Eos Llyfnwy'; *DWB*, 1038 under WILLIAMS, FOULK ROBERT). He was baptised at Llanllyfni, 6 Dec. 1782; an elder brother of the same name was buried on 16 July 1780. He m. his cousin, Catherine Williams, at Llanberis on 6 Aug. 1800.

Information from Huw Roberts, Pwllheli.

ROBERTS, HOWELL ('Hywel Tudur'; 1840-1922), poet, preacher and inventor; b. 21 Aug. 1840 at Bron-yr-haul, (Blaenau) Llangernyw, Denbs., the third of eight children. The family moved often as their father's occupation was building and selling houses. He began to take an interest in land surveying and became skilled in the craft. When he was aged thirteen he made an attempt at preaching. He attended a school at Abergele for a short time and it is said that he was for a while at the Mechanics Institute, Liverpool. Around 1853 a Literary

Society was established at the Pandy, and it was there that he learnt Caledfryn's grammar (see William Williams, *DWB*, 1083). In 1861 he won a certificate in Welsh at the Caernarfon Training College, but was unable to be admitted to the Normal College due to a lack of places. He regarded himself as 'Bardd Mawr y Pandy, B.B.D.' ('The Great Poet of Pandy'). He decided to settle in Clynnog where Eben Fardd (Ebenezer Thomas, *DWB*, 944-5), 'aged patriarch', kept a school and post office. He was invited to design a new school for the village which could be adapted as houses, should that be necessary. He is referred to as running a school in Llanllyfni but his interests turned increasingly towards inventions, and especially to the principle of 'perpetual motion'. He designed and built an airship (according to his daughter, in some of the buildings of the present St. Beuno's Hotel). A number of local craftsmen assisted him and he was visited by some important persons. His designs were frustrated by lack of money. His design (no. 110,201) for 'A propeller or driving wheel to put in motion vehicles, boats and flying machines' was accepted by the Patent Office on 14 Oct. 1916. He designed and built Bryn Eisteddfod (his home in Clynnog). A leisurely and unruffled man, he used to stay up until the small hours and was proverbial for missing trains! He assisted many in drafting their wills. He was one of the prime movers behind the Clynnog and Trefor Motor Company in 1912. He is said to have designed a gadget which would enable a railway guard to open and shut doors; he also designed a candlestick which had a pincers attached to it to hold the candle. He foresaw an invention that would enable people to see pictures of distant lands. He was an acceptable preacher, and wrote to denominational (CM) journals and newspapers. He adjudicated mainly in local *eisteddfodau* such as *Cylchwyl Lenydddol a Cherddorol Capel Uchaf* – a chapel which he had designed.

He m. the daughter of Hafod-y-wern, Clynnog, where he farmed and was pastor at Seion, Gyrn Coch and Capel Uchaf (CM) churches. They had five children. After his wife's death he m. the sister of the Rev. R. Dewi Williams (see above), a son and daughter were born to them. He d. suddenly on 3 June 1922 and was buried in the cemetery of Clynnog church, though it had been his wish to be interred in the place where he had spent his youth. He was the editor of *Gweithiau Barddonol Eben Fardd* (with Wm. Jones, junior 1873?); and author of *Llyfr Genesis ar Gân; Tlysau Beuno* (1902).

Gen., 32 (1914); *Gol.*, 7.6.1922; *Blwyddiadur* (MC), 1923; *Drys.*, 71; Catrin Parri Huws, *Sul, Gŵyl a Gwaith* (1981); Patent Office, London; [Catrin Parri Huws, ed., *Hywel Tudur, bardd, pregethwr, dyfeisydd* (1993)].

G.A.J.

ROBERTS, JOHN (1731-1806; *DWB*, 865). He was summoned before Bangor consistory court in Aug. 1765 for keeping a school in Llaniestyn without a licence.

Bangor diocesan papers, B/CC/C(G)/69 at N.L.W.; *Tr.*, 1870, 464.

Ll.G.C.

ROBERTS, RICHARD (harpist); *DWB*, 875). Read (1769-1855) (not '1796'). Since John Parry ('Bardd Alaw'; *DWB*, 736) referred to him in 1808 as a very good harpist who had been collecting the works of the poets for many years, 1769 should be accepted as his year of birth, as given by R. Griffith in *Cerdd Dannau*. [Llanbeblig register of burials, Richard Roberts, Bangor St., was buried 4 July 1855 aged 86].

ROBERTS, RICHARD (1810-83; *DWB*, 875). The Hen Gapel, Llanbryn-mair register (NLW MS. 488B) and *Cofiant y Tri Brawd* give 5 Nov. 1809 as his date of birth.

ROBERTS, THOMAS (1760-1811; *DWB*, 880-1). He was the eldest s. of Thomas Roberts (1735-1804; *DWB*, 880). He was b. prematurely on 13 Mar. 1760, in the 'little parlour' at Trefeca, when his mother was visiting her father-in-law, William Roberts (of Plas Bach) in his last illness. As mentioned in the article on Thomas Roberts (1735-1804), his father later moved with the family to Talgarth. He is referred to more than once in his father's diaries. He went to Talgarth school in 1775 and was sent to London, c. 1782, to be under the supervision of the well-known Moravian Benjamin La Trobe, and to learn the printer's trade. After La Trobe's d. in 1786 he returned to Trefeca (June 1787) to superintend the printing of '*y Beibl bach*' – the small Bible. However, by 1797 he was printing at Caernarfon. He printed both of the only two numbers of the periodical *Trysorfa Gwybodaeth, neu Eurgrawn Cymraeg* (see David Thomas, 'Dafydd Ddu Eryri'; *DWB*, 941). He m., at Caernarfon, Mary (Williams), a rich widow.

N.W. Gazette, 2 May 1811; notes taken by R. Idloes Owen, Bangor, from the diaries of Thomas Roberts (senior) at N.L.W. and from family documents.

R.T.J.

ROBERTS, WILLIAM (1773-1857), minister (Presb.). He hailed from the Clynnog Fawr area, Caerns. Having been with the Baptists for some time, he began preaching with the Calvinistic Methodists in 1804 and was ord. in 1819. He was reckoned to be well-versed in the scriptures and sustained an effective teaching ministry. More than anyone he was instrumental in establishing 'Mr Charles's Sunday schools' (*DWB*, 73-4) in the districts around Clynnog. In 1818 he published his handbook for teachers - *Arweinydd i Athrawon* - and in 1845 *Traethawd ar yr Ordinhad o Fedydd*, an essay on the sacrament of baptism. For some years he was blind; he would open the Bible, but recite Scripture from memory. He d. at Hendre Bach, 14 Oct 1857, aged 84.

Trys., 1858, 387; W. Hobley, *Hanes Meth. Arfon*, i, 34-5.

R.T.

ROBERTS, WILLIAM ('Nefydd'; 1813-72; *DWB*, 884). Read Llanefydd (not 'Llannefydd').

ROBERTS, WILLIAM JOHN (*DWB*, 885). B. in 1828 (not '1827'); he founded his '*Gorsedd*' in 1863 (not '1865').

RODERICK, JOHN (*DWB*, 888-9). On p. 7b of

B.L. Add. MS. 14874 (which he had owned) is written 'Llyfr Cywyddau Siôn Rhydderch, 1709; b. April 11, 1675'.

E.P.R.

He published a paper on arithmetic *c.* 1716. This may have been the first discussion of arithmetic in Welsh but there is no copy extant. It is mentioned in John William Thomas, *Elfennau Rhifyddiaeth* (Caerfyrddin, 1832), 6 (1805-40; *DWB*, 955-6), and John Roberts, *Rhyfyddeg neu Arithmetic* (Dublin, 1768), iii (1731-1806; *DWB*, 865).

Ll.G.C.

ROWLAND, NATHANIEL (*DWB*, 894). He was ordained deacon at Oxford, 26 May 1771, and a priest in London 21 Sept. 1773. He was curate of Stock (Essex) from 1771 until his marriage (1776). (*Cylch. Cymd. Hanes M.C.*, 1960, 69-70; see also 60-6). His will was published in the same periodical, 1954, 11-13.

ROWLANDS, GRIFFITH (1761-1828), surgeon; born in the parish of Llanfair near Harlech, Mer. on 9 April 1761. Having spent his apprenticeship as a surgeon in Liverpool, he succeeded in obtaining a place at St. Bartholomew's Hospital, London. Following completion of seven years of medical education, he was accepted, on 1 August 1782, as a member of the Company of Surgeons, the predecessor of the Royal College of Surgeons. He was a house surgeon in the hospital in London for two years before establishing himself as a surgeon in Chester. In 1785 he was appointed surgeon to the city hospital, a post he occupied for 43 years. Griffith Rowlands was one of the first in Europe to treat a broken hip by sawing away both ends of the bone each side of the fracture in order to seek a better bond – and that over fifty years before the time of anaesthetic. Under his treatment, the left thumb of Thomas Charles of Bala (*DWB*, 73-4) was amputated in 1799. The thumb had frozen as Thomas Charles travelled on a frosty night over the Migneint mountains between the counties of Caernarfon and Merioneth. With Rowlands's help also, a stone weighing two and a quarter ounces was removed from the gall bladder of Thomas Jones of Denbigh (1756-1820; *DWB*, 516) in 1802.

Although he spent the greater part of his life in England, he never lost his knowledge of the Welsh language and he was prominent in the activities of the Chester Cymrodorion Soc.

He died on 29 March 1828, a few days before his 66th birthday.

J.T.J., II, 526-7; G.P. Jones, *Newyn a Haint yng Nghymru* (1963), 161-63; T. Jones, *Hunangofiant* (ed. Idwal Jones, 1937), 41-43.

M.R.W.

ROWLANDS, Sir HUGH (1828-1909), general, and the first Welshman to be awarded the Victoria Cross; b. on 6 May 1928 at Plastirion, Llanrug, Caerns., the second son of John and Elizabeth Rowlands. His father was the heir to the Plastirion estate which amounted to approx. 1,200 acres. The family claimed descent from Bleddyn ap Cynfyn, Prince of Powys and were also descended from Dafydd, brother of Llywelyn ap Gruffydd; they had resided in the

Caernarfon area for nearly two hundred years. Hugh was educated at Beaumaris Grammar School and, at the age of 21, purchased a commission in the 41st Foot, the Welch Regiment. He served with the regiment in Ireland, the Ionian Island and Malta before going to Turkey in 1854 for the Eastern Campaign against Russia. From there he went to Varna and then, as Captain of the Grenadier Company took part in the invasion of the Crimea. He first saw action at the Battle of the Alma but it was at Inkerman on 5 Nov. that his name first came to prominence. For his action during that battle, in which he was severely wounded in the arm, he was later awarded the Victoria Cross, the first Welshman to be so decorated. He served throughout the siege of Sebastopol and took part in both attacks on the Redan. During the first attack he was again nominated for the Victoria Cross, but the regulations at the time made a second award impossible. At the end of the hostilities he was promoted Brevet Major, in recognition of his services, appointed Town Major of Sebastopol and later Brigade Major to the 2nd Brigade of the 2nd Division. He was created a Knight of the Legion of Honour by the French and a Knight of the Order of the Medjidie by the Turks. He also received the Crimean Medal with three clasps and the Turkish Crimean Medal. During the course of the war his name appeared in despatches on numerous occasions and one officer, when asked to name one person who did more than any other during the war, named Hugh Rowlands of the 41st. On his return from the war he received a civic reception from the people of Caernarfon who also presented him with a handsome Sword of Honour in the castle. He served afterwards in the West Indies, England, Scotland and Ireland before embarking for India where, in 1865, he took command of the Welch Regiment. Two years later he m. Isabella Jane Barrow, the grand-daughter of William Glynne Griffith of Rhosfawr and Bodegroes, Pwllheli and they had two children.

In 1875 he returned to Britain and had command of the 34th Foot, the Border Regiment and then returned to India where he remained until 1878 when he was sent as a special service officer to Cape Colony. In Africa he first served as ADC to Lt. General Thesiger (later Lord Chelmsford) and was then appointed inspector of forces in the Transvaal. In July he was appointed commandant of the Transvaal and immediately led an abortive assault on the Bapedi Chief, Sekukuni. During this campaign he came into conflict with Redvers Buller and Evelyn Wood, two of the most dominant officers of the late 19th century. In early 1879 Rowlands took command of the town of Pretoria which was being threatened by several thousand Boers who were demanding independence. The defences were such that the threat passed without any violence (only to reappear the following year as the First Boer War). He was then promoted to local Brigadier General and given the command of a brigade in Zululand where he remained until the end of that war when he returned to Britain and another great welcome from the people of Caernarfon. Rowlands was given various commands (Aldershot and Peshawar on the northwest frontier of India) before being appointed

to command the Bangalore Division of the Madras Army in 1884 (having been promoted Major General three years earlier). He remained in this post until 1889 when he left India for the last time and returned to Britain. In 1890 he was promoted Lieutenant General and in 1893 was appointed Lieutenant of the Tower of London by the Queen. The following year he took up his last command as C-in-C Scottish District where he remained until retiring in 1896 with the rank of General.

On retiring he returned to Plastirion, Llanrug, where he lived until his death in 1909. Amongst the honours which he received after 1896 was the rank of Knight Military Commander of the Order of the Bath in 1898 and Colonel of the Duke of Wellington's Regiment in 1897. He was also created a Deputy Lieutenant for Caernarfonshire and J.P. (he had already been a J.P. for the Transvaal).

His only son, Hugh Barrow Rowlands, d. of wounds received in Somaliland where he was serving as a major in the King's African Rifles in 1903.

Sir Hugh Rowlands d. on 1 Aug. 1909 and was buried in the parish churchyard at Llanrug.

Y Genedl Gymreig, 3 Aug. 1909; personal research.
W.A.W.

ROWLAND(S), JOHN ('Giraldus'; *DWB*, 894). By his own testimony, he was b. at Nanteos Arms, Llanbadarn Fawr, Cards. He was baptized in the parish church, 20 Mar. 1824, by William Herbert, curate, as the s. of Lewis Rowland, Tynewydd, and Anne his wife, daughter of John Griffiths, steward of Nanteos estate. His grandfather, Thomas Rowland, Ffynnon-wen, was a well-known huntsman and on friendly terms with the Pryse family of Gogerddan (*DWB*, 808). His father d. when John was only 4 years old, and he was then brought up by his grandmother at Ffynnon-wen. He worked as a shepherd during the summer months, receiving some education during the winter in a school held by Isaac Jenkins (*DWB*, 433) at Caeau Bach on the Hafodau estate. He left Ffynnon-wen after his grandmother's d. and went to his grandfather John Griffiths, thereby becoming friendly with the Powell family of Nanteos (*DWB*, 772-3). His mother re-m. Her second husband, David James of Llanddewibrefi, was a carpenter and builder. The family later moved to Pontlotyn. David James's family were staunch Anglicans in Cardiganshire and Glamorganshire. The boy was for 3 years apprenticed as a carpenter by his step-father. By this time he had taken to reading and at the age of 15 he was a local reporter for the *Carmarthen Journal*, being dubbed *Brutus bach* since his style resembled that of David Owen, 'Brutus', (*DWB*, 700-1). In 1848 he entered the new teachers' training college at Carmarthen, where he came to the notice of Harry Longueville Jones (*DWB*, 465-6). His first school was at Llangynnwr, in 1850. He moved to Llandybïe in 1851, and thence to Llanelli and Dinas Powys. Towards the end of 1864 he became Welsh secretary to Sir Thomas Phillipps (*DWB*, 756) at Cheltenham, for whom he had been copying monumental inscriptions in Wales since Aug. 1863. Giraldus described himself as Welsh librarian to Sir Thomas

Phillipps, and there is no doubt that he did assist in this splendid library, but on 4 Sept. 1865 he left Thirlestaine House. Phillipps complained of his inaccuracy; Rowland of low pay. In an article in *Yr Haul*, Oct. 1873, Rowland offers his side of the story of his service in the employ of the eccentric bookworm. To scrape a meagre living from his pay he would have to transcribe very rapidly in view of the low rates offered him. Other than that he turned to journalism, his subsequent movements are unclear. According to an article on him by one 'Gwyn o Went' in *Yr Haul*, 1881, 201-3, based, apparently, on information supplied by Rowland himself, he secured a post in the library of Llandaff House (the property of Colonel Bennett, better known as Major Richards) which was sold by Sotheby's, 20 and 21 Apr. 1871 (*Cardiff Times*). According to John Davies (1860-1939; *DWB*, 137-8) a catalogue by Rowland of the contents of this library was published in 1864. There is no known copy of this catalogue nor of the first catalogue of Cardiff Public Library which Davies says he made during the same period. He may have gone to Carmarthen as a schoolmaster. In any case, on the d. of Brutus in Jan. 1866 he became assistant editor of *Yr Haul*. There is evidence that he turned yet again to teaching, this time at an endowed school in Bedwas. He left to join Hugh Williams ('Cadfan'; *DWB*, 1042) to begin publication of *Y Dywysogaeth* in 1870, and moved to Carmarthen to devote his time entirely to the Church press. His *Historical Notes on ... Glamorgan, Carmarthen, and Cardigan, by John Rowlands, late librarian* (1866) was published in Cardiff, and it may be surmised that he lived in the neighbourhood of Cardiff at the time. It is not known when he left Carmarthen. A short note in *Y Llan*, 10 July 1891, testifies that he had been 'a faithful and interesting reporter for *Y Llan* and other Welsh Church papers for many years. He was cheerful and very contented, and a zealous churchman'.

To the sources named, add: NLW MS. 8705; A.N.L. Munby, *Phillipps Studies No. IV*; for an extensive list of his booklets and articles see Glyn Lewis Jones, *Llyfryddiaeth Ceredigion* (Aberystwyth, 1967), iii, 809-12.
E.D.J.

ROWLANDS, JOHN ('Giraldus'; 1824-91) – see ROWLAND(S), JOHN above.

ROWLANDS, JOHN (1841-1904) – see STANLEY, Sir HENRY MORTON below.

ROWLANDS, ROBERT PUGH (1874-1933), chief surgeon of Guy's Hospital; born at Tywyn, Mer. on 27 Sep. 1874, the son of John Rowlands. When he was two years old the family moved to Abaty Cymer, Dolgellau. He was educated at Llanelltyd school and at Dolgellau grammar school. At the end of his time there, he succeeded in securing a place for himself as an apprentice for a year with Dr. Hugh Pugh Rowlands. He went up to Guy's Hospital medical school, London, in October 1892. He had an exceptionally brilliant career there. In his first year he won the Arthur Durham prize, the Michael Harris prize for anatomy in 1894 and the first prize in 1895 and 1896. The following year he was awarded the Treasurer gold medal

for surgery and medicine. After further training as a house surgeon in the hospital he resolved to obtain surgical qualifications. After obtaining a place at the University of London he went on to win the gold medal in anatomy at the end of his first year. In 1902 he graduated with an M.B. and he was awarded the University scholarship and gold medal in medicine. He became an F.R.C.S. in 1901; he obtained a B.S. degree in 1902 and an M.S. in 1903.

Throughout the whole period of his studies for his examinations in the University of London he was also teaching in the medical school. In 1899 he was appointed a demonstrator in anatomy and biology, in which post he remained until 1905. In the same year he was promoted to become a surgical registrar and in 1906 to become a lecturer and demonstrator in practical surgery and Professor of pathological surgery. Before the end of the year he fulfilled his lifelong dream when he was appointed assistant surgeon at the hospital.

During the years leading up to World War I his reputation as a surgeon grew and in 1914 his work and responsibilities increased markedly. As he was a member of the Territorial Army, he was attached as a surgeon to the second London general hospital and he also took the post of surgeon to Hall Walker hospital and the Russian hospital in the city. He had to work exceptionally hard during the war years and this affected his health. During one air raid he walked from Queen Anne St to Chelsea, and having arrived at the hospital, he worked throughout the night. Having finished his work there, he walked back, and performed twenty-seven operations the following day.

In July 1918, aged only 44 years, he was promoted to become a full surgeon at Guy's Hospital and a lecturer in surgery. In 1922 he was elected to the council of the Royal College of Surgeons and in 1927 he was the co-editor of the seventh edition of Jacobson's work, *Operations of Surgery*. He had already co-edited the volume in 1907 and 1915. In 1929 he was appointed Bradshaw lecturer to the Royal College of Surgeons and his chosen subject was surgery to the bile duct and gall bladder. In July 1930 he was appointed vice-president of the Royal College of Surgeons which appointment he held until July 1932. For his work in his profession he was awarded the O.B.E.

He developed exceptional speed in his craft by perfecting his surgical style, an essentially simple technique, based on his instinctive and thorough knowledge of anatomy and his firm judgement. He was always ready to confront the unexpected by rearranging the normal pattern of parts of the body. He believed firmly, contrary to the practice at the time, that not too many bandages should be used after surgery and he encouraged his patients to sit up in bed very soon and to get up as soon as it was possible. He was the most talented and well-known surgeon of Guy's Hospital. He contributed extensively to medical journals on a variety of subjects: e.g. 'When and how to operate for appendicitis', *British Medical Journal*, 1910; 'Time in Surgery', 1916; 'Cancer of the colon', 1927; 'The surgery of the gall bladder and bile ducts', 1929; and 'Cancer of the stomach', 1933.

According to his contemporaries, Robert Pugh Rowlands was born a Welshman and died a Welshman, because he himself confessed to thinking in Welsh while speaking English. He married Alice Maude, the daughter of Edward Piper, Bodiam Manor, Susssex in 1905 and they had two children. He died on 6 Dec. 1933 after a short illness.

Guy's Hospital Gazette, 47 (1933); Guy's Hospital Reports, 84 (1933); H.C. Cameron, Mr. Guy's Hospital (1954); Www, 1929-40, 1176.

M.R.W.

SALUSBURY, FAMILY, of Lleweni and Bachygraig, DWB, 889. Second paragraph: Thomas, killed at the battle of Barnet (1741) . . . According to Gutun Owain, he d. 1490, not at the battle of Barnet, and Ffowc Salusbury was his eldest (not his second) son, and Thomas Salusbury 9d. 1505) was the second (not the eldest) son.

E. Bachellery, L'Oeuvre Poetique de Gutun Owain, 293-7.

E.P.R., T.Ro.

SALUSBURY, THOMAS (DWB, 902). He was b. 1561 (not '1564'). His year of birth is found in an englyn by William Cynwal, NLW MS. 1553. His brother (Sir) John was b. in 1566 (englyn by William Cynwal in NLW MS. 6495, facing p. 1); in the same MS., englynion by various poets name five of his children.

E.P.R.

SAMUEL, DAVID (DWB, 903). Read Ashbourn (not 'Ashburn').

SANDERS, IOAN (fl. 1786), Methodist exhorter and hymn writer. He was an exhorter with the Calvinistic Methodists near Pembrey, Carms. In 1786 he published a hymnbook under the title Hymnau a Chaniadau Duwiol, ar fesurau hen a newydd; gyd a phrofiadau ysgrythurol er cadarn-had i'r gwirionedd (Carmarthen, 1786).

W. A. Griffiths, Hanes Emynwyr Cymru; Llyfryddiaeth y Cymry.

K.M.D.

SAUNDERSON, ROBERT (DWB, 906-7). Saunderson's small diary is kept at N.L.W. (NLW MS. 16370). Frances, his unmarried sister, was buried in St. John's churchyard, Chester, 29 Nov. 1801. See also Y Faner, 1864; Charles Saunderson was b. 15 March 1809 and christened 28 March. See also Y Gwyliedydd, x, 1833, 218.

R.F.R.

SHANKLAND, THOMAS (DWB, 909). Read J.T. Griffith (not 'Griffiths').

SIÔN ap HOWEL ab OWAIN (1550?-1626/7), translator; son of Howel ab Owain, Cefn Treflaeth, Llanystumdwy, Caerns., and Catherine, daughter of Rhisiart ap Dafydd of Cefn Llanfair. He was, therefore, a nephew of Huw ap Rhisiart ap Dafydd (DWB, 398) and a cousin of Richard Hughes (DWB, 388-9). At his father's death in 1583 he became head of the family at Cefn Treflaeth, and he was one of those prosecuted by the Earl of Leicester during the troubles relating to Snowdon Forest. There

is a copy of the beginning of Siôn ap Howel's Welsh translation of Rhetorica ad Herennium in Llanfair and Brynodol MS. 2 at the National Library of Wales. He d. in 1626/7 and was buried in the choir of Llanystumdwy church.

Trans. Caerns. Hist. Soc., 1958, 20-21; 1960, 54-60 and 63-9.

B.L.J.

SIÔN BRWYNOG (DWB, 912-3). He d. in 1562, according to an elegy by Gr. Hiraethog – Bodleian MS. 31440, f. 4, 176-80.

E.P.R.

SIÔN CERI (DWB, 913). His full name was Siôn ap y Bedo ap Dafydd ap Hywel ap Tudur. (Bodl. Welsh, c.4, 27b).

SKENE, WILLIAM FORBES (1809-92), Scottish historian and Celtic scholar; b. 7 June 1809 at Irvine, Inverness-shire, and d. 29 Aug. 1892 in Edinburgh. In 1868 he published The Four Ancient Books of Wales, containing Welsh verse from 'The Book of Aneirin', 'The Book of Taliesin', 'the Black Book of Carmarthen' and part of 'The Red Book of Hergest'; the verse was translated for him by D. Silvan Evans and Robert Williams (DWB, 223-4 and 1067-8). This work was an attempt at separating the historical element from the imagined and fictitious in old Welsh poetry.

D.N.B.

T.I.J.

STANLEY, Sir HENRY MORTON, formerly ROWLANDS, JOHN (DWB, 922-3). Recent research has revealed the complexity of Stanley's personality and has cast doubt on many biographical details. He was a fantasist and pathological liar and many of the so-called 'facts' in his autobiography cannot be accepted. Though his date of birth can be confirmed as 28 Jan. 1841 his parents were not John Rowlands (jun.), Y Llys, and his 'wife' Elizabeth Parry. It is argued in NLWJ 28 that the father was James Vaughan Horne, a Denbigh solicitor. There is no basis for the story of his rejection by his 'father', John Rolant, nor for the account of hardship and cruelty in the Workhouse, the beating he gave his hated schoolmaster and the escape afterwards with a friend. John Rowlands d. 24 May 1854 (not 1843) aged 39. The biographer Cadwalader Rowlands was not related to Stanley and his biography has greater value than has been asserted.

See Emyr Wyn Jones, Sir Henry M. Stanley: the enigma (1989); Henry M. Stanley, pentewyn tân a'i gymhlethdod phaetonaidd (1992); Flint. Hist. Soc. Jnl., 33 (on the schoolmaster, James Francis); Tr., 1991 (on Cadwalader Rowlands); NLWJ 28 (on his presumed father); Richard Hall, Stanley: an adventurer explored (1974).

STRADLING FAMILY (DWB, 925-7). In the second column on p. 925 add 1389 as the year of Sir Edward Stradling's birth, and 3 May 1453 as the date of his death. His son, Sir Harri Stradling, d. 31 Aug. 1476. Sir Thomas Stradling d. 27 Jan. 1571, (not '1573'). Add to the bibliography the detailed article by Ralph Griffiths, 'The rise of the

Stradling of St. Donats', *Morgannwg*, VII, 15-47, and Ceri W. Lewis, 'Syr Edward Stradling, (1529-1609', *Ysgrifau Beirniadol*, 19 (1993), 139-207.

TEGWYN – see THOMAS DAVIES, 1831-1924, under DAVIES, JOHN BREESE, *DWB*, 138 and above in the Supplement.

TELYNOR WAUN OER – see EVAN JONES under JONES, HUGH (1789-1858; *DWB*, 467).

THELWALL, JOHN (1764-1834), reformer, lecturer and poet; son of Joseph Thelwall (1731-72), silk merchant of London, descended from a branch of the Thelwall family of Plas y Ward (*DWB*, 932-3) which settled in Crosby, Lancashire. He was b. at Chandos Street, Covent Garden, 27 July 1764. He published *Poems upon various subjects* (London, 1787), and became editor of *Biographical and Imperial Magazine*. He came under the spell of the French Revolution, and joined the Society of the Friends of the People. Because of his extreme radical views, he had to stand trial, 1-5 Dec. 1794, having been imprisoned in the Tower of London since the previous May; however, he was found not guilty. Soon afterwards he published *Poems written in close confinement in the Town and Newgate* (London, 1795). He took a farm near Llyswen, Breck., *c*. 1798, but returned to London within two years to lecture mainly on oratory and elocution. He was a friend of Southy, Hazlitt, Coleridge, and Lamb. *Poems chiefly written in retirement . . . with a prefatory memoir of the life of the author* (Hereford, 1801) contains several poems relating to Wales. Thelwall also wrote a number of works on political matters and oratory.

He d. at Bath, 17 Feb. 1834. He m. (1), Susan Vellum, (2) Cecil Boyle.

Poems (1801); *D.N.B.*

D.J.

THOMAS PENLLYN (*DWB*, 934). He was a descendant of Tudur Penllyn (*DWB*, 987).

THOMAS, DAVID (1813-94; *DWB*, 942). Second par., read chairman (not 'president').

THOMAS, DAVID (?-1780?), minister (Congl.) at Llanedi, Carms. The only extant source of knowledge about him is in *H. Egl. Ann.*, iii, 503-4, where it is said that he hailed from Cilgwyn, Cards., that he lived at Ffos-yr-efail, Llandeilo Fach [Llandeilo Tal-y-bont], Glam., was prosperous, and that he was ord. minister of Llanedi *c*. 1739. Although his name is not (for some reason) on W. D. Jeremy's list (copy in NLW MS. 362), a few crumbs of information about him can be gathered from other manuscripts. It is evident from the scornful references made by Edmund Jones (*DWB*, 455; diary 1773) that he associated with Arians; it is also suggested that he was not a teetotaller. Edmund Jones's words, 'old David Thomas', support the fact that Evan Davies was ord. there (3 Aug. 1775) – as co-pastor, according to *H. Egl. Ann.* – in Thomas's presence; however, in the only church book extant for Llanedi (at Somerset House; commencing with 1745), Davies is called 'minister', and it was he who had custody of the meeting-house lease. Under 28 March 1778 the church

book records that 'the major part of the congregation' undertook to pay £5 annually for life to 'the Rev. David Thomas, our old Pastor', but accompanying this is a list of patrons of the church with '£100 given by the Rev. Mr. David Thomas, Pastor of this Congregation' - would this be a loan, at an annual interest to be remitted on Thomas's death? Among the papers of Thomas Morgan 'Henllan' (*DWB*, 653-4) is a list (NLW MS. 5453) of ministers in Wales who d. after 1760. The last but one is 'Mr. David Thomas of Llanedy'; no date is given, as it happens, but the list is chronological, and Thomas's name lies between 1779 and 1781.

R.T.J.

THOMAS, DAVID VAUGHAN (*DWB*, 943-4). He took the name Vaughan in 1911 when he became a member of the *Gorsedd* of Bards in Carmarthen *eisteddfod*. He attended Watcyn Wyn's school in Ammanford before entering Llandovery College, and from 1873 to 1883 the family lived in Ystalyfera, Llantrisant, Maesteg, Llangennech and Dowlais. He graduated 3rd class at Oxford in 1895, M.A. 1905, B.Mus. 1906, D.Mus. 1911. After leaving Oxford he taught mathematics in the United Services College, Westward Ho! He made an unsuccessful application for the post of Music Director of the University of Wales in 1919.

Times, 17 Sept. 1934; T. Haydn Thomas, *Welsh Music*, 4 (1973), 2; Ifor ap Gwilym, *Y Traddodiad Cerddorol yng Nghymru* (1978), 35.

LI.G.C.

THOMAS, EVAN (1733-1814; *DWB*, 946). His wife was *not* the sister of Thomas Richards; his wife was Ellen Parry, sister of William Parry of Cae Ceirch, Dolgellau, Warden of Ruthin School (*Bye-Gones*, 6.3.1901, 4.6.1902, 21.1.1903); according to the parish register of St. Chad, Shrewsbury, they m. there on 15 June 1766. He d. at Shrewsbury workhouse, 12 Jan. (not 'March') 1814 – *Shrewsbury Chronicle*, 14 Jan. 1814; 2s. 10d. was paid to the bearers at his funeral, as in the workhouse accounts at Shrewsbury Record Office.

Information from Mrs. Brenda Parry-Jones.

THOMAS, GEORGE (*DWB*, 947). He d. 30 Aug. 1859 aged 73 so his dates should be altered to 1786-1859.

THOMAS, IFOR (1877-1918), geologist and inspector of schools; b. at Commercial Place, Glanaman, Carms., on 24 Nov. 1877, son of Dafydd Thomas ('Trumor'; 1844-1916) and his wife Margaret. His father, who was a miner at Gelliceidrim colliery in the Aman Valley, was a poet, a local historian and a regular contributor to Welsh-language newspapers. His prize-winning essay *Hen Gymeriadau Plwyf y Betws* was published in 1894 (reprinted 1912). Ifor Thomas was educated at the Board school, Glanaman, where he was also a pupil-teacher and at the University College of Wales, Aberystwyth, where he graduated B.Sc. After a short period as a teacher at Wellington College and at Brynmawr secondary school, he went to the University of Marburg in Germany to study geology and palaeontology under Professor Emanuel Kayser. He learnt German during this time and graduated with a Ph.D. in 1905. He returned to London in the same year when he was appointed to the staff of the Geological Survey in Jermyn Street and he was elected a Fellow of the Royal Geological Society. He gained the degree of D.Sc. from the University of Wales in 1911. He had a great interest in education and when his health deteriorated in 1912 he returned to Wales on his appointment as one of His Majesty's Inspectors of Schools, setting up home in Swansea. He placed great emphasis on the teaching of Welsh in schools at a time when that was not fashionable and he won the respect and admiration of Sir Owen M. Edwards (*DWB*, 192-3) for his work on behalf of the language. He wrote many scholarly articles on geological subjects in *The Geological Magazine* and he also contributed articles to *Seren Gomer* and *Y Genhinen*. He was among the first to discuss in Welsh the geological interests of Edward Lhuyd (*DWB*, 565-7). Among his principal published works are: *The British Carboniferous Orthotetinae* (1910); *The British Carboniferous Producti* (1914); *The Trilobite Fauna of Devon and Cornwall* (1909); *A New Devonian Trilobite and Lamellibranch from Cornwall* (1909); *A Note on Phacops (Trimerocephalus) Laevis (Münst)* (1909); *Neue Beiträge zur Kenntnis der Devonischen Fauna Argentiniens* (1905). His health was always indifferent; he returned to his old home in Glanaman in the spring of 1918, where he died, unmarried, on 30 March in the same year. He was buried in the graveyard of Bethesda Baptist church, Glanaman.

Seren Gomer, May 1918, 136-148; *Quarterly Journal of the Geological Society*, 75 (1919), xvii-xviii; *South Wales Guardian*, 30 Mar. 1975.

H.Wa.

THOMAS, JOHN (1730-1804?; *DWB*, 950-1). He was christened 25 Apr. and not 25 March. He m. Miss Elizabeth Jones of Dyffryn Cothi, parish of Llanfynydd. *Rhad Râs*, 1810, and *Cylch. Cymd. Hanes M.C.*, March 1967.

G.M.R.

THOMAS, JOHN WILLIAM (1805-40; *DWB*, 955-6). In 1832 he published a primer on reading English, *Ffordd anffaeledig I Gymro uniaith ddarllen Saesneg yn gywir*, one of the earliest books of instruction. On *Elfennau Rhifyddiaeth* see *Gwyddonydd*, 11 (1973), 128.

Ll.G.C.

THOMAS, THOMAS HENRY ('Arlunydd Penygarn'; *DWB*, 967). There are further collections of his MSS. lodged at the Museum of Welsh Life, St. Fagans: 688, 741, 2435/1-395, 2492/1-2, 2591/1-24, 2810 and 3617/1-132. In the main they reflect his interest in the National *Eisteddfod* (especially the *Gorsedd* of Bards), heraldry and folklore.

A.Ll.H.

THOMAS, THOMAS LLEWELYN (1840-97), scholar, teacher and linguist; b. 14 Nov. 1840 at the old vicarage Caernarfon; the eldest son of a

family of three daughters and five sons of Canon Thomas Thomas (1804-77) and his wife. The father was appointed vicar of Caernarfon in 1835 and he threw himself into the religious and educational life of the town which suffered heavily at the time from poverty and visitations of the cholera. 'Thomas of Caernarfon', as he was known, succeeded in starting elementary schools and laying the foundation for training teachers in the town. Thomas Llewelyn, who was not a strong boy, was educated privately until the age of nine. After six years of schooling and attending a Welsh-medium Sunday school, he became in Oct. 1860 a scholar of Jesus College, Oxford. The college did not have a good academic reputation at the time. J.R. Green, the historian, had drawn attention to this and emphasised that the college showed little respect towards Wales. In 1863 Thomas won the Newdigate prize (and the praise of Matthew Arnold) for an English poem on the subject of 'Coal mines'. He graduated B.A. in 1864 and M.A. in 1868. He taught for a while at Rossall School and after two years at Llandovery College moved to Ruthin schoool where he stayed for five years. He was ordained deacon in 1867 and in 1868 received holy orders from the Bishop of St. Asaph. He spent time as a curate in Llanfwrog, Vale of Clwyd. He accepted the rectorship of Nutfield which was a college benefice and stayed there for two years. He won a prize at the national *eisteddfod* in Ruthin for a poem, 'The Harpist's Grave' for which Brinley Richards (*DWB*, 852) composed the music. In March 1872 Llewelyn Thomas was elected, despite keen competition, a fellow of his old college. He remained in post for a quarter of a century, teaching and instructing generation after generation of students as senior tutor, vice-principal and Welsh reader. He was regarded as an exceptionally popular tutor. He acted as university examiner and adjudicator of the Newdigate prize. On the strength of his distinction as a classicist he was invited to deliver the Latin sermon. He could compose verses in the classical languages, Welsh and English with ease. He ensured that Jesus College's closed scholarships were earmarked for boys from Wales who could not afford to pay for their education. He held that from the start the college was intended for students from Wales; he gave special support to the Meyrick Trust. Thomas laboured to promote the church's mission on Welsh soil. It was thought that he had qualities which could have led to his becoming a bishop. He strongly supported the establishment of a chair of Celtic. He could be harsh in his criticism as well as a hard but kind disciplinarian. He was an interesting conversationalist in the common room, and there was no curbing his Welsh rhymes in the college's annual concerts. He was especially fond of the works of Virgil, Dante, Goethe and Tennyson. He contributed a chapter on the history of his college to *Colleges of Oxford* (1891). During Dr. Hugo Harper's illness he acted as principal between 1887 and 1895, but it was John Rhŷs (*DWB*, 844-5) who succeeded Harper. In 1897 he accepted the canonry of St. Asaph from the Crown. Llewelyn Thomas contributed scholarly articles on the Basque language to *The Academy*, 21 Jan. 1893, 23 June 1894, 1 Feb. 1896, and 8 Feb. 1896. His treatise on the Basque manuscripts shows that he had a mastery of that language. It was he who edited Pierre D'Urte's version of his translation into Basque, based on the Geneva French Bible, of the Old Testament. It was he also who compared it to Licarrague's translation of the New Testament. Thomas called for a popular version of the Old Testament in Basque which ordinary folk could read. His efforts did not pass without criticism but it is agreed that his contribution was very considerable. In March 1893 he published in the series *Anecdota Oxonienis, The Earliest Translation of the Old Testament into the Basque Language.* In May 1897 he was struck by pneumonia and d. on the 12th of the month aged fifty-seven. He was buried next to his father's grave in Llanbeblig cemetery, Caernarfon. There is a pulpit erected in that church in memory of his father. The choral funeral service was conducted in Welsh.

Harriet Thomas (ed.), *Father and Son* (1898); *Alumni Oxon.; Carn. and Denb. Herald*, 14 May 1897.
G.A.J.

THOMAS, WILLIAM (d. 1554; *DWB*, 969). 969b, l. 6, Writtle is the present-day form of Wretyll.

TOMAS ab IEUAN ap RHYS (*DWB*, 975). He. d. 1617.

TOMOS ap TITUS – see JOHN THOMAS EVANS (1869-1940) under WADE-EVANS, ARTHUR WADE above.

TOUT, THOMAS FREDERICK (1855-1929), historian, who is fully treated by V. H. Galbraith in *D.N.B.*, 1922-30 and by Sir Maurice Powicke in *Proceedings of the British Academy*, 1929. Although Tout did most of his work in Manchester he is noted here since much of his work dealt with Wales and it was in Wales that it was begun. He was professor of history at St. David's College, 1881-90. In the words of Galbraith, 'his years at Lampeter were the making of him'; and Powicke says, 'at Lampeter, Tout found himself'. He learnt Welsh, and immersed himself not only in the work of the college but also in the life of the town of Lampeter; when it became a borough in 1884, Tout was one of its first aldermen, and he often presided over the town council. He also took an interest in the history of Wales. He wrote very many of the articles relating to Wales in *D.N.B.* Before Sir John Lloyd in 1893 undertook the work, Tout wrote mostly on the Welsh of the Middle Ages; but his knowledge was not confined to that period - it was he e.g. who wrote the article on Charles of Bala; note also his paper 'Wales under the Stuarts' in *Liverpool Welsh Nat. Soc. Trans.*, 1891-2, 24-41. The main result of his study of Welsh history was to realise (as he demonstrated quite clearly in his books) that the history of England in the 13th c. cannot be understood without giving full weight to the 'Welsh problem'. He did not write a book specifically on the history of Wales, but some of his papers which are of Welsh interest can be cited here: 'The Welsh Shires' (*Cymm.*, ix), 'Wales and the March during the Barons' Wars, 1258-67' (in *Historical Essays by Members of Owens College*, 1902, 76-136), 'Flintshire, its History and Records' (*Flints. Hist. Soc. Proc.*, i,

1-38), *The Captivity and Death of Edward of Caernarvon*, 1920, the treatment of the old boroughs of Wales in his *Mediaeval Town Planning*, 1917, and the Welsh sections of his important book *The Place of the Reign of Edward II in English History*, 1914. Tout was b. in London, 28 Sept. 1855, and d. there, 23 Oct. 1929.

R.T.J.

TRAHERNE, JOHN MONTGOMERY (*DWB*, 976-7). The manuscript biography of Traherne contains some new information. See Roy Denning, *Glam. Hist.*, 4 (1967), 46-55.

TREGELLES, SAMUEL PRIDEAUX (*DWB*, 977-8). Read Darby (not 'Derby') in l. 10.

TURNER, SHARON (1768-1847), solicitor and historian; b. in London 24 Sept. 1768 and d. there 13 Feb. 1847. His career and work are fully discussed in *D.N.B.* His chief work was his *History of England ... to the Norman Conquest*, 1799-1805. In the course of this book (which broke new ground in this subject) he made use of the ancient poetry of Britain, for which he was criticised by those who disputed the genuineness of the poems. He replied, in 1803, by publishing *A Vindication of the Genuineness of the Ancient British Poems of Aneurin, Taliesin, Llywarch Hen, and Merdhin, with Specimens of the Poems.* He was the first to discuss their antiquity, demonstrating the ignorance of the sceptics; see John Morris-Jones, *Taliesin* (=*Cymm.*, xxviii). His letters to William Owen Pughe (*DWB*, 815-6) are in the National Library of Wales (NLW MSS. 13222-4); he also corresponded with John Hughes of Brecon (1776-1843; *DWB*, 381), praising the work of the latter.

D.N.B.

E.P.R.

VAUGHAN, ARTHUR OWEN (*DWB*, 1001). This was an adopted name; his baptismal name was Robert Scourfield, s. of Robert Mills and Jane Ann, daughter of Joseph Scourfield; b. at Southport, 6 Sept. 1863. His father was buried less than a month later. His mother moved to Manchester and remarried. Her second husband, Luke Etchells, d. in 1869. The child was brought up by his grandmother who came originally from Tremeirchion. She called him Owen. He himself adopted the name Arthur Owen Vaughan and formed his pseudonym 'Owen Rhoscomyl' from Rho[bert] Sco[urfield] Myl[ne] using the Middle English word for mill. He m. Catherine Lois (Katherine Louisa) de Geere on the bank of the river Vaal c. 21 Dec. 1900. His certificate of marriage was lost when he was admitted to hospital. She d. at Penarth in 1927. The regiment in which he served during the South African War was the 14th Northumberland Fusiliers.

Information from his daughter.

He was the author of two other novels, *Old Fireproof* (1906) and *Battlement and Tower* [1896].

T.G.J.

His papers are at the National Library of Wales, uncatalogued. See further Hywel Teifi Edwards, *I godi'r hen wlad yn ei hôl* (1989), 246-50; also *Hel Achau*, 34 (1991).

VAUGHAN, JOHN (d. 1824; *DWB*, 1005). Hugh Wynn had a LL.D. degree (not 'D.D.').

VAUGHAN, RICE (*DWB*, 1005). As his will was proved in 1670 (P.C.C.), the date of death should be corrected to 1670.

VINCENT, THOMAS (1677-1738), priest; see VINCENT (FAMILY) (*DWB*, 1008-9) and WYNN PRYSE, and CORBET (FAMILIES), (*DWB*, 1101).

WARDLE, GWILYM LLOYD (*DWB*, 1012-3). Gwilym Lloyd Wardle's father, Francis Wardle, m. Catherine Lloyd Gwyllym, daughter and heiress of Richard Lloyd Gwyllym of Hersedd (Hartsheath).

WATKINS, WILLIAM (*fl.* 1750-62), a cleric in Breconshire and author of the first published book on trees of Wales. He is on record as a pensioner at Trinity Hall, Cambridge, from June 1750 to 1754, but he regularly signed the registers of Hay as a curate assisting an absent vicar during 1750-52. He left Hay soon after his wife and daughter died there of smallpox in 1752, and published *A Treatise on Forest-Trees* (London, 1753), which is now a very rare book. In 1762 he was appointed vicar of Llaneleu, but no more is known about him.

Jnl. W.B.S., 11 (1975-76), 247-50.

W.L.

WAYNE (FAMILY; *DWB*, 1015). Matthew Wayne was b. in Stogursey, Somerset, in 1780. By 1806 he resided in Ivy House, Nantygwenith St., Merthyr Tydfil, and although he had bought a lease of the ironworks in Nant-y-glo, Mon. in 1811, his daughter Mary was b. in Merthyr in 1816. After establishing iron works and sinking the first deep coal mine in Aberdare, Glam., he made his home in Glandare House. He d. 1854 aged 73 yrs. Note that Crawshay Bailey was Sir Joseph Bailey's brother, not his son.

D.L.D.

WILKS, JOHN (1764 or 1765-1854), London attorney and Member of Parliament - see under DAVIES, JOHN (1781-1848), of Fronheulog, *DWB*, 1117.

WILKINSON, JOHN (*DWB*, 1019-20). Read Caleb Rotheram (not 'Rotherham') in l. 6.

WILLIAM, THOMAS (1717-65; *DWB*, 1022). In the bibliography read Bennett (not 'Bennet').

WILLIAMS (FAMILY), of Marl (*DWB*, 1024-5). The will of William ap William ap Gruffydd was proved in 1559 (not '1589'); see WILLIAMS (FAMILY) of Cochwillan, *DWB*, 1154-6, par. 3.

WILLIAMS, CHARLES (1807-77; *DWB*, 1027-8). He received a M.A. degree in 1830, B.D. in 1837, and D.D. in 1858. He was an honorary canon of Bangor from 1857 until his d.

WILLIAMS, DAVID (1709-84; *DWB*, 1030-1). He m. twice. His first wife, Mary, d. 27 Sept. 1745, aged 24. His second wife was also called Mary, and she d. 24 Dec. 1787 aged 67.

Information from memorial tablets.

WILLIAMS, DAVID DAVID (1862-1938), minister (Presb.) and author; b. at Garth Lwynog, Croesor, Mer., son of David and Grace Williams. He was educated at Gelli-gaer Grammar School, Bala College, and at the university colleges of Aberystwyth and Cardiff. He was ord. in 1891, and served his ministry at Peniel, Ffestiniog (1890-96); Oswestry (1896-1906); Moss Side, Manchester (1906-15); and David St. (later Belvidere Rd.), Liverpool (1915-38). He m., *c.* 1896-97, Clara A. Jones, Ashlands; they had no children. He lived at Prestatyn after retiring, and d. there 3 July 1938.

He was a prominent figure in his Connexion, being Moderator of the North Wales Association (1931). He was an assiduous researcher and received a M.A. degree of the Univ. of Liverpool for his thesis on 'Vaticination in Welsh literature'. For a period he edited *The Journal of the Historical Society of the Presbyterian Church in Wales* (1930-34). He competed regularly at the National *Eisteddfod*, submitting essays on literary and historical subjects. Many of his prize-winning essays were published by the National *Eisteddfod* Society. He contributed articles to *Y Brython*, *Y Beirniad*, *Y Genhinen*, *Yr Efrydydd*, and *The Journal of the Historical Society of the Presbyterian Church in Wales*. He published the following books: *Dyfyniadau llên Cymru* (1909); *Deuddeg o feirdd y Berwyn* (1910); *Twm o'r Nant* (1911); *Geirfa Prifeirdd* (1911); *Dylanwad y Rhufeiniaid ar iaith, gwareiddiad a gwaedoliaeth y Cymry* (1912); *Hanes mynachdai gogledd Cymru* (1914); *Cymru enwog cyfnod y Tuduriaid* (1914); *Addysg Cymru yn y Canol Oesoedd* (1914); *Hanes dirwest yng Ngwynedd* (1921); *Thomas Charles Edwards* (1921); *Cofiant T. J. Wheldon* (1925); *Hanes Cyfundeb y Methodistiaid Calfinaidd* (1927).

WwW (1921), 504; *Drys.*, 1931, 336-9; *Cylch. Cymd. Hanes MC*, 1928, 51-3; *Gol.*, 13, 20 July 1938; *Blwyddiadur MC*, 1939, 215-6.

G.M.R.

WILLIAMS, EDWARD (1750-1813; *DWB*, 1034-5). End of par. 1, 1035a, Joseph (not 'S') Gilbert was his biographer. See further W.T. Owen, *Edward Williams, D.D: his life, thought and influence* (Cardiff, 1963).

WILLIAMS, HENRY PARRY – see PARRY-WILLIAMS, HENRY above.

WILLIAMS, JOHN (1582-1650; *DWB*, 1045-6). In the last par. and bibliography read Hacket (not 'Hackett').

WILLIAMS, JOHN (1745/6-1818; *DWB*, 1049). He was ordained by Bishop Moss (not 'Ross').

WILLIAMS, JOHN ('Ab Ithel'; 1811-62; *DWB*, 1052-3). B. 7 Apr. 1811. He took his M.A. in 1838. He was the first priest to serve the new parish of Rhosygwaliau. He was co-editor of

Archaeologia Cambrensis with H. Longueville Jones until 1851, and then sole editor until he resigned in 1853. His widow, Elizabeth, received a civil pension, 18 June 1873.

WILLIAMS, OWEN (1774-1839; *DWB*, 1062). He d. in London 23 May 1839. See Huw Williams, *Owen Williams o Fôn* (1993).

WILLIAMS, PETER ('Pedr Hir'; *DWB*, 1064). His father, Thomas Williams, was a cousin of Sir Charles James Watkin Williams (*DWB*, 1028).

W.R.Wi.

WILLIAMS, PETER BAILEY (1763-1836; *DWB*, 1064-5). In 1798 he led the first recorded rock climb in Britain, probably the east Terrace of Clogwyn Du'r Arddu (a 'moderate' climb according to the first climbing guides: 'easy' today). He was acting as guide for the botanist Bingley at the time but it was his idea to venture up the rock: he was wearing nailed boots and when Bingley failed to follow him he extended his belt to assist him. On another occasion he took Bingley across to Cwm Idwal and then to the summits of Tryfan, y Gluder Fawr and Gluder Fach: on the summit of Tryfan he frightened him by leaping from Adam to Eve, as the two rocks above the eastern precipice are called. He did not make much comment on the mountains in his Caernarfonshire travel-book but it is difficult to believe that he would have acted a guide for a stranger had he not been familiar with the difficult places. Evan Roberts suggested that he was the 'fabled parson' immortalized in the name Clogwyn y Person ('Parson's Precipice'): that may be so but it was in the 1840s, after Williams's death, that J.H. Cliffe met the unknown 'climbing parson' whom he describes.

William Bingley, *North Wales, etc* (1804); G.A. Lister, in *The mountains of Snowdonia* (2 ed., 1948), 51-2; Evan Roberts, 'Natural History Notes' in H.I. Banner and P. Crew, *Clogwyn Du'r Arddu* (1963); Alan Hankinson, *The mountain men* (1977).

I.B.R.

WILLIAMS, RICHARD ('Gwydderig'; 1842-1917; *DWB*, 1066-7). B. 16 Feb. 1842 in a cottage called Pen-y-graig, Brynaman. His parents moved to Bryn Hafod later. (Information from John Jenkin Morgan, Glanaman.)

WILLIAMS, ROBERT (*DWB*, 1157). Baptised 27 Oct. 1782, s. of Owen Williams and Mary (née Davies) of Mynydd Ithel farm, Llanfechell, Anglesey. His burial is recorded in Llanfechell parish register under the name Robert Owen, 15 July 1818, though he is said to have been buried in Llanrhwydrys churchyard. See Huw Williams, *Cofio Robert Williams, Mynydd Ithel* (1990).

H.W.

WILLIAMS, ROGER (*DWB*, 1069). In l. 5, 1069b, read 1698 (not '1798').

WILLIAMS, THOMAS ('Capelulo'; *c*. 1782-1855), reformed drunkard, itinerant bookseller, 'character'; b. in Llanrwst, Denbs., about 1782 the son of a hatter and baking-woman. His father came from Capelulo, Dwygyfylchi, Conwy, which is how he gained his nickname. He was a hostler and carriage driver for a while before enlisting as a soldier, seeing service in the Napoleonic wars and then in South Africa, South America and India. His predeliction for drink got him into trouble frequently both in the army and after returning home, and he lived by begging, entertaining, singing and recounting his escapades and adventures. Granted his lifestyle as a drunkard and adulterer, there can be no doubt about his skill as an oral storyteller and this is what characterized his life after his religious conversion about 1840. He became a zealous teetotaller and a dangerously witty speaker for the cause. He became a well-known character, famed for his memorable sayings, his simple-minded attitudes (probably more feigned than real as he revealed a sharp wit when provoked), his humour and his ability to entertain audiences with accounts both of his reformed and his dissipated life.

His chief patron was John Jones, the Llanrwst printer (1786-1865, see above) who helped him to make a living by selling songs and ballads, almanacks and books.

Most of what is known of 'Capelulo' is found in his autobiography published by John Jones in 1854. This is a literary version of what the author said 'in his own words' and its honesty is a remarkable feature. Robert Owen Hughes 'Elfyn' (*DWB*, 390) based his memoir on the autobiography but also brought together many stories in oral circulation or found in magazines, succeeding in capturing the flavour of Capelulo's lively oral style. He d. in Llanrwst and was buried there, aged 73, 14 Feb. 1855.

The autobiography was reprinted with an introduction by Gerald Morgan, *Lle diogel i sobri* (1982); 'Elfyn', *Capelulo* (1907, 1927).

B.F.R.

WILLIAMS, WILLIAM (1747-1812; *DWB*, 1080). He has been confused with two others of the same name. He was not educated at Magdalene College, Cambridge and he was not from Cowbridge.

D.E.W.

WILLIAMS, WILLIAM WYN (1876-1936), minister and poet; b. in Blaenau Ffestiniog, Mer., 12 July 1876, of a religious family from the district of Bowydd. He was a pupil-teacher in Tanygrisiau before entering Bangor Normal College. He then became a teacher in the neighbourhood of Wrexham. He began to preach and went to University College and Theological College, both at Aberystwyth. In 1909 he was inducted minister of Moriah (Presb.), Llanystumdwy; in 1921 he moved to Salem, Dolgellau, and thence to Glan-rhyd, Llanwnda in 1925. He published two volumes of poems *Wrth Borth yr Awen* (1909) and *Caniadau* (1911). A shy and musical person, he suffered ill health, and spent a year travelling through U.S.A. and Patagonia and climbing the Andes to recover his health. He m. Kate Pritchard of Betws Garmon in 1927 and they had a son. He d. 12 Nov. 1936.

Blwyddiadur MC, 1938, 211-2; *Gol.*, 25 Nov. 1936, 8.

B.L.J.

WILLIAMS-ELLIS, JOHN CLOUGH (1833-1913), scholar, clergyman, poet and possibly the first Welshman to climb one of the highest mountains in the Alps; b. 11 Mar. 1833 in Bangor, Caerns., second son of John Williams-Ellis, clergyman, and his wife Harriet Ellen Clough of Denbigh. He was brought up in Brondanw, Llanfrothen, and later, when his father was inducted rector of Llanaelhaearn, at Glasfryn, Llangybi. He was educated in Rossall School and Sidney Sussex College, Cambridge, where he graduated 3rd Wrangler and was elected a fellow of the college in 1856. Being a brilliant mathematician and a successful tutor he did as much as anyone to promote the good name of the college. When the Cambridge chair in mechanics became vacant all the eminent workers in the field supported him but another person was elected as a result of the influence of the larger colleges. He turned to the church, becoming vicar of Madingley, Cambs., in 1865 and rector of Gayton, Northants., in 1876. Meanwhile he had invested his earnings as a tutor in expanding his Glasfryn estate, where he retired in 1888. He was appointed J.P. in 1890.

He won prizes for poetry in Cambridge and later. Although he was proficient in Welsh and assumed the pen-name, 'Shon Pentyrch', he seems to have written in English only. He was a good oarsman and swimmer and in 1855 won the Royal Humane Society medal for rescuing a friend from drowning in the River Cam. He was familiar with the mountains of Snowdonia as a follower of the Ynysfor hounds and in 1857 went on a tour in the Alps with J.F. Hardy. On 13 Aug., accompanied by William and St. John Mathews, E.S. Kennedy, Hardy and five guides, he climbed the Finsteraarhorn (4,274 m.), the highest peak in Bern Oberland. The mountain had been scaled earlier, possibly as early as 1812, but this first British climb motivated William Mathews and Kennedy to establish an Alpine Club. Williams-Ellis did not join the Club and there is no mention of him visiting the Alps again but the family still has his alpenstock.

On 2 Jan. 1877 he m. Ellen Mabel Greaves. They had 6 sons: Sir Clough Williams-Ellis, the architect (1883-1978), was the 4th. He d. 27 May 1913 and was buried in a glade near Glasfryn.

J.F. Hardy, 'Ascent of the Finsteraar Horn' in J. Ball (ed.) *Peaks, passes and glaciers* (first series, 1859); 'Recollections' (1904), a short MS. autobiography (copy in Gwynedd Record Office); Cybi, *Beirdd gwerin Eifionydd* (1911) includes three of his poems; *Haul*, Sept. 1913; *Burke* (1952); E.A. Williams-Ellis, 'A Merioneth boyhood in the 1830's', *Jnl. Merioneth Hist. Soc.*, IV, 4 (1964); Ioan Bowen Rees, *Mynyddoedd* (1975).

I.B.R.

WILSON (FAMILY), Bwlch-y-llyn, Monts. - see WILSON, RICHARD, *DWB*, 1087.

WOODING, DAVID LEWIS (1828-91), genealogist, historian, bibliophile and shopkeeper; b. 13 Dec. 1828 at Penybont Cottage, Llanfihangel Abergwesyn, Breck., eldest son of Benjamin Wooding (d. 1861) of Beulah, near Builth Wells, Breck., a shopkeeper and farmer, and his wife Susannah (née Davies). He was educated at Beulah Chapel school, 1834-36, and then boarded at a small school at Cefnllanddewi run by Thomas Price, 'Twm Cork', 1837-38, after which he attended Ffrwdfâl Academy, Carms., under the direction of Dr. William Davies (*DWB*, 159), 1838-44, with a brief interval at Hay Academy in 1842. In 1844 he moved to a school in Hills Lane, Mardol, Shrewsbury for one term. At the age of 16 he was apprenticed to a draper in Newtown, Mont., for one year but did not complete his period due to the draper not fulfilling the conditions of his agreement. He moved briefly back to Ffrwdfâl Academy but left Oct. 1845 to assist his father in the family business, travelling extensively in both England and Wales. He m. Marianne, dau. of Peter Jones, at Llanddewi Abergwesyn parish church on 18 June 1858. He d. on 2 May 1891 after a brief illness and was buried in Beulah (Congl.) cemetery.

In 1861 he took over responsibility for the shop. This enabled him to develop what had already become his life-long interest. He was a contemporary of David Lloyd Isaac, vicar of Llangamarch and author (*DWB*, 418), eventually purchasing all of his MS works and notes. He was nominated by Egerton G.B. Phillimore (*DWB*, 755) and became a member of the Hon. Soc. of Cymmrodorion. Wooding corresponded with Morris Davies of Bangor, a noted hymnologist and musician (*DWB*, 144), and he became a leading authority on the authorship of Welsh hymns. His library was given into the care of John Ballinger, chief librarian of Cardiff Free Library (and later of the National Library of Wales, *DWB*, 23-24), by councillor Ben Davies of Beulah. In addition, a proportion of his MSS, in particular his note-books, were handed over to the care of the library. His work is characterised by attention to detail and an endeavour to obtain information first-hand. He was renowned for his knowledge of Welsh history and in particular of matters relating to the Hundred of Builth. According to Evans' *Guide to Wales* (1888), 'His library is good and select, but Mr. Woodings' real library is carried a little above his neck. He is much admired and respected in all circles'. He contributed to *Yr Haul* and assisted in other publications. Regrettably he left no published books of his own and those few MSS that remain in private hands indicate what has been lost to the public by his failure to go to print. The MSS are of special value in that they furnish ample material for describing Wales and especially Mid-Wales. He succeeded in recording information from people of all classes. He was a close friend of James Rhys Jones ('Kilsby'; *DWB*, 470) and although he was no match for him in imaginative genius, he was incomparably his superior in historical accomplishments. After an encounter with him in Llangamarch Wells he was heard to say that 'truth is life's a torch, the more it's shook, the more it shines'. His main MSS are: the trial and execution of Lewis Lewis; autobiographical works; Jemal; historical pedigrees of gentry in Builth Hundred; Welsh hymn authorship.

MSS of D.L. Wooding in Cardiff Central Library and private hands; *Brecon and Radnorshire Express*, 8 and 15 May 1891 and other papers; Evans, *Guide to Wales* (1888); autobiographical material and letters.

B.A.M.W.

WYNDHAM-QUIN, WINDHAM THOMAS (1841-1926), 4th EARL of DUNRAVEN AND MOUNT-EARL in the Irish peerage and 2nd Baron KENRY of the United Kingdom, K.P. 1872, C.M.G. 1902, Glamorgan landowner and politician, sportsman and author; b. 12 Feb. 1841 at Adare, county Limerick, but spent his childhood at his father's home, Dunraven Castle, on the Glamorgan coast near Porthcawl. He was descended from the ancient Irish family of Quin, one of the few families of genuinely native origin in the Irish peerage and from the Gloucestershire family of Wyndham, who had been Glamorgan landowners since the 17th century. They were connected by marriage with the Carnes of Ewenny, the Thomases of Llanfihangel and the Vivians of Swansea. His father, Edwin Richard Windham Wyndham-Quin, 3rd Earl of Dunraven, was M.P. for Glamorgan, 1837-1850. His mother was Augusta, daughter of Thomas Goold, master in chancery in Ireland. Owing to his father's conversion to Roman Catholicism (although the son remained a Protestant), he was educated abroad in Paris and Rome before being sent to Christ Church, Oxford, in 1858. In the Life Guards as a cornet in 1862. In 1867 he obtained leave to go as a war correspondent with the British expedition to Abyssinia, commanded by General Sir Robert Napier, later Lord Napier of Magdala, the brother of Captain Napier, the first Chief Constable of Glamorgan. While on the expedition he shared a tent with another Welshman, Henry Morton Stanley (see above), then the correspondent of the *New York Herald* and wrote some of his copy for him. In 1869, Lord Adare, as he then was, married Florence Elizabeth, daughter of Lord Charles Lennox Kerr, and visited America for the first time. He constantly returned to that country and even bought a ranch in Colorado. His insatiable curiosity led him to investigate many things, including spiritualism. He succeeded to the earldom and other titles on the death of his father in 1871 but did not immediately take his seat in the House of Lords. In Dec. 1877, while staying in the United States with a party which included Lord Rosebery, he wrote an article for *The World* on the state of Europe which attracted attention. He made his maiden speech in the Lords in Feb. 1878. In June 1885 he became under-secretary at the Colonial Office in Lord Salisbury's first administration and returned to that position when the Conservatives resumed office in Aug. 1886 but resigned in Feb. 1887. This was partly in sympathy with his close friend, Lord Randolph Churchill, who had resigned a few weeks earlier, partly because he feared that the British government's attitude to the Newfoundland fishery question breached the autonomy of the Newfoundland assembly. He never held office again but he remained in the public eye as an active campaigner for tariff reform, the first President of the Fair Trade League and a leading signatory of the minority Report of the Royal Commission on the Depression in Trade and Industry of 1885-86, which advocated moderate protection and imperial preference. He chaired the parliamentary committee which investigated sweated labour, 1888-90. Dunraven opposed Gladstone's Irish Home Rule measure of 1886 because he saw it as tantamount to separatism but he was a strong advocate of devolution, arguing that if it worked for the Channel Islands and the Isle of Man, it must work for larger units like Scotland and Wales. Ireland was the great cause of Dunraven's later years. He helped to secure the passage of the Irish Land Act in 1903 and the following year joined with other moderate Unionist landlords in the Irish Reform Association to suggest, unsuccessfully, a new scheme for Irish devolution. In Dec. 1921 he seconded John Morley in replying to the King's Speech announcing the setting up of the Irish Free State. He did not, however, abandon his Welsh interests. He entertained many prominent politicians, including Joseph Chamberlain, at Dunraven Castle. He was a J.P. for Glamorgan and honorary Colonel of the Glamorgan Royal Garrison Artillery. He became president of the Cardiff Tariff Reform League and frequently addressed political meetings in the county. He was a wealthy man. In 1883 he owned 39,756 acres in various parts of the country and had an annual income of £35,478. A large part of his income derived from his Welsh estates, which consisted of farmland in the Vale of Glamorgan and mineral rights in the south Wales coalfield. Most of the town of Bridgend lay on the estate. He was a prominent sportsman, who owned racehorses in partnership with Lord Randolph Churchill, but he was best known as a yachtsman who made two gallant but unsuccessful attempts to bring the America Cup back to Britain with *Valkyrie II* and *III* in 1893 and 1895. During the World War I, although aged over seventy, he turned his steam yacht, the *Grianaig*, into a hospital ship and served in her himself. He d. in London, 14 June 1926. He had three daughters, two of whom predeceased him. He was succeeded in his titles by his cousin, Windham Henry Wyndham-Quin, MP for South Glamorgan, 1895-1906 (see above).

Publications: *Experiences in spiritualism* with D.D. Home, 1871; *The Great divide: Travels in the Upper Yellowstone*, 1876; *The Irish Question*, 1880; *The Soudan: its history, geography and characteristics*, 1884; *The Labour Question*, 1885; *Self-instruction in the practice and theory of Navigation*, 1900; *No Army, No Empire*, 1901; *Ireland and Scotland under the Unions: failure and success*, 1905; *Devolution in the British Empire*, 1906; *The Outlook in Ireland: the case for devolution and conciliation*, 1907; *Irish Land Purchase*, 1909; *The Legacy of past years*, 1911; *The New spirit in Ireland*, 1912; *The Finances of Ireland*, 1912; *Canadian Nights ... reminiscences of life and sport in the Rockies etc.*, 1914; *The Crisis in Ireland – Federal Union through devolution*, 1920; *Past times and pastimes* (autobiography), 1922; *Dunraven Castle, Glamorgan: some notes on its history and associations*, 1926.

Past times and pastimes, 1922; Dunraven Castle ...,1926; DNB Supplement, 1922-30; Times, 15 June 1926; West. Mail, 15 June 1926; Burke, 4, 549; Dunraven Papers, N.L.W. Aberystwyth.

M.E.C.

WYNN (FAMILY), Cesail Gyfarch (*DWB*, 1096). Change the date of death of Ann, daughter of Humphrey Humphreys to 1 Jan. 1699/1700.

WYNN (FAMILY), Rug (*DWB*, 1099-1100). Par. 3, the Ket rebellion was in 1549 (not '1594').

WYNN (FAMILY), Wynnstay (*DWB*, 1100), Sir William Williams (1634-1700) was Solicitor-General (not Attorney-General).

WYNN (FAMILY), Wynnstay. See above. All *after 1940* except Sir Watkin Williams Wynn (1820-85).

WYNN, Sir WATKIN WILLIAMS (1820-85) – see WYNN (FAMILY), Wynnstay above.

WYNNE, EDWARD (1685-1745) - see under WYNNE, ROBERT, *DWB*, 1108.

WYNNE, ELLIS (*DWB*, 1105). Y Lasynys is in the parish of Llandanwg, not Llanfihangel y Traethau.

YALE (*DWB*, 1110). Plâs-yn-Iâl is in the parish of Bryneglwys, and not in Llanelidan, which is outside the boudary of Iâl.

YARDLEY, EDWARD (1698-1769; *DWB*, 1110). On 5 Nov. 1731 he was elected preacher for St. Michael's chapel, the old chapel of Highgate School which was a chapel of ease in the parish of St. Mary, Hornsey, a position which he held for the remainder of his life. He d. at the age of 71 on 26 Dec. 1769 (not 1770). Upon the demolition of the chapel the gravestones were removed to S. Mary's.

Information supplied by the Rev. D.H. Matthews from a booklet entitled *Old Highgate* quoted from F.T. Cansick, *Epitaphs of Hornsey, St Pancras &c* (3 vols., 1872-75).

E.D.J.

YONG, JOHN – see MORGAN alias YONG, JOHN above.

INDEX to CONTRIBUTORS and their ARTICLES

The locations of articles in the current volume are not given.

1 = *The Dictionary of Welsh Biography down to 1940* (1959).
Only articles in the Appendix are given a page number.
2 = The current volume.

FITZSTEPHEN, ROBERT, ?-1183	1
GIBSON, JOHN, Sir, 1841-1915	1
HARRY, GEORGE OWEN (or OWEN, GEORGE), c.1553-c.1614	1
LAWS, EDWARD, 1837-1913	1
MARSHAL, Family, earls of Pembroke	1
MORGAN(N), MAURICE, c.1725-1802	1
OWEN, GEORGE, Henllys, c.1552-1613	1
OWEN, HENRY, 1844-1919	1
OWEN, MARGARET, 'Peggy', 1742-1816	1
PHILIPPS, Family, Picton, Pembs.	1
PHILLIMORE, EGERTON GRENVILLE BAGOT, 1856-1937	1
PHILLIPS, JAMES, 1847-1907	1
SKEEL, CAROLINE ANNE JAMES, 1872-1951	2
STEPNEY, or STEPNETH, Family, Prendergast, Pembs.	1
WOGAN, Families, Pembrokeshire	1
CLEARY, JOHN MARTIN	**J.M.C.**
BEDLOE, WILLIAM, 1650-80	1: 1113
CADWALADR, ROGER, 1566-1610	1: 1113
CLYNNOG, MORGAN, 1558->1619	1: 1114
EVANS, PHILIP, 1645-79	1: 1120
JONES, ROBERT, 1560-1615	1: 1136-7
LLOYD, JOHN, ?-1679	1: 1141
MORRIS, DAVID, 1630-1703	1: 1143
POWELL, PHILIP, 1594-1646	1: 1146
CLEMENT, MARY	**M.C.**
BEVAN, BRIDGET, 1698-1779	1
GOUGE, THOMAS, 1605?-81	1
JONES, GRIFFITH, 1683-1761	1
PHILIPPS, JOHN, Sir, 1666?-1737	1
VAUGHAN, JOHN, Derllys Court, Carms., 1663-1722	1
COLE, MAIR ELIZABETH	**Ma.E.C.**
LEWIS, THOMAS ARNOLD, 1893-1952	2
COLLINS, WILLIAM JOHN TOWNSEND	**W.J.T.C.**
JOHNS, WILLIAM NICHOLAS, 1834-98	1
COX, IDRIS	**I.C.**
JONES, LEWIS, 1897-1939	1
DAVIES, ALED LLOYD	**A.Ll.D.**
DAVIES, HUGH THOMAS, 1881-1969	2
JONES, WATKIN, 1882-1967	2
LLOYD, WILLIAM, 1901-1967	2
ROBERTS, DAVID JOHN, 1883-1956	2
ROBERTS, DAVID, 'Telynor Mawddwy', 1875-1956	2
DAVIES, DANIEL	**D.D.**
JONES, HENRY, Sir, 1852-1922	1
JONES, WILLIAM TUDOR, 1865-1946	2
DAVIES, DANIEL T.	**D.T.D.**
DAVIES, WILLIAM ANTHONY, 1886-1962	2
DAVIES, DAVID ELWYN JAMES	**D.E.J.D.**
JONES, REES CRIBIN, 1841-1927	2
JONES, WATCYN SAMUEL, 1877-1964	2
THOMAS, JOSEPH MORGAN LLOYD, 1868-1955	2
WILLIAMS, THOMAS OSWALD, 1888-1965	2
DAVIES, DAVID JACOB	**D.J.D. (vol. 1)**
STEPHENS, THOMAS, 1821-75	1
THOMAS, THOMAS EMLYN, 'Taliesin Craig-y-felin', 1822-46	1
THOMAS, WILLIAM, 'Gwilym Marles', 1834-79	1
DAVIES, DAVID JAMES LLEWELFRYN	**D.J.Ll.D.**
EVANS, SAMUEL THOMAS, Sir, 1859-1918	1
JENKINS, LEOLINE, Sir, 1625-85	1
DAVIES, DAVID JOSEPH	**D.J.D. (vol. 2)**
JONES, JOSEPH, 1877-1950	2
DAVIES, DAVID LESLIE	**D.L.D.**
ELLIOT, GEORGE, Sir, 1815-1893	2
JONES, DAVID BEVAN, 1807-1863	2
MATTHEWS, ABRAHAM, 1832-1899	2
PRICE, WATKIN WILLIAM, 1873-1967	2
STONELAKE, EDMUND WILLIAM, 1873-1960	2
WAYNE, Family, industrialists, Glam.	2
DAVIES, DAVID MYRDDIN	**D.M.D.**
DAVIES, CHARLES, 1849-1927	1
DAVIES, DEWI ALED EIRUG	**D.A.E.D.**
RICHARDS, DAVID THOMAS GLYNDWR, 1879-1956	2
STEPHENS, JOHN OLIVER, 1880-1957	2

DAVIES, EBENEZER CURIG — E.C.D.
    GRIFFITHS, DAVID, Madagascar, 1792-1863 — 1
    GRIFFITHS, JAMES, 1782-1858 — 1
DAVIES, EDWARD — Ed.D.
    LLOYD (LLWYD), ROBERT, Plas Ashpool, 1716-92 — 1
    OWEN, JOHN, Berthen Gron, 1733-76 — 1
    PARRY, EDWARD, hymn-writer, 1723-86 — 1
DAVIES, EDWARD TEGLA — E.T.D.
    DAVIES, JOHN, 1784-1845 — 1
    DAVIES, JOHN CADVAN, 1846-1923 — 1
    EVANS, JOHN, Eglwys Bach, 1840-97 — 1
    EVANS, JOHN HUGH, 'Cynfaen', 1833-86 — 1
    EVANS, WILLIAM HUGH, 'Gwyllt y Mynydd', 1831-1909 — 1
    HUGHES, JOHN, 'Glanystwyth', 1842-1902 — 1
    HUGHES, THOMAS, 1854-1928 — 1
    HUMPHREYS, ROBERT, 1779-1832 — 1
    ISAAC, EVAN, 1865-1938 — 1
    JONES, HUGH, 1837-1919 — 1
DAVIES, ELLIS — E.D.
    FISHER, JOHN, 1862-1930 — 1
    HUGHES, HENRY HAROLD, 1864-1940 — 1
    OWEN, ELIAS, 1833-99 — 1
    PENNANT, THOMAS, 1726-98 — 1
DAVIES, EMLYN — Em.D.
    HOWELLS, GEORGE, 1871-1955 — 2
DAVIES, EVAN THOMAS — E.Th.D.
    OWEN, MORFYDD LLWYN, 1891-1918 — 1
DAVIES, GWILYM — G.D.; also Gw.D.
    DAVIES, DAVID, baron, 1880-1944 — 2
    JONES, GARETH RICHARD VAUGHAN, 1905-35 — 1
DAVIES, JAMES ARTHUR — J.A.D.
    HAMER, GEORGE FREDERICK, Sir, 1885-1965 — 2
DAVIES, JOHN — J.D.
    DAGGAR, GEORGE, 1879-1950 — 2
    DAVIES, JOHN, 1882-1937 — 2
    EDWARDS, NESS, 1897-1968 — 2
DAVIES, KATHARINE MONICA — K.M.D.
    DAVIES, EDWARD OWEN, 1864-1936 — 1
    EVANS, WILLIAM, 1838-1921 — 1
    NEWELL, RICHARD, 1785-1852 — 1
    SANDERS, IOAN, fl. 1786 — 2
    WILLIAMS, OWEN (GAIANYDD), 1865-1928 — 1
DAVIES, LORRAINE — L.D.
    WILLIAMS, ROBERT JOHN (PRYSOR), 1891-1967 — 2
DAVIES, MARGARET BEATRICE — M.B.D.
    DAVIES, WILLIAM LEWIS, 1896-1941 — 2
    JONES, ALICE GRAY, 1852-1943 — 2
    JONES, DAVID OWEN, 1856-1903 — 1: 1131-2
    JONES, HUGH, 1831-83 — 1: 1133
    WILLIAMS, WILLIAM, 'Creuddynfab', 1814-69 — 1: 1157
    WILLIAMS, WILLIAM JONES, 1863-1949 — 2
DAVIES, MARGARET HELEN — M.H.D.
    EMANUEL, HYWEL DAVID, 1921-1970 — 2
DAVIES, MARY BEYNON — Ma.B.D.
    JONES, JOHN ROBERT, 1911-1970 — 2
DAVIES, OWEN PICTON — O.P.D.
    CARR, HENRY LASCELLES, 1841-1902 — 1
    DAVIES, WILLIAM, Sir, 1863-1935 — 1
    EVANS, DAVID TUDOR, 1822-96 — 1
    THOMAS, WILLIAM JAMES, Sir, 1867-1945 — 2
DAVIES, THOMAS EIRUG — T.E.D.
    CHARLES, JAMES, 1846-1920 — 1
    DAVIES, BEN, Trelech, 1840-1930 — 1
    DAVIES, JOHN, 'Siôn Gymro', 1804-84 — 1
    EDWARDS, DAVID, c.1654-1716 — 1
    EVANS, BENJAMIN, Trewen, 1740-1821 — 1
    GRIFFITHS, SAMUEL, 1783-1860 — 1
    LEWIS, JAMES, 1674-1747 — 1
    PUGH, PHILIP, 1679-1760 — 1
    REES, WILLIAM, 'Gwilym Hiraethog', 1802-83 — 1
DAVIES, THOMAS GRUFFYDD — T.G.D.
    JONES, ALFRED ERNEST, 1879-1958 — 2

DAVIES, THOMAS MAELGWYN	**T.M.D.**
EVANS, DAVID OWEN, 1876-1945	2
DAVIES, THOMAS TEGRYN	**T.T.D.**
EVANS, HENRY TOBIT, 1844-1908	1
DAVIES, WALFORD	**W.D.**
THOMAS, DYLAN MARLAIS, 1914-1953	2
DAVIES, WILLIAM BEYNON	**W.B.D.**
LEWIS, TIMOTHY, 1877-1958	2
DAVIES, WILLIAM CARADOC	**W.C.D.**
LEWIS, JOHN GOMER, 1844-1914	1
DAVIES, WILLIAM HOPKIN	**W.H.D.**
JOHANNES WALLENSIS (GALLENSIS, WALEYS) or 'John of Wales', fl. c.1260-83	1
MAELGWN GWYNEDD, ?-c.547	1
NENNIUS (NEMNIUS, NEMNIUUS), fl. c.800	1
RHUN ap MAELGWN GWYNEDD, fl. 55O	1
RHYGYFARCH (RICEMARCHUS), 1056/7-99	1
SULIEN, 'Sulgenus', 'The Wise', 1011-91	1
DAVIES, WILLIAM JOHN	**W.J.D.**
GRUFFUDD ap MAREDUDD ap DAFYDD, fl. 1352-82	1
DAVIES, WILLIAM LLEWELYN	**W.Ll.D.**
ADAMS, ROGER, ?-1741	1
ANWYL, LEWIS, 1705?-1776	1
ASHTON, CHARLES, 1848-99	1
BAKER, ELIZABETH, c.1720-89	1
BALLINGER, JOHN, Sir, 1860-1933	1
BARRINGTON, DAINES, 1727-1800	1
BAUGH, ROBERT, 1748?-1832	1
BLACKWELL, HENRY, 1851-1928	1
BRADNEY, JOSEPH ALFRED, Sir, 1859-1933	1
BROSTER, Family, printers, Chester and Bangor	1
BROWN, JAMES CONWAY, 1838-1908	1
BRYDGES, HARFORD JONES, Sir, 1764-1847	1
BUTE, marquesses of, Cardiff Castle	1
CARNES, EDWARD, 1772?-1828	1
CARTER, ISAAC, ?-1741	1
CHALONER, THOMAS, ?-1598	1
CHAPPELL, EDGAR LEYSHON, 1879-1949	2
CLARK, Family, printers, Monmouthshire	1
CLOUGH, RICHARD, Sir, ?-1570	1
COX, JOHN, ?-1870	2
DAFYDD TREFOR, 'Syr', ?-1528?	1
DANIEL, JOHN, 1755?-1823	1
DAVIES, DAVID, Sir, 1792-1865	1
DAVIES, HUGH, 1739-1821	1
DAVIES, HUGH TUDWAL, 1847-1915	1
DAVIES, JOHN, of Kidwelly, 1627?-93	1
DAVIES, MORGAN, ?-1857	1
DAVIES, RICHARD, 'Isgarn', 1887-1947	2
DAVIES, WILLIAM, 1756-1823	1
DAVIES, WILLIAM, 1874-1949	2
DAVIS, WILLIAM, 'Golden Farmer', 1627-90	1
DIVERRES, POL, 1880-1946	2
DONNE, JAMES, 1764-1844	1
DURSTON, THOMAS, ?-1767	1
EDDOWES, JOSHUA, 1724-1811	1
EDWARDS, JOHN HUGH, 1869-1945	2
EDWIN, ?-1073	1
ELLIS, Family, Bron y Foel and Ystumllyn, Caerns.	1
ELLIS, ELLIS OWEN, 1813-61	1
ELLIS, RICHARD, (not 1869) 1865-1928	1
EVANS, Family, printers, Machynlleth, Barmouth and Carmarthen	1
EVANS, GRIFFITH, and OAKELEY, Families, Tanybwlch, Mer.	1
EVANS, EVAN WILLIAM, 1860-1925	1
EVANS, WILLIAM, 'Alaw Afan', 1836-1900	1
GLENN, THOMAS ALLEN, 1864-1948	2
GRIFFITH, Family, Garn and Plasnewydd, Denbs.	1
GRUFFYDD, ROBERT, 'Patrobas', 1832-63	1
GRUFFYDD ap IEUAN ap LLYWELYN FYCHAN, c.1485-1550	1
HAINES, WILLIAM, 1852-1922	1
HOARE, RICHARD COLT, Sir, 1758-1838	1
HOLLAND, SAMUEL, 1803-92	1
HOWELL, JOHN, 1774-1830	1

HOWELL, THOMAS, Spain, ?-1540? 1
HUGHES, MICHAEL, 1752-1825 1
HUW ap RHISIART ap DAFYDD, 16c. 1
IEUAN FYCHAN ap IEUAN ab ADDA, ?-c.1458 1
JAMES, ANGHARAD, fl. 1680?-1730? 1
JAMES, FRANK TREHARNE, 1861-1942 2
JAMES, IVOR, 1840-1909 1
JONES, DAFYDD, 1743-1831 1
JONES, EVAN DAVIES, Sir, 1859-1949 2
JONES, JOHN, Gelli Lyfdy, c.1578-1658? 1
JONES, JOHN, Llanddeiniolen, 18c. 1
JONES, LEWIS, 'Rhuddenfab', 1835-1915 1
JONES, MOSES OWEN, 1842-1908 1
JONES, OWEN, London, 1809-74 1
JONES (JOHNES), RICHARD, printer, fl. 1564-c.1602 1
JONES, RICHARD, printer, 1787-1855? 1
JONES, THOMAS, almanack maker, 1648?-1713 1
JONES, THOMAS, Llanfaethlu, 1818-98 1
JONES, THOMAS JESSE, 1873-1950 2
JONES, THOMAS LLECHID, 1867-1946 2
JONES, WILLIAM COLLISTER, 1772-? 1
JONES, WILLIAM HENRY, 1860-1932 1
KATHERYN of BERAIN, 1534/5-91 1
KINSEY, WILLIAM MORGAN, 1788-1851 1
LATHROP, RICHARD, ?-1764 1
LEATHART, WILLIAM DAVIES, ?->1840 1
LEE (LEGH), ROWLAND, ?-1543 1
LEWES, ERASMUS, 1663?-1745 2
LEWIS, ERASMUS, 1670-1754 1
LEWIS, JOHN, Llynwene, ?-1616 1
LEWIS, WILLIAM, Cardiff printer, 1835?-1918 1
LLOYD, Family, Rhiwaedog, Mer. 1
LLOYD, JOHN, 'The Philosopher', 1749-1815 1
LLOYD-OWEN, DAVID CHARLES, 1843-1925 1
LLWYD, RICHARD, 'Bard of Snowdon', 1752-1835 1
LLYWARCH ap BRAN, fl. c.1137 1
MANSEL, Family, Oxwich, Penrice and Margam abbey, Glam. 1
MANSEL, BUSSY, 1623-99 1
MANSEL, ROBERT, Sir, 1573-1656 1
MARSH, RICHARD, 1710?-92 1
MATHEWS, JOHN HOBSON, 1858-1914 1
MAURICE and OWEN, Families, Clenennau, Penmorfa, Caerns. and Glyn
   (Cywarch), Mer. 1
MEYRICK, SAMUEL RUSH, Sir, 1783-1848 1
MILLINGCHAMP, BENJAMIN, 1756-1829 1
MORGAN, CHARLES OCTAVIUS SWINNERTON, 1803-88 1
MORGAN, THOMAS OWEN, 1799-1878 1
MORRIS, ROBERT PRYS, 1831?-90 1
MOSTYN, Family, Mostyn Hall, Flints. 1
MOSTYN, Family, Talacre, Flints. 1
NICHOLAS, THOMAS, 1816-79 1
OSBWRN WYDDEL, fl. 1293 1
OWEN, Family, Peniarth, Mer. 1
OWEN, ANEURIN, 1792-1851 1
OWEN, EDWARD HUMPHREY, 1850-1904 1
OWEN, EDWARD PRYCE, 1788-1863 1
OWEN, HUGH, 1761-1827 1
OWEN, RICHARD, fl. 1552 1
OWEN, ROBERT, 1858-85 1
PAINTER, Family, Wrexham, Denbs. 1
PARKER, JOHN, 1798-1860 1
PARRY, GEORGE, 1613?-78 1
PARRY, HENRY, 1766?-1854 1
PARRY, JAMES RHYS, fl. 1570?-1625? 1
PARRY, ROBERT, fl. 1540?-1612? 1
PAYNE, HENRY THOMAS, 1759-1832 1
PENNY, ANNE, fl. 1729-80 1
PHILLIPPS, THOMAS, Sir, 1792-1872 1
PHYLIP, Family, Ardudwy, Mer. - see PHYLIPIAID ARDUDWY 1
PIERCE, THOMAS MORDAF, 1867?-1919 1
PIOZZI, HESTER LYNCH, 1741-1821 1
POWELL, Family, Nanteos (Llechwedd-dyrus), Cards. 1
PRICE, ROBERT, 1655-1733 1

WILLIAMS, JOHN, 1825-1904 | 1
WILLIAMS, JOHN, Sir, 1840-1926 | 1
WILLIAMS, MATHEW, 1732-1819 | 1
WILLIAMS, PHILIP, ?-1717 | 1
WILLIAMS, RICHARD, 'Gwydderig', 1842-1917 | 1
WILLIAMS, ROGER, Sir, 1540?-95 | 1
WILLIAMS, THOMAS, 'Twm Pedrog', 1774-1814 | 1
WILLIAMS, WILLIAM, fl. 1648-77 | 1
WILLIAMS, WILLIAM, 'Y Lefiad', fl. 1853 | 1
WILLIAMSON, ROBERT (MONA), 1807-52 | 1
WYNN, Family, Cesail Gyfarch, Caerns.
WYNN and OWEN, Families, Glyn (Glyn Cywarch), Mer., and
Brogyntyn, Salop | 1
WYNN, NANNEY, and VAUGHAN, Families, Maesyneuadd, Mer. | 1
WYNN, Family, Rug, Mer., and Boduan (Bodfean), Caerns. | 1
WYNN, PRYSE and CORBET, Families, Ynysmaengwyn, Mer., and
GWYN and NANNEY, Dolau Gwyn, Mer., | 1
WYNN, GRIFFITH, 1669?-1736 | 1
WYNNE, Family, Peniarth, Mer. | 1
WYNNE (WYNNE-FINCH), Family, Voelas, Denbs. | 1
WYNNE, ELLIS, 1670/1-1734 | 1
YARDLEY, EDWARD, 1698-1769 (not 1770) | 1
DAVIES, WILLIAM THOMAS PENNAR | **W.T.P.D.**
EVANS, JOHN, 1858-1963 | 2
LEWIS, THOMAS, 1868-1953 | 2
ROBERTS, DAVID OWEN, 1888-1958 | 2
DAVIES, WILLIAM WATKIN | **W.W.D.**
DAVIES, JOHN GWYNORO, 1855-1935 | 1
DIGNAM, CHRISTOPHER | **C.D.**
RHYS, WALTER FITZURYAN, 1873-1956 | 2
DODD, ARTHUR HERBERT | **A.H.D.**
ALMER (or ALMOR), Family, Almer and Pant Iocyn, Denbs. | 1
ARNOLD, Family, Llanthony and Llanfihangel Crucorney, Mon. | 1
AUBREY, WILLIAM, c.1529-95 | 1
BAKER, DAVID, (Ven. AUGUSTINE BAKER), 1575-1641 | 1
BODVEL, Family, Bodfel, Caerns., and Caerfryn, Anglesey | 1
BODWRDA (BODURDA), Family, Bodwrda, Caerns. | 1
BROUGHTON, Family, Marchwiel, Denbs. | 1
CARNE, EDWARD, Sir, c.1500-61 | 1
CECIL, Family, Alltyrynys, Herefs., Burghley, Northants. and
Hatfield, Herts. | 1
CLOUGH, Family, Plas Clough, Glan-y-wern, Bathafarn and Hafodunos,
Denbs. | 1
DAVIES (DAVYS), MATTHEW, fl. 1620 | 1
DAVIES (DAVIS or DAVYES), THOMAS, bishop of S. Asaph, 1512?-73 | 1
DAVIES, WILLIAM, martyr, ?-1593 | 1
DEVEREUX, Family, Lamphey, Ystrad Ffin, Vaynor, Nantariba,
Pencoyd, etc. | 1
DOLBEN (DOULBEN, DOULBIN, DAULBIN), Family, Segrwyd, Denbs. | 1
EDISBURY, Family, Bedwal, Marchwiel, Pentreclawdd and Erddig, Denbs. | 1
EDWARDS (EDWARDES), Family, Chirkland, Denbs., Pembrokeshire,
and Kensington | 1
EDWARDS, Family, Cilhendre and Plas Iolyn, Salop | 1
EDWARDS, Family, Stansty, Denbs. | 1
ELLICE (ELLIS), ROBERT, fl. 1640 | 1
EVANS, JOHN, schoolmaster, 1628-1700 | 1
EVANS, JOHN, c.1680-1730 | 1
GLYN, THOMAS, ?-1648 - see under GLYN, Family, Glynllifon | 1
GRIFFITH, JOHN, Oxford, fl. 1548-87 | 1
GRIFFITH, THOMAS TAYLOR, 1795-1876 | 1
GWYN (GWYNN, GWYNNE or WYNN), JOHN, ?-1574 | 1
GWYNNE (GWINNE, GWYN or WYNNE), ROBERT (JOHNS), fl. 1568-91 | 1
HANMER, Family, Hanmer, Bettisfield, Fens, and Halton, Flints., and
Pentrepant, Salop | 1
HERBERT, Family, earls of Pembroke (2nd creation) | 1
HERBERT, Family, Montgomery, Parke, Blackhall, Dolguog, Cherbury,
Aston | 1
HERBERT, HENRY, 1617-56 | 1
HERBERT, JOHN, Sir, 1550-1617 | 1
HERBERT, WILLIAM, Sir, ?-1593 | 1
HEYLIN, ROWLAND, 1562?-1631 | 1
JEFFREYS, GEORGE, 1645-89 | 1
JONES, EDWARD, ?-1586 | 1: 1132

EDWARDS, OWEN	O.E.
DAVIES, ANNIE (NAN), 1910-1970	2
DAVIES, HYWEL, 1919-1965	2
ELIS, ISLWYN FFOWC	I.Ff.E.
DAVIES, EDWARD TEGLA, 1880-1967	2
ELLIS, EDWARD LEWIS	E.L.El.
EVANS, IFOR (IVOR) LESLIE, 1897-1952	2
ELLIS, MARY GWENDOLINE	M.G.E.
DAFYDD NANCONWY, fl. 17c.	1
EDWARD ap HYWEL ap GRUFFYDD, fl. 15c.	1
ELIS ap SION ap MORYS, 15c.	1
ELLIS, THOMAS IORWERTH, 1899-1970	2
EVANS, JOHN SILAS, 1864-1953	2
HARRIS, WILLIAM HENRY, 1884-1956	2
HAVARD, WILLIAM THOMAS, 1889-1956	2
JONES, MAURICE, 1863-1957	2
LLAWDDEN or IEUAN LLAWDDEN, fl. 1450	1
MATTHEWS, NORMAN GREGORY, 1904-1964	2
MORGAN, JOHN, 1886-1957	2
RHYS NANMOR, fl. 1480-1513	1
ROBERTS, GRIFFITH JOHN, 1912-1969	2
THOMAS, LAWRENCE, 1889-1960	2
TREE, RONALD JAMES, 1914-1970	2
WILLIAMSON, EDWARD WILLIAM, 1892-1953	2
ELLIS, MEGAN	M.E.
BRIGSTOCKE, THOMAS, 1809-81	1
EDWARDS, JOSEPH, 1814-82	1
EDWARDS, SYDENHAM TEAK, 1768-1819	1
EDWARDS, WILLIAM CAMDEN, 1777-1855	1
FRANCIS, JOHN DEFFETT, 1815-1901	1
GEORGE, THOMAS, fl. 1829-40	1
GIBBON, BENJAMIN PHELPS, 1802-51	1
GIBSON, JOHN, 1790-1866	1
GRIFFITH, MOSES, 1747-1819	1
INNES, JAMES DICKSON, 1887-1914	1: 1129-30
JONES, THOMAS, 1742-1803	1
JONES-DAVIES, HENRY, 1870-1955	2
JONES-DAVIES, THOMAS ELLIS, 1906-1960	2
PARRY, WILLIAM, c.1742-91	1
PRICHARD, JOHN, 1817-86	1
PUGH, EDWARD, c.1761-1813	1
REDMOND, THOMAS, 1745?-85	1
ROOS, WILLIAM, 1808-78	1
VAUGHAN, ROWLAND, Caer-gai, c.1590-1667	1
WILLIAMS, CHRISTOPHER DAVID, 1873-1934	1
WILLIAMS, PENRY, 1800-85	1
WILLIAMS, WILLIAM, 'Ap Caledfryn', 1837-1915	1
ELLIS, ROBERT	R.E.
JENKINS, JOSEPH, (not 1861) 1859-1929	1
ELLIS, TECWYN	T.E.
JONES, EDWARD, 'Bardd y Brenin', 1752-1824	1
ELLIS, THOMAS IORWERTH	T.I.E.
BEBB, LLEWELLYN JOHN MONTFORT, 1862-1915	2
BEVAN, WILLIAM LATHAM, 1821-1908	1
BURGESS, THOMAS, 1756-1837	1
CHARLES, DAVID, II, 1803-80	1
CHARLES, DAVID, III, 1812-78	1
DANIEL, DAVID ROBERT, 1859-1931	1
DARLINGTON, THOMAS, 1864-1908	1
DAVIES, EVAN THOMAS, 1847-1927	1
DAVIES, JOHN HUMPHREYS, 1871-1926	1
DAVIES, ROBERT, Aberystwyth, 1790-1841	1
EDWARDS, ALFRED GEORGE, 1848-1937	1
EDWARDS, THOMAS, 'Gwynedd', 1844-1924	1
ELLIS, THOMAS EDWARD, 1859-99	1
EVANS, HOWELL THOMAS, 1877-1950	2
EVANS-WILLIAMS, LAURA, 1883-1944	2
GREEN, CHARLES ALFRED HOWELL, 1864-1944	2
GRIFFITHS, JOHN, cleric, educationalist, 1820-97	1
HERBERT, DAVID, 1762-1835	1
HUGHES, DAVID, Llanfyllin, 1785-1850	1
HUGHES, HUGH PRICE, 1847-1902	1
HUGHES, THOMAS JOHN, 'Adfyfr', 1853-1927	1

HUGHES, THOMAS JONES, 1822-91	1
JAMES, HERBERT ARMITAGE, 1844-1931	1
JAYNE, FRANCIS JOHN, 1845-1921	1
JOHNES, ARTHUR JAMES, 1809-71	1
JONES, EDMUND OSBORNE, 1858-1931	1
JONES, EDWARD, 1790-1860	2
JONES, GRIFFITH ARTHUR, 1827-1906	1
JONES, ISAAC, 1804-50	1
JONES, JOHN, Llandaff, 1645-1709	1
JONES, JOHN, archdeacon of Merioneth, 1775-1834	1
JONES, LEWIS DAVIES, Llew Tegid, 1851-1928	1
JONES, ROBERT, Rotherhithe, 1810-79	1
JONES, THOMAS, ?-1676	1
JONES, THOMAS, 1752-1845	1
JONES, WILLIAM BASIL TICKELL, 1822-97	1
JOYCE, GILBERT CUNNINGHAM, 1866-1942	2
LEWELLIN, LLEWELYN, 1798-1878	1
LEWIS (LEWES), DAVID, Oxford, 1520?-84	1
LEWIS, DAVID, 1760-1850	1
LEWIS, DAVID, 'Ap Ceredigion', 1870-1948	2
LEWIS, GEORGE, c.1640?-1709?	1
LLOYD, DANIEL LEWIS, 1843-99	1
LLOYD, THOMAS RICHARD, 1820-91	1
MATTHEWS, JOHN, 1773-1848	1
MORGAN, HECTOR DAVIES, 1785-1850	1
MORGAN, HENRY, ?-1559	1
NEWCOME, RICHARD, 1779-1857	1
OLLIVANT, ALFRED, 1798-1882	1
OWEN, HUGH, Sir, 1804-81	1
OWEN, JOHN, bishop of S. David's, 1854-1926	1
OWEN, MORGAN, 1585?-1645	1
PARRY, DAVID, 'Y Gloch Arian', 1794-1877	1
PHILLIPS, SAMUEL LEVI, c.1730-1812	1
PROSSER, DAVID LEWIS, 1868-1950	2
REES, TIMOTHY, 1874-1939	1
RENDEL, STUART, 1834-1913	1
RICHARD, HENRY, 1812-88	1
RICHARDS, THOMAS, 1754-1837	1
ROBERTS, ROBERT, scholar, 1834-85	1
ROBERTS, THOMAS FRANCIS, 1860-1919	1
ROWLAND(S), DAVID, 'Dewi Brefi', 1782-1820	1
ROWLAND, JOHN, Sir, 1877-1941	2
SANKEY, JOHN, 1866-1948	2
SHIPLEY, WILLIAM DAVIES, 1745-1826	1
THOMAS, DAVID WALTER, 1829-1905	1
THOMAS, MESAC, 1816-92	1
THOMAS, THOMAS, 1804-77	1
THOMAS, WILLIAM, bishop, 1613-89	1
WADE, GEORGE WOOSUNG, 1858-1941	2
WILLIAMS, ELIEZER, 1754-1820	1
WILLIAMS, JOHN, 'Yr Hen Syr', 1745/6-1818	1
WILLIAMS, JOHN, 1792-1858	1
WILLIAMS, MORRIS, 'Nicander', 1809-74	1
WILLIAMS, PETER, 1756-1837	1
WILLIAMS, ROBERT ARTHUR, 1854-1926	1
WILLIAMS, ROWLAND, 1779-1854	1
WILLIAMS, ROWLAND, 1817-70	1
WILLIAMS, THOMAS, 1658-1726	1
WORTHINGTON, WILLIAM, 1704-78	1
EMANUEL, HYWEL DAVID	**H.D.E.**
AIDAN, 6c.	1
BRIOG, 6c.	1
BRYCHAN, 5c.	1
BRYNACH, 5c.	1
CYNGAR, 6c.	1
CYNIDR, 6c.	1
DOGMAEL (DOGFAEL, DOGWEL), fl. 6c.	1
DUNAWD, fl. 6c.	1
DYFRIG (DUBRICIUS), fl. 475?	1
ELLI, fl. 6c.	1
FINIAN, fl. 6c.	1
GWYNLLYW (GUNDLEIUS, GUNLYU), fl. 5c.-6c.	1
HODGES, JOHN, 1700?-77	1

INNES, JOHN, 1853?-1923   1: 1130
JUSTINIAN, SAINT (Stinan Sant), fl. 6c.   1
KEYNE (CAIN), fl. 5c.-6c.   1
LLAWDDOG, or LLEUDDAD, fl. 600?   1: 1140
MALO (MACHU, MACHUTES, MACLOVIUS, MECHELL), 6c.   1
NONN (NONNA, NONNITA), fl. 5c.   1
OLIVER, JOHN, 1838-66   1
OUDOCEUS (EUDDOGWY), fl. late 6c.   1
OWEN, OWEN, 'Celatus', 1806-74   1
OWEN, RICHARD JONES, 1831-1909   1
OWEN, THOMAS, 1748-1812   1
PARRY, DAVID, 'Dewi Moelwyn', 1835-70   1
PARRY, JOHN, Llanelian, 1770-1820   1
PARRY, THOMAS, 'Llanerchydd', c.1809-1874   1
PAUL AURELIAN, 5c.   1
PAULINUS (PEULIN), 5c.   1
PETROC (PEDROG), 6c.   1
PRICE, WILLIAM, 1597-1646   1
PRICHARD, THOMAS, 1764-1843   1
THOMAS, WILLIAM, antiquary, 1734-99   1
WILLIAM, LODWICK, fl. 1689?   1
WILLIAMS, ARTHUR WYNN, 1819-86   1
WILLIAMS, BENJAMIN THOMAS, 1832-90   1
WILLIAMS, HUGH, 'Cadfan', 1807?-70   1
WILLIAMS (alias PENROSE), LLEWELLIN, 1725-?   1
ETHALL, HUW   H.E.
THOMAS, LEWIS JOHN, 1883-1970   2
EVANS, DANIEL   D.E.
JAMES, JOHN, 'Ioan ap Iago', 18c.-19c.   1
EVANS, DAVID EMRYS   D.E.E.
EVANS, FREDERICK, 'Ednyfed', 1840-97   1
EVANS, TOM VALENTINE, 1861-1935   1
REICHEL, HARRY (HENRY RUDOLF), Sir, 1856-1931   1
EVANS, DAVID TECWYN   D.T.E.
DAVIES, SAMUEL, 1818-91   1
HUGHES, HUGH, 'Tegai', 1805-64   1
EVANS, DAVID TUDWAL   D.Td.E.
WILLIAMS, HUGH, 'Hywel Cernyw', 1843-1937   1
EVANS, DYFED OSWALD   D.O.E.
OWEN, ROBERT, Croesor, 1885-1962   2
EVANS, EDWARD WILLIAM PRICE   E.W.P.E.
EDWARDS, MILES, 1743-1808   1
EDWARDS, MORGAN, 1722-95   1
HARRY, MILES, 1700-76   1
LEWIS, THOMAS, 1859-1929   1: 1140
RICHARD, TIMOTHY, 1845-1919   1
THOMAS, MICAH, 1778-1853   1
THOMAS, THOMAS, Pontypool, 1805-81   1
EVANS, ELWYN   E.E.
BAXTER, GEORGE ROBERT WYTHEN, (not 1815) 1814-54   1
BLAYNEY, Family, Gregynog, Mont.   1
BREEZE, EVAN, 'Ieuan Cadfan', 1798-1855   1
CADWALADR, ELLIS, fl. 1707-40   1
DAVIES, THOMAS, fl. 1700   1
EDGEWORTH, ROGER, ?-1560   1
EDWARDS, JONATHAN, 1629-1712   1
EDWARDS, RICHARD FOULKES, 1836-70   1
EDWARDS, ROBERT, 'Robin Ddu o Feirion', 1775-1805   1
ELLIS, SAMUEL, 1803-52   1
EVANS, DAVID, poet, fl. 1750   1
EVANS, JOHN RHAIADORE, 1790?-1850?   2
HINDE, CHARLES THOMAS EDWARD, 1820-70   1
HUMPHREYS, JAMES, c.1768-1830   1
HUXLEY, THOMAS, fl. 1765-88   1
IEUAN ap HYWEL SWRDWAL, fl. 1430-80   1
JENKINS, JOHN, Llanidloes, 1821-96   1
JONES, HUGH, Maesglasau, 1749-1825   1
JONES, JOHN, 'Myllin', 1800-26   1
JONES, JOHN, 'Idrisyn', 1804-87   1
JONES, THOMAS, 1720?-90   1
POWEL(L), RICHARD, 1769-95   1
PRITCHARD, EDWARD, 1839-1900   1
PUGH, Family, Mathafarn, Mont.   1

RHYS, DAVID, THOMAS and MARY, Llanbryn-mair   1
EVANS, EMLYN WYNNE   E.W.E.
    DAVIES, STEPHEN, 1790-1858   1
    DRISCOLL, JAMES, 1880-1925   1
EVANS, EMRYS PEREGRYN   E.P.E.
    EVANS, DAVID EMLYN, 1843-1913   2
    EVANS, EVAN KERI, 1860-1941   2
EVANS, EVAN GWYNDAF   E.G.E.
    THOMAS, LEWIS, 1877-1955   2
EVANS, EVAN LEWIS   E.L.E.
    BEVAN, THOMAS, 1796?-1819   1
    DAVIES, EVAN, missionary, 1805-64   1
    DAVIES, JACOB, 1816-49   1
    DAVIES, JOHN, Tahiti, 1772-1855   1
    EVANS, JOHN CEREDIG, 1855-1936   1
    GRIFFITH, RICHARD DAVIES, 1813-56   1
    GRIFFITHS, GRIFFITH, Jamaica, 1799-1845   1
    JEHU, DAVID, 1812-40   1
    JOHN, GRIFFITH, 1831-1912   1
    JOHNS, DAVID, Madagascar, 1796-1843   1
    JONES, DANIEL, Khasi Hills, 1813-46   1
    JONES, DAVID, Madagascar, 1797-1841   1
    JONES, THOMAS JERMAN, 1833-90   1
    JONES, WILLIAM JENKYN, 1852-1925   1
    LEWIS, JOHN, missionary, 1792?-1816   1
    LEWIS, JOHN DANIEL VERNON, 1879-1970   2
    LEWIS, WILLIAM, Khasia Hills, 1814-91   1
    LLWYD (LLOYD), MORGAN, 1619-59   1
    MORGAN, THOMAS, missionary, ?-1833   1
    PENRY, DAVID, 1660?-1721?   1
    PENRY, JOHN, 1854-83   1
    PRICE, ROGER, 1834-1900   1
    REES, WILLIAM HOPKYN, 1859-1924   1
    THOMAS, ROBERT JERMAIN, 1840-66   1
    WILLIAM, THOMAS, Mynydd-bach, Carm., 1697-1778   1
EVANS, GRUFFYDD GLYN   G.G.E.
    KADWALADR (CADWALADR), SION (JOHN, SIONYN), fl. 1750-65   1
    ROBERTS, ELIS, ?-1789   1
EVANS, GWILYM   G.E.
    BLIGH, STANLEY PRICE MORGAN, 1870-1949   2
    WILLIAMS, WILLIAM EMYR, 1889-1958   2
EVANS, GWYNFOR   Gw.E.
    JONES, JOHN EDWARD, 1905-1970   2
EVANS, HOWELL THOMAS   H.T.E.
    DAFYDD ab IFAN ab EINION, fl. 1440-68   1
    GOUGH (GOCH), MATHEW (MATHAU), c.1390-1450   1
    HERBERT, WILLIAM, earl of Pembroke, ?-1469   1
    HERBERT, WILLIAM, earl of Pembroke, 1460-91   1
EVANS, JANET   J.E. (vol. 1)
    EVANS, THOMAS JOHN, 1863-1932   1
EVANS, JOHN   J.E. (vol. 2)
    JONES, DANIEL EVAN, 1860-1941   2
EVANS, JOHN JAMES   J.J.E.
    GREEN, FRANCIS, 1854-1942   2
    JONES, DAVID, 'Welsh Freeholder', 1765-1816   1
    LEWES, WATKIN, Sir, 1740-1821   1
    RHYS, MORGAN JOHN, 1760-1804   1
EVANS, JOHN KEITH   J.K.E.
    JONES, JOHN JAMES, 1892-1957   2
EVANS, JOHN ROBERTS   J.R.E.
    AUBREY, WILLIAM, 1759-1827   1
EVANS, MEREDYDD   Me.E.
    JONES, JOHN WILLIAM, 1883-1954   2
    WILLIAMS, WILLIAM MORRIS, 1883-1954   2
EVANS, PERCY CYRIL CONNICK   P.C.C.E.
    PERROT, Family, Haroldston, Pembs.   1
EVANS, RAYMOND WALLIS   R.W.E.
    ADDA FRAS, 1240?-1320?   1
    BERGAM, Y, 14c.   2
    DAFYDD GORLECH, 1410?-90?   1
    HININ FARDD, 1360?-1420?   1
EVANS, TREBOR LLOYD   T.Ll.E.
    EDWARDS, LEWIS, 1809-87   1

EVANS, WILLIAM	W.E.
JONES, THOMAS, 'Taliesin o Eifion', 1820-76	1
THOMAS, DAVID JOHN, 'Afan', 1881-1928	1
EVANS, WILLIAM GARETH	W.G.E.
LLOYD, DAVID JOHN, 1886-1951	2
PHILLIPS, MORGAN HECTOR, 1885-1953	2
EVANS, WILLIAM LLEWELYN	W.Ll.E.
THOMAS, OWEN, 1812-91	1
FORRESTER, DOROTHY ELWYN	D.E.F.
ROBERTS, JOHN, missionary in Assam, 1842-1908	1
FOSTER, IDRIS LLEWELYN	I.Ll.F.
BAXTER, WILLIAM, 1650-1723	1
DAVIES, ELLIS WILLIAM, 1871-1939	2
GEOFFREY of MONMOUTH, 1090?-1155	1
POWELL, GRIFFITH, 1561-1620	1
PRICE, HUGH, 1495?-1574	1
GEORGE, WILLIAM RICHARD PHILIP	W.R.P.G.
GEORGE, WILLIAM, 1865-1967	2
LLOYD GEORGE, Family, Cricieth	2
GIBBS, FRANCIS MICHAEL	F.M.G.
HARRY, GEORGE OWEN, c.1553-1614	2
GRAY-JONES, ARTHUR	A.G.-J.; also A.Gr.-J.
JOHN, HENRY, or HARRI SION, 1664-1754	1
JONES, EDMUND, 1702-93	1
WILLIAMS, EDMUND, 1717-42	1
GRESHAM, COLIN ALISTAIR	C.A.G.
EVANS, ROBERT, 'Cybi', 1871-1956	2
HEMP, WILFRID JAMES, 1882-1962	2
GRIFFITH, GRIFFITH WYNNE	G.W.G.
REES, HENRY, 1798-1869	1
GRIFFITH, LLEWELYN WYN	Ll.W.G.
GRIFFITH, JOHN, 1863-1933	1
GRIFFITH, ROBERT DAVID	R.D.G.
ANTHONY, GRIFFITH, 1846-97	1
ASHTON, JOHN, 1830-96	1
BARRETT, WILLIAM LEWIS, 1847-1927	1
BENNETT, NICHOLAS, 1823-99	1
BEYNON, ROSSER, 1811-76	1
BLAYNEY, THOMAS, 1785-c.1829	1
BRYANT, JOHN, 1832-1926	1
BRYANT, TOM, 1882-1946	2
BWTTING, RHYS, 15c.	1
CADWGAN DELYNOR, fl. 14c.	1
CRYTHOR LLWYD MARCHEDD, 16c.	1
CYNWRIG BENCERDD, c.1451	1
DAFYDD ap HYWEL GRYTHOR, fl. 1568	1
DAI LLWYD of CWM BYCHAN, fl. c.1485	1
DAI MAESMOR, 16c.	1
DAVIES, BENJAMIN, 1858-1943	2
DAVIES, CLARA NOVELLO, 1861-1943	2
DAVIES, DAVID, musician, 1810-75	1
DAVIES, DAVID, harpist, 1817-55	1
DAVIES, DAVID THOMAS FFRANGCON, 1855-1918	1
DAVIES, EVAN CYNFFIG, 1843-1908	1
DAVIES, HUGH, 1844-1907	1
DAVIES, JOHN, composer, 1787-1855	1
DAVIES, JOHN ELIAS, 1847-83	1
DAVIES, MARY, 1855-1930	1
DAVIES, MATTHEW WILLIAM, 1882-1947	2
DAVIES, MOSES, 1799-1866	1
DAVIES, OLIVER, fl. 1820	1
DAVIES, OWEN HUMPHREY, 1828-98	1
DAVIES, ROBERT, 'Cyndeyrn', 1814-67	1
DAVIES, ROBERT, 'Asaph Llechid', 1834-58	1
DAVIES, THOMAS, 'Trithyd', 1810?-73?	1
DAVIES, WILLIAM, musician, 1859-1907	1
DEVONALD, JOHN, 1863-1936	1
EAMES, ROLANT, fl. 18c.	2
EDNYFED, SION, fl. 1568	1
EDNYFED, WILLIAM, fl. 1568	1
EDWARD ab IFAN, fl. 1568	1
EDWARD GRYTHOR, fl. 1523	1
EDWARDS, EDWARD, 'Pencerdd Ceredigion', 1816-97	1

EDWARDS, EVAN, 1734-66   1
EDWARDS, JOHN, musician, 1799-1873?   1
EDWARDS, JOHN DAVID, 1805-85   1
EDWARDS, PETER, 1854-1934   1
EDWARDS, ROBERT, 1796-1862   1
EDWARDS, THOMAS DAVID, (not 1875) 1874-1930   1
EDWARDS, WILLIAM, 'Cymro Gwyllt', 1826-84   1
ELLIS, HUW, 1714-74   1
ELLIS, JOHN, musician, 1760-1839   1
ELLIS, LEWIS, 1761-1823   1
ELLIS, RICHARD, musician, 1775-1855   1
ELLIS, RICHARD, musician, 1784-1824   1
ELLIS, ROBERT, 1817-93   1
ELLIS SION SIAMS, fl. 17c.   1
EVANS, DANIEL, 'Eos Dâr', 1846-1915   1
EVANS, DAVID, 1705-88   1
EVANS, DAVID LLOYD, 1861-1912   1
EVANS, DAVID PUGH, 1866-97   1
EVANS, EDWARD, 'Heman Gwent', 1823-78   1
EVANS, EVAN, harpist, 18c.   1
EVANS, HARRY, 1873-1914   1
EVANS, HUGH, 1790-1853   1
EVANS, JOHN, land surveyor, 1770-1851   1
EVANS, RHYS, 1835-1917   1
EVANS, WILLIAM JOHN, 1866-1947   2
FOULKES, ROBERT, 1743-1841   1
FRANCIS, GRIFFITH, 1876-1936 and OWEN, 1879-1936   1
FRANCIS, JOHN, 1789-1843   1
FROST, WILLIAM FREDERICK, 1846-91   1
GRIFFITH, MORGAN WILLIAM, 1855-1925   1
GRIFFITH, OWEN, 'Eryr Eryri', 1839-1903   1
GRIFFITH, ROBERT, 1847-1909 (not 1911)   1
GRIFFITH, ROWLAND, fl. 18c.   1
GRIFFITH, WILLIAM, 'Gwilym Caledffrwd', 1832-1913   1
GRIFFITHS, ROBERT, 1824-1903   1
GRUFFYDD, ROBERT, 1753-1820   1
GWALCHMAI ap DAFYDD, fl. 16c.   1
HARRIES, DAVID, 1747-1834   1
HARRIS, GRIFFITH, (not 1813) 1811-92   1
HAYDEN, HENRY SAMUEL, 1805-60   1
HENRY, JOHN, 1859-1914   1
HOWELLS, THOMAS, 'Hywel Cynon', 1839-1905   1
HUGHES, DAVID, 'Cristiolus Môn', 1810-81   1
HUGHES, EDWARD, 'Eos Maldwyn', ?-1862   2
HUGHES, GRIFFITH WILLIAM, 1861-1941   2
HUGHES, JAMES BILSLAND, 'Iago Bencerdd', 1831-78   1
HUGHES, JOHN, 1791-?   2
HUGHES, MEGAN WATTS, 1842-1907   1
HUGHES, RICHARD SAMUEL, 1855-93   1
HUGHES, WILLIAM, harpist, 1798-1866   1
HUGHES, WILLIAM JOHN, 1833-79   1
HUMPHREYS, HENRY, fl. 1819-24   1
HUW ap MORUS, fl. 1568   1
HUW DAI, fl. 1568   1
HUW MENAI, fl. 1523   2
JACOB, WILLIAM, 1777-1845   1
JAMES, CHARLES, 1820-90?   1
JAMES, DAVID, 1787-1862   1
JAMES, ROBERT, 'Jeduthyn', 1825-79   1
JEFFREYS, JOHN, 1718?-98   1
JONES, CADWALADR, 1794-1883   1
JONES, DAVID, emynydd, 1770-1831   1
JONES, DAVID, 'Dewi Wyllt', 1836-78?   2
JONES, EDWARD, 1749-79   1
JONES, EDWARD, 1768-1813   1
JONES, GRIFFITH HUGH, 1849-1919   1
JONES, GRIFFITH RHYS, 'Caradog', 1834-97   1
JONES, JOHN, musician, 1725?-96   2
JONES, JOHN, 'Idris Fychan', 1825-87   1
JONES, JOHN, 'Eos Bradwen', 1831-99   1
JONES, JOHN EDWARD, 'Iorwerth Twrog', 1886-1934   1: 1134
JONES, JOSEPH DAVID, 1827-70   1
JONES, MOSES OWEN, 1842-1908   1

JONES, ROBERT (WILFRID), 1862-1929	1
JONES, THOMAS, 'Gogrynwr', 1822-54	2
JONES, THOMAS, 'Canrhawdfardd', 1823-1904	1
JONES, THOMAS GRUFFYDD, 1832-98	1
LEWIS, DAVID, musician, 1828-1908	1
LEWIS, DAVID WILLIAM, 1845-1920	1
LEWIS, JOSEPH RHYS, 1860-1920	1
LEWIS, REES, 'Eos Ebrill', 1828-80	1
LLEWELYN, THOMAS DAVID, 1828-79	1
LLOYD, CHARLES FRANCIS, 1852-1917	1
LLOYD (FLOYD), JOHN, musician, 1480-1523	1
LLOYD, JOHN AMBROSE, 1815-74	1
LLWYD, HWLCYN, fl. 1523	1
LLWYD, STEPHEN, 1794-1854	1
LOWE, RICHARD, 1810-53	1
MARKS, DAVID, 1788-1871	1
MORGAN, ALFRED PHILLIPS, 1857-1942	2
MORGAN, DAFYDD SIENCYN, 1752-1844	1
MORGAN, EVAN, 1846-1920	1
OWEN, DAVID, 1711/12-1741	1
OWEN, HUGH, musician, 1832-97	1
OWEN, JOHN, 'Owain Alaw', 1821-83	1
OWEN, JOHN JONES, 1876-1947	2
OWEN, RICHARD GRIFFITH, 1869-1930	1
OWEN, WILLIAM, Gwilym Ddu Glan Hafren, 1788-1838	1
OWEN, WILLIAM, Prysgol, 1813-93	1
OWEN, WILLIAM, musician, 1830-65	1
PARRY, JOHN, 'The Blind Harpist', 1710?-82	1
PARRY, JOHN, 'Bardd Alaw', 1776-1851	1
PRICE, JOHN, musician, 1857-1930	1
PRICE, THOMAS, musician, 1809-92	1
PRITCHARD, JOHN THOMAS, 1859-90	1
PRITCHARD, ROWLAND HUW, 1811-87	1
PROTHERO, DANIEL, 1866-1934	1
RANDLES, EDWARD, 1763-1820	1
RANDLES, ELIZABETH, 1801?-29	1
REES, GEORGE, (GEORGE REES HEYCOCK), 1873-1950	2
REES, ROBERT, 'Eos Morlais', 1841-92	1
REES, WILLIAM THOMAS, 1838-1904	1
RICHARDS, DAVID, 1822-1900	1
RICHARDS, HENRY BRINLEY, 1819-85	1
RICHARDS, JOHN, 'Isalaw', 1843-1901	1
ROBERTS, CARADOG, 1878-1935	1
ROBERTS, DAVID, 'Alawydd', 1820-72	1
ROBERTS, ELEAZAR, 1825-1912	1
ROBERTS, JOHN, musician, 1806-79	1
ROBERTS, JOHN, musician, 1807-76	1
ROBERTS, JOHN, 'Alaw Elwy', 1816-94	1
ROBERTS, JOHN, 'Ieuan Gwyllt', 1822-77	1
ROBERTS, JOHN HENRY, 1848-1924	1
ROBERTS, LEWIS, 'Eos Twrog', 1756-1844	1
ROBERTS, RICHARD, 'Y Telynor Dall', (not 1796) 1769-1855	1
ROBERTS, ROBERT, musician, 1840-71	1
ROBERTS, THOMAS OSBORNE, 1879-1948	2
ROBERTS, WILLIAM, 'Wil Brych', fl. c.1825	1
ROBERTS, WILLIAM MORGAN, 1853-1923	1
ROGERS, ROLAND, 1847-1927	1
SAMUEL, WILLIAM THOMAS, 1852-1917	1
STEPHEN, EDWARD JONES, 1822-85	1
STEPHEN, THOMAS, musician, 1856-1906	1
THOMAS, EDWARD WILLIAM, 1814-92	1
THOMAS, JOHN, 'Ieuan Ddu', 1795-1871	1
THOMAS, JOHN, 'Pencerdd Gwalia', 1826-1913	1
THOMAS, JOHN, Llanwrtyd, 1839-1921	1
WILLIAMS, BENJAMIN MORRIS, 1832-1903	1
WILLIAMS, DAVID CHRISTMAS, 1871-1926	1
WILLIAMS, EVAN, harpist, 1706-?	1
WILLIAMS, FOULK ROBERT, (not 1774) c.1782-1870	1
WILLIAMS, JOHN, 'Ioan Rhagfyr', 1740-1821	1
WILLIAMS, JOHN, 'Siôn Singer', c.1750-1807	1
WILLIAMS, JOHN, 'Gorfyniawc o Arfon', 1814-78	1
WILLIAMS, JOHN, 1856-1917	1: 1156-7
WILLIAMS, MARIA JANE, 'Llinos', 1795-1873	1

WILLIAMS, OWEN, 1774->1827 [to 1839]   1
WILLIAMS, ROBERT HERBERT, 'Corfanydd', 1805-76   1
WILLIAMS, THOMAS, 'Hafrenydd', 1807-94   1
WILLIAMS, WILLIAM AUBREY, 1838-91   1
WYNNE, SARAH EDITH, 'Eos Cymru', 1842-97   1
GRIFFITH, WILLIAM   **W.G.**
ELLIS, JOHN GRIFFITH, 1723/4-1805   1: 1119
JONES, WILLIAM, 1718->1778 (not 1773?)   1
THOMAS, RICHARD, 1718-1807   1
GRIFFITHS, DAVID GORONWY   **D.G.G.**
EVANS, DAVID, 'Dewi Dawel', 1814-91   1
GRIFFITHS, DAVID JOHN   **D.J.G.**
PHILIPPS, LAURENCE RICHARD, 1874-1962   2
GRIFFITHS, GRIFFITH MILWYN   **G.M.G.**
BARKER, THOMAS WILLIAM, 1861-1912   1
BEFIS, n.d.   2
BEVAN, EVAN, 'Ianto'r Castell', 1803-66   1
BRACE, WILLIAM, 1865-1947   2
BRERETON, JANE, 'Melissa', 1685-1740   1
BULKELEY, HUGH, fl. 17c.   1
BULKELEY, RICHARD, fl. 16c.-17c.   1
CRADOCK, MATHEW or MATHIAS, Sir, 1468?-1531   1
EDWARD ap ROGER, 16c.   1: 1118
EDWARDS, FRANCIS, Sir, 1852-1927   1
EDWARDS, THOMAS, 'Arfona', fl. c.1824   1
EDWARDS, WILLIAM, 'Gwilym Padarn', 1786-1857   1
EDWART URIEN, fl. 17c.   1
EVANS, JOHN, 'Ioan Tachwedd', 1790-1856   1
FOULKES, HENRY POWELL, 1815-86   2
FOULKES, HUMPHREY, 1673-1737 (not 1747)   1
FOULKES, PETER, 1676-1747   1
FOULKES, WILLIAM, fl. 1699 - see under FOULKES, WILLIAM (?-1691)   1
GILBERTSON, LEWIS, 1815-96   1
GRIFFITH, ROBERT ARTHUR, 1860-1936   1
GRIFFITHS, EVAN THOMAS, 1886-1967   2
GRIFFITHS, ROBERT, inventor, 1805-83   1
GRIFFITHS, WILLIAM, 1898-1962   2
GROVE, WILLIAM ROBERT, Sir, 1811-96   1
GRUFFYDD, JEREMY (or IEUAN), 'Teiliwr Llawen', 17c.   1
GRUFFYDD, OWEN, c.1643-1730   1
HOLLAND, Family, Berw, Anglesey   1
HUGHES, WILLIAM, engineer, 1779-1836   2
HUW ARWYSTLI, fl. 1550   1
JAMES, DAVID, 'Dewi o Ddyfed', 1803-71   1
JAMES, JAMES, 'Iago Emlyn', 1800-79   1
JAMES, JENKIN, 1875-1949   2
JAMES, MARIA, 1793-1868   2
JAMES, THOMAS EVAN, 1824-70   1
JENKINS, JABEZ EDMUND, 1840-1903   1
JENKINS, LLEWELYN, 1810-78   1
JONES, ALFRED LEWIS, Sir, 1845-1909   1
JONES, DANIEL ANGELL, 1861-1936   2
JONES, DAVID, of Trefriw, 1708?-85   1
JONES, EDMUND DAVID, 1869-1941   2
JONES, JOHN, classical scholar, 1766?-1827   1
JONES, JOHN, printer, 1807-75   1
JONES, JOHN MORGAN, Merthyr Tydfil, 1861-1935   1
JONES, JOHN SHARE, 1873-1950   2
JONES, MARGARET, 'Y Gymraes o Ganaan', ?-1902   2
JONES, RICHARD, Llanfair Caereinion, 1603-55/6?   1
JONES, RICHARD, 1603?-73   1
JONES, WILLIAM, 'Gwilym Myrddin', 1863-1946   2
KEMEYS and KEMEYS-TYNTE, Family, Cefn Mabli, Mon.   1
LEWIS, DAVID, lawyer, 1848-97   1
LEWIS, MATHEW, 1817?-60   1
LEWIS, RICHARD, 1817-65   1
LEWIS, ROBERT EDWARD, 18c.   1
LEWIS, WILFRID HUBERT POYER, Sir, 1881-1950   2
LEWIS, WILLIAM MORTIMER, 1840-80   1
LLOYD, DAVID, ?-1747?   1
LLOYD, EVAN, of Maes-y-porth, 1728-1801   1: 1140-1
LLOYD, HANNIBAL EVANS, 1771-1847   1
LLWYD, Yr USTUS, fl. 14c.   1

LUCAS, RICHARD, 1648-1715 — 1
MANUEL, DAVID, 1624?-1726 — 1
MORGAN, HERBERT, 1875-1946 — 2
MORTIMER, Family, Wigmore, Herefs. — 1
MORTIMER, ROGER de, 1256?-1326 — 1
NORTH, HERBERT LUCK, 1871-1941 — 2
PARRY, MORRIS, fl. 1661-83 — 1: 1145
RHYS, HYWEL, 1715?-99 — 1
RHYS, IFAN THOMAS, fl. 18c. — 1
RHYS ap HARRI o EUAS, fl. 16c. — 1
RICHARDS, THOMAS, 1859-1931 — 2
ROBERTS, EDWARD, fl. 18c. — 1
ROBERTS, RICHARD ARTHUR, 1851-1943 — 2
ROBERTS, WILLIAM, writer of interludes, fl. 1745 — 1
ROBERTS, WILLIAM, 'Gwilym Eryri', 1844-95? — 1
SION ap HYWEL ap LLYWELYN FYCHAN, fl. c.1526 — 1
SION CERI, fl. 1500?-30? — 1
SION CLYWEDOG (SION IEUAN CLYWEDOG), fl. c.1610-30 — 1
SION DAFYDD ap SIENCYN, 16c.-17c. — 1
SION TREFOR (JOHN TREFOR), n.d. — 1
THOMAS, DAVID, 'Dewi Hefin', 1828-1909 — 1
THOMAS, HUMPHREY, 1745-1805 - see under THOMAS, DAVID
  (1759-1822) — 1
THOMAS, JOHN, of Bodedern, fl. 1719 — 1
THOMAS BRWYNLLYS, fl. c.1580-90 — 1
THOMAS DERLLYS, fl. 15c. — 1
THOMAS GRYTHOR, 17c. — 1
THOMAS GWYNEDD, fl. 16c. — 1
THOMAS PENLLYN, ?-1623 — 1
THOMAS TEIFI, fl. 16c. — 1
WILIAM EGWAD, c.1450 — 1
WILLIAMS, EVAN JAMES, 1903-1945 — 2
GRIFFITHS, RHIDIAN — Rh.G.
DAVIES, WILLIAM HUBERT, 1893-1965 — 2
PARR-DAVIES, HARRY, (HARRY PARR DAVIES), 1914-1955 — 2
REES-DAVIES, IEUAN, 1894-1967 — 2
SNELL, DAVID JOHN, 1880-1957 — 2
THOMAS, DAVID FFRANGCON, 1910-1963 — 2
WALTERS, THOMAS GLYN, (WALTER GLYNNE), 1890-1970 — 2
GRIFFITHS, RHYS LEWIS — R.L.G.
BOWEN, Family, Llwyngwair, Pembs. — 1
GRIFFITHS, THOMAS ELWYN — T.E.G.
JONES, THOMAS OWEN, 1875-1941 — 2
GRUFFUDD, CERIS — C.G.
EVANS, WILLIAM MEIRION, 1826-83 — 2
GRUFFYDD, ROBERT GERAINT — G.G.
DAVIES, JOHN GLYN, 1870-1953 — 2
SMYTH, ROGER, 1541-1625 — 1
HABAKKUK, JOHN HROTHGAR — J.H.H.
JONES, EDGAR WILLIAM, 1868-1953 — 2
HARRIES, LESLIE — L.H.
GWERFUL MECHAIN, 1462?-1500 — 1
HUW CAE LLWYD, fl. 1431-1504 — 1
IEUAN ap HUW CAE LLWYD, 1477?-1500 — 1
IEUAN DYFI, 1461?-1500 — 1
HARTMANN, EDWARD GEORGE — E.G.H.
WILLIAMS, DANIEL JENKINS, 1874-1952 — 2
HAVARD, WILLIAM THOMAS — W.T.H.
HUGHES, JOSHUA, 1807-89 — 1
SHORT, THOMAS VOWLER, 1790-1872 — 1
HOCKEY, LAWRENCE WILLIAM — L.W.H.
DAVIES, WILLIAM HENRY, 1871-1940 — 1
HOLMES, GRAEME — G.H.
WILLIAMS, EVAN, Sir, 1871-1959 — 2
HOOSON, HUGH EMLYN — H.E.H.
HOOSON, JOHN, 1883-1969 — 2
HOPKIN, DEIAN R. — D.R.Ho.
MACDONALD, GORDON, 1888-1966 — 2
HOPKINS, DONALD WALTER — D.W.H.
EDWARDS, CHARLES ALFRED, 1882-1960 — 2
HOPKINS, THOMAS JAMES — T.J.H.
GRAY, THOMAS, 1847-1924 — 1: 1123
JONES, DAVID, 1834-90 — 1: 1131

HOPPER, L. N.   L.N.H.
    CRAWSHAY, GEOFFREY CARTLAND HUGH, Sir, 1892-1954   2
HUDSON-WILLIAMS, THOMAS   T.H.-W.
    ROBERTS, WILLIAM RHYS, 1858-1929   1
    WILLIAMS, WILLIAM PRICHARD, 1848-1916   1
HUGH, RICHARD LEONARD   R.L.H.
    PARCELL, GEORGE HENRY, 1895-1967   2
HUGHES, ALFRED ERNEST   A.E.H.
    HUGHES, WILLIAM, Dolgellau, 1838-1921   1
HUGHES, ARWYN LLOYD   A.Ll.H.
    DAVIES, MORRIS, 1891-1961   2
    EDWARDS, FANNY WINIFRED, 1876-1959   2
    EVANS, THOMAS CHRISTOPHER, Cadrawd, 1846-1918   2
    HOOSON, ISAAC DANIEL, 1880-1948   2
    JONES, EVAN, 'Ieuan Buallt', 1850-1928   2
    JONES, RICHARD, 1848-1915   2
    JONES, ROBERT LLOYD, 1878-1959   2
    LLOYD, JOHN, 1885-1964   2
    OWEN, HUGH JOHN, 1880-1961   2
    ROWLANDS, EDWARD DAVID, 1880-1969   2
    THOMAS, THOMAS HENRY, 'Arlunydd Penygarn, 1839-1915   2
HUGHES, DAVID ROWLAND   D.R.H.
    JONES, JOHN, 'Jac Glanygors', 1766-1821   1
HUGHES, GARFIELD HOPKIN   G.H.H.
    DAVIES, JAMES, 'Iaco ap Dewi', 1648-1722   1
    DWNN, GRUFFYDD, c.1500-1570   1
    DWNN, JAMES, c.1570-1660   1
    DWNN, LEWYS, c.1550-1616   1
    DWNN, OWAIN, c.1400-1460   1
    EDWARDS, JOHN, 'Siôn y Potiau', c.1700-76   1
    ELIAS, WILLIAM, 1708-87   1
    JOHNS, DAVID, Llanfair Dyffryn Clwyd, fl. 1569-86 (instead of 1573-87)   1
    PERRI (PARRY), HENRY, 1560/1-1617   1
    POWELL, THOMAS, 1608?-60   1
    SIMON, BEN, c.1703-93   1
HUGHES, GLYN RHYS   G.R.H.
    BOWEN, DAVID, 'Myfyr Hefin', 1874-1955   2
HUGHES, GLYN TEGAI   G.T.H.
    DAVIES, GWENDOLINE ELIZABETH, 1882-1951   2
    DAVIES, MARGARET SIDNEY, 1884-1963   2
HUGHES, HOWELL HARRIS   H.H.H.
    HUGHES, JOHN RICHARD, 1828-93   1
HUGHES, JOHN   J.H.
    JONES, DAVID JOHN TAWE, 1885-1949   2
    ROBERTS, OWEN OWENS, 1847-1926   1
    WILLIAMS, WILLIAM ALBERT, 1909-46   2
HUGHES, JOHN EDWARD   J.E.H.
    ELIAS, JOHN, 1774-1841   1
    WILLIAMS, HUGH, church historian, 1843-1911   1
    WILLIAMS, JOHN, Brynsiencyn, 1854-1921   1
    WILLIAMS, THOMAS CHARLES, 1868-1927   1
HUGHES, JOHN WILLIAMS   J.W.H.
    DAVIES, DAVID, author, 1849-1926   1
    EDWARDS, WILLIAM, 1848-1929   1
HUGHES, NORMA GWYNETH   N.G.H.
    BEDO HAFESP, fl. 1568   1
    BEDO PHYLIP BACH, fl. 1480   1
    CADWALADR, RHYS, Sir, ?-1690   1
    CADWALADR ap RHYS TREFNANT, fl. 1600   1
    CADWALADR CESAIL, fl. 1620   1
HUGHES, RICHARD EDMUND   R.E.H.
    EVANS, DANIEL SILVAN, 1818-1903   1
HUGHES, ROBERT GWILYM   R.G.H.
    WYNN, WILLIAM, 1709-60   1
HUGHES, ROBERT RICHARD   R.R.H.
    JONES, JOHN PULESTON, 1862-1925   1
HUGHES, ROBERT WILLIAM   R.W.H.
    HUGHES, EDWARD, 'Y Dryw', 1772-1850   1
HUGHES, THOMAS MICHAEL   T.M.H.
    HUGHES, HUGH MICHAEL, 1858-1933   1
HUGHES, WILLIAM ROGER   W.R.H.
    SAUNDERS, WILLIAM, 1806-51   1

HUMFREY, BELINDA	**B.H.**
POWYS, JOHN COWPER, 1872-1963	2
HUMPHREYS, CHARLES HEBER	**C.H.H.**
GRIFFITHS, JOHN, artist, Bombay, 1837-1918	1
HUMPHREYS, EDWARD MORGAN	**E.M.H.**
APPERLEY, CHARLES JAMES, 1779-1843	1
ARMSTRONG-JONES, ROBERT, Sir, 1857-1943	2
BRYAN, ROBERT, 1858-1920	1
DAVIES, JOHN, 'Gwyneddon', 1832-1904	1
DAVIES, OWEN, 1840-1929	1
ELLIS-GRIFFITH, ELLIS JONES, Sir, 1860-1926	1
EVANS, BERIAH GWYNFE, 1848-1927	1
EVANS, JOHN EMRYS, 1853-1931	1
EVANS, SAMUEL, 1859-1935	1
EVANS, TIM, 1877-1939	1
GEE, THOMAS, 1815-98	1
GRIFFITH, WILLIAM JOHN, 1875-1931	1
HOBLEY, WILLIAM, 1858-1933	1
HUGHES, HENRY BAILEY, 1833-87	1
HUGHES, JOHN EVAN, 1865-1932	1
HUGHES, JOHN JAMES, 'Alfardd', 1842-75	1
HUGHES, THOMAS, 'Glan Pherath', 1803-98	1
HUMPHREYS, HUGH, 1817-96	1
HUMPHREYS, RICHARD, 1790-1863	1
JONES, EVAN, 1836-1915	1
JONES, GRIFFITH HARTWELL, 1859-1944	2
JONES, JOHN EVANS, 1839-93	1
JONES, JOHN HUGH, 1843-1910	1
JONES, SAMUEL MAURICE, 1853-1932	1
JONES, WILLIAM RICHARD, 'Goleufryn', 1840-98	1
LEWIS, ALFRED EDWARD, Sir, 1868-1940	1
LEWIS, HUGH DAVIES, 1866-1937 – see under LEWIS, Sir ALFRED (EDWARD)	1
LLOYD, MORGAN, 1820-93	1
LLOYD, RICHARD, Cricieth, 1834-1917	1
LLOYD GEORGE, DAVID, 1863-1945	2
MORGAN, EDWARD, 1817-71	1
MORGAN, GEORGE OSBORNE, 1826-97	1
MORGAN, RICHARD HUMPHREYS, 1850-99	1
MYTTON, JOHN, 1796-1834	1
OWEN, OWEN GRIFFITH, 'Alafon', 1847-1916	1
PARRY, ROBERT, 'Robyn Ddu Eryri', 1804-92	1
PRICE, JOHN ARTHUR, 1861-1942	2
REES, DANIEL, 1855-1931	1
ROBERTS, THOMAS ROWLAND, 1857?-1940	1
ROWLAND, ROBERT DAVID, 1853?-1944	2
THOMAS, EDWARD, 'Idriswyn', 1847-1906	1
WILLIAMS, CHARLES JAMES WATKIN, Sir, 1828-84	1
WILLIAMS, EVAN, 'the limner', 1816?-78	1
WILLIAMS, RICHARD HUGHES, 1878?-1919	1
WILLIAMS, THOMAS MARCHANT, Sir, 1845-1914	1
HUWS, RICHARD E.	**Ri.E.H.**
WILLIAMS, DANIEL, 1878-1968	2
IORWERTH, DYLAN	**D.I.**
ROBERTS, EDWARD STANTON, 1878-1938	2
JAMES, E. WYN	**E.Wy.J.**
HUGHES, JANE, 1811-c.1880	2
JAMES, JOHN WILLIAMS	**J.W.J.**
ALLEN, JAMES, 1802-97	1
BEYNON, THOMAS, 1744-1835 (not 1833)	1
BRISCOE, THOMAS, 1813-95	1
COTTON, JAMES HENRY, 1780-1862	1
DAVIES, JOHN, Durham, 1795-1861	1
DAVIES, RANDOLF, ?-1695	1
DAVIES, TIMOTHY, 1802-62	1
DEINIOL, ?-584	1
EVANS, JOHN, 1815-91	1
SAMSON, c.485-565	1
SEIRIOL, c.500-550	1
JAMES, MARY AURONWY	**M.A.J.**
ALBAN DAVIES, DAVID, 1873-1951	2
ALBAN DAVIES, JENKIN, 1901-1968	2
BERRY, Family, [Merthyr Tudful, Glam.]	2

JENKINS, A. DAVID FRASER	A.D.F.J.
JOHN, GWENDOLEN MARY, 1876-1939	2
JENKINS, DAFYDD	Da.J.
JOHNES, THOMAS, 1748-1816	1
JENKINS, DAVID (Aberystwyth; Penrhyn-coch)	D.J.
BIRCHINSHAW, WILLIAM, fl. 1584-1617	1
BRWMFFILD (BROMFIELD), MATTHEW, fl. 1520-60	1
DAVIES, ROGER, 'Syr', fl. c.1500	1
DAVIES-COOKE, Family, Gwysaney, Flints., successors of DAVIES Family, of Llannerch, and Gwysaney , 13c., 16c.-1824	1
DEIO ab IEUAN BWL, fl. c.1530	1
EDWARDES, DAVID EDWARD, 1832-98	1
EDWARDS, JOHN, 'Meiriadog', 1813-1906	1
ELLIS, DAVID, 1736-95	1
GLYNNE, Family, Hawarden, Flints.	1
GRIFFITH, Family, Carreglwyd, Anglesey	1
GWGON ap MEURIG, ?-871	1: 1127
HANSON, CARL AUGUST, 1872-1961	2
IEUAN ap RHYDDERCH ap IEUAN LLWYD, fl. 1430-70	1
JACOB, SARAH, 1857-69	1
JONES, DANIEL, 1725?-1806	1: 1131
JONES, GEORGE DANIEL, 1877-1955	2
LEWIS, SAMUEL SAVAGE, 1836-91, under LEWIS, GEORGE (1763-1822)	1
MORYS, HUW, 'Eos Ceiriog', 1622-1709	1
OWEN, FOULKE, fl. 1686	1
PHILLIPS, DANIEL, U.S.A., 1826-1905	2
PRYSE, Family, Gogerddan, Cards.	2
PUDDICOMBE, ANNE ADALISA, 1836-1908	1
THELWALL, Family, Plas y Ward, Bathafarn, Plas Coch and Llanbedr, Denbs.	1
THOMAS, ROBERT, poet, ?-1774	1
WILLIAMS, ISAAC, 1802-65	1
WILLIAMS, JOHN, 'Ioan Mai', 1823-87	1
WILLIAMS, ROBERT ROLFE, 1870-1948	2
JENKINS, DAVID (Aberystwyth)	D.Je.
JONES, ELIZABETH MARY, 'Moelona', 1877-1953	2
JONES, JOHN TYWI, 1870-1948	2
JENKINS, EMLYN GLASNANT	E.G.Je.
LEWIS, HOWELL ELVET, 1860-1953	2
JENKINS, GERAINT HUW	G.H.J.
MEREDITH, WILLIAM (BILLY), 1874-1958	2
JENKINS, GWYN	G.Je.
ORMSBY-GORE, WILLIAM GEORGE ARTHUR, 1885-1964	2
JENKINS, ISLWYN	I.Je.
DAVIES, IDRIS, 1905-1953	2
JENKINS, ROBERT THOMAS	R.T.J.
ABEL, JOHN, 1770-1819	2
ALLEN, EVAN OWEN, 1805-52	2
ALLEN, LANCELOT BAUGH, 1774-1845 - see under ALLEN, JOHN ROMILLY	1
AMBROSE, WILLIAM ROBERT, 1832-78	1
ANDREWS, JOSHUA, 1708?-93	1
ANWYL, EDWARD, 1786-1857	1
BADDY, THOMAS, ?-1729	1
BANKES, JOHN ELDON, Sir, 1854-1946	2
BARNWELL, EDWARD LOWRY, 1813-87	1
BEAUMONT, JAMES, ?-1750	1
BENNETT, RICHARD, 1860-1937	1
BEVAN, LLEWELYN DAVID, 1842-1918	1
BEVAN, SILVANUS, 1691-1765	1
BEYNON, THOMAS, ?-1729	1
BIRCH, JAMES, ?-1795?	1
BLOOM, MILBOURN, ?-1766	1
BOLD, HUGH, 1731-1809	1; 2
BRERETON, ANDREW JONES, 1827-85	1
BRERETON, OWEN SALUSBURY, 1715-98	1
BRIDGEMAN, GEORGE THOMAS ORLANDO, 1823-95	1
BROMLEY, HUMPHREY, fl. 1826	1
BRYAN, ROBERT, 1858-1920	1
BULMER, JOHN, 1784-1857	1
CADWALADR, DAFYDD, 1752-1834	1
CAMPBELL (later MORRIESON), ELIZA CONSTANTIA, 1796-1864	1
CARTER, Family, Kinmel, Denbs.	1: 1113-4

JOB, ENAF MORRICE   E.M.J.
     JOB, JOHN THOMAS, 1867-1938   1
JOHN, JAMES MANSEL   J.M.J.
     JENKINS, JOHN, Hengoed, 1779-1853   1
JOHNSTON, SAMUEL HENRY FERGUS   S.H.F.J.
     LLOYD, HENRY, c.1720-83   1
     MORGAN, THOMAS, Sir, c.1542-95   1
     NOTT, WILLIAM, Sir, 1782-1845   1
     PICTON, THOMAS, Sir, 1758-1815   1
JONES, ALWYN RICE   Al.R.J.
     JONES, ROBERT EVAN, 1869-1956   2
JONES, ANNIE GWENLLIAN   A.G.J.
     HUGHES, JOHN, pioneer of iron-works in Russia, 1814-89   1
JONES, ARTHUR ROCYN   A.R.J.
     JONES, ROBERT, Sir, 1857-1933   1
     JONES, THOMAS ROCYN, 1822-77   1
     LYNN-THOMAS, JOHN, Sir, 1861-1939   1
     THOMAS, HUGH OWEN, 1834-91   1
JONES, BEDWYR LEWIS   B.L.J.
     CEMLYN-JONES, ELIAS WYNNE, Sir, 1888-1966   2
     FISHER, FRANCIS GEORGE, 1909-1970   2
     FOULKES, ANNIE, 1877-1962   2
     HUMPHREYS, EDWARD OWEN, 1899-1959   2
     JONES, EDWARD OWEN, 1871-1953   2
     LEWIS, LEWIS WILLIAM, 'Llew Llwyfo', 1831-1901   2
     PIERCE, JOHN, 1889-1955   2
     RADMILOVIC, PAUL, 1886-1968   2
     SION ap HOWEL ab OWAIN, 1550?-1626/7   2
     WATKIN-JONES, ELIZABETH, 1887-1966   2
     WILLIAMS, WILLIAM WYN, 1876-1936   2
JONES, BENJAMIN GEORGE   B.G.J.
     CECIL-WILLIAMS, JOHN LIAS CECIL, Sir, 1892-1964   2
JONES, DAFYDD   Da.Jo.
     JENKINS, EVAN, 1895-1959   2
JONES, DANIEL BERTRAM   D.B.J.
     JONES, EDWARD, 'Iorwerth Goes Hir', 1824-80   1
JONES, DAVID BRINLEY CLAY   D.B.C.J.
     RUSSON, WILLIAM CLAYTON, Sir, 1895-1968   2
JONES, DAVID GWENALLT   D.G.J.
     DERFEL, ROBERT JONES, 1824-1905   1
     EDMUNDS, WILLIAM, 1827-75   1
     EVANS, DANIEL, 'Daniel Ddu', 1792-1846   1
     EVANS, EVAN, 'Ieuan Glan Geirionydd', 1795-1855   1
     EVANS, WILLIAM EILIR, 1852-1910   1
     HOWELL, DAVID, 'Llawdden', 1831-1903   1
     HUGHES, JOHN CEIRIOG, 'Ceiriog', 1832-87   1
     HUGHES, RICHARD, ?-1618   1
     JAMES, EDWARD, 1569?-1610?   1
     JENKINS, JOHN, 'Ifor Ceri', 1770-1829   1
     JONES, JOHN, 'Talhaiarn', 1810-69   1
     JONES, OWEN WYNNE, 'Glasynys', 1828-70   1
     JONES, RICHARD IDWAL MERVYN, 1895-1937   1
     JONES, RHYS (or RICE), 1713-1801   1
     JONES, WILLIAM, 'Ehedydd Iâl', 1815-99   1
     LANGFORD, JOHN, 1650?-1715/6?   1
     LEWIS, LEWIS WILLIAM, 'Llew Llwyfo', 1831-1901   1
     OWEN, GORONWY, 1723-69   1
     PRICHARD, RHYS, 'Yr Hen Ficer', 1579?-1644   1
     RICHARD, EDWARD, 1714-77   1
     RICHARDS, DAVID, 'Dafydd Ionawr', 1751-1827   1
     THOMAS, WILLIAM, 'Islwyn', 1832-78   1
JONES, DAVID PEREGRINE   D.P.J.
     LEWIS, DAVID JOHN, 'Lewis Tymbl', 1879-1947   2
JONES, DAVID THOMAS   D.T.J.
     JONES, JOSIAH TOWYN, 1858-1925   1
JONES, DERWYN (Bangor; also Colwyn Bay)   D.Jo.; also De.J.
     DAVIES, GLYNNE GERALLT, 1916-1968   2
     HOWARD, JAMES HENRY, 1876-1947   2
     JONES, DAVID HUGH, 'Dewi Arfon', 1833-1869   2
     ROBERTS, JOHN, 'Minimus', 1808-80   1: 1148
     ROBERTS, RICHARD, 1874-1945   2
     STEPHEN, ROBERT, 1878-1966   2
     THOMAS, MORRIS, 1874-1959   2

JONES, DERWYN MORRIS   D.M.J.
  DAVIES, DAVID TEGFAN, 1883-1968   2
  MORRIS, ROBERT DAVID, 1871-1948   2
JONES, EDGAR   E.J.
  EDWARDS, WILLIAM, inspector of schools, 1851-1940   1
  JONES, JOHN VIRIAMU, 1856-1901   1
  OWEN, OWEN, 1850-1920   1
JONES, EDWARD   Ed.J.
  HUMPHREYS, DAVID, 1813-66   2
  HUMPHREYS, GEORGE, 1747?-1813   1
  JONES, JAMES, 'Iago Mochnant', 19c.   1
JONES, EDWYN HENRY STUART   E.H.S.J.
  HASSALL, CHARLES, 1754-1814   1
JONES, ELIS GWYN   El.G.J.
  MORRIS, CAREY, 1882-1968   2
  WILLIAMS, HUGH DOUGLAS, 1917-1969   2
JONES, ELIZABETH (BETHAN) EIRLIW LOUIS   E.E.L.J.
  JONES, ELIZABETH JANE LOUIS, 1889-1952   2
JONES, EMRYS WYNN   Em.W.J.
  JONES, FRANCIS WYNN, 1898-1970   2
JONES, EMYR GWYNNE   E.G.J.
  CONWAY or CONWY, Family, Botryddan, Flints.   1: 1115-6
  FYNES-CLINTON, OSBERT HENRY, 1869-1941   2
  GOODEN, JAMES, 1670-1730   1
  GRIFFITH, Family, Cefn Amwlch, Caerns.   1; 2
  GRIFFITH, JOHN, Llanddyfnan, fl. 1649-69   1
  GWYN, RICHARD, (or RICHARD WHITE), c.1557-84   1
  HUGHES, HUGH ROBERT, 1827-1911   1
  HUGHES, JOHN, (or HUGH OWEN), 1615-86   1
  HUGHES, WILLIAM BULKELEY, 1797-1882   1
  IRBY, GEORGE FLORANCE, 1860-1941   2
  JONES, ELIAS HENRY, 1883-1942   2
  JONES, JOHN, 'Leander a Sancto Marino', 1575-1636   1
  LEWIS, OWEN, 1533-95   1
  LLOYD, HUMPHREY, bishop of Bangor, 1610-88/9   1
  MEREDITH, RICHARD, ?-1597   1
  MEYRICK, Family, Bodorgan, Anglesey   1
  MORGAN, WILLIAM, Sir, ?-1584   1
  MORGAN, WILLIAM, Jesuit, 1623-89   1
  OWEN, HUGH, Gwenynog, 1575?-1642   1
  OWEN, LEWIS, 1572-1629?   1
  OWEN, WILLIAM, antiquary, 1785-1864   1
  PAGET, Family, Plas Newydd, Anglesey   1
  PHILLIPS, MORGAN, ?-1570   1
  POWELL, EDWARD, 1478?-1540   1
  PULESTON, Family, Emral, Plas-ym-mers, Hafod-y-wern, Caernarfon   1
  PULESTON, JOHN HENRY, Sir, 1829-1908   1
  ROBERTS, JOHN, Benedictine monk, 1576-1610   1
  SALUSBURY, SALISBURY, SALESBURY, Family, Lleweni, and Bachygraig   1
  SALUSBURY, Family, Rug, Mer., and Bachymbyd, Denbs.   1
  SALUSBURY, JOHN, 1575-1625   1
  SALUSBURY, THOMAS, (not 1564) 1561-86   1
  SALUSBURY, THOMAS, Sir, 1612-43   1
  SMITH, THOMAS ASSHETON, 1752-1828   1
  WILLIAMS, JOHN, Treffos, 1784-1876 - see under WILLIAMS, JAMES   1
  WILLIAMS, JOHN, Beaumaris, 1833-72   1
  WILLIAMS, WILLIAM, antiquary, c.1625-84   1
  WYNN, Family, Wynnstay, Denbs.   1
JONES, EMYR WYN   E.W.J.
  DAVIES, HUGH MORRISTON, 1879-1965   2
  EVANS, GRIFFITH IFOR, 1889-1966   2
  JONES, ENID WYN, 1909-1967   2
  LEWIS, EMLYN EVANS, 1905-1969   2
  PARRY, CALEB HILLIER, 1755-1822 - see under PARRY, JOSHUA   2
  REES, JOHN MILSOM, Sir, 1866-1952   2
  ROCYN-JONES, DAVID THOMAS, Sir, 1862-1953   2
  THOMAS, WILLIAM THELWALL, 1865-1927   1: 1152-3
  WILLIAMS, OWEN HERBERT, 1884-1962   2
JONES, EVAN DAVID   E.D.J.
  ALBAN, FREDERICK JOHN, Sir, 1882-1965   2
  ALBAN DAVIES, JENKIN, 1901-1968   2
  ALIS verch GRUFFUDD, 1540-70   1
  BARSTOW, GEORGE LEWIS, Sir, 1874-1966   2

JONES, HENRY PARRY	H.P.J.
ROBERTS, WILLIAM JOHN, (not 1827) 1828-1904	1
JONES, HUGH DAVID	H.D.J.
MARTIN, RICHARD, Sir, 1843-1922	1: 1141-2
JONES, IDWAL	I.J.
JONES, THOMAS, Denbigh, 1756-1820	1
LEWIS, JOHN HERBERT, Sir, 1858-1933	1
JONES, IEUAN SAMUEL	I.S.J.
EVANS, WILLIAM, 1869-1948	2
JONES, DANIEL OWEN, 1880-1951	2
JONES, JOHN THOMAS, 1889-1952	2
JONES, IORWERTH	Io.J.
DAVIES, BEN, 1878-1958	2
DAVIES, DANIEL JOHN, 1885-1970	2
JONES, IWAN MEICAL	I.M.J.
JONES, CALVERT RICHARD, 1802-1877	2
JONES, JOHN CHARLES	J.C.J.
JONES, EVAN, 'Ieuan Buallt', 1850-1928	1
JONES, JOHN DAVID	J.D.J.
JEREMY, JOHN DAVID, 1782-1860	1
JEREMY, WALTER DAVID, 1825-93	1
JONES, REES JENKIN, 1835-1924	1
JONES, JOHN GRAHAM	J.G.J.
AWBERY, STANLEY STEPHEN, 1888-1969	2
BEVAN, ANEURIN, 1897-1960	2
DEAKIN, ARTHUR, 1890-1955	2
EDWARDS, HUW THOMAS, 1892-1970	2
HUGHES, EMRYS DANIEL, 1894-1969	2
JONES, LEWIS, Sir, 1884-1968	2
JONES, WILLIAM, Sir, 1888-1961	2
MARDY-JONES, THOMAS ISAAC, 1879-1970	2
MATHIAS, RONALD CAVILL, 1912-1968	2
MORGAN, IWAN JAMES, 1904-1966	2
MORRIS, PERCY, 1893-1967	2
MYRDDIN-EVANS, GUILDHAUME, Sir, 1894-1964	2
OWEN, GORONWY, Sir, 1881-1963	2
ROBERTS, GEORGE FOSSETT, Sir, 1870-1954	2
ROCH, WALTER FRANCIS, 1880-1965	2
THOMAS, DAVID EMLYN, 1892-1954	2
THOMAS, IORWERTH RHYS, 1895-1966	2
THOMAS, ROBERT JOHN, Sir, 1873-1951	2
VAUGHAN, JOHN, 1871-1956	2
WILLIAMS, CHRISTMAS PRICE, 1881-1965	2
WILLIAMS, EDWARD JOHN (TED), Sir, 1890-1963	2
WILLIAMS, WILLIAM JOHN, 1878-1952	2
WILLIS, ALBERT CHARLES, 1876-1954	2
WYNDHAM-QUIN, WINDHAM HENRY, 1857-1952	2
JONES, JOHN GWILYM	Jo.G.J.
YORKE, SIMON, 1903-1966	2
JONES, JOHN HENRY	J.H.J.
OWEN, JOHN, epigrammatist, 1564?-1628?	1
JONES, JOHN IDWAL	J.Id.J.
JONES, WILLIAM, 1762-1846	1
JONES, JOHN ISLAN	J.I.J.
DAVIES, JOHN PARK, 1879-1937	1
JONES, JOHN JAMES	J.J.J.
DAVIES, MYLES (or MILES), 1662-1715?	1
DEE, JOHN, 1527-1608	1
EVANS, WILLIAM, Rhymney, 1823-1900	1
GWENT, RICHARD, ?-1543	1
GWYNNETH, JOHN, 1490?-1562?	1
HUGHES, HENRY MALDWYN, 1875-1940	1
HUGHES, JANE, fl. c.1840-80	1
HUMPHREYS, RICHARD GRIFFITH, 1848-1924	1
LLOYD, DAVID, dean of S. Asaph, 1597-1663	1
LLOYD, DAVID, biographer, 1635-92	1
LLOYD, DAVID, Llanbister, 1752-1838	1
LLOYD, HUGH, master of Winchester college, 1546-1601	1
LLOYD, LUDOVIC, fl. 1573-1610	1
LLOYD (or LLOYDE), OLIVER, 1570/1-1625	1
LLUELYN (or LLEWELLIN), MARTIN, 1616-82	1
MAURICE, DAVID, 1626-1702	1
MEURIG, fl. 1210	1

OWEN, EDWARD, 1729?-1807	1
OWEN, WILLIAM, lawyer, fl. c.1486-1574	1
PHAER (or PHAYER), THOMAS, 1510?-60	1
PHILIPPS, JENKIN THOMAS, ?-1755	1
PHILLIPS, JAMES, 1703-83	1
POWEL, CHARLES, 1712-96	1
PRICE (PRICAEUS), JOHN, c.1600-76	1
PRICE, JOHN, Bodley's librarian, 1734-1813	1
ROGER, of Conway, ?-1360	1
SPARK, THOMAS, 1655-92	1
THOMAS, LEWIS, 1565-1619	1
THOMAS, NATHANIEL, 1730->1760	1
WILLIAMS, JOHN, Oxford, ?-1613	1
JONES, JOHN LEWIS	J.L.J.
ROBERTS, DAFYDD, 1892-1965	2
JONES, JOHN MORGAN	J.M.J.
JONES, CADWALADR BRYNER, Sir, 1872-1954	2
JONES, JOHN THOMAS (Rhiwabon)	J.T.J.
ELLIS, ROBERT, (Cynddelw) 1812-75	1
EVANS, CHRISTMAS, 1766-1838	1
JONES, JOHN RICHARD, 1765-1822	1
JONES, THOMAS, Rhydwilym, 1769-1850	1
JONES, JOHN THOMAS (Porthmadog)	J.T.Jo.
MORGAN, JOHN, 1662-1701	1
JONES, JOHN TYSUL	J.Ty.J.
LEWIS, Family, Llandysul, Cards.	2
LEWIS, JOHN DAVID, 1859-1914	1: 1139-40
JONES, JOHN WILLIAM	J.W.Jo.
DAVIES, JOHN DANIEL, 1874-1948	2
EDWARDS, JOHN KELT, 1875-1934	1
EDWARDS, WILLIAM THOMAS, 1863-1940	1
HUGHES, ROBERT OWEN, 'Elfyn', 1858-1919	1
JONES, JOHN, 'Ioan Brothen', 1868-1940	1
JONES, WILLIAM OWEN, Eos y Gogledd, 1868-1928	1
WILLIAMS, GRIFFITH JOHN, 1854-1933	1
JONES, KEITH WILLIAMS	K.W.J.
WILLIAMS, WILLIAM OGWEN, 1924-1969	2
JONES, KENNETH EMLYN	K.E.J.
WOOD, MARY MYFANWY, 1882-1967	2
JONES, MARIAN HENRY	M.H.J.
HUGHES, EDWARD ERNEST, 1877-1953	2
JONES, MOSES JOHN	M.J.J.
WILLIAMS, BENJAMIN HAYDN, 1902-1965	2
JONES, NANSI CERIDWEN	N.C.J.
BLEDDYN DDU, c.1200	1
CADWALADR, EDWARD, 16c.	1
CADWALADR, HUW, 17c.	1
CADWGAN FFOL, 13c.	1
CROPPER, THOMAS, 1869-1923	1
CYNFRIG ap DAFYDD GOCH, c.1420	1
DAFYDD PENNANT, 16c.	1
DAVIES, JOHN LLOYD, 1801-60	1
ELLIS, REES, fl. 1714	1
ELLIS, THOMAS, 'Eos Tegeingl', fl. 1824	1
EUTUN, OWAIN, c.15c.	1
EVANS, EVAN, Nantyglo, 1804-86	1
HARDING, JOHN DORNEY, Sir, 1809-68	1
HOPKINS, WILLIAM, 1706-86	1
JONES, JOHN MATHER, 1826-74	2
MEREDITH, BENJAMIN, 1700-49	1
MORGAN, RICHARD WILLIAMS, c.1815-1889	1
RHYS BRYCHAN, fl. c.1500	1
RHYS WYN ap CADWALADR, fl. c.1600	1
ROBERT ap HARRY, c.1580	1
THOMAS, THOMAS MORGAN, 1828-84	1
THOMAS, WILLIAM, poet, 1790-1861	1
JONES, OWAIN WILLIAM	O.W.J.
WHITEHEAD, LEWIS STANLEY, 1889-1956	2
JONES, RICHARD LESLIE	R.L.J.
JOSHUA, SETH, 1858-1925	2
JONES, ROBERT (BOBI) MAYNARD	R.M.J.
JONES, IDWAL, 1899-1966	2

JONES, WILLIAM EMRYS — W.E.J.
    JONES, HUMPHREY, 'Bryfdir', 1867-1947 — 2
JONES, WILLIAM PHILIP — W.P.J.
    JONES, JOHN HARRIS, 1827-85 — 1
JONES, WILLIAM ROSSER — W.R.J.
    JONES, THOMAS, Trealaw, 1871-1938 — 1
JOYNER, PAUL — P.J.
    JOHN, WILLIAM GOSCOMBE, Sir, 1860-1952 — 2
KENYON, Arglwydd — K.
    KENYON, Family, Gredington, Flints., and Peel Hall, Lancs. — 1
LAWSON, PHILIP HUGH — P.H.L.
    ANWYL, Family, Park, Llanfrothen, Mer. — 1
LEE, ARCHIBALD HENRY — A.H.L.
    JAMES, FRANK TREHARNE, 1861-1942 — 2
    WARD, JOHN, 1856-1922 — 1
    WILLIAMS, ISAAC JOHN, 1874-1939 — 1
LERRY, GEORGE GEOFFREY — G.G.L.
    DENNIS, HENRY, 1825-1906 — 1
    HUGHES, EDWARD, 1856-1925 — 1
    KENRICK, SAMUEL LLEWELYN, 1848-1933 - see under KENRICK, Family — 1
    ROBERTSON, HENRY, 1816-88 — 1
    TRAINER, JAMES, footballer, 1863-1915? — 1
LEVI, THOMAS ARTHUR — T.A.L.
    ATKIN, JAMES RICHARD, 1867-1944 — 2
    LEVI, THOMAS, 1825-1916 — 1
LEWIS, ANEIRIN — A.L.
    EVANS, EVAN, 'Ieuan Fardd', 1731-88 — 1
    WILLIAMS, GRIFFITH JOHN, 1892-1963 — 2
LEWIS, DAVID HUGHES — D.H.L.
    GRIFFITHS, WILLIAM, 'Ifander', 1830-1910 — 1
LEWIS, DAVID WYRE — D.W.L.
    LEWIS, JOHN, 'Eos Glyn Wyre', 1836-92 — 1
LEWIS, HENRY — H.L.
    EDWARDS, THOMAS, 'Caerfallwch', 1779-1858 — 1
    IOLO GOCH, c.1320-98 — 1
    POWEL, THOMAS, 1845-1922 — 1
    SION CENT, 1367?-1430? — 1
    THOMAS, WILLIAM, 'Glanffrwd', 1843-90 — 1
LEWIS, HYWEL DAVID — H.D.L.
    EDWARDS, DAVID MIALL, 1873-1941 — 2
LEWIS, IDWAL — I.L.
    BEDO AEDDREN, fl. c.1500 — 1
    CROWTHER, JOHN NEWTON, 1847-1928 — 1
    DAVIES, MARY, 'Mair Eifion', 1846-82 — 1
    EDWARDS, WILLIAM RICE, Sir, 1862-1923 — 1
    ELIAS, JOHN ROOSE, 1819-81 — 1
    EVAN-THOMAS, HUGH, Sir, 1862-1928 — 1
    EVANS, DAVID TREHARNE, Sir, 1849-1907 — 1
    GRIFFITH, WILLIAM, 1853-1918 — 1
    HUGHES, ALFRED WILLIAM, 1861-1900 — 1
    HUGHES, HUGH (BRYTHON), 1848-1913 — 1
    HUGHES, ISAAC, 1852-1928 — 1
    JONES, HUMPHREY ROWLAND, 1832-95 — 1
    JONES, JOHN, 'Mephiboseth', 1850-1926 — 1
    JONES, NATHANIEL CYNHAFAL, 1832-1905 — 1
    JONES, WILLIAM OWEN, 1861-1937 — 1
    LLOYD, WILLIAM VALENTINE, 1825-96 — 1
    OWEN, JOHN, 'Ap Glaslyn', 1857-1934 - see under OWEN,
        RICHARD JONES — 1
    PARRY, EDWARD, 1798-1854 — 1
    PRYSE, JOHN, 1826-83 — 1
    PUGHE, JOHN, (not 1815) 1814-74 — 1
    WILLIAMS, JOHN OWEN, 'Pedrog', 1853-1932 — 1
LEWIS, JOHN DANIEL VERNON — J.D.V.L.
    HUGHES, THOMAS HYWEL, 1875-1945 — 2
    TREGELLES, SAMUEL PRIDEAUX, 1813-75 — 1
LEWIS, MARY GWYNETH — M.G.L.
    ANTHONY, HENRY MARK, 1817-86 — 1
    CATHERALL, JONATHAN, 1761-1833 — 1
    EVANS, DAVID, glass stainer, 1793-1861 — 1
    EVANS, LEWIS, c.1700-56 — 2
    NASH, DAVID WILLIAM, ?-1876/7 — 1
    PARRY, JOSEPH, painter, 1744-1826 — 1

LEWIS, MEGAN	M.L.
HUGHES, ELIZABETH PHILLIPS, 1851-1925	1
LEWIS, MEILIR PENNANT	M.P.L.
ROBERTS, RICHARD, 1823-1909	1: 1149
LEWIS, THOMAS	T.L.
LEWIS, GEORGE, 1763-1822	1
LEWIS, THOMAS HARRIS	T.H.L.
DAVIES, EVAN, 1750-1806	1
DAVIES, JOHN, Allt Wen, 1737-1821	1
DAVIES, JOHN, 1823-74	1
DAVIES, JOHN, Taihirion, 1825-1904	2
WILLIAMS, THOMAS, 'Brynfab', 1848-1927	1
LEWIS, VYRNWY JOHN	V.J.L.
JONES, THOMAS IVOR, 1896-1969	2
LINNARD, WILLIAM	W.L.
WATKINS, WILLIAM, fl. 1750-62	2
LLOYD, DAVID MYRDDIN	D.M.Ll.
ABEL, SION, 18c.	1
ALEN, RHISIART ap RHISIART, <17c.	1
ASSER, ?-909	1
BARNES, EDWARD, 18c.	1
CASNODYN, fl. 1320-40	1
CNEPPYN GWERTHRYNION, 13c.	1
CYNDDELW BRYDYDD MAWR, fl. 1155-1200	1
CYNWRIG HIR, c.1093	1
DAFYDD LLWYD ap LLYWELYN ap GRUFFUDD, c.1420-1500	1
DANIEL ap LLOSGWRN MEW, ?-1170	1
EINION ap GWALCHMAI, fl. 1203-23	1
EINION WAN, fl. 1230-45	1
ELIDIR SAIS, 12c.-13c.	1
ENDERBIE, PERCY, fl. 1661	1
EVANS, THOMAS CHRISTOPHER, Cadrawd, 1846-1918	1
GRUFFUDD ap GWRGENAU, fl. c.1200	1
GWALCHMAI ap MEILYR, fl. 1130-80	1
GWILYM RYFEL, 12c.	1
HYWEL YSTORM (or YSTORYN), 14c.	1
IORWERTH BELI, 14c.	1
JAMES, DANIEL, 'Gwyrosydd', 1847-1920	1
JONES, BASSETT, 17c.	1
JONES, ROBERT AMBROSE, (not 1851) 1848-1906	1
JONES, THOMAS MORRIS, 1859-1933	1
LEWIS, HENRY, 1889-1968	2
LLYGAD GWR, fl. 1268	1
LLYWARCH ap LLYWELYN, fl. 1173-1220	1
LLYWARCH HEN, 6c.	1
LLYWELYN FARDD, fl. c.1150-75	1
MADOG ap GWALLTER, 13c.	1
MEILYR BRYDYDD, fl. c.1100-37	1
MORRIS, WILLIAM, printer, 1812?-86	1
OWAIN CYFEILIOG, c.1130-97	1
OWEN, MATTHEW, 1631?-1679	1
PERYF ap CEDIFOR WYDDEL, fl. 1170	1
PHYLIP BRYDYDD, fl. 1222	1
PRYDYDD BYCHAN, Y, fl. 1220-70	1
RHISIART FYNGLWYD, fl. 1510-70	1
RHISIERDYN, 14c.	1
RHYS GOCH ap RHICCERT, 12c.	1
RICHARDS, THOMAS, Australian journalist, 1800-77	1
SEFNYN, 14c.	1
SEISYLL BRYFFWRCH, fl. 1155-75	1
SYPYN CYFEILIOG (II), fl. 1340-90	1
TRAHAEARN BRYDYDD MAWR, 14c.	1
WILLIAMS, WILLIAM, 'Myfyr Wyn', 1849-1900	1
LLOYD, DAVID TECWYN	D.T.Ll.
JONES, JOHN, 1773-1853	2
LLOYD, ROBERT, 'Llwyd o'r Bryn', 1888-1961	2
LLOYD, ISAAC	I.Ll.
JONES, RICHARD, 'Gwyndaf Eryri', 1785-1848	1
JONES, RICHARD, 'Glan Alaw', 1838-1925	2
LLOYD, JOHN	J.Ll.
WILLIAMS, DAVID JOHN, 1886-1950	2

LLOYD-JOHNES, HERBERT JOHN	H.J.Ll.-J.
EVANS, GRIFFITH HUMPHREY PUGH, Sir, 1840-1902	1
HERBERT, WILLIAM REGINALD, 1841-1929	2
HILLS-JOHNES, JAMES, Sir, 1833-1919	1
JOHNES, JOHN, 1800-76	1
LLOYD, Family, Maesyfelin, Cards.	1
LLOYD, Family, Peterwell, Cards.	1
LLOYD, THOMAS DAVIES, Sir, 1820-77	1
LLOYD, WALTER, Sir, 1580-1662?	1
LLOYD-MORGAN, CERIDWEN	C.Ll.-M.
JOHN, AUGUSTUS EDWIN, 1878-1961	2
LLYWELYN-WILLIAMS, ALUN	A.Ll.-W.
WILLIAMS, DAVID LLEWELYN, 1870-1949	2
LOOKER, RAY	R.L.
CATRIN ferch GRUFFYDD ab IEUAN, fl. 16c.	1
CYFFIN, ROGER, fl. c.1587-1609	1
CYNWAL, RICHARD, ?-1634	1
CYNWAL, WILLIAM, ?-1587?	1
DAFYDD ap DAFYDD LLWYD, 1549-?	1
DAFYDD ap MAREDUDD ab EDNYFED, fl. c.1460	1
DAFYDD ap PHYLIP ap RHYS, 'Syr', fl. 1500-40	1
DAFYDD ap RHYS o FENAI (or O'R FENNI), fl. c.1550	1
DAFYDD BAENTIWR, fl. 1500-30?	1
DAFYDD EPYNT, fl. c.1460	1
DAFYDD FYNGLWYD, fl. 1500-50	1
DAFYDD GOCH BRYDYDD o FUALLT, 16c.	1
DAFYDD LLWYD ap HUW, fl. 17c.	1
DAFYDD LLWYD of HENBLAS, ?-1619	1
DAFYDD LLWYD SYBYLLTIR, fl. c.1610	1
DAFYDD MEIFOD, fl. c.1600	1
DAFYDD WILIAM PYRS, fl. c.1660	1
DAVIES, ROLAND, fl. c.1730	1
EDWARD MAELOR, fl. 1580-1620	1
ELIS CYNFRIG, fl. 1580-1620	1
ELIS DRWYNHIR, c.1600?	1
ELIS GOCH, n.d.	2
ELISE JOHN y GWEHYDD, n.d.	2
GORONWY GYRIOG, fl. c.1310-60	1
GRUFFUDD, RHISIART, (Rhisiart Gruffudd ap Huw?), fl. c.1569	1
GRUFFUDD ap DAFYDD ap TUDUR, fl. c.1300	1
GRUFFUDD ap DAFYDD FYCHAN, 15c.	1
GRUFFUDD ap GRONW GETHIN, fl. c.1380-1420	1
GRUFFUDD BENRHAW, or PENRHAW, 15c.	1
GRUFFUDD DAFYDD DDU, fl. c.1500?	1
GRUFFUDD HAFREN, fl. c.1600	1
GRUFFUDD LEIAF, 15c.	1
GRUFFUDD LLWYD ab IFAN, fl. c.1564	1
GRUFFUDD LLWYD ap DAFYDD ab EINION LLYGLIW, fl. c.1380-1410	1
GRUFFUDD LLWYD ap DAFYDD GAPLAN, fl. c.1400?	1
GRUFFUDD LLWYD ap RHOBERT, n.d.	1
GRUFFUDD NANNAU, (not c.1654) fl. 1460	1
GRUFFYDD, SION, Sir, ?-1586?	1
GRUFFYDD, THOMAS, 1815-87	1
GUTUN GOCH BRYDYDD, fl. c.1550?	1
GWGON BRYDYDD, fl. c.1240	1
GWILYM ab IEUAN HEN, fl. 1440-80	1
GWILYM ap SEFNYN, fl. c.1440	1
GWILYM DDU o ARFON, fl. c.1280-1320	1
GWILYM GWYN, fl. end of 15c. (not c.1560-1600)	1
GWYNN, HARRI, fl. c.1627	1
HARRI, Mastr or 'Syr', 15c.	1
HUMPHREYS, ROBERT (or RHOBERT RHAGAT), fl. c.1720	1
HUW, THOMAS, fl. c.1574-1606	1
HUW ap DAFYDD, fl. 1550-1628	1
HUW ap DAFYDD ap LLYWELYN, fl. c.1526-80	1
HUW ap RHYS WYN, fl. c.1550	1
HUW CEIRIOG, fl. c.1560-1600	1
HUW DAFI, 15c.-16c.	1
HUW LLIFON, fl. c.1570-1607	1
HUW LLYN, fl. c.1552-94	1
HUW PENNAL, fl. 15c.	1
HUW PENNANT, 'Syr', 15c.	1
HUW PENNANT, fl. c.1565-1619	1

HUW TALAI, fl. c.1550-80	1
HWMFFRE ap HYWEL, 17c.	1
HYWEL ab EINION LLYGLIW, fl. c.1330-70	1
HYWEL AERDDREN, fl. c.1540-70?	1
HYWEL ap DAFYDD ap IEUAN, fl. c.1450-80	1
HYWEL ap DAFYDD LLWYD ab y GOF, fl. c.1500	1
HYWEL ap LLYWELYN ap MAREDUDD, fl. c.1500?	1
HYWEL ap RHEINALLT, fl. c.1471-94	1
HYWEL ap 'Syr' MATHEW, ?-1581	1
HYWEL CILAN, 15c.	1
HYWEL FOEL ap GRIFFRI ap PWYLL GWYDDEL, fl. c.1240-1300	1
HYWEL GETHIN, 'of Celynnog', fl. c.1485	1
HYWEL HEILIN, 'Heilin Fardd', 15c.	2
HYWEL HIR, fl. 1600-40	1
IEUAN ap BEDO GWYN, or IEUAN BEDO GWYN, fl. c.1530-90?	1
IEUAN ap GRUFFUDD LEIAF, 15c.	1
IEUAN ap LLYWELYN FYCHAN, ?-1532	1
IEUAN ap MADOG ap DAFYDD, fl. c.1500	1
IEUAN ap RHYS ap LLYWELYN, 16c.	1
IEUAN (IFAN) ap SION, fl. c.1612-36	1
IEUAN ap TUDUR PENLLYN, fl. c.1480	1
IEUAN BRECHFA, c.1430-15OO	1
IEUAN BRYDYDD HIR HYNAF, fl. c.1450	1
IEUAN CLYWEDOG, fl. c.1577-96	1
IEUAN DDU ap DAFYDD ab OWAIN, fl. c.1440-80	1
IEUAN DEULWYN, fl. c.1460	1
IEUAN DRWCH y DARAN, fl. c.1370-1400?	1
IEUAN DU'R BILWG, fl. c.1470	1
IEUAN GETHIN ap IEUAN ap LLEISION, fl. c.1450	1
IEUAN GYFANNEDD, fl. c.1450-60 (not fl. 1570-1600)	1
IEUAN LLAFAR, fl. c.1594-1610	1
IEUAN LLWYD ab y GARGAM, 14c.	1
IEUAN LLWYD BRYDYDD, fl. c.1460-90	1
IEUAN LLWYD SIEFFRAI, fl. 1599-1619	1
IEUAN MON (or IEUAN MON HEN), fl. 1460-80	1
IEUAN (IFAN) o GARNO, 'Syr', fl. c.1530-70	1
IEUAN RHAEADR, fl. c.1480	1
IEUAN TEW, 15c.; 16c.	1
IEUAN TUDUR OWEN, fl. c.1627	1
INCO BRYDYDD, fl. c.1480	1
IOCYN DDU ab ITHEL GRACH, fl. c.1380	1
IORWERTH ab y CYRIOG, fl. c.1380	1
IORWERTH FYCHAN ap IORWERTH ap ROTPERT, fl. c.1300	1
JONES, ARTHUR, fl. 18c.	1
JONES, HUGH, 'Gwyndaf Ieuanc', fl. 1812	2
JONES, JOHN, 'Humilis', 1818-69	1
JONES, JOHN, barrister, translator, 1772-1837	1
JONES, LEWIS, Pandy, fl. 1703	1
JONES, OWEN, 'Manoethwy', 1838-66	1
JONES, PETER, 'Pedr Fardd', 1775-1845	1
JONES, ROBERT, 'Trebor Aled', 1866-1917	1
JONES, THOMAS, 'Y Bardd Cloff', 1768-1828	1
KENWARD, JAMES, 'Elfynydd', fl. 1868	1
LEWIS, DAVID, 1683?-1760	1
LEWIS, THOMAS, hymn-writer, 18c.	1
LEWYS ap HYWEL (or POWEL), fl. c.1560-1600	1
LLEWELYN, MARY PENDRILL, 1811-74	1
LLWYD, FFOWC, fl. c.1580-1620	1
LLYWARCH LLAETY, fl. 1140-60	1
LLYWELYN ab EDNYFED, fl. c.1400-60?	1
LLYWELYN ab OWAIN ap CYNFRIG MOEL, fl. c.1480?	1
LLYWELYN ap CYNFRIG DDU o FON, fl. c.1460-1500?	2
LLYWELYN ap GUTUN (ap IEUAN LYDAN), fl. c.1480	1
LLYWELYN ap GWILYM ap RHYS, 16c.	1
LLYWELYN ap HYWEL ap IEUAN ap GRONW, fl. c.1480?	1
LLYWELYN ap MOEL y PANTRI, ?-1440	1
LLYWELYN BRYDYDD HODDNANT, fl. c.1300-50	1
LLYWELYN DDU ab y PASTARD, fl. 14c.	1
LLYWELYN GOCH ap MEURIG HEN, fl. c.1360-90	1
MAB y CLOCHYDDYN, fl. c.1380	1
MADOG BENFRAS, fl. c.1320-60	1
MADOG DWYGRAIG, fl. c.1370	1
MAREDUDD ap RHOSER, fl. c.1530	1

MATHEW ap LLYWELYN GOCH, fl. c.1550 (not 1360-1400)   1
MEURUG ab IORWERTH, fl. c.1320-70   1
MORGAN ap HUW LEWYS, fl. c.1550-1600   1
MORGAN ELFAEL, fl. c.1528-63 (not 1541)   1
MORUS BERWYN, fl. 1553-1615   1
MORUS DWYFECH, fl. c.1523-90   1
MORUS GETHIN, fl. c.1525   1
MORUS MAWDDWY, fl. c.1540-70   1
MORYS ap HYWEL ap TUDUR, fl. c.1530   1
OWAIN GWYNEDD, fl. c.1550-90   1
PARRY, RHISIART, poet, 1665?-1749   1
PARRY, RICHARD, poet, of Newborough, 1710-63   1
POWEL, JOHN or SION, [1731]-1767   1
POWEL, MORGAN, fl. c.1563   1
PRYS, JOHN PRICHARD, fl. c.1704-21   1
PRYS, SION, ?-1640?   1
RHISIART OWEN ap RHISIART, fl. c.1622   1
RHOBERT ap DAFYDD LLWYD, fl. 1550-90   1
RHYS DEGANWY, fl. c.1480   1
RHYS PENNARDD, fl. c.1480   1
ROBERTS, HUW, 'Syr', fl. 1555-1619   1
ROBERTS, MORRIS, ?-1723   1
SIANCYN FYNGLWYD, fl. c.1470   1
SION LEIAF, 'Syr', fl. c.1480   1
LORD, PETER   P.L.
    WILLIAMS, LUCY GWENDOLEN, 1870-1955   2
    WILLIAMS, MARGARET LINDSAY, 1888-1960   2
LUMLEY, G. I.   G.I.L.
    PRICE, THOMAS WALTER (GWALLTER), 'Cuhelyn'   2
McLEAN, JOHN CHARLES   J.C.McL.
    DAVIES, HENRY WALFORD, Sir, 1869-1941   2
MARTIN, AUBREY JOHN   A.J.M.
    EVANS, DAVID DELTA, 1866-1948   2
MATHEW, DAVID   D.M.
    MATHEW, Family, Llandaff, Radyr and Castell y Mynach, Glam.   1
MATHEW, HUGH PAWLEY   H.P.M.
    MATHEW, Family, Llandaff   2
MATHIAS, ROLAND G.   R.M.
    FREEMAN, KATHLEEN, 'Mary Fitt', 1897-1959   2
    HAYCOCK, BLODWEN MYFANWY, 1913-1963   2
    WATKINS, VERNON PHILLIPS, 1906-1967   2
MATHIAS, WILLIAM ALUN   W.A.M.
    SALESBURY, WILLIAM, 1520?-84?   1
MEREDITH, JOHN ELLIS   J.E.M.
    DAVIES, GEORGE MAITLAND LLOYD, 1880-1949   2
    ROBERTS, DAVID FRANCIS, 1882-1945   2
MILES, DILLWYN   Dil.M.
    OWEN, JOHN, 1836-1915   1
MOORE, DONALD   Don.M.
    O'NEILL, BRYAN HUGH ST. JOHN, 1905-1954   2
    PHILLIPS, PHILIP ESMONDE, 1888-1960   2
    WALKER-HENEAGE-VIVIAN, ALGERNON, 1871-1952   2
    WALTERS, EVAN JOHN, 1893-1951   2
    WILLIAMS, IOLO ANEURIN, 1890-1962   2
MORGAN, DAVID JAMES   D.J.M.
    EVANS, WILLIAM DAVIES, 1790-1872   2
MORGAN, GERALD   Ge.M.
    JONES, JOHN, printer and inventor, 1786-1865   2
MORGAN, GWYNETH   G.M.
    MORGAN, TREFOR RICHARD, 1914-1970   2
MORGAN, PRYS   P.M.
    HARRY, GEORGE OWEN, c.1553-1614   2
    JAMES, IVOR, 1840-1909   2
    LOUGHER, LEWIS, Sir, 1871-1955   2
MORGAN, RICHARD HARDING   R.H.M.
    JAMES, DAVID JOHN, Sir, 1887-1967   2
MORGAN, THOMAS JOHN   T.J.M.
    ANTHONY, DAVID BRYNMOR, 1886-1966   2
    DAVIES, JOHN, 'Ossian Gwent', 1839-92   1
    DAVIES (or DAVID), THOMAS ESSILE, 1820-91   1
    WILLIAMS, THOMAS, 'Gwilym Morgannwg', 1778-1835   1

MORGAN, WALTER THOMAS	W.T.M.
COX, LEONARD, fl. 1572	1
DAVIES, RHYS JOHN, 1877-1954	2
ELLIS, ROWLAND, Aberdeen, 1841-1911	1
EVANS, EDWARD, 1582-?	2
EVANS, HENRY, 'Harri Evan William', fl. 17c.	1
EVANS, JOHN VICTOR, 1895-1957	2
EVANS, PETER MAELOR, 1817-78	1
EVANS, ROBERT, fl. c.1750	1
EVANS, SAMUEL, 'Gomerydd', 1793-1856	1
EVANS, STEPHEN, 1818-1905	1
EVANS, THOMAS, 'Telynog', 1840-65	1
EVANS, THOMAS, 1897-1963	2
FARR, HARRY, 1874-1968	2
GIBBS, SION, 'the Ludlow lawyer', fl. 1643	1
GITTINS, EDWARD, 1843-84, Iorwerth Pentyrch	1
GRIFFITH, EDWARD, 1832-1918	1
GRIFFITHS, EVAN, 'Ieuan Ebblig', 1795-1873	1
GRUFFUDD ab ADDA ap DAFYDD, fl. 1340-70	1
GRUFFUDD ap DAFYDD ap HYWEL, fl. 1480-1520	1
GRUFFUDD ap TUDUR ap HYWEL, fl. 1500-40	1
GWYN, FRANCIS, 1648?-1734	1
HALL, GEORGE HENRY, 1881-1965	2
JAMES, CHARLES HERBERT, 1817-90	1
JAMES, WILLIAM MILBOURNE, Sir, 1807-81	1
JONES, JAMES IFANO, 1865-1955	2
LEWIS, TITUS, 1822-87	1
LEWIS of CAERLEON, fl. 1491	1
LLOYD, JOHN, Oxford, 1638-87	1
LLOYD, MEREDITH, fl. 1655-77	1
MORGAN, Family, Tredegar Park, Mon.	1
MORGAN, JOHN, 1827-1903	1
MORGAN, PHILIP, ?-1435	1
MORGAN, WALTER, fl. 1695	1
PETTINGALL, JOHN, 1708-81	1
POWELL, THOMAS, attorney, 1572?-1635?	1
POWELL, THOMAS, 1779?-1863	1: 1146
PRYCE, THOMAS, 1833-1904	1
REYNOLDS, JOHN, fl. 1739	1
ROBERTS, JOHN, billiards player, 1823-93	1
ROWLAND, JOHN, 'Yr Undodwr', 1816?-88	1
WILLIAMS, EDWARD, iron-master, 1826-86	1
MORRIS, EDWARD RONALD	E.R.M.
HAMER, EDWARD, 1840-1911	2
HORSFALL TURNER, ERNEST RICHMOND, 1870-1936	2
JERMAN, HUGH, 1836-1895	2
MORRIS, WILLIAM	W.M.
EVANS, ELLIS HUMPHREY, 1887-1917	1
HUGHES, JOHN GRUFFYDD MOELWYN, 1866-1944	2
MORRIS, RICHARD ROBERTS, 1852-1935	1
MORRIS-JONES, HUW	H.M.-J.
ABLETT, NOAH, 1883-1935	1: 1113
ABRAHAM, WILLIAM, 'Mabon', 1842-1922	1
BELL, RICHARD, 1859-1930	1
COOK, ARTHUR JAMES, 1884-1931	1
STANTON, CHARLES BUTT, 1873-1946	2
THOMAS, JAMES HENRY, 1874-1949	2
WINSTONE, JAMES, 1863-1921	1
MULLINS, DANIEL JOSEPH	D.J.Mu.
McGRATH, MICHAEL JOSEPH, 1882-1961	2
NICHOLAS, WILLIAM RHYS	W.R.N.
WILLIAMS, WILLIAM, 'Crwys', 1875-1968	2
NORTH, FREDERICK JOHN	F.J.N.
CONYBEARE, WILLIAM DANIEL, 1787-1857	1
DAVID, TANNATT WILLIAM EDGEWORTH, Sir, 1858-1934	1
DAVIES, DAVID CHRISTOPHER, 1827-85	1
DAVIES, THOMAS, 1837-92	1
DAVIES, WILLIAM, palaeontologist, 1814-91	1
DAWKINS, WILLIAM BOYD, Sir, 1837-1929	1
EVANS, JOHN, cartographer, 1723-95	1
EVANS, JOHN, surgeon, 1756-1846	1
EVANS, JOHN, topographical writer, 1768-c.1812	1
FENTON, RICHARD, 1747-1821	1

HICKS, HENRY, 1837-99	1
HUGHES, THOMAS McKENNY, 1832-1917	1
JEHU, THOMAS JOHN, 1871-1943	2
LLWYD (LHUYD), HUMPHREY, 1527-68	1
MORGAN, JOHN BICKERTON, 1859-94	1
ODDY, JOHN A.	J.A.O.
RICHARDS, WILLIAM, 1749-1818	2
OLIVER, REGINALD CAMPBELL BURN	R.C.B.O.
JONES, JOHN, 1820-1907	2
OWEN, EDWIN AUGUSTINE	E.A.O.
EVANS, EVAN JENKIN, 1882-1944	2
GRIFFITHS, ERNEST HOWARD, 1851-1932	1
HUGHES, DAVID EDWARD, 1831-1900	1
OWEN, GWILYM, 1880-1940	1: 1145
PREECE, WILLIAM HENRY, Sir, 1834-1913	1
OWEN, EMYR HYWEL	E.H.O.
ROBERTS, OWEN OWEN, 1793-1866	1
OWEN, GWILYM BEYNON	G.B.O.
RICHARDS, THOMAS, 1878-1962	2
OWEN, HUGH	H.O.
MORRIS, MORRIS ap RHISIART, or MORRIS PRICHARD, 1674-1763	1
OWEN, EDWARD, 1853-1943	2
OWEN, IFOR	I.O.
DAVIES, GRIFFITH, 'Gwyndaf', 1868-1962	2
JONES, MEIRION, 1907-1970	2
OWEN, JOHN	J.O.
HUGHES, JOHN, 1827-93	1
ROBERTS, THOMAS, 1835-99	1
OWEN, JOHN DYFNALLT	J.D.O.
BERRY, ROBERT GRIFFITH, 1869-1945	2
BEVAN, LLYWELYN, 1661-1723	1
BRACE, DAVID ONLLWYN, 1848-91	1
DAVIES, BEN, Panteg, 1864-1937	1
DAVIES, THOMAS, Llandeilo, 1820-73	1
EDWARDS, THOMAS, 'Cynonfardd', 1848-1927	1
EVANS, DANIEL, 1774-1835	1
EVANS, DAVID, 1842-1914	1
EVANS, EVAN HERBER, 1836-96	1
EVANS, JENKIN, 1674-1709	1
EVANS, JONAH, 1836-96	2
EVANS, OWEN, 1829-1920	1
EVANS, THOMAS, 'Tomos Glyn Cothi', 1764-1833	1
EVANS, THOMAS, 1844-1922	1
EVANS, THOMAS PENRY, 1839-88	1
EVANS, WILLIAM, 1716-70	1
GRIFFITH-JONES, EBENEZER, 1860-1942	2
GRIFFITHS, GRIFFITH PENNAR, 1860-1918	1
GRIFFITHS, JOHN, Glandwr, 1731-1811	1
GRIFFITHS, WILLIAM, 1777-1825	1
HUGHES, DAVID, 1800-49	2
HUGHES, GRIFFITH, Groeswen, 1775-1839	1
JAMES, JOHN, ?-1705	1
JAMES, JOHN LLOYD, 'Clwydwenfro', 1835-1919	1
JARDINE, DAVID, 1732-66	1
JARDINE, JAMES, ?-1737	1
JONES, HUGH, 'Cromwell o Went', 1800-72	1
JONES, JAMES RHYS (KILSBY), 1813-89	1
JONES, JOHN BOWEN, 1829-1905	1
JONES, MORGAN, Cefnarthen, 1717?-80	1
JONES, MORGAN, Tre-lech, 1768-1835	1
JONES, SAMUEL, Brynllywarch, 1628-97	1
JONES, SAMUEL, fl. 1715-1767 (not 1764)	1
LEWIS, WILLIAM HOWELL, 1793?-1868	2
MEYLER, JAMES, 1761-1825	2
MORGAN, WILLIAM, 1818-84	1
MORRIS, CALEB, 1800-65	1
PERKINS, WILLIAM, fl. 1745-76	1
PETER, DAVID, 1765-1837	1
PHILLIPS, THOMAS, Neuadd-lwyd, 1772-1842	1
POWELL, HOWELL, ?-1716	1
POWELL, THOMAS, 1781-1842	1
PRICE, ISAAC, 1735?-1805	1
PRICE, RHYS, 1807-69	1

PRYDDERCH, RHYS, 1620?-99	1
REES, DAVID, Llanelly, 1801-69	1
REES, LEWIS, 1710-1800	1
ROBERTS, EDWARD, 1816-87	1
ROWLANDS, DAVID, 'Dewi Môn', 1836-1907	1
SAMUEL, CHRISTMAS, 1674-1764	1
THOMAS, DAVID, 1813-94	1
THOMAS, JOHN, hymnist, 1730-1804?	1
THOMAS, WILLIAM, 1832-1911	1
THOMAS, WILLIAM THEOPHILUS, 1824-99	1
WILLIAMS, DAVID, Troedrhiwdalar, 1779-1874	1
WILLIAMS, EVAN, Cwmllynfell, 1719-48	1
OWEN, JOHN THOMAS	**J.T.O.**
DAVIES, WALTER, 1761-1849	1
OWEN, MORRIS BRYNLLWYN	**M.B.O.**
BOWEN, DAVID, 1774-1853	2
BREEZE, SAMUEL, 1772-1812	1
DAVIES, DANIEL, Felinfoel, 1756-1837	1
DAVIES, DANIEL, 'Y Dyn Dall', 1797-1876	1
DAVIES, THOMAS, Llanelli, 1823-98	1
OWEN, RICHARD GRIFFITH	**R.G.O.**
AMBROSE, WILLIAM, 'Emrys', 1813-73	1
BOWEN, SAMUEL, 1799-1887	1
BOWEN, THOMAS, 1756-1827	1
BREESE, JOHN, 1789-1842	1
BREWER, JEHOIADA, 1752-1817	1
DAVIDS, THOMAS WILLIAM, 1816-84	1
DAVIES, ELLIS THOMAS, 1822-95	1
DAVIES, EVAN, 'Eta Delta', 1794-1855	1
DAVIES, RHYS, 'Y Glun Bren', 1772-1847	1
EVERETT, ROBERT, 1791-1875 and LEWIS, 1799-1863	1
GIBBON, JAMES MORGAN, 1855-1932	1
GRIFFITH, DAVID, 1792?-1873	1
GRIFFITHS, WILLIAM ALONZO, 1842-93	1
HARRY, NUN MORGAN, 1800-42	1
HUWS, RHYS JONES, 1862-1917	1
HUWS, WILLIAM PARI, 1853-1936	1
JARVICE (JERVIS), WILLIAM, ?-1743	1
JENKYN, THOMAS WILLIAM, 1794-1858	1
JONES, ARTHUR, Bangor, 1776-1860	1
JONES, BENJAMIN, 1756-1823	1
JONES, CADWALADR, 1783-1867	1
JONES, DAVID STANLEY, 1860-1919	1: 1132
JONES, EVAN (PAN), 1834-1922	1
JONES, JOHN, of Llangollen, 1801-56	1
JONES, JOHN DANIEL, 1865-1942	2
JONES, JOSIAH, 1830-1915	1
JONES, MICHAEL, Bala, 1787-1853	1
JONES, MICHAEL DANIEL, 1822-98	1
JONES, RICHARD, Llwyngwril, 1780-1853	1
LEWIS, THOMAS, Bala, 1837-92	1
MORGAN, DAVID, 1779-1858	1
NICHOLSON, WILLIAM, 1844-85	1
NICHOLSON, WILLIAM JOHN, 1866-1943	2
OWENS, OWEN, 1792-1862	1
PARRY, RICHARD, 'Gwalchmai', 1803-97	1
POWELL, JONATHAN, 1764-1823	1
POWELL, LEWIS, 1788-1869	1
PROBERT, LEWIS, 1837-1908	1
PUGH, HUGH, 1779-1809	1
PUGH, HUGH, schoolmaster, 1803-68	1
REES, THOMAS, 1869-1926	1
ROBERTS, DAVID, 'Dewi Ogwen', 1818-97	1
ROBERTS, JOHN, Llanbryn-mair, 1767-1834	1
ROBERTS, JOHN, 'J. R.', 1804-84	1
ROBERTS, MORRIS, 1799-1878	1
ROBERTS, RICHARD, (not 1810) 1809-83	1
ROBERTS, THOMAS, 'Scorpion', 1816-87	1
THOMAS, HUGH EVAN, 'Huwco Meirion', 1830-89	1
THOMAS, JOHN, Liverpool, 1821-92	1
THOMAS, ROBERT, 'Ap Vychan', 1809-80	1
THOMAS, ROBERT DAVID, 1817-88	1
THOMAS, WILLIAM, publisher, 1749-1809	1

WILLIAMS, EDWARD, Dinas Mawddwy, 1818-80	1
WILLIAMS, ROWLAND, 'Hwfa Môn', 1823-1905	1
WILLIAMS, WILLIAM, of Wern, 1781-1840	1
OWEN, ROBERT	**R.O.**
BOWEN, D. E., fl. 1840-80	2
CHIDLAW, BENJAMIN WILLIAM, 1811-92	1
DAFYDD GLYN DYFRDWY, fl. c.1575	1
DAVIES, DAVID, 'Dewi Emlyn', 1817-88	1
DAVIES, DAVID LLOYD, ?-1881	1
DAVIES, EDWARD, U.S.A., 1827-1905	1
DAVIES, JOHN IDRIS, 'Ioan Idris', 1821-89	1
DAVIES, JOSEPH E., 1812-81	2
DAVIES, MORRIS, 'Meurig Ebrill', 1780-1861	1
DAVIES, RACHEL, 'Rahel o Fôn', 1846-1915	1
DAVIES, ROBERT HUMPHREY, 1856-1947	2
DAVIES, WILLIAM DANIEL, 1838-1900	1
EDWARDS, EBENEZER, 1824-1901	1
EDWARDS, GEORGE ROWLAND, 1810-94	2
EDWARDS, JOHN, 'Eos Glan Twrch', 1806-87	1
EDWARDS, RICHARD, fl. 1840-84	1
ELLIS, EDWARD, 1842?-92	1
ELLIS, MORGAN ALBERT, 1832-1901	1
ELLIS, ROWLAND, Bryn Mawr, U.S.A., 1650-1731	1
EVANS, CADWALADR, 1664-1745	1
EVANS, DAVID, Pennsylvania, fl. 1710?-45?	2
EVANS, EVAN WILLIAM, 1827?-74	1
EVANS, HENRY WILLIAM, 1840-1919	1
EVANS, HUGH, 'Hywel Eryri', 1767-1841?	1
EVANS, ROBERT TROGWY, 1824-1901	1
EVANS, WILLIAM MEIRION, 1826-83	1
GOODWIN, JOHN, 1681-1763	1
GRIFFITH, JOHN, Quaker, 1713-76	1
GRIFFITH, OWEN, 'Giraldus', 1832-96	1
GRIFFITH, RICHARD, 'Carneddog', 1861-1947	2
GRIFFITHS, JOHN THOMAS, 1824-95	2
HOWEL, HARRI, fl. 1637-71	1
HOWELL, LLEWELYN DAVID, 1812-64	1
HUGHES, DAVID, 'Eos Iâl', 1794?-1862	1: 1129
HUGHES, EVAN, 'Hughes Fawr', ?-1800	1
HUGHES, HUGH JOHN, 1828?-72	1
HUGHES, JOSEPH TUDOR, 1827-41	1
HUGHES, WILLIAM ROBERT, 1798?-1879	2
HUW BODWRDA, fl. 1566	1
HUW CORNWY, fl. 1580-96	1
HUWS, MORIEN MON, 1856-1932	1
IEUAN (IFAN) DYLYNIWR, fl. 1520-67	1
JONES, DAVID RICHARD, 1832-1916	1
JONES, ERASMUS, 1817-1909	1
JONES, JOHN WILLIAM, U.S.A., 1827-84	1
JONES, RHYS GWESYN, 1826-1901	1
LEWIS, ELLIS, fl. 1640-61	1
LLOYD, THOMAS, 'Crych Elen', 1841-1909	1
LLWYD, HUW, 1568?-1630?	1
MEREDITH, ROBERT, 1823-93	1
MILLS, SEBASTIAN BACH, 1838-98	1
MORGAN, THOMAS REES, 1834-97	1
OWEN, IFAN TUDUR, ?-1625?	1
POWELL, HOWELL, 1819-75	1
PRICE, Family, Rhiwlas, Mer.	1
PRICE, DAVID, 'Dewi Dinorwig', 1804-74	1
PRICE, THOMAS WALTER, 'Cuhelyn', 1829-69	1
PUGH, ELLIS, 1656-1718	1
ROBERTS, HUGH, 1644?-1702	1
ROBERTS, JOHN, 'Siôn Lleyn', 1749-1817	1
ROBERTS, WILLIAM, Utica, 1809-87	1
ROBERTS, WILLIAM CHARLES, 1832-1903	1
ROWLANDS, WILLIAM, U.S.A., 1807-66	1
THOMAS, DAVID, U.S.A., 1794-1882	1
THOMAS, ELLIS, 1823-78 - see under THOMAS, ROBERT (1809-80)	1
THOMAS, JOHN, 'Eos Gwynedd', 1742-1818	1
THOMAS, JOHN, Penfforddwen, 1757-1835	1
THOMAS, JOHN, 'Eifionydd', 1848-1922	1
TREHARNE, BRYCESON, 1879-1948	2

THOMAS, BENJAMIN, 'Myfyr Emlyn', 1836-93   1
THOMAS, TIMOTHY, I, 1720-68   1
THOMAS, ZACHARIAS, 1727-1816   1
WILLIAMS, DAVID PRYSE, 1878-1952   2
WILLIAMS, ERNEST LLWYD, 1906-1960   2
WILLIAMS, JOHN, 'Ioan ap Ioan', 1800-71   1
WILLIAMS, JOHN CEULANYDD, 1847?-99   1
WILLIAMS, JOHN (RUFUS), 1833-77   1
WILLIAMS, RICHARD, ?-1724   1
PARRY, ENID   En.P.
DAVIES, OWEN PICTON, 1882-1970   2
PARRY, GLYN   Gl.P.
OWEN, HUGH, 1880-1953   2
PARRY, GRUFFYDD   G.P.
JONES, RICHARD ROBERT, 'Dic Aberdaron', 1780-1843   1
PARRY, R. PALMER   R.P.P.
PARRY, SARAH WINIFRED, 1870-1953   2
PARRY, ROBERT IVOR   R.I.P.
ROBERTS, SAMUEL, 'S. R.', 1800-85   1
PARRY, THOMAS   T.P.
BEBB, WILLIAM AMBROSE, 1894-1955   2
BELL, ERNEST DAVID, 1915-1959   2
BELL, HAROLD IDRIS, Sir, 1879-1967   2
BLACKWELL, JOHN, 'Alun', 1797-1840   1
DAFYDD ap GWILYM, fl. 1340-70   1
DAFYDD BENFRAS, fl. 1230-60   1
DAVIES, JOSEPH, ?-1831?   1
DAVIES, RICHARD, 'Tafolog', 1830-1904   1
DAVIES, ROBERT, 'Bardd Nantglyn', 1769-1835   1
DEIO ab IEUAN DU, fl. 1460-80   1
EDWARDS, GRIFFITH, 'Gutyn Padarn', 1812-93   1
EDWARDS, THOMAS, 'Twm o'r Nant', 1739-1810   1
EVANS, DAVID EMRYS, Sir, 1891-1966   2
GRUFFUDD ab Yr YNAD COCH, fl. 1280   1
GRUFFUDD ap CYNAN, c.1055-1137   1
GRUFFUDD HIRAETHOG, ?-1564   1
GRUFFYDD, WILLIAM JOHN, 1881-1954   2
HOOSON, ISAAC DANIEL, 1880-1948   2
HUDSON-WILLIAMS, THOMAS, 1873-1961   2
HUGHES, JOHN HENRY, 'Ieuan o Leyn', 1814-93   1
HUGHES, JONATHAN, 1721-1805   1
HUGHES, WILLIAM ROGER, 1898-1958   2
JONES, CYNAN ALBERT EVANS, Sir, 1895-1970   2
JONES, THOMAS TUDNO, 1844-95   1
JONES, WILLIAM ELLIS, 'Cawrdaf', 1795-1848   1
LLOYD-JONES, JOHN, 1885-1956   2
MORRIS-JONES, JOHN, Sir, (formerly JONES, JOHN MORRIS) 1864-1929   1
PARRY, ROBERT WILLIAMS, 1884-1956   2
PARRY-WILLIAMS, HENRY, 1858-1925   2
PRITCHARD, EVAN, 1769-1832   1
RHYS, JOHN DAVID, 1534-1609?   1
ROBERTS, THOMAS, 1884-1960   2
ROBIN CLIDRO, fl. 1580   1
THOMAS, EBENEZER, 1802-63   1
WILLIAMS, IFOR, Sir, 1881-1965   2
PARRY-WILLIAMS, THOMAS HERBERT   T.H.P.-W.
ANWYL, EDWARD, Sir, 1866-1914   1
ANWYL, JOHN BODVAN, 1875-1949   2
GUEST (née BERTIE; later SCHREIBER), CHARLOTTE ELIZABETH, Lady, 1812-95   1
SALESBURY (SALISBURY), HENRY, 1561-1637?   1
SAMUEL, DAVID, 1856-1921   1
WILLIAMS, ELISEUS, 1867-1926   1
PEATE, IORWERTH CYFEILIOG   I.C.P.
DAVIES, Family, Bersham, Denb.   1: 1116-7
DAVIES, JOHN, Peirianydd Gwynedd, 1783-1855   1: 1117
DAVIES, JOHN BREESE, 1893-1940   2
DAVIES, LEONARD TWISTON, Sir, 1894-1953   2
FOX, CYRIL FRED, Sir, 1882-1967   2
WILSON, RICHARD, 1713-82   1
PHILLIPS, EDGAR   E.P.
JONES, ANEURIN, 1822-1904   1

WILLIAMS, DAVID, 'Alaw Goch', 1809-63	1
WILLIAMS, GWILYM, 1839-1906	1
RAMAGE, HELEN MYFANWY	H.M.R.
JONES, WILLIAM, 'Gwrgant' 1803-86	1
THOMAS, JOHN, antiquary, 1736-69	1
RANDALL, HENRY JOHN	H.J.R.
CLARK, GEORGE THOMAS, 1809-98	1
CORBETT, JOHN STUART, 1845-1921	1
FRANCIS, GEORGE GRANT, 1814-82	1
HARTLAND, EDWIN SIDNEY, 1848-1927	1
JENKINS, DAVID, 'Judge Jenkins', 1582-1663	1
LEWIS, Family, Van, Glam.	1
NICHOLL, JOHN, Sir, 1759-1838	1
NICHOLL, JOHN, 1797-1853	1
NICHOLLS, JOHN, 1555-84?	1
THOMAS, Family, Wenvoe, Glam.	1
TRAHERNE, JOHN MONTGOMERY, 1788-1860	1
TURBERVILLE, Family, Coity, Glam.	1
TURBERVILLE, Family, Crickhowell, Brecs.	1
TURBERVILLE, EDWARD, c.1648-81	1
REES, BRINLEY	B.R.
PRICE, THOMAS, 'Carnhuanawc', 1787-1848	1
WILIAM LLYN, 1534?-80	1
WILLIAMS, JANE, 'Ysgafell', 1806-85	1
WILLIAMS, WATKIN HEZEKIAH, 1844-1905	1
REES, GARNET	Ga.R.
JONES, PERCY MANSELL, 1889-1968	2
REES, GRAHAM LLOYD	G.L.R.
COOMBE TENNANT, WINIFRED MARGARET, 1874-1956	2
REES, IOAN BOWEN	I.B.R.
BRUCE, CHARLES GRANVILLE, 1866-1939	2
DAVIES, JOHN LLEWELYN, 1826-1916	2
EDWARDS, JOHN MENLOVE, 1910-1958	2
JONES, HUMPHREY OWEN, 1878-1912	2
JONES, OWEN GLYNNE, 1867-1899	2
LEWIS LLOYD, EMMELINE, 1827-1913	2
LLOYD, WILLIAM, Sir, 1782-1857	2
REES, BOWEN, 1857-1929	2
WILLIAMS, PETER BAILEY, 1763-1836	2
WILLIAMS-ELLIS, JOHN CLOUGH, 1833-1913	2
REES, IVOR GLYN	I.Gl.R.
REES, THOMAS, 1825-1908	2
REES, IVOR GWYNFIL	I.G.R.
JENKINS, DANIEL, 1856-1946	2
REES, JAMES FREDERICK	J.F.R.
BRUCE, HENRY AUSTIN, 1815-95	1
BRUCE, WILLIAM NAPIER, 1858-1936	1
DAVIES, DAVID, Barkham, 1741-1819	1
DAVIES, GETHIN, 1846-96	1
GREVILLE, CHARLES FRANCIS, 1749-1809	1
LAUGHARNE, ROWLAND, ?-1676?	1
OWEN, Family, Orielton, Pembs.	1
OWEN, ROBERT, Utopian socialist, 1771-1858	1
POWELL, RICE, fl. 1641-65	1
POYER, JOHN, ?-1649	1
RECORDE, ROBERT, ?-1558	1
RHYS ap THOMAS, Sir, 1449-1525	1
TUCKER, JOSIAH, 1712-99	1
VAUGHAN, Family, Golden Grove, Carms.	1
WALTER, LUCY, 1630?-58	1
REES, JOHN RODERICK	J.R.R.
REES, THOMAS, 1862-1951	2
REES, THOMAS MARDY	T.M.R.
ADAMS, WILLIAM, 1813-86	1
BARKER, Family, Pontypool, Mon. and Bath	1
BEADLES, ELISHA, 1670-1734	1
BELLEROCHE, ALBERT de, 1864-1944	2
BIRD, JOHN, 1768-1829	1
BOYDELL, JOSIAH, 1752-1817	1
BROWN, MIA ARNESBY, ?-1931	2
CHARLES, JAMES, 1851-1906	1
CONWAY, CHARLES, 1820-84	1
DAVIES, JOHN OSSIAN, 1851-1916	1

WILLIAMS, Family, Cochwillan, Caerns.	1: 1154-6
WILLIAMS, WILLIAM, Sir, 1634-1700	1
WYNN, Family, Gwydir, Caerns.	1
YOUNG, GRUFFYDD, c.1370-1435	1
ROBERTS, GOMER MORGAN	**G.M.R.**
BARHAM (formerly NOEL, née MIDDLETON), DIANA, peeress, 1763-1823	1
BASSETT, CHRISTOPHER, 1753-84	1
BASSETT, RICHARD, 1777-1852	1
BELCHER, JOHN, fl. 1721-63	1
BEVAN, HOPKIN, 1765-1839	1
BEYNON, ROBERT, 1881-1953	2
BEYNON, TOM, 1886-1961	2
CHARLES, DAVID, I, 1762-1834	1
COSLET, EDWARD, 1750-1828	1
DAFYDD, JOHN and MORGAN, fl. 1747	1
DAFYDD, OWEN, 1751-1814?	1: 1116
DAFYDD, RICHARD WILLIAM, fl. 1740-52	1
DAVIES, DAVID, Methodist cleric, 1753-1820	1
DAVIES, DAVID, Rhydcymerau, 1814-91	1
DAVIES, HOWEL, c.1716-70	1
DAVIES, HUGH EMYR, 1878-1950	2
DAVIES, JOHN, 1750-1821	1
DAVIES, TREVOR OWEN, 1895-1966	2
DAVIES, WILLIAM, 1729?-87	1
DAVIES, WILLIAM, 'Gwilym Teilo', 1831-92	1
DAVIES, WILLIAM DAVID [P.], 1897-1969	2
EDWARDS, GWILYM ARTHUR, 1881-1963	2
ELLIS, ROBERT MORTON STANLEY, 1898-1966	2
ELLIS, WILLIAM, 'Gwilym ab Elis', 1752-1810	1
EVAN, EVAN DAFYDD, fl. 1771-79	1
EVANS, DAVID JOHN, 1884-1965	2
EVANS, EBENEZER GWYN, 1898-1958	2
EVANS, EVAN, 1758-1828	1
EVANS, JOHN, Cil-y-cwm, 1737?-84	1
EVANS, JOHN, 'Old Llwynffortun', 1779-1847	1
EVANS, JOHN RICHARDS, 1882-1969	2
EVANS, WILLIAM, Tonyrefail, 1795-1891	1
GRIFFITH, GRACE WYNNE, 1888-1963	2
GRIFFITH, GRIFFITH WYNNE, 1883-1967	2
GRIFFITHS, ANN, 1776-1805	1
GRIFFITHS, DAVID, 1756-1834	1
GRIFFITHS, DAVID REES, 'Amanwy', 1882-1953	2
GRIFFITHS, MORRIS, 1721-69	1
GRIFFITHS, MORRIS, hymn-writer, fl. 1766-1805	1
GRIFFITHS, PETER HUGHES, 1871-1937	1
GRIFFITHS, WILLIAM, 1788-1861	1
HARRIES, EVAN, 1786-1861	1
HARRIS, HOWEL(L), 1714-73	1
HOWELL, DAVID, 1797-1873	1
HOWELLS, ELISEUS, 1893-1969	2
HOWELLS, HOWELL, 1750-1842	1
HOWELLS, MORGAN, 1794-1852	1
HOWELS, WILLIAM, 1778-1832	1
HUGHES, HOWEL HARRIS, 1873-1956	2
HUGHES, JAMES, 'Iago Trichrug', 1779-1844	1
HUGHES, JOHN, Pontrobert, 1775-1854	1
HUGHES, JOHN, 1850-1932	1
HUGHES, JOHN EDWARD, 1879-1959	2
HUGHES, RICHARD SAMUEL, 1888-1952	2
HUGHES, ROBERT RICHARD, 1871-1957	2
JAMES, JAMES, 1760-1831	1
JAMES, THOMAS, Llanelli, 1827-99	1
JOHN, THOMAS, 1816-62	1
JONES, DAFYDD, Caeo, 1711-77	1
JONES, DANIEL, 1757-1821	1
JONES, DAVID, Llan-gan, 1736-1810	1
JONES, DAVID MORRIS, 1887-1957	2
JONES, GRIFFITH, 'Glan Menai', 1836-1906	1: 1132-3
JONES, GWILYM CERI, 1897-1963	2
JONES, JOHN, 'Old Blaenannerch', 1807-75	1
JONES, LLEWELYN, 1894-1960	2
JONES, PHILIP, 1855-1945	2

WILLIAMS, THOMAS, 'Tom Nefyn', 1895-1958	2
WILLIAMS, WILLIAM, Pantycelyn, 1717-91	1
WILLIAMS, WILLIAM, 1817-1900	1
WILLIAMS, WILLIAM NANTLAIS, 1874-1959	2
WILLIAMS, WILLIAM RICHARD, 1896-1962	2
ROBERTS, GRIFFITH THOMAS (Llanrug)	G.T.R.
EDWARDS, HUMPHREY, 1730-88	1
GRIFFITH, JOHN OWEN, 1828-81	1
HUGHES, ROBERT, 'Robin Ddu yr Ail o Fôn', 1744-85	1
JONES, JOHN EIDDON, 1841-1903	1
JONES, ROBERT, Rhos-lan, 1745-1829	1
JONES, ROBERT, Pencae'r-waun, 1806-96	1
THOMAS, DAVID, 'Dafydd Ddu Eryri', 1759-1822	1
THOMAS, JOHN, 'Siôn Wyn o Eifion', 1786-1859	1
WILLIAMS, ABRAHAM, 1755-1828	1
WILLIAMS, GRIFFITH, bishop, 1587?-1673	1
WILLIAMS, GRIFFITH, 'Gutyn Peris', 1769-1838	1
WILLIAMS, OWEN, 'Owain Gwyrfai', 1790-1874	1
WILLIAMS, WILLIAM, 'Gwilym Peris', 1769-1847	1
ROBERTS, GRIFFITH THOMAS (The Rev., Talsarnau)	G.T.Ro.; also G.T.R.
DAVIES, WILLIAM, Sierra Leone, 1785-1851	1
DAVIES, WILLIAM, 1820-75	1
DYKINS, WILLIAM, 'Dirwynydd', 1831-72	1
EVANS, DAVID, 'the second', 1814-47	1
EVANS, EDMUND, 'Utgorn Meirion', 1791-1864	2
EVANS, WILLIAM, 1779-1854	1
HUGHES, HUGH, 1778-1855	1
HUGHES, LOT, 1787-1873	1
HUGHES, ROWLAND, 1811-61	1
HUGHES, THOMAS, 1814-84	1
HUGHES, THOMAS ISFRYN, 1865-1942 (G.T.R. = G.T.Ro.)	2
HUMPHREYS, THOMAS JONES, 1841-1934	1
JENKINS, ISAAC, 1812-77	1
JONES, EDWARD, 'the second', 1775-1838	1
JONES, JOHN, 'Vulcan', 1825-89	1
LLWYD (LLOYD), HARRI, ?-1799	1
MEREDITH, LEWIS, 'Lewys Glyn Dyfi', 1826-91	1
PHILLIPS, EDWARD, 1716-c.1776	1
PRICHARD, RICHARD, 1811-82	1
ROGERS, DAVID, 1783-1824	1
WILLIAMS, PETER BAILEY, 1763-1836	1
YOUNG, DAVID, 1844-1913	1
ROBERTS, JOHN	J.R.
CHARLES, THOMAS, of Bala, 1755-1814	1
ROBERTS, JOHN WYN	J.W.R.
PRYS, EDMWND, 1544-1623	1
ROBERTS, KATE (Mrs KATHERINE WILLIAMS)	K.R.
EVANS, JOHN JOHN, 1862-1942	2
HUGHES, THOMAS ROWLAND, 1903-49	2
OWEN, DANIEL, 1836-95	1
RHYS, EDWARD PROSSER, 1901-45	2
ROBERTS, OWEN ELIAS	O.E.R.
EDWARDS, ARTHUR TUDOR, 1890-1946	2
LEWIS, THOMAS, Sir, 1881-1945	2
ROBERTS, ROBERT	R.R.
ROBERTS, ABSALOM, 1780?-1864	1
ROBERTS, ROBERT ALUN	R.A.R.
ROBINSON, GILBERT WOODING, 1888-1950	2
WILLIAMS, JOHN LLOYD, 1854-1945	2
ROBERTS, RHIANNON FRANCIS	R.F.R.
BEDO BRWYNLLYS, c.1460	1
DAFYDD ALAW, fl. 1550	1
DAFYDD ap GRUFFYDD of DREWYN, c.1600	1
DAFYDD ap HYWEL ab IEUAN FYCHAN, fl. 1480-1510	1
DAFYDD ap IEUAN LLWYD, fl. 1500	1
DAFYDD ap MAREDUDD ap TUDUR, fl. 1460	1
DAVIES, JOHN, Mallwyd, c.1567-1644	1
EDWART ap RAFF, fl. 1578-1606	1
EVANS, JAMES, 'Carneinion', 1814-42	1
EVANS, MORGAN, 'Cynllo Maesyfed', 1777?-1843	1
HUGHES, HUGH, 'Y Bardd Coch o Fôn' 1693-1776	1
JONES, DAVID, linguist, 1793-1825	1

LEWYS, DAFYDD, Llanllawddog, ?-1727 — 1
RAFF ap ROBERT, fl. 1550 — 1
ROBERT ab IFAN, fl. 1572-1603 — 1: 1147-8
ROBERT (ROBIN) DYFI, c.1620 — 1
SAUNDERSON, ROBERT, 1780-1863 — 2
THOMAS, SAMPSON, 1739-1807 — 1
WILLIAMS, MORGAN, c.1750-1830 — 1
ROBERTS, THOMAS — T.Ro.
DAFYDD ab EDMWND, fl. 1450-90 — 1
DAFYDD ap SIANCYN (SIENCYN) ap DAFYDD ap y CRACH, fl. mid 15c. — 1
EDMUNDS, MARY ANNE, 1813-58 — 1
GUTUN OWAIN, or GRUFFUDD ap HUW ab OWAIN, fl. c.1460-c.1498 — 1
HUGHES, WILLIAM JOHN, 1891-1945 — 2
MEREDUDD ap RHYS, fl. 1450-85 — 1
PRICE, JOHN, Bangor, 1830-1906 — 1
ROWLANDS, DANIEL, 1827-1917 — 1
SALUSBURY, Family, Lleweni, Denb., and Bachygraig — 2
ROBERTS, WILBERT LLOYD — W.Ll.R.
EVANS, JOHN, 'I. D. Ffraid', 1814-75 — 1
RODERICK, ARTHUR JAMES — A.J.R.
HYWEL ab OWAIN GWYNEDD, ?-1170 — 1
ROGERS, WILLIAM C. — W.C.R.
SEYLER, CLARENCE ARTHUR, 1866-1959 — 2
ROGERS, WILLIAM MORGAN — W.M.R.
WILDE, WILLIAM JAMES (JIMMY), 1892-1969 — 2
ROSSER, DAVID GLANVILLE — D.G.R.
CUDLIPP, PERCY, 1905-1962 — 2
HOWELL, THOMAS FRANCIS, 1864-1953 — 2
JENKINS, WILLIAM ALBERT, Sir, 1878-1968 — 2
LLEWELYN, WILLIAM CRAVEN, 1892-1966 — 2
MERRETT, HERBERT HENRY, Sir, 1886-1959 — 2
OWEN, DAVID JOHN, Sir, 1874-1941 — 2
PASCOE, FREDERICK JOHN, Sir, 1893-1963 — 2
REES, THOMAS WYNFORD, 1898-1959 — 2
WILLIAMS, WILLIAM RICHARD, Sir, 1879-1961 — 2
ROWLANDS, ERYL WYN — E.W.R.
THOMAS, IFOR OWEN, 1892-1956 — 2
ROWLANDS, WILLIAM — W.Ro.
JONES, JOHN, 'Myrddin Fardd', 1836-1921 — 1
JONES, ROBERT ISAAC, 1815-1905 — 1
JONES, ROWLAND, 1722-74 — 1
OWEN, DAVID, 'Dewi Wyn o Eifion', 1784-1841 — 1
OWEN, ELLIS, Cefn-y-meysydd Isaf, 1789-1868 — 1
PHILLIPS, JOHN, 'Tegidon', 1810-77 — 1
PRYS (PRICE), ELIS, 'Y Doctor Coch', 1512?-94? — 1
PRYS (PRICE), THOMAS, of Plas Iolyn, 1564?-1634 — 1
SALMON, H. MORREY — H.M.S.
RANDALL, HENRY JOHN (HARRY), 1877-1964 — 2
SANDERS, IVOR JOHN — I.J.S.
CHERLETON or CHARLTON, Family, Wrockwardine, Salop — 1
FITZ ALAN, Family, Oswestry and Clun, Salop and Arundel — 1
FITZ WARIN, lords of Whittington and Alderbury, Salop, Alveston, Gloucs. — 1
LESTRANGE, Family, Great Ness, Cheswardine and Knockin, Salop — 1
PECOCK, REGINALD, c.1390-1461 — 1
PETER of LEE, 'de Leia', ?-1198 — 1
SAUNDERS, EVAN JOHN — E.J.S.
LEWYS MORGANNWG, fl. 1520-65 — 1
LLEISION ap THOMAS, fl. 1513-41 — 1
SMITH, WILLIAM JAMES — W.J.S.
SALUSBURY, Family, Lleweni, Denb. and Bachygraig — 1
SALUSBURY, Family, Rug, Mer. and Bachymbyd, Denb. — 1
STEEGMAN, JOHN — J.S.
WILSON, RICHARD, 1713-82 — 1
STEPHEN, ROBERT — R.S.
ALLGOOD, Family, Pontypool and Usk, Mon. — 1
HANBURY, Family, Pontypool, Mon. — 1
JONES, EVAN, 1790-1860 — 1
PYRKE, JOHN, 1755-1834 — 1
STEPHENS, JOHN OLIVER — J.O.S.
ADAMS, DAVID, 1845-1922 (not 1923) — 1
DAVIES, OWEN, 1719-92 — 1
EVANS, EVAN KERI, 1860-1941 — 2
GRIFFITH, JAMES MILO, 1843-97 — 1

GRIFFITH, SAMUEL WALKER, Sir, 1845-1920	1
LEWIS, RICHARD MORRIS, 1847-1918	1
LOYD, LEWIS, 1767-1858	1
PHILLIPS, DAVID, fl. 1814 - see under PHILLIPS, DAVID (1751-1825)	1
THOMAS, LEWIS, Australia, 1832-1913	1
STEVENS, DENNIS WILLIAM	D.W.S.
PHILIP ap RHYS, fl. 1530	1
STREATHER, G. T.	G.T.S.
MAURICE, MATHIAS, 1684-1738	2
THOMAS, ARTHUR SPENCER VAUGHAN	A.S.V.T.
HOLLAND, HUGH, 1569-1633	1
THOMAS, DAVID VAUGHAN, 1873-1934	1
THOMAS, BENJAMIN BOWEN	B.B.T.
BOWEN, BEN, 1878-1903	1
JONES, THOMAS, 1870-1955	2
ROBERTS, ROBERT DAVIES, 1851-1911	1
THOMAS, BRINLEY	B.T.
THOMAS, DAVID ALFRED, 1856-1918	1
THOMAS, CEINWEN HANNAH	C.H.T.
DAVIES, DAVID JAMES, 1893-1956	2
FITZOSBERN, WILLIAM, ?-1071	1
IESTYN ap GWRGANT, fl. 1081-93	1
THOMAS, DAVID	D.T.
JONES, JOHN, 'Ioan Bryngwyn Bach', 1818-98	1
JONES, ROBERT THOMAS, 1874-1940	1
MADOCKS, WILLIAM ALEXANDER, 1773-1828	1
PARRY, JOHN, 1835-97	1
PARRY, WILLIAM JOHN, 1842-1927	1
PRITCHARD, ROBERT, fl. 1730-38	1
PUGH, HUGH, master mariner, 1794/5-1865	1
ROBERTS, ROBERT (SILYN), 1871-1930	1
SPOONER, JAMES, 1789-1856	1
THOMAS, JOHN EVAN, 1884-1941	2
WILLIAMS, JOHN HUW, 1871-1944	2
WILLIAMS, WILLIAM HUGH, 'Arafon', 1848-1917	1
THOMAS, IVOR	I.T.
DAVIES, DAVID, Llandinam, 1818-90	1
THOMAS, JOHN LLOYD	J.Ll.T.
MOSES-EVANS, DAVID LEWIS, 1822-1893	2
THOMAS, LAWRENCE	L.T.
BLETHIN, WILLIAM, ?-1590	1
DAVIES, FRANCIS, 1605-75	1
HARRIS, JOHN, 1680-1738	1
KITCHIN (alias Dunstan), ANTHONY, 1477-1563	1
KNIGHT, WILLIAM BRUCE, 1785-1845	1
LLOYD, HUGH, bishop of Llandaff, 1586-1667	1
NEWELL, EBENEZER JOSIAH, 1853-1916	1
THOMAS, MARGARET ETHELWYNNE	M.E.T.
THOMAS, ROGER, Sir, 1886-1960	2
THOMAS, MORRIS	M.T.
HUGHES, HENRY, 1841-1924	1
THOMAS, NORMAN PERCY	N.T.
THOMAS, PERCY EDWARD, Sir, 1883-1969	2
THOMAS, ONFEL	O.T.
PRICE, EDWARD MEREDITH, 1816-98	1
THOMAS, RICHARD	R.T.
JONES, DAVID, Treborth, 1805-68	1
JONES, GRIFFITH, Tre-garth, 1808-86	1
JONES, JOHN, of Edern, 1761-1822	1
JONES, JOHN OGWEN, 1829-84	1
JONES, RICHARD, of Wern, 1771?-1833	1
MARC, SIARL, 1720-95	1
OWEN, RICHARD, 'Y diwygiwr', 1839-87	1
OWEN, ROBERT, Pennal, 1834-99	1
PARRY, JOHN, 1775-1846	1
PRICHARD, WILLIAM, Clwchdernog, 1702-73	1
ROBERTS, JOHN, 1753-1834	1
ROBERTS, MICHAEL, Pwllheli, 1780-1849	1
ROBERTS, ROBERT, Clynnog, 1762-1802	1
ROBERTS, WILLIAM, Clynnog, 1773-1857	2
ROBERTS, WILLIAM, 1784-1864	1

THOMAS, ROGER	Ro.T.
WILLIAMS, JOHN, 1727-98	1
THOMAS, ROLAND	Rol.T.
PRICE, RICHARD, 1723-91	1
THOMAS, RHYS MALDWYN	R.M.T.
JAMES, JAMES, 'Iago ap Iago', 1818-43	2
THOMAS, W. GWYN	W.G.T.
LEACH, ARTHUR LEONARD, 1869-1957	2
THOMAS, WILLIAM JENKYN	W.J.T.
ROBERTS, BARTHOLOMEW (originally JOHN), 1682?-1721/2	1
TURNER, EDWARD (NED), 1792-1826	1
THOMAS, WILLIAM JOHN	Wm.J.T.
JONES, JOHN FOULKES, 1826-80	1
TIBBOTT, GILDAS	G.T.
DAVIES, JOHN, bibliographer, 1860-1939	1
DAVIES, WILLIAM LLEWELYN, Sir, 1887-1952	2
EDWARDS, WILLIAM ROBERT, 'Glanllafar', 1858-1921	1
EINION ap GWGON, c.1215	1
EINION ap MADOG ap RHAHAWD, c.1237	1
ELLIS, ELLIS ab, fl. 1685-1726	1
ELLIS, JOHN, antiquary, 1674-1735	1
EVANS, SAMUEL JAMES, 1870-1938	1
KYFFIN, EDWARD, c.1558-1603	1
LEWIS, DAVID MORGAN, 1851-1937	1
MORGAN, DAVID, Ysbyty Ystwyth, 1814-83	1
TIBBOTT, Family, Llanbrynmair, Mont.	1
TILSLEY, GWILYM RICHARD	G.R.T.
DAVIES, DAVID JOSHUA, 1877-1945	2
EVANS, DAVID TECWYN, 1876-1957	2
JENKINS, JOSEPH, 1886-1962	2
JONES, DAVID GWYNFRYN, 1867-1954	2
JONES, RICHARD, 'Dofwy', 1863-1956	2
LEWIS, DAVID EMRYS, 1887-1954	2
LLOYD, HENRY, 'Ap Hefin', 1870-1946	2
ROBERTS, EMMANUEL BERWYN, 1869-1951	2
TUDUR, GWILYM	G.Tu.
DAVIES, JAMES KITCHENER, 1902-1952	2
USHER, GWILYM ARTHUR	G.A.U.
MUTTON, PETER, Sir, 1565-1637	1: 1144
VALENTINE, LEWIS EDWARD	L.E.V.
DAVIES, THOMAS RHYS, 1790-1859	1
DAVIES, THOMAS WITTON, 1851-1923	1
VAUGHAN-JONES, GERAINT	G.V.-J.
JONES, ROBERT WILLIAM, 'Erfyl Fychan', 1899-1968	2
WALTERS, HUW	H.Wa.
DAVIES, DAVID THOMAS, 1876-1962	2
HOWELLS, REES, 1879-1950	2
JONES, THOMAS ROBERT, 1802-1856	2
MORGAN, JOHN JENKYN, 1875-1961	2
OWEN, WILLIAM, 'Gwilym Meudwy', 1841-1902	2
REES, EBENEZER, 1848-1908	2
THOMAS, IFOR, 1877-1918	2
WATKINS, HAROLD MOSTYN	H.M.W.
EDWARDS, DOROTHY, 1903-34	1
WHELDON, WYNN POWELL	W.P.W.
WATKINS, PERCY EMERSON, Sir, 1871-1946	2
WHELDON, THOMAS JONES, 1841-1916	1
WILLIAMS, ALBERT HUGHES	A.H.W.
AUBREY, THOMAS, 1808-67	1
BRYAN, JOHN, 1770-1856	1
CARTER, HUGH, 1784-1855	1
COKE, THOMAS, 1747-1814	1
DAVIES, OWEN, 1752-1830	1
DAVIES, SAMUEL, 1788-1854	1
HARRISON, RICHARD, 1743-1830	1
JONES, EDWARD, Bathafarn, 1778-1837	1
WILLIAMS, B. A. MARK	B.A.M.W.
WOODING, DAVID LEWIS, 1828-1891	2
WILLIAMS, DANIEL	Dl.W.
DAVIES, JOHN, 1700?-92	1
DAVIES, WILLIAM EDWARDS, 1851-1927	1
EVANS, JOHN, 'the parson of Portsmouth', ?-1779?	1
EVANS, MAURICE, 1765-1831	1

GLASCOTT, CRADOCK, 1743-1831	1
GRIFFITH, DAVID, 'Clwydfardd', 1800-94	1
HUGHES, JOHN, archdeacon, 1787-1860	1
HUGHES, JOSEPH, 'Carn Ingli', 1803-63	1
JAMES, THOMAS, 'Llallawg', 1817-79	1
JONES, JOHN, 'the vicar of Alconbury', 1700-70	1
JONES, LEWIS, 'the church building parson', 1793-1866	1
MORGAN, EDWARD, 1783-1869	1
OWEN, JOHN, 1788-1867	1
OWEN, WILLIAM, 1750-1830	1
PUGH, DAVID, 1739-1816	1
PUGH, JOHN, 1744-99	1
PUGH, ROBERT, 1749-1825	1
REES, ROBERT OLIVER, 1819-81	1
WILLIAMS, WILLIAM, Waterbeach, 1747-1812	1
WILLIAMS, WILLIAM, Cornwall, 1748-1820	1
WILLIAMS, DANIEL EMRYS	**D.E.W.**
WILLIAMS, WILLIAM, 1747-1812	2
WILLIAMS, DAVID	**D.W.**
CHAMBERS, WILLIAM, 1774-1855	1
DAVIES, DAVID, 'Dai'r Cantwr', 1812?-74	1
EVANS, JOHN, explorer, 1770-99	1
FROST, JOHN, 1784-1877	1
HALL, BENJAMIN, 1778-1817	1
HALL, BENJAMIN, 1802-67	1
JONES, DANIEL, Salt Lake City, 1811-61	1
JONES, JOHN, of Ystrad, 1777-1842	1: 1133-4
JONES, JOHN, 'Shoni Sguborfawr', fl. 1811-58	1
LEWIS, FRANCIS, 1713-1802	1
LEWIS, GEORGE CORNEWALL, Sir, 1806-63	1
LEWIS, LEWIS, 'Lewsyn yr Heliwr', 1793-?	1
LEWIS, RICHARD, 'Dic Penderyn', 1807/8-1831	1
LEWIS, THOMAS FRANKLAND, Sir, 1780-1855	1
MACKWORTH, HUMPHREY, Sir, 1657-1727	1
MORGAN, DAVID THOMAS, c.1695-1746	1
MORGAN, HENRY, 1635?-88	1
PHILLIPS, DANIEL THOMAS, 1842-1905	1
PHILLIPS, JOHN ROLAND, 1844-87	1
PHILLIPS, THOMAS, Sir, 1801-67	1
PHILLIPS, THOMAS, principal of Cardiff (B) college, 1868-1936	1
POWELL, THOMAS, chartist, fl. 1832-41	1
REES, ABRAHAM, 1743-1825	1
ROBERTS, THOMAS, Llwyn'rhudol, 1765/6-1841	1
SALMON, DAVID, 1852-1944	2
SAUNDERS, ERASMUS, 1670-1724	1
THOMAS, DANIEL (LLEUFER), Sir, 1863-1940	1
WAITHMAN, ROBERT, 1764-1833	1
WHITE, JOHN, 1590-1645	1
WILLIAMS, CHARLES HANBURY, Sir, 1708-59	1
WILLIAMS, DAVID, littérateur, 1738-1816	1
WILLIAMS, HUGH, solicitor, 1796-1874	1
WILLIAMS, WILLIAM, Member of Parliament, 1788-1865	1
WILLIAMS, ZEPHANIAH, 1795-1874	1
WILLIAMS, DAVID ALUN	**D.A.W.**
MORRIS, RHYS HOPKIN, Sir, 1888-1956	2
WILLIAMS, DAVID EWART PARRY	**D.E.P.W.**
EVANS, DAVID, 1874-1948	2
EVANS, DAVID EMLYN, 1843-1913	1
EVANS, THOMAS HOPKIN, 1879-1940	1: 1120-1
REES, JOHN THOMAS, 1857-1949	2
WILLIAMS, EDWARD IVOR	**E.I.W.**
EDWARDS, WILLIAM, builder of bridges, 1719-89	1
JOHN, DAVID, 1782?-1853	1
REYNOLDS, JONATHAN OWAIN, 1814-91	1
WILKINS, CHARLES, 'Catwg', 1831-1913	1
WILLIAMS, MORGAN, chartist, 1808-83	1
WILLIAMS, EURYN OGWEN	**E.O.W.**
WILLIAMS, ALUN OGWEN, 1904-1970	2
WILLIAMS, GARETH HAULFRYN	**G.H.W.**
FOXWIST, WILLIAM, 1610-c.1673	2
WILLIAMS, WILLIAM GILBERT, 1874-1966	2

WILLIAMS, GARETH W.	**G.W.W.**
BANCROFT, WILLIAM JOHN, 1871-1959	2
BUSH, PERCY FRANK, 1879-1955	2
GABE, RHYS THOMAS, 1880-1967	2
JENKINS, ALBERT EDWARD, 1895-1953	2
LYNE, HORACE SAMPSON, 1860-1949	2
MORGAN, EDWARD, 'E.T.', 1880-1949	2
REES, WALTER ENOCH, 1863-1949	2
VILE, THOMAS HENRY, 1882-1958	2
WILLIAMS, GLANMOR	**G.W.**
BARLOW, WILLIAM, 1499?-1568	1
CONSTANTINE, GEORGE, c.1500-1560?	1: 1114-5
DAVIES, RICHARD, biblical translator, 1501?-81	1
FERRAR, ROBERT, ?-1555	1
GORE, HUGH, 1613-91	1: 1123
HUET, THOMAS, ?-1591	1
HUGHES, WILLIAM, bishop of S. Asaph, ?-1600	1
KYFFIN, MORRIS, c.1555-98	1
LLWYD, ROBERT, of Chirk, 1565-1655	1
MORGAN (alias YOUNG), JOHN, ?-1504	1
MORGAN, WILLIAM, biblical translator, c.1545-1604	1; 2
PARRY, RICHARD, biblical translator, 1560-1623	1
PARRY, WILLIAM, ?-1585	1
PHILIPPS, GRISMOND PICTON, Sir, 1898-1967	2
VAUGHAN, EDWARD, bishop of S. David's, ?-1522	1
YOUNG, THOMAS, 1507-68	1
WILLIAMS, GRIFFITH JOHN	**G.J.W.**
BRADFORD, JOHN, 1706-85	1
DAFYDD, EDWARD, c.1600-78?	1
DAFYDD BENWYN, 16c.	1
DAFYDD DDU ATHRO o HIRADDUG, <1400	1
DAVIES, EDWARD, 'Y Celtic Ddafis', 1756-1831	1
DAVIES, EVAN, 'Myfyr Morganwg', 1801-88	1
DAVIES, MARGARET, c.1700-85?	1
EDERN DAFOD AUR, 15c.?	1
EDWARDS, CHARLES, 1628->1691	1
EDWARDS, JOHN, 'Siôn Treredyn', 1606?-1660?	1
EDWARDS, JOHN, 'Siôn Ceiriog', 1747-92	1
EINION OFFEIRIAD, ?-1353	1
GWILYM TEW, fl. c.1470	1
HOPCYN, WILIAM, 'Wil Hopcyn', 1700-41	1
HOPCYN ap TOMAS, c.1330- >1403	1
HOPKIN, LEWIS, c.1708-71	1
HUGHES, STEPHEN, 1622-88	1
IEUAN RUDD, fl. 1470	1
IORWERTH FYNGLWYD, fl. c.1480-1527	1
JONES, OWEN, 'Owain Myfyr', 1741-1814	1
LLYWELYN, TOMAS, fl. c.1580-1610	1
MERRICK, RICE, (RHYS MEURUG), ?-1586/7	1
MIDLETON (MYDDELTON), WILLIAM, c.1550-1600	1
MORGAN, RHYS, c.1700-1775	1
NICOLAS, DAFYDD, 1705?-74	1
POWEL, ANTHONY, c.1560-1618/9	1
POWEL, WATCYN, c.1600-55	1
PUGHE, WILLIAM OWEN, 1759-1835	1
RICHARDS, THOMAS, lexicographer, 1710-90	1
ROBERT, GRUFFYDD, c.1522-1610	1
SILS ap SION, 16c.	1
SIMWNT FYCHAN, c.1530-1606	1
TOMAS ab IEUAN ap RHYS, c.1510-60)	1
WALTERS, JOHN, lexicographer, 1721-97	1
WALTERS, JOHN, 1760-89	1
WARING, ELIJAH, c.1788-1857	1
WILLIAMS, EDWARD, 'Iolo Morganwg', 1747-1826	1
WILLIAMS, TALIESIN, 1787-1847	1
WILLIAMS, GWILYM	**Gw.W.**
JONES, JOHN MORGAN, Cardiff, 1838-1921	1
WILLIAMS, GWILYM OWEN	**G.O.W.**
PHILLIPS, THOMAS, surgeon, 1760-1851	1
WILLIAMS, HAROLD	**Ha.W.**
DAVIES, DAVID JOHN, (or DYER), 1870-? [H.W. = Ha.W.]	1

WILLIAMS, HUW   **H.W.**

BRAZELL, DAVID, 1875-1959	2
CARRINGTON, THOMAS (TOM), 1881-1961	2
DAVIES, DAVID JOHN (DYER) [not by H.W.; see Ha.W. above]	1
DAVIES, EVAN THOMAS, 1878-1969	2
DAVIES, TUDOR, 1892-1958	2
EDWARDS, THOMAS DAVID, 1874-1930	2
ELLIS, JOHN, 1760-1839	2
FOSTER, IVOR LLEWELYN, 1870-1959	2
GRIFFITH, ROBERT DAVID, 1877-1958	2
HARRIS, GRIFFITH, 1811-1892	2
HUGHES, JOHN, 1896-1968	2
HUGHES, (ROBERTS), MARGARET, 'Leila Megáne', 1891-1960	2
JONES, GWILYM GWALCHMAI, 1921-1970	2
JONES, MAI, 1899-1960	2
JONES, WILLIAM ARTHUR, William Bradwen Jones, 1892-1970	2
JONES, WILLIAM JOHN PARRY, 1891-1963	2
LEWIS, IDRIS, 1889-1952	2
LLOYD, DAVID GEORGE, 1912-1969	2
LLOYD, JOHN MORGAN, 1880-1960	2
MORRIS, HAYDN, 1891-1965	2
WILLIAMS, ROBERT, 1782-1818	2

WILLIAMS, IFOR   **I.W.**

ANEIRIN, 6c.	1
DAFYDD NANMOR, 15c.	1
GILDAS, 6c.	1
GRUFFUDD GRYG, 14c.	1
GUTO'R GLYN, fl. 1440-93	1
GWRTHEYRN (VORTIGERN), 5c.	1
HUGHES, HUGH DERFEL, 1816-90	1
IFOR HAEL (Ifor the Generous), 14c.	1
RHYS, JOHN, Sir, 1840-1915	1
RHYS GOCH ERYRI, fl. 15c.	1
TALIESIN, 6c.	1

WILLIAMS, JOHN ELLIS CAERWYN   **J.E.C.W.**

BONAPARTE, LOUIS-LUCIEN, 1813-91	1
GWYNFARDD BRYCHEINIOG, fl. c.1180	1
HYWEL SWRDWAL, fl. 1430-60	1
JEFFREYS-JONES, THOMAS IEUAN, 1909-1967	2
OWEN, ROBERT, 'Eryron Gwyllt Walia', 1803-70	1
TUDUR ALED, fl. 1480-1526	1
TUDUR PENLLYN, c.1420-90	1

WILLIAMS, JOHN GWYNN   **J.G.W.**

JENKINS, ROBERT THOMAS, 1881-1969	2
ROBERTS, GLYN, 1904-1962	2
VAUGHAN, JOHN, Sir, 1603-74	1
WATERHOUSE, THOMAS, 1878-1961	2
WHELDON, WYN POWELL, Sir, 1879-1961	2

WILLIAMS, JOHN JOHN   **J.J.W.**

JONES, WILLIAM GARMON, 1884-1937	1

WILLIAMS, JOHN ROBERTS   **J.R.W.**

ROWLANDS, ROBERT JOHN, 1880-1967	2

WILLIAMS, MARGARET MITFORD   **M.M.W.**

DAVIES, WILFRED MITFORD, 1895-1966	2

WILLIAMS, MELFYN RICHARD   **M.R.W.**

DAVIES, RICHARD OWEN, 1894-1962	2
DAVIES, RHISIART MORGAN, 1903-1958	2
HUGHES, EDWARD DAVID, 1906-1963	2
JONES, THOMAS, 1777-1847	2
ROBERTS, ROBERT ALUN, 1894-1969	2
ROBERTS, ROBERT ELLIS VAUGHAN, 1888-1962	2
ROWLANDS, GRIFFITH, 1761-1828	2
ROWLANDS, ROBERT PUGH, 1874-1933	2

WILLIAMS, MENAI   **M.W.**

DAVIES, HUMFFREY, fl. 1600-64?	1
DAVIES, JOHN, ?-1694	1

WILLIAMS, MOELWYN IDWAL   **M.I.W.**

BEYNON, WILLIAM, 1884?-1932	1
BIGGS, NORMAN, 1870-1908	1
BOOTS, JOHN GEORGE, 1874-1928	1
EVANS, DAVID, 'Dewi Haran', 1812-85	1
GIBBS, REGINALD ARTHUR, 1872-1938	1
GOULD, ARTHUR JOSEPH, 1864-1919	1

HODGES, JEHOIADA, 1877?-1930   1
JAMES, DAVID, 1863-1929, and EVAN, ?-c.1920   1
JAMES, JOHN, 1815-69   1
JENKINS, THOMAS JOHN PRICE, 1864-1922   1
JONES, DAVID WATKIN, 1832-1905   1
JONES, PERCY, 1891-1922   1
JONES, ROBERT, 1706?-42   1
LEWIS, BENJAMIN, ?-1749   1
LEWIS, CHARLES PRYTHERCH, 1853-1923   1
MOSES, DAVID (not DANIEL) LEWIS, 1822-93   1
MOSES, WILLIAM, 1742-1824   1
NICHOLLS, ERITH GWYN, 1875-1939   1
OWEN, RICHARD MORGAN, 1877-1932   1
PHILLIPS, JOHN, 1810-67   1
POWELL, EVAN, 1721?-1785   1
PRITCHARD, CHARLES MEYRICK, 1882-1916   1
PRITCHARD, MICHAEL, c.1709-33   1
PROPERT, JOHN, 1793-1867   1
REES, JAMES, 1803-80   1
REES, JOHN CONWAY, 1870-1932   1
REES, REES ARTHUR, 1837-66   1
THOMAS, DAVID, bone-setter, 1739?-88   1
THOMAS, FREDERICK HALL, 1886-1927   1
THOMAS, THOMAS, boxing champion, 1880-1911   1
TREW, WILLIAM JOHN, 1878-1926   1
WILLIAMS, JOHN LEWIS, 1882-1916   1
WINFIELD, HERBERT BENJAMIN, 1879-1919   1
WILLIAMS, MORGAN JOHN   M.J.W.
JOHN, WALTER PHILLIPS, 1910-1967   2
WILLIAMS, NIA HALL   N.H.W.
JONES, FRANCIS WYNN, 1898-1970   2
WILLIAMS, RICHARD BRYN   R.B.W.
BERWYN, RICHARD JONES, 1836-1917   1
DAVIES, DAVID STEPHEN, 1841-98   1
EVANS, JOHN DANIEL, 1862-1943   2
HUGHES, ANNIE HARRIET, Gwyneth Vaughan, 1852-1910   1
HUGHES, ARTHUR, 1878-1965   2
HUGHES, HUGH, 'Cadfan Gwynedd', 1824-98   1
HUGHES, WILLIAM MELOCH, 1860-1926   1: 1129
JONES, LEWIS, Patagonia, 1836-1904   1
MATHEWS, ABRAHAM, 1832-99   1
MORGAN, ELUNED, 1870-1938   1
ROGERS, RICHARD SAMUEL, 1882-1950   2
THOMAS, RICHARD, 1871-1950   2
WILLIAMS, ROBIN O. G.   R.O.G.W.
ROBERTS, ROBERT, 1870-1951   2
WILLIAMS, SIAN RHIANNON   S.R.W.
OWEN, OWEN JOHN, 1867-1960   2
WILLIAMS, STEPHEN JOSEPH   S.J.W.
BLEGYWRYD, fl. c.945   1
ELLIS, THOMAS PETER, 1873-1936   1
HYWEL DDA (Hywel the Good), ?-950   1
WILLIAMS, ROBERT, 'Robert ap Gwilym Ddu', 1766-1850   1
WILLIAMS, THOMAS OSWALD   T.O.W.
DAVIES, JOHN, Adpar, 1795-1858   1
DAVIES, REUBEN, 1808-33   1
DAVIES, WILLIAM JENKIN, 1858-1919   1
DAVIS, DAVID, Castellhywel, 1745-1827   1
EVANS, DAVID LEWIS, 1813-1902   1
EVANS, GEORGE EYRE, 1857-1939   1
EVANS, OWEN, 1808-65   1
EVANS, TITUS, 1809-64   1
EVANS, WALTER JENKIN, 1856-1927   1
GRIFFITHS, THOMAS JEREMY, 'Tau Gimel', 1797?-1871   1
GRIFFITHS, WILLIAM, 1859-1940   1
HARRIS, SOLOMON, 1726-85   1
HOWELL, WILLIAM, 1740-1822   1
JAMES, JOHN, Gellionnen, 1779-1864   1
JAMES, WILLIAM, 1848-1907   1
JONES, DAVID LEWIS, 1788-1830   1
JONES, JENKIN, Llwynrhydowen, 1700?-42   1
JONES, JOHN, Aberdare, 1802-63   1
JONES, JOHN EDWARD, 1801-66   1